Pre-Registration Segment

THE REAL ESTATE TRANSACTION—GENERAL

The Real Estate Transaction—General
© 2016 Real Estate Council of Ontario

DISCLAIMERS

This publication, including all third party material and all schedules, appendices, pre-printed forms, standard clauses, processes, facts, information and any other material contained therein (the "Publication"), is summary in nature and not intended to replace direct research of original source documents and expert advice. Real estate registrants and consumers should seek appropriate counsel in matters relating to real estate. At all times, diligence and prudence should be uppermost as all real estate transactions are unique. This Publication is strictly intended for educational purposes only. RECO reserves the right to change or revise this Publication without notice, and will not be liable for any loss or damage incurred by you as a result of such changes or revisions.

RECO, the Ontario Real Estate Association (Designate), service providers and others associated with this Publication and offering of this program (collectively referred to as the "Program Providers") are not responsible for any deficiencies, defects, errors, omissions, or for the adequacy, sufficiency, completeness, suitability, accuracy, currency or applicability of the contents of this Publication. This disclaimer, and all that follow, applies regardless of whether this Publication is made available to you in paper or electronic form.

In the event that you access this Publication by means of the internet or other electronic transmission, you expressly agree that the Program Providers are not responsible for any damage to hardware or software, loss or corruption of data, or any other loss or damage, that may result from your use of this Publication or from your accessing any web site related to this Publication or utilizing any other means of electronic transmission owned or operated by, or on behalf of, the Program Providers. The Program Providers make no warranty or representation that any such web site, electronic document or electronic transmission will meet your requirements, will be uninterrupted, timely, secure or error-free or that defects, if any, will be corrected.

The Program Providers disclaim all warranties of any kind, whether express or implied, including without limitation any warranties of merchantability or fitness for a particular purpose, related to this Publication. Further, the Program Providers are not liable for loss or damage, whether direct, indirect or consequential, and whether or not it was foreseeable, arising from the utilization of this Publication.

This Course Has Been Approved By The Registrar Under The *Real Estate And Business Brokers Act, 2002*.

Real Estate Council of Ontario
3300 Bloor Street West
Suite 1200, West Tower
Toronto, ON M8X 2X2

International Standard Book Number: 978-0-9780344-2-9
Content Development: Ontario Real Estate Association and Acronamic Learning Systems Inc.
Design and Graphics: Automation Plus Ltd.

Printing and Binding: MediaLinx Printing Group

Reprint: June, 2016

ROLE OF THE REGISTRAR UNDER REBBA 2002 IN EDUCATION

The Registrar under the *Real Estate and Business Brokers Act, 2002* (REBBA 2002) is responsible for setting the educational requirements for individuals who wish to obtain and maintain registration as a real estate broker or salesperson. In order to trade in real estate in Ontario, real estate brokerages, brokers and salespersons must be registered with the Real Estate Council of Ontario (RECO) under REBBA 2002. Before beginning a career as a real estate salesperson, individuals are required to complete the required pre-registration courses.

The Registrar, through an Educational Services Agreement, had designated the Ontario Real Estate Association as the organization authorized to provide the pre-registration, articling and broker educational program. All registration-related courses of study, including associated course content, must be approved by the Registrar prior to being offered to students.

DESIGNATE

The Ontario Real Estate Association, through its OREA Real Estate College, takes great pleasure in delivering this program on behalf of the Registrar pursuant to an Educational Services Agreement between the Real Estate Council of Ontario and the Ontario Real Estate Association.

The course curriculum supports the Real Estate Council of Ontario's mandate to protect the public interest through the development of skilled and educated real estate professionals by providing students with timely, comprehensive, accurate and up-to-date education that will allow them to succeed in the real estate marketplace. The OREA Real Estate College fulfills many of its responsibilities to the Registrar, the public of Ontario and the real estate profession by providing learning opportunities so that individuals, either contemplating registration or currently holding registration, can receive appropriate and timely training.

The real estate profession makes a valuable contribution to the economy of Canada and the welfare of its people. Congratulations on taking the first step towards real estate registration in Ontario. The Real Estate Council of Ontario and the Ontario Real Estate Association hope that the successful completion of *The Real Estate Transaction* course will inspire and motivate you to pursue advanced educational offerings throughout your new career.

ACKNOWLEDGEMENTS

A course of this scope is only possible with the assistance of many dedicated professionals committed to the advancement of real estate skills and knowledge. A special note of thanks is owed to the Ontario Real Estate Association for its ongoing forty-year commitment to excellence in real estate education.

A further debt of gratitude is owed to various government departments and agencies who assisted with information and published materials. Appropriate references are included within text materials.

The terms REALTOR® and MLS® are identified as design marks in this publication. No attempt has been made to designate all words or terms in which proprietary rights might exist. The inclusion, definition, or description of a word or term is provided for general information purposes only and is not intended to affect any legal status associated with the word or term as a trademark, service mark or proprietary item.

BEFORE YOU BEGIN...

Course Materials

Check that all required course materials are included. Contents vary based on course delivery selection.

	CORRESPONDENCE	ONLINE	CLASSROOM
The Real Estate Transaction—General Text	●		●

If any materials are missing, call Course Administration Services at (416) 391-6732 or (866) 411-6732.

The Hewlett Packard 10BII

Real Estate as a Professional Career, Land, Structures and Real Estate Trading, The Real Estate Transaction—General, The Residential Real Estate Transaction and *The Commercial Real Estate Transaction,* as well as various advanced programs, require detailed financial calculations. Calculations are illustrated using **HP 10BII** keystrokes. The use of the **HP 10BII** is not an endorsement of the product, but a practical decision for consistent content presentation. Students may select other calculators, but no assistance or support is provided. Students using such calculators are well advised to compare computational capabilities with required course calculations.

Examination

An examination follows completion of *The Real Estate Transaction—General.* See College Program Standards in the *Student Handbook* for full details regarding examination locations, rules, policies and procedures.

Other Resources

Instructor Support Line   (866) 444-5557
Clarification regarding *course content only.*

Missing Course Materials   (416) 391-6732 (866) 411-6732
Course Administration Services

College Education Centre   (866) 411-6732 (Toronto)

My OREA Community—Education Forums

OREA encourages the use of the Education Forums as a learning tool. This can be found on our website at **www.orea.com**. Log in to "My Portfolio" using your student ID and password. Once logged in, click on the *My OREA Community (Discussion Forum for Courses)* link. If you do not already have a "My Portfolio" password, please contact the College Education Centre. This positive exchange of content information with an expert who will answer posted questions can be practical and extensive. Participation in the forum is specific to each course and fellow students are encouraged to join the discussions. Privacy is protected.

THE REAL ESTATE TRANSACTION—GENERAL

CONTENTS AT A GLANCE

TABLE OF CONTENTS

TABLE OF CONTENTS (continued)

TABLE OF CONTENTS (continued)

TABLE OF CONTENTS (continued)

CHAPTER 6
Marketing The Property   200

CHAPTER 7
Analyzing The Agreement   234

TABLE OF CONTENTS (continued)

TABLE OF CONTENTS (continued)

CHAPTER 8
Drafting Offers: Part 1   288

TABLE OF CONTENTS (continued)

TABLE OF CONTENTS (continued)

INTRODUCTION

 ## LEARNING FEATURES

Chapter content summaries and **learning outcomes** detail the learning journey in each chapter.

Key terms are boldfaced with the most significant glossary terms highlighted in page margins. All glossary terms and associated definitions are found in the *Appendix: Glossary*.

Illustrations simplify and summarize complex topics. A picture is worth a thousand words. Detailed subject matter often requires visual enhancements to ensure complete understanding.

Curiosities offer novel ideas or explanatory details, while satisfying the inquisitive nature in us all. The element of discovery can expand awareness and consolidate subject matter.

Market Memos are interspersed to bring reality to the subject matter. If a topic involves value, the memo may address new technologies that are revolutionizing the valuation process. If the topic details economic trends, the memo may highlight a specific indicator together with statistical data.

Perspectives bring fresh outlooks and consolidate complex topics, usually using a story line. Everyday occurrences of registrants often complement the subject matter.

Cautions identify special concerns including situations where prudence is required and practices that can lead to dire consequences if pursued.

Each **Focus** concentrates on additional details for a particular topic. These informative descriptions bridge the gap between academic discussions and today's realities.

STUDY AIDS

Notables highlight key topics in each chapter to assist students with review and study efforts, along with a summary of key glossary terms.

Strategic Thinking questions are included to assist in preparing for a new sales career.

A **Chapter Mini-Review** is provided with each chapter for personal review and assessment. The mini-review is a warm up for active learning exercises.

Active Learning Exercises are included at the end of each chapter. Various testing formats are used including multiple choice, fill-in-the-blanks, matching, short answer and form completion exercises.

The **Appendix** contains the *Glossary,* as well as *all* solutions (for chapter mini-reviews and active learning exercises). In addition, the Appendix contains other reference material including *Mortgage Payment Factors, Forms* and *Clauses.*

ADDITIONAL RESOURCES

 Web Links are provided for general interest regarding selected chapter topics. Knowledge of website content is not required for examination purposes.

Forms included in this text are copyrighted by the Ontario Real Estate Association and are included for illustration purposes. These forms have been developed by OREA for the use and reproduction of its members and licensees only and are reproduced with permission of the Ontario Real Estate Association. OREA forms, or portions thereof, are illustrated in various chapters. All OREA forms used in this course are reprinted in the *Appendix.*

TIPS & GUIDELINES

Registration courses emphasize *learning by doing* through the mastery of practical real estate skills and knowledge. The course combines formal instruction, self evaluation and problem-solving with fictional characters and scenarios. Students must evaluate circumstances, make suggestions, correct errors and learn important lessons in preparation for the marketplace. Questions are posed that require introspection, strategic thinking, application of techniques and explanation of procedures.

HOW TO MAXIMIZE LEARNING

Make the Text Priority One	• Carefully review each chapter including every topic, illustration and example.
Follow the Learning Path	• Topics are logically sequenced by section and topics within chapters. • While creativity is encouraged, most students are advised to follow the pre-set order.
Access Additional Resources	• *Web Links* can be very helpful in clarifying and expanding chapter topics. *These resources are not required for examination purposes.*
Study Key Terms	• Clearly understand all boldfaced terms included in the primary text. These are also summarized at the end of each chapter and detailed in *Appendix: Glossary*.
Complete all Questions/ Exercises	• Practice makes perfect. Complete all chapter mini-reviews and exercises. Solutions are provided in the *Appendix*. • Suggestion: Use a blank sheet of paper as an answer sheet where feasible, leaving the chapter mini-reviews and exercises blank for follow-up review.
Continuously Review	• When in doubt, review. Repeat readings, mini-reviews and active learning exercises as often as required. • Don't move forward without fully understanding all content. • Learning has a lot in common with building blocks. Start with a good foundation and a sound structure will emerge. • Remember, knowledge is cumulative. Don't skip any chapters.
Prepare for the Exam	• The examination tests subject matter covered in the primary text. No surprises...if you diligently study the materials. • Exam questions vary, but not the underlying purpose. Emphasis is on understanding concepts, techniques and procedures. • Don't expect a mere recital of facts.

THE REAL ESTATE TRANSACTION—GENERAL

ABOUT THIS TEXT

The Real Estate Transaction—General provides detailed knowledge of the real estate transaction, from listing agreement to final sale. Course content also sets the stage for advanced residential and commercial real estate transactions addressed in *The Residential Real Estate Transaction* and *The Commercial Real Estate Transaction*. The general component consists of eleven chapters, each highlighting different dimensions of the real estate transaction. The program begins with an indepth discussion of contract law, followed by an analysis of REBBA 2002 regulatory requirements affecting real estate transactions, with particular emphasis on the Code of Ethics.

The course then outlines key considerations when documenting seller and buyer representation, including negotiating commissions and common errors/omission. This is followed by a discussion of procedures relating to multiple representation, customer services and effective marketing techniques. The focus then shifts to a clause-by-clause review of the agreement of purchase and sale and how to effectively draft offers. Chapter materials emphasize different types of offers typically encountered in the marketplace, along with associated clauses.

The Real Estate Transaction—General concludes with offer negotiations, including acceptances, counter offers and other sale-related documents such as amending offers and removing conditions. The final chapter highlights closing the transaction from buyer and seller perspectives, title conveyancing and commission disbursement. Various text features and study aids are included to make this a rewarding learning experience, while building a solid foundation for advanced residential and commercial courses.

CHAPTER 1

Understanding Contract Law

Introduction

A contract is a legally binding agreement between two or more parties that must have certain essential elements to be enforceable. This chapter reviews the six essential elements and expands on selected topic areas associated with each. For example, registrants must understand the consequences of not having these elements and the fact that such contracts can either be voidable or void.

Emphasis is placed on selected elements, such as the capacity of parties including various considerations focusing on the issue of a person's legal capacity. Detailed examples are provided with various contract elements to ensure thorough understanding. Knowledge acquired in this chapter is essential for subsequent chapters dealing with documentation (e.g., representation agreements and agreements of purchase and sale).

The issue of mistakes and misrepresentations are also detailed. In particular, misrepresentations have resulted in considerable litigation involving registrants. Breaches of contracts along with five remedies are also outlined, along with five common methods of contract termination. The chapter concludes with a discussion of representation agreements and agreements of purchase and sale from a contractual perspective, including regulatory requirements impacting such agreements.

Learning Outcomes

At the conclusion of this chapter, students will be able to:

- Define a contract and identify the essential elements of a contract.
- Outline factors that can render a contract void or voidable and differentiate between these two terms.
- Describe a person's capacity to enter into a contract in terms of persons with mental incompetence, intoxicated persons, illiterates and minors.
- Define lawful object and list examples of contracts having illegality (no lawful object).
- Discuss the contractual element of consideration with specific reference to value, lawful consideration, past consideration and the use of a seal.
- Identify general rules that apply in the offer and acceptance of a contract.
- Discuss genuine intention including four ways by which parties may be misled by improper inducements including mistakes, misrepresentations, undue influence and lack of disclosure.
- Discuss the importance of the terms of an agreement being definite and clear.
- Outline how a breach of contract can occur along with five remedies for such a breach.
- Outline five common methods to terminate a contract involving real property.
- Discuss contract documents usual to real estate transactions with reference to the parol evidence rule and privity.
- Define and discuss types of representation agreements and discuss REBBA 2002 requirements in regard to such agreements.
- Define and discuss the agreement of purchase in sale with regard to the Statute of Frauds, the *Vendors and Purchasers Act* and REBBA 2002 Requirements.

CONTRACT

A **contract** is broadly defined as a legally binding agreement between two or more persons, competent at law to enter into such agreement, for consideration or value, to do or refrain from doing some lawful and genuinely intended act.

A contract is a binding promise of one person made to another or others. It is more than a mere offer to do something or a simple statement of intention. A contract requires a meeting of the minds whereby a legal rather than a moral obligation is created, imposing an enforceable duty to fulfill the promise on the one party and conferring a legal right on the other to claim its fulfillment. The underlying intention of any contract is that it shall be binding on the parties.

Contract

A legally binding agreement between two or more capable persons.

Contract Form

The law enforces a binding promise or set of promises made by one person to another or others. Contracts may exist in many forms; e.g., verbal contracts (word of mouth), contracts made by exchanging letters or contracts drawn up as long, detailed legal documents. All contracts and, therefore, agreements of purchase and sale are affected by contract law.

A document, such as an agreement of purchase and sale, is not technically a contract, but rather evidence of a contract. The contract is the legal relationship created between the parties. If any of the elements essential to the contracting process are absent, it will matter very little how well the document has been prepared. An agreement cannot give evidence of a contract that does not exist at law.

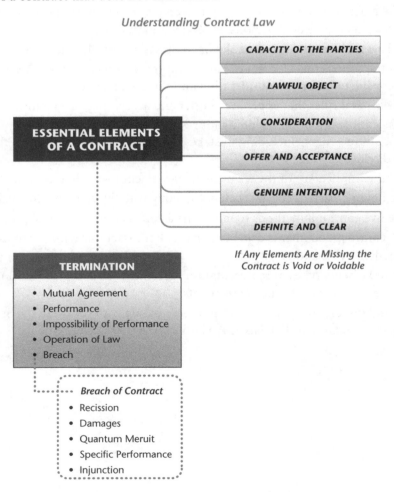

Understanding Contract Law

ESSENTIAL ELEMENTS OF A CONTRACT

- CAPACITY OF THE PARTIES
- LAWFUL OBJECT
- CONSIDERATION
- OFFER AND ACCEPTANCE
- GENUINE INTENTION
- DEFINITE AND CLEAR

If Any Elements Are Missing the Contract is Void or Voidable

TERMINATION
- Mutual Agreement
- Performance
- Impossibility of Performance
- Operation of Law
- Breach

Breach of Contract
- Recission
- Damages
- Quantum Meruit
- Specific Performance
- Injunction

Contract Elements

Certain elements must be present to make the contract enforceable.

- The parties entering into a contract must be legally competent to contract (*capacity of the parties*).
- The contractual arrangement must be lawful (*lawful object* or *legality of object*).
- Each party must receive something (*consideration*).
- There must be offer and acceptance (*mutual agreement*).
- Both parties must consent to the terms of the contract (*genuine intention*).
- The agreement must be certain (*definite and clear*).

If Elements Missing

A contract, not fulfilling all requirements, may be either **void** or **voidable**:

- Void (never came into existence);
- Voidable (originally valid but capable of being rejected by the offended parties at a later time); or
- Illegal (not enforceable by the courts).

Void
Of no legal effect; a nullity.

VOID VS. VOIDABLE

A void contract has no force or effect. A contract that is void is said to be a nullity at law. As far as the law is concerned, the agreement does not exist. Neither party can enforce it and neither party has any obligations under it.

Voidable
One party to a contract is entitled to rescind the contract at his or her option.

> **EXAMPLE**   *Void Contract*
>
> A void contract can occur when the agreement is impossible to perform. For example, Seller Smith and Buyer Jones enter into an agreement of purchase and sale for the acquisition of an isolated cottage owned by Smith. Unknown to either party, Smith's cottage was destroyed by fire during the winter. All of the elements of the contract are in existence, but the structure is not. Both buyer and seller are mistaken as to this essential fact and the contract is impossible to perform and would undoubtedly be judged void.

Conversely, a voidable contract is enforceable, valid and binding until rendered void. A contract that is voidable is one where the offended party may make a choice. The person may choose to avoid the contract and treat it as being at an end, or to treat it as subsisting and enforce it against the offending party. A good example of a voidable contract involves minors (see subsequent topic).

> **EXAMPLE**   *Voidable Contract*
>
> An example of a voidable contract involving undue influence can include a situation where one party, by virtue of a special relationship to the other, is in a position of confidence and abuses that position. In cases such as relations between parent and child or solicitor and client, presumption of undue influence may arise that can be rebutted by showing that, in fact, the person susceptible to influence was able to form a decision free of any sort of control.
>
> The fact that the person claiming undue influence received independent legal advice or independent valuations of the property are excellent ways of establishing that no undue influence occurred. Where undue influence is shown, the contract is voidable, not void. That is, the person claiming undue influence must go to court to have the contract adjudged void.

The question of void and voidable contracts relates to much larger issues concerning avoidance of a contract. In other words, cases may arise where the elements of a valid contract are present (i.e., not void) but where the promise of one or both parties has been given on the basis of or affected by some misunderstanding, false inducement, force, or the like, so that the offended party has rights of redress. Usually the two types of redress for grievances of this kind are either to allow avoidance of the contract altogether or to obtain damages for the conduct of the other party. Such instances involve voidable contracts as opposed to void contracts; i.e., contracts that do not exist. Other issues relating to void and voidable contracts go beyond the scope of this text and legal advice is strongly recommended.

CAPACITY OF THE PARTIES

Parties to a contract must, at the time when the contract is made, have the legal **capacity** to make the contract.

Persons

Capacity

The legal ability to enter into an enforceable contract.

While contractual promises are enforceable against anyone having legal capacity, some persons are deemed by law as either incapable of contracting or having only limited capacity to contract. In cases involving limited capacity, the contract is usually considered voidable; that is, the contract is valid until the individual goes to court to void it. As long as the person of limited capacity allows the contract to exist, it may not be voided. Some examples of those with limited capacity to enter a contract include:

- mentally incompetent persons (those having diminished mental capacity);
- intoxicated persons (incapable of understanding the nature of a contract by virtue of excessive use of drugs or chemicals);
- illiterates (unable to read or write); and
- minors (those under the age of majority).

MENTAL INCOMPETENCE

For purposes of parties to a contract, any person declared to be mentally incompetent is incapable of contracting. Any representation agreement or agreement of purchase and sale entered into by such a person for the purchase, sale, exchange or other disposition of property is voidable. If a person does not declare his/her mental incompetency and the other party knows of this mental incompetency, then the contract may be voidable by the undeclared mentally incompetent person. Expert advice is required on such matters.

INTOXICATED PERSONS

Under contract law, two conditions must generally exist in order that a buyer or seller can avoid a contract based on the fact that he or she was intoxicated. First, the individual must have been so inebriated when the contract was signed that he or she did not understand what was taking place. Second, the condition of that party must be known to the other party to the contract. If these two conditions are satisfied, then such a contract would be considered to be voidable.

ILLITERATE

An **illiterate** is a person who is unable to read or write. In terms of a contract, the question about an illiterate person and whether the contract is binding rests on whether the person knew what was being signed (a rule known as *non est factum*).

Illiterate

Unable to read or write.

EXAMPLE   *The Main Street Offer*

Buyer Jones, having practically no knowledge of reading or writing, inspected a property on Main Street with his wife and daughter. The salesperson was unaware of the buyer's limitations as he was able to converse freely on a wide range of topics, particularly concerning house construction and design.

The salesperson drafted an agreement based on instructions from the buyer and delivered it for signature. Once signed by Jones (he was capable of affixing his signature only), the agreement/contract was accepted by the sellers. However, only two days before closing, Jones refused to close, arguing that he was unable to read or write and, therefore, the contract was not binding.

While the ultimate decision by a court concerning Jones' illiteracy would depend on circumstances, several arguments can be put forth against his claim. Jones displayed a working knowledge of houses and was capable of carrying on a full and complete discussion with the salesperson. His family was present to assist (assuming they were literate) and, lastly, he provided the salesperson with details of how the offer was to be drafted.

MINOR

A **minor** is a person in Ontario who is under the age of legal competence (age of majority). Simply put, all contracts with minors for the sale or purchase of land are generally voidable, sometimes void and not usually considered valid and binding on the minor.

In the case of a voidable contract, the minor would be entitled to avoid the contract at any time until a reasonable time after age of majority. However, if the contract is ratified after majority, the right to avoid it generally disappears. Avoidance is the privilege of the minor and the other side is bound until the minor repudiates the contract.

Minor

A person who is under the age of legal competence.

- All contracts of minors for the purchase or sale of land are voidable by the minor. It is immaterial whether or not the minor has purported to be over the age of majority. In rare circumstances the court could hold that a reasonable purchase of a home was a necessity and a contract for such was binding on the minor.

- A minor may avoid a contract made during the age of minority for a reasonable time after majority, providing that nothing occurs after majority that might be deemed to be ratification of the contract, such as making an additional deposit or payment.

- The contract is binding upon the other party until avoided by the minor, but it is doubtful if the minor can obtain specific performance unless the other party has received all the benefits given under the contract.

- Should the minor avoid the contract, any benefits obtained must be returned, but it is not clear whether this must be done at the time of avoidance.

- The minor, in the absence of any fraud by the other side, cannot recover any payment made upon the contract.

- If the contract contains a penalty or is otherwise to the disadvantage of the minor, it is probably void. In that case, the minor can always recover payments that have been made, at least if no consideration has been received under the contract.

Literally translated as *it is not his deed*, the phrase identifies the legal rule that a person who was induced innocently or fraudulently by another to sign a written document, which is fundamentally different from that which he/she contemplated, is not bound by that document. The document is invalid on the grounds that the mind of the signer did not accompany the signature. He/she never intended to sign and, therefore, in contemplation of the law, the individual never did sign the document to which his/her name is appended.

Non est factum cannot be pleaded where a person misunderstands something that he/she intended to sign. If a person believes that the contract says one thing, but does not read it and then finds out that the contract says something else, he/she has no defence. In this situation, the person has simply been negligent in not reading the contract. Similarly, a blind or illiterate person, who knows the general nature and effect of the contract, would be bound by it unless the contract was falsely read to the individual or it was not read when he/she requested that it be.

From a real estate perspective, where a person is induced by the fraud of another to sign a written document, such as a representation agreement, agreement of purchase and sale, amendment or notice, which is materially or fundamentally different from that which was expected, the person signing may successfully plead that the document is not valid. Pleading of non est factum in regards to a contract is not a simple matter and expert legal advice should be obtained.

EXAMPLE

Buyer Jones signed an agreement to buy a lot on Main Street owned by Smith. He intended to build a new home. At time of inspection and signing of the agreement, Smith was not involved, but rather another person representing Smith.

Smith ultimately discovered that the individual representing his interests had done so fraudulently and without proper authority. As a result, Smith argued successfully that the agreement was non est factum and he was not bound in any way by that agreement.

Non Est Factum

A person is not bound by a fraudulent contract that he or she unwittingly entered into.

Corporation

A corporation usually has the rights, powers and privileges to enter into contracts concerning the purchase and sale of real property, unless specific restrictions are located in the articles of incorporation or the corporation has not enacted empowering provisions in its by-laws.

A corporation can be described as a business entity created by statute law and established by articles of incorporation. Corporations vary from small *privately-held* operations to large *offering* or *public* companies that actively trade shares in the marketplace. Two important cautions are necessary concerning corporations involved in acquisition or disposition of real estate. First, does the corporation exist and secondly, does it have the right to enter into such contracts?

Partnership

A partnership exists when two or more individuals or entities pool their personal and financial resources to carry on a business with the view to profit. In a partnership, any partner may bind the other partners in a transaction during the ordinary course of business, as all partners are viewed as agents of the business.

Condominium/Co-operative

Condominium corporations and co-operatives are permitted to enter into contracts for the purchase and sale of real property in line with incorporation documents or statutory regulations limiting the scope of such organizations.

Non-Profit Organization

Non-profit organizations have the rights, powers and privileges to enter into contracts for the purchase and sale of real property. For example, incorporation documents of a real estate board often specifically mention the right to acquire and dispose of real estate.

LAWFUL OBJECT

Lawful object can be broadly defined as *within the bounds of the law*. If the object of the contract is illegal by statute or common law, the contract will be void and **unenforceable** in the courts. For example, a contract would not be considered lawful if the acquisition involved criminal activity or was a direct violation of competition policy (*Competition Act*) or deliberate evasion of taxes (*Income Tax Act*). In such instances, the contract would be totally void. Examples of illegality or no lawful object would include contracts:

> *Unenforceable*
> That which cannot be imposed; e.g., not enforceable by the court.

- contrary to public policy or good morals;
- injurious or prejudicial to the safety of the state or to the public service;
- tending to pervert justice or abuse the legal process;
- in restraint of trade such as price fixing;
- in restraint of personal liberty or marriage; and
- for the commission of a criminal offence or civil wrong, or relating to gambling or wagering (unless authorized by means of provincial statutes).

Often, buyers and sellers believe that a sale made on a Sunday is illegal and void. The Supreme Court of Canada held that the particular section of the *Lord's Day Act* relating to this issue was unconstitutional in view of the Canadian Charter of Rights and Freedoms.

EXAMPLE   *Lawful Object*

The showing on Smith's property was proceeding smoothly. Salesperson Ward had just completed touring the upper floors with Buyer Jones and was currently viewing the main floor rooms. Smith, while patiently following the salesperson and buyer, was frequently excusing himself to answer incoming telephone calls on a cellular phone. When reaching the basement, the salesperson discovered a flurry of activity. Instead of the traditional family room, the area was buzzing with activity. A full off-track betting operation unfolded before his eyes. The seller, noticing the salesperson's look of amazement, simply turned to the buyer and said:

> *Don't worry, we've had this operation going for two years. If you want to make some big money, why not join in. We'll continue to rent the basement. Just get Ward to put in an appropriate clause in the agreement.*

Ward is now contemplating an unlawful act that affects the lawful object of the contract.

CONSIDERATION

The element of consideration is what each party receives or is to receive in exchange for promises to act in a certain manner and is something of value that is given by a promisee to a promisor to make the promise binding. The law will not enforce a purely gratuitous promise. The essence of a valid, binding contract is the idea of a bargain between the parties. The bargain is the **consideration** of a contract and may consist of an act in return for an act, a promise in return for a promise or an act in return for a promise. As a result, each side receives something from the other. In real estate transactions, consideration usually takes the form of a promise from the seller to sell in return for a sum of money to be received from the buyer. Consideration is best viewed in terms of the following three headings.

> **Consideration**
>
> Something given by one party to another to make a contract binding and viewed as one of six elements required in a legally binding agreement.

Value

Value is what either party receives of some worth. Interestingly, the court does not assess the adequacy of this value, but only its existence. Sometimes, registrants misunderstand the concept of valuable consideration. This does not mean that the consideration given has some extraordinary worth associated with it.

However, if the consideration was so minimal as to make the contract one-sided, the courts might act based on the unconscionability of the agreement. Further, the court might review the adequacy of the consideration if undue influence, fraud, duress or misrepresentation exists.

Lawful

The consideration under the contract must be lawful. If the buyer and seller knowingly agree to transact business based on stolen money or goods, the contract does not have lawful consideration.

Past Consideration

To quote an old phrase: *Old consideration is no consideration.* For example, the buyer enters into an agreement to purchase a cottage for $85,000. Subsequent to that agreement, the seller mentions that he will include the boat. No documentation is prepared and no consideration is given. At closing, the boat has been removed by the seller. As consideration does not exist and past consideration ($85,000) did not include the boat, the buyer does not have an enforceable contract concerning the boat.

Using A Seal   FOCUS

A contract can be made binding without consideration if a seal is used. Where a promise is made under seal, no consideration is required since the law presumes the act of sealing replaces consideration. Therefore, in the case of an agreement involving real estate, if legal seals are affixed at the time of signing, no consideration is required. This is only valid if the parties are clearly aware of the legal effect that a seal has on the contract.

The ancient method of sealing by wax and swearing a solemn oath has been replaced in modern legal practice by a variety of methods to indicate that the document has been signed under seal. Generally, the courts will now accept anything from red wafers to preprinted or hand written seals as long as it is clear the parties signing knew, or were directed to the fact, that they were signing under seal.

While, in many instances, the corporate seal is unnecessary for signing documents, any document signed on behalf of a company under its corporate seal and indicating the authority of the person signing by inserting that person's position above the signature would be good business practice. If a corporate seal is not used, the following words should be used:

I have the authority to bind the corporation.

The act of placing a mark or symbol on a document is evidence and assurance of the intent to carry out promises contained therein. A sealed document provides added confirmation of intent of the parties to perform a contract. Under old conveyancing law, an official seal was often used as a substitute for consideration. Where a promise is made under seal, no consideration is required since the law presumes that the solemn act of sealing replaces consideration.

THE REAL ESTATE TRANSACTION—GENERAL

OFFER AND ACCEPTANCE (MUTUAL AGREEMENT)

A contract is formed when the offer (made by the offeror) is accepted by the other party (the offeree). The following items are general rules concerning basic requirements for **offer and acceptance:**

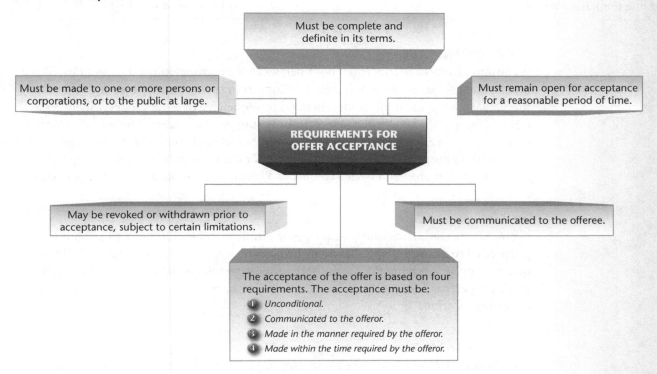

Must be complete and definite in its terms.

Must be made to one or more persons or corporations, or to the public at large.

Must remain open for acceptance for a reasonable period of time.

REQUIREMENTS FOR OFFER ACCEPTANCE

May be revoked or withdrawn prior to acceptance, subject to certain limitations.

Must be communicated to the offeree.

The acceptance of the offer is based on four requirements. The acceptance must be:
1. *Unconditional.*
2. *Communicated to the offeror.*
3. *Made in the manner required by the offeror.*
4. *Made within the time required by the offeror.*

Where the communication of acceptance is permitted by mail, telegram or fax, such acceptance is deemed to be completed upon the letter having been mailed, the telegram sent or the fax transmitted. The contract is binding even if the letter, telegram or fax is not received. Further, if an offer is made in the form of a promise upon the performance of a future act, the process of carrying out that act can constitute acceptance.

GENUINE INTENTION

The agreement must have **genuine intention** and give more than the outward appearance of a contract. In other words, one of the parties may have been induced to enter into the agreement by improper means and the document does not express what was intended. Inducements by improper means are caused by four different circumstances.

Mistake

The word *mistake*, in legal terms as it applies to real estate contracts, has a narrow meaning. Not every mistake or simple error affects a contract and is considered a legal mistake of fact. The law does not simply declare a contract void simply because one or other of the parties makes a mistake. Only certain types of mistakes give rise to a remedy. Obviously, the determination of a mistake and its impact on a contract is a legal issue and appropriate advice should be obtained.

As a guideline for registrants, mistakes can be grouped under the following three common headings.

COMMON MISTAKE	MUTUAL MISTAKE	UNILATERAL MISTAKE
Both parties make the same mistake; that is, each is mistaken about some underlying fundamental fact.	The parties misunderstand each other and are at cross purposes.	One of the parties is mistaken concerning a fundamental character of the contract.

COMMON MISTAKE

A common mistake occurs when both parties to the contract know the intention of the other, accept it, but are somehow mistaken concerning some underlying material or fundamental fact. As an example, both seller and buyer believe that the property includes a right-of-way to the beach, but in fact nothing supports this belief. The buyer and seller enter into an agreement/contract that, among other terms, describes a specific right-of-way along with appropriate measurements. The error does not in fact create an easement or any beneficial interest and is viewed only as a common mistake between the parties.

MUTUAL MISTAKE

A mutual mistake arises when the parties misunderstand each other and are at cross purposes. For example, the seller owns two lots on opposite sides of a lake. The buyer believes he/she is buying the south shore property, while the seller believes the north shore property is being sold. The parties would be agreeing based on a mutual mistake regarding location.

UNILATERAL MISTAKE

A unilateral mistake occurs when one party is mistaken and the other party knows of this mistake concerning a fundamental aspect of a contract. As an example, the buyer believes that the lot is approximately one acre in size and the seller is clearly aware of this mistaken belief and does not make the buyer aware of the situation. The buyer then proceeds with the purchase based on the mistaken fact.

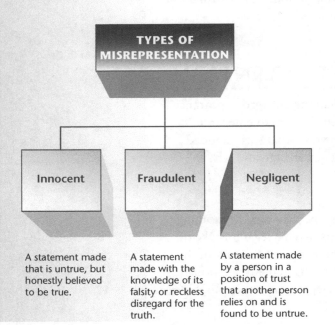

Misrepresentation

A representation may be defined as a statement or assertion made by one party to the other, before or at the time of contracting, regarding some existing fact matter or circumstance affecting the contract or its object. Simply put, **misrepresentation** is a false statement of fact. Misrepresentations are viewed as innocent, fraudulent or negligent.

Distinguishing between a representation and a mere exaggeration or statement of intention or opinion can be difficult. The statement *"this is the best deal in town"* may be treated as an exaggeration, not giving rise to legal rights, although it might be false or misleading pursuant to the *Competition Act*. If, however, a specific statement is made to the effect that a property can be put to a certain type of use, this statement is a representation. If proven false, a misrepresentation has been made.

Misrepresentation is a complicated area of law that is usually categorized as innocent, fraudulent or negligent. The following is provided as a general guideline only.

INNOCENT MISREPRESENTATION

An innocent misrepresentation is a statement by one party of a material fact that is untrue, but is honestly believed to be true. If the victim of misrepresentation is induced into a contract based on such a statement, he/she may refuse to complete the contract, attempt to have it set aside and attempt to recover anything paid or delivered under it. He/she can also defend any action brought against him/her under the contract, but as a general rule cannot recover **damages** if the misrepresentation was innocent.

> **EXAMPLES**   *Innocent Misrepresentation*
>
> *Example 1*
>
> Seller Smith is offering his home for sale through the local real estate board's MLS® service. A buyer, upon inspecting the property, asks if the nearby school offers grades K–8. The seller, unable to reach the school, calls a neighbour and confirms that fact. The buyer relies upon this statement and purchases the property only to discover that both his children could not attend this school, but would have to travel five miles by bus. The school now provides only junior grades K–4. He refuses to close the transaction arguing that a misrepresentation, no matter how innocent, has occurred.
>
> . . . .
>
> *Example 2*
>
> Salesperson Lee, when asked if the basement had any leakage, informed the buyer that the seller had clearly stated to him at the time of listing that there were no leakage problems whatsoever in the basement area. The salesperson did, however, suggest to the buyer that he could place a condition in the offer or require a warranty from the seller regarding his concern. The buyer elected to place a warranty in the agreement. Following closing, water seepage occurred in the property. Salesperson Lee had innocently misrepresented this situation, based on what he believed were sincere, honest representations made by the seller.

FRAUDULENT MISREPRESENTATION

A fraudulent misrepresentation has three elements:

- The misrepresentation must be made with the knowledge of its falsity or with reckless disregard for its truth on the part of the person making it.
- The purpose must have been to induce the other party to enter a contract.
- The misrepresentation must have been acted on to the other party's prejudice.

Where such **fraud** exists, the party deceived may resist enforcement of the contract and that party has the right to recover damages for deceit.

A principal is liable for misrepresentations made by his agent, if made with express or implied authority. Authority will be implied where the misrepresentation is made in the course of and within the scope of, duties of the agent; e.g., when showing the property.

The owner may be liable for representations about the property made by the broker or sales representative. With fraudulent misrepresentation made by an agent, both the person making it and the principal will be liable for damages.

Fraud

A false representation of fact knowingly made by an individual that induces another person to act upon the representation.

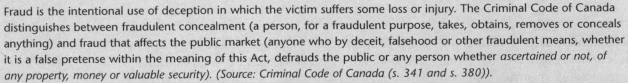

NEGLIGENT MISREPRESENTATION

If there is a special relationship between the parties and a misrepresentation is made negligently, then the person who is misled will have an action for damages. When it is clear that the statement was made with intention that it be relied on and that the person did rely on it, then a claim for damages may arise. This could occur in situations where the buyer has relied on a real estate salesperson, who is agent for the seller. For example, the agent may have misrepresented the seller's financial statements when marketing the seller's business to a buyer.

An agent has also been held liable for negligent misrepresentation as to the quantity of property included in a transaction, for failing to confirm information in a listing and making wrongful representations of the property carrying costs, knowing that the buyer was relying on his/her expertise and advice. It is negligent to misrepresent that the property may be used for a specific purpose if, in fact, that use may be illegal under the zoning by-laws of that municipality. Appraisers have been held responsible for inaccuracies in their reports that were relied upon by lenders. In all these situations an assumption is made that care, as well as honesty, is demanded.

EXAMPLES *Negligent Misrepresentation*

Example 1

A mortgagee employed an appraiser to appraise a property for mortgage loan purposes. The appraiser relied on statements of the mortgagor and gave a high value based on the property having been approved for a subdivision. Such approval had not been given. A mortgage was subsequently registered, a default occurred and a deficiency also arose on a subsequent sale. The court held that the appraiser was liable to the mortgagee for the deficiency for failing to make enquiries that a reasonable, careful and prudent appraiser would have made.

Example 2

Salesperson Lee listed a two-storey home backing onto a new housing development. When securing the listing, the seller admitted that he could not locate the rear boundary of the property. To complicate matters, no recent survey existed. Lee showed the property to a prospective buyer. When asked about the size of the property, Lee confidently pointed to two iron bars at the extreme rear left and right corners of the lot, then paced off the distance and informed the buyer that the depth was around 250 feet.

Based on this representation, the buyer bought the property, only to discover that the two survey pins related to the development area and not to the property. In fact, the lot had a depth of 150 feet. The buyer sued the brokerage and the seller for negligent misrepresentation arguing that the salesperson owed a duty of care in providing information that misled and injured the buyer.

NEGLIGENT MISREPRESENTATION AND TORT LIABILITY

As previously discussed, a client can sue for damages if a breach of a promise in a contract occurs and resulting in harm or loss. However, additional liability arises given the duty of care imposed on professionals when providing advice. In other words, a person acting in a professional capacity has certain duties that extend beyond the contractual relationship. In other words, tort liability can arise given a breach of duty *other than under a contract.*

The most common **tort** is that of negligence. A negligent misrepresentation can result in a common law action for damages. The primary role of tort law is to compensate individuals for wrongs endured, not to punish the offender. While the most common tort involves negligence, others include deceit or fraudulent misrepresentation, invasion of privacy, false imprisonment, malicious prosecution and defamation (i.e., libel and slander).

> **Tort**
>
> A breach of duty involving a civil wrong (other than a breach of contract) that can lead to common law action for damages.

Special Relationships

Any person in a special relationship of trust can incur tort liability, even if the services performed were free of charge. An agreement to provide professional services to a client contains a promise, whether stated or not, to perform those services with due care. A duty of care is owed to both clients and customers. In the case of clients, this duty extends to all activities performed on behalf of the client. For customers, the duty of care is limited to the giving of information, responding to questions and doing anything (i.e., performing functions) that the salesperson has agreed to for the customer.

Complexities

Tort liability is a growing area of law given today's increasingly complex society and heavy reliance on real estate as well as other professionals. As such, instances can arise where the injury is not only addressed from a criminal law perspective, but also from a tort law. For example, an individual causing a car accident may not only face criminal charges arising from his or her actions, but also a lawsuit from the injured parties. In real estate brokerage, a brokerage or its representatives may misrepresent key facts about a property that results not only in legal action for injury caused to an innocent party (i.e., the customer), but also regulatory sanctions under REBBA 2002 taken by the Real Estate Council of Ontario.

Duty of Care—Watch What You Say!   CAUTION

Real estate negotiations were never the same after May 28th, 1963. That day represented a legal benchmark for those providing information and advice. The Hedley Byrne v. Heller case (Hedley Byrne & Co Ltd v. Heller & Partners Ltd. [1964] AC 465) had progressed through complex, time-consuming appeals in England, ultimately leading to the House of Lords. The final judgment reverberated across the ocean, substantively impacting how registrants in Canada, as well as anyone in a position of trust, must conduct themselves.

Canadian Courts have refined, but always reaffirmed, the essentials of Hedley Byrne. A representation (written or spoken), no matter how honestly provided, can give rise to action for damages, apart from any contract or fiduciary relationship. Simply put, a duty of care is implied when:

- one party seeks information from another who has special skills;
- that party trusts the person to exercise due care; and
- the other party giving the advice knows or ought to know that reliance is being placed on such advice.

If the person receiving such information suffers economic loss, damages can result due to negligent misrepresentation.

Hedley Byrne, along with many other legal and ethical considerations guide today's registrant in the complex world of representing others, performing agency duties and negotiating contracts. Seasoned brokers and salespersons go about daily activities helping thousands of consumers achieve personal goals and dreams with the proven benchmarks of knowledge and competence. After all, the essence of professionalism is not in seeking a destination, but rather in continuously pursuing the journey.

Duress or Undue Influence

Duress involves the threat of violence, force or pressure to coerce a person into an action against his or her will. Duress occurs when a person does not act with his/her free will, but instead through fear of personal suffering.

> **EXAMPLE**   *Duress*
>
> Smith is attempting to sell his vacant property to Jones, an adjacent neighbour. While the discussion has centred on verbal promises, Smith is getting anxious and wants to put the agreement on paper, but Jones is hesitant. Smith, in a bout of anger, tells Jones that if the sale doesn't go through, he will contaminate the property and ultimately affect Jones' water supply. While uncertain whether or not Smith's threat is real, Jones elects to sign an agreement for fear that Smith's actions will affect his land value and ability to use the property. Smith is exerting duress on Jones and the contract may be voidable.

Undue influence is the improper use of one person's power over another to induce that person into a contract. Following are examples that might fall under undue influence.

- One party is knowledgeable and experienced while the other is ill-informed and inexperienced.
- A gift is made by a child to an adult, guardian or ward; a beneficiary to a trustee; a patient to a doctor; a person to a spiritual advisor; or, a client to a solicitor.
- A real estate salesperson purchases property from his/her client.

The person appearing to have exerted undue influence must prove that the transaction was reasonable and fair and that no advantage was gained due to his/her position. The fact that the person claiming undue influence received independent legal advice or valuation of a property is valid to establish that a reasonable transaction occurred.

Failure to Disclose

The non-disclosure of *material* latent defects might invalidate a contract. A latent defect is generally described as a physical deficiency or defect not readily observable through reasonable vigilance by the person inspecting a property. A material latent defect is one that is judged material to enjoyment of the property and would include defects that:

- render the property dangerous or potentially dangerous to the occupants;
- render the property unfit for habitation;
- render the property unfit for the purpose for which the buyer is acquiring it where the buyer has made this purpose known to the seller or broker;
- concern local authority and similar notices received by the seller that affect the property; or
- concern the lack of appropriate municipal building and other permits.

Source: William Foster, *Agency Law and Real Estate Brokerage: Current Issues*, (McGill University, January 2003).

A buyer might not have entered into the contract had he/she been aware of the defect. An example could be the presence of ground contamination given a prior owner's use and spillage/seepage of hazardous products.

A material latent defect should be clearly differentiated from a patent defect. A patent defect is readily observable assuming reasonable diligence. However, caution is advised given that what is or is not a patent defect can depend on the specific individual conducting the inspection. As a general guideline, the brokerage and its representatives are not required to disclose patent defects.

When discussing patent and latent defects, registrants are reminded that a real estate brokerage and its representatives are required to make full disclosure of all factors that would impact the *client* in his or her decision-making process. However, brokerages do not owe this general obligation of disclosure to *customers*. The obligation to customers extends only to material latent defects, not patent defects or other latent defects.

DEFINITE AND CLEAR

The terms of an agreement must be definite and clear and if the essential terms have not been agreed upon, a binding contract does not exist. However, this does not mean that the terms have to be decided. A term of a contract can be established through arbitration by a third party.

Some terms of a contract will, if necessary, be implied by law. A contract in which no date was specified for possession might be held to be invalid for lack of certainty, particularly if the phrase *time is of the essence* is contained in the agreement. If the terms, conditions and other provisions of the agreement establish with reasonable certainty that the parties intended possession to occur within reasonable time limits, then the court might interpret the contract so as to give effect to the intent of the parties as determined from the additional circumstances.

A frequent cause of uncertainty is the agreement to negotiate some time in the future. A sale at a price to be fixed by arbitration through a third party is one thing, but a sale at a price to be fixed by subsequent negotiations between seller and buyer is not a concluded contract until these negotiations have resulted in an agreed price. This problem frequently arises with a right to renew a lease or with a right given to a tenant to purchase property during or at the end of a lease. If the rent or price is simply left to be agreed upon, no agreement exists.

In summary, if a vital and material condition of the contract is undetermined, no contract exists, but merely an undertaking to seek a contract at a future time.

BREACH

A breach involves a failure to fulfill an obligation under a contract. Breach of a contract, by one of the parties, results in the imposition of a new obligation in place of the broken one by conferring a right of legal action on the party injured by the breach. A breach may discharge the injured party from further obligations to perform his/her side of the bargain. Breach may occur through an express refusal to perform the contract, making it impossible to perform through one's own act or through the failure to perform.

If a breach goes to the root of a contract, the injured party has the option to either accept the breach and treat himself/herself as relieved or discharged from performance or to treat the contract as subsisting and, if available, seek other remedies such as specific performance. If the breach does not go to the root of the contract, it will give rise only to a right of the other party to sue for damages, not to an option to discharge the contract.

If there are several promises, only some of which are broken or if there is only a partial failure to perform or complete the contract, a question may arise as to whether the other party can put an end to the contract or sue for damages. The answer will depend on the expressed or implied intention of the parties and whether the breach was substantial enough to go to the root of the contract.

> **EXAMPLE**   *The Unsold Home*
>
> Despite warnings from his real estate brokerage and lawyer, Buyer Jones insisted that the salesperson present an unconditional offer on a large home owned by Smith. Jones was confident that his present home would sell before the July closing of the new residence. By July, Jones was unable to sell his home and was declined interim financing to close the purchase. Smith sued for breach of contract and received damages to compensate for losses incurred in placing the property back on the market to secure another buyer.

Remedies

Five remedies are available in relation to a breach of contract involving real property.

RESCISSION

Rescission

Setting aside a contract.

Rescission involves the revocation or cancellation of a contract and that contract is then set aside; e.g., the buyer requests the court to set aside a contract because the builder has encountered financial difficulties, has only begun renovation work and is apparently unable to complete the job.

DAMAGES

Damages involve compensation for losses incurred. The most common remedy is monetary damages awarded by a court to recompense an injured party for a loss suffered by reason of a breach. Every breach gives rise to a right to this remedy and the measure of damages recoverable is the amount that may fairly and reasonably be considered either:

- Arising naturally, (i.e., according to the usual course of events occurring from such breach of contract itself); or
- As may reasonably be supposed to have been in the contemplation of the parties at the time the contract was made.

Damages are given as financial compensation and not as a punishment for the breach or for the motive or manner of the breach and so the plaintiff in a damage action must prove the actual amount of the damages. The plaintiff also has a duty to mitigate those damages by taking any reasonable steps available following the breach in order to reduce the extent of the loss.

> **EXAMPLE**   *Insufficient Funds*
>
> Seller Smith sells his property unconditionally and Buyer Jones refuses to close due to insufficient funds. Smith places the property back on the market to find a new buyer. The damages normally sought would include the cost of re-marketing and disposing of the property, incidental costs incurred by the seller (e.g., cost of borrowing funds if a subsequent purchase was affected), any loss incurred if the property sold at a lesser price than originally agreed to with Jones, and a sum of money for inconvenience and related matters.

QUANTUM MERUIT

Quantum meruit is a determination by the courts of a reasonable sum of money for work or services performed. If a contract has been discharged by breach after the injured party has done part but not all of what was promised under the contract, that person is entitled to the reasonable value (**quantum meruit**) of what was done from the party who committed the breach.

> **EXAMPLE**   *The Property Management Contract*
>
> ABC Realty Inc. enters into an exclusive, two-year agreement to manage a building with a contract where compensation is received semi-annually for units rented during the preceding six-month period. Owner Smith breaches the contract eight months into the contract period and refuses to pay for ten units rented during the first six-month period. ABC Realty Inc. is entitled to compensation for the work performed.

Quantum Meruit
Remedy for breach of contract based on court determination of work/services performed.

SPECIFIC PERFORMANCE

Specific performance takes the form of a decree or order of the court that the party in breach must do the specific thing that was promised. This is a discretionary remedy and not an absolute right. It will be awarded only where damages are not an adequate remedy, the contract is fair and just, and the injured party acts promptly and fairly in claiming a right to specific performance.

> **EXAMPLE**   *The Adjacent Land*
>
> Buyer Jones has a binding contract to purchase adjacent lands to his property for the purpose of expanding his business enterprise. The acquisition of this property is vital to meet local zoning regulations and environmental requirements. Prior to closing, Jones has already started expansion/renovation work in anticipation of the closing. The owner of the land refuses to close and lacks any substantive reason for doing so. Jones sues for specific performance.

Specific Performance
A court remedy for breach of contract compelling a defendant to carry out the terms of an agreement or contract.

An agreement to sell land is an example of the sort of contract that may be specifically enforceable, given the character of the particular land or its importance to the buyer. It may be that damages would be insufficient compensation.

INJUNCTION

Where the broken promise was to refrain from doing something, the court may award an injunction to restrain the offending party from doing that act. More simply put, an **injunction** is a court order stopping a party from continuing a breach.

The court will not compel the performance of a contract for personal service or employment, but may award an injunction to prevent the offending party from serving or performing elsewhere. The granting of an injunction, also a discretionary remedy, will be subject to the same conditions as in the case of specific performance.

A common case involves the breach of a covenant not to use the premises in a particular manner. A case might involve the tenant in a shopping plaza who agrees under the lease not to offer a specific service within the plaza and then proceeds to breach the agreement by offering that service. Another instance might involve a tenant in a large industrial building who has specifically agreed not to store, process or otherwise handle certain hazardous waste products on the premises and then breaches that agreement following occupancy.

Injunction
A judicial process or order requiring the person to whom it is directed to do, or refrain from doing, something.

In discussing remedies for breach of contract, the issues of costs and interest frequently arise. The successful litigant may be awarded interest on the amounts given. That interest may be calculated from the date of the breach and can vary depending on the prime rate. The court can also award costs that normally involve all disbursements paid to court officials and others involved in the litigation and a proportion of the costs that are payable to the litigant's own lawyer. The award will vary with the amount of the claim and the particular court jurisdiction. In rare situations, the judge can order full compensation of all costs.

TERMINATION

Five common methods to terminate a contract involving real property are detailed.

By Mutual Agreement	A contract may be discharged by mutual agreement of the parties that it shall no longer bind them, or that it shall be replaced by another contract in altered terms, which are substituted for discharge within itself.
By Performance	A contract may be discharged by performance or tender of performance of the contract, in which case the obligations of the performing party are fulfilled and the rights of the other party are satisfied.
By Impossibility of Performance	A contract may be discharged because of the impossibility of performance or frustration, whereby supervening and unanticipated circumstances arising after the making of the contract are held to absolve the parties from their obligations.
By Operation of Law	A contract may be discharged by operation of law; e.g., discharge from bankruptcy, alteration by one party without consent of the other.
By Breach	Breach or the breaking of the contract by one of the parties, results in the imposition of a new obligation by conferring a right of legal action on the party injured by the breach.

Contract Law—Summary

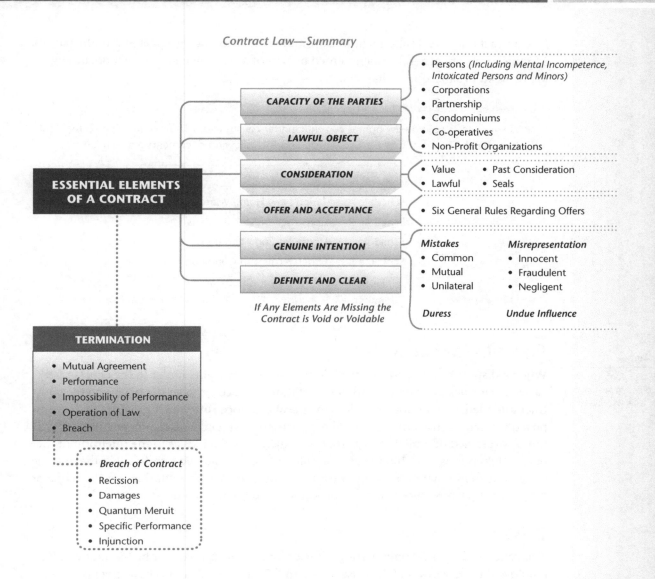

ESSENTIAL ELEMENTS OF A CONTRACT

CAPACITY OF THE PARTIES
- Persons (Including Mental Incompetence, Intoxicated Persons and Minors)
- Corporations
- Partnership
- Condominiums
- Co-operatives
- Non-Profit Organizations

LAWFUL OBJECT

CONSIDERATION
- Value   • Past Consideration
- Lawful   • Seals

OFFER AND ACCEPTANCE
- Six General Rules Regarding Offers

GENUINE INTENTION

DEFINITE AND CLEAR

If Any Elements Are Missing the Contract is Void or Voidable

Mistakes
- Common
- Mutual
- Unilateral

Misrepresentation
- Innocent
- Fraudulent
- Negligent

Duress   Undue Influence

TERMINATION
- Mutual Agreement
- Performance
- Impossibility of Performance
- Operation of Law
- Breach

Breach of Contract
- Recission
- Damages
- Quantum Meruit
- Specific Performance
- Injunction

CONTRACT DOCUMENTS

The term *contract documents* generally refers to preprinted agreement forms along with necessary schedules and addenda relating to that specific agreement. Contract documents apply to the agreement of purchase and sale as well as leases.

- In residential real estate, contract documents for the purchase of a new home might include items that substantiate the contract terms such as drawings, specifications, plans, schedules, descriptions and warranties. Typical documents attached to a new home purchase are illustrated.

- In commercial real estate, contract documents normally consist of the agreement/contract along with drawings, specifications, survey, buyer and seller covenants, conditions, additional contract terms and assumption of mortgage.

- With a lease, the documents would include the preprinted offer to lease and the layout of the premises, landlord's and tenant's work, conditions and additional details.

Contract documents also include any modifications following agreement of the parties. Modifications are generally documented by way of amendments. Contract documents are detailed in subsequent chapters.

EXAMPLE   *New Home Agreement*

ABC Realty Inc. is selling new homes currently under construction. To provide a complete package for the buyer, the brokerage is including the following documents and schedules.

> **Agreement of Purchase and Sale**
> Schedule A: Tarion New Home Warranty*
> Schedule B: Construction Specifications
> Schedule C: Upgrades and Alterations
> Schedule D: Other Terms and Conditions

*NOTE: Tarion New Home Warranty coverage is discussed in *The Residential Real Estate Transaction.*

Parol Evidence Rule

Parol Evidence Rule

A completed written contract can only be modified in writing, subject to certain legal exceptions.

When a dispute arises as to a contract's meaning or the rights under it, the courts apply varied legal rules of evidence and interpretation to discover what the parties to the contract intended. One important rule is the **parol evidence rule** which provides that a completed written contract may not be altered, varied or amended except in writing and may not be explained or added to by verbal agreement or evidence, as to the intention of the parties. Exceptions exist, but the general rule must be considered significant in the drafting of agreements so that every term, warranty, condition or representation on which one or other of the parties relies will be incorporated into the written document.

Privity

The general rule is that only parties to the contract can enforce it or be bound by it. If A employs B to do work on C's house in return for payment, A and B have certain rights against each other that can be enforced at law, but C has no legal rights against B for non-performance of the work because he/she is not a party to or privy to the contract between A and B. (C does have legal rights against A for non-performance of the work because of the contract between C and A.)

Similarly, a brokerage (or its representative) is only a witness to the signing of a contract for a property sale. Therefore, if a breach of the contract occurs, the seller can only sue the buyer and vice versa. The brokerage, acting on the seller's behalf, cannot be sued by either of the contracting parties under the terms of the contract since he/she is not privy to the contract.

However, the brokerage may be sued independent of the contract if he/she encouraged the seller or the buyer to enter into the contract by the provision of misleading information or as a consequence of negligence or error. Only the brokerage, not the salesperson, can sue the seller for a real estate commission as the salesperson is not a party to the contract—he/she is only representing the brokerage.

An assumed but invalid exception is the case of a contract entered into by a broker who makes it known to the other party that he/she was in fact acting on behalf of an undisclosed principal. The principal can step in and enforce the contract since, according to the law of agency, he/she was really a party to the contract and the broker (or agent) was a mere extension of the principal.

REPRESENTATION AGREEMENT

A representation agreement can be generally described as an oral or written agreement under which the owner appoints a real estate brokerage, for a designated period of time, to sell, lease or exchange a property based on the owner's stated terms and under which the owner agrees to pay the brokerage a commission. *Reminder:* REBBA 2002 does not require a signed representation agreement, but does require that the registrant prepare a written agreement for presentation to the prospective client.

Seller and Buyer Representation Agreements

A seller representation agreement is defined in REBBA 2002 as *an agreement between a brokerage and a seller and includes a listing agreement that is a representation agreement* (Code of Ethics, Subsec. 1(1)). The buyer representation agreement is defined as *a representation agreement between a brokerage and a buyer* (Code of Ethics, Subsec. 1(1)).

The representation agreement performs several basic functions. For example, the seller representation agreement establishes well-defined limitations on the brokerage's authority, provides detailed information regarding the property and assists when answering inquiries from prospective buyers. This representation agreement also provides the foundation for offer negotiations, the drafting of an agreement of purchase and sale and, if necessary, a mortgage application.

Seller and buyer representation agreement formats and wordings can vary, as no standardized form is used throughout Ontario. However, as with agreements of purchase and sale, the Ontario Real Estate Association's representation agreements (or variations thereof) are widely used by organized real estate.

Most seller representation agreements consist of two parts:

- The authority involves the appointment of the agent, disclosures, remuneration provisions and related matters.
- The data input form is used for detailed information on the property.

Buyer representation agreements are also fairly standardized with an authority granted to the brokerage to locate real property within a certain geographic location that meets the buyer's specifications. As with seller forms, various more or less standard clauses are included highlighting key considerations about topics such as commission arrangements, representation, multiple representation and customer service.

Accuracy and care in completing a representation agreement is crucial, not only for regulatory purposes, but also legal considerations. The representation agreement is a legal document and must always be prepared with due regard and consideration for its completeness and accuracy.

Types of Agreements

Three basic types of seller representation agreements (listing agreements) are found in Ontario.

OPEN	EXCLUSIVE	MLS®
Generally described as relatively loose verbal arrangements in which the owner gives one or more brokerages authority to find a buyer for the property. Occasionally, the owner may agree to the placing of the brokerages' signs on the property (more common with vacant land). The seller reserves the right to sell the property himself/herself and avoid any commission. The terms of an open representation arrangement must be committed to written form by the registrant, but in practice, most sellers who will not agree to an exclusive or MLS® arrangement, will also typically refuse to sign a written open agreement. Since most are verbal, they are usually avoided or at least very cautiously handled, by most real estate brokerages.	An exclusive representation agreement gives one brokerage the authority to offer a property for sale, lease or exchange, during a specified time period. The seller agrees to pay the listing brokerage a commission, even if he/she sells the property directly. A variety of exclusive representation agreements and data input forms (used for property particulars) exist in the marketplace.	An MLS® listing agreement is an exclusive agreement with an added marketing feature. The Multiple Listing Service® is operated by local real estate boards. A signed multiple listing agreement contains an authority from the seller permitting the listing brokerage to employ the services of co-operating brokerages who are members of the real estate board. The responsibility regarding promotion, negotiations and payment of commission to co-operating brokerages rests with the listing brokerage. An MLS® listing is always in writing. *Note:* ICX is the commercial counterpart of MLS®.

Buyer representation agreements can be generally grouped under the first two types described above (i.e., open and exclusive).

REBBA 2002 Requirements

The *Real Estate and Business Brokers Act, 2002* and *Regulations* include various requirements involving agreements for the purpose of trading in real estate (buyer and seller representation agreements). The Code of Ethics requires that such agreements are reduced to writing, signed by the brokerage and submitted to the seller or buyer for signature (Code of Ethics, Sec. 13 and 14).

The Code also requires that specific content be set out in written agreements for the purpose of trading in real estate (Code of Ethics, Sec. 11) and that copies of representation agreements be immediately given to the buyer or seller (Code of Ethics, Sec. 12). Disclosure requirements relating to buyer and seller representation agreements (including multiple representation scenarios) have been previously discussed in *Land, Structures and Real Estate Trading*.

AGREEMENT OF PURCHASE AND SALE

A contract for the sale of property in Ontario (i.e., an agreement of purchase and sale) must be in writing and signed by the parties in order to be enforceable. While no standard forms are mandated, the residential agreement of purchase and sale developed by the Ontario Real Estate Association (OREA Form 100) is widely used by organized real estate in the province.

This agreement of purchase and sale is analyzed later in the course, as are other agreements designed for other property types (e.g., condominium resale and co-operative). Commercial forms are also not standardized and registrants will encounter different formats and wordings than is the case with residential, particularly regarding specialized commercial transactions. Course materials focus on OREA commercial forms, as these are widely used in the marketplace.

Statute of Frauds

The *Statute of Frauds* provides that certain contracts, including real estate contracts, must be in writing to be enforceable at law.

> *No action shall be brought. . .upon any contract or sale of lands, tenements or heredita-ments, or any interest in or concerning them, unless the agreement upon which the action is brought, or some memorandum or note thereof is in writing and signed by the party to be charged therewith or some person thereunto lawfully authorized by the party. (Statute of Frauds, Sec. 4).*

The Statute of Frauds, although requiring written evidence of a contract for the sale of an interest in land, does not require that any particular form be used. More specifically, this statute prohibits the bringing of any actions under certain circumstances, including any contract or sale of lands, unless some memorandum or note thereof is in writing and signed by the party to be charged.

The Courts of Equity, however, have modified the strict reliance on this statute by the Doctrine of Part Performance. This doctrine applies to contracts of land that are not in writing, where one party has actually performed part of the bargain, so as to suggest very clearly the existence of a contract for land. In such instances, where the person will suffer a loss if the contract is not performed, the courts will enforce the agreement.

However, this part performance must be very clear (e.g., the building of a house on the land or renovating the property) and the plaintiff must clearly suffer loss if no contract exists. If the contract is ambiguous as to whether a sale or leasing of the land occurred under which the party renovated the premises, then the agreement may be unenforceable depending on the interpretation of the court given the evidence presented. As mentioned previously, organized real estate in Ontario uses standard preprinted agreements in the interest of accuracy and consistency.

Vendors and Purchasers Act

This statute sets out provisions that are deemed statutorily to be included in an agreement of purchase and sale involving the sale of lands. Under contract law, an agreement must be complete and describe accurately all essential terms. However, given that no standard form of agreement exists for the sale of land, certain provisions are obviously required and these are codified in the *Vendors and Purchasers Act.*

Every contract for the sale and purchase of land is deemed, *unless otherwise stipulated,* to include the following:

- The seller is not bound to produce any abstract of title, deed, copy of a deed or other evidence of title except as are in the seller's possession or control.
- The buyer shall search the title at the buyer's own expense and shall make any objections thereto in writing within 30 days from the making of the contract.
- The seller has 30 days in which to remove any objection made to the title, but if the seller is unable or unwilling to remove any objection that the buyer is not willing to waive, the seller may cancel the contract and return any deposit made, but is not otherwise liable to the buyer.

- Taxes, local improvements, insurance premiums, rents and interest shall be adjusted as at the date of closing.
- The conveyance shall be prepared by the seller and the mortgage, if any, by the buyer, the buyer shall bear the expense of registration of the transfer/deed and the seller shall bear the expense of the discharge of the mortgage, if any.
- The buyer is entitled to possession or the receipt of rents and profits upon the closing of the transaction.

A registrant who prepares an agreement does not rely on the provisions of the *Vendors and Purchasers Act* nor on any brief note or memorandum. He/she is bound to prepare a properly documented contract that satisfies legal requirements and fulfills the instructions of his/her principal. Registrants are also required to comply with the provisions of the *Real Estate and Business Brokers Act, 2002* and the Code of Ethics. If a broker or salesperson is a member of organized real estate in Canada, he/she must also comply with The Canadian Real Estate Association Code of Ethics and Standards of Business Practice.

REBBA 2002 Requirements

The *Real Estate and Business Brokers Act, 2002* and *Regulations* focus on registrant duties involving agreements for the conveyance of real estate (agreement of purchase and sale) and agreements for the purpose of trading in real estate (buyer and seller representation agreements).

In terms of agreements for conveyancing real estate, the Code of Ethics requires that registrants use their best efforts to ensure that such agreements are in writing and legible (Code, Sec. 27). Registrants must also use their best efforts to ensure that all parties to an agreement receive a copy as soon as practicably possible (Code, Sec. 28) and ensure that deposits and other documents relating to the agreement (e.g., notice removing conditions) be delivered (Code, Sec. 29).

REBBA 2002 also sets out requirements concerning the purchase and sale of a business, particularly concerning documents required before a binding agreement and selected written disclosure are made by the buyer. Sale of business requirements are discussed in *The Commercial Real Estate Transaction.*

The *Real Estate and Business Brokers Act, 2002* details regulatory requirements regarding the handling of documents (including the agreement of purchase and sale) when processing trades in the brokerage on behalf of buyers and sellers. Lastly, REBBA 2002 sets out various requirements concerning offer negotiations that are detailed in a subsequent chapter.

Electronic Contracts   FOCUS

The *Electronic Commerce Act, 2000* (ECA) allows contracts to be created and signed electronically. For real estate, these contracts have included seller and buyer representation agreements and, as of July 1, 2015, now include agreements of purchase and sale, and leases. The Act and its Regulations govern the creation, recording, transmission, and storage of contracts electronically.

Due to the critical nature of real estate contracts, registrants should seek guidance from their brokerage to ensure the proper procedures and appropriate software are used when using electronic agreements.

Contract Q & A

Registrants must be aware of essential contract elements when preparing agreements of purchase and sale. The following Q & A is an added perspective on capacity, consideration and offers.

Q Is 'capacity' a major issue for registrants in negotiating real estate contracts?

A Fortunately not. Most of us have the capacity to enter contracts. In fact, we do it every day. But, the law protects those who are not legally able to do so and registrants must exercise appropriate caution.

Minors are a good example. One would think that it's cut and dried; i.e., the contract is not enforceable as the party is under 18. But things can get complicated when the contract involves the necessities of life. Such a contract might be enforceable if it was clearly for that individual's benefit. The bottom line… if you think a minor is involved…get legal advice.

Mentally incapacitated persons are generally responsible for contracts involving necessities. Any other contract is binding unless it can be shown that the party was mentally incapacitated and the other person contracting knew it. If such is proven, the contract is voidable. A similar approach is taken in the case of an intoxicated person. If you suspect a capacity problem, get advice.

Q Why is consideration necessary?

A The concept of a bargain between parties is fundamental to any contract. Each party gets something from the other. Consideration is essential to make a contract enforceable.

Valuable consideration may consist of some right, interest, profit or benefit to one party, with forbearance, detriment, loss or responsibility by the other. In other words, the promise of one party is the price (i.e., consideration) for which the promise of another is given.

Q What guidelines exist concerning consideration?

A • Consideration must have some value whether it's funds, an act for an act or a promise for a promise. The courts do not assess the adequacy of that value. Whether or not the contract represents a good deal for the parties is somewhat academic.
 • If the consideration given contravenes the law, then the contract is unenforceable; e.g., if drug money is used to purchase a property.
 • Consideration must be executory; i.e., the promise to do, pay or give something is in the future. For example, the seller agrees to pay a commission when the house is sold. The contract is executory. When the house is sold, the contract is executed.

Q What exceptions apply regarding consideration?

A An important exception to consideration involves seals. The sealed contract provides a way to make enforceable contracts with no consideration (i.e., a promise without consideration).

Another use of the seal involves an offer held open for a time period and binding upon the party making the offer. Essentially, an offer made can be withdrawn by the party making the offer any time to the point of presentation. However, by using the seal, the promise is made binding as if consideration had been given.

Q What is NOT an offer?

A • If a seller says that he is thinking of selling and advises the broker accordingly, no offer is being made.
 • If a buyer asks a seller what price he expects from the house sale and the seller says $250,000, that statement is not an offer, but merely the giving of information in response to a request.
 • Placing a house for sale on the MLS® service is not an offer, but merely an invitation to the general public to make offers. The offer arises when the buyer elects to buy and submits an offer to the seller.

Q When is an offer terminated?

A Registrants should note that an offeror's irrevocable instruction in an agreement (i.e., a written statement that the offer is irrevocable by the offeror), signed under seal may not be withdrawn by that offeror. However, common law principles support the concept that an offeror (person making the offer) may withdraw the offer at any time prior to acceptance (if not under seal).

The law requires that the withdrawal be communicated to the offeree (person receiving the offer). For example, the buyer agrees to buy a home and submit an offer. The offer doesn't simply disappear because the buyer changes his or her mind. That fact must be communicated to the seller. Generally, notice of withdrawal brought to the offeree's attention is sufficient. If a written letter is sent, receipt of that letter is notice.

Contract Q & A

MARKET PERSPECTIVE

Q When is an offer rejected?

A In real estate, a buyer's offer is ended upon rejection of that offer by the seller. However, the buyer may revive the original offer, which could then be subsequently accepted by the seller.

Q What happens in a counter offer situation?

A If a seller counters a buyer's offer, that offer is valid and the buyer may accept such offer, for example:

- Buyer A submits offer which is not accepted by Seller B.
- Seller B makes a counter offer, which is accepted by Buyer A.
- Seller B's counter offer becomes a valid and enforceable contract.

In the marketplace, negotiations may involve several offers and counter offers. Procedures are detailed in later chapters.

Q When does an offer lapse?

A An offer lapses when not accepted within the time period provided for in that offer.

Q What constitutes acceptance of an offer?

A Acceptance must:

- *Correspond exactly with the terms of the offer.* However, if a qualifier is added (e.g., provided that my spouse consents), acceptance has not occurred.
- *Be communicated to the offeror.* In other words, such acceptance must be brought to his/her notice. Certain exceptions do apply. The buyer may waive his or her right to notice or specify how notice is deemed to have been received, e.g., when something is mailed and the date of mailing is deemed notice.
- *Be in the manner described.* For example, if acceptance can be made by mailed notice only, a faxed acceptance will not suffice.
- *Be made within the time limit set out in the offer.*

KNOWLEDGE INTEGRATION

Notables

- A contract is a binding agreement between two or more parties.

- Enforceable contracts have six essential elements which, if not fulfilled, render a contract void, voidable or unenforceable.

- If any essential elements are missing, the contract may be void or voidable.

- Capacity of the parties is an important contract element, particularly as it relates to persons.

- The contract element of genuine intention can be impacted by misunderstandings that can render contracts unenforceable. Most relate to misrepresentations, mistakes, fraud and duress.

- Registrants should be cautious in making representations. Negligent misrepresentations can arise from tort liability given special skills of the salesperson acting in a professional capacity.

- Five remedies are possible for a breach: rescission, damages, quantum meruit, specific performance and injunction.

- Contracts can be terminated in five ways: mutual agreement, performance, impossibility of performance, operation of law or breach.

- Privity and the parol evidence rule are important factors when analyzing contract documents.

- Seller representation agreements can be open, exclusive or MLS® (exclusive plus the added marketing feature of the Multiple Listing Service®).

- The agreement of purchase and sale is subject to regulatory provisions including those found in the *Statute of Frauds*, the *Vendors and Purchasers Act* and REBBA 2002.

- The *Statute of Frauds* requires that all real estate contracts, to be enforceable, must be in writing.

- The *Vendors and Purchasers Act* sets out terms which are implied in real estate contracts, unless otherwise specified.

- Representation agreements are subject to provisions set out in REBBA 2002.

Glossary

Capacity

Consideration

Contract

Damages

Fraud

Genuine Intention

Illiterate

Injunction

Lawful Object

Minor

Misrepresentation

Non Est Factum

Offer and Acceptance

Parol Evidence Rule

Quantum Meruit

Rescission

Specific Performance

Tort

Unenforceable

Void

Voidable

Strategic Thinking For Your Career

Questions are included to assist in developing your new career. No answers are provided.

1. How will I handle a situation in which a suspected minor comes to an open house or calls on an advertisement for a listed property?

2. Consideration is key to most real estate transactions. What is a reasonable deposit in the local marketplace, as a sign of good faith during negotiations?

3. What policies does my intended employing brokerage have regarding offer negotiations, counter offers and acceptance?

4. What happens if a seller knowingly misrepresents something about his/her property? How can I best protect both myself and the buyer client's interests?

Chapter Mini-Review

Solutions are located in the Appendix.

1. A void contract has no legal status.

   ◯ True   ◯ False

2. Mistakes are commonly grouped under three categories: common, mutual and bilateral.

   ◯ True   ◯ False

3. If consideration contravenes the law, then the contract is unenforceable.

   ◯ True   ◯ False

4. If a seller counters a buyer's offer, the original buyer's offer may still be accepted by the seller (despite the counter offer) if proper notice of his/her intent is given.

   ◯ True   ◯ False

5. Fraud not only destroys the contract, but also can give rise to damages.

   ◯ True   ◯ False

6. A contract cannot be binding without consideration.

   ◯ True   ◯ False

7. Innocent misrepresentation involves a statement by one party of a material fact that is known to be untrue.

   ◯ True   ◯ False

8. Various remedies are provided for a breach of contract including rescission, damages and specific performance.

   ◯ True   ◯ False

9. The court will assess both the existence and adequacy of consideration when a dispute arises concerning contract enforceability.

   ◯ True   ◯ False

10. Privity of contract refers to the legal concept that, generally, only parties to the contract can enforce it or be bound by it.

    ◯ True   ◯ False

11. The *Statute of Frauds* requires that all contracts involving real estate must be drafted on an agreement of purchase and sale approved by the Real Estate Council of Ontario.

    ◯ True   ◯ False

12. Tort liability is defined as a breach of duty involving a contract, such as an accepted agreement of purchase and sale.

   ○ True   ○ False

13. A contract can only be terminated by the mutual agreement of the parties.

   ○ True   ○ False

14. Non est factum can be pleaded by a person who misunderstands a contract but nevertheless signs it. However, such a pleading may not have merit if that individual was negligent in not reading the contract. Therefore, he or she has no real defence.

   ○ True   ○ False

15. The *Vendors and Purchasers Act* sets out provisions that are deemed statutorily to be included within an agreement of purchase and sale.

   ○ True   ○ False

16. A seller representation agreement is a standard form approved by the Real Estate Council of Ontario.

   ○ True   ○ False

17. Failure to disclose a material latent defect could invalidate a contract. A material latent defect is one that is readily observable to the casual observer.

   ○ True   ○ False

Active Learning Exercises

Solutions are located in the Appendix.

▣ Exercise 1   Contract Terms (Fill-in-the-Blanks)

Complete the following eight statements relating to contracts. Use the appropriate term from the list provided below.

unilateral mistake	mutual mistake	consideration
capacity of the parties	no consideration	mutual agreement
duress or undue influence	voidable	void
failure to disclose	damages	no lawful object
		rescission

1.1   Smith signs an agreement that amounts to price fixing, this contract has

   ....

1.2   The fact that parties must be legally capable of entering into contracts is

   referred to as ....

1.3   An agreement set aside by the court is referred to as

   ....

1.4 When an offended party can make a choice between performing or not performing a contract, the contract is said to be ....

1.5 When parties misunderstand each other and are at cross purposes when it comes to a contract, this situation is referred to as a

....

1.6 Compensation for losses arising from a breach of contract is referred to as

....

1.7 Complete the following phrase: Old consideration is

....

1.8 When a person does not act with free will, he/she is often said to be under

....

■ Exercise 2   Consideration

Identify whether consideration is present or not in the following situations.

2.1 Seller Smith pays $68,750 for home renovations to Builder Anderson.

◯ Present   ◯ Not Present

2.2 Seller Smith agrees not to open a pizza business to compete with Buyer Jones' newly acquired pizza business that was sold by Smith to Jones. In return for this agreement, Jones pays Smith $20,000.

◯ Present   ◯ Not Present

2.3 Assume Jones paid Smith $1.00 rather than the $20,000 in Question 2.2. Is consideration present or not present?

◯ Present   ◯ Not Present

2.4 Assume no money changed hands in Question 2.2, but the agreement was signed under seal. Is consideration present or not present?

◯ Present   ◯ Not Present

2.5 Seller Smith sells his home for $225,000 to Buyer Jones, but does not include any chattels. Subsequently, Jones and Smith agree that all recreation room furniture will be included, but do not sign an agreement to that effect. Is consideration present or not present regarding the furniture?

◯ Present   ◯ Not Present

2.6 Seller Smith sells his auto for $16,400 to Jones and agrees to be paid in shares from an illegal business venture in which Jones is involved.

◯ Present   ◯ Not Present

■ Exercise 3   Multiple Choice

3.1 Mutual agreement in a contract requires that there must be an offer, an acceptance and a communication of that acceptance. Which of the following is NOT a requirement of acceptance?

a. Unconditional.
b. Communicated by personal delivery to the offeror.
c. Made in the manner required by offeror.
d. Made within the time limit of the offeror.

3.2 Which of the following does NOT result in a lack of genuine intention during a contractual undertaking?

a. Duress.
b. Undue influence.
c. Mistake.
d. Specific Performance.

3.3 If a contract has been terminated by breach and the injured party has done part of what was promised, that individual is entitled to reasonable value for what has been done. Which of the following best describes this right?

a. Right to damages.
b. Right to specific performance.
c. Right to quantum meruit.
d. None of the above.

3.4 Which of the following is a correct statement regarding consideration?

a. Consideration is not an important element in contracting.
b. Consideration must be equal to what is received in return.
c. If a promise is made under seal, no consideration is necessary to make it binding.
d. Consideration must always be monetary.

3.5 Which of the following is NOT a correct statement?

   a. A minor's right to avoid a contract is extinguished immediately once he/she reaches the age of majority.

   b. Contracts with infants for the sale of land are generally voidable by the infant.

   c. Specific performance is a discretionary remedy for breach of contract and will not normally be granted if an award of damages would be adequate.

   d. An action for negligence can involve a circumstance in which a salesperson provides information to a customer and that individual relies on such information to his/her detriment.

3.6 A salesperson has a prospect interested in a property. The buyer notices water stains on the basement walls. Without any further investigation, the salesperson assures the buyer that there is no problem. After closing, the buyer discovers a major leakage problem that will prove costly to repair. How is the salesperson's representation best described?

   a. Innocent misrepresentation.

   b. Negligent misrepresentation.

   c. Fraudulent misrepresentation.

   d. Common mistake.

■ Exercise 4   Minors

Salesperson Lee of ABC Realty Inc. recently conducted an open house for his principal, Seller Smith. A young couple inspected the property and then made a subsequent appointment at the brokerage office. Several salespersons, following that visit, remarked that the couple looked barely out of their teens. Lee dismissed the comments and proceeded to obtain an offer which was subsequently accepted by Seller Smith. If the couple were in fact under 18, comment on the following:

4.1 Can the contract be enforced? Briefly support your answer with reference to contract law.

4.2 What would occur if either or both buyers turned 18 prior to closing? Be specific.

4.3 If the couple lied to Lee, saying that they were over 18, but in reality were minors, describe how this would or would not change your answer to 4.1.

▣ Exercise 5   Scenarios

5.1 An offer is presented to Seller Smith on his rental property. Smith and his son have never lived in the property. Smith accepts the offer but adds the words adjacent to his signature: *I accept the above offer subject to approval by my son.* The son does not agree with the price and an argument ensues that continues well past the irrevocable date. The buyer argues that, despite the disagreement, a valid contract exists because the offer was signed within the irrevocable period, the son was not on title and Smith's written words do not constitute a formal condition in the offer. Does a valid contract exist? Support your answer with reference to contract law.

5.2   Salesperson Garcia of ABC Realty Inc. presents an offer for $233,500 to Seller Smith who refuses the price but counters with a signback at $242,000. The counter offer has an irrevocable date to the buyer of 11:59 p.m. that same evening. Garcia returns to the buyer who ultimately agrees verbally at 11:55 p.m. to the counter offer. Garcia gets the buyer's initials on the agreement just after midnight. Is this a valid contract? Support your answer with reference to contract law.

5.3   Seller Smith receives an offer for $239,500 on his two-storey residence in Anycity. While anxious to sell, Smith wants to test the market. He countersigns the offer from Buyer Jones for $245,500 with an irrevocable date for the next day. Jones immediately rejects the counter offer. Smith, realizing that he may have lost the buyer, retracts the counter offer and signs the original agreement of purchase and sale at $239,500. Discuss whether Smith has a valid contract. Support your argument with specific reference to contract law.

CHAPTER 2

REBBA 2002 and the Real Estate Transaction

Introduction

Regulatory controls extend into all aspects of the real estate transaction, including adherence to the Code of Ethics. Representation and related issues involving the Code were introduced in *Land Structures and Real Estate Trading*. This chapter extends the discussion to Code requirements, as well as other regulatory provisions, from the point at which a representation agreement or service agreement is signed to the point of completing the transaction.

The chapter is divided into topic areas beginning with working with clients and progressing through sequential steps as the typical real estate transaction unfolds; i.e., dealing with others, advertising and promotion, showing properties and related disclosures, drafting an agreement of purchase and sale, negotiating and presenting offers, delivery of documents, handling deposits, understanding how trust accounts operate and, lastly, concluding the transaction.

Most key topics are highlighted with direct excerpts from the Code of Ethics and with practical examples involving both residential and commercial activities. Other regulatory requirements under REBBA 2002 are also referred to in the discussion, as the need arises to fully describe selected topics.

Learning Outcomes

At the conclusion of this chapter, students will be able to:

- Describe Code of Ethics requirements when providing services and offering opinions.
- Outline Code requirements when dealing with others, including other registrants.
- Identify specific advertising provisions in the Code that relate to false advertising/falsifying information, promises/inducements, registrant name, identifying property, parties and agreement particulars, inaccurate representations, and error, misrepresentation and fraud.
- Outline property-related disclosures when showing properties and discuss key compliance issues relating to seller property information statements and material facts.
- Discuss various ethical requirements regarding the drafting of agreements.
- Identify and discuss ethical requirements that impact the negotiating and presenting of offers including conveying offers, agreements relating to commission, handling competing offers, providing copies of agreements, delivery of deposits and documents, and informing the client of key steps taken when representing that client.
- Discuss the retention requirements for both successful and unsuccessful offers, including the potential retention of a summary document.
- Discuss deposit-handling procedures as set out in the Code, the Act and the General Regulation.
- Discuss the handling of funds placed in the trust account and the need to prepare a trade record sheet when concluding the transaction.

REBBA 2002: FROM LISTING TO SALE

REBBA 2002 addresses major stages in negotiations and elements of a transaction. For study purposes, this chapter includes summary details about key activities and obligations leading from the point at which the buyer or seller enters into a representation agreement to the conclusion of the sale. Numerous activities are involved in arriving at a successful real estate transaction that extends beyond the mere paperwork.

Registrants work with clients and customers, market and demonstrate property, respond to questions and perform other duties that advance the real estate buying and selling process. Topics are presented as they typically occur from point of listing and selling property to drafting of an agreement, final negotiations and ultimate completion of the transaction.

Requirements concerning seller and buyer representation agreements have already been covered in *Land, Structures and Real Estate Trading*.

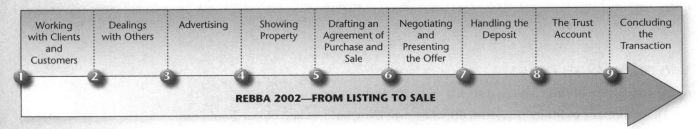

Working with Clients and Customers	Dealings with Others	Advertising	Showing Property	Drafting an Agreement of Purchase and Sale	Negotiating and Presenting the Offer	Handling the Deposit	The Trust Account	Concluding the Transaction
1	2	3	4	5	6	7	8	9

REBBA 2002—FROM LISTING TO SALE

WORKING WITH CLIENTS AND CUSTOMERS

Providing Services

Successful registrants work hard at making transactions happen. Activities begin long before an offer is made. The Code of Ethics provides important guidelines in that process. The Code requires that all registrants treat every person in the course of a trade in real estate fairly, honestly and with integrity. This requirement, set out in Sec. 3 of the Code, should be read in conjunction with Sec. 5 of the Code which states that clients and customers must receive conscientious and competent service.

FAIRNESS, HONESTY, ETC.   `CODE`

3.   A registrant shall treat every person the registrant deals with in the course of a trade in real estate fairly, honestly and with integrity. O. Reg. 580/05, s. 3.

. . . .

CONSCIENTIOUS AND COMPETENT SERVICE, ETC.   `CODE`

5.   A registrant shall provide conscientious service to the registrant's clients and customers and shall demonstrate reasonable knowledge, skill, judgment and competence in providing those services. O. Reg. 580/05, s. 5.

EXAMPLE   *The New Home*

A salesperson is representing a buyer contemplating a new home on the outskirts of Anycity. The home is located in a new subdivision and the buyer, who has young children, is very pleased about a nearby park, as well as a regional shopping centre scheduled to open within a few months. During casual conversation, the buyer asks about where the children will be attending school. The salesperson is aware that children are currently being bused to an adjacent community until such time as a new facility is built. The salesperson honestly conveys that known information, seeks out contact information for appropriate school officials so that the buyer may research this matter further and generally assists the buyer in getting the necessary information.

Offering Opinions

Buyers and sellers often seek out advice or ask questions of registrants. The Code of Ethics requires that all registrants demonstrate reasonable knowledge, skill, judgement and competence when responding to such questions. In particular, brokerages, brokers and salespersons must ensure that registrants, providing opinions or advice on value, have education or experience (and hopefully both) related to real estate valuation.

PROVIDING OPINIONS, ETC.　　　　　　　　　　　　　　　　`CODE`

6.　(1)　A registrant shall demonstrate reasonable knowledge, skill, judgment and competence in providing opinions, advice or information to any person in respect of a trade in real estate. O. Reg. 580/05, s. 6 (1).

　　(2)　Without limiting the generality of subsection (1) or section 5,

　　　　(a)　a brokerage shall not provide an opinion or advice about the value of real estate to any person unless the opinion or advice is provided on behalf of the brokerage by a broker or salesperson who has education or experience related to the valuation of real estate; and

　　　　(b)　a broker or salesperson shall not provide an opinion or advice about the value of real estate to any person unless the broker or salesperson has education or experience related to the valuation of real estate. O. Reg. 580/05, s. 6 (2).

EXAMPLE　　　*The Commercial Site*

A salesperson was approached by a developer to list a commercial lot zoned for mixed use on a major arterial street in Anycity. The developer wanted to know the salesperson's opinion as to the property's value in today's market. The salesperson immediately informed the seller that he was not experienced in commercial properties and could not provide any input as to value. The salesperson also advised the seller that his brokerage had a commercial division who could assist further, provided the developer with contact information for the commercial division manager and did a follow-up with the manager.

Client's Best Interests

REBBA 2002 requires that a registrant always work in the best interest of the registrant's client and to actively promote and protect that interest. The client places his or her trust and confidence in the brokerage and its representatives. While the Act and Regulations do not specifically address fiduciary obligations, such are deemed to be included in the term *represent*. As such, the registrant must ensure that personal interests never take precedent over the client's interests.

BEST INTERESTS　　　　　　　　　　　　　　　　　　　`CODE`

4.　A registrant shall promote and protect the best interests of the registrant's clients. O. Reg. 580/05, s. 4.

EXAMPLE   *Confidential Information*

The buyer client informs the salesperson in confidence that he will offer $365,000 for the resale condominium unit (which is currently listed through another brokerage for $385,000) but admits that this is simply a starting point. He is quite prepared to pay the full listing price if necessary. He divulges this information, as he has trust and confidence in the relationship with the salesperson. The listing salesperson, when presented with the offer, asks if the buyer will 'go any higher,' as the seller will not accept the offer as presented. The salesperson, fearing that negotiations may fall apart, admits that the buyer is anxious to buy and will probably pay full list price. The salesperson has breached Sec. 4 of the Code of Ethics.

DEALINGS WITH OTHERS

Other Registrants

Brokers and salespersons must be careful to not interfere with client relationships established by other registrants. Registrants cannot directly communicate with the client of another registrant, unless the applicable registrant consents in writing. An additional provision makes it a violation to in any way induce a buyer or seller to break an existing contract.

DEALINGS WITH OTHER REGISTRANTS   `CODE`

7.   (1) A registrant who knows or ought to know that a person is a client of another registrant shall communicate information to the person for the purpose of a trade in real estate only through the other registrant, unless the other registrant has consented in writing. O. Reg. 580/05, s. 7 (1).

      (2) If a broker or salesperson knows or ought to know that a buyer or seller is a party to an agreement in connection with a trade in real estate with a brokerage other than the brokerage that employs the broker or salesperson, the broker or salesperson shall not induce the buyer or seller to break the agreement. O. Reg. 580/05, s. 7 (2).

EXAMPLE   *The Luncheon*

A salesperson attends a commercial luncheon attended by various builders and developers. During the social time leading up to the meal and guest speaker, the salesperson is approached by a developer who currently has a new multi-unit, industrial building listed with another brokerage. During the conversation, the developer is discussing market conditions in Anycity and mentions that he is not getting much 'action' on the building, which is presently only 20% leased. He then tells the salesperson that he is not happy with services being provided by the listing brokerage and wants to cancel the representation agreement. The salesperson immediately advises the developer that he, as a salesperson, should not get involved with this situation given that it involves a client relationship with another brokerage. The salesperson advises the developer to speak directly with the listing brokerage and hopefully resolve any problems.

Services from Others

Registrants must be careful not to overstep their abilities when providing services to clients and customers. Situations may arise that require knowledge and skills that exceed that of the particular broker or salesperson. The Code of Ethics requires that registrants must advise a client or customer to obtain such services from others better qualified and, under no circumstances, should clients or customers be dissuaded from seeking such services.

SERVICES FROM OTHERS   `CODE`

8. (1) A registrant shall advise a client or customer to obtain services from another person if the registrant is not able to provide the services with reasonable knowledge, skill, judgment and competence or is not authorized by law to provide the services. O. Reg. 580/05, s. 8 (1).

    (2) A registrant shall not discourage a client or customer from seeking a particular kind of service if the registrant is not able to provide the service with reasonable knowledge, skill, judgment and competence or is not authorized by law to provide the service. O. Reg. 580/05, s. 8 (2).

EXAMPLE   *Mortgage Options*

The buyer client has looked at several properties and now has narrowed his focus to an older, rural home needing some repairs. He wants to make an offer on the property and feels confident that financing will be readily available at an attractive rate of interest. The salesperson explains that the amount of mortgage and interest rate charged might be affected given the age, location and general condition of the property. Accordingly, he inserts an appropriate condition in the offer and then directs the buyer client to seek out the services of a mortgage broker to assist in securing acceptable financing.

ADVERTISING

Registrants involved in marketing properties and promoting their services in the marketplace must fully comply with advertising requirements, as set out in REBBA 2002. The Act does not define the term *advertising*, but the Registrar has adopted the following definition for purposes of developing advertising guidelines:

> *"Advertising" means any notice, announcement or representation directed at the public that is authorized, made by or on behalf of a registrant and that is intended to promote a registrant or the business, services or real estate trades of a registrant in any medium including, but not limited to, print, radio, television, electronic media or publication on the internet (including websites and social media sites). Business cards, letterhead or fax cover sheets that contain promotional statements may be considered as "advertising".*

Advertising is given extensive treatment both in REBBA 2002 and various published guidelines given its focal role in many listing and selling activities.

Promotion and Advertising

Promotion can be broadly defined as the sum of favourable communication delivered by specific advertising tools. Registrants are actively involved in various promotional activities including personal publicity, institutional material to bolster image, maintenance of a particular marketing plan and classified advertising to advance specific properties. REBBA 2002 addresses both personal or brokerage promotion, including day-to-day advertising requirements and responsibilities.

FALSE ADVERTISING/FALSIFYING INFORMATION

Registrants are prohibited under the Act from making false, misleading or deceptive advertising statements, as well as furnishing false information (including inducing or counselling others to do so). The Registrar can order the cessation of false advertising, as well as requiring registrants to retract statements and publish corrections. A *Registrar's Bulletin* regarding falsifying information can be found on the following page.

FALSIFYING INFORMATION   REBBA

34. No registrant shall falsify, assist in falsifying or induce or counsel another person to falsify or assist in falsifying any information or document relating to a trade in real estate. 2002, c. 30, Sched. C, s. 34.

FURNISHING FALSE INFORMATION

35. No registrant shall furnish, assist in furnishing or induce or counsel another person to furnish or assist in furnishing any false or deceptive information or documents relating to a trade in real estate. 2002, c. 30, Sched. C, s. 35.

FALSE ADVERTISING

37. No registrant shall make false, misleading or deceptive statements in any advertisement, circular, pamphlet or material published by any means relating to trading in real estate. 2002, c. 30, Sched. C, s. 37.

ORDER OF REGISTRAR RE: FALSE ADVERTISING

38. (1) If the registrar believes on reasonable grounds that a registrant is making a false, misleading or deceptive statement in any advertisement, circular, pamphlet or material published by any means, the registrar may,

(a) order the cessation of the use of such material;

(b) order the registrant to retract the statement or publish a correction of equal prominence to the original publication; or

(c) order both a cessation described in clause (a) and a retraction or correction described in clause (b). 2002, c. 30, Sched. C, s. 38 (1).

Procedures

(2) Section 14 applies with necessary modifications to an order under this section in the same manner as to a proposal by the registrar to refuse a registration. 2002, c. 30, Sched. C, s. 38 (2).

Effect

(3) The order of the registrar shall take effect immediately, but the Tribunal may grant a stay until the registrar's order becomes final. 2002, c. 30, Sched. C, s. 38 (3).

Pre-approval

(4) If the registrant does not appeal an order under this section or if the order or a variation of it is upheld by the Tribunal, the registrant shall, upon the request of the registrar, submit all statements in any advertisement, circular, pamphlet or material to be published by any means to the registrar for approval before publication for such period as the registrar specifies. 2002, c. 30, Sched. C, s. 38 (4); 2004, c. 19, s. 18 (23).

Specified period

(5) The registrar shall not specify under subsection (4) a period,

(a) that exceeds such period as may be prescribed; or

(b) any part of which falls outside such period as may be prescribed. 2004, c. 19, s. 18 (24).

Published by the Real Estate Council of Ontario

Falsifying information

The *Real Estate and Business Brokers Act, 2002* (the "Act") which came into force on March 31, 2006 contained two new offences related to falsifying information. Sec. 34 and 35 of the Act state:

Falsifying information

34. No registrant shall falsify, assist in falsifying or induce or counsel another person to falsify or assist in falsifying any information or document relating to a trade in real estate.

Furnishing false information

35. No registrant shall furnish, assist in furnishing or induce or counsel another person to furnish or assist in furnishing any false or deceptive information or documents relating to a trade in real estate.

These provisions make it an explicit offence under the Act to falsify information, assist another person in falsifying information or furnish false information related to real estate transactions.

Registrants who contravene this section of the Act may have their registration suspended or revoked or be charged under the statute. If convicted of an offence under the Act, individual registrants may be fined up to $50,000 and are subject to prison terms of up to 2 years. Corporations are subject to fines of up to $250,000 for offences under the Act. In addition, a court may order a convicted person to pay compensation or restitution to affected parties.

These measures reflect the fact that falsifying information related to real estate transactions is a serious issue. Any registrant, for example, who counseled an individual to lie with respect to a mortgage application, would be guilty of an offence under these clauses.

Registrants also have an obligation not to provide any false information about a property during a transaction or to counsel a seller to falsify any information about a property.

These measures also strengthen the ability of enforcement officials to deal with real estate scams. Most if not all real estate scams, involve, at some point in the process, the falsification of information related to a real estate transaction. In some real estate scams individuals have sold properties without the true owners consent. Registrants or any persons who participate in this type of activity are obviously operating in violation of the Act.

Real Estate Council of Ontario
Tel: 416-207-4800 Toll Free: 1-800-245-6910 Fax: 416-207-4820

Office of the Registrar
AsktheRegistrar@reco.on.ca

REBBA 2002
Real Estate & Business Brokers Act, 2002

For more information about RECO,
visit: www.reco.on.ca

PROMISES/INDUCEMENTS

The General Regulation details requirements concerning promises/inducements and the need for a written contract regarding such matters. Carefully review the following excerpt from the General Regulation 567/05 and note that *Subsec. (2), (3) and (4) do not apply to a representation or promise if the registrant has entered into a written contract with the person to whom the representation or promise is made.*

INDUCEMENTS   GEN

25. (1) The definitions of "sell" and "seller" in section 1 and the definitions of "buy" and "buyer" in section 2 do not apply to this section. O. Reg. 567/05, s. 25 (1).

     (2) A registrant shall not, as an inducement to purchase, lease or exchange real estate, make any representation or promise that the registrant or any other person will sell, lease or exchange the real estate. O. Reg. 567/05, s. 25 (2).

     (3) A registrant shall not, as an inducement to purchase real estate, make any representation or promise that the registrant or any other person will,

         (a) purchase or sell any of the purchaser's real estate;

         (b) procure for the purchaser a mortgage or extension of a mortgage or a lease or extension of a lease; or

         (c) purchase or sell a mortgage or procure a loan. O. Reg. 567/05, s. 25 (3).

     (4) A registrant shall not, as an inducement to sell real estate, make any representation or promise that the registrant or any other person will,

         (a) purchase any of the seller's real estate;

         (b) procure a mortgage, extension of a mortgage, lease or extension of a lease; or

         (c) purchase or sell a mortgage or procure a loan. O. Reg. 567/05, s. 25 (4).

     (5) Subsections (2), (3) and (4) do not apply to a representation or promise if the registrant has entered into a written contract with the person to whom the representation or promise is made that obligates the registrant to ensure that the promise or representation is complied with. O. Reg. 567/05, s. 25 (5).

REGISTRANT NAME

Both the General Regulation 567/05 (Sec. 8) and the Code of Ethics (Sec. 36) address compliance issues concerning use of a registrant's name . The General Regulation focuses on requirements at time of registration, with the Code highlighting the need for clear and prominent name disclosure in all advertisements. The Code provisions are highlighted.

ADVERTISING   CODE

36. (1) A registrant shall clearly and prominently disclose the name in which the registrant is registered in all the registrant's advertisements. O. Reg. 580/05, s. 36 (1).

     (2) A brokerage that identifies a broker or salesperson by name in an advertisement shall use the name in which the broker or salesperson is registered. O. Reg. 580/05, s. 36 (2).

     (3) A broker or salesperson shall not advertise in any manner unless the advertisement clearly and prominently identifies the brokerage that employs the broker or salesperson, using the name in which the brokerage is registered. O. Reg. 580/05, s. 36 (3).

     (4) A registrant who advertises shall,

         (a) use the term "brokerage", "real estate brokerage", "maison de courtage" or "maison de courtage immobilier" to describe any brokerage that is referred to in the advertisement;

         (b) use the term "broker of record", "real estate broker of record", "courtier responsable" or "courtier immobilier responsable" to describe any broker of record who is referred to in the advertisement;

continued...

ADVERTISING (continued)   `CODE`

   (c) use the term "broker", "real estate broker", "courtier" or "courtier immobilier" to describe any broker who is referred to in the advertisement; and

   (d) use the term "salesperson", "real estate salesperson", "sales representative", "real estate sales representative", "agent immobilier", "représentant commercial" or "représentant immobilier" to describe any salesperson who is referred to in the advertisement. O. Reg. 580/05, s. 36 (4).

(5) Despite clause (4) (c), a registrant who advertises may, before April 1, 2008, use the term "associate broker", "associate real estate broker", "courtier associé" or "courtier immobilier associé" to describe any broker who is referred to in the advertisement. O. Reg. 580/05, s. 36 (5).

EXAMPLE   *The Advertisement*

A commercial registrant wrote a classified advertisement which appeared in the paper. The ad, relating to a small retail business, ended with the following sentence: *Call Salesperson Smith, Sales Associate, ABC Realty Inc.* The use of *'sales associate'* is in violation of the Code of Ethics, Subsec. 36(4), which provides that salespersons are only permitted to use the following terms: *salesperson, sales representative* or *real estate representative* (or their French equivalents).

PROPERTY, PARTIES AND AGREEMENT PARTICULARS

The Code of Ethics provides that registrants must not identify specific information unless appropriate consent is obtained; e.g., a party cannot be identified in an ad unless that party has consented.

ADVERTISING   `CODE`

36. (7) A registrant shall not include anything in an advertisement that could reasonably be used to identify a party to the acquisition or disposition of an interest in real estate unless the party has consented in writing. O. Reg. 580/05, s. 36 (7).

   (8) A registrant shall not include anything in an advertisement that could reasonably be used to identify specific real estate unless the owner of the real estate has consented in writing. O. Reg. 580/05, s. 36 (8).

   (9) A registrant shall not include anything in an advertisement that could reasonably be used to determine any of the contents of an agreement that deals with the conveyance of an interest in real estate, including any provision of the agreement relating to the price, unless the parties to the agreement have consented in writing. O. Reg. 580/05, s. 36 (9).

EXAMPLE   *The Address*

A salesperson has a representation agreement signed by the seller for a detached home in the west end of Anycity. She prepares advertisements for both the website and the newspaper. In both, the advertising text provides the property address. The seller did not give his consent in writing to this disclosure. The salesperson is in violation of the Code of Ethics, Subsec. 36 (8).

INACCURATE REPRESENTATIONS

Registrants must not knowingly make inaccurate representations about either trades in real estate or services being provided.

INACCURATE REPRESENTATIONS   CODE

37. (1) A registrant shall not knowingly make an inaccurate representation in respect of a trade in real estate. O. Reg. 580/05, s. 37 (1).

    (2) A registrant shall not knowingly make an inaccurate representation about services provided by the registrant. O. Reg. 580/05, s. 37 (2).

EXAMPLE   *The Wiring*

A salesperson, when showing an older residential property, is asked by the buyer client about the knob-and-tube wiring clearly evident in the basement. The salesperson assures her that all older homes have this wiring and that it in no way will affect the sale of the property or its future use. The buyer is anxious to close within a few weeks so that her children can begin classes in their new school.

   The buyer arranges financing, but only after meeting the lender's requirement that the electrical panel be updated, along with a thorough assessment to determine that all existing knob-and-tube wiring is safe. Any new circuits added would then be fed through the new panel. The total cost of the assessment and related wiring improvements amounted to $4,300. The buyer files a complaint with the Real Estate Council of Ontario regarding this misrepresentation pursuant to Sec. 37 of the Code of Ethics.

ERROR, MISREPRESENTATION AND FRAUD

Registrants must not only avoid error, misrepresentation, fraud or any unethical practice but must also take necessary steps to prevent them.

ERROR, MISREPRESENTATION, FRAUD, ETC.   CODE

38. A registrant shall use the registrant's best efforts to prevent error, misrepresentation, fraud or any unethical practice in respect of a trade in real estate. O. Reg. 580/05, s. 38.

EXAMPLE   *The Fraudulent Act*

The seller informs the salesperson of a known problem that impacts water quality. The rural home has a well with unsafe drinking water, but the seller does not want anyone to know this fact. He maintains that the problem is 'seasonal' due to spring water runoff. At present, during the summer, there is no problem. The salesperson agrees to not disclose this matter.

   Following closing, the buyer and his family become ill due to the drinking water problem, only to discover that the seller had repeatedly tried to fix the problem in the past. The lawyer for the buyer takes legal action arguing that this is a material latent defect (a dangerous or potentially dangerous situation) that was known and should have been disclosed. The lawyer, on behalf of his client also files a complaint with the Real Estate Council of Ontario for a violation of Article 38: Error, Misrepresentation, Fraud, Etc. (Note: Additional requirements regarding material facts are discussed later in this chapter.)

SHOWING PROPERTY

Properties That Meet Buyer's Criteria

This ethical requirement provides that the registrant must inform the buyer client about any property meeting the client's criteria, regardless of commission or other remuneration.

PROPERTIES THAT MEET BUYER'S CRITERIA | CODE |

19. If a brokerage has entered into a representation agreement with a buyer, a broker or salesperson who acts on behalf of the buyer pursuant to the agreement shall inform the buyer of properties that meet the buyer's criteria without having any regard to the amount of commission or other remuneration, if any, to which the brokerage might be entitled. O. Reg. 580/05, s. 19.

EXAMPLE   *The Unknown Opportunity*

The buyer was attempting to locate a suitable retail site for his expanding business. He signed a buyer representation agreement which specified that the brokerage would seek out smaller retail businesses in the $650,000 to $750,000 range within an area near a specific east/west arterial road. The salesperson became aware of two properties being offered with differing commission rates. He showed the client the property which offered the higher commission, but did not mention the second possibility, as the commission would be significantly less. The salesperson, in doing so, is in violation of Section 19.

Seller Property Information Statement

Seller Property Information Statements (SPISs) are widely used with residential properties in Ontario and can provide useful additional information about the listed property that is not typically included in a seller representation agreement. If a broker or salesperson knows that the client has completed such a statement, he or she is obligated to inform every interested buyer of its existence and make it available upon request, unless directed otherwise by the seller.

SELLER PROPERTY INFORMATION STATEMENT | CODE |

20. If a broker or salesperson has a seller as a client and knows that the seller has completed a written statement that is intended to provide information to buyers about the real estate that is available for acquisition, the broker or salesperson shall, unless the seller directs otherwise,

  (a) disclose the existence of the statement to every buyer who expresses an interest in the real estate; and

  (b) on request, make the statement available to a buyer at the earliest practicable opportunity after the request is made. O. Reg. 580/05, s. 20.

EXAMPLE   *The Missing Evidence*

A salesperson listed a property and inadvertently misplaced the Seller Property Information Statement completed by her client. Several weeks passed before the first showing and the misplaced SPIS was forgotten. The prospective buyer viewed the property through a co-operating brokerage and made an acceptable offer. Subsequent to closing, he discovered that the property had significant drainage issues that required remedial work amounting to $18,000. He took legal action against the seller for repair costs. The seller produced his copy of the missing SPIS which made reference to similar problems in the past. The salesperson was not only in violation of Sec. 20, but also probably faced litigation.

Material Facts

A material fact can be generally described as any fact that would affect a reasonable person's decision to acquire or dispose of an interest in real estate. The Code of Ethics requires disclosure of pertinent facts both to clients and customers. For clients, the obligation is to take reasonable steps to determine and disclose such facts. With customers, the obligation is more limited to disclosing only those material facts that are known, or ought to be known, by the registrant. This obligation supersedes any direction otherwise from the seller.

MATERIAL FACTS   `CODE`

21. (1) A broker or salesperson who has a client in respect of the acquisition or disposition of a particular interest in real estate shall take reasonable steps to determine the material facts relating to the acquisition or disposition and, at the earliest practicable opportunity, shall disclose the material facts to the client. O. Reg. 580/05, s. 21 (1).

    (2) A broker or salesperson who has a customer in respect of the acquisition or disposition of a particular interest in real estate shall, at the earliest practicable opportunity, disclose to the customer the material facts relating to the acquisition or disposition that are known by or ought to be known by the broker or salesperson. O. Reg. 580/05, s. 21 (2).

EXAMPLE   *The Foundation*

The salesperson, when showing a property in suburban Anycity to his client, noticed a number of rusty staples in the baseboard and wall panelling in the finished basement. This minor item went unnoticed by the client. The salesperson then casually looked in the unfinished basement areas suspecting that moisture might be an issue. Upon closer inspection, he found some efflorescence on the concrete block wall and advised his client accordingly. The seller was asked about the potential problem and told the salesperson and buyer that there had been some leakage from a basement window a couple of years ago but that no further problems had occurred once the external window well was repaired. The client, based on this input, did decide to make an offer conditional upon a home inspection, including a detailed reporting of this particular situation. The salesperson complied with both the intent and wording of Sec. 21.

DRAFTING AN AGREEMENT OF PURCHASE AND SALE

The Code sets out selected compliance requirements relating to an agreement for the conveyance of an interest in real estate; i.e., an agreement of purchase and sale.

Written and Legible

This Code of Ethics provision, requiring that agreements be in writing and legible, applies to both clients and customers.

WRITTEN AND LEGIBLE AGREEMENTS   `CODE`

27. (1) A registrant who represents a client in respect of a trade in real estate shall use the registrant's best efforts to ensure that,

    (a) any agreement that deals with the conveyance of an interest in real estate is in writing; and

    (b) any written agreement that deals with the conveyance of an interest in real estate is legible. O. Reg. 580/05, s. 27 (1).

    (2) Subsection (1) applies, with necessary modifications, if a brokerage and a customer have an agreement that provides for the brokerage to provide services to the customer in respect of any agreement that deals with the conveyance of an interest in real estate. O. Reg. 580/05, s. 27 (2).

Current Forms

Registrants must use current forms and be fully informed about such forms.

CURRENT FORMS   `CODE`

34. A registrant shall ensure that forms used by the registrant in the course of a trade in real estate are current. O. Reg. 580/05, s. 34.

NEGOTIATING AND PRESENTING THE OFFER

Offers to Purchase Real Estate

When a registrant is acting on behalf of a buyer, only written offers may be presented. For a written offer to be valid, the offer must be signed. A registrant cannot indicate that an offer has been received unless it is in writing.

The seller's brokerage must retain a copy of every written offer it receives from a buyer, including any counter offer and any unsuccessful offer. The brokerage may retain an equivalent summary document (e.g., the OREA Form 801, included in the appendix for reference purposes only) for each offer rather than retaining a copy of the offer in its entirety providing:

- The seller's brokerage receives the offer on behalf of the seller;
- The offer is made through a brokerage on behalf of the buyer;
- The offer did not result in a transaction (i.e., the offer was unsuccessful/not accepted); and
- The summary contains all the required information.

The seller's brokerage must retain a copy of an unsuccessful offer or an equivalent summary document for that unsuccessful offer for at least one year from the date it is received. Offers that have been accepted and result in a purchase of real estate must be kept for at least six years.

The offer retention provisions in the Act enable the Registrar to determine the number of offers received by a seller's brokerage for a property in the event that the Registrar receives a request from a buyer who made a written offer on the property, or a registrant acting on behalf of such a buyer. When requested by the Registrar, the seller's brokerage must provide the Registrar with a copy of every written offer received for the property, or the equivalent summary documents, as applicable.

OFFERS TO PURCHASE REAL ESTATE   `REBBA`

35.1 (1) No registrant shall,

   (a) while acting on behalf of a purchaser, present an offer to purchase real estate except if the offer is in writing;

   (b) represent to any person that a written offer to purchase real estate exists except if the offer is in writing. 2013, c. 13, Sched. 3, s. 1.

Records

(2) A brokerage acting on behalf of a seller shall retain, for the period of time prescribed, copies of all written offers that it receives to purchase real estate or copies of all other prescribed documents related to those offers. 2013, c. 13, Sched. 3, s. 1.

Request for inquiry by registrar

(3) A person who has made a written offer to purchase real estate or a registrant acting on behalf of such a person may request that the registrar make an inquiry to determine the number of written offers that the brokerage acting for a seller has received to purchase the real estate. 2013, c. 13, Sched. 3, s. 1.

Inquiry

(4) On receiving a request under subsection (3), the registrar may make an inquiry of the brokerage and the brokerage shall,

   (a) respond within a reasonable period of time, or within the time that is prescribed; and

   (b) at the request o8f the registrar, provide the registrar with copies of the written offers or other documents that it is required to retain under subsection (2). 2013, c. 13, Sched. 3, s. 1.

Disclosure by registrar

(5) The registrar shall determine the number of written offers that the brokerage has received to purchase the real estate and shall disclose the number of the offers as soon as practicable, or within the period of time that is prescribed, to the person who requested the inquiry under subsection (3), but shall not disclose the substance of any of the offers or the identity of the person making any of the offers. 2013, c. 13, Sched. 3, s. 1.

Other action by registrar

(6) Nothing in this section limits the authority of the registrar to take any other action against a registrant that this Act authorizes the registrar to take. 2013, c. 13, Sched. 3, s. 1.

RECORDS — OFFERS TO PURCHASE   `OTH`

Retention of offers that are not accepted

19.1 (1) Despite section 18, for the purposes of subsection 35.1 (2) of the Act, this section applies when a brokerage acting on behalf of a seller received a written offer to purchase real estate for the purposes of presenting it to the seller, but the offer did not result in the purchase of the real estate. O. Reg. 307/14, s. 1.

(2) If the written offer was made by a person who was a client or customer of a registrant, then the brokerage acting on behalf of the seller shall keep, for at least one year after the date the brokerage received the written offer for the purposes of presenting it to the seller, either a copy of the written offer or a copy of a document that includes the following information:

   1. The name and signature of the person who made the offer to purchase the real estate.

   2. The name and contact information of the seller of the real estate.

continued...

RECORDS — OFFERS TO PURCHASE (continued)   [OTH]

3.   The name of the brokerage and of the broker or salesperson who acted for the seller.

4.   The name of the brokerage and of the broker or salesperson who acted for the person who made the offer.

5.   The address, legal description or other identifier of the real estate on which the offer was made.

6.   The date and time the offer was made.

7.   The date and time the offer was received by the brokerage for the purposes of presenting it to the seller, and the means by which the offer was received, such as in person or by fax.

8.   If the brokerage presented the offer to the seller, the date of presentation.

9.   The date and time, if any, until which the offer was irrevocable. O. Reg. 307/14, s. 1.

(3)   If the written offer was made by a person who was not a client or customer of a registrant, then the brokerage acting on behalf of the seller shall keep a copy of the written offer for at least one year after the date the brokerage received the written offer for the purposes of presenting it to the seller. O. Reg. 307/14, s. 1.

Conveying Offers

The Code of Ethics sets out various requirements, which essentially centre on the need to present offers (including all written amendments thereto) to the client as soon as is practicably possible. Registrants must also ensure that in their absence procedures must be in place so that others ensure the timely delivery. This section of the Code provides that these requirements also apply to customers, assuming that the customer and the brokerage have a written agreement for the brokerage to receive offers.

CONVEYING OFFERS   [CODE]

24.   (1)   A registrant shall convey any written offer received by the registrant to the registrant's client at the earliest practicable opportunity. O. Reg. 580/05, s. 24 (1).

(2)   A broker or salesperson shall establish a method of ensuring that,

(a)   written offers are received by someone on behalf of the broker or salesperson, if the broker or salesperson is not available at the time an offer is submitted; and

(b)   written offers are conveyed to the client of the broker or salesperson at the earliest practicable opportunity, even if the broker or salesperson is not available at the time an offer is submitted. O. Reg. 580/05, s. 24 (2).

(3)   Without limiting the generality of subsections (1) and (2), those subsections apply regardless of the identity of the person making the offer, the contents of the offer or the nature of any arrangements for commission or other remuneration. O. Reg. 580/05, s. 24 (3).

(4)   Subsections (1) to (3) are subject to any written directions given by a client. O. Reg. 580/05, s. 24 (4).

(5)   Subsections (1) to (4) also apply, with necessary modifications, to,

(a)   written amendments to written offers and any other written document directly related to a written offer; and

(b)   written assignments of agreements that relate to interests in real estate, written waivers of conditions in agreements that relate to interests in real estate, and any other written document directly related to a written agreement that relates to an interest in real estate. O. Reg. 580/05, s. 24 (5).

(6)   Subsections (1) to (5) apply, with necessary modifications, if a brokerage and a customer have an agreement that provides for the brokerage to receive written offers. O. Reg. 580/05, s. 24 (6).

(7)   Subsections (1) to (5) apply, with necessary modifications, to brokers and salespersons employed by a brokerage, if the brokerage and a customer have an agreement that provides for the brokerage to receive written offers. O. Reg. 580/05, s. 24 (7).

EXAMPLE   *The Missing Salesperson*

The listing salesperson went on a much needed, four-day vacation with her family. During her absence, she arranged with another salesperson in the brokerage to handle any matters relating to her listings and associated activities and made the broker of record aware of this arrangement. An offer was submitted on one of her listings by a co-operating brokerage during her absence. The salesperson ensured that the offer was presented in a timely fashion and assisted the client during the negotiations. As such, the vacationing salesperson has generally complied with requirements of Section 24.

Agreement Relating to Commission

This provision deals with negotiations and specifically targets the impact of differing commission rates on the seller's net proceeds. For example, two offers may have identical offering prices, but one commission due could be less than the other. Consequently, the seller's net would fluctuate based on which offer was accepted. If such was not disclosed, the seller would not be fully informed in making a decision. Further, the offering parties would not be aware of pertinent facts relating to their competitive position and would not be competing on an even playing field. This provision is directed both to clients and customers.

AGREEMENTS RELATING TO COMMISSION   `CODE`

25. (1) If a brokerage has a seller as a client and an agreement between the brokerage and the seller contains terms that relate to a commission or other remuneration and that may affect whether an offer to buy is accepted, the brokerage shall disclose the existence of and the details of those terms to any person who makes a written offer to buy, at the earliest practicable opportunity and before any offer is accepted. O. Reg. 580/05, s. 25 (1).

(2) Subsection (1) applies, with necessary modifications, to a brokerage that has a seller as a customer, if the brokerage and the seller have an agreement that provides for the brokerage to receive written offers to buy. O. Reg. 580/05, s. 25 (2).

Competing Offers

A registrant must disclose the existence of competing offers to every person who is making one of the competing offers, but not disclose the substance of such offers.

COMPETING OFFERS   `CODE`

26. (1) If a brokerage that has a seller as a client receives a competing written offer, the brokerage shall disclose the number of competing written offers to every person who is making one of the competing offers, but shall not disclose the substance of the competing offers. O. Reg. 580/05, s. 26 (1).

(2) Subsection (1) applies, with necessary modifications, to a brokerage that has a seller as a customer, if the brokerage and the seller have an agreement that provides for the brokerage to receive written offers to buy. O. Reg. 580/05, s. 26 (2).

Copies of Agreements

A registrant must use his best efforts to ensure that all parties to an agreement, involving a conveyance of an interest in real estate, receive a copy of the agreement at the earliest practicable opportunity. This requirement applies to clients and also to customers (with necessary modifications) assuming that the applicable customer has an agreement with the brokerage to provide services.

COPIES OF AGREEMENTS   `CODE`

28. (1) If a registrant represents a client who enters into a written agreement that deals with the conveyance of an interest in real estate, the registrant shall use the registrant's best efforts to ensure that all parties to the agreement receive a copy of the agreement at the earliest practicable opportunity. O. Reg. 580/05, s. 28 (1).

(2) Subsection (1) applies, with necessary modifications, if a brokerage and a customer have an agreement that provides for the brokerage to provide services to the customer in respect of any agreement that deals with the conveyance of an interest in real estate. O. Reg. 580/05, s. 28 (2).

EXAMPLE   *The Delayed Delivery*

The seller client accepted an offer on his commercial property. The offer presentation and acceptance occurred on a Friday evening. Copies of the accepted offer were delivered by the listing salesperson to the buyer's representative late that same evening. The buyer's representative was planning a trip away for the weekend and called the buyer to inform him that the offer was accepted. He promised to provide a copy to the buyer within a few days after his return. The intent of Sec. 28 is that copies should be delivered at the earliest practicable opportunity and not *within a few days.*

Delivery of Deposits and Documents

This section of the Code requires that registrants deliver the deposit or documents in accordance with the agreement. This requirement applies both when representing a client or providing services to a customer.

DELIVERY OF DEPOSITS AND DOCUMENTS   `CODE`

29. Except as otherwise provided by law, if a registrant is representing a client or providing services to a customer in connection with a trade in real estate, and the client or customer has entered into an agreement in connection with the trade that requires the registrant to deliver a deposit or documents, the registrant shall deliver the deposit or documents in accordance with the agreement. O. Reg. 580/05, s. 29.

EXAMPLE   *The Financing Condition*

The salesperson has successfully negotiated an agreement on behalf of his buyer client for the purchase of a home listed through a co-operating brokerage. The offer is subject to obtaining a new first mortgage of not less than $247,000. The buyer elects to obtain financing through a specific lender. When the mortgage commitment is signed, the salesperson assists by preparing the required notice concerning the removal of the condition, promptly delivers the notice to the appropriate parties and generally assists the buyer client as needed.

Steps Taken by Registrant

Sec. 23 of the Code is of particular note, as it not only applies to negotiations and preparation of offers, but to all significant activities undertaken on behalf of a client, be it buyer or seller.

STEPS TAKEN BY REGISTRANT   `CODE`

23. A registrant shall inform a client of all significant steps that the registrant takes in the course of representing the client. O. Reg. 580/05, s. 23.

The salesperson is completing a buyer representation agreement for the buyer client. The buyer wants to make certain that he is fully informed of the salesperson's activities after the agreement is signed. His focal concern is that he be made aware of all properties meeting his requirements. The salesperson assures the client that not only will he be made aware of all such properties, but the salesperson will also maintain ongoing contact as to significant activities when searching for property and advise him of key market trends. When a suitable property is found, the salesperson will draft an agreement for the client, handle all negotiations and, if accepted, track the deal until closing and address any problems as the need arises. Most importantly, the salesperson will keep the buyer client fully informed throughout the process.

HANDLING THE DEPOSIT

REBBA 2002 sets out various requirements regarding the handling of deposits by brokerages, brokers and salespersons. Key provisions are highlighted.

Deposits: The Five-Day Provision

Under REBBA 2002, a brokerage is allowed five business days to deposit funds received into the real estate trust account (**GEN, Subsec. 17(1)**). Business days exclude Saturdays, Sundays and statutory holidays. All registrants are reminded that time is of the essence in handling deposits. The five-day provision is a minimum standard. Funds should be deposited as soon as is practically possible.

DEPOSIT WITHIN FIVE BUSINESS DAYS   `GEN`

17. (1) If an amount of money comes into a brokerage's hands in trust for another person in connection with the brokerage's business, the brokerage shall deposit the amount in the trust account maintained under section 27 of the Act within five business days. O. Reg. 567/05, s. 17 (1).

(2) In subsection (1), "business day" means a day that is not,
   (a) Saturday, or
   (b) a holiday within the meaning of subsection 29 (1) of the *Interpretation Act*. O. Reg. 567/05, s. 17 (2).

ABC Realty Inc., the listing brokerage, finalizes an agreement stating that the deposit is submitted herewith. The assumption is that ABC Realty Inc. is in receipt of the funds, which must then be placed in trust within the five-day period.

XYZ Real Estate Ltd., the co-operating brokerage, drafts and successfully concludes an agreement on ABC Realty Inc.'s listing, which states that the deposit is to be received on acceptance. The five-day rule applies to ABC Realty Inc. from when it comes into the brokerage's hands.

DELAY BY CO-OPERATING BROKERAGE

The five-day provision applies to the brokerage actually placing the deposit in trust. However, a co-operating brokerage's tardiness in delivering a buyer's deposit to the listing brokerage will be closely scrutinized and appropriate action taken (see **CODE, Sec. 29: Delivery of Deposits and Documents** on a previous page).

EXAMPLE   *The Misplaced Cheque*

XYZ Real Estate Ltd. concludes an agreement with the deposit due on acceptance. However, the cheque was not given immediately to the listing brokerage, as it was misplaced for several days. Located six business days later, the cheque is immediately delivered to the listing brokerage, who in turn deposits the funds that same day. An inspector, on a routine inspection, discovers the violation, reviews the matter with the listing brokerage and recommends further action be taken by the Registrar against the co-operating brokerage.

FAILED AGREEMENT: RETURN OF DEPOSIT

A brokerage can only return a deposit when a deal falls through if:

- A mutual consent or direction is signed by the parties (i.e., buyer and seller) agreeing to the disbursement.
- A Court Order authorizes the disbursement.

Further, REBBA 2002 requires that disbursements from the trust account must be made as soon as is practicably possible. Delays will be closely scrutinized by RECO and appropriate action taken. A *Registrar's Bulletin* regarding failed agreements of purchase and sale and the return of deposits can be found on a subsequent page.

EXAMPLE   *The Cancelled Sale*

ABC Realty Inc. is holding a deposit in trust for the sale of 123 Main Street, Anycity. The sale is cancelled due to unfulfilled conditions. Both parties immediately sign a mutual release. The broker of record for ABC Realty Inc. receives the documentation, agrees to disburse the funds, but delays for a week as the brokerage only disburses trust monies on the 15th and 30th of the month. This office policy is not in keeping with the requirement to disburse funds as soon as is practicably possible.

Handling Unclaimed Trust Funds (i.e., Deposits)

The Act sets out specific procedures if a deposit placed in trust remains unclaimed for various reasons (**REBBA, Subsec. 27(4) to (7)**). For example, funds held in the trust account must be forwarded to RECO if the brokerage is unsuccessful in locating the person within one year. If the situation involves a dispute and entitlement to the funds is not clear, the brokerage must forward those funds if unclaimed for two years. The above procedures do not apply if funds held are less that $25.00.

TRUST ACCOUNT   REBBA

Entitlement unclear

27. (4) If a brokerage holds money in trust for a period of two years and entitlement to the money has not been determined or is unclear, the brokerage shall pay the money to,

    (a) the administrative authority; or

    (b) if there is no designated administrative authority, the Minister of Finance. 2002, c. 30, Sched. C, s. 27 (4).

Unclaimed trust money

(5) If a brokerage holds money in trust for a period of one year after the person for whom it is held first became entitled to payment of the money and the person cannot be located, the brokerage shall pay the money to,

    (a) the administrative authority; or

    (b) if there is no designated administrative authority, the Minister of Finance. 2002, c. 30, Sched. C, s. 27 (5).

Attempt to locate person entitled to payment of money

(6) Before the brokerage pays the money under subsection (5), the brokerage shall use reasonable efforts to locate the person entitled to the money being held in trust. 2002, c. 30, Sched. C, s. 27 (6).

Information on entitlement

(7) When a brokerage pays money over under subsection (4) or (5), the brokerage shall provide to the administrative authority or to the Minister of Finance, as the case may be, as much information as the brokerage has in order to determine who is entitled to the trust money. 2002, c. 30, Sched. C, s. 27 (7)..

Handling Deposits Properly   MARKET MEMO

Be fully aware of responsibilities regarding handling of deposit cheques from prospective buyers. Important points to remember about the deposit cheque:

- Amounts must be exactly as spelled out in the agreement.
- Cheques must be currently dated and capable of being accepted for payment.
- Cheques are usually made out to the listing brokerage "in trust", but never, under any circumstances, to the salesperson. In some instances, the deposit may be made payable to a party other than the listing brokerage; e.g., seller or seller's lawyer.
- Where a brokerage receives a deposit that is directed to another party (e.g., the listing brokerage), a receipt from that brokerage must be obtained.
- No legal requirement exists concerning the amount of deposit, but 5% or more is strongly recommended.
- Two options are available when submitting the deposit: either at time of offer or upon acceptance.

Life Cycle of a Deposit

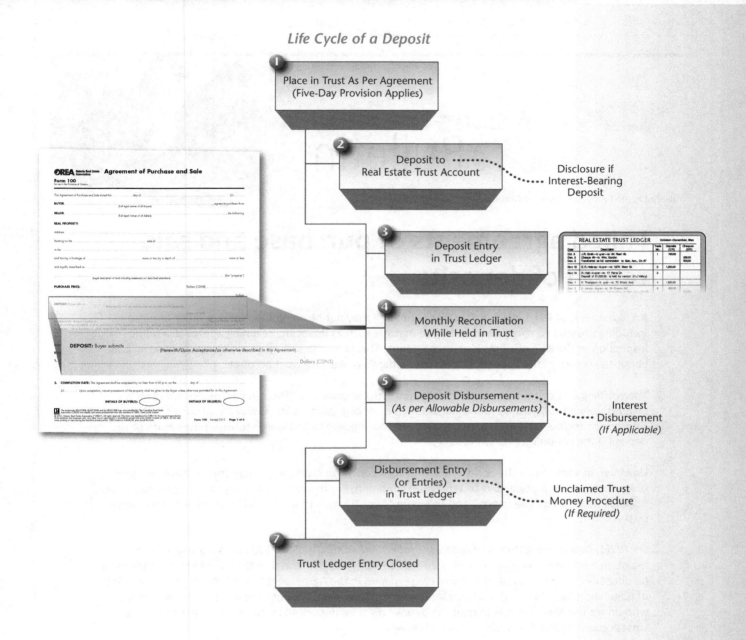

Published by the Real Estate Council of Ontario

Failed agreements of purchase and sale return of deposits

An Agreement of Purchase and Sale ("Agreement") may not be completed for a number of reasons, including unsatisfied conditions relating to matters such as financing, rezoning approval, a home inspection or the sale of a buyer's current home. This failure to satisfy a condition may raise an issue about the return of the deposit held in a brokerage's real estate trust account.

The wording of a condition clause in an Agreement, for example, *"This offer is conditional upon the buyer obtaining satisfactory financing within five banking days, failing which the deposit shall be returned to the buyer in full without deduction"* may appear to be clear in terms of the return of the deposit if the condition isn't waived.

However, in some cases the courts, in reviewing a condition clause in an Agreement, have imposed obligations on the party who is to satisfy the condition. For this reason, a party to the Agreement may dispute the return of the deposit and the issue of entitlement to the deposit may have to be resolved by the courts.

Sec. 27(1) of the *Real Estate and Business Brokers Act, 2002* (the "Act") requires a brokerage to maintain a properly designated trust account at a recognized financial institution. All trust funds must be deposited in the account of the brokerage named in the Agreement to hold the deposit. Sec. 17(1) of Regulation 567/05 (GEN) made under the Act requires that a deposit received by the brokerage who under the Agreement is to hold the deposit must be deposited in that brokerage's real estate trust account within five business days of receipt.

A brokerage may only disburse the funds held in the real estate trust account in accordance with the terms of the trust. This is important to the purposes of the Act – consumer protection and regulation of trading in real estate. Breach of trust is an offence contrary to Sec. 27(1) of the Act; a criminal offence under the Criminal Code of Canada; and may create a civil cause of action against the trustee, i.e. the brokerage.

Brokerages as trustees of a consumer's money have important responsibilities, including a legal duty to observe a high standard of care and to act impartially when dealing with potential beneficiaries of a trust. The proper course of action in the case of a failed Agreement is to disburse the trust money in accordance with a release or direction signed by the parties to the Agreement or pursuant to a court order. The parties to the Agreement are the seller and buyer. If the parties to the Agreement are or become involved in a court action it may be possible to arrange to have the deposit money held in trust paid into court. The advice of a lawyer may be advisable in any of these situations.

In summary, in the case of a failed transaction, a brokerage should only disburse the deposit in two circumstances:

1. In accordance with a release or direction signed by all parties to the Agreement (Mutual Release) or;
2. Upon receipt of a direction from the Court (Court Order).

TRUST ACCOUNT
Section 27(1) of the Act

27.   (1) Every brokerage shall,

    (a) maintain in Ontario an account designated as a trust account, in,

        (i)   a bank, or an authorized foreign bank, within the meaning of section 2 of the Bank Act (Canada),

        (ii)   a loan or trust corporation, or

        (iii)   a credit union, as defined in the Credit Unions and Caisses Populaires Act, 1994;

    (b) deposit into the account all money that comes into the brokerage's hands in trust for other persons in connection with the brokerage's business;

    (c) at all times keep the money separate and apart from money belonging to the brokerage; and

    (d) disburse the money only in accordance with the terms of the trust. 2004, c. 19, s. 18 (18).

TRUST FUNDS
Section 17 of Regulation 567/05

17.   (1) If an amount of money comes into a brokerage's hands in trust for another person in connection with the brokerage's business, the brokerage shall deposit the amount in the trust account maintained under section 27 of the Act within the five business days.

    (2) In Subsection (1), "business day" means a day that is not,

    (a) Saturday, or

    (b) a holiday within the meaning of Subsection 29(1) of the Interpretation Act.

Real Estate Council of Ontario
Tel: 416-207-4800 Toll Free: 1-800-245-6910 Fax: 416-207-4820

Office of the Registrar
AsktheRegistrar@reco.on.ca

For more information about RECO,
visit: www.reco.on.ca

REBBA 2002
Real Estate & Business Brokers Act, 2002

THE TRUST ACCOUNT

Basic regulatory requirements for trust accounts and deposits are outlined. Salespersons need not understand all the intricacies of trust account management, but should be aware of basic components and requirements.

Real Estate Trust Account

A brokerage is required to maintain a trust account designated as a real estate trust account into which all monies coming into the possession of the brokerage for other persons must be deposited.

TRUST ACCOUNT ADMINISTRATION

Trust funds must be kept separate, a trust ledger must be maintained, such funds must be apart from other monies at all times and disbursements can only be made within the terms of the trust. The trust account imposes grave fiduciary and legal responsibilities on the brokerage. REBBA 2002 requirements include:

- The trust account must be designated as a real estate trust account.
- Only one trust account may be used, unless otherwise approved by the Registrar.
- No bank charges can be paid. If any are incurred, these must be settled using the general account.
- Payments to salespersons and co-operating brokerages are not paid directly from the trust account but rather through the commission trust account, as required by the RECO insurance policy.

The trust account must be clearly identifiable from the general account (day-to-day banking for the brokerage). All cheques, deposits and general banking records must state the brokerage's name as registered followed by *real estate trust account.*

The general account is similarly titled *real estate general account.* Monies held in trust must never be co-mingled with other finances of the brokerage and must never be referred to in a financial statement nor pledged, either directly or indirectly, as part of the normal brokerage business operation.

DISCLOSURE OF INTEREST EARNED

REBBA 2002 requires detailed disclosure regarding interest earned on trust funds. When funds are deposited in an interest bearing account, the interest rate received must be disclosed to the person for whom the deposit is made. The current rate at the time of deposit must be disclosed for variable interest accounts.

Interest accruing must be paid to the owner of the trust money, typically the buyer, unless otherwise specified in the agreement.

EXAMPLES   *Interest Calculations*

ABC Realty Inc. deposits the buyer's funds in a fixed interest-bearing account at 2%. The brokerage must disclose this rate and pay accrued interest to the beneficial owner of the trust money, unless otherwise agreed.

ABC Realty Inc. deposits the buyer's funds in a variable interest rate account currently at 2.75%, but several interest fluctuations occur during the term. The brokerage must disclose the 2.75% rate at inception, but not the fluctuations. ABC Realty Inc. must pay the buyer whatever interest accrues (unless otherwise agreed).

ABC Realty Inc. deposits the buyer's funds in an interest-bearing account at 2.5%, but agrees to only pay 1.5% to the buyer. The brokerage must obtain agreement to the 1.5% payment, disclose the true rate of 2.5% received by the brokerage and pay the buyer the 1.5% interest accrued.

RECORDKEEPING

All trust money transactions must be authorized by the broker of record. That individual is also responsible for the full review and signing of the monthly trust reconciliation, making certain that all records are maintained in accordance with the Act and generally ensuring brokerage compliance with the legislation.

Monthly Bank Reconciliation

The Regulations contain specific procedures for trust account reconciliations. The monthly reconciliation must be prepared no later than 30 days after the monthly bank account statement is received or, in any other case, 30 days after the last day of the month.

For example, a brokerage receives the real estate trust account bank statement on April 11, 20xx for the period March 1–31st. The broker of record must prepare, review and sign the reconciliation within 30 days of receipt.

Trust Ledger

As with reconciliations, the Regulations include specific requirements for trust ledger preparation and the recording of trust money transactions. Each deposit must be entered in the ledger as a single entry. The entry is closed when appropriate disbursements equal to that amount are entered.

As an example, the broker of record for a new brokerage is establishing a trust ledger. Each deposit appears as a single entry showing the amount received, the date received, the person's name from whom the money was received and the property to which the trust funds relate.

In addition, any payment of interest on money held must indicate which trust funds that the interest relates to, the payment amount, the disbursement date and the person who authorized the payment.

Remedy Shortfalls Immediately

The Regulations are very clear regarding irregularities in the real estate trust account. Any shortfall must be immediately remedied. For example, a broker of record might possibly issue a trust cheque in error; i.e., the payment should have been made from the general account but, due to staff oversight, a trust cheque was issued and signed by mistake. The problem is not discovered until the monthly reconciliation. The broker of record must immediately deposit the full amount to offset funds disbursed in error and make appropriate notations so that complete records of the incident are available for any subsequent RECO Inspection.

Can a Brokerage Have More Than One Real Estate Trust Account?

The Registrar's approval is required for more than one real estate trust account. The most frequent requirement for a second trust account relates to property management. The establishment of this trust account typically involves setting up required books of record, creation of appropriate property records, the use of a property management trust ledger and related administrative procedures.

Brokerages may have a commission trust account depending on the real estate board they belong to.

Who Has Signing Authority for the Real Estate Trust Account?

REBBA 2002 requires that all trust money transactions must be authorized by the brokerage's broker of record and all trust cheques signed by the broker of record. If the broker of record is absent, another broker under the brokerage's employ may exercise signing authority. The Registrar must be notified of any such designations. A designation is not possible in a sole proprietorship as the broker is also the broker of record.

Can Property Other Than Funds Be Held in Trust?

Yes, REBBA 2002 contemplates such a possibility. The wording of OTH, Sec. 15 specifically addresses Records of Trust Property; e.g., investment certificates or similar valuable documents.

CONCLUDING THE TRANSACTION

Trade Record Sheet

Trade record sheets must be completed for all agreements that involve the conveyance of an interest in real estate. Specific information must be included as set out in Regulation 579/05 (**OTH, Sec. 17**). Procedures are also detailed concerning how trade record sheets must be prepared, reviewed and signed.

Trade record sheet preparation is covered in more detail later in this course when discussing form completion and outlining transaction closing procedures.

Overall Conduct and Compliance

As a final note, the Code contains two important provisions that apply to the conduct of all registrants when carrying out their activities in the marketplace.

UNPROFESSIONAL CONDUCT, ETC.   CODE

39. A registrant shall not, in the course of trading in real estate, engage in any act or omission that, having regard to all of the circumstances, would reasonably be regarded as disgraceful, dishonourable, unprofessional or unbecoming a registrant. O. Reg. 580/05, s. 39.

EXAMPLE   *Unprofessional Conduct, Etc.*

A salesperson was provided a key to the seller's property in order to hold open houses during the seller's extended absence from Canada. Unknown to the brokerage, the salesperson was involved in certain illegal activities and was using the seller's house as a rendezvous point. Unknown to the salesperson, the seller had contacted a neighbour to 'keep an eye on the place' during his absence. The neighbour reported these happenings to the seller, the police were called and subsequent charges laid. The Real Estate Council of Ontario also took disciplinary action under Section 39 of the Code.

ABUSE AND HARASSMENT   CODE

40. A registrant shall not abuse or harass any person in the course of trading in real estate. O. Reg. 580/05, s. 40.

EXAMPLE   *Abuse and Harassment*

The buyers, clients of a co-operating brokerage, refused the counter offer made by the salesperson's seller client and abruptly ended all negotiations. The salesperson representing the seller couldn't understand why the buyers wouldn't want the property at the counter-offered price. On her own initiative, she sought out the buyers and tried to convince them to resume negotiations. After a heated discussion in the local mall and several calls to the buyers' home, the buyers lodged a complaint with the Real Estate Council of Ontario stating that the salesperson was harassing them.

KNOWLEDGE INTEGRATION

Notables

- The Code of Ethics includes requirements that address major steps leading to a real estate transaction.
- Registrants must meet ethical requirements when working with clients, customers and others.
- The Code includes various provisions concerning false advertising/falsifying information, promises/inducements, inaccurate representations and errors, misrepresentations and fraud.
- Registrants must adhere to various regulatory requirements regarding the use of a registered name.
- The Code of Ethics requires that registrants disclose the existence of known seller property information statements.
- Material (pertinent) facts must be disclosed to clients and customers.
- Registrants must ensure that agreements are written and legible and on current forms.

- Various ethical provisions are set out in the Code regarding negotiating and presenting offers.
- REBBA 2002 contains requirements relating to the retention of copies of all written offers received by a seller's brokerage.
- Timely delivery of agreements and other documents is required.
- Registrants must ensure that clients are made fully aware of significant activities undertaken on behalf of those clients.
- Deposit requirements are found in the Code, REBBA 2002 and the General Regulation (567/05).
- Salespersons need not know all the intricacies of trust account management, but should understand basic trust account operation.
- Registrants must complete a trade record sheet for each transaction in accordance with requirements set out in REBBA 2002.
- The Code requires that registrants must not engage in unprofessional conduct.

Glossary

Glossary terms are not included in this chapter. Students should, however, review the following defined terms included in the Code of Ethics, Sec. 1: Interpretations.

Buy

Buyer

Buyer Representation Agreement

Material Fact

Seller Representation Agreement

Strategic Thinking For Your Career

Questions are included to assist in developing your new career. No answers are provided.

1. What books are available that can assist me in developing effective, accurate advertising?

2. What advertising guidelines can my intended employing brokerage provide to assist me in my new career?

3. What office policies have been developed in my intended employing brokerage regarding handling of deposits?

4. What plan can I put into place to ensure that my future clients are always kept fully informed in accordance with Code of Ethics, Sec. 23: Steps Taken by the Registrant?

Chapter Mini-Review

Solutions are located in the Appendix.

1. Registrants must provide conscientious and competent service to clients, but not to customers.

   ◯ True ◯ False

2. A registrant who offers an opinion about the value of a client's property must have appropriate education or experience to provide such an opinion.

   ◯ True ◯ False

3. Brokers and salespersons must be careful not to interfere with client relationships of other registrants.

   ◯ True ◯ False

4. A salesperson who contravenes Sec. 34: Falsifying Information can face a fine of up to $50,000.

   ◯ True ◯ False

5. A seller does not have to give his or her written consent in order for a salesperson to include the following heading on a classified advertisement: New Listing: 84 Weston Court.

   ◯ True ◯ False

6. A seller must complete a seller property information statement when offering a property for sale, failing which the registrant acting for that seller client would be in violation of Code of Ethics, Sec. 20: Seller Property Information Statement.

   ◯ True ◯ False

7. A salesperson must disclose the existence and substance of competing offers to every person who is making one of the competing offers.

   ◯ True ◯ False

8. A registrant must advise a buyer client of all significant activities undertaken on behalf of that client when representing that client.

   ◯ True ◯ False

9. A deposit received from a buyer involving a transaction must be placed in the real estate trust account within two days.

   ◯ True ◯ False

Chapter Mini-Review (continued)

10. Trust funds need not be kept separate from other funds within a brokerage, provided that the brokerage maintains a trust ledger and carries out monthly reconciliation for such funds.

    ◯ True   ◯ False

11. If monies are dispersed from the trust fund in error, the broker of record must ensure that sufficient funds are immediately deposited in the trust account to offset this error.

    ◯ True   ◯ False

12. A brokerage is only permitted to have one trust account.

    ◯ True   ◯ False

13. A seller's brokerage has the option to retain, for a period of one year only, either a summary document of an accepted offer that results in the purchase of real estate or an actual copy of the accepted offer.

    ◯ True   ◯ False

Active Learning Exercises

Solutions are located in the Appendix.

▣ Exercise 1   Multiple Choice

1.1   A salesperson, acting on behalf of his brokerage, is representing both buyer and seller. He advises his seller client to accept an offer from his buyer client, while knowing that a competing offer will net more to his seller client. Which of the following Code of Ethics provisions best applies to this situation?

   a.   Sec. 3: Fairness, Honesty, Etc.
   b.   Sec. 4: Best Interests
   c.   Sec. 5: Conscientious and Competent Service, Etc.
   d.   Sec. 7: Dealings with Other Registrants

1.2   A salesperson, acting on behalf of her brokerage, represents a buyer client and has three available properties that meet the buyer's requirements. The commission rates offered to a co-operating brokerage for the sale of these properties varies; i.e., 1.5%, 2.5% and 3%. According to the Code of Ethics, she should:

   a.   Introduce the client only to the property that most closely meets the buyer's requirements.
   b.   Introduce the client to the property that provides the highest commission rate.
   c.   Introduce the client to all three available properties.
   d.   Introduce the client only to the property that provides the lowest commission rate.

1.3   A salesperson, acting on behalf of his brokerage, has received an offer for his seller client's home from a salesperson with a co-operating brokerage. The registrant delays the presentation of this offer for one day hoping to secure a better offer from another prospective buyer.

   a.   This delay is in contravention of the Code of Ethics, Sec. 24: Conveying Offers.

   b.   This delay is acceptable, as the salesperson may obtain a better offer from another prospective buyer.

   c.   This situation is not addressed in the Code of Ethics.

   d.   This delay is acceptable provided that the delay is not more than 24 hours.

1.4   Which of the following statements is correct?

   a.   A registrant must ensure that the client receives a copy of the signed agreement of purchase and sale at the earliest practicable opportunity, but this requirement does not extend to customers.

   b.   A registrant is permitted to make an inaccurate representation provided that no damages arise from that representation.

   c.   A registrant may offer services even though he or she does not have the necessary skills and knowledge, provided that a written consent is obtained from the person receiving those services.

   d.   A registrant must disclose known or ought to be known material facts to a customer.

1.5   According to the Code of Ethics, a Seller Property Information Statement:

   a.   Must be completed by the registrant when preparing a seller representation agreement for a prospective client.

   b.   Is intended to provide information to buyers about the real estate that is being offered for sale.

   c.   Must be attached to any agreement for the conveyance of an interest in real estate to which it applies.

   d.   Is a confidential document that must not be disclosed to prospective buyers.

1.6   A listing salesperson is presenting two offers, one for $397,000 that he obtained from a buyer and a second offer for $399,000 obtained by a salesperson from a co-operating brokerage. The listing salesperson agrees to reduce commission by $4,000 to make his offer more attractive, but does not disclose this fact to the other brokerage or its respective buyer.

   a.   The listing salesperson does not have to disclose this commission reduction, as it is a private matter between the salesperson and the seller client.

   b.   The listing salesperson, by not disclosing this fact, is in violation of Sec. 24: Conveying Offers.

   c.   The listing salesperson, by not disclosing this fact, is in violation of Sec. 25: Agreement Relating to Commission.

   d.   The listing salesperson cannot reduce commission during negotiations.

1.7   A salesperson is showing a property to a prospective buyer. During the showing, the buyer remarks about the vacant land behind the property. The salesperson informs the buyer that this is 'green space' even though he knows that a re-zoning application for the land is being finalized. The buyer purchases the property only to discover that a 12-unit apartment complex is scheduled for the site. The buyer takes legal action, as well as filing a complaint with the Real Estate Council of Ontario.

    a.   The salesperson is not responsible for inaccurate statements concerning matters that exist beyond the specific property being shown.

    b.   The salesperson innocently made a mistake and would not be subject to any disciplinary action.

    c.   The salesperson would not be subject to disciplinary action, as the matter is being addressed by the Courts.

    d.   The salesperson has made an inaccurate representation and, more particularly, is in violation of Sec. 37 of the Code of Ethics.

1.8   A salesperson places a classified ad for a listed property and includes his registered name and telephone number, but fails to also include the registered name of the brokerage in the ad. Which of the following options best addresses this situation?

    a.   The salesperson is in violation of Sec. 38: Error, Misrepresentation, Fraud, etc.

    b.   The salesperson made an innocent mistake and is not in violation of the Code of Ethics.

    c.   The salesperson is in violation of Sec. 36: Advertising.

    d.   The salesperson is not required to include the brokerage name within the ad, as long as the brokerage telephone number is inserted in the ad.

■ Exercise 2   The Countered Counter Offer

A salesperson prepared an offer for the buyer client, which was subsequently counter offered by the seller who wanted different terms, including a higher price. The buyer client, upon reviewing the counter offer made on his original offer form, made further changes and countered the counter offer. As a result, the offer form was difficult to read given all the changes. What guidance does the Code of Ethics give in regard to this situation?

▓ Exercise 3   The Incentive

A salesperson requested an appraiser to value a property for mortgage purposes on behalf of a buyer client. The appraiser, a personal friend of the salesperson, arrived at a $387,000 value estimate following an inspection of the property being purchased by the buyer client. The salesperson, needing a higher valuation in order to obtain the necessary mortgage financing for his client, offered a cash incentive to the appraiser to *up the value estimate to $425,000.* Comment on the salesperson's actions in terms of the *Real Estate and Business Brokers Act, 2002,* including the Code of Ethics.

▓ Exercise 4   The Commission

A salesperson is working with a buyer client in finding a suitable home. He finds a suitable property, but is not content with the commission being offered for this particular home and does not introduce that home to his client. What specific provision in the Code of Ethics best addresses this situation?

◼ Exercise 5   The Presentation

A salesperson obtains an offer from his buyer client, who is very anxious to have the offer presented to the seller before any competing offers appear. He instructs the salesperson to call the seller directly and not communicate through the seller's brokerage, as this will *simply slow down the process*. If the salesperson complies with this instruction, what section in the Code of Ethics has been violated?

CHAPTER 3

Documenting Seller Representation

Introduction

Representation agreements are fundamental to real estate brokerage. No other document is more frequently encountered in day-to-day activities. The listing is the foundation on which a successful residential or commercial sale is built.

Registrants must fully understand preprinted wordings, accurately complete documentation and be knowledgeable about representation agreement requirements set out in the *Real Estate and Business Brokers Act, 2002*.

Ontario Real Estate Association forms are highlighted for instructional purposes. All OREA forms used in this course are reprinted in the *Appendix*. Wordings and formats may vary depending on the particular brokerage and real estate board. Registrants must fully acquaint themselves with all local wording/procedural variations. This text highlights MLS® listings when discussing residential representation, as the vast majority of residential property is marketed through this service.

Learning Outcomes

At the conclusion of this chapter, students will be able to:

- Describe and explain the structure of seller representation agreements, including the authority and data input form components.
- Briefly describe clauses in a residential *Listing Agreement: Authority to Offer for Sale* (OREA Form 200).
- Briefly outline significant differences between the OREA residential and commercial listing agreements.
- Describe the legal obligations owed by a seller client to the real estate brokerage (agent).
- Outline commission negotiations with particular reference to the seller's legal obligations and regulatory requirements set out in REBBA 2002 regarding commission and commission-related disclosures.
- Discuss the operation of a holdover clause including legal perspectives in the enforcement of such a provision.
- Analyze support documents commonly associated with residential listing agreements including the seller property information statement (SPIS), mortgage verification form, amendment to listing agreement form, suspension of listing agreement form, cancellation of listing agreement form and assignment of listing agreement form.
- Outline common errors and omissions when listing property and preparing associated representation agreements.
- Briefly discuss errors and omissions insurance claims relating to urban and rural properties.

SELLER REPRESENTATION AGREEMENT

A seller representation agreement (listing agreement) is an **authority** granted by a seller to a real estate brokerage to act on his/her behalf in offering a property for sale (or lease) on terms and conditions set forth in the representation agreement. The listing agreement performs several functions:

- Establishes the seller/brokerage agency relationship with defined limitations on the agent's authority.
- Provides property specifics for paper and electronic distribution.
- Furnishes information for negotiations and drafting offers.
- Outlines services being performed.

The terms *seller representation agreement* and *listing agreement* are viewed as synonymous and are used interchangeably in this text.

Types of Listings

Major listing types include the **open listing**, the **exclusive listing** and the **MLS® listing**. An open listing is given to any number of brokers without liability to compensate any, except the one who first acquires a buyer ready, willing and able to meet the terms of the listing, or secures the acceptance by the seller of a satisfactory offer.

An exclusive listing involves the giving of the sole right to sell the described property according to the terms of the representation agreement. Under this arrangement, one brokerage is authorized by the seller to sell the property during a specific time. If the property is sold during that time, the brokerage receives a commission. With this form of representation agreement, only the brokerage with whom the agreement is signed may sell the property and receive the commission. However, the brokerage has the option of co-operating with other brokerages.

An MLS® listing is viewed in the marketplace as a distinct type of listing. However, it is actually a special form of exclusive listing where co-operation with other brokerages is specifically authorized by the seller.

Authority vs. Data Input Form

Most representation agreements, including those developed by the Ontario Real Estate Association, contain two parts: the authority (legal relationship) and the data input form (property particulars).

AUTHORITY

The representation agreement sets out the legal relationship, obligations of the parties and time limits concerning such authority. The authority is granted in the brokerage's name, never the salesperson's. While the seller's authority can be verbal, the Code of Ethics requires that the authority be put in writing and signed by the registrant prior to any offer being made. The seller is not obligated to sign the agreement.

This express authority delegated by the principal clearly sets forth in exact, plain, direct and well-defined limits those acts and duties that the agent is empowered to perform on behalf of the principal. If there is a definite understanding between the principal and agent, then the agency relationship has been established by express agreement.

The property is fully identified with the authority granted until 11:59 p.m. on a specified date. The document generally sets out commission arrangements including a **holdover**

Authority

The legal power or right given by a principal and accepted by the agent to act on the principal's behalf in business transactions with a third party.

Holdover Provision

A provision in a listing agreement extending the broker's right to commission beyond the expiration date for persons introduced to the property during the currency of the listing.

provision. A listing price is established, but the authority is typically extended to include any other price or terms that the seller may accept.

Ultimately, the responsibility to set a listing price rests with the seller, not the salesperson. The seller is entitled to the salesperson's professional opinion regarding property value and listing price. A comparative market analysis (CMA) is usually prepared for that purpose.

Representation agreement wordings and formats used by real estate boards are generally similar across Ontario. However, registrants must carefully study local forms to identify and fully understand any significant text differences. Brokerages may also use different forms when processing exclusive, non-MLS® listings.

DATA INPUT FORMS

Data input forms typically are used with all listings. Real estate board data input forms (sometimes referred to as data information forms) vary across the province given differing MLS® providers, local market needs and traditional practices within different boards.

Input forms used by real estate boards typically include mandatory and optional data fields. Brokerages are responsible for the completeness and accuracy of all listing information.

Processing the MLS® Representation Agreement   **CURIOSITY**

Brokerages forward listed property details to the real estate board by way of board load (the data input form is forwarded to the board for inputting) or broker load (the information is electronically transmitted to the board's MLS® database). The latter is most commonly found in the marketplace. With broker load, boards do not typically require original documentation, but reserve the right to audit the brokerage's paper trail. Brokerages are subject to strict time requirements for inputting MLS® data following the commencement date of the seller representation agreement.

Photographs are forwarded or transmitted electronically. Selected boards maintain a photo library or members can request a new photo provided by the board photo service (if available). Alternatively, selected listings may specify *No Photo Required* or *No Photo Available*. Specific requirements for data-related input and usage policies are set out in the MLS® Rules and Regulations.

Information contained on the MLS® database is then available to authorized users (i.e., brokers and salespersons within that board) to assist in representing their clients. Some boards may still offer paper-based (property catalogues), but electronic (online) access to listed property is by far the most common method, given costs associated with print productions. Further, Boards establish electronic links to a national database (**www.realtor.ca**), and also typically provide links to member Internet sites.

REBBA 2002: Agreement Preparation

Sec. 11 of the Code of Ethics sets out minimum requirements for all written seller representation agreements including:

- effective date of the agreement;
- amount of commission/other remuneration;
- amount payable to a co-operating brokerage (for seller-related agreements);
- how commission is paid;
- services being provided under the agreement;
- provision for agreements exceeding six months (i.e., the date is to be prominently displayed on the first page with space for the required buyer or seller initials); and
- agreement must contain only one expiry date.

CONTENTS OF WRITTEN AGREEMENTS `CODE`

11. (1) A brokerage shall not enter into a written agreement with a buyer or seller for the purpose of trading in real estate unless the agreement clearly, comprehensibly and prominently,

    (a) specifies the date on which the agreement takes effect and the date on which it expires;

    (b) specifies or describes the method for determining,

        (i) the amount of any commission or other remuneration payable to the brokerage, and

        (ii) in the case of an agreement with a seller, the amount of any commission or other remuneration payable to any other brokerage;

    (c) describes how any commission or other remuneration payable to the brokerage will be paid; and

    (d) sets out the services that the brokerage will provide under the agreement. O. Reg. 580/05, s. 11 (1).

  (2) A brokerage shall not, for the purpose of trading in real estate, enter into a written agreement with a buyer or seller that provides that the date on which the agreement expires is more than six months after the date on which the agreement takes effect unless,

    (a) the date on which the agreement expires is prominently displayed on the first page of the agreement; and

    (b) the buyer or seller has initialled the agreement next to the date referred to in clause (a). O. Reg. 580/05, s. 11 (2).

  (3) A brokerage shall ensure that a written agreement that is entered into between the brokerage and a buyer or seller for the purpose of trading in real estate contains only one date on which the agreement expires. O. Reg. 580/05, s. 11 (3).

The Code of Ethics also requires that the representation agreement be in writing and that copies of written agreements must be given to the applicable person(s).

COPIES OF WRITTEN AGREEMENTS `CODE`

12. If a brokerage and one or more other persons enter into a written agreement in connection with a trade in real estate, the brokerage shall ensure that each of the other persons is immediately given a copy of the agreement. O. Reg. 580/05, s. 12.

SELLER REPRESENTATION AGREEMENTS `CODE`

13. If a brokerage enters into a seller representation agreement with a seller and the agreement is not in writing, the brokerage shall, at the earliest practicable opportunity and before any buyer makes an offer, reduce the agreement to writing, have it signed on behalf of the brokerage and submit it to the seller for signature. O. Reg. 580/05, s. 13.

Authority vs. Introduction   RESIDENTIAL CASE LAW

The seller initially listed a rural property on March 13th, granting an authority to sell the property, which involved a commission of 5% and an expiry date of September 30th of the same year. The second listing agreement, executed on September 27th (also at 5% commission) had an altered authority which provided that:

> Vendor may sell privately @ 2.5% if purchaser is not introduced to property by listing broker/agent or any M.L.S. advertising (or) other real estate agents through M.L.S.

On November 6th, the seller sold the property with the transaction being completed in April of the following year. At that point, the seller paid a commission of 2.5%, but refused to pay the balance arguing that the buyer had not been introduced by the brokerage.

As further background, at or about the time of signing the second listing, the seller prepared two signs: one indicating that the property was for sale and the other for Saturday and Sunday open houses (no dates were specified—only times, that being 2:00–4:00 p.m.). The seller had an open house on Saturday, September 30th and the brokerage advertised an open house for Sunday, October 1st.

The buyers, who passed the property frequently, first became aware of its availability from seeing the brokerage signs, probably within the initial listing period. They attended the listing brokerage's open house on October 1st. Consequently, the issue revolved around whose open house was conducted on that date: the seller's or the brokerage's. A complicating matter involved the fact that the seller insisted on being in attendance at all open houses.

The Court found that the October 1st open house was that of the listing brokerage, as the company had placed a number of signs and advertised the property at its own expense. Further, a registry sheet was provided at the open house and the future buyer's name appeared on that registry. When the buyers appeared, the salesperson invited the seller to assist in the inspection of the property by the buyers, as she was involved with another prospect. The listing salesperson knew the buyers and did a follow up call following the open house.

The Court found that the listing brokerage had introduced the property in two ways: First, the listing brokerage's For Sale signs were on the property up to and including October 1st and seen by the future buyers. Secondly, the listing brokerage made efforts to attract prospects for the open house on October 1st which was attended by the buyers. A judgment was granted in favour of the brokerage for $8,292.53, being the equivalent of 2.5% of the sale price, plus costs.

Reference   Capital Real Estate Services Inc. v. Patrick and Rosemary Evangelisto.

COMMENTARY

The word *introduction* has received considerable attention by the Courts over the years. The Judge determined that the issue at trial was whether the brokerage had introduced the property, as opposed to the effort put forward to effect the sale. In rendering a decision, the Judge referred to a leading Ontario case (Terry Martel Real Estate Ltd. v. Lovette Investments Ltd. et al (1998) 20 R.P.R. 133 (O.C.A)) in which the Appeal Court awarded commission based on who originally introduced the property, as opposed to the broker who ultimately listed the property or the broker that sold the property during a holdover period relating to that listing.

According to the Appeal Court, the word *introduce* should be given its ordinary and accepted meaning. As such, the word carries a connotation of initial or first presentation. In this instance, evidence showed that the buyers had seen the property first, previous to the listing being taken.

Registrants should also note the importance of maintaining a registry of all individuals who attend an open house. This document may be key in a dispute involving commission.

PREPARATION GUIDELINES

Form 200 — Listing Agreement (Authority to Offer for Sale)

A **Listing Authority**   Seller(s) initials required for applicable option. (Authorized individual's initials for a limited corporation.)

B **Brokerage**   Insert full registered brokerage name. A salesperson's name is never entered.

C **Seller(s)**   Insert full name(s) of registered owner(s). Non-owner spousal consent is located on Page 3.

D **Address**   Insert municipal address for urban properties. Use acceptable rural address as per local practice. *Note:* The detailed legal description for offer drafting is typically included on the data input form.

E **Effective/Termination Dates** A commencement date must be inserted, as well as a termination date pursuant to the Code of Ethics, Sec. 11: Contents of Written Agreements. *Note:* A new MLS® listing cannot commence before the expiry of an existing MLS® listing. Some exceptions may apply depending on the MLS® system. For example, two listings may exist concurrently for sale and leasing purposes. The board, in this case, would treat sale and lease as separate trading functions.

F **Six-Month Provision**   The date cannot exceed six months without the seller's informed consent and initials, as per the Code of Ethics, Sec. 11: Contents of Written Agreements.

G **Price**   Include both words and figures.

H **Seller Representation/Warranty**   This clause is bolded for emphasis, as this warranty relates to the property not being currently listed with any other brokerage.

I **Commission**   Include commission percentage rate, agreed amount or a combination of both (See REBBA, Sec. 36).

J **Holdover Period**   Typically 60–90 days or a reasonable time period as agreed by the parties.

K **Co-operating Brokerage Commission**   Include commission percentage rate, agreed amount or a combination of both (See REBBA, Sec. 36).

L **Initials**   Initials of an authorized representative of the brokerage is required, as well as the seller's. In the case of a corporation, an authorized individual's initials are required.

The Seller understands that unless the Seller is otherwise informed, the co-operating brokerage is representing the interests of the buyer in the transaction. The Seller further acknowledges that the Listing Brokerage may be listing other properties that may be similar to the Seller's Property and the Seller hereby consents to the Listing Brokerage listing other properties that may be similar to the Seller's Property without any claim by the Seller of conflict of interest. The Seller hereby appoints the Listing Brokerage as the Seller's agent for the purpose of giving and receiving notices pursuant to any offer or agreement to purchase the property. Unless otherwise agreed in writing between Seller and Listing Brokerage, any commission payable to any other brokerage shall be paid out of the commission the Seller pays the Listing Brokerage, said commission to be disbursed in accordance with the Commission Trust Agreement.

MULTIPLE REPRESENTATION: The Seller hereby acknowledges that the Listing Brokerage may be entering into buyer representation agreements with buyers who may be interested in purchasing the Seller's Property. In the event that the Listing Brokerage has entered into or enters into a buyer representation agreement with a prospective buyer for the Seller's Property, the Listing Brokerage will obtain the Seller's written consent to represent both the Seller and the buyer for the transaction at the earliest practicable opportunity and in all cases prior to any offer to purchase being submitted or presented.

The Seller understands and acknowledges that the Listing Brokerage must be impartial when representing both the Seller and the buyer and equally protect the interests of the Seller and buyer. The Seller understands and acknowledges that when representing both the Seller and the buyer, the Listing Brokerage shall have a duty of full disclosure to both the Seller and the buyer, including a requirement to disclose all factual information about the Property known to the Listing Brokerage.

However, the Seller further understands and acknowledges that the Listing Brokerage shall not disclose:
- that the Seller may or will accept less than the listed price, unless otherwise instructed in writing by the Seller;
- that the buyer may or will pay more than the offered price, unless otherwise instructed in writing by the buyer;
- the motivation of or personal information about the Seller or buyer, unless otherwise instructed in writing by the party to which the information applies or unless failure to disclose would constitute fraudulent, unlawful or unethical practice;
- the price the buyer should offer or the price the Seller should accept; and
- the Listing Brokerage shall not disclose to the buyer the terms of any other offer.

However, it is understood that factual market information about comparable properties and information known to the Listing Brokerage concerning potential uses for the Property will be disclosed to both Seller and buyer to assist them to come to their own conclusions.

Where a Brokerage represents both the Seller and the Buyer (multiple representation), the Brokerage shall not be entitled or authorized to be agent for either the Buyer or the Seller for the purpose of giving and receiving notices.

MULTIPLE REPRESENTATION AND CUSTOMER SERVICE: The Seller understands and agrees that the Listing Brokerage also provides representation and customer service to other sellers and buyers. If the Listing Brokerage represents or provides customer service to more than one seller or buyer for the same trade, the Listing Brokerage shall, in writing, at the earliest practicable opportunity and before any offer is made, inform all sellers and buyers of the nature of the Listing Brokerage's relationship to each seller and buyer.

4. **FINDERS FEES:** The Seller acknowledges that the Brokerage may be receiving a finder's fee, reward and/or referral incentive, and the Seller consents to any such benefit being received and retained by the Brokerage in addition to the commission as described above.

5. **REFERRAL OF ENQUIRIES:** The Seller agrees that during the Listing Period, the Seller shall advise the Listing Brokerage immediately of all enquiries from any source whatsoever, and all offers to purchase submitted to the Seller shall be immediately submitted to the Listing Brokerage before the Seller accepts or rejects the same. If any enquiry during the Listing Period results in the Seller accepting a valid offer to purchase during the Listing Period or within the Holdover Period after the expiration of the Listing Period, the Seller agrees to pay the Listing Brokerage the amount of commission set out above, payable within five (5) days following the Listing Brokerage's written demand therefor.

6. **MARKETING:** The Seller agrees to allow the Listing Brokerage to show and permit prospective buyers to fully inspect the Property during reasonable hours and the Seller gives the Listing Brokerage the sole and exclusive right to place "For Sale" and "Sold" sign(s) upon the Property. The Seller consents to the Listing Brokerage including information in advertising that may identify the Property. The Seller further agrees that the Listing Brokerage shall have sole and exclusive authority to make all advertising decisions relating to the marketing of the Property for sale during the Listing Period. The Seller agrees that the Listing Brokerage will not be held liable in any manner whatsoever for any acts or omissions with respect to advertising by the Listing Brokerage or any other party, other than by the Listing Brokerage's gross negligence or wilful act.

7. **WARRANTY:** The Seller represents and warrants that the Seller has exclusive authority and power to execute this Authority to offer the Property for sale and that the Seller has informed the Listing Brokerage of any third party interests or claims on the Property such as rights of first refusal, options, easements, mortgages, encumbrances or otherwise concerning the Property, which may affect the sale of the Property.

8. **INDEMNIFICATION AND INSURANCE:** The Seller will not hold the Listing Brokerage and representatives of the Brokerage responsible for any loss or damage to the Property or contents occurring during the term of this Agreement caused by the Listing Brokerage or anyone else by any means, including theft, fire or vandalism, other than by the Listing Brokerage's gross negligence or wilful act. The Seller agrees to indemnify and save harmless the Listing Brokerage and representatives of the Brokerage and any co-operating brokerage from any liability, claim, loss, cost, damage or injury, including but not limited to loss of the commission payable under this Agreement, caused or contributed to by the breach of any warranty or representation made by the Seller in this Agreement or the accompanying data form. The Seller warrants the Property is insured, including personal liability insurance against any claims or lawsuits resulting from bodily injury or property damage to others caused in any way on or at the Property and the Seller indemnifies the Brokerage and all of its employees, representatives, salespersons and brokers (Listing Brokerage) and any co-operating brokerage and all of its employees, representatives, salespersons and brokers (co-operating brokerage) for and against any claims against the Listing Brokerage or co-operating brokerage made by anyone who attends or visits the Property.

9. **FAMILY LAW ACT:** The Seller hereby warrants that spousal consent is not necessary under the provisions of the Family Law Act, R.S.O. 1990, unless the Seller's spouse has executed the consent hereinafter provided.

10. **VERIFICATION OF INFORMATION:** The Seller authorizes the Listing Brokerage to obtain any information affecting the Property from any regulatory authorities, governments, mortgagees or others and the Seller agrees to execute and deliver such further authorizations in this regard as may be reasonably required. The Seller hereby appoints the Listing Brokerage or the Listing Brokerage's authorized representative as the Seller's attorney to execute such documentation as may be necessary to effect obtaining any information as aforesaid. The Seller hereby authorizes, instructs and directs the above noted regulatory authorities, governments, mortgagees or others to release any and all information to the Listing Brokerage.

11. **USE AND DISTRIBUTION OF INFORMATION:** The Seller consents to the collection, use and disclosure of personal information by the Brokerage for the purpose of listing and marketing the Property including, but not limited to: listing and advertising the Property using any medium including the Internet; disclosing Property information to prospective buyers, brokerages, salespersons and others who may assist in the sale of the Property; such other use of

INITIALS OF LISTING BROKERAGE: ⟨   ⟩   INITIALS OF SELLER(S): ⟨   ⟩

Form 200   Revised 2015   **Page 2 of 3**

 Representation   Carefully review all Clause 3 provisions with the seller concerning representation, multiple representation, and multiple representation and customer service.

 Finder's Fee   Consent by seller for the listing brokerage or co-operating brokerage to receive and retain a finder's fee relating to financing for the property, over and above commission received in relation to this agreement. This consent is required pursuant to the Code of Ethics, Sec. 18: Disclosure of Interest.

 Spousal Consent   The seller warrants that spousal consent is not required, unless an appropriate signature is affixed (see Item).

 Initials   Initials of an authorized representative of the brokerage is required, as well as the seller's. In the case of a corporation, an authorized individual's initials are required.

the Seller's personal information as is consistent with listing and marketing of the Property. The Seller consents, if this is an MLS® Listing, to placement of the listing information and sales information by the Brokerage into the database(s) of the MLS® System of the appropriate Board, and to the posting of any documents and other information (including, without limitation, photographs, images, graphics, audio and video recordings, virtual tours, drawings, floor plans, architectural designs, artistic renderings, surveys and listing descriptions) provided by or on behalf of the Seller into the database(s) of the MLS® System of the appropriate Board. The Seller hereby indemnifies and saves harmless the Brokerage and/or any of its employees, servants, brokers or sales representatives from any and all claims, liabilities, suits, actions, losses, costs and legal fees caused by, or arising out of, or resulting from the posting of any documents or other information (including, without limitation, photographs, images, graphics, audio and video recordings, virtual tours, drawings, floor plans, architectural designs, artistic renderings, surveys and listing descriptions) as aforesaid. The Seller acknowledges that the database, within the board's MLS® System is the property of the real estate board(s) and can be licensed, resold, or otherwise dealt with by the board(s). The Seller further acknowledges that the real estate board(s) may: during the term of the listing and thereafter, distribute the information in the database, within the board's MLS® System to any persons authorized to use such service which may include other brokerages, government departments, appraisers, municipal organizations and others; market the Property, at its option, in any medium, including electronic media; during the term of the listing and thereafter, compile, retain and publish any statistics including historical data within the board's MLS® System and retain, reproduce and display photographs, images, graphics, audio and video recordings, virtual tours, drawings, floor plans, architectural designs, artistic renderings, surveys and listing descriptions which may be used by board members to conduct comparative analyses; and make such other use of the information as the Brokerage and/or real estate board(s) deem appropriate, in connection with the listing, marketing and selling of real estate during the term of the listing and thereafter. The Seller acknowledges that the information, personal or otherwise ("information"), provided to the real estate board or association may be stored on databases located outside of Canada, in which case the information would be subject to the laws of the jurisdiction in which the information is located.

In the event that this Agreement expires or is cancelled or otherwise terminated and the Property is not sold, the Seller, by initialling:

consent to allow other real estate board members to contact the Seller after expiration or other termination of this Agreement to discuss listing or otherwise marketing the Property.

Does   **Does Not**   [Q]

12. SUCCESSORS AND ASSIGNS: The heirs, executors, administrators, successors and assigns of the undersigned are bound by the terms of this Agreement.

13. CONFLICT OR DISCREPANCY: If there is any conflict or discrepancy between any provision added to this Agreement (including any Schedule attached hereto) and any provision in the standard pre-set portion hereof, the added provision shall supersede the standard pre-set provision to the extent of such conflict or discrepancy. This Agreement, including any Schedule attached hereto, shall constitute the entire Agreement between the Seller and the Listing Brokerage. There is no representation, warranty, collateral agreement or condition which affects this Agreement other than as expressed herein.

14. ELECTRONIC COMMUNICATION: This Listing Agreement and any agreements, notices or other communications contemplated thereby may be transmitted by means of electronic systems, in which case signatures shall be deemed to be original. The transmission of this Agreement by the Seller by electronic means shall be deemed to confirm the Seller has retained a true copy of the Agreement.

15. SCHEDULE(S): .... [R] .... and data form attached hereto form(s) part of this Agreement. [S]

THE LISTING BROKERAGE AGREES TO MARKET THE PROPERTY ON BEHALF OF THE SELLER AND REPRESENT THE SELLER IN AN ENDEAVOUR TO OBTAIN A VALID OFFER TO PURCHASE THE PROPERTY ON THE TERMS SET OUT IN THIS AGREEMENT OR ON SUCH OTHER TERMS SATISFACTORY TO THE SELLER.

[T]
.... DATE.................................. ....
(Authorized to bind the Listing Brokerage)   (Name of Person Signing)

THIS AGREEMENT HAS BEEN READ AND FULLY UNDERSTOOD BY ME AND I ACKNOWLEDGE THIS DATE I HAVE SIGNED UNDER SEAL. Any representations contained herein or as shown on the accompanying data form respecting the Property are true to the best of my knowledge, information and belief.

SIGNED, SEALED AND DELIVERED I have hereunto set my hand and seal:

[U]
.... ● DATE ....
(Signature of Seller)   (Seal)   (Tel. No.)

.... ● DATE ....
(Signature of Seller)   (Seal)

[V] **SPOUSAL CONSENT:** The undersigned spouse of the Seller hereby consents to the listing of the Property herein pursuant to the provisions of the Family Law Act, R.S.O. 1990 and hereby agrees that he/she will execute all necessary or incidental documents to further any transaction provided for herein.

.... ● DATE ....
(Spouse)   (Seal)

[W]
DECLARATION OF INSURANCE

The broker/salesperson..
(Name of Broker/Salesperson)

hereby declares that he/she is insured as required by the Real Estate and Business Brokers Act (REBBA) and Regulations.

....
(Signature(s) of Broker/Salesperson)

ACKNOWLEDGEMENT

[X] The Seller(s) hereby acknowledge that the Seller(s) fully understand the terms of this Agreement and have received a true copy of this Agreement

on the .... day of ...., 20 ....

.... Date: ....
(Signature of Seller)

.... Date: ....
(Signature of Seller)

Form 200   Revised 2015   **Page 3 of 3**

[Q] **Seller Consent to Contact**   Seller's initials required indicating whether other real estate board members can contact the seller following expiration of the listing.

[R] **Schedules**   Additional provisions (e.g., detailed chattels list, survey, etc.) should be identified in sequential order as Schedule A, Schedule B and so forth. Make certain that cross-references, such as property address and listing date, are included on all schedules. Seller(s) initials required on each schedule.

[S] **Data Input Form**   Seller's initials required on data input form.

[T] **Signature—Brokerage**   A person authorized to bind the brokerage (a broker or salesperson employed by that brokerage) must sign and date his or her signature.

[U] **Signature—Seller**   Seller's usual signature required. For corporations, an authorized signature is required along with the individual's title and corporate seal. If the seal is not used, insert the words: *I have the authority to bind the corporation.*

[V] **Spousal signature**   Follows guidelines set out in previous clause.

[W] **Insurance**   A declaration of insurance is signed by the applicable broker or salesperson.

[X] **Acknowledgement**   Seller acknowledges understanding and receipt of the agreement.

Other Listing Forms

All OREA forms relating to buyer representation, as well as other OREA forms, are reprinted in the *Appendix*.

RESIDENTIAL LEASING FORMS

The Ontario Real Estate Association has a listing agreement for leasing properties referred to as the *Listing Agreement: Authority to Offer for Lease* (OREA Form 210) which is not illustrated in this chapter, but is included in the *Appendix*. The residential leasing form generally parallels the sale form, with necessary *landlord/tenant* wording changes.

COMMERCIAL FORMS

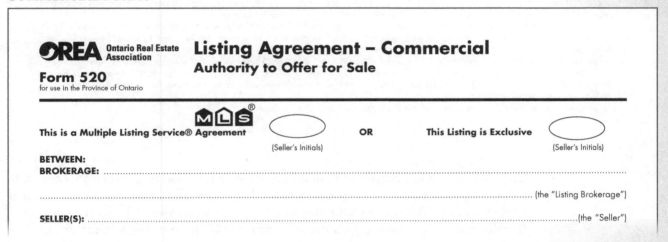

The *Listing Agreement —Commercial: Authority to Offer for Sale* (OREA Form 520) generally follows the structure and wording of its residential counterpart, but important differences require highlighting. Present discussion is limited to three notable differences only. Students contemplating commercial listing and sale activities should fully review both forms to identify all wording variations.

Clause 1: Definitions and Interpretations

The commercial listing form expands the definition of a purchase to include an option to purchase, exercising a First Right of Refusal, and the selling or transferring of shares or assets. Further, real property includes real estate as defined in the *Real Estate and Business Brokers Act, 2002* and property is deemed to include any part thereof or interest therein.

1. **DEFINITIONS AND INTERPRETATIONS:** For the purposes of this Listing Agreement ("Authority" or "Agreement"), "Seller" includes vendor and a "buyer" includes a purchaser or a prospective purchaser. A purchase shall be deemed to include the entering into of any agreement to exchange, or the obtaining of an option to purchase which is subsequently exercised, or the causing of a First Right of Refusal to be exercised, or an agreement to sell or transfer shares or assets. "Real property" includes real estate as defined in the Real Estate and Business Brokers Act (2002). The "Property" shall be deemed to include any part thereof or interest therein. A "real estate board" includes a real estate association. This Agreement shall be read with all changes of gender or number required by the context. For purposes of this Agreement, anyone introduced to or shown the Property shall be deemed to include any spouse, heirs, executors, administrators, successors, assigns, related corporations and affiliated corporations. Related corporations or affiliated corporations shall include any corporation where one half or a majority of the shareholders, directors or officers of the related or affiliated corporation are the same person(s) as the shareholders, directors, or officers of the corporation introduced to or shown the Property.

Clause 2: Commission

Clause 2 has an added provision that pertains to an instance where a deposit becomes forfeited, awarded, directed or released by the seller. If such occurs, the listing brokerage is authorized by the seller to retain 50% of the deposit for services rendered (but not to exceed commission that would have been payable had the sale been consummated).

The Seller further agrees to pay such commission as calculated above if an agreement to purchase is agreed to or accepted by the Seller or anyone on

the Seller's behalf within .... days after the expiration of the Listing Period (**Holdover Period**), so long as such agreement is with anyone who was introduced to the Property from any source whatsoever during the Listing Period or shown the Property during the Listing Period. If, however, the offer for the purchase of the Property is pursuant to a new agreement in writing to pay commission to another registered real estate brokerage, the Seller's liability for commission shall be reduced by the amount paid by the Seller under the new agreement.

The Seller further agrees to pay such commission as calculated above even if the transaction contemplated by an agreement to purchase agreed to or accepted by the Seller or anyone on the Seller's behalf is not completed, if such non-completion is owing or attributable to the Seller's default or neglect, said commission to be payable on the date set for completion of the purchase of the Property.

Any deposit in respect of any agreement where the transaction has been completed shall first be applied to reduce the commission payable. Should such amounts paid to the Listing Brokerage from the deposit or by the Seller's solicitor not be sufficient, the Seller shall be liable to pay to the Listing Brokerage on demand, any deficiency in commission and taxes owing on such commission.

In the event the buyer fails to complete the purchase and the deposit or any part thereof becomes forfeited, awarded, directed or released to the Seller, the Seller then authorizes the Listing Brokerage to retain as commission for services rendered, fifty (50%) per cent of the amount of the said deposit forfeited, awarded, directed or released to the Seller (but not to exceed the commission payable had a sale been consummated) and to pay the balance of the deposit to the Seller.

All amounts set out as commission are to be paid plus applicable taxes on such commission.

Clause 7: Indemnification and Insurance

The indemnification clause found in the commercial form has been expanded to include liability, claim, loss, cost, damage or injury resulting from contaminants or environmental problems. The seller is also warranting that the property is insured, including personal liability insurance against any claims or lawsuits resulting from bodily injury or property damage to others.

7. **INDEMNIFICATION AND INSURANCE:** The Seller will not hold the Listing Brokerage and representatives of the Brokerage responsible for any loss or damage to the Property or contents occurring during the term of this Agreement caused by the Listing Brokerage or anyone else by any means, including theft, fire or vandalism, other than by the Listing Brokerage's gross negligence or wilful act. The Seller agrees to indemnify and save harmless the Listing Brokerage and representatives of the Brokerage and any co-operating brokerage from any liability, claim, loss, cost, damage or injury, including but not limited to loss of the commission payable under this Agreement, caused or contributed to by the breach of any warranty or representation made by the Seller in this Agreement or the accompanying data form. The Seller agrees to indemnify and save harmless the Listing Brokerage and representatives of the Brokerage and any co-operating brokerage from any liability, claim, loss, cost, damage or injury as a result of the Property being affected by any contaminants or environmental problems. The Seller warrants the Property is insured, including personal liability insurance against any claims or lawsuits resulting from bodily injury or property damage to others caused in any way on or at the Property and the Seller indemnifies the Brokerage and all of its employees, representatives, salespersons and brokers (Listing Brokerage) and any co-operating brokerage and all of its employees, representatives, salespersons and brokers (co-operating brokerage) for and against any claims against the Listing Brokerage or co-operating brokerage made by anyone who attends or visits the Property.

In addition, a commercial leasing form is available that generally parallels the residential listing sale form, titled: *Listing Agreement: Authority to Offer for Lease (OREA Form 525)*, as well as forms for sub-leasing. See the *Appendix*.

Data Input Forms

Forms, data fields and codes vary by real estate boards for MLS® listings, and by brokerages for exclusive listings. Residential and commercial data input forms vary significantly in the marketplace. Selected topics are highlighted concerning residential data input for general guidance only. Accuracy and completeness are essential. Include additional information/schedules as required.

OREA
Ontario
Real Estate
Association

ONTARIO REAL ESTATE ASSOCIATION

RESIDENTIAL/RECREATIONAL

MLS # _____   ☐ EXISTING   ☐ TO BE BUILT   ☐ NEW   ☐ UNDER CONSTRUCTION

Effective Date:_____ Expiry Date:_____ Completion/Possession Date:_____ Price:_____ Terms:_____

Commission to Selling Broker:_____   Matrimonial Home: ☐ Yes   ☐ No   Easement and/or Encroachment: ☐   Yes   ☐ No   ☐ Unk

Holdover Period_____days   SPIS Completed: ☐ Yes   ☐ No   Listing Authority Modification: ☐ Yes   ☐ No

Special Provisions:_____   Applicable Schedules:_____

Property Address:_____   Municipality/Township:_____   Postal Code:_____

Roll #:_____ PIN #:_____ Legal Description: /Plan, Lot #, County, Town]:_____

Side of Road:_____ Area/Map Locator:_____ Near_____ Property Size:_____

Seller/Owners [s]:_____   Phone:_____

Assessment:_____ Taxes:_____ Year_____ Local Improvement: ☐ Yes ☐ No

Directions: _____

Broker: 1)_____ ID#_____ Phone #_____ Fax #:_____ email: _____
    2)_____ ID#_____ Phone #_____ Fax #:_____ email: _____

Salesperson: 1)_____ ID#_____ Phone #_____ Fax #:_____ email: _____
    2)_____ ID#_____ Phone #_____ Fax #:_____ email: _____

Occupant: (Select ___ only)	Indicate whether Property is: (Select ___ only)	Water Meter: ☐ yes ☐ no Water Supply: (Select ___ only) (indicate in remarks section if supply is not connected)	UFFI: ☐ yes ☐ no ☐ removed ☐ unknown
☐ Owner	☐ For Lease Only	☐ cistern ☐ municipal	Building Location Survey: ☐ yes ☐ no
☐ Tenant	☐ For Sale Only	☐ drilled well ☐ well	
☐ Vacant	☐ For Sale or Lease	☐ river/lake ☐ none	Single Family ☐ yes ☐ no
	☐ Exchange	☐ dug-well ☐ other_____	
Showings: (Select ___ only)	Age of Dwelling: _____	Sewer Type:	Multi-Unit - 2 units ☐ yes ☐ no
☐ Direct		☐ Sanitary Connected ☐ Sanitary Not Connected	Comments: _____
☐ Lock Box	(Use NE for New Construction or indicate	☐ Septic Installed ☐ Storm Connected	
☐ Call LBO	the age in years or use UN for unknown)	☐ See Remarks ☐ Storm Not Connected	
	Zoning		

Room Sizes and Levels: all room sizes are approximate and are to be verified by the Purchaser. Use only the abbreviation listed below to describe each room. Insert the level abbreviation and insert the room size. Please indicate if measurement is in ☐ imperial or ☐ metric.

Foyer	FO	Recreation Room	RR	Utility	UT	Great Room	GR	4 pce. Bathroom	B4
Living Room	LR	Recreation Room w/FP	RF	Fruit Cellar	FC	Great Room w/FP	GF	5 pce. Bathroom	B5
Living Room/Dining Room	LD	Play Room	PR	Games Room	GR	Cold Room	CR	6 pce. Bathroom	B6

Legal Description   Confirm with source documents; e.g., deed or survey. Watch for mutual driveways, easements and rights-of-way.

Lot Size   Confirm with source document. Include:
- frontage and depth for rectangular lots;
- full dimensions for irregular lots; and
- dimensions and/or exact acreage for larger tracts.

Retain survey on file and/or attach as schedule.

Age   Useful for buyer inquiries, but caution is advised. Actual age is usually available from the seller, original owner, builder or sometimes municipal records. If unknown, state so clearly. Don't guess.

Room Sizes   Measure rooms with seller assistance where possible. Never use previous listing information. Note any irregular rooms.

Rental Equipment   Get specifics. Rental equipment now goes well beyond rental hot water tanks; e.g., water softeners, satellite dishes and security systems. Details are ultimately required in the agreement.

Living Area   No standardized method is universally accepted regarding **living area measurements**. Some input forms may request square footage based on exterior measurements. In all instances, check with brokerage and/or real estate board for relevant guidelines.

Living Area Measurements

A measurement method, endorsed by the Alliance for Canadian Real Estate Education, setting out living area calculations for various styles of houses; e.g., one-storey, 1½ storey, bi-level and 2-storey.

Assessment/Taxes   Verify with seller's most recent assessment and tax notices. Board MLS® systems typically provide electronic links to tax information. Ensure full year's taxes are shown, not interim taxes. Watch for **special assessments**.

Zoning	Confirm current zoning. Zoning manuals are typically available for sale through local municipalities, but registrants should be aware that there may be site specific variances.
Wiring	Current rating (e.g., 60, 100 or 200 amp) is usually printed on the electrical panel, but confusion can arise. Ensure that main fuse capacity matches printed rating. Seek additional guidance as required.
Fixtures/Chattels	Clearly identify fixtures excluded and chattels included. To avoid potential confusion and problems, have the seller remove/replace any excluded items prior to showings.

COMMISSION NEGOTIATIONS

Seller's Legal Obligations

The seller, as principal, has three obligations to the agent (brokerage) under agency law when entering into a representation relationship: indemnification, remuneration and any additional obligations set out in the representation agreement. For additional discussion, see *Land, Structures and Real Estate Trading, Chapter 15: Trading and Agency Relationships.*

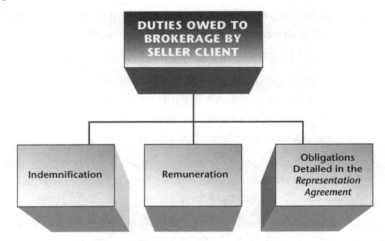

INDEMNIFICATION

Indemnification involves the obligation to compensate the brokerage for loss or damage in carrying out lawful acts. Indemnification also involves the reimbursement to the brokerage for expenses incurred when carrying out specific duties for the client. This right does not typically apply when a brokerage is receiving a commission for efforts expended in securing an acceptable offer for the seller client (unless this obligation is set out in the representation agreement).

EXAMPLE   *The Commercial Representation Agreement*

A brokerage enters into an agreement to lease a multi-unit retail complex in Anycity on behalf of a seller client. The brokerage will be remunerated based on a commission rate (% of the negotiated lease), but will pay its own expenses in regard to marketing the property. However, the seller client wants additional advertising targeted to selected potential renters and agrees to reimburse the brokerage for these specific costs. A schedule is added to the representation agreement setting out the terms of this reimbursement.

REMUNERATION

The seller client is obligated to remunerate the brokerage for carrying out duties as stated in the representation agreement. Exact wordings may vary, but typically the client agrees to pay a commission for a valid agreement to purchase the property, from any source whatsoever, obtained during the listing period.

The commission is due if the terms and conditions set out in the representation agreement are met or on such other terms or conditions, as the seller may accept. Further, the client agrees to pay such commission for a specified number of days after the expiration of the representation agreement to anyone introduced to the property during the currency of the agreement (see subsequent discussion on the holdover clause).

OTHER OBLIGATIONS

Exact wordings regarding additional obligations can vary in the marketplace. Generally, these focus on six primary areas:

If Sale Does Not Complete	The seller is typically obligated to pay commission if the transaction contemplated by the agreement is not completed, if such non-completion is due to the seller's default or neglect.
Deposit	The brokerage has the right to first apply the deposit to reduce the commission owed.
Deficiency	The seller agrees to pay the brokerage on demand any deficiency in commission (and taxes owing on such commission) when the deposit is insufficient to cover the commission.
Taxes	The seller agrees to pay applicable harmonized sales tax on the total commission payable to the brokerage.
Referral of Enquiries	The seller agrees to notify the brokerage immediately of any enquiries. If such is not done and a sale is negotiated directly with the seller, the brokerage is owed commission, as set out in the representation agreement.
Offers Presented Directly to Seller	The seller agrees to notify the brokerage of any offers submitted directly to the seller. If such is not done and a sale is negotiated directly with the seller, the brokerage is owed commission as set out in the representation agreement.

Regulatory Requirements

Various commission provisions are set out in REBBA 2002 regarding how commission is to be calculated and entitlement to commission.

COMMISSION CALCULATION

Commission or other remuneration can be an agreed amount, a percentage of the sale price/rental price, or a combination of both. If a percentage is used, the remuneration may include several percentages that decrease as the sale price or rental price increases. A commission must never be calculated based on the difference between the listing price and the actual sale price.

If no amount is agreed upon between seller and brokerage, the prevailing rate in the community will be used. Registrants must NOT indicate directly or indirectly that commissions are fixed or approved by administrative or government authorities, real estate boards or real estate associations.

COMMISSION AND REMUNERATION   `REBBA`

36. (1) All commission or other remuneration payable to a brokerage in respect of a trade in real estate shall be an agreed amount or percentage of the sale price or rental price, as the case may be, or a combination of both. 2013, c. 13, Sched. 3, s. 2.

If no agreement

(1.1) If there is no agreement as to the amount of the commission or other remuneration, the rate of it or other basis for determining it shall be that generally prevailing in the community where the real estate is located. 2013, c. 13, Sched. 3, s. 2.

Percentages

(2) If the commission payable in respect of a trade in real estate is expressed as a percentage of the sale price or rental price, the percentage does not have to be fixed but may be expressed as a series of percentages that decrease at specified amounts as the sale price or rental price increases. 2002, c. 30, Sched. C, s. 36 (2).

Prohibition

(3) No registrant shall request or enter into an arrangement for the payment of a commission or any other remuneration based on the difference between the price at which real estate is listed for sale or rental and the actual sale price or rental price, as the case may be, of the real estate, nor is a registrant entitled to retain any commission or other remuneration computed upon any such basis. 2002, c. 30, Sched. C, s. 36 (3).

COMMISSIONS, ETC.   `CODE`

9.   A registrant shall not indicate to any person, directly or indirectly, that commissions or other remuneration are fixed or approved by the administrative authority, any government authority, or any real estate board or real estate association. O. Reg. 580/05, s. 9.

ENTITLEMENT TO COMMISSION

A registrant is not entitled to a commission or other remuneration unless a written agreement is signed by the party paying the commission or the registrant has shown the property to the buyer (or introduced the buyer and seller to one another in relation to the buying or selling of an interest in real estate).

COMMISSIONS   `GEN`

23. (1) Subject to subsection 33 (3) of the Act and subsection (2), a registrant shall not charge or collect a commission or other remuneration in respect of a trade in real estate unless,

(a) the entitlement to the commission or other remuneration arises under a written agreement that is signed by or on behalf of the person who is required to pay the commission or other remuneration; or

(b) the entitlement to the commission or other remuneration arises under an agreement that is not referred to in clause (a) and,

(i) the registrant has conveyed an offer in writing that is accepted, or

(ii) the registrant,

(A) shows the property to the buyer, or

(B) introduces the buyer and the seller to one another for the purpose of discussing the proposed acquisition or disposition of an interest in real estate. O. Reg. 567/05, s. 23 (1).

LEGAL ACTION FOR COMMISSION

No legal action can be taken for the collecting of a commission involving a trade in real estate unless the person bringing such action was either registered or exempt from registration. Sec. 9 is cited below. Additional references to registration, refusals and suspensions are found in Sec. 10, 11, 14 and 15.

REGISTRATION A REQUIREMENT TO BRING ACTION   `REBBA`

9. No action shall be brought for commission or other remuneration for services in connection with a trade in real estate unless at the time of rendering the services the person bringing the action was registered or exempt from registration under this Act and the court may stay any such action upon motion. 2002, c. 30, Sched. C, s. 9.

UNEXPIRED LISTING AGREEMENT

A brokerage is not entitled to claim commission or other remuneration if the registrant knows that an unexpired listing agreement exists, unless the seller agrees in writing to pay such commission.

---

33. Commission   `REBBA`

(3) Unless agreed to in writing by the seller, no brokerage is entitled to claim commission or other remuneration from the seller in respect of a trade in real estate if the real estate is, to the knowledge of the brokerage, covered by an unexpired listing agreement with another brokerage. 2002, c. 30, Sched. C, s. 33 (3); 2004, c. 19, s. 18 (22).

The Need for Bold Print	CURIOSITY

The OREA *Listing Agreement* ensures that no confusion exists as to whether or not the seller has another listing agreement for the property or an agreement to pay commission to any other real estate brokerage. Following are bolded words from the current OREA form to ensure that the brokerage is in compliance with REBBA, Subsec. 33(3):

> **The Seller hereby represents and warrants that the Seller is not a party to any other listing agreement for the property or agreements to pay commission to any other real estate brokerage for the sale of the property.**

PAYMENT OF COMMISSION

Brokerages are not permitted to pay any commission or other remuneration to brokers or salespersons employed by another brokerage, nor to any unregistered person. Brokers and salespersons can only accept commission or other remuneration from their employing brokerage.

RESTRICTIONS RE: EMPLOYEES   `REBBA`

30. No brokerage shall,

    (a) employ another brokerage's broker or salesperson to trade in real estate or permit such broker or salesperson to act on the brokerage's behalf;

    (b) employ an unregistered person to perform a function for which registration is required; or

    (c) pay any commission or other remuneration to a person referred to in clause (a) or (b). 2002, c. 30, Sched. C, s. 30.

RESTRICTIONS RE: BROKERS AND SALESPERSONS   `REBBA`

31. (1) No broker or salesperson shall trade in real estate on behalf of any brokerage other than the brokerage which employs the broker or salesperson. 2002, c. 30, Sched. C, s. 31 (1).

Same

(2) No broker or salesperson is entitled to or shall accept any commission or other remuneration for trading in real estate from any person except the brokerage which employs the broker or salesperson. 2002, c. 30, Sched. C, s. 31 (2).

Holdover Provision

A holdover provision can be looked at from two dimensions. First, the term 'holdover' technically refers to a provision in an agreement that remains after expiration of the original agreement. Interestingly, the payment of a commission after expiration of the representation agreement would constitute one form of holdover. Fortunately, the courts have long recognized that commissions are due and payable even though the representation agreement may have expired before the property actually closes.

The more crucial issue when discussing holdover provisions involves a second dimension, that of a buyer introduced to the seller's property during the term of the representation agreement, but an agreement of purchase and sale is not concluded for the seller's property. What happens if the buyer subsequently buys the seller's property after expiration of the representation agreement? The holdover provision provides that the seller agrees to pay the commission (as set out in the representation agreement) if an agreement to purchase is agreed to or accepted by the seller or anyone on the seller's behalf within a stated number of days after the expiration of the listing period, unless the property is listed with another brokerage. The typical time period for such a holdover is 60–90 days, but longer periods may be found particularly when dealing with commercial properties.

The exact wording and time limit of a holdover period in a listing agreement can vary. Under current practices, the holdover provision usually states that the amount of commission payable to the brokerage is reduced by the amount of commission payable to the subsequent brokerage.

EXAMPLE   *Buyer Introduced During Listing Period*

Seller Smith signs a 90-day representation agreement with ABC Realty Inc. that contains a holdover provision. Following expiration, a buyer originally introduced to the property by a salesperson in ABC Realty's employ returns to negotiate directly with Smith. The buyer clearly wants a lower price to gain the benefit from the fact that Smith is not paying any commission. Smith, uncertain as to his position, takes the exclusive agreement to his lawyer. The lawyer confirms that if Smith sells the property to this buyer, then a commission is payable to ABC Realty Inc. pursuant to the holdover clause.

EXAMPLE   *Subsequent Listing and Holdover Clause*

Seller Smith was unhappy with Salesperson Lee because the property did not sell within the 60-day listing period despite several showings. While Lee insisted that a price reduction was necessary, Smith elected not to renew the representation agreement but rather to select XYZ Real Estate Ltd.

Interestingly, within the first month of this new 120-day authority, Smith agreed to reduce the price. Two months later, it was sold unconditionally by a co-operating brokerage to a buyer who was originally introduced to the property when ABC Realty Inc. was the listing agent. Smith, alluding to the holdover clause, expressed concerns that he might have to pay two commissions. XYZ Real Estate Ltd. assured him that such was not the case. The holdover provision in the original representation agreement provided that the liability for commission would be reduced by the amount paid to the new brokerage under a subsequent representation agreement.

Right to Commission: Holdover Clause	RESIDENTIAL CASE LAW

An owner invested in excess of $1 million when building a home in 1992. In 1994, personal circumstances had changed and the property was put up for sale, but failed to attract a buyer during successive years despite marketing efforts by various brokerages. In March of 1998, the owner listed the home with the plaintiff (the listing brokerage). From March 3, 1998 to July 15, 1999, the listing brokerage marketed the property unsuccessfully.

In early June, a potential buyer, when driving her children to school, noticed that the sign had disappeared from the property. The buyer inquired from a friend as to the status of the home and discovered that the property was still available for sale. The buyer, upon learning this fact, went directly to the seller. Interestingly, during testimony, the seller argued that the buyer did not initially approach her to purchase, but rather merely dropped in to see the home (as others had done in the past). Credible evidence revealed, however, that the buyer had dropped in on three occasions and had a clear intention of purchasing the property. Ultimately, an offer was drafted by the purchaser dated July 16, 1999. The listing expired on July 15, 1999.

The Judge, based on the evidence, confirmed that a valid listing agreement existed pursuant to the *Real Estate and Business Brokers Act,* Sec. 23 (the Act that immediately preceded REBBA 2002). Secondly, clearly a meeting between the buyer and seller had occurred during the currency of the listing agreement. Lastly, while the seller argued that the meetings with the buyer did not constitute an introduction to the property, the Judge found that the second meeting (occurring on June 6, 1999) was for the purpose of negotiating a sale. Consequently, the conditions set out in the holdover clause had been breached, regardless of whether or not the broker was the effective cause of the sale. The listing brokerage was awarded $96,300, plus pre-judgment interest at six percent.

Reference   Prudential Lorimer Realty v. Odette Barnes. Digested from full text judgment.

COMMENTARY

The holdover clause, an important component in any representation agreement, is enforceable in Court. The Judge found that the buyer and seller had met on several occasions and clearly such meetings constituted an introduction to the property. His exact comment from the full text judgment is noteworthy:

> *"...I [the Judge] have used the ordinary meaning of 'introduced' in the overholding clause and find that any initiation for [the buyer] which led her to the property, whether it involved the agent or broker, is an introduction satisfying the terms of this clause."*

The seller signed an MLS® listing (referred to as the first listing) for a 24-acre parcel of land on February 24, 1999. The listing agreement provided for a 5% commission along with a 90-day holdover provision. A buyer, seeking development property, submitted an acceptable offer through a co-operating broker but the deal fell through due to the inability to satisfy zoning conditions. The seller, prior to that event, decided to also sell the landscaping business that occupied the 24-acre parcel.

On May 13th, he signed an ICI MLS® agreement (referred to as the second listing) for the sale of the business. This agreement provided for a 5% commission with a six-month holdover provision. The holdover provision, in effect until the end of April of the following year, included a requirement that the broker notify the seller in writing of any persons introduced to the property prior to agreement expiration. The first listing agreement did not require written notice.

After the land sale fell through, the seller and buyer resumed negotiations later in 1999 without involving the brokerages from the original agreement. The parties concluded an asset agreement for the sale of both land and business sometime in March/April 2000, with the deal closing on April 11, 2000. In ensuing litigation, the listing and co-operating brokerages claimed commission, but the seller argued that no commission was due as the brokerages were not the 'effective cause of the concluded sale.' (Note: The buyer was also included as a defendant to the action, but was removed at point of trial.)

The buyer admitted that he learned of the property through the listing broker. However, both buyer and seller believed that the brokerages did not put the ultimate deal together. The sale, according to them, was successful only after the lawyers and accountants drafted and concluded the asset agreement. The seller did acknowledge that some commission might be warranted, but that it should be commensurate with the limited work done.

The Court found that the listing and co-operating brokerages were the true cause of the sale. However, the written notice provision regarding the sale of the business was not fulfilled. The brokerages argued that written documents conveyed between the parties during the listing period constituted such notice. The Court, however, found that such items did not constitute formal notice as contemplated in the listing agreement. The listing document specifically required that the seller be informed in writing of any persons introduced to the property. Such written notice specifically informed the seller of ongoing commission liability.

Accordingly, commission was due on the land sale (first listing), but not the business (second listing). The listing brokerage was awarded $48,150 commission (plus GST) based on 5% of $900,000. The balance of the $1,500,000 sale price was attributed to the business. The co-operating brokerage could then rely on its agreement with the listing brokerage to receive commission due.

Reference   First City Realty Limited v. Herman, Superior Court of Justice, Court File #00-BN-4179.

COMMENTARY

The Courts carefully review contractual wordings when arriving at a decision. In this instance, the holdover provision in the second listing required that written notice be provided. The Court reasoned that such notice was expressly included to ensure that the seller was aware of ongoing liability (when provided a list of buyers introduced to the property). The fact that various written documents were circulated during the listing period was not sufficient.

Commission-Related Disclosures

ADDITIONAL FEES

As part of remuneration paid to brokerages, the topic of additional monies received from others must be addressed. Agency law requires that an agent cannot make any secret profit or receive remuneration from anyone other than the client, without his or her fully informed consent. Section 18 of the Code of Ethics reinforces this requirement by stating that a registrant must disclose any direct or indirect financial benefit received from another person arising from services provided to the client.

DISCLOSURE OF INTEREST   `CODE`

18. (4) A registrant shall disclose in writing to a client, at the earliest practicable opportunity, any direct or indirect financial benefit that the registrant or a person related to the registrant may receive from another person in connection with services provided by the registrant to the client, including any commission or other remuneration that may be received from another person. O. Reg. 580/05, s. 18 (4).

For example, the OREA *Listing Agreement* includes a provision regarding finder's fees:

The Seller consents to the Listing Brokerage or co-operating brokerage receiving and retaining, in addition to the commission provided for in this Agreement, a finder's fee for any financing of the property.

DISCLOSURE: TWO COMMISSIONS/SAME TRADE

The Code of Ethics addresses a potential situation that might arise in which a brokerage could potentially receive two commissions on one trade. The Code provides that the brokerage cannot collect a commission from a buyer or seller and then collect a second commission pursuant to an agreement with another party, unless full written disclosure is made to both the buyer or seller and the other party (see example for possible scenario).

DISCLOSURE OF INTEREST   `CODE`

18. (5) A brokerage that has entered into an agreement with a buyer or seller that requires the buyer or seller to pay the brokerage a commission or other remuneration in respect of a trade in real estate shall not charge or collect any commission or other remuneration under another agreement entered into with another person in respect of the same trade unless,

(a) the brokerage discloses at the earliest practicable opportunity to the other person, in writing, the terms of the agreement with the buyer or seller that require the payment of a commission or other remuneration; and

(b) the brokerage discloses at the earliest practicable opportunity to the buyer or seller, in writing, the terms of the agreement with the other person that require the payment of a commission or other remuneration. O. Reg. 580/05, s. 18 (5).

EXAMPLE   *The Clients*

A residential seller has entered into a representation agreement with ABC Realty Inc., which provides for payment of commission upon the seller receiving an offer on terms and conditions set out in the agreement or on other terms that are acceptable to the seller. The listing salesperson circulates information about the property and another salesperson with the same brokerage contacts a buyer client who has been anxiously waiting for a property such as the seller's. The buyer client has also signed an agreement with ABC Realty Inc. agreeing to pay a commission if a suitable home is located for the buyer. If neither party was aware of the other agreement, the brokerage could possibly collect two commissions on the same trade. The Code requires that the terms of such agreements be fully disclosed in writing to both parties.

Commission disputes often arise out of lack of communication. Problems can develop if commission arrangements are not fully detailed. Many sellers think that commission is only due when the property sells and closes, but technically the typical wording provides that commission is due upon an acceptable offer being presented and does not address the closing of the transaction. Further, the seller should understand the implications of the holdover provision.

While holdover wordings vary, a key provision is that a commission is due if *an agreement of purchase and sale is accepted by the seller or anyone on the seller's behalf to anyone who was introduced to the property from any source whatsoever during the listing period or shown the property during the listing period.* Of course, such does not apply if the property is subsequently listed and sold through another brokerage. In that instance, the seller's obligation to the original brokerage is reduced by the amount paid under the subsequent representation agreement.

SUPPORT DOCUMENTS

Seller Property Information Statement (Form 220)

The Code of Ethics contains specific provisions related to the Seller Property Information Statement (SPIS). However, it does not oblige a seller to complete one. The Code requires that if a seller has completed an SPIS or similar written statement providing information about the real estate being offered, the representing broker or salesperson must disclose the existence of this statement to any buyer expressing interest in the property, unless the seller has instructed otherwise. On request, the broker or salesperson must make the statement available to a buyer as soon as is practicably possible.

OREA Ontario Real Estate Association   **Seller Property Information Statement**
Residential

Form 220
for use in the Province of Ontario

ANSWERS MUST BE COMPLETE AND ACCURATE This statement is designed in part to protect Sellers by establishing that correct information concerning the property is being provided to buyers. All of the information contained herein is provided by the Sellers to the brokerage/broker/salesperson. Any person who is in receipt of and utilizes this Statement acknowledges and agrees that **the information is being provided for information purposes only and is not a warranty as to the matters recited hereinafter even if attached to an Agreement of Purchase and Sale.** The brokerage/broker/salesperson shall not be held responsible for the accuracy of any information contained herein.

BUYERS MUST STILL MAKE THEIR OWN ENQUIRIES Buyers must still make their own enquiries notwithstanding the information contained on this statement. Each question and answer must be considered and where necessary, keeping in mind that the Sellers' knowledge of the property may be inaccurate or incomplete, additional information can be requested from the Sellers or from an independent source such as the municipality. Buyers can hire an independent inspector to examine the property to determine whether defects exist and to provide an estimate of the cost of repairing problems that have been identified. **This statement does not provide information on psychological stigmas that may be associated with a property.**

For the purposes of this Seller Property Information Statement, a "Seller" includes a landlord or a prospective landlord and a "buyer" includes a tenant, or a prospective tenant.

PROPERTY:		SELLER(S) TO **INITIAL** EACH APPLICABLE BOX			
SELLER(S):					
GENERAL: (Provide Applicable ADDITIONAL COMMENTS)		YES	NO	UNKNOWN	NOT APPLICABLE
1.	I have occupied the property from.........................to............................				
2.	Does any other party have an ownership or spousal interest in the property?				
3.	Is the property a condominium or a freehold property that includes an interest in a common elements condominium, (POTL)? (If yes, Schedule 221 to be completed.)				
4.	Does ownership of this property require membership in an Association and payment of				

COMMENTARY

- The SPIS is designed for residential purposes. No commercial version presently exists. Additional schedules (not illustrated) can be used for condominium (OREA Form 221: *Schedule for Condominium*) and rural properties (OREA Form 222: *Schedule for Water Supply, Waste Disposal, Access and Shoreline*).

- The statement does not provide information on psychological stigmas that may be associated with a property.

- The seller initials appropriate boxes: *Yes, No, Unknown* or *Not Applicable.*

- The seller states that information contained in the SPIS is true, *based on their current actual knowledge* as of the date that the form is signed.

- Any important changes known to the sellers prior to closing must be disclosed.

- An authorization is given to the brokerage to post the SPIS in the MLS® database.

- An authorization is given to the brokerage to deliver the SPIS to prospective buyers (or their agents or representatives).

- The buyer, when acknowledging receipt of the SPIS, acknowledges that the information contained in the form is not a warranty.

LEGAL DEBATE

Seller property information statements have undoubtedly gained popularity amongst registrants by limiting potential liability for defects that might otherwise go unnoticed during the listing process. Buyers have demonstrated a keen willingness to pursue legal action against both the brokerage and the seller when defects are discovered following closing. However, the merits of the SPIS vary depending on one's perspective.

BUYER'S PERSPECTIVE	SELLER'S PERSPECTIVE
The SPIS is advantageous in that detailed information is provided to them which they might not otherwise become aware of when viewing the property and negotiating a sale. However, the buyer should be cautioned not to rely on this statement, but rather to seek expert advice. The SPIS is not a warranty and only provides information based on the seller's actual knowledge. Other unknown defects or issues may impact the property. The bottom line: Caveat Emptor (*Let the Buyer Beware*).	The seller, when entering into a representation agreement, creates an agency relationship with the brokerage. The brokerage has a fiduciary duty to protect and promote the seller client's interests. However, when asking the seller to complete an SPIS, the brokerage is seeking certain information that the seller does not have to legally disclose including certain **patent defects**; i.e., those defects that are readily visible upon reasonable inspection. The seller's only obligation is to disclose material **latent defects** to the prospective buyer. A latent defect is a hidden flaw, weakness or imperfection known to the seller, but one which the buyer cannot discover by reasonable inspection. A *material* latent defect is a latent defect that, for example, renders the property dangerous or potentially dangerous to the occupants, unfit for habitation or unfit for the purpose for which the buyer is acquiring the property. The SPIS goes well beyond that minimum disclosure requirement. As such, the brokerage's promotion of the SPIS may be viewed as a fundamental conflict with the brokerage's duty to protect the seller's interests. Ironically, the SPIS can sometimes improve the seller's marketing stance by the client's open and forthright disclosure of relevant property information.

THE FULLY INFORMED SELLER

The best course of action lies in ensuring that the seller client is fully informed about the SPIS and the implications of completing this form. In doing so, the brokerage is protecting and promoting the client's interests by making him or her aware of all relevant factors in the decision-making process.

YOU, THE SELLER . . .

No Legal Requirement to Complete Form	. . . are not legally required to complete the form or sign it, but its contents can provide relevant information and conditions about the property.
No Legal Requirement to Disclose Certain Information	. . . are not legally obligated to answer questions in the SPIS.
Disclose Material Latent Defects Only	. . . are only required to disclose material latent defects; that is, those defects that: • render the property dangerous or potentially dangerous; • render the property unfit for habitation; • render the property unfit for the buyer's purposes (assuming that those purposes are known to the seller or the brokerage); • concern local authority or similar notices received by the seller that affect the property; and • concern the lack of municipal building or other permits.
Information Provided is Not a Warranty	. . . must ensure that information provided reflects your current actual knowledge, but the information that you provide is not a warranty.
Providing Copies	. . . are agreeing that the brokerage can provide a copy of the SPIS to interested buyers.

The Lowered Basement   RESIDENTIAL CASE LAW

Registrants still debating the merits of using the Seller Property Information Statement or comparable form in their day-to-day practices should carefully ponder the outcome of the following case.

The buyers purchased an older home for $570,000 that had undergone renovations including lowering the basement floor to accommodate a family room. A home inspection was conducted pursuant to the agreement of purchase and sale. The home inspector clearly advised the buyers of the inability to inspect various electrical and water fixtures that were situated behind walls or otherwise inaccessible. During the inspection, the home inspector noted evidence of possible water seepage in the basement. The buyers discussed the matter with the seller and received verbal assurances that there was no problem. They proceeded with the sale feeling that the identified problem was not significant. (The seller, during testimony, disputed this statement saying that he made no such representation.)

continued...

The buyers encountered basement water problems several months after closing and contacted a company for a repair estimate. Interestingly, the seller had contacted the same company to carry out repairs approximately two years earlier (but the contract was subsequently cancelled, as the seller claimed to have taken other steps to remedy the problem). Ultimately, the buyers' problem, which arose due to the lowered basement floor, was corrected for $9,800.

Evidence presented by both buyers and seller was somewhat contradictory. However, the situation was clarified by the salesperson's testimony during which a seller property information statement was produced. Two questions on the completed form related directly to the basement (history of any water, cracks, etc.) and any structural problems. The word 'no' was circled for both questions. The document was executed by the seller and witnessed by the salesperson. Apparently, even the seller's solicitor was unaware of the form until introduced at trial.

Based on evidence presented, the Judge ruled that the buyers were entitled to recover damages of $12,572.40 from the seller, which included costs of work performed by the basement specialist, replacement of affected carpet and cleaning.

Reference   Swayze v. Robertson, (2001) 39 R.P.R. (3d) 114)

Mortgage Verification (OREA Form 261)

A mortgage verification form does not have to be used but, when it is, the information must be accurate. A seller representation agreement should set out mortgage particulars if a mortgage is being assumed. Details would include mortgagee full name (lender holding the mortgage), priority (1st, 2nd and so on), approximate balance outstanding, interest rate, repayment terms, term expiry (don't confuse *term* with *amortization*) and special privileges. Otherwise, if the mortgage is not being assumed, registrants commonly insert the phrase *treat as clear*.

If mortgage details are required, these can often be confirmed based on the mortgage document, failing which the *Mortgage Verification* (OREA Form 261) can be forwarded to the mortgagee to obtain all relevant information.

OREA Ontario Real Estate Association   **Mortgage Verification**

Form 261
for use in the Province of Ontario

TO: ....   Date: ...., 20......................
        (Name of Mortgagee)

....   RE: Mortgage No. ....
        (Address)

....

The mortgage on the following property is held by you.

        Address ....

        Owners. ....

This property has been listed for sale and it would be appreciated if you would give my agent, ...
                                                                                (Name of Brokerage)

....
                (Address)

COMMENTARY

- **Special Privileges**   Any special privileges should be described in detail. The existence or non-existence of such privileges as prepayment, non-transferability or demolition may prove vital to the eventual sale. Many variations of mortgage privileges exist. The exact wording of such privileges should be included in the representation agreement. If a mortgage is to be assumed as part of a sale, the exact wording will be needed when the offer is being drafted. It is also vital to be aware of whether the ability to assume the mortgage is subject to prior approval by the mortgagee.

- **Contacting the Mortgagee**   The listing salesperson might consider contacting the existing mortgagee directly to explore whether the mortgagee would be amenable to refinancing the property for a new buyer if necessary and if so, what terms would likely be quoted.

- **Improved Knowledge/Rapport**   The importance of this initial contact with an existing mortgagee cannot be overemphasized. This contact provides the listing sales representative with a better knowledge of the flexibility of available financing and also keeps the mortgagee aware of what is happening with respect to the property, avoids unpleasant surprises and establishes a rapport that could be essential to refinancing at point of sale.

Amendment to Listing Agreement (OREA Form 240)

This form is typically used for changes such as altered listing price, extended expiry date and corrections/updating. Both the seller and listing brokerage sign the form. The listing brokerage must notify the real estate board (if applicable) within the required notice period as set out in the MLS® Rules and Regulations.

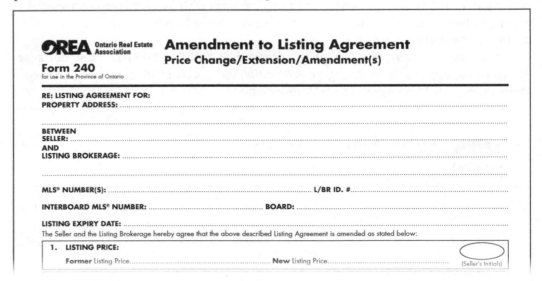

Suspension of Listing Agreement (OREA Form 241)

Suspension (not a cancellation) of listed property results in the cessation of all marketing/negotiations concerning the listed property for a specified time period. The listing brokerage must notify the real estate board (if applicable) within the required notice period as set out in the MLS® Rules and Regulations.

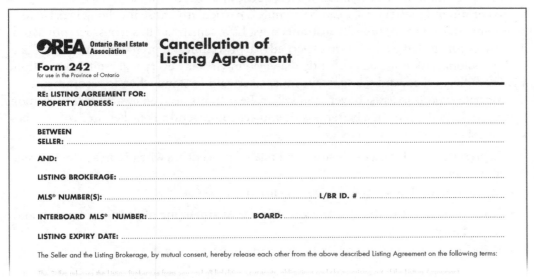

Cancellation of Listing Agreement (OREA Form 242)

The cancellation represents a release by both the seller and the listing brokerage, except for persons introduced to the property during the currency of the listing. The listing brokerage must notify the real estate board (if applicable) within the required notice period set out in the MLS® Rules and Regulations.

Assignment of Listing Agreement (OREA Form 243)

To be effective, the assignment must be executed by the seller and the assignee and a copy returned to the listing brokerage prior to the effective date. The listing brokerage must notify the real estate board (if applicable) within the required notice period as set out in the MLS® Rules and Regulations.

OREA Ontario Real Estate Association   **Assignment of Listing Agreement**

Form 243
for use in the Province of Ontario

RE: LISTING AGREEMENT FOR:
PROPERTY ADDRESS: ....

....

BETWEEN
SELLER: ....
AND:
LISTING BROKERAGE: ....

MLS® NUMBER(S): ....   **L/BR ID. #** ....

INTERBOARD MLS® NUMBER: ....   **BOARD:** ....

LISTING EXPIRY DATE: ....
The Listing Brokerage for the above described Listing Agreement assigns, transfers and sets over to:

....(the "Assignee")
any and all interest in the Listing Agreement, including all rights, duties and obligations pursuant to the Agreement. The Listing Brokerage releases the Seller
from any claims of remuneration or compensation with respect to this Listing Agreement.

COMMON ERRORS AND OMISSIONS

Risk and liability are constant companions in any profession and real estate is no exception. The listing process involves details, facts and figures, all of which are vital both for accuracy in representation agreements and subsequent offer negotiations.

To compound matters, risks can be complex, particularly those involving legislative requirements and procedures. Registrants must have sensitivity to such issues, but avoid any involvement that extends into expert advice or technical representations.

Professional risk must be prudently managed in virtually every real estate transaction. For example, brokers and salespersons must clearly understand when to recommend appropriate experts to assist buyers and sellers. Registrants need an awareness of common sources of liability to be in a better position to act competently. Four key areas of concern warrant special attention:

- Representation duties, disclosures and related procedures when representing buyers and sellers.
- Misrepresentation of facts concerning listed properties.
- Document errors in the preparation, delivery or amending of listings, contracts and related forms.
- Verbal misunderstandings with buyers and sellers.

Common representation agreement errors leading to disputes and litigation include:

- failing to carefully read/analyze source documents;
- transposing information from source materials to the representation agreement (including the data input form);
- size errors in listings; e.g., building and lot sizes;
- lack of knowledge and/or improper document preparation regarding **taxation**; e.g., property taxes and HST;
- incorrect or incomplete information regarding wells and septic systems;
- inaccurate details relating to overall property condition; e.g., age of various components, water leakage, roof problems and whether mechanical systems are fully functioning;

- structural defects including leaks/moisture in basement areas;
- representations concerning unverified property boundaries;
- zoning and land designations; e.g., restricted uses applying to property;
- encroachments or easements not identified or improperly described;
- failure to recognize the importance of patent and latent defects when listing property; and
- vague or incomplete listing of items included/excluded leading to negotiation and sale problems.

Take the prudent path. Get corroboration for key information included in representation agreements and insist on further investigation where necessary. Additional guidelines concerning errors and omissions are provided in subsequent chapters involving drafting and negotiating agreements.

CLAIMS EXPERIENCE: E & O INSURANCE

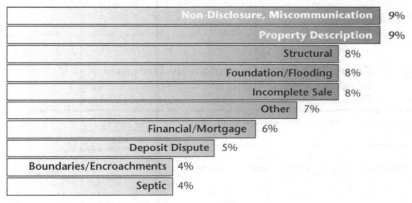

*Top Ten **Residential** Sources of Loss*
% Frequency, September 2000 – November 2011

Non-Disclosure, Miscommunication	9%
Property Description	9%
Structural	8%
Foundation/Flooding	8%
Incomplete Sale	8%
Other	7%
Financial/Mortgage	6%
Deposit Dispute	5%
Boundaries/Encroachments	4%
Septic	4%

As the above graph reveals, non-disclosure of relevant information is a key source of claims under the RECO insurance policy, followed by property description and physical components, most notably matters concerning structural components and the foundation (including flooding).

Below, claims experience over the eleven-year reporting span is broken down into urban and rural cases.

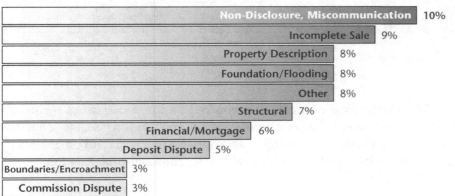

*Top Ten **Urban** Sources of Loss*
% Frequency, September 2000 – November 2011

Non-Disclosure, Miscommunication	10%
Incomplete Sale	9%
Property Description	8%
Foundation/Flooding	8%
Other	8%
Structural	7%
Financial/Mortgage	6%
Deposit Dispute	5%
Boundaries/Encroachment	3%
Commission Dispute	3%

Top Ten *Rural* Sources of Loss
% Frequency, September 2000 – November 2011

Well	15%
Non-Disclosure/Miscommunication	11%
Property Description	10%
Septic	9%
Foundation/Flooding	7%
Structural	6%
Other	6%
Boundaries/Encroachment	4%
Taxes (Including GST & HST)	4%
Incomplete Sale	4%

Based on the previous graph, well and septic systems tanks accounted for 24% of rural sources of loss. Clearly, registrants should seriously consider using the Seller Property Information Statement, along with the associated schedule (OREA Form 222: *Schedule for Water Supply, Waste Disposal, Access, Shoreline, Utilities*). The relevant questions from that form are reprinted below.

OREA Ontario Real Estate Association

Form 222
for use in the Province of Ontario

Seller Property Information Statement
Schedule for Water Supply, Waste Disposal, Access, Shoreline, Utilities

This Schedule is attached to and forms part of the Seller Property Information Statement (Form 220) for:

PROPERTY:	SELLER(S) TO **INITIAL** EACH APPLICABLE BOX
SELLER(S):	

WATER SUPPLY AND WASTE DISPOSAL: (Provide Applicable ADDITIONAL COMMENTS)	YES	NO	UNKNOWN	NOT APPLICABLE
1. (a) What is your water source? ☐ Municipal ☐ Drilled ☐ Bored ☐ Dug ☐ Cistern ☐ Lake ☐ Community ☐ Shared ☐ Other........				
(b) If your water source is Community/Shared, is there a transferrable written agreement?				
(c) Are you aware of any problem re: quantity of water? (If yes, explain below)				
(d) Are you aware of any problems re: quality of water? (If yes, explain below)				
(e) Do you have any water treatment devices?...				
(f) Is your water system operable year round? Heated lines? ☐Yes ☐No				
(g) Date and result of most recent water test..				
(h) Are any documents available for the well?				
If yes, specify				
(i) Does the property have any abandoned well(s)?				
2. (a) What kind of sewage disposal system services the property? ☐ Municipal ☐ Septic tank with tile bed ☐ Holding tank ☐ Other (Explain below)				
(b) Are you aware of any problems with the sewage system? Date septic/holding tank last pumped........................... Age of system..................				
(c) What documentation for the sewage system is available? ☐ Use Permit ☐ Location Sketch ☐ Maintenance Records ☐ Inspection Certificate ☐ Other				
3. Are all the well(s), water line(s) and waste disposal system(s) within the boundaries of the subject property?				

ACCESS, SHORELINE, UTILITIES: (Provide Applicable ADDITIONAL COMMENTS)	YES	NO	UNKNOWN	NOT APPLICABLE

While the SPIS is helpful in assessing water supply and waste disposal issues, registrants should include relevant clauses in agreements of purchase and sale when selling properties with wells and/or septic tanks. The drafting of appropriate conditions and other related provisions are discussed later in this course, as well as in *The Residential Real Estate Transaction*.

KNOWLEDGE INTEGRATION

Notables

- A well-listed property sets the stage for marketing, offer drafting, negotiations and the ultimate property sale.

- Primary listing documents include two components: the representation authority and the data input form.

- Precise knowledge of all preprinted clauses in the representation agreement is essential to fully inform the seller client regarding requirements and obligations.

- OREA forms are used for illustration purposes. Brokerage and/or real estate board wordings and formats may vary.

- Care must be taken in completing the representation agreement, particularly regarding property specifics.

- The seller has certain legal obligations regarding brokerage remuneration.

- REBBA 2002 contains regulatory requirements concerning commission calculations, entitlement to commission and payment arrangements.

- Both the commission arrangements and holdover provision should be fully discussed with the seller client.

- REBBA 2002 also has regulatory requirements regarding additional fees and two commissions involving the same trade.

- Various supporting documents are associated with seller representation (see the illustration below).

- The Seller Property Information Statement can be an effective tool, if used properly and with the seller's informed consent.

- Common errors and omissions relating to representation agreements, along with claims experience from the RECO insurance program, provide important insight into potential problem areas.

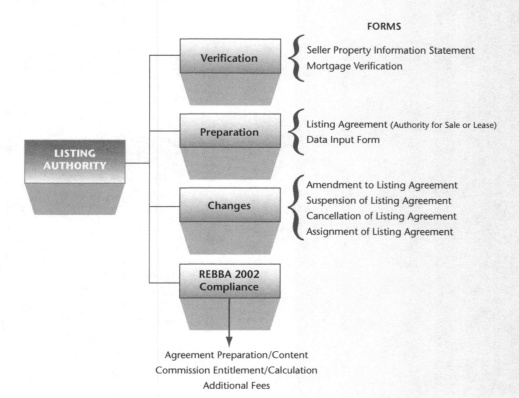

FORMS

Verification
{ Seller Property Information Statement
Mortgage Verification

Preparation
{ Listing Agreement (Authority for Sale or Lease)
Data Input Form

LISTING AUTHORITY

Changes
{ Amendment to Listing Agreement
Suspension of Listing Agreement
Cancellation of Listing Agreement
Assignment of Listing Agreement

REBBA 2002 Compliance

Agreement Preparation/Content
Commission Entitlement/Calculation
Additional Fees

Glossary

Authority

Exclusive Listing

Holdover Provision

Latent Defect

Living Area Measurement

MLS® Listing

Open Listing

Patent Defect

Special Assessment (Taxation)

Strategic Thinking For Your Career

Questions are included to assist in developing your new career. No answers are provided.

1. Can I fully explain all preprinted listing agreement clauses to a seller?

2. What significant differences exist between the OREA forms discussed in this chapter and those used by my intended employing brokerage?

3. How do the forms in this course compare with those supplied by the local real estate board?

4. What office policies in my intended brokerage specifically address the obtaining and processing of listings?

5. Are the SPIS form and schedules widely used in the local marketplace? What strategy will I develop regarding their use when listing property?

6. Are mortgage verification forms routinely sent out to confirm mortgage details for incoming listings in the local marketplace?

Chapter Mini-Review

Solutions are located in the Appendix.

1. A data input form establishes the legal relationship between seller and brokerage, while also setting out property details.

   ○ True   ○ False

2. The amount payable to a co-operating brokerage must be included in a seller representation agreement, according to requirements set out in REBBA 2002.

   ○ True   ○ False

3. Listing salespersons are well advised to suggest that sellers remove excluded fixtures prior to showings to avoid misunderstandings.

   ○ True   ○ False

4. The OREA *Listing Agreement* requires a holdover provision not to exceed 60 days.

   ○ True   ○ False

5. According to the Code of Ethics, if a listing exceeds three months, the listing brokerage must have the seller's initials in close proximity to the expiry date set out in the representation agreement.

   ○ True   ○ False

6. A registrant authorized to bind the listing brokerage must sign and date his or her signature on the representation agreement.

   ○ True   ○ False

7. According to REBBA 2002, a brokerage cannot collect a commission based on the difference between the asking and selling prices.

   ○ True   ○ False

8. Brokerages are permitted to pay commission or other remuneration to salespersons employed by another brokerage, provided that consent is obtained from that other brokerage pursuant to requirements set out in REBBA 2002.

   ○ True   ○ False

9. The seller must complete a Seller Property Information Statement (SPIS) at the time that a representation agreement is signed with a brokerage.

   ○ True   ○ False

10. The OREA SPIS Schedule for condominium can also be used for access and shoreline issues.

    ○ True   ○ False

11. Transposing information from an original source document to the representation agreement (including the data input form) is a potential source for error in the listing process.

    ○ True   ○ False

12. According to errors and omissions claims experience involving rural property, problems with wells and septic systems have been a significant issue over the past few years.

    ○ True   ○ False

Active Learning Exercises

Solutions are located in the Appendix.

◼ Exercise 1   Matching

Match the phrase/word in the left column with the appropriate description in the right column (not all descriptions are used).

____	*Broker Load*
____	*SPIS*
____	*Family Law Act*
____	*Cancellation of Listing Agreement*
____	*Amendment to Listing Agreement*
____	*Mortgage Verification*
____	*Express Authority*
____	*Exclusive Listing*

a. *Written Confirmation of Principal Outstanding*

b. *Seller and Listing Brokerage Release Each Other by Agreement*

c. *Electronic Transmission to Real Estate Board*

d. *Not a Warranty Even if Attached to an Agreement*

e. *Discover Pertinent Facts*

f. *Spousal Consent*

g. *Extend the Expiry Date*

h. *Holdover Provision*

i. *Sole Right to Sell Property*

j. *Disclosure of Role*

k. *A Precise Instruction*

■ Exercise 2   The Home at 36 Longmore Drive

Complete the listing agreement and data input sheet provided. Mr. and Mrs. Johnson have decided to list their bungalow at 36 Longmore Drive for $297,900 effective March 30th. Complete a 90-day MLS® listing based on the following particulars.

Legal Description	Lot 22, Plan 470, City of Westville, Region of Anyregion
Taxes	Assessment—$265,000; Taxes—$4,482.81 (current year)
Zoning	R-1
Location	Rosewood District
Type	Bungalow (private side drive, no garage)
Room Sizes	Kitchen: 17' x 12' 3"
	Dining Room: 13' 6" x 11' 8"
	Living Room: 14' 8" x 19'
	Master Bedroom: 14' 10" x 13' 9"
	Bedroom: 13' x 13' 8"
	Bedroom: 11' x 12'
	Recreation Room: 16' x 10' (basement level, fully finished)
Listing Brokerage	ABC Realty Inc.
Listing Salesperson	Albert Lee

The hot water tank is rented, while the gas-fired forced air furnace is owned. Annual heating costs are estimated at $1,450. The rectangular lot, 50 feet frontage by 120 feet depth, is connected to city water and sewer. The property has a cable TV connection. The door chimes and dining room chandelier are excluded. The garden shed is included.

The property is registered in the names of Wilma Jane Johnson and John Henry Johnson. A first mortgage has a remaining balance of approximately $73,600 payable at $469.97 per month including principal and interest. The interest rate is 7.75% through Lender Inc. The mortgage is assumable with mortgagee approval and is due June 1st, two years from now. Commission rate is 6% with 3% payable to the co-operating broker. Possession is 90 days. Insert additional information as required to fully complete the listing agreement and data input form.

OREA Ontario Real Estate Association

Listing Agreement
Authority to Offer for Sale

Form 200
for use in the Province of Ontario

This is a **Multiple Listing Service® Agreement** ⬭ **OR** **Exclusive Listing Agreement** **EXCLUSIVE** ⬭
(Seller's Initials)   (Seller's Initials)

BETWEEN:
BROKERAGE: ....

....(the "Listing Brokerage") Tel.No. (...............)...

SELLER(S): ....(the "Seller")

In consideration of the Listing Brokerage listing the real property **for sale** known as...

....(the "Property")

the Seller hereby gives the Listing Brokerage the **exclusive and irrevocable** right to act as the Seller's agent, **commencing** at 12:01 a.m. on the .... day

of ...., 20..........., **until** 11:59 p.m. on the .... day of ...., 20......... (the "Listing Period"),

{ Seller acknowledges that the length of the Listing Period is negotiable between the Seller and the Listing Brokerage and, if an
MLS® listing, may be subject to minimum requirements of the real estate board, however, in accordance with the Real Estate
and Business Brokers Act (2002), **if the Listing Period exceeds six months, the Listing Brokerage must obtain the Seller's initials.** }   ⬭
(Seller's Initials)

to offer the property **for sale** at a price of: Dollars (CDN$) ....

....Dollars

and upon the terms particularly set out herein, or at such other price and/or terms acceptable to the Seller. It is understood that the price and/or terms set
out herein are at the Seller's personal request, after full discussion with the Listing Brokerage's representative regarding potential market value of the Property.

**The Seller hereby represents and warrants that the Seller is not a party to any other listing agreement for the Property or agreement to pay commission to
any other real estate brokerage for the sale of the property.**

1. **DEFINITIONS AND INTERPRETATIONS:** For the purposes of this Listing Agreement ("Authority" or "Agreement"), "Seller" includes vendor, a
"buyer" includes a purchaser, or a prospective purchaser and a "real estate board" includes a real estate association. A purchase shall be deemed to
include the entering into of any agreement to exchange, or the obtaining of an option to purchase which is subsequently exercised. This Agreement shall
be read with all changes of gender or number required by the context. For purposes of this Agreement, anyone introduced to or shown the Property
shall be deemed to include any spouse, heirs, executors, administrators, successors, assigns, related corporations and affiliated corporations. Related
corporations or affiliated corporations shall include any corporation where one half or a majority of the shareholders, directors or officers of the related
or affiliated corporation are the same person(s) as the shareholders, directors, or officers of the corporation introduced to or shown the Property.

2. **COMMISSION:** In consideration of the Listing Brokerage listing the Property, the Seller agrees to pay the Listing Brokerage a commission of

..............% of the sale price of the Property or .... for any valid
offer to purchase the Property from any source whatsoever obtained during the Listing Period and on the terms and conditions set out in this Agreement
OR such other terms and conditions as the Seller may accept.

The Seller further agrees to pay such commission as calculated above if an agreement to purchase is agreed to or accepted by the Seller or anyone

on the Seller's behalf within .... days after the expiration of the Listing Period **(Holdover Period)**, so long as such agreement is with
anyone who was introduced to the Property from any source whatsoever during the Listing Period or shown the Property during the Listing Period.
If, however, the offer for the purchase of the Property is pursuant to a new agreement in writing to pay commission to another registered real estate
brokerage, the Seller's liability for commission shall be reduced by the amount paid by the Seller under the new agreement.

The Seller further agrees to pay such commission as calculated above even if the transaction contemplated by an agreement to purchase agreed to
or accepted by the Seller or anyone on the Seller's behalf is not completed, if such non-completion is owing or attributable to the Seller's default or
neglect, said commission to be payable on the date set for completion of the purchase of the Property.

Any deposit in respect of any agreement where the transaction has been completed shall first be applied to reduce the commission payable. Should
such amounts paid to the Listing Brokerage from the deposit or by the Seller's solicitor not be sufficient, the Seller shall be liable to pay to the Listing
Brokerage on demand, any deficiency in commission and taxes owing on such commission.

All amounts set out as commission are to be paid plus applicable taxes on such commission.

3. **REPRESENTATION:** The Seller acknowledges that the Listing Brokerage has provided the Seller with information explaining agency relationships,
including information on Seller Representation, Sub-agency, Buyer Representation, Multiple Representation and Customer Service. The Seller authorizes
the Listing Brokerage to co-operate with any other registered real estate brokerage (co-operating brokerage), and to offer to pay the co-operating

brokerage a commission of................% of the sale price of the Property or...

.... out of the commission the Seller pays the Listing Brokerage.

INITIALS OF LISTING BROKERAGE: ⬭   **INITIALS OF SELLER(S):** ⬭

Exercise 2   Listing Agreement, Page 2 of 3

The Seller understands that unless the Seller is otherwise informed, the co-operating brokerage is representing the interests of the buyer in the transaction. The Seller further acknowledges that the Listing Brokerage may be listing other properties that may be similar to the Seller's Property and the Seller hereby consents to the Listing Brokerage listing other properties that may be similar to the Seller's Property without any claim by the Seller of conflict of interest. The Seller hereby appoints the Listing Brokerage as the Seller's agent for the purpose of giving and receiving notices pursuant to any offer or agreement to purchase the property. Unless otherwise agreed in writing between Seller and Listing Brokerage, any commission payable to any other brokerage shall be paid out of the commission the Seller pays the Listing Brokerage, said commission to be disbursed in accordance with the Commission Trust Agreement.

MULTIPLE REPRESENTATION: The Seller hereby acknowledges that the Listing Brokerage may be entering into buyer representation agreements with buyers who may be interested in purchasing the Seller's Property. In the event that the Listing Brokerage has entered into or enters into a buyer representation agreement with a prospective buyer for the Seller's Property, the Listing Brokerage will obtain the Seller's written consent to represent both the Seller and the buyer for the transaction at the earliest practicable opportunity and in all cases prior to any offer to purchase being submitted or presented.

The Seller understands and acknowledges that the Listing Brokerage must be impartial when representing both the Seller and the buyer and equally protect the interests of the Seller and buyer. The Seller understands and acknowledges that when representing both the Seller and the buyer, the Listing Brokerage shall have a duty of full disclosure to both the Seller and the buyer, including a requirement to disclose all factual information about the Property known to the Listing Brokerage.

However, the Seller further understands and acknowledges that the Listing Brokerage shall not disclose:
- that the Seller may or will accept less than the listed price, unless otherwise instructed in writing by the Seller;
- that the buyer may or will pay more than the offered price, unless otherwise instructed in writing by the buyer;
- the motivation of or personal information about the Seller or buyer, unless otherwise instructed in writing by the party to which the information applies or unless failure to disclose would constitute fraudulent, unlawful or unethical practice;
- the price the buyer should offer or the price the Seller should accept; and
- the Listing Brokerage shall not disclose to the buyer the terms of any other offer.

However, it is understood that factual market information about comparable properties and information known to the Listing Brokerage concerning potential uses for the Property will be disclosed to both Seller and buyer to assist them to come to their own conclusions.

Where a Brokerage represents both the Seller and the Buyer (multiple representation), the Brokerage shall not be entitled or authorized to be agent for either the Buyer or the Seller for the purpose of giving and receiving notices.

MULTIPLE REPRESENTATION AND CUSTOMER SERVICE: The Seller understands and agrees that the Listing Brokerage also provides representation and customer service to other sellers and buyers. If the Listing Brokerage represents or provides customer service to more than one seller or buyer for the same trade, the Listing Brokerage shall, in writing, at the earliest practicable opportunity and before any offer is made, inform all sellers and buyers of the nature of the Listing Brokerage's relationship to each seller and buyer.

4. **FINDERS FEES:** The Seller acknowledges that the Brokerage may be receiving a finder's fee, reward and/or referral incentive, and the Seller consents to any such benefit being received and retained by the Brokerage in addition to the commission as described above.

5. **REFERRAL OF ENQUIRIES:** The Seller agrees that during the Listing Period, the Seller shall advise the Listing Brokerage immediately of all enquiries from any source whatsoever, and all offers to purchase submitted to the Seller shall be immediately submitted to the Listing Brokerage before the Seller accepts or rejects the same. If any enquiry during the Listing Period results in the Seller accepting a valid offer to purchase during the Listing Period or within the Holdover Period after the expiration of the Listing Period, the Seller agrees to pay the Listing Brokerage the amount of commission set out above, payable within five (5) days following the Listing Brokerage's written demand therefor.

6. **MARKETING:** The Seller agrees to allow the Listing Brokerage to show and permit prospective buyers to fully inspect the Property during reasonable hours and the Seller gives the Listing Brokerage the sole and exclusive right to place "For Sale" and "Sold" sign(s) upon the Property. The Seller consents to the Listing Brokerage including information in advertising that may identify the Property. The Seller further agrees that the Listing Brokerage shall have sole and exclusive authority to make all advertising decisions relating to the marketing of the Property for sale during the Listing Period. The Seller agrees that the Listing Brokerage will not be held liable in any manner whatsoever for any acts or omissions with respect to advertising by the Listing Brokerage or any other party, other than by the Listing Brokerage's gross negligence or wilful act.

7. **WARRANTY:** The Seller represents and warrants that the Seller has the exclusive authority and power to execute this Authority to offer the Property for sale and that the Seller has informed the Listing Brokerage of any third party interests or claims on the Property such as rights of first refusal, options, easements, mortgages, encumbrances or otherwise concerning the Property, which may affect the sale of the Property.

8. **INDEMNIFICATION AND INSURANCE:** The Seller will not hold the Listing Brokerage and representatives of the Brokerage responsible for any loss or damage to the Property or contents occurring during the term of this Agreement caused by the Listing Brokerage or anyone else by any means, including theft, fire or vandalism, other than by the Listing Brokerage's gross negligence or wilful act. The Seller agrees to indemnify and save harmless the Listing Brokerage and representatives of the Brokerage and any co-operating brokerage from any liability, claim, loss, cost, damage or injury, including but not limited to loss of the commission payable under this Agreement, caused or contributed to by the breach of any warranty or representation made by the Seller in this Agreement or the accompanying data form. The Seller warrants the Property is insured, including personal liability insurance against any claims or lawsuits resulting from bodily injury or property damage to others caused in any way on or at the Property and the Seller indemnifies the Brokerage and all of its employees, representatives, salespersons and brokers (Listing Brokerage) and any co-operating brokerage and all of its employees, representatives, salespersons and brokers (co-operating brokerage) for and against any claims against the Listing Brokerage or co-operating brokerage made by anyone who attends or visits the Property.

9. **FAMILY LAW ACT:** The Seller hereby warrants that spousal consent is not necessary under the provisions of the Family Law Act, R.S.O. 1990, unless the Seller's spouse has executed the consent hereinafter provided.

10. **VERIFICATION OF INFORMATION:** The Seller authorizes the Listing Brokerage to obtain any information affecting the Property from any regulatory authorities, governments, mortgagees or others and the Seller agrees to execute and deliver such further authorizations in this regard as may be reasonably required. The Seller hereby appoints the Listing Brokerage or the Listing Brokerage's authorized representative as the Seller's attorney to execute such documentation as may be necessary to effect obtaining any information as aforesaid. The Seller hereby authorizes, instructs and directs the above noted regulatory authorities, governments, mortgagees or others to release any and all information to the Listing Brokerage.

11. **USE AND DISTRIBUTION OF INFORMATION:** The Seller consents to the collection, use and disclosure of personal information by the Brokerage for the purpose of listing and marketing the Property including, but not limited to: listing and advertising the Property using any medium including the Internet; disclosing Property information to prospective buyers, brokerages, salespersons and others who may assist in the sale of the Property; such other use of

INITIALS OF LISTING BROKERAGE: ( )   **INITIALS OF SELLER(S):** ( )

Form 200   Revised 2015   **Page 2 of 3**

the Seller's personal information as is consistent with listing and marketing of the Property. The Seller consents, if this is an MLS® Listing, to placement of the listing information and sales information by the Brokerage into the database(s) of the MLS® System of the appropriate Board, and to the posting of any documents and other information (including, without limitation, photographs, images, graphics, audio and video recordings, virtual tours, drawings, floor plans, architectural designs, artistic renderings, surveys and listing descriptions) provided by or on behalf of the Seller into the database(s) of the MLS® System of the appropriate Board. The Seller hereby indemnifies and saves harmless the Brokerage and/or any of its employees, servants, brokers or sales representatives from any and all claims, liabilities, suits, actions, losses, costs and legal fees caused by, or arising out of, or resulting from the posting of any documents or other information (including, without limitation, photographs, images, graphics, audio and video recordings, virtual tours, drawings, floor plans, architectural designs, artistic renderings, surveys and listing descriptions) as aforesaid. The Seller acknowledges that the database, within the board's MLS® System is the property of the real estate board(s) and can be licensed, resold, or otherwise dealt with by the board(s). The Seller further acknowledges that the real estate board(s) may: during the term of the listing and thereafter, distribute the information in the database, within the board's MLS® System to any persons authorized to use such service which may include other brokerages, government departments, appraisers, municipal organizations and others; market the Property, at its option, in any medium, including electronic media; during the term of the listing and thereafter, compile, retain and publish any statistics including historical data within the board's MLS® System and retain, reproduce and display photographs, images, graphics, audio and video recordings, virtual tours, drawings, floor plans, architectural designs, artistic renderings, surveys and listing descriptions which may be used by board members to conduct comparative analyses; and make such other use of the information as the Brokerage and/or real estate board(s) deem appropriate, in connection with the listing, marketing and selling of real estate during the term of the listing and thereafter. The Seller acknowledges that the information, personal or otherwise ("information"), provided to the real estate board or association may be stored on databases located outside of Canada, in which case the information would be subject to the laws of the jurisdiction in which the information is located.

In the event that this Agreement expires or is cancelled or otherwise terminated and the Property is not sold, the Seller, by initialling:

consent to allow other real estate board members to contact the Seller after expiration or other termination of this Agreement to discuss listing or otherwise marketing the Property.

Does   **Does Not**

12. **SUCCESSORS AND ASSIGNS:** The heirs, executors, administrators, successors and assigns of the undersigned are bound by the terms of this Agreement.

13. **CONFLICT OR DISCREPANCY:** If there is any conflict or discrepancy between any provision added to this Agreement (including any Schedule attached hereto) and any provision in the standard pre-set portion hereof, the added provision shall supersede the standard pre-set provision to the extent of such conflict or discrepancy. This Agreement, including any Schedule attached hereto, shall constitute the entire Agreement between the Seller and the Listing Brokerage. There is no representation, warranty, collateral agreement or condition which affects this Agreement other than as expressed herein.

14. **ELECTRONIC COMMUNICATION:** This Listing Agreement and any agreements, notices or other communications contemplated thereby may be transmitted by means of electronic systems, in which case signatures shall be deemed to be original. The transmission of this Agreement by the Seller by electronic means shall be deemed to confirm the Seller has retained a true copy of the Agreement.

15. **SCHEDULE(S):** .... and data form attached hereto form(s) part of this Agreement.

THE LISTING BROKERAGE AGREES TO MARKET THE PROPERTY ON BEHALF OF THE SELLER AND REPRESENT THE SELLER IN AN ENDEAVOUR TO OBTAIN A VALID OFFER TO PURCHASE THE PROPERTY ON THE TERMS SET OUT IN THIS AGREEMENT OR ON SUCH OTHER TERMS SATISFACTORY TO THE SELLER.

....   DATE.........................   ....
(Authorized to bind the Listing Brokerage)   (Name of Person Signing)

THIS AGREEMENT HAS BEEN READ AND FULLY UNDERSTOOD BY ME AND I ACKNOWLEDGE THIS DATE I HAVE SIGNED UNDER SEAL. Any representations contained herein or as shown on the accompanying data form respecting the Property are true to the best of my knowledge, information and belief.

SIGNED, SEALED AND DELIVERED I have hereunto set my hand and seal:

....   ● DATE ....
(Signature of Seller)   (Seal)   (Tel. No.)

....   ● DATE ....
(Signature of Seller)   (Seal)

SPOUSAL CONSENT: The undersigned spouse of the Seller hereby consents to the listing of the Property herein pursuant to the provisions of the Family Law Act, R.S.O. 1990 and hereby agrees that he/she will execute all necessary or incidental documents to further any transaction provided for herein.

....   ● DATE ....
(Spouse)   (Seal)

DECLARATION OF INSURANCE

The broker/salesperson..
                                        (Name of Broker/Salesperson)
hereby declares that he/she is insured as required by the Real Estate and Business Brokers Act (REBBA) and Regulations.

....
                                (Signature(s) of Broker/Salesperson)

ACKNOWLEDGEMENT

The Seller(s) hereby acknowledge that the Seller(s) fully understand the terms of this Agreement and have received a true copy of this Agreement

on the .... day of ...., 20 ....

....   Date: ....
(Signature of Seller)

....   Date: ....
(Signature of Seller)

Exercise 2 Data Input Form, Page 1 of 2

OREA
Ontario
Real Estate
Association

ONTARIO REAL ESTATE ASSOCIATION

| RESIDENTIAL/RECREATIONAL |

MLS #_____   ❏ EXISTING   ❏ TO BE BUILT   ❏ NEW   ❏ UNDER CONSTRUCTION

Effective Date:_____ Expiry Date:_____ Completion/Possession Date:_____ Price_____ Terms:_____

Commission to Selling Broker:_____   Matrimonial Home: ❏ Yes   ❏ No   Easement and/or Encroachment: ❏ Yes   ❏ No   ❏ Unk

Holdover Period_____days   SPIS Completed: ❏ Yes   ❏ No   Listing Authority Modification: ❏ Yes   ❏ No

Special Provisions:_____   Applicable Schedules:_____

Property Address:_____ Municipality/Township:_____ Postal Code:_____

Roll #:_____ PIN #:_____ Legal Description: /Plan, Lot #, County, Town]:_____

Side of Road:_____ Area/Map Locator:_____ Near_____ Property Size:_____

Seller/Owners [s]:_____ Phone: _____

Assessment:_____ Taxes:_____ Year_____ Local Improvement: ❏ Yes ❏ No

Directions: _____

Broker: 1)_____ ID#_____ Phone #_____ Fax #:_____ email: _____
2)_____ ID#_____ Phone #_____ Fax #:_____ email: _____

Salesperson: 1)_____ ID#_____ Phone #_____ Fax #:_____ email: _____
2)_____ ID#_____ Phone #_____ Fax #:_____ email: _____

Occupant: (Select ____ only)
❏ Owner
❏ Tenant
❏ Vacant

Showings: (Select ____ only)
❏ Direct
❏ Lock Box
❏ Call LBO

Indicate whether Property is. (Select ____ only)
❏ For Lease Only
❏ For Sale Only
❏ For Sale or Lease
❏ Exchange

Age of Dwelling: _____
(Use NE for New Construction or indicate the age in years or use UN for unknown)

Zoning _____

Water Meter: ❏ yes ❏ no
Water Supply: (Select ____ only)
(Indicate in remarks section if supply is not connected)
❏ cistern   ❏ municipal
❏ drilled well   ❏ well
❏ river/lake   ❏ none
❏ dug-well   ❏ other_____

Sewer Type:
❏ Sanitary Connected   ❏ Sanitary Not Connected
❏ Septic Installed   ❏ Storm Connected
❏ See Remarks   ❏ Storm Not Connected

UFFI: ❏ yes   ❏ no   ❏ removed ❏ unknown

Building Location Survey: ❏ yes   ❏ no

Single Family   ❏ yes   ❏ no

Multi-Unit - 2 units   ❏ yes   ❏ no

Comments: _____

Room Sizes and Levels: all room sizes are approximate and are to be verified by the Purchaser. Use only the abbreviation listed below to describe each room. Insert the level abbreviation and insert the room size. Please indicate if measurement is in ❏ **imperial** or ❏ **metric**.

Foyer	FO	Recreation Room	RR	Utility	UT	Great Room	GR	4 pce. Bathroom	B4
Living Room	LR	Recreation Room w/FP	RF	Fruit Cellar	FC	Great Room w/FP	GF	5 pce. Bathroom	B5
Living Room/Dining Room	LD	Play Room	PR	Games Room	GR	Cold Room	CR	6 pce. Bathroom	B6
Living Room w/FP	LF	Family Room	FR	Sunroom	SR	Porch Enclosed	PE	2 pce. Ensuite	E2
Dining Room	DR	Family Room w/FP	FF	Attic	AT	Other	OT	3 pce. Ensuite	E3
Kitchen	K1	Master Bedroom	MB	Hobby Room	HR	1 pce. Bathroom	B1	4 pce. Ensuite	E4
Lower Kitchen	K2	Bedroom	BR	Workshop	WK	2 pce. Bathroom	B2	5 pce. Ensuite	E5
Eating Area	EA	Laundry	LA	Media Room	MR	3 pce. Bathroom	B3		
Den	DE								

# of Bedrooms: _____ # of Kitchens: _____ # of Baths: _____ R-In Baths: ❏ yes ❏ no   Ensuite Baths: ❏ yes ❏ no

LEVEL	ROOM	DIMENSIONS	LEVEL	ROOM	DIMENSIONS
		x			x
		x			x
		x			x
		x			x
		x			x
		x			x
		x			x
		x			x

BATHROOMS	LEVEL

Levels	
Main	M
2nd Level	2
3rd Level	3
4th Level	4
Lower	L
Basement	B
Other	O

Water Front
❏ yes   ❏ no
Type of Dwelling (Select ____ only)
❏ Carriage House
❏ Cottage
❏ Detached
❏ Link
❏ Mobile/Modular
❏ Row
❏ Semi Detached
❏ Stacked
❏ Townhouse
❏ Townhouse End-unit
❏ See Remarks
❏ Other
Style (Select ____ only)
❏ 1 ½ Storey
❏ 1 ¾ Storey
❏ 1 Storey
❏ 1 Storey Raised
❏ 2 ½ Storey
❏ 2 Storey
❏ 3 Level Back Split
❏ 3 Level Side Split
❏ 3 Storey
❏ 4 Level Back Split
❏ 4 Level Side Split
❏ 5 Level Back Split
❏ 5 Level Side Split
❏ Bi-Level
❏ See Remarks
Rental Equipment (Select ____ only)
❏ Conversion Burner
❏ Conversion Burner & Water Heater
❏ Conversion Burner, Water Heater & Water Softener
❏ Fireplace
❏ Water Filter
❏ Water Heater
❏ Water Softener
❏ See Remarks
Fireplace & Type (Select ____ only)
❏ yes   ❏ no
❏ # of units _____
❏ Electric
❏ Gas (natural)
❏ Propane
❏ Rough-in
❏ Wood
❏ Woodstove
❏ Other
❏ See Remarks

Garage (Select ____ only)
❏ Attached
❏ Auto. Gar.Opener
❏ Carport
❏ Detached
❏ Double
❏ Inside Entry
❏ One one-half
❏ Single
❏ Triple
❏ See Remarks
Parking (Select ____ only)
❏ Double
❏ Front Drive
❏ Gravel
❏ Mutual
❏ No Drive
❏ Rear Drive
❏ Side Drive
❏ Single
❏ Surfaced
❏ See Remarks
Foundation (Select ____ only)
❏ Block
❏ Concrete (Poured)
❏ Pillar/Piers
❏ Stone/Brick
❏ Wood
❏ None
❏ See Remarks
Basement (Select ____ only)
❏ Crawl
❏ Full
❏ Partial
❏ Slab
❏ See Remarks
❏ None
Basement Develop. (Select ____ only)
❏ Finished
❏ Partly Finished
❏ Unfinished
❏ See Remarks

Fuel (Select ____ only)
❏ Electricity
❏ Gas (natural)
❏ Oil
❏ Pellets
❏ Propane
❏ Solar
❏ Wood
❏ Other
❏ See Remarks
Heating and Cooling (Select ____ only)
❏ Baseboard
❏ Central Air Cond.
❏ Electric Air Cleaner
❏ Energy Efficient
❏ Forced Air
❏ Fresh Air Exchange
❏ Furnace
❏ Gravity
❏ Heat Pump
❏ Hot Water/Steam
❏ Radiant
❏ Solar
❏ Space Heater
❏ Wall Furnace
❏ Other
❏ See Remarks
Insulation (Select ____ only)
❏ Basement
❏ Ceilings
❏ Floors
❏ Perimeter Walls
❏ Walls
Square Footage (Select ____ only)
❏ 0-750
❏ 751-1000
❏ 1001-1200
❏ 1201-1500
❏ 1501-2000
❏ over 2000
Est. Sq. Ft: _____

Indoor Features (Select ____ only)
❏ Alarm System
❏ Cable TV connected
❏ Cable TV not connected
❏ Central vacuum
❏ Compactor
❏ Dishwasher
❏ Dryer
❏ Electric Air Cleaner
❏ Freezer
❏ Garburetor
❏ In-Law Suite
❏ Intercom
❏ Microwave
❏ Oven built-in
❏ Refrigerator
❏ Stove
❏ Washer
❏ Water Filter
❏ Water Softener
❏ Whirlpool tub
❏ Window A/Conditioner
❏ See Remarks
Other Features (Select ____ only)
❏ Above Ground Pool
❏ Balcony
❏ Barbeque Equipment
❏ Boat House
❏ Boat Lift
❏ Dock
❏ Greenhouse
❏ Hot Tub Pool
❏ Indoor Pool
❏ Inground Pool
❏ Patio
❏ Satellite Dish
❏ Sauna
❏ Skylight
❏ Sleeping Cabin
❏ Smoke Detector
❏ Solarium
❏ Sprinkler System
❏ Storage Shed
❏ Storm Doors
❏ Storm Windows
❏ Sundeck
❏ TV Antenna
❏ Wet Bar
❏ Workbench

Roof (Select ____ only)
❏ Asphalt
❏ Wood Shingle
❏ Metal
❏ Tar & Gravel
❏ Tile
❏ Concrete
❏ Other
Flooring (Select ____ only)
❏ Carpet w/w
❏ Ceramic
❏ Hardwood
❏ Lino/Vinyl
❏ Softwood
❏ Other
❏ See Remarks
Exterior Finish (Select ____ only)
❏ Aluminum
❏ Brick
❏ Concrete Block
❏ Hard Bd.
❏ Insulbrick
❏ Log
❏ Stone
❏ Stucco
❏ Vinyl
❏ Wood
❏ Other
❏ See Remarks
Acreage (Select ____ only)
❏ .99 or less
❏ 1-1.99 acres
❏ 2-4.99 acres
❏ 5-9.99 acres
❏ 10-24.99 acres
❏ 25 + acres
Water Access (Select ____ only)
❏ Waterfront Owned
❏ Waterfront Not Owned
❏ Deeded Access
❏ Public Access Nearby
❏ Island
_____

Topography (Select ____ only)
❏ Cons./Green Belt
❏ Escarpment
❏ Fenced
❏ Flood Plain
❏ Golf Course
❏ Hardwood Bush
❏ Level
❏ Open Space
❏ Partially cleared
❏ Pond
❏ Ravine
❏ Rolling
❏ Sand Beach
❏ Sea Wall
❏ Sloping/Terraced
❏ Softwood Bush
❏ Stream/River
❏ Waterfront
❏ Wooded/Treed
❏ Other
Road Access (Select ____ only)
❏ Private
❏ Private-Mtnce Fee
❏ Public
❏ Right of Way
❏ Seasonal
❏ Water Access
❏ Year Round
Right of Way
❏ Yes ❏ No ❏ Unk
❏ subject to
❏ benefit of
Advertising
For Sale Sign
❏ Yes   ❏ No
Listing Broker Only
❏ Yes   ❏ No
Broker Loaded
❏ Yes ❏ No
Broker Load #:_____

Seller[s] Initials

OREA
Ontario
Real Estate
Association

ONTARIO REAL ESTATE ASSOCIATION

RESIDENTIAL/RECREATIONAL

Page 2

1st Mortgage Information:

❑ Clear

Mortgagee	Amount	Rate	Due Date	Pmt (P&I)	Additional Information

[Select all applicable options]

❑ May be assumed with approval   ❑ May be paid off without penalty   ❑ Must be paid off
❑ May be assumed without approval   ❑ May be paid off with penalty   ❑ Seller may buy down
❑ May be increased   ❑ Seller may take back   ❑ Mortgage information verified
❑ Must be assumed   ❑ Buyer to arrange own financing   ❑ See remarks

2nd Mortgage Information:

❑ Clear

Mortgagee	Amount	Rate	Due Date	Pmt (P&I)	Additional Information

[Select all applicable options]

❑ May be assumed with approval   ❑ May be paid off without penalty   ❑ Must be paid off
❑ May be assumed without approval   ❑ May be paid off with penalty   ❑ Seller may buy down
❑ May be increased   ❑ Seller may take back   ❑ Mortgage information verified
❑ Must be assumed   ❑ Buyer to arrange own financing   ❑ See remarks

Other Mortgage Information:
❑ Clear

Mortgagee	Amount	Rate	Due Date	Pmt (P&I)	Additional Information

[Select all applicable options]

❑ May be assumed with approval   ❑ May be paid off without penalty   ❑ Must be paid off
❑ May be assumed without approval   ❑ May be paid off with penalty   ❑ Seller may buy down
❑ May be increased   ❑ Seller may take back   ❑ Mortgage information verified
❑ Must be assumed   ❑ Buyer to arrange own financing   ❑ See remarks

Chattels Included:[___ characters including spaces are available] [The MLS® reserves the right to abbreviate if content exceeds space allowed]

_____
_____
_____

Fixtures Excluded:[___ characters including spaces are available] [The MLS® reserves the right to abbreviate if content exceeds space allowed]

_____
_____
_____

REMARKS:[The MLS® reserves the right to abbreviate if content exceeds space allowed]

_____
_____
_____
_____
_____
_____
_____

I ACKNOWLEDGE HAVING CAREFULLY READ THIS ENTIRE FORM AND, AS OF THIS DATE, CONFIRM THE ACCURACY OF THE ABOVE INFORMATION CONCERNING MY PROPERTY. I AGREE TO ALLOW CHANGES TO ITEMS SUCH AS TAXES, ASSESSMENT, LEGAL DESCRIPTION AND LOT SIZE AS MAY BE NECESSARY. I FURTHER AGREE THAT THE LISTING BROKER, AS DEEMED APPROPRIATE, MAY AMEND THE ADVERTISEMENT COPY FOR THE INTERNET.

_____
[SIGNATURE OF SELLER]   [DATE]

_____
[SIGNATURE OF SELLER]   [DATE]

■■■

PLEASE COMPLETE THE APPROPRIATE SPACE[S]
❑ Photo Attached
❑ Sketch Attached   ❑ Take Photo #1-View _____
❑ New Picture   ❑ Take Photo #2-View _____
❑ Use Previous Picture

                          MLS# _____

If special photographic instructions are required, please indicate:

_____
_____
_____
_____

Page 2 of 2

▣ Exercise 3   Regulatory Requirements

For each of the following scenarios, insert a checkmark to indicate whether the *Real Estate and Business Brokers Act, 2002* or the Code of Ethics (CODE) Regulation (Reg. 580/05) applies and support your answer with the appropriate section.

3.1 An unexpired listing agreement existed at the time that a different registrant had the seller sign a second listing agreement. The registrant then attempted to collect commission pursuant to this second agreement. The seller did not agree in writing to pay two commissions, but forgot that the first agreement had not expired.

REBBA ◯   CODE ◯

Section or Subsection _____

3.2 The Anycity market is slow and the salesperson requires a nine-month listing period for the seller's residential property. The listing is completed and signed by the seller, but no initials are included regarding the extended listing period, as required under the Act and Regulations.

REBBA ◯   CODE ◯

Section or Subsection _____

3.3 The salesperson had a listing signed on March 14th, but forgot to provide copies. Realizing his mistake several days later, he called the sellers. Unconcerned, the sellers told him not to bother. The salesperson took no further action.

REBBA ◯   CODE ◯

Section or Subsection _____

3.4 The seller requests that the expiry date on a representation agreement be July 31st, or alternatively June 30th, if he elects to take holidays during July. The salesperson agrees and inserts the two dates in the agreement.

REBBA ◯   CODE ◯

Section or Subsection _____

3.5 The brokerage receives a finder's fee relating to arranging a mortgage for the buyer, but does not disclose this fact to the seller client.

REBBA ◯   CODE ◯

Section or Subsection _____

3.6   The salesperson completes a representation agreement that includes both the payment of a commission based on a percentage of sale price, along with a flat fee of $2,000.

REBBA ◯   CODE ◯

Section or Subsection _____

■ **Exercise 4   SPIS: 287 Westvale Crescent**

A Seller Property Information Statement is illustrated for 287 Westvale Crescent, Anycity. Identify eight possible problems or areas of concern (in point form) that may require further clarification or additional information, from either the seller's or buyer's perspective. Provide a short explanation or brief action plan for each.

SECTION	LINE	CONCERN	BRIEF EXPLANATION/ACTION PLAN
e.g., General	6	No Plan of Survey	Buyer will probably incur survey costs.

Exercise 4   SPIS—287 Westvale Crescent, Page 1 of 3

 **OREA** Ontario Real Estate Association

Seller Property Information Statement
Residential

Form 220
for use in the Province of Ontario

ANSWERS MUST BE COMPLETE AND ACCURATE This statement is designed in part to protect Sellers by establishing that correct information concerning the property is being provided to buyers. All of the information contained herein is provided by the Sellers to the brokerage/broker/salesperson. Any person who is in receipt of and utilizes this Statement acknowledges and agrees that **the information is being provided for information purposes only and is not a warranty as to the matters recited hereinafter even if attached to an Agreement of Purchase and Sale.** The brokerage/broker/salesperson shall not be held responsible for the accuracy of any information contained herein.

BUYERS MUST STILL MAKE THEIR OWN ENQUIRIES Buyers must still make their own enquiries notwithstanding the information contained on this statement. Each question and answer must be considered and where necessary, keeping in mind that the Sellers' knowledge of the property may be inaccurate or incomplete, additional information can be requested from the Sellers or from an independent source such as the municipality. Buyers can hire an independent inspector to examine the property to determine whether defects exist and to provide an estimate of the cost of repairing problems that have been identified. **This statement does not provide information on psychological stigmas that may be associated with a property.**

For the purposes of this Seller Property Information Statement, a "Seller" includes a landlord or a prospective landlord and a "buyer" includes a tenant, or a prospective tenant.

PROPERTY: 287 Westvale Crescent, Anycity	SELLER(S) TO **INITIAL** EACH APPLICABLE BOX			
SELLER(S): Steven M. Costa				

GENERAL: (Provide Applicable ADDITIONAL COMMENTS)	YES	NO	UNKNOWN	NOT APPLICABLE
1. I have occupied the property from.......**19xx**..........to......**present**..........				
2. Does any other party have an ownership or spousal interest in the property?	SC			
3. Is the property a condominium or a freehold property that includes an interest in a common elements condominium, (POTL)? (If yes, Schedule 221 to be completed.)		SC		
4. Does ownership of this property require membership in an Association and payment of Association fees? If yes, specify..		SC		
5. Is the property subject to first right of refusal, option, lease, rental agreement or other listing?	SC			
6. Are there any encroachments, registered easements, or rights-of-way?		SC		
7. Is there a plan of survey? Date of survey...		SC		
8. Are there any disputes concerning the boundaries of the property? **Fence Dispute**	SC			
9. Are you aware of any non-compliance with zoning regulations?		SC		
10. Are you aware of any pending developments, projects or rezoning applications in the neighbourhood?		SC		
11. Are there any public projects planned for the neighbourhood? eg: road widenings, new highways, expropriations etc.	SC			
12. Are there any restrictive covenants that run with the land?		SC		
13. Are there any drainage restrictions?		SC		
14. Are there any local levies or unusual taxes being charged at the present time or contemplated? If so, at what cost? ....**Unknown**.................... Expiry date........**Unknown**..........	SC			
15. Have you received any notice, claim, work order or deficiency notice affecting the property from any person or any public body?		SC		
16. (a) Is the property connected to municipal water? (If not, Schedule 222 to be completed.)	SC			
(b) Is the property connected to municipal sewer? (If not, Schedule 222 to be completed.)	SC			
17. Are there any current or pending Heritage restrictions for the property or the area?	SC			

INITIALS OF BUYER(S): *VS ES*

GENERAL (cont'd): (Provide Applicable ADDITIONAL COMMENTS)	YES	NO	UNKNOWN	NOT APPLICABLE
18. Are there any conditional sales contracts, leases, rental agreements or service contracts? eg: furnace, alarm system, hot water tank, propane tank, etc. Specify.. Are they assignable or will they be discharged?...		SC		
19. Are there any defects in any appliances or equipment included with the property?		SC		
20. Do you know the approximate age of the building(s)?Age...**80+**............................... Any additions: Age..				
21. Are you aware of any past or pending claims under the Tarion Warranty Corporation (formerly ONHWP)? Tarion Warranty Corporation/ONHWP Registration No......................................				SC
22. Will the sale of this property be subject to HST?		SC		

ADDITIONAL COMMENTS: **Q. 2: Spouse, Marlene Costa, not on title**

Rental : Two student renters occupying upper level at $425.00 per month each

ENVIRONMENTAL: (Provide Applicable ADDITIONAL COMMENTS)	YES	NO	UNKNOWN	NOT APPLICABLE
1. Are you aware of possible environmental problems or soil contamination of any kind on the property or in the immediate area? eg: radon gas, toxic waste, underground gasoline or fuel tanks etc.		SC		
2. Are there any existing or proposed waste dumps, disposal sites or land fills in the immediate area?		SC		
3. Are there any hydro generating projects planned for the immediate area? eg: Wind Turbines		SC		
4. Is the property subject to flooding?		SC		
5. Is the property under the jurisdiction of any Conservation Authority or Commission?		SC		
6. Are you aware of any excessive erosion, settling, slippage, sliding or other soil problems?		SC		
7. Does the property have any abandoned or de-commissioned ☐ well ☐ septic system ☐ swimming pool ☐ foundation ☐ other, specify................................		SC		
8. (a) Is there a fuel oil tank on the property? If yes, complete the following: ☑ Underground. Date for required upgrading or removal........**Unknown**............................. ☐ Aboveground. Age of tank...**Unknown**...... Date of last inspection..**Unknown**.........			SC	
(b) Does the fuel oil tank comply with the Technical Standards and Safety Authority requirements and any other requirements for fuel to be delivered?			SC	
9. Has the use of the property ever been for the growth or manufacture of illegal substances?		SC		

ADDITIONAL COMMENTS:...

INITIALS OF BUYER(S): *VS ES*

Form 220   Revised 2016   **Page 2 of 3**

Exercise 4   SPIS—287 Westvale Crescent, Page 3 of 3

IMPROVEMENTS AND STRUCTURAL: (Provide Applicable ADDITIONAL COMMENTS)	YES	NO	UNKNOWN	NOT APPLICABLE
1. Are you aware of any structural problems?		SC		
2. (a) Have you made any renovations, additions or improvements to the property?	SC			
(b) Was a building permit obtained?		SC		
(c) Has the final building inspection been approved or has a final occupancy permit been obtained?		SC		
3. To the best of your knowledge have the building(s) ever contained ureaformaldehyde insulation?				
4. Is there vermiculite insulation on the property? If yes, has it been tested for asbestos?....................			SC	
5. (a) Are you aware of any deficiencies or non-compliance with the Ontario Fire Code?			SC	
(b) Is your property equipped with operational smoke detectors?	SC			
(c) Is the property equipped with operational carbon monoxide detectors?	SC			
6. (a) Is the woodstove(s)/chimney(s)/fireplace(s)/insert(s) in good working order?	SC			
(b) Has the wood energy system been **WETT** inspected? (Wood Energy Technology Transfer)			SC	
7. Are you aware of any problems with the central air conditioning system?		SC		
8. Are you aware of any problems with the heating system?		SC		
9. (a) Are you aware of any moisture and/or water problems?		SC		
(b) Are you aware of any roof leakage or unrepaired damage? Age of roof covering ..... **25 years**	SC			
(c) Are you aware of any damage due to wind, fire, flood, insects, termites, rodents, pets or wood rot?		SC		
(d) Have any repairs been carried out to correct any past or present problems related to (a), (b) and/or (c)? If yes, explain in additional comments below.	SC			
10. (a) Are you aware of any problems with the electrical system? Size of service..... **60 amp**		SC		
(b) Type of wiring: ☐ copper ☐ aluminium ☑ knob-and-tube ☐ other................................				
11. Are you aware of any problems with the plumbing system?		SC		
12. Is there any lead, galvanized metal, cast iron or Kitec plumbing on the property?			SC	
13. Are you aware of any problems with the swimming pool, sauna, hot tub, jet bathtub or lawn sprinkler system?		SC		

ADDITIONAL COMMENTS: Re: Q. 2 (Improvements): No building permit; only minor change made by the seller to accommodate rental arrangement (e.g., washroom and free-standing gas fireplace on upper level).

Re: Q. 9 (Roof): Minor leakage on upper level repaired last year.

Schedule(s) attached hereto and forming part of this Statement include:..

The Sellers state that the above information is true, based on their current actual knowledge as of the date below. Any important changes to this information known to the Sellers will be disclosed by the Sellers prior to closing. Sellers are responsible for the accuracy of all answers. Sellers further agree to indemnify and hold the Brokerage/Broker/Salesperson harmless from any liability incurred as a result of any buyer relying on this information. The Sellers hereby authorize the Brokerage to post a copy of this Seller Property Information Statement into the database(s) of the appropriate MLS® system and that a copy of this Seller Property Information Statement be delivered by their agent or representative to prospective buyers or their agents or representatives. The Sellers hereby acknowledge receipt of a true copy of this statement.

Steven Costa .... DATE... *May 20, 20xx* .... DATE...............
(Signature of Seller)   (Signature of Seller)

I acknowledge that the information provided herein is not warranted and hereby acknowledge receipt of a copy of the above information including any applicable Schedule(s).

Valerie Sawyer ....   DATE... *May 30, 20xx* ....
(Signature of Buyer or Authorized Representative)

Eric Sawyer ....   DATE... *May 30, 20xx* ....
(Signature of Buyer)

Form 220   Revised 2016   **Page 3 of 3**

■ Exercise 5   The Basement Apartment

This exercise involves topics discussed in both Chapters 2 and 3. The following case has been summarized from a CCD Hearing under the previous Real Estate and Business Brokers Act. For all published cases go to **www.reco.on.ca**.

Salesperson A listed a basement apartment for rent, showed the unit to a client, obtained an acknowledgement of multiple representation and had a one-year lease signed. Upon moving in, the tenant was informed by neighbours that the apartment was illegal pursuant to a city by-law. Following an investigation by the city, the owners received a notice confirming that fact and indicating that the tenant must be evicted.

Salesperson A advised the renter that he was unaware of the blanket prohibition of basement apartments in the city. Further, his suggestion to find alternate accommodation or amend the lease to month-to-month was rejected. The tenant refused to pay further rent payments and cancelled all post-dated cheques. The owners served the tenant with a termination notice and the tenant eventually moved out approximately three months later (with no rent paid for three months).

Salesperson A did not know that the apartment was not legal. In fact, evidence suggested that registrants generally appear to lack awareness of the basement apartment prohibition relating to that city. However, information posted on the MLS® system raises the issue of legal vs. illegal apartments. Among the listings submitted by counsel for Salesperson A at the hearing, two of them clearly noted that apartments within the listed properties were not legal.

The salesperson, in further defense of his actions, stated that he had received conflicting information concerning this issue from the city. Further, he felt that even if the owners had advertised the property themselves, the tenant would have found herself in the same situation.

a.   Based on your knowledge of the current *Real Estate and Business Brokers Act, 2002,* what specific section of the Code of Ethics has been violated in this seller representation?

b.   Comment on the validity of Salesperson A's defense concerning his lack of awareness.

CHAPTER 4

Documenting Buyer Representation

Introduction

Buyer representation has rapidly gained prominence in Ontario's real estate market-place, due in no small part to increasing transaction complexities and consumer demand for skilled representation. Presently, regulatory and professional organizations are refining procedures and guidelines to assist buyer representatives in carrying out duties. Further, litigation and court cases involving buyer representation are occurring more frequently, thereby furnishing additional insight regarding prudent practices.

As with seller representation, OREA forms are used for instructional purposes. Wordings and format may vary in broker-ages and real estate boards. Registrants should fully acquaint themselves with such variations, as the need arises. Selected OREA forms are reprinted in the *Appendix*.

Learning Outcomes

At the conclusion of this chapter, students will be able to:

- Describe and explain the structure of a buyer representation agreement and the authority granted in a typical exclusive representation agreement.
- Briefly describe clauses in the OREA residential *Buyer Representation Agreement* (Form 300).
- Briefly outline significant differences between the OREA residential and commercial representation agreements.
- Detail the legal obligations owed by the buyer client (principal) to the real estate brokerage (agent).
- Outline REBBA 2002 requirements concerning buyer representation with particular reference to minimum required content, commission calculation, entitlement and payment.
- Discuss the operation of a holdover clause as it applies to buyer representation agreements.
- Discuss disclosures relating to commission.
- Analyze support documents associated with the cancellation, assignment and amendment to the OREA *Buyer Representation Agreement*.
- Outline common errors and omissions involved with buyer representation.

BUYER REPRESENTATION AGREEMENT

A **buyer representation agreement** is an authority granted by a buyer to a real estate brokerage to act on his/her behalf in locating a suitable property for that buyer on terms and conditions set forth in the representation agreement.

A buyer representation agreement, similar to the seller representation agreement, typically grants an exclusive authority to a real estate brokerage to represent that party. This chapter focuses solely on exclusive buyer representation agreements. The representation agreement performs several functions:

- Establishes an exclusive **buyer representation** relationship.
- Sets out duties and responsibilities of both parties.
- Details commission arrangements and buyer responsibilities should commission not be paid by the seller.

> **Buyer Representation Agreement**
>
> An agreement setting out the representation relationship between a brokerage and a buyer.

The Exclusive Agreement

An exclusive buyer representation agreement gives the brokerage the sole right to locate real property that meets a specific buyer's requirements. Most importantly, the form details a general description of the property desired and geographic location, as well as setting out commission arrangements for locating such property.

AUTHORITY

As with the seller representation agreement, the buyer representation agreement sets out the legal relationship, obligations of the parties and time limits concerning such authority. Unlike the seller agreement, the buyer representation form is an authority both for the purchase of property and the leasing of property.

The authority is granted in the brokerage's name, never the salesperson's. While the buyer's authority can be verbal, the Code of Ethics requires that the authority be put in writing and signed by the brokerage or its representative prior to any offer being made. The buyer is not obligated to sign the agreement.

Exclusive written representation agreements require that an express, signed authority be given. This express authority delegated by the principal clearly sets forth in exact, plain, direct and well-defined limits those acts and duties that the agent is empowered to perform on behalf of the principal. If there is a definite understanding between the principal and agent, then the relationship has been established by express agreement.

KEY PROVISIONS: RESIDENTIAL REPRESENTATION AGREEMENT

Residential representation agreement wordings and formats can vary. The OREA *Buyer Representation Agreement: Authority for Purchase or Lease* (Form 300) is illustrated later in this chapter when discussing detailed preparation guidelines. Forms used for buyer representation are generally similar across Ontario. However, registrants must carefully study local forms to identify and fully understand any significant text differences.

The residential OREA *Buyer Representation Agreement* broadly parallels provisions set out in the OREA *Listing Agreement*. Certain key clauses warrant emphasis.

Property Type/Location   Form 300 provides for a general description of the property being sought, while granting the brokerage full authority to seek out all relevant properties. An important qualifier should be noted (see Clause 3: Representation).

The buyer acknowledges that the buyer may not be shown or offered all properties that may be of interest to the buyer.

Commission   The OREA *Buyer Representation Agreement* provides for payment either by the listing brokerage or by the seller, however, such payment does not create a representation (agency) relationship with the seller. The buyer remains responsible for the entire commission if no commission is to be paid by the seller or listing brokerage. However, the brokerage must inform the buyer of the amount of commission that will be paid, as the buyer is responsible for any deficiency between the contracted amount and the amount actually paid by the seller or listing brokerage. A holdover provision is also included.

Representation   As with the listing agreement, the buyer representation agreement sets out disclosure and related procedures concerning representation, multiple representation and customer service.

The agreement also provides a buyer acknowledgement that multiple representation may occur and details procedural specifics in that event. Further, the buyer understands that the broker may be entering into other buyer representation relationships. Negotiations may arise with more than one buyer client regarding the same property.

Indemnification   An important disclaimer is included regarding the physical condition of the land or improvements. The brokerage and its representatives are not qualified regarding the physical condition of either land or improvements and the buyer indemnifies the brokerage regarding liability for defects—latent or patent. Further, information supplied by a seller/landlord or listing brokerage is not warranted as accurate. Such matters fall to the buyer's risk (**caveat emptor**) and appropriate inquiries must be made.

> **Caveat Emptor**
>
> Let the buyer beware. The buyer must examine the goods or property being acquired and, therefore, buys at his/her own risk.

Consumer Report   The *Consumer Reporting Act* requires that every person be notified if a consumer report may be referred to in connection with a transaction. An appropriate clause is inserted in the *Buyer Representation Agreement* to that effect (see Clause 7: Consumer Reports), as such information may be required in order to secure financing.

Buyer Registry Service (BRS)   CURIOSITY

The Toronto Real Estate Board (TREB) has created a Buyer Registry Service that somewhat parallels the Multiple Listing Service® for sellers, in that buyers can be registered under this service if a *Buyer Representation Agreement* is signed, which has a term of five (5) days or longer. Only the buyer's salesperson representative or broker of record can enter details in the system. The Toronto Real Estate Board has established procedures to operate the BRS that are separate from the Multiple Listing Service® and are enforced under the By-laws of the Board.

TREB members are able to search the BRS to find out if a particular buyer is registered in the system or not, thereby avoiding any potential problems arising out of multiple representation agreements. The BRS also offers a unique reverse search by which TREB members can type in criteria concerning a newly listed property and the BRS will return contact information for members who have buyer profiles that may be interested in the property. The buyers' information is not made available, as this information is personal and subject to privacy protection.

RESPONSIBILITIES TO THE CLIENT

The OREA *Buyer Representation Agreement* generally addresses responsibilities owed to the buyer by the registrant, but does not set out specifics. Buyer client expectations of brokerages and their representatives in everyday market activities are gradually evolving. An illustrative list is provided for general discussion only. Policies and procedures can vary by brokerage. Duties may include:

- Assisting the buyer in setting out property preferences.
- Developing a property profile for guidance.
- Seeking out property in a timely manner that meet the buyer's criteria, without regard for commission or other remuneration to which the brokerage may be entitled.
- Preparing a comparative market analysis (CMA) or analyzing a seller-provided CMA or other documentation (i.e., Seller Property Information Statement) to assist the buyer in making an informed decision and taking appropriate action.
- Accurately and professionally preparing and conveying offers, counter offers and other written documentation.
- Taking reasonable steps to determine and disclose to the buyer material facts relating to the acquisition of a specific property.
- Assisting with buyer negotiations with strategies/options to advance the client's interests.
- Negotiating for the client to obtain the lowest price and best possible terms.
- Assisting the buyer with mortgage lenders, home inspectors and other professionals as required.
- Reviewing or otherwise assisting the client, as appropriate, with reports received and other documentation arising from the property buying process.
- Informing the client of all significant steps taken in the course of representing that client.

REBBA 2002: Agreement Preparation

Sec. 11 of the Code of Ethics, as discussed regarding sellers in Chapter 3, sets out minimum requirements for all written buyer representation agreements as well. These include:

- Effective date of the agreement.
- Amount of commission/other remuneration.
- Amount payable to a co-operating brokerage (for seller-related agreements).
- How commission is paid.
- Services being provided under the agreement.
- Provision for agreements exceeding six months (i.e., the date is to be prominently displayed on the first page with space for the required buyer or seller initials).
- Agreement must contain only one expiry date.

CONTENTS OF WRITTEN AGREEMENTS   CODE

11. (1) A brokerage shall not enter into a written agreement with a buyer or seller for the purpose of trading in real estate unless the agreement clearly, comprehensibly and prominently,

     (a) specifies the date on which the agreement takes effect and the date on which it expires;

     (b) specifies or describes the method for determining,

         (i) the amount of any commission or other remuneration payable to the brokerage, and

         (ii) in the case of an agreement with a seller, the amount of any commission or other remuneration payable to any other brokerage;

     (c) describes how any commission or other remuneration payable to the brokerage will be paid; and

     (d) sets out the services that the brokerage will provide under the agreement. O. Reg. 580/05, s. 11 (1).

   (2) A brokerage shall not, for the purpose of trading in real estate, enter into a written agreement with a buyer or seller that provides that the date on which the agreement expires is more than six months after the date on which the agreement takes effect unless,

     (a) the date on which the agreement expires is prominently displayed on the first page of the agreement; and

     (b) the buyer or seller has initialled the agreement next to the date referred to in clause (a). O. Reg. 580/05, s. 11 (2).

   (3) A brokerage shall ensure that a written agreement that is entered into between the brokerage and a buyer or seller for the purpose of trading in real estate contains only one date on which the agreement expires. O. Reg. 580/05, s. 11 (3).

The Code of Ethics also states the representation agreement be in writing prior to any offer being made and that copies of written agreements must be given to the applicable person(s).

COPIES OF WRITTEN AGREEMENTS   CODE

12. If a brokerage and one or more other persons enter into a written agreement in connection with a trade in real estate, the brokerage shall ensure that each of the other persons is immediately given a copy of the agreement. O. Reg. 580/05, s. 12.

BUYER REPRESENTATION AGREEMENTS   CODE

14. If a brokerage enters into a buyer representation agreement with a buyer and the agreement is not in writing, the brokerage shall, before the buyer makes an offer, reduce the agreement to writing, have it signed on behalf of the brokerage and submit it to the buyer for signature. O. Reg. 580/05, s. 14.

PREPARATION GUIDELINES

OREA Ontario Real Estate Association

Buyer Representation Agreement
Authority for Purchase or Lease

Form 300
for use in the Province of Ontario

This is an Exclusive Buyer Representation Agreement

BETWEEN:

BROKERAGE: .... **A** ...., Tel.No. (...........)................................

ADDRESS: ....

.... Fax.No. (...........).....................

hereinafter referred to as the Brokerage.

AND:

BUYER(S):............................ **B** ...., hereinafter referred to as the Buyer,

ADDRESS: ....
               Street Number   Street Name

MUNICIPALITY: .... **POSTAL CODE:** ....

The Buyer hereby gives the Brokerage the **exclusive and irrevocable authority** to act as the Buyer's agent

commencing at .... a.m./p.m. on the .... **C** .... day of ...., 20................,

and expiring at 11:59 p.m. on the .... day of ...., 20.............(Expiry Date),

{ Buyer acknowledges that the time period for this Agreement is negotiable between the Buyer and the Brokerage, however, in accordance with the Real Estate and Business Brokers Act of Ontario (2002), **if the time period for this Agreement exceeds six months, the Brokerage must obtain the Buyer's initials.** } ( ) **D**
                                                                (Buyer's Initials)

for the purpose of locating a real property meeting the following general description:

E Property Type (Use): ....

....

Geographic Location: ....

....

F **The Buyer hereby warrants that the Buyer is not a party to a buyer representation agreement with any other registered real estate brokerage for the purchase or lease of a real property of the general description indicated above.**

1. **DEFINITIONS AND INTERPRETATIONS:** For the purposes of this Buyer Representation Agreement ("Authority" or "Agreement"), "Buyer" includes purchaser and tenant, a "seller" includes a vendor, a landlord or a prospective seller, vendor or landlord and a "real estate board" includes a real estate association. A purchase shall be deemed to include the entering into of any agreement to exchange, or the obtaining of an option to purchase which is subsequently exercised, and a lease includes any rental agreement, sub-lease or renewal of a lease. This Agreement shall be read with all changes of gender or number required by the context. For purposes of this Agreement, Buyer shall be deemed to include any spouse, heirs, executors, administrators, successors, assigns, related corporations and affiliated corporations. Related corporations or affiliated corporations shall include any corporation where one half or a majority of the shareholders, directors or officers of the related or affiliated corporation are the same person(s) as the shareholders, directors, or officers of the corporation introduced to or shown the property.

G 2. **COMMISSION:** In consideration of the Brokerage undertaking to assist the Buyer, the Buyer agrees to pay commission to the Brokerage as follows: If, during the currency of this Agreement, the Buyer enters into an agreement to purchase or lease a real property of the general description indicated above, the Buyer agrees the Brokerage is entitled to receive and retain any commission offered by a listing brokerage or by the seller. The Buyer understands that the amount of commission offered by a listing brokerage or by the seller may be greater or less than the commission stated below. The Buyer understands that the Brokerage will inform the Buyer of the amount of commission to be paid to the Brokerage by the listing brokerage or the seller at the earliest practical opportunity. The Buyer acknowledges that the payment of any commission by the listing brokerage or the seller will not make the Brokerage either the agent or sub-agent of the listing brokerage or the seller.

INITIALS OF BROKERAGE: ( ) ← **H** → INITIALS OF BUYER(S): ( )

The trademarks REALTOR®, REALTORS® and the REALTOR® logo are controlled by The Canadian Real Estate Association (CREA) and identify real estate professionals who are members of CREA. Used under license.

© 2016, Ontario Real Estate Association ("OREA"). All rights reserved. This form was developed by OREA for the use and reproduction of its members and licensees only. Any other use or reproduction is prohibited except with prior written consent of OREA. Do not alter when printing or reproducing the standard pre-set portion. OREA bears no liability for your use of this form.

Form 300   Revised 2015   **Page 1 of 3**

A **Brokerage** Insert full registered brokerage name. A salesperson's name is never entered. Complete address of brokerage is also required.

B **Buyer(s)** Insert full name(s) of buyer(s) and address(es).

C **Commencement/Expiration Date** A commencement date must be inserted, as well as a termination date pursuant to the Code of Ethics, Sec. 11: Contents of Written Agreements.

D **Six-Month Provision** The date cannot exceed six months without the buyer's informed consent and initials, as per the Code of Ethics, Sec. 11: Contents of Written Agreements.

E **Property Description** Ensure that sufficient detail is provided to identify both the property type desired and geographic location.

F **Buyer Representation/ Warranty** This clause is bolded for emphasis, as this warranty relates to the buyer not being a party to a buyer representation agreement with any other registered real estate brokerage.

G **Commission** Fully review commission provisions with the buyer, including the obligation to pay any deficiency between the amount stated in this agreement and the amount received from the listing brokerage. Include commission percentage rate, agreed amount or a combination of both (See REBBA, Sec. 36).

H **Initials** Initials of an authorized representative of the brokerage is required, as well as the buyer's. In the case of a corporation, an authorized individual's initials are required.

If, during the currency of this Agreement, the Buyer enters into an agreement to purchase any property of the general description indicated above,

the Buyer agrees that the Brokerage is entitled to be paid a commission of .... % of the sale price of the property

or ....

or for a lease, a commission of ....

The Buyer agrees to pay directly to the Brokerage any deficiency between this amount and the amount, if any, to be paid to the Brokerage by a listing brokerage or by the seller. The Buyer understands that if the Brokerage is not to be paid any commission by a listing brokerage or by the seller, the Buyer will pay the Brokerage the full amount of commission indicated above.

The Buyer agrees to pay the Brokerage such commission if the Buyer enters into an agreement within .... days after the expiration of this Agreement (Holdover Period) to purchase or lease any real property shown or introduced to the Buyer from any source whatsoever during the term of this Agreement, provided, however, that if the Buyer enters into a new buyer representation agreement with another registered real estate brokerage after the expiration of this Agreement, the Buyer's liability to pay commission to the Brokerage shall be reduced by the amount paid to the other brokerage under the new agreement.

The Buyer agrees to pay such commission as described above even if a transaction contemplated by an agreement to purchase or lease agreed to or accepted by the Buyer or anyone on the Buyer's behalf is not completed, if such non-completion is owing or attributable to the Buyers default or neglect. Said commission, plus any applicable taxes, shall be payable on the date set for completion of the purchase of the property or, in the case of a lease or tenancy, the earlier of the date of occupancy by the tenant or the date set for commencement of the lease or tenancy. All amounts set out as commission are to be paid plus applicable taxes on such commission.

This Agreement applies for the purchase or lease of one real property. Notwithstanding the foregoing, in the event that the Buyer leases a property, this agreement remains in force as set out herein for the purchase of the leased property or a property of the general description indicated above. The leasing of a property by the Buyer does not terminate this Agreement with respect to the purchase of a property.

3. REPRESENTATION: The Buyer acknowledges that the Brokerage has provided the Buyer with written information explaining agency relationships, including information on Seller Representation, Sub-Agency, Buyer Representation, Multiple Representation and Customer Service. The Brokerage shall assist the Buyer in locating a real property of the general description indicated above and shall represent the Buyer in an endeavour to procure the acceptance of an agreement to purchase or lease such a property.

The Buyer acknowledges that the Buyer may not be shown or offered all properties that may be of interest to the Buyer. The Buyer hereby agrees that the terms of any buyer's offer or agreement to purchase or lease the property will not be disclosed to any other buyer. The Buyer further acknowledges that the Brokerage may be entering into buyer representation agreements with other buyers who may be interested in the same or similar properties that the Buyer may be interested in buying or leasing and the Buyer hereby consents to the Brokerage entering into buyer representation agreements with other buyers who may be interested in the same or similar properties without any claim by the Buyer of conflict of interest. The Buyer hereby appoints the Brokerage as agent for the purpose of giving and receiving notices pursuant to any offer or agreement to purchase or lease a property negotiated by the Brokerage.

MULTIPLE REPRESENTATION: The Buyer hereby acknowledges that the Brokerage may be entering into listing agreements with sellers of properties the Buyer may be interested in buying or leasing. In the event that the Brokerage has entered into or enters into a listing agreement with the seller of a property the Buyer may be interested in buying or leasing, the Brokerage will obtain the Buyer's written consent to represent both the Buyer and the seller for the transaction at the earliest practicable opportunity and in all cases prior to any offer to purchase or lease being submitted or presented.

The Buyer understands and acknowledges that the Brokerage must be impartial when representing both the Buyer and the seller in the transaction. The Buyer understands and acknowledges that when representing both the Buyer and the seller, the Brokerage shall have a duty of full disclosure to both the Buyer and the seller, including a requirement to disclose all factual information about the property known to the Brokerage.

However, The Buyer further understands and acknowledges that the Brokerage shall not disclose:
* that the seller may or will accept less than the listed price, unless otherwise instructed in writing by the seller;
* that the Buyer may or will pay more than the offered price, unless otherwise instructed in writing by the Buyer;
* the motivation of or personal information about the Buyer or seller, unless otherwise instructed in writing by the party to which the information applies or unless failure to disclose would constitute fraudulent, unlawful or unethical practice;
* the price the Buyer should offer or the price the seller should accept; and
* the Brokerage shall not disclose to the Buyer the terms of any other offer.

However, it is understood that factual market information about comparable properties and information known to the Brokerage concerning potential uses for the property will be disclosed to both Buyer and seller to assist them to come to their own conclusions.

Where a Brokerage represents both the Seller and the Buyer (multiple representation), the Brokerage shall not be entitled or authorized to be agent for either the Buyer or the Seller for the purpose of giving and receiving notices.

MULTIPLE REPRESENTATION AND CUSTOMER SERVICE: The Buyer understands and agrees that the Brokerage also provides representation and customer service to other buyers and sellers. If the Brokerage represents or provides customer service to more than one seller or buyer for the same trade, the Brokerage shall, in writing, at the earliest practicable opportunity and before any offer is made, inform all sellers and buyers of the nature of the Brokerage's relationship to each seller and buyer.

4. REFERRAL OF PROPERTIES: The Buyer agrees that during the currency of this Buyer Representation Agreement the Buyer will act in good faith and work exclusively with the Brokerage for the purchase or lease of a real property of the general description indicated above. The Buyer agrees that, during the currency of this Agreement, the Buyer shall advise the Brokerage immediately of any property of interest to the Buyer that came to the Buyer's attention from any source whatsoever, and all offers to purchase or lease submitted by the Buyer shall be submitted through the Brokerage to the seller. If the Buyer arranges a valid agreement to purchase or lease any property of the general description indicated above that came to the attention of the Buyer during the currency of this Agreement and the Buyer arranges said agreement during the currency of this Agreement or within the Holdover Period after expiration of this Agreement, the Buyer agrees to pay the Brokerage the amount of commission set out above in Paragraph 2 of this Agreement, payable within (5) days following the Brokerage's written demand therefor.

INITIALS OF BROKERAGE: ( )   **INITIALS OF BUYER(S):** ( )

Form 300   Revised 2015   **Page 2 of 3**

I Holdover Period   Typically 60–90 days or reasonable time period as agreed by the parties.

J Representation   Carefully review all Clause 3 provisions with the buyer concerning representation, multiple representation, and multiple representation and customer service.

K Initials   Initials of an authorized representative of the brokerage is required, as well as the buyer's. In the case of a corporation, an authorized individual's initials are required.

L 5. **INDEMNIFICATION:** The Brokerage and representatives of the Brokerage are trained in dealing in real estate but are not qualified in determining the physical condition of the land or any improvements thereon. The Buyer agrees that the Brokerage and representatives of the Brokerage will not be liable for any defects, whether latent or patent, to the land or improvements thereon. All information supplied by the seller or landlord or the listing brokerage may not have been verified and is not warranted by the Brokerage as being accurate and will be relied on by the Buyer at the Buyer's own risk. The Buyer acknowledges having been advised to make their own enquiries to confirm the condition of the property.

M 6. **FINDERS FEE:** The Buyer acknowledges that the Brokerage may be receiving a finder's fee, reward and/or referral incentive, and the Buyer consents to any such benefit being received and retained by the Brokerage in addition to the commission as described above.

N 7. **CONSUMER REPORTS:** The Buyer is hereby notified that a Consumer Report containing credit and/or personal information may be referred to in connection with this Agreement and any subsequent transaction.

8. **USE AND DISTRIBUTION OF INFORMATION:** The Buyer consents to the collection, use and disclosure of personal information by the Brokerage for such purposes that relate to the real estate services provided by the Brokerage to the Buyer including, but not limited to: locating, assessing and qualifying properties for the Buyer; advertising on behalf of the Buyer; providing information as needed to third parties retained by the Buyer to assist in a transaction (e.g. financial institutions, building inspectors, etc...); and such other use of the Buyer's information as is consistent with the services provided by the Brokerage in connection with the purchase or prospective purchase of the property.

The Buyer agrees that the sale and related information regarding any property purchased by the Buyer through the Brokerage may be retained and disclosed by the Brokerage and/or real estate board(s) (if the property is an MLS® Listing) for reporting, appraisal and statistical purposes and for such other use of the information as the Brokerage and/or board deems appropriate in connection with the listing, marketing and selling of real estate, including conducting comparative market analyses.

The Buyer acknowledges that the information, personal or otherwise ("information"), provided to the real estate board or association may be stored on databases located outside of Canada, in which case the information would be subject to the laws of the jurisdiction in which the information is located.

9. **CONFLICT OR DISCREPANCY:** If there is any conflict or discrepancy between any provision added to this Agreement and any provision in the standard pre-set portion hereof, the added provision shall supersede the standard pre-set provision to the extent of such conflict or discrepancy. This Agreement, including any provisions added to this Agreement, shall constitute the entire Agreement between the Buyer and the Brokerage. There is no representation, warranty, collateral agreement or condition, which affects this Agreement other than as expressed herein.

10. **ELECTRONIC COMMUNICATION:** This Buyer Representation Agreement and any agreements, notices or other communications contemplated thereby may be transmitted by means of electronic systems, in which case signatures shall be deemed to be original. The transmission of this Agreement by the Buyer by electronic means shall be deemed to confirm the Buyer has retained a true copy of the Agreement.

O 11. **SCHEDULE(S):**.. attached hereto form(s) part of this Agreement.

THE BROKERAGE AGREES TO REPRESENT THE BUYER IN LOCATING A REAL PROPERTY OF THE GENERAL DESCRIPTION INDICATED ABOVE IN AN ENDEAVOUR TO OBTAIN THE ACCEPTANCE OF AN AGREEMENT TO PURCHASE OR LEASE A PROPERTY ON TERMS SATISFACTORY TO THE BUYER.

P ....   DATE.............................   ....
(Authorized to bind the Brokerage)   (Name of Person Signing)

THIS AGREEMENT HAS BEEN READ AND FULLY UNDERSTOOD BY ME AND I ACKNOWLEDGE THIS DATE I HAVE SIGNED UNDER SEAL. Any representations contained herein are true to the best of my knowledge, information and belief.

SIGNED, SEALED AND DELIVERED I have hereunto set my hand and seal:

Q ....   ● DATE.............................   ....
(Signature of Buyer)   (Seal)   (Tel. No.)

....   ● DATE.............................   ....
(Signature of Buyer)   (Seal)

R **DECLARATION OF INSURANCE**

The broker/salesperson ....
                                               (Name of Broker/Salesperson)
hereby declares that he/she is insured as required by the Real Estate and Business Brokers Act (REBBA) and Regulations.

....
                                               (Signature(s) of Broker/Salesperson)

ACKNOWLEDGEMENT

S The Buyer(s) hereby acknowledge that the Buyer(s) fully understand the terms of this Agreement and have received a true copy of this Agreement

on the .... day of ...., 20 ....

....   Date:.......................................
(Signature of Buyer)

....   Date:.......................................
(Signature of Buyer)

The trademarks REALTOR®, REALTORS® and the REALTOR® logo are controlled by The Canadian Real Estate Association (CREA) and identify real estate professionals who are members of CREA. Used under license.

© 2016, Ontario Real Estate Association ("OREA"). All rights reserved. This form was developed by OREA for the use and reproduction of its members and licensees only. Any other use or reproduction is prohibited except with prior written consent of OREA. Do not alter when printing or reproducing the standard pre-set portion. OREA bears no liability for your use of this form.

Form 300   Revised 2015   **Page 3 of 3**

L Indemnification   Carefully review with buyer including the need for the buyer to make their own enquiries to confirm the condition of the property.

M Finder's Fee   Consent by buyer for the brokerage to receive and retain a finder's fee relating to financing for the property, over and above commission received in relation to this agreement. This consent is required pursuant to the Code of Ethics, Sec. 18: Disclosure of Interest.

N Consumer Report   This provision is bolded to emphasize that a consumer report may be referred to in connection with this agreement and any subsequent purchase. This provision complies with requirements set out in the *Consumer Reporting Act.*

O Schedules   Additional provisions should be identified in sequential order as Schedule A, Schedule B and so forth. Make certain that cross-references, such as buyer's name and agreement date are included on all schedules. Buyer(s) initials required.

P Brokerage Signature   A person authorized to bind the brokerage (a broker or salesperson employed by that brokerage) must sign and date his or her signature.

Q Buyer Signature   Buyer's usual signature required. For corporations, an authorized signature is required along with the individual's title and corporate seal. If the seal is not used, insert the words: I have the authority to bind the corporation.

R Insurance   A declaration of insurance is signed by the applicable broker or salesperson.

S Acknowledgement   Buyer acknowledges understanding and receipt of agreement.

Commercial Buyer Representation

The *Buyer Representation Agreement—Commercial: Mandate for Purchase or Lease* (OREA Form 540) generally follows the structure and wording of its residential counterpart, but important differences require highlighting. Present discussion is limited to notable differences only. Students contemplating commercial listing and sale activity should fully review both forms to identify all wording variations. Registrants should review the specific forms that will be used in their brokerage.

OREA Ontario Real Estate Association

Buyer Representation Agreement – Commercial
Mandate for Purchase or Lease

Form 540
for use in the Province of Ontario

This is an Exclusive Buyer Representation Agreement

BETWEEN:
BROKERAGE: ...., Tel.No. (..........)....................................

ADDRESS: ....

.... Fax.No. (..........)....................................

Clause 1: Definitions and Interpretations

The commercial form expands the definition of a purchase to include an option to purchase and the transfer of shares or assets. Further, real property includes real estate as defined in the *Real Estate and Business Brokers Act, 2002*.

estate brokerage for the purchase or lease of a real property of the general description indicated above.

1. **DEFINITIONS AND INTERPRETATIONS:** For the purposes of this Buyer Representation Agreement ("Mandate"), "Buyer" includes purchaser, lessee and tenant and a "seller" includes a vendor, a lessor, a landlord or a prospective seller, vendor, lessor or landlord. A "real property" includes real estate as defined in the Real Estate and Business Brokers Act (2002). A purchase shall be deemed to include the entering into of any agreement to exchange, or the obtaining of an option to purchase which is subsequently exercised, or an agreement to purchase or transfer shares or assets, and a lease includes any rental agreement, sub-lease or renewal of a lease. A "real estate board" includes a real estate association. This Agreement shall be read with all changes of gender or number required by the context. For the purposes of this Agreement, the definition of "Buyer" in the phrase "any property of interest to the Buyer that came to the Buyer's attention from any source whatsoever" shall be deemed to include any spouse, heirs, executors, administrators, successors, assigns, related corporations and affiliated corporations. Related corporations or affiliated corporations shall include any corporation where one half or a majority of the shareholders, directors or officers of the related or affiliated corporation are the same person(s) as the shareholders, directors, or officers of the corporation introduced to or shown the property.

2. SERVICES PROVIDED BY THE BROKERAGE: It is understood that the Brokerage may assist the Buyer with any or all of the following services

Clause 2: Services Provided by Brokerage

This clause is an added provision relating to specific services that may assist the buyer. Space is provided for other services as agreed between the parties (including the possibility of a separate schedule).

include any corporation where one half or a majority of the shareholders, directors or officers of the related or affiliated corporation are the same person(s) as the shareholders, directors, or officers of the corporation introduced to or shown the property.

2. **SERVICES PROVIDED BY THE BROKERAGE:** It is understood that the Brokerage may assist the Buyer with any or all of the following services, and any other services, as agreed to between the Buyer and the Brokerage:
   - to identify the needs of the Buyer.
   - to locate available properties that may meet the Buyer's needs.
   - to assist the Buyer in negotiations for the purchase or lease of any property of interest to the Buyer (subject to the special provisions for Multiple Representation described below).
   - Other: (Attach Schedule if additional space is required) ....

INITIALS OF BROKERAGE: ( )   **INITIALS OF BUYER(S):** ( )

Clause 3: Responsibilities of the Buyer

Clause 3 sets out specific duties owed by the buyer to the brokerage during the currency of the agreement.

---

3. RESPONSIBILITIES OF THE BUYER: In consideration of the Brokerage undertaking to assist the Buyer, the Buyer agrees to:

- co-operate with the Brokerage with respect to the Brokerage providing any or all of the services described above, as agreed to between the Buyer and the Brokerage.
- work exclusively with the Brokerage for the purchase or lease of a real property that meets the Buyer's needs.
- advise the Brokerage immediately of any property of interest to the Buyer that came to the Buyer's attention from any source whatsoever during the currency of this Agreement.
- submit through the Brokerage all offers by the Buyer during the currency of this Agreement to purchase or lease a real property of the general description indicated above.
- submit through the Brokerage all offers by the Buyer within .... days after expiration of this Agreement for the purchase or lease of any property that came to the Buyer's attention from any source whatsoever during the currency of this Agreement.

The Buyer agrees the Brokerage is entitled to be paid a commission of ....
....
....

The Buyer authorizes the Brokerage to receive payment of commission from the seller of the property or the seller's agent. Should the Brokerage be unable to obtain an agreement in writing from the seller or the seller's agent to pay the full commission described above, the Buyer will be so informed in writing prior to submitting an offer to purchase or lease and the Buyer will pay the commission for the transaction, or any deficiency in the amount of commission described above, directly to the Brokerage.

The Buyer agrees to pay such commission as described above even if a transaction contemplated by an agreement to purchase or lease agreed to or accepted by the Buyer or anyone on the Buyer's behalf is not completed, if such non-completion is owing or attributable to the Buyer's default or neglect. The Buyer understands that a failure to negotiate and submit offers through the Brokerage as described herein will make the Buyer liable for payment of commission to the Brokerage. The payment of commission by the seller to the Brokerage will not make the Brokerage the agent for the seller. All amounts set out as commission are to be paid plus applicable taxes on such commission.

4. REPRESENTATION: The Buyer acknowledges that the Brokerage has provided the Buyer with written information explaining agency relationships

---

In addition, the *Amendment to Buyer Representation Agreement—Commercial* (Form 541), a commercial amendment form, is provided that serves much the same purpose as its residential counterpart to provide written confirmation of changes to the agreement.

 **OREA** Ontario Real Estate Association

Amendment to Buyer Representation Agreement — Commercial

Form 541
for use in the Province of Ontario

RE: BUYER REPRESENTATION AGREEMENT— COMMERCIAL BETWEEN:

BUYER: ....
AND
BROKERAGE: ....

BUYER REGISTRATION NUMBER(S) (if applicable): ....

EXPIRY DATE: ....

The Buyer and the Brokerage hereby agree that the above described Buyer Representation Agreement— Commercial is amended as stated below:

 # COMMISSION NEGOTIATIONS

Buyer's Legal Obligations

The buyer, as a principal, has three obligations to the agent (brokerage) under agency law when entering into a buyer representation relationship: remuneration, indemnification and any additional obligations set out in the representation agreement, as with seller representation agreements, discussed in the last chapter.

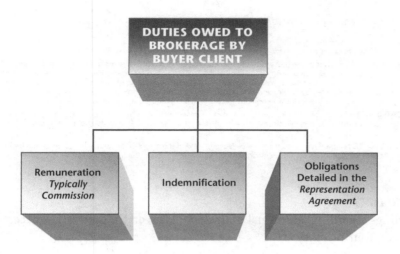

REMUNERATION

The buyer agrees that the brokerage is entitled to a commission based on a percentage of the sale price of the property, a specific amount or a combination of both as set out in the agreement. At the same time, the buyer client agrees that the brokerage is entitled to receive and retain a commission paid by a listing brokerage or a client. If such does occur, the buyer agrees to pay any deficiency between the amount received from a listing brokerage or a client and the commission agreed upon in the buyer representation agreement. If no commission is received from a listing brokerage or a seller, then the amount as set out in the agreement is due and payable.

Further, the client agrees to pay such commission for a specified number of days after the expiration of the representation agreement if he or she enters into an agreement to purchase or lease any real property shown or introduced to him or her during the term of the agreement (see subsequent discussion on the holdover clause).

INDEMNIFICATION

Indemnification involves the obligation to compensate the brokerage for loss or damage in carrying out lawful acts. Indemnification, for purposes of buyer representation, is set out in the agreement and specifically focuses on liability for defects (latent or patent). The applicable clause from the residential *Buyer Representation Agreement (*Form 300*)* is reprinted, along with the variation found in the *Buyer Representation Agreement —Commercial (*Form 540*)*.

Indemnification—Buyer Representation Agreement

5. **INDEMNIFICATION:** The Brokerage and representatives of the Brokerage are trained in dealing in real estate but are not qualified in determining the physical condition of the land or any improvements thereon. The Buyer agrees that the Brokerage and representatives of the Brokerage will not be liable for any defects, whether latent or patent, to the land or improvements thereon. All information supplied by the seller or landlord or the listing brokerage may not have been verified and is not warranted by the Brokerage as being accurate and will be relied on by the Buyer at the Buyer's own risk. The Buyer acknowledges having been advised to make their own enquiries to confirm the condition of the property.

6. **FINDERS FEE:** The Buyer acknowledges that the Brokerage may be receiving a finder's fee, reward and/or referral incentive, and the Buyer consents to any such benefit being received and retained by the Brokerage in addition to the commission as described above.

Indemnification—Buyer Representation Agreement, Commercial

5. **FINDERS FEES:** The Buyer acknowledges that the Brokerage may be receiving a finder's fee, reward and/or referral incentive, and the buyer consents to any such benefit being received and retained by the Brokerage in addition to the commission as described above.

6. **INDEMNIFICATION:** The Brokerage and representatives of the Brokerage are trained in dealing in real estate but are not qualified in determining the physical condition of the land or any improvements thereon. The Buyer agrees that the Brokerage and representatives of the Brokerage will not be liable for any defects, whether latent or patent, to the land or improvements thereon. All information supplied by the seller or landlord or the listing brokerage may not have been verified and is not warranted by the Brokerage as being accurate and will be relied on by the Buyer at the Buyer's own risk. The Buyer acknowledges having been advised to make their own enquiries to confirm the condition of the property.

7. **ENVIRONMENTAL INDEMNIFICATION:** The Buyer agrees to indemnify and save harmless the Brokerage and representatives of the Brokerage from any liability, claim, loss, cost, damage or injury as a result of any property of interest to the Buyer being affected by any contaminants or environmental problems.

8. **USE AND DISTRIBUTION OF INFORMATION:** The Buyer consents to the collection, use and disclosure of personal information by the Brokerage for such purposes that relate to the real estate services provided by the Brokerage to the Buyer including, but not limited to: locating, assessing and qualifying properties for the Buyer; advertising on behalf of the Buyer; providing information as needed to third parties retained by the Buyer to assist

OTHER OBLIGATIONS

Exact wordings regarding additional obligations can vary in the marketplace. Generally, these focus on four primary areas:

If Sale Does Not Complete	Assuming that the buyer is to pay the commission, the buyer is typically obligated to pay such commission if the transaction contemplated by the agreement is not completed, if this non-completion is due to the buyer's default or neglect.
Deficiency	The buyer agrees to pay the brokerage on demand any deficiency in commission (and taxes owing on such commission) when the commission received from a brokerage or a seller is less than agreed to in the buyer representation agreement.
Taxes	The buyer agrees to pay applicable harmonized sales tax on the total commission payable to the brokerage by the buyer.
Referral of Properties	The buyer agrees to notify the brokerage immediately of any properties of interest to the buyer. If such is not done and a sale is negotiated directly with a seller in relation to such a property, the brokerage is owed the commission as per the representation agreement.

Regulatory Requirements

Various commission provisions are set out in REBBA 2002 regarding entitlement to commission and how commission is to be calculated.

COMMISSION CALCULATION

Commission or other remuneration can be an agreed amount or percentage of the sale price/rental price, or a combination of both. If a percentage is used, the remuneration may include several percentages that decrease as the sale price or rental price increases. A commission must never be calculated based on the difference between the listing price and the actual sale price.

If no amount is agreed upon, the prevailing rate in the community will prevail. Registrants must NOT indicate directly or indirectly that commissions are fixed or approved by administrative or government authorities, real estate boards or real estate associations.

COMMISSION AND REMUNERATION

REBBA

36. (1) All commission or other remuneration payable to a brokerage in respect of a trade in real estate shall be an agreed amount or percentage of the sale price or rental price, as the case may be, or a combination of both. 2013, c. 13, Sched. 3, s. 2.

If no agreement

(1.1) If there is no agreement as to the amount of the commission or other remuneration, the rate of it or other basis for determining it shall be that generally prevailing in the community where the real estate is located. 2013, c. 13, Sched. 3, s. 2.

Percentages

(2) If the commission payable in respect of a trade in real estate is expressed as a percentage of the sale price or rental price, the percentage does not have to be fixed but may be expressed as a series of percentages that decrease at specified amounts as the sale price or rental price increases. 2002, c. 30, Sched. C, s. 36 (2).

Prohibition

(3) No registrant shall request or enter into an arrangement for the payment of a commission or any other remuneration based on the difference between the price at which real estate is listed for sale or rental and the actual sale price or rental price, as the case may be, of the real estate, nor is a registrant entitled to retain any commission or other remuneration computed upon any such basis. 2002, c. 30, Sched. C, s. 36 (3).

COMMISSIONS, ETC.

CODE

9. A registrant shall not indicate to any person, directly or indirectly, that commissions or other remuneration are fixed or approved by the administrative authority, any government authority, or any real estate board or real estate association. O. Reg. 580/05, s. 9.

ENTITLEMENT TO COMMISSION

A registrant is not entitled to a commission or other remuneration unless a written agreement is signed by the party paying the commission or the registrant has shown the property to the buyer (or introduced the buyer and seller to one another in relation to the buying or selling of an interest in real estate).

COMMISSIONS

GEN

23. (1) Subject to subsection 33 (3) of the Act and subsection (2), a registrant shall not charge or collect a commission or other remuneration in respect of a trade in real estate unless,

(a) the entitlement to the commission or other remuneration arises under a written agreement that is signed by or on behalf of the person who is required to pay the commission or other remuneration; or

(b) the entitlement to the commission or other remuneration arises under an agreement that is not referred to in clause (a) and,

(i) the registrant has conveyed an offer in writing that is accepted, or

(ii) the registrant,

(A) shows the property to the buyer, or

(B) introduces the buyer and the seller to one another for the purpose of discussing the proposed acquisition or disposition of an interest in real estate. O. Reg. 567/05, s. 23 (1).

LEGAL ACTION FOR COMMISSION

No legal action can be taken for the collecting of a commission involving a trade in real estate unless the person bringing such action was either registered or exempt from registration.

REGISTRATION A REQUIREMENT TO BRING ACTION   REBBA

9.   No action shall be brought for commission or other remuneration for services in connection with a trade in real estate unless at the time of rendering the services the person bringing the action was registered or exempt from registration under this Act and the court may stay any such action upon motion. 2002, c. 30, Sched. C, s. 9.

UNEXPIRED AGREEMENT

A brokerage is not entitled to claim commission or other remuneration if the registrant knows than an unexpired buyer representation agreement exists with a different brokerage, unless the buyer agrees in writing to pay such commission.

COMMISSIONS   GEN

23.   (2)   Unless agreed to in writing by the buyer, a registrant shall not charge or collect a commission or other remuneration from a buyer in respect of a trade in real estate if the registrant knows that there is an unexpired buyer representation agreement between the buyer and another registrant. O. Reg. 567/05, s. 23 (2).

The Need for Bold Print   **CURIOSITY**

The OREA *Buyer Representation Agreement* (both residential and commercial versions) ensures that no confusion exists as to whether or not the buyer has a representation with another brokerage. Following are bolded words from the current OREA representation form to ensure that the brokerage is in compliance with GEN, Subsec. 23(2):

The Buyer hereby warrants that the Buyer is not a party to a buyer representation agreement with any other registered real estate brokerage for the purchase or lease of a real property of the general description indicated above.

PAYMENT OF COMMISSION

Brokerages are not permitted to pay any commission or other remuneration to brokers or salespersons employed by another brokerage, nor to any unregistered person. Brokers and salespersons can only accept commission or other remuneration from their employing brokerage.

RESTRICTIONS RE: EMPLOYEES   REBBA

30.   No brokerage shall,

(a)   employ another brokerage's broker or salesperson to trade in real estate or permit such broker or salesperson to act on the brokerage's behalf;

(b)   employ an unregistered person to perform a function for which registration is required; or

(c)   pay any commission or other remuneration to a person referred to in clause (a) or (b). 2002, c. 30, Sched. C, s. 30.

RESTRICTIONS RE: BROKERS AND SALESPERSONS

31.   (1)   No broker or salesperson shall trade in real estate on behalf of any brokerage other than the brokerage which employs the broker or salesperson. 2002, c. 30, Sched. C, s. 31 (1).

Same

(2)   No broker or salesperson is entitled to or shall accept any commission or other remuneration for trading in real estate from any person except the brokerage which employs the broker or salesperson. 2002, c. 30, Sched. C, s. 31 (2).

Holdover Provision

As discussed in Chapter 3 relating to seller representation, a holdover provision can be looked at from two dimensions. First, the term *holdover* technically refers to a provision in an agreement that remains after expiration of the original agreement. Interestingly, the payment of a commission after expiration of the representation agreement would constitute one form of holdover. Fortunately, the courts have long recognized that commissions are due and payable even though the representation agreement may have expired before the property actually closes.

The more crucial issue when discussing holdover provisions involves a second dimension, that of a buyer introduced to a property during the term of the representation agreement, but an agreement of purchase and sale is not concluded for that property. What happens if the buyer subsequently buys the property after expiration of the representation agreement? The holdover provision provides that the buyer agrees to pay the commission (as set out in the representation agreement) if an agreement to purchase is agreed to in relation to the introduced property within a stated number of days after the expiration of the representation agreement. The typical time period for such a holdover is 60–90 days, but longer periods may be found particularly when dealing with commercial buyers.

EXAMPLE   *Buyer Introduced to Property During Term of Representation Agreement*

Buyer Smith signs a 90-day representation agreement with ABC Realty Inc., which contains a holdover provision. Following expiration, the owner of a property originally introduced to Buyer Smith by a salesperson in ABC Realty's employ returns to negotiate directly with Smith. Smith clearly wants a lower price to gain the benefit given that he would not be paying any commission. Smith, uncertain as to his position, takes the exclusive agreement to his lawyer. The lawyer confirms that if Smith buys the property, then a commission is payable to ABC Realty Inc. pursuant to the holdover clause.

EXAMPLE   *Subsequent Representation Agreement and Holdover Clause*

Buyer Smith was unhappy with Salesperson Lee of ABC Realty Inc. because a suitable property was not introduced to him within the 60-day representation agreement, despite several showings. Interestingly, within the first month of signing a new 20-day representation agreement with XYZ Real Estate Ltd., Smith decided to offer on the same property introduced previously by ABC Realty Inc. Smith, alluding to the holdover clause, expressed concerns that he might have to pay two commissions. XYZ Real Estate Ltd. assured him that such was not the case as the original representation agreement provided that the liability for commission would be reduced by the amount paid to the new brokerage under a subsequent representation agreement.

Right to Commission: Holdover Clause   RESIDENTIAL CASE LAW

In June, the sales representative of a real estate brokerage met with buyers to discuss housing needs and offered to find a house for them without compensation. Several homes were shown to the buyers in early July and an offer was drafted, but was subsequently refused on a signback from the seller. On July 31st, a buyer representation agreement was signed. The salesperson explained the agreement and, according to testimony, felt that he had secured the buyers' understanding of its content—a point under dispute within the trial. Over ensuing months, the salesperson persuaded the buyers to look at resale homes. The buyers suggested seeing both new and resale, but did not insist.

Following a number of showings, an offer was drafted for one particular home on October 5th, but that offer was not accepted by the seller. Near the end of October, the buyers decided to purchase a new home and concluded a sale without the knowledge or assistance of the salesperson with a closing in February of the next year. The salesperson received no commission relating to the new home purchase.

While various arguments were put forward by the buyers and their solicitor, the Judge found that the actions of the salesperson were reasonable, that while properties shown were not exactly suitable such were inspected to give the buyer an idea of the market, that he showed at least eight properties and had a buyer representation agreement signed and that no unreasonable efforts by the salesperson would allow the buyer to avoid the agreement on any grounds.

The Judge awarded the real estate brokerage the sum of $5,705.71, which represented an agreed upon amount, plus pre-judgment interest at the rate of six percent plus costs.

Reference   Homelife Performance Realty v. Reynold Gayadeen

COMMENTARY

This case has several interesting perspectives both about the activities of salespersons and the use of a buyer representation agreement.

One of the issues at trial was whether or not the salesperson had in some manner misrepresented the buyer representation agreement and, therefore, induced the buyer into signing the agreement. Consistency on the part of the salesperson was clearly an issue in the decision. To quote from the transcript:

> 'I [the Judge] find it unusual and difficult to accept that [the salesperson] would explain both offers to purchase to the defendant and his wife and allow them to read and understand them, but would not afford the defendant and his wife the opportunity of same for the [Representation] Agreement.'

Registrants should always clearly explain all clauses in agreements and get confirmation from buyers and sellers that they understand such clauses.

- In support of the buyer representation agreement, the Judge did not find the agreement unusual, no language contained in the document was difficult to read or understand and no language was used to confuse potential buyers. Further, the commission arrangements were clearly spelled out in the agreement. Such commission was due on the purchase of any real property of the general description indicated [in the buyer representation agreement].

- Further, the obligation to pay commission and under what circumstances such commission would be paid are clear; i.e., the representation relationship was exclusive, the commission arrangement was firmly established and the broker's role in the process was properly described.

- The buyers also understood from the terms of the agreement that they may not be shown or offered all properties (in this instance, new homes) that may be of interest to that buyer.

A potential tenant seeking expanded premises for a packaging/distributor operation signed an exclusive authority with a commercial brokerage to act as a buyer/tenant representative. The buyer representation agreement (and supporting descriptive document) set forth various requirements, one of the most notable for purposes of this case stated:

> It is our [the prospective tenant's] understanding that we shall not incur any expenses by this appointment and that the owners of properties shall be responsible for any fees payable as a result of a lease or purchase transaction resulting from our commitment to their property.

A second reference to this arrangement was located in other marketing material:

> There is no financial obligation to the purchaser or tenant. The broker will be paid a commission by the Vendor or Landlord of the property which is purchased or leased by the client.

The brokerage drafted two leases on behalf of the tenant, but negotiations ended with no agreement. An offer to lease for the first property (Property A) was rejected by the tenant following a landlord signback on price and the second property (Property B) was rejected given the lack of mezzanine space overlooking the production floor. Following the failed negotiations, the tenant concluded a lease directly with the owner of Property A after the expiration of the representation agreement. Testimony indicated that the landlord had been advised that the brokerage was no longer involved in the negotiations.

The Judge found in favour of the brokerage and awarded commission at 6% for the first year and 2½% for subsequent years, along with interest at the prescribed rate and GST.

Reference   Royal LePage Commercial Inc. v. 1237742 Ontario Inc. carrying on business as F. P. Canada—Digested from Full Text Judgment.

COMMENTARY

This case has several interesting perspectives for registrants:

- Damages were awarded despite the tenant's argument that the representation agreement (and supporting descriptive document) clearly stated that no expenses or financial obligation would result as a consequence of signing. According to the Judge, such statements do not constitute a waiver of claim for damages by the brokerage, but merely reflect common practice where payment is usually received from the landlord or seller.

- The award was made based on commission rates generally in effect for the local market.

- The timing of the lease execution (signed following expiration of the representation agreement) was irrelevant, as the brokerage had negotiated the original offer within the currency of that agreement.

- The tenant also argued unsuccessfully that the brokerage had breached its obligations under the agreement.

Commission-Related Disclosures

ADDITIONAL FEES

As part of remuneration paid to brokerages, the topic of additional monies received from others must be addressed. Agency law requires that an agent cannot make any secret profit or receive remuneration from anyone other than the client, without his or her fully informed consent. Section 18 of the Code of Ethics reinforces this requirement by stating that a registrant must disclose any direct or indirect financial benefit received from another person arising from services provided to the client.

DISCLOSURE OF INTEREST   CODE

18. (4) A registrant shall disclose in writing to a client, at the earliest practicable opportunity, any direct or indirect financial benefit that the registrant or a person related to the registrant may receive from another person in connection with services provided by the registrant to the client, including any commission or other remuneration that may be received from another person. O. Reg. 580/05, s. 18 (4).

For example, the OREA *Buyer Representation Agreement* includes a provision regarding finder's fees:

> *The Buyer acknowledges that the Brokerage may be receiving a finder's fee from a lender in the event that a new mortgage or an increase in financing is required for a transaction contemplated by this Agreement and the Buyer consents to any such fee being retained by the Brokerage in addition to the commission as described above.*

DISCLOSURE: TWO COMMISSIONS/SAME TRADE

The Code of Ethics addresses a potential situation that might arise in which a brokerage could potentially receive two commissions on one trade. The Code provides that the brokerage cannot collect a commission from a buyer or seller and then collect a second commission pursuant to an agreement with another party, unless full written disclosure is made to both the buyer or seller and the other party (see example on next page for possible scenario).

DISCLOSURE OF INTEREST   CODE

18. (5) A brokerage that has entered into an agreement with a buyer or seller that requires the buyer or seller to pay the brokerage a commission or other remuneration in respect of a trade in real estate shall not charge or collect any commission or other remuneration under another agreement entered into with another person in respect of the same trade unless,

    (a) the brokerage discloses at the earliest practicable opportunity to the other person, in writing, the terms of the agreement with the buyer or seller that require the payment of a commission or other remuneration; and

    (b) the brokerage discloses at the earliest practicable opportunity to the buyer or seller, in writing, the terms of the agreement with the other person that require the payment of a commission or other remuneration. O. Reg. 580/05, s. 18 (5).

DISCLOSURE: PROPERTIES THAT MEET BUYER'S CRITERIA

The Code of Ethics requires that the brokerage shall inform the buyer client of properties that meet the buyer's criteria, regardless of the amount of commission or other remuneration to which the brokerage might be entitled.

PROPERTIES THAT MEET BUYER'S CRITERIA   CODE

19. If a brokerage has entered into a representation agreement with a buyer, a broker or salesperson who acts on behalf of the buyer pursuant to the agreement shall inform the buyer of properties that meet the buyer's criteria without having any regard to the amount of commission or other remuneration, if any, to which the brokerage might be entitled. O. Reg. 580/05, s. 19.

EXAMPLE   *The Buyer and Seller Clients*

A residential buyer has entered into a representation agreement at ABC Realty Inc., which provides for payment of commission upon the buyer entering into an agreement of purchase and sale for any property of the general description outlined in the buyer representation agreement. The salesperson representing the buyer circulates information about the desired property and another salesperson with the same brokerage contacts a seller who has a suitable property and the seller signs a listing agreement. If neither party was aware of the other agreement, the brokerage could possibly collect two commissions on the same trade. The Code requires that the terms of such agreements be fully disclosed in writing to both parties.

The Fine Print	CAUTION

Commission disputes often arise out of lack of communication. Problems can develop if commission arrangements are not fully detailed. Buyers may mistakenly believe that commission is only due when the property is acquired, but technically the wording of a buyer representation agreement provides that commission is due upon the buyer entering into an agreement and does not address the completion of the transaction. Further, the buyer should understand the implications of the holdover provision.

While holdover wordings vary, a key provision is that a commission is due if *the buyer enters into an agreement and the property was shown or introduced to the buyer during the term of the agreement.* Of course, such does not apply if a subsequent representation agreement is signed by the buyer and a property introduced during the prior agreement is sold to that buyer. In that instance, the buyer's obligation to the original brokerage is reduced by the amount paid under the subsequent representation agreement.

SUPPORT DOCUMENTS

Cancellation of Buyer Representation Agreement (OREA Form 301)

The cancellation represents a release by both the buyer and the brokerage, except concerning properties introduced to the buyer during the currency of the agreement.

OREA Ontario Real Estate Association
Cancellation of Buyer Representation Agreement
Form 301
for use in the Province of Ontario

TO:

BROKERAGE: ....

FROM:

BUYER: ....

RE: Buyer Representation Agreement between the Buyer and the Brokerage signed by the Buyer on the .... day of ....,

20............ and that was to continue in effect until the.................day of ....,20................

I hereby request the cancellation of this Buyer Representation Agreement for the following reasons:

....

....

Assignment of Buyer Representation Agreement (OREA Form 302)

A brokerage may require an assignment of representation for an existing buyer representation agreement. For example, a salesperson has an independent contractor agreement with a brokerage, which states if that salesperson leaves the brokerage and, if the buyer client agrees, the brokerage will assign the buyer representation agreement to the salesperson's new brokerage (the assignee). The assignment must be executed by the buyer and the assignee, and a copy returned to the original brokerage prior to the effective date.

OREA Ontario Real Estate Association
Assignment of Buyer Representation Agreement
Form 302
for use in the Province of Ontario

RE: BUYER REPRESENTATION AGREEMENT BETWEEN:

BUYER: ....

AND:

BROKERAGE: ....

AGREEMENT EXPIRY DATE: ....

The Brokerage for the above described Buyer Representation Agreement assigns, transfers and sets over to:

.... (the "Assignee")
any and all interest in the Buyer Representation Agreement, including all rights, duties and obligations pursuant to the Agreement. The Brokerage releases the Buyer from any claims of remuneration or compensation with respect to this Buyer Representation Agreement.

For the purposes of this Assignment of Buyer Representation Agreement, "Buyer" includes purchaser, tenant and lessee.

This Assignment of Buyer Representation Agreement is to be effective at 12:01 a.m. the .... day of ....20........

Amendment to Buyer Representation Agreement (OREA Form 305)

This form is typically used for changes such as an extended expiry date and corrections/updating. Both the buyer and brokerage sign the form.

OREA Ontario Real Estate Association

Amendment to Buyer Representation Agreement

Form 305
for use in the Province of Ontario

RE: BUYER REPRESENTATION AGREEMENT

BETWEEN:

BUYER: ....
AND
BROKERAGE: ....

BUYER REGISTRATION NUMBER(S) (if applicable): ....

EXPIRY DATE: ....

The Buyer and the Brokerage hereby agree that the above described Buyer Representation Agreement is amended as stated below:

1. **EXPIRY DATE:**

   New Expiry Date .... **Former** Expiry Date ....

   Buyer acknowledges that the length of the Agreement is negotiable between the Buyer and the Brokerage, however, in accordance with the Real Estate and Business Brokers Act of Ontario (2002), if the Agreement exceeds six months

---

COMMON ERRORS AND OMISSIONS

While document errors are most commonly associated with listing agreements, the spoken word is a major consideration when addressing errors and omissions involving buyer representation. What is said and how it is said are vital. Here's some tips:

- Avoid making statements that advance opinions or promote comparisons; e.g., *best property, worst investment, most sought after location, newest features, greatest return, smallest down payment* and *largest lot*. Stick to the facts.
- Don't make predictions or give absolute assurances. No one knows the future. Words such as *guarantee, great investment* and *real bargain* can be problematic.
- Avoid words that are vague or could cause confusion; e.g., *We can get that approval right away!*
- Learn to qualify statements that might mislead. Consider the difference: *The roof is new* and t*he seller said that the shingles were replaced approximately six months ago.*
- Seek confirmation that the client fully understands; e.g., *Replacing the five excluded ceiling fixtures could be costly. Does this pose a problem for you?*
- Expand your vocabulary: The more precise your wordings, the less chance of confusion.
- Use operative words carefully. Consider a simple example; the important differences between *can, will, might, should* and *must*. The well *can* be tested, *will* need testing, *might* need testing, *should* be tested and *must* be tested.
- Shift risk when appropriate. Defer to other professionals; e.g., *I can't answer that question. I think you should contact your lawyer. I can insert an appropriate condition in the offer.*

- Be wary of times when you think that a verbal agreement is achieved, when in fact it has not. Often communication reflects cultural background, age, education level and prior experience. Reading verbal signals incorrectly can have disastrous results.

Proper representation is also essential. The registrant must protect and promote the interests of the client at all times. Litigation can arise if duties owed to principals are not performed correctly. Several common problems areas are detailed below.

- Incorrect form preparation.
- Exceeding the scope of authority granted by the client.
- Failure to demonstrate property to a buyer client in a diligent manner.
- Failure to fully investigate matters regarding property that are material to the client or, alternatively, not referring the client to appropriate experts.
- Problems arising during negotiations and multiple offer presentations.
- Nondisclosure or misrepresentation of material information to the client.
- Breach of duties as specified in the agreement with the client.
- Failure to carry out obligations in a conscientious and competent manner.

Protecting the Buyer Client's Interests   **RECO DISCIPLINE DECISION**

The buyers expressed interest in a property needing some work, including debris that had to be removed from the home. The home had a basement apartment rented out for $1,750 a month. An offer was successfully negotiated at $280,000 with several conditions including financing and an inspection. Subsequently, the buyers signed waivers relating to these conditions, but discovered that there was no provision for apartments in the township in which the property was located. To compound matters, certain problems arose regarding the ability to obtain insurance on the property.

Ultimately, in the midst of discussions and needed documents, communications broke down between the registrant and the buyer clients, but the sale did close. Without delving into all the particulars, the Discipline Committee found that the registrant acted unprofessionally when she:

- Failed to protect her clients' interest by not including a clause in the Offer for a final "walk through" of the Property;

- Failed to protect her clients by not verifying and researching the legality of the basement apartment and placing her clients at risk of violating a municipal zoning by-law and/or obtaining adequate home insurance and/or having an adequate provision in her offer;

- Blamed the Complainants for the failure to have the transaction completed in an appropriate manner;

- Failed to procure an executed copy of a buyer representation agreement.

The salesperson was ordered to pay a penalty of $3,500 for not protecting and promoting the clients' interests, not fulfilling disclosure requirements and not meeting requirements regarding document preparation and delivery. The broker was also ordered to pay a penalty of $2,500 for not properly overseeing the registrant and not maintaining appropriate records in regard to the matter at hand.

Source: Discipline Decision, Wildeboer, Sept. 20, 2007. This report is a summary only. Detailed Discipline and Appeals Decisions are published on the RECO Website (**www.reco.on.ca**). This case was heard pursuant to Complaints, Compliance and Discipline procedures established under the previous _Real Estate and Business Brokers Act_.

The Grow House	RECO DISCIPLINE DECISION

A registrant represented a buyer client in acquiring a property in 2003 that had previously been used for the cultivation of marijuana plants (i.e., a grow house). The registrant included a disclosure to that effect in the agreement of purchase and sale, which also stated that the buyer was acquiring the building and structures thereon in their present state and in an 'as is ' condition.

In 2005, this property was listed by the same registrant, who also represented the interested buyers. An agreement was prepared and accepted in April 2005 with a completion date of June 17, 2005. In June, prior to the completion date, the buyers became aware of the prior use as a grow house. The registrant had not disclosed this fact to them, nor did she give them a copy or disclose the existence of the written disclosure relating to the 2003 transaction. The buyers requested a mutual release and the return of their deposit and this was agreed to. The property was subsequently resold and the registrant provided disclosure regarding the grow house to the ultimate buyers.

The registrant was ordered to pay a penalty of $15,000 for various breaches of the Code of Ethics, including failure to protect and promote the best interests of the client and misrepresentation of relevant facts.

Source: Discipline Decision, Burgess, June 21, 2007. This report is a summary only. Detailed Discipline and Appeals Decisions are published on the RECO Website (**www.reco.on.ca**). This case was heard pursuant to Complaints, Compliance and Discipline procedures established under the previous *Real Estate and Business Brokers Act*.

Additional Tips and Guidelines

Providing conscientious competent service not only helps to minimize risk, but also better ensures that clients receive the professional help needed to make an informed decision about property.

- Carefully review the *Buyer Representation Agreement* with every buyer client. Build a solid working relationship right from the start.
- Make a planned presentation. Discuss the specific buyer services being offered by the brokerage. Build an effective flyer and/or have detailed information on the brokerage website.
- Interview the buyer carefully. Analyze their needs and wants. Pre-qualification is vital.
- Select homes carefully based on the client's preferences and know all comparable sales.
- Seriously consider a homebuyer's package for every client. Data on neighbourhood trends, features/benefits of living in the particular community, school locations, market reports and press releases can be interesting, informative and right on point.
- Sometimes, only limited property information is readily available. Do your homework and get other professionals involved as needed.
- Put well-worded conditions in any offers.
- Critically analyze every property in which your client expresses sincere interest. Identify features and drawbacks. Seek the help of other professionals as needed.
- When available, thoroughly review the Seller Property Information Statement and recommend action as appropriate.
- Remember, it's the client's obligation to conduct further investigation, but guidance is helpful.
- Explain to the client how to effectively negotiate in the marketplace.

- Illustrate the difference between excitement at first inspection and rational analysis afterwards. Always be matching needs and wants with properties shown.
- When demonstrating older homes, point out the true impact of depreciation and obsolescence, and carefully compare properties making note of seller upgrades.
- Accentuate the benefits, but balance these with a factual discussion of drawbacks that affect market value and may impact future disposition. At the same time, don't overlook opportunities that were missed by others. Some drawbacks may be largely cosmetic and/or easily remedied.
- Be honest and forthright with the buyer at all times. Your role is to protect his or her interests.

THE REAL ESTATE TRANSACTION—GENERAL

KNOWLEDGE INTEGRATION

Notables

- A buyer representation agreement typically provides for an express, written authority to locate suitable property for a buyer client.

- Precise knowledge of all preprinted clauses in the buyer representation agreement is essential to fully inform the buyer client regarding requirements and obligations.

- OREA forms are used for illustration purposes. Brokerage and/or real estate board wordings and formats may vary.

- Care must be taken in completing the representation agreement, particularly regarding what type of property is being sought by the client.

- REBBA 2002 sets out minimum content requirements for buyer representation agreements.

- The OREA *Buyer Representation Agreement—Commercial* varies somewhat from its residential counterpart.

- The buyer, as the principal, has three primary obligations to the brokerage: indemnification, remuneration and other obligations as set out in the buyer representation agreement.

- REBBA 2002 contains regulatory requirements concerning commission calculations, entitlement to commission and payment arrangements.

- Both the commission arrangements and holdover provision should be fully discussed with the buyer client.

- REBBA 2002 also has regulatory requirements regarding additional fees, two commissions involving the same trade and disclosure regarding properties meeting the buyer's criteria.

- Three supporting documents regarding cancellation, assignment and amendment are associated with the buyer representation agreement.

- The spoken word is a major consideration when addressing errors and omissions involving buyer representation.

Glossary

Buyer Representation
Buyer Representation Agreement
Caveat Emptor

Strategic Thinking For Your Career

Questions are included to assist in developing your new career. No answers are provided.

1. What services can I promote with potential buyer clients to highlight my abilities and develop a strong marketing package to attract other potential clients?

2. What unique knowledge or expertise do I have that sets me apart from the competition?

3. What buyer profile(s) are typical for my local area and what are typical buyers looking for in new and resale homes within my local community?

4. What community information is readily available that will complement my presentation to potential buyer clients?

5. What additional research should I undertake to be more fully informed about the expanding role of buyer representation in real estate negotiations? (Note: As a first step, search the Internet for the terms *buyer representation* and *buyer agency*.)

Chapter Mini-Review

Solutions are located in the Appendix.

1. The OREA *Buyer Representation Agreement* provides for commission payment either by the listing brokerage or the seller.

   ○ True   ○ False

2. A buyer representation agreement must prominently display the date and provide space for the buyer's initials if the term of the agreement exceeds four months.

   ○ True   ○ False

3. The *Consumer Reporting Act* requires that every person be notified if a consumer report may be referred to in connection with a transaction.

   ○ True   ○ False

4. The residential OREA *Buyer Representation Agreement* contains an expanded definition of *purchase* to include the transfer of shares or assets.

   ○ True   ○ False

5. Indemnification involves the obligation to pay a commission to a real estate brokerage.

   ○ True   ○ False

6. A registrant authorized to bind the brokerage must sign and date his or her signature on the buyer representation agreement.

   ○ True   ○ False

7. According to REBBA 2002, no legal action can be taken to claim commission or other remuneration unless the person bringing such action was either registered or exempt.

   ○ True   ○ False

8. If a buyer is introduced to a property by a brokerage during the listing period, but buys the property following expiration of the holdover period, a commission is due and payable according to the wording of the OREA *Buyer Representation Agreement*.

   ○ True   ○ False

9. A brokerage cannot receive money from anyone other than the client regarding services being provided to that client without his or her consent.

   ○ True   ○ False

10. In the commercial court case involving tenant representation the Judge awarded a commission of 6% for the first year and 2½% for subsequent years, based on his determination that these were commission rates generally in effect for the local market.

    ○ True   ○ False

11. Registrants are well advised to avoid making any statements to a buyer client that involve making a prediction or giving absolute assurance.

    ○ True   ○ False

12. Failure to disclose the known existence of a past grow operation, within a property being seriously considered by a client, would be a violation of the Code of Ethics.

    ○ True   ○ False

Active Learning Exercises

Solutions are located in the Appendix.

▣ Exercise 1   Matching

Match the phrase/word in the left column with the appropriate description in the right column (not all descriptions are used).

____ Buyer Registry Service	*a.* Let the Buyer Beware
____ Consumer Report	*b.* Buyer and Brokerage Release Each Other by Agreement
____ Change Expiry Date	*c.* Toronto Real Estate Board
____ Cancellation of Buyer Representation Agreement	*d.* Notification Required if Report May be Referred to
____ Holdover	*e.* Discover Pertinent Facts
____ Caveat Emptor	*f.* Amendment to Representation Agreement
____ Express Authority	*g.* Remains after Expiration of Agreement
____ Exclusive Buyer Representation Agreement	*h.* Indemnification
	i. Sole Right to Locate Suitable Property
	j. Disclosure of Role
	k. A Precise Instruction

■ Exercise 2   The Altered Buyer Representation Agreement

Mr. and Mrs. Howell are looking for a property in Anycity. They would prefer a Ridgeway location (small neighbourhood within Anycity) but are realistic that a suitable property might not be located in this particular locale. They want to view listed and private for sale properties that meet their general criteria; i.e., 3 bedroom houses with a pool (or large yard) in the $335,000 to $360,000 range. The agreed commission is 2.5% of the selling price and the agreement will expire in approximately 45 days.

A buyer representation agreement is prepared and the Howells subsequently take the document to their lawyer for review. The resulting altered agreement is illustrated on the following pages. Briefly outline the impact of such changes on the agency relationship and any additional concerns arising from these changes.

 **Ontario Real Estate Association**

Buyer Representation Agreement
Authority for Purchase or Lease

Form 300
for use in the Province of Ontario

This is an Exclusive Buyer Representation Agreement

BETWEEN:

BROKERAGE: ABC Realty Inc. , Tel.No. (905) 555-1212

ADDRESS: 397 West Front Street

Anycity   K2P 3J7   Fax.No. (905) 555-2121

hereinafter referred to as the Brokerage.

AND:

BUYER(S): Terry J. Howell and Judy Kathryn Howell , hereinafter referred to as the Buyer,

ADDRESS: 1575   Faircourt Boulevard

Street Number   Street Name

MUNICIPALITY: Anycity   **POSTAL CODE:** K2J 4M9

The Buyer hereby gives the Brokerage the ~~exclusive and~~ *TH JH* irrevocable authority to act as the Buyer's agent

commencing at 1:00 ~~a.m.~~/p.m. on the 15th day of June , 20 XX ,

and expiring at 11:59 p.m. on the 30th day of July , 20 XX (Expiry Date),

{ Buyer acknowledges that the time period for this Agreement is negotiable between the Buyer and the Brokerage, however, in accordance with the Real Estate and Business Brokers Act of Ontario (2002), **if the time period for this Agreement exceeds six months, the Brokerage must obtain the Buyer's initials.** }

(Buyer's Initials)

for the purpose of locating a real property meeting the following general description:

Property Type (Use): Single Family Residential

Geographic Location: **Ridgeway** *TH JH* ~~Anycity, Anyregion~~

The Buyer hereby warrants that the Buyer is not a party to a buyer representation agreement with any other registered real estate brokerage for the purchase or lease of a real property of the general description indicated above.

1. **DEFINITIONS AND INTERPRETATIONS:** For the purposes of this Buyer Representation Agreement ("Authority" or "Agreement"), "Buyer" includes purchaser and tenant, a "seller" includes a vendor, a landlord or a prospective seller, vendor or landlord and a "real estate board" includes a real estate association. A purchase shall be deemed to include the entering into of any agreement to exchange, or the obtaining of an option to purchase which is subsequently exercised, and a lease includes any rental agreement, sub-lease or renewal of a lease. This Agreement shall be read with all changes of gender or number required by the context. For purposes of this Agreement, Buyer shall be deemed to include any spouse, heirs, executors, administrators, successors, assigns, related corporations and affiliated corporations. Related corporations or affiliated corporations shall include any corporation where one half or a majority of the shareholders, directors or officers of the related or affiliated corporation are the same person(s) as the shareholders, directors, or officers of the corporation introduced to or shown the property.

2. **COMMISSION:** In consideration of the Brokerage undertaking to assist the Buyer, the Buyer agrees to pay commission to the Brokerage as follows: If, during the currency of this Agreement, the Buyer enters into an agreement to purchase or lease a real property of the general description indicated above, the Buyer agrees the Brokerage is entitled to receive and retain any commission offered by a listing brokerage or by the seller. The Buyer understands that the amount of commission offered by a listing brokerage or by the seller may be greater or less than the commission stated below. The Buyer understands that the Brokerage will inform the Buyer of the amount of commission to be paid to the Brokerage by the listing brokerage or the seller at the earliest practical opportunity. The Buyer acknowledges that the payment of any commission by the listing brokerage or the seller will not make the Brokerage either the agent or sub-agent of the listing brokerage or the seller.

INITIALS OF BROKERAGE: JP   **INITIALS OF BUYER(S):** TH JH

Form 300   Revised 2015   **Page 1 of 3**

Exercise 2   Buyer Representation Agreement—Page 2 of 3

If, during the currency of this Agreement, the Buyer enters into an agreement to purchase any property of the general description indicated above,

the Buyer agrees that the Brokerage is entitled to be paid a commission of ....2.5...................... % of the sale price of the property

or ....

or for a lease, a commission of ....

~~The Buyer agrees to pay directly to the Brokerage any deficiency between this amount and the amount, if any, to be paid to the Brokerage by a listing~~
TH JH ~~brokerage or by the seller. The Buyer understands that if the Brokerage is not to be paid any commission by a listing brokerage or by the seller, the~~
~~Buyer will pay the Brokerage the full amount of commission indicated above.~~   **10** *TH JH*

The Buyer agrees to pay the Brokerage such commission if the Buyer enters into an agreement within ....~~60~~............... days after the expiration of this Agreement (Holdover Period) to purchase or lease any real property shown or introduced to the Buyer from any source whatsoever during the term of this Agreement, provided, however, that if the Buyer enters into a new buyer representation agreement with another registered real estate brokerage after the expiration of this Agreement, the Buyer's liability to pay commission to the Brokerage shall be reduced by the amount paid to the other brokerage under the new agreement.

The Buyer agrees to pay such commission as described above even if a transaction contemplated by an agreement to purchase or lease agreed to or accepted by the Buyer or anyone on the Buyer's behalf is not completed, if such non-completion is owing or attributable to the Buyers default or neglect. Said commission, plus any applicable taxes, shall be payable on the date set for completion of the purchase of the property or, in the case of a lease or tenancy, the earlier of the date of occupancy by the tenant or the date set for commencement of the lease or tenancy. All amounts set out as commission are to be paid plus applicable taxes on such commission.

This Agreement applies for the purchase or lease of one real property. Notwithstanding the foregoing, in the event that the Buyer leases a property, this agreement remains in force as set out herein for the purchase of the leased property or a property of the general description indicated above. The leasing of a property by the Buyer does not terminate this Agreement with respect to the purchase of a property.

3. **REPRESENTATION:** The Buyer acknowledges that the Brokerage has provided the Buyer with written information explaining agency relationships, including information on Seller Representation, Sub-Agency, Buyer Representation, Multiple Representation and Customer Service. The Brokerage shall assist the Buyer in locating a real property of the general description indicated above and shall represent the Buyer in an endeavour to procure the acceptance of an agreement to purchase or lease such a property.

TH JH ~~The Buyer acknowledges that the Buyer may not be shown or offered all properties that may be of interest to the Buyer.~~ The Buyer hereby agrees that the terms of any buyer's offer or agreement to purchase or lease the property will not be disclosed to any other buyer. The Buyer further acknowledges that the Brokerage may be entering into buyer representation agreements with other buyers who may be interested in the same or similar properties that the Buyer may be interested in buying or leasing and the Buyer hereby consents to the Brokerage entering into buyer representation agreements with other buyers who may be interested in the same or similar properties without any claim by the Buyer of conflict of interest. The Buyer hereby appoints the Brokerage as agent for the purpose of giving and receiving notices pursuant to any offer or agreement to purchase or lease a property negotiated by the Brokerage.

MULTIPLE REPRESENTATION: ~~The Buyer hereby acknowledges that the Brokerage may be entering into listing agreements with sellers of properties~~
~~the Buyer may be interested in buying or leasing. In the event that the Brokerage has entered into or enters into a listing agreement with the seller of~~
TH JH ~~a property the Buyer may be interested in buying or leasing, the Brokerage will obtain the Buyer's written consent to represent both the Buyer and the~~
~~seller for the transaction at the earliest practicable opportunity and in all cases prior to any offer to purchase or lease being submitted or presented.~~

The Buyer understands and acknowledges that the Brokerage must be impartial when representing both the Buyer and the seller and equally protect the interests of the Buyer and the seller in the transaction. The Buyer understands and acknowledges that when representing both the Buyer and the seller, the Brokerage shall have a duty of full disclosure to both the Buyer and the seller, including a requirement to disclose all factual information about the property known to the Brokerage.   *Buyer shall have right to purchase direct from seller if property not introduced by brokerage.*   *TH JH*

However, The Buyer further understands and acknowledges that the Brokerage shall not disclose:
- that the seller may or will accept less than the listed price, unless otherwise instructed in writing by the seller;
- that the Buyer may or will pay more than the offered price, unless otherwise instructed in writing by the Buyer;
- the motivation of or personal information about the Buyer or seller, unless otherwise instructed in writing by the party to which the information applies or unless failure to disclose would constitute fraudulent, unlawful or unethical practice;
- the price the Buyer should offer or the price the seller should accept; and
- the Brokerage shall not disclose to the Buyer the terms of any other offer.

However, it is understood that factual market information about comparable properties and information known to the Brokerage concerning potential uses for the property will be disclosed to both Buyer and seller to assist them to come to their own conclusions.

Where a Brokerage represents both the Seller and the Buyer (multiple representation), the Brokerage shall not be entitled or authorized to be agent for either the Buyer or the Seller for the purpose of giving and receiving notices.

MULTIPLE REPRESENTATION AND CUSTOMER SERVICE: The Buyer understands and agrees that the Brokerage also provides representation and customer service to other buyers and sellers. If the Brokerage represents or provides customer service to more than one seller or buyer for the same trade, the Brokerage shall, in writing, at the earliest practicable opportunity and before any offer is made, inform all sellers and buyers of the nature of the Brokerage's relationship to each seller and buyer.

4. **REFERRAL OF PROPERTIES:** The Buyer agrees that during the currency of this Buyer Representation Agreement the Buyer will act in good faith and work exclusively with the Brokerage for the purchase or lease of a real property of the general description indicated above. The Buyer agrees that, during the currency of this Agreement, the Buyer shall advise the Brokerage immediately of any property of interest to the Buyer that came to the Buyer's attention from any source whatsoever, and all offers to purchase or lease submitted by the Buyer shall be submitted through the Brokerage to the seller. If the Buyer arranges a valid agreement to purchase or lease any property of the general description indicated above that came to the attention of the Buyer during the currency of this Agreement and the Buyer arranges said agreement during the currency of this Agreement or within the Holdover Period after expiration of this Agreement, the Buyer agrees to pay the Brokerage the amount of commission set out above in Paragraph 2 of this Agreement, payable within (5) days following the Brokerage's written demand therefor.

INITIALS OF BROKERAGE: (JP)   **INITIALS OF BUYER(S):** (TH JH)

Form 300   Revised 2015   **Page 2 of 3**

5. **INDEMNIFICATION:** ~~The Brokerage and representatives of the Brokerage are trained in dealing in real estate but are not qualified in determining the physical condition of the land or any improvements thereon. The Buyer agrees that the Brokerage and representatives of the Brokerage will not be liable for any defects, whether latent or patent, to the land or improvements thereon. All information supplied by the seller or landlord or the listing brokerage may not have been verified and is not warranted by the Brokerage as being accurate and will be relied on by the Buyer at the Buyer's own risk. The Buyer acknowledges having been advised to make their own enquiries to confirm the condition of the property.~~

TH JH

6. **FINDERS FEE:** The Buyer acknowledges that the Brokerage may be receiving a finder's fee, reward and/or referral incentive, and the Buyer consents to any such benefit being received and retained by the Brokerage in addition to the commission as described above.

7. **CONSUMER REPORTS:** The Buyer is hereby notified that a Consumer Report containing credit and/or personal information may be referred to in connection with this Agreement and any subsequent transaction.

8. **USE AND DISTRIBUTION OF INFORMATION:** The Buyer consents to the collection, use and disclosure of personal information by the Brokerage for such purposes that relate to the real estate services provided by the Brokerage to the Buyer including, but not limited to: locating, assessing and qualifying properties for the Buyer; advertising on behalf of the Buyer; providing information as needed to third parties retained by the Buyer to assist in a transaction (e.g. financial institutions, building inspectors, etc...); and such other use of the Buyer's information as is consistent with the services provided by the Brokerage in connection with the purchase or prospective purchase of the property.

   The Buyer agrees that the sale and related information regarding any property purchased by the Buyer through the Brokerage may be retained and disclosed by the Brokerage and/or real estate board(s) (if the property is an MLS® Listing) for reporting, appraisal and statistical purposes and for such other use of the information as the Brokerage and/or board deems appropriate in connection with the listing, marketing and selling of real estate, including conducting comparative market analyses.

   The Buyer acknowledges that the information, personal or otherwise ("information"), provided to the real estate board or association may be stored on databases located outside of Canada, in which case the information would be subject to the laws of the jurisdiction in which the information is located.

9. **CONFLICT OR DISCREPANCY:** If there is any conflict or discrepancy between any provision added to this Agreement and any provision in the standard pre-set portion hereof, the added provision shall supersede the standard pre-set provision to the extent of such conflict or discrepancy. This Agreement, including any provisions added to this Agreement, shall constitute the entire Agreement between the Buyer and the Brokerage. There is no representation, warranty, collateral agreement or condition, which affects this Agreement other than as expressed herein.

10. **ELECTRONIC COMMUNICATION:** This Buyer Representation Agreement and any agreements, notices or other communications contemplated thereby may be transmitted by means of electronic systems, in which case signatures shall be deemed to be original. The transmission of this Agreement by the Buyer by electronic means shall be deemed to confirm the Buyer has retained a true copy of the Agreement.

11. **SCHEDULE(S):** .... attached hereto form(s) part of this Agreement.

THE BROKERAGE AGREES TO REPRESENT THE BUYER IN LOCATING A REAL PROPERTY OF THE GENERAL DESCRIPTION INDICATED ABOVE IN AN ENDEAVOUR TO OBTAIN THE ACCEPTANCE OF AN AGREEMENT TO PURCHASE OR LEASE A PROPERTY ON TERMS SATISFACTORY TO THE BUYER.

Justin Perrilli .... DATE *June 15/xx* .... *Justin Perrilli* ....
(Authorized to bind the Brokerage)   (Name of Person Signing)

THIS AGREEMENT HAS BEEN READ AND FULLY UNDERSTOOD BY ME AND I ACKNOWLEDGE THIS DATE I HAVE SIGNED UNDER SEAL. Any representations contained herein are true to the best of my knowledge, information and belief.

SIGNED, SEALED AND DELIVERED I have hereunto set my hand and seal:

Terry Howell .... ● DATE *June 15/xx* .... **(905) 777-1212** ....
(Signature of Buyer)   (Seal)   (Tel. No.)

Judy Howell .... ● DATE *June 15/xx* ....
(Signature of Buyer)   (Seal)

DECLARATION OF INSURANCE

The broker/salesperson .... **Justin Perrilli** ....
                                             (Name of Broker/Salesperson)

hereby declares that he/she is insured as required by the Real Estate and Business Brokers Act (REBBA) and Regulations.

                                  Justin Perrilli ....
                                             (Signature(s) of Broker/Salesperson)

ACKNOWLEDGEMENT

The Buyer(s) hereby acknowledge that the Buyer(s) fully understand the terms of this Agreement and have received a true copy of this Agreement

on the .... *15th* .... day of .... *June* ...., 20 *xx* ....

Terry Howell .... Date: *June 15/xx* ....
(Signature of Buyer)

Judy Howell .... Date: *June 15/xx* ....
(Signature of Buyer)

Exercise 3   SPIS—36 Windward Avenue, Gateway Estates

A Seller Property Information Statement is illustrated for a recreational property. Identify areas of concern along with a brief action plan (e.g., seek professional assistance, place condition in offer, obtain/verify additional source information etc.).

NOTE: Registrants are reminded that while the buyer representation agreement contains an indemnification clause regarding property defects, the Code of Ethics requires that the registrant provide services in a competent and conscientious manner (Code, Sec. 5), and also take reasonable steps to determine material facts (Code, Sec. 21).

SECTION	LINE	CONCERN	BRIEF EXPLANATION/ACTION PLAN

Seller Property Information Statement
Residential

Form 220
for use in the Province of Ontario

ANSWERS MUST BE COMPLETE AND ACCURATE This statement is designed in part to protect Sellers by establishing that correct information concerning the property is being provided to buyers. All of the information contained herein is provided by the Sellers to the brokerage/broker/salesperson. Any person who is in receipt of and utilizes this Statement acknowledges and agrees that **the information is being provided for information purposes only and is not a warranty as to the matters recited hereinafter even if attached to an Agreement of Purchase and Sale.** The brokerage/broker/salesperson shall not be held responsible for the accuracy of any information contained herein.

BUYERS MUST STILL MAKE THEIR OWN ENQUIRIES Buyers must still make their own enquiries notwithstanding the information contained on this statement. Each question and answer must be considered and where necessary, keeping in mind that the Sellers' knowledge of the property may be inaccurate or incomplete, additional information can be requested from the Sellers or from an independent source such as the municipality. Buyers can hire an independent inspector to examine the property to determine whether defects exist and to provide an estimate of the cost of repairing problems that have been identified. **This statement does not provide information on psychological stigmas that may be associated with a property.**

For the purposes of this Seller Property Information Statement, a "Seller" includes a landlord or a prospective landlord and a "buyer" includes a tenant, or a prospective tenant.

PROPERTY: 36 Windward Avenue, Gateway Estates, RR #2, Anycity	**SELLER(S) TO INITIAL EACH APPLICABLE BOX**			
SELLER(S): Patricia Ellen Burke				
GENERAL: (Provide Applicable ADDITIONAL COMMENTS)	**YES**	**NO**	**UNKNOWN**	**NOT APPLICABLE**
1. I have occupied the property from........19xx........to.....present........				
2. Does any other party have an ownership or spousal interest in the property?		PEB		
3. Is the property a condominium or a freehold property that includes an interest in a common elements condominium, (POTL)? (If yes, Schedule 221 to be completed.)		PEB		
4. Does ownership of this property require membership in an Association and payment of Association fees? If yes, specify....................		PEB		
5. Is the property subject to first right of refusal, option, lease, rental agreement or other listing?		PEB		
6. Are there any encroachments, registered easements, or rights-of-way? **See below**	PEB			
7. Is there a plan of survey? Date of survey........1986...................	PEB			
8. Are there any disputes concerning the boundaries of the property?				
9. Are you aware of any non-compliance with zoning regulations?		PEB		
10. Are you aware of any pending developments, projects or rezoning applications in the neighbourhood?	PEB			
11. Are there any public projects planned for the neighbourhood? **See #14 below** eg: road widenings, new highways, expropriations etc.	PEB			
12. Are there any restrictive covenants that run with the land?		PEB		
13. Are there any drainage restrictions?		PEB		
14. Are there any local levies or unusual taxes being charged at the present time or contemplated? If so, at what cost? .Main road upgrade for municipal services. Expiry date........................	PEB			
15. Have you received any notice, claim, work order or deficiency notice affecting the property from any person or any public body?		PEB		
16. (a) Is the property connected to municipal water? (If not, Schedule 222 to be completed.)	PEB			
(b) Is the property connected to municipal sewer? (If not, Schedule 222 to be completed.)	PEB			
17. Are there any current or pending Heritage restrictions for the property or the area?		PEB		

INITIALS OF BUYER(S):

Form 220   Revised 2016   **Page 1 of 3**

GENERAL (cont'd): (Provide Applicable ADDITIONAL COMMENTS)	YES	NO	UNKNOWN	NOT APPLICABLE
18. Are there any conditional sales contracts, leases, rental agreements or service contracts? eg: furnace, alarm system, hot water tank, propane tank, etc. Specify.. Are they assignable or will they be discharged?.... **Water softener $19/month**	PEB			
19. Are there any defects in any appliances or equipment included with the property?		PEB		
20. Do you know the approximate age of the building(s)?Age.... **38 years** Any additions: Age..				
21. Are you aware of any past or pending claims under the Tarion Warranty Corporation (formerly ONHWP)? Tarion Warranty Corporation/ONHWP Registration No..........................		PEB		
22. Will the sale of this property be subject to HST?		PEB		

ADDITIONAL COMMENTS: Right of way on 36 & 38 Windward Ave. Path leading to new area being developed with recreational park. Main road cost to be assessed to all homes in Gateway Estates.

ENVIRONMENTAL: (Provide Applicable ADDITIONAL COMMENTS)	YES	NO	UNKNOWN	NOT APPLICABLE
1. Are you aware of possible environmental problems or soil contamination of any kind on the property or in the immediate area? eg: radon gas, toxic waste, underground gasoline or fuel tanks etc.			PEB	
2. Are there any existing or proposed waste dumps, disposal sites or land fills in the immediate area?	PEB			
3. Are there any hydro generating projects planned for the immediate area? eg: Wind Turbines				
4. Is the property subject to flooding?		PEB		
5. Is the property under the jurisdiction of any Conservation Authority or Commission?			PEB	
6. Are you aware of any excessive erosion, settling, slippage, sliding or other soil problems?		PEB		
7. Does the property have any abandoned or de-commissioned ☐ well ☐ septic system ☐ swimming pool ☐ foundation ☐ other, specify..............................		PEB		
8. (a) Is there a fuel oil tank on the property? If yes, complete the following: ☐ Underground. Date for required upgrading or removal.............................. ☐ Aboveground. Age of tank.................... Date of last inspection....................		PEB		
(b) Does the fuel oil tank comply with the Technical Standards and Safety Authority requirements and any other requirements for fuel to be delivered?				PEB
9. Has the use of the property ever been for the growth or manufacture of illegal substances?		PEB		

ADDITIONAL COMMENTS:...

INITIALS OF BUYER(S): ⬭

Form 220   Revised 2016   **Page 2 of 3**

IMPROVEMENTS AND STRUCTURAL: (Provide Applicable ADDITIONAL COMMENTS)	YES	NO	UNKNOWN	NOT APPLICABLE
1. Are you aware of any structural problems? **Minor cracks in brick exterior, south side**	PEB			
2. (a) Have you made any renovations, additions or improvements to the property?	PEB			
(b) Was a building permit obtained?		PEB		
(c) Has the final building inspection been approved or has a final occupancy permit been obtained?				PEB
3. To the best of your knowledge have the building(s) ever contained ureaformaldehyde insulation?			PEB	
4. Is there vermiculite insulation on the property? If yes, has it been tested for asbestos?....................................		PEB		
5. (a) Are you aware of any deficiencies or non-compliance with the Ontario Fire Code?		PEB		
(b) Is your property equipped with operational smoke detectors?	PEB			
(c) Is the property equipped with operational carbon monoxide detectors?	PEB			
6. (a) Is the woodstove(s)/chimney(s)/fireplace(s)/insert(s) in good working order? **In basement rec room**	PEB			
(b) Has the wood energy system been **WETT** inspected? (Wood Energy Technology Transfer)				
7. Are you aware of any problems with the central air conditioning system?		PEB		
8. Are you aware of any problems with the heating system?		PEB		
9. (a) Are you aware of any moisture and/or water problems? **Installed sump pump 1991**		PEB		
(b) Are you aware of any roof leakage or unrepaired damage? Age of roof covering ....**14 years**.............................		PEB		
(c) Are you aware of any damage due to wind, fire, flood, insects, termites, rodents, pets or wood rot?		PEB		
(d) Have any repairs been carried out to correct any past or present problems related to (a), (b) and/or (c)? If yes, explain in additional comments below.	PEB			
10. (a) Are you aware of any problems with the electrical system? Size of service..................................		PEB		
(b) Type of wiring: ☐ copper ☐ aluminium ☐ knob-and-tube ☐ other.....**Unknown**..........				
11. Are you aware of any problems with the plumbing system? **Well repaired 1994**				
12. Is there any lead, galvanized metal, cast iron or Kitec plumbing on the property?		PEB		
13. Are you aware of any problems with the swimming pool, sauna, hot tub, jet bathtub or lawn sprinkler system?	PEB	*See below		

ADDITIONAL COMMENTS: **Moved support post in basement for larger rec room. In-ground pool - minor leaks.**

....

....

Schedule(s) attached hereto and forming part of this Statement include:...

The Sellers state that the above information is true, based on their current actual knowledge as of the date below. Any important changes to this information known to the Sellers will be disclosed by the Sellers prior to closing. Sellers are responsible for the accuracy of all answers. Sellers further agree to indemnify and hold the Brokerage/Broker/Salesperson harmless from any liability incurred as a result of any buyer relying on this information. The Sellers hereby authorize the Brokerage to post a copy of this Seller Property Information Statement into the database(s) of the appropriate MLS® system and that a copy of this Seller Property Information Statement be delivered by their agent or representative to prospective buyers or their agents or representatives. The Sellers hereby acknowledge receipt of a true copy of this statement.

Patricia Ellen Burke   DATE *June 12, 20xx* .... DATE...............
(Signature of Seller)   (Signature of Seller)

I acknowledge that the information provided herein is not warranted and hereby acknowledge receipt of a copy of the above information including any applicable Schedule(s).

....   DATE...
(Signature of Buyer or Authorized Representative)

....   DATE...
(Signature of Buyer)

Exercise 3   Seller Property information Statement (Schedule)—Page 1 of 1

Form 222
for use in the Province of Ontario

Seller Property Information Statement
Schedule for Water Supply, Waste Disposal, Access, Shoreline, Utilities

This Schedule is attached to and forms part of the Seller Property Information Statement (Form 220) for:

PROPERTY: 36 Windward Avenue, Gateway Estates, RR #2, Anycity	**SELLER(S) TO INITIAL EACH APPLICABLE BOX**			
SELLER(S): Patricia Ellen Burke				

WATER SUPPLY AND WASTE DISPOSAL: (Provide Applicable ADDITIONAL COMMENTS)	YES	NO	UNKNOWN	NOT APPLICABLE
1. **(a)** What is your water source? ☐ Municipal ☑ Drilled ☐ Bored ☐ Dug ☐ Cistern ☐ Lake ☑ Community ☐ Shared ☐ Other..........				
(b) If your water source is Community/Shared, is there a transferrable written agreement?	*PEB*			
(c) Are you aware of any problem re: quantity of water? (If yes, explain below)			*PEB*	
(d) Are you aware of any problems re: quality of water? (If yes, explain below) Drilled well is 45 feet deep, 7 gallons per minute (1986)			*PEB*	
(e) Do you have any water treatment devices?..........		*PEB*		
(f) Is your water system operable year round? Heated lines? ☐ Yes ☐ No	*PEB*			
(g) Date and result of most recent water test..........			*PEB*	
(h) Are any documents available for the well? If yes, specify		*PEB*		
(i) Does the property have any abandoned well(s)?		*PEB*		
2. **(a)** What kind of sewage disposal system services the property? ☐ Municipal ☐ Septic tank with tile bed ☐ Holding tank ☐ Other (Explain below)				
(b) Are you aware of any problems with the sewage system? **Increased size of tile bed 1987** Date septic/holding tank last pumped.......... Age of system..........		*PEB*		
(c) What documentation for the sewage system is available? ☐ Use Permit ☐ Location Sketch ☐ Maintenance Records ☐ Inspection Certificate ☐ Other			*PEB*	
3. Are all the well(s), water line(s) and waste disposal system(s) within the boundaries of the subject property?	*PEB*			

ACCESS, SHORELINE, UTILITIES: (Provide Applicable ADDITIONAL COMMENTS)	YES	NO	UNKNOWN	NOT APPLICABLE
1. **(a)** Is property access by municipal road? If yes; ☑ Open all year ☐ Seasonally open	*PEB*			
(b) Is the property serviced by a private road? Cost $.......... per year.				
2. If your access is across private property, access is: ☐ Right of way ☐ Deeded ☐ Other .... Cost $.......... per year.				*PEB*
3. **(a)** If water access only, access is: ☐ Deeded ☐ Leased ☐ Other (Explain below)				*PEB*
(b) Water access cost of: Parking $.......... Dock $.......... per year.				*PEB*
4. **(a)** Is the original Shore Road Allowance owned?				*PEB*
(b) Are there any pending applications for shoreline improvement?				*PEB*
(c) Are there any disputes concerning the shoreline or improvements on the shoreline?				*PEB*
(d) Are there any structures or docks on the original Shore Road Allowance?				*PEB*
(e) Is the original Road Allowance included in the lot size?				*PEB*
5. Does the boundary of the property extend beyond the water line? If yes, explain below.				*PEB*
6. **(a)** Is hydro available to the property?				
(b) Is the owner responsible for the installation, replacement/maintenance of any utility poles/ equipment?				

ADDITIONAL COMMENTS:..
....
....

INITIALS OF BUYER(S): ⬭

Form 222   Revised 2011   **Page 1 of 1**

CHAPTER 5

Multiple Representation and Customer Service Agreements

Introduction

Multiple representation involves a situation in which two or more clients are represented by a brokerage in the same transaction. The ability to properly represent two clients has been criticized by some as mere legal fiction, but the practice is widespread particularly given the double end sales in the marketplace; i.e., brokerage sales involving listed property and buyers of the same brokerage concluding sales involving those properties.

As chapter materials will emphasize, while such activity is not prohibited, it is strictly regulated under the *Real Estate and Business Brokers Act, 2002* and associated Regulations. Practical issues faced by registrants are highlighted, along with detailed analysis of both statutory requirements and associated listing and buyer representation forms that are widely used in the marketplace.

Customer service agreements are also discussed including regulatory requirements concerning such forms and preparation guidelines for both the *Seller Customer Service Agreement* (OREA Form 201) and the *Buyer Customer Service Agreement* (OREA Form 310).

Learning Outcomes

At the conclusion of this chapter, students will be able to:

- Outline key issues to consider regarding multiple representation including competing interests, imputed knowledge, defined duties, impartiality and limited disclosure, and practical issues faced by registrants.

- Detail statutory requirements concerning Step 1: Disclosure Before Agreement and explain key wordings provided in the *Listing Agreement* (OREA Form 200).

- Detail statutory requirements concerning Step 2: Disclosure Before Offer and discuss use of the *Confirmation of Co-operation and Representation* (OREA Form 320) for written confirmation.

- Explain regulatory requirements concerning customer service including disclosure information, minimum content and duties owed to the customer.

- Explain key wordings and adhere to preparation guidelines when completing a *Seller Customer Service Agreement* (OREA Form 201) or a *Buyer Customer Service Agreement* (OREA Form 310).

- Outline common errors and omissions relating to preparation of representation forms and customer service forms.

- Analyze selected case law as it applies to representation and the offering of customer services.

MULTIPLE REPRESENTATION

Multiple representation involves any situation where two or more **clients** in a real estate transaction are represented by a single brokerage. Scenarios can include:

- a single broker or salesperson representing both the buyer and seller;
- different brokers or salespersons employed by the same brokerage (same office or different offices) representing both the buyer and seller; or
- one or more brokers or salespersons employed by the same brokerage representing multiple buyers negotiating over the same property.

A discussion of key issues surrounding multiple representation is necessary prior to discussing disclosure procedures and form preparation.

> **Multiple Representation**
>
> Two or more clients in a real estate transaction are represented by the same real estate brokerage.

Competing Interests

Brokerages, in a fiduciary relationship, must always act in the client's best interests. However, a brokerage practising multiple representation, represents the interests of two or more parties (i.e., the buyer and the seller) that are invariably diametrically opposed. Multiple representation places the brokerage in a difficult situation, as competing interests of the buyer and the seller, or of competing buyers, cannot be simultaneously fulfilled given that the brokerage in a fiduciary relationship must always act in the best interests of the client, give undivided loyalty to the client and obey the client's legal instructions.

> It is an untenable situation for, as observed in one case, [brokerages] cannot be the loyal, obedient and trusted advisor of both clients, providing the level of professional and confidential service that each would be entitled to expect if the brokerage were the agent solely for one or the other.

Source: Professor W. Foster, *Agency Law and Real Estate Brokerage: Current Issues* (January, 2003).

Imputed Knowledge

Multiple representation is inherent in various, commonly-encountered situations within real estate brokerages. At the heart of the problem lies **imputed knowledge**. The representation agreement, be it with buyer or seller, effectively makes the brokerage and all brokers and salespersons representatives of the client.

The underlying legal assumption is that all representatives in a brokerage share each other's confidences; i.e., knowledge of confidential matters is imputed to all other representatives.

> **Imputed Knowledge**
>
> Knowledge or notice of facts known by one party that are deemed to also be known by another. For real estate purposes, knowledge of a broker or salesperson is deemed to be known by all other salespersons/brokers and the employing brokerage.

Defining Duties

The challenge with multiple representation as currently practised, lies in defining precise duties owed to the respective clients. As often said: *the devil is in the details when you serve two masters.* Danger lurks as even a minor advantage, given one over the other, can dramatically tip the negotiating scale.

Critics argue that those practising multiple representation attempt to define general and fiduciary obligations in what is at best a murky mixture of limited loyalty, obedience and disclosure to address clients' divergent interests. Legal experts point out that limitations in one's general and fiduciary obligations are at best an artificial line in the sand with inevitable confrontation in the courts.

CONCURRENT REPRESENTATION
Multiple Representation Possibilities

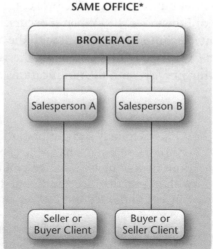

* Multiple representation may also occur between employees with differing responsibilities
(e.g., a salesperson and an appraiser within the same brokerage representing different parties in the transaction).
Source: © Alliance for Canadian Real Estate Education, 2006. *Agency Fundamentals: The National Perspective.*

Further, while forms used clearly require the client's informed consent, many question whether brokerages or their clients truly understand the process, not to mention the ramifications. Little wonder that organized real estate has issued dire warnings about its use.

Impartiality and Limited Disclosure

The brokerage agrees to act impartially and equally protect the interests of both clients, while agreeing to abide by a limited duty of disclosure. However, the ability to be even-handed, objective and impartial is hampered by inevitable risks given the inherent conflict of interest that exists. Limits to such disclosure are then set out with the understanding that identified items cannot be disclosed to either client, unless instructed in writing to do so by the respective client.

A clause is taken from the *Listing Agreement* (OREA Form 200):

disbursed in accordance with the Commission Trust Agreement.

MULTIPLE REPRESENTATION: The Seller hereby acknowledges that the Listing Brokerage may be entering into buyer representation agreements with buyers who may be interested in purchasing the Seller's Property. In the event that the Listing Brokerage has entered into or enters into a buyer representation agreement with a prospective buyer for the Seller's Property, the Listing Brokerage will obtain the Seller's written consent to represent both the Seller and the buyer for the transaction at the earliest practicable opportunity and in all cases prior to any offer to purchase being submitted or presented.

The Seller understands and acknowledges that the Listing Brokerage must be impartial when representing both the Seller and the buyer and equally protect the interests of the Seller and buyer. The Seller understands and acknowledges that when representing both the Seller and the buyer, the Listing Brokerage shall have a duty of full disclosure to both the Seller and the buyer, including a requirement to disclose all factual information about the Property known to the Listing Brokerage.

However, the Seller further understands and acknowledges that the Listing Brokerage shall not disclose:
• that the Seller may or will accept less than the listed price, unless otherwise instructed in writing by the Seller;
• that the buyer may or will pay more than the offered price, unless otherwise instructed in writing by the buyer;
• the motivation of or personal information about the Seller or buyer, unless otherwise instructed in writing by the party to which the information applies or unless failure to disclose would constitute fraudulent, unlawful or unethical practice;
• the price the buyer should offer or the price the Seller should accept; and
• the Listing Brokerage shall not disclose to the buyer the terms of any other offer.

However, it is understood that factual market information about comparable properties and information known to the Listing Brokerage concerning potential uses for the Property will be disclosed to both Seller and buyer to assist them to come to their own conclusions.

Where a Brokerage represents both the Seller and the Buyer (multiple representation), the Brokerage shall not be entitled or authorized to be agent for either the Buyer or the Seller for the purpose of giving and receiving notices.

MULTIPLE REPRESENTATION AND CUSTOMER SERVICE: The Seller understands and agrees that the Listing Brokerage also provides representation and customer service to other sellers and buyers. If the Listing Brokerage represents or provides customer service to more than one seller or buyer for the same trade, the Listing Brokerage shall, in writing, at the earliest practicable opportunity and before any offer is made, inform all sellers and buyers of the nature of the Listing Brokerage's relationship to each seller and buyer.

4.   FINDERS FEES: The Seller acknowledges that the Brokerage may be receiving a finder's fee, reward and/or referral incentive, and the Seller

Practical Issues

Multiple representation typically arises after a single representation arrangement has been established with either buyer or seller. The brokerage must first inform the client of this possibility (Code of Ethics, Sec. 10). When it occurs, both clients must be informed of that fact before entering into an agreement with the brokerage obtaining their consent (GEN, Sec. 22 and CODE, Sec. 16). In doing so, the salesperson must accurately convey the limitations being imposed and the ramifications of such limitations from the clients' perspectives.

Understanding Procedures	While seemingly straightforward in theory, critics question whether or not the salespersons or the clients truly understand the ramifications of serving two masters, much less how limitations are dealt with in practice. See additional discussion regarding informed consent under *REBBA 2002 Compliance* later in this chapter.
Second Client Advantage	Does the salesperson acquire more confidential and/or negotiating information from the first client (e.g., the seller client with a lengthy listing) as opposed to the second client (e.g., the buyer client considering the seller's property)? Is the risk higher, therefore, that such information could be imparted to the recently-encountered buyer client and prove detrimental to the original client?
Client Instructions	How can a salesperson obey conflicting instructions from clients? Which should be followed and which not?
Loyalty/ Allegiance	While an apparent conflict can be resolved by disbanding the multiple representation, do salespersons readily acknowledge all conflicts or attempt to smooth over these differences to make the deal? Which client suffers in the process?
Salesperson Conduct	Does the salesperson's actual conduct fully align with the stated procedure? Remember, the substance of representation (i.e., an agency relationship) is judged legally on the facts, not the forms and the words. If a breach occurs, liability and litigation may well follow.
Impartiality	Can a salesperson ever be completely impartial and without bias when representing two clients, particularly when personal interests are also at stake; i.e., making the deal?

Walking the Fine Line

Salesperson Martin listed a residential property for $329,000. At time of listing, the seller readily admitted that the reason for selling involved his wife wanting to return to Western Canada (their original home), as she missed the three grandchildren. However, urgency did not initially appear to be the driving issue, but rather a high selling price.

INITIAL NEGOTIATIONS

A buyer submitted an offer following Martin obtaining informed written consent to multiple representation involving both clients. The buyer's initial offer of $280,000 was countered at $320,000, but the buyer took no further action. Three weeks later, with no other offers forthcoming, the seller asked if the original prospective buyer was still interested. Salesperson Martin called and suggested that the buyer should perhaps restart negotiations.

THE SECOND OFFER

At Martin's urging, the buyer submitted a second offer of $290,000. The seller, clearly conflicted between getting the best price and addressing his wife's growing insistence on selling, signed back the offer at $310,000, but candidly admitted that the counter was more 'show' than 'substance' and, in fact, he would probably accept the low $290,000s if things came to 'push and shove.'

THE DEAL

Martin approached the buyer and presented the $310,000 counter-offer, but by his manner of presentation he was clearly giving subtle signals to the buyer that a tough negotiating stand would probably produce results. Also, Martin emphasized that the seller had seen no other action on the property and that he was getting anxious. The buyer, sensing some weakness in the seller's negotiating position, confidently drafted a new offer at $292,500 which was ultimately accepted.

THE FINE LINE

The deal was made but were the clients' interests equally protected?

FACTORS TO CONSIDER

- The seller indicated to Martin that the low $290s would probably be acceptable. Martin didn't disclose this fact to the buyer, but implied that further negotiations would produce results. Has Martin violated his responsibilities to the seller?

- Martin argues that he did the right thing by bringing the parties together in the best interests of both clients. After all, the seller wanted to re-open negotiations, did say that he would take less and his urgency was clearly more apparent than when originally listed. Has Martin worked in the best interests of his seller client?

MULTIPLE REPRESENTATION: DISCLOSURE

Multiple representation disclosure involves two steps. Each step is detailed in relation to REBBA 2002 and applicable wordings taken from the *Working with a REALTOR®* (OREA Form 810), the *Listing Agreement* (OREA Form 200) and the *Confirmation of Co-operation and Representation* (OREA Form 320) to illustrate how the representation is explained and disclosure is confirmed. Commentary includes multiple representation and other related disclosures, as both are intertwined in regulatory and form wordings.

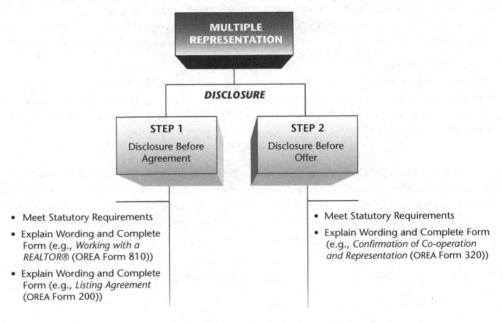

Step 1: Disclosure Before Agreement

STATUTORY REQUIREMENT

Registrants must meet minimum disclosure requirements as set out in the Code of Ethics (Sec. 10) to buyers and sellers prior to entering into an agreement in respect of trading in real estate. Registrants must describe services that will be provided and alternatives available to the potential client or **customer**. Part of that disclosure includes the fact that multiple representation could occur in which the brokerage provides representation to more than one client or provides services to more than one customer.

INFORMATION BEFORE AGREEMENTS

CODE

10. (1) Before entering into an agreement with a buyer or seller in respect of trading in real estate, a brokerage shall, at the earliest practicable opportunity, inform the buyer or seller of the following:

1. The types of service alternatives that are available in the circumstances, including a representation agreement or another type of agreement.

2. The services that the brokerage would provide under the agreement.

3. The fact that circumstances could arise in which the brokerage could represent more than one client in respect of the same trade in real estate, but that the brokerage could not do this unless all of the clients represented by the brokerage in respect of that trade consented in writing.

4. The nature of the services that the brokerage would provide to each client if the brokerage represents more than one client in respect of the same trade in real estate.

5. The fact that circumstances could arise in which the brokerage could provide services to more than one customer in respect of the same trade in real estate.

6. The fact that circumstances could arise in which the brokerage could, in respect of the same trade in real estate, both represent clients and provide services to customers.

7. The restricted nature of the services that the brokerage would provide to a customer in respect of a trade in real estate if the brokerage also represents a client in respect of that trade. O. Reg. 580/05, s. 10 (1).

(2) The brokerage shall, at the earliest practicable opportunity and before an offer is made, use the brokerage's best efforts to obtain from the buyer or seller a written acknowledgement that the buyer or seller received all the information referred to in subsection (1). O. Reg. 580/05, s. 10 (2).

WORKING WITH A REALTOR® (OREA FORM 810)

The *Working with a REALTOR®* form provides information on seller and buyer representation, multiple representation and customer service in line with the Code of Ethics, Subsec. 10(1). An acknowledgement is provided confirming that the buyer or seller has read and understood the form.

- Ask the seller to read the form and sign the acknowledgement. Provide a copy to the seller and retain a copy for the brokerage records.

- Ask the buyer, at first point of substantial contact, to read the form and sign the acknowledgement. Provide a copy to the buyer and retain a copy for the brokerage records.

- Provide explanations as required.

The *Working with a REALTOR®* (OREA Form 810) is highlighted given its wide use in the marketplace. However, individual brokerages may have developed alternate wordings and graphics that complement their corporate image.

 **Ontario Real Estate Association**

Working with a REALTOR®

Form 810
for use in the Province of Ontario

The REALTOR® Consumer Relationship

In Ontario, the real estate profession is governed by the Real Estate and Business Brokers Act, 2002, and Associated Regulations (REBBA 2002 or Act), administered by the Real Estate Council of Ontario (RECO). All Ontario REALTORS® are registered under the Act and governed by its provisions. REBBA 2002 is consumer protection legislation, regulating the conduct of real estate brokerages and their salespeople/brokers. The Act provides consumer protection in the form of deposit insurance and requires every salesperson/broker to carry errors & omission (E&O) insurance.

When you choose to use the services of a REALTOR®, it is important to understand that this individual works on behalf of a real estate brokerage, usually a company. The brokerage is operated by a Broker of Record, who has the ultimate responsibility for the employees registered with the brokerage. When you sign a contract, it is with the brokerage, not with the salesperson/broker employee.

The Act also requires that the brokerage (usually through its REALTORS®) explain the types of service alternatives available to consumers and the services the brokerage will be providing. The brokerage must document the relationship being created between the brokerage and the consumer, and submit it to the consumer for his/her approval and signature. The most common relationships are "client" and "customer", but other options may be available in the marketplace.

Client

A "client" relationship creates the highest form of obligation for a REALTOR® to a consumer. The brokerage and its salespeople/brokers have a fiduciary (legal) relationship with the client and represent the interests of the client in a real estate transaction. The REALTOR® will establish this relationship with the use of a representation agreement, called a Listing Agreement with the seller and a Buyer Representation Agreement with the buyer. The agreement contains an explanation of the services the brokerage will be providing, the fee arrangement for those services, the obligations the client will have under the agreement, and the expiry date of the agreement. Ensure that you have read and fully understand any such agreement before you sign the document.

Once a brokerage and a consumer enter into a client relationship, the brokerage must protect the interests of the client and do what is best for the client. A brokerage must strive for the benefit of the client and must not disclose a client's confidential information to others. Under the Act, the brokerage must also make reasonable efforts to determine any material facts relating to the transaction that would be of interest to the client and must inform the client of those facts. Although they are representing the interests of their client, they must still treat all parties to the transaction with fairness, honesty, and integrity.

Customer

A buyer or seller may not wish to be under contract as a client with the brokerage but would rather be treated as a customer. A REALTOR® is obligated to treat every person in a real estate transaction with honesty, fairness, and integrity, but unlike a client, provides a customer with a restricted level of service. Services provided to a customer may include showing the property or properties, drafting the offer, presenting the offer, etc. Brokerages use a Customer Service Agreement to document the services they are providing to a buyer or seller customer.

Under the Act, the REALTOR® has disclosure obligations to a customer and must disclose material facts known to the brokerage that relate to the transaction.

What Happens When...

Buyer(s) and the seller(s) are sometimes under contract with the same brokerage when properties are being shown or an offer is being contemplated. There can also be instances when there is more than one offer on a property and more than one buyer and seller are under a representation agreement with the same brokerage. This situation is referred to as multiple representation. Under the Act, the REALTORS® and their brokerage must make sure all buyers, sellers, and their REALTORS® confirm in writing that they acknowledge, understand, and consent to the situation before their offer is made. REALTORS® typically use what is called a Confirmation of Co-operation and Representation form to document this situation.

Offer negotiations may become stressful, so if you have any questions when reference is made to multiple representation or multiple offers, please ask your REALTOR® for an explanation.

Critical Information

REALTORS® are obligated to disclose facts that may affect a buying or selling decision. It may be difficult for a REALTOR® to judge what facts are important. They also may not be in a position to know a fact. You should communicate to your REALTOR® what information and facts about a property are important to you in making a buying or selling decision, and document this information to avoid any misunderstandings and/or unpleasant surprises.

Similarly, services that are important to you and are to be performed by the brokerage, or promises that have been made to you, should be documented in your contract with the brokerage and its salesperson/broker.

To ensure the best possible real estate experience, make sure all your questions are answered by your REALTOR®. You should read and understand every contract before you finalize it.

Acknowledgement by: ....
(Names)

I/we have read, understand, and have received a copy of Working with a REALTOR®

Sellers: As seller(s), I/we understand that

(initial one)

_____
(Name of Brokerage)

| | Is representing my interests, to be documented in a separate written agency representation agreement, and I understand the brokerage may represent and/or provide customer service to other sellers and buyers. |

| | Is not representing my interests, to be documented in a separate written customer service agreement, but will act in a fair, ethical and professional manner. |

_____   _____
(Signature)   (Date)

_____   _____
(Signature)   (Date)

Buyers: As buyer(s), I/we understand that

(initial one)

_____
(Name of Brokerage)

| | Is representing my interests, to be documented in a separate written agency representation agreement, and I understand the brokerage may represent and/or provide customer service to other buyers and sellers. |

| | Is not representing my interests, to be documented in a separate written customer service agreement, but will act in a fair, ethical and professional manner. |

_____   _____
(Signature)   (Date)

_____   _____
(Signature)   (Date)

Please note that Federal legislation requires REALTORS® to verify the identity of sellers and buyers with whom they are working.
For the purposes of this information, the term "seller" can be interpreted as "landlord" and "buyer" can mean "tenant." This form is for information only and is not a contract.

Form 810   New 2015   **Page 1 of 1**

FORM WORDING (LISTING AGREEMENT, OREA FORM 200)

All amounts set out as commission are to be paid plus applicable taxes on such commission.

A **3. REPRESENTATION:** The Seller acknowledges that the Listing Brokerage has provided the Seller with information explaining agency relationships, including information on Seller Representation, Sub-agency, Buyer Representation, Multiple Representation and Customer Service. The Seller authorizes the Listing Brokerage to co-operate with any other registered real estate brokerage (co-operating brokerage), and to offer to pay the co-operating

brokerage a commission of................% of the sale price of the Property or..

.... out of the commission the Seller pays the Listing Brokerage.

B The Seller understands that unless the Seller is otherwise informed, the co-operating brokerage is representing the interests of the buyer in the transaction. The Seller further acknowledges that the Listing Brokerage may be listing other properties that may be similar to the Seller's Property and the Seller hereby consents to the Listing Brokerage listing other properties that may be similar to the Seller's Property without any claim by the Seller of conflict of interest. The Seller hereby appoints the Listing Brokerage as the Seller's agent for the purpose of giving and receiving notices pursuant to any offer or agreement to purchase the property. Unless otherwise agreed in writing between Seller and Listing Brokerage, any commission payable to any other brokerage shall be paid out of the commission the Seller pays the Listing Brokerage, said commission to be disbursed in accordance with the Commission Trust Agreement.

C **MULTIPLE REPRESENTATION:** The Seller hereby acknowledges that the Listing Brokerage may be entering into buyer representation agreements with buyers who may be interested in purchasing the Seller's Property. In the event that the Listing Brokerage has entered into or enters into a buyer representation agreement with a prospective buyer for the Seller's Property, the Listing Brokerage will obtain the Seller's written consent to represent both the Seller and the buyer for the transaction at the earliest practicable opportunity and in all cases prior to any offer to purchase being submitted or presented.

The Seller understands and acknowledges that the Listing Brokerage must be impartial when representing both the Seller and the buyer and equally protect the interests of the Seller and buyer. The Seller understands and acknowledges that when representing both the Seller and the buyer, the Listing Brokerage shall have a duty of full disclosure to both the Seller and the buyer, including a requirement to disclose all factual information about the Property known to the Listing Brokerage.

D However, the Seller further understands and acknowledges that the Listing Brokerage shall not disclose:
- that the Seller may or will accept less than the listed price, unless otherwise instructed in writing by the Seller;
- that the buyer may or will pay more than the offered price, unless otherwise instructed in writing by the buyer;
- the motivation of or personal information about the Seller or buyer, unless otherwise instructed in writing by the party to which the information applies or unless failure to disclose would constitute fraudulent, unlawful or unethical practice;
- the price the buyer should offer or the price the Seller should accept; and
- the Listing Brokerage shall not disclose to the buyer the terms of any other offer.

However, it is understood that factual market information about comparable properties and information known to the Listing Brokerage concerning potential uses for the Property will be disclosed to both Seller and buyer to assist them to come to their own conclusions.

Where a Brokerage represents both the Seller and the Buyer (multiple representation), the Brokerage shall not be entitled or authorized to be agent for either the Buyer or the Seller for the purpose of giving and receiving notices.

E **MULTIPLE REPRESENTATION AND CUSTOMER SERVICE:** The Seller understands and agrees that the Listing Brokerage also provides representation and customer service to other sellers and buyers. If the Listing Brokerage represents or provides customer service to more than one seller or buyer for the same trade, the Listing Brokerage shall, in writing, at the earliest practicable opportunity and before any offer is made, inform all sellers and buyers of the nature of the Listing Brokerage's relationship to each seller and buyer.

4. FINDERS FEES: The Seller acknowledges that the Brokerage may be receiving a finder's fee, reward and/or referral incentive, and the Seller consents to any such benefit being received and retained by the Brokerage in addition to the commission as described above.

A **Acknowledgement**
Clause 3 provides an acknowledgement regarding disclosure of relationships discussed with the client, and confirms that representation and other services have been fully described.

B **Competing Sellers**
This clause involves the client's confirmation that any co-operating brokerage would be representing the buyer, unless the client is otherwise notified. In addition, the client confirms that the listing brokerage may list other properties similar to the seller's and that such is not a conflict of interest.

C **Seller's Written Consent Required**
This clause confirms the possibility of multiple representation, including a description of the services the brokerage would provide in such situations. The client must clearly understand that the brokerage cannot represent multiple clients in a transaction unless all of the clients and potential clients involved consent in writing.

D **Multiple Representation Procedure**
The highlighted wording sets out specific duties owed to the seller and the buyer under multiple representation including those matters than cannot be disclosed, or can only be disclosed if so instructed in writing by the seller. It also states that in a multiple representation situation, the brokerage shall not be entitled or authorized to act as an agent for either party to give or receive notices.

E **Representation and Customer Service to Other Sellers and Buyers**
In accordance with the Code of Ethics, Sec. 10, the seller acknowledges that the brokerage may provide representation and customer service to other sellers and buyers for the same trade. If so, written disclosure will be given before any offer is made (See *Step 2: Disclosure Prior to Offer*).

Step 2: Disclosure Before Offer

The registrant cannot represent more than one party to a trade without the written consent of all parties being represented. Informed consent must be obtained at the point that the registrant wants to represent more than one client in a real estate transaction. The Ontario Real Estate Association has developed a form that addresses such disclosure prior to offer presentation. The *Confirmation of Co-operation and Representation* (OREA Form 320) is illustrated highlighting multiple representation disclosures, as well as other representation and customer service options that this versatile form addresses. If a client refuses to grant such consent, the brokerage must release one or more of its clients to seek alternate representation with respect to the transaction.

STATUTORY REQUIREMENT

Sec. 16 and 17 of the Code of Ethics details this further disclosure requirement, which must be read in conjunction with Sec. 22 of the General Regulation 567/05.

DISCLOSURE BEFORE MULTIPLE REPRESENTATION   `CODE`

16. A brokerage shall not represent more than one client in respect of the same trade in real estate unless it has disclosed the following matters to the clients or prospective clients at the earliest practicable opportunity:

   1. The fact that the brokerage proposes to represent more than one client in respect of the same trade.

   2. The differences between the obligations the brokerage would have if it represented only one client in respect of the trade and the obligations the brokerage would have if it represented more than one client in respect of the trade, including any differences relating to the disclosure of information or the services that the brokerage would provide. O. Reg. 580/05, s. 16.

NATURE OF RELATIONSHIP

17. If a registrant represents or provides services to more than one buyer or seller in respect of the same trade in real estate, the registrant shall, in writing, at the earliest practicable opportunity and before any offer is made, inform all buyers and sellers involved in that trade of the nature of the registrant's relationship to each buyer and seller. O. Reg. 580/05, s. 17.

MULTIPLE REPRESENTATION   `GEN`

22. A registrant shall not represent more than one client in respect of the same trade in real estate unless all of the clients represented by the registrant in respect of that trade consent in writing. O. Reg. 567/05, s. 22.

FORM WORDING (CONFIRMATION OF CO-OPERATION AND REPRESENTATION, OREA FORM 320)

The *Confirmation of Co-operation and Representation* (OREA Form 320) is designed to address various matters prior to an offer including multiple representation, buyer brokerage, customer service, service agreements (discussed later in this chapter) and representation/commission issues involving a co-operating brokerage.

The form is prepared and signed prior to the presentation of an offer. The signatories include the listing brokerage, co-operating brokerage (if applicable), seller and buyer. This ensures that all parties clearly understand who is being represented by whom and the commission payable to the co-operating brokerage. Space is provided for additional comments as the need arises.

Confirmation of Co-operation and Representation, Page 1 of 2

OREA Ontario Real Estate Association

Confirmation of Co-operation and Representation

Form 320
for use in the Province of Ontario

BUYER: ....

SELLER: ....

For the transaction on the property known as: ....

For the purposes of this Confirmation of Co-operation and Representation, "Seller" includes a vendor, a landlord, or a prospective, seller, vendor or landlord and "Buyer" includes a purchaser, a tenant, or a prospective, buyer, purchaser or tenant, "sale" includes a lease, and "Agreement of Purchase and Sale" includes an Agreement to Lease.

The following information is confirmed by the undersigned salesperson/broker representatives of the Brokerage(s). If a Co-operating Brokerage is involved in the transaction, the brokerages agree to co-operate, in consideration of, and on the terms and conditions as set out below.

DECLARATION OF INSURANCE: The undersigned salesperson/broker representative(s) of the Brokerage(s) hereby declare that he/she is insured as required by the Real Estate and Business Brokers Act, 2002 (REBBA 2002) and Regulations.

1. LISTING BROKERAGE

A   **a)** ☐ The Listing Brokerage represents the interests of the Seller in this transaction. It is further understood and agreed that:

   1) ☐ The Listing Brokerage is not representing or providing Customer Service to the Buyer.
   (If the Buyer is working with a Co-operating Brokerage, Section 3 is to be completed by Co-operating Brokerage)

   2) ☐ The Listing Brokerage is providing Customer Service to the Buyer.

B   **b)** ☐ **MULTIPLE REPRESENTATION:** The Listing Brokerage has entered into a Buyer Representation Agreement with the Buyer and represents the interests of the Seller and the Buyer, with their consent, for this transaction. The Listing Brokerage must be impartial and equally protect the interests of the Seller and the Buyer in this transaction. The Listing Brokerage has a duty of full disclosure to both the Seller and the Buyer, including a requirement to disclose all factual information about the property known to the Listing Brokerage. However, the Listing Brokerage shall not disclose:

   - That the Seller may or will accept less than the listed price, unless otherwise instructed in writing by the Seller;
   - That the Buyer may or will pay more than the offered price, unless otherwise instructed in writing by the Buyer;
   - The motivation of or personal information about the Seller or Buyer, unless otherwise instructed in writing by the party to which the information applies, or unless failure to disclose would constitute fraudulent, unlawful or unethical practice;
   - The price the Buyer should offer or the price the Seller should accept;
   - And; the Listing Brokerage shall not disclose to the Buyer the terms of any other offer.

   However, it is understood that factual market information about comparable properties and information known to the Listing Brokerage concerning potential uses for the property will be disclosed to both Seller and Buyer to assist them to come to their own conclusions.

C   Additional comments and/or disclosures by Listing Brokerage: (e.g. The Listing Brokerage represents more than one Buyer offering on this property.)

....

....

....

D   **2. PROPERTY SOLD BY BUYER BROKERAGE – PROPERTY NOT LISTED**

   ☐ The Brokerage .... represent the Buyer and the property is not listed with any real estate brokerage. The Brokerage will be paid
   (does/does not)

   ☐ by the Seller in accordance with a Seller Customer Service Agreement

   or: ☐ by the Buyer directly

   Additional comments and/or disclosures by Buyer Brokerage: (e.g. The Buyer Brokerage represents more than one Buyer offering on this property.)

....

....

....

INITIALS OF BUYER(S)/SELLER(S)/BROKERAGE REPRESENTATIVE(S) (Where applicable)

⬭   ⬭   ⬭   ⬭

A **Single Agency**
This option confirms that the listing brokerage represents the interests of the seller. The buyer may be a customer of the listing brokerage or represented by a co-operating brokerage.

B **Multiple Representation—Description**
This option confirms that the listing brokerage is involved in multiple representation and sets out specific requirements in that regard.

C **Other Situations**
Additional space is provided for other comments or disclosures by the listing brokerage.

D **Property Not Listed**
This section focuses on situations where the property is not listed. It indicates whether the brokerage does or does not represent the buyer and how the brokerage will be paid for services provided. The brokerage or its representative would check the appropriate box and include any additional comments or disclosures in the space provided.

E **3. Co-operating Brokerage completes Section 3 and Listing Brokerage completes Section 1.**

CO-OPERATING BROKERAGE- REPRESENTATION:

a) ☐ The Co-operating Brokerage represents the interests of the Buyer in this transaction.

b) ☐ The Co-operating Brokerage is providing Customer Service to the Buyer in this transaction.

c) ☐ The Co-operating Brokerage is not representing the Buyer and has not entered into an agreement to provide customer service(s) to the Buyer.

CO-OPERATING BROKERAGE- COMMISSION:

a) ☐ The Listing Brokerage will pay the Co-operating Brokerage the commission as indicated in the MLS® information for the property

.... to be paid from the amount paid by the Seller to the Listing Brokerage.
(Commission As Indicated In MLS® Information)

b) ☐ The Co-operating Brokerage will be paid as follows:

....

....

....

Additional comments and/or disclosures by Co-operating Brokerage: (e.g., The Co-operating Brokerage represents more than one Buyer offering on this property.)

....

....

....

Commission will be payable as described above, plus applicable taxes.

COMMISSION TRUST AGREEMENT: If the above Co-operating Brokerage is receiving payment of commission from the Listing Brokerage, then the agreement between Listing Brokerage and Co-operating Brokerage further includes a Commission Trust Agreement, the consideration for which is the Co-operating Brokerage procuring an offer for a trade of the property, acceptable to the Seller. This Commission Trust Agreement shall be subject to and governed by the MLS® rules and regulations pertaining to commission trusts of the Listing Brokerage's local real estate board, if the local board's MLS® rules and regulations so provide. Otherwise, the provisions of the OREA recommended MLS® rules and regulations shall apply to this Commission Trust Agreement. For the purpose of this Commission Trust Agreement, the Commission Trust Amount shall be the amount noted in Section 3 above. The Listing Brokerage hereby declares that all monies received in connection with the trade shall constitute a Commission Trust and shall be held, in trust, for the Co-operating Brokerage under the terms of the applicable MLS® rules and regulations.

SIGNED BY THE BROKER/SALESPERSON REPRESENTATIVE(S) OF THE BROKERAGE(S) (Where applicable)

F

....
(Name of Co-operating/Buyer Brokerage)

....

Tel:.................................. Fax: ....

.... Date:...............................
(Authorized to bind the Co-operating/Buyer Brokerage)

....
(Print Name of Broker/Salesperson Representative of the Brokerage)

....
(Name of Listing Brokerage)

....

Tel:.................................. Fax: ....

.... Date:...............................
(Authorized to bind the Listing Brokerage)

....
(Print Name of Broker/Salesperson Representative of the Brokerage)

CONSENT FOR MULTIPLE REPRESENTATION (To be completed only if the Brokerage represents more than one client for the transaction)

The Buyer/Seller consent with their initials to their Brokerage representing more than one client for this transaction.

⬭ BUYER'S INITIALS   ⬭ SELLER'S INITIALS

ACKNOWLEDGEMENT

G I have received, read, and understand the above information.

.... Date: ....
(Signature of Buyer)

.... Date: ....
(Signature of Buyer)

.... Date: ....
(Signature of Seller)

.... Date: ....
(Signature of Seller)

E **Co-operating Brokerage—Various Situations**
This section details various situations involving the co-operating brokerage; i.e., whether or not the buyer is being represented and how commission will be paid. The co-operating brokerage checks off the applicable option and provides any additional comments or disclosures in the space provided.

F **Signatures—Brokerages**
The listing brokerage and the co-operating brokerage, or their respective representatives, sign the Confirmation of Co-operation and Representation prior to the offer presentation.

G **Signatures—Sellers & Buyers**
The seller and buyer sign an acknowledgement that they have received, read and understood information provided in the *Confirmation of Co-operation and Representation* prior to the offer presentation.

The Unsophisticated Buyers

RESIDENTIAL CASE LAW

The buyers, unsophisticated neighbours and friends of Salesperson A, informed Salesperson A that they were interested in buying a condominium unit. The buyers were shown a unit and advised that the seller would take no less than $160,000 and that this was a good price.

The buyers proceeded to acquire the condominium and, upon discovering after the sale was closed that the price paid exceeded market value, pursued legal action and sought damages. They did not ask the salesperson for his opinion regarding the price nor did they enquire of other available properties. Further, Salesperson A did not inform the buyers that he was not representing their interests or that they should retain independent legal counsel. The buyers asserted: *He was supposed to be our salesperson. He was supposed to help us. We believed and trusted him.*

The seller, a niece of Salesperson A, accepted the offer of $160,000 and agreed to a 6% commission without the property ever having been listed or advertised for sale. Salesperson A had sold her the unit two years earlier for $150,000. Expert opinion established the market value of $125,000 at the time of the sale to the buyers, who ultimately resold the property five years later for $110,000.

The Judge found that Salesperson A had a duty to the buyers and should have disclosed the conflict of also acting for the seller. This lack of disclosure deprived the buyers of the opportunity to retain an independent agent. Salesperson A was held liable for the buyers' overpayment. The court awarded $17,500.

Reference Mucci v. CMF Realty, Supreme Court of Justice; Court File No. 96-CU-114018.

COMMENTARY

Registrants must understand their obligations when representing others. While typically granted by express agreement, agency (representation) may also be created by words or conduct from which a reasonable person would infer that a principal/agent relationship has been established.

What and how something is said becomes focal. Salesperson A clearly overstepped the limited boundaries of answering questions and showing the property. Potential difficulties are often avoided if the broker or salesperson has a clear understanding of obligations owed and ensures timely, forthright and complete disclosure to both buyer and seller.

On the matter of pricing, the Judge said that the buyers' expectation of advice on price was reasonable and that Salesperson A should have appreciated that expectation. The Judge had the following comment:

> "While real estate agents are not appraisers they should know the general range of the market. They regularly advise vendors on listing prices and hold themselves out as being able to do so. They have a comparable obligation to purchasers to whom they owe a duty to advise on whether the asking price is unrealistically high. If the agent lacks such expertise or market knowledge... (he)...has a duty to warn his principal that he cannot and will not advise on the adequacy of the price. The agent for a purchaser has a duty to advise the purchaser of a market price range or to inform himself by independently assessing the market or obtaining appraisal advice."

A registrant treating a buyer as a client has higher obligations to the client than those owed to a customer. At the very least, every buyer's representative should prepare a comprehensive comparative market analysis of the subject property. As the Judge suggested, the value estimate does not require the precision as one would expect in an appraisal report. An appropriate range may be sufficient. Buyers' representatives are then expected to use their negotiation skills within that market range.

Seller A bought two apartment buildings for $775,000 and sold them four months later for $975,000 to Buyers B and C under an agreement where that seller retained title until payment was made. Buyers B and C went into default on their payments and Seller A sent a notice terminating the agreement.

Seller A then instructed the real estate salesperson to sell the properties for $1.3 million. Buyers B and C also signed a listing agreement with the brokerage for $1.25 million. An *as is* offer for $1 million was received, presented to Buyers B and C, but was rejected. The salesperson forwarded copies of the offer to Seller A, who advised him to replace the name of the seller in the offer from Buyers B and C to Seller A. The transaction was successfully closed.

Buyers B and C subsequently sued Seller A for relief from forfeiture and damages. The Judge decided that no breach of the original agreement had occurred and that Buyers B and C had the right to sell the buildings. Seller A's actions were judged unconscionable and the seller was ordered to repay $100,000 to the buyers for payments made.

While the trial judge found that the salesperson did not breach any of his duties to Buyers B and C and allowed him to recover commission, the Court of Appeal reversed that finding and stated that a fiduciary relationship existed with Buyers B and C based on the listing. The Court of Appeal determined that Buyers B and C trusted the salesperson and were unsophisticated and inexperienced investors.

The breach of duty arose from delivering a copy of the offer to Seller A, changing the name of the seller and not disclosing that change to Buyers B and C. The salesperson's loyalty and duty lay with the buyers and he compromised both by acting for Seller A at the same time. The salesperson was found liable for the $100,000, an additional $25,000 for the equity in the building and was not entitled to commission.

Reference   Spence v. Suechris and Harvey; 15 R.P.R. (3d) 39.

COMMENTARY

Representation involving both a buyer and seller requires proper disclosure. The brokerage through its representatives must advise the seller and the buyer of multiple representation and obtain their informed consent.

Often, issues concerning multiple representation are complex and not subject to easy resolution. Failing to understand correct procedures can have unfortunate results. All registrants are reminded of disclosure requirements clearly set out in the Code of Ethics, Sec. 10, 16 and 17.

Full and complete disclosure, combined with a written representation agreement, goes a long way to minimize risk. However, a strong cautionary note is warranted. Commercial registrants, in particular, should be aware of potential pitfalls involving multiple representation and always exercise prudence in its use.

 # CUSTOMER SERVICE

REBBA 2002, as previously discussed, clearly distinguishes between a client and a customer. A customer is someone who has entered into some form of service agreement with a brokerage, but is not represented by the brokerage. A customer, while not owed fiduciary duties, must be dealt with honestly and with integrity.

Historically, agency law provided certain protections to customers by way of duty of care. Recall that the duty of care owed to clients applies to everything that is done and that ought to be done for a client. The duty owed to customers is limited to the giving of information, responding to questions and doing anything (i.e., performing functions) that the salesperson, on behalf of the brokerage, has agreed to for the customer.

However, regulatory requirements have expanded the scope of obligations to a customer. Various Code of Ethics provisions apply both to clients and customers. For example, registrants owe both clients and customers conscientious and competent service (Sec. 5) and must:

- demonstrate reasonable knowledge, skill, judgment and competence in offering opinions (Sec. 6);
- meet various disclosure requirements in advance of agreements (Sec. 10);
- meet minimum requirements concerning agreements (Sec. 11);
- disclose material defects (Sec. 21);
- ensure compliance with regulatory requirements concerning the conveying of offers (Sec. 24);
- provide disclosure of competing offers (Sec. 26); and
- deliver copies of agreements, deposits and documents in accordance with Code requirements (Sec. 28 and 29).

Customer Service Agreements

General Regulation (GEN, Subsec. 1(2)) refers to agreements other than representation agreements in which the brokerage provides services to a customer, as distinct from a representation agreement with a client. Wordings may vary, but a **service agreement** typically:

- States that the brokerage is representing the client and the buyer or seller is a customer.
- Confirms that no representation exists in relation to the customer and that regulatory and limited general obligations are owed, but no fiduciary obligations.
- Identifies specific services that may be provided to the customer.
- Provides for written consent by the customer.

Service Agreement

An agreement in which the brokerage provides services to the customer, as distinct from a representation agreement with a client.

IMPORTANT: A customer service agreement involving the seller normally includes a provision regarding commission payable to the brokerage. However, the wording clearly states that the payment of such commission by the seller does not create or constitute representation by the brokerage of the seller as a client. In the case of a service agreement for the buyer, there is no require-ment for the buyer to pay a commission for services rendered, unless the parties agree otherwise.

EXAMPLE   *The Seller's Perspective*

Salesperson Martin of XYZ Real Estate Ltd. is attempting to locate an acceptable commercial property for his investor client, Buyer Jones. Jones has signed a buyer representation agreement, which provides that Martin can receive remuneration from the seller.

Martin approaches a For Sale by Owner who will provide remuneration, but does not want to be represented by way of a seller representation agreement. This arrangement also suits XYZ Real Estate Ltd., as Martin and the brokerage can avoid multiple representation. Accordingly, the seller signs a *Seller Customer Service Agreement*.

> **EXAMPLE**   *The Buyer's Perspective*
>
> Mr. and Mrs. Jones arrive at an open house held by Salesperson Lee of ABC Realty Inc. on behalf of his client, Seller Smith. Lee, at the first practical opportunity, advises the buyers that ABC Realty Inc. is the seller's agent. The buyers are knowledgeable, having sold several homes and do not want to be represented. They inform Lee that they will seek legal advice should any contentious issues arise.
>
> Salesperson Lee, to avoid any possible confusion, has the buyers sign a buyer customer service agreement. In doing so, Lee does not disturb his seller representation agreement by choosing to represent the buyers. The *Buyer Customer Service Agreement* provides that duties will include:
>
> - the ethical duty to deal fairly, honestly and with integrity;
> - the legal duty to exercise due care when answering questions and providing information; and
> - the legal duty to avoid misrepresentation.
>
> Source: ©OREA 2010, Form 310: *Buyer Customer Service Agreement.*

REBBA 2002 Compliance

Provisions in REBBA 2002 regarding service agreements are intended to minimize potential problems by ensuring that registrants and customers are both clear about the nature of services being provided.

INFORMATION BEFORE AGREEMENT

As with representation agreements, Sec. 10 of the Code of Ethics provides that the buyer or seller be informed regarding various matters at the earliest practicable opportunity. These include the type of service alternatives available, services provided, the fact that circumstances could arise in which the brokerage provides services to more than one customer and also that the brokerage could represent clients and provide services to customers. Applicable portions of Sec. 10 referring to service agreements are highlighted.

INFORMATION BEFORE AGREEMENTS   `CODE`

10. (1) Before entering into an agreement with a buyer or seller in respect of trading in real estate, a brokerage shall, at the earliest practicable opportunity, inform the buyer or seller of the following:

  1. The types of service alternatives that are available in the circumstances, including a representation agreement or another type of agreement.

  2. The services that the brokerage would provide under the agreement.

  3. The fact that circumstances could arise in which the brokerage could represent more than one client in respect of the same trade in real estate, but that the brokerage could not do this unless all of the clients represented by the brokerage in respect of that trade consented in writing.

  4. The nature of the services that the brokerage would provide to each client if the brokerage represents more than one client in respect of the same trade in real estate.

  5. The fact that circumstances could arise in which the brokerage could provide services to more than one customer in respect of the same trade in real estate.

  6. The fact that circumstances could arise in which the brokerage could, in respect of the same trade in real estate, both represent clients and provide services to customers.

  7. The restricted nature of the services that the brokerage would provide to a customer in respect of a trade in real estate if the brokerage also represents a client in respect of that trade. O. Reg. 580/05, s. 10 (1).

  (2) The brokerage shall, at the earliest practicable opportunity and before an offer is made, use the brokerage's best efforts to obtain from the buyer or seller a written acknowledgement that the buyer or seller received all the information referred to in subsection (1). O. Reg. 580/05, s. 10 (2).

MINIMUM CONTENT

The Code of Ethics (Sec. 11) sets out minimum information that must be contained in service agreements between brokerages and buyers/sellers, as was the case with representation agreements. These include:

- effective date of the agreement;
- amount of commission/other remuneration;
- amount payable to a co-operating brokerage;
- how commission will be paid;
- services being provided under the agreement;
- provision for agreement exceeding six months (i.e., date to be prominently displayed on first page with space for required buyer or seller initials); and
- agreement contains only one expiry date.

CONTENTS OF WRITTEN AGREEMENTS   `CODE`

11. (1) A brokerage shall not enter into a written agreement with a buyer or seller for the purpose of trading in real estate unless the agreement clearly, comprehensibly and prominently,

    (a) specifies the date on which the agreement takes effect and the date on which it expires;

    (b) specifies or describes the method for determining,

        (i) the amount of any commission or other remuneration payable to the brokerage, and

        (ii) in the case of an agreement with a seller, the amount of any commission or other remuneration payable to any other brokerage;

    (c) describes how any commission or other remuneration payable to the brokerage will be paid; and

    (d) sets out the services that the brokerage will provide under the agreement. O. Reg. 580/05, s. 11 (1).

(2) A brokerage shall not, for the purpose of trading in real estate, enter into a written agreement with a buyer or seller that provides that the date on which the agreement expires is more than six months after the date on which the agreement takes effect unless,

    (a) the date on which the agreement expires is prominently displayed on the first page of the agreement; and

    (b) the buyer or seller has initialled the agreement next to the date referred to in clause (a). O. Reg. 580/05, s. 11 (2).

(3) A brokerage shall ensure that a written agreement that is entered into between the brokerage and a buyer or seller for the purpose of trading in real estate contains only one date on which the agreement expires. O. Reg. 580/05, s. 11 (3).

COPIES OF AGREEMENTS

As with representation agreements, the Code of Ethics requires that each person entering into a written service agreement must immediately receive a copy of that agreement.

COPIES OF WRITTEN AGREEMENTS   `CODE`

12. If a brokerage and one or more other persons enter into a written agreement in connection with a trade in real estate, the brokerage shall ensure that each of the other persons is immediately given a copy of the agreement. O. Reg. 580/05, s. 12.

WRITTEN AGREEMENT

The Code of Ethics requires that an agreement in respect of a trade in real estate must be reduced to writing, signed by the brokerage and submitted to the customer for signature. The Code does not require the customer's signature, but registrants are once again cautioned regarding verbal agreements and problems that can arise, particularly concerning commission.

AGREEMENTS WITH CUSTOMERS

CODE

15. If a brokerage enters into an agreement with a customer in respect of a trade in real estate and the agreement is not in writing, the brokerage shall, at the earliest practicable opportunity, reduce the agreement to writing, have it signed on behalf of the brokerage and submit it to the customer for signature. O. Reg. 580/05, s. 15.

EXAMPLE   *The Service Agreement*

Salesperson Wendell is discussing provisions included in a *Buyer Customer Service Agreement*. The buyer does not want to be represented, but is seeking customer services. Wendell emphasizes the following wording in the agreement that addresses representation and customer service, along with requirements as set out in REBBA 2002.

REPRESENTATION AND CUSTOMER SERVICE: The Buyer acknowledges that the Brokerage has provided the Buyer with written information explaining agency relationships, including information on Seller Representation, Sub-Agency, Buyer Representation, Multiple Representation and Customer Service.

The Buyer acknowledges that the Brokerage will be providing customer service to the Buyer and will not be representing the interests of the Buyer in a transaction.

The Brokerage may be representing the interests of the seller as an agent or sub-agent. When the Brokerage is representing the seller, the seller is considered to be the Brokerage's client and the Brokerage's primary duties are to protect and promote the interests of the seller/client. The Brokerage will disclose all pertinent information to a seller/client obtained from or about the Buyer.

Even though the Brokerage's primary duties may be to the seller, the Brokerage may provide many valuable customer services to the Buyer.

When providing customer service to the Buyer, the Brokerage's duties to the Buyer include:

- *the **Ethical** duty to deal fairly, honestly and with integrity;*
- *the **Legal** duty to exercise due care when answering questions and providing information; and*
- *the **Legal** duty to avoid misrepresentation.*

The Buyer acknowledges that the Buyer may not be shown or offered all properties that may be of interest to the Buyer.

The Buyer hereby agrees that the terms of any buyer's offer or agreement to purchase or lease the property will not be disclosed to any other buyer.

The Buyer understands and agrees that the Brokerage also provides representation and customer service to other buyers and sellers. If the Brokerage represents or provides customer service to more than one seller or buyer for the same trade, the Brokerage shall, in writing, at the earliest practicable opportunity and before any offer is made, inform all sellers and buyers of the nature of the Brokerage's relationship to each seller and buyer.

Source: ©OREA 2010, Form 310: Buyer Customer Service Agreement.

CUSTOMER SERVICE FORMS

Customer service forms currently published by the Ontario Real Estate Association include:

- **OREA Form 201 (Residential)**
  Seller Customer Service Agreement, Commission Agreement for Property Not Listed.

- **OREA Form 310 (Residential)**
  Buyer Customer Service Agreement, For Use When the Buyer is Not Represented by the Brokerage.

- **OREA Form 545 (Commercial)**
  Buyer Customer Service Agreement—Commercial, For Use When the Buyer is Not Represented By the Brokerage.

Seller Customer Service Agreement

The *Seller Customer Service Agreement* (OREA Form 201) establishes a contract between the brokerage and the seller for customer services only. The form design for property not listed achieves several objectives:

- Details commission including amount and terms under which remuneration is paid.
- Confirms in writing that the brokerage is not the representative of the seller.
- Assigns the deposit to the payment of the commission.
- Provides the brokerage with the authority to obtain additional information about the property.

OREA Ontario Real Estate Association   **Seller Customer Service Agreement**
Commission Agreement For Property Not Listed

Form 201
for use in the Province of Ontario

This Is A Non-Exclusive Seller Customer Service Agreement
BETWEEN:
BROKERAGE: ....

....(the "Brokerage") Tel.No. (............)..................................

SELLER(S): .... (the "Seller")

....

for the property known as: .... (the "Property")

and for the following Buyer: .... (the "Buyer")
The Brokerage agrees to provide customer service to the Seller for the sale or lease of the above described property to the Buyer and the Seller acknowledges and agrees to the terms as stated in this Agreement. **This non-exclusive Seller Customer Service Agreement:**

commences at .... a.m./p.m. on the .... day of ...., 20............,

and expires at 11:59 p.m. on the .... day of .... 20 .... (Expiry Date).

EXAMPLE   *The Seller's Perspective*

Salesperson Wilson is seeking property for a buyer client. The client has signed a Buyer Representation Agreement providing that a commission can be collected from that buyer, but also when offered by a co-operating brokerage or seller.

A suitable unlisted home is located. The seller agrees to the showing and will pay a commission, but wants no further involvement; i.e., a representation relationship.

A *Seller Customer Service Agreement* is signed acknowledging the arrangement, while confirming that a representation relationship does not exist and that an agreement of purchase and sale will be negotiated with the brokerage representing the buyer.

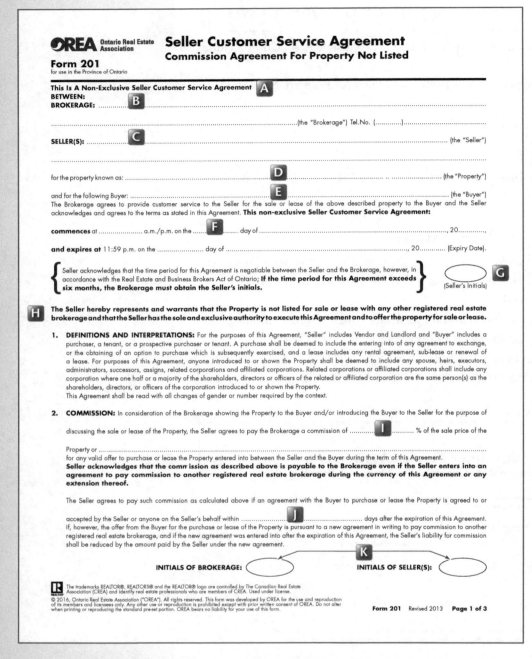

PREPARATION GUIDELINES

A This is a non-exclusive agreement, but note that the seller represents and warrants that the property is not listed for sale or lease with any other brokerage (see H).

B Insert full registered brokerage name. A broker's or salesperson's name is never inserted.

C Insert full names of registered owner(s). Non-owner spousal consent is located on page 3.

D Insert municipal address for urban properties. Use acceptable rural address as per local practice. It is advisable to include the full legal description for offer drafting purposes.

E Insert full names of buyer or buyers.

F A commencement and termination date must be included pursuant to requirements set out in REBBA 2002 (see Code of Ethics, Sec. 11: Contents of Written Agreements).

G The date on the service agreement cannot exceed six months without the seller's informed consent and initials (see Code of Ethics, Sec. 11: Contents of Written Agreements).

H This clause is bolded for emphasis, as this warranty relates to the property not being current-

ly listed with any other brokerage and that the seller has the right to sign this agreement. The seller should be aware that a commission is payable even if the seller enters into a listing agreement or commission agreement with another registered real estate broker (see bolded section in *Clause 2: Commission*).

I Include commission percentage rate, agreed amount or a combination of both (See REBBA, Sec. 36).

J Include time period, typically 60 to 90 days for residential property or as agreed by the parties.

K Initials of an authorized representative of the brokerage and the seller's initials must be included. Further, an authorized individual's initials are required in the case of a corporation.

An important clause that should be carefully reviewed with the seller following explanation of various services provided by the brokerage (e.g., *Working with a REALTOR®* OREA Form 810). Emphasize that the seller is not represented and that the brokerage's client is the buyer and primary duties to protect and promote that buyer/client are uppermost.

 Limited duties to seller are outlined, as well as an acknowledgement that payment of commission does not create or constitute representation of the seller as a client. Also, an appropriate disclosure is provided regarding representing other sellers or providing customer services to more than one seller or buyer for the same trade.

The seller warrants that spousal consent is not necessary. If spousal consent is required, an appropriate signature line is provided (see **R**).

The Seller agrees to pay such commission as described above even if the transaction contemplated by an agreement to purchase or lease agreed to or accepted by the Seller or anyone on the Seller's behalf is not completed, if such non-completion is owing or attributable to the Seller's default or neglect. The commission as described above shall be payable on the date set for completion of the purchase of the Property or, in the case of a lease or tenancy, the earlier of the date of occupancy by the tenant or the execution of the lease or the date set for commencement of the lease or tenancy. Any deposit in respect of any agreement where the transaction has been completed shall first be applied to reduce the commission payable. Should such amounts paid to the Brokerage from the deposit or by the Seller's solicitor not be sufficient, the Seller shall be liable to pay to the Brokerage on demand, any deficiency in commission and taxes owing on such commission. All amounts set out as commission are to be paid plus applicable taxes on such commission.

3. **REPRESENTATION AND CUSTOMER SERVICE:** The Seller acknowledges that the Brokerage has provided the Seller with written information explaining agency relationships, including information on Seller Representation, Sub-Agency, Buyer Representation, Multiple Representation and Customer Service. The Seller acknowledges that the Brokerage will be providing customer service to the Seller and will not be representing the interests of the Seller in a transaction.

The Brokerage may be representing the interests of the Buyer for the transaction. When the Brokerage is representing the Buyer, the Buyer is considered to be the Brokerage's client, and the Brokerage's primary duties are to protect and promote the interests of the Buyer/client. The Brokerage will disclose all pertinent information to a Buyer/client obtained from or about the Seller.

Even though the Brokerage's primary duties may be to the Buyer, the Brokerage may provide many valuable customer services to the Seller. When providing customer service to the Seller, the Brokerage's duties to the Seller include:
   - the **Ethical** duty to deal fairly, honestly and with integrity;
   - the **Legal** duty to exercise due care when answering questions and providing information; and
   - the **Legal** duty to avoid misrepresentation.

The Seller further acknowledges and agrees that the payment of commission by the Seller to the Brokerage will not create or constitute representation by the Brokerage of the Seller as a client.

The Seller understands and agrees that the Brokerage also provides representation and customer service to other sellers and buyers.

If the Brokerage represents or provides customer service to more than one seller or buyer for the same trade, the Brokerage shall, in writing, at the earliest practicable opportunity and before any offer is made, inform all sellers and buyers of the nature of the Brokerage's relationship to each seller and buyer.

4. **DEPOSIT:** The Seller and Brokerage agree that the deposit for a transaction shall be held in trust by the Brokerage.

Any deposit in respect of any agreement where the transaction has been completed shall be first applied to reduce the commission payable. Should such amounts paid to the Brokerage from the deposit or by the Seller's solicitor not be sufficient, the Seller shall be liable to pay the Brokerage on demand, any deficiency in commission and taxes owing on such commission.

5. **FINDERS FEES:** The Seller acknowledges that the Brokerage may be receiving a finder's fee, reward and/or referral incentive, and the Seller consents to any such benefit being received and retained by the Brokerage in addition to the commission as described above.

6. **INSURANCE:** The Seller warrants the Property is insured, including personal liability insurance against any claims or lawsuits resulting from bodily injury or property damage to others caused in any way on or at the Property and the Seller indemnifies the Brokerage and all of its employees, representatives, salespersons and brokers for and against any claims against the Brokerage made by anyone who attends or visits the Property.

7. **VERIFICATION OF INFORMATION:** The Seller authorizes the Brokerage to obtain any information from any regulatory authorities, governments, mortgagees or others affecting the Property and the Seller agrees to execute and deliver such further authorizations in this regard as may be reasonably required.

8. **USE AND DISTRIBUTION OF INFORMATION:** The Seller consents to the collection, use and disclosure of personal information by the Brokerage for the purpose of compiling, retaining and publishing any statistics including data which may be used by the Brokerage to conduct comparative market analyses; and make such other use of information as the Brokerage deems appropriate in connection with the listing, marketing, selling or leasing of real estate.

9. **FAMILY LAW ACT:** The Seller hereby warrants that spousal consent is not necessary under the provisions of the Family Law Act, R.S.O. 1990, unless the Seller's spouse has executed the consent hereinafter provided.

10. **SUCCESSORS AND ASSIGNS:** The heirs, executors, administrators, successors and assigns of the undersigned are bound by the terms of this Agreement.

11. **CONFLICT OR DISCREPANCY:** If there is any conflict or discrepancy between any provision added to this Agreement (including any Schedule attached hereto) and any provision in the standard pre-set portion hereof, the added provision shall supersede the standard pre-set provision to the extent of such conflict or discrepancy. This Agreement, including any Schedule attached hereto, shall constitute the entire Agreement between the Seller and the Brokerage. There is no representation, warranty, collateral agreement or condition, which affects this Agreement other than as expressed herein.

INITIALS OF BROKERAGE: ⬭   INITIALS OF SELLER(S): ⬭

 Form 201   Revised 2013   **Page 2 of 3**

12. ELECTRONIC COMMUNICATION: This Agreement and any agreements, notices or other communications contemplated thereby may be transmitted by means of electronic systems, in which case signatures shall be deemed to be original. The transmission of this Agreement by the Seller by electronic means shall be deemed to confirm the Seller has retained a true copy of the Agreement.

O **13. SOLD SIGN:** The Seller hereby agrees and consents by the Seller initialling this term of the Agreement that, upon the Seller entering into a binding Agreement to sell or lease the property with the Buyer, the Brokerage is authorized to place the Brokerage's Sold/Leased sign on the property.

(Seller's Initials)

14. SCHEDULE(S) .... attached hereto form(s) part of this Agreement.

THE BROKERAGE AGREES TO PROVIDE CUSTOMER SERVICE TO THE SELLER IN AN ENDEAVOUR TO OBTAIN THE ACCEPTANCE OF AN AGREEMENT TO PURCHASE OR LEASE BETWEEN THE SELLER AND THE BUYER.

P

.... DATE.................................. ....
(Authorized to bind the Brokerage)   (Name of Person Signing)

THIS AGREEMENT HAS BEEN READ AND FULLY UNDERSTOOD BY ME AND I ACKNOWLEDGE THIS DATE I HAVE SIGNED UNDER SEAL.
SIGNED, SEALED AND DELIVERED I have hereunto set my hand and seal:

Q

.... ● DATE ....
(Signature of Seller)   (Seal)   (Tel. No.)

.... ● DATE ....
(Signature of Seller)   (Seal)

SPOUSAL CONSENT: The undersigned spouse of the Seller hereby consents to the listing of the Property herein pursuant to the provisions of the Family Law Act, R.S.O. 1990 and hereby agrees that he/she will execute all necessary or incidental documents to further any transaction provided for herein.

R

.... ● DATE ....
(Spouse)   (Seal)

S   **DECLARATION OF INSURANCE**

The broker/salesperson ....
                                           (Name of Broker/Salesperson)

hereby declares that he/she is insured as required by the Real Estate and Business Brokers Act (REBBA) and Regulations.

....
                               (Signature(s) of Broker/Salesperson)

T   **ACKNOWLEDGEMENT**

The Seller(s) hereby acknowledge that the Seller(s) fully understand the terms of this Agreement and have received a true copy

of this Agreement on the .... day of ...., 20 ....

.... Date: ....
(Signature of Seller)

.... Date: ....
(Signature of Seller)

Form 201   Revised 2013   **Page 3 of 3**

O The seller must approve the use of a sold/leased sign by affixing his or her initials.

P A person authorized to bind the brokerage (a broker or salesperson employed by that brokerage) must sign and date his or her signature.

Q Usual signature required. For corporations, an authorized signature is required, along with the individual's title and corporate seal. If the seal is not used, insert the words: *I have the authority to bind the corporation.*

R Spousal signature follows guidelines set out previously.

S A declaration of insurance is prepared and signed by the applicable broker or salesperson.

T Seller acknowledges understanding and receipt of the agreement.

Buyer Customer Service Agreement

The *Buyer Customer Service Agreement* (OREA Form 310) establishes a contract between the brokerage and the buyer for customer services only. The form, designed for situations when the buyer is not represented by the brokerage, achieves several objectives:

- Confirms that no commission is paid for customer service provided by the brokerage, unless specifically set out in writing.
- Confirms in writing that the brokerage is not the representative of the buyer.
- States that the brokerage is not liable for any defects, whether latent or patent to the land or improvements. Information provided by the seller may not have been verified and is not warranted by the brokerage.
- The buyer acknowledges having been advised to make his or her own enquiries to confirm the condition of the property.

OREA Ontario Real Estate Association

Form 310
for use in the Province of Ontario

Buyer Customer Service Agreement
For Use When the Buyer is Not Represented By the Brokerage

This Is A Non-Exclusive Buyer Customer Service Agreement

BETWEEN:
BROKERAGE:.., Tel.No. (..........)....................................

ADDRESS:...

.... Fax.No. (..........)....................................
hereinafter referred to as the Brokerage.

AND:
BUYER(S):.., hereinafter referred to as the
Buyer, for the purpose of locating a real property meeting the following general description:

Property Type (Use):...

....

Geographic Location:..

....
In consideration of the Brokerage providing customer service to the Buyer for the purchase or lease of a real property of the general description indicated
above, the Buyer acknowledges and agrees to the terms as stated in this Agreement.

EXAMPLE   *The Buyer's Perspective*

The buyers arrive at an open house to view the property. The salesperson in attendance represents the seller and explains his or her role at the earliest practicable point in the conversation.

The buyers, having bought and sold several properties, feel comfortable receiving only customer service and sign the *Buyer Customer Service Agreement*.

The salesperson answers questions posed by the buyers, points out the home's features and honestly assists where possible in the decision-making process. The salesperson also carries out any other duties for that customer, as dictated by REBBA 2002; e.g., prompt delivery of documents.

At no time does the salesperson undertake any activities or negotiate on the buyer's behalf. The salesperson must protect and promote the interests of the seller client.

PREPARATION GUIDELINES

Preparation guidelines generally follow those described for the *Seller Customer Service Agreement* (OREA Form 201), with appropriate modifications. However, take particular note of the following clauses:

OREA Ontario Real Estate Association

Buyer Customer Service Agreement

For Use When the Buyer is Not Represented By the Brokerage

Form 310
for use in the Province of Ontario

This Is A Non-Exclusive Buyer Customer Service Agreement

BETWEEN:

BROKERAGE:.., Tel.No. (..........)................................

ADDRESS:...

.... Fax.No. (..........)................................

hereinafter referred to as the Brokerage.

AND:

BUYER(S):.., hereinafter referred to as the

Buyer, for the purpose of locating a real property meeting the following general description:

Property Type (Use):...

....

Geographic Location:...

In consideration of the Brokerage providing customer service to the Buyer for the purchase or lease of a real property of the general description indicated above, the Buyer acknowledges and agrees to the terms as stated in this Agreement.

This non-exclusive Buyer Customer Service Agreement:

commences at......................a.m./p.m. on the................................day of.., 20............,

and expires at 11:59 p.m. on the................................day of......................................, 20.............(Expiry Date).

{ Buyer acknowledges that the time period for this Agreement is negotiable between the Buyer and the Brokerage, however, in accordance with the Real Estate and Business Brokers Act of Ontario (2002), **if the time period for this Agreement exceeds six months, the Brokerage must obtain the Buyer's initials.** } (Buyer's Initials)

The Buyer hereby warrants that the Buyer is not a party to a buyer representation agreement with any other registered real estate brokerage for the purchase or lease of a real property of the general description indicated above.

1. **DEFINITIONS AND INTERPRETATIONS:** For the purposes of this Buyer Customer Service Agreement ("Authority" or "Agreement"), "Buyer" includes purchaser and tenant, a "seller" includes a vendor, a landlord or a prospective seller, vendor or landlord and a "real estate board" includes a real estate association. A purchase shall be deemed to include the entering into of any agreement to exchange, or the obtaining of an option to purchase which is subsequently exercised, and a lease includes any rental agreement, sub-lease or renewal of a lease. This Agreement shall be read with all changes of gender or number required by the context.

2. **COMMISSION:** For a Buyer Customer Service Agreement between Buyer and Brokerage, there is no requirement for the Buyer to pay the Brokerage compensation for the customer service provided by the Brokerage, unless otherwise agreed to in writing.

3. **REPRESENTATION AND CUSTOMER SERVICE:** The Buyer acknowledges that the Brokerage has provided the Buyer with written information explaining agency relationships, including information on Seller Representation, Sub-Agency, Buyer Representation, Multiple Representation and Customer Service. The Buyer acknowledges that the Brokerage will be providing customer service to the Buyer and will not be representing the interests of the Buyer in a transaction. The Brokerage may be representing the interests of the seller as an agent or sub-agent. When the Brokerage is representing the seller, the seller is considered to be the Brokerage's client, and the Brokerage's primary duties are to protect and promote the interests of the seller/client. The Brokerage will disclose all pertinent information to a seller/client obtained from or about the Buyer.

   Even though the Brokerage's primary duties may be to the seller, the Brokerage may provide many valuable customer services to the Buyer.

   When providing customer service to the Buyer, the Brokerage's duties to the Buyer include:
   - the **Ethical** duty to deal fairly, honestly and with integrity;
   - the **Legal** duty to exercise due care when answering questions and providing information; and
   - the **Legal** duty to avoid misrepresentation.

   The Buyer acknowledges that the Buyer may not be shown or offered all properties that may be of interest to the Buyer. The Buyer hereby agrees that the terms of any buyer's offer or agreement to purchase or lease the property will not be disclosed to any other buyer.

   The Buyer understands and agrees that the Brokerage also provides representation and customer service to other buyers and sellers. If the Brokerage represents or provides customer service to more than one seller or buyer for the same trade, the Brokerage shall, in writing, at the earliest practicable opportunity and before any offer is made, inform all sellers and buyers of the nature of the Brokerage's relationship to each seller and buyer.

   INITIALS OF BROKERAGE: ( )   **INITIALS OF BUYER(S):** ( )

The trademarks REALTOR®, REALTORS® and the REALTOR® logo are controlled by The Canadian Real Estate ...

A **Commission** *(no commission is due unless agreed to in writing)*

The buyer is not responsible to compensate the brokerage for services provided under this agreement, unless specifically agreed to in writing.

Buyer Customer Service Agreement, Page 2 of 2

4. INDEMNIFICATION: The Brokerage and representatives of the Brokerage are trained in dealing in real estate but are not qualified in determining the physical condition of the land or any improvements thereon. The Buyer agrees that the Brokerage and representatives of the Brokerage will not be liable for any defects, whether latent or patent, to the land or improvements thereon. All information supplied by the seller or landlord or the listing brokerage may not have been verified and is not warranted by the Brokerage as being accurate and will be relied on by the Buyer at the Buyer's own risk. The Buyer acknowledges having been advised to make their own enquiries to confirm the condition of the property.

5. FINDERS FEE: The Buyer acknowledges that the Brokerage may be receiving a finder's fee, reward and/or referral incentive, and the Buyer consents to any such benefit being received and retained by the Brokerage in addition to the commission as described above.

6. CONSUMER REPORTS: The Buyer is hereby notified that a Consumer Report containing credit and/or personal information may be referred to in connection with this Agreement and any subsequent transaction.

7. USE AND DISTRIBUTION OF INFORMATION: The Buyer consents to the collection, use and disclosure of personal information by the Brokerage for such purposes that relate to the real estate services provided by the Brokerage to the Buyer including, but not limited to: locating, assessing and qualifying properties for the Buyer; advertising on behalf of the Buyer; providing information as needed to third parties retained by the Buyer to assist in a transaction (e.g., financial institutions, building inspectors, etc...); and such other use of the Buyer's information as is consistent with the services provided by the Brokerage in connection with the purchase or prospective purchase of the property.

The Buyer agrees that the sale and related information regarding any property purchased by the Buyer through the Brokerage may be retained and disclosed by the Brokerage and/or real estate board(s) (if the property is an MLS® Listing) for reporting, appraisal and statistical purposes and for such other use of the information as the Brokerage and/or board deems appropriate in connection with the listing, marketing and selling of real estate, including conducting comparative market analyses.

The Buyer acknowledges that the information, personal or otherwise ("information"), provided to the real estate board or association may be stored on databases located outside of Canada, in which case the information would be subject to the laws of the jurisdiction in which the information is located.

8. CONFLICT OR DISCREPANCY: If there is any conflict or discrepancy between any provision added to this Agreement and any provision in the standard pre-set portion hereof, the added provision shall supersede the standard pre-set provision to the extent of such conflict or discrepancy. This Agreement, including any provisions added to this Agreement, shall constitute the entire Agreement between the Buyer and the Brokerage. There is no representation, warranty, collateral agreement or condition, which affects this Agreement other than as expressed herein.

9. ELECTRONIC COMMUNICATION: This Buyer Customer Service Agreement and any agreements, notices or other communications contemplated thereby may be transmitted by means of electronic systems, in which case signatures shall be deemed to be original. The transmission of this Agreement by the Buyer by electronic means shall be deemed to confirm the Buyer has retained a true copy of the Agreement.

10. SCHEDULE(S): .... attached hereto form(s) part of this Agreement.

THE BROKERAGE AGREES TO ASSIST THE BUYER IN LOCATING A REAL PROPERTY OF THE GENERAL DESCRIPTION INDICATED ABOVE AND TO PROVIDE CUSTOMER SERVICE TO THE BUYER IN AN ENDEAVOUR TO PROCURE THE ACCEPTANCE OF AN AGREEMENT TO PURCHASE OR LEASE A PROPERTY ACCEPTABLE TO THE BUYER.

.... DATE.. ....
(Authorized to bind the Brokerage)   (Name of Person Signing)

THIS AGREEMENT HAS BEEN READ AND FULLY UNDERSTOOD BY ME AND I ACKNOWLEDGE THIS DATE I HAVE SIGNED UNDER SEAL. Any representations contained herein are true to the best of my knowledge, information and belief.

SIGNED, SEALED AND DELIVERED I have hereunto set my hand and seal:

....   ● DATE...
(Signature of Buyer)   (Seal)

....   ● DATE...
(Signature of Buyer)   (Seal)

Address..

(...............)..   (...............)..
Tel. No.   FAX No.

DECLARATION OF INSURANCE

The broker/salesperson..
                                                                (Name of Broker/Salesperson)
hereby declares that he/she is insured as required by the Real Estate and Business Brokers Act (REBBA) and Regulations.

B **Indemnification** *(brokerage not liable regarding patent or latent defects)*

The buyer agrees that the brokerage is not responsible for latent or patent defects and further highlights the fact that information provided by the seller is not verified, nor warrantied by the brokerage and that the buyer should take appropriate action to independently confirm the condition of the property.

C **Provision Regarding Consumer Reports**

This disclosure is mandated under the *Consumer Reporting Act* in situations where credit and/or personal information may be referred to in regard to services provided under this agreement or a subsequent transaction.

D **Expanded Provision Regarding Use and Distribution of Information**

This clause sets out the buyer's agreement to the collection of personal information in relation to services provided under this agreement, as well as consenting to the sharing of sale and related information about a purchased property, either by the brokerage or by the real estate board (if the property is sold on MLS®).

COMMON ERRORS AND PROBLEMS

Representation problems typically arise from:

- Not discussing representation with buyers and sellers at the earliest practicable opportunity.
- Lack of, or incomplete disclosure, to clients and customers as required by REBBA 2002.
- Failure to complete proper documentation and incorrect form preparation.
- Exceeding the scope of authority granted by the client.
- Failure to market property in a diligent manner for a seller client or failure to diligently pursue all suitable properties on behalf of a buyer client.
- Failing to recognize conflicts of interest arising when acquiring property for personal use and not making complete disclosure as required under REBBA, Sec. 32.
- Failure to document services.
- Failure to document promises/commitments.
- Failure to disclose additional remuneration obtained (e.g., finder's fees) to the client.
- Nondisclosure or misrepresentation of material information.
- Breach of duties as set out in the representation or service agreement.
- Failure to precisely carry out multiple representation responsibilities, including disclosure requirements for both buyer and seller.

The Four D's	MARKET MEMO

How can a registrant best advance professionalism and adhere to disclosure provisions? While disclosure requirements may appear complex, registrants are best to follow a handy disclosure reminder based on the four D's:

DECIDE	Make your decision regarding who you will be representing in the transaction.
DISCLOSE	Ensure that the disclosure is made as soon as is practically possible.
DOCUMENT	Put the disclosure in writing.
DO	Do what you said you were going to do!

The buyer was seeking suitable property to develop a greenhouse/nursery operation based on five criteria. The desired property would require three-phase electric power, natural gas, have good drainage, be roughly square and be level. During the search, a property advertised by a real estate brokerage was identified as a possibility. The ad described the property as a fabulous horse farm with gravel based land [that] provides the best possible drainage.

The listing salesperson and the prospective buyer visited the property on several occasions. Various conversations occurred during these showings, as well as in separate instances when the buyer went directly to discuss specifics with the seller. As a consequence, a number of issues arose; e.g., a leaking roof, an odour in one of the rooms of the main house and the matter of water supply. In regard to the latter, the seller confirmed that the water supply was adequate for its present purpose, that is, servicing a 60-horse farm. The buyer made his own investigation concerning soil type and drainage issues. Following negotiations, an offer of $1,600,000 was accepted with the option to purchase either the property or shares of the controlling company.

The buyer sued for negligence on the salesperson's part given problems following closing. While negotiations and contacts between the parties were somewhat complex, the evidence supported the fact that the salesperson had been diligent in regard to disclosure of his dual agency (referred to statutorily as multiple representation) status, had attempted to honestly represent both parties and had made the buyers aware of property conditions. The Court was satisfied, given the ongoing efforts and assistance provided by the listing salesperson, that most of the allegations of negligence were unfounded. This was due in no small way to the fact that full disclosure of the dual relationship was given and supported by appropriate documentation. Claims of misrepresentation and negligence (including vicarious liability on the part of the brokerage) were dismissed. The only representation found false involved the seller's statements concerning the room odour and $2,000 was awarded to remedy that problem.

Reference   Houweling v. Imperial Equestrian Centre Ltd., 47 R.P.R. (3d) 151

COMMENTARY

The important message for registrants centres on actions, representations, documentation and follow-up required on complex transactions. In this situation, the buyer visited the premises on numerous occasions, discussed various features and drawbacks, and was involved in several offers and counter offers prior to negotiating a sale.

The salesperson's conduct was central to the finding of no negligence. This individual provided a brochure explaining agency (representation) services provided, obtained written acknowledgement, correctly advertised the property and allowed the buyer ample latitude to investigate and satisfy himself on various issues.

KNOWLEDGE INTEGRATION

Notables

- Multiple representation involves any situation where two or more parties in a real estate transaction are represented by a single brokerage.

- Multiple representation is always inherently dangerous, as competing interests are involved.

- The key to successfully working in a multiple representation situation is to ensure that the brokerage (and its representatives) act in an impartial manner, equally protecting the interests of multiple clients.

- Multiple representation disclosure is best viewed in two steps: Step 1—Disclosure Before Agreement and Step 2—Disclosure Before Offer.

- The *Listing Agreement* (OREA Form 200) provides various wordings to align with statutory requirements for Step 1, set out in the Code of Ethics, Sec. 10.

- Sec. 16 and 17 of the Code of Ethics detail further disclosure requirements for Step 2.

- The *Confirmation of Co-operation and Representation* (OREA Form 320) is used to confirm both representation and co-operation between brokerages.

- A customer is someone who has entered into some form of service agreement with a brokerage, but is not represented as a client by that brokerage.

- Customer service agreements must meet many of the same requirements as set out for representation agreements.

- The *Seller Customer Service Agreement* (OREA Form 201) is designed for property not listed.

- The *Buyer Customer Service Agreement* (OREA Form 310) is designed for situations in which a buyer is not being represented as a client, but seeks selected services from the brokerage.

- Common errors and omissions relating to representation typically focus on failure to disclose in a timely manner and not fully documenting such disclosure.

- The best guideline for registrants in the marketplace is the Four D's: Decide, Disclose, Document and Do.

Glossary

Client

Customer

Imputed Knowledge

Multiple Representation

Service Agreement

Strategic Thinking For Your Career

Questions are included to assist in developing your new career. No answers are provided.

1. What procedures are currently in place at my intended employing brokerage concerning representation disclosure and adherence to the Code of Ethics provisions?

2. If I am holding open houses for a seller client, what representation-related information should be readily available when discussing the home with prospective buyers?

3. Can I readily and clearly outline the concepts and details presented in *Working with a REALTOR®* (OREA Form 810) and the *Listing Agreement* (OREA Form 200) to prospective sellers?

4. Is the *Confirmation of Co-operation and Representation* (OREA Form 320) or similar form commonly used in the local marketplace?

5. Can I clearly differentiate between representation agreements and customer service agreements when discussing these options with buyers and sellers?

Chapter Mini-Review

Solutions are located in the Appendix.

1. The issue of competing interests is a major source of conflict for a brokerage when attempting to represent more than one client.

   ○ True   ○ False

2. Under multiple representation, as set out in the *Listing Agreement,* (OREA Form 200) the listing brokerage can disclose what the seller may or will accept, if written instruction to do so is given by the seller.

   ○ True   ○ False

3. A key question should litigation arise over multiple representation is: *Did the salesperson's actual conduct align with the stated procedure as set out in the representation form?*

   ○ True   ○ False

4. According to the Code of Ethics, a brokerage need only disclose to a client the services provided to that client when discussing a representation agreement.

   ○ True   ○ False

5. *Working with a REALTOR®* (OREA Form 810), published by the Ontario Real Estate Association, provides a description of services potentially provided by a brokerage, but does not include an acknowledgement.

   ○ True   ○ False

6. The *Confirmation of Co-operation and Representation* (OREA Form 320) is typically signed at the time that the listing agreement or buyer representation agreement is signed.

   ○ True   ○ False

7. The *Listing Agreement* (OREA Form 200) contains a provision relating to the seller's consent to obtaining a finder's fee, but such a provision is not included in the *Buyer Representation Agreement* (OREA Form 300).

   ○ True   ○ False

8. A seller customer service agreement does not typically include any reference to the payment of commission to the brokerage.

   ○ True   ○ False

9. A customer service agreement with a buyer may require that the brokerage protect and promote the interests of that customer.

   ○ True   ○ False

10. Minimum content requirements for agreements apply equally to representation agreements and service agreements.

    ○ True   ○ False

11. The *Confirmation of Co-operation and Representation* (OREA Form 320) can be used for situations involving multiple representation or co-operating brokerages, but does not apply to circumstances involving single representation.

    ○ True   ○ False

12. The *Buyer Customer Service Agreement* (OREA Form 310) provides that the buyer must pay compensation to the brokerage for services rendered.

    ○ True   ○ False

Active Learning Exercises

Solutions are located in the Appendix.

■ Exercise 1   Fill-in-the-Blanks

Seller Watson selects Salesperson James of ABC Realty Inc. to represent her in the sale of a property. Salesperson Janson of XYZ Real Estate Ltd. arranges an appointment to show the property to Mrs. Williams, who has signed a buyer representation agreement with Janson.

AVAILABLE TERMS/PHRASES	
client	Step 2: Disclosure Before Offer
Confirmation of Co-operation and Representation	*Working with a REALTOR® Form*
James	Watson
Janson	Williams
listing	

1.1   Salesperson James provides the *Working with a REALTOR®* form to the seller client and receives written acknowledgement of .... status.

1.2   Salesperson James then has Watson sign a (an) .... agreement, which sets out the agreement between them and details such things as representation procedures and commission payment.

1.3   Salesperson Janson provides a (an) .... to the buyer to comply with the Code of Ethics, Sec 10 regarding the types of service alternatives available to the buyer.

1.4   Salesperson Janson, who drafts the agreement of purchase and sale, also completes a (an) .... to confirm the roles of both listing and co-operating brokerages.

1.5   The form, prepared under 1.4, is then signed by

.... ,

.... ,

.... and

....

1.6   The signing of this form meets requirements as set out in this chapter under ....

■ Exercise 2   Questions, Questions

Mr. and Mrs. Jones are interested in purchasing a home and have just arrived at your brokerage. You provide the *Working with a REALTOR®* form (OREA Form 810) to clearly establish options available through the brokerage by way of representation and customer services. The potential clients have three questions. Provide a short answer for each.

2.1   Why is a form necessary to disclose the type of services available?

2.2   If we sign the acknowledgement in this form, are we obligated in any way to ABC Realty Inc. and why is an acknowledgement needed?

2.3   Why do we have to decide at this point whether we want to work with you on a customer or client basis? Couldn't we wait until we find the right house and then decide?

▣ Exercise 3   The Listing Agreement

John and Mary Smith have signed a listing agreement with ABC Realty Inc. using the *Listing Agreement* (OREA Form 200). See illustration provided on the following pages. Answer the following questions based on that completed form.

3.1   If Mr. and Mrs. Jones view the Smith property through a co-operating brokerage and purchase it on April 30, 20xx directly from Smith, what rights does ABC Realty Inc. have concerning commission?

3.2   Mr. and Mrs. Smith accept an offer of $444,500, but the transaction does not close due to the buyer's financial difficulties. Can ABC Realty Inc. collect the commission? Explain.

3.3   Mr. Smith receives a late evening call from an acquaintance on January 24, 20xx. This individual may be interested in purchasing the home. According to the terms of the listing, what procedures should Smith follow?

3.4   If another buyer, as a client of ABC Realty Inc., is introduced to the property and is competing with Mr. and Mrs. Jones to purchase that property, what must be done by ABC Realty Inc.?

3.5   What happens if the seller refuses to allow multiple representation?

Exercise 3   Listing Agreement—Page 1 of 3

OREA Ontario Real Estate Association   **Listing Agreement**
Authority to Offer for Sale

Form 200
for use in the Province of Ontario

This is a Multiple Listing Service® Agreement    JS MS   OR   Exclusive Listing Agreement   **EXCLUSIVE**
(Seller's Initials)   (Seller's Initials)

BETWEEN:
BROKERAGE: .... ABC Realty Inc. ....

..........(the "Listing Brokerage") Tel.No. (..416..) 555-1212 ....

SELLER(S): .... Mary Smith and John Smith ....(the "Seller")

In consideration of the Listing Brokerage listing the real property **for sale** known as.......... 124 Main Street, Anycity ....

.... Lot 96, Plan M 314 ....(the "Property")

the Seller hereby gives the Listing Brokerage the **exclusive and irrevocable** right to act as the Seller's agent, **commencing** at 12:01 a.m. on the ....15th.... day

of .... January ...., 20..XX.., **until** 11:59 p.m. on the ..30th.. day of .... April ...., 20..XX.. (the "Listing Period"),

{ Seller acknowledges that the length of the Listing Period is negotiable between the Seller and the Listing Brokerage and, if an MLS® listing, may be subject to minimum requirements of the real estate board, however, in accordance with the Real Estate and Business Brokers Act (2002), **if the Listing Period exceeds six months, the Listing Brokerage must obtain the Seller's initials.** }
(Seller's Initials)

to offer the property **for sale** at a price of: Dollars (CDN$) $449,000.00

.... Four Hundred and Forty-Nine Thousand--Dollars

and upon the terms particularly set out herein, or at such other price and/or terms acceptable to the Seller. It is understood that the price and/or terms set out herein are at the Seller's personal request, after full discussion with the Listing Brokerage's representative regarding potential market value of the Property.

The Seller hereby represents and warrants that the Seller is not a party to any other listing agreement for the Property or agreement to pay commission to any other real estate brokerage for the sale of the property.

1. **DEFINITIONS AND INTERPRETATIONS:** For the purposes of this Listing Agreement ("Authority" or "Agreement"), "Seller" includes vendor, a "buyer" includes a purchaser, or a prospective purchaser and a "real estate board" includes a real estate association. A purchase shall be deemed to include the entering into of any agreement to exchange, or the obtaining of an option to purchase which is subsequently exercised. This Agreement shall be read with all changes of gender or number required by the context. For purposes of this Agreement, anyone introduced to or shown the Property shall be deemed to include any spouse, heirs, executors, administrators, successors, assigns, related corporations and affiliated corporations. Related corporations or affiliated corporations shall include any corporation where one half or a majority of the shareholders, directors or officers of the related or affiliated corporation are the same person(s) as the shareholders, directors, or officers of the corporation introduced to or shown the Property.

2. **COMMISSION:** In consideration of the Listing Brokerage listing the Property, the Seller agrees to pay the Listing Brokerage a commission of

   ..6.0..% of the sale price of the Property or .... N/A .... for any valid offer to purchase the Property from any source whatsoever obtained during the Listing Period and on the terms and conditions set out in this Agreement **OR** such other terms and conditions as the Seller may accept.

   The Seller further agrees to pay such commission as calculated above if an agreement to purchase is agreed to or accepted by the Seller or anyone

   on the Seller's behalf within ....60.... days after the expiration of the Listing Period (**Holdover Period**), so long as such agreement is with anyone who was introduced to the Property from any source whatsoever during the Listing Period or shown the Property during the Listing Period.

   If, however, the offer for the purchase of the Property is pursuant to a new agreement in writing to pay commission to another registered real estate brokerage, the Seller's liability for commission shall be reduced by the amount paid by the Seller under the new agreement.

   The Seller further agrees to pay such commission as calculated above even if the transaction contemplated by an agreement to purchase agreed to or accepted by the Seller or anyone on the Seller's behalf is not completed, if such non-completion is owing or attributable to the Seller's default or neglect, said commission to be payable on the date set for completion of the purchase of the Property.

   Any deposit in respect of any agreement where the transaction has been completed shall first be applied to reduce the commission payable. Should such amounts paid to the Listing Brokerage from the deposit or by the Seller's solicitor not be sufficient, the Seller shall be liable to pay to the Listing Brokerage on demand, any deficiency in commission and taxes owing on such commission.

   All amounts set out as commission are to be paid plus applicable taxes on such commission.

3. **REPRESENTATION:** The Seller acknowledges that the Listing Brokerage has provided the Seller with information explaining agency relationships, including information on Seller Representation, Sub-agency, Buyer Representation, Multiple Representation and Customer Service. The Seller authorizes the Listing Brokerage to co-operate with any other registered real estate brokerage (co-operating brokerage), and to offer to pay the co-operating

   brokerage a commission of....3.0....% of the sale price of the Property or.......... N/A ....

   .... out of the commission the Seller pays the Listing Brokerage.

INITIALS OF LISTING BROKERAGE: (AL)   **INITIALS OF SELLER(S):** (JS MS)

Form 200   Revised 2015   **Page 1 of 3**

The Seller understands that unless the Seller is otherwise informed, the co-operating brokerage is representing the interests of the buyer in the transaction. The Seller further acknowledges that the Listing Brokerage may be listing other properties that may be similar to the Seller's Property and the Seller hereby consents to the Listing Brokerage listing other properties that may be similar to the Seller's Property without any claim by the Seller of conflict of interest. The Seller hereby appoints the Listing Brokerage as the Seller's agent for the purpose of giving and receiving notices pursuant to any offer or agreement to purchase the property. Unless otherwise agreed in writing between Seller and Listing Brokerage, any commission payable to any other brokerage shall be paid out of the commission the Seller pays the Listing Brokerage, said commission to be disbursed in accordance with the Commission Trust Agreement.

MULTIPLE REPRESENTATION: The Seller hereby acknowledges that the Listing Brokerage may be entering into buyer representation agreements with buyers who may be interested in purchasing the Seller's Property. In the event that the Listing Brokerage has entered into or enters into a buyer representation agreement with a prospective buyer for the Seller's Property, the Listing Brokerage will obtain the Seller's written consent to represent both the Seller and the buyer for the transaction at the earliest practicable opportunity and in all cases prior to any offer to purchase being submitted or presented.

The Seller understands and acknowledges that the Listing Brokerage must be impartial when representing both the Seller and the buyer and equally protect the interests of the Seller and buyer. The Seller understands and acknowledges that when representing both the Seller and the buyer, the Listing Brokerage shall have a duty of full disclosure to both the Seller and the buyer, including a requirement to disclose all factual information about the Property known to the Listing Brokerage.

However, the Seller further understands and acknowledges that the Listing Brokerage shall not disclose:
- that the Seller may or will accept less than the listed price, unless otherwise instructed in writing by the Seller;
- that the buyer may or will pay more than the offered price, unless otherwise instructed in writing by the buyer;
- the motivation of or personal information about the Seller or buyer, unless otherwise instructed in writing by the party to which the information applies or unless failure to disclose would constitute fraudulent, unlawful or unethical practice;
- the price the buyer should offer or the price the Seller should accept; and
- the Listing Brokerage shall not disclose to the buyer the terms of any other offer.

However, it is understood that factual market information about comparable properties and information known to the Listing Brokerage concerning potential uses for the Property will be disclosed to both Seller and buyer to assist them to come to their own conclusions.

Where a Brokerage represents both the Seller and the Buyer (multiple representation), the Brokerage shall not be entitled or authorized to be agent for either the Buyer or the Seller for the purpose of giving and receiving notices.

MULTIPLE REPRESENTATION AND CUSTOMER SERVICE: The Seller understands and agrees that the Listing Brokerage also provides representation and customer service to other sellers and buyers. If the Listing Brokerage represents or provides customer service to more than one seller or buyer for the same trade, the Listing Brokerage shall, in writing, at the earliest practicable opportunity and before any offer is made, inform all sellers and buyers of the nature of the Listing Brokerage's relationship to each seller and buyer.

4. **FINDERS FEES:** The Seller acknowledges that the Brokerage may be receiving a finder's fee, reward and/or referral incentive, and the Seller consents to any such benefit being received and retained by the Brokerage in addition to the commission as described above.

5. **REFERRAL OF ENQUIRIES:** The Seller agrees that during the Listing Period, the Seller shall advise the Listing Brokerage immediately of all enquiries from any source whatsoever, and all offers to purchase submitted to the Seller shall be immediately submitted to the Listing Brokerage before the Seller accepts or rejects the same. If any enquiry during the Listing Period results in the Seller accepting a valid offer to purchase during the Listing Period or within the Holdover Period after the expiration of the Listing Period, the Seller agrees to pay the Listing Brokerage the amount of commission set out above, payable within five (5) days following the Listing Brokerage's written demand therefor.

6. **MARKETING:** The Seller agrees to allow the Listing Brokerage to show and permit prospective buyers to fully inspect the Property during reasonable hours and the Seller gives the Listing Brokerage the sole and exclusive right to place "For Sale" and "Sold" sign(s) upon the Property. The Seller consents to the Listing Brokerage including information in advertising that may identify the Property. The Seller further agrees that the Listing Brokerage shall have sole and exclusive authority to make all advertising decisions relating to the marketing of the Property for sale during the Listing Period. The Seller agrees that the Listing Brokerage will not be held liable in any manner whatsoever for any acts or omissions with respect to advertising by the Listing Brokerage or any other party, other than by the Listing Brokerage's gross negligence or wilful act.

7. **WARRANTY:** The Seller represents and warrants that the Seller has the exclusive authority and power to execute this Authority to offer the Property for sale and that the Seller has informed the Listing Brokerage of any third party interests or claims on the Property such as rights of first refusal, options, easements, mortgages, encumbrances or otherwise concerning the Property, which may affect the sale of the Property.

8. **INDEMNIFICATION AND INSURANCE:** The Seller will not hold the Listing Brokerage and representatives of the Brokerage responsible for any loss or damage to the Property or contents occurring during the term of this Agreement caused by the Listing Brokerage or anyone else by any means, including theft, fire or vandalism, other than by the Listing Brokerage's gross negligence or wilful act. The Seller agrees to indemnify and save harmless the Listing Brokerage and representatives of the Brokerage and any co-operating brokerage from any liability, claim, loss, cost, damage or injury, including but not limited to loss of the commission payable under this Agreement, caused or contributed to by the breach of any warranty or representation made by the Seller in this Agreement or the accompanying data form. The Seller warrants the Property is insured, including personal liability insurance against any claims or lawsuits resulting from bodily injury or property damage to others caused in any way on or at the Property and the Seller indemnifies the Brokerage and all of its employees, representatives, salespersons and brokers (Listing Brokerage) and any co-operating brokerage and all of its employees, representatives, salespersons and brokers (co-operating brokerage) for and against any claims against the Listing Brokerage or co-operating brokerage made by anyone who attends or visits the Property.

9. **FAMILY LAW ACT:** The Seller hereby warrants that spousal consent is not necessary under the provisions of the Family Law Act, R.S.O. 1990, unless the Seller's spouse has executed the consent hereinafter provided.

10. **VERIFICATION OF INFORMATION:** The Seller authorizes the Listing Brokerage to obtain any information affecting the Property from any regulatory authorities, governments, mortgagees or others and the Seller agrees to execute and deliver such further authorizations in this regard as may be reasonably required. The Seller hereby appoints the Listing Brokerage or the Listing Brokerage's authorized representative as the Seller's attorney to execute such documentation as may be necessary to effect obtaining any information as aforesaid. The Seller hereby authorizes, instructs and directs the above noted regulatory authorities, governments, mortgagees or others to release any and all information to the Listing Brokerage.

11. **USE AND DISTRIBUTION OF INFORMATION:** The Seller consents to the collection, use and disclosure of personal information by the Brokerage for the purpose of listing and marketing the Property including, but not limited to: listing and advertising the Property using any medium including the Internet; disclosing Property information to prospective buyers, brokerages, salespersons and others who may assist in the sale of the Property; such other use of

INITIALS OF LISTING BROKERAGE: ⟨ AL ⟩   **INITIALS OF SELLER(S):** ⟨ JS MS ⟩

Form 200   Revised 2015   **Page 2 of 3**

Exercise 3 Listing Agreement—Page 3 of 3

the Seller's personal information as is consistent with listing and marketing of the Property. The Seller consents, if this is an MLS® Listing, to placement of the listing information and sales information by the Brokerage into the database(s) of the MLS® System of the appropriate Board, and to the posting of any documents and other information (including, without limitation, photographs, images, graphics, audio and video recordings, virtual tours, drawings, floor plans, architectural designs, artistic renderings, surveys and listing descriptions) provided by or on behalf of the Seller into the database(s) of the MLS® System of the appropriate Board. The Seller hereby indemnifies and saves harmless the Brokerage and/or any of its employees, servants, brokers or sales representatives from any and all claims, liabilities, suits, actions, losses, costs and legal fees caused by, or arising out of, or resulting from the posting of any documents or other information (including, without limitation, photographs, images, graphics, audio and video recordings, virtual tours, drawings, floor plans, architectural designs, artistic renderings, surveys and listing descriptions) as aforesaid. The Seller acknowledges that the database, within the board's MLS® System is the property of the real estate board(s) and can be licensed, resold, or otherwise dealt with by the board(s). The Seller further acknowledges that the real estate board(s) may: during the term of the listing and thereafter, distribute the information in the database, within the board's MLS® System to any persons authorized to use such service which may include other brokerages, government departments, appraisers, municipal organizations and others; market the Property, at its option, in any medium, including electronic media; during the term of the listing and thereafter, compile, retain and publish any statistics including historical data within the board's MLS® System and retain, reproduce and display photographs, images, graphics, audio and video recordings, virtual tours, drawings, floor plans, architectural designs, artistic renderings, surveys and listing descriptions which may be used by board members to conduct comparative analyses; and make such other use of the information as the Brokerage and/or real estate board(s) deem appropriate, in connection with the listing, marketing and selling of real estate during the term of the listing and thereafter. The Seller acknowledges that the information, personal or otherwise ("information"), provided to the real estate board or association may be stored on databases located outside of Canada, in which case the information would be subject to the laws of the jurisdiction in which the information is located.

In the event that this Agreement expires or is cancelled or otherwise terminated and the Property is not sold, the Seller, by initialling:	⬭	(JS MS)
consent to allow other real estate board members to contact the Seller after expiration or other termination of this Agreement to discuss listing or otherwise marketing the Property.	**Does**	**Does Not**

12. SUCCESSORS AND ASSIGNS: The heirs, executors, administrators, successors and assigns of the undersigned are bound by the terms of this Agreement.

13. CONFLICT OR DISCREPANCY: If there is any conflict or discrepancy between any provision added to this Agreement (including any Schedule attached hereto) and any provision in the standard pre-set portion hereof, the added provision shall supersede the standard pre-set provision to the extent of such conflict or discrepancy. This Agreement, including any Schedule attached hereto, shall constitute the entire Agreement between the Seller and the Listing Brokerage. There is no representation, warranty, collateral agreement or condition which affects this Agreement other than as expressed herein.

14. ELECTRONIC COMMUNICATION: This Listing Agreement and any agreements, notices or other communications contemplated thereby may be transmitted by means of electronic systems, in which case signatures shall be deemed to be original. The transmission of this Agreement by the Seller by electronic means shall be deemed to confirm the Seller has retained a true copy of the Agreement.

15. SCHEDULE(S): ...... N/A .... and data form attached hereto form(s) part of this Agreement.

THE LISTING BROKERAGE AGREES TO MARKET THE PROPERTY ON BEHALF OF THE SELLER AND REPRESENT THE SELLER IN AN ENDEAVOUR TO OBTAIN A VALID OFFER TO PURCHASE THE PROPERTY ON THE TERMS SET OUT IN THIS AGREEMENT OR ON SUCH OTHER TERMS SATISFACTORY TO THE SELLER.

Albert Lee .... DATE *Jan. 14/xx* .... *Albert Lee* ....
(Authorized to bind the Listing Brokerage)   (Name of Person Signing)

THIS AGREEMENT HAS BEEN READ AND FULLY UNDERSTOOD BY ME AND I ACKNOWLEDGE THIS DATE I HAVE SIGNED UNDER SEAL. Any representations contained herein or as shown on the accompanying data form respecting the Property are true to the best of my knowledge, information and belief.

SIGNED, SEALED AND DELIVERED I have hereunto set my hand and seal:

John Smith .... ● DATE *Jan. 14/xx* *416-444-1212*
(Signature of Seller)   (Seal)   (Tel. No.)

Mary Smith .... ● DATE *Jan. 14/xx* ....
(Signature of Seller)   (Seal)

SPOUSAL CONSENT: The undersigned spouse of the Seller hereby consents to the listing of the Property herein pursuant to the provisions of the Family Law Act, R.S.O. 1990 and hereby agrees that he/she will execute all necessary or incidental documents to further any transaction provided for herein.

.... ● DATE ....
(Spouse)   (Seal)

DECLARATION OF INSURANCE

The broker/salesperson............................... Albert Lee ....
(Name of Broker/Salesperson)

hereby declares that he/she is insured as required by the Real Estate and Business Brokers Act (REBBA) and Regulations.

Albert Lee
....
(Signature(s) of Broker/Salesperson)

ACKNOWLEDGEMENT

The Seller(s) hereby acknowledge that the Seller(s) fully understand the terms of this Agreement and have received a true copy of this Agreement

on the ...... 14th ...... day of .... January ...., 20 ...xx......

John Smith .... Date: *Jan. 14/xx* ....
(Signature of Seller)

Mary Smith .... Date: *Jan. 14/xx* ....
(Signature of Seller)

Form 200 Revised 2015 **Page 3 of 3**

■ Exercise 4   The Confirmation of Co-operation and Representation

Salesperson Ward of XYZ Real Estate Ltd. is representing a buyer as a client. The client is interested in development land in the general area of Anycity. Ward has located a property that meets the client's specifications. It is currently listed by Salesperson Lee of ABC Realty Inc., with a total commission of 3.25%. Broker/Owner Brown insists that Ward obtain a *Confirmation of Co-operation and Representation* (OREA Form 320) from ABC Realty Inc. The MLS® listing information states the co-operating brokerage will be paid 1.625%.

4.1   Salesperson Lee is on a 65/35 split and Ward is on a 60/40 split, how much commission will the brokerages and salespersons receive if the property sells for $495,000?

4.2   Complete the *Confirmation of Co-operation and Representation* (OREA Form 320) based on the facts presented (see illustrated form on following page). Insert fictitious names and dates where applicable.

Exercise 4   *Confirmation of Co-operation and Representation—Page 1 of 2*

 **Ontario Real Estate Association**

Form 320
for use in the Province of Ontario

Confirmation of Co-operation and Representation

BUYER: ....

SELLER: ....

For the transaction on the property known as: ....

For the purposes of this Confirmation of Co-operation and Representation, "Seller" includes a vendor, a landlord, or a prospective, seller, vendor or landlord and "Buyer" includes a purchaser, a tenant, or a prospective, buyer, purchaser or tenant, "sale" includes a lease, and "Agreement of Purchase and Sale" includes an Agreement to Lease.

The following information is confirmed by the undersigned salesperson/broker representatives of the Brokerage(s). If a Co-operating Brokerage is involved in the transaction, the brokerages agree to co-operate, in consideration of, and on the terms and conditions as set out below.

DECLARATION OF INSURANCE: The undersigned salesperson/broker representative(s) of the Brokerage(s) hereby declare that he/she is insured as required by the Real Estate and Business Brokers Act, 2002 (REBBA 2002) and Regulations.

1. LISTING BROKERAGE

    a) ☐   The Listing Brokerage represents the interests of the Seller in this transaction. It is further understood and agreed that:

         1) ☐   The Listing Brokerage is not representing or providing Customer Service to the Buyer.
               (If the Buyer is working with a Co-operating Brokerage, Section 3 is to be completed by Co-operating Brokerage)

         2) ☐   The Listing Brokerage is providing Customer Service to the Buyer.

    b) ☐   **MULTIPLE REPRESENTATION:** The Listing Brokerage has entered into a Buyer Representation Agreement with the Buyer and represents the interests of the Seller and the Buyer, with their consent, for this transaction. The Listing Brokerage must be impartial and equally protect the interests of the Seller and the Buyer in this transaction. The Listing Brokerage has a duty of full disclosure to both the Seller and the Buyer, including a requirement to disclose all factual information about the property known to the Listing Brokerage. However, the Listing Brokerage shall not disclose:

- That the Seller may or will accept less than the listed price, unless otherwise instructed in writing by the Seller;
- That the Buyer may or will pay more than the offered price, unless otherwise instructed in writing by the Buyer;
- The motivation of or personal information about the Seller or Buyer, unless otherwise instructed in writing by the party to which the information applies, or unless failure to disclose would constitute fraudulent, unlawful or unethical practice;
- The price the Buyer should offer or the price the Seller should accept;
- And; the Listing Brokerage shall not disclose to the Buyer the terms of any other offer.

However, it is understood that factual market information about comparable properties and information known to the Listing Brokerage concerning potential uses for the property will be disclosed to both Seller and Buyer to assist them to come to their own conclusions.

Additional comments and/or disclosures by Listing Brokerage: (e.g. The Listing Brokerage represents more than one Buyer offering on this property.)

....

....

....

....

2. PROPERTY SOLD BY BUYER BROKERAGE – PROPERTY NOT LISTED

    ☐   The Brokerage .... represent the Buyer and the property is not listed with any real estate brokerage. The Brokerage will be paid
                 (does/does not)

                         ☐   by the Seller in accordance with a Seller Customer Service Agreement

         or: ☐   by the Buyer directly

Additional comments and/or disclosures by Buyer Brokerage: (e.g. The Buyer Brokerage represents more than one Buyer offering on this property.)

....

....

....

....

INITIALS OF BUYER(S)/SELLER(S)/BROKERAGE REPRESENTATIVE(S) (Where applicable)

    ⬭   ⬭   ⬭   ⬭

    BUYER   **CO-OPERATING/BUYER BROKERAGE**   **SELLER**   **LISTING BROKERAGE**

Form 320   Revised 2015   **Page 1 of 2**

3. **Co-operating Brokerage completes Section 3 and Listing Brokerage completes Section 1.**

   CO-OPERATING BROKERAGE- REPRESENTATION:

   a) ☐ The Co-operating Brokerage represents the interests of the Buyer in this transaction.

   b) ☐ The Co-operating Brokerage is providing Customer Service to the Buyer in this transaction.

   c) ☐ The Co-operating Brokerage is not representing the Buyer and has not entered into an agreement to provide customer service(s) to the Buyer.

   CO-OPERATING BROKERAGE- COMMISSION:

   a) ☐ The Listing Brokerage will pay the Co-operating Brokerage the commission as indicated in the MLS® information for the property

   .... to be paid from the amount paid by the Seller to the Listing Brokerage.
   (Commission As Indicated In MLS® Information)

   b) ☐ The Co-operating Brokerage will be paid as follows:

   ....
   ....
   ....

Additional comments and/or disclosures by Co-operating Brokerage: (e.g., The Co-operating Brokerage represents more than one Buyer offering on this property.)

....
....
....

Commission will be payable as described above, plus applicable taxes.

COMMISSION TRUST AGREEMENT: If the above Co-operating Brokerage is receiving payment of commission from the Listing Brokerage, then the agreement between Listing Brokerage and Co-operating Brokerage further includes a Commission Trust Agreement, the consideration for which is the Co-operating Brokerage procuring an offer for a trade of the property, acceptable to the Seller. This Commission Trust Agreement shall be subject to and governed by the MLS® rules and regulations pertaining to commission trusts of the Listing Brokerage's local real estate board, if the local board's MLS® rules and regulations so provide. Otherwise, the provisions of the OREA recommended MLS® rules and regulations shall apply to this Commission Trust Agreement. For the purpose of this Commission Trust Agreement, the Commission Trust Amount shall be the amount noted in Section 3 above. The Listing Brokerage hereby declares that all monies received in connection with the trade shall constitute a Commission Trust and shall be held, in trust, for the Co-operating Brokerage under the terms of the applicable MLS® rules and regulations.

SIGNED BY THE BROKER/SALESPERSON REPRESENTATIVE(S) OF THE BROKERAGE(S) (Where applicable)

....
(Name of Co-operating/Buyer Brokerage)   (Name of Listing Brokerage)

....

Tel:. .... Fax: ....   Tel:. .... Fax: ....

.... Date:..................   .... Date:..................
(Authorized to bind the Co-operating/Buyer Brokerage)   (Authorized to bind the Listing Brokerage)

....
(Print Name of Broker/Salesperson Representative of the Brokerage)   (Print Name of Broker/Salesperson Representative of the Brokerage)

CONSENT FOR MULTIPLE REPRESENTATION (To be completed only if the Brokerage represents more than one client for the transaction)

The Buyer/Seller consent with their initials to their Brokerage representing more than one client for this transaction.

⬭ **BUYER'S INITIALS**   ⬭ **SELLER'S INITIALS**

ACKNOWLEDGEMENT

I have received, read, and understand the above information.

.... Date: .... Date: ....
(Signature of Buyer)   (Signature of Seller)

.... Date: .... Date: ....
(Signature of Buyer)   (Signature of Seller)

4.3 What would happen if Salesperson Lee does not sign the form and payment is not made? Based on your knowledge to date, discuss XYZ Real Estate Ltd.'s options.

CHAPTER 6

Marketing The Property

Introduction

Registrants quickly discover: *A well-listed property is half sold!* But listing activity goes well beyond basic document preparation. Marketing strategy and effective promotion are essential. The listing salesperson who leaves the seller's home with complete, accurate property details, a listing price at or close to market value and a well-formulated promotional plan is well on the way to earning a commission and providing a valuable service in the marketplace.

The route to a successful sale is not assured. Flexibility and ongoing seller communication are key. Even the best laid plans may not produce results, as minimal buyer interest can arise simply due to fluctuating market demand. Subsequent discussions, altered strategies and price adjustments may be necessary. Representing a seller demands your constant attention.

This chapter delves into what constitutes a saleable listing, how to make effective listing presentations for residential property, developing market proposals in the case of commercial property and establishing a practical strategy that includes both print and electronic marketing.

Learning Outcomes

At the conclusion of this chapter, students will be able to:

- List and discuss six characteristics of a saleable listing.
- Demonstrate how listing price can be used as a sales tool including various techniques when presenting a comparative market analysis (i.e., the *Residential Market Comparison Guide* (OREA Form 260)) to the seller.
- Identify methods to improve a listing presentation, along with specific guidelines when counselling the seller regarding the marketing and servicing of a listing.
- Summarize key considerations when gathering property details in order to avoid potential problems, errors and omissions.
- Itemize various marketing methods open to the registrant and explain the fundamentals of both print and electronic marketing strategies.
- Outline key advertising requirements set out in the *Competition Act* regarding abbreviations, advertised price, contests, coupons/market evaluation certificates, fine print/ disclaimers, free offerings, MLS® agreements, pictures/illustrations and promotional claims.
- Outline key advertising requirements set out in REBBA 2002 concerning false advertising, identifying property/parties/agreements and inaccurate representations.
- Discuss working definitions for advertising provided by the Registrar, along with associated guidelines involving advertising claims, promises and statements and required written consents involving information about parties, properties and transactions.

THE SALEABLE LISTING

The saleable listing sets the foundation for productive negotiations and a successful sale. Certain features and/or qualities are associated with saleable listings. These characteristics refer both to property issues and professional skills of the salesperson.

Exclusive	An exclusive listing indicates that the sales representative, on behalf of the brokerage, has obtained a measure of confidence from the seller and has obtained a degree of understanding with the seller as to marketing the property and services to be performed. The brokerage and salesperson have reasonable assurances of commission payment. If an MLS® listing (that is an exclusive listing with special features), the seller has the added advantage of other brokerages' services. Simply put, a written, signed and valid listing is fundamental to a saleable listing.
Reasonable Time Period	Listings require adequate exposure to the market. A reasonable time will vary based on market conditions prevalent at the time of marketing the property, typically available from real estate board reports. Most boards also have a minimum time period for placing a listing on the Multiple Listing Service®.
Accurate Information	The listing is a contract and information must be complete and accurate. Ask the seller to produce documents concerning the property. Verify all information, including the mortgage (using a mortgage verification form). Inaccurate or incomplete information can have disastrous consequences.
Price	Have all the necessary information to establish price. The sellers must understand that the issue is not what they wish to get, but what a willing and informed buyer will likely pay. Experienced salespersons know that listing too high above the market value estimate will only frighten off genuine prospects who would have otherwise made reasonable offers. Generally, the greater the disparity between market value and listing price, the less chance of a sale within a reasonable period of time.
Rapport with the Seller	The salesperson has the responsibility to instill confidence in the relationship with the seller. The best way to do that is by demonstrating knowledge, ability, resourcefulness and a positive attitude. Fully discuss the marketing plan and develop a rapport with the seller early in the relationship.
Knowledge of the Property	A working knowledge of the property is essential. Simple procedures such as opening closet doors, checking the location of light switches, finding out about the neighbours and discovering why the seller purchased the home in the first place, will pay dividends during subsequent showings to prospective buyers.

Listing Price as a Sales Tool

Competitive pricing is uppermost when working with motivated sellers. An attractive listing price begins with a properly prepared comparative market analysis (CMA). The CMA's format is roughly patterned after the direct comparison approach. However, **listing price,** not market value, is being determined based on current market information.

The CMA can be generally described as an analysis to assist the seller in comparing his or her property with others in the marketplace in order to establish a listing price. The CMA helps assess how the seller's property stacks up against the competition based on other similar properties now for sale, sold or expired/removed from the market. Comparable property specifics are limited and no detailed adjustments are made.

In reality, both market value and listing price are inextricably interwoven. Experienced salespersons come equipped to discuss both. That's where client strategy comes into play: *Obtain the highest dollar value for the seller, while positioning the property correctly in the marketplace.* True professionals routinely strike the delicate balance.

The Listing Price	CURIOSITY

The listing price is a price at which a property is offered for sale in the market, frequently referred to as the *asking price*. The listing price may equal market value depending on circumstances surrounding a particular property and seller. Listing price is usually established based on information concerning current sales, available inventory in the market of a comparable nature and properties recently for sale that did not sell and were removed from the market.

Ideally, the listing price is established to attract informed buyers, while being competitive with other properties now on the market that offer similar features and/or benefits. Experience and judgement are required in establishing a realistic listing price that will attract willing buyers and result in the highest price assuming a reasonable exposure of the property to the market. A salesperson's ability to properly establish listing price, given market conditions and supply/demand forces, can directly impact the final selling price of a property.

PRESENTING THE CMA

CMA preparation was addressed in *Land Structures and Real Estate Trading*. The current discussion focuses on how to effectively present the CMA to a seller. A copy of the *Residential Market Comparison Guide* (OREA Form 260) is included in the *Appendix*.

OREA Ontario Real Estate Association

Residential Market Comparison Guide

Form 260 for use in the Province of Ontario

Subject Property:...

Prepared for:...

Prepared by:...   Date:...

COMPARABLES FOR SALE NOW:

Address	Price	Features/Comments

(Use back of form for additional features/comments if required)

When presenting the CMA, be properly prepared with supporting information when reviewing details with the seller.

- **Comparables** Provide detailed information concerning comparables used, particularly the top two or three in each category.

- **Current Trends** Be prepared to discuss major market trends occurring within the immediate neighbourhood and surrounding community.

- **Past Trends**   Have historical information concerning the average length of time properties are on the market until sold, turnover of property in the immediate area, listing to sale price ratios and other relevant indicators.

- **Strengths/Weaknesses**   Objectively evaluate the strengths and weaknesses of the seller's home in relation to comparables in the guide using factors such as location, extras, buyer appeal, special neighbourhood amenities, site features, functional room layout and attractive financing.

- **Avoid Overpricing**   Discuss problems of overpricing a property:
  - Difficulty in getting other brokers or salespersons enthused about the property.
  - The possibility of the property remaining unsold and becoming market stale.
  - The risk of appearing in the wrong price category and thereby restricting the number of qualified buyers who might otherwise seriously consider the property (e.g., buyers in the $300,000–$400,000 not looking above the $400,000 price level).
  - The risk of becoming a 'comparison house' that may be actively shown, but only to sell other well-priced property.

- **Recommendations**   The CMA provides space for recommendations concerning both maximum list price, probable selling price and estimate of selling costs. Completion of any/all of these, including the salesperson's signature, is optional. Often salespersons complete information on comparables only and then use this form as a guide for general discussions with the seller. If the net proceeds portion is completed, registrants must ensure that details regarding mortgage balance and selling costs are accurate.

- **Not an Appraisal**   Make certain to point out the bolded statement in the OREA Residential Market Comparison Guide: *The above information is NOT an appraisal and is to be used for marketing purposes only.*

- **Privacy**   To address the issue of privacy, the seller should be advised that the information on the form is not to be shared with anyone else without the prior written consent of the registrant supplying the information.

Overpricing: A Costly Mistake	MARKET MEMO

Overpricing can have far reaching negative impact, is difficult to overcome and can prove costly for everyone involved.

The Seller	Doesn't sell the property within a reasonable time.
Potential Buyers	Avoid the overpriced property or at best use it for comparison purposes.
The Right Buyer	The property is often overlooked by the ideal buyer given an unrealistic asking price.
The Property	The unsold home is ultimately price adjusted downward. Market staleness creeps in, but few notice the lowered price. Still nothing occurs. Buyers may wrongfully assume that something is wrong with the property. The seller might even have to reduce the listing price below actual value just to regain market momentum.
The Brokerage and the Broker or Salesperson	Negative advertising as the for sale sign ages, amidst the competitions' sold signs. A commission is not earned and an unhappy client is the result.

Listing Presentations

PREPARATION	PRESENTATION	FLEXIBILITY
Do your homework. • Why is the owner selling? • What comparables have recently sold? • How much did they sell for? • What market factors affect saleability? • What brokerage services best fit the seller's needs? • What selling strategy will I use? • How can I best prepare myself for the seller?	Build a framework that works for you: flip sheets, booklet or computer presentation. Answer the important questions: • Why list? • Why list with me? • Why list with my brokerage?	Think planned, not canned. Fit your presentation to the seller's needs and personality.

Several successive steps are recommended before meeting with a potential seller and making a listing presentation.

- Get backup information from available sources; e.g., office files and MLS® records.
- Make certain that the listing kit is complete; e.g., forms, presentation manual, listing book and handouts.
- Be prepared to establish the most competitive listing price for the seller. Develop a comparative market analysis detailing all available inventory, sold listings and expired listings within the immediate area that are comparable to the seller's property.
- Be able to complete and fully discuss the comparative market analysis with the seller.
- Develop an overall strategy for establishing a listing price and marketing the property.
- Have a range of suggestions concerning how the seller will get the best price.
- Be prepared to answer the seller's concerns and demonstrate all marketing services.
- Bring supporting documentation; e.g., other listings, market trend information and related analysis, to assist in the discussion.

Counselling the Seller

Successful salespersons carefully plot their course of action when servicing and marketing listings. Open and candid discussion at the time of listing will give the seller a better understanding of what is involved in the actual procedures of showing and offer presentation. The seller can greatly assist in the marketing process by:

- Having the home ready for showings. Any necessary repairs, cleaning or decorating should be discussed and agreed upon.
- Being flexible for showing appointments. Assure the owners that as much advance notice as possible will be given. Also discuss those times when short notice may be required and gain the seller's agreement.
- Avoiding involvement in the showing process. Many representatives prefer that the owner not be present to enable more frank discussions with buyers who are viewing the property. If present, the owner should be advised to stay in the background and participate only if questions are asked of them by the sales representative.
- Allowing an open house. Discuss this option candidly, including the responsibilities of the seller and the brokerage, procedures and benefits when inviting the public to inspect a home by open house.
- Referring direct contacts by buyers to the listing salesperson. Circumstances may occur when prospects and/or sales representatives will attempt to circumvent the courtesies of dealing through the listing representative and contact the seller directly.

The seller should be instructed to call the listing salesperson immediately if such a contact takes place. An adequate supply of the listing salesperson's business cards should be left with the owner for this possibility.

- Dealing with offer presentations. The salesperson should clearly set out the various scenarios in which offers may be presented (e.g., working with co-operating brokerages as buyer brokerages), the implications of multiple representation, dealings with customers and explaining in detail the listing salesperson's role in the offer presentation.

Accurate Details a Must   **RESIDENTIAL CASE LAW**

The seller listed his cottage with the following description: Home has many improvements...new septic, new well, 200 amp serv. When inspecting the property, the buyer was not informed that the seller had installed an underground water line to the neighbour's well to obtain water.

The well went dry after closing. The buyer contracted a well driller and paid $8,774 for a new drilled well. He also discovered that the neighbours knew the original well was defective and that the seller had told them previously of his plans to ultimately install a new one. In the meantime, he had continually used the neighbours' wells and water lines. The seller had retained a well driller and obtained a quotation, but this was not disclosed to the buyer. One neighbour gave evidence that when he asked the seller whether he was going to tell the proposed buyer that the well had gone dry, his reply was simple: No!

The Judge determined that the buyer relied on the listing representation to his detriment. Sellers are required to disclose major latent defects of which they are aware. Silence regarding a known, latent defect is the equivalent of an intention to deceive. The Judge determined that the withholding of information was intentional. The buyer was awarded $7,000.

Reference   Frost v. Stewart 19 R.P.R. (3d) 281

COMMENTARY

Sellers need to clearly understand that withholding information regarding material defects when listing property can lead to litigation. An accurate and complete listing is the best defence. In this instance, the listing data went beyond mere promotion and was intended to convey the fact that the water supply was normal. The descriptive words *new well* were intended to give the impression that the water supply was adequate. Caveat emptor does not help a deceitful seller who hides a major defect.

Gathering Property Details

Significant problems can be avoided if care is taken when listing property and completing listing details. Common issues associated with residential property are emphasized below, along with highlighted items relating to commercial activities.

THE RESIDENTIAL PERSPECTIVE

- Rely on original source documents whenever possible such as surveys, permits, financial statements, tax statements and the like. Take particular care when reading any source document to ensure that information used is accurate; i.e., no transpositions, missing descriptive words and so forth. Make certain that such documents are returned to the seller.

- Pay particular attention to accuracy when describing lot size (front/depth) and lot irregularities.
- Be prepared to go to the Land Registry Office or municipal offices to confirm information about the property.
- Watch for significant problem areas that warrant further analysis and do not hesitate to seek appropriate help and expertise as the need arises.

THE RESIDENTIAL PERSPECTIVE (CONTINUED)

- Look at the entire property, not just the main structure. Too many real estate people concentrate on interior matters without due regard for exterior surfaces, land characteristics (e.g., drainage) and adjacent properties that can directly impact the value of the listed property.

- When viewing the land, make certain that any rights-of-way, easements and encroachments are identified by the seller and corroborated. Have there been any disputes with neighbours about such matters or other boundary-related disputes?

- If the seller wants certain factual information included (e.g., new shingles installed last year) confirm through visual inspection and don't hesitate to ask for corroborating documents as the need arises. Support documents can include receipts, warranties, permits and so forth.

- Watch for alterations or additions. Ask pertinent questions about when the work was done, was a building permit issued and are there any additional changes that are not readily observable?

- Check for general deterioration, water stains, moisture, mould, sagging and other signs of neglect and damage. Watch for any indications that the property may have been used as a grow house.

- Look for out-of-date systems, particularly involving wiring (e.g., knob-and-tube).

- Make certain that your information is current and complete. When was the survey completed? When does the warranty expire? Is the tax bill for the current year or a prior year? Is the document provided to me an interim tax notice or a final tax notice? Are there any known tax increases, local improvements pending and the like.

- Is the property connected to both municipal water and/or sewage services? What documentation is available regarding an existing well or septic system? Is a community well involved? Is the well dug or drilled? Is there a cistern? Is the water pumped from a lake/river?

- What heat sources are used; e.g., electric, gas, ground source, oil, propane, solar and/or wood? What about air conditioning?

- Pay particular attention to environmental considerations including flood plains, flooding potential, any environmental problems or soil contamination and underground fuel tanks.

- Clearly set out chattels that are included in the sale and fixtures that are excluded from the sale.

- What about special designations impacting the property such as a heritage designation?

- Use a Seller Property Information Statement to ensure a higher degree of accuracy and completeness when gathering property details.

- When in doubt regarding any uncertain issues concerning a property, seek expert advice.

- Above all, if unknowns about the property cannot be resolved and your concerns about property details persist, you are well advised to not pursue the listing.

- Condominium requires additional careful analysis involving such matters as the type (e.g., common element, phased and leasehold), parking spaces/type (common, exclusive, rental, owned, etc.), storage units and common expenses. Condominiums as well as unique characteristics associated with rural/recreational properties are discussed in detail in *The Residential Real Estate Transaction*.

THE COMMERCIAL PERSPECTIVE

Registrants focusing on commercial activities have further issues to consider when gathering property details. Selected items are highlighted. More detailed discussions are provided in *The Commercial Real Estate Transaction*.

- Key measurements must be carefully noted and double-checked. What is the clear height of the building interior? What are the bay sizes (if applicable)? What are the door heights and widths for truck level doors, drive-in level doors and shipping doors?

- What is the square footage or square metre measurements of the office, industrial, retail or other applicable areas and are these areas divisible?

- Are there freight and/or public elevators? What about rail access, parking/parking garage, cranes, sprinklers, electrical services and any unique features?

- What financial and related information is available; e.g., financial statements, chattels, franchise agreement(s), operating hours, number of employees and detailed expenses (actual or estimated)?

MARKETING THE LISTING

A fair price alone rarely sells a property. The well priced home can languish in relative obscurity without creative **marketing**. While the market for listed property extends to anyone capable of purchasing that property, the trick lies in attracting the right buyer's attention.

That's where research and strategy fit in. Brokerages and salespersons continuously refine plans that target prospects, promote property and maximize advertising dollars. Many marketing options are available. The following is a short list to help with your personal strategy. Students seeking detailed discussions of marketing strategies should revisit *Real Estate as a Professional Career, Chapter 6: Marketing and Customer Service.*

Marketing Methods—Options

• direct mail	• video
• classified ads	• radio and television
• web site	• display ads
• for sale/sold signs	• special client services
• social media	• public relations
• newsletters	• e-mail
• open houses	• personal contact

Print and Electronic Marketing Strategies

Advertising is commonly associated with newspaper classified ads, institutional ads in other print media and web pages. However, promotion extends to any method that informs and persuades. Hundreds of advertising options are available. Select those that produce a creative, unique and effective **marketing plan** for promoting property and advancing the client's best interests.

Uniqueness is key, as it leads to competitive advantage. Savvy brokerages and salespersons continuously seek and refine their distinct **market positions**. By standing out, potential sellers can then differentiate between competing services. A powerful, exclusive sales plan can reap significant rewards. The following flowchart highlights typical marketing possibilities. Options, services and activities vary by brokerage and real estate board jurisdiction.

Marketing Plan

An action plan developed by a brokerage or a salesperson flowing from a marketing strategy to promote property and secure potential prospects.

Print and Electronic Marketing

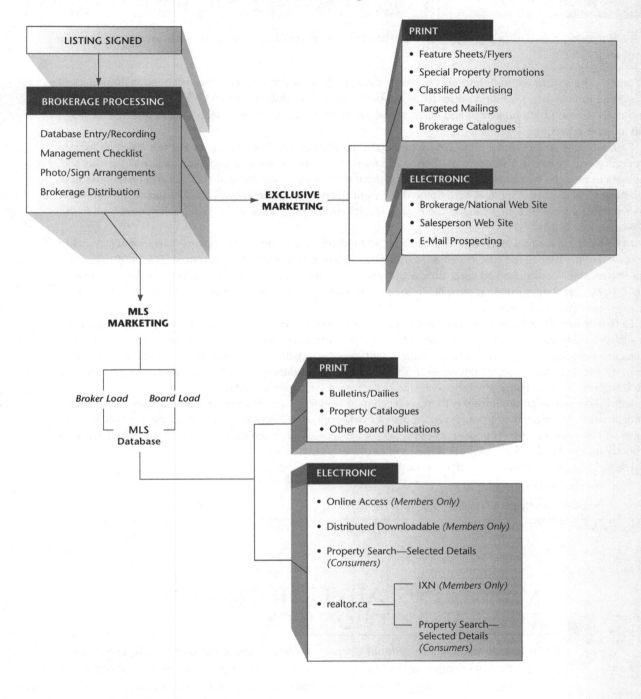

James is discussing his personal marketing strategy with another salesperson. His ideas may help in establishing your future plans.

For me...the structured marketing plan is everything. Clients know immediately what will happen from point of signing to final sale. My listing presentation is jammed with facts, testimonials and advertising examples. I use a flow chart showing both brokerage and MLS® marketing options. The seller sees exactly what's planned for print and Internet advertising.

First, I'll focus on low tech basics...before getting to the electronic bells and whistles. For example, the for sale sign is first and foremost. This silent salesperson is a must. If the seller objects to signage, I review all benefits and show them how the best prospect might be lost without one. Signs create demand and demand usually translates into better selling price. Simple as that. Some don't want the neighbours to know. With me, the neighbours will always know–sign or no sign. I canvass the entire area. It's part of my plan. After all, many sales come from friends or relatives of neighbours.

My advertising is straightforward. No fancy stuff, just location, price and major features. That's what buyers want to know. For my money the time-tested AIDA (Attention, Interest, Desire and Action) formula is best. An effective heading and well-constructed ad copy attracts the attention and interest of qualified readers. The property features, if effectively described, increase desirability in the prospect's mind. Lastly, a proactive request or instruction for action makes the telephone ring.

Electronic marketing is the new wave and I'm solidly into Internet promotions. All my ads, flyers and feature sheets are readily available online. The site is really dynamic with a mortgage calculator, down payment estimator, municipal links and various local market statistics that I've compiled. Buyers can also go on my site and do basic property searches. What does all this mean to sellers? As I tell them during the listing interview: Half my marketing job is to promote your home; the other half is to make it easy for buyers to find it.

Lastly, I constantly communicate with my sellers. I'm in contact either by e-mail or telephone on a weekly basis. Sometimes, the conversation is nothing more than a market update. Other times, we may discuss specifics; e.g., buyer comments on showings or open house results. If the topic is more sensitive; e.g., lower the price to make a property more competitive, a personal visit is in order.

For me, the best marketing is straightforward:

- Have a plan and stick to it.
- Continuously communicate with your clients.

MARKETING, ADVERTISING AND THE COMPETITION ACT

In *Real Estate as a Professional Career*, marketing and **advertising** tactics were discussed regarding sold signs, open houses, direct mail, e-mail, Internet push-pull technologies, tips on co-ordinating print/electronic marketing, lead generation/customer contact software and the various marketing features associated with the Multiple Listing Service®.

However, regardless of the advertising vehicle used, federal and provincial regulatory requirements come into play. Key federal and provincial regulatory controls are outlined, along with practical guidelines to avoid problems and errors when developing print and electronic advertising content.

The Competition Bureau has established helpful technical guidelines on advertising practice; e.g., use of disclaimers and promotional claims. Real estate advertising standards are most directly regulated by the Real Estate Council of Ontario through enforcement of REBBA 2002 provisions and, most notably, the Code of Ethics.

WEB LINKS

Competition Bureau   For more information concerning federal advertising requirements and the operation of the Competition Bureau, go to *www.competitionbureau.gc.ca*.

Avoiding Problem Areas

The *Competition Act*, while enforcing various matters, prohibits misleading advertising and deceptive business practices in the promotion of a service or the supply/use of a product. Industry Canada is responsible for the Act with enforcement and administration undertaken by the Competition Bureau. An excerpt of the *Competition Act* is illustrated.

False and Misleading Advertising–Competition Act

The *Competition Act*, although dictating procedures on a number of trading activities, is particularly broad in its approach to false or deceptive advertising practices. In particular, Section 52 of the *Competition Act* should be noted:

52 (1)   "No person shall, for the purpose of promoting, directly or indirectly, the supply or use of a product or for the purpose of promoting, directly or indirectly, any business interest, by any means whatever, knowingly or recklessly make a representation to the public that is false or misleading in a material respect."

The following are three important factors involving offences under this statute.

- The term *material* refers to any information which could affect a purchasing decision. In other words, any representation that might influence a consumer in the marketplace can fall under the Act. Consequently, the *Competition Act* touches upon practically every activity involving the day-to-day trading of real estate and related purchasing decisions.

- Proof of intention to deceive is not necessarily a prerequisite for charges under this statute. In fact, it is not a proper defence to argue that the misrepresentation was never intended. However, Subsection 60 (2) does state that a proper defence can be *due diligence* to correct the error.

- The definition of "misleading" is deliberately expanded to include non-literal impressions given by the advertisements. This is commonly referred to as the *general impression test*.

52 (4)   "In any prosecution for a contravention of this section, the general impression conveyed by the representation as well as the literal meaning thereof shall be taken into account in determining whether or not the representation is false or misleading in a material respect."

The actual wording of an advertisement may be technically correct, but the general impression can still be false.

Selected topics are included for general guidance and to avoid potential problems when advertising properties and services. Registrants are advised to access current information from appropriate authorities, the brokerage and/or legal counsel, prior to the development of any marketing materials. This descriptive material, based on the *Competition Act* materials, should be read in conjunction with provincial advertising requirements set out in the *Real Estate and Business Brokers Act, 2002* and related Regulations (see subsequent topic in this chapter). Clearly, regardless of the regulatory control, accuracy and clarity are fundamental to all advertising.

ABBREVIATIONS

The cost of classified advertising is a primary rationale for using abbreviations. Also, a host of codes and contractions are frequently used when completing seller representation forms. As a general rule, those found in local trading areas are acceptable provided that they do not confuse or mislead.

> **EXAMPLE**   *Abbreviations*
>
> A reader in Toronto would understand the DVP as the Don Valley Parkway and a buyer would correctly decipher 3 BR TH as a three-bedroom townhouse. However, ASSUME 1ST, 2ND, MIN DN, QUALF. could present problems. Abbreviations should be avoided whenever uninformed or innocent parties could misunderstand. This is particularly true when describing property uses, zoning, mortgaging or other specific attributes of a property.

ADVERTISED PRICE

Subsection 58(3) of the *Competition Act* does permit sales above the advertised price in the case of private real estate transactions. Specifically, the actual reference in the Act excludes the sale of a product by or on behalf of the person who is not engaged in the business of dealing in that product (e.g., private real estate sales).

However, other representations concerning price come under scrutiny. Any reduction or other alteration of price should be clearly identified and not be materially misleading. Further, the suggestion of a bargain that is not substantiated can have legal ramifications. Consider the following case involving a property listed below market value.

> **EXAMPLE**   *Advertised Price (Hypothetical)*
>
> The accused (a house builder in Anycity) promoting the sale of new homes in a brochure, stated that his homes were priced $10,000 below market value and published the prices of homes recently sold in the market area for comparison purposes. An investigation revealed that the builder's homes were not priced below market value and that the comparison homes differed from those of the accused in several respects. The accused plead guilty to one charge under Subsection 52(1) of the *Competition Act,* was convicted and fined $10,000.

CONTESTS

The *Competition Act* outlines basic rules for the operation of contests. Section 59 focuses primarily on adequate and fair disclosure of certain key facts:

- Approximate number and value of prizes included in the contest.
- Allocation of prizes by region, if applicable.
- Chances of winning (if it is within the knowledge of the advertiser).
- Whether or not a skill testing question is required to win the contest.
- Place where the contest rules may be obtained.
- The closing date of the contest.
- Any unusual restrictions or conditions relating to the promotional contest.

Registrants are strongly encouraged to seek expert advice when developing contests, particularly those involving games of chance, to ensure compliance with the lottery provisions of the Criminal Code and other applicable provincial and federal statutes.

COUPONS/MARKET EVALUATION CERTIFICATES

Certificates and coupons must clearly identify the service being provided. Disclaimers and limiting conditions should be consistent with the overall impression conveyed.

FINE PRINT/DISCLAIMERS

Classified advertising and other promotional materials often contain additional information in small print that either qualifies or otherwise expands the message being conveyed. Registrants, in order to save space, may relegate certain information to the fine print. Generally, this text will not arouse concern if it is additive and complementary to the main message. However, if the fine print in any way contradicts or otherwise limits the general impression conveyed by the main message, then a violation under the *Competition Act* may arise.

Fine print should be clearly visible, readable and relative to the print size used throughout other portions of the advertisement and take into account the needs of the targeted audience (e.g., age of reader and ability to read). While general impression remains the ultimate test, the Director has indicated the acceptability of 7 point print size as a minimum.

This sentence is printed in 7 point Arial Regular.

However, such a minimum measurement is subject to the qualifiers mentioned above. Disclaimers are frequently found in fine print. As a rule, such disclaimers should not contain information that materially limits or contradicts the main text or have any significant effect on the general impression being conveyed in the ad. The Canadian Code of Advertising Standards, Clause 1(d) provides guidance on the issues of disclaimers and asterisked fine print information.

FREE OFFERINGS

If a product or service is advertised as free, then such an offering shall not include any condition or other requirement of which the prospective customer would be unable to comply. An example of a false representation would be: *Buy one real estate lot and receive your next choice absolutely free*, where the price of the first lot is inflated to cover the cost of the free lot.

MULTIPLE LISTING AGREEMENTS

All MLS® listings are viewed as advertisements and consequently fall under the *Competition Act*. All members must ensure that listing information is accurate and correct. As a rule, registrants are advised to include nothing on a listing agreement that cannot be verified by source documentation. Information concerning items such as lot size, legal description, mortgage financing, taxes, chattels and fixtures, current zoning and rentals, to mention a few, come under scrutiny. In fact, inaccurate representations are normally not only actionable under the federal statute but also under common law as either innocent or fraudulent misrepresentation.

The importance of accurate listing information and representations relating thereto is obviously a notable factor in brokerage liability in the marketplace. Legal entanglements between buyers and brokers undoubtedly arise from matters pertaining to the accuracy and adequacy of listing information.

PICTURES/ILLUSTRATIONS

Erroneous impressions can be conveyed when a picture or illustration accompanies and forms part of an overall advertisement. For example, if homes are being sold in the $300,000–$350,000 price range and the house pictured in the advertisement is a model other than that offered, an offence could arise under the *Competition Act*. Further, the fine print in such advertisements requires careful wording.

In the case of illustrations, it is common to see various asterisked statements in new home sales such as:

- *Illustrations are artist's concept only, prices and specifications subject to change without notice.*
- *Limited quantities available in some price ranges.*
- *Illustration only. Prices and specifications subject to change without notice, E. & O. E.*

If a complaint is lodged under provisions of the *Competition Act*, the content of such statements including the respective sizes and locations in relation to other advertised information would all be taken into consideration.

PROMOTIONAL CLAIMS

Registrants must be careful to correctly represent any claims concerning personal performance levels. The general impression of the marketing piece and the actual text must agree and the statement must be accurate and not misleading. Caution is strongly advised when contemplating claim statements such as:

> The best....in the area,
> The first....in production,
> The most popular choice for...,
> The most...respected.......,
> The largest..., etc.

While such claims may be substantiated, each case will be viewed by the Competition Bureau on its own merits. Ensure that performance claims are correct and accurate. Consider the following decision under the *Competition Act*:

> *The accused, in promoting a real estate service, made the following representation in newspaper advertisements: For maximum exposure and results...over 90% of [Name of Brokerage (Agent)] Realty team listings have sold in 12 days or less. Investigation revealed that the representation was untrue.*

If testimonials are utilized in promotional material, ensure that any statements printed are accurate, not taken out of context from a larger statement and the person providing such statement has in fact received the services outlined in the testimonial. As a matter of policy, the signed statements of individuals should be kept on file in case their authenticity is ever questioned.

WEB LINKS

Competition Bureau   For more information concerning Competition Bureau activities and policies relating to advertising, go to **www.competitionbureau.gc.ca**.

MARKETING/ADVERTISING METHODS AND REBBA 2002

REBBA 2002 and the Regulations address various advertising requirements. This Act prohibits registrants from making false, misleading or deceptive statements in advertising. Key provisions are outlined below. Topics from the Act/Regulations are listed by their sequential order in the legislation.

False Advertising

REBBA 2002 contains a provision prohibiting registrants from making false, misleading or deceptive advertising statements.

FALSE ADVERTISING   REBBA

37. No registrant shall make false, misleading or deceptive statements in any advertisement, circular, pamphlet or material published by any means relating to trading in real estate. 2002, c. 30, Sched. C, s. 37.

The new Act allows the Registrar to not only order the cessation of false advertising, but also order registrants to retract statements or publish corrections. The Registrar may also require pre-approval of a registrant's advertising for a period up to one year if the registrant is found in violation of the false advertising prohibition.

ORDER OF REGISTRAR RE: FALSE ADVERTISING   REBBA

38. (1) If the registrar believes on reasonable grounds that a registrant is making a false, misleading or deceptive statement in any advertisement, circular, pamphlet or material published by any means, the registrar may,

    (a) order the cessation of the use of such material;

    (b) order the registrant to retract the statement or publish a correction of equal prominence to the original publication; or

    (c) order both a cessation described in clause (a) and a retraction or correction described in clause (b). 2002, c. 30, Sched. C, s. 38 (1).

Pre-approval

    (4) If the registrant does not appeal an order under this section or if the order or a variation of it is upheld by the Tribunal, the registrant shall, upon the request of the registrar, submit all statements in any advertisement, circular, pamphlet or material to be published by any means to the registrar for approval before publication for such period as the registrar specifies. 2002, c. 30, Sched. C, s. 38 (4); 2004, c. 19, s. 18 (23).

REGISTRAR'S ORDER RE: FALSE ADVERTISING   GEN

41. For the purpose of clause 38 (5) of the Act, the prescribed period is one year from the date the registrar makes the request referred to in subsection 38 (4) of the Act. O. Reg. 567/05, s. 41.

Identifying Property/Parties/Agreements

The Code of Ethics provides that a registrant cannot include anything in advertising that could be used to identify a specific property, unless the owner of that real estate has consented in writing.

Similarly, a party cannot be identified in an ad, unless that party has consented. Lastly, nothing can be included in an advertisement that would identify details relating to an agreement involving a conveyance of real estate unless the parties to that agreement have consented in writing.

ADVERTISING

CODE

36. (1) A registrant shall clearly and prominently disclose the name in which the registrant is registered in all the registrant's advertisements. O. Reg. 580/05, s. 36 (1).

(2) A brokerage that identifies a broker or salesperson by name in an advertisement shall use the name in which the broker or salesperson is registered. O. Reg. 580/05, s. 36 (2).

(3) A broker or salesperson shall not advertise in any manner unless the advertisement clearly and prominently identifies the brokerage that employs the broker or salesperson, using the name in which the brokerage is registered. O. Reg. 580/05, s. 36 (3).

(4) A registrant who advertises shall,

(a) use the term "brokerage", "real estate brokerage", "maison de courtage" or "maison de courtage immobilier" to describe any brokerage that is referred to in the advertisement;

(b) use the term "broker of record", "real estate broker of record", "courtier responsable" or "courtier immobilier responsable" to describe any broker of record who is referred to in the advertisement;

(c) use the term "broker", "real estate broker", "courtier" or "courtier immobilier" to describe any broker who is referred to in the advertisement; and

(d) use the term "salesperson", "real estate salesperson", "sales representative", "real estate sales representative", "agent immobilier", "représentant commercial" or "représentant immobilier" to describe any salesperson who is referred to in the advertisement. O. Reg. 580/05, s. 36 (4).

(5) Despite clause (4) (c), a registrant who advertises may, before April 1, 2008, use the term "associate broker", "associate real estate broker", "courtier associé" or "courtier immobilier associé" to describe any broker who is referred to in the advertisement. O. Reg. 580/05, s. 36 (5).

(6) A registrant who advertises shall not use a term to describe any registrant that is referred to in the advertisement if the term could reasonably be confused with a term that is required or authorized by subsection (4) or (5). O. Reg. 580/05, s. 36 (6).

(7) A registrant shall not include anything in an advertisement that could reasonably be used to identify a party to the acquisition or disposition of an interest in real estate unless the party has consented in writing. O. Reg. 580/05, s. 36 (7).

(8) A registrant shall not include anything in an advertisement that could reasonably be used to identify specific real estate unless the owner of the real estate has consented in writing. O. Reg. 580/05, s. 36 (8).

(9) A registrant shall not include anything in an advertisement that could reasonably be used to determine any of the contents of an agreement that deals with the conveyance of an interest in real estate, including any provision of the agreement relating to the price, unless the parties to the agreement have consented in writing. O. Reg. 580/05, s. 36 (9).

INACCURATE REPRESENTATIONS

The Code also clearly states that a registrant must not knowingly make inaccurate representations about service provided and must use his or her best efforts to avoid error and misrepresentation.

INACCURATE REPRESENTATIONS

CODE

37. (1) A registrant shall not knowingly make an inaccurate representation in respect of a trade in real estate. O. Reg. 580/05, s. 37 (1).

(2) A registrant shall not knowingly make an inaccurate representation about services provided by the registrant. O. Reg. 580/05, s. 37 (2).

EXAMPLE   *The Sub-Standard Footing*

A salesperson, when showing a cottage property, advises the buyer client that a crack in an exterior wall is only minor and the buyer need not be concerned. He assures the buyer that this sort of thing is common with non-winterized cottages as the perimeter foundation may move slightly, but things would return to normal in the spring. Following closing, the buyer discovers that the crack actually widens during the warmer months and has the structure inspected by an appropriate expert. The culprit involved a substandard footing requiring $8,500 in repairs. A complaint was lodged against the registrant for inaccurate representation and appropriate disciplinary action was taken.

ERROR, MISREPRESENTATION, FRAUD, ETC.   `CODE`

38. A registrant shall use the registrant's best efforts to prevent error, misrepresentation, fraud or any unethical practice in respect of a trade in real estate. O. Reg. 580/05, s. 38.

EXAMPLE   *Prudent Advice to the Client*

A salesperson registrant showing an industrial property was asked by the client as to the exact square footage within the structure and the current electrical service size entering the building. The salesperson checked this listing information and informed the buyer that the building contained 10,500 square feet and a 400-amp service according to the listing information. He then advised the buyer to seek independent confirmation of both facts, as well as other material matters, by contacting appropriate experts. The salesperson also inserted a clause in the offer allowing the buyer reasonable time to check out all relevant matters to ensure that this building met his particular needs. In doing so, the salesperson has taken reasonable steps to avoid error and misrepresentation when advising the client.

ADVERTISING: WORKING DEFINITIONS

Registrants should be aware that statutory requirements and Code of Ethics requirements span a broad range of activities including advertising, direct mail and the Internet. Following are key definitions provided by the Registrar regarding what constitutes an advertisement and associated terminologies.

Advertising	"Advertising" means any notice, announcement or representation directed at the public that is authorized, made by or on behalf of a registrant and that is intended to promote a registrant or the business, services or real estate trades of a registrant in any medium including, but not limited to, print, radio, television, electronic media or publication on the internet (including websites and social media sites). Business cards, letterhead or fax cover sheets that contain promotional statements may be considered as "advertising".
Broadcast and Electronic	Broadcast and electronic when used to describe advertising or an advertisement means any advertisement in any electronic medium, including the Internet, radio and television.
Disclaimer	A disclosure (see definition of disclosure below) that must be included in an advertisement to explain, modify or qualify a claim or promise made in that advertisement to provide accurate and complete information and avoid ambiguity, confusion, deception or misrepresentation that might be caused by the omission of the disclaimer.

Disclosure	Any and all information, including disclaimers (see definition above) that must be included in an advertisement in order to provide accurate and complete information and to avoid ambiguity, confusion, deception or misrepresentation that might otherwise be caused by the omission of information or by information that, without the disclosure, is inaccurate, incomplete, unclear or unverifiable.
	In many advertisements, it is necessary to provide disclosure with respect to a number of statements that appear in the advertisement and in those cases "disclosure" is used to refer to all the information that is required to be disclosed in that advertisement.

Registrar Advertising Guidelines

These guidelines have been developed to assist registrants in complying with the advertising requirements and prohibitions found in the *Real Estate and Business Brokers Act, 2002* (the "Act") and Ontario Regulation 580/05 under the Act (known as the Code of Ethics).

These guidelines cannot hope to encompass every situation and every type of advertising material being used or contemplated by registrants. It does, however, convey many of the principles that the Registrar will consider in determining whether an advertisement complies with the Act and/or the Code of Ethics. Should a complaint about advertising be referred to the Discipline Committee, a Discipline Panel might also take these principles into consideration.

These guidelines are not intended as a comprehensive description of all applicable advertising laws. Many statutes impact advertising and related conduct in the marketplace. These include federal laws such as the *Competition Act*, the *Personal Information Protection and Electronic Documents Act* (PIPEDA), and trademark and copyright statutes, provincial laws including consumer protection legislation, and municipal by-laws regarding things such as signage. The enforcement of these various statutes is outside of RECO's jurisdiction.

Minimum Requirements For Advertisements

Section 36 of the Code of Ethics sets out four minimum requirements that must appear in all advertising. Those requirements are as follows:

A) IDENTIFICATION OF REGISTRANT

All advertising by a registrant, including a brokerage, a broker or a salesperson, must clearly and prominently include the name of the registrant that is placing the advertisement. The name used in the advertisement must be the name (legal name or trade name) in which the registrant is registered with RECO. Registrants with a common last name and designation may be identified jointly (e.g., Tom & Rita McIntyre, Sales Representatives).

There are no formal criteria for what constitutes "clearly and prominently". Registrant identification information must be sufficiently sized and placed within the advertisement so that it can reasonably be noticed and understood by the intended audience. For the purpose of determining if an advertisement appears to be in violation of the Code of Ethics, the Registrar will consider, among other things, the following characteristics of the advertisement:

1) For visually-based advertising, the size and legibility of the printed name, and the location of the name relative to the other elements of the advertisement;

2) For aurally-based advertising (i.e., radio), the frequency with which the name is used, the point in the advertisement when the name is used, and the speed with which the name is mentioned.

B) IDENTIFICATION OF INDIVIDUALS

If an individual broker or salesperson is identified by name, the name used must be the name in which the broker or salesperson is registered with RECO. Registrants with a common last name and designation may be identified jointly (e.g., Keiko & Jordan Smith, Brokers).

C) IDENTIFICATION OF BROKERAGE

Every advertisement by a broker or a salesperson must clearly and prominently identify the brokerage that employs the broker or salesperson. The brokerage name used in the advertisement must be the name in which the brokerage is registered with RECO.

As noted in "Identification of registrant", "clearly and prominently" will be assessed by the Registrar (or the Discipline Committee if an advertising complaint is referred to them) based on various characteristics of the advertisement.

A sole proprietorship brokerage must take special care to ensure that it is clear that the individual is both a registered brokerage and the broker of record.

D) DESCRIPTION OF REGISTRANT

Where an advertisement identifies a registrant, the specific description of the registrant must be noted. Specifically:

i. Salesperson	The terms "salesperson", "real estate salesperson", "sales representative" or "real estate sales representative", or the French language equivalents "agent immobilier", "représentant commercial" or "représentant immobilier", must be used to describe any salesperson who is referred to in the advertisement;
ii. Broker	The terms "broker" or "real estate broker", or the French language equivalents "courtier" or "courtier immobilier", must be used to describe any broker who is referred to in the advertisement;
iii. Broker of record	The terms "broker of record" or "real estate broker of record", or the French language equivalents "courtier responsable" or "courtier immobilier responsable", must be used to describe any broker of record who is referred to in the advertisement; and
iv. Brokerage	The terms "brokerage" or "real estate brokerage", or the French language equivalents "maison de courtage" or "maison de courtage immobilier", must be used to describe any brokerage that is referred to in the advertisement.
v. Other issues	In larger advertisements where multiple registrants are identified, there may be a desire to eliminate the costs or visual clutter associated with repetition of terms such as "salesperson" and "broker" throughout the advertisement. Registrants are permitted to use a clear and visible symbol (such as an asterisk) to denote a description throughout the page. The symbol and associated reference must be clearly visible in the medium in question. In multiple page advertisements, or on multi-page websites, both the symbol and accompanying designation reference must appear on every page that refers to registrants.

If a registrant placing an advertisement is uncertain about the registered name or designation of a brokerage, broker or salesperson that is to be identified or described in the advertisement, they may confirm the information on MyWeb or through RECO's website at **www.reco.on.ca**.

Prohibitions

Section 36 and 37 of the Code of Ethics and other sections of REBBA 2002 contain specific prohibitions related to advertising (i.e., things that are not allowed in advertising, or are only allowed in specific circumstances). Those prohibitions are as follows:

A) CONFUSING TERMS

Registrants must not use any terms to describe a registrant in an advertisement if the term could reasonably be confused with registration status terms described in Section II(d) of these guidelines. Without limiting the generality of this prohibition, terms such as "sales agent", "sales associate" or "sales consultant" are not permitted. Subject to other advertising guidelines and requirements, registrants are permitted to use terms denoting an affiliation with a real estate group or association, but such terms must not appear as a substitute for the description of registrant noted previously.

B) IDENTIFICATION OF A PARTY WITHOUT CONSENT

Registrants must not include anything in an advertisement (such as an image or text) that could reasonably be used to identify any party to a real estate transaction, unless the registrant has the written consent of that party to do so.

A registrant may, within the terms of a representation agreement or a customer service agreement, include wording that provides consent to allow advertising which includes the type of information noted above. Alternatively, separate written consent can be obtained. In a situation where a consent is required from a party to the transaction that was not represented by the registrant, communication must go through that party's brokerage to seek written consent.

C) IDENTIFICATION OF A PROPERTY WITHOUT CONSENT

Registrants must not include anything in an advertisement (such as an image or text) that could reasonably be used to identify a specific property, unless the brokerage has the written consent of the owner of the property to do so. The provisions of a listing agreement signed by the seller are typically drafted to give authority to the listing brokerage to advertise the property and may include permission for that property to be advertised on a real estate board Multiple Listing Service (MLS®) system and/or other media. Registrants should be familiar with the terms of their standard listing agreements in this regard.

A registrant, with the seller's written consent, may advertise that a property has sold, for example using a sold sign or distribution of sold cards, once a transaction has been entered into, provided that no information related to terms of the agreement are included in the advertisement and provided that the seller is the owner of the property at the time of the advertisement (see item (D) on the following page). Once title to the property has transferred to the buyer (i.e. once the transaction has completed), a registrant would need the buyer's written consent to make any reference to the property in sold cards or other advertisements.

As noted in (B), consent can be obtained through specific wording in a representation or service agreement, and a registrant must communicate through the appropriate brokerage to seek consent.

D) IDENTIFICATION OF AGREEMENT DETAILS WITHOUT CONSENT

Registrants must not include anything in an advertisement (such as an image or text) that could reasonably be used to determine any of the contents of an agreement (such as price) regarding a real estate transaction, unless the registrant has the written consent of all the parties to the agreement to do so. For example, a registrant wishing to distribute sold cards that indicate a property sold for 95 % of asking price, would need the written consent of both the buyer and seller, regardless of who was the owner of the property at the time of the advertisement.

As noted in (B), consent can be obtained through specific wording in a representation or service agreement, and a registrant must communicate through the appropriate brokerage to seek consent.

E) FALSE, MISLEADING OR DECEPTIVE STATEMENTS, AND INACCURATE REPRESENTATIONS

Consistent with RECO's principal objective of fostering public confidence and upholding integrity in real estate transactions, Section 37 of REBBA 2002 contains a general prohibition against false, misleading or deceptive statements in advertising by registrants. Section 37 of the Code of Ethics further prohibits a registrant from knowingly making an inaccurate representation in respect of the services provided by the registrant and in respect of a trade in real estate. This would include inaccurate representations made in an advertisement.

The issues giving rise to these prohibitions generally relate to claims, promises and statements made in advertising, such as comparative rankings (e.g., "#1 brokerage in town"), claims about business volume or trading activity (e.g., "Over 100 transactions last year"), promises of savings or rebates ("$1,000 cash back"), and honours or awards received by the registrant.

False statements are those than can be shown to be factually incorrect. Generally, there is little room for interpretation in these situations. The assessment of statements that may be misleading, deceptive or inaccurate, however, is more subjective in nature.

A misleading statement is one that causes someone to have a wrong idea or impression. It does not require that all readers of the statement be misled in order for the statement or claim to be considered misleading.

Similarly, a deceptive statement is one that causes something to be easily mistaken for something else, or causes the reader to believe something that is not true. It is a statement that is purposefully misleading.

An inaccurate representation is one that is imprecise. It would be inaccurate to make a statement that is true, but to make it in a vague or incomplete manner in circumstances where specificity is required to understand its truth. An inaccurate statement may or may not be misleading and/or deceptive.

It is not possible for these guidelines to address all the types of potentially false, misleading, deceptive or inaccurate statements that may appear in real estate advertising. RECO cannot provide a prescriptive set of rules that, if followed, will ensure that an advertisement will not breach REBBA 2002 or the Code of Ethics.

In general, registrants should assume that all statements in an advertisement will be taken at face value and interpreted based on their plain meaning (consistent with the "reasonable bystander" test used in legal cases). If the registrant's intent is to imply something else, or is aware that the statement could be interpreted in different ways, it would be better to spell out the intended meaning in plain language, or to provide some form of disclaimer within the advertisement. Failure to do so could result in the statement being deemed misleading, deceptive or inaccurate.

In assessing whether a statement might represent a breach of REBBA 2002 or the Code, the Registrar will apply a form of the "reasonable bystander" test noted above.

By way of guidance, however, there are a number of good practices which, if followed, should minimize the risk that a registrant's advertising will face scrutiny regarding these concerns. These practices are as follows:

i. Comparative Claims	An advertisement that expressly, or by implication, makes a comparative claim regarding a registrant's business performance, should disclose the basis of that comparison or claim including disclosure of the details of the information used to make the claim and the source of the information.
ii. Statements Re: Business Volume/ Trading Activity	An advertisement that includes statements or claims that state, imply, allude or refer to a volume of business or trading activity should be accompanied by disclosure of how that claim has been determined, including the relevant time period. By way of illustration, reference to terms such as "transaction" or "transaction side" or "end" or similar concepts should be accompanied by disclosure of how those terms are being used in that advertisement, including whether a transaction in which the brokerage, broker or salesperson, as applicable, represents more than one party to a particular transaction is being counted as one or two "sides", ends or transactions. Further, claims that refer to volume of business or trading activity should disclose the identity of the registrant, registrants or brokerage about whom that reference is made. If the basis of the claim concerns more than one registrant, including where the information concerns the brokerage activity or other registrant(s) activities within the brokerage cooperating as a team, then the claim should clearly disclose such brokerage or team activity as applicable. When a "team" claim is used, the size of the team should be noted or the identities of the members of the team should be provided.
iii. Promises and Statements Re: Commission or Savings	All claims within advertisements that refer to commission rates should be accompanied by disclosure of any conditions or circumstances in which that commission rate would not in fact be charged, unless the commission rate referred to is in fact charged in all transactions. This applies even when qualifying language, including for example "as low as" or similar language accompanies the claim. All claims of savings or comparisons regarding commission or other remuneration should be accompanied by sufficient information to enable an informed comparison to be made. Comparative claims between an advertised and hypothetical commission rate should be accompanied by information that clearly indicates the hypothetical rate as such and discloses that the hypothetical rate is not a fixed rate that is charged by all real estate brokerages. Advertisements must not indicate or suggest, directly or indirectly, that commissions or other fees are fixed or approved by RECO or any other government authority, real estate board or real estate association.

THE REAL ESTATE TRANSACTION—GENERAL

iv. Statements or Indications of Honours and Awards	If an advertisement refers to an award or honour, then the source and date of that award or honour should be indicated. Registrant advertising should not refer to an award or honour that was shared amongst other registrants without clearly indicating that fact. Registrant advertising should not, directly or by inference, refer to anything as an award or honour if that thing was in any way purchased or paid for by, or on behalf of, the registrant.

WEB LINKS

Advertising Guidelines   The full text of the Advertising Guidelines and the Advertising Checklist can be accessed on the RECO website at *www.reco.on.ca*.

The Special Designation   **RECO DISCIPLINE DECISION**

Salesperson A, employed by ABC Realty Inc., showed a property, but did not know of a proposed designation in the regional official plan (High Potential Mineral Aggregate Resource Area (HPMARA)) which potentially impacted the property. The listing broker, XYZ Realty Inc., failed to disclose the HPMARA under the Special Designation listing category. Further, the listing stated that a Seller Property Information Statement was available—such was not the case.

Salesperson A, following the property sale, learned of the designation and official plan amendment (OPA). She immediately informed the buyer and told him to see his lawyer. The buyer did close the sale (despite his dislike for the Special Designation) because he did not want to lose his $10,000 deposit or become embroiled in litigation. The buyer also stated that he would not have signed the agreement and purchased had he been aware of the designation.

As background information, the HPMARA could restrict future land use. Further, adjacent properties might be used for a pit or a quarry. Generally, the proposed official plan amendment was intended to restrict new land uses, including severance and subdivision plans, to preserve areas for aggregate extraction. The designation would not give anyone the automatic right regarding gravel or other aggregate extraction. Further, the time frame for such activity could extend beyond 2021. The official plan amendment, approved by the regional government and the Minister of Municipal Affairs, was pending before the Ontario Municipal Board. Therefore, it was still a proposed official plan amendment under the *Planning Act*.

COMMENTARY

The Broker of XYZ Realty Inc. was found in violation of selected provisions under the previous RECO Code of Ethics (prior to REBBA 2002). An administrative penalty of $3,000 (plus $900 in costs) was imposed. The salesperson of ABC Realty Inc. was found in violation of the RECO Code of Ethics and an administrative penalty of $1,000 (plus $300 in costs) was imposed.

Reference   Abstracted from published cases. Go to *www.reco.on.ca*.

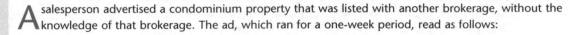

The Unauthorized Ad	RECO DISCIPLINE DECISION

A salesperson advertised a condominium property that was listed with another brokerage, without the knowledge of that brokerage. The ad, which ran for a one-week period, read as follows:

Harbour Front Corner 2 bdrm, facing lake, firepl., balc., stunning lake
view, S. exp., 9' ceilings, 1,700 sq. ft. $XXX,000. (416) XXX-XXXX

The telephone number on the ad turned out to be the salesperson's cell phone. The listing salesperson confirmed that, at all material times, he was the listing salesperson for the property and that the multiple listing agreement with the sellers gave that brokerage the exclusive right to advertise the property.

COMMENTARY

The Discipline Hearing Panel found the salesperson in violation of selected Rules under the previous RECO Code of Ethics (prior to REBBA 2002). An administrative penalty of $3,000 (plus $1,550 in costs) was imposed along with one year's probation. The Panel decided that her conduct was unfair to the sellers, the general public, the listing brokerage and sales representative. This conduct was also dishonourable and unprofessional.

Reference   Abstracted from published cases. Go to ***www.reco.on.ca***.

A Final Note

Marketing property has become an increasingly complex facet of real estate trading. Salespersons must consider both legal issues and statutory requirements that surround the promotion of property. The demand for accuracy is neither isolated to real estate sales nor solely directed to salespersons' activities. Brokerages are increasingly focused on avoiding potential problems by ensuring that factual information is obtained and correctly conveyed to consumers. Listing forms, once half-page documents, now consume three or more pages. Proper disclaimers and qualifiers, once the exception, are now commonplace in all types of advertising.

The future undoubtedly will demand even clearer delineation of facts, responsibilities and representations in the interest of fair marketing practices and consumer protection. Regulatory bodies are already confronting new issues surrounding private versus public information, direct mail and telephone canvassing procedures, and increasingly detailed advertising requirements spanning both print and electronic worlds. Ironically, for all the complexities of modern real estate trading, the registrant looking to the future is best served by following the simple, unencumbered guidelines already established in REBBA 2002 including the Code of Ethics and detailed guidelines published by the Registrar. All individuals, upon becoming registered with a real estate brokerage, should also inquire about and fully review all brokerage policies regarding marketing and advertising.

KNOWLEDGE INTEGRATION

Notables

- The saleable listing sets the foundation for productive negotiations and a successful sale.

- Listing price can be an effective sales tool in competitively marketing property and promoting the best interests of the seller client.

- The comparative market analysis establishes recommended listing price, not market value.

- Overpricing negatively impacts everyone involved with the listing: the seller, the buyers and the registrants.

- Think planned, not canned. Make listing presentations informative but be flexible.

- Carefully prepare property details to ensure that no significant issues are overlooked.

- When marketing a listing, ensure that your marketing plan takes into consideration both print and electronic strategies.

- Avoid common problems when marketing property by diligently avoiding misleading headlines and wordings. Be particularly cautious when developing custom advertising materials; e.g., coupons, flyers and free offerings.

- Comply fully with all advertising standards found in the *Competition Act* and REBBA 2002 including the Code of Ethics.

- The Registrar applies a very broad definition of advertising to include all print material, however distributed, as well as electronic media including the Internet, radio and television.

- The Registrar has established helpful guidelines that address advertising claims, promises and statements, as well as consent procedures regarding information about parties, properties and transactions.

- Selected RECO discipline decisions provide further guidelines for registrants.

- Carefully review brokerage marketing and advertising policies.

Glossary

Advertising   Marketing

Listing Price   Marketing Plan

Market Position

Web Links

Web links are included for general interest regarding selected chapter topics.

Competition Bureau   For more information concerning federal advertising requirements, the operation of the Competition Bureau and policies relating to advertising go to *www.competitionbureau.gc.ca*.

Advertising Guidelines   The full text of the Advertising Guidelines and the Advertising Checklist can be accessed on the RECO website at *www.reco.on.ca*.

Strategic Thinking For Your Career

Questions are included to assist in developing your new career. No answers are provided.

1. What properties have remained unsold in my local market for an extended period of time? Is overpricing the culprit?

2. What information should I include in my listing presentation? What do successful salespersons use in the local area to market their skills?

3. Can I provide solid benefits when asked the question: Why should I list with you?

4. What type of Internet advertising is available at my intended employing brokerage and/or in the local marketplace that will give me an effective electronic presence?

5. Will I be joining a local real estate board and, if so, what online advertising/marketing facilities do they offer brokerages, brokers and salespersons?

Chapter Mini-Review

Solutions are located in the Appendix.

1. Two characteristics of a saleable listing are exclusivity and a reasonable listing time period.

   ○ True   ○ False

2. A comparative market analysis is used to establish market value when listing a property for sale.

   ○ True   ○ False

3. The seller's motivation for selling is not highly relevant when preparing for a listing presentation.

   ○ True   ○ False

4. A property that is frequently shown to prospective buyers is the most likely property to sell in a short period of time.

   ○ True   ○ False

5. A brokerage is always responsible for deceitful statements made by a seller client regarding his or her property that result in litigation.

   ○ True   ○ False

6. If a seller states that he has installed new shingles on a residential structure within the last six months, the salesperson listing the property should investigate further to substantiate this statement.

   ○ True   ○ False

7. Rail access, cranes and sprinkler systems are three of many factors that should be taken into consideration when listing property used for industrial purposes.

   ○ True   ○ False

8. The *Competition Act* sets out various guidelines concerning advertising, one of which relates to the use of abbreviations when promoting property through print and electronic media.

   ○ True   ○ False

9. Based on the requirements of the *Competition Act*, a disclaimer cannot be included in the fine print for an advertisement, but must be prominently displayed within the ad instead.

   ○ True   ○ False

10. The Registrar cannot only order the cessation of false advertising, but can also require the registrant to retract statements or publish corrections.

    ○ True   ○ False

11. Advertising, for purposes of guidelines published by the Registrar, can include print as well as electronic media.

    ○ True   ○ False

12. A registrant cannot make an advertising claim regarding volume of business conducted, as such is not in keeping with the Code of Ethics.

    ○ True   ○ False

Active Learning Exercises

Solutions are located in the Appendix.

■ Exercise 1   Multiple Choice

1.1   A brokerage advertises that the organization is 'Number One'. This is acceptable to the Registrar provided that:

    a. The brokerage places the advertisement in all local papers.

    b. The brokerage refers only to transactions and does not address dollar volume.

    c. The brokerage discloses the basis upon which the comparison or claim is made.

    d. The brokerage seeks the permission of the local real estate board to publish this information.

1.2   A brokerage, when advertising a commission rate:

    a. Must include a statement in the advertisement that the rate advertised is not fixed, set or mandated by law.

    b. Must include a description of any situation in which the commission rate advertised is not in fact charged.

    c. Must include the phrase 'as low as' to indicate that higher rates may apply.

    d. Must include the amount of commission paid to co-operating brokerages.

1.3   A registrant receives an award for outstanding sales performance by her employing brokerage. The registrant:

    a. Cannot advertise this award, as it relates to internal sales performance within the brokerage, as opposed to performance within the general marketplace.

    b. Can only advertise this award if the award was purchased by the registrant or her employing brokerage.

    c. Must include the phrase 'Award available for inspection upon request.'

    d. Must include the source and date of that award in any advertising.

1.4   A registrant may use property 'sold' cards to advertise a seller client's property that has just sold, provided that:

    a. The seller gives his or her written consent and is the owner of the property at the time of the consent.

    b. The transaction has closed and the seller gives his or her written consent.

    c. The buyer and seller give written consent regardless of whether the sale has closed or not.

    d. The sold card used includes the terms of the agreement under which the property was sold.

1.5   Which of the following statements is correct regarding guidelines set out under the *Competition Act*?

    a.   Disclaimers and limiting conditions must be consistent with the overall impression given in advertising.

    b.   With contests, the advertiser need only disclose the closing date and where contest rules can be obtained.

    c.   Five point print size is acceptable for fine print.

    d.   Only registrants in organized real estate need to comply with Competition Bureau guidelines.

1.6   Which of the following is a correct statement?

    a.   A model home pictured in an advertisement doesn't necessarily have to resemble the actual home or homes being offered at the construction site.

    b.   With a promotional claim, the actual text and the general impression need not agree.

    c.   Promotional claims can be used in print advertising, but not Internet marketing.

    d.   All MLS® listings are viewed as advertisements for purposes of the *Competition Act*.

1.7   According to guidelines provided under the *Competition Act*:

    a.   Brokerages should not use the terms *best, first, largest* or *most popular* when describing real estate.

    b.   Abbreviations found in the local trading place are generally acceptable provided that they do not confuse or mislead.

    c.   A property cannot sell above the advertised price.

    d.   Disclaimers are not permitted when including property details in a seller representation agreement.

■ Exercise 2   The CMA

Mr. and Mrs. Hanson have decided to list their older townhome. Similar properties in the immediate vicinity, with few exceptions, have sold around $200,000. A partially-completed Residential Market Comparison Guide is illustrated.

Mr. Hanson is convinced that the home, while somewhat small, should be in the $225,000 range. Prices in the immediate area have remained relatively stable over the past eight months.

2.1   What maximum list price and estimated selling price would you recommend? Assume the local listing to selling ratio is 96%.

2.2   Complete the bottom of the form (see the following page) including estimated selling cost and anticipated net proceeds. Assume a 5.25% commission rate, a selling price of $197,000 and three months' interest penalty on an existing $127,300 (balance outstanding) mortgage at 6.5%.

NOTE   An approximate estimate (three month's interest) is adequate for learning purposes. Interest penalty calculations are addressed in Principles of Mortgage Financing. No mortgage discount fees or miscellaneous costs apply. Legal costs for the seller are estimated at $650.

Exercise 2   Residential Market Comparison Guide—Page 1 of 1

 **OREA** Ontario Real Estate Association   # Residential Market Comparison Guide

Form 260
for use in the Province of Ontario

SUBJECT PROPERTY: .... 39 Springdale Road

PREPARED FOR: .... Dorothy Hanson and Douglas Hanson

PREPARED BY: ...... Albert Lee, ABC Realty Inc. ...... **DATE :** ...... June 16, 20xx

COMPARABLES FOR SALE NOW:

Address	Price	Features/Comments
132 Springdale Road	$209,900	Similar home
39 Cedar Avenue	$208,900	Finished 4th bedroom
206 Ridge Road	$219,850	Superior lot; view
29 Centre Street	$198,900	Required decorating and some minor repairs

(Use back of form for additional features/comments if required)

COMPARABLES SOLD PAST 12 MONTHS:

Address	Price	Features/Comments
34 Springdale Road	$189,900	Similar home, sold 8 months ago
29 Oak St.	$181,500	Inferior, required decorating, sold 2 months ago
196 Falcon Street	$208,700	Extensive landscaping, some upgrades, sold 3 months ago
1296 Cartier Boulevard	$218,500	Inground pool, extensive decking and landscaping, sold 2 months ago

(Use back of form for additional features/comments if required)

COMPARABLES EXPIRED PAST 12 MONTHS:

Address	Price	Features/Comments
238 Springdale Road	$219,000	Similar home, unsold, now rented
38 Westway Avenue	$209,000	Renovations required, corner lot
1305 Cartier Boulevard	$209,900	Corner lot, busy intersection

(Use back of form for additional features/comments if required)

ESTIMATED SELLING COSTS :

Brokerage Fee	$ ....
Mortgage Payout Penalty	$ ....
Mortgage Discount	$ ....
Approximate Legal Costs	$ ....
Miscellaneous	$ ....
Total	$ ....

Recommendations: as of ....

I recommend a maximum list price of: $ ....

With estimated selling price of: $ ....

With estimated outstanding mortgage balance of: $ ....

With estimated selling costs of: $ ....

Anticipated net proceeds would be: $ ....

Signature ....

NB: The recipient of the above information acknowledges by reading, reviewing or receiving such information that the information may not be accurate or current or correct and agrees to indemnify, save harmless and release, the Brokerage, sales representative or broker by whom the information was prepared, from all manner of actions, causes of action, suits or claims of any kind whatsoever.

NB: The above information is the property of the Brokerage, sales representative or broker by whom it was prepared and is not to be shared, distributed, published, transmitted, assigned, communicated or transferred in any way whatsoever without the prior written consent of the Brokerage, sales representative or broker named above.

NB: The above information is NOT an appraisal and is to be used for marketing purposes only.

Form 260   Revised 2012   **Page 1 of 1**

◼ Exercise 3   The Overpriced Property

The seller is adamant concerning listing price. Despite research indicating a $395,000 maximum listing price, the client insists on no less than $449,000. Itemize seven possible problems that could impact the seller, the brokerage, the broker or salesperson when overpricing a property? Creative answers are encouraged.

■ Exercise 4   The Anxious Seller

Salesperson Lee has just listed vacant land measuring 100' x 200' in a rural setting approximately five miles from Westville. The seller lists at $149,900 and will consider a first mortgage with 50% down. Confidentially, the seller admits that the property sale will provide much needed cash. Lee's first ad appears below. Comment with direct reference to advertising guidelines described in this chapter under the *Competition Act* and REBBA 2002. Additional commentary is also encouraged regarding other aspects of REBBA 2002 that are not addressed in this chapter, but were covered in previous chapters and courses.

Building Lot—Seller Anxious

Can't wait to build that new country home? Don't miss the best building lot north of Westville. Priced to sell quickly. Don't delay. Seller will take back mortgage—easy terms. A real buy in the low $140,000s. Call Salesperson Lee at 555–1212.

CHAPTER 7

Analyzing The Agreement

Introduction

The agreement of purchase and sale represents the most complex document used in real estate. Understanding the agreement and providing competent discussions of wordings with buyers and sellers is focal in real estate negotiations. The agreement contains an intricate interplay of legislative requirements, common law principles and generally-accepted practices.

The analysis includes both new topics and a review of selected subject matter covered in previous chapters and courses with relation to pre-printed text. Registrants are expected to be conversant with all agreement wordings but should direct clients to expert legal advice as appropriate. Particular emphasis is placed on drafting accurate, complete offers and avoiding common errors and omissions.

Nothing replaces a solid working knowledge gained through clause-by-clause review. Salespersons build careers on client trust. Providing informed guidance advances that trust-building process.

Picture yourself as a consumer purchasing a home. Something is troubling you about the preprinted wordings. For example, how is the sale registered or what adjustments are made? Rather than assisting, the salesperson evades the question. What is the lasting impression?

Be pro-active when discussing agreements. Know what every sentence means and be able to explain each clause in simple, understandable terms. Buyers and sellers look to you for guidance. Respect is not achieved by accident, but by hard work, professional knowledge and continuously updated skills. When legal questions arise, direct them to appropriate experts.

Learning Outcomes

At the conclusion of this chapter, students will be able to:

- Describe the essential components and overall structure of the *Agreement of Purchase and Sale* (Form 100).
- Identify and discuss key contractual provisions and preprinted clauses contained on pages 1 through 4 of the *Agreement of Purchase and Sale.*
- Identify and discuss methods to avoid errors and omissions when drafting agreements.
- Identify and discuss all signature lines including acceptable practices for their completion.
- Describe guidelines and acceptable procedures for the insertion of selected non-signature details involving confirmations, acknowledgements and the commission trust agreement.
- Identify and discuss key differences between the *Agreement of Purchase and Sale* (OREA Form 100) and the *Agreement of Purchase and Sale—Commercial* (OREA Form 500).

REMINDER: This chapter builds on topics covered in previous chapters and courses. Appropriate review is encouraged.

THE AGREEMENT OF PURCHASE AND SALE

The **Agreement of Purchase and Sale** (OREA Form 100) is widely used in the Ontario marketplace and is used for instructional purposes in this text. The residential offer is reviewed in detail, followed at the end of the chapter with key differences in the commercial counterpart (OREA Form 500).

Preprinted agreements of purchase and sale developed by the Ontario Real Estate Association are best viewed in four sections:

CONTRACT DETAILS   **PAGE 1**

> **OREA** Ontario Real Estate Association **Agreement of Purchase and Sale**
>
> **Form 100**
> for use in the Province of Ontario
>
> This Agreement of Purchase and Sale dated this .... day of .... 20...........
>
> **BUYER,** ...., agrees to purchase from
> (Full legal names of all Buyers)
>
> **SELLER,** ...., the following
> (Full legal names of all Sellers)
>
> **REAL PROPERTY:**
>
> Address ....
>
> fronting on the .... side of ....

PREPRINTED CLAUSES   **PAGES 2, 3 AND 4**

> 3.   **NOTICES:** The Seller hereby appoints the Listing Brokerage as agent for the Seller for the purpose of giving and receiving notices pursuant to this
>
> 8.   **TITLE SEARCH:** Buyer shall be allowed until 6:00 p.m. on the .... day of ...., 20..........., (Requisition Date)
>
> 15. **PLANNING ACT:** This Agreement shall be effective to create an interest in the property only if Seller complies with the subdivision control provisions of the Planning Act by completion and Seller covenants to proceed diligently at Seller's expense to obtain any necessary consent by completion.
>
> 16. **DOCUMENT PREPARATION:** The Transfer/Deed shall, save for the Land Transfer Tax Affidavit, be prepared in registrable form at the expense of Seller, and any Charge/Mortgage to be given back by the Buyer to Seller at the expense of the Buyer. If requested by Buyer, Seller covenants that the Transfer/Deed to be delivered on completion shall contain the statements contemplated by Section 50(22) of the Planning Act, R.S.O.1990.
>
> 17. **RESIDENCY:** (a) Subject to (b) below, the Seller represents and warrants that the Seller is not and on completion will not be a non-resident under the non-residency provisions of the Income Tax Act which representation and warranty shall survive and not merge upon the completion of this transaction and the Seller shall deliver to the Buyer a statutory declaration that Seller is not then a non-resident of Canada; (b) provided that if the Seller is a non-resident under the non-residency provisions of the Income Tax Act, the Buyer shall be credited towards the Purchase Price with the amount, if any, necessary for Buyer to pay to the Minister of National Revenue to satisfy Buyer's liability in respect of tax payable by Seller under the non-residency provisions of the Income Tax Act by reason of this sale. Buyer shall not claim such credit if Seller delivers on completion the prescribed certificate.
>
> 18. **ADJUSTMENTS:** Any rents, mortgage interest, realty taxes including local improvement rates and unmetered public or private utility charges and unmetered cost of fuel, as applicable, shall be apportioned and allowed to the day of completion, the day of completion itself to be apportioned to Buyer.

SIGNATURES, CONFIRMATIONS AND ACKNOWLEDGEMENTS   **PAGE 5**

> 28. **SUCCESSORS AND ASSIGNS:** The heirs, executors, administrators, successors and assigns of the undersigned are bound by the terms herein.
>
> SIGNED, SEALED AND DELIVERED in the presence of: IN WITNESS whereof I have hereunto set my hand and seal:
>
> .... ● .... DATE ....
> (Witness)   (Buyer)   (Seal)
>
> .... ● .... DATE ....
> (Witness)   (Buyer)   (Seal)
>
> I, the Undersigned Seller, agree to the above offer. I hereby irrevocably instruct my lawyer to pay directly to the brokerage(s) with whom I have agreed to pay commission, the unpaid balance of the commission together with applicable Harmonized Sales Tax (and any other taxes as may hereafter be applicable), from the proceeds of the sale prior to any payment to the undersigned on completion, as advised by the brokerage(s) to my lawyer.
>
> SIGNED, SEALED AND DELIVERED in the presence of: IN WITNESS whereof I have hereunto set my hand and seal:
>
> .... ● .... DATE ....
> (Witness)   (Seller)   (Seal)
>
> .... ● .... DATE ....
> (Witness)   (Seller)   (Seal)
>
> **SPOUSAL CONSENT:** The Undersigned Spouse of the Seller hereby consents to the disposition evidenced herein pursuant to the provisions of the Family

SCHEDULE A   **PAGE 6**

> **OREA** Ontario Real Estate Association **Schedule A**
>
> **Form 100**   **Agreement of Purchase and Sale**
> for use in the Province of Ontario
>
> This Schedule is attached to and forms part of the Agreement of Purchase and Sale between:
>
> **BUYER,** ...., and
>
> **SELLER,** ....
>
> for the purchase and sale of ....

When properly prepared, the agreement must clearly represent the intentions of both parties and fully provide for all agreed terms.

The *Agreement of Purchase and Sale* (Form 100) is intended for resale residential properties only, not including resale condominiums and co-operatives. Other forms (i.e., OREA Forms 101 and 102) address these specialty ownership types. Further, an **Agreement to Lease–Residential** (Form 400) applies to residential tenancies. An OREA new house agreement is not currently available in Ontario.

The residential agreement of purchase and sale is also not intended for other complex situations; e.g., multi-residential buildings and commercial buildings. Procedures concerning the *Agreement of Purchase and Sale—Commercial* (Form 500) are addressed in *The Commercial Real Estate Transaction*.

Agreement of Purchase and Sale vs. Agreement for Sale

An agreement of purchase and sale should be clearly distinguished from an agreement for sale. An **agreement for sale** is an agreement for the purchase of real property wherein the seller retains title to the property, while permitting the buyer to occupy the premises without becoming the owner. Unlike the agreement of purchase and sale, title is not conveyed until some future stipulated date or until some future event occurs.

- When payment for the property is made in full.
- When sufficient payments are made to pay the difference between the price and the existing mortgage.
- When the buyer has built up sufficient downpayment and the seller feels comfortable in taking back a mortgage on the property.

Until one of these occurrences takes place, the buyer is said to have a contractual interest in the property. If payment default occurs, the buyer immediately relinquishes any right to the property. The seller has no need to foreclose as title still rests with that individual. No standard form exists for an agreement for sale to be used by registrants in Ontario, but forms are provided by legal publishers.

An agreement for sale is infrequently used but could be viewed as a financing alternative for a buyer with limited downpayment when the seller is seeking the best possible security. The agreement for sale can be used in various circumstances: where existing mortgages cannot be discharged for a specified period, when the deposit is small or where it is impractical to have a sale with a mortgage back to the seller.

EXAMPLE   *Agreement For Sale*

Buyer Jones agrees to pay $4,000 downpayment with 12 installment payments of $4,000 and takes possession of the property. Upon receipt of the full $52,000, Seller Smith takes back the balance of the purchase price as a seller-take-back mortgage. Once Jones has made all payments in full, he will get the normal transfer/deed. If Jones defaults in payment prior to Smith receiving the full sum of $52,000, Seller Smith can terminate the agreement and proceed with eviction, unless a court orders the reinstatement of the agreement.

Agreement Structure

CONTRACT DETAILS

Registrants are required to complete selected contract specifics; e.g., buyer, seller, real property, purchase price, deposit and identification of schedules. Detailed guidelines are provided in this chapter to ensure accuracy and completeness.

Page 1 also includes preprinted Clauses 1 and 2. Both have space for additional details to be completed as the need arises. Note: Not all blanks must be filled in. Some registrants insert N/A if a specific blank is not applicable, but this is more a personal preference than a required practice.

PREPRINTED CLAUSES

Clauses 3 through 7 also contain selected clauses for additional details as well as preprinted provisions. Registrants must be capable of fully discussing such wordings with buyers and sellers. Preprinted wordings have been carefully drafted to address specific circumstances surrounding residential sales. Negotiations, in rare instances, may involve additions and deletions to such wordings. If such occurs, discuss the matter directly with the broker of record or manager and seek expert legal advice as required.

PREPRINTED CLAUSES

Clauses 8 to 14 are contained on page 3. Clauses 15 through 27 are contained on page 4. As with page 2, preprinted wordings have been carefully drafted, but changes may be necessary to suit specific circumstances. Once again, discuss the matter directly with the broker of record or manager and seek expert legal advice as required

SIGNATURES, CONFIRMATIONS AND ACKNOWLEDGEMENTS

Page 5 contains a final preprinted clause, but the page is devoted primarily to the agreement of the parties and with various legal, statutory and confirming requirements. The page flows logically from buyer(s) signature, seller(s) signature of acceptance, spousal consent (if required), confirmation of acceptance (i.e., when offer was finally accepted by all parties), information on brokerages and acknowledgements regarding receipt of true copies.

SCHEDULE A

Schedule A is an integral part of the agreement. Other schedules may be attached if additional space is required. Buyer, seller and property identification are included for cross-reference purposes.

Extreme care must be taken in drafting clauses for insertion in the Schedule. Numerous court cases attest to this responsibility and liability that can be incurred for incorrectly prepared agreements and supporting documents.

PAGE 1: CLAUSE-BY-CLAUSE REVIEW

OREA Ontario Real Estate Association   **Agreement of Purchase and Sale**

Form 100
for use in the Province of Ontario

This Agreement of Purchase and Sale dated this .... day of .... 20..........

BUYER, ... **A** ...., agrees to purchase from
(Full legal names of all Buyers)

SELLER, ..., the following
(Full legal names of all Sellers)

REAL PROPERTY: **B**

Address ....

fronting on the .... side of ....

in the ....

and having a frontage of .... more or less by a depth of .... more or less

---

A Buyer and Seller Lines

Individuals must be clearly identified as buyers/sellers; i.e., full legal names. If more than one buyer, treat each party individually; i.e., *John William Smith and Mary Jane Smith*, NOT Mr. and Mrs. John Smith. *Note:* A person can be named as a buyer but his or her name may not ultimately appear on title at registration. Conversely, an offer may be made in one buyer's name but the transaction closes with a second or third buyer also on title.

Always confirm ownership details. The transfer/deed of land provides ownership information and confirms legal description, including any limitations and ownership extent (e.g., joint tenancy or tenancy in common).

CORPORATIONS

Confirm and insert the full corporate legal name. Appropriate officers must be identified and the corporate seal used with their signatures (see Page 5). In lieu of the corporate seal, individual(s) signing may include *I/We have the authority to bind the corporation* on the signature lines on Page 5. Insist on confirming corporate officer(s) status, having appropriate signatures and including the corporate seal. Avoid possible legal problems— for example, a corporate employee executes the contract and a dispute ensues regarding authority to do so.

MINORS

Age of majority is 18 in Ontario. If any doubt, seek confirming evidence.

NON-OWNERS

- **Estate Trustees** (formally referred to as **Executors** or **Administrators** depending on whether a will existed or not) may sign as non-owners assuming proper authority. While legal issues concerning estate trustees (executors) go beyond normal real estate practice, certain guidelines should be followed. In dealing with estate trustees, registrants must be sure that all trustees sign the agreement. Should only one of two (or more) do so and even though such person may purport to have the authority to do so, a valid and enforceable contract may not exist.

> *Estate Trustees*
>
> An individual either appointed by the court (Estate Trustee Without a Will—previously known as an administrator), or appointed in a will (Estate Trustee With a Will—previously known as an executor).

- To ensure validity, an agent should insist that all estate trustees sign and should seek a notarized copy of probate documents to ensure that all have signed. As well, the trustees must have a power to sell under the will, since in certain circumstances the beneficiaries under the will may have to sign as well. Whenever doubt exists, the salesperson should request the solicitor for the estate to confirm who the representatives of the deceased are and who is empowered to sign all contracts, including listings and agreements.

- If a person dies leaving no estate trustee, the court will make an appointment. When a death occurs and no will exists (dying intestate), the court will confirm arrangements by appropriate documentation. If a valid will exists but an estate trustee was not named, the court will address this situation. The distribution of the deceased's assets can then proceed subject to various statutory regulations and provisions. Legal advice is strongly recommended on all matters concerning executors.

- An individual may have **power of attorney** to act on behalf of another in a real estate transaction. Seek confirming evidence. Legal advice is strongly encouraged to ensure that such authority has been granted.

Power of Attorney CURIOSITY

A power of attorney is a delegated written authority to a person to act legally, including the signing of documents, on behalf of another. A power of attorney must be executed and witnessed. A power of attorney may involve a very general power to act on behalf of another or it can be precisely described and limited in scope.

EXAMPLE
Seller Smith will be out of the country for several months while his property is being offered for sale. To avoid various problems if an offer were presented, Smith signs a power of attorney with his lawyer. The power of attorney addresses various issues that must be attended to in his absence. The specific reference to the marketing of his home provides that the lawyer shall sign on Smith's behalf any offer that meets or exceeds the minimum acceptable price of $190,000. The power of attorney also states that the lawyer shall have full power to negotiate other terms and conditions leading to the sale of the property.

- Registrants may encounter *in trust* arrangements; e.g., *William Smith (In Trust)* or *William Smith (In Trust for a Corporation Yet to be Formed)*. The seller typically has no recourse against the individual, with the ultimate owner being a corporation with few or no assets. A person signing in trust is not generally held liable for contracts signed under seal. Get expert advice on this matter.

- A builder may sign an agreement for a new house yet to be constructed while not presently owning the land. Technically, the builder does not have lot title at time of signing, but does have the right to purchase the lot from the developer.

PARTNERS
Fully identify and obtain signatures of all partners.

SPOUSES
Both owner spouses must sign if title is held jointly; e.g., joint tenancy or tenancy in common. If only one spouse holds title and the property is a **matrimonial home**, the non-owner spouse signs under Spousal Consent (Page 5). If the spouse does not sign

consent, problems may arise pursuant to the *Family Law Act*. Both buyer spouses also typically sign. However, a spouse who does not sign can be added subsequently by way of direction.

ESTATE SALE

Registrants require confirming evidence that the person(s) signing on behalf of an estate has the explicit authority to do so. The issue often involves timing. In Registry, the Will or a Certificate of Appointment of the Estate Trustee must be registered. In Land Titles, a Certificate of Appointment must be registered. (Note: The Land Titles Registrar may waive this requirement if the Estate does not exceed a prescribed limit.)

The representation agreement is then prepared showing the estate; i.e., *The Estate of John Doe*, with the Estate Trustee Mary Doe signing appropriately on the listing agreement. Obtaining a Certificate can involve several weeks and registrants may be under pressure to get the property on the market. What can be done in the interim? Some might consider inserting the following: *Mary Doe as Applicant for a Certificate of Appointment of the Estate Trustee* both on the listing and any accepted offer. This strategy is strongly discouraged. Legal and practical difficulties can arise; e.g., a legal issue unfolds regarding Mary Doe's application resulting in a prolonged delay extending well beyond the intended closing date. Alternatively, a dispute can arise concerning who will administer the estate and/or another party becomes involved who also provides instructions to list and sell the property.

As with all non-owner situations, the best policy is to get appropriate authority and seek confirming evidence. Anything less can result in misunderstandings, poor service and possibly litigation.

B Real Property

Identification of real property must be accurate and easily distinguish the property from others. No standard form can possibly contemplate all property descriptions. The OREA Form 100 agreement includes four dimensions to best ensure a unique description for each property.

ADDRESS

- Full civic address; e.g., *1271 Main Street, 20371 Leslie Street* and so forth. Rural areas can prove challenging. Rural route number may be the only locator information available (in addition to legal description).

- Ontario rural areas have adopted the 911 address program to more accurately identify remote properties. If lacking specific information, include mailing address and other details (e.g., location, size of property, etc.) so as to clearly distinguish the property from others.

FRONTING ON

- Include North, West, East or South as applicable along with street name. Property may have an address on one street but front onto another.

FRONTAGE/DEPTH

- Precise imperial or metric measurements required. The preprinted words '**more or less**' are intended for minor discrepancies only and should not be relied upon.

- Confirm using source documents. Include an up-to-date survey, if available, for irregularly-shaped properties and/or when confusion might arise. If appropriate, attach the survey as a schedule.

More or Less

Slight or unimportant inaccuracies that both parties are willing to accept.

LEGAL DESCRIPTION

- The complete **legal description** is required as found in a valid source document. Insert any easements unless described elsewhere in the agreement. Registrants should note that the preprinted Clause 10 addresses compliance with easements but there is an exception for those that materially affect the present use of the property (e.g., mutual driveways). A separate acknowledgement of major easements should be included in the agreement.

What Does 'More or Less' Mean	RESIDENTIAL CASE LAW

Is there any room for minor variation and when does a difference become significant? This case involves a significant variance between what was represented and what existed on the ground.

The buyers entered into an agreement to buy an irregularly-shaped residential lot using the Toronto Real Estate Board agreement of purchase and sale form. The agreement described the property as having a frontage of AS PER SURVEY and approximately 1.5 acres in size. The offer of $1,110,000 was also conditional on obtaining a building permit.

The seller did not furnish the survey that he agreed to provide within 72 hours. The buyers therefore had a survey completed and discovered, just a few days prior to the requisition date, that the property was only 1.15 acres. As a consequence, they would be unable to build a large home (16,000 square feet) due to lot coverage restrictions set out in local zoning by-laws.

Given that the property was significantly less than represented, the buyers essentially took the position that the lot was other than described and did nothing further, allowing both the requisition and closing dates to go by with no further action. The issue at trial involved the return of the deposit and the matter of whether or not the buyers could rescind the contract based on the incorrect lot size. Given evidence submitted, the Judge found that the smaller than promised lot size was a material and substantial fact. Accordingly, the Court declared that the agreement was void ab initio (Latin for from the beginning) and ordered that the deposit money (plus accumulated interest) be released to the buyers.

Reference: Olszewski v. Trapman, Manchella and Re/Max (2000) 35 R.P.R. (3d) 316

COMMENTARY

The lot was 23.33% smaller than represented and the Judge deemed this to be a significant variation. As a point of interest, another case cited involved a lot that was 6.541% smaller than promised and was also judged to be substantial. While very minor variations might be legally tolerated, the issue becomes one of interpretation by the Courts. Prudent registrants should always strive for complete accuracy.

.... (the "property")
(Legal description of land including easements not described elsewhere)

PURCHASE PRICE: C   Dollars (CDN$) ....

.... Dollars

DEPOSIT: Buyer submits .... D
     (Herewith/Upon Acceptance/as otherwise described in this Agreement)

.... Dollars (CDN$) ....

by negotiable cheque payable to .... "Deposit Holder" to be held in trust pending completion or other termination of this Agreement and to be credited toward the Purchase Price on completion. For the purposes of this Agreement, "Upon Acceptance" shall mean that the Buyer is required to deliver the deposit to the Deposit Holder within 24 hours of the acceptance of this Agreement. The parties to this Agreement hereby acknowledge that, unless otherwise provided for in this Agreement, the Deposit Holder shall place the deposit in trust in the Deposit Holder's non-interest bearing Real Estate Trust Account and no interest shall be earned, received or paid on the deposit.

Buyer agrees to pay the balance as more particularly set out in Schedule A attached.

C Purchase Price

AMOUNT

Purchase price represents the total money that the seller is to receive in return for transferring title on the completion date. Insert words/numbers (as in writing a cheque) for purchase price and **deposit**. If a purchase price is not entered, the agreement does not comply with the Statute of Frauds and is, therefore, invalid.

ACREAGE/FRONTAGE

If the price is based on acreage calculation, for example at $5,300 per acre, make certain that the exact acreage is stated as part of the description. If working acres are involved, such as a cash crop farm where price might be established by working acres, include both total acreage and working acreage. Failure to do so can result in confusion when buyer and seller are negotiating price.

UNIT PRICE

In some instances, the purchase price for a vacant lot might be established based on a price per front foot (e.g., a new house lot or waterfront lot) with exact dimensions yet to be determined. The purchase price is stated as *$x.xx per front foot* with an appropriate offer clause regarding obtaining a survey—including at whose expense.

 Make certain that the clause trail within the offer properly reflects the parties' understanding.

D Deposit

DEPOSIT HOLDER

The deposit is typically held by the listing brokerage; e.g., *ABC Realty Inc.* If circumstances vary; e.g., buyer requests that the selling brokerage or lawyer hold the deposit (e.g., *John Q. Solicitor, In Trust*), seek guidance from your broker of record or manager. Registrants should note that new homes covered by the Tarion Warranty Corporation have special deposit protection. New homes are discussed in *The Residential Real Estate Transaction*.

ADDITIONAL/MULTIPLE DEPOSITS

The initial deposit is inserted on Page 1 with subsequent deposit descriptions on Schedule A (Page 6). Brokerage policies concerning interest on deposits and handling of supplemental deposits may vary. No minimum deposit requirements exist, as such funds are a sign of good faith. Five to ten percent is encouraged.

Deposit

Payment of money or other valuable consideration as pledge for fulfillment of a contract.

DEPOSITING FUNDS

The *Real Estate and Business Brokers Act, 2002* requires that monies received be deposited into a trust account within five business days of receipt. Insert the appropriate term: *Herewith, Upon Acceptance* or *as otherwise described in this agreement.*

INTEREST ON DEPOSIT

Wording provides that no interest is paid for funds held in trust. If the arrangement is otherwise, an appropriate clause must be inserted in Schedule A.

RETURN OF DEPOSIT

A mutual release is required from both parties for a deposit to be released by a brokerage following acceptance. The only other acceptable instruction to a brokerage is a direction by the Court.

RECEIPT OF FUNDS/IDENTIFICATION

Registrants are required under the federal *Proceeds of Crime (Money Laundering) and Terrorist Financing Act* to prepare a receipt of funds form for money received (i.e., deposits) in the course of a real estate transaction. Identification verification is also required for each transaction. FINTRAC (Financial Transactions and Reports Analysis Centre of Canada) oversees all matters concerning this Act and has set out specific requirements concerning real estate brokerages, brokers and salespersons. Detailed procedures are provided in Chapter 8: Drafting Offers: Part 1.

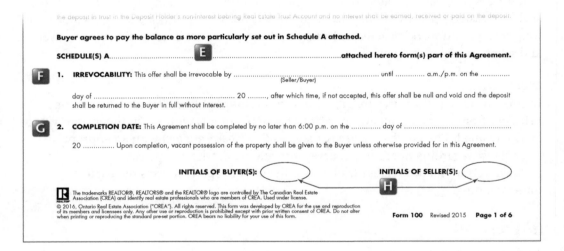

E Schedule A

Offer terms, conditions and other miscellaneous clauses are inserted on Schedule A (Page 6). Clause construction is detailed in a subsequent chapter.

BUYER AGREES TO PAY THE BALANCE

Balance due on completion is inserted following the preprinted text on Schedule A which reads: *Buyer agrees to pay the balance as follows.* (See subsequent chapter on clause drafting). The inserted clause includes the phrase *subject to adjustments*. Registrants should generally explain to clients how adjustments are made to avoid misunderstandings at closing.

INITIALING

Schedules must be initialed by all parties to the contract.

ADDITIONAL SCHEDULES

Additional schedules are sequentially identified; e.g., B, C, D, etc. A standard additional schedule format is provided (Schedule _____ *Agreement of Purchase and Sale*, OREA Form 105) but not mandated. Make certain that additional schedules are listed on Page 1. Additional schedules are commonly used for complex legal descriptions, detailed lists and additional clauses.

CUSTOM SCHEDULES

Custom schedules may be required to suit specific circumstances that are in a format not readily adaptable to the standard schedule (i.e., OREA Form 105). For example, a schedule could be a survey, a lengthy list of chattels/fixtures prepared by the seller on his or her letterhead, a rent roll from a property management company detailing all tenants along with rental specifics or a new home warranty description as detailed by the Tarion Warranty Corporation.

- Schedules are attached to the agreement in their sequential order and typically parallel reference order found in the agreement.
- Read all schedules carefully and be particularly sensitive to wordings that directly impact preprinted, numbered agreement clauses. Remember that text added or schedules inserted take priority over pre-printed provisions when conflict exists.
- Salespersons using schedules other than OREA Form 105 should include appropriate cross-references; e.g., buyer, seller and property address.

F Clause 1. Irrevocability

Insert **irrevocable** by buyer or seller as appropriate:

> *This offer shall be irrevocable by the Buyer until 8:00 p.m. on the 10th day of February, 2015.*

No minimum irrevocable is mandated, but the time period should be reasonable. Emphasize to the signing party that he/she is signing under seal and that an irrevocable instruction is being given to which the individual is bound until the stated time and date.

The agreement provides that the deposit is returned if the offer is not accepted. A mutual release (or direction by the Court) is required for deposit return after acceptance.

Irrevocable refers to that which is incapable of being recalled or revoked, unchangeable or unalterable. Agreements for the purchase and sale of real estate typically provide for an irrevocable date by either the buyer or seller until a specific time on a specified date, after which time, if the offer is not accepted, it becomes null and void and the deposit is returned to the buyer in full without deduction. Irrevocable dates also apply in the case of counter offers.

It is fundamental to contract law that a person making an offer to purchase real estate may withdraw that offer at any time prior to the communication of acceptance of the offer back to the offeror (unless otherwise provided for in the agreement). Once communication has taken place the offer becomes a legally binding contract and thus is irrevocable.

A question always arises as to whether a prospective buyer is actually bound by the word irrevocable, as there is no contract until the seller accepts the offer and the buyer generally receives no consideration for his/her promise not to withdraw the offer. However a promise made under seal is generally binding on the person making the promise, even in the absence of consideration. This is one of the main reasons for having the seals on agreements.

However, no unanimous agreement exists among members of the legal profession as to the effectiveness of the seal in binding the buyer to the irrevocable date. Sales representatives must do everything possible to make sure the offers they present are free of legal loopholes. Prudent sales representatives should always have the offer signed under seal and clearly advise the person signing that they are doing so under seal and, as such, the offer is irrevocable for the time period stated in the agreement. If a dispute arises, advise the parties to refer the matter to their respective solicitors.

The person making the offer has the right to specify the length of the irrevocable time. The irrevocable period is undoubtedly one of the most potent pressuring devices available in making an offer or a counter offer. Some buyers and sellers will attempt to keep the irrevocable time extremely short to swing negotiations in their favour. The prudent salesperson should negotiate a reasonable time period so that the parties can make an informed decision and complete the agreement/contract within the required time period.

G Clause 2. Completion Date

Completion Date

Date set for transfer of title.

The preprinted form provides for completion no later than 6 p.m. with the **completion date** inserted by the salesperson.

- Ensure that the date does not fall on a Saturday, Sunday or legal holiday, as land registry offices are closed. Vacant possession is given.
- If tenants occupy the property, an appropriate clause must be inserted overriding the preprinted text.

H Initials

Buyer(s) and seller(s) initials are required at the bottom of Page 1 and every other page where the signatures of the parties are not affixed. Initialing confirms the understanding of the parties regarding both preprinted clauses and inserted information. Always instruct buyer and seller to initial once they have had the opportunity to review the page, ask any questions and obtain explanations or clarifications.

PAGE 2: CLAUSE-BY-CLAUSE REVIEW

3. NOTICES: The Seller hereby appoints the Listing Brokerage as agent for the Seller for the purpose of giving and receiving notices pursuant to this Agreement. Where a Brokerage (Buyer's Brokerage) has entered into a representation agreement with the Buyer, the Buyer hereby appoints the Buyer's Brokerage as agent for the purpose of giving and receiving notices pursuant to this Agreement. **Where a Brokerage represents both the Seller and the Buyer (multiple representation), the Brokerage shall not be appointed or authorized to be agent for either the Buyer or the Seller for the purpose of giving and receiving notices.** Any notice relating hereto or provided for herein shall be in writing. In addition to any provision contained herein and in any Schedule hereto, this offer, any counter-offer, notice of acceptance thereof or any notice to be given or received pursuant to this Agreement or any Schedule hereto (any of them, "Document") shall be deemed given and received when delivered personally or hand delivered to the Address for Service provided in the Acknowledgement below, or where a facsimile number or email address is provided herein, when transmitted electronically to that facsimile number or email address, respectively, in which case, the signature(s) of the party (parties) shall be deemed to be original.

FAX No.: .... FAX No.: ....
(For delivery of Documents to Seller) (For delivery of Documents to Buyer)

Email Address: .... Email Address: ....
(For delivery of Documents to Seller) (For delivery of Documents to Buyer)

Clause 3. Notices

LISTING BROKERAGE

The listing brokerage is provided authority to give and receive written **notices** on the seller's behalf involving matters concerning an offer, counter offer or other negotiations (e.g., condition removal). OREA provides various notice forms relating to residential negotiations, which are highlighted in subsequent chapters on offer drafting and negotiations. This authority is only extended to facsimile or email if a fax number and/or an email address is inserted. Fax numbers and email addresses should not be inserted in a multiple representation situation in order to avoid any conflict of interest.

> **Notices**
> Information or knowledge brought to a party's attention.

CO-OPERATING BROKERAGE

A similar authority is granted if the co-operating brokerage represents the buyer. Once again, this authority is only extended to facsimile or email if a fax number and/or email address is inserted. Without such authorities to listing and co-operating brokerages, direct communication with buyer and seller clients would be required.

- This clause does not extend authority to the co-operating brokers, if the buyer is a customer; i.e., not represented in an agency capacity.
- Similarly, the co-operating broker's fax number and/or email address should not be included if the buyer is a customer as this would imply a representation relationship where one did not exist.

DELIVERY

Notices are deemed to be given and received when delivered to the address for service or transmitted electronically to the fax number(s) and/or email address(es) (if inserted in the Notice clause).

CAUTION: Care must be taken to ensure that the email has been sent to the correct email address. If the delivery of a document must be made within a definite time period, registrants should verify that the document has in fact been received and verify the status of a transaction and related documentation based on the required time periods and other provision(s) set out in the Agreement.

J   **4.   CHATTELS INCLUDED:**...

....

....

....

....

Unless otherwise stated in this Agreement or any Schedule hereto, Seller agrees to convey all fixtures and chattels included in the Purchase Price free from all liens, encumbrances or claims affecting the said fixtures and chattels.

K   **5.   FIXTURES EXCLUDED:**...

....

....

....

....

L   **6.   RENTAL ITEMS (Including Lease, Lease to Own):** The following equipment is rented and **not** included in the Purchase Price. The Buyer agrees to assume the rental contract(s), if assumable:

....

....

....

The Buyer agrees to co-operate and execute such documentation as may be required to facilitate such assumption.

M   **7.   HST:** If the sale of the Property (Real Property as described above) is subject to Harmonized Sales Tax (HST), then such tax shall be

.... the Purchase Price. If the sale of the Property is not subject to HST, Seller agrees to certify on or before
            (included in/in addition to)

closing, that the sale of the Property is not subject to HST. Any HST on chattels, if applicable, is not included in the Purchase Price.

N

INITIALS OF BUYER(S): ⬭   INITIALS OF SELLER(S): ⬭

J Clause 4. Chattels Included

Be specific. Include identifying characteristics such as name, model and serial number wherever possible.

> *Easywash Cyclone Washer–Serial # MNW19381718 and*
> *Easywash Cyclone Dryer–Serial # MND32618129.*

Alternatively, clearly specify chattels including location if applicable.

> *All existing living room drapes, valances and decorator rods and QuickFire Model 800, 80,000 BTU Gas Barbecue including attachments, lines and cover.*

Place lengthy chattel lists on an attached schedule. Providing detailed descriptions helps avoid potential problems should sellers substitute or remove items prior to closing.

K Clause 5. Fixtures Excluded

Be specific. Avoid troublesome chattel/fixture debates by discussing all relevant items including **built-ins** with the seller on a room-by-room basis. Problems arise more from confusion and incomplete documentation than from wrongful intent. Be particularly cautious with significant chattel/fixture inclusions and exclusions; e.g., a large recreational property sale with furnishings, appliances, equipment and recreational items. If necessary, insert an appropriate condition to fully identify such items at a later time. Listing sales-persons should encourage sellers to remove/replace any excluded fixtures if possible, prior to the property being shown, to minimize confusion.

Chattels/Fixtures: A Less Than Perfect World	CAUTION

Legally, a seller has the right to remove all chattels while all items, which are considered fixtures (at law), remain with the land. But complications arise. What is or what is not a fixture or chattel is a matter of circumstance. Articles not otherwise attached to the land by their own weight are not considered part of the land, unless circumstances reveal otherwise:

- What about the remote control unit for an automatic garage door opener? Is it a chattel or a fixture?
- Consider the dishwasher which is enclosed by kitchen cabinets, but not technically affixed other than by a simple water disconnect value?

The best solution–make certain that all questionable items are reviewed. Sellers often fail to appreciate the legal significance between a chattel and a fixture or for that matter the legal right to remove something.

Custom complicates the situation. For example, while many sellers assume that an ornate crystal chandelier would not be included, what about the special decorator rods in the living room? Assumptions are dangerous things. Many sales have been lost over seemingly insignificant items. Include/exclude any item that might be misunderstood. Don't leave such matters for the lawyers to settle. Take affirmative action and avoid frustration.

As a matter of interest, keys to buildings are deemed at law to be constructive fixtures, the ownership of which passes to the buyer on the transfer of land and buildings.

BUILT-INS

Built-in appliances and furniture (e.g., a built-in shelving unit) or other equipment can cause problems if not addressed properly. While a built-in may fulfill the legal requirements of a fixture, the seller may be under the impression that certain items will be removed at closing due to an emotional attachment (e.g., a gift from someone) or simply by assuming that such is the case (e.g., a personally crafted, but attached, book shelf). Don't assume anything. The ultimate objective is to clearly identify items that are included and excluded from the sale.

Clause 6. Rental Items

ASSUMPTION OF AGREEMENTS

Check with the seller regarding assumability of rental equipment. Clause 6 only applies to assumable rental contracts. If otherwise, the seller must:

- Remove such equipment;
- Perform requirements set out in the rental agreement; e.g., required buyout at end of lease term; or
- Fully detail obligations for the new buyer in the listing document (for subsequent negotiations leading to an agreement).

BE SPECIFIC

Rental items were once confined to rental hot water tanks, typically cancellable on notice. Traditionally, the common insertion was simply: *Rental hot water tank.* Recent years have witnessed an explosion of rental contracts, options and equipment. Rental items can include furnaces, water purification equipment, air conditioning units, satellite receivers, in-home theatre installations and alarm systems.

- Carefully detail rental arrangements wherever possible; e.g., Rental hot water tank, Union Energy, $36.40 quarterly rental.
- Descriptions may be more complex depending on circumstances such as rent-to-own contracts and shared rental/ownership plans.

> *XYZ Alarm, Focus D99 Model—Seller owned LCD Fixed KeyPads (3) and 2 Remote Controls, $36.80 per month.*

Clause 7. HST

INCLUDED IN

Most residential resale transactions do not attract HST. However, inserting the phrase *included in* places the risk on the seller should the property be subject to HST. Registrants should note the second preprinted statement which states that, if not subject to HST, the seller will certify accordingly prior to closing.

IN ADDITION TO

Inserting *in addition to* places the HST onus on the buyer. Problems can arise over complexities involving HST. Registrants need awareness of basic procedures, while appreciating that HST rules are complex. Avoid providing guidance beyond instructing buyers and sellers to seek expert advice. An appropriate condition may be required to override the preprinted clause, if HST issues arise during negotiations.

> **WEB LINKS**
> **Harmonized Sales Tax**   Go to the Canada Revenue Agency (*www.cra.gc.ca*) for detailed information regarding HST.

N Initials

Buyer(s) and seller(s) initials are required at the bottom of Page 2. Initialing confirms the understanding of the parties regarding both preprinted clauses and inserted information. Always instruct buyer and seller to initial once they have had the opportunity to review the page, ask any questions and obtain explanations or clarifications.

GST and the Bottom Line   COMMERCIAL CASE LAW

Registrants encounter tort liability particularly with complex transactions. An obvious remedy is to avoid offering opinions regarding matters that are better directed to professional advice and to ensure that appropriate conditions are inserted in agreements. While this case is about GST, the lesson learned would have equally applied if the tax had been HST.

The owner operated a day care business in renovated residential premises and initially sought to sell the property including the business at a listing price of $198,000. Remaining unsold, a year later the owner decided to relist with a brokerage (excluding the business as it was being closed) for $177,000. Ultimately, the property sold for $130,000 as a result of an offer and negotiations involving a co-operating broker—an amount the seller clearly indicated was her bottom line.

In court proceedings, both the listing salesperson and the owner acknowledged that a discussion had occurred regarding what the seller would receive at closing. The salesperson, aware of the bottom line $130,000 negotiating point, informed the seller that the only deductions would be the real estate commission and legal fees. On the matter of GST, the offer did state:

Unless otherwise agreed in writing, the Purchase Price includes any applicable Goods and Services Tax.

The Judge noted that both parties may have believed that the sale would not attract GST. Recollections of both salesperson and owner differed as to whether or not GST was openly discussed during the negotiation process. Regardless, subsequent investigation by the seller's solicitor revealed that the sale was not GST exempt.

The Judge, in awarding damages to the seller for $8,505 {GST on sale of $121,495 ($121,495 + $8,505 = $130,000)}, did not rely upon GST discussions between salesperson and seller, but rather upon the representation by the listing salesperson that only legal fees and real estate commission would be deducted from the selling price. The salesperson, in holding himself out as a specialist, should have special skill or knowledge of factors that could affect monies received by the client.

A direct quote from the Reasons for Judgment bears special emphasis:

In my view, the duty to provide the vendor with a reasonably accurate assessment of what will be received from the transaction can readily be implied in the contract arising from the listing agreement. This would include the duty to warn the vendor of potential monetary hazards such as the GST, of which the REALTOR® was, or ought to have been, aware.

Reference: Top Realty (GP) Ltd. v. 388204 Alberta Ltd., 2000 ABPC 106

COMMENTARY

The Judge relied on the landmark Hedley Byrne & Co. v. Heller [1964] case regarding duty of care and negligent misrepresentation. An individual possessing special skill or knowledge may be found in tort (breach of duty other than responsibilities arising out of a contract) and liable for common law action for damages. In this instance, the actions of the salesperson fell within tort liability; i.e.,

- A false statement was made negligently.

- A duty of care arose as the salesperson possessed special skills and knowledge on the matter in question and the recipient (the seller) relied on these skills and knowledge.

- The seller suffered loss as a consequence of this reliance.

PAGE 3: CLAUSE-BY-CLAUSE REVIEW

[O] 8. TITLE SEARCH: Buyer shall be allowed until 6:00 p.m. on the .... day of ...., 20..........., (Requisition Date) to examine the title to the Property at Buyer's own expense and until the earlier of: (i) thirty days from the later of the Requisition Date or the date on which the conditions in this Agreement are fulfilled or otherwise waived or; (ii) five days prior to completion, to satisfy Buyer that there are no outstanding

work orders or deficiency notices affecting the Property, and that its present use (...) may be lawfully continued and that the principal building may be insured against risk of fire. Seller hereby consents to the municipality or other governmental agencies releasing to Buyer details of all outstanding work orders and deficiency notices affecting the property, and Seller agrees to execute and deliver such further authorizations in this regard as Buyer may reasonably require.

[P] 9. FUTURE USE: Seller and Buyer agree that there is no representation or warranty of any kind that the future intended use of the property by Buyer is or will be lawful except as may be specifically provided for in this Agreement.

[Q] 10. TITLE: Provided that the title to the property is good and free from all registered restrictions, charges, liens, and encumbrances except as otherwise specifically provided in this Agreement and save and except for (a) any registered restrictions or covenants that run with the land providing that such are complied with; (b) any registered municipal agreements and registered agreements with publicly regulated utilities providing such have been complied with, or security has been posted to ensure compliance and completion, as evidenced by a letter from the relevant municipality or regulated utility; (c) any minor easements for the supply of domestic utility or telephone services to the property o adjacent properties; and (d) any easements for drainage, storm or sanitary sewers, public utility lines, telephone lines, cable television lines or other services which do not materially affect the use of the property. If within the specified times referred to in paragraph 8 any valid objection to title or to any outstanding work order or deficiency notice, or to the fact the said present use may not lawfully be continued, or that the principal building may not be insured against risk of fire is made in writing to Seller and which Seller is unable or unwilling to remove, remedy or satisfy or obtain insurance save and except against risk of fire (Title Insurance) in favour of the Buyer and any mortgagee, (with all related costs at the expense of the Seller), and which Buyer will not waive, this Agreement notwithstanding any intermediate acts or negotiations in respect of such objections, shall be at an end and all monies paid shall be returned without interest or deduction and Seller, Listing Brokerage and Co-operating Brokerage shall not be liable for any costs or damages. Save as to any valid objection so made by such day and except for any objection going to the root of the title, Buyer shall be conclusively deemed to have accepted Seller's title to the property.

[O] Clause 8. Title Search

REQUISITION DATE—TITLE SEARCH

Allow sufficient time for **title** search. The time period should extend beyond any conditions inserted in the agreement. *Root of title* issues and *matters of title* must be reported by legal counsel within the requisition period.

- *Root of title* objections relate to fundamental title issues; e.g., a seller is unable to transfer title as a previous severance did not comply with the *Planning Act* or a former owner had not signed off thereby potentially nullifying the current seller's right to own.

  · As a further example, a buyer's solicitor undertakes a title search in the registry system and discovers a mortgage affecting the land that originated in 1950, but apparently had not been paid off. This objection is made to the seller's solicitor, who will either undertake to ensure that the mortgagee is paid in full, or if already paid, undertake to have a discharge recorded on title.

- *Matters of title* involve title issues that the seller cannot remove; e.g., a right-of-way granted to another party and registered on title.

Statutory provisions also exist (e.g., *Vendor and Purchasers Act*) to address title problems through the Courts, for example, the seller's lawyer responds to a requisition, but the buyer's lawyer is not satisfied with that response. Resolution of title objections goes beyond the scope of this course.

OTHER SEARCHES

Additional time is provided regarding work orders, deficiency notices, continuation of present use and capability of being insured against fire. Two time frames are provided, the earliest of which applies:

- **Option 1:** Thirty days past the Requisition Date or date on which offer conditions are fulfilled or waived; OR
- **Option 2:** Five days prior to completion.

PRESENT USE

Insert the current use (e.g., single-family residential) but do not insert zoning. Current zoning may conflict with present use. For example, a property zoned for commercial might be presently used for residential purposes. Registrants may elect to leave this line blank. If nothing is inserted, the preprinted wording provides: …*that its present use may be lawfully continued*… Even though the present use is not described, the statement allows the buyer to ensure that the present use currently being carried on by the seller is legal. If it is not legal, the buyer may be able to use it as an objection to completing the transaction.

Ⓟ Clause 9. Future Use

If intended future use is other than specified under Present Use (Clause 8), a condition is typically inserted to protect the buyer; e.g., buyer seeking to expand use beyond single-family to two or more self contained rental units or a commercial conversion.

Conditional wording would typically focus on the buyer obtaining re-zoning or confirming that present zoning would accommodate the intended purposes.

Ⓠ Clause 10. Title

The buyer is assured that title is good and free from restrictions, charges, liens and encumbrances save and except for:

- Items specifically set out in the agreement such as a mortgage being assumed.
- Registered restrictions or covenants which are complied with. Examples would include house size limitation, restriction on use and non-storage of recreational vehicles, etc.
- Minor utility easements such as telephone and hydro service for the subject or adjoining properties. The wording is intended to avoid frivolous title objections regarding usual utilities servicing residential properties.
- Easements (drainage, sewer, utility lines, etc.) that do not materially affect the property.

TITLE ISSUES—SALESPERSON'S PERSPECTIVE

Source Documents	Registrants are not responsible for title issues, but can assist by reviewing the seller's deed at point of listing and identifying significant issues that materially affect the property; e.g., a large drainage easement or mutual drive.
Seller Property Information Statement (SPIS)	The Seller Property Information Statement, completed by the seller, is useful in identifying title-related issues. Always inform both buyers and sellers that title problems or related questions should be directed to legal counsel.
Buyer Plans/Uses	Salespersons must exercise caution with buyers. Assume a buyer plans property renovations and the resulting increased size exceeds zoning square footage restrictions. The preprinted wording provides that the buyer must accept title if registered restrictions are complied with. The existing home complies, the renovated one does not. An appropriate condition is required to permit time for the buyer and his/her legal counsel to investigate.

TITLE ACCEPTANCE

The buyer is deemed to accept title save and except for any valid objection. Should objections arise, written notice to the seller is required. The agreement is at an end if the seller is unwilling (e.g., high cost to remedy) or unable (i.e., material restriction cannot be removed from title) to resolve such objections. The deposit is then returned. The seller, listing broker and co-operating broker are not normally liable for any costs or damages.

TITLE INSURANCE

The preprinted wording provides that insurance (i.e., **title insurance**) can be obtained to remove, remedy or satisfy an objection. The term 'insurance' in the title clause specifically EXCLUDES fire insurance, which must always be obtained by the buyer. Title insurance is discussed in more detail in a subsequent chapter.

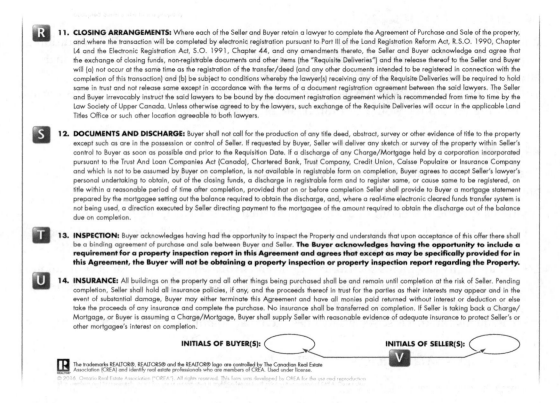

R 11. CLOSING ARRANGEMENTS: Where each of the Seller and Buyer retain a lawyer to complete the Agreement of Purchase and Sale of the property, and where the transaction will be completed by electronic registration pursuant to Part III of the Land Registration Reform Act, R.S.O. 1990, Chapter L4 and the Electronic Registration Act, S.O. 1991, Chapter 44, and any amendments thereto, the Seller and Buyer acknowledge and agree that the exchange of closing funds, non-registrable documents and other items (the "Requisite Deliveries") and the release thereof to the Seller and Buyer will (a) not occur at the same time as the registration of the transfer/deed (and any other documents intended to be registered in connection with the completion of this transaction) and (b) be subject to conditions whereby the lawyer(s) receiving any of the Requisite Deliveries will be required to hold same in trust and not release same except in accordance with the terms of a document registration agreement between the said lawyers. The Seller and Buyer irrevocably instruct the said lawyers to be bound by the document registration agreement which is recommended from time to time by the Law Society of Upper Canada. Unless otherwise agreed to by the lawyers, such exchange of the Requisite Deliveries will occur in the applicable Land Titles Office or such other location agreeable to both lawyers.

S 12. DOCUMENTS AND DISCHARGE: Buyer shall not call for the production of any title deed, abstract, survey or other evidence of title to the property except such as are in the possession or control of Seller. If requested by Buyer, Seller will deliver any sketch or survey of the property within Seller's control to Buyer as soon as possible and prior to the Requisition Date. If a discharge of any Charge/Mortgage held by a corporation incorporated pursuant to the Trust And Loan Companies Act (Canada), Chartered Bank, Trust Company, Credit Union, Caisse Populaire or Insurance Company and which is not to be assumed by Buyer on completion, is not available in registrable form on completion, Buyer agrees to accept Seller's lawyer's personal undertaking to obtain, out of the closing funds, a discharge in registrable form and to register same, or cause same to be registered, on title within a reasonable period of time after completion, provided that on or before completion Seller shall provide to Buyer a mortgage statement prepared by the mortgagee setting out the balance required to obtain the discharge, and, where a real-time electronic cleared funds transfer system is not being used, a direction executed by Seller directing payment to the mortgagee of the amount required to obtain the discharge out of the balance due on completion.

T 13. INSPECTION: Buyer acknowledges having had the opportunity to inspect the Property and understands that upon acceptance of this offer there shall be a binding agreement of purchase and sale between Buyer and Seller. **The Buyer acknowledges having the opportunity to include a requirement for a property inspection report in this Agreement and agrees that except as may be specifically provided for in this Agreement, the Buyer will not be obtaining a property inspection or property inspection report regarding the Property.**

U 14. INSURANCE: All buildings on the property and all other things being purchased shall be and remain until completion at the risk of Seller. Pending completion, Seller shall hold all insurance policies, if any, and the proceeds thereof in trust for the parties as their interests may appear and in the event of substantial damage, Buyer may either terminate this Agreement and have all monies paid returned without interest or deduction or else take the proceeds of any insurance and complete the purchase. No insurance shall be transferred on completion. If Seller is taking back a Charge/Mortgage, or Buyer is assuming a Charge/Mortgage, Buyer shall supply Seller with reasonable evidence of adequate insurance to protect Seller's or other mortgagee's interest on completion.

INITIALS OF BUYER(S):   INITIALS OF SELLER(S):

R Clause 11. Closing Arrangements

This clause details closing procedures when lawyers are retained and electronic registration is used.

DOCUMENT DELIVERY

Various documents and their release to either buyer or seller; i.e., closing funds, non-registrable documents and other items, do not coincide with the e-registration of the Deed/Transfer of Land.

DOCUMENT EXCHANGE

Requisite documents are held in trust and exchanged between lawyers in accordance with a document registration agreement (DRA) and related procedures set out by the Law

Society of Upper Canada. The DRA is a trust agreement between the lawyers setting out procedures for document forwarding in relation to an electronic closing. Unless otherwise agreed, the exchange occurs in the applicable land titles office.

⑤ Clause 12. Documents and Discharge

TITLE

The seller is only required to produce the title deed, abstract or evidence of title documents that are in his/her possession or control. Registrants are not normally involved in forwarding title documents to lawyers—the seller should take all property documents to the solicitor, once an acceptable offer is concluded.

SURVEY

Any survey (or sketch) in the seller's control must be delivered. Registrants must be cautious concerning surveys supplied by sellers. Completeness can vary based on document age. Older surveys may contain limited information concerning boundaries and building locations. Recent surveys contain more elaborate detail mandated by current Ontario Land Surveyor standards and statutory requirements.

If the seller furnishes a survey, registrants should make it readily available to the buyer; i.e., attach as a schedule to the offer, but caution the buyer to seek legal advice as it may not be up-to-date. The buyer has several options regarding surveys. He or she can:

- Accept the existing survey acknowledging its historical nature and limitations.
- Ask the seller to provide a new survey. An appropriate clause is then inserted in the offer.
- Order a new survey at the buyer's expense.
- Title insurance can be obtained. A survey may not be required depending on the insurer.
- The buyer may elect to purchase without a survey.

Assuming the last option, the buyer's solicitor would undoubtedly require written confirmation that a survey is not available and the lawyer's title opinion on the final reporting letter would reflect that fact.

MORTGAGE DISCHARGE

Mortgages not being assumed by the buyer must be discharged. Few buyers and sellers realize that such mortgages are often not discharged for several days following closing. If a discharge is not available in registrable form at closing, the buyer agrees to accept the seller's lawyer's personal undertaking (promise) to discharge the mortgage(s) within a reasonable time, using funds received at closing. The seller agrees to furnish a mortgage statement setting out the exact balance for discharge purposes.

This provision avoids a potentially awkward situation in which the seller would be forced to pay off any outstanding mortgage (i.e., those not being assumed by the buyer) out of his/her funds, prior to receipt of closing funds. Such an arrangement would prove unworkable for most residential transactions.

A mortgage is legally discharged under the *Registry Act* and *Land Titles Act* using Form 3: *Discharge of Charge/Mortgage.*

▣ Clause 13. Inspection

OPPORTUNITY TO INSPECT ONLY

Clause 13 is limited in scope. The wording confirms only that the buyer has had the opportunity to inspect the property, including observing any patent defects.

The seller provides an opportunity to inspect, but nothing more. Proponents of this wording argue that lack of further inspection avoids any subsequent negotiations with buyers, requests for repairs and any associated problems. Following acceptance, the seller must maintain the property in good repair until closing, nothing more.

OPPORTUNITY FOR PROPERTY INSPECTION REPORT

Home inspections are commonplace in today's marketplace. Recently, a bolded statement was added to Clause 13 confirming that the buyer has had the opportunity to include a requirement for a home inspection report within the agreement.

Pre-Closing Inspection   PERSPECTIVE

Buyers must clearly understand that no right exists to re-inspect the premises prior to closing unless:

- the seller, at his/her sole discretion, grants such permission;
- an appropriate clause is inserted in the offer expressly providing access for one or more times following acceptance ; and/or
- substantial damage occurs between signing the agreement and closing. (See Clause 14. Insurance.)

Buyer clients require adequate time to carefully inspect the property. Increasingly, knowledgeable buyers are relying on detailed notes, photo and video recordings as evidence should changes occur prior to closing.

A re-inspection is often advisable prior to offer submission. This second inspection opportunity confirms facts and consolidates impressions gathered in the initial showing. Sellers are usually motivated to grant this privilege in anticipation of an offer.

The issue of pre-closing inspection is significant. In some jurisdictions beyond Ontario, a further right of inspection prior to closing is set out in agreements. Proponents argue that a re-inspection avoids potential problems should buyers discover discrepancies between what was purchased often months earlier and what is delivered on closing.

▣ Clause 14. Insurance

SELLER RESPONSIBILITY

All buildings and other things being purchased remain at the seller's risk. He/she holds insurance policies, if any, in trust pending completion.

BUYER'S OPTIONS

Should substantial damage (a term not defined in the agreement) occur, the buyer may either terminate the agreement or take any insurance proceeds and complete the transaction.

NEW COVERAGE

No insurance coverages are transferred at closing. The seller cancels any existing property insurance (e.g., homeowner's policy) and the new buyer purchases a new policy.

Recently, buyers have encountered difficulties securing insurance for selected properties; e.g., outdated wiring and underground oil tanks. In most instances, insurance coverage is granted subject to appropriate modifications, but outright refusals can occur.

While insurance underwriting rules differ, property age and overall condition are primary concerns. If problems are anticipated, recommend that the buyer insert an appropriate condition. Additional clause drafting guidelines are provided in a later chapter.

MORTGAGING

The buyer agrees to provide proof of adequate insurance to the seller if a seller take back mortgage is involved and/or to the mortgagee with a mortgage assumption.

Initials

Buyer(s) and seller(s) initials are required at the bottom of Page 3. Initialing confirms the understanding of the parties regarding both preprinted clauses and inserted information. Always instruct buyer and seller to initial once they have had the opportunity to review the page, ask any questions and obtain explanations or clarifications.

PAGE 4: CLAUSE-BY-CLAUSE REVIEW

 15. PLANNING ACT: This Agreement shall be effective to create an interest in the property only if Seller complies with the subdivision control provisions of the Planning Act by completion and Seller covenants to proceed diligently at Seller's expense to obtain any necessary consent by completion.

 16. DOCUMENT PREPARATION: The Transfer/Deed shall, save for the Land Transfer Tax Affidavit, be prepared in registrable form at the expense of Seller, and any Charge/Mortgage to be given back by the Buyer to Seller at the expense of the Buyer. If requested by Buyer, Seller covenants that the Transfer/Deed to be delivered on completion shall contain the statements contemplated by Section 50(22) of the Planning Act, R.S.O.1990.

 17. RESIDENCY: (a) Subject to (b) below, the Seller represents and warrants that the Seller is not and on completion will not be a non-resident under the non-residency provisions of the Income Tax Act which representation and warranty shall survive and not merge upon the completion of this transaction and the Seller shall deliver to the Buyer a statutory declaration that Seller is not then a non-resident of Canada; (b) provided that if the Seller is a non-resident under the non-residency provisions of the Income Tax Act, the Buyer shall be credited towards the Purchase Price with the amount, if any, necessary for Buyer to pay to the Minister of National Revenue to satisfy Buyer's liability in respect of tax payable by Seller under the non-residency provisions of the Income Tax Act by reason of this sale. Buyer shall not claim such credit if Seller delivers on completion the prescribed certificate.

 18. ADJUSTMENTS: Any rents, mortgage interest, realty taxes including local improvement rates and unmetered public or private utility charges and unmetered cost of fuel, as applicable, shall be apportioned and allowed to the day of completion, the day of completion itself to be apportioned to Buyer.

 19. PROPERTY ASSESSMENT: The Buyer and Seller hereby acknowledge that the Province of Ontario has implemented current value assessment and properties may be re-assessed on an annual basis. The Buyer and Seller agree that no claim will be made against the Buyer or Seller, or any Brokerage, Broker or Salesperson, for any changes in property tax as a result of a re-assessment of the property, save and except any property taxes that accrued prior to the completion of this transaction.

20. TIME LIMITS: Time shall in all respects be of the essence hereof provided that the time for doing or completing of any matter provided for herein may be extended or abridged by an agreement in writing signed by Seller and Buyer or by their respective lawyers who may be specifically authorized in that regard.

Clause 15. Planning Act

INVALID IF NOT COMPLIANT

The agreement is invalid if the property does not comply with the *Planning Act*. For example, no effective interest in land has been created if a rural lot is severed and does not meet statutory subdivision control provisions.

REQUIRED PRIOR TO COMPLETION

Planning compliance is not required at offer acceptance, but is necessary prior to completion. In other words, an offer can be accepted conditional on receiving consent.

SELLER INVOLVEMENT

The seller must proceed diligently at his/her expense to obtain such consent. Consents involve detailed applications and processing costs. The approval process can be time consuming. A consent can take three to six months, but much longer periods may be necessary if difficulties arise. A review of planning procedures and subdivision control provisions is recommended.

⊠ Clause 16. Document Preparation

WHO PAYS

The deed is prepared at the seller's cost with the buyer paying for the land transfer affidavit and mortgages taken back.

PLANNING ACT STATEMENTS

The buyer or buyer's solicitor can require the seller to sign a compliance statement concerning the *Planning Act*. Section 50(22), specifically referred to in this clause, sets out in legislative terms what the statement must contain.

The necessary statement can be found on the preprinted Transfer/Deed of Land. Box 14 (normally an optional statement) states:

> *The transferor (seller) verifies that to the best of the transferor's knowledge and belief, this transfer does not contravene Section 50 of the Planning Act.*

A solicitor's statement is also included outlining that he/she has reviewed the effect of Section 50 with the seller and made appropriate inquiries to confirm that the sale does not contravene the Act. Lastly, the buyer's solicitor also confirms no contravention through his/her research (see Box 14). Completing Boxes 13 and 14 effectively renders any prior contravention of Section 50 of no effect.

 **WEB LINKS**
Planning Act   Go to ***www.e-laws.gov.on.ca*** and search under *Consolidated Statutes and Regulations.*

⊡ Clause 17. Residency

This clause is directed to non-resident sellers disposing of Canadian property. Tax calculation is based on capital gain realized.

BUYER'S LIABILITY

Section 116 of the *Income Tax Act* imposes the tax obligation on the buyer. Consequently, the clause provides that a credit must be given to the buyer at closing by the seller. The buyer must remit a percentage of the purchase price to the Minister of National Revenue, which is then applied to the seller's account pending a final tax determination.

 WEB LINKS
Income Tax Act   Go to the Canada Revenue Agency website (***www.cra.gc.ca***) for detailed information on income tax.

SELLER OBTAINS CERTIFICATE

Alternatively, no credit need be applied if the seller delivers a Ministry Certificate at completion. This Certificate is issued following the seller's filing of necessary documents and payment of required taxes. The actual tax owing is calculated using the estimated sale proceeds and the property's adjusted cost base.

DECLARATION

The seller can sign a statutory declaration that he/she is not a non-resident (both at time of signing the offer and upon sale completion).

REASONABLE INQUIRY

Buyers are expected to make reasonable inquiry as to the seller's residency status, as the ultimate onus rests with them. Non-residency is particularly relevant in recreational areas where cottages and other vacation properties are located.

Z Clause 18. Adjustments

The completion date is the buyer's responsibility. Registrants can generally discuss residential resale adjustments but should leave specifics to legal counsel. Mortgage interest and taxes tend to be the largest adjustments. No adjustment is made for home insurance, as the buyer obtains new coverage. Similarly, no adjustments typically occur for metered utilities (assuming a reading is taken on completion date).

AA Clause 19. Property Assessment

No claim can be made by the buyer or seller against each other or any brokerage or salesperson for reassessments. Go to the Municipal Property Assessment Corporation website (**www.mpac.ca**) for additional information and procedures regarding assessments.

BB Clause 20. Time Limits

ALTERED TIME LIMITS

Time is of the essence applies. All time limits must be strictly adhered to. Only parties to the contract (or their authorized agents) can alter such limits by mutual agreement.

AMENDMENTS

Registrants must ensure that time limit changes are properly documented, mutually agreed upon and appropriate notices delivered; e.g., *Amendment to Agreement* (Form 120).

ACCURATE PAPER TRAILS

Agreements of purchase and sale are driven by exact time limits. The brokerage paper trail must be complete, accurate and sequentially correct; i.e., dates flow logically through agreements, amendments, etc. Registrants should always double check dates. As many as 16 dates can be found in an accepted agreement, not to mention additional ones found in clauses.

NOTICES/COMMUNICATION

Notice periods must be strictly followed and confirming documentation properly dated.

DEFAULT ON TIMING

Buyers and sellers are expected to be ready, willing and able to close the transaction on the completion date. Failure by one party can result in default action taken by the other (see Clause 21, Tender).

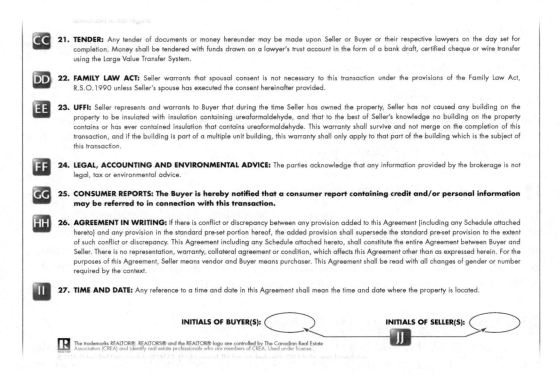

CC **21. TENDER:** Any tender of documents or money hereunder may be made upon Seller or Buyer or their respective lawyers on the day set for completion. Money shall be tendered with funds drawn on a lawyer's trust account in the form of a bank draft, certified cheque or wire transfer using the Large Value Transfer System.

DD **22. FAMILY LAW ACT:** Seller warrants that spousal consent is not necessary to this transaction under the provisions of the Family Law Act, R.S.O.1990 unless Seller's spouse has executed the consent hereinafter provided.

EE **23. UFFI:** Seller represents and warrants to Buyer that during the time Seller has owned the property, Seller has not caused any building on the property to be insulated with insulation containing ureaformaldehyde, and that to the best of Seller's knowledge no building on the property contains or has ever contained insulation that contains ureaformaldehyde. This warranty shall survive and not merge on the completion of this transaction, and if the building is part of a multiple unit building, this warranty shall only apply to that part of the building which is the subject of this transaction.

FF **24. LEGAL, ACCOUNTING AND ENVIRONMENTAL ADVICE:** The parties acknowledge that any information provided by the brokerage is not legal, tax or environmental advice.

GG **25. CONSUMER REPORTS: The Buyer is hereby notified that a consumer report containing credit and/or personal information may be referred to in connection with this transaction.**

HH **26. AGREEMENT IN WRITING:** If there is conflict or discrepancy between any provision added to this Agreement (including any Schedule attached hereto) and any provision in the standard pre-set portion hereof, the added provision shall supersede the standard pre-set provision to the extent of such conflict or discrepancy. This Agreement including any Schedule attached hereto, shall constitute the entire Agreement between Buyer and Seller. There is no representation, warranty, collateral agreement or condition, which affects this Agreement other than as expressed herein. For the purposes of this Agreement, Seller means vendor and Buyer means purchaser. This Agreement shall be read with all changes of gender or number required by the context.

II **27. TIME AND DATE:** Any reference to a time and date in this Agreement shall mean the time and date where the property is located.

INITIALS OF BUYER(S):   INITIALS OF SELLER(S):   **JJ**

The trademarks REALTOR®, REALTORS® and the REALTOR® logo are controlled by The Canadian Real Estate Association (CREA) and identify real estate professionals who are members of CREA. Used under license.

CC Clause 21. Tender

PROCESS

By tendering required documents and funds, that party confirms that he/she is ready, willing and able to complete the transaction. Both buyer and seller have the option to **tender** on the day set for completion should unresolved closing difficulties arise. Tendering involves one of the contract parties providing an unconditional offer to perform what has been agreed upon, even if the other party will not close. Money may be tendered by bank draft or certified cheque drawn on a lawyer's trust account (as outlined in the clause).

BREACH OF CONTRACT

If documents and funds are tendered by one party and the other party refuses to close for unjustified reasons, the party tendering is then in a position to seek remedies under breach of contract including recision, damages, quantum meruit, specific performance and injunction.

> **Tendering**
>
> An unconditional offer to perform as in a buyer or seller tendering regarding a real estate agreement by presenting the necessary documentation and funds at the Land Registry office on the date set for completion.

EXAMPLE	Buyer Tendering

A buyer tendering would normally present the exact funds owing and the statement of adjustments at the Land Registry office during normal business hours. Exceptions and special circumstances regarding the tendering process go beyond this discussion.

DD Clause 22. Family Law Act

The seller provides a warrant to the buyer that consent of the seller's spouse is not required. Alternatively, the spouse signs the appropriate line under Spousal Consent, granting such consent.

EE Clause 23. UFFI

SELLER DISCLOSURE

Disclosure regarding this low density foam used in the 1970's involves two seller warrants:

- That the seller has not insulated the building with material containing urea formaldehyde; and
- To his/her best knowledge and belief the building now, or in the past, has not contained UFFI.

UFFI is covered in the *The Residential Real Estate Transaction* when discussing environmental issues.

> **UFFI**
>
> Urea formaldehyde foam insulation (UFFI) was blown into place under pressure, but banned in 1980 due to health concerns.

FF Clause 24. Legal, Accounting and Environmental Advice

Both buyer and seller are acknowledging that the brokerage is not providing legal, tax or environmental advice.

GG Clause 25. Consumer Reports

This disclosure is mandated under the *Consumer Reporting Act*.

HH Clause 26. Agreement in Writing

PREPRINTED VS. INSERTED

Items inserted take precedence over pre-set wordings if a conflict or discrepancy arises.

> **EXAMPLE**
>
> A salesperson might incorrectly insert the words: *The seller agrees to execute and register a discharge of any mortgages prior to closing.* This statement would override the preprinted wording in Clause 12 which allows for mortgage discharge after closing, using proceeds from that closing.

ENTIRE AGREEMENT

No representation, warranty, **collateral agreement** or condition affects the agreement—other than those which are included. Registrants are well advised to emphasize this wording when parties sign the agreement. Essentially the parties are agreeing that nothing has been said or done, other than specifically stated in the agreement, to bring them to a mutual agreement.

VENDOR/PURCHASER

This is a necessary reference given the gradual shifting of Canadian real estate terminology away from vendor and purchaser to buyer and seller. Western Canadian jurisdictions and the United States typically reference only buyer and seller. While OREA forms are converted, many statutes still use original British references; e.g., *Vendors and Purchasers Act*.

GENDER/NUMBER

This more or less standard clause is commonly found in contracts. For example, when two (or more) buyers are signing, the phrase:

> *In Witness whereof I have hereunto set my hand and seal*
>
> can legally be read as:
>
> *In Witness whereof we have hereunto set our hands and seals.*

▐▐ Clause 27. Time and Date

The time and date refer to where the property is located, not the location where the buyer or seller may sign; e.g., a buyer living in Hong Kong but purchasing property in Ontario.

▐▐ Initials

Buyer(s) and seller(s) initials are required at the bottom of Page 4. Initialing confirms understanding of the parties regarding both preprinted clauses and inserted information. Always instruct buyer and seller to initial once they have had the opportunity to review the page, ask any questions and obtain explanations or clarifications.

PAGE 5: CLAUSE-BY-CLAUSE REVIEW

KK **28. SUCCESSORS AND ASSIGNS:** The heirs, executors, administrators, successors and assigns of the undersigned are bound by the terms herein.

LL SIGNED, SEALED AND DELIVERED in the presence of: IN WITNESS whereof I have hereunto set my hand and seal:

.... ● DATE ....
(Witness)   (Buyer)   (Seal)

.... ● DATE ....
(Witness)   (Buyer)   (Seal)

I, the Undersigned Seller, agree to the above offer. I hereby irrevocably instruct my lawyer to pay directly to the brokerage(s) with whom I have agreed to pay commission, the unpaid balance of the commission together with applicable Harmonized Sales Tax (and any other taxes as may hereafter be applicable), from the proceeds of the sale prior to any payment to the undersigned on completion, as advised by the brokerage(s) to my lawyer.

LL SIGNED, SEALED AND DELIVERED in the presence of: IN WITNESS whereof I have hereunto set my hand and seal:

.... ● DATE ....
(Witness)   (Seller)   (Seal)

.... ● DATE ....
(Witness)   (Seller)   (Seal)

MM **SPOUSAL CONSENT:** The Undersigned Spouse of the Seller hereby consents to the disposition evidenced herein pursuant to the provisions of the Family Law Act, R.S.O.1990, and hereby agrees with the Buyer that he/she will execute all necessary or incidental documents to give full force and effect to the sale evidenced herein.

.... ● DATE ....
(Witness)   (Spouse)   (Seal)

▐▐ Clause 28. Successors and Assigns

Heirs, **executors**, **administrators**, **successors** and **assigns** are bound by the agreement in the event one of the buyers or sellers dies before closing.

LL Buyer/Seller Signatures

WITNESS

- Any competent individual can **witness** a signature.
- Salespersons should witness wherever possible to confirm attendance at time of signing.
- Every signature should be witnessed. The witness does not date his/her signature.
- Witnesses can be called upon to testify should a dispute arise.
- His or her usual signature is acceptable; i.e., as opposed to his/her full legal name.

SIGNING GUIDELINES

- A party to a contract should sign with his/her usual signature (in lieu of full legal name inserted on Page 1).
- Signing date must be inserted by buyer/seller.
- Numbers and words are preferred; e.g., May 12, 20xx. Numbers only can cause confusion—is 05/12/xx May 12, 20xx or December 5, 20xx?
- The date affixed is the date on which the party actually affixes his or her signature.
- If more than two buyers or sellers are involved, add additional lines as required.
- If a corporation, affix seal and/or insert appropriate words.

    I have the authority to bind the corporation.

- Include the signing person's name and position; e.g., *John J. McKay, President, Anycity Holdings Inc.* The Confirmation of Acceptance requires only one signature.
- For non-owner signatures, include the appropriate status; e.g., *Mary Doe, Estate Trustee.*
- Inform all parties that they are signing under seal and that the irrevocable date is binding.

MM Spousal Consent

- Follow procedures described above regarding signing, witnessing and dating.
- Spousal consent is confined to non-owner spouses of matrimonial property.
- If no spousal consent is required, leave blank.
- Signing by a non-owner spouse should be completed once an agreement has been reached between the seller and buyer(s).
- Brokerages may have standard policies regarding transactions that involve a non-owner spouse in a trade involving their matrimonial home. Registrants should seek advice from their brokerage in this regard.

(Witness)   (Spouse)   (Seal)

NN CONFIRMATION OF ACCEPTANCE: Notwithstanding anything contained herein to the contrary, I confirm this Agreement with all changes both typed and written was finally accepted by all parties at .... a.m./p.m. this .... day of..., 20...........

....
(Signature of Seller or Buyer)

OO   INFORMATION ON BROKERAGE(S)

Listing Brokerage .... Tel.No.(...............)...............

....
(Salesperson / Broker Name)

Co-op/Buyer Brokerage .... Tel.No.(...............)...............

....
(Salesperson / Broker Name)

ACKNOWLEDGEMENT

PP I acknowledge receipt of my signed copy of this accepted Agreement of Purchase and Sale and I authorize the Brokerage to forward a copy to my lawyer. | I acknowledge receipt of my signed copy of this accepted Agreement of Purchase and Sale and I authorize the Brokerage to forward a copy to my lawyer.

.... DATE .... | .... DATE ....
(Seller) | (Buyer)

.... DATE .... | .... DATE ....
(Seller) | (Buyer)
Address for Service .... | Address for Service ....

.... Tel.No.(..........)....... | .... Tel.No.(..........).......

Seller's Lawyer .... | Buyer's Lawyer ....

Address .... | Address ....

Email .... | Email ....

(..........)........... (..........)..... | (..........)........... (..........).....
Tel.No.   FAX No. | Tel.No.   FAX No.

FOR OFFICE USE ONLY   **COMMISSION TRUST AGREEMENT   QQ**

To: Co-operating Brokerage shown on the foregoing Agreement of Purchase and Sale:
In consideration for the Co-operating Brokerage procuring the foregoing Agreement of Purchase and Sale, I hereby declare that all moneys received or receivable by me in connection with the Transaction as contemplated in the MLS® Rules and Regulations of my Real Estate Board shall be receivable and held in trust. This agreement shall constitute a Commission Trust Agreement as defined in the MLS® Rules and shall be subject to and governed by the MLS® Rules pertaining to Commission Trust.
DATED as of the date and time of the acceptance of the foregoing Agreement of Purchase and Sale.   Acknowledged by:

....
(Authorized to bind the Listing Brokerage)   (Authorized to bind the Co-operating Brokerage)

The trademarks REALTOR®, REALTORS® and the REALTOR® logo are controlled by The Canadian Real Estate Association (CREA) and identify real estate professionals who are members of CREA. Used under license.
© 2016, Ontario Real Estate Association ("OREA"). All rights reserved. This form was developed by OREA for the use and reproduction of its members and licensees only. Any other use or reproduction is prohibited except with prior written consent of OREA. Do not alter when printing or reproducing the standard pre-set portion. OREA bears no liability for your use of this form.   **Form 100**   Revised 2015   **Page 5 of 6**

NN Confirmation of Acceptance

- Establishes the exact time that an accepted agreement occurred. Don't confuse this with the *Acknowledgement*, which may happen at a different time. For example, the last person receiving a copy of the offer is not necessarily the last person who signed the offer.
- The last person signing or initialing has responsibility to accurately complete the confirmation.
- Buyer or seller, as appropriate, should enter time, date and signature.
- The time stated is key when establishing time limits for certain types of conditions and placing deposit funds in trust (e.g., buyer submits deposit upon acceptance).

OO Information on Brokerages

- Insert full name and contact information for both brokerages and the name of the broker or salesperson.

PP Acknowledgement

- Provides proof that parties to the contract received true copies, while granting authority to forward copies to lawyers.
- Complete full lawyer details. Details are used when the transaction is processed by the brokerage.

Commission Trust Agreement

The commission trust protects commissions of co-operating brokerages in MLS® trans-actions should the listing brokerage become insolvent or bankrupt. A **commission trust account** is in addition to the statutory **real estate trust account** maintained by all brokerages.

Salespersons are authorized representatives to sign for the brokerages in the space provided. The listing brokerage declares that funds will be held in trust and, consequently, the agreement constitutes a commission trust agreement.

How Commission Trust Works   FOCUS

A commission trust account is separate and apart from the statutory trust account maintained by a brokerage. When a transaction closes, the listing brokerage typically issues a cheque to the commission trust account from the statutory real estate trust account (assuming that the deposit is applied in full against commission earned). Secondly, a cheque is forwarded by the solicitor for the balance. This cheque is also deposited in the commission trust account.

The listing brokerage then disperses funds to the co-operating brokerage, salespersons within the brokerage and lastly to the brokerage general account.

The co-operating brokerage, in turn, deposits funds received from the listing brokerage into a commission trust account and then disperses first to the salesperson and second to the co-operating brokerage general account.

PAGE 6: SCHEDULE A

OREA Ontario Real Estate Association
Form 100
for use in the Province of Ontario

Schedule A
Agreement of Purchase and Sale

This Schedule is attached to and forms part of the Agreement of Purchase and Sale between:

BUYER, ... RR ...., and

SELLER, ... SS ....

TT for the purchase and sale of ....

.... dated the .... day of ...., 20..........

UU Buyer agrees to pay the balance as follows:

Buyer

Insert buyers' names exactly as they appear on Page 1 of the *Agreement of Purchase and Sale*.

SS Seller

Insert sellers' names exactly as they appear on Page 1 of the *Agreement of Purchase and Sale*.

🆃🆃 For the Purchase and Sale of

Property address as detailed on Page 1 is usually sufficient for cross-reference purposes. Regardless, description should be sufficient to avoid any possible confusion in the event that Page 6 becomes detached from the balance of the agreement.

🆄🆄 Buyer Agrees to Pay The Balance As Follows

The *pay the balance* line on Schedule A describes the amount due to the seller on the completion date. The six key elements in the *pay the balance* clause are:

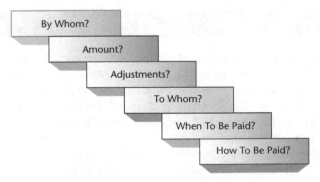

The amount can always be calculated as:

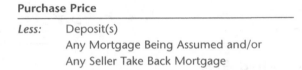

Purchase Price
_____

Less: Deposit(s)
          Any Mortgage Being Assumed and/or
          Any Seller Take Back Mortgage

If the buyer is arranging a new mortgage from an outside source, these monies are included in the balance due to the seller. Detailed clause construction is discussed in a subsequent chapter.

🆅🆅 Initials

Buyer(s) and seller(s) initials are required at the bottom of Schedule A. Initialing confirms understanding of the parties regarding information within the schedule. Always instruct buyer and seller to initial once they have had the opportunity to review the page, ask any questions and obtain explanations or clarifications.

AGREEMENT OF PURCHASE
AND SALE—COMMERCIAL

The commercial counterpart of the residential *Agreement of Purchase and Sale* has a limited number of significant differences. Key clauses are reprinted from the *Agreement of Purchase and Sale—Commercial* (OREA Form 500).

Harmonized Sales Tax (Revised/Added Wording)

The harmonized sales tax is in *addition* to the purchase price. The seller will not collect HST provided that the buyer is registered under the *Excise Tax Act*, the buyer provides a copy of that registration, the buyer will warranty that he or she will remit the HST payable and indemnify the seller in that regard.

The Buyer agrees to co-operate and execute such documentation as may be required to facilitate such assumption.

7. **HST: If the sale of the property (Real Property as described above) is subject to Harmonized Sales Tax (HST), then such tax shall be in addition to the Purchase Price.** The Seller will not collect HST if the Buyer provides to the Seller a warranty that the Buyer is registered under the Excise Tax Act ("ETA"), together with a copy of the Buyer's ETA registration, a warranty that the Buyer shall self-assess and remit the HST payable and file the prescribed form and shall indemnify the Seller in respect of any HST payable. The foregoing warranties shall not merge but shall survive the completion of the transaction. If the sale of the property is not subject to HST, Seller agrees to certify on or before closing, that the transaction is not subject to HST. Any HST on chattels, If applicable, is not included in the Purchase Price.

Inspection (Deleted Wording)

The inspection clause in the *Agreement of Purchase and Sale—Commercial* is significantly shorter than the residential version, as the provision concerning *the opportunity to include a requirement for a property inspection report* has been deleted.

Clause 13, Agreement of Purchase and Sale—Commercial

13. **INSPECTION:** Buyer acknowledges having had the opportunity to inspect the property and understands that upon acceptance of this offer there shall be a binding agreement of purchase and sale between Buyer and Seller.

Clause 13, Agreement of Purchase and Sale—Residential

13. **INSPECTION:** Buyer acknowledges having had the opportunity to inspect the Property and understands that upon acceptance of this offer there shall be a binding agreement of purchase and sale between Buyer and Seller. **The Buyer acknowledges having the opportunity to include a requirement for a property inspection report in this Agreement and agrees that except as may be specifically provided for in this Agreement, the Buyer will not be obtaining a property inspection or property inspection report regarding the Property.**

Highlighted words appearing in the *Agreement of Purchase and Sale* (OREA Form 100) have been deleted in the commercial version (OREA Form 500).

Legal, Accounting and Environmental Advice

Registrants must ensure that this clause is discussed during negotiations and prior to signing. Unlike the residential version, the clause states that it has been recommended to the parties to the agreement to obtain independent professional advice prior to signing due to the typically complex nature of a commercial transaction.

Clause 24, Agreement of Purchase and Sale—Commercial

24. LEGAL, ACCOUNTING AND ENVIRONMENTAL ADVICE: The parties acknowledge that any information provided by the brokerage is not legal, tax or environmental advice, and that it has been recommended that the parties obtain independent professional advice prior to signing this document.

Clause 24, Agreement of Purchase and Sale—Residential

24. LEGAL, ACCOUNTING AND ENVIRONMENTAL ADVICE: The parties acknowledge that any information provided by the brokerage is not legal, tax or environmental advice.

25. CONSUMER REPORTS: The Buyer is hereby notified that a consumer report containing credit and/or personal information

---

Electronic Signatures and the Agreement of Purchase and Sale   MARKET MEMO

On July 1, 2015, amendments to the *Electronic Commerce Act, 2000* (ECA) allowed agreements of purchase and sale to be signed electronically. Previously, other contracts used by a brokerage could be signed electronically (e.g., a seller or a buyer representation agreement). However, certain documents covered under the *Statute of Frauds*, including agreements of purchase and sale, were specifically excluded. Registrants who choose a technology for electronic signatures must ensure the technology meets specific criteria, including:

- *Authentication:* the ability to confirm the signature is from the person from whom it is supposed to be
- *Unauthorized use:* the signature must be permanent and tamper-proof to prevent fraudulent use of the signature

All parties to an agreement must consent to the use of electronic signatures. While consent can be implied, it is recommended that the consent be in writing to avoid future disputes. If any party to an agreement insists on using written signatures, registrants must oblige. Mortgage providers and financial institutions may also insist on paper documents with written signatures. Registrants should seek guidance from their brokerage when contemplating the use of electronic signatures because of specific procedures and audit trails that must take place. Working electronically does not change any obligation a registrant has under REBBA 2002.

AGREEMENT OF PURCHASE AND SALE— RESIDENTIAL EXAMPLE

A fully completed residential Agreement of Purchase and Sale is illustrated on the following pages. Additional discussion of its commercial counterpart including examples are found in *The Commercial Real Estate Transaction*.

Fully Completed Sample   Agreement of Purchase and Sale—Residential, Page 1 of 6

OREA Ontario Real Estate Association   # Agreement of Purchase and Sale

Form 100
for use in the Province of Ontario

This Agreement of Purchase and Sale dated this ....**8th**........ day of ....**February**........................ 20.**XX**.....

BUYER, ...**James E. Jones and Judy W. Jones**.................., agrees to purchase from
(Full legal names of all Buyers)

SELLER, ...**Mary Rose Smith and John Michael Smith**.................., the following
(Full legal names of all Sellers)

REAL PROPERTY:

Address ....**123 Main Street**..................................

fronting on the ....**East**.................. side of ....**Main Street**..................

in the ....**City of Anycity, Regional Municipality of Anyregion**..................

and having a frontage of ....**61.24 feet**.......... more or less by a depth of ....**107.50 feet**.......... more or less

and legally described as ....**Lot 94, Plan M 314**..................

.... (the "property")
(Legal description of land including easements not described elsewhere)

PURCHASE PRICE: Dollars (CDN$) ....**$230,000.00**..........

..**Two Hundred and Thirty-Thousand**-- Dollars

DEPOSIT: Buyer submits ....**Herewith**..................
(Herewith/Upon Acceptance/as otherwise described in this Agreement)

..**Twenty Thousand**-- Dollars (CDN$) ....**$20,000.00**..........

by negotiable cheque payable to ....**ABC Realty Inc.**.................. "Deposit Holder" to be held in trust pending completion or other termination of this Agreement and to be credited toward the Purchase Price on completion. For the purposes of this Agreement, "Upon Acceptance" shall mean that the Buyer is required to deliver the deposit to the Deposit Holder within 24 hours of the acceptance of this Agreement. The parties to this Agreement hereby acknowledge that, unless otherwise provided for in this Agreement, the Deposit Holder shall place the deposit in trust in the Deposit Holder's non-interest bearing Real Estate Trust Account and no interest shall be earned, received or paid on the deposit.

Buyer agrees to pay the balance as more particularly set out in Schedule A attached.

SCHEDULE(S) A..**attached hereto form(s) part of this Agreement.**

1. **IRREVOCABILITY:** This offer shall be irrevocable by ....**Buyer**.................. until **10:00** ~~a.m.~~/p.m. on the **10th**
(Seller/Buyer)

    day of ....**February**.......... 20 **XX**....., after which time, if not accepted, this offer shall be null and void and the deposit shall be returned to the Buyer in full without interest.

2. **COMPLETION DATE:** This Agreement shall be completed by no later than 6:00 p.m. on the ..**30th**.. day of ....**May**..............

    20 **XX**........ Upon completion, vacant possession of the property shall be given to the Buyer unless otherwise provided for in this Agreement.

INITIALS OF BUYER(S): (JJ JJ)   **INITIALS OF SELLER(S):** (MS JS)

3. **NOTICES:** The Seller hereby appoints the Listing Brokerage as agent for the Seller for the purpose of giving and receiving notices pursuant to this Agreement. Where a Brokerage (Buyer's Brokerage) has entered into a representation agreement with the Buyer, the Buyer hereby appoints the Buyer's Brokerage as agent for the purpose of giving and receiving notices pursuant to this Agreement. **Where a Brokerage represents both the Seller and the Buyer (multiple representation), the Brokerage shall not be appointed or authorized to be agent for either the Buyer or the Seller for the purpose of giving and receiving notices.** Any notice relating hereto or provided for herein shall be in writing. In addition to any provision contained herein and in any Schedule hereto, this offer, any counter-offer, notice of acceptance thereof or any notice to be given or received pursuant to this Agreement or any Schedule hereto (any of them, "Document") shall be deemed given and received when delivered personally or hand delivered to the Address for Service provided in the Acknowledgement below, or where a facsimile number or email address is provided herein, when transmitted electronically to that facsimile number or email address, respectively, in which case, the signature(s) of the party (parties) shall be deemed to be original.

FAX No.: ..... **(416) 555-1212**   FAX No.: ..... **(416) 444-1212**
(For delivery of Documents to Seller)   (For delivery of Documents to Buyer)

Email Address: ..... **admin@abcrealty.com**   Email Address: ..... **notices@xyzrealestate.com**
(For delivery of Documents to Seller)   (For delivery of Documents to Buyer)

4. **CHATTELS INCLUDED:** QuietTone dishwasher (Model 300), ABC central vaccum and all hoses/ accessories, brass fireplace screen in family room including accessories, garage door opener with two remote controls

Unless otherwise stated in this Agreement or any Schedule hereto, Seller agrees to convey all fixtures and chattels included in the Purchase Price free from all liens, encumbrances or claims affecting the said fixtures and chattels.

5. **FIXTURES EXCLUDED:** Dining room chandelier

6. **RENTAL ITEMS (Including Lease, Lease to Own):** The following equipment is rented and **not** included in the Purchase Price. The Buyer agrees to assume the rental contract(s), if assumable:

Hot water tank - Anycity Energy - payable $33.50 quarterly (plus applicable taxes).

The Buyer agrees to co-operate and execute such documentation as may be required to facilitate such assumption.

7. **HST:** If the sale of the Property (Real Property as described above) is subject to Harmonized Sales Tax (HST), then such tax shall be ..... included in ..... the Purchase Price. If the sale of the Property is not subject to HST, Seller agrees to certify on or before
(included in/in addition to)
closing, that the sale of the Property is not subject to HST. Any HST on chattels, if applicable, is not included in the Purchase Price.

INITIALS OF BUYER(S): (JJ JJ)   INITIALS OF SELLER(S): (MS JS)

Form 100   Revised 2015   **Page 2 of 6**

Fully Completed Sample   *Agreement of Purchase and Sale—Residential, Page 3 of 6*

8. **TITLE SEARCH:** Buyer shall be allowed until 6:00 p.m. on the 31st day of .... March ...., 20..XX.., (Requisition Date) to examine the title to the Property at Buyer's own expense and until the earlier of: (i) thirty days from the later of the Requisition Date or the date on which the conditions in this Agreement are fulfilled or otherwise waived or; (ii) five days prior to completion, to satisfy Buyer that there are no outstanding

   work orders or deficiency notices affecting the Property, and that its present use (.................. single family residential ....) may be lawfully continued and that the principal building may be insured against risk of fire. Seller hereby consents to the municipality or other governmental agencies releasing to Buyer details of all outstanding work orders and deficiency notices affecting the property, and Seller agrees to execute and deliver such further authorizations in this regard as Buyer may reasonably require.

9. **FUTURE USE:** Seller and Buyer agree that there is no representation or warranty of any kind that the future intended use of the property by Buyer is or will be lawful except as may be specifically provided for in this Agreement.

10. **TITLE:** Provided that the title to the property is good and free from all registered restrictions, charges, liens, and encumbrances except as otherwise specifically provided in this Agreement and save and except for (a) any registered restrictions or covenants that run with the land providing that such are complied with; (b) any registered municipal agreements and registered agreements with publicly regulated utilities providing such have been complied with, or security has been posted to ensure compliance and completion, as evidenced by a letter from the relevant municipality or regulated utility; (c) any minor easements for the supply of domestic utility or telephone services to the property or adjacent properties; and (d) any easements for drainage, storm or sanitary sewers, public utility lines, telephone lines, cable television lines or other services which do not materially affect the use of the property. If within the specified times referred to in paragraph 8 any valid objection to title or to any outstanding work order or deficiency notice, or to the fact the said present use may not lawfully be continued, or that the principal building may not be insured against risk of fire is made in writing to Seller and which Seller is unable or unwilling to remove, remedy or satisfy or obtain insurance save and except against risk of fire (Title Insurance) in favour of the Buyer and any mortgagee, (with all related costs at the expense of the Seller), and which Buyer will not waive, this Agreement notwithstanding any intermediate acts or negotiations in respect of such objections, shall be at an end and all monies paid shall be returned without interest or deduction and Seller, Listing Brokerage and Co-operating Brokerage shall not be liable for any costs or damages. Save as to any valid objection so made by such day and except for any objection going to the root of the title, Buyer shall be conclusively deemed to have accepted Seller's title to the property.

11. **CLOSING ARRANGEMENTS:** Where each of the Seller and Buyer retain a lawyer to complete the Agreement of Purchase and Sale of the property, and where the transaction will be completed by electronic registration pursuant to Part III of the Land Registration Reform Act, R.S.O. 1990, Chapter L4 and the Electronic Registration Act, S.O. 1991, Chapter 44, and any amendments thereto, the Seller and Buyer acknowledge and agree that the exchange of closing funds, non-registrable documents and other items (the "Requisite Deliveries") and the release thereof to the Seller and Buyer will (a) not occur at the same time as the registration of the transfer/deed (and any other documents intended to be registered in connection with the completion of this transaction) and (b) be subject to conditions whereby the lawyer(s) receiving any of the Requisite Deliveries will be required to hold same in trust and not release same except in accordance with the terms of a document registration agreement between the said lawyers. The Seller and Buyer irrevocably instruct the said lawyers to be bound by the document registration agreement which is recommended from time to time by the Law Society of Upper Canada. Unless otherwise agreed to by the lawyers, such exchange of the Requisite Deliveries will occur in the applicable Land Titles Office or such other location agreeable to both lawyers.

12. **DOCUMENTS AND DISCHARGE:** Buyer shall not call for the production of any title deed, abstract, survey or other evidence of title to the property except such as are in the possession or control of Seller. If requested by Buyer, Seller will deliver any sketch or survey of the property within Seller's control to Buyer as soon as possible and prior to the Requisition Date. If a discharge of any Charge/Mortgage held by a corporation incorporated pursuant to the Trust And Loan Companies Act (Canada), Chartered Bank, Trust Company, Credit Union, Caisse Populaire or Insurance Company and which is not to be assumed by Buyer on completion, is not available in registrable form on completion, Buyer agrees to accept Seller's lawyer's personal undertaking to obtain, out of the closing funds, a discharge in registrable form and to register same, or cause same to be registered, on title within a reasonable period of time after completion, provided that on or before completion Seller shall provide to Buyer a mortgage statement prepared by the mortgagee setting out the balance required to obtain the discharge, and, where a real-time electronic cleared funds transfer system is not being used, a direction executed by Seller directing payment to the mortgagee of the amount required to obtain the discharge out of the balance due on completion.

13. **INSPECTION:** Buyer acknowledges having had the opportunity to inspect the Property and understands that upon acceptance of this offer there shall be a binding agreement of purchase and sale between Buyer and Seller. **The Buyer acknowledges having the opportunity to include a requirement for a property inspection report in this Agreement and agrees that except as may be specifically provided for in this Agreement, the Buyer will not be obtaining a property inspection or property inspection report regarding the Property.**

14. **INSURANCE:** All buildings on the property and all other things being purchased shall be and remain until completion at the risk of Seller. Pending completion, Seller shall hold all insurance policies, if any, and the proceeds thereof in trust for the parties as their interests may appear and in the event of substantial damage, Buyer may either terminate this Agreement and have all monies paid returned without interest or deduction or else take the proceeds of any insurance and complete the purchase. No insurance shall be transferred on completion. If Seller is taking back a Charge/ Mortgage, or Buyer is assuming a Charge/Mortgage, Buyer shall supply Seller with reasonable evidence of adequate insurance to protect Seller's or other mortgagee's interest on completion.

INITIALS OF BUYER(S): (JJ JJ)   INITIALS OF SELLER(S): (MS JS)

15. **PLANNING ACT:** This Agreement shall be effective to create an interest in the property only if Seller complies with the subdivision control provisions of the Planning Act by completion and Seller covenants to proceed diligently at Seller's expense to obtain any necessary consent by completion.

16. **DOCUMENT PREPARATION:** The Transfer/Deed shall, save for the Land Transfer Tax Affidavit, be prepared in registrable form at the expense of Seller, and any Charge/Mortgage to be given back by the Buyer to Seller at the expense of the Buyer. If requested by Buyer, Seller covenants that the Transfer/Deed to be delivered on completion shall contain the statements contemplated by Section 50(22) of the Planning Act, R.S.O.1990.

17. **RESIDENCY:** (a) Subject to (b) below, the Seller represents and warrants that the Seller is not and on completion will not be a non-resident under the non-residency provisions of the Income Tax Act which representation and warranty shall survive and not merge upon the completion of this transaction and the Seller shall deliver to the Buyer a statutory declaration that Seller is not then a non-resident of Canada; (b) provided that if the Seller is a non-resident under the non-residency provisions of the Income Tax Act, the Buyer shall be credited towards the Purchase Price with the amount, if any, necessary for Buyer to pay to the Minister of National Revenue to satisfy Buyer's liability in respect of tax payable by Seller under the non-residency provisions of the Income Tax Act by reason of this sale. Buyer shall not claim such credit if Seller delivers on completion the prescribed certificate.

18. **ADJUSTMENTS:** Any rents, mortgage interest, realty taxes including local improvement rates and unmetered public or private utility charges and unmetered cost of fuel, as applicable, shall be apportioned and allowed to the day of completion, the day of completion itself to be apportioned to Buyer.

19. **PROPERTY ASSESSMENT:** The Buyer and Seller hereby acknowledge that the Province of Ontario has implemented current value assessment and properties may be re-assessed on an annual basis. The Buyer and Seller agree that no claim will be made against the Buyer or Seller, or any Brokerage, Broker or Salesperson, for any changes in property tax as a result of a re-assessment of the property, save and except any property taxes that accrued prior to the completion of this transaction.

20. **TIME LIMITS:** Time shall in all respects be of the essence hereof provided that the time for doing or completing of any matter provided for herein may be extended or abridged by an agreement in writing signed by Seller and Buyer or by their respective lawyers who may be specifically authorized in that regard.

21. **TENDER:** Any tender of documents or money hereunder may be made upon Seller or Buyer or their respective lawyers on the day set for completion. Money shall be tendered with funds drawn on a lawyer's trust account in the form of a bank draft, certified cheque or wire transfer using the Large Value Transfer System.

22. **FAMILY LAW ACT:** Seller warrants that spousal consent is not necessary to this transaction under the provisions of the Family Law Act, R.S.O.1990 unless Seller's spouse has executed the consent hereinafter provided.

23. **UFFI:** Seller represents and warrants to Buyer that during the time Seller has owned the property, Seller has not caused any building on the property to be insulated with insulation containing ureaformaldehyde, and that to the best of Seller's knowledge no building on the property contains or has ever contained insulation that contains ureaformaldehyde. This warranty shall survive and not merge on the completion of this transaction, and if the building is part of a multiple unit building, this warranty shall only apply to that part of the building which is the subject of this transaction.

24. **LEGAL, ACCOUNTING AND ENVIRONMENTAL ADVICE:** The parties acknowledge that any information provided by the brokerage is not legal, tax or environmental advice.

25. **CONSUMER REPORTS: The Buyer is hereby notified that a consumer report containing credit and/or personal information may be referred to in connection with this transaction.**

26. **AGREEMENT IN WRITING:** If there is conflict or discrepancy between any provision added to this Agreement (including any Schedule attached hereto) and any provision in the standard pre-set portion hereof, the added provision shall supersede the standard pre-set provision to the extent of such conflict or discrepancy. This Agreement including any Schedule attached hereto, shall constitute the entire Agreement between Buyer and Seller. There is no representation, warranty, collateral agreement or condition, which affects this Agreement other than as expressed herein. For the purposes of this Agreement, Seller means vendor and Buyer means purchaser. This Agreement shall be read with all changes of gender or number required by the context.

27. **TIME AND DATE:** Any reference to a time and date in this Agreement shall mean the time and date where the property is located.

INITIALS OF BUYER(S): (JJ JJ)   INITIALS OF SELLER(S): (MS JS)

Form 100   Revised 2015   **Page 4 of 6**

28. SUCCESSORS AND ASSIGNS: The heirs, executors, administrators, successors and assigns of the undersigned are bound by the terms herein.

SIGNED, SEALED AND DELIVERED in the presence of: IN WITNESS whereof I have hereunto set my hand and seal:

Linda Ward _____   James E. Jones _____   ● DATE ..... Feb. 8/xx
(Witness)   (Buyer)   (Seal)

Linda Ward _____   Judy W. Jones _____   ● DATE ..... Feb. 8/xx
(Witness)   (Buyer)   (Seal)

I, the Undersigned Seller, agree to the above offer. I hereby irrevocably instruct my lawyer to pay directly to the brokerage(s) with whom I have agreed to pay commission, the unpaid balance of the commission together with applicable Harmonized Sales Tax (and any other taxes as may hereafter be applicable), from the proceeds of the sale prior to any payment to the undersigned on completion, as advised by the brokerage(s) to my lawyer.

SIGNED, SEALED AND DELIVERED in the presence of: IN WITNESS whereof I have hereunto set my hand and seal:

Albert Lee _____   Mary R. Smith _____   ● DATE ..... Feb. 9/xx
(Witness)   (Seller)   (Seal)

Albert Lee _____   John M. Smith _____   ● DATE ..... Feb. 9/xx
(Witness)   (Seller)   (Seal)

SPOUSAL CONSENT: The Undersigned Spouse of the Seller hereby consents to the disposition evidenced herein pursuant to the provisions of the Family Law Act, R.S.O.1990, and hereby agrees with the Buyer that he/she will execute all necessary or incidental documents to give full force and effect to the sale evidenced herein.

_____   _____   ● DATE _____
(Witness)   (Spouse)   (Seal)

CONFIRMATION OF ACCEPTANCE: Notwithstanding anything contained herein to the contrary, I confirm this Agreement with all changes both typed and written was finally accepted by all parties at 2:00 ~~a.m.~~/p.m. this 9th day of.......February........, 20XX

                                          Mary R. Smith
                                          (Signature of Seller or Buyer)

INFORMATION ON BROKERAGE(S)	
Listing Brokerage ..... ABC Realty Inc.	Tel.No.(416) 253-0910
25 Main Street, Anycity M4C 2A9 Albert Lee	
	(Salesperson / Broker Name)
Co-op/Buyer Brokerage ..... XYZ Real Estate Ltd.	Tel.No.(416) 257-0800
815 First Street, Anycity M4C 1C7 Linda Ward	
	(Salesperson / Broker Name)

ACKNOWLEDGEMENT

I acknowledge receipt of my signed copy of this accepted Agreement of Purchase and Sale and I authorize the Brokerage to forward a copy to my lawyer. | I acknowledge receipt of my signed copy of this accepted Agreement of Purchase and Sale and I authorize the Brokerage to forward a copy to my lawyer.

Mary R. Smith .... DATE Feb. 9/xx | James E. Jones .... DATE Feb. 9/xx
(Seller) | (Buyer)
John M. Smith .... DATE Feb. 9/xx | Judy W. Jones .... DATE Feb. 9/xx
(Seller) | (Buyer)
Address for Service *123 Main Street, Anycity M4C 2A9* | Address for Service 16 Pine Court, Anycity M5E 2J6

Tel.No.(*416*) *777-1212* | Tel.No.(905) 222-1212

Seller's Lawyer *Brooks and Dunn* | Buyer's Lawyer Marchand and Jenkins
Address *19 Centre Street, Anycity M5E 6T9* | Address 25 First Street, Anycity M4J 3C4
Email _____ | Email _____
(*416*) *666-1212*   (*416*) *999-1212* | (*416*) 333-1212   (*416*) 444-1212
Tel.No.   FAX No. | Tel.No.   FAX No.

FOR OFFICE USE ONLY	**COMMISSION TRUST AGREEMENT**

To: Co-operating Brokerage shown on the foregoing Agreement of Purchase and Sale:
In consideration for the Co-operating Brokerage procuring the foregoing Agreement of Purchase and Sale, I hereby declare that all moneys received or receivable by me in connection with the Transaction as contemplated in the MLS® Rules and Regulations of my Real Estate Board shall be receivable and held in trust. This agreement shall constitute a Commission Trust Agreement as defined in the MLS® Rules and shall be subject to and governed by the MLS® Rules pertaining to Commission Trust.

DATED as of the date and time of the acceptance of the foregoing Agreement of Purchase and Sale.   Acknowledged by:

Albert Lee _____   *Linda Ward* _____
(Authorized to bind the Listing Brokerage)   (Authorized to bind the Co-operating Brokerage)

Form 100   Revised 2015   **Page 5 of 6**

Fully Completed Sample   *Agreement of Purchase and Sale—Residential, Page 6 of 6*

 **Ontario Real Estate Association**

Schedule A
Agreement of Purchase and Sale

Form 100
for use in the Province of Ontario

This Schedule is attached to and forms part of the Agreement of Purchase and Sale between:

BUYER, ... James E. Jones and Judy W. Jones ...., and

SELLER, ... Mary Rose Smith and John Michael Smith ....

for the purchase and sale of .... 123 Main Street, City of Anycity, Regional Municipality of Anyregion ....

.... dated the ...8th... day of .... February ...., 20.XX

Buyer agrees to pay the balance as follows:

The Buyer agrees to pay a further sum of Two Hundred and Ten Thousand Dollars ($210,000.00) subject to adjustments, to the Seller on completion of this transaction, with funds drawn on a lawyer's trust account in the form of a bank draft, certified cheque, or wire transfer using the Large Value Transfer System.

This Offer is conditional upon the Buyer arranging, at the Buyer's own expense, a new first charge/ mortgage for not less than One Hundred and Forty Thousand Dollars ($140,000.00), bearing interest at a rate of not more than 6.25% per annum, calculated semi-annually not in advance, repayable in blended monthly payments of about Nine Hundred Sixteen Dollars and Sixty-Four Cents ($916.64), including principal and interest, and to run for a term of not less than 5 years from the date of completion of this transaction. Unless the Buyer gives notice in writing, delivered to the Seller personally or in accordance with any other provisions for the delivery of notice in this Agreement of Purchase and Sale or any Schedule thereto not later than 5:00 p.m. on the 25th day of February, 20xx, that this condition is fulfilled, this Offer shall be null and void and the deposit shall be returned to the Buyer in full without deduction. This condition is included for the benefit of the Buyer and may be waived at the Buyer's sole option by notice in writing to the Seller, as aforesaid, within the time period stated herein.

The Seller acknowledges that there may be a penalty to discharge the existing Charge/ Mortgage and agrees to pay any costs, expenses or penalties incurred in discharging the existing Charge/Mortgage.

This form must be initialed by all parties to the Agreement of Purchase and Sale.

INITIALS OF BUYER(S): (JJ JJ)   **INITIALS OF SELLER(S):** (MS JS)

Form 100   Revised 2015   **Page 6 of 6**

KNOWLEDGE INTEGRATION

Notables

- An agreement of purchase and sale is clearly differentiated from an agreement for sale.

- The OREA *Agreement of Purchase and Sale* (Form 100) is used for resale residential property only, excluding condominiums and co-operatives.

- Individuals must be clearly identified as buyers or sellers. For corporations, confirm full corporate name and signing officers.

- Be cautious when dealing with non-owners; e.g., estate trustees and powers of attorney. Seek confirming evidence and legal advice as necessary.

- The OREA agreement provides four levels of description to ensure property distinctiveness.

- Schedule A forms part of the agreement. Subsequent schedules are identified and attached in sequential order.

- Be specific regarding all fixtures excluded, chattels included and rental equipment. Avoid vague descriptions that often lead to poor service, delayed or cancelled sales and possible litigation.

- Inform all buyers and sellers that they are signing under seal and that the offer cannot be revoked until the stated expiration.

- Be aware of general HST provisions only. HST rules are complex. Direct buyers and sellers to expert advice.

- Be cautious with out-of-date surveys.

- The inspection provision in the preprinted wording is limited. The agreement only states that the buyer has had the opportunity to inspect the property.

- Time is of the essence. Registrants must ensure accurate paper trails and proper date sequencing in all documentation.

- Text inserted by way of contract particulars and clauses override preprinted agreement wordings.

- Adhere to all guidelines concerning signature lines. Accuracy and completeness is vital in all agreements.

Glossary

Administrator

Agreement for Sale

Agreement of Purchase and Sale

Agreement to Lease

Assigns

Built-Ins

Collateral Agreement

Commission Trust Account

Completion Date

Deposit

Estate Trustee

Executor

Heir

Irrevocable

Legal Description

Matrimonial Home

More or Less

Notice

Power of Attorney

Real Estate Trust Account

Successors

Tender

Time is of the Essence

Title

Title Insurance

UFFI

Witness

Web Links

Web links are included for general interest regarding selected chapter topics.

Harmonized Sales Tax   Go to the Canada Revenue Agency (*www.cra.gc.ca*) for detailed information regarding HST.

Planning Act   Go to *www.e-laws.gov.on.ca* and search under *Consolidated Statutes and Regulations.*

Income Tax Act   Go to the Canada Revenue Agency website (*www.cra.gc.ca*) for detailed information on income tax.

Strategic Thinking For Your Career

Questions are included to assist in developing your new career. No answers are provided.

1. How is rural property identified in the local marketplace? Are specific addresses provided or simply rural routes?

2. How does my intended employing brokerage handle initial and supplemental deposits for residential transactions?

3. Can I effectively explain to clients how adjustments are made at closing?

4. Can I simply and effectively describe to buyers and sellers what is contained in preprinted clauses within the *Agreement of Purchase and Sale* (OREA Form 100)?

5. What types of rental equipment are typically found in my local marketplace?

6. Does my intended brokerage use the *Agreement of Purchase and Sale* (OREA Form 100)? If not, how does it differ in terms of wordings and layout?

7. What length of time is typically required to obtain a severance in the local market?

8. Will I encounter many non-resident sellers in my planned trading area?

9. Does my intended employing brokerage have a commission trust account?

10. What schedules does my intended employing brokerage have available that are used to suit particular local circumstances or specific types of property (e.g., new homes)?

Chapter Mini-Review

Solutions are located in the Appendix.

1. An agreement for sale provides that title is retained by the seller until some future stipulated date or until some future event occurs.

    ◯ True   ◯ False

2. A non-owner, for purposes of an agreement of purchase and sale, could be an individual having power of attorney or a person being an estate trustee (executor) to an estate.

    ◯ True   ◯ False

3. A Certificate of Appointment is required by a corporation in order to sign an agreement of purchase and sale when acquiring or disposing of real property.

    ◯ True   ◯ False

4. A survey can be attached as a schedule to an agreement of purchase and sale only if a proper legal description is not available.

    ◯ True   ◯ False

5. Minor variations in lot dimensions might be tolerated by the courts if such were slight and unimportant.

    ◯ True   ◯ False

6. All deposits relating to the *Agreement of Purchase and Sale* (OREA Form 100) must be deposited within two banking days of receipt.

    ◯ True   ◯ False

7. A seller has the right to remove all chattels, while all fixtures remain with the land (unless otherwise specified in the agreement).

    ◯ True   ◯ False

8. Rental equipment located on the property must be assumed by the buyer according to the *Agreement of Purchase and Sale* (OREA Form 100).

    ◯ True   ◯ False

9. The term *irrevocable* broadly refers to any instruction that is incapable of being recalled or revoked.

    ◯ True   ◯ False

10. The fax number and/or email address of the co-operating brokerage should be inserted in the appropriate space under *Notices* when that co-operating broker is not representing the buyer.

    ◯ True   ◯ False

11. Most residential resale transactions do not attract harmonized sales tax.

    ◯ True   ◯ False

12. The requisition period in the *Agreement of Purchase and Sale* (OREA Form 100) provides the opportunity to examine title, including matters that go to the root of that title.

    ◯ True   ◯ False

13. A lawyer's personal undertaking may be required to delay discharging a mortgage until after the completion date.

    ◯ True   ◯ False

14. No right of reinspection is included in the *Agreement of Purchase and Sale* (OREA Form 100), but a buyer may negotiate such a right with the seller.

    ◯ True   ◯ False

15. If substantial damage occurs to a house prior to the completion date, the agreement will be automatically terminated.

   ○ True   ○ False

16. The deed in a real estate transaction is typically prepared at the buyer's cost.

   ○ True   ○ False

17. Section 116 of the *Income Tax Act* imposes a tax liability on the buyer.

   ○ True   ○ False

18. If a property is a matrimonial home, the non-owner spouse must sign both the spousal consent and also sign as one of the sellers.

   ○ True   ○ False

19. Contracts are generally assignable at common law.

   ○ True   ○ False

20. The salesperson who drafts the agreement of purchase and sale must witness all signatures affixed to that agreement.

   ○ True   ○ False

21. Commission to a co-operating brokerage is the first disbursement made from the commission trust account when a listing brokerage processes commission funds received relating to a closed transaction.

   ○ True   ○ False

Active Learning Exercises

Solutions are located in the Appendix.

■ Exercise 1   Scenarios

Various scenarios are provided with salespersons taking certain actions. For each of the following, identify which is acceptable or not acceptable, along with a brief reason for your selection.

1.1   The Jones' are signing an offer concerning their home in Westville. Jim is the owner and Ruth, his spouse, is not on title but paid for half of the home when they were married. *James R. Jones and Ruth B. Jones* has been inserted on the line for Seller.

◯ **Acceptable**   ◯ **Not Acceptable**

Reason:

1.2   Mary Sanchez intends to act as a trustee for her sister's estate. The salesperson inserts the following on the Seller line: *Mary Sanchez—Estate Trustee Status Pending.*

◯ **Acceptable**   ◯ **Not Acceptable**

Reason:

1.3   Salesperson Sanjay attaches a schedule to the offer dated October 3, 20xx between Seller Wellington and Buyer Chin. He writes the following at the top of the schedule: *Schedule B Attached and Forming Part of an Agreement of Purchase and Sale dated October 3, 20xx*; Seller: *Wellington*; Buyer: *Chin*. He has both parties affix their initials.

◯ **Acceptable**   ◯ **Not Acceptable**

Reason:

1.4   Salesperson Smith describes chattels included with the sale as follows: *Fridge, stove and dishwasher.*

◯ **Acceptable**   ◯ **Not Acceptable**

Reason:

1.5   Salesperson Lee prepares an offer with a condition expiring on March 15th and a requisition date of March 12th.

◯ Acceptable   ◯ Not Acceptable

Reason:

1.6   Neither the buyer nor the seller are certain whether HST applies. The salesperson in a multiple representation inserts the following in Clause 7: *Included In.*

◯ Acceptable   ◯ Not Acceptable

Reason:

1.7   The salesperson insists that the buyers and sellers initial at the bottom of page 1 of the *Agreement of Purchase and Sale* (OREA Form 100).

◯ Acceptable   ◯ Not Acceptable

Reason:

1.8   The buyer signs an agreement on April 23, 200x with an irrevocable date of April 25th. The agreement is subsequently accepted verbally by Mr. Chung, the seller, on April 23rd at 2 p.m. However, his spouse (also an owner) cannot be reached until the following day. At 3 p.m. on April 24th, she signs acceptance and Mr. Chung is reached at his office where he signs an hour later confirming his verbal acceptance of April 23rd. The Confirmation of Acceptance reads as follows: …*was finally executed by all parties at 3 p.m. on this 24th day of April, 200x.*

◯ Acceptable   ◯ Not Acceptable

Reason:

1.9   The buyer hears from a friend that the seller has no intention of moving out of the home, despite the fact that only three days remain until completion date. Firmly believing that the property will not close, the buyer drops by the seller's house and demands access to see if the rumours are true. If so, he will instruct the lawyer to tender documents the next morning.

◯ Acceptable   ◯ Not Acceptable

Reason:

1.10   The salesperson drafts an agreement including a seller take back mortgage. He advises the seller that the buyer must provide evidence of adequate insurance relating to the mortgagee's (seller's) interest on completion.

◯ Acceptable   ◯ Not Acceptable

Reason:

1.11   The seller is married but her spouse does not have joint ownership in the matrimonial home, which is now being sold. When presenting an offer on OREA Form 100, the buyer representative insists that a clause be inserted in the agreement. The clause would provide a warranty by the seller to the buyer that the consent of the seller's spouse is not required.

◯ Acceptable   ◯ Not Acceptable

Reason:

1.12   The sellers insist that the OREA *Agreement of Purchase and Sale* is technically wrong and wants the salesperson to stroke out all references to '*I*' and insert '*We*'. The salesperson agrees.

◯ Acceptable   ◯ Not Acceptable

Reason:

1.13   The buyer has not yet selected a lawyer and the salesperson inserts the words '*To be Advised*' in the acknowledgement space, but emphasizes that the buyer make the selection as soon as possible.

◯ Acceptable   ◯ Not Acceptable

Reason:

▣ Exercise 2   Multiple Choice

2.1   Which one of the following statements is correct with respect to the *Notices* clause in OREA's Agreement of Purchase and Sale?

a.   A Listing Brokerage's fax number must not be entered into the *Notices* clause if the brokerage also represents the buyer.

b.   Fax numbers must always be entered into the *Notices* clause in OREA's Agreement of Purchase and Sale.

c.   A co-operating brokerage's fax number can only be entered into the *Notices* clause if the buyer is a customer of that brokerage.

d.   A brokerage's fax number must never be entered into the *Notices* clause since the clause specifically states that only the buyer/seller's fax number can be entered.

2.2   An irrevocable instruction regarding how long an offer remains open for acceptance is:

a.   Generally binding if signed under seal.

b.   Established by legal counsel for the buyer and seller after offer acceptance.

c.   Not applicable for most offers involving residential property.

d.   Mandated to be no more than 48 hours from signing of the agreement.

2.3   According to the *Agreement of Purchase and Sale* (OREA Form 100) the buyer accepts title subject to certain exceptions. Which is NOT one of them?

a.   Relevant items specifically set out in the agreement.

b.   Ownership issues that go to the root of title.

c.   Registered restrictions or covenants which are complied with.

d.   Minor utility easements.

2.4   Which of the following statements is correct?

a.   Root of title issues and matters of title are the same thing and the terms can be used interchangeably.

b.   The current zoning must always be inserted under present use in Clause 8 of the *Agreement of Purchase and Sale.*

c.   Inserting the word *included* in Clause 7 (HST) places the risk on the seller should the property be subject to HST.

d.   The preprinted wording of the OREA *Agreement of Purchase and Sale* provides for a completion no later than 11:59 p.m. on the completion date set out.

2.5   In setting out details concerning buyers and sellers in an agreement of purchase and sale, which of the following is NOT correct?

a.   Insert full identity of all partners when including a partnership as a buyer or seller.

b.   Use legal names for buyers and sellers when completing the offer.

c.   Use the corporate seal or insert the words: I/We have the authority to bind the corporation.

d.   Always include both spouses as sellers when dealing with a married couple.

2.6   Clause 3–Notices generally provides:

a.   Authority for the listing brokerage and co-operating brokerage to give and receive notices on behalf of their respective clients.

b.   Authority for the listing brokerage and co-operating brokerage to give and receive notices on behalf of their respective customers.

c.   Authority for the listing brokerage and co-operating brokerage to sign agreements of purchase and sale on behalf of their clients.

d.   Authority for the listing brokerage and co-operating brokerage to amend agreements on behalf of their clients.

2.7   Which of the following statements is NOT correct?

a.   A person signing in trust is not generally liable for contracts signed under seal.

b.   All legally authorized estate trustees of a property should sign the agreement of purchase and sale when selling that property.

c.   The deposit is typically held by the listing brokerage.

d.   The title search clause in the *Agreement of Purchase and Sale* (OREA Form 100) provides only one time period for title and related searches.

■ Exercise 3   Errors and Omissions

Mr. and Mrs. Metzger, the buyers, and Michael Sandhu, the seller, have reached agreement on the sale of 238 Main Street in Anycity. The initial offer by the Metzgers was accepted. The irrevocable date on this accepted offer was September 23, 200x.

Identify at least five errors on Page 5 of the agreement.

Exercise 3   Agreement of Purchase and Sale—Page 5

28. SUCCESSORS AND ASSIGNS: The heirs, executors, administrators, successors and assigns of the undersigned are bound by the terms herein.

SIGNED, SEALED AND DELIVERED in the presence of: IN WITNESS whereof I have hereunto set my hand and seal:

Judith Powers   C.E. Metzger   ● DATE *Sept. 22/xx*
(Witness)   (Buyer)   (Seal)

                                         A.L. Metzger   ● DATE ....
(Witness)   (Buyer)   (Seal)

I, the Undersigned Seller, agree to the above offer. I hereby irrevocably instruct my lawyer to pay directly to the brokerage(s) with whom I have agreed to pay commission, the unpaid balance of the commission together with applicable Harmonized Sales Tax (and any other taxes as may hereafter be applicable), from the proceeds of the sale prior to any payment to the undersigned on completion, as advised by the brokerage(s) to my lawyer.

SIGNED, SEALED AND DELIVERED in the presence of: IN WITNESS whereof I have hereunto set my hand and seal:

....   *Michael Sandhu*   ● DATE *Sept. 25/xx*
(Witness)   (Seller)   (Seal)

.... ● DATE ....
(Witness)   (Seller)   (Seal)

SPOUSAL CONSENT: The Undersigned Spouse of the Seller hereby consents to the disposition evidenced herein pursuant to the provisions of the Family Law Act, R.S.O.1990, and hereby agrees with the Buyer that he/she will execute all necessary or incidental documents to give full force and effect to the sale evidenced herein.

.... ● DATE ....
(Witness)   (Spouse)   (Seal)

CONFIRMATION OF ACCEPTANCE: Notwithstanding anything contained herein to the contrary, I confirm this Agreement with all changes both typed and written was finally accepted by all parties at *3:00* ~~a.m.~~/p.m. this *24th* day of.......*September*........., 20.*XX*

                                         C.E. Metzger
                                         (Signature of Seller or Buyer)

INFORMATION ON BROKERAGE(S)

Listing Brokerage ....**ABC Realty Inc.**............................ Tel.No.(.*416*..) **555-1212**
328 Main Street, Anycity M4C 2J2   **Albert Lee**
                                         (Salesperson / Broker Name)

Co-op/Buyer Brokerage ....**XYZ Realty Inc.**...................... Tel.No.(.*416*..) **555-2121**
28 Norfield Drive, Anycity M4X 6U7   **Judith Powers**
                                         (Salesperson / Broker Name)

ACKNOWLEDGEMENT

I acknowledge receipt of my signed copy of this accepted Agreement of Purchase and Sale and I authorize the Brokerage to forward a copy to my lawyer.	I acknowledge receipt of my signed copy of this accepted Agreement of Purchase and Sale and I authorize the Brokerage to forward a copy to my lawyer.
Michael Sandhu DATE *Sept. 25/xx* (Seller)	A.L. Metzger DATE *Sept. 25/xx* (Buyer)
.... DATE .... (Seller)	.... DATE .... (Buyer)
Address for Service *238 Main Street, Anycity M4C 2J6* Tel.No.(.*800*.) *555-1234*	Address for Service *Apt. 808, 300 Grand Avenue,* *Anycity M4H 2N3* Tel.No.(.*416*.) **555-5678**
Seller's Lawyer *A. J. Woods*	Buyer's Lawyer *Ms. Jane Willis*
Address *201-3762 Parkside Drive*	Address *7361 Bennett Avenue*
Email	Email ....
(.*416*.) *555-1313* (.*416*.) *555-3131* Tel.No. FAX No.	(.*416*.) **555-1414** (.*416*.) **555-4141** Tel.No. FAX No.

FOR OFFICE USE ONLY   **COMMISSION TRUST AGREEMENT**
To: Co-operating Brokerage shown on the foregoing Agreement of Purchase and Sale: In consideration for the Co-operating Brokerage procuring the foregoing Agreement of Purchase and Sale, I hereby declare that all moneys received or receivable by me in connection with the Transaction as contemplated in the MLS® Rules and Regulations of my Real Estate Board shall be receivable and held in trust. This agreement shall constitute a Commission Trust Agreement as defined in the MLS® Rules and shall be subject to and governed by the MLS® Rules pertaining to Commission Trust.   DATED as of the date and time of the acceptance of the foregoing Agreement of Purchase and Sale.   Acknowledged by:
....   (Authorized to bind the Listing Brokerage)   (Authorized to bind the Co-operating Brokerage)

Form 100   Revised 2015   **Page 5 of 6**

■ **Exercise 4   The Fine Print**

In a sense, all offers are conditional. Explain this statement with direct reference to appropriate preprinted portions of the residential *Agreement of Purchase and Sale.*

CHAPTER 8

Drafting Offers: Part 1

Introduction

Mastery in drafting offers requires continuous practice. No two real estate transactions are identical. Exercises cannot possibly contemplate all the possibilities and potential problem areas, but they lay the groundwork. This chapter includes the first building blocks leading to more advanced drafting in *The Residential Real Estate Transaction* and *The Commercial Real Estate Transaction*.

As part of the offer drafting and negotiating process, all registrants must ensure that they are in compliance with federal identification verification and receipt of funds documentation. Detailed procedures are outlined along with applicable forms. Following this discussion, the basic all cash offer is highlighted. Six handy steps help guide you from identifying required information to final offer completion and the check/proof stage. Chapter materials introduce increasingly complex circumstances and clause structures. Carefully review examples and complete all exercises. Lay a solid foundation for your future.

Emphasis in this chapter is on basic offers and associated clauses that apply both to the *Agreement of Purchase and Sale* (OREA Form 100) and the *Agreement of Purchase and Sale—Commercial* (OREA Form 500). The residential version is used for illustration purposes. Advanced clause preparation relating to commercial transactions is addressed in *The Commercial Real Estate Transaction*.

Learning Outcomes

At the conclusion of this chapter, students will be able to:

- Detail and apply a six-step offer plan to organize information when drafting residential offers.
- Outline specifics concerning compliance with identification and receipt of funds requirements pursuant to the *Proceeds of Crime (Money Laundering) and Terrorist Financing Act*.
- Accurately draft an all cash offer with no conditions based on OREA clause wordings.
- Analyze and draft clauses regarding handling of deposits and briefly highlight legal issues concerning deposits not paid.
- Analyze and draft clauses to properly include facts and assurances clearly reflecting what the party(ies) intended in regard to acknowledgements, representations and warranties, actions, agreed facts and rights.
- Discuss wording fundamentals underlying the preparation of clauses in this chapter.
- Detail methods to avoid errors and omissions when drafting offers and preparing clauses.

GETTING READY TO DRAFT OFFERS

Offers can be straightforward when planned correctly. No mystery surrounds writing the basic all cash offer or, for that matter, more complex offers. Salespeople merely have to adapt a basic structure to differing circumstances. If the fundamentals are grasped quickly, adaptations will readily follow.

The Offer Plan: Avoiding Common Problems

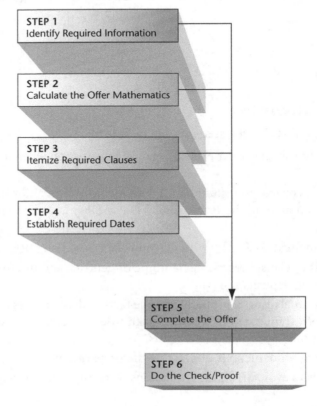

STEP 1
Identify Required Information

STEP 2
Calculate the Offer Mathematics

STEP 3
Itemize Required Clauses

STEP 4
Establish Required Dates

STEP 5
Complete the Offer

STEP 6
Do the Check/Proof

Proper preparation can avoid problems, ensure accurate mathematics (particularly balance due on completion), and establish correct sequential time for condition fulfilment, title search and a realistic completion date.

CLAUSES

OREA has developed recommended clauses that are provided solely for guidance and do not in any way constitute required wordings. The Ontario Real Estate Association does not warrant and assumes no liability concerning such clauses. All clauses have been reprinted with permission and can be found in the *Appendix*.

Alternate recommended clause wordings may be provided for the same topic. Carefully read all possibilities, revise as required to suit individual circumstances and seek expert advice as needed.

GETTING STARTED

Cheat Sheets	Registrants encounter many brokerages using cheat sheets, which include basic offer information and a list of common clauses. The term *cheat sheet* came from earlier decades when salespeople were expected to hand-write clauses and instead cheated by using these handy references. The user merely had to fill in the blanks (e.g., buyers and sellers names, legal description, etc.), check off appropriate clauses, insert other details as necessary and the brokerage would prepare the offer ready for signing. Cheat sheets simply sped up the internal process, but the responsibility still rested with the salesperson to ensure that the offer was accurate and complete. The responsibility remains today: *Always double check the final document.*
Clause Wordings	Brokerages may use different clause wordings than those recommended by OREA. In some instances, brokerages may also insist on selected clauses being included in all offers as a matter of brokerage policy (e.g., due to local circumstances). Review such matters with the broker of record and/or manager.
Offer Software	In the electronic age, the cheat sheet took on new stature within the introduction of software programs. Brokerages now rely on automated offer software. Fully review any clauses included with the package, given the likelihood of variations and unique clauses to suit local circumstances. Be prepared to knowledgeably discuss such wordings with clients.
Agreement of Purchase and Sale	Real estate boards typically use the OREA agreement form imprinted with the appropriate board logo. In some instances, slight wording differences may occur. Identify all such differences and fully discuss with the broker of record and/or manager. Brokerages who are not members of organized real estate will use agreements and related documentation which are significantly different from the OREA format. Registrants must fully review and be able to knowledgeably discuss such forms with clients and customers.

IDENTIFICATION/FUNDS COMPLIANCE: OFFER DRAFTING AND NEGOTIATIONS

The *Proceeds of Crime (Money Laundering) and Terrorist Financing Act*, administered by the Financial Transactions and Reports Analysis Centre of Canada (**FINTRAC**), sets out requirements concerning receipt of funds (i.e., receiving deposits relating to real estate transactions) and client identification of those involved in the transaction. The Act details both procedural matters, as well as forms to be completed. Responsibilities under the Act extend to all real estate brokerages, brokers and salespersons.

This description is focused on client identification requirements and receipt of funds in relation to offer drafting and negotiations. Additional information about the Act, including procedures concerning suspicious transactions and terrorist property are highlighted in *The Residential Real Estate Transaction*, along with related topics including fraud, mortgage fraud and other illegal activities that may be encountered by registrants.

Overview

Real estate brokerages, brokers and salespeople have had to comply with various requirements under the *Proceeds of Crime (Money Laundering) and Terrorist Financing Act* since 2001. These remain in force at the current time.

Compliance Officer	Every real estate brokerage must appoint a Compliance Officer to implement and oversee compliance with the Act.
Training	Every real estate brokerage must implement a training program concerning obligations under the Act for persons designated for such responsibilities.
Office Policies	Every real estate brokerage must develop a compliance program to include office policies and procedures. These policies have to be updated as required.
Suspicious Transactions	Every real estate brokerage must report suspicious transactions.
Large Cash Transactions	Every real estate brokerage must report large cash transactions ($10,000 or more).
Terrorist Property	Every real estate brokerage must report property in their possession or control that is owned or controlled by (or on behalf of) a terrorist organization. A list of known terrorist groups and individuals is available on the FINTRAC website.
Verification	Every brokerage must verify that the names of their clients are NOT on the Canadian or United Nations list of known terrorists or terrorist organizations.

The new requirements concerning identification verification and receipt of funds were effective June 23, 2008. The following discussion includes forms developed by The Canadian Real Estate Association and published by the Ontario Real Estate Association for use by members of organized real estate. These forms are illustrated for general educational purposes. Registrants should contact their intended employing brokerage regarding specific policies and procedures, including any custom forms being used.

Records/Policies

Real estate brokerages are required to have necessary forms to meet all requirements as set out in the *Proceeds of Crime (Money Laundering) and Terrorist Financing Act* which is overseen by the Financial Transactions and Reports Analysis Centre of Canada (FINTRAC). Brokerages must also maintain all records relating to identification verification and receipt of funds for a period of five years. Records can be kept in a machine-readable or electronic format. The record must be immediately retrievable in paper form upon request by FINTRAC.

Brokerages must develop and apply ongoing compliance policies including appropriate training for all employees (staff, brokers and salespersons). As well, a Risk Assessment Form must be completed by the brokerage every two years and kept on file for five years.

Privacy

FINTRAC compliance regarding the collection of additional personal information places greater responsibility on the brokerage, brokers and salespersons to ensure that such details are diligently collected and adequately protected pursuant to the *Personal Information Protection and Electronic Documents Act* (PIPEDA). Privacy legislation was covered in *Real Estate as a Professional Career*.

Be Fully Informed FOCUS

Registrants must be fully informed on all matters relating to the *Proceeds of Crime (Money Laundering) and Terrorist Financing Act*. Identification verification and receipt of funds forms are detailed in this chapter, with additional information regarding suspicious transactions and terrorist property located in *The Residential Real Estate Transaction*.

Detailed information and guidance is available from FINTRAC. For those individuals who will become members of organized real estate, the Money Laundering Compliance Centre developed by The Canadian Real Estate Association is an excellent resource. Member access is available through REALTORLink®. Registrants should also discuss all compliance matters with the intended employing brokerage regarding forms used and specific procedures to be followed.

 WEB LINKS

FINTRAC   Go to the Financial Transactions and Reports Analysis Centre of Canada website (*www.fintrac.ca*) for detailed information regarding compliance issues.

REALTORLink®   Members of organized real estate can access the Money Laundering Compliance Centre through the REALTORLink® website. Go to *www.realtorlink.ca.*

IDENTIFICATION VERIFICATION

An identification record must be kept for every real estate transaction in which a brokerage is involved. When more than one brokerage is involved (e.g., a listing brokerage and a selling (co-operating) brokerage), both must have applicable forms signed for the seller and buyer respectively. These forms must be retained for a five-year period.

Two identification forms have been developed by organized real estate and are included for illustration purposes: one for individuals and the other for other entities (e.g., corporations, partnerships and charities).

General Guidelines

Selected guidelines will assist in completing the applicable form. Either the *Individual Identification Information Record* or the *Corporate/Entity Identification Information Record* should be completed.

Form Completion	Whenever a broker or salesperson is acting in respect of a purchase or sale of real estate.
Timing	At minimum, identification must be made for the buyer client, when the offer is submitted and/or a deposit is taken and for the seller client, when the offer is accepted. Identification can be made earlier if appropriate. Salespersons are strongly encouraged to discuss FINTRAC requirements as soon as possible to avoid any confusion or problems.

Listing Brokerage	Identify the client that is being represented.
Selling Brokerage	Identify the client that is being represented.
Multiple Clients	In a multiple representation situation within one brokerage, complete applicable forms for all clients.
Unrepresented Persons	In the case of unrepresented buyers and sellers (e.g., for sale by owners), registrants must take reasonable measures to ascertain their identities. If an individual refuses, note this refusal on the form and proceed with the transaction.
Third Parties	Third parties are individuals or entities other than the individual or entity conducting the business. For example, an employee of a company may give instructions regarding how to handle the deposit or other matters concerning the sale on behalf of the company. The employer would be viewed as a third party.
Receipt of Funds	If a deposit is involved, a *Receipt of Funds Record* must be completed (see later discussion).
Previously Identified Clients	Registrants do not have to re-verify the identity of a client that they recognize and have previously identified in a past transaction. While making a notation in the transaction file (that a previous identification is on file) may be adequate, the prudent registrant is well advised to include a photocopy of the original identification record in the applicable transaction file. If any information has changed regarding the individual or entity, then the registrant should complete the applicable form once again.
Excluded Activities	Property management activities (i.e., rentals) are excluded from these requirements, as are sales of a businesses (provided that no real property is included).

Client Refusal   CAUTION

What happens if a client refuses to supply the necessary information? You are well advised not to proceed with the transaction, as doing so could lead to a violation under federal legislation. Based on circumstances surrounding this refusal, this refusal may constitute a suspicious transaction and an appropriate report should be filed with FINTRAC. See *The Residential Real Estate Transaction* for further discussion.

Individual Identification: Form Completion

The *Individual Identification Information Record* (OREA Form 630) details required information about the transaction and individual verification.

PART A: VERIFICATION OF INDIVIDUAL (ACCEPTABLE DOCUMENTS)
Registrants should take particular note of procedures set out in Part A regarding refusals to provide verification information. Following are a list of acceptable documents* for Ontario residents when completing Part A:

- birth certificate;
- driver's licence;
- passport;
- record of landing;
- permanent resident card;

- old age security card;
- certificate of Indian status; and
- SIN card (not recommended, as SIN numbers are not to be included on any report sent to FINTRAC).

*NOTE: Keeping photocopies of ID's is not necessary. Acceptable documents vary by province. See lower portion of form (page 1) for details.

PART B: VERIFICATION OF THIRD PARTIES

Part B must be completed when a client or customer is acting on behalf of a third party. The salesperson should verify the third party's identification. If the registrant is unable to determine if a third party is involved, but there are reasonable grounds to suspect that such is the case, a record of that fact must be kept.

PART C: CLIENT RISK

Real estate brokerages have an obligation to conduct a risk assessment of every client with respect to the possibility of money laundering or terrorist financing. One way to satisfy this obligation with respect to a client who is an individual is to ask the broker/salesperson involved in a purchase or sale transaction to conduct the necessary risk analysis by completing Part C of OREA Standard Form 630. (Please note that brokerages can use their own form. The OREA form is included for illustration purposes only.)

When completing Part C, the broker/salesperson must identify whether the client is a low, medium, or high risk for terrorist financing or money laundering activities. To enable the broker/salesperson to do this, the brokerage would have developed a series of clusters (categories) in their policies/procedures manual. Each cluster (category) would detail the profile/features of a client that would fit into that cluster (category).

Currently, OREA Standard Form 630 identifies four clusters or categories of clients who are low risk and one cluster for high risk. A brokerage's policy will most likely contain a more detailed profile of the type of client that would fit within each cluster and the policies/procedures manual may contain additional clusters that can be checked off as "other." When determining which box to check off in the relevant level of risk, a broker/salesperson should refer to the brokerage's profile of the type of client that fits within each cluster and match it to the client they are currently identifying.

PART D: BUSINESS RELATIONSHIP

Whenever a brokerage has a "business relationship" with a client, FINTRAC requires that brokerage, among other things:

1. Keep a record of the purpose and intended nature of the business relationship.
2. Ensure client information is kept up to date.
3. Keep a record of the measures taken to monitor the business relationship. This could be accomplished by simply keeping pertinent records and correspondence on file.

A business relationship is effectively established whenever a brokerage conducts two or more transactions (i.e., a purchase and/or sale) with a client within a five-year period. The business relationship expires if there are less than two transactions within a five-year period.

With respect to a client who is an individual, one way to satisfy the obligations noted above would be for the brokerage to ask the broker/salesperson involved in a purchase or sale transaction to complete Part D in OREA Standard Form 630. Where the client in question is high risk, the brokerage may ask the broker/salesperson to conduct enhanced measures to monitor the business relationship and document those measures in Part D.2.3. Enhanced measures may include, among other things:

- Obtaining additional information on the client (e.g., occupation, volume of assets, information available through public databases, Internet, etc.).
- Obtaining information on the source of funds or source of wealth of the client.
- Obtaining information on the reasons for intended or conducted transactions.
- Obtaining the approval of senior management to enter into or maintain the business relationship .

Brokerage policies may require that a broker/salesperson complete Part D every time there is a transaction regardless of whether a business relationship has been established.

A broker/salesperson must report to his/her compliance officer something suspicious that occurs during a transaction even if the transaction is never completed.

Parts C and D do not have to be completed for an unrepresented person or for an individual who is acting on behalf of a corporation.

No Face-to-Face Meeting

Special procedures apply if the broker or salesperson does not meet directly with the client.

CLIENT RESIDES IN CANADA		CLIENT RESIDES OUTSIDE OF CANADA
Two of five resources can be used (but exercise caution, as some cannot be done in combination).		The brokerage must have a contracted agent (mandatary) who can meet the person, review required identification and forward a report for filing. The agent can be a broker or salesperson, lawyer or notary. An agent arrangement *must be used* outside Canada and *can be used* inside Canada. Check with your intended employing brokerage for the form used when engaging the services of a contracted agent/mandatary. A form for a contracted agent relating to a *no face-to-face meeting* and associated consent is included in the *Appendix*. See *Identification Mandatary/Agent Agreement* (OREA Form 632).
1. Independent ID Product	Verify an independent ID (such as a bus pass or club membership card). The ID must have a photo and registration number.	
2. Credit File	Verify a credit file (e.g., Equifax or TransUnion).	
3. Attestation	Obtain an attestation from a Commissioner of Oaths or guarantor (see FINTRAC site for list of guarantors).	
4. Cleared Cheque	Cleared cheque drawn on a deposit account from a Canadian financial institution.	
5. Account Confirmation	Confirm existence of a deposit account from a Canadian financial institution.	
NOTE: 1 & 2 and 4 & 5 cannot be combined.		
Alternatively, an attestation by an agent (**mandatary**) can be used. See *Client Resides Outside of Canada.*		

OREA Form 630—Individual Identification Information Record, Page 1 of 4

 **OREA** Ontario Real Estate Association

Form 630
for use in the Province of Ontario

Individual Identification Information Record

NOTE: An Individual Identification Information Record is required by the *Proceeds of Crime (Money Laundering) and Terrorist Financing Act*. This Record must be completed by the REALTOR® member whenever they act in respect to the purchase or sale of real estate.
It is recommended that the Individual Identification Information Record be completed:
    (i) for a buyer when the offer is submitted and/or a deposit made, and
    (ii) for a seller when the seller accepts the offer.

Transaction Property Address: ....

....

....

Sales Representative/Broker Name: ....

Date: ....

A. Verification of Individual

NOTE: This section must be completed for clients that are individuals or unrepresented individuals who are not clients, but are parties to the transaction (e.g. unrepresented buyer or seller). Where an unrepresented individual refuses to provide identification after reasonable efforts are made to verify that identification, a REALTOR® member must keep a record of that refusal and consider sending a Suspicious Transaction Report to FINTRAC if there are reasonable grounds to suspect that the transaction involves property from the proceeds of crime, or terrorist activity. Where you are using an agent or mandatary to verify an individual, see procedure described in CREA's FINTRAC Compliance manual.

1. **Full legal name of individual:** ....

2. **Address:** ....

....

....

....

3. **Date of Birth:** ....

4. **Nature of Principal Business or Occupation:** ....

5. **Type of Identification Document*:** ....
                            (must view the original, see below for list of acceptable documents)

6. **Document Identifier Number:** ....

7. **Issuing Jurisdiction:** ....
             (insert name of the applicable Province, Territory, Foreign Jurisdiction or "Federal Government of Canada")

8. **Document Expiry Date:** ....
                     (must be valid and not expired)

*Acceptable identification documents: birth certificate, driver's licence, provincial health insurance card (not acceptable if from Ontario, Nova Scotia, Manitoba or Prince Edward Island), passport, record of landing, permanent resident card, old age security card, a certificate of Indian status, or SIN card (although SIN numbers are not to be included on any report sent to FINTRAC). Other acceptable identification documents: provincial or territorial identification card issued by the Insurance Corporation of British Columbia, Alberta Registries, Saskatchewan Government Insurance, the Department of Service Nova Scotia and Municipal Relations, the Department of Transportation and Infrastructure Renewal of the Province of Prince Edward Island, Service New Brunswick, the Department of Government Services and Lands of the Province of Newfoundland and Labrador, the Department of Transportation of the Northwest Territories or the Department of Community Government and Transportation of the Territory of Nunavut. If identification document is from a foreign jurisdiction, it must be equivalent to one of the above identification documents.

 This document has been prepared by The Canadian Real Estate Association to assist members in complying with requirements of Canada's *Proceeds of Crime (Money Laundering) and Terrorist Financing Regulations*. © 2014-2015. **1** of 4

Individual Identification Information Record

Form 630
for use in the Province of Ontario

B. Verification of Third Parties *(if applicable)*

NOTE: Complete this section of the form when a client or unrepresented individual is acting on behalf of a third party. Where you cannot determine if there is a third party, but there are reasonable grounds to suspect the individual is acting on behalf of a third party, you must keep a record of that fact.

1. **Name of third party:** ....

2. **Address:** ....

   ....

   ....

   ....

3. **Date of Birth:** ....

4. **Nature of Principal Business or Occupation:** ....

5. **Incorporation number and place of issue** *(if applicable)*: ....

6. **Relationship between third party and client:** ....

   ....

   ....

   ....

---

2 of 4

 **Ontario Real Estate Association**

Individual Identification Information Record

Form 630
for use in the Province of Ontario

Only complete Sections C and D for your clients.

C. Client Risk *(ask your Compliance Officer if this section is applicable)*

Determine the level of risk of a money laundering or terrorist financing offence for this client by determining the appropriate cluster of client in your policies and procedures manual this client falls into and checking one of the checkboxes below:

Low Risk

☐ Canadian Citizen or Resident Physically Present

☐ Canadian Citizen or Resident Not Physically Present

☐ Canadian Citizen or Resident – High Crime Area – No Other Higher Risk Factors Evident

☐ Foreign Citizen or Resident that does not Operate in a High Risk Country (physically present or not)

☐ Other, explain:

Medium Risk

☐ Explain:

High Risk

☐ Foreign Citizen or Resident that operates in a High Risk Country (physically present or not)

☐ Other, explain:

If you determined that the client's risk was high, tell your brokerage's Compliance Officer. They will want to consider this when conducting the overall brokerage risk assessment, which occurs every two years. It will also be relevant in completing Section D below. Note that your brokerage may have developed other clusters not listed above. If no cluster is appropriate, the agent will need to provide a risk assessment of the client, and explain their assessment, in the relevant space above.

3 of 4

 **Ontario Real Estate Association**

Individual Identification Information Record

Form 630
for use in the Province of Ontario

D. Business Relationship
(ask your Compliance Officer when this section is applicable if you don't know)

D.1. Purpose and Intended Nature of the Business Relationship

Check the appropriate boxes.

Acting as an agent for the purchase or sale of:

☐ Residential property   ☐ Residential property for income purposes

☐ Commercial property   ☐ Land for Commercial Use

☐ Other, please specify:. . . . .

D.2. Measures Taken to Monitor Business Relationship and Keep Client Information Up-To-Date

D.2.1. Ask the Client if their name, address or principal business or occupation has changed and if it has include the updated information on page one.

D.2.2 Keep all relevant correspondence with the client on file in order to maintain a record of the information you have used to monitor the business relationship with the client. Optional - if you have taken measures beyond simply keeping correspondence on file, specify them here:

```



```

D.2.3. If the client is high risk you must conduct enhanced measures to monitor the brokerage's business relationship and keep their client information up to date. Optional - consult your Compliance Officer and document what enhanced measures you have applied:

```



```

D.3 Suspicious Transactions

Don't forget, if you see something suspicious during the transaction report it to your Compliance Officer. Consult your policies and procedures manual for more information.

REALTOR®

This document has been prepared by The Canadian Real Estate Association to assist members in complying with requirements of Canada's *Proceeds of Crime (Money Laundering) and Terrorist Financing Regulations*. © 2014-2015.

 4 of 4

Corporation/Entity Identification: Form Completion

An alternate form, titled *Corporation/Entity Identification Information Record* (OREA Form 631), is required for identification verification involving corporations or other entities.

PART A.1: VERIFICATION OF CORPORATION

Part A requires information to confirm that the corporation exists, including the name of the corporation, corporate address, nature of principal business, name of directors, verification record (paper or electronic), registration number and copy of corporate record showing authority to bind the corporation.

The existence of the corporation must be confirmed either by paper copy (which must be retained with the verification form) or by electronic confirmation from a public source (e.g., obtain federal corporation details including directors names from the Corporations Canada website (**http://corporationscanada.ic.gc.ca**)). An electronic search of provincial corporations is available through search services.

A copy of the corporate record showing authority to bind the corporation regarding the transaction must also be retained (e.g., articles of incorporation or by-law setting out officers duly authorized to sign on behalf of the corporation).

PART A.2: VERIFICATION OF OTHER ENTITY

When the transaction involves an entity other than a corporation, the articles of association, partnership agreement or similar document is needed to confirm the entity's existence. A paper copy must be retained. As with corporations, if the record is electronic, it must be from a public source and must include the entity's registration number and type/source of record.

PART B: VERIFICATION OF THIRD PARTIES

This section is used when a client is acting on behalf of a third party and closely resembles a similar verification required for individuals. When the registrant is unable to determine if there is a third party, but there are reasonable grounds to suspect that such is the case, a record of that fact must be kept.

NOTE: A *Consent Agreement* (OREA Form 633) can be used to obtain the necessary information from a lawyer or other party familiar with the corporation (or other entity). A *Consent Agreement* (OREA Form 633) is reprinted, along with other forms in the *Appendix*.

PART C: CLIENT RISK

The rationale behind and purpose of Part C is the same as previously outlined for Part C of OREA Standard Form 630 (the Individual Identification Information Record), and the wording of the two forms are similar. However, given the differences between an individual and a corporation/entity, the clusters and the profiles of the clients within those clusters will be different for a corporation/entity compared to an individual. Currently, OREA Standard Form 631 identifies two clusters or categories of clients who are low risk and one cluster who is high risk.

A brokerage's policy will most likely contain a more detailed profile of the type of client that would fit within each cluster and the policies/procedures manual may well contain additional clusters that can be checked off as "other."

PART D: BUSINESS RELATIONSHIP

The rationale behind and purpose of Part D is the same as previously outlined for Part D of OREA Standard Form 630 (the Individual Identification Information Record). There are some differences in the wording and information required that reflect the differences between a corporation/entity and an individual (e.g., for a corporation, confirm the name and address, and the name of its directors). Where a corporate client is high risk, an enhanced measure of monitoring might include obtaining additional information on the client (e.g., business products/services, volume of assets, information available through public databases, Internet, etc.)

Brokerage policies may require that a broker/salesperson complete Part D every time there is a transaction regardless of whether a business relationship has been established.

A broker/salesperson must report to his/her compliance officer something suspicious that occurs during a transaction even if the transaction is never completed.

RECEIPT OF FUNDS: FORM COMPLETION

A receipt of funds is required for every real estate transaction, subject to certain exceptions:

- when funds are received from a financial entity or a public body that is buying or selling;
- if a **large cash transaction** ($10,000 or more) is involved and an appropriate record is prepared (see below); or
- if the deposit does not go into the trust account of a real estate brokerage; e.g., paid directly to a builder or a lawyer.

When both buyer and seller are being represented, the agent of the buyer must prepare this record and retain it for a period of five years. In instances where only a listing brokerage is involved, the responsibility rests with that brokerage. The agent, when completing the Receipt of Funds Record, must make reasonable effort to obtain information about the listing brokerage's trust account, as required on the form (see Item #3).

The *Receipt of Funds Record* (OREA Form 635) (see page 307) provides detailed information on form completion. Salespersons should consult with the broker of record and/or manager regarding internal brokerage policies regarding the handling of *Receipt of Funds Records* and related questions.

Large Cash Transactions

A *Large Cash Transaction Report* is required when funds received are $10,000 or more (or successive amounts are paid by the same client within a 24-hour consecutive period totalling $10,000 or more). This report, as with the *Receipt of Funds Report*, must include details of the amount, how funds were received, the transaction date and purpose. The *Large Cash Transactions Report* is available on the FINTRAC website.

Large cash transactions must be reported within 15 days of the cash being offered by the client or potential client. As with the *Receipt of Funds Report*, no report is required if the funds are from a financial entity or a public body; e.g., government agency. The large cash transaction requirement has been in effect since 2001.

 **Ontario Real Estate Association**

Corporation/Entity Identification Information Record

Form 631
for use in the Province of Ontario

NOTE: A Corporation/Entity Identification Information Record is required by the *Proceeds of Crime (Money Laundering) and Terrorist Financing Act*. This Record must be completed by the REALTOR® member whenever they act in respect to the purchase or sale of real estate.

It is recommended that the Corporation/Entity Identification Information Record be completed:

    (i) for a buyer when the offer is submitted and/or a deposit made, and

    (ii) for a seller when the seller accepts the offer.

Transaction Property Address: ....

....

....

Sales Representative/Broker Name: ....

Date: ....

A.1. Verification of Corporation

1. **Name of corporation:** ....

2. **Corporate Address:** ....

....

....

3. **Nature of Principal Business:** ....

4. **Name of Directors:** As set out in certificate of corporate status or other record confirming corporation's existence.

....

....

5. **Type and Source of Verification Record:**

Must confirm existence of the corporation (e.g., certificate of corporate status, published annual report, government notice of assessment). If record is in paper format, a copy must be kept. If record is an electronic version, a record of the corporation's registration number and type and source of record (e.g., Corporations Canada website) must be kept.

....

....

6. **Registration number of corporation:** ....

7. **Copy of corporate record showing authority to bind corporation regarding transaction:**

(e.g., certificate of incumbency, articles of incorporation, by-laws setting out officers duly authorized to sign on behalf of corporation)

....

....

 1 of 4

Form 631
for use in the Province of Ontario

Corporation/Entity Identification Information Record

A.2. Verification of Other Entity *(if applicable)*

1. **Name of other entity:** ....

2. **Address:** ....

    ....

    ....

3. **Nature of Principal Business:** ....

4. **Type of Verification Record:** Must confirm existence of other entity (e.g., partnership agreement, articles of association).

    ....

5. **Source of Record:** ....

    Record may be paper or an electronic version. If record is in paper format, a copy must be kept. If record is an electronic version, a record of the entity's registration number and type and source of record must be kept.

6. **Registration number:** ....

B. Verification of Third Parties *(if applicable)*

NOTE: Complete this section of the form when a client is acting on behalf of a third party. Where you cannot determine if there is a third party, but there are reasonable grounds to suspect the client is acting on behalf of a third party, you must keep a record of that fact.

1. **Name of other entity:** ....

2. **Address:** ....

    ....

    ....

3. **Date of Birth:** ....

4. **Nature of Principal Business or Occupation:** ....

    ....

5. **Incorporation number and place of issue** *(if applicable)*: ....

    ....

6. **Relationship between third party and client:** ....

    ....

    ....

This document has been prepared by The Canadian Real Estate Association to assist members in complying with requirements of Canada's *Proceeds of Crime (Money Laundering) and Terrorist Financing Regulations.* © 2014-2015.

2 of 4

OREA Ontario Real Estate
Association

Form 631
for use in the Province of Ontario

Corporation/Entity Identification
Information Record

Only complete Sections C and D for your clients.

C. Client Risk *(ask your Compliance Officer if this section is applicable)*

Determine the level of risk of a money laundering or terrorist financing offence for this client by determining the appropriate cluster of client in your policies and procedures manual this client falls into and checking one of the checkboxes below:

Low Risk

☐ Canadian Corporation or Entity

☐ Foreign Corporation or Entity that does not operate in a High Risk Country

☐ Other, explain:

Medium Risk

☐ Explain:

High Risk

☐ Foreign Corporation or Entity that operates in a High Risk Country

☐ Other, explain:

If you determined that the client's risk was high, tell your brokerage's Compliance Officer. They will want to consider this when conducting the overall brokerage risk assessment, which occurs every two years. It will also be relevant in completing Section D below. Note that your brokerage may have developed other clusters not listed above. If no cluster is appropriate, the agent will need to provide a risk assessment of the client, and explain their assessment, in the relevant space above.

3
of 4

 **Ontario Real Estate Association**

Corporation/Entity Identification Information Record

Form 631
for use in the Province of Ontario

D. Business Relationship
(ask your Compliance Officer when this section is applicable if you don't know)

D.1. Purpose and Intended Nature of the Business Relationship

Check the appropriate boxes.

Acting as an agent for the purchase or sale of:

☐ Land for Commercial Use

☐ Commercial property

☐ Other, please specify:. . . . .

D.2. Measures Taken to Monitor Business Relationship and Keep Client Information Up-To-Date

D.2.1. If the client is a corporation, ask if its name and address and name of its directors have changed and if they have include the updated information on page one. If the client is an entity other than a corporation, ask if its name, address and principal place of business has changed and if they have include the updated information on page one.

D.2.2 Keep all relevant correspondence with the client on file in order to maintain a record of the information you have used to monitor the business relationship with the client. Optional - if you have taken measures beyond simply keeping correspondence on file, specify them here:

D.2.3. If the client is high risk you must conduct enhanced measures to monitor the brokerage's business relationship and keep their client information up to date. Optional - consult your Compliance Officer and document what enhanced measures you have applied:

D.3 Suspicious Transactions

Don't forget, if you see something suspicious during the transaction report it to your Compliance Officer. Consult your policies and procedures manual for more information.

 This document has been prepared by The Canadian Real Estate Association to assist members in complying with requirements of Canada's *Proceeds of Crime (Money Laundering) and Terrorist Financing Regulations.* © 2014-2015.

 4 of 4

OREA Form 635—Receipt of Funds Record, Page 1 of 1

 **Ontario Real Estate Association**   **Receipt of Funds Record**

Form 635
for use in the Province of Ontario

NOTE: A Receipt of Funds record is required by the *Proceeds of Crime (Money Laundering) and Terrorist Financing Act* for every amount of funds that a REALTOR® member receives in the course of a single purchase or sale real estate transaction.
A REALTOR® does NOT have to complete a Receipt of Funds Record if:

    (i)   the funds are received from a financial entity or a public body that is buying or selling; or,

    (ii) a Large Cash Transaction Record must be completed; or,

    (iii) the deposit does not go into the trust account of a licensed practitioner. In other words, if the deposit goes directly into the account of a builder, lawyer or notary, or developer, a Receipt of Funds Record does not have to be completed by a member acting as the buyers' agent.

When this Record is completed, it is the responsibility of the broker to ensure that a record is kept for five years from the date it was created.

    (i)   When a REALTOR® member completes a Receipt of Funds Record, they must also complete an Identification Information Record at the same time, unless the Identification Information Record was completed prior to the receipt of funds.

    (ii) When both the buyer and seller are represented, it is the agent of the buyer who is required to complete and retain a Receipt of Funds Record in respect of the deposit made, regardless of who retains the deposit.

Transaction Property Address: ....

....

....

Sales Representative/Broker Name:...

Date: ....

1. **Amount of Funds Received:** .... **Currency:**.................................

    ☐ **Cheque** ☐ **Certified Cheque** ☐ **Cash** ☐ **Bank Draft**

    ☐ **Other, explain:** ....

(a) **If cash, indicate method of receipt** *(in person, mail, courier, other (explain))* ....

(b) **If cheque, indicate: Number of account:** ....

    Financial Institution:...................... **Name of account holder:**.................................

2. **Date of receipt of funds:**..

3. **Account where funds were deposited** *(eg. Broker's trust account)*: ....

Where there are two agents involved in a transaction and the funds are deposited in the listing agent's account the buyer's agent is responsible for completing the receipt of funds record. However, the buyer's agent is not required to include the number and type of the listing agent's account or the name of the person or entity that is the holder of that account if, after taking reasonable measures, they are unable to do so. Further, if dealing with trust accounts, although the buyer's agent must indicate that the funds were deposited into the listing agent's trust account, the buyer's agent would not be required to include the number of the trust account or the name or entity that holds the trust account.

Note that if multiple accounts are affected, information on all accounts affected needs to be recorded. For example, assuming the buyer's agent transfers funds from their account into the listing agent's account, both accounts are affected by the transaction and therefore both numbers are to be recorded on the Receipt of Funds Record. However, the features noted in the previous paragraph with respect to the listing agent's accounts still apply.

    Indicate type of account where deposit has been made: ☐ **Trust** ☐ **Other**

    Number of account:.................... **Name of account holder:** ....

4. **Purpose of funds (e.g., deposit for purchase):**..

5. **Other details concerning receipt of funds:** ....

....

DRAFTING THE ALL CASH OFFER

A detailed case study is provided to assist in drafting the first offer. The offer plan is highlighted, including detail instructions for each of the six steps.

NOTE: The term 'all cash' does not refer to cash as discussed under the previous topic. Cash for FINTRAC reporting concerns the deposit.

The All Cash Offer   *CASE STUDY*

Your clients, James Edwin Harari and Betty Jane Westcott, want to draft an offer to buy 219 Centre Street owned by Harry S. Wilkins and Rose A. Wilkins. The property:

- is located on the south side of Centre Street;
- has a frontage of 55.34 feet and a depth of 110.37 feet; and
- is described as Lot 3, Registered Plan 1392, City of Anycity, Regional Municipality of Anyregion.

The offered price is $329,000, with a deposit of $30,000 and the balance due on completion date. The deposit is provided upon acceptance of the offer with the listing brokerage, ABC Realty Inc. No mortgage is required.

The dining room chandelier, a family heirloom, is to be excluded but all drapes and gold decorator rods in the living room and dining room are included, along with an EasyUse Washer and Dryer (Neptune Models). A rental hot water tank from Anycity Energy @ $33.50 per quarter (plus tax) is assumable.

The offer, dated at Anycity, will be irrevocable for two days, with a title search period of approximately 30 days from today's date. Completion will be approximately 60 days from today. The present use is single-family residential. Notices cannot be delivered by fax or email and HST is deemed to be included in the purchase price. Assume today's date is March 5, 20xx. The listing brokerage, ABC Realty Inc., represents the seller. The co-operating brokerage, XYZ Real Estate Limited, represents the buyer. Include any additional information required for a complete offer.

OFFER PLAN

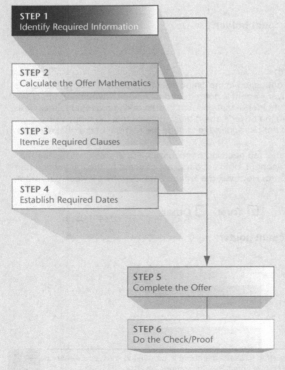

STEP 1
Identify Required Information

STEP 2
Calculate the Offer Mathematics

STEP 3
Itemize Required Clauses

STEP 4
Establish Required Dates

STEP 5
Complete the Offer

STEP 6
Do the Check/Proof

STEP 1   Identify Information

Buyer	James Edwin Harari and Betty Jane Westcott
Seller	Harry S. Wilkins and Rose A. Wilkins
Real Property	219 Centre Street, South Side, 55.34' x 110.37', Lot 3 Reg. Plan 1392, City of Anycity, Regional Municipality of Anyregion
Purchase Price	$329,000
Deposit	$30,000
Schedules	A
Chattels Included	Living room and dining room drapes, including gold decorator rods
Fixtures Excluded	Dining room chandelier
Irrevocable	Two days (assume today's date is March 5, 20xx)
Completion Date	Approximately 60 days (assume May 5, 20xx)
Notices	No fax provisions
HST	Included in purchase price
Title Search	Approximately 30 days (assume April 5, 20xx)
Brokerages	ABC Realty Inc. is the listing brokerage. XYZ Real Estate Limited is the co-operating brokerage.

The All Cash Offer

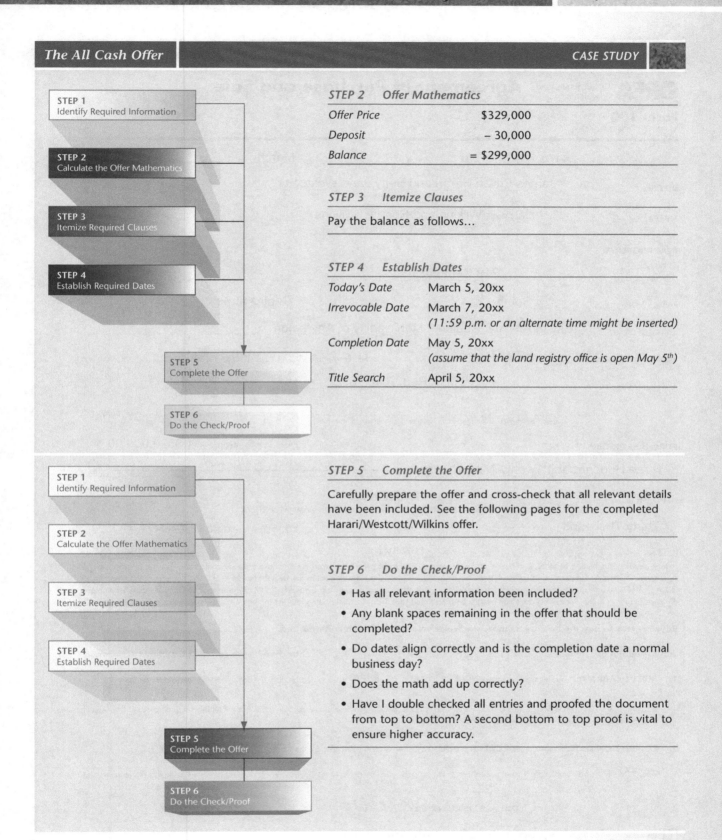

STEP 1
Identify Required Information

STEP 2
Calculate the Offer Mathematics

STEP 3
Itemize Required Clauses

STEP 4
Establish Required Dates

STEP 5
Complete the Offer

STEP 6
Do the Check/Proof

STEP 2   Offer Mathematics

Offer Price	$329,000
Deposit	− 30,000
Balance	= $299,000

STEP 3   Itemize Clauses

Pay the balance as follows...

STEP 4   Establish Dates

Today's Date	March 5, 20xx
Irrevocable Date	March 7, 20xx
	(11:59 p.m. or an alternate time might be inserted)
Completion Date	May 5, 20xx
	(assume that the land registry office is open May 5th)
Title Search	April 5, 20xx

STEP 1
Identify Required Information

STEP 2
Calculate the Offer Mathematics

STEP 3
Itemize Required Clauses

STEP 4
Establish Required Dates

STEP 5
Complete the Offer

STEP 6
Do the Check/Proof

STEP 5   Complete the Offer

Carefully prepare the offer and cross-check that all relevant details have been included. See the following pages for the completed Harari/Westcott/Wilkins offer.

STEP 6   Do the Check/Proof

- Has all relevant information been included?
- Any blank spaces remaining in the offer that should be completed?
- Do dates align correctly and is the completion date a normal business day?
- Does the math add up correctly?
- Have I double checked all entries and proofed the document from top to bottom? A second bottom to top proof is vital to ensure higher accuracy.

OREA Ontario Real Estate Association   # Agreement of Purchase and Sale

Form 100
for use in the Province of Ontario

This Agreement of Purchase and Sale dated this ..... 5th .... day of .... March .... 20 XX .....

BUYER, ... James Edwin Harari and Betty Jane Westcott ...., agrees to purchase from
(Full legal names of all Buyers)

SELLER, ... Harry S. Wilkins and Rose A. Wilkins ...., the following
(Full legal names of all Sellers)

REAL PROPERTY:

Address .... 219 Centre Street ....

fronting on the .... South .... side of .... Centre Street ....

in the .... City of Anycity, Regional Municipality of Anyregion ....

and having a frontage of .... 55.34 feet .... more or less by a depth of .... 110.37 feet .... more or less

and legally described as .... Lot 3, Reg. Plan 1392 ....

.... (the "property")
(Legal description of land including easements not described elsewhere)

PURCHASE PRICE: Dollars (CDN$) ...... $329,000.00 ......

Three Hundred and Twenty-Nine Thousand--- Dollars

DEPOSIT: Buyer submits .... Upon Acceptance ....
(Herewith/Upon Acceptance/as otherwise described in this Agreement)

Thirty Thousand--- Dollars (CDN$) ...... $30,000.00 ......

by negotiable cheque payable to .... ABC Realty Inc. .... "Deposit Holder" to be held
in trust pending completion or other termination of this Agreement and to be credited toward the Purchase Price on completion. For the purposes of this
Agreement, "Upon Acceptance" shall mean that the Buyer is required to deliver the deposit to the Deposit Holder within 24 hours of the acceptance of
this Agreement. The parties to this Agreement hereby acknowledge that, unless otherwise provided for in this Agreement, the Deposit Holder shall place
the deposit in trust in the Deposit Holder's non-interest bearing Real Estate Trust Account and no interest shall be earned, received or paid on the deposit.

Buyer agrees to pay the balance as more particularly set out in Schedule A attached.

SCHEDULE(S) A...**attached hereto form(s) part of this Agreement.**

1. **IRREVOCABILITY:** This offer shall be irrevocable by .... Buyer .... until 11:59 ~~a.m.~~/p.m. on the 7th
    (Seller/Buyer)

    day of .... March .... 20 XX ...., after which time, if not accepted, this offer shall be null and void and the deposit
    shall be returned to the Buyer in full without interest.

2. **COMPLETION DATE:** This Agreement shall be completed by no later than 6:00 p.m. on the ... 5th .... day of .... May ....

    20 XX .... Upon completion, vacant possession of the property shall be given to the Buyer unless otherwise provided for in this Agreement.

INITIALS OF BUYER(S): (*JH BW*)   **INITIALS OF SELLER(S):** (   )

Form 100   Revised 2015   Page 1 of 6

Sample All Cash Offer—Page 2 of 6

3. NOTICES: The Seller hereby appoints the Listing Brokerage as agent for the Seller for the purpose of giving and receiving notices pursuant to this Agreement. Where a Brokerage (Buyer's Brokerage) has entered into a representation agreement with the Buyer, the Buyer hereby appoints the Buyer's Brokerage as agent for the purpose of giving and receiving notices pursuant to this Agreement. **Where a Brokerage represents both the Seller and the Buyer (multiple representation), the Brokerage shall not be appointed or authorized to be agent for either the Buyer or the Seller for the purpose of giving and receiving notices.** Any notice relating hereto or provided for herein shall be in writing. In addition to any provision contained herein and in any Schedule hereto, this offer, any counter-offer, notice of acceptance thereof or any notice to be given or received pursuant to this Agreement or any Schedule hereto (any of them, "Document") shall be deemed given and received when delivered personally or hand delivered to the Address for Service provided in the Acknowledgement below, or where a facsimile number or email address is provided herein, when transmitted electronically to that facsimile number or email address, respectively, in which case, the signature(s) of the party (parties) shall be deemed to be original.

FAX No.: ....
(For delivery of Documents to Seller)

FAX No.: ....
(For delivery of Documents to Buyer)

Email Address: ....
(For delivery of Documents to Seller)

Email Address: ....
(For delivery of Documents to Buyer)

4. CHATTELS INCLUDED: Living room and dining room drapes including gold decorator rods, and EasyUse washer and EasyUse dryer (2000 Neptune models)

Unless otherwise stated in this Agreement or any Schedule hereto, Seller agrees to convey all fixtures and chattels included in the Purchase Price free from all liens, encumbrances or claims affecting the said fixtures and chattels.

5. FIXTURES EXCLUDED: Dining room chandelier

6. RENTAL ITEMS (Including Lease, Lease to Own): The following equipment is rented and **not** included in the Purchase Price. The Buyer agrees to assume the rental contract(s), if assumable:

Rental hot water tank, Anycity Energy, payable $33.50 quarterly (plus applicable taxes)

The Buyer agrees to co-operate and execute such documentation as may be required to facilitate such assumption.

7. HST: If the sale of the Property (Real Property as described above) is subject to Harmonized Sales Tax (HST), then such tax shall be

included in the Purchase Price. If the sale of the Property is not subject to HST, Seller agrees to certify on or before
(included in/in addition to)

closing, that the sale of the Property is not subject to HST. Any HST on chattels, if applicable, is not included in the Purchase Price.

INITIALS OF BUYER(S): (*JH BW*)   **INITIALS OF SELLER(S):** ( )

Form 100   Revised 2015   **Page 2 of 6**

8.   TITLE SEARCH: Buyer shall be allowed until 6:00 p.m. on the .....5th..... day of ....April........................., 20..xx...., (Requisition Date) to examine the title to the Property at Buyer's own expense and until the earlier of: (i) thirty days from the later of the Requisition Date or the date on which the conditions in this Agreement are fulfilled or otherwise waived or; (ii) five days prior to completion, to satisfy Buyer that there are no outstanding

work orders or deficiency notices affecting the Property, and that its present use (...............single family residential..................) may be lawfully continued and that the principal building may be insured against risk of fire. Seller hereby consents to the municipality or other governmental agencies releasing to Buyer details of all outstanding work orders and deficiency notices affecting the property, and Seller agrees to execute and deliver such further authorizations in this regard as Buyer may reasonably require.

9.   FUTURE USE: Seller and Buyer agree that there is no representation or warranty of any kind that the future intended use of the property by Buyer is or will be lawful except as may be specifically provided for in this Agreement.

10. TITLE: Provided that the title to the property is good and free from all registered restrictions, charges, liens, and encumbrances except as otherwise specifically provided in this Agreement and save and except for (a) any registered restrictions or covenants that run with the land providing that such are complied with; (b) any registered municipal agreements and registered agreements with publicly regulated utilities providing such have been complied with, or security has been posted to ensure compliance and completion, as evidenced by a letter from the relevant municipality or regulated utility; (c) any minor easements for the supply of domestic utility or telephone services to the property or adjacent properties; and (d) any easements for drainage, storm or sanitary sewers, public utility lines, telephone lines, cable television lines or other services which do not materially affect the use of the property. If within the specified times referred to in paragraph 8 any valid objection to title or to any outstanding work order or deficiency notice, or to the fact the said present use may not lawfully be continued, or that the principal building may not be insured against risk of fire is made in writing to Seller and which Seller is unable or unwilling to remove, remedy or satisfy or obtain insurance save and except against risk of fire (Title Insurance) in favour of the Buyer and any mortgagee, (with all related costs at the expense of the Seller), and which Buyer will not waive, this Agreement notwithstanding any intermediate acts or negotiations in respect of such objections, shall be at an end and all monies paid shall be returned without interest or deduction and Seller, Listing Brokerage and Co-operating Brokerage shall not be liable for any costs or damages. Save as to any valid objection so made by such day and except for any objection going to the root of the title, Buyer shall be conclusively deemed to have accepted Seller's title to the property.

11. CLOSING ARRANGEMENTS: Where each of the Seller and Buyer retain a lawyer to complete the Agreement of Purchase and Sale of the property, and where the transaction will be completed by electronic registration pursuant to Part III of the Land Registration Reform Act, R.S.O. 1990, Chapter L4 and the Electronic Registration Act, S.O. 1991, Chapter 44, and any amendments thereto, the Seller and Buyer acknowledge and agree that the exchange of closing funds, non-registrable documents and other items (the "Requisite Deliveries") and the release thereof to the Seller and Buyer will (a) not occur at the same time as the registration of the transfer/deed (and any other documents intended to be registered in connection with the completion of this transaction) and (b) be subject to conditions whereby the lawyer(s) receiving any of the Requisite Deliveries will be required to hold same in trust and not release same except in accordance with the terms of a document registration agreement between the said lawyers. The Seller and Buyer irrevocably instruct the said lawyers to be bound by the document registration agreement which is recommended from time to time by the Law Society of Upper Canada. Unless otherwise agreed to by the lawyers, such exchange of the Requisite Deliveries will occur in the applicable Land Titles Office or such other location agreeable to both lawyers.

12. DOCUMENTS AND DISCHARGE: Buyer shall not call for the production of any title deed, abstract, survey or other evidence of title to the property except such as are in the possession or control of Seller. If requested by Buyer, Seller will deliver any sketch or survey of the property within Seller's control to Buyer as soon as possible and prior to the Requisition Date. If a discharge of any Charge/Mortgage held by a corporation incorporated pursuant to the Trust And Loan Companies Act (Canada), Chartered Bank, Trust Company, Credit Union, Caisse Populaire or Insurance Company and which is not to be assumed by Buyer on completion, is not available in registrable form on completion, Buyer agrees to accept Seller's lawyer's personal undertaking to obtain, out of the closing funds, a discharge in registrable form and to register same, or cause same to be registered, on title within a reasonable period of time after completion, provided that on or before completion Seller shall provide to Buyer a mortgage statement prepared by the mortgagee setting out the balance required to obtain the discharge, and, where a real-time electronic cleared funds transfer system is not being used, a direction executed by Seller directing payment to the mortgagee of the amount required to obtain the discharge out of the balance due on completion.

13. INSPECTION: Buyer acknowledges having had the opportunity to inspect the Property and understands that upon acceptance of this offer there shall be a binding agreement of purchase and sale between Buyer and Seller. **The Buyer acknowledges having the opportunity to include a requirement for a property inspection report in this Agreement and agrees that except as may be specifically provided for in this Agreement, the Buyer will not be obtaining a property inspection or property inspection report regarding the Property.**

14. INSURANCE: All buildings on the property and all other things being purchased shall be and remain until completion at the risk of Seller. Pending completion, Seller shall hold all insurance policies, if any, and the proceeds thereof in trust for the parties as their interests may appear and in the event of substantial damage, Buyer may either terminate this Agreement and have all monies paid returned without interest or deduction or else take the proceeds of any insurance and complete the purchase. No insurance shall be transferred on completion. If Seller is taking back a Charge/Mortgage, or Buyer is assuming a Charge/Mortgage, Buyer shall supply Seller with reasonable evidence of adequate insurance to protect Seller's or other mortgagee's interest on completion.

INITIALS OF BUYER(S): (*JH BW*)   INITIALS OF SELLER(S): (   )

Sample All Cash Offer—Page 4 of 6

15. **PLANNING ACT:** This Agreement shall be effective to create an interest in the property only if Seller complies with the subdivision control provisions of the Planning Act by completion and Seller covenants to proceed diligently at Seller's expense to obtain any necessary consent by completion.

16. **DOCUMENT PREPARATION:** The Transfer/Deed shall, save for the Land Transfer Tax Affidavit, be prepared in registrable form at the expense of Seller, and any Charge/Mortgage to be given back by the Buyer to Seller at the expense of the Buyer. If requested by Buyer, Seller covenants that the Transfer/Deed to be delivered on completion shall contain the statements contemplated by Section 50(22) of the Planning Act, R.S.O.1990.

17. **RESIDENCY:** (a) Subject to (b) below, the Seller represents and warrants that the Seller is not and on completion will not be a non-resident under the non-residency provisions of the Income Tax Act which representation and warranty shall survive and not merge upon the completion of this transaction and the Seller shall deliver to the Buyer a statutory declaration that Seller is not then a non-resident of Canada; (b) provided that if the Seller is a non-resident under the non-residency provisions of the Income Tax Act, the Buyer shall be credited towards the Purchase Price with the amount, if any, necessary for Buyer to pay to the Minister of National Revenue to satisfy Buyer's liability in respect of tax payable by Seller under the non-residency provisions of the Income Tax Act by reason of this sale. Buyer shall not claim such credit if Seller delivers on completion the prescribed certificate.

18. **ADJUSTMENTS:** Any rents, mortgage interest, realty taxes including local improvement rates and unmetered public or private utility charges and unmetered cost of fuel, as applicable, shall be apportioned and allowed to the day of completion, the day of completion itself to be apportioned to Buyer.

19. **PROPERTY ASSESSMENT:** The Buyer and Seller hereby acknowledge that the Province of Ontario has implemented current value assessment and properties may be re-assessed on an annual basis. The Buyer and Seller agree that no claim will be made against the Buyer or Seller, or any Brokerage, Broker or Salesperson, for any changes in property tax as a result of a re-assessment of the property, save and except any property taxes that accrued prior to the completion of this transaction.

20. **TIME LIMITS:** Time shall in all respects be of the essence hereof provided that the time for doing or completing of any matter provided for herein may be extended or abridged by an agreement in writing signed by Seller and Buyer or by their respective lawyers who may be specifically authorized in that regard.

21. **TENDER:** Any tender of documents or money hereunder may be made upon Seller or Buyer or their respective lawyers on the day set for completion. Money shall be tendered with funds drawn on a lawyer's trust account in the form of a bank draft, certified cheque or wire transfer using the Large Value Transfer System.

22. **FAMILY LAW ACT:** Seller warrants that spousal consent is not necessary to this transaction under the provisions of the Family Law Act, R.S.O.1990 unless Seller's spouse has executed the consent hereinafter provided.

23. **UFFI:** Seller represents and warrants to Buyer that during the time Seller has owned the property, Seller has not caused any building on the property to be insulated with insulation containing ureaformaldehyde, and that to the best of Seller's knowledge no building on the property contains or has ever contained insulation that contains ureaformaldehyde. This warranty shall survive and not merge on the completion of this transaction, and if the building is part of a multiple unit building, this warranty shall only apply to that part of the building which is the subject of this transaction.

24. **LEGAL, ACCOUNTING AND ENVIRONMENTAL ADVICE:** The parties acknowledge that any information provided by the brokerage is not legal, tax or environmental advice.

25. **CONSUMER REPORTS: The Buyer is hereby notified that a consumer report containing credit and/or personal information may be referred to in connection with this transaction.**

26. **AGREEMENT IN WRITING:** If there is conflict or discrepancy between any provision added to this Agreement (including any Schedule attached hereto) and any provision in the standard pre-set portion hereof, the added provision shall supersede the standard pre-set provision to the extent of such conflict or discrepancy. This Agreement including any Schedule attached hereto, shall constitute the entire Agreement between Buyer and Seller. There is no representation, warranty, collateral agreement or condition, which affects this Agreement other than as expressed herein. For the purposes of this Agreement, Seller means vendor and Buyer means purchaser. This Agreement shall be read with all changes of gender or number required by the context.

27. **TIME AND DATE:** Any reference to a time and date in this Agreement shall mean the time and date where the property is located.

INITIALS OF BUYER(S): (*JH BW*)   **INITIALS OF SELLER(S):** ( )

Form 100   Revised 2015   **Page 4 of 6**

28. SUCCESSORS AND ASSIGNS: The heirs, executors, administrators, successors and assigns of the undersigned are bound by the terms herein.

SIGNED, SEALED AND DELIVERED in the presence of: IN WITNESS whereof I have hereunto set my hand and seal:

Linda Ward   *James Harari*   ●   DATE   *March 5/xx*
(Witness)   (Buyer)   (Seal)

Linda Ward   *Betty Westcott*   ●   DATE   *March 5/xx*
(Witness)   (Buyer)   (Seal)

I, the Undersigned Seller, agree to the above offer. I hereby irrevocably instruct my lawyer to pay directly to the brokerage(s) with whom I have agreed to pay commission, the unpaid balance of the commission together with applicable Harmonized Sales Tax (and any other taxes as may hereafter be applicable), from the proceeds of the sale prior to any payment to the undersigned on completion, as advised by the brokerage(s) to my lawyer.

SIGNED, SEALED AND DELIVERED in the presence of: IN WITNESS whereof I have hereunto set my hand and seal:

....   ●   DATE ....
(Witness)   (Seller)   (Seal)

....   ●   DATE ....
(Witness)   (Seller)   (Seal)

SPOUSAL CONSENT: The Undersigned Spouse of the Seller hereby consents to the disposition evidenced herein pursuant to the provisions of the Family Law Act, R.S.O.1990, and hereby agrees with the Buyer that he/she will execute all necessary or incidental documents to give full force and effect to the sale evidenced herein.

....   ●   DATE ....
(Witness)   (Spouse)   (Seal)

CONFIRMATION OF ACCEPTANCE: Notwithstanding anything contained herein to the contrary, I confirm this Agreement with all changes both typed and written was finally accepted by all parties at .... a.m./p.m. this .... day of.., 20..........

....
(Signature of Seller or Buyer)

INFORMATION ON BROKERAGE(S)

Listing Brokerage ...... **ABC Realty Inc.** .... Tel.No.(.. **416** ..) **444-1212**
    123 Main Street, Anycity   M3X 3C1   **Albert Lee**
                            (Salesperson / Broker Name)

Co-op/Buyer Brokerage ...... **XYZ Real Estate Limited** ...... Tel.No.(.. **416** ..) **333-1212**
    15 Centre Street, Anycity   M5E 6T8   **Linda Ward**
                            (Salesperson / Broker Name)

ACKNOWLEDGEMENT

I acknowledge receipt of my signed copy of this accepted Agreement of Purchase and Sale and I authorize the Brokerage to forward a copy to my lawyer.   I acknowledge receipt of my signed copy of this accepted Agreement of Purchase and Sale and I authorize the Brokerage to forward a copy to my lawyer.

.... DATE .... DATE ....
(Seller)   (Buyer)

.... DATE .... DATE ....
(Seller)   (Buyer)
Address for Service ....   Address for Service ....

.... Tel.No.(...........) .... Tel.No.(...........) ......

Seller's Lawyer ....   Buyer's Lawyer ....

Address ....   Address ....

Email ....   Email ....

(.........)........... (.........)...........   (.........)........... (.........)...........
   Tel.No.   FAX No.   Tel.No.   FAX No.

FOR OFFICE USE ONLY   **COMMISSION TRUST AGREEMENT**

To: Co-operating Brokerage shown on the foregoing Agreement of Purchase and Sale:
In consideration for the Co-operating Brokerage procuring the foregoing Agreement of Purchase and Sale, I hereby declare that all moneys received or receivable by me in connection with the Transaction as contemplated in the MLS® Rules and Regulations of my Real Estate Board shall be receivable and held in trust. This agreement shall constitute a Commission Trust Agreement as defined in the MLS® Rules and shall be subject to and governed by the MLS® Rules pertaining to Commission Trust.
DATED as of the date and time of the acceptance of the foregoing Agreement of Purchase and Sale.   Acknowledged by:

....
(Authorized to bind the Listing Brokerage)   (Authorized to bind the Co-operating Brokerage)

Form 100   Revised 2015   **Page 5 of 6**

Sample All Cash Offer—Page 6 of 6

OREA Ontario Real Estate Association

Form 100
for use in the Province of Ontario

Schedule A
Agreement of Purchase and Sale

This Schedule is attached to and forms part of the Agreement of Purchase and Sale between:

BUYER, James Edwin Harari and Betty Jane Westcott ...., and

SELLER, Henry S. Wilkins and Rose A. Wilkins ....

for the purchase and sale of 219 Centre Street, City of Anycity, Regional Municipality of Anyregion

.... dated the 5th day of March , 20 XX

Buyer agrees to pay the balance as follows:

The Buyer agrees to pay a further sum of Two Hundred and Ninety-Nine Thousand Dollars ($299,000.00), subject to adjustments, to the Seller on completion of this transaction with funds drawn on a lawyer's trust account in the form of a bank draft, certified cheque, or wire transfer using the Large Value Transfer System.

This form must be initialed by all parties to the Agreement of Purchase and Sale.

INITIALS OF BUYER(S): JH BW

INITIALS OF SELLER(S):

Form 100   Revised 2015   **Page 6 of 6**

OFFERS WITH ALTERNATE DEPOSIT(S)

A deposit, a sign of good faith, is integral to the agreement and forms part of the purchase price. In an all cash offer:

price – deposit(s) = balance of purchase price

which is the amount inserted in the *pay the balance as follows* (balance due on completion) clause on Schedule A. This formula is applicable to all cash offers, but not other offers. For example, when a mortgage is being assumed, the balance of the purchase price is the price *less* the deposit and *less* the mortgage being assumed. See the next chapter regarding arranging new financing or assuming financing.

Timing

The *Agreement of Purchase and Sale* (OREA Form 100) calls for a deposit *herewith, upon acceptance* or *as otherwise described in the agreement.* Timing to receive the deposit from a buyer for *herewith* offers is when the agreement is signed. For *upon acceptance* offers, timing to receive the deposit from the buyer begins when the *Confirmation of Acceptance* is signed. REBBA 2002 statutory requirements dictate the deposit be deposited by the brokerage (designated as the "Deposit Holder") into their real estate trust account within five business days of receipt. Receipt of the money by an employee of the brokerage would constitute receipt by the brokerage.

The preprinted wording calls for a negotiable cheque. Deposits must be capable of being presented immediately for payment at the banking institution on which they are drawn. In certain board jurisdictions and brokerages, accepted practice may dictate a certified cheque, but this is not required under the Act and Regulations.

When a co-operating brokerage gives the buyer's deposit to the listing brokerage, a receipt is issued to the co-operating brokerage for paper trail purposes. See *Deposit Focus* to follow the typical deposit to closing.

Tracking the Deposit: From Buyer to Final Closing   **DEPOSIT FOCUS**

Salesperson Garcia of XYZ Real Estate Limited receives a $15,000 deposit from Buyers Smith and Jones. The offer provides for the deposit *upon acceptance*. The Wilsons, sign the agreement at 4 p.m. on Oct. 5th, along with the Confirmation of Acceptance, in the presence of both Garcia and Salesperson James (the listing salesperson) of ABC Realty Inc. Garcia hands James the deposit made out to ABC Realty Inc. and receives a deposit receipt from James.

James returns to ABC Realty Inc., processes the transaction and gives the deposit cheque to the broker of record. The broker of record prepares a bank deposit for these funds, along with any other deposit funds received. She makes the deposit on Oct. 6th into the brokerage's *Real Estate Trust Account*. No interest will be paid on this deposit.

NOTE: If an interest-bearing certificate (IBC) was required, the broker of record would issue a trust cheque for the IBC and then return the funds, plus interest, to the real estate trust account prior to completion date.

Following completion, ABC Realty Inc. obtains written confirmation that the sale has closed and then issues a cheque to the Commission Trust Account for commission earned. Subsequent disbursements from that account are made to the co-operating brokerage (XYZ Real Estate Limited) who in turn pays Salesperson Garcia. Any excess funds remaining in the *Real Estate Trust Account* after commission earned amounts are dispersed, are forwarded to the seller.

Deposit Variations

Most offers contain a straight-forward deposit, but circumstances can dictate otherwise.

DEPOSIT VARIATIONS

Additional Payment The buyer has additional investments, not readily convertible to cash on signing date.	**Multiple Payments** Make additional scheduled payments to align with construction stages in the building of a custom home.
On Removal of Condition(s) Buyer submits smaller deposit with larger amount to follow when sale is firm; i.e., conditions are removed.	**Interest Bearing** Buyer provides large deposit with long closing and wants interest paid on funds held.

For interest-bearing deposits, the buyer's social insurance number is required as the brokerage holding the deposit will issue a T5 for earned interest. Brokerage policies vary regarding minimum deposit amounts and administration fees for interest-bearing accounts.

The following pages illustrate excerpts from the Harari/Westcott/Wilkins offer with an alternate deposit approach.

Sample Offer With Alternate Deposit Clauses—Page 1

OREA Ontario Real Estate Association   **Agreement of Purchase and Sale**

Form 100
for use in the Province of Ontario

This Agreement of Purchase and Sale dated this ...... **5th** ...... day of .... **March** .... 20 **XX** ....

BUYER, ... **James Edwin Harari and Betty Jane Westcott** ...., agrees to purchase from
(Full legal names of all Buyers)

SELLER, ... **Harry S. Wilkins and Rose A. Wilkins** ...., the following
(Full legal names of all Sellers)

REAL PROPERTY:

Address .... **219 Centre Street** ....

fronting on the .... **South** .... side of .... **Centre Street** ....

in the .... **City of Anycity, Regional Municipality of Anyregion** ....

and having a frontage of .... **55.34 feet** .... more or less by a depth of .... **110.37 feet** .... more or less

and legally described as .... **Lot 3, Reg. Plan 1392** ....

.... (the "property")
(Legal description of land including easements not described elsewhere)

PURCHASE PRICE: Dollars (CDN$) ...... **$329,000.00** ......

.... **Three Hundred and Twenty-Nine Thousand** --- Dollars

DEPOSIT: Buyer submits .... **Upon Aceptance** ....
(Herewith/Upon Acceptance/as otherwise described in this Agreement)

.... **Ten Thousand** --- Dollars (CDN$) ...... **$10,000.00** ......

by negotiable cheque payable to .... **ABC Realty Inc.** .... "Deposit Holder" to be held
in trust pending completion or other termination of this Agreement and to be credited toward the Purchase Price on completion. For the purposes of this Agreement, "Upon Acceptance" shall mean that the Buyer is required to deliver the deposit to the Deposit Holder within 24 hours of the acceptance of this Agreement. The parties to this Agreement hereby acknowledge that, unless otherwise provided for in this Agreement, the Deposit Holder shall place the deposit in trust in the Deposit Holder's non-interest bearing Real Estate Trust Account and no interest shall be earned, received or paid on the deposit.

Buyer agrees to pay the balance as more particularly set out in Schedule A attached.

SCHEDULE(S) A .... **attached hereto form(s) part of this Agreement.**

1. **IRREVOCABILITY:** This offer shall be irrevocable by .... **Buyer** .... until **11:59** a.m./p.m. on the **7th**
(Seller/Buyer)

day of .... **March** .... 20 **XX** ...., after which time, if not accepted, this offer shall be null and void and the deposit shall be returned to the Buyer in full without interest.

2. **COMPLETION DATE:** This Agreement shall be completed by no later than 6:00 p.m. on the ...... **5th** ...... day of .... **May** ....

20 **XX** ...... Upon completion, vacant possession of the property shall be given to the Buyer unless otherwise provided for in this Agreement.

INITIALS OF BUYER(S): (*JH BW*)   **INITIALS OF SELLER(S):** ( )

Form 100   Revised 2015   **Page 1 of 6**

Sample Offer With Alternate Deposit Clauses—Page 6

 **Ontario Real Estate Association**

Form 100
for use in the Province of Ontario

Schedule A
Agreement of Purchase and Sale

This Schedule is attached to and forms part of the Agreement of Purchase and Sale between:

BUYER, ... James Edwin Harari and Betty Jane Westcott ...., and

SELLER, ... Harry S. Wilkins and Rose A. Wilkins ....

for the purchase and sale of ..... 219 Centre Street, City of Anycity, Regional Municipality of Anyregion .....

.... dated the ....5th.... day of .... March ...., 20..XX....

Buyer agrees to pay the balance as follows:

The Buyer agrees to pay a further sum of Twenty Thousand Dollars ($20,000.00) to ABC Realty Inc., by negotiable cheque not later than 5:00 p.m. on the 20th day of March, 20xx, as a supplementary deposit to be held in trust in the same manner as the initial deposit pending completion or other termination of this Agreement. This amount is to be credited towards the purchase price on completion of this transaction.

The Buyer agrees to pay a further sum of Two Hundred and Ninety-Nine Thousand Dollars ($299,000.00), subject to adjustments, to the Seller on completion of this transaction, with funds drawn on a lawyer's trust account in the form of a bank draft, certified cheque, or wire transfer using the Large Value Transfer System.

This form must be initialed by all parties to the Agreement of Purchase and Sale.

INITIALS OF BUYER(S): (*JH BW*)　　　　**INITIALS OF SELLER(S):** ( )

Form 100　Revised 2015　**Page 6 of 6**

DRAFTING FACTS AND ASSURANCES CLAUSES

Real estate negotiations hinge on each party's understanding of what exactly is being bought and sold. Unfortunately, seemingly innocent assumptions can lead to disappointment at minimum, or escalate to serious disputes and potential litigation.

Clarity is uppermost. Avoid obscure, convoluted or entangled language. Draft clauses in a straightforward manner, so that ordinary persons can reasonably understand what is meant.

Many issues present themselves in a real estate transaction that require clarification. For example, does the buyer understand that no express warranty is being given by the seller concerning whether or not the chattels are in good working order?

What about the swimming pool? Are there leaks not readily visible? More importantly, if the seller warrants that no leaks exist, does the warranty extend beyond closing? To complicate matters further, does he give this warranty when the property was inspected by the buyer or as of the completion date? Buyers and sellers want certainty.

Acknowledgements

> **Acknowledgement**
>
> An admission or affirmation that some circumstance exists, as in a fact, situation or liability. Acknowledgements are found in standard agreements (i.e., acknowledging receipt of a true copy) and in clauses where buyer and/or seller confirm certain facts.

An **acknowledgement** is useful to obtain admission or affirmation that something exists. In clause writing, an acknowledgement places emphasis on matters that might be misunderstood or misconstrued.

> **EXAMPLE**
>
> Buyer Smith is pleased that the seller is including all outboard motors, boats, accessories and cottage furnishings. The listing salesperson, to avoid confusion regarding their overall condition, inserts the following clause:
>
> ---
> *The buyer acknowledges that there are no express or implied warranties on chattels included in this Agreement of Purchase and Sale.*
>
> ---

In other words, caveat emptor (*let the buyer beware*) generally applies. All listed items will be included as promised, but their condition, working order or other related circumstances are not in any way warranted.

When both parties to the contract are involved, the wording typically reads either as:

> *The buyer(s) and the seller(s) acknowledge…*
>
> **or**
>
> *the parties to the transaction acknowledge….*

Representations/Warranties

> **Representation**
>
> A statement made regarding some existing fact or event that induces a contract and could be the basis for rescinding that agreement, if found false.

The inclusion of a **representation** and/or **warranty** extends beyond mere acknowledgement to an assurance, typically concerning facts key to negotiations.

The terms *represents* and *warrants* have somewhat different meanings and consequent legal implications. Clause drafting has understandably embraced both; i.e., *the seller represents and warrants to* fully encompass assurances made, should subsequent legal action ensue.

SURVIVE CLOSING/CURRENT STATE

Most *represents and warrants* clauses include a subsequent statement that defines the scope and timing of the assurance. All matters in an agreement are merged (extinguished) when title passes, unless otherwise provided. Therefore, a clause is typically required to ensure that the representation and warranty survives the closing. Note that the wording only applies to the condition of the property at completion.

> **EXAMPLE**
>
> The seller represents and warrants that no known water damage has occurred to the basement by water seepage or flooding. The parties agree that this representation and warranty shall survive and not merge on completion of this transaction, but apply only to the state of the property at completion of this transaction.

Registrants should also contemplate including a provision as to how far past the completion date the representation/warranty applies, if that is the intention.

BEST KNOWLEDGE AND BELIEF

Buyers and sellers may feel uncomfortable providing absolute assurances. Registrants may encounter the phrase *to the best of my knowledge and belief* inserted in the clause. Loosely translated: *I believe it to be true, as far as I know, but it's not a 100% assurance.* The legal merits of this phrase will be left to judicial interpretation.

Such clauses may also contain a provision that the agreement may be terminated by the buyer should the representation/warranty prove false prior to completion date.

Action to be Taken

Many circumstances arise in which buyers or sellers must take some action in furtherance of the contract. Selected introductory words are provided:

> *The buyer authorizes and directs the seller to...*

This phrase not only gives the seller *authority*, but also provides a *direct instruction* to do something on the buyer's behalf; e.g., deliver tenant notices regarding the new owner when the sale becomes firm and binding.

This wording should be distinguished from a simple authority; i.e., *The seller authorizes the Ministry of the Environment to release to the buyer any and all documentation on record concerning the said property.*

SIGN AND DELIVER

Another commonly used action phrase is for the buyer or seller to sign and deliver something:

> *The seller will execute and deliver to the buyer...*

The assumption underlying the following phraseology is that the action will be done in a timely fashion; i.e., time is of the essence.

> *The buyer agrees to (pay, provide, assume, abide by, allow access to, complete, etc.)...*

THE REAL ESTATE TRANSACTION—GENERAL

Agreed Facts

Precise statements of fact are vital to promote correct understanding of the parties. Such clauses are typically associated with complex agreements in which specific terms must be isolated and detailed.

> **EXAMPLE**
>
> Salesperson Chong wants to ensure the parties' understanding regarding purchase price calculation based on total acreage:
>
> ---
> *It is understood and agreed that the purchase price for the said property will be established based on $4,900 per acre. The seller agrees to provide an up-to-date survey at his expense....*
> ---

Alternatively, a direct statement would also suffice: *The purchase price of the said property will be established based on $4,900 per acre...*

Right(s) Given

This is a positive authority given to a buyer or seller to perform some function; e.g., a right to enter the premises for inspection purposes prior to closing.

> **EXAMPLE**
>
> Salesperson Jennings is negotiating a vacant land sale and the buyer wants property access for soil testing prior to construction.
>
> ---
> *The seller agrees to grant the buyer and the buyer's authorized agent the right to enter the property for the purpose of...*
> ---

The full clause typically includes a provision that such access shall not in any way alter the current state of the land.

This clause might be found in an agreement in which the buyer is contemplating the subdividing of the property and/ or the erection of some structure(s) and, consequently, requires permission to enter the property for the purpose of surveying and conducting soil tests before the completion of the transaction.

Such permission is normally worded so that the right does not extend to any alteration of the lands, servicing work, removal of trees, soil or any other activity that would alter the current state of the property.

EXAMPLE

Developer Reed has recently purchased, but not yet closed, the sale for a large tract of vacant land. However, he would like access to the property for purposes of surveying and conducting soil samples. Following is the clause inserted in the offer:

> *The seller agrees to grant the buyer and his/her authorized agent the right to enter the property for the purpose of surveying and conducting soil tests prior to the completion of this transaction. Such permission does not extend to any alteration of the lands, servicing work, removal of trees, soil or any other activity which would alter the current state of the property.*

The following form excerpt shows the original Harari/Westcott/Wilkins offer with additional clauses regarding facts and assurances.

Sample Offer With Clauses Regarding Facts and Assurances—Page 6

 **OREA** Ontario Real Estate Association

Schedule A
Agreement of Purchase and Sale

Form 100 for use in the Province of Ontario

This Schedule is attached to and forms part of the Agreement of Purchase and Sale between:

BUYER,............................ James Edwin Harari and Betty Jane Wescott ...., and

SELLER,............................ Harry S. Wilkins and Rose A. Wilkins ....

for the purchase and sale of ..219 Centre Street, City of Anycity, Regional Municipality of Anyregion ....

.... dated the ....5th............... day of ....March........., 20XX..... .

Buyer agrees to pay the balance as follows:

The Buyer agrees to pay a further sum of Two Hundred and Ninety-Nine Thousand Dollars ($299,000.00), subject to adjustments, to the Seller on completion of this transaction, with funds drawn on a lawyer's trust account in the form of a bank draft, certified cheque, or wire transfer using the Large Value Transfer System.

The Buyer acknowledges that there are no express or implied warranties by the Seller on the chattels included in the Agreement of Purchase and Sale.

The Seller represents and warrants that no known damage has occurred to the basement due to water seepage or flooding. The parties agree that this representation and warranty shall survive and not merge on completion of this transaction, but apply only to the state of the property at completion of this transaction.

The following questions were posed to a broker of record on one of the online forums provided by the OREA Real Estate College. Here are her responses:

Q   I heard that brokerages in my marketplace require certified deposit cheques when presenting offers. Is that true?

A   The *Agreement of Purchase and Sale* (OREA Form 100) requires a negotiable cheque only; i.e., one capable of being presented to the lending institution upon which it was drawn. Local trading practices and/or brokerage policies have sometimes dictated certified cheques. In fact, in my market area, it was fairly commonplace in the 1980s and 1990s, but seems to have largely disappeared at present. Check with your broker of record or manager.

Q   Why does the co-operating brokerage need a receipt for the deposit?

A   From my perspective as the broker of record, I need written proof that the cheque was given to the listing brokerage. Otherwise, our company's paper trail would be missing a key link. I don't like to think in negatives, but prudence is uppermost. Suppose the cheque went missing? Besides, when we are inspected by the Real Estate Council of Ontario, a full document trail is required.

Q   When must I get the cheque from the buyer and do I have five business days to get it to the other brokerage, if it's not my brokerage's listing?

A   You've actually asked two distinct questions. First, if the offer states *herewith*, then the cheque must accompany the offer at time of signing. If *upon acceptance*, the cheque must be available when the *Confirmation of Acceptance* is completed. Of course, the agreement also provides that other deposit arrangements can be made *as otherwise described in the agreement*.

continued...

A   Now the second question. What about the five business days? REBBA 2002 does not contemplate whether a deposit is *herewith, upon acceptance* or *otherwise*. The Act only states that funds received shall be deposited to the real estate trust account within five business days. Timing begins when the brokerage receives the money in trust. Receipt of the money by an employee of the brokerage constitutes receipt by the brokerage.

Q   I've heard that sometimes an offer is faxed for acceptance by the other party. What happens to the deposit?

A   Faxing is acceptable, if the *Notices* clause in the agreement is correctly completed. While no specific rule exists regarding your question, our brokerage faxes the cheque with the offer to confirm the buyer's good faith. The cheque is then forwarded by mail or delivered. Other brokerages may have different policies.

Q   An experienced buyer representative told me that she asks for a small deposit from clients, followed by a subsequent larger deposit when conditions are removed. Does this make good sense?

A   I have no problem with that strategy. Good faith is ultimately provided through sequential deposits and the buyer need not commit significant dollars until a firm sale. Further, the buyer client is in a better position should some dispute arise regarding release of the deposit. Keep in mind that I'm looking at this from the buyer's perspective. Seller representatives might take a different viewpoint when protecting their clients.

CLAUSE FUNDAMENTALS

The following highlights major clause elements reviewed to this point. Clauses illustrated are summary only and do not constitute detailed wordings as found in the *Appendix*.

PAY THE BALANCE AS FOLLOWS

By Whom   *Amount*   *Adjustments*

The buyer agrees to pay   a further sum of _____   subject to adjustments

to the seller   on completion of this transaction   with funds drawn on a lawyer's trust account in
To Whom   *When*   *How*

the form of a bank draft, certified cheque or wire transfer using the Large Value Transfer system.
How

DEPOSITS

By Whom   *Amount*

The buyer agrees to pay   a further sum of _____.

This amount is to be credited toward the purchase price.
Where Applied

ACKNOWLEDGEMENT

By Whom   *Admission/Affirmation*

The buyer acknowledges   that _____.

REPRESENTS/WARRANTS

By Whom   *Assurance(s)*

The buyer/seller represents and warrants   that _____

shall survive and not merge on closing   and apply only to the state of the property _____.
No Merge   *State at Completion*

ACTION TO BE TAKEN

By Whom   *To Whom*

The buyer/seller authorizes and directs   the buyer/seller

to _____.
Action Specifics
(e.g., pay..., provide..., assume..., etc.)

AGREED FACTS

By Whom   *Statement(s) of Fact*

The parties agree   that the _____.

RIGHTS TO BE GIVEN

By Whom   *Description of Right(s)*

The buyer/seller agrees   that _____.

AVOIDING ERRORS AND OMISSIONS

This chapter, as with previous ones, emphasizes techniques to minimize the possibility of making errors or omitting key information when preparing documentation. For purposes of drafting agreements of purchase and sale:

- Make certain that forms for identification verification and receipt of funds are fully completed, as per compliance guidelines when drafting and negotiating offers.

- Always rely on the six-step offer plan to organize your thoughts and your offer.

- Carefully review clause wordings used by your intended employing brokerage, clarify any concerns with the broker of record or manager and be prepared to fully explain wordings to clients and customers.

- Make certain that all relevant information is included. Are all blank spots in the *Agreement of Purchase and Sale* filled-in (or alternatively, left blank depending on circumstances)?

- Assess if deposit terms are as agreed with the party making the offer.

- Does the math add up: price – deposit = balance of purchase price?

- Confirm that all dates are in the correct, sequential order; e.g., current date, irrevocable date, title search date and completion date?

- Don't take any shortcuts. Follow all six steps and take extra time to check/proof (Step 6).

- Get to the facts: Use acknowledgements to affirm and representations/warranties to assure.

- Do clients and customers clearly understand what is meant by represent and warrant?

- Find the right words: Is this an action to be taken, a fact to be agreed or a right to be given?

- Always read the offer from the top down and then review from the bottom up. It may seem redundant, but it's amazing what errors go unnoticed the first time.

- If changes have to be made and a new offer drafted, go through a full review once again. A seemingly minor change in one portion of an offer can affect other terms in that offer.

- Computers only print out what is inputted. Remember: *Garbage In—Garbage Out.*

KNOWLEDGE INTEGRATION

Notables

- Mastery in drafting offers results from continuous practice. No two transactions are ever exactly identical.

- Make certain that you fully comply with identification verification and receipt of funds requirements.

- OREA recommended clauses are for guidance only. Review and adapt wordings to meet circumstances.

- Use the resources and knowledge available to you. Check with the broker of record or manager as needed.

- Paper/electronic cheat sheets are widely used. Just make certain that the right clauses are being used to suit particular circumstances.

- The *Agreement of Purchase and Sale* (OREA Form 100) is widely, but not universally, used by brokerages in Ontario.

- The *Agreement of Purchase and Sale— Commercial* (OREA Form 500) closely parallels its residential counterpart.

- A deposit is a sign of good faith, an integral part of the agreement and forms part of the purchase price.

- Check the *pay the balance as follows* (balance due on completion) clause. Make certain it contains the six key elements.

- Deposits must be placed in the Real Estate Trust Account within five business days of receipt.

- Brokerage policies vary regarding interest payments on deposits.

- An acknowledgement clause in an agreement is a written admission or affirmation that something exists.

- Avoid legal complexities concerning represents versus warrants by including both in appropriate clauses.

- Represents and warrants clauses typically state that such assurances survive closing, but apply only to the state of the property as of the completion date.

- A deposit receipt from the listing brokerage should be issued to the co-operating broker to ensure a proper brokerage paper trail.

- Make certain that facts and assurances clauses are accurately worded to reflect what is intended.

Glossary

Acknowledgement
FINTRAC
Large Cash Transaction

Mandatary
Representation
Warranty

THE REAL ESTATE TRANSACTION—GENERAL

Web Links

Web links are included for general interest regarding selected chapter topics.

FINTRAC	Go to the Financial Transactions and Reports Analysis Centre of Canada website (*www.fintrac.ca*) for detailed information regarding compliance issues.
REALTORLink®	Members of organized real estate can access the Money Laundering Compliance Centre through the REALTORLink® website. Go to *www.realtorlink.ca*.
Corporation Verification	The existence of a corporation can be confirmed by obtaining federal corporation details from the Corporations Canada website (*http://corporationscanada.ic.gc.ca*).

Strategic Thinking For Your Career

Questions are included to assist in developing your new career. No answers are provided.

1. What type of offer software (if any) do local brokerages use and what different offer drafting methods exist in the local area; e.g., salespersons using offer software, broker preparation of offers using cheat sheets and so forth?

2. Based on materials covered in this chapter, what questions should I prepare to ask my intended employing brokerage concerning handling of deposits?

3. What procedures and forms does my intended employing brokerage use to be in compliance with identification verification and receipt of funds requirements set out by FINTRAC.

4. Are there certain clause wordings used in the local marketplace that are not found in the OREA recommended clauses?

Chapter Mini-Review

Solutions are located in the Appendix.

1. All brokerages in Ontario must use the *Agreement of Purchase and Sale* (OREA Form 100).

   ◯ True   ◯ False

2. Cheat sheets are seldom used and have been discouraged by the Real Estate Council of Ontario and real estate boards.

   ◯ True   ◯ False

3. When two brokerages are involved with respective clients in a real estate transaction, the *Individual Identification Information Form* must be completed by the co-operating brokerage, but not by the listing brokerage.

   ◯ True   ◯ False

4. The Receipt of Funds Record must be prepared for every amount of funds received by a real estate brokerage.

   ◯ True   ◯ False

5. A mandatary is required for identification verification of a buyer client from another country, when a face-to-face meeting is not possible.

   ◯ True   ◯ False

6. The deposit is always the difference between the agreed price and the amount inserted in the *pay the balance as follows* line.

   ◯ True   ◯ False

7. The completion date normally follows the title search date by two or three days.

   ◯ True   ◯ False

8. Deposit increases can be accomplished through multiple payments provided that times, dates and amounts are stated in the agreement.

   ◯ True   ◯ False

9. A buyer who deliberately withholds a deposit may be in breach of the contract.

   ◯ True   ◯ False

10. The decision to use a representation/warranty or other clause; e.g., acknowledgement or statement of agreed facts, is typically dictated by circumstances.

    ◯ True   ◯ False

11. A delay in the delivery of a deposit by a co-operating brokerage can jeopardize the listing brokerage's ability to satisfy depositing requirements set out in the *Real Estate and Business Brokers Act, 2002*.

    ◯ True   ◯ False

12. A right to access clause must always include a provision that such access by the buyer shall be at reasonable times and only upon sufficient notice to the seller.

    ◯ True   ◯ False

13. An acknowledgement clause cannot be inserted that overrides the pre-printed portion of an agreement of purchase and sale.

    ◯ True   ◯ False

14. In drafting any action to be taken, the words *authorizes* and *directs* must always be inserted.

    ◯ True   ◯ False

15. The order of acknowledgements, representations and agreed facts clauses within an agreement of purchase and sale is normally at the option of the person drafting the offer.

   ◯ True   ◯ False

16. FINTRAC deems that a business relationship is effectively established whenever a brokerage conducts three or more transactions with a client within a two-year period.

   ◯ True   ◯ False

17. Real estate brokerages have an obligation to conduct a risk assessment of all corporate clients with respect to the possibility of money laundering or terrorist financing. The obligation to conduct a risk assessment does not extend to clients who are private individuals.

   ◯ True   ◯ False

Active Learning Exercises

Solutions are located in the Appendix.

■ Exercise 1   Matching

Match the words in the right column with the appropriate descriptions in the left column (not all descriptions are used).

____	*Represents/Warrants Clause*	*a. Agreed Facts*
____	*Admission or Affirmation That Something Exists*	*b. False Representation*
____	*Purchase Price Minus Deposit, Mortgage Assumptions and Seller Take Backs*	*c. Offer Mathematics*
____	*It is Understood and Agreed*	*d. Deposit Receipt*
____	*Potential Basis for Rescinding a Contract*	*e. Acknowledgement*
____	*Offer Plan*	*f. Pay the Balance as Follows: Amount*
____	*Co-operating Brokerage*	*g. Commission Trust Account*
		h. Survive Closing
		i. Five Business Days

■ Exercise 2   Six Components

List the six components of a *pay a further sum of* clause.

1.	
2.	
3.	
4.	
5.	
6.	

■ Exercise 3   Clause Analysis

Identify whether the following clauses are acceptable or not acceptable based on recommended OREA wordings and, if not acceptable, detail the reason(s) for your decision.

3.1 The buyer agrees to pay a further sum of Ten Thousand Dollars to ABC Realty Inc., by cheque, at the time of notification or fulfillment or removal of the condition pertaining to arranging a new first mortgage, as an additional deposit to be held in trust pending completion of this agreement. This amount is to be credited toward the deposit on completion of this transaction.

◯ **Acceptable**   ◯ **Not Acceptable**

Reasons (If Not Acceptable):

3.2 The buyer represents and warrants that on completion, the satellite receiver and associated equipment, as further detailed under Chattels in this agreement, shall be in good working order. The parties agree that this representation and warranty shall survive and not merge on completion of this transaction, but apply only to the state of the property existing at completion of this transaction.

◯ **Acceptable**   ◯ **Not Acceptable**

Reasons (If Not Acceptable):

3.3   The buyer and seller agree that the representations and warranties stated herein shall survive and merge on completion of this transaction.

○ Acceptable   ○ Not Acceptable

Reasons (If Not Acceptable):

3.4   The buyer shall have the right to inspect the property one further time at completion, provided that notice is given to the seller. The seller agrees to provide access to the property for the purpose of this inspection.

○ Acceptable   ○ Not Acceptable

Reasons (If Not Acceptable):

▣ Exercise 4   The Jones/Brown All Cash Offer

Ronald A. Jones and Cathy W. Brown are interested in a property located at 224 Stevenson Avenue in Anycity. As buyer clients, they want you to draft an offer for this property owned by Yvonne J. Racine and Scott P. Racine listed by ABC Realty Inc. Various information is described on the following page.

The property, located on the south side of Stevenson Avenue, has a frontage of 39.55 feet and a depth of 120.20 feet, and is described as *Lot 12, Registered Plan 4332, City of Anycity, Regional Municipality of Anyregion*. The property has a mutual rear drive that is shared with two adjacent owners.

The offered price is $231,000 with a deposit of $10,000, a supplemental deposit of $10,000 payable 12 days from the offer date and the balance due on completion date. The deposit is to be provided herewith the offer to the listing brokerage. No mortgage is required. The built-in bookcase in the family room is excluded. The buyers want the sellers to repair any damage and repaint the entire family room wall where the bookcase is now located. Draperies and decorator rods in the master bedroom, living room and dining room will remain with the property. A rental hot water tank from Anycity Energy @ $33.50 per quarter (plus tax) is assumable.

The buyers have expressed some concerns about the swimming pool and its compliance with local by-laws and want the sellers' assurance that, to the best of their knowledge, the pool is in compliance. Swimming pool accessories include the PoolClean vacuum, hoses and hand skimmer.

The offer, dated at Anycity, will be irrevocable for two days and expires at 6 p.m. on that day. Allow a title search period of approximately 45 days from today's date. Completion will be approximately 60 days from today's date. The present use is single-family residential. Notices cannot be delivered by fax or email and HST is deemed to be included in the purchase price. Assume that today's date is July 16, 20xx and the completion date is a normal business day. Insert necessary dates and signatures as required for a fully-completed agreement ready for presentation.

4.1   Draft an offer and insert any additional details necessary to full complete the offer. You work for XYZ Real Estate Limited. A blank *Agreement of Purchase and Sale* (OREA Form 100) is provided.

4.2   Prepare an *Individual Identification Information Record* and *Receipt of Funds Record*. Insert additional details as necessary to fully complete each form. Blank copies are provided.

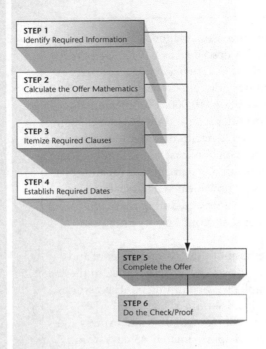

STEP 1 Identify Required Information

STEP 2 Calculate the Offer Mathematics

STEP 3 Itemize Required Clauses

STEP 4 Establish Required Dates

Exercise 4   Agreement of Purchase and Sale—Page 1 of 6

OREA Ontario Real Estate Association   **Agreement of Purchase and Sale**

Form 100
for use in the Province of Ontario

This Agreement of Purchase and Sale dated this .... day of .... 20............

BUYER, ..., agrees to purchase from
(Full legal names of all Buyers)

SELLER, ..., the following
(Full legal names of all Sellers)

REAL PROPERTY:

Address ....

fronting on the .... side of ....

in the ....

and having a frontage of .... more or less by a depth of .... more or less

and legally described as ....

.... (the "property")
(Legal description of land including easements not described elsewhere)

PURCHASE PRICE: Dollars (CDN$) ....

.... Dollars

DEPOSIT: Buyer submits ....
(Herewith/Upon Acceptance/as otherwise described in this Agreement)

.... Dollars (CDN$) ....

by negotiable cheque payable to .... "Deposit Holder" to be held
in trust pending completion or other termination of this Agreement and to be credited toward the Purchase Price on completion. For the purposes of this
Agreement, "Upon Acceptance" shall mean that the Buyer is required to deliver the deposit to the Deposit Holder within 24 hours of the acceptance of
this Agreement. The parties to this Agreement hereby acknowledge that, unless otherwise provided for in this Agreement, the Deposit Holder shall place
the deposit in trust in the Deposit Holder's non-interest bearing Real Estate Trust Account and no interest shall be earned, received or paid on the deposit.

Buyer agrees to pay the balance as more particularly set out in Schedule A attached.

SCHEDULE(S) A..**attached hereto form(s) part of this Agreement.**

1.   **IRREVOCABILITY:** This offer shall be irrevocable by .... until .... a.m./p.m. on the ....
(Seller/Buyer)

    day of .... 20 ...., after which time, if not accepted, this offer shall be null and void and the deposit
    shall be returned to the Buyer in full without interest.

2.   **COMPLETION DATE:** This Agreement shall be completed by no later than 6:00 p.m. on the .... day of ....

    20 .... Upon completion, vacant possession of the property shall be given to the Buyer unless otherwise provided for in this Agreement.

INITIALS OF BUYER(S): ◯   **INITIALS OF SELLER(S):** ◯

Form 100   Revised 2015   **Page 1 of 6**

3. **NOTICES:** The Seller hereby appoints the Listing Brokerage as agent for the Seller for the purpose of giving and receiving notices pursuant to this Agreement. Where a Brokerage (Buyer's Brokerage) has entered into a representation agreement with the Buyer, the Buyer hereby appoints the Buyer's Brokerage as agent for the purpose of giving and receiving notices pursuant to this Agreement. **Where a Brokerage represents both the Seller and the Buyer (multiple representation), the Brokerage shall not be appointed or authorized to be agent for either the Buyer or the Seller for the purpose of giving and receiving notices.** Any notice relating hereto or provided for herein shall be in writing. In addition to any provision contained herein and in any Schedule hereto, this offer, any counter-offer, notice of acceptance thereof or any notice to be given or received pursuant to this Agreement or any Schedule hereto (any of them, "Document") shall be deemed given and received when delivered personally or hand delivered to the Address for Service provided in the Acknowledgement below, or where a facsimile number or email address is provided herein, when transmitted electronically to that facsimile number or email address, respectively, in which case, the signature(s) of the party (parties) shall be deemed to be original.

FAX No.: ....   FAX No.: ....
        (For delivery of Documents to Seller)   (For delivery of Documents to Buyer)

Email Address: ....   Email Address: ....
        (For delivery of Documents to Seller)   (For delivery of Documents to Buyer)

4. **CHATTELS INCLUDED:**...

....

....

....

Unless otherwise stated in this Agreement or any Schedule hereto, Seller agrees to convey all fixtures and chattels included in the Purchase Price free from all liens, encumbrances or claims affecting the said fixtures and chattels.

5. **FIXTURES EXCLUDED:**...

....

....

....

....

6. **RENTAL ITEMS (Including Lease, Lease to Own):** The following equipment is rented and **not** included in the Purchase Price. The Buyer agrees to assume the rental contract(s), if assumable:

....

....

....

The Buyer agrees to co-operate and execute such documentation as may be required to facilitate such assumption.

7. **HST:** If the sale of the Property (Real Property as described above) is subject to Harmonized Sales Tax (HST), then such tax shall be

.... the Purchase Price. If the sale of the Property is not subject to HST, Seller agrees to certify on or before
        (included in/in addition to)

closing, that the sale of the Property is not subject to HST. Any HST on chattels, if applicable, is not included in the Purchase Price.

INITIALS OF BUYER(S): ⬭   **INITIALS OF SELLER(S):** ⬭

Form 100   Revised 2015   **Page 2 of 6**

8. **TITLE SEARCH:** Buyer shall be allowed until 6:00 p.m. on the .... day of ...., 20..........., (Requisition Date) to examine the title to the Property at Buyer's own expense and until the earlier of: (i) thirty days from the later of the Requisition Date or the date on which the conditions in this Agreement are fulfilled or otherwise waived or; (ii) five days prior to completion, to satisfy Buyer that there are no outstanding

work orders or deficiency notices affecting the Property, and that its present use (...) may be lawfully continued and that the principal building may be insured against risk of fire. Seller hereby consents to the municipality or other governmental agencies releasing to Buyer details of all outstanding work orders and deficiency notices affecting the property, and Seller agrees to execute and deliver such further authorizations in this regard as Buyer may reasonably require.

9. **FUTURE USE:** Seller and Buyer agree that there is no representation or warranty of any kind that the future intended use of the property by Buyer is or will be lawful except as may be specifically provided for in this Agreement.

10. **TITLE:** Provided that the title to the property is good and free from all registered restrictions, charges, liens, and encumbrances except as otherwise specifically provided in this Agreement and save and except for (a) any registered restrictions or covenants that run with the land providing that such are complied with; (b) any registered municipal agreements and registered agreements with publicly regulated utilities providing such have been complied with, or security has been posted to ensure compliance and completion, as evidenced by a letter from the relevant municipality or regulated utility; (c) any minor easements for the supply of domestic utility or telephone services to the property or adjacent properties; and (d) any easements for drainage, storm or sanitary sewers, public utility lines, telephone lines, cable television lines or other services which do not materially affect the use of the property. If within the specified times referred to in paragraph 8 any valid objection to title or to any outstanding work order or deficiency notice, or to the fact the said present use may not lawfully be continued, or that the principal building may not be insured against risk of fire is made in writing to Seller and which Seller is unable or unwilling to remove, remedy or satisfy or obtain insurance save and except against risk of fire (Title Insurance) in favour of the Buyer and any mortgagee, (with all related costs at the expense of the Seller), and which Buyer will not waive, this Agreement notwithstanding any intermediate acts or negotiations in respect of such objections, shall be at an end and all monies paid shall be returned without interest or deduction and Seller, Listing Brokerage and Co-operating Brokerage shall not be liable for any costs or damages. Save as to any valid objection so made by such day and except for any objection going to the root of the title, Buyer shall be conclusively deemed to have accepted Seller's title to the property.

11. **CLOSING ARRANGEMENTS:** Where each of the Seller and Buyer retain a lawyer to complete the Agreement of Purchase and Sale of the property, and where the transaction will be completed by electronic registration pursuant to Part III of the Land Registration Reform Act, R.S.O. 1990, Chapter L4 and the Electronic Registration Act, S.O. 1991, Chapter 44, and any amendments thereto, the Seller and Buyer acknowledge and agree that the exchange of closing funds, non-registrable documents and other items (the "Requisite Deliveries") and the release thereof to the Seller and Buyer will (a) not occur at the same time as the registration of the transfer/deed (and any other documents intended to be registered in connection with the completion of this transaction) and (b) be subject to conditions whereby the lawyer(s) receiving any of the Requisite Deliveries will be required to hold same in trust and not release same except in accordance with the terms of a document registration agreement between the said lawyers. The Seller and Buyer irrevocably instruct the said lawyers to be bound by the document registration agreement which is recommended from time to time by the Law Society of Upper Canada. Unless otherwise agreed to by the lawyers, such exchange of the Requisite Deliveries will occur in the applicable Land Titles Office or such other location agreeable to both lawyers.

12. **DOCUMENTS AND DISCHARGE:** Buyer shall not call for the production of any title deed, abstract, survey or other evidence of title to the property except such as are in the possession or control of Seller. If requested by Buyer, Seller will deliver any sketch or survey of the property within Seller's control to Buyer as soon as possible and prior to the Requisition Date. If a discharge of any Charge/Mortgage held by a corporation incorporated pursuant to the Trust And Loan Companies Act (Canada), Chartered Bank, Trust Company, Credit Union, Caisse Populaire or Insurance Company and which is not to be assumed by Buyer on completion, is not available in registrable form on completion, Buyer agrees to accept Seller's lawyer's personal undertaking to obtain, out of the closing funds, a discharge in registrable form and to register same, or cause same to be registered, on title within a reasonable period of time after completion, provided that on or before completion Seller shall provide to Buyer a mortgage statement prepared by the mortgagee setting out the balance required to obtain the discharge, and, where a real-time electronic cleared funds transfer system is not being used, a direction executed by Seller directing payment to the mortgagee of the amount required to obtain the discharge out of the balance due on completion.

13. **INSPECTION:** Buyer acknowledges having had the opportunity to inspect the Property and understands that upon acceptance of this offer there shall be a binding agreement of purchase and sale between Buyer and Seller. **The Buyer acknowledges having the opportunity to include a requirement for a property inspection report in this Agreement and agrees that except as may be specifically provided for in this Agreement, the Buyer will not be obtaining a property inspection or property inspection report regarding the Property.**

14. **INSURANCE:** All buildings on the property and all other things being purchased shall be and remain until completion at the risk of Seller. Pending completion, Seller shall hold all insurance policies, if any, and the proceeds thereof in trust for the parties as their interests may appear and in the event of substantial damage, Buyer may either terminate this Agreement and have all monies paid returned without interest or deduction or else take the proceeds of any insurance and complete the purchase. No insurance shall be transferred on completion. If Seller is taking back a Charge/ Mortgage, or Buyer is assuming a Charge/Mortgage, Buyer shall supply Seller with reasonable evidence of adequate insurance to protect Seller's or other mortgagee's interest on completion.

INITIALS OF BUYER(S): ( )   INITIALS OF SELLER(S): ( )

Form 100   Revised 2015   **Page 3 of 6**

15. **PLANNING ACT:** This Agreement shall be effective to create an interest in the property only if Seller complies with the subdivision control provisions of the Planning Act by completion and Seller covenants to proceed diligently at Seller's expense to obtain any necessary consent by completion.

16. **DOCUMENT PREPARATION:** The Transfer/Deed shall, save for the Land Transfer Tax Affidavit, be prepared in registrable form at the expense of Seller, and any Charge/Mortgage to be given back by the Buyer to Seller at the expense of the Buyer. If requested by Buyer, Seller covenants that the Transfer/Deed to be delivered on completion shall contain the statements contemplated by Section 50(22) of the Planning Act, R.S.O.1990.

17. **RESIDENCY:** (a) Subject to (b) below, the Seller represents and warrants that the Seller is not and on completion will not be a non-resident under the non-residency provisions of the Income Tax Act which representation and warranty shall survive and not merge upon the completion of this transaction and the Seller shall deliver to the Buyer a statutory declaration that Seller is not then a non-resident of Canada; (b) provided that if the Seller is a non-resident under the non-residency provisions of the Income Tax Act, the Buyer shall be credited towards the Purchase Price with the amount, if any, necessary for Buyer to pay to the Minister of National Revenue to satisfy Buyer's liability in respect of tax payable by Seller under the non-residency provisions of the Income Tax Act by reason of this sale. Buyer shall not claim such credit if Seller delivers on completion the prescribed certificate.

18. **ADJUSTMENTS:** Any rents, mortgage interest, realty taxes including local improvement rates and unmetered public or private utility charges and unmetered cost of fuel, as applicable, shall be apportioned and allowed to the day of completion, the day of completion itself to be apportioned to Buyer.

19. **PROPERTY ASSESSMENT:** The Buyer and Seller hereby acknowledge that the Province of Ontario has implemented current value assessment and properties may be re-assessed on an annual basis. The Buyer and Seller agree that no claim will be made against the Buyer or Seller, or any Brokerage, Broker or Salesperson, for any changes in property tax as a result of a re-assessment of the property, save and except any property taxes that accrued prior to the completion of this transaction.

20. **TIME LIMITS:** Time shall in all respects be of the essence hereof provided that the time for doing or completing of any matter provided for herein may be extended or abridged by an agreement in writing signed by Seller and Buyer or by their respective lawyers who may be specifically authorized in that regard.

21. **TENDER:** Any tender of documents or money hereunder may be made upon Seller or Buyer or their respective lawyers on the day set for completion. Money shall be tendered with funds drawn on a lawyer's trust account in the form of a bank draft, certified cheque or wire transfer using the Large Value Transfer System.

22. **FAMILY LAW ACT:** Seller warrants that spousal consent is not necessary to this transaction under the provisions of the Family Law Act, R.S.O.1990 unless Seller's spouse has executed the consent hereinafter provided.

23. **UFFI:** Seller represents and warrants to Buyer that during the time Seller has owned the property, Seller has not caused any building on the property to be insulated with insulation containing ureaformaldehyde, and that to the best of Seller's knowledge no building on the property contains or has ever contained insulation that contains ureaformaldehyde. This warranty shall survive and not merge on the completion of this transaction, and if the building is part of a multiple unit building, this warranty shall only apply to that part of the building which is the subject of this transaction.

24. **LEGAL, ACCOUNTING AND ENVIRONMENTAL ADVICE:** The parties acknowledge that any information provided by the brokerage is not legal, tax or environmental advice.

25. **CONSUMER REPORTS: The Buyer is hereby notified that a consumer report containing credit and/or personal information may be referred to in connection with this transaction.**

26. **AGREEMENT IN WRITING:** If there is conflict or discrepancy between any provision added to this Agreement (including any Schedule attached hereto) and any provision in the standard pre-set portion hereof, the added provision shall supersede the standard pre-set provision to the extent of such conflict or discrepancy. This Agreement including any Schedule attached hereto, shall constitute the entire Agreement between Buyer and Seller. There is no representation, warranty, collateral agreement or condition, which affects this Agreement other than as expressed herein. For the purposes of this Agreement, Seller means vendor and Buyer means purchaser. This Agreement shall be read with all changes of gender or number required by the context.

27. **TIME AND DATE:** Any reference to a time and date in this Agreement shall mean the time and date where the property is located.

INITIALS OF BUYER(S): ⬭   **INITIALS OF SELLER(S):** ⬭

Form 100   Revised 2015   **Page 4 of 6**

28. SUCCESSORS AND ASSIGNS: The heirs, executors, administrators, successors and assigns of the undersigned are bound by the terms herein.

SIGNED, SEALED AND DELIVERED in the presence of: IN WITNESS whereof I have hereunto set my hand and seal:

.... ● DATE ....
(Witness)   (Buyer)   (Seal)

.... ● DATE ....
(Witness)   (Buyer)   (Seal)

I, the Undersigned Seller, agree to the above offer. I hereby irrevocably instruct my lawyer to pay directly to the brokerage(s) with whom I have agreed to pay commission, the unpaid balance of the commission together with applicable Harmonized Sales Tax (and any other taxes as may hereafter be applicable), from the proceeds of the sale prior to any payment to the undersigned on completion, as advised by the brokerage(s) to my lawyer.

SIGNED, SEALED AND DELIVERED in the presence of: IN WITNESS whereof I have hereunto set my hand and seal:

.... ● DATE ....
(Witness)   (Seller)   (Seal)

.... ● DATE ....
(Witness)   (Seller)   (Seal)

SPOUSAL CONSENT: The Undersigned Spouse of the Seller hereby consents to the disposition evidenced herein pursuant to the provisions of the Family Law Act, R.S.O.1990, and hereby agrees with the Buyer that he/she will execute all necessary or incidental documents to give full force and effect to the sale evidenced herein.

.... ● DATE ....
(Witness)   (Spouse)   (Seal)

CONFIRMATION OF ACCEPTANCE: Notwithstanding anything contained herein to the contrary, I confirm this Agreement with all changes both typed and written was finally accepted by all parties at .... a.m./p.m. this .... day of.., 20..........

....
(Signature of Seller or Buyer)

INFORMATION ON BROKERAGE(S)

Listing Brokerage .... Tel.No.(..............)..............................

....
(Salesperson / Broker Name)

Co-op/Buyer Brokerage .... Tel.No.(..............)..............................

....
(Salesperson / Broker Name)

ACKNOWLEDGEMENT

I acknowledge receipt of my signed copy of this accepted Agreement of Purchase and Sale and I authorize the Brokerage to forward a copy to my lawyer.   I acknowledge receipt of my signed copy of this accepted Agreement of Purchase and Sale and I authorize the Brokerage to forward a copy to my lawyer.

.... DATE .... DATE ....
(Seller)   (Buyer)

.... DATE .... DATE ....
(Seller)   (Buyer)
Address for Service ....   Address for Service ....

.... Tel.No.(..........)..............   .... Tel.No.(..........)..............

Seller's Lawyer ....   Buyer's Lawyer ....

Address ....   Address ....

Email ....   Email ....

(..........)..............   (..........)..............   (..........)..............   (..........)..............
       Tel.No.   FAX No.   Tel.No.   FAX No.

FOR OFFICE USE ONLY   **COMMISSION TRUST AGREEMENT**

To: Co-operating Brokerage shown on the foregoing Agreement of Purchase and Sale:
In consideration for the Co-operating Brokerage procuring the foregoing Agreement of Purchase and Sale, I hereby declare that all moneys received or receivable by me in connection with the Transaction as contemplated in the MLS® Rules and Regulations of my Real Estate Board shall be receivable and held in trust. This agreement shall constitute a Commission Trust Agreement as defined in the MLS® Rules and shall be subject to and governed by the MLS® Rules pertaining to Commission Trust.

DATED as of the date and time of the acceptance of the foregoing Agreement of Purchase and Sale.   Acknowledged by:

....
(Authorized to bind the Listing Brokerage)   (Authorized to bind the Co-operating Brokerage)

Form 100   Revised 2015   **Page 5 of 6**

Schedule A
Agreement of Purchase and Sale

Form 100
for use in the Province of Ontario

This Schedule is attached to and forms part of the Agreement of Purchase and Sale between:

BUYER, ..., and

SELLER, ...

for the purchase and sale of ....

.... dated the .... day of ...., 20...............

Buyer agrees to pay the balance as follows:

This form must be initialed by all parties to the Agreement of Purchase and Sale.

INITIALS OF BUYER(S): ⬭   INITIALS OF SELLER(S): ⬭

Form 100   Revised 2015   **Page 6 of 6**

OREA Ontario Real Estate Association

Individual Identification Information Record

Form 630
for use in the Province of Ontario

NOTE: An Individual Identification Information Record is required by the *Proceeds of Crime (Money Laundering) and Terrorist Financing Act*. This Record must be completed by the REALTOR® member whenever they act in respect to the purchase or sale of real estate.

It is recommended that the Individual Identification Information Record be completed:

(i)   for a buyer when the offer is submitted and/or a deposit made, and

(ii) for a seller when the seller accepts the offer.

Transaction Property Address: ....

....

....

Sales Representative/Broker Name: ....

Date: ....

A. Verification of Individual

NOTE: This section must be completed for clients that are individuals or unrepresented individuals who are not clients, but are parties to the transaction (e.g. unrepresented buyer or seller). Where an unrepresented individual refuses to provide identification after reasonable efforts are made to verify that identification, a REALTOR® member must keep a record of that refusal and consider sending a Suspicious Transaction Report to FINTRAC if there are reasonable grounds to suspect that the transaction involves property from the proceeds of crime, or terrorist activity. Where you are using an agent or mandatary to verify an individual, see procedure described in CREA's FINTRAC Compliance manual.

1. **Full legal name of individual:** ....

2. **Address:** ....

....

....

....

3. **Date of Birth:** ....

4. **Nature of Principal Business or Occupation:** ....

5. **Type of Identification Document*:** ....
    (must view the original, see below for list of acceptable documents)

6. **Document Identifier Number:** ....

7. **Issuing Jurisdiction:** ....
    (insert name of the applicable Province, Territory, Foreign Jurisdiction or "Federal Government of Canada")

8. **Document Expiry Date:** ....
    (must be valid and not expired)

*Acceptable identification documents: birth certificate, driver's licence, provincial health insurance card (not acceptable if from Ontario, Nova Scotia, Manitoba or Prince Edward Island), passport, record of landing, permanent resident card, old age security card, a certificate of Indian status, or SIN card (although SIN numbers are not to be included on any report sent to FINTRAC). Other acceptable identification documents: provincial or territorial identification card issued by the Insurance Corporation of British Columbia, Alberta Registries, Saskatchewan Government Insurance, the Department of Service Nova Scotia and Municipal Relations, the Department of Transportation and Infrastructure Renewal of the Province of Prince Edward Island, Service New Brunswick, the Department of Government Services and Lands of the Province of Newfoundland and Labrador, the Department of Transportation of the Northwest Territories or the Department of Community Government and Transportation of the Territory of Nunavut. If identification document is from a foreign jurisdiction, it must be equivalent to one of the above identification documents.

REALTOR®

This document has been prepared by The Canadian Real Estate Association to assist members in complying with requirements of Canada's *Proceeds of Crime (Money Laundering) and Terrorist Financing Regulations*. © 2014-2015.

1 of 4

Individual Identification Information Record

OREA Ontario Real Estate Association

Form 630
for use in the Province of Ontario

B. Verification of Third Parties *(if applicable)*

NOTE: Complete this section of the form when a client or unrepresented individual is acting on behalf of a third party. Where you cannot determine if there is a third party, but there are reasonable grounds to suspect the individual is acting on behalf of a third party, you must keep a record of that fact.

1. **Name of third party:** ....

2. **Address:** ....

   ....

   ....

   ....

3. **Date of Birth:** ....

4. **Nature of Principal Business or Occupation:** ....

5. **Incorporation number and place of issue** *(if applicable)*: ....

6. **Relationship between third party and client:** ....

   ....

   ....

   ....

2
of 4

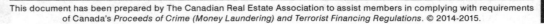

 **Ontario Real Estate Association**

Individual Identification Information Record

Form 630
for use in the Province of Ontario

Only complete Sections C and D for your clients.

C. Client Risk *(ask your Compliance Officer if this section is applicable)*

Determine the level of risk of a money laundering or terrorist financing offence for this client by determining the appropriate cluster of client in your policies and procedures manual this client falls into and checking one of the checkboxes below:

Low Risk

☐ Canadian Citizen or Resident Physically Present

☐ Canadian Citizen or Resident Not Physically Present

☐ Canadian Citizen or Resident – High Crime Area – No Other Higher Risk Factors Evident

☐ Foreign Citizen or Resident that does not Operate in a High Risk Country (physically present or not)

☐ Other, explain:

Medium Risk

☐ Explain:

High Risk

☐ Foreign Citizen or Resident that operates in a High Risk Country (physically present or not)

☐ Other, explain:

If you determined that the client's risk was high, tell your brokerage's Compliance Officer. They will want to consider this when conducting the overall brokerage risk assessment, which occurs every two years. It will also be relevant in completing Section D below. Note that your brokerage may have developed other clusters not listed above. If no cluster is appropriate, the agent will need to provide a risk assessment of the client, and explain their assessment, in the relevant space above.

REALTOR®   This document has been prepared by The Canadian Real Estate Association to assist members in complying with requirements of Canada's *Proceeds of Crime (Money Laundering) and Terrorist Financing Regulations.* © 2014-2015.   **3** of 4

 **Ontario Real Estate Association**

Individual Identification Information Record

Form 630
for use in the Province of Ontario

D. Business Relationship
(ask your Compliance Officer when this section is applicable if you don't know)

D.1. Purpose and Intended Nature of the Business Relationship

Check the appropriate boxes.

Acting as an agent for the purchase or sale of:

☐ Residential property   ☐ Residential property for income purposes

☐ Commercial property   ☐ Land for Commercial Use

☐ Other, please specify:...

D.2. Measures Taken to Monitor Business Relationship and Keep Client Information Up-To-Date

D.2.1. Ask the Client if their name, address or principal business or occupation has changed and if it has include the updated information on page one.

D.2.2 Keep all relevant correspondence with the client on file in order to maintain a record of the information you have used to monitor the business relationship with the client. Optional - if you have taken measures beyond simply keeping correspondence on file, specify them here:

```



```

D.2.3. If the client is high risk you must conduct enhanced measures to monitor the brokerage's business relationship and keep their client information up to date. Optional - consult your Compliance Officer and document what enhanced measures you have applied:

```



```

D.3 Suspicious Transactions

Don't forget, if you see something suspicious during the transaction report it to your Compliance Officer. Consult your policies and procedures manual for more information.

   This document has been prepared by The Canadian Real Estate Association to assist members in complying with requirements of Canada's *Proceeds of Crime (Money Laundering) and Terrorist Financing Regulations*. © 2014-2015.   **4** of 4

Exercise 4   Receipt of Funds Record, Page 1 of 1

 **OREA** Ontario Real Estate Association   # Receipt of Funds Record

Form 635
for use in the Province of Ontario

NOTE: A Receipt of Funds record is required by the *Proceeds of Crime (Money Laundering) and Terrorist Financing Act* for every amount of funds that a REALTOR® member receives in the course of a single purchase or sale real estate transaction.
A REALTOR® does NOT have to complete a Receipt of Funds Record if:

    (i)   the funds are received from a financial entity or a public body that is buying or selling; or,

    (ii) a Large Cash Transaction Record must be completed; or,

    (iii) the deposit does not go into the trust account of a licensed practitioner. In other words, if the deposit goes directly into the account of a builder, lawyer or notary, or developer, a Receipt of Funds Record does not have to be completed by a member acting as the buyers' agent.

When this Record is completed, it is the responsibility of the broker to ensure that a record is kept for five years from the date it was created.

    (i)   When a REALTOR® member completes a Receipt of Funds Record, they must also complete an Identification Information Record at the same time, unless the Identification Information Record was completed prior to the receipt of funds.

    (ii) When both the buyer and seller are represented, it is the agent of the buyer who is required to complete and retain a Receipt of Funds Record in respect of the deposit made, regardless of who retains the deposit.

Transaction Property Address: ....

....

....

Sales Representative/Broker Name:...

Date: ....

1. Amount of Funds Received: .... **Currency:**........................

    ☐ **Cheque** ☐ **Certified Cheque** ☐ **Cash** ☐ **Bank Draft**

    ☐ **Other, explain:** ....

(a) If cash, indicate method of receipt *(in person, mail, courier, other (explain))* ....

(b) If cheque, indicate: Number of account: ....

    Financial Institution:....................... **Name of account holder:**...............................

2. Date of receipt of funds:..

3. Account where funds were deposited *(eg. Broker's trust account)*: ....

Where there are two agents involved in a transaction and the funds are deposited in the listing agent's account the buyer's agent is responsible for completing the receipt of funds record. However, the buyer's agent is not required to include the number and type of the listing agent's account or the name of the person or entity that is the holder of that account if, after taking reasonable measures, they are unable to do so. Further, if dealing with trust accounts, although the buyer's agent must indicate that the funds were deposited into the listing agent's trust account, the buyer's agent would not be required to include the number of the trust account or the name or entity that holds the trust account.

Note that if multiple accounts are affected, information on all accounts affected needs to be recorded. For example, assuming the buyer's agent transfers funds from their account into the listing agent's account, both accounts are affected by the transaction and therefore both numbers are to be recorded on the Receipt of Funds Record. However, the features noted in the previous paragraph with respect to the listing agent's accounts still apply.

    Indicate type of account where deposit has been made: ☐ **Trust** ☐ **Other**

    Number of account:..................... **Name of account holder:** ....

4. Purpose of funds (e.g., deposit for purchase):..

5. Other details concerning receipt of funds: ....

....

 This document has been prepared by The Canadian Real Estate Association to assist members in complying with requirements of Canada's *Proceeds of Crime (Money Laundering) and Terrorist Financing Regulations.* © 2014-2015.   **1** of 1

CHAPTER 9

Drafting Offers: Part 2

Introduction

A conditional offer sets out stipulations that can result in a binding contract upon either the occurrence or non-occurrence of a specific event. Conditions are either *condition precedent* or *condition subsequent*. The vast majority of conditions found in agreements of purchase and sale are condition precedent.

Most conditions involve buyers activities; e.g., conditional on the sale of buyer's existing home. This does not preclude seller conditions, but their use is more limited in scope. An example might involve an offer conditional on the seller's release from a previous agreement. Escape clauses are also discussed. Escape clauses are typically used when the seller wants to continue to offer a property for sale given a lengthy condition relating to the sale of the buyer's property.

Conditions in this chapter focus on common circumstances encountered by residential registrants; e.g., home inspection, sale of buyer's property and mortgage financing. For mortgage financing purposes, real estate transactions typically involve one or more mortgages with most agreements of purchase and sale requiring new financing conditions, but assumptions of existing mortgages are also possible.

Learning Outcomes

At the conclusion of this chapter, students will be able to:

- Describe and differentiate between condition precedent and condition subsequent clauses.
- Draft both condition precedent and condition subsequent clauses involving various situations typically encountered in residential real estate.
- Describe the use of escape clauses and draft appropriate wordings for use with condition precedent clauses.
- Organize multiple conditions and review miscellaneous clauses encountered in residential negotiations.
- Draft conditional clauses when arranging a new mortgage, assuming an existing mortgage or structuring a seller take back arrangement.
- Describe clauses involving typical mortgage privileges including prepayment, renewal and postponement.

CONDITIONAL CLAUSES

Many circumstances necessitate conditions; e.g., arranging a mortgage, sale of existing property and home inspection. Two drafting methods have evolved: **condition precedent** and **condition subsequent.** The vast majority of residential conditions are condition precedent, but registrants may encounter condition subsequent in local marketplaces. Conditions typically contain more complex wordings than those concerning facts and assurances.

Condition Precedent vs. Subsequent

A condition precedent provides that if the condition is not fulfilled or waived no binding contract has been formed. In other words, whether or not the agreement is binding is subject to a future event.

Condition subsequent assumes a binding contract unless a described event occurs. In effect, an option is allowed providing for termination of the agreement under specific circumstances. Clause wordings for both condition precedent and condition subsequent are illustrated on a subsequent page.

CONDITION PRECEDENT

- No fully binding agreement exists at point of offer acceptance.
- Upon acceptance, the parties are placed under some degree of obligation. For example, a buyer is undertaking to arrange a mortgage and the seller is under an obligation to keep the property available to that buyer pending a future outcome.
- A binding contract is formed if the condition is fulfilled or waived.
- No contract has been formed if the condition is not fulfilled or waived.
- Most conditions precedent follow the same pattern:

Steps in Condition Precedent

1. Who Is To Do It?
2. Who Is To Pay For It?
3. What Is To Be Done?
4. Within What Time Limit?
5. What Is To Happen In The Event That It Is Not Done?
6. That It May Be Waived.

Condition Precedent

A condition in an agreement calling for the happening of some event, or performance of some act, before the agreement becomes binding on the parties.

Condition Subsequent

A condition referring to a future event upon the happening of which the contract becomes no longer binding on the parties.

Waiver Provision

Over the years, the courts have firmly established that, unless specified otherwise in the agreement, a condition precedent can be used by either party to the transaction and no one has the automatic and unilateral right to waive the condition.

The inclusion of a **waiver** provision allows the party for whose protection the condition was included to remove that condition entirely, rendering the agreement firm and binding regardless of whether the specific terms of the condition have been fulfilled.

The waiver provides the party with the condition to give up their conditional protection and proceed with the agreement.

A major consideration in using waivers is the fact that circumstances can arise which are different from those contemplated by the condition. In these instances, the protection and/or benefit envisaged by the inclusion of the condition is achieved but not in accordance with the exact terms as expressed in the agreement. The result is the same but the circumstances or terms giving rise to that result are different from those originally contemplated. For example, a buyer makes an agreement conditional on arranging a new mortgage but before arranging that mortgage, receives a windfall and no longer requires the benefit and/or protection of this condition.

The waiver form allows the buyer to waive the condition (again emphasizing that the right of waiver must be part of the original condition) and complete the contract without reference to the fulfillment of the condition. As a consequence, rarely are condition precedents seen in the marketplace without corresponding waiver provisions.

> **Waiver**
>
> The relinquishment of some right. More specifically, a wording within an agreement providing that the party may waive a condition at his/her sole option.

True Condition Precedent

Certain conditions are true condition precedent and must be fulfilled as written. No waiver provision is possible, because the condition must be fulfilled for the contract to be created.

EXAMPLE   *Severance*

Buyer Smith makes an offer to Seller Jones conditional on severing the described lot. Neither party can waive the condition, as only fulfillment (i.e., a successful severance) will produce an interest in land pursuant to the *Planning Act*.

EXAMPLE   *Clause: Seller Release from Previous Agreement*

Seller Smith wants to accept an offer, but must be released from a previous offer. A condition precedent is drafted regarding the release with no waiver provision, as neither party can waive the provision because obtaining the release is essential.

> *This Offer is conditional upon the Seller obtaining a release from a prior Agreement of Purchase and Sale. Unless the Seller gives notice in writing delivered to the Buyer personally or in accordance with any other provisions for the delivery of notice in this Agreement of Purchase and Sale or any Schedule thereto not later than 11:59 p.m. on the 12th day of January, 20xx, that this condition is fulfilled, this Offer shall be null and void and the deposit shall be returned to the Buyer in full without deduction.*

This clause is a true condition precedent and neither the seller nor a buyer is entitled to waive this condition.

CONDITION SUBSEQUENT

- Allows for contract termination under defined circumstances.
- No waiver necessary as a binding contract is in place subject to termination provision(s).
- The party protected by the condition can demand sale completion by not exercising the option to terminate.
- The key issue centres on whether or not notice of termination is sent within the specified time limit.

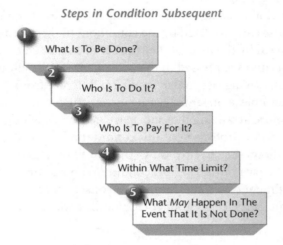

Steps in Condition Subsequent

1. What Is To Be Done?
2. Who Is To Do It?
3. Who Is To Pay For It?
4. Within What Time Limit?
5. What *May* Happen In The Event That It Is Not Done?

Regardless of the condition format used, real estate registrants must ensure proper follow up. Keep involved regarding the timely satisfaction or failure of a condition precedent. Make certain the client is aware that termination notice is only possible within a specified time period when a condition subsequent is involved. At all times, ensure that clients remain fully informed as to their rights and obligations. The diagram on the following page illustrates the key differences between condition subsequent and condition precedent.

 # FREQUENTLY DRAFTED CONDITIONS

Conditions can be drafted to cover virtually unlimited marketplace circumstances. In reality, residential registrants are most frequently involved with five topics:

- Sale of Buyer's Property
- Inspections
- Approvals
- Multiple Conditions
- Mortgages

Within each topic, important wording variations have evolved to suit particular buyer and seller needs. As with other chapters, examples highlight OREA clause wordings (see *Appendix*) but many variations are found in the marketplace.

CONDITION ANATOMY: PRECEDENT VS. SUBSEQUENT

Condition Precedent (Including Waiver Provision):

This offer is conditional upon the inspection of the subject property by a home inspector at the buyer's own expense, and the obtaining of a report satisfactory to the buyer in the buyer's sole and absolute discretion. Unless the buyer gives notice in writing, delivered to the seller personally or in accordance with any other provisions for the delivery of notice in this Agreement of Purchase and Sale or any Schedule thereto not later than 11:59 p.m. on the 1st day of May, 20xx, that this condition is fulfilled, this offer shall be null and void and the deposit shall be returned to the buyer in full without deduction. The seller agrees to co-operate in providing access to the property for the purposes of this inspection. This condition is included for the benefit of the buyer and may be waived at the buyer's sole option by notice in writing to the seller as aforesaid within the time period stated herein.

Condition Subsequent:

The buyer may terminate this agreement in the event that a home inspection report satisfactory to the buyer in the sole and absolute discretion of the buyer is not obtained from a home inspector who inspects the subject property at the buyer's expense. The buyer may notify the seller in writing personally or in accordance with any other provisions for the delivery of notice in this Agreement of Purchase and Sale or any Schedule thereto by 11:59 p.m. on the 1st day of May, 20xx of the inability to obtain a satisfactory home inspection report thus rendering this agreement null and void and the deposit shall be returned to the buyer in full without interest. If no such notification is received, this term of contract shall be deemed to be waived by the buyer and the agreement shall remain valid and binding whether or not such satisfactory home inspection report has been obtained.

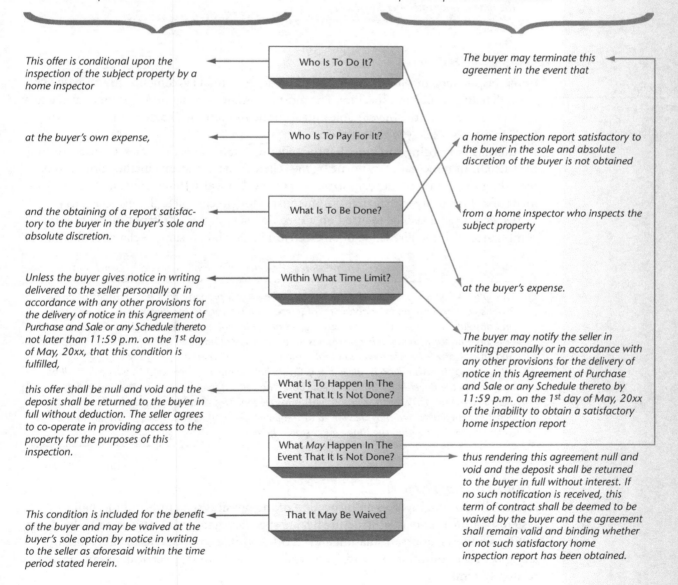

This offer is conditional upon the inspection of the subject property by a home inspector

Who Is To Do It?

The buyer may terminate this agreement in the event that

at the buyer's own expense,

Who Is To Pay For It?

a home inspection report satisfactory to the buyer in the sole and absolute discretion of the buyer is not obtained

and the obtaining of a report satisfactory to the buyer in the buyer's sole and absolute discretion.

What Is To Be Done?

from a home inspector who inspects the subject property

Unless the buyer gives notice in writing delivered to the seller personally or in accordance with any other provisions for the delivery of notice in this Agreement of Purchase and Sale or any Schedule thereto not later than 11:59 p.m. on the 1st day of May, 20xx, that this condition is fulfilled,

Within What Time Limit?

at the buyer's expense.

this offer shall be null and void and the deposit shall be returned to the buyer in full without deduction. The seller agrees to co-operate in providing access to the property for the purposes of this inspection.

What Is To Happen In The Event That It Is Not Done?

The buyer may notify the seller in writing personally or in accordance with any other provisions for the delivery of notice in this Agreement of Purchase and Sale or any Schedule thereto by 11:59 p.m. on the 1st day of May, 20xx of the inability to obtain a satisfactory home inspection report

What *May* Happen In The Event That It Is Not Done?

thus rendering this agreement null and void and the deposit shall be returned to the buyer in full without interest. If no such notification is received, this term of contract shall be deemed to be waived by the buyer and the agreement shall remain valid and binding whether or not such satisfactory home inspection report has been obtained.

This condition is included for the benefit of the buyer and may be waived at the buyer's sole option by notice in writing to the seller as aforesaid within the time period stated herein.

That It May Be Waived

Sale of Buyer's Property

One use of a condition precedent clause involves the offer being conditional on the sale of the buyer's property for a specified period of time, failing which the offer is null and void and the deposit returned. A common variation involves the ultimate removal of conditions relating to the buyer's property (which has already been sold subject to conditions).

SAMPLE CLAUSE *Condition—Buyer's Property*

---

*This Offer is conditional upon the sale of the Buyer's property known as _____.
Unless the Buyer gives notice in writing delivered to the Seller personally or in accordance with any other provisions for the delivery of notice in this Agreement of Purchase and Sale or any Schedule thereto not later than ____p.m. on the _____day of _____, 20____, that this condition is fulfilled, this Offer shall be null and void and the deposit shall be returned to the Buyer in full without deduction. This condition is included for the benefit of the Buyer and may be waived at the Buyer's sole option by notice in writing to the Seller as aforesaid within the time period stated herein.*

Inspections

Home inspection conditions are found in most residential agreements. Exercise due care when detailing inspection specifics. The most common wording provides for a satisfactory inspection report at the buyer's sole and absolute discretion. The decision as to what is satisfactory rests solely with the buyer.

Alternative wordings provide that the seller may remedy deficiencies. Clause wordings may also limit remedial costs borne by the seller. Other variations include limitations regarding inspection scope; e.g., structural or mechanical systems only and the involvement of a third party (other than a home inspector) to complete the inspection.

Inspections can also be focused on a specific issue, such as a retrofit inspection for compliance with the Fire Code or an electrical inspection. A sample clause is illustrated.

SAMPLE CLAUSE *Condition—Inspection of Property by a Home Inspector—General Inspection*

This Offer is conditional upon the inspection of the subject property by a home inspector at the Buyer's own expense and the obtaining of a report satisfactory to the Buyer in the Buyer's sole and absolute discretion. Unless the Buyer gives notice in writing delivered to the Seller personally or in accordance with any other provisions for the delivery of notice in this Agreement of Purchase and Sale or any Schedule thereto not later than _____ p.m. on the _____day of _____, 20____, that this condition is fulfilled, this Offer shall be null and void and the deposit shall be returned to the Buyer in full without deduction. The Seller agrees to co-operate in providing access to the property for the purpose of this inspection. This condition is included for the benefit of the Buyer and may be waived at the Buyer's sole option by notice in writing to the Seller as aforesaid within the time period stated herein.

SCOPE OF INSPECTION

A home inspection involves an inspection of the physical structure and mechanical systems within a residential structure having specific regard to the roof, attic, walls, floors, ceiling, windows, doors, insulation and all other visible components of the structure, along with the condition of heating, central air conditioning, electrical, plumbing and related systems.

Home inspections are typically requested by buyers seeking to assess the condition of property prior to a planned purchase. A written report is provided by the home inspector who identifies both positive and negative aspects of the home under consideration. Home inspections are also sometimes requested by owners in contemplation of offering property for sale. The report can assist in effecting repairs and generally placing the house in a better condition for marketing purposes.

A home inspection should not be confused with a municipal inspection involving compliance with local codes. In the latter, a municipal inspector is concerned solely with whether or not structural and mechanical components meet minimum specifications as set out in the Ontario Building Code (OBC). Lack of compliance can result in sanctions pursuant to the OBC. The home inspector is concerned with overall condition and the identification of items that may need repair or replacement.

Typical Home Inspection Report

THE HOME INSPECTION REPORT

- Physical structure and mechanical systems
- Written report—both positive and negative features

SCOPE OF INSPECTION

- Components
- Exterior
- Interior
- Electrical
- Air Conditioning
- General Comments
- Structural
- Roofing
- Plumbing
- Heating
- Insulation/Ventilation

- Observe condition.
- Describe selected components.
- Detail damage (if applicable).
- Discuss operability (if applicable).
- Comment as required (both positive and negative).
- May provide estimate for suggested repairs.

GENERAL LIMITING CONDITIONS

- Visual inspection of accessible features, not a technical report.
- Declaration of adherence to specific inspection standards.
- Not a warranty or guarantee.

- No representations concerning extent of any identified problems.
- Not an Ontario Building Code Inspection.
- Specific exclusions; e.g., latent defects and environmental concerns.

HOUSE-SPECIFIC LIMITING CONDITIONS (Examples)

- Inability to inspect basement walls due to finishing.
- Well and septic beyond scope of report.

- Older home with inherent deficiencies given lack of standardized construction methods and limited building codes.

THE REAL ESTATE TRANSACTION—GENERAL

Home Inspection: Q & A   PERSPECTIVE

Home inspections have become an indispensable tool these days. While older properties have been primary targets, today's inspections include most residential properties regardless of age. Currently, research suggests that upwards of 60–70% of all residential resale homes undergo an inspection. Broker of record Jones is conducting an orientation meeting for new salespersons. This fictitious Q & A at that meeting may give you more insight into home inspections.

Q   Should we encourage sellers to have a pre-listing home inspection?

A   Some sellers think the pre-inspection makes the home more marketable. Buyers are naturally suspicious and want to do their own thing. Besides, if they pay for the report, they own it. Don't get me wrong—the idea is sound. We just don't see it happening often. That said, other brokerages have had success with this approach, as problems can be corrected by the seller.

Q   How many home inspectors should I recommend to a buyer?

A   At least three or four. Beyond that, don't get involved in the selection process. Let the buyer make contact and satisfy themselves. I also remind all of you that you must comply with the Code of Ethics and not steer any client or customer to a particular home inspector.

Q   How do I select home inspectors for my list?

A   Check them out. Get background information, talk with other salespersons and ask about memberships in professional associations, errors and omissions insurance and specific services. Find out what an average residential home inspection entails (2–3 hours is typical) and get an estimate of typical costs.

Q   Should I be present for the home inspection?

A   I recommend that you be present. How else can you see problems first hand and learn more about construction? Besides, it's a great way to better understand the process, while demonstrating your commitment to the client.

Q   What happens if I see something that the home inspector missed? What should I do?

A   We represent the client and must protect and promote his or her interests at all times. If there's a problem, discuss it with the client. Remember, a poor inspection report can come back to haunt you and me. What happens if a serious problem goes unnoticed, only to appear two years later? Both you and the brokerage could face litigation.

Q   What happens if the market is active, several buyers are interested and my client doesn't want to include a home inspection condition?

A   Ultimately, that decision rests with the client. We must encourage buyers to obtain home inspections and if they elect against that, then we should also explain the possible ramifications of that decision. Have the client carefully read Clause 13 in the *Agreement of Purchase and Sale* (OREA Form 100).

Q   A buyer just received a favourable home inspection and was elated. He made a point of calling and thanking me this morning for finding a home with no problems. We're waiving the home inspection condition later today.

A   His comment concerns me. A home inspection is not a warranty nor does it assess all property components. He needs to carefully read the full report, duly noting disclaimers and limitations. Some people have the faulty impression that a home inspection is some sort of guarantee. It is not! When you take the waiver provision to the buyer, review the report before anything gets signed. Keep me posted.

Approvals

OREA recommended clauses also provide for conditions subject to the approval of either the buyer's or seller's solicitor. For example, the offer may be subject to the buyer's solicitor reviewing and approving of condominium documents or that a property meets required environmental standards. Alternatively, a third party may be involved such as an accountant, who must approve of financial statements provided by the seller.

SAMPLE CLAUSE   *Condition—Lawyer's Approval —Buyer*

This Offer is conditional upon the approval of the terms hereof by the Buyer's Solicitor. Unless the Buyer gives notice in writing delivered to the Seller personally or in accordance with any other provisions for the delivery of notice in this Agreement of Purchase and Sale or any Schedule thereto not later than __ p.m. on the _____ day of _____, 20___, that this condition is fulfilled, this Offer shall be null and void and the deposit shall be returned to the Buyer in full without deduction. This condition is included for the benefit of Buyer and may be waived at the Buyer's sole option by notice in writing to the Seller as aforesaid within the time period stated herein.

Escape Clause

> **Escape Clause**
>
> A clause in an agreement permitting the seller to continue to offer the property for sale during conditional period; e.g., an existing offer conditional on the sale of the buyer's home.

An **escape clause** allows the seller to continue to offer the property for sale when accepting an offer containing a condition, typically the sale of the buyer's property. Otherwise, the length of time normally required for condition fulfillment effectively removes the seller's property from the market.

The escape clause provides that the seller may continue to offer the property for sale. If another acceptable offer is received, the original buyer has a specified time (typically 48 hours, but varies based on circumstances) to remove his/her condition. An alternative wording involves waiving all conditions; e.g., the original offer may be conditional on financing as well as sale of the buyer's property.

WHEN TO USE

Obviously, an escape clause should be considered for any lengthy condition. But many factors impact its use, for example:

- If the buyer wants 60 days to sell his/her property, the seller must carefully weigh the impact on saleability. Is it better to reject the offer, hoping for a shorter condition (e.g., conditional on financing in 10 days or an all cash offer from someone else)?
- Will qualified prospects eliminate the property knowing that an accepted offer could be negotiated, only to have their hopes dashed when the original buyer removes the condition?

No easy rules exist. As a general guideline, escape clauses are more frequently used in buyer's markets where abundant housing choices exist and sellers must seriously consider all offers.

Certain obstacles can emerge with conditional offers, particularly for the seller. For example, in the sale of property, the seller, when agreeing to a condition may have to place the property back on the market if the condition is not fulfilled or waived by the buyer. For some conditions, this problem is not a major factor. It is unlikely that a competent sales-person would negotiate an offer conditional upon arranging a first mortgage unless:

- There was reasonable assurance that a lender would consider the buyer's mortgage application; and
- The time limit involved to secure the approval did not involve a lengthy period.

With respect to the sale of the buyer's property, the condition is usually for a longer period. Further, the decision to sell the property rests with that buyer during the conditional period. In most instances, an escape clause (also referred to as a time clause) usually improves the acceptability of such conditions by the seller.

DRAFTING GUIDELINES—CONDITIONS

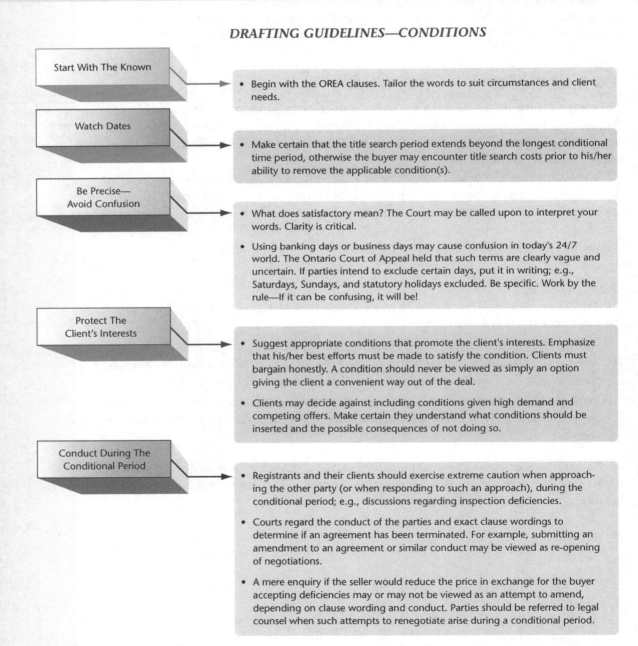

Start With The Known

- Begin with the OREA clauses. Tailor the words to suit circumstances and client needs.

Watch Dates

- Make certain that the title search period extends beyond the longest conditional time period, otherwise the buyer may encounter title search costs prior to his/her ability to remove the applicable condition(s).

Be Precise— Avoid Confusion

- What does satisfactory mean? The Court may be called upon to interpret your words. Clarity is critical.
- Using banking days or business days may cause confusion in today's 24/7 world. The Ontario Court of Appeal held that such terms are clearly vague and uncertain. If parties intend to exclude certain days, put it in writing; e.g., Saturdays, Sundays, and statutory holidays excluded. Be specific. Work by the rule—If it can be confusing, it will be!

Protect The Client's Interests

- Suggest appropriate conditions that promote the client's interests. Emphasize that his/her best efforts must be made to satisfy the condition. Clients must bargain honestly. A condition should never be viewed as simply an option giving the client a convenient way out of the deal.
- Clients may decide against including conditions given high demand and competing offers. Make certain they understand what conditions should be inserted and the possible consequences of not doing so.

Conduct During The Conditional Period

- Registrants and their clients should exercise extreme caution when approaching the other party (or when responding to such an approach), during the conditional period; e.g., discussions regarding inspection deficiencies.
- Courts regard the conduct of the parties and exact clause wordings to determine if an agreement has been terminated. For example, submitting an amendment to an agreement or similar conduct may be viewed as re-opening of negotiations.
- A mere enquiry if the seller would reduce the price in exchange for the buyer accepting deficiencies may or may not be viewed as an attempt to amend, depending on clause wording and conduct. Parties should be referred to legal counsel when such attempts to renegotiate arise during a conditional period.

Source: Modified from original text, OREA Legal Pamphlets, www.orea.com

DRAFTING MULTIPLE CONDITIONS

Registrants encounter circumstances requiring multiple conditions. Individual conditional clauses with differing dates are legally correct, but can be lengthy and cumbersome.

- Wherever possible, stack multiple conditions under one mega-condition setting out a single fulfillment date and a waiver provision.
- Construct the stack based on the typical sequence for activities included within the condition.
- Use schedule(s) for additional space and have all parties initial those schedules.

EXAMPLE   *Multiple Conditions*

This offer is conditional upon:

- *the inspection of the subject property by a home inspector at the buyer's own expense and the obtaining of a report satisfactory to the buyer in the buyer's sole and absolute discretion.*

- *the buyer receiving notification of the removal of all conditions in an existing agreement of purchase and sale for the property known as 123 Main Street, Anycity, Ontario.*

Unless the buyer gives notice in writing delivered to the seller personally or in accordance with any other provisions for the delivery of notice in this Agreement of Purchase and Sale or any Schedule thereto not later than 11:59 p.m. on the 11th day of March, 20xx, that these conditions are fulfilled, this offer shall be null and void and the deposit shall be returned to the buyer in full without deduction. These conditions are included for the benefit of the buyer and may be waived at the buyer's sole option by notice in writing to the seller as aforesaid within the time period stated herein.

Complex Offers: Avoiding Problems

Situations can arise where a large variety of clauses are required involving several attached schedules.

Review Clauses	Carefully review clauses to assess impact on pre-printed wordings. Buyers and sellers may want to include provisions not fully understanding preprinted clauses and the impact of such wordings on those clauses.
Avoid Vague Wordings	If either or both parties want various unacceptable (i.e., vague) clause wordings—be diplomatic but insist on precision.
Group Where Possible	Simplify where possible. Several provisions or requirements can be grouped under one condition. For example, a buyer may wish to review tenant records, confirm rental amounts, check with the fire department regarding safety issues, confirm building code compliance and seek selected documents from the seller. The condition may simply provide that the property meets all regulatory requirements and tenant records are accurate, complete and meet the buyer's requirements. Exact wordings will vary.
Insist on the Right Order	Make certain that multiple schedules are correctly sequenced, cross-referenced and initialled by all parties.

Follow-up When Appropriate	If the negotiation includes detailed listings of chattels included and fixtures excluded, consider inserting a condition to have a fully detailed list approved by the parties within an acceptable time frame, rather than attempting to quantify these items in the midst of negotiations.
Be Succinct	Beware of wordy, vague conditions and other clauses—they often cause problems.
Redraft When Necessary	Don't hesitate to redraft an offer several times to clarify and present clauses in a logical sequence. Your client will appreciate it and your negotiations will be more productive.

A Matter of Words   RESIDENTIAL CASE LAW

The Court carefully analyzes conditions given their focal role in agreements. Make certain your words stand up to close scrutiny.

The buyers entered into an agreement to purchase a renovated mid-town house for $1,510,000. The $150,000 deposit was held by the listing brokerage. The initial offer included the following condition:

This Agreement is conditional upon the inspection of the Property by a home inspector of the Purchaser's choice and at the Purchaser's own expense and receipt of a report satisfactory to him in his sole and absolute discretion. Unless the Purchaser/Cooperating Broker[age] gives notice in writing, delivered to the Vendor/Listing Broker[age] within two weeks from acceptance of this offer [subsequently amended on countersign to read: on or before 3:00 p.m. Wednesday, August 19, 1998], that this condition is fulfilled, this Agreement shall be null and void and the deposit shall be returned to the Purchaser in full, without interest or deduction. The Vendor agrees to cooperate in providing access to the property for the purpose of this inspection at reasonable times upon reasonable notice given by the Purchaser. This condition is included for the sole benefit of the Purchaser and may be waived at his sole option by notice in writing to the Vendor/Listing Broker[age] within the time period stated herein.

The buyers engaged the services of a home inspector on August 14th who submitted a report the same day. They advised the co-operating brokerage on August 17th that the report had been received, that they would not remove their condition and asked for the return of the deposit. The seller refused, arguing that the deficiencies were minor in nature, that the buyers failed to act reasonably, honestly and in good faith, and failed to give the seller a copy of the inspection report. The buyers commenced the action for the return of the deposit. The listing brokerage holding the deposit was initially a defendant, but paid the deposit to the Court and had the action against the brokerage dismissed.

The Judge found that the buyers acted neither arbitrarily nor capriciously or other than in honesty and in good faith. The buyers had the right to decide not to go through with the transaction and have their deposit returned to them. As put succinctly in the full text judgment: The condition clause clearly says so.

Reference Marshall v. Bernard Place Corporation and Chestnut Park Real Estate Limited—Digested from Full Text Judgment. See also (2000), 36 R.P.R. (3d) 153. Appeal by Bernard Place Corporation dismissed by the Court of Appeal for Ontario. Released February 13, 2002

(continued on next page)

COMMENTARY

Sole Discretion   The Judge addressed the term sole discretion and found that the conditional clause contained clear words that permitted the buyer to waive the condition. The wording:

> *clearly excludes any participation by the Vendor in the property inspection or the decision whether the report is satisfactory or should be satisfactory to the Purchaser.*

Clear Words   The selling salesperson, during testimony, submitted that she wanted to know the problems related to the inspection report so that resolution might be effected. The Judge commented as follows:

> *In effect, [the salesperson] would have interpreted the inspection condition along these lines: If the Purchaser intends not to waive this condition, the Purchaser shall state his reasons and forward a copy of the inspection report to the Vendor. If the report discloses a substantial defect in the property which the Vendor is unable or unwilling to remedy prior to the date set for closing, the Purchaser shall have the right to declare the Agreement null and void and to call for return of the deposit.*

Such an interpretation was judged untenable as it suggests an intention that is in opposition to the clear words in the agreement.

Onus of Proof   The court also addressed the issue of onus, as the seller argued that the buyers must prove that they acted reasonably and in good faith. As the Judge commented:

> *To place an onus on a party exercising 'a sole and absolute discretion' to deliver a copy of the inspection report and to give reasons for his decision, renders meaningless the clear words of the condition clause.*

However, considerable comment was directed to the issue of honesty and good faith on the part of the buyers and the need to avoid capricious or arbitrary conduct. The buyers in this case acted in good faith, obtained the necessary report and relied upon the clear wording of the condition. Alternate conduct, while not in evidence in this case, is obviously a significant factor. In other words, the terms of the condition should be diligently performed.

Discretion, Opinion and Satisfaction   Provisions that refer to the discretion, the opinion or the satisfaction of a party fall broadly into two categories: application of subjective standards (e.g., taste, personal compatibility and personal judgement); and objective standards (e.g., operative fitness, structural completion and mechanical utility). In any given transaction, the appropriate category will depend on the explicit wording of the condition. If no clear indication is given; i.e., in the absence of explicit language, the tendency is to require that the discretion or dissatisfaction be reasonable and measured against some standard.

MORTGAGE CONDITIONS

Today's financial marketplace boasts an unending variety of home financing packages. Salespersons must properly structure clauses to assist clients in securing suitable mortgaging that meets their needs and wants. Most mortgage clauses involve new financing to replace existing mortgages.

Condition Precedent

The typical mortgage condition precedent closely resembles previous conditional clauses, but with additional financing specifics.

Mortgage Condition Precedent (Including Waiver Provision)

This offer is conditional upon the buyer arranging at the buyer's own expense, a new first mortgage for not less than Two Hundred Thousand Dollars ($200,000.00) bearing interest at a rate of not more than 5.5% per annum, calculated semi-annually not in advance, repayable in blended monthly payments of about One Thousand Two Hundred and Twenty Dollars and Seventy-Eight Cents ($1,220.78) including principal and interest, and to run for a term of not less than five years from the date of completion of this transaction. Unless the buyer gives notice in writing delivered to the seller personally or in accordance with any other provisions for the delivery of notice in this Agreement of Purchase and Sale or any Schedule thereto not later than 11:59 p.m. on the 1st day of May, 20xx, that this condition is fulfilled, this offer shall be null and void and the deposit shall be returned to the buyer in full without deduction. This condition is included for the benefit of the buyer and may be waived at the buyer's sole option by notice in writing to the seller as aforesaid within the time period stated herein.

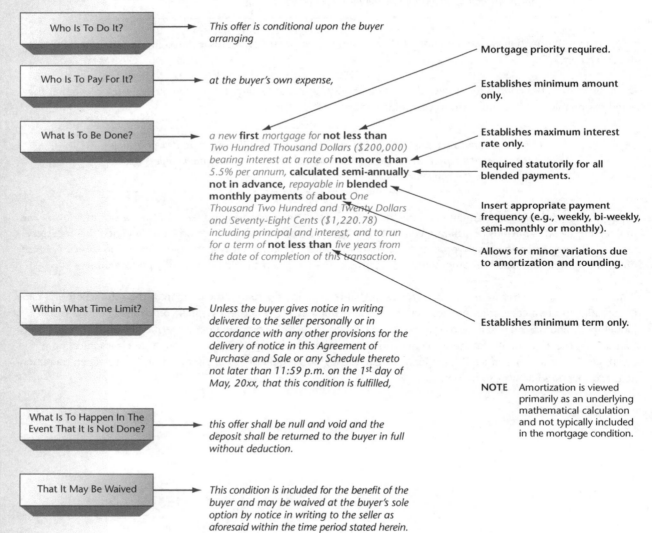

Percentage Clause

This clause variation involves stating a percentage of the sale price rather than a specific amount; e.g., 90% of the purchase price. In this instance, amortization is included in order to establish the monthly payment once offer negotiations are finalized.

SAMPLE CLAUSE   *Condition—Arranging a New Mortgage as Percentage of Purchase Price*

This Offer is conditional upon the Buyer arranging, at the Buyer's own expense, a new_____ Charge/Mortgage for not less than ____% of the purchase price, bearing interest at a rate of not more than ____% per annum, calculated semi-annually not in advance, repayable in equal blended monthly payments, amortized over a period of not less than__ years and to run for a term of not less than___ years from the date of completion of this transaction. Unless the Buyer gives notice in writing delivered to the Seller personally or in accordance with any other provisions for the delivery of notice in this Agreement of Purchase and Sale or any Schedule thereto not later than _____p.m. on the ____day of_____, 20 ____, that this condition is fulfilled, this Offer shall be null and void and the deposit shall be returned to the Buyer in full without deduction. This condition is included for the benefit of the Buyer and may be waived at the Buyer's sole option by notice in writing to the Seller as aforesaid within the time period stated herein.

Condition Subsequent

The condition subsequent for new financing includes the same mortgage specifics as the condition precedent.

SAMPLE CLAUSE   *Condition—Arranging New Mortgage (Condition Subsequent)*

The Buyer may terminate this Agreement through written notice delivered to the Seller personally or in accordance with any other provisions for the delivery of notice in this Agreement of Purchase and Sale or any Schedule thereto not later than _____ p.m. on the _____ day of _____, 20____, if a new first Charge/Mortgage cannot be arranged by the Buyer, at the Buyer's expense. This Charge/Mortgage is to be for a sum of not less than _____, ($_____) bearing interest at a rate of not more than _____% per annum, calculated semi-annually, not in advance, repayable in blended monthly payments of about _____, ($_____), including both principal and interest, and to run for a term of not less than _____ year(s) from the date of completion of this transaction. Upon receipt of the above notice, this Agreement shall be null and void and the deposit shall be returned to the Buyer in full without deduction. If no such notice is received within the above time limit, then this term of contract shall be deemed waived by the Buyer and this Agreement shall remain valid and binding whether or not such Charge/Mortgage has been arranged.

Waiver   CAUTION

Do not include the waiver if the mortgage is to be arranged through the seller's existing mortgagee (in order for the seller to save all or part of a prepayment penalty). If so, clearly state that fact in the clause. If a waiver was provided, the buyer might obtain other financing, waive the condition and the seller would then be required to discharge the existing mortgage, with a potentially significant discharge penalty.

ASSUMPTIONS/SELLER TAKE BACKS

Real estate markets and financial markets are inextricably tied. Fortunately, real estate registrants have benefited from strong financial market conditions, diverse mortgage products and low interest rates. A seller's market has generally persisted for the past decade.

However, history presents a much different picture. Previous decades witnessed dramatic swings in housing demand, interest rates, access to mortgage funds and financial product diversity. In such times, mortgage assumptions and seller take backs had greater prominence.

Market dynamics present both challenges and opportunities. For example, existing longer-term mortgages take on greater appeal when interest rates rise. In some instances, seller take backs are the only viable method to finance when funds are scarce. Registrants must be equipped with appropriate knowledge to handle all circumstances.

Mortgage Assumptions

Existing mortgage financing may be assumed by the buyer provided that the mortgagee agrees and, in most instances, the buyer qualifies by being eligible to obtain a loan of this nature from the lender, just as the original mortgagor did. When a buyer assumes the mortgage, he/she takes over the mortgage balance and becomes responsible for the payments, terms and all monies owed. By assuming an existing mortgage, the buyer may save appraisal fees, some legal costs and survey costs. The advantage to the seller may be a savings of any payout penalty or interest differential that may apply.

CLAUSE DRAFTING

Mortgage assumptions typically involve two clause structures: assumption with or without mortgagee approval. If approval is required, the lender will require the new buyer to meet current lending criteria for the amount being assumed. The *subject to approval assumption* clause is a true condition precedent.

In a mortgage assumption, unless otherwise agreed, the original mortgagor's personal covenant applies, despite the fact that the new buyer has taken over payments.

SAMPLE CLAUSE *Condition—Approval to Assume Existing Mortgage (Condition Precedent)*

The Buyer agrees to assume the existing _____Charge/Mortgage held by _____ for approximately _____, ($_____), bearing interest at the rate of _____% per annum, calculated semi-annually not in advance, repayable in blended monthly payments of _____ ($_____), including both principal and interest, and due on the _____day of _____, 20 ____. This Offer is conditional upon the Buyer obtaining the approval of the Chargee/Mortgagee to assume the existing Charge/Mortgage. Unless the Buyer gives notice in writing delivered to the Seller personally or in accordance with any other provisions for the delivery of notice in this Agreement of Purchase and Sale or any Schedule thereto not later than _____ p.m. on the _____day of _____, 20____, that this condition is fulfilled, this Offer shall be null and void and the deposit shall be returned to the Buyer in full without deduction. The Buyer hereby agrees to proceed immediately to make an application and provide such material as may be required by the Chargee/Mortgagee for approval of the Buyer as the Chargor/Mortgagor.

NOTE: This clause is a true Condition Precedent and neither a Seller nor a Buyer is entitled to waive this condition.

MORTGAGE ASSUMPTION MATHEMATICS

Double check math calculations when drafting mortgage assumptions. (Note: This also applies to seller take back offers.) The *pay the balance as follows* line is impacted. Consider the following example.

39 Westchester Blvd. — Calculating The Balance

	CONDITIONAL ON NEW FINANCING	ASSUME EXISTING MORTGAGE	SELLER TAKE BACK
Purchase Price	$309,500	$309,500	$309,500
Deposit	20,000	20,000	20,000
Conditional on New First Mortgage	200,000		
Assume Existing First Mortgage		200,000	
Seller Take Back			200,000
PAY THE BALANCE AS FOLLOWS:	$289,500	$89,500	$89,500

Seller Take Backs (STBs)

Most conventional lenders provide streamlined approval processes and standardized financing packages. The **seller take back** offers an opportunity for creative packaging to suit the client's needs.

Seller take backs are positive negotiating tools that can serve both buyer's and seller's interests. The buyer may avoid certain costs and paperwork typically associated with conventional lenders. The seller can improve marketability through attractive terms and/or achieve certain personal investment objectives. STBs are particularly effective with older or unique properties, situations where sellers have adequate financial reserves to assist and buyers bring significant down payments to the negotiating table.

CLAUSE DRAFTING

Specific clauses for a seller take back mortgage will vary based on circumstances. The basic clause is highlighted, but additional provisions may be required.

SAMPLE CLAUSE   *Seller Take Back Mortgage*

The Seller agrees to take back a _____ Charge/Mortgage in the amount of _____ ($_____), bearing interest at the rate of _____% per annum, calculated semi-annually not in advance, repayable in blended monthly payments of _____ ($_____), including both principal and interest, and to run for a term of _____ years from the date of completion of this transaction. (See Prepayment Privileges, Clauses MORT–23, MORT–24, MORT–25 & MORT–26.)

NOTE: Without a prepayment privilege, the borrower does not have any automatic right to early discharge of the Charge/Mortgage or prepayment of principal.

Various mortgage privileges and provisions can be added to customize the STB from both seller and buyer perspectives.

Creditworthiness	What about a credit check and some form of warranty regarding the downpayment?
Prepayment	What privileges should be included: fully open, subject to a bonus, etc? How will this impact my client?
Renewal	Should I insert a renewal provision; i.e., same terms except for a further renewal or a further renewal at the then current interest rate?
Postponement	What about an existing mortgage if, for example, the STB is a second mortgage? Does it expire prior to the STB?
Sale of STB	Will the seller want to sell the STB prior to closing?

Creditworthiness

Every seller should be given the opportunity to take back a mortgage and, at the same time, be provided with sufficient information to make a well-informed decision on the matter. An example is provided in which the seller is seeking further information about the buyer when considering a STB.

> **EXAMPLE**   *Credit Worthiness*
>
> Seller Smith is considering a STB with Buyer Jones. The salesperson has explained the basic steps in such an arrangement. Jones requires a $200,000 mortgage and has a downpayment of $80,000 that will come from the sale of his existing home. Accordingly, the salesperson drafted a clause in the agreement concerning the STB but Smith wants to be assured that he can fully investigate Jones' credit worthiness. The additional clause relating to credit worthiness follows:
>
> > *This Offer is conditional upon the Seller being satisfied concerning the personal and/or credit worthiness of the Buyer. Unless the Seller gives notice in writing to the Buyer personally or in accordance with any other provisions for the delivery of notice in this Agreement of Purchase and Sale or any Schedule thereto not later than _____p.m. on the _____day of _____, 20 ___, that this condition is fulfilled, this Offer shall be null and void and the deposit shall be returned to the Buyer in full without deduction. This condition is included for the benefit of the Seller and may be waived at the Seller's sole option by notice in writing to the Buyer as aforesaid within the time period stated herein.*

Prepayment

The concept of **prepayment** is not a right under the mortgage document, but a privilege. Unless otherwise specified, the mortgagor has agreed to make payments according to a specified schedule and the contract is written to run for a specified period. Prepayment privileges vary significantly. For example, the mortgage might be:

- Fully open.
- Open but prepayments must equal the principal amounts next falling due under the mortgage.
- Open on anniversary date only.
- Prepayment subject to a bonus (e.g., one or more month's interest).

Prepayment

A right given to a mortgagor to pay all or part of the mortgage debt in advance of the maturity date, on stipulated terms.

Renewal

When drafting a **renewal** privilege, registrants must clearly delineate the terms and conditions for the further renewal period. For example, a renewal clause might permit the mortgagor to renew the mortgage when not in default, on the same terms and conditions save and except for a further renewal. A more restrictive renewal clause might include a requirement that the interest rate be set 30 days prior to the expiration, based on a pre-determined formula, that the term be specifically identified; e.g., one, two or three years and that such renewal be subject to the continued credit worthiness of the mortgagor.

> **Renewal**
>
> A right given to the mortgagor to renew the mortgage at maturity date, on stipulated terms.

> **EXAMPLE**   *Renewal*
>
> Seller Smith has agreed to a seller take back mortgage to facilitate a sale to Buyer Jones. Jones is uncertain whether he will require the mortgage for one year, or at most, two years. He has other property that may be sold and these funds would be used to discharge the mortgage completely. Accordingly, the following clause is inserted in the agreement:
>
> > *This Charge/Mortgage shall contain a clause permitting the Chargor/Mortgagor, when not in default, the privilege of renewing this Charge/Mortgage on its maturity, for a further term of one year on the same terms and conditions save and except for the right to any further renewal.*

Postponement

Registrants may encounter situations where the seller takes back a second mortgage that would expire after the existing first mortgage. Assume the property has a $200,000 first mortgage and a $30,000 STB. Upon expiration of the first mortgage, the second mortgage of $30,000 could move into first position. The buyer would face the unfavourable position of having to raise $200,000 to pay off the existing first mortgage at maturity.

The **postponement** clause, which forms part of the second mortgage, gives the buyer the right to arrange a new first mortgage or renew the existing one in priority to the second. The second mortgagee is protected in that any excess monies raised on a new first mortgage must be used to reduce or pay off the second.

> **Postponement**
>
> The agreement by a mortgagee to maintain a subsequent priority during the refinancing or re-registration of another mortgage in higher priority.

> **EXAMPLE**   *Postponement*
>
> Seller Smith has agreed to a seller take back second mortgage to facilitate a sale to Buyer Jones. The existing first mortgage expires before the STB and a postponement clause is inserted as follows:
>
> > *This Charge/Mortgage shall contain a clause permitting the renewal or replacement of the existing first Charge/Mortgage at any time, provided that any increase in the principal amount of the new first Charge/ Mortgage over the amount of principal owing under the first Charge/Mortgage at the time of renewal or replacement shall be applied in reduction of the principal amount of this Charge/Mortgage; and the Chargee/Mortgagee hereunder shall execute and deliver to the Chargor/Mortgagor such postponement agreement, Charge/Mortgage Statement or other documents as the new first Chargee/ Mortgagee may reasonably require, forthwith upon request.*
>
> **NOTE:** If Charge/Mortgage being arranged is a third, etc., change clause to read: "*replacement of the first and/or second Charge(s)/Mortgage(s)*" and "*principal owing under the first and/or second Charge(s)/Mortgage(s)*".

Sale of STB

The range of underwriting criteria used by lenders in buying mortgages is quite broad. Sellers contemplating the sale of a seller take back mortgage should be fully informed concerning lender guidelines on such matters. Yield is usually a major consideration along with information concerning the mortgagor's personal covenant, condition of the property and general degree of risk associated with the mortgage.

Registrants should be aware that lenders involved in purchasing STBs normally require:

- The seller to declare that there is good title other than encumbrances declared in the purchase agreement (e.g., additional mortgages) and allow a time limit to check out that title. It should be noted that title insurance can be required in support of title.
- The seller to sell at a discounted value, to increase the rate of return to the investor, unless the mortgage already has terms that are very favourable compared with current market.
- The seller to supply a duly executed assignment of mortgage document.
- The seller to supply an affidavit attesting to the balance of the mortgage and that such mortgage is up-to-date and not in default.
- The agreement to be subject to the buyer of the mortgage making an inspection of the property.

The mortgage is fully described in an agreement between the seller and the lender, a deposit is held pending closing, and the seller and buyer warrant and agree to perform certain items. The actual document used will vary considerably in the marketplace.

EXAMPLE   *Sale of STB*

Smith is willing to take back a mortgage on Jones' purchase of the property, provided that he can sell the $200,000 mortgage @ 5.5% for a discounted value of $195,000 (which effectively increases the ultimate yield to the lender). The salesperson, after fully discussing seller take back mortgages, drafts an appropriate condition.

This Offer is conditional upon the Seller obtaining at the Seller's own expense, a commitment for the sale of the aforementioned first Charge/Mortgage for an amount of not less than One Hundred and Ninety-Five Thousand Dollars ($195,000). Unless the Seller gives notice in writing delivered to the Buyer personally or in accordance with any other provisions for the delivery of notice in this Agreement of Purchase and Sale or any Schedule thereto not later than 11:59 p.m. on the 1st day of June, 20xx, that this condition is fulfilled, this Offer shall be null and void and the deposit shall be returned to the Buyer in full without deduction. This condition is included for the benefit of the Seller and may be waived at the Seller's sole option by notice in writing to the Buyer as aforesaid within the time period stated herein.

STB Tax Considerations   **MARKET MEMO**

The seller should be aware that the decision to participate in a STB can affect personal tax position. The real estate salesperson should not provide advice, however, a general knowledge of tax implications is useful. As a guideline, the *Income Tax Act* is quite precise regarding the collection of interest. Normally, it is deemed to be income for the year in which it was received. Consequently, the mortgagee will have to report this interest as income.

If capital gains tax applies in the transaction and part of the gain is involved in the seller take back, then the seller is permitted to set up mortgage reserves. Essentially, the government's position is that part of the gain has not been received but will ultimately be in the seller's possession. The reserve fund takes into account this deferral and delays some tax on the taxable gain. In such circumstances, the seller should contact his/her accountant directly as the reserve structure will impact tax position.

KNOWLEDGE INTEGRATION

Notables

- A *condition precedent* provides that if a condition is not fulfilled or waived, no binding contract has been formed.

- A *condition subsequent* assumes a binding contract unless a described event occurs.

- An escape clause provides that the seller may continue to offer the property for sale, while accepting an offer containing condition(s).

- No simple guidelines exist concerning escape clause use and the length of notice period regarding removal of the condition(s).

- Use clear, precise wording when constructing conditions.

- Exercise caution regarding any negotiations within the conditional period. Seek legal advice.

- A home inspection is not a warranty or a guarantee.

- Wherever possible, stack multiple conditions under one mega-condition.

- In a mortgage condition, the *what is to be done* portion is key. Make certain exact amounts and wordings are included.

- Mortgage assumptions typically involve two wordings: assumption with or without approval. The vast majority of mortgages require approval.

- Seller take back arrangements provide for creative packaging and can be an effective negotiating tool.

- When customizing an STB, make certain to carefully consider options that best align with the client's interests.

- A postponement clause can be used when an existing mortgage (e.g., a first mortgage) expires before a second mortgage.

- Sellers should be aware that certain tax consequences arise with a seller take back.

Glossary

Condition Precedent
Condition Subsequent
Escape Clause
Home Inspection
Postponement

Prepayment
Renewal
Seller Take Back
Waiver

Strategic Thinking For Your Career

Questions are included to assist in developing your new career. No answers are provided.

1. Is condition subsequent used in the local marketplace or does condition precedent dominate?

2. The text refers to selected examples of true condition precedent clauses that cannot be waived by either buyer or seller. Can you think of others?

3. How do OREA's recommended conditional clauses compare with those used in my intended brokerage or elsewhere in the local marketplace?

4. Under what circumstances do salespersons typically use escape clauses in the local marketplace?

5. What home inspection companies operate locally and what information is available about them to start building my home inspector list and information file?

6. Can I effectively customize a seller take back mortgage to suit buyers' and sellers' needs?

Chapter Mini-Review

Solutions are located in the Appendix.

1. A condition precedent would normally include a reference as to who is to perform the condition and at whose expense?

    ◯ True   ◯ False

2. In a condition precedent, neither party has the right to waive the condition, unless a waiver provision is included.

    ◯ True   ◯ False

3. An escape clause may result in a buyer waiving a condition before it is fulfilled.

    ◯ True   ◯ False

4. A waiver provision can be used with condition subsequent.

    ◯ True   ◯ False

5. Any condition relating to a home inspection must not include a waiver provision.

    ◯ True   ◯ False

6. An escape clause allows the seller to continue to offer the property for sale following acceptance of a conditional offer.

    ◯ True   ◯ False

7. A typical residential home inspection takes between two and three hours to complete.

    ◯ True   ◯ False

8. A pre-listing home inspection can be helpful as it provides the seller with information to remedy potential problem areas prior to offering the property for sale.

    ◯ True   ◯ False

9. A stacked multiple condition can potentially avoid lengthy and cumbersome individual conditions, each with its respective time period and waiver provision.

    ◯ True   ◯ False

10. Mortgage assumptions for residential property do not typically require the mortgagee's approval.

    ◯ True   ◯ False

11. If the purchase price is $300,000, the deposit is $30,000 and a mortgage taken back by the seller is $200,000, the *pay the balance as follows* amount is $70,000.

    ◯ True   ◯ False

12. A postponement provision in a second mortgage is normally included if the expiry date of the second mortgage precedes the expiry of the first mortgage.

    ◯ True   ◯ False

Active Learning Exercises

Solutions are located in the Appendix.

■ **Exercise 1   Multiple Choice**

1.1   Which of the following statements is correct?

    a.   With condition subsequent, a binding contract is created if the condition is fulfilled or waived.

    b.   A condition precedent involving a land severance is typically a true condition precedent.

    c.   In an agreement, the title search period must be shorter than the longest conditional period.

    d.   The waiver provision provides that the seller may continue to offer the property for sale.

1.2   One of the most notable benefits of a professional home inspection is:

    a.   The determination of the presence or absence of hazardous substances.

    b.   The assistance given in estimating market value.

    c.   The assessment of the strength of internal structural components.

    d.   A report including systems or components in need of immediate repair.

1.3   Based on legal issues reviewed in this chapter, which of the following is NOT correct?

    a.   Clear words are vital when developing conditional clauses.

    b.   Buyers should act honestly in performing conditions and not in a capricious manner.

    c.   Terms of a condition should be diligently performed.

    d.   The Court has little regard for specific condition wordings if a dispute arises.

1.4   An escape clause:

    a.   Must be inserted if the conditional period exceeds 30 days.

    b.   Must have a 48-hour time limit for waiving condition(s) after receiving notice.

    c.   Is always used with a condition precedent involving the sale of the buyer's property.

    d.   Might be included with a condition based on market circumstances and the length of the conditional period.

1.5 A mortgage condition requiring that the buyer be approved for a mortgage through the same lender who currently has a first mortgage on the property:

a. Would include a waiver provision.

b. Would not include a waiver provision.

c. Must include both a waiver provision and an escape clause.

d. None of the above.

1.6 Which of the following is a correct statement?

a. A typical postponement clause provides that if additional monies are advanced by way of a new first mortgage, the excess must be paid to reduce the second mortgage.

b. A renewal clause must only provide for a single renewal of a mortgage.

c. Seller take backs require the same approval process, as would be undertaken had the buyer secured financing through a lending institution.

d. A seller who decides to take back a mortgage is not typically required to report interest received on that mortgage until the mortgage term has ended.

■ Exercise 2   Offer Drafting

Douglas M. Huber and Ella C. Huber want you to draft an offer for 832 Wentworth Drive owned by Betty W. Favreau and Denise B. Strauss. Various information is described below. Insert any additional details necessary to complete the offer. A blank *Agreement of Purchase and Sale* (OREA Form 100) is provided.

The property, located on the south side of Wentworth Drive, has a frontage of 46.50 feet and a depth of 109.30 feet and is described as Pt. Lot 7, Concession IV, more specifically as Part 1, Reference Plan 99R 3816, City of Anycity, Regional Municipality of Anyregion. The property is located in a relatively undeveloped area in the southwest quadrant of the city.

The offered price is $289,500 with a deposit of $15,000, a supplemental deposit of $10,000 payable 14 days from the offer date, with the balance due on completion date. The $15,000 is to be deposited upon acceptance of the agreement with the listing brokerage. No mortgage is required. However, the Hubers are requesting a home inspection condition, as well as making the offer conditional on the sale of their home at 320 Maple Lane in West City within 60 days. The 60-day time frame is sufficient for both conditions precedent. The buyers understand that they may have to waive both conditions if a competing offer is submitted pursuant to an escape clause.

The buyers also noticed damage to the garage doors resulting in one door being unworkable with the other making a noticeable clanging noise during the opening/closing process. The buyers want the sellers' assurance that such items will be repaired before closing.

The DigiScan satellite receiver, Model 5000 and two converters are included in the purchase price. A rental hot water tank from Anycity Energy @ $33.50 per quarter (plus tax) is assumable, as well as a water softener from AquaClean, Model 2200 @ 18.00 per month (plus tax).

The offer, dated at Anycity, will be irrevocable for two days and expiring at 6 p.m. on that day. Allow an appropriate title search period. Completion will be approximately 90 days from today's date. The present use is single-family residential. Notices cannot be delivered by fax or email and HST is deemed to be included in the purchase price. Assume that today's date is September 1, 20xx and the completion date is a normal business day. Insert necessary dates and signatures as required for a fully completed agreement ready for presentation. The listing brokerage is ABC Realty Inc. representing the seller and the co-operating brokerage is XYZ Real Estate Limited representing the buyer.

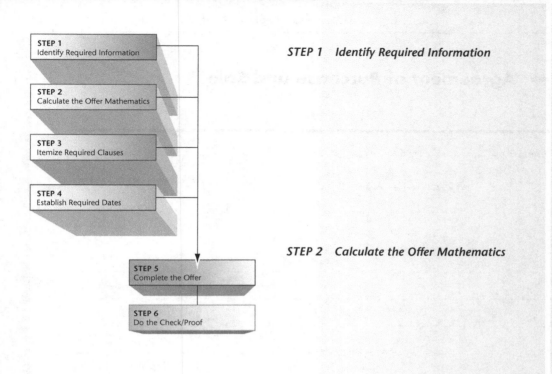

STEP 1   *Identify Required Information*

STEP 2   *Calculate the Offer Mathematics*

STEP 3   *Itemize Required Clauses*

STEP 4   *Establish Required Dates*

OREA Ontario Real Estate Association

Agreement of Purchase and Sale

Form 100
for use in the Province of Ontario

This Agreement of Purchase and Sale dated this .... day of .... 20............

BUYER, ..., agrees to purchase from
(Full legal names of all Buyers)

SELLER, ..., the following
(Full legal names of all Sellers)

REAL PROPERTY:

Address ....

fronting on the .... side of ....

in the ....

and having a frontage of .... more or less by a depth of .... more or less

and legally described as ....

.... (the "property")
(Legal description of land including easements not described elsewhere)

PURCHASE PRICE: Dollars (CDN$) ....

.... Dollars

DEPOSIT: Buyer submits .... Dollars (CDN$) ....
(Herewith/Upon Acceptance/as otherwise described in this Agreement)

.... Dollars (CDN$) ....

by negotiable cheque payable to .... "Deposit Holder" to be held
in trust pending completion or other termination of this Agreement and to be credited toward the Purchase Price on completion. For the purposes of this
Agreement, "Upon Acceptance" shall mean that the Buyer is required to deliver the deposit to the Deposit Holder within 24 hours of the acceptance of
this Agreement. The parties to this Agreement hereby acknowledge that, unless otherwise provided for in this Agreement, the Deposit Holder shall place
the deposit in trust in the Deposit Holder's non-interest bearing Real Estate Trust Account and no interest shall be earned, received or paid on the deposit.

Buyer agrees to pay the balance as more particularly set out in Schedule A attached.

SCHEDULE(S) A..**attached hereto form(s) part of this Agreement.**

1.   **IRREVOCABILITY:** This offer shall be irrevocable by .... until .... a.m./p.m. on the ....
(Seller/Buyer)

    day of .... 20 ...., after which time, if not accepted, this offer shall be null and void and the deposit
    shall be returned to the Buyer in full without interest.

2.   **COMPLETION DATE:** This Agreement shall be completed by no later than 6:00 p.m. on the .... day of ....

    20 .... Upon completion, vacant possession of the property shall be given to the Buyer unless otherwise provided for in this Agreement.

    INITIALS OF BUYER(S): (   )   **INITIALS OF SELLER(S):** (   )

Form 100   Revised 2015   **Page 1 of 6**

3. **NOTICES:** The Seller hereby appoints the Listing Brokerage as agent for the Seller for the purpose of giving and receiving notices pursuant to this Agreement. Where a Brokerage (Buyer's Brokerage) has entered into a representation agreement with the Buyer, the Buyer hereby appoints the Buyer's Brokerage as agent for the purpose of giving and receiving notices pursuant to this Agreement. **Where a Brokerage represents both the Seller and the Buyer (multiple representation), the Brokerage shall not be appointed or authorized to be agent for either the Buyer or the Seller for the purpose of giving and receiving notices.** Any notice relating hereto or provided for herein shall be in writing. In addition to any provision contained herein and in any Schedule hereto, this offer, any counter-offer, notice of acceptance thereof or any notice to be given or received pursuant to this Agreement or any Schedule hereto (any of them, "Document") shall be deemed given and received when delivered personally or hand delivered to the Address for Service provided in the Acknowledgement below, or where a facsimile number or email address is provided herein, when transmitted electronically to that facsimile number or email address, respectively, in which case, the signature(s) of the party (parties) shall be deemed to be original.

    FAX No.: ....   FAX No.: ....
    (For delivery of Documents to Seller)   (For delivery of Documents to Buyer)

    Email Address: ....   Email Address: ....
    (For delivery of Documents to Seller)   (For delivery of Documents to Buyer)

4. **CHATTELS INCLUDED:** ....

    ....

    ....

    ....

    ....

    Unless otherwise stated in this Agreement or any Schedule hereto, Seller agrees to convey all fixtures and chattels included in the Purchase Price free from all liens, encumbrances or claims affecting the said fixtures and chattels.

5. **FIXTURES EXCLUDED:** ....

    ....

    ....

    ....

    ....

6. **RENTAL ITEMS (Including Lease, Lease to Own):** The following equipment is rented and **not** included in the Purchase Price. The Buyer agrees to assume the rental contract(s), if assumable:

    ....

    ....

    ....

    The Buyer agrees to co-operate and execute such documentation as may be required to facilitate such assumption.

7. **HST:** If the sale of the Property (Real Property as described above) is subject to Harmonized Sales Tax (HST), then such tax shall be

    .... the Purchase Price. If the sale of the Property is not subject to HST, Seller agrees to certify on or before
    (included in/in addition to)

    closing, that the sale of the Property is not subject to HST. Any HST on chattels, if applicable, is not included in the Purchase Price.

    INITIALS OF BUYER(S): ( )   **INITIALS OF SELLER(S):** ( )

8. **TITLE SEARCH:** Buyer shall be allowed until 6:00 p.m. on the .... day of .... , 20.........., (Requisition Date) to examine the title to the Property at Buyer's own expense and until the earlier of: (i) thirty days from the later of the Requisition Date or the date on which the conditions in this Agreement are fulfilled or otherwise waived or; (ii) five days prior to completion, to satisfy Buyer that there are no outstanding

work orders or deficiency notices affecting the Property, and that its present use (..) may be lawfully continued and that the principal building may be insured against risk of fire. Seller hereby consents to the municipality or other governmental agencies releasing to Buyer details of all outstanding work orders and deficiency notices affecting the property, and Seller agrees to execute and deliver such further authorizations in this regard as Buyer may reasonably require.

9. **FUTURE USE:** Seller and Buyer agree that there is no representation or warranty of any kind that the future intended use of the property by Buyer is or will be lawful except as may be specifically provided for in this Agreement.

10. **TITLE:** Provided that the title to the property is good and free from all registered restrictions, charges, liens, and encumbrances except as otherwise specifically provided in this Agreement and save and except for (a) any registered restrictions or covenants that run with the land providing that such are complied with; (b) any registered municipal agreements and registered agreements with publicly regulated utilities providing such have been complied with, or security has been posted to ensure compliance and completion, as evidenced by a letter from the relevant municipality or regulated utility; (c) any minor easements for the supply of domestic utility or telephone services to the property or adjacent properties; and (d) any easements for drainage, storm or sanitary sewers, public utility lines, telephone lines, cable television lines or other services which do not materially affect the use of the property. If within the specified times referred to in paragraph 8 any valid objection to title or to any outstanding work order or deficiency notice, or to the fact the said present use may not lawfully be continued, or that the principal building may not be insured against risk of fire is made in writing to Seller and which Seller is unable or unwilling to remove, remedy or satisfy or obtain insurance save and except against risk of fire (Title Insurance) in favour of the Buyer and any mortgagee, (with all related costs at the expense of the Seller), and which Buyer will not waive, this Agreement notwithstanding any intermediate acts or negotiations in respect of such objections, shall be at an end and all monies paid shall be returned without interest or deduction and Seller, Listing Brokerage and Co-operating Brokerage shall not be liable for any costs or damages. Save as to any valid objection so made by such day and except for any objection going to the root of the title, Buyer shall be conclusively deemed to have accepted Seller's title to the property.

11. **CLOSING ARRANGEMENTS:** Where each of the Seller and Buyer retain a lawyer to complete the Agreement of Purchase and Sale of the property, and where the transaction will be completed by electronic registration pursuant to Part III of the Land Registration Reform Act, R.S.O. 1990, Chapter L4 and the Electronic Registration Act, S.O. 1991, Chapter 44, and any amendments thereto, the Seller and Buyer acknowledge and agree that the exchange of closing funds, non-registrable documents and other items (the "Requisite Deliveries") and the release thereof to the Seller and Buyer will (a) not occur at the same time as the registration of the transfer/deed (and any other documents intended to be registered in connection with the completion of this transaction) and (b) be subject to conditions whereby the lawyer(s) receiving any of the Requisite Deliveries will be required to hold same in trust and not release same except in accordance with the terms of a document registration agreement between the said lawyers. The Seller and Buyer irrevocably instruct the said lawyers to be bound by the document registration agreement which is recommended from time to time by the Law Society of Upper Canada. Unless otherwise agreed to by the lawyers, such exchange of the Requisite Deliveries will occur in the applicable Land Titles Office or such other location agreeable to both lawyers.

12. **DOCUMENTS AND DISCHARGE:** Buyer shall not call for the production of any title deed, abstract, survey or other evidence of title to the property except such as are in the possession or control of Seller. If requested by Buyer, Seller will deliver any sketch or survey of the property within Seller's control to Buyer as soon as possible and prior to the Requisition Date. If a discharge of any Charge/Mortgage held by a corporation incorporated pursuant to the Trust And Loan Companies Act (Canada), Chartered Bank, Trust Company, Credit Union, Caisse Populaire or Insurance Company and which is not to be assumed by Buyer on completion, is not available in registrable form on completion, Buyer agrees to accept Seller's lawyer's personal undertaking to obtain, out of the closing funds, a discharge in registrable form and to register same, or cause same to be registered, on title within a reasonable period of time after completion, provided that on or before completion Seller shall provide to Buyer a mortgage statement prepared by the mortgagee setting out the balance required to obtain the discharge, and, where a real-time electronic cleared funds transfer system is not being used, a direction executed by Seller directing payment to the mortgagee of the amount required to obtain the discharge out of the balance due on completion.

13. **INSPECTION:** Buyer acknowledges having had the opportunity to inspect the Property and understands that upon acceptance of this offer there shall be a binding agreement of purchase and sale between Buyer and Seller. **The Buyer acknowledges having the opportunity to include a requirement for a property inspection report in this Agreement and agrees that except as may be specifically provided for in this Agreement, the Buyer will not be obtaining a property inspection or property inspection report regarding the Property.**

14. **INSURANCE:** All buildings on the property and all other things being purchased shall be and remain until completion at the risk of Seller. Pending completion, Seller shall hold all insurance policies, if any, and the proceeds thereof in trust for the parties as their interests may appear and in the event of substantial damage, Buyer may either terminate this Agreement and have all monies paid returned without interest or deduction or else take the proceeds of any insurance and complete the purchase. No insurance shall be transferred on completion. If Seller is taking back a Charge/Mortgage, or Buyer is assuming a Charge/Mortgage, Buyer shall supply Seller with reasonable evidence of adequate insurance to protect Seller's or other mortgagee's interest on completion.

INITIALS OF BUYER(S): ( )   INITIALS OF SELLER(S): ( )

Form 100   Revised 2015   **Page 3 of 6**

Exercise 2   Agreement of Purchase and Sale—Page 4 of 6

15. **PLANNING ACT:** This Agreement shall be effective to create an interest in the property only if Seller complies with the subdivision control provisions of the Planning Act by completion and Seller covenants to proceed diligently at Seller's expense to obtain any necessary consent by completion.

16. **DOCUMENT PREPARATION:** The Transfer/Deed shall, save for the Land Transfer Tax Affidavit, be prepared in registrable form at the expense of Seller, and any Charge/Mortgage to be given back by the Buyer to Seller at the expense of the Buyer. If requested by Buyer, Seller covenants that the Transfer/Deed to be delivered on completion shall contain the statements contemplated by Section 50(22) of the Planning Act, R.S.O.1990.

17. **RESIDENCY:** (a) Subject to (b) below, the Seller represents and warrants that the Seller is not and on completion will not be a non-resident under the non-residency provisions of the Income Tax Act which representation and warranty shall survive and not merge upon the completion of this transaction and the Seller shall deliver to the Buyer a statutory declaration that Seller is not then a non-resident of Canada; (b) provided that if the Seller is a non-resident under the non-residency provisions of the Income Tax Act, the Buyer shall be credited towards the Purchase Price with the amount, if any, necessary for Buyer to pay to the Minister of National Revenue to satisfy Buyer's liability in respect of tax payable by Seller under the non-residency provisions of the Income Tax Act by reason of this sale. Buyer shall not claim such credit if Seller delivers on completion the prescribed certificate.

18. **ADJUSTMENTS:** Any rents, mortgage interest, realty taxes including local improvement rates and unmetered public or private utility charges and unmetered cost of fuel, as applicable, shall be apportioned and allowed to the day of completion, the day of completion itself to be apportioned to Buyer.

19. **PROPERTY ASSESSMENT:** The Buyer and Seller hereby acknowledge that the Province of Ontario has implemented current value assessment and properties may be re-assessed on an annual basis. The Buyer and Seller agree that no claim will be made against the Buyer or Seller, or any Brokerage, Broker or Salesperson, for any changes in property tax as a result of a re-assessment of the property, save and except any property taxes that accrued prior to the completion of this transaction.

20. **TIME LIMITS:** Time shall in all respects be of the essence hereof provided that the time for doing or completing of any matter provided for herein may be extended or abridged by an agreement in writing signed by Seller and Buyer or by their respective lawyers who may be specifically authorized in that regard.

21. **TENDER:** Any tender of documents or money hereunder may be made upon Seller or Buyer or their respective lawyers on the day set for completion. Money shall be tendered with funds drawn on a lawyer's trust account in the form of a bank draft, certified cheque or wire transfer using the Large Value Transfer System.

22. **FAMILY LAW ACT:** Seller warrants that spousal consent is not necessary to this transaction under the provisions of the Family Law Act, R.S.O.1990 unless Seller's spouse has executed the consent hereinafter provided.

23. **UFFI:** Seller represents and warrants to Buyer that during the time Seller has owned the property, Seller has not caused any building on the property to be insulated with insulation containing ureaformaldehyde, and that to the best of Seller's knowledge no building on the property contains or has ever contained insulation that contains ureaformaldehyde. This warranty shall survive and not merge on the completion of this transaction, and if the building is part of a multiple unit building, this warranty shall only apply to that part of the building which is the subject of this transaction.

24. **LEGAL, ACCOUNTING AND ENVIRONMENTAL ADVICE:** The parties acknowledge that any information provided by the brokerage is not legal, tax or environmental advice.

25. **CONSUMER REPORTS: The Buyer is hereby notified that a consumer report containing credit and/or personal information may be referred to in connection with this transaction.**

26. **AGREEMENT IN WRITING:** If there is conflict or discrepancy between any provision added to this Agreement (including any Schedule attached hereto) and any provision in the standard pre-set portion hereof, the added provision shall supersede the standard pre-set provision to the extent of such conflict or discrepancy. This Agreement including any Schedule attached hereto, shall constitute the entire Agreement between Buyer and Seller. There is no representation, warranty, collateral agreement or condition, which affects this Agreement other than as expressed herein. For the purposes of this Agreement, Seller means vendor and Buyer means purchaser. This Agreement shall be read with all changes of gender or number required by the context.

27. **TIME AND DATE:** Any reference to a time and date in this Agreement shall mean the time and date where the property is located.

INITIALS OF BUYER(S): (   )   **INITIALS OF SELLER(S):** (   )

Form 100   Revised 2015   **Page 4 of 6**

28. SUCCESSORS AND ASSIGNS: The heirs, executors, administrators, successors and assigns of the undersigned are bound by the terms herein.

SIGNED, SEALED AND DELIVERED in the presence of: IN WITNESS whereof I have hereunto set my hand and seal:

.... ● DATE ....
(Witness)   (Buyer)   (Seal)

.... ● DATE ....
(Witness)   (Buyer)   (Seal)

I, the Undersigned Seller, agree to the above offer. I hereby irrevocably instruct my lawyer to pay directly to the brokerage(s) with whom I have agreed to pay commission, the unpaid balance of the commission together with applicable Harmonized Sales Tax (and any other taxes as may hereafter be applicable), from the proceeds of the sale prior to any payment to the undersigned on completion, as advised by the brokerage(s) to my lawyer.

SIGNED, SEALED AND DELIVERED in the presence of: IN WITNESS whereof I have hereunto set my hand and seal:

.... ● DATE ....
(Witness)   (Seller)   (Seal)

.... ● DATE ....
(Witness)   (Seller)   (Seal)

SPOUSAL CONSENT: The Undersigned Spouse of the Seller hereby consents to the disposition evidenced herein pursuant to the provisions of the Family Law Act, R.S.O.1990, and hereby agrees with the Buyer that he/she will execute all necessary or incidental documents to give full force and effect to the sale evidenced herein.

.... ● DATE ....
(Witness)   (Spouse)   (Seal)

CONFIRMATION OF ACCEPTANCE: Notwithstanding anything contained herein to the contrary, I confirm this Agreement with all changes both typed and written was finally accepted by all parties at .... a.m./p.m. this .... day of.., 20..........

....
(Signature of Seller or Buyer)

INFORMATION ON BROKERAGE(S)

Listing Brokerage .... Tel.No.(...............)..........

....
(Salesperson / Broker Name)

Co-op/Buyer Brokerage .... Tel.No.(...............)..........

....
(Salesperson / Broker Name)

ACKNOWLEDGEMENT

I acknowledge receipt of my signed copy of this accepted Agreement of Purchase and Sale and I authorize the Brokerage to forward a copy to my lawyer.	I acknowledge receipt of my signed copy of this accepted Agreement of Purchase and Sale and I authorize the Brokerage to forward a copy to my lawyer.
.... DATE .... (Seller)	.... DATE .... (Buyer)
.... DATE .... (Seller)	.... DATE .... (Buyer)
Address for Service	Address for Service ....
.... Tel.No.(..........)...........	.... Tel.No.(..........)...........
Seller's Lawyer	Buyer's Lawyer ....
Address	Address ....
Email	Email ....
(..........)............... (..........)............... Tel.No. FAX No.	(..........)............... (..........)............... Tel.No. FAX No.

FOR OFFICE USE ONLY   **COMMISSION TRUST AGREEMENT**

To: Co-operating Brokerage shown on the foregoing Agreement of Purchase and Sale:
In consideration for the Co-operating Brokerage procuring the foregoing Agreement of Purchase and Sale, I hereby declare that all moneys received or receivable by me in connection with the Transaction as contemplated in the MLS® Rules and Regulations of my Real Estate Board shall be receivable and held in trust. This agreement shall constitute a Commission Trust Agreement as defined in the MLS® Rules and shall be subject to and governed by the MLS® Rules pertaining to Commission Trust.

DATED as of the date and time of the acceptance of the foregoing Agreement of Purchase and Sale.   Acknowledged by:

....
(Authorized to bind the Listing Brokerage)   (Authorized to bind the Co-operating Brokerage)

Exercise 2   Agreement of Purchase and Sale—Page 6 of 6

 **Ontario Real Estate Association**

Form 100
for use in the Province of Ontario

Schedule A
Agreement of Purchase and Sale

This Schedule is attached to and forms part of the Agreement of Purchase and Sale between:

BUYER, ..., and

SELLER, ...

for the purchase and sale of ....

.... dated the .... day of ...., 20...............

Buyer agrees to pay the balance as follows:

This form must be initialed by all parties to the Agreement of Purchase and Sale.

INITIALS OF BUYER(S):   INITIALS OF SELLER(S):

Form 100   Revised 2015   **Page 6 of 6**

Assume that the Hubers' conditional offer was accepted by the sellers and five days later, the home inspection condition was removed. One month after that, a second offer is submitted on the sellers' property by another buyer. If the sellers want to accept the second offer, what clause must be included to prevent the home from being sold to two different buyers (see *Appendix*)?

Clause [_____]

■ Exercise 3   Identifying Errors and Omissions

Salesperson Lee of ABC Realty Inc. drafted an offer for Mr. and Mrs. Selznick as potential buyers of 3216 Bayside Drive, in the City of Anycity, Regional Municipality of Anyregion. Critically analyze the offer illustrated on the following pages and identify at least 12 errors or omissions.

Exercise 3   Agreement of Purchase and Sale—Page 1 of 6

OREA Ontario Real Estate Association   **Agreement of Purchase and Sale**

Form 100
for use in the Province of Ontario

This Agreement of Purchase and Sale dated this ..... **21st** ..... day of ..... **May** ..... 20 **XX** ....

BUYER, ... **James and Stella Selznick** ..... , agrees to purchase from
(Full legal names of all Buyers)

SELLER, ... **Arthur T. Osland and Jenny B. Osland** ..... , the following
(Full legal names of all Sellers)

REAL PROPERTY:

Address ..... **3216 Bayside Drive** .....

fronting on the ..... **North** ..... side of ..... **Bayside Drive** .....

in the ..... **City of Anycity** .....

and having a frontage of ..... **55 feet** ..... more or less by a depth of ..... **110 feet** ..... more or less

and legally described as ..... **Part of Lot 12 subject to a mutual side drive** .....

..... (the "property")
(Legal description of land including easements not described elsewhere)

PURCHASE PRICE: Dollars (CDN$) ..... **$238,000.00** .....

Two Hundred and Thirty-Eight Thousand--- Dollars

DEPOSIT: Buyer submits ..... **Upon Acceptance** .....
(Herewith/Upon Acceptance/as otherwise described in this Agreement)

One Thousand--- Dollars (CDN$) ..... **$1,000.00** .....

by negotiable cheque payable to ..... **XYZ Real Estate Limited** ..... "Deposit Holder" to be held
in trust pending completion or other termination of this Agreement and to be credited toward the Purchase Price on completion. For the purposes of this
Agreement, "Upon Acceptance" shall mean that the Buyer is required to deliver the deposit to the Deposit Holder within 24 hours of the acceptance of
this Agreement. The parties to this Agreement hereby acknowledge that, unless otherwise provided for in this Agreement, the Deposit Holder shall place
the deposit in trust in the Deposit Holder's non-interest bearing Real Estate Trust Account and no interest shall be earned, received or paid on the deposit.

Buyer agrees to pay the balance as more particularly set out in Schedule A attached.

SCHEDULE(S) A ..... **attached hereto form(s) part of this Agreement.**

1. **IRREVOCABILITY:** This offer shall be irrevocable by ..... **Seller** ..... until ..... **5:00** ..... ~~a.m.~~/p.m. on the ..... **22nd** .....
(Seller/Buyer)

   day of ..... **May** ..... 20 **XX** ..... , after which time, if not accepted, this offer shall be null and void and the deposit
   shall be returned to the Buyer in full without interest.

2. **COMPLETION DATE:** This Agreement shall be completed by no later than 6:00 p.m. on the ..... **30th** ..... day of ..... **June** .....

   20 **XX** ..... Upon completion, vacant possession of the property shall be given to the Buyer unless otherwise provided for in this Agreement.

INITIALS OF BUYER(S): ( )   **INITIALS OF SELLER(S):** (*JS SS*)

3. **NOTICES:** The Seller hereby appoints the Listing Brokerage as agent for the Seller for the purpose of giving and receiving notices pursuant to this Agreement. Where a Brokerage (Buyer's Brokerage) has entered into a representation agreement with the Buyer, the Buyer hereby appoints the Buyer's Brokerage as agent for the purpose of giving and receiving notices pursuant to this Agreement. **Where a Brokerage represents both the Seller and the Buyer (multiple representation), the Brokerage shall not be appointed or authorized to be agent for either the Buyer or the Seller for the purpose of giving and receiving notices.** Any notice relating hereto or provided for herein shall be in writing. In addition to any provision contained herein and in any Schedule hereto, this offer, any counter-offer, notice of acceptance thereof or any notice to be given or received pursuant to this Agreement or any Schedule hereto (any of them, "Document") shall be deemed given and received when delivered personally or hand delivered to the Address for Service provided in the Acknowledgement below, or where a facsimile number or email address is provided herein, when transmitted electronically to that facsimile number or email address, respectively, in which case, the signature(s) of the party (parties) shall be deemed to be original.

FAX No.: .... **(888) 555-1212** ....
(For delivery of Documents to Seller)

FAX No.: .... **(888) 555-2121** ....
(For delivery of Documents to Buyer)

Email Address: ....
(For delivery of Documents to Seller)

Email Address: ....
(For delivery of Documents to Buyer)

4. **CHATTELS INCLUDED:** Hot Sizzle barbecue Model 3000 including cover and five stainless steel Magnolia utensils, eight EZ Comfort patio chairs and matching table/umbrella

Unless otherwise stated in this Agreement or any Schedule hereto, Seller agrees to convey all fixtures and chattels included in the Purchase Price free from all liens, encumbrances or claims affecting the said fixtures and chattels.

5. **FIXTURES EXCLUDED:** None

6. **RENTAL ITEMS (Including Lease, Lease to Own):** The following equipment is rented and **not** included in the Purchase Price. The Buyer agrees to assume the rental contract(s), if assumable:

Rental hot water tank, Anycity Energy @$42.15 per month (plus taxes)

The Buyer agrees to co-operate and execute such documentation as may be required to facilitate such assumption.

7. **HST:** If the sale of the Property (Real Property as described above) is subject to Harmonized Sales Tax (HST), then such tax shall be

.... not applicable .... the Purchase Price. If the sale of the Property is not subject to HST, Seller agrees to certify on or before
(included in/in addition to)

closing, that the sale of the Property is not subject to HST. Any HST on chattels, if applicable, is not included in the Purchase Price.

INITIALS OF BUYER(S): ( )
INITIALS OF SELLER(S): (*JS SS*)

Form 100   Revised 2015   **Page 2 of 6**

8. **TITLE SEARCH:** Buyer shall be allowed until 6:00 p.m. on the ...15th... day of ....June.............................., 20...XX..., (Requisition Date) to examine the title to the Property at Buyer's own expense and until the earlier of: (i) thirty days from the later of the Requisition Date or the date on which the conditions in this Agreement are fulfilled or otherwise waived or; (ii) five days prior to completion, to satisfy Buyer that there are no outstanding work orders or deficiency notices affecting the Property, and that its present use (...........single family residential.....................) may be lawfully continued and that the principal building may be insured against risk of fire. Seller hereby consents to the municipality or other governmental agencies releasing to Buyer details of all outstanding work orders and deficiency notices affecting the property, and Seller agrees to execute and deliver such further authorizations in this regard as Buyer may reasonably require.

9. **FUTURE USE:** Seller and Buyer agree that there is no representation or warranty of any kind that the future intended use of the property by Buyer is or will be lawful except as may be specifically provided for in this Agreement.

10. **TITLE:** Provided that the title to the property is good and free from all registered restrictions, charges, liens, and encumbrances except as otherwise specifically provided in this Agreement and save and except for (a) any registered restrictions or covenants that run with the land providing that such are complied with; (b) any registered municipal agreements and registered agreements with publicly regulated utilities providing such have been complied with, or security has been posted to ensure compliance and completion, as evidenced by a letter from the relevant municipality or regulated utility; (c) any minor easements for the supply of domestic utility or telephone services to the property or adjacent properties; and (d) any easements for drainage, storm or sanitary sewers, public utility lines, telephone lines, cable television lines or other services which do not materially affect the use of the property. If within the specified times referred to in paragraph 8 any valid objection to title or to any outstanding work order or deficiency notice, or to the fact the said present use may not lawfully be continued, or that the principal building may not be insured against risk of fire is made in writing to Seller and which Seller is unable or unwilling to remove, remedy or satisfy or obtain insurance save and except against risk of fire (Title Insurance) in favour of the Buyer and any mortgagee, (with all related costs at the expense of the Seller), and which Buyer will not waive, this Agreement notwithstanding any intermediate acts or negotiations in respect of such objections, shall be at an end and all monies paid shall be returned without interest or deduction and Seller, Listing Brokerage and Co-operating Brokerage shall not be liable for any costs or damages. Save as to any valid objection so made by such day and except for any objection going to the root of the title, Buyer shall be conclusively deemed to have accepted Seller's title to the property.

11. **CLOSING ARRANGEMENTS:** Where each of the Seller and Buyer retain a lawyer to complete the Agreement of Purchase and Sale of the property, and where the transaction will be completed by electronic registration pursuant to Part III of the Land Registration Reform Act, R.S.O. 1990, Chapter L4 and the Electronic Registration Act, S.O. 1991, Chapter 44, and any amendments thereto, the Seller and Buyer acknowledge and agree that the exchange of closing funds, non-registrable documents and other items (the "Requisite Deliveries") and the release thereof to the Seller and Buyer will (a) not occur at the same time as the registration of the transfer/deed (and any other documents intended to be registered in connection with the completion of this transaction) and (b) be subject to conditions whereby the lawyer(s) receiving any of the Requisite Deliveries will be required to hold same in trust and not release same except in accordance with the terms of a document registration agreement between the said lawyers. The Seller and Buyer irrevocably instruct the said lawyers to be bound by the document registration agreement which is recommended from time to time by the Law Society of Upper Canada. Unless otherwise agreed to by the lawyers, such exchange of the Requisite Deliveries will occur in the applicable Land Titles Office or such other location agreeable to both lawyers.

12. **DOCUMENTS AND DISCHARGE:** Buyer shall not call for the production of any title deed, abstract, survey or other evidence of title to the property except such as are in the possession or control of Seller. If requested by Buyer, Seller will deliver any sketch or survey of the property within Seller's control to Buyer as soon as possible and prior to the Requisition Date. If a discharge of any Charge/Mortgage held by a corporation incorporated pursuant to the Trust And Loan Companies Act (Canada), Chartered Bank, Trust Company, Credit Union, Caisse Populaire or Insurance Company and which is not to be assumed by Buyer on completion, is not available in registrable form on completion, Buyer agrees to accept Seller's lawyer's personal undertaking to obtain, out of the closing funds, a discharge in registrable form and to register same, or cause same to be registered, on title within a reasonable period of time after completion, provided that on or before completion Seller shall provide to Buyer a mortgage statement prepared by the mortgagee setting out the balance required to obtain the discharge, and, where a real-time electronic cleared funds transfer system is not being used, a direction executed by Seller directing payment to the mortgagee of the amount required to obtain the discharge out of the balance due on completion.

13. **INSPECTION:** Buyer acknowledges having had the opportunity to inspect the Property and understands that upon acceptance of this offer there shall be a binding agreement of purchase and sale between Buyer and Seller. **The Buyer acknowledges having the opportunity to include a requirement for a property inspection report in this Agreement and agrees that except as may be specifically provided for in this Agreement, the Buyer will not be obtaining a property inspection or property inspection report regarding the Property.**

14. **INSURANCE:** All buildings on the property and all other things being purchased shall be and remain until completion at the risk of Seller. Pending completion, Seller shall hold all insurance policies, if any, and the proceeds thereof in trust for the parties as their interests may appear and in the event of substantial damage, Buyer may either terminate this Agreement and have all monies paid returned without interest or deduction or else take the proceeds of any insurance and complete the purchase. No insurance shall be transferred on completion. If Seller is taking back a Charge/Mortgage, or Buyer is assuming a Charge/Mortgage, Buyer shall supply Seller with reasonable evidence of adequate insurance to protect Seller's or other mortgagee's interest on completion.

INITIALS OF BUYER(S): ( )   **INITIALS OF SELLER(S):** (JS SS)

Form 100   Revised 2015   **Page 3 of 6**

15. **PLANNING ACT:** This Agreement shall be effective to create an interest in the property only if Seller complies with the subdivision control provisions of the Planning Act by completion and Seller covenants to proceed diligently at Seller's expense to obtain any necessary consent by completion.

16. **DOCUMENT PREPARATION:** The Transfer/Deed shall, save for the Land Transfer Tax Affidavit, be prepared in registrable form at the expense of Seller, and any Charge/Mortgage to be given back by the Buyer to Seller at the expense of the Buyer. If requested by Buyer, Seller covenants that the Transfer/Deed to be delivered on completion shall contain the statements contemplated by Section 50(22) of the Planning Act, R.S.O.1990.

17. **RESIDENCY:** (a) Subject to (b) below, the Seller represents and warrants that the Seller is not and on completion will not be a non-resident under the non-residency provisions of the Income Tax Act which representation and warranty shall survive and not merge upon the completion of this transaction and the Seller shall deliver to the Buyer a statutory declaration that Seller is not then a non-resident of Canada; (b) provided that if the Seller is a non-resident under the non-residency provisions of the Income Tax Act, the Buyer shall be credited towards the Purchase Price with the amount, if any, necessary for Buyer to pay to the Minister of National Revenue to satisfy Buyer's liability in respect of tax payable by Seller under the non-residency provisions of the Income Tax Act by reason of this sale. Buyer shall not claim such credit if Seller delivers on completion the prescribed certificate.

18. **ADJUSTMENTS:** Any rents, mortgage interest, realty taxes including local improvement rates and unmetered public or private utility charges and unmetered cost of fuel, as applicable, shall be apportioned and allowed to the day of completion, the day of completion itself to be apportioned to Buyer.

19. **PROPERTY ASSESSMENT:** The Buyer and Seller hereby acknowledge that the Province of Ontario has implemented current value assessment and properties may be re-assessed on an annual basis. The Buyer and Seller agree that no claim will be made against the Buyer or Seller, or any Brokerage, Broker or Salesperson, for any changes in property tax as a result of a re-assessment of the property, save and except any property taxes that accrued prior to the completion of this transaction.

20. **TIME LIMITS:** Time shall in all respects be of the essence hereof provided that the time for doing or completing of any matter provided for herein may be extended or abridged by an agreement in writing signed by Seller and Buyer or by their respective lawyers who may be specifically authorized in that regard.

21. **TENDER:** Any tender of documents or money hereunder may be made upon Seller or Buyer or their respective lawyers on the day set for completion. Money shall be tendered with funds drawn on a lawyer's trust account in the form of a bank draft, certified cheque or wire transfer using the Large Value Transfer System.

22. **FAMILY LAW ACT:** Seller warrants that spousal consent is not necessary to this transaction under the provisions of the Family Law Act, R.S.O.1990 unless Seller's spouse has executed the consent hereinafter provided.

23. **UFFI:** Seller represents and warrants to Buyer that during the time Seller has owned the property, Seller has not caused any building on the property to be insulated with insulation containing ureaformaldehyde, and that to the best of Seller's knowledge no building on the property contains or has ever contained insulation that contains ureaformaldehyde. This warranty shall survive and not merge on the completion of this transaction, and if the building is part of a multiple unit building, this warranty shall only apply to that part of the building which is the subject of this transaction.

24. **LEGAL, ACCOUNTING AND ENVIRONMENTAL ADVICE:** The parties acknowledge that any information provided by the brokerage is not legal, tax or environmental advice.

25. **CONSUMER REPORTS: The Buyer is hereby notified that a consumer report containing credit and/or personal information may be referred to in connection with this transaction.**

26. **AGREEMENT IN WRITING:** If there is conflict or discrepancy between any provision added to this Agreement (including any Schedule attached hereto) and any provision in the standard pre-set portion hereof, the added provision shall supersede the standard pre-set provision to the extent of such conflict or discrepancy. This Agreement including any Schedule attached hereto, shall constitute the entire Agreement between Buyer and Seller. There is no representation, warranty, collateral agreement or condition, which affects this Agreement other than as expressed herein. For the purposes of this Agreement, Seller means vendor and Buyer means purchaser. This Agreement shall be read with all changes of gender or number required by the context.

27. **TIME AND DATE:** Any reference to a time and date in this Agreement shall mean the time and date where the property is located.

INITIALS OF BUYER(S): (   )   INITIALS OF SELLER(S): (*JS SS*)

Form 100   Revised 2015   **Page 4 of 6**

Exercise 3   Agreement of Purchase and Sale—Page 5 of 6

28. SUCCESSORS AND ASSIGNS: The heirs, executors, administrators, successors and assigns of the undersigned are bound by the terms herein.

SIGNED, SEALED AND DELIVERED in the presence of: IN WITNESS whereof I have hereunto set my hand and seal:

Albert Lee ....   *J. Selznick* ....   ● DATE ...*May 21/xx*......
(Witness)   (Buyer)   (Seal)

....   *S. Selznick* ....   ● DATE ...*May 21/xx*......
(Witness)   (Buyer)   (Seal)

I, the Undersigned Seller, agree to the above offer. I hereby irrevocably instruct my lawyer to pay directly to the brokerage(s) with whom I have agreed to pay commission, the unpaid balance of the commission together with applicable Harmonized Sales Tax (and any other taxes as may hereafter be applicable), from the proceeds of the sale prior to any payment to the undersigned on completion, as advised by the brokerage(s) to my lawyer.

SIGNED, SEALED AND DELIVERED in the presence of: IN WITNESS whereof I have hereunto set my hand and seal:

....   ● DATE ....
(Witness)   (Seller)   (Seal)

....   ● DATE ....
(Witness)   (Seller)   (Seal)

SPOUSAL CONSENT: The Undersigned Spouse of the Seller hereby consents to the disposition evidenced herein pursuant to the provisions of the Family Law Act, R.S.O.1990, and hereby agrees with the Buyer that he/she will execute all necessary or incidental documents to give full force and effect to the sale evidenced herein.

....   ● DATE ....
(Witness)   (Spouse)   (Seal)

CONFIRMATION OF ACCEPTANCE: Notwithstanding anything contained herein to the contrary, I confirm this Agreement with all changes both typed and written was finally accepted by all parties at .... a.m./p.m. this .... day of.. , 20..........

....
(Signature of Seller or Buyer)

INFORMATION ON BROKERAGE(S)

Listing Brokerage .... Tel.No.(................)...

....
(Salesperson / Broker Name)

Co-op/Buyer Brokerage .... Tel.No.(................)...

....
(Salesperson / Broker Name)

ACKNOWLEDGEMENT	
I acknowledge receipt of my signed copy of this accepted Agreement of Purchase and Sale and I authorize the Brokerage to forward a copy to my lawyer.	I acknowledge receipt of my signed copy of this accepted Agreement of Purchase and Sale and I authorize the Brokerage to forward a copy to my lawyer.
.... DATE .... (Seller)	.... DATE .... (Buyer)
.... DATE .... (Seller)	.... DATE .... (Buyer)
Address for Service	Address for Service ....
.... Tel.No.(...........).................	.... Tel.No.(...........).................
Seller's Lawyer	Buyer's Lawyer ....
Address	Address ....
Email	Email ....
(...........).................... (...........)................. Tel.No. FAX No.	(...........).................... (...........)................. Tel.No. FAX No.

FOR OFFICE USE ONLY   **COMMISSION TRUST AGREEMENT**

To: Co-operating Brokerage shown on the foregoing Agreement of Purchase and Sale:
In consideration for the Co-operating Brokerage procuring the foregoing Agreement of Purchase and Sale, I hereby declare that all moneys received or receivable by me in connection with the Transaction as contemplated in the MLS® Rules and Regulations of my Real Estate Board shall be receivable and held in trust. This agreement shall constitute a Commission Trust Agreement as defined in the MLS® Rules and shall be subject to and governed by the MLS® Rules pertaining to Commission Trust.
DATED as of the date and time of the acceptance of the foregoing Agreement of Purchase and Sale.   Acknowledged by:

....
(Authorized to bind the Listing Brokerage)   (Authorized to bind the Co-operating Brokerage)

Form 100   Revised 2015   **Page 5 of 6**

Schedule A
Agreement of Purchase and Sale

Form 100
for use in the Province of Ontario

This Schedule is attached to and forms part of the Agreement of Purchase and Sale between:

BUYER, ... James and Stella Selznick ...., and

SELLER, ... Arthur T. Osland and Jenny B. Osland ....

for the purchase and sale of .... 3216 Bayside Drive, City of Anycity ....

.... dated the ..21st.. day of .... May ...., 20.XX......

Buyer agrees to pay the balance as follows:

The Buyer agrees to pay a further sum of Two Hundred and Twenty-Seven Thousand Dollars ($227,000.00), to the Seller on completion of this transaction, with funds drawn on a lawyer's trust account in the form of a bank draft, certified cheque, or wire transfer using the Large Value Transfer System.

The Offer is conditional upon the inspection of the subject property by a home inspector and the obtaining of a report satisfactory to the Buyer in the Buyer's sole and absolute discretion. Unless the Buyer gives notice in writing delivered to the Seller personally or in accordance with any other provisions for the delivery of notice in this Agreement of Purchase and Sale or any Schedule thereto not later than 6:00 p.m. on the 21st day of June, 20xx, that this condition is fulfilled, this Offer shall be null and void and the deposit shall be returned to the Buyer. The Seller agrees to co-operate in providing access to the property for the sole purpose of this inspection. This condition is included for the benefit of the Buyer and may be waived at the Buyer's sole option by notice in writing to the Seller as aforesaid within the time period stated herein.

In the event the foregoing condition is not fulfilled or waived by the Buyer, the Buyer agrees to provide the Seller with a true copy of the Inspection Report and all estimates related thereto prior to the return of the deposit herein.

The Seller represents and warrants that the gas barbecue and all accessories are now, and on the completion date shall be, in good working order. The Parties agree that this representation and warranty shall survive and not merge on completion of this transaction, but apply only to the state of the property existing at completion of this transaction.

This form must be initialed by all parties to the Agreement of Purchase and Sale.

INITIALS OF BUYER(S): ( )   **INITIALS OF SELLER(S):** (JS SS)

Form 100   Revised 2015   **Page 6 of 6**

■ Exercise 4 Critically Analyze Clauses

The following clauses were inserted in an offer dated January 5, 20xx. The Anycity market has been a seller's market for the past year. This offer was received three days after the property appeared on MLS®.

Based on your knowledge of clause drafting, critically comment on these clauses from the buyer's and seller's perspectives. For example, are their interests adequately protected, are any important phrases missing and what might be better worded? Be specific. Insert comments in the space provided.

Condition/Escape Clause

This offer is conditional on the sale of the buyer's property known as 238 Winchester Drive. Unless the buyer gives notice in writing to the seller personally or in accordance with any other provisions for the delivery of notice in this Agreement of Purchase and Sale or any Schedule thereto not later than 5 p.m. on the 30th day of May, 20xx that this condition is fulfilled, this offer shall be null and void and the deposit shall be returned to the buyer in full without deduction. This condition is included for the benefit of the buyer and may be waived at the buyer's sole option by notice in writing to the seller, within the time period stated herein.

Provided further that the seller may continue to offer the property for sale and, in the event the seller receives another offer satisfactory to the seller, the seller may so notify the buyer in writing by delivery to the buyer personally or in accordance with any other provisions for the delivery of notice in this Agreement of Purchase and Sale or any Schedule thereto. The buyer shall have 18 hours from the giving of such notice to waive this condition.

BUYER'S PERSPECTIVE	SELLER'S PERSPECTIVE

Represents and Warrants Clause

The seller represents and warrants that the hot tub is working satisfactorily, and that this representation and warranty shall survive and not merge on completion of this transaction.

BUYER'S PERSPECTIVE	SELLER'S PERSPECTIVE

Home Inspection Clause

The buyer agrees that the seller shall provide a home inspection report upon removal of the above-noted condition and furnish said report within 10 business days.

BUYER'S PERSPECTIVE	SELLER'S PERSPECTIVE

Re-Inspection Clause

The buyer shall have the right to re-inspect the property on reasonable notice.

BUYER'S PERSPECTIVE	SELLER'S PERSPECTIVE

▣ Exercise 5   Clause Order

Buyer Shaughnessy wants you to draft an offer conditional on arranging a new first mortgage (three-year term), along with a seller take back that will expire in four years. Number the following items in the order they would appear in the agreement of purchase and sale.

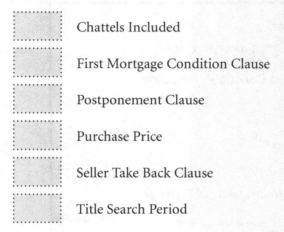

Chattels Included

First Mortgage Condition Clause

Postponement Clause

Purchase Price

Seller Take Back Clause

Title Search Period

▣ Exercise 6   Amending the Offer

The Fergusons (your seller clients), when reviewing the illustrated offer, express concern about the buyer's ability to pay the mortgage. Further, upon closer inspection, you are not satisfied with the prepayment and renewal provisions given their lack of precision. Amend Schedule A by adding, ruling out or amending clauses in the interests of your client. The Fergusons are willing to contemplate a renewal for a further three-year term.

OREA Ontario Real Estate Association   **Agreement of Purchase and Sale**

Form 100
for use in the Province of Ontario

This Agreement of Purchase and Sale dated this ...... 15th ...... day of .... April .... 20 .. XX ..

BUYER, ... Mary J. O'Hara and Christopher P. O'Hara ...., agrees to purchase from
(Full legal names of all Buyers)

SELLER, ... William C. Ferguson and Darlene P. Ferguson ...., the following
(Full legal names of all Sellers)

REAL PROPERTY:

Address .... 3281 River Parkway ....

fronting on the .... East .... side of .... River Parkway ....

in the .... City of Anycity, Regional Municipality of Anyregion ....

and having a frontage of .... 82.45 feet .... more or less by a depth of .... 165.55 feet .... more or less

and legally described as .... Lots 1 and 2, Registered Plan 535 ....

.... (the "property")
(Legal description of land including easements not described elsewhere)

PURCHASE PRICE: Dollars (CDN$) ...... $295,000.00 ......

Two Hundred and Ninety-Five Thousand-- Dollars

DEPOSIT: Buyer submits .... Upon Acceptance ....
(Herewith/Upon Acceptance/as otherwise described in this Agreement)

Twenty-Five Thousand-- Dollars (CDN$) ...... $25,000.00 ......

by negotiable cheque payable to .... ABC Realty Inc. .... "Deposit Holder" to be held
in trust pending completion or other termination of this Agreement and to be credited toward the Purchase Price on completion. For the purposes of this
Agreement, "Upon Acceptance" shall mean that the Buyer is required to deliver the deposit to the Deposit Holder within 24 hours of the acceptance of
this Agreement. The parties to this Agreement hereby acknowledge that, unless otherwise provided for in this Agreement, the Deposit Holder shall place
the deposit in trust in the Deposit Holder's non-interest bearing Real Estate Trust Account and no interest shall be earned, received or paid on the deposit.

Buyer agrees to pay the balance as more particularly set out in Schedule A attached.

SCHEDULE(S) A .... **attached hereto form(s) part of this Agreement.**

1. **IRREVOCABILITY:** This offer shall be irrevocable by .... Buyer .... until ...... 5:00 ...... a.m./p.m. on the ...... 16th ......
    (Seller/Buyer)

    day of .... April .... 20 .. XX .., after which time, if not accepted, this offer shall be null and void and the deposit
    shall be returned to the Buyer in full without interest.

2. **COMPLETION DATE:** This Agreement shall be completed by no later than 6:00 p.m. on the ...... 31st ...... day of .... May ......

    20 .. XX .... Upon completion, vacant possession of the property shall be given to the Buyer unless otherwise provided for in this Agreement.

INITIALS OF BUYER(S): (*MO CO*)   INITIALS OF SELLER(S): ( )

3. **NOTICES:** The Seller hereby appoints the Listing Brokerage as agent for the Seller for the purpose of giving and receiving notices pursuant to this Agreement. Where a Brokerage (Buyer's Brokerage) has entered into a representation agreement with the Buyer, the Buyer hereby appoints the Buyer's Brokerage as agent for the purpose of giving and receiving notices pursuant to this Agreement. **Where a Brokerage represents both the Seller and the Buyer (multiple representation), the Brokerage shall not be appointed or authorized to be agent for either the Buyer or the Seller for the purpose of giving and receiving notices.** Any notice relating hereto or provided for herein shall be in writing. In addition to any provision contained herein and in any Schedule hereto, this offer, any counter-offer, notice of acceptance thereof or any notice to be given or received pursuant to this Agreement or any Schedule hereto (any of them, "Document") shall be deemed given and received when delivered personally or hand delivered to the Address for Service provided in the Acknowledgement below, or where a facsimile number or email address is provided herein, when transmitted electronically to that facsimile number or email address, respectively, in which case, the signature(s) of the party (parties) shall be deemed to be original.

FAX No.: ....   FAX No.: ....
(For delivery of Documents to Seller)   (For delivery of Documents to Buyer)

Email Address: ....   Email Address: ....
(For delivery of Documents to Seller)   (For delivery of Documents to Buyer)

4. **CHATTELS INCLUDED:** None

....

....

....

....

Unless otherwise stated in this Agreement or any Schedule hereto, Seller agrees to convey all fixtures and chattels included in the Purchase Price free from all liens, encumbrances or claims affecting the said fixtures and chattels.

5. **FIXTURES EXCLUDED:** None

....

....

....

....

6. **RENTAL ITEMS (Including Lease, Lease to Own):** The following equipment is rented and **not** included in the Purchase Price. The Buyer agrees to assume the rental contract(s), if assumable:

Hot water tank, Union Energy, $36.50 quarterly (plus applicable taxes)

....

....

The Buyer agrees to co-operate and execute such documentation as may be required to facilitate such assumption.

7. **HST:** If the sale of the Property (Real Property as described above) is subject to Harmonized Sales Tax (HST), then such tax shall be

.... included in .... the Purchase Price. If the sale of the Property is not subject to HST, Seller agrees to certify on or before
(included in/in addition to)

closing, that the sale of the Property is not subject to HST. Any HST on chattels, if applicable, is not included in the Purchase Price.

INITIALS OF BUYER(S): (*MO CO*)   **INITIALS OF SELLER(S):** ( )

Form 100   Revised 2015   **Page 2 of 6**

8. **TITLE SEARCH:** Buyer shall be allowed until 6:00 p.m. on the ....10th.... day of ....May......................., 20 ..xx...., (Requisition Date) to examine the title to the Property at Buyer's own expense and until the earlier of: (i) thirty days from the later of the Requisition Date or the date on which the conditions in this Agreement are fulfilled or otherwise waived or; (ii) five days prior to completion, to satisfy Buyer that there are no outstanding

    work orders or deficiency notices affecting the Property, and that its present use (.............single family residential.............) may be lawfully continued and that the principal building may be insured against risk of fire. Seller hereby consents to the municipality or other governmental agencies releasing to Buyer details of all outstanding work orders and deficiency notices affecting the property, and Seller agrees to execute and deliver such further authorizations in this regard as Buyer may reasonably require.

9. **FUTURE USE:** Seller and Buyer agree that there is no representation or warranty of any kind that the future intended use of the property by Buyer is or will be lawful except as may be specifically provided for in this Agreement.

10. **TITLE:** Provided that the title to the property is good and free from all registered restrictions, charges, liens, and encumbrances except as otherwise specifically provided in this Agreement and save and except for (a) any registered restrictions or covenants that run with the land providing that such are complied with; (b) any registered municipal agreements and registered agreements with publicly regulated utilities providing such have been complied with, or security has been posted to ensure compliance and completion, as evidenced by a letter from the relevant municipality or regulated utility; (c) any minor easements for the supply of domestic utility or telephone services to the property or adjacent properties; and (d) any easements for drainage, storm or sanitary sewers, public utility lines, telephone lines, cable television lines or other services which do not materially affect the use of the property. If within the specified times referred to in paragraph 8 any valid objection to title or to any outstanding work order or deficiency notice, or to the fact the said present use may not lawfully be continued, or that the principal building may not be insured against risk of fire is made in writing to Seller and which Seller is unable or unwilling to remove, remedy or satisfy or obtain insurance save and except against risk of fire (Title Insurance) in favour of the Buyer and any mortgagee, (with all related costs at the expense of the Seller), and which Buyer will not waive, this Agreement notwithstanding any intermediate acts or negotiations in respect of such objections, shall be at an end and all monies paid shall be returned without interest or deduction and Seller, Listing Brokerage and Co-operating Brokerage shall not be liable for any costs or damages. Save as to any valid objection so made by such day and except for any objection going to the root of the title, Buyer shall be conclusively deemed to have accepted Seller's title to the property.

11. **CLOSING ARRANGEMENTS:** Where each of the Seller and Buyer retain a lawyer to complete the Agreement of Purchase and Sale of the property, and where the transaction will be completed by electronic registration pursuant to Part III of the Land Registration Reform Act, R.S.O. 1990, Chapter L4 and the Electronic Registration Act, S.O. 1991, Chapter 44, and any amendments thereto, the Seller and Buyer acknowledge and agree that the exchange of closing funds, non-registrable documents and other items (the "Requisite Deliveries") and the release thereof to the Seller and Buyer will (a) not occur at the same time as the registration of the transfer/deed (and any other documents intended to be registered in connection with the completion of this transaction) and (b) be subject to conditions whereby the lawyer(s) receiving any of the Requisite Deliveries will be required to hold same in trust and not release same except in accordance with the terms of a document registration agreement between the said lawyers. The Seller and Buyer irrevocably instruct the said lawyers to be bound by the document registration agreement which is recommended from time to time by the Law Society of Upper Canada. Unless otherwise agreed to by the lawyers, such exchange of the Requisite Deliveries will occur in the applicable Land Titles Office or such other location agreeable to both lawyers.

12. **DOCUMENTS AND DISCHARGE:** Buyer shall not call for the production of any title deed, abstract, survey or other evidence of title to the property except such as are in the possession or control of Seller. If requested by Buyer, Seller will deliver any sketch or survey of the property within Seller's control to Buyer as soon as possible and prior to the Requisition Date. If a discharge of any Charge/Mortgage held by a corporation incorporated pursuant to the Trust And Loan Companies Act (Canada), Chartered Bank, Trust Company, Credit Union, Caisse Populaire or Insurance Company and which is not to be assumed by Buyer on completion, is not available in registrable form on completion, Buyer agrees to accept Seller's lawyer's personal undertaking to obtain, out of the closing funds, a discharge in registrable form and to register same, or cause same to be registered, on title within a reasonable period of time after completion, provided that on or before completion Seller shall provide to Buyer a mortgage statement prepared by the mortgagee setting out the balance required to obtain the discharge, and, where a real-time electronic cleared funds transfer system is not being used, a direction executed by Seller directing payment to the mortgagee of the amount required to obtain the discharge out of the balance due on completion.

13. **INSPECTION:** Buyer acknowledges having had the opportunity to inspect the Property and understands that upon acceptance of this offer there shall be a binding agreement of purchase and sale between Buyer and Seller. **The Buyer acknowledges having the opportunity to include a requirement for a property inspection report in this Agreement and agrees that except as may be specifically provided for in this Agreement, the Buyer will not be obtaining a property inspection or property inspection report regarding the Property.**

14. **INSURANCE:** All buildings on the property and all other things being purchased shall be and remain until completion at the risk of Seller. Pending completion, Seller shall hold all insurance policies, if any, and the proceeds thereof in trust for the parties as their interests may appear and in the event of substantial damage, Buyer may either terminate this Agreement and have all monies paid returned without interest or deduction or else take the proceeds of any insurance and complete the purchase. No insurance shall be transferred on completion. If Seller is taking back a Charge/Mortgage, or Buyer is assuming a Charge/Mortgage, Buyer shall supply Seller with reasonable evidence of adequate insurance to protect Seller's or other mortgagee's interest on completion.

INITIALS OF BUYER(S): (MO CO)   **INITIALS OF SELLER(S):** (   )

Form 100   Revised 2015   **Page 3 of 6**

Exercise 6   Agreement of Purchase and Sale—Page 4 of 6

15. PLANNING ACT: This Agreement shall be effective to create an interest in the property only if Seller complies with the subdivision control provisions of the Planning Act by completion and Seller covenants to proceed diligently at Seller's expense to obtain any necessary consent by completion.

16. DOCUMENT PREPARATION: The Transfer/Deed shall, save for the Land Transfer Tax Affidavit, be prepared in registrable form at the expense of Seller, and any Charge/Mortgage to be given back by the Buyer to Seller at the expense of the Buyer. If requested by Buyer, Seller covenants that the Transfer/Deed to be delivered on completion shall contain the statements contemplated by Section 50(22) of the Planning Act, R.S.O.1990.

17. RESIDENCY: (a) Subject to (b) below, the Seller represents and warrants that the Seller is not and on completion will not be a non-resident under the non-residency provisions of the Income Tax Act which representation and warranty shall survive and not merge upon the completion of this transaction and the Seller shall deliver to the Buyer a statutory declaration that Seller is not then a non-resident of Canada; (b) provided that if the Seller is a non-resident under the non-residency provisions of the Income Tax Act, the Buyer shall be credited towards the Purchase Price with the amount, if any, necessary for Buyer to pay to the Minister of National Revenue to satisfy Buyer's liability in respect of tax payable by Seller under the non-residency provisions of the Income Tax Act by reason of this sale. Buyer shall not claim such credit if Seller delivers on completion the prescribed certificate.

18. ADJUSTMENTS: Any rents, mortgage interest, realty taxes including local improvement rates and unmetered public or private utility charges and unmetered cost of fuel, as applicable, shall be apportioned and allowed to the day of completion, the day of completion itself to be apportioned to Buyer.

19. PROPERTY ASSESSMENT: The Buyer and Seller hereby acknowledge that the Province of Ontario has implemented current value assessment and properties may be re-assessed on an annual basis. The Buyer and Seller agree that no claim will be made against the Buyer or Seller, or any Brokerage, Broker or Salesperson, for any changes in property tax as a result of a re-assessment of the property, save and except any property taxes that accrued prior to the completion of this transaction.

20. TIME LIMITS: Time shall in all respects be of the essence hereof provided that the time for doing or completing of any matter provided for herein may be extended or abridged by an agreement in writing signed by Seller and Buyer or by their respective lawyers who may be specifically authorized in that regard.

21. TENDER: Any tender of documents or money hereunder may be made upon Seller or Buyer or their respective lawyers on the day set for completion. Money shall be tendered with funds drawn on a lawyer's trust account in the form of a bank draft, certified cheque or wire transfer using the Large Value Transfer System.

22. FAMILY LAW ACT: Seller warrants that spousal consent is not necessary to this transaction under the provisions of the Family Law Act, R.S.O.1990 unless Seller's spouse has executed the consent hereinafter provided.

23. UFFI: Seller represents and warrants to Buyer that during the time Seller has owned the property, Seller has not caused any building on the property to be insulated with insulation containing ureaformaldehyde, and that to the best of Seller's knowledge no building on the property contains or has ever contained insulation that contains ureaformaldehyde. This warranty shall survive and not merge on the completion of this transaction, and if the building is part of a multiple unit building, this warranty shall only apply to that part of the building which is the subject of this transaction.

24. LEGAL, ACCOUNTING AND ENVIRONMENTAL ADVICE: The parties acknowledge that any information provided by the brokerage is not legal, tax or environmental advice.

25. CONSUMER REPORTS: The Buyer is hereby notified that a consumer report containing credit and/or personal information may be referred to in connection with this transaction.

26. AGREEMENT IN WRITING: If there is conflict or discrepancy between any provision added to this Agreement (including any Schedule attached hereto) and any provision in the standard pre-set portion hereof, the added provision shall supersede the standard pre-set provision to the extent of such conflict or discrepancy. This Agreement including any Schedule attached hereto, shall constitute the entire Agreement between Buyer and Seller. There is no representation, warranty, collateral agreement or condition, which affects this Agreement other than as expressed herein. For the purposes of this Agreement, Seller means vendor and Buyer means purchaser. This Agreement shall be read with all changes of gender or number required by the context.

27. TIME AND DATE: Any reference to a time and date in this Agreement shall mean the time and date where the property is located.

INITIALS OF BUYER(S): (*MO CO*)   INITIALS OF SELLER(S): (   )

28. SUCCESSORS AND ASSIGNS: The heirs, executors, administrators, successors and assigns of the undersigned are bound by the terms herein.

SIGNED, SEALED AND DELIVERED in the presence of: IN WITNESS whereof I have hereunto set my hand and seal:

Albert Lee ....   *Mary O'Hara* ....   ● ...   DATE ....*April 15/xx*....
(Witness)   (Buyer)   (Seal)

Albert Lee ....   *Chris O'Hara* ....   ● ...   DATE ....*April 15/xx*....
(Witness)   (Buyer)   (Seal)

I, the Undersigned Seller, agree to the above offer. I hereby irrevocably instruct my lawyer to pay directly to the brokerage(s) with whom I have agreed to pay commission, the unpaid balance of the commission together with applicable Harmonized Sales Tax (and any other taxes as may hereafter be applicable), from the proceeds of the sale prior to any payment to the undersigned on completion, as advised by the brokerage(s) to my lawyer.

SIGNED, SEALED AND DELIVERED in the presence of: IN WITNESS whereof I have hereunto set my hand and seal:

....   ● ...   DATE ....
(Witness)   (Seller)   (Seal)

....   ● ...   DATE ....
(Witness)   (Seller)   (Seal)

SPOUSAL CONSENT: The Undersigned Spouse of the Seller hereby consents to the disposition evidenced herein pursuant to the provisions of the Family Law Act, R.S.O.1990, and hereby agrees with the Buyer that he/she will execute all necessary or incidental documents to give full force and effect to the sale evidenced herein.

....   ● ...   DATE ....
(Witness)   (Spouse)   (Seal)

CONFIRMATION OF ACCEPTANCE: Notwithstanding anything contained herein to the contrary, I confirm this Agreement with all changes both typed

and written was finally accepted by all parties at .... a.m./p.m. this .... day of..., 20..........

....
(Signature of Seller or Buyer)

INFORMATION ON BROKERAGE(S)

Listing Brokerage ....**ABC Realty Inc.**................   Tel.No.(..**416**..) **444-1212**

123 Main Street, Anycity M3X 3C1   **Albert Lee**
                                               (Salesperson / Broker Name)

Co-op/Buyer Brokerage ....   Tel.No.(.............)......................

....
(Salesperson / Broker Name)

ACKNOWLEDGEMENT

I acknowledge receipt of my signed copy of this accepted Agreement of Purchase and Sale and I authorize the Brokerage to forward a copy to my lawyer.	I acknowledge receipt of my signed copy of this accepted Agreement of Purchase and Sale and I authorize the Brokerage to forward a copy to my lawyer.
.... DATE .... (Seller)	.... DATE .... (Buyer)
.... DATE .... (Seller)	.... DATE .... (Buyer)
Address for Service	Address for Service ....
.... Tel.No.(..........)...........	.... Tel.No.(..........)...........
Seller's Lawyer	Buyer's Lawyer ....
Address	Address ....
Email	Email ....
(..........)........................... (..........)...........	(..........)........................... (..........)...........
Tel.No. FAX No.	Tel.No. FAX No.

FOR OFFICE USE ONLY	**COMMISSION TRUST AGREEMENT**

To: Co-operating Brokerage shown on the foregoing Agreement of Purchase and Sale:
In consideration for the Co-operating Brokerage procuring the foregoing Agreement of Purchase and Sale, I hereby declare that all moneys received or receivable by me in connection with the Transaction as contemplated in the MLS® Rules and Regulations of my Real Estate Board shall be receivable and held in trust. This agreement shall constitute a Commission Trust Agreement as defined in the MLS® Rules and shall be subject to and governed by the MLS® Rules pertaining to Commission Trust.
DATED as of the date and time of the acceptance of the foregoing Agreement of Purchase and Sale.   Acknowledged by:

....
(Authorized to bind the Listing Brokerage)   (Authorized to bind the Co-operating Brokerage)

Exercise 6   Agreement of Purchase and Sale—Page 6 of 6

 **OREA** Ontario Real Estate Association

Form 100
for use in the Province of Ontario

Schedule A
Agreement of Purchase and Sale

This Schedule is attached to and forms part of the Agreement of Purchase and Sale between:

BUYER, ... Mary J. O'Hara and Christopher P. O'Hara ...., and

SELLER, ... William C. Ferguson and Darlene P. Ferguson ....

for the purchase and sale of ..... 3281 River Parkway, City of Anycity, Regional Municipality of Anyregion ....

.... dated the ...15th... day of .... April ...., 20.. XX ....

Buyer agrees to pay the balance as follows:

The Buyer agrees to pay a further sum of Seventy Thousand Dollars ($70,000.00), subject to adjustments, to the Seller on completion of this transaction, with funds drawn on a lawyer's trust account in the form of a bank draft, certified cheque, or wire transfer using the Large Value Transfer System.

The Seller agrees to take back a first Charge/Mortgage in the amount of Two Hundred Thousand Dollars ($200,000.00), bearing interest at the rate of 5.00% per annum, calculated semi-annually not in advance, repayable in blended monthly payments of One Thousand One Hundred and Sixty-Three Dollars and Twenty-One Cents ($1,163.21), including both principal and interest, and to run for a term of three years from the date of completion of this transaction. This Charge/Mortgage shall contain a clause permitting the prepaying of any or all of the principal sum outstanding at any time or times without notice or bonus. Said Charge/Mortgage shall be renewable at the sole option of the Buyer on the same terms and conditions.

This form must be initialed by all parties to the Agreement of Purchase and Sale.

INITIALS OF BUYER(S): (*MO CO*)   INITIALS OF SELLER(S): ( )

Form 100   Revised 2015   **Page 6 of 6**

CHAPTER 10

Negotiating Agreements

Introduction

Offer presentations are never hit and miss affairs. Savvy registrants understand the importance of buyer and seller preparations, long before the offer appears. Use strategies that get the best results for clients. Nothing replaces advance preparation, follow through and positive negotiating tactics.

No two negotiations are ever the same. Unpredictable factors and different personalities come into play. A selling salesperson must successfully guide his or her client in drafting an effective offer, presenting the offer and negotiating the best deal. At the same time, he or she must build a solid paper trail. Negotiating successful deals is a complex matter. This chapter sets out the basics. Experience will refine these techniques.

Salespersons understandably concentrate on negotiations and securing signed agreements. However, sale-related forms are equally vital and an integral part of the overall negotiating process including after-sale service. While many transactions proceed smoothly from acceptance to closing, inevitable changes and challenges await others.

What must be done when the buyer can't arrange financing in the agreed conditional period? What if the seller reconsiders and wants to keep chattels currently included in the sale? What if the sale of the buyer's home is delayed or worse, cancelled?

While the objective is to always successfully guide the sale to a win-win conclusion, many factors can impact the outcome. Be prepared for inevitable fall throughs. Sale cancellations happen despite all the positive attitudes, conscientious efforts and persistence that you can muster.

Learning Outcomes

At the conclusion of this chapter, students will be able to:

- Describe basic real estate negotiating techniques and principles.
- Explain typical steps involved in presenting an offer, a counter offer and ultimate acceptance including ethical responsibilities.
- Complete appropriate portions of an accepted agreement of purchase and sale.
- Describe and analyze typical steps involved in competing offer presentations.
- Complete appropriate portions of a counter offer when amending the initial offer and detail steps in completing a counter offer form.
- Detail regulatory procedures and accepted guidelines for trade record sheet preparation.
- Analyze and complete selected sale-related documents such as amending an offer, removing conditions and waiving conditions.
- Analyze and complete selected forms to terminate a contract and release the parties regarding liabilities, obligations and claims.
- Briefly outline privacy considerations as they relate to processing sale-related documents.

DEVELOPING A NEGOTIATING STRATEGY

Most of our day-to-day experiences are shaped by negotiations. Often, the impact is relatively insignificant: What television program two people decide to watch or what paint to select for a remodelled room. But others, including real estate purchases and sales, can be life changing.

Negotiation Outcomes

Bookstore shelves are crammed with how to guides on achieving personal objectives. Negotiation is always a key element. Negotiations typically result in three possible outcomes:

Win-Win	Everyone's objectives are met in a positive manner. The seller obtains market value, the buyer receives the sought-after property.
Win-Lose (or Lose-Win)	The seller wins by successfully selling his home, at or close to asking price. The buyer, disregarding certain problems with the property, must make significant repairs after taking possession.
Lose-Lose	Both buyer and seller fail to achieve a meeting of the minds and everyone loses. The seller misses the opportunity to sell to the best buyer; the buyer fails to get the desired property.

Of course, as go the fortunes of the buyer and seller so go the salesperson's. A win-win leads to satisfied clients and a commission, a win-lose can result in disputes or litigation, a lose-lose benefits no one.

THE FOURTH OPTION: NO OUTCOME

Just as some things in life may be non-negotiable; e.g., personal convictions and religious beliefs, some negotiations become stalemated having no result. The seller decides not to sell and the buyer exits having second thoughts about the financial commitment. Don't confuse this with a lose-lose. It's just a no outcome. Both parties may re-negotiate at a later time or advance to other win-wins.

The challenge for new salespeople is readily identifying the no outcome. Motivated parties are key. Remember, negotiating power increases as motivation decreases. The buyer or seller who doesn't have to make a decision wields power. Why? He or she can walk away at any time.

QUESTION POWER

Buyers and sellers want to deal with people they like and trust. Build rapport through genuine interest and commitment. The more you know about the client, the better the relationship and the more productive the negotiations. Fill in the information gaps. Don't leave stones unturned.

Compliment your clients by taking the time to clearly understand their objectives, hopes and plans. A strong relationship will unfold, one that can stand the heat of negotiations and the test of time.

Solution Listening

Say less and listen more. Become a creative listener. The solution to roadblocks often lay hidden within the prospect's needs and wants. Be a solution maker. When in doubt—ask more questions. Get into the prospect's mind. What is a definite *no* versus a negotiable *maybe*? Listen closely to responses, as often the solution rests within the answer.

Other Than the Price

Selling price is focal to most negotiations, but other terms can be equally important. Don't let clients get sidetracked on price alone. Negotiating thrives on interlocking issues, not isolating a single circumstance. The few thousand dollars separating buyer and seller is just one piece of the puzzle.

- Is the seller justified in demanding those dollars?
- Has the buyer carefully weighed the benefits of the earlier closing date, better mortgage terms, extras in the home as compared to other properties viewed?

Often, the most relevant question to ask anyone reviewing an offer is:

Other than the price, do the other terms meet your needs?

Negotiations rarely hinge on a single item.

Today Business, Not Maybe Business	MARKET MEMO

For me, negotiations start long before the offer. Over the years, I've discovered the two **M's** when it comes to buyers: motivation and money. I'm direct with clients. I want to know what they want and how they're going to pay for it. I need to mentally connect with the prospect. How else can I do a professional job, meet their objective and find the right home? We need to think like a team. That way, when the negotiations begin, we're on the same page.

I invest a lot of time discussing wants, needs, housing alternatives, neighbourhoods and market trends. I provide a detailed package called *Buying Smart* to prepare them for inevitable negotiations. Building trust is the name of the game. But the M's are always lurking in the background. Sooner or later, I pop the big question.

If we found the perfect home for you today, are you in a position to buy it?

Sometimes, I phrase it differently. You know…a little more direct or a little less…but the underlying objective is always there: Can you buy today? It's amazing how these simple words bring out the M's. I've heard all the possibilities.

> - *Sure, but we have a house to sell.*
> - *Oh, we'd have to get our down payment together.*
> - *Oh no, we're just thinking about buying.*
> - *Yes, if it's a real deal! Otherwise, we're prepared to wait.*
> - *Absolutely. But we couldn't move immediately, we'd have to give notice to the landlord.*

See how easy it is! We're already getting on the same page. I'm setting the stage for productive, positive negotiations. For me, it's *today* business, not *maybe* business.

PREPARING FOR THE OFFER PRESENTATION

Preparation for an offer presentation cannot be a hit and miss affair. The following guidelines assume a relationship in which the listing brokerage and salespersons are representing the seller and the co-operating brokerage is representing the buyer. Descriptive text is limited to a typical residential transaction, but general guidelines apply equally to commercial presentations.

Initial Preparation

Once an offer has been signed by the buyers and is ready for presentation, the listing sales-person requires certain information to assist the seller in making an informed decision. Buyer representatives may also contemplate selected items discussed below in preparing for their role in the presentation process.

Review the Listing File	Any offer should be examined in light of the terms under which the sellers agreed to market the property. Circumstances may have changed since the property was originally listed.
Summarize Marketing Activity	Summarize information such as frequency of advertising, responses, number of showings, previous offers and open houses conducted. Relevant comments from buyers can be helpful.
Update CMA	Prepare or update the comparative market analysis showing recent sales or properties that remain unsold.
Review Buyer's Information	Information, if provided by the selling brokerage concerning the buyer, can provide important background details that will assist the seller in making a decision.
Prepare for Seller's Net	Advance preparation of financial information can assist the seller regarding approximate selling costs and net proceeds if the offer is accepted.

The Offer Preparation Checklist

In addition to price, any offer to purchase contains a variety of terms, each of which can have an impact on the seller's decision. The offer should also be reviewed in light of the seller's circumstances in contemplation of a broad range of questions that might arise during the presentation. The following is provided as a checklist only. Practical considerations will vary with specific negotiations.

1. THE DEPOSIT	2. CLOSING/COMPLETION DATE
• Is the deposit sufficient and, if by cheque, has its validity been verified in any way?	• Non-alignment of the buyer's completion date with that of the seller's can be a focal point of discussion. Be prepared.
• The larger the deposit, the greater the practical security for the seller.	• The question of interim financing can loom if the seller must complete his/her new purchase prior to closing of the currently-owned property now under negotiations.
• A substantial deposit adds credibility and integrity to the buyer's offer.	• In the opposite situation, the seller may be asked to vacate the premises prior to a new property being ready for occupancy. This will initiate questions concerning such items as interim accommodations, costs and furniture storage.
• A substantial deposit is a strong plus in any offer presentation.	
• A small deposit can show lack of commitment.	• Preparation to discuss associated costs can make the presentation more effective.

3. CHATTELS INCLUDED/FIXTURES EXCLUDED	4. FINANCING
• Often the buyer's offer does not exactly match the seller's plans regarding chattels and fixtures as indicated on the listing. Such discrepancies can detract from the offered price. • Excluded items may hold emotional value to the seller and as such are non-negotiable.	• If a mortgage is being taken back by the seller, then a seller take back (STB) presentation should be anticipated. Be prepared to fully discuss this option and assist the seller in making a decision. • In some instances, the seller contemplating an STB may require cash for a subsequent transaction. Consideration must be given to the possible sale of the mortgage, associated costs and procedures and final net to the seller. • Sometimes a seller is required to discharge an existing mortgage as part of the transaction. The salesperson should be aware of approximate discharge costs, be prepared to confirm exact costs with the lender and advise the client accordingly. • The salesperson may wish to develop alternate scenarios to show the seller what he/she would net from other hypothetical offers including different financing options.
5. PRICE	**6. OTHER ISSUES**
Sellers tend to look at the price on an offer and react emotionally to it without examining the other terms and how they impact the overall price. Obviously price is important, but other factors such as closing date, terms of financing and items included or excluded, can directly affect bottom line considerations for the seller.	Various other questions are often worthy of exploring prior to any presentation. • How does this offer compare with the salesperson's original advice provided to the sellers as to what they could expect? Is this a reasonable offer? • How does the offer compare to others that the seller has rejected? How much activity has there been since listing? • The salesperson should ask himself/herself: *If I were the seller, would I accept this offer?* • Is it, in all honesty, the best possible offer that can be obtained from this buyer? • Are there any other serious prospects who might be prepared to make a better offer? • What is likely to happen if the seller rejects or counters this offer?

Making the Appointment

Since every offer sets a time limit for acceptance and the offer may no longer be accepted upon the expiration of that set time, the buyer who executes such an offer has a right to expect that the real estate salesperson involved will present it at the earliest possible time. Time is of the essence and it is obviously in the salesperson's own interests to present the offer for acceptance as promptly as possible and to expediently communicate acceptance, if given, back to the buyer.

The listing salesperson may have the broker of record, the manager or another salesperson in the listing brokerage make the appointment. The salesperson is not put in the awkward position of having to discuss the details of the offer over the telephone. Most real estate board jurisdictions have precise rules regarding registering an offer and the presentation process involving listing and selling brokerages.

The presentation should take place when sufficient time is available to deal with the offer in a relaxed atmosphere and where all of the parties who are involved in the decision-making process can be present. When the offer is presented to the seller, the salesperson should provide explanations of fundamental terms. Failure to make these explanations might be considered negligence that could result in a lawsuit, the loss of the real estate commission or both.

Right to Legal Advice

Sellers and buyers must be protected from accepting terms in an offer that they are not able to perform or terms over which they have no control. A lawyer is in the best position to advise a seller whether he/she can freely accept an offer and is in a position to fulfill terms stipulated in the offer.

Such legal counsel should be independent representation. Several points concerning legal advice follow.

- The seller and buyer have an absolute right to independent legal advice and salespersons must in no way attempt to deprive them of such advice.
- In certain instances, in fact, the salesperson should insist that the client obtain legal advice; e.g., complex transactions involving environmental issues.
- A salesperson should not hesitate to advise the seller of a concern about a condition or other matter that is not completely understood and should suggest that the seller consult his/her solicitor.
- The seller has the right to full disclosure of any and all information known by the seller's representative that could affect the decision regarding offer acceptance.
- Based on the Code of Ethics, while a salesperson may act in an advisory capacity to the extent of his/her abilities and suggest alternatives, he or she should advise the client or customer to obtain services from an appropriate expert.

SERVICES FROM OTHERS   `CODE`

8.   (1)   A registrant shall advise a client or customer to obtain services from another person if the registrant is not able to provide the services with reasonable knowledge, skill, judgment and competence or is not authorized by law to provide the services. O. Reg. 580/05, s. 8 (1).

     (2)   A registrant shall not discourage a client or customer from seeking a particular kind of service if the registrant is not able to provide the service with reasonable knowledge, skill, judgment and competence or is not authorized by law to provide the service. O. Reg. 580/05, s. 8 (2).

Upon occasion, inexperienced salespersons have difficulty dealing with a request by the seller or buyer to see a lawyer. Usually, concerns are more imagined than real:

- Agree with the wisdom of seeking legal counsel at the outset of the transaction.
- Ask to be present to answer any questions that might concern their solicitor. Offer to drive the individual to the solicitor's office or fax a copy of the agreement with a follow-up telephone call.
- During the conversation or direct meeting, do not attempt to argue points of law. Remember that the individual is the solicitor's client and the solicitor has a duty to advise the client as to whether or not the offer properly sets out his/her intentions.
- Provide input as appropriate. When it comes to matters within the salesperson's expertise, such as price negotiations and financing, the knowledgeable salesperson should have no trouble in assisting both solicitor and buyer or seller.

In short, salespersons who have confidence in their own knowledge, ability and integrity and who are prepared for such a meeting or telephone conversation will welcome a lawyer's scrutiny without concern. However, do make both the lawyer and the client aware of practical limitations and time concerns.

Debating Best Offer Strategies — MARKET MEMO

How will you advise clients when drafting an offer? Should they submit the best offer or hold back dollars hoping for give and take with the seller. No magic answer exists, but here's a few factors to consider:

- If you inform the seller that the offer is your client's best offer...then it should be! However, even though they say it is—it may not be! After all, if the right house is slipping away, who knows how the buyer will respond. The only thing at stake when making such statements is your credibility.

- A variation found in strong buyer markets is the *my only offer* tactic when sellers are anxiously awaiting willing buyers in a slow market. This take it or leave it attitude is a powerful negotiating tool. But remember, the individual having the least motivation has the most negotiating power. Conversely, the seller may be insulted by the offer and elect not to consider it further. Re-establishing negotiations after a rejection can be challenging.

- The best offer first strategy is also associated with strong seller markets where demand for housing is high. Going in strong is almost a given, as it may be the only opportunity to catch the seller's attention amidst competing offers. But prepare the buyer. His or her best may not be good enough.

- As a word of caution, you can advise but do not make the decision for your client. Buyers and sellers must decide on the price that they should offer or accept.

The bottom line: no single strategy works all the time. Remember the basics. Understand your prospects, prepare them properly for negotiations and seek a positive conclusion for all concerned.

OFFER PRESENTATION AND ACCEPTANCE

Offer presentations are often a challenge for new salespeople. Make certain that local methods and policies are fully understood. Be particularly cautious with multiple offer presentations. In some areas, well-established presentation procedures have evolved. For those joining organized real estate, real estate board rules and regulations apply. Further, brokerages establish guidelines and policies. Fully investigate such matters.

Representing the Client

The client's interests must always be promoted. The client may make the final decision regarding offer acceptance or rejection, but the sales representative's duty is to make him or her aware of relevant facts and assist in rendering an informed, rational decision.

Many negotiations fail due to inadequate or poor preparation. In particular, knowledge is vital. Sales representatives who consistently find themselves saying *I don't know* during offer presentations in response to legitimate questions are simply not doing the job.

Working with Other Salespersons

The typical real estate negotiation involves opposing interests. The listing salesperson advances the seller's interest and negotiating stance. The selling salesperson drafts an agreement to advance the buyer's position and, as such, may conflict with the seller's best interests. The selling salesperson usually brings the buyer's offer to the listing salesperson and the seller and the listing salesperson presents the offer. Ultimately any decision regarding its merit falls to the listing salesperson and his/her client.

While fiduciary duties are owed to clients, all discussions and negotiations between listing and selling salespersons must be dealt with fairly, honestly and with integrity. Salespeople must also respect the client relationship that exists with other salespersons and communicate information to that person through the other salesperson.

DEALINGS WITH OTHER REGISTRANTS   CODE

7.   (1)   A registrant who knows or ought to know that a person is a client of another registrant shall communicate information to the person for the purpose of a trade in real estate only through the other registrant, unless the other registrant has consented in writing. O. Reg. 580/05, s. 7 (1).

     (2)   If a broker or salesperson knows or ought to know that a buyer or seller is a party to an agreement in connection with a trade in real estate with a brokerage other than the brokerage that employs the broker or salesperson, the broker or salesperson shall not induce the buyer or seller to break the agreement. O. Reg. 580/05, s. 7 (2).

ATTENDING THE PRESENTATION

The relationship between a client and the brokerage is uppermost and must be respected at all times. Discussions often centre on who should be in attendance at the offer presentation. The co-operating brokerage wants to be present when the offer is presented to the listing brokerage's client in order to advance the buyer client's interests. Conversely, the listing brokerage and seller client have the right for private discussions concerning the offer.

While local practices may differ somewhat, a rule from a typical MLS® Rules and Regulations highlights one approach:

> The co-operating brokerage shall have the right to be present when the offer is presented by the listing brokerage to the seller and the listing brokerage shall have the right to be present when any counter-offer is presented by the co-operating brokerage to the buyer. However, this does not mean that the [board] member may be present during subsequent discussions between the other [board] member and his or her client.

Keep in mind that this procedure is set out in a real estate board by-law and is not a legal requirement. Ultimately, the client decides what will or will not occur in the presentation process involving an agreement relating to his or her property.

Disclosures

Disclosure relating to the preparation of agreements has been detailed in previous chapters. Three key requirements are highlighted for emphasis and review purposes. Selected OREA forms were detailed in prior chapters to achieve these disclosure requirements including the *Working with a REALTOR®* form, the *Listing Agreement* or *Buyer Representation Agreement* and the *Confirmation of Co-operation and Representation*. Registrants are also reminded that brokerages may use different forms to meet these disclosure requirements.

INFORMATION BEFORE AGREEMENT	MULTIPLE REPRESENTATION	DISCLOSURE OF INTEREST
Registrants must provide certain information as soon as is practicably possible and before an agreement is entered into in respect to trading in real estate (e.g., seller or buyer representation agreement).	Registrants must disclose matters concerning multiple representation both when entering into an agreement in respect of trading in real estate and also prior to an offer to purchase being made.	Registrants must disclose matters concerning any personal interest in the acquisition or disposition of property or any direct or indirect financial benefit (i.e., a finder's fee).
`CODE` Sec. 10	`CODE` Sec. 10, 16 and 17 `GEN` Sec. 22	`CODE` Sec. 18

Offers to Purchase Real Estate

Given the requirements of REBBA 2002, only written offers to purchase real estate may be presented by a buyer's representative. A registrant cannot represent to anyone that an offer has been received unless it is in writing. A written offer must be signed to be valid.

OFFERS TO PURCHASE REAL ESTATE   `REBBA`

35.1 (1) No registrant shall,

    (a) while acting on behalf of a purchaser, present an offer to purchase real estate except if the offer is in writing;

    (b) represent to any person that a written offer to purchase real estate exists except if the offer is in writing. 2013, c. 13, Sched. 3, s. 1.

Conveying Offers

The Code of Ethics requires that offers be presented at the earliest practicable opportunity and also stipulates that another registrant must be available should the broker or salesperson be unable to attend the presentation.

CONVEYING OFFERS   `CODE`

24. (1) A registrant shall convey any written offer received by the registrant to the registrant's client at the earliest practicable opportunity. O. Reg. 580/05, s. 24 (1).

  (2) A broker or salesperson shall establish a method of ensuring that,

    (a) written offers are received by someone on behalf of the broker or salesperson, if the broker or salesperson is not available at the time an offer is submitted; and

    (b) written offers are conveyed to the client of the broker or salesperson at the earliest practicable opportunity, even if the broker or salesperson is not available at the time an offer is submitted. O. Reg. 580/05, s. 24 (2).

  (3) Without limiting the generality of subsections (1) and (2), those subsections apply regardless of the identity of the person making the offer, the contents of the offer or the nature of any arrangements for commission or other remuneration. O. Reg. 580/05, s. 24 (3).

  (4) Subsections (1) to (3) are subject to any written directions given by a client. O. Reg. 580/05, s. 24 (4).

  (5) Subsections (1) to (4) also apply, with necessary modifications, to,

    (a) written amendments to written offers and any other written document directly related to a written offer; and

    (b) written assignments of agreements that relate to interests in real estate, written waivers of conditions in agreements that relate to interests in real estate, and any other written document directly related to a written agreement that relates to an interest in real estate. O. Reg. 580/05, s. 24 (5).

  (6) Subsections (1) to (5) apply, with necessary modifications, if a brokerage and a customer have an agreement that provides for the brokerage to receive written offers. O. Reg. 580/05, s. 24 (6).

continued...

THE REAL ESTATE TRANSACTION—GENERAL

CONVEYING OFFERS (continued)   `CODE`

    (7)   Subsections (1) to (5) apply, with necessary modifications, to brokers and salespersons employed by a brokerage, if the brokerage and a customer have an agreement that provides for the brokerage to receive written offers. O. Reg. 580/05, s. 24 (7).

Presentation Order/Acceptance

Salesperson Lee of ABC Realty Inc. lists Mr. and Mrs. McGill's property and Salesperson Martin of XYZ Real Estate Ltd. prepares an offer for his clients, Mr. and Mrs. Reddick. Typical presentation steps are illustrated for general instructional purposes only. Circumstances and local procedures will vary.

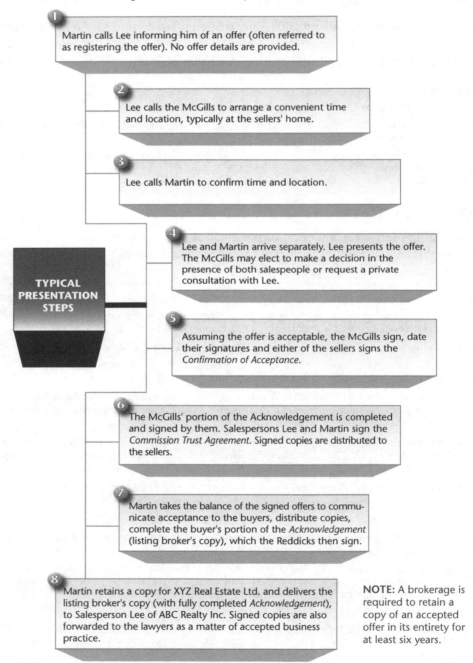

TYPICAL PRESENTATION STEPS

1. Martin calls Lee informing him of an offer (often referred to as registering the offer). No offer details are provided.

2. Lee calls the McGills to arrange a convenient time and location, typically at the sellers' home.

3. Lee calls Martin to confirm time and location.

4. Lee and Martin arrive separately. Lee presents the offer. The McGills may elect to make a decision in the presence of both salespeople or request a private consultation with Lee.

5. Assuming the offer is acceptable, the McGills sign, date their signatures and either of the sellers signs the *Confirmation of Acceptance*.

6. The McGills' portion of the Acknowledgement is completed and signed by them. Salespersons Lee and Martin sign the *Commission Trust Agreement*. Signed copies are distributed to the sellers.

7. Martin takes the balance of the signed offers to communicate acceptance to the buyers, distribute copies, complete the buyer's portion of the *Acknowledgement* (listing broker's copy), which the Reddicks then sign.

8. Martin retains a copy for XYZ Real Estate Ltd. and delivers the listing broker's copy (with fully completed *Acknowledgement*), to Salesperson Lee of ABC Realty Inc. Signed copies are also forwarded to the lawyers as a matter of accepted business practice.

NOTE: A brokerage is required to retain a copy of an accepted offer in its entirety for at least six years.

COMPETING OFFERS

A registrant must disclose the existence of other offers, without divulging the substance of such offers, to any person making an offer.

COMPETING OFFERS   CODE

26. (1) If a brokerage that has a seller as a client receives a competing written offer, the brokerage shall disclose the number of competing written offers to every person who is making one of the competing offers, but shall not disclose the substance of the competing offers. O. Reg. 580/05, s. 26 (1).

(2) Subsection (1) applies, with necessary modifications, to a brokerage that has a seller as a customer, if the brokerage and the seller have an agreement that provides for the brokerage to receive written offers to buy. O. Reg. 580/05, s. 26 (2).

Multiple offers present both an opportunity and a risk. The best approach is to openly and fully discuss options, benefits and drawbacks with the client. Also, fully discuss brokerage policies regarding multiple offers and the sequencing of offer presentations.

Notification/Presentation Order

Offers are typically presented in the order that they are received by the listing brokerage (i.e., notification by the co-operating brokerage or from within the listing brokerage). This is a matter of accepted custom, rather than a requirement. The seller client has the right to decide in which order the competing offers will be presented.

Formal notification (sometimes referred to as *registering an offer*) involves a written, signed offer. Registrants must always ensure that only written offers should be represented as such and that any promises of interest must be clearly distinguished from a written offer.

Negotiating Strategies

Three possible actions and consequences are highlighted, but other negotiating strategies are possible.

- If the seller accepts one offer, the remaining buyers may look for other properties. If the accepted offer is conditional and the condition is not met, a lost transaction may result.
- If the seller counters an offer in any manner, the buyer may wait until the last minute and decide not to accept that counter offer.
- If the seller rejects all offers and advises all buyers to reconsider their positions and bring their best offers at a specific time, some or all buyers may decide not to participate.

A Dangerous Option   CAUTION

If the seller contemplates countering several offers, a real risk exists that several buyers may accept at the same time resulting in competing contracts and litigation. This strategy should never be seriously considered.

Registrants may suggest other negotiating strategies, but caution is strongly advised. Advantages and disadvantages should be clearly set out for clients to make an informed decision. Market volatility often drives such creative endeavours.

Negotiations and Risk

Clients need full awareness of pitfalls regarding certain innovative marketing techniques that are attempted to take advantage of multiple offer situations. Sharp bids (i.e., willingness to pay a stated sum higher than any other offer presented) and other creative pricing clauses may be dangerous and should not be considered without independent legal advice. An unhappy client is a potentially litigious client.

At the same time, buyers can improve their negotiating position by impacting factors within their immediate control. Buyers may forego chattels, make a higher than usual deposit, provide a certified cheque with the offer, adjust the completion date or offer other concessions that would make their offer more appealing to the seller.

Buyers are often tempted to delete conditions in order to make their offers more competitive in a sellers' market. For example, they may want to delete a financing clause given that they have a pre-approval from a lending institution. A pre-approval is not typically a lending commitment and does not eliminate the need for a proper financing condition. Alternatively, buyers may remove a home inspection and assume the associated risk. Caution is strongly advised.

COMPETING OFFERS—DISCLOSURE

Sec. 26 of the Code of Ethics prohibits the disclosure of the substance of the competing offers, but other sections of the Code require that certain situations and circumstances must be disclosed.

Section 17—Disclosure of Multiple Representation

A registrant is required to disclose a dual representation situation in writing and at the earliest practical opportunity to all parties involved in a trade. Therefore, a seller representative that is also representing a buyer in a competing offer situation must disclose this relationship in writing to every person involved in the competing offer situation.

A seller representative must also disclose if a competing offer has been made by a buyer representative within their brokerage or if two buyer representatives from the same co-operating brokerage have submitted offers.

Sec. 25—Disclosure of Agreements Relating to Commission

A brokerage representing a seller is required to also disclose to all persons making an offer, any agreements relating to commission or other remuneration (such as rebates) that could create a financial incentive for the seller to accept a certain offer.

The Acceptance

If an offer from a buyer is acceptable, the seller will sign, date his or her signature and sign the Confirmation of Acceptance. The *Acknowledgement* is completed and signed and then the *Commission Trust Agreement* is filled out (assuming a co-operating brokerage). A copy of the agreement is provided to the seller immediately and the balance of the signed agreements are taken to the buyer. The buyer's portion of the Acknowledgement is then filled in and signed. A fully completed *Agreement of Purchase and Sale* (OREA Form 100) is illustrated.

Sample Fully Completed and Signed Agreement of Purchase and Sale—Page 1 of 6

OREA Ontario Real Estate Association

Agreement of Purchase and Sale

Form 100
for use in the Province of Ontario

This Agreement of Purchase and Sale dated this ..... **23rd** ..... day of ..... **January** ..... 20**XX** .....

BUYER, ... **James T. Reddick and Eleanor B. Reddick** ....., agrees to purchase from
(Full legal names of all Buyers)

SELLER, ... **Gordon K. McGill and Nancy C. McGill** ....., the following
(Full legal names of all Sellers)

REAL PROPERTY:

Address ..... **328 Prospect Point** .....

fronting on the ..... **North** ..... side of ..... **Prospect Point** .....

in the ..... **City of Anycity , Regional Municipality of Anyregion** .....

and having a frontage of ..... **58.50 feet** ..... more or less by a depth of ..... **110 feet** ..... more or less

and legally described as ..... **Lot 38, Registered Plan M-297** .....

..... (the "property")
(Legal description of land including easements not described elsewhere)

PURCHASE PRICE: Dollars (CDN$) ..... **$320,000.00** .....

..... **Three Hundred Twenty Thousand--** Dollars

DEPOSIT: Buyer submits ..... **Upon Acceptance** .....
(Herewith/Upon Acceptance/as otherwise described in this Agreement)

..... **Twenty-Five Thousand--** Dollars (CDN$) ..... **$25,000.00** .....

by negotiable cheque payable to ..... **ABC Realty Inc.** ..... "Deposit Holder" to be held in trust pending completion or other termination of this Agreement and to be credited toward the Purchase Price on completion. For the purposes of this Agreement, "Upon Acceptance" shall mean that the Buyer is required to deliver the deposit to the Deposit Holder within 24 hours of the acceptance of this Agreement. The parties to this Agreement hereby acknowledge that, unless otherwise provided for in this Agreement, the Deposit Holder shall place the deposit in trust in the Deposit Holder's non-interest bearing Real Estate Trust Account and no interest shall be earned, received or paid on the deposit.

Buyer agrees to pay the balance as more particularly set out in Schedule A attached.

SCHEDULE(S) A ..... **attached hereto form(s) part of this Agreement.**

1. **IRREVOCABILITY:** This offer shall be irrevocable by ..... **Buyer** ..... until **11:59** a.m./p.m. on the **24th**
(Seller/Buyer)

day of ..... **January** ..... 20 **XX** ..., after which time, if not accepted, this offer shall be null and void and the deposit shall be returned to the Buyer in full without interest.

2. **COMPLETION DATE:** This Agreement shall be completed by no later than 6:00 p.m. on the ..... **28th** day of ..... **February**

20 **XX** ..... Upon completion, vacant possession of the property shall be given to the Buyer unless otherwise provided for in this Agreement.

INITIALS OF BUYER(S): (JR ER)   **INITIALS OF SELLER(S):** (GM NM)

Form 100   Revised 2015   Page 1 of 6

3. NOTICES: The Seller hereby appoints the Listing Brokerage as agent for the Seller for the purpose of giving and receiving notices pursuant to this Agreement. Where a Brokerage (Buyer's Brokerage) has entered into a representation agreement with the Buyer, the Buyer hereby appoints the Buyer's Brokerage as agent for the purpose of giving and receiving notices pursuant to this Agreement. **Where a Brokerage represents both the Seller and the Buyer (multiple representation), the Brokerage shall not be appointed or authorized to be agent for either the Buyer or the Seller for the purpose of giving and receiving notices.** Any notice relating hereto or provided for herein shall be in writing. In addition to any provision contained herein and in any Schedule hereto, this offer, any counter-offer, notice of acceptance thereof or any notice to be given or received pursuant to this Agreement or any Schedule hereto (any of them, "Document") shall be deemed given and received when delivered personally or hand delivered to the Address for Service provided in the Acknowledgement below, or where a facsimile number or email address is provided herein, when transmitted electronically to that facsimile number or email address, respectively, in which case, the signature(s) of the party (parties) shall be deemed to be original.

FAX No.: .... 416-555-1215 ....   FAX No.: .... 416-444-1215 ....
                    (For delivery of Documents to Seller)   (For delivery of Documents to Buyer)

Email Address: .... admin@abcrealty.com ....   Email Address: .... notices@xyzrealestate.com ....
                    (For delivery of Documents to Seller)   (For delivery of Documents to Buyer)

4. CHATTELS INCLUDED: ... All existing draperies in living room, dining room, family room, and four upper bedrooms. ....

Unless otherwise stated in this Agreement or any Schedule hereto, Seller agrees to convey all fixtures and chattels included in the Purchase Price free from all liens, encumbrances or claims affecting the said fixtures and chattels.

5. FIXTURES EXCLUDED: ... None ....

6. RENTAL ITEMS (Including Lease, Lease to Own): The following equipment is rented and **not** included in the Purchase Price. The Buyer agrees to assume the rental contract(s), if assumable:

Hot water tank, $16.50 per month (plus applicable taxes)

The Buyer agrees to co-operate and execute such documentation as may be required to facilitate such assumption.

7. HST: If the sale of the Property (Real Property as described above) is subject to Harmonized Sales Tax (HST), then such tax shall be .... included in .... the Purchase Price. If the sale of the Property is not subject to HST, Seller agrees to certify on or before
            (included in/in addition to)
closing, that the sale of the Property is not subject to HST. Any HST on chattels, if applicable, is not included in the Purchase Price.

INITIALS OF BUYER(S): (JR ER)   INITIALS OF SELLER(S): (GM NM)

Form 100   Revised 2015   **Page 2 of 6**

Sample Fully Completed and Signed Agreement of Purchase and Sale—Page 3 of 6

8. **TITLE SEARCH:** Buyer shall be allowed until 6:00 p.m. on the ....20th.... day of ....February..................., 20..xx...., (Requisition Date) to examine the title to the Property at Buyer's own expense and until the earlier of: (i) thirty days from the later of the Requisition Date or the date on which the conditions in this Agreement are fulfilled or otherwise waived or; (ii) five days prior to completion, to satisfy Buyer that there are no outstanding

work orders or deficiency notices affecting the Property, and that its present use (..............single family residential...............) may be lawfully continued and that the principal building may be insured against risk of fire. Seller hereby consents to the municipality or other governmental agencies releasing to Buyer details of all outstanding work orders and deficiency notices affecting the property, and Seller agrees to execute and deliver such further authorizations in this regard as Buyer may reasonably require.

9. **FUTURE USE:** Seller and Buyer agree that there is no representation or warranty of any kind that the future intended use of the property by Buyer is or will be lawful except as may be specifically provided for in this Agreement.

10. **TITLE:** Provided that the title to the property is good and free from all registered restrictions, charges, liens, and encumbrances except as otherwise specifically provided in this Agreement and save and except for (a) any registered restrictions or covenants that run with the land providing that such are complied with; (b) any registered municipal agreements and registered agreements with publicly regulated utilities providing such have been complied with, or security has been posted to ensure compliance and completion, as evidenced by a letter from the relevant municipality or regulated utility; (c) any minor easements for the supply of domestic utility or telephone services to the property or adjacent properties; and (d) any easements for drainage, storm or sanitary sewers, public utility lines, telephone lines, cable television lines or other services which do not materially affect the use of the property. If within the specified times referred to in paragraph 8 any valid objection to title or to any outstanding work order or deficiency notice, or to the fact the said present use may not lawfully be continued, or that the principal building may not be insured against risk of fire is made in writing to Seller and which Seller is unable or unwilling to remove, remedy or satisfy or obtain insurance save and except against risk of fire (Title Insurance) in favour of the Buyer and any mortgagee, (with all related costs at the expense of the Seller), and which Buyer will not waive, this Agreement notwithstanding any intermediate acts or negotiations in respect of such objections, shall be at an end and all monies paid shall be returned without interest or deduction and Seller, Listing Brokerage and Co-operating Brokerage shall not be liable for any costs or damages. Save as to any valid objection so made by such day and except for any objection going to the root of the title, Buyer shall be conclusively deemed to have accepted Seller's title to the property.

11. **CLOSING ARRANGEMENTS:** Where each of the Seller and Buyer retain a lawyer to complete the Agreement of Purchase and Sale of the property, and where the transaction will be completed by electronic registration pursuant to Part III of the Land Registration Reform Act, R.S.O. 1990, Chapter L4 and the Electronic Registration Act, S.O. 1991, Chapter 44, and any amendments thereto, the Seller and Buyer acknowledge and agree that the exchange of closing funds, non-registrable documents and other items (the "Requisite Deliveries") and the release thereof to the Seller and Buyer will (a) not occur at the same time as the registration of the transfer/deed (and any other documents intended to be registered in connection with the completion of this transaction) and (b) be subject to conditions whereby the lawyer(s) receiving any of the Requisite Deliveries will be required to hold same in trust and not release same except in accordance with the terms of a document registration agreement between the said lawyers. The Seller and Buyer irrevocably instruct the said lawyers to be bound by the document registration agreement which is recommended from time to time by the Law Society of Upper Canada. Unless otherwise agreed to by the lawyers, such exchange of the Requisite Deliveries will occur in the applicable Land Titles Office or such other location agreeable to both lawyers.

12. **DOCUMENTS AND DISCHARGE:** Buyer shall not call for the production of any title deed, abstract, survey or other evidence of title to the property except such as are in the possession or control of Seller. If requested by Buyer, Seller will deliver any sketch or survey of the property within Seller's control to Buyer as soon as possible and prior to the Requisition Date. If a discharge of any Charge/Mortgage held by a corporation incorporated pursuant to the Trust And Loan Companies Act (Canada), Chartered Bank, Trust Company, Credit Union, Caisse Populaire or Insurance Company and which is not to be assumed by Buyer on completion, is not available in registrable form on completion, Buyer agrees to accept Seller's lawyer's personal undertaking to obtain, out of the closing funds, a discharge in registrable form and to register same, or cause same to be registered, on title within a reasonable period of time after completion, provided that on or before completion Seller shall provide to Buyer a mortgage statement prepared by the mortgagee setting out the balance required to obtain the discharge, and, where a real-time electronic cleared funds transfer system is not being used, a direction executed by Seller directing payment to the mortgagee of the amount required to obtain the discharge out of the balance due on completion.

13. **INSPECTION:** Buyer acknowledges having had the opportunity to inspect the Property and understands that upon acceptance of this offer there shall be a binding agreement of purchase and sale between Buyer and Seller. **The Buyer acknowledges having the opportunity to include a requirement for a property inspection report in this Agreement and agrees that except as may be specifically provided for in this Agreement, the Buyer will not be obtaining a property inspection or property inspection report regarding the Property.**

14. **INSURANCE:** All buildings on the property and all other things being purchased shall be and remain until completion at the risk of Seller. Pending completion, Seller shall hold all insurance policies, if any, and the proceeds thereof in trust for the parties as their interests may appear and in the event of substantial damage, Buyer may either terminate this Agreement and have all monies paid returned without interest or deduction or else take the proceeds of any insurance and complete the purchase. No insurance shall be transferred on completion. If Seller is taking back a Charge/Mortgage, or Buyer is assuming a Charge/Mortgage, Buyer shall supply Seller with reasonable evidence of adequate insurance to protect Seller's or other mortgagee's interest on completion.

INITIALS OF BUYER(S): JR ER   INITIALS OF SELLER(S): GM NM

Form 100   Revised 2015   **Page 3 of 6**

Sample Fully Completed and Signed Agreement of Purchase and Sale—Page 4 of 6

15. PLANNING ACT: This Agreement shall be effective to create an interest in the property only if Seller complies with the subdivision control provisions of the Planning Act by completion and Seller covenants to proceed diligently at Seller's expense to obtain any necessary consent by completion.

16. DOCUMENT PREPARATION: The Transfer/Deed shall, save for the Land Transfer Tax Affidavit, be prepared in registrable form at the expense of Seller, and any Charge/Mortgage to be given back by the Buyer to Seller at the expense of the Buyer. If requested by Buyer, Seller covenants that the Transfer/Deed to be delivered on completion shall contain the statements contemplated by Section 50(22) of the Planning Act, R.S.O.1990.

17. RESIDENCY: (a) Subject to (b) below, the Seller represents and warrants that the Seller is not and on completion will not be a non-resident under the non-residency provisions of the Income Tax Act which representation and warranty shall survive and not merge upon the completion of this transaction and the Seller shall deliver to the Buyer a statutory declaration that Seller is not then a non-resident of Canada; (b) provided that if the Seller is a non-resident under the non-residency provisions of the Income Tax Act, the Buyer shall be credited towards the Purchase Price with the amount, if any, necessary for Buyer to pay to the Minister of National Revenue to satisfy Buyer's liability in respect of tax payable by Seller under the non-residency provisions of the Income Tax Act by reason of this sale. Buyer shall not claim such credit if Seller delivers on completion the prescribed certificate.

18. ADJUSTMENTS: Any rents, mortgage interest, realty taxes including local improvement rates and unmetered public or private utility charges and unmetered cost of fuel, as applicable, shall be apportioned and allowed to the day of completion, the day of completion itself to be apportioned to Buyer.

19. PROPERTY ASSESSMENT: The Buyer and Seller hereby acknowledge that the Province of Ontario has implemented current value assessment and properties may be re-assessed on an annual basis. The Buyer and Seller agree that no claim will be made against the Buyer or Seller, or any Brokerage, Broker or Salesperson, for any changes in property tax as a result of a re-assessment of the property, save and except any property taxes that accrued prior to the completion of this transaction.

20. TIME LIMITS: Time shall in all respects be of the essence hereof provided that the time for doing or completing of any matter provided for herein may be extended or abridged by an agreement in writing signed by Seller and Buyer or by their respective lawyers who may be specifically authorized in that regard.

21. TENDER: Any tender of documents or money hereunder may be made upon Seller or Buyer or their respective lawyers on the day set for completion. Money shall be tendered with funds drawn on a lawyer's trust account in the form of a bank draft, certified cheque or wire transfer using the Large Value Transfer System.

22. FAMILY LAW ACT: Seller warrants that spousal consent is not necessary to this transaction under the provisions of the Family Law Act, R.S.O.1990 unless Seller's spouse has executed the consent hereinafter provided.

23. UFFI: Seller represents and warrants to Buyer that during the time Seller has owned the property, Seller has not caused any building on the property to be insulated with insulation containing ureaformaldehyde, and that to the best of Seller's knowledge no building on the property contains or has ever contained insulation that contains ureaformaldehyde. This warranty shall survive and not merge on the completion of this transaction, and if the building is part of a multiple unit building, this warranty shall only apply to that part of the building which is the subject of this transaction.

24. LEGAL, ACCOUNTING AND ENVIRONMENTAL ADVICE: The parties acknowledge that any information provided by the brokerage is not legal, tax or environmental advice.

25. CONSUMER REPORTS: The Buyer is hereby notified that a consumer report containing credit and/or personal information may be referred to in connection with this transaction.

26. AGREEMENT IN WRITING: If there is conflict or discrepancy between any provision added to this Agreement (including any Schedule attached hereto) and any provision in the standard pre-set portion hereof, the added provision shall supersede the standard pre-set provision to the extent of such conflict or discrepancy. This Agreement including any Schedule attached hereto, shall constitute the entire Agreement between Buyer and Seller. There is no representation, warranty, collateral agreement or condition, which affects this Agreement other than as expressed herein. For the purposes of this Agreement, Seller means vendor and Buyer means purchaser. This Agreement shall be read with all changes of gender or number required by the context.

27. TIME AND DATE: Any reference to a time and date in this Agreement shall mean the time and date where the property is located.

INITIALS OF BUYER(S): (JR ER)   INITIALS OF SELLER(S): (GM NM)

Sample Fully Completed and Signed Agreement of Purchase and Sale—Page 5 of 6

28. SUCCESSORS AND ASSIGNS: The heirs, executors, administrators, successors and assigns of the undersigned are bound by the terms herein.

SIGNED, SEALED AND DELIVERED in the presence of: IN WITNESS whereof I have hereunto set my hand and seal:

Allen Martin   James Reddick   ● DATE *Jan. 23/xx*
(Witness)   (Buyer)   (Seal)

Allen Martin   Eleanor Reddick   ● DATE *Jan. 23/xx*
(Witness)   (Buyer)   (Seal)

I, the Undersigned Seller, agree to the above offer. I hereby irrevocably instruct my lawyer to pay directly to the brokerage(s) with whom I have agreed to pay commission, the unpaid balance of the commission together with applicable Harmonized Sales Tax (and any other taxes as may hereafter be applicable), from the proceeds of the sale prior to any payment to the undersigned on completion, as advised by the brokerage(s) to my lawyer.

SIGNED, SEALED AND DELIVERED in the presence of:

James Lee   *Gordon McGill*   ● DATE *Jan. 24/xx*
(Witness)   (Seller)   (Seal)

James Lee   *Nancy McGill*   ● DATE *Jan. 24/xx*
(Witness)   (Seller)   (Seal)

SPOUSAL CONSENT: The Undersigned Spouse of the Seller hereby consents to the disposition evidenced herein pursuant to the provisions of the Family Law Act, R.S.O.1990, and hereby agrees with the Buyer that he/she will execute all necessary or incidental documents to give full force and effect to the sale evidenced herein.

(Witness)   (Spouse)   ● DATE
                                                          (Seal)

CONFIRMATION OF ACCEPTANCE: Notwithstanding anything contained herein to the contrary, I confirm this Agreement with all changes both typed and written was finally accepted by all parties at *9:30* a.m./p.m. this *24th* day of *January*, 20*XX*.

                                                          Gordon McGill
                                                          (Signature of Seller or Buyer)

INFORMATION ON BROKERAGE(S)

Listing Brokerage .... ABC Realty Inc. .... Tel.No.(416) 555-1212
328 Main Street, Anycity   James Lee
                                  (Salesperson / Broker Name)

Co-op/Buyer Brokerage ..... XYZ Real Estate Limited .... Tel.No.(416) 444-1212
28 Norfield Drive, Anycity   Allen Martin
                                  (Salesperson / Broker Name)

ACKNOWLEDGEMENT

I acknowledge receipt of my signed copy of this accepted Agreement of Purchase and Sale and I authorize the Brokerage to forward a copy to my lawyer.	I acknowledge receipt of my signed copy of this accepted Agreement of Purchase and Sale and I authorize the Brokerage to forward a copy to my lawyer.
Gordon McGill DATE *Jan. 24/xx* (Seller)	*Jamie Reddick* DATE *Jan. 24/xx* (Buyer)
Nancy McGill DATE *Jan. 24/xx* (Seller)	*Eleanor Reddick* DATE *Jan. 24/xx* (Buyer)
Address for Service *328 Prospect Point, Anycity*	Address for Service *Apt. 417, 3000 Weston Avenue, Anycity K0V 1Z2*
Tel.No.(416) 333-1212	Tel.No.(416) 666-1212
Seller's Lawyer *James McLennon*	Buyer's Lawyer *Wendy Kolalski*
Address *1275 Main Street, Anycity K07 1T3*	Address *Suite 301, Eastern Parkway, Anycity K0V 3C7*
Email	Email
(416) 222-1212 (416) 222-2121 Tel.No. FAX No.	(416) 777-1212 (416) 777-2121 Tel.No. FAX No.

FOR OFFICE USE ONLY   **COMMISSION TRUST AGREEMENT**

To: Co-operating Brokerage shown on the foregoing Agreement of Purchase and Sale:
In consideration for the Co-operating Brokerage procuring the foregoing Agreement of Purchase and Sale, I hereby declare that all moneys received or receivable by me in connection with the Transaction as contemplated in the MLS® Rules and Regulations of my Real Estate Board shall be receivable and held in trust. This agreement shall constitute a Commission Trust Agreement as defined in the MLS® Rules and shall be subject to and governed by the MLS® Rules pertaining to Commission Trust.
DATED as of the date and time of the acceptance of the foregoing Agreement of Purchase and Sale.   Acknowledged by:

James Lee   *Allen Martin*
(Authorized to bind the Listing Brokerage)   (Authorized to bind the Co-operating Brokerage)

Form 100   Revised 2015   **Page 5 of 6**

OREA Ontario Real Estate Association

Form 100
for use in the Province of Ontario

Schedule A
Agreement of Purchase and Sale

This Schedule is attached to and forms part of the Agreement of Purchase and Sale between:

BUYER, ... James T. Reddick and Eleanor B. Reddick ...., and

SELLER, ... Gordon K. McGill and Nancy C. McGill ....

for the purchase and sale of ...... 328 Prospect Point, City of Anycity, Regional Municipality of Anyregion ......

.... dated the ...23rd. day of .... January ...., 20. **xx** ......

Buyer agrees to pay the balance as follows:

The Buyer agrees to pay a further sum of Two Hundred and Ninety-Five Thousand Dollars ($295,000.00), subject to adjustments, to the Seller on completion of this transaction, with funds drawn on a lawyer's trust account in the form of a bank draft, certified cheque, or wire transfer using the Large Value Transfer System.

This Offer is conditional upon the inspection of the subject property by a home inspector at the Buyer's own expense, and the obtaining of a report satisfactory to the Buyer in the Buyer's sole and absolute discretion. Unless the Buyer gives notice in writing delivered to the Seller personally or in accordance with any other provisions for the delivery of notice in this Agreement of Purchase and Sale or any Schedule thereto not later than 11:59 p.m. on the 31st day of January, 20xx, that this condition is fulfilled, this Offer shall be null and void and the deposit shall be returned to the Buyer in full without deduction. The Seller agrees to co-operate in providing access to the property for the purpose of this inspection. This condition is included for the benefit of the Buyer and may be waived at the Buyer's sole option by notice in writing to the Seller as aforesaid within the time period stated herein.

This form must be initialed by all parties to the Agreement of Purchase and Sale.

INITIALS OF BUYER(S): JR ER

INITIALS OF SELLER(S): GM NM

Form 100   Revised 2015   **Page 6 of 6**

COUNTER OFFERS

Counter offers can be made by either party. Typically, the buyer offers and, if the original offer is not acceptable, the seller can make a counter offer with changes to unacceptable conditions or terms; e.g., price, possession date, financing or other terms. A counter offer is an offer to sell with the seller and buyer roles reversed. The seller is now the offeror. Three types of counter offer strategies are possible.

Amend Original Offer

Prior to making any changes to the buyer's offer, the seller's brokerage should ensure it has retained a copy of the unsuccessful offer as received from the buyer. If the buyer is a client or customer of a brokerage, then the seller's brokerage may retain an equivalent summary document instead of a copy of the offer. The original offer is countered by ruling out or changing appropriate sections and initialling at the rule-out point(s). The irrevocable clause is also changed to indicate that a counter offer is being made. The *Confirmation of Acceptance* and *Acknowledgement* sections are not completed until an accepted agreement is finalized. See the following page for steps relating to an amended offer presentation.

THE ACCEPTED COUNTER OFFER

Based on the McGill offer, discussed previously in this chapter, assume that the offer presented was not acceptable due to price, chattels included and closing date. The McGills counter on January 24th and the Reddicks accept late that same day. See the following page for amended offer presentation steps (steps 1 through 4 remain as per earlier discussion). An accepted, amended original offer is illustrated.

STEPS: AMENDED OFFER PRESENTATION

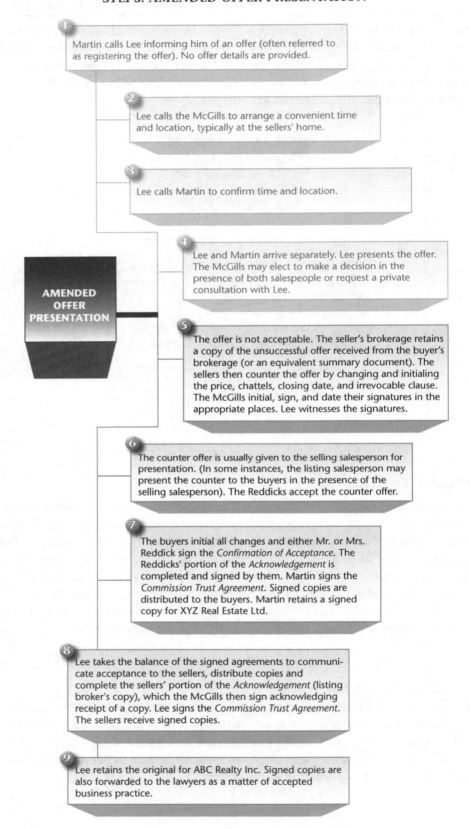

1 Martin calls Lee informing him of an offer (often referred to as registering the offer). No offer details are provided.

2 Lee calls the McGills to arrange a convenient time and location, typically at the sellers' home.

3 Lee calls Martin to confirm time and location.

4 Lee and Martin arrive separately. Lee presents the offer. The McGills may elect to make a decision in the presence of both salespeople or request a private consultation with Lee.

AMENDED OFFER PRESENTATION

5 The offer is not acceptable. The seller's brokerage retains a copy of the unsuccessful offer received from the buyer's brokerage (or an equivalent summary document). The sellers then counter the offer by changing and initialing the price, chattels, closing date, and irrevocable clause. The McGills initial, sign, and date their signatures in the appropriate places. Lee witnesses the signatures.

6 The counter offer is usually given to the selling salesperson for presentation. (In some instances, the listing salesperson may present the counter to the buyers in the presence of the selling salesperson). The Reddicks accept the counter offer.

7 The buyers initial all changes and either Mr. or Mrs. Reddick sign the *Confirmation of Acceptance.* The Reddicks' portion of the *Acknowledgement* is completed and signed by them. Martin signs the *Commission Trust Agreement.* Signed copies are distributed to the buyers. Martin retains a signed copy for XYZ Real Estate Ltd.

8 Lee takes the balance of the signed agreements to communicate acceptance to the sellers, distribute copies and complete the sellers' portion of the *Acknowledgement* (listing broker's copy), which the McGills then sign acknowledging receipt of a copy. Lee signs the *Commission Trust Agreement.* The sellers receive signed copies.

9 Lee retains the original for ABC Realty Inc. Signed copies are also forwarded to the lawyers as a matter of accepted business practice.

NOTE: A brokerage is required to retain a copy of an accepted offer in its entirety for at least six years.

Sample Amended Agreement of Purchase and Sale—Page 1 of 6

OREA Ontario Real Estate Association   **Agreement of Purchase and Sale**

Form 100
for use in the Province of Ontario

This Agreement of Purchase and Sale dated this ......**23rd**...... day of ....**January**........................ 20 **XX**......

BUYER, ...**James T. Reddick and Eleanor B. Reddick**........................, agrees to purchase from
(Full legal names of all Buyers)

SELLER, ...**Gordon K. McGill and Nancy C. McGill**........................, the following
(Full legal names of all Sellers)

REAL PROPERTY:

Address ....**328 Prospect Point**........................

fronting on the ....**North**........................ side of ....**Prospect Point**........................

in the ....**City of Anycity , Regional Municipality of Anyregion**........................

and having a frontage of ....**58.50 feet**........................ more or less by a depth of ....**110 feet**........................ more or less

and legally described as ....**Lot 38, Registered Plan M-297**........................

.... (the "property")
(Legal description of land including easements not described elsewhere)

JRER **$330,000.00** *GM NM*

PURCHASE PRICE: *JRER GM NM*   Dollars (CDN$) ...... ~~$320,000.00~~

Three Hundred and Thirty Thousand
~~Three Hundred and Twenty Thousand~~-- Dollars

DEPOSIT: Buyer submits ....**Upon Acceptance**........................
(Herewith/Upon Acceptance/as otherwise described in this Agreement)

......**Twenty-Five Thousand**-- Dollars (CDN$) **$25,000.00**

by negotiable cheque payable to ....**ABC Realty Inc.**........................ "Deposit Holder" to be held in trust pending completion or other termination of this Agreement and to be credited toward the Purchase Price on completion. For the purposes of this Agreement, "Upon Acceptance" shall mean that the Buyer is required to deliver the deposit to the Deposit Holder within 24 hours of the acceptance of this Agreement. The parties to this Agreement hereby acknowledge that, unless otherwise provided for in this Agreement, the Deposit Holder shall place the deposit in trust in the Deposit Holder's non-interest bearing Real Estate Trust Account and no interest shall be earned, received or paid on the deposit.

Buyer agrees to pay the balance as more particularly set out in Schedule A attached.

SCHEDULE(S) A........................**attached hereto form(s) part of this Agreement.**

JRER **Seller** *GM NM*

1. **IRREVOCABILITY:** This offer shall be irrevocable by .... **Buyer** .... until **11:59** ~~a.m.~~/p.m. on the **24th**
(Seller/Buyer)

day of ....**January**........................ 20 **XX**..., after which time, if not accepted, this offer shall be null and void and the deposit shall be returned to the Buyer in full without interest.

JRER **31st** *GM NM*   *JRER* **March** *GM NM*

2. **COMPLETION DATE:** This Agreement shall be completed by no later than 6:00 p.m. on the ......~~28th~~...... day of ....~~February~~........................

20 **XX**........ Upon completion, vacant possession of the property shall be given to the Buyer unless otherwise provided for in this Agreement.

INITIALS OF BUYER(S): (*JRER*)   **INITIALS OF SELLER(S):** (*GM NM*)

Form 100   Revised 2015   **Page 1 of 6**

3. **NOTICES:** The Seller hereby appoints the Listing Brokerage as agent for the Seller for the purpose of giving and receiving notices pursuant to this Agreement. Where a Brokerage (Buyer's Brokerage) has entered into a representation agreement with the Buyer, the Buyer hereby appoints the Buyer's Brokerage as agent for the purpose of giving and receiving notices pursuant to this Agreement. **Where a Brokerage represents both the Seller and the Buyer (multiple representation), the Brokerage shall not be appointed or authorized to be agent for either the Buyer or the Seller for the purpose of giving and receiving notices.** Any notice relating hereto or provided for herein shall be in writing. In addition to any provision contained herein and in any Schedule hereto, this offer, any counter-offer, notice of acceptance thereof or any notice to be given or received pursuant to this Agreement or any Schedule hereto (any of them, "Document") shall be deemed given and received when delivered personally or hand delivered to the Address for Service provided in the Acknowledgement below, or where a facsimile number or email address is provided herein, when transmitted electronically to that facsimile number or email address, respectively, in which case, the signature(s) of the party (parties) shall be deemed to be original.

FAX No.: ...... 416-555-1215 ......
(For delivery of Documents to Seller)

FAX No.: ...... 416-444-1215 ......
(For delivery of Documents to Buyer)

Email Address: ...... admin@abcrealty.com ......
(For delivery of Documents to Seller)

Email Address: ...... notices@xyzrealestate.com ......
(For delivery of Documents to Buyer)

JR ER   GM NM

4. **CHATTELS INCLUDED:** ~~All existing draperies in living room, dining room, family room, and four upper bedrooms.~~

Unless otherwise stated in this Agreement or any Schedule hereto, Seller agrees to convey all fixtures and chattels included in the Purchase Price free from all liens, encumbrances or claims affecting the said fixtures and chattels.

5. **FIXTURES EXCLUDED:** None

6. **RENTAL ITEMS (Including Lease, Lease to Own):** The following equipment is rented and **not** included in the Purchase Price. The Buyer agrees to assume the rental contract(s), if assumable:

Hot water tank, $16.50 per month (plus applicable taxes)

The Buyer agrees to co-operate and execute such documentation as may be required to facilitate such assumption.

7. **HST:** If the sale of the Property (Real Property as described above) is subject to Harmonized Sales Tax (HST), then such tax shall be ...... included in ...... the Purchase Price. If the sale of the Property is not subject to HST, Seller agrees to certify on or before
(included in/in addition to)
closing, that the sale of the Property is not subject to HST. Any HST on chattels, if applicable, is not included in the Purchase Price.

INITIALS OF BUYER(S): (*JR ER*)   INITIALS OF SELLER(S): (*GM NM*)

Form 100   Revised 2015   **Page 2 of 6**

Sample Amended Agreement of Purchase and Sale—Page 3 of 6

8. **TITLE SEARCH:** Buyer shall be allowed until 6:00 p.m. on the ...20th... day of ....February......................., 20..XX..., (Requisition Date) to examine the title to the Property at Buyer's own expense and until the earlier of: (i) thirty days from the later of the Requisition Date or the date on which the conditions in this Agreement are fulfilled or otherwise waived or; (ii) five days prior to completion, to satisfy Buyer that there are no outstanding

   work orders or deficiency notices affecting the Property, and that its present use (..................single family residential..............) may be lawfully continued and that the principal building may be insured against risk of fire. Seller hereby consents to the municipality or other governmental agencies releasing to Buyer details of all outstanding work orders and deficiency notices affecting the property, and Seller agrees to execute and deliver such further authorizations in this regard as Buyer may reasonably require.

9. **FUTURE USE:** Seller and Buyer agree that there is no representation or warranty of any kind that the future intended use of the property by Buyer is or will be lawful except as may be specifically provided for in this Agreement.

10. **TITLE:** Provided that the title to the property is good and free from all registered restrictions, charges, liens, and encumbrances except as otherwise specifically provided in this Agreement and save and except for (a) any registered restrictions or covenants that run with the land providing that such are complied with; (b) any registered municipal agreements and registered agreements with publicly regulated utilities providing such have been complied with, or security has been posted to ensure compliance and completion, as evidenced by a letter from the relevant municipality or regulated utility; (c) any minor easements for the supply of domestic utility or telephone services to the property or adjacent properties; and (d) any easements for drainage, storm or sanitary sewers, public utility lines, telephone lines, cable television lines or other services which do not materially affect the use of the property. If within the specified times referred to in paragraph 8 any valid objection to title or to any outstanding work order or deficiency notice, or to the fact the said present use may not lawfully be continued, or that the principal building may not be insured against risk of fire is made in writing to Seller and which Seller is unable or unwilling to remove, remedy or satisfy or obtain insurance save and except against risk of fire (Title Insurance) in favour of the Buyer and any mortgagee, (with all related costs at the expense of the Seller), and which Buyer will not waive, this Agreement notwithstanding any intermediate acts or negotiations in respect of such objections, shall be at an end and all monies paid shall be returned without interest or deduction and Seller, Listing Brokerage and Co-operating Brokerage shall not be liable for any costs or damages. Save as to any valid objection so made by such day and except for any objection going to the root of the title, Buyer shall be conclusively deemed to have accepted Seller's title to the property.

11. **CLOSING ARRANGEMENTS:** Where each of the Seller and Buyer retain a lawyer to complete the Agreement of Purchase and Sale of the property, and where the transaction will be completed by electronic registration pursuant to Part III of the Land Registration Reform Act, R.S.O. 1990, Chapter L4 and the Electronic Registration Act, S.O. 1991, Chapter 44, and any amendments thereto, the Seller and Buyer acknowledge and agree that the exchange of closing funds, non-registrable documents and other items (the "Requisite Deliveries") and the release thereof to the Seller and Buyer will (a) not occur at the same time as the registration of the transfer/deed (and any other documents intended to be registered in connection with the completion of this transaction) and (b) be subject to conditions whereby the lawyer(s) receiving any of the Requisite Deliveries will be required to hold same in trust and not release same except in accordance with the terms of a document registration agreement between the said lawyers. The Seller and Buyer irrevocably instruct the said lawyers to be bound by the document registration agreement which is recommended from time to time by the Law Society of Upper Canada. Unless otherwise agreed to by the lawyers, such exchange of the Requisite Deliveries will occur in the applicable Land Titles Office or such other location agreeable to both lawyers.

12. **DOCUMENTS AND DISCHARGE:** Buyer shall not call for the production of any title deed, abstract, survey or other evidence of title to the property except such as are in the possession or control of Seller. If requested by Buyer, Seller will deliver any sketch or survey of the property within Seller's control to Buyer as soon as possible and prior to the Requisition Date. If a discharge of any Charge/Mortgage held by a corporation incorporated pursuant to the Trust And Loan Companies Act (Canada), Chartered Bank, Trust Company, Credit Union, Caisse Populaire or Insurance Company and which is not to be assumed by Buyer on completion, is not available in registrable form on completion, Buyer agrees to accept Seller's lawyer's personal undertaking to obtain, out of the closing funds, a discharge in registrable form and to register same, or cause same to be registered, on title within a reasonable period of time after completion, provided that on or before completion Seller shall provide to Buyer a mortgage statement prepared by the mortgagee setting out the balance required to obtain the discharge, and, where a real-time electronic cleared funds transfer system is not being used, a direction executed by Seller directing payment to the mortgagee of the amount required to obtain the discharge out of the balance due on completion.

13. **INSPECTION:** Buyer acknowledges having had the opportunity to inspect the Property and understands that upon acceptance of this offer there shall be a binding agreement of purchase and sale between Buyer and Seller. **The Buyer acknowledges having the opportunity to include a requirement for a property inspection report in this Agreement and agrees that except as may be specifically provided for in this Agreement, the Buyer will not be obtaining a property inspection or property inspection report regarding the Property.**

14. **INSURANCE:** All buildings on the property and all other things being purchased shall be and remain until completion at the risk of Seller. Pending completion, Seller shall hold all insurance policies, if any, and the proceeds thereof in trust for the parties as their interests may appear and in the event of substantial damage, Buyer may either terminate this Agreement and have all monies paid returned without interest or deduction or else take the proceeds of any insurance and complete the purchase. No insurance shall be transferred on completion. If Seller is taking back a Charge/Mortgage, or Buyer is assuming a Charge/Mortgage, Buyer shall supply Seller with reasonable evidence of adequate insurance to protect Seller's or other mortgagee's interest on completion.

INITIALS OF BUYER(S): (JR ER)　　　　　INITIALS OF SELLER(S): (GM NM)

Form 100　Revised 2015　**Page 3 of 6**

15. PLANNING ACT: This Agreement shall be effective to create an interest in the property only if Seller complies with the subdivision control provisions of the Planning Act by completion and Seller covenants to proceed diligently at Seller's expense to obtain any necessary consent by completion.

16. DOCUMENT PREPARATION: The Transfer/Deed shall, save for the Land Transfer Tax Affidavit, be prepared in registrable form at the expense of Seller, and any Charge/Mortgage to be given back by the Buyer to Seller at the expense of the Buyer. If requested by Buyer, Seller covenants that the Transfer/Deed to be delivered on completion shall contain the statements contemplated by Section 50(22) of the Planning Act, R.S.O.1990.

17. RESIDENCY: (a) Subject to (b) below, the Seller represents and warrants that the Seller is not and on completion will not be a non-resident under the non-residency provisions of the Income Tax Act which representation and warranty shall survive and not merge upon the completion of this transaction and the Seller shall deliver to the Buyer a statutory declaration that Seller is not then a non-resident of Canada; (b) provided that if the Seller is a non-resident under the non-residency provisions of the Income Tax Act, the Buyer shall be credited towards the Purchase Price with the amount, if any, necessary for Buyer to pay to the Minister of National Revenue to satisfy Buyer's liability in respect of tax payable by Seller under the non-residency provisions of the Income Tax Act by reason of this sale. Buyer shall not claim such credit if Seller delivers on completion the prescribed certificate.

18. ADJUSTMENTS: Any rents, mortgage interest, realty taxes including local improvement rates and unmetered public or private utility charges and unmetered cost of fuel, as applicable, shall be apportioned and allowed to the day of completion, the day of completion itself to be apportioned to Buyer.

19. PROPERTY ASSESSMENT: The Buyer and Seller hereby acknowledge that the Province of Ontario has implemented current value assessment and properties may be re-assessed on an annual basis. The Buyer and Seller agree that no claim will be made against the Buyer or Seller, or any Brokerage, Broker or Salesperson, for any changes in property tax as a result of a re-assessment of the property, save and except any property taxes that accrued prior to the completion of this transaction.

20. TIME LIMITS: Time shall in all respects be of the essence hereof provided that the time for doing or completing of any matter provided for herein may be extended or abridged by an agreement in writing signed by Seller and Buyer or by their respective lawyers who may be specifically authorized in that regard.

21. TENDER: Any tender of documents or money hereunder may be made upon Seller or Buyer or their respective lawyers on the day set for completion. Money shall be tendered with funds drawn on a lawyer's trust account in the form of a bank draft, certified cheque or wire transfer using the Large Value Transfer System.

22. FAMILY LAW ACT: Seller warrants that spousal consent is not necessary to this transaction under the provisions of the Family Law Act, R.S.O.1990 unless Seller's spouse has executed the consent hereinafter provided.

23. UFFI: Seller represents and warrants to Buyer that during the time Seller has owned the property, Seller has not caused any building on the property to be insulated with insulation containing ureaformaldehyde, and that to the best of Seller's knowledge no building on the property contains or has ever contained insulation that contains ureaformaldehyde. This warranty shall survive and not merge on the completion of this transaction, and if the building is part of a multiple unit building, this warranty shall only apply to that part of the building which is the subject of this transaction.

24. LEGAL, ACCOUNTING AND ENVIRONMENTAL ADVICE: The parties acknowledge that any information provided by the brokerage is not legal, tax or environmental advice.

25. CONSUMER REPORTS: The Buyer is hereby notified that a consumer report containing credit and/or personal information may be referred to in connection with this transaction.

26. AGREEMENT IN WRITING: If there is conflict or discrepancy between any provision added to this Agreement (including any Schedule attached hereto) and any provision in the standard pre-set portion hereof, the added provision shall supersede the standard pre-set provision to the extent of such conflict or discrepancy. This Agreement including any Schedule attached hereto, shall constitute the entire Agreement between Buyer and Seller. There is no representation, warranty, collateral agreement or condition, which affects this Agreement other than as expressed herein. For the purposes of this Agreement, Seller means vendor and Buyer means purchaser. This Agreement shall be read with all changes of gender or number required by the context.

27. TIME AND DATE: Any reference to a time and date in this Agreement shall mean the time and date where the property is located.

INITIALS OF BUYER(S): (*JR ER*)   INITIALS OF SELLER(S): (*GM NM*)

Form 100   Revised 2015   **Page 4 of 6**

Sample Amended Agreement of Purchase and Sale—Page 5 of 6

28. SUCCESSORS AND ASSIGNS: The heirs, executors, administrators, successors and assigns of the undersigned are bound by the terms herein.

SIGNED, SEALED AND DELIVERED in the presence of: IN WITNESS whereof I have hereunto set my hand and seal:

Allen Martin
(Witness)

Jamie Reddick   ● (Seal)   DATE *Jan. 23/xx*
(Buyer)

Allen Martin
(Witness)

Eleanor Reddick   ● (Seal)   DATE *Jan. 23/xx*
(Buyer)

I, the Undersigned Seller, agree to the above offer. I hereby irrevocably instruct my lawyer to pay directly to the brokerage(s) with whom I have agreed to pay commission, the unpaid balance of the commission together with applicable Harmonized Sales Tax (and any other taxes as may hereafter be applicable), from the proceeds of the sale prior to any payment to the undersigned on completion, as advised by the brokerage(s) to my lawyer.

SIGNED, SEALED AND DELIVERED in the presence of: IN WITNESS whereof I have hereunto set my hand and seal:

James Lee
(Witness)

Gordon McGill   ● (Seal)   DATE *Jan. 24/xx*
(Seller)

James Lee
(Witness)

Nancy McGill   ● (Seal)   DATE *Jan. 24/xx*
(Seller)

SPOUSAL CONSENT: The Undersigned Spouse of the Seller hereby consents to the disposition evidenced herein pursuant to the provisions of the Family Law Act, R.S.O.1990, and hereby agrees with the Buyer that he/she will execute all necessary or incidental documents to give full force and effect to the sale evidenced herein.

(Witness)   (Spouse)   ● (Seal)   DATE

CONFIRMATION OF ACCEPTANCE: Notwithstanding anything contained herein to the contrary, I confirm this Agreement with all changes both typed and written was finally accepted by all parties at 9:30 ~~a.m.~~/p.m. this 24th day of .... Janaury ...., 20 **XX**

Jamie Reddick
(Signature of Seller or Buyer)

INFORMATION ON BROKERAGE(S)

Listing Brokerage .... **ABC Realty Inc.**   Tel.No.(416) 555-1212
 328 Main Street, Anycity   **James Lee**
                                     (Salesperson / Broker Name)

Co-op/Buyer Brokerage .... **XYZ Real Estate Limited**   Tel.No.(416) 444-1212
 28 Norfield Drive, Anycity   **Allen Martin**
                                     (Salesperson / Broker Name)

ACKNOWLEDGEMENT

I acknowledge receipt of my signed copy of this accepted Agreement of Purchase and Sale and I authorize the Brokerage to forward a copy to my lawyer.	I acknowledge receipt of my signed copy of this accepted Agreement of Purchase and Sale and I authorize the Brokerage to forward a copy to my lawyer.
Gordon McGill DATE *Jan. 24/xx* (Seller)	*Jamie Reddick* DATE *Jan. 24/xx* (Buyer)
Nancy McGill DATE *Jan. 24/xx* (Seller)	*Eleanor Reddick* DATE *Jan. 24/xx* (Buyer)
Address for Service **328 Prospect Point, Anycity**	Address for Service *Apt. 417, 3000 Weston Avenue, Anycity*
Tel.No.(416) 333-1212	*K0V 1Z2* Tel.No.(416) 666-1212
Seller's Lawyer **James McLennon**	Buyer's Lawyer *Wendy Kolalski*
Address **1275 Main Street, Anycity K07 1T3**	Address *Suite 301, Eastern Parkway, Anycity K0V 3C7*
Email	Email
(416) 222-1212 (416) 222-2121 Tel.No. FAX No.	(416) 777-1212 (416) 777-2121 Tel.No. FAX No.

FOR OFFICE USE ONLY   **COMMISSION TRUST AGREEMENT**

To: Co-operating Brokerage shown on the foregoing Agreement of Purchase and Sale:
In consideration for the Co-operating Brokerage procuring the foregoing Agreement of Purchase and Sale, I hereby declare that all moneys received or receivable by me in connection with the Transaction as contemplated in the MLS® Rules and Regulations of my Real Estate Board shall be receivable and held in trust. This agreement shall constitute a Commission Trust Agreement as defined in the MLS® Rules and shall be subject to and governed by the MLS® Rules pertaining to Commission Trust.

DATED as of the date and time of the acceptance of the foregoing Agreement of Purchase and Sale.   Acknowledged by:

James Lee   *Allen Martin*
(Authorized to bind the Listing Brokerage)   (Authorized to bind the Co-operating Brokerage)

 **Ontario Real Estate Association**

Form 100
for use in the Province of Ontario

Schedule A
Agreement of Purchase and Sale

This Schedule is attached to and forms part of the Agreement of Purchase and Sale between:

BUYER, ... James T. Reddick and Eleanor B. Reddick ...., and

SELLER, ... Gordon K. McGill and Nancy C. McGill ....

for the purchase and sale of ...... 328 Prospect Point, City of Anycity, Regional Municipality of Anyregion ......

.... dated the ...... 23rd .. day of .... January .... , 20 .. XX ......

Buyer agrees to pay the balance as follows:

JR ER **Three Hundred and Five Thousand** *GM NM*

JR ER The Buyer agrees to pay a further sum of ~~Two Hundred and Ninety-Five Thousand~~ Dollars
GM NM **$305,000.00**
(~~$295,000.00~~ subject to adjustments, to the Seller on completion of this transaction, with funds
drawn on a lawyer's trust account in the form of a bank draft, certified cheque, or wire transfer
using the Large Value Transfer System.

This Offer is conditional upon the inspection of the subject property by a home inspector at the
Buyer's own expense, and the obtaining of a report satisfactory to the Buyer in the Buyer's sole
and absolute discretion. Unless the Buyer gives notice in writing delivered to the Seller personally
or in accordance with any other provisions for the delivery of notice in this Agreement of Purchase
and Sale or any Schedule thereto not later than 11:59 p.m. on the 31st day of January, 20xx, that
this condition is fulfilled, this Offer shall be null and void and the deposit shall be returned to the
Buyer in full without deduction. The Seller agrees to co-operate in providing access to the property
for the purpose of this inspection. This condition is included for the benefit of the Buyer and may
be waived at the Buyer's sole option by notice in writing to the Seller as aforesaid within the time
period stated herein.

This form must be initialed by all parties to the Agreement of Purchase and Sale.

INITIALS OF BUYER(S): *JR ER*   **INITIALS OF SELLER(S):** *GM NM*

 Form 100   Revised 2015   **Page 6 of 6**

Retaining Copies of Offers

Copies of each offer received by the seller's brokerage must be retained by that brokerage. If the buyer is a client or customer of a brokerage and the offer is not accepted, then that seller's brokerage may retain a summary document of the offer rather than a copy in its entirety.

An example of a summary document (OREA Form 801) is provided in the appendix for reference purposes only.

OFFERS TO PURCHASE REAL ESTATE   REBBA

35.1 (1) No registrant shall,

    (a) while acting on behalf of a purchaser, present an offer to purchase real estate except if the offer is in writing;

    (b) represent to any person that a written offer to purchase real estate exists except if the offer is in writing. 2013, c. 13, Sched. 3, s. 1.

Records

(2) A brokerage acting on behalf of a seller shall retain, for the period of time prescribed, copies of all written offers that it receives to purchase real estate or copies of all other prescribed documents related to those offers. 2013, c. 13, Sched. 3, s. 1.

Request for inquiry by registrar

(3) A person who has made a written offer to purchase real estate or a registrant acting on behalf of such a person may request that the registrar make an inquiry to determine the number of written offers that the brokerage acting for a seller has received to purchase the real estate. 2013, c. 13, Sched. 3, s. 1.

Inquiry

(4) On receiving a request under subsection (3), the registrar may make an inquiry of the brokerage and the brokerage shall,

    (a) respond within a reasonable period of time, or within the time that is prescribed; and

    (b) at the request o8f the registrar, provide the registrar with copies of the written offers or other documents that it is required to retain under subsection (2). 2013, c. 13, Sched. 3, s. 1.

Disclosure by registrar

(5) The registrar shall determine the number of written offers that the brokerage has received to purchase the real estate and shall disclose the number of the offers as soon as practicable, or within the period of time that is prescribed, to the person who requested the inquiry under subsection (3), but shall not disclose the substance of any of the offers or the identity of the person making any of the offers. 2013, c. 13, Sched. 3, s. 1.

Other action by registrar

(6) Nothing in this section limits the authority of the registrar to take any other action against a registrant that this Act authorizes the registrar to take. 2013, c. 13, Sched. 3, s. 1.

RECORDS — OFFERS TO PURCHASE   OTH

Retention of offers that are not accepted

19.1 (1) Despite section 18, for the purposes of subsection 35.1 (2) of the Act, this section applies when a brokerage acting on behalf of a seller received a written offer to purchase real estate for the purposes of presenting it to the seller, but the offer did not result in the purchase of the real estate. O. Reg. 307/14, s. 1.

(2) If the written offer was made by a person who was a client or customer of a registrant, then the brokerage acting on behalf of the seller shall keep, for at least one year after the date the brokerage received the written offer for the purposes of presenting it to the seller, either a copy of the written offer or a copy of a document that includes the following information:

    1. The name and signature of the person who made the offer to purchase the real estate.

    2. The name and contact information of the seller of the real estate.

continued...

RECORDS — OFFERS TO PURCHASE (continued)   OTH

3. The name of the brokerage and of the broker or salesperson who acted for the seller.

4. The name of the brokerage and of the broker or salesperson who acted for the person who made the offer.

5. The address, legal description or other identifier of the real estate on which the offer was made.

6. The date and time the offer was made.

7. The date and time the offer was received by the brokerage for the purposes of presenting it to the seller, and the means by which the offer was received, such as in person or by fax.

8. If the brokerage presented the offer to the seller, the date of presentation.

9. The date and time, if any, until which the offer was irrevocable. O. Reg. 307/14, s. 1.

(3) If the written offer was made by a person who was not a client or customer of a registrant, then the brokerage acting on behalf of the seller shall keep a copy of the written offer for at least one year after the date the brokerage received the written offer for the purposes of presenting it to the seller. O. Reg. 307/14, s. 1.

As at July 1, 2015, brokerages acting on behalf of sellers must meet new requirements for handling offers. Questions and answers related to written offers and the retention of unaccepted offers are provided on the pages that follow.

Q&As

Q1: I received three unsuccessful offers, along with one successful offer. Only two of the unsuccessful offers included summary documents. What should I do?

A: For the unsuccessful offer that did not include a summary document, you have to retain the offer. For the two unsuccessful offers that included the summary, you could choose to retain the offer or the summary document. The successful offer must always be retained in its entirety (Agreement of Purchase and Sale) for at least six years.

Q2: What about counter offers that amend the original offer?

A: Every written offer to a seller, including changes in the course of negotiating, is considered a separate offer. The brokerage must retain a record for every offer, including those made in any negotiations. So, if a buyer puts in an offer, and later makes two more offers in negotiations, the seller's brokerage will need to retain a record for all three of the offers. You could retain summary documents, or the offers in their entirety.

Q3: Can one summary document be used to cover all counter offers from one buyer?

A: The summary document could be designed to accommodate several offers. OREA expects to have a form available by July 1, 2015. Alternately, your brokerage may create a form for you to use.

Q4: What about offers that come directly from a buyer, and not through a brokerage?

A: The summary document can only be used when the buyer is making an offer through a brokerage. For offers coming from a buyer directly, you must retain the offer in its entirety. Keeping the full offer is necessary in case RECO needs to contact the buyer that made the offer, since the summary document does not contain contact information.

Q5: If RECO asks for documentation for the offers on a property, how much time will I have to provide it?

A: Generally RECO will expect to receive the documentation upon request, but no later than two weeks, unless otherwise directed.

Q6: How long will it take for RECO to determine the number of written offers that a brokerage received?

A: RECO will aim to determine the number of written offers as quickly as possible. Each situation is unique, so it is not possible to offer a typical timeline. The volume of requests we receive will also be a factor.

Q7: If a buyer or seller is delivering or receiving offers directly, or through a lawyer, do I still have to retain records for the offers?

A: Your brokerage has to retain the offers it receives on the seller's behalf. If the seller or some other party receives offers directly, you do not have to retain the offers.

Q8: How long do I have to retain the record of each offer?

A: For unsuccessful offers, you must retain either the offer in its entirety, or a suitable summary document, for at least one year from the day the offer is signed by the buyer. You must retain the successful offer in its entirety for six years.

Q9: Can I retain records for offers beyond one year?

A: You may retain records beyond the minimum one year. It is imperative that you ensure the confidentiality of those documents for as long as you retain them.

Q10: What happens to a failed offer presentation (no transaction occurs)?

A: All offers that a listing brokerage receives must be retained, whether the property in question was sold or not. If no transaction occurred, the brokerage may retain the summary document instead of the actual offer, if it was submitted through a brokerage.

Q11: What happens to collected paperwork/information when the transaction completes?

A: The offer that resulted in a successful transaction must be retained in its entirety for the required six years, a summary document cannot be used. The summary may be used only for unsuccessful offers.

Q12: When can I retain a summary document instead of a full offer?

A: The seller's brokerage may retain a summary document if:
- The seller's brokerage receives the offer on behalf of the seller;
- The offer is made through a brokerage on behalf of the buyer;
- The offer did not result in a transaction; and
- The summary contains all the required information.

Q13: What information must be included in the summary document?

A: The summary document must include:
- The name and signature of the buyer.
- The name and contact information of the seller.
- The name of the buyer's brokerage and their representative.
- The name of the seller's brokerage and their representative.
- The address, legal description or other identifier of the property.
- The date and time the offer was made.
- The date and time the offer was received by the brokerage, and how the offer was received, such as in person or by fax.
- The date of presentation, if the brokerage presented the offer to the seller.
- The date and time, if any, until which the offer was irrevocable.

Q14: Will RECO return the written offers that it obtains from the brokerage?

A: When RECO requests that a brokerage provide offers, it will identify whether the brokerage should provide originals or copies, and upon request return any original documents after the process is complete.

Q15: Does this only apply to competing offer situations?

A: No, the regulations apply to *all* offers received through a brokerage.

Q16: If I have a letter of intent from a buyer, can I indicate that I have received an offer?

A: If the letter is binding on the part of the buyer, you would then indicate that you have received an offer.

Q17: Does this apply to offers to lease?

A: No, the regulations only apply to offers to purchase real estate.

THE REAL ESTATE TRANSACTION—GENERAL

Q18: Can my brokerage start retaining records of offers any time, or do we have to wait for July 1?

A: You can begin retaining records at any time, but you must retain records as of July 1. However, RECO will only be able to determine the number of offers on a property for transactions that occurred as of July 1.

Prepare Counter Offer Form

A counter offer form can be used as an alternative to amending an original offer. A completed counter offer form is provided (*Counter Offer*, OREA Form 107) on the following page based on the Reddick agreement of purchase and sale not being acceptable. The Reddick agreement is illustrated earlier in this chapter.

In preparing the counter offer form, itemized changes are detailed in preparation for the seller's signature. The seller signs the counter offer form, NOT the original offer. The buyer, if the offer terms are acceptable, signs the counter offer form. The listing and selling salespersons sign the *Commission Trust Agreement* on the original agreement.
The buyers receive copies of both the agreement of purchase and sale and the counter offer. The acknowledgement is signed.

The selling salesperson retains one signed copy of the agreement and the counter offer for the co-operating brokerage's records and returns the balance of the copies to the listing salesperson. The listing salesperson delivers copies to the sellers and has the sellers sign the *Acknowledgement*. The sellers receive copies of the agreement and the counter offer. The agreement containing both acknowledgements is retained by the listing brokerage.

 # SALE-RELATED DOCUMENTS

Sale-related forms can be involved at various points from listing to final closing or mutual release in the case of cancellation. OREA forms are used for illustration purposes. Registrants may encounter offers in the marketplace.

- Brokerage policy may require a *Confirmation of Co-operation and Representation* in advance of offer presentation.
- A trade record sheet must be prepared for the transaction (formally referred to as a trade).
- Following the sale, amendments may be required and conditions fulfilled (or waived).
- If the sale falls through, appropriate forms must be used to terminate the contract.

Sample Counter Offer—Page 1 of 1

OREA Ontario Real Estate Association   **Counter Offer**

Form 107
for use in the Province of Ontario

Attached to and forming part of Offer to Purchase between between .... **James T. Reddick and Eleanor B. Reddick** ....
(Buyer)

and ...... **Gordon K. McGill and Nancy C. McGill** ...., for the property known as: ...... **328 Prospect Point, Anycity** .....
(Seller)

...... **Regional Municipality of Anyregion** ...... dated the .... **23rd** .... day of ...... **January** ......, 20**xx** ......
(Description of Property)

The Seller accepts the attached offer and all its terms and conditions subject to the following amendments, exceptions and/or additions:

Purchase price to be Three Hundred and Thirty Thousand Dollars ($330,000.00).

Buyer agrees to pay a further sum of Three Hundred and Five Thousand Dollars ($305,000.00), subject to adjustments.

Chattels included: None

The completion date is March 31, 20xx.

This Counter Offer shall be irrevocable by the Seller until the .... **24th** .... day of .... **January** ...., 20 **xx** ......
after which time, if not accepted by the Buyer and a copy delivered to the Seller or the Seller's agent, this counter offer shall be null and void and all deposit monies shall be returned to the Buyer, without interest. If this Counter Offer is accepted by the Buyer, the Seller agrees, in consideration for the brokerage's services in procuring said Offer, to pay the brokerage(s) on the date of completion the commission set out in the agreement to pay commission together with applicable HST (and any other taxes as may hereafter be applicable), which commission and taxes may be deducted from the deposit. The Seller hereby irrevocably instructs the Seller's solicitor to pay directly to the brokerage(s) with whom I have agreed to pay commission, the unpaid balance of the commission and such taxes from the proceeds of the sale prior to any payment to the undersigned on completion, as advised by the brokerage(s) to the solicitor.

SIGNED, SEALED AND DELIVERED in the presence of: IN WITNESS whereof I have hereunto set my hand and seal:

James Lee ....   *Gordon McGill* ....   ⬤ DATE *Jan. 24/xx* ......
(Witness)   (Seller)   (Seal)

James Lee ....   *Nancy McGill* ....   ⬤ DATE *Jan. 24/xx* ......
(Witness)   (Seller)   (Seal)

SPOUSAL CONSENT: The Undersigned Spouse of the Seller hereby consents to the disposition evidenced herein pursuant to the provisions of the Family Law Act, R.S.O.1990, and hereby agrees with the Buyer that he/she will execute all necessary or incidental documents to give full force and effect to the sale evidenced herein.

....   ⬤ DATE ....
(Witness)   (Spouse)   (Seal)

APPROVED FAX No. ....   APPROVED FAX No. ....
(For delivery of notices to Seller)   (For delivery of notices to Buyer)

The above Counter Offer of the Seller to my Offer dated........................ *January 23, 20xx* ....is hereby accepted

SIGNED, SEALED AND DELIVERED in the presence of: IN WITNESS whereof I have hereunto set my hand and seal:

Allen Martin ....   *Jamie Reddick* ....   ⬤ DATE *Jan. 24/xx* ......
(Witness)   (Buyer)   (Seal)

Allen Martin ....   *Eleanor Reddick* ....   ⬤ DATE *Jan. 24/xx* ......
(Witness)   (Buyer)   (Seal)

SELLER SIGNING THIS FORM SHOULD NOT SIGN THE ORIGINAL OFFER.

Common Sale-Related Forms

Confirmation of Co-operation and Representation (OREA Form 320)	See previous chapter for detailed discussion.
Trade Record Sheet (OREA Form 640)	Completed following accepted agreement. Sets out trade details, deposit particulars and commission splits.
Amendment to Agreement (OREA Form 120)	Deletes specific agreement wording(s) and adds amended wording(s). Signed by both parties.
Notice to Remove Condition (OREA Form 121)	Seller notice to buyer to remove condition(s); e.g., sale of buyer's property.
Waiver (OREA Form 123)	Buyer or seller waiver of condition.
Notice of Fulfillment of Condition (OREA Form 124)	Notice that condition has been fulfilled as written; e.g., a true condition precedent.
Termination of Agreement (OREA Form 125–126)	Written termination notice by one party to the other.
Mutual Release (OREA Form 122)	Formal release of obligations, covenants, etc.

Trade Record Sheet

Trade

Disposition or acquisition of or transaction in real estate by sale, purchase, agreement for purchase and sale, exchange, option, lease, rental or otherwise and any offer or attempt to list real estate for the purpose of such a disposition, acquisition or transaction, and any act, advertisement, conduct or negotiation, directly or indirectly, in furtherance of any disposition, acquisition, transaction, offer or attempt, and the verb trade has a corresponding meaning; (Source: *Real Estate and Business Brokers Act.*

The *Real Estate and Business Brokers Act, 2002* requires that a trade record sheet (TRS) be prepared for every **trade**. Trade records must be completed regardless of whether a deposit is received or not. Both listing and co-operating brokerages complete trade record sheets for a single trade.

The *Trade Record Sheet* (OREA Form 640) meets all statutory requirements. Brokerages may use expanded computer generated versions, provided that they contain statutorily required information. Trade record sheets are focal both for regulatory control and also as data sources for management summary reports and brokerage tracking systems, concerning everything from commission receivables to trust account status.

INITIAL PROCESSING

Completed trade record sheets are signed by salespersons along with the broker of record (or his/her designate). Practices vary concerning copies for salespersons. Some include all salespersons' splits on one trade record, while others print separate trade record sheets for each salesperson, as a matter of confidentiality.

Trades are numbered consecutively and are usually assigned automatically by brokerage software. Banking records (e.g., deposits) relating to the trade are cross-referenced to assigned trade numbers. Real estate commissions are subject to harmonized sales tax. Selected questions are included in the *Knowledge Integration* component of this chapter.

Sample Trade Record Sheet—Page 1 of 2

OREA Ontario Real Estate Association — **Trade Record Sheet**

Form 640
for use in the Province of Ontario

Sale No:	4291
MLS® No:	32874

.... **ABC Realty Inc.** ....
(Name of Brokerage)

Dated: ...... **February 10** ......, 20 **XX** ......

I, ... **Jennifer Lancaster** ...., have today sold (leased or rented, exchanged, optioned):
(Name of Broker/Salesperson)

Property .... **123 Main St., Anycity** ....

SELLER/LANDLORD:	BUYER/TENANT:
Alfred J. Romano and Betty C. Romano	John M. Robinson and Mary R. Preston
Address **123 Main St., Anycity K9C 4B2**	Address **16 Pine Court, Anycity K8B 4C3**
Tel **(519) 555-1212**	Tel **(519) 777-1212**
Fax	Fax
Lawyer **James Brooks**	Lawyer **Sylvia Marchand**
Brooks and Dunn	**Marchand & Jenkins**
19 Centre Street, Anycity M5E 6T9	**25 Main Street, Anycity M2T 3C4**
Tel **(519) 666-1212**	Tel **(519) 444-1212**
Fax **(516) 666-2121**	Fax **(516) 444-2121**

CO-OPERATING/LISTING BROKERAGE (If applicable): ☐ Listing Brokerage ☑ Co-operating Brokerage

XYZ Real Estate Limited

Address **2037 Eastern Drive, Anycity M5T 2Z3**

Tel **(519) 222-1212**   Fax **(519) 222-2121**

Co-op Brokerage HST Number **1128796977 RT**

REFERRAL BROKERAGE   Tel

Address   Fax

REFERRAL BROKERAGE   Tel

Address   Fax

Total Consideration For Transaction $ .... **$238,000** ....
(sale price, rent, exchange value, option price, fee (other))

Completion Date .... **June 30, 20xx**

Deposit $ .... **$20,000** .... ☐ cash ☑ cheque

If cheque, payable to .... **ABC Realty Inc.** ...., in trust.

Additional Deposit $ .... **N/A** .... ☐ cash ☐ cheque

If cheque, payable to ...., in trust.

Property Other Than Money Held In Trust ....

Total Commission $	14,280	**Total HST $**	1,856.40	**Total Receivable Comm $**	16,136.40

Jennifer Lancaster

(Broker/Salesperson)   (Broker/Salesperson)

Form 640   Revised 2015   **Page 1 of 2**

Property	123 Main Street, Anycity	Sale No.:	4291
Seller/Landlord	Alfred J. Romano and Betty C. Romano	MLS® No.:	32874
Buyer/Tenant	John M. Robinson and Mary R. Preston		

THE FOLLOWING TO BE COMPLETED BY THE BROKERAGE:

	COMMISSION	HST	TOTAL	DATE PAID	CHEQUE NO.
Total Receivable Commission:	$14,280.00	$1,856.40	$16,136.40		
Listing Brokerage: ABC Realty Inc.	$2,142.00	$278.46	$2,420.46	Jul 3/xx	00915
Listing #1 Jennifer Lancaster Salesperson/ Broker #2	$4,998.00	$649.74	$5,647.74	Jul 3/xx	00914
Co-op Brokerage: XYZ Real Estate Limited	$7,140.00	$928.20	$8,068.20	Jul 3/xx	00913
Selling #1 Salesperson/ Broker #2					
Referral Fee:					
Referral Fee:					
Real Estate Board:					
Other:					

Received deposit from (Salesperson/Broker) .... Jennifer Lancaster .... DATE Feb. 10/xx

Additional deposit from (Salesperson/Broker) .... N/A .... DATE

Deposited in Real Estate Trust Acc. (Amount) .... $20,000 .... DATE Feb. 10/xx

Additional deposit to Real Estate Trust Acc. (Amount) .... N/A .... DATE

Statement to Seller DATE .... May 14/xx

Interest bearing deposit transferred to .... N/A

Instrument # .... N/A .... DATE .... Cheque #

Interest bearing deposit returned

to Real Estate Trust Acc. (Amount) .... N/A .... DATE .... Cheque #

If applicable, Interest earned (Amount) .... N/A

If applicable, interest paid to ....

Cheque # ....

If applicable, SIN of interest recipient .... N/A

If applicable, Business # of Corporation ....

Remitted to Seller/Buyer (Amount) .... $3,863.60 .... DATE Jul. 3/xx .... Cheque # 02296

Transferred to Commission Trust (Amount) .... $16,136.40 .... DATE Jul. 3/xx .... Cheque # 02297

Transferred Commission to Gen. Acct. (Amount) .... $2,420.46 .... DATE Jul. 3/xx .... Cheque # 00915

Additional Necessary Information ....

To the best of my knowledge and belief the above information is correct.

DATED at .... Anycity .... Ontario, this .... 11th .... day of .... February ...., 20.. xx

.... R. A. Johnson
(Signature of Broker of Record)

FOR OFFICE USE ONLY   **COMMISSION TRUST AGREEMENT**

To: The Salesperson(s) shown on the foregoing Trade Record Sheet:

In consideration of the Salesperson(s) having successfully completed a trade in real estate on behalf of the Brokerage with respect to the property more particularly dened in the foregoing Trade Record Sheet, I hereby declare that all moneys received or receivable by me in connection with the transaction as contemplated in the Office Policy shall be receivable and held in trust. This agreement shall constitute a Commission Trust Agreement as defined in the Office Policy and shall be subject to and governed by the Office Policy pertaining to Commission Trust. DATED as of the date and time of the acceptance of the foregoing Trade Record Sheet.   Acknowledged by:

R. A. Johnson
(Signature of Broker of Record/Manager)

Jennifer Lancaster
(Signature of Broker/Salesperson)

Form 640   Revised 2015   **Page 2 of 2**

PENDING SALE FILING

A file is opened for every trade. All associated documents are filed with the agreement; e.g., trade record sheet, amendments and letters.

The brokerage typically attaches a trade checklist as a guide for deal processing, follow-up on conditions and closing procedures. Trades are placed in a pending sale file and re-filed once closed.

HANDLING THE DEPOSIT

Deposit details are recorded on the trade record sheet; i.e., the date funds are received from the salesperson, date deposited in the statutory trust account, arrangements made for an interest-bearing trust account (if applicable) and disbursement details at closing.

CLOSING PROCEDURE

The trade remains in the pending file until verification is received that the sale has closed. Administrative staff remove the trade file, update all brokerage records and issue/distribute cheques to the co-operating broker (if applicable) and salespersons within the brokerage. The completed file is then archived, usually in sequential trade number order.

What's a Transaction Report	CURIOSITY

Historically, salespeople completed a draft trade record sheet, which was processed, typed and returned for signature(s). Today, many brokerages have salespeople complete transaction reports detailing information required for the TRS as well as for internal tracking/accounting systems.

Staff transfer details into administrative software to generate the formal trade record sheet. The transaction report does NOT replace the trade record sheet.

Amendment to Agreement

> **OREA** Ontario Real Estate Association
> **Form 120**
> for use in the Province of Ontario
>
> **Amendment to Agreement of Purchase and Sale**
>
> **BETWEEN BUYER,** ....
>
> **AND SELLER,** ....
>
> **RE:** Agreement of Purchase and Sale between the Seller and Buyer, dated the .... day of ...., 20............,
>
> concerning the property known as...
>
> .... as more particularly described in the aforementioned Agreement.
>
> **The Buyer(s) and Seller(s) herein agree to the following Amendments to the aforementioned Agreement:**
>
> Delete:

DRAFTING GUIDELINES

- Fully cross-reference to agreement.
- Insert clause or words being deleted along with exact replacement clause (if applicable). Registrants should avoid abbreviated instructions (e.g., delete financing clause) which can cause confusion.
- Insert irrevocable date.

- Complete signatures as per agreement; i.e., if spousal consent is required on agreement, the same consent is required on the amendment.
- Fully complete the *Acknowledgement* for filing with the listing brokerage and a copy to the co-operating brokerage.
- Distribute signed copies to all parties and solicitors.

REMINDER   Exercise caution when discussing any amendment during a conditional period in an agreement. Actions of the parties and clause wordings may be interpreted by the courts as a re-opening of negotiations.

Notice to Remove Condition

OREA Ontario Real Estate Association   **Notice to Remove Condition(s)**

Form 121
for use in the Province of Ontario

BETWEEN:

BUYER:.., agrees to purchase from
AND
SELLER:..., the following

RE: Agreement of Purchase and Sale between the Buyer and Seller dated the .... day of...,

20................., concerning the property known as:...

as more particularly described in the aforementioned Agreement of Purchase and Sale.

In accordance with the terms and conditions of the above Agreement of Purchase and Sale, I/we hereby advise that I/we have received another offer to

DRAFTING GUIDELINES
- Fully cross-reference to agreement.
- Insert specific time limit to remove condition(s).
- Copies are distributed following buyer and seller signatures.
- Make certain both parties clearly understand what condition(s) are involved. Are all conditions being removed or only selected ones?

Waiver

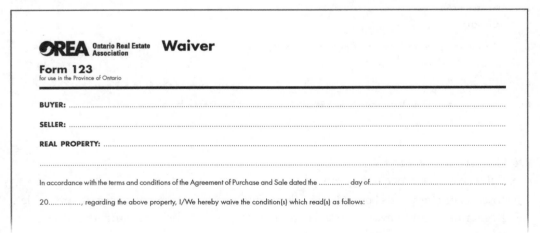

OREA Ontario Real Estate Association   **Waiver**

Form 123
for use in the Province of Ontario

BUYER: ....

SELLER: ....

REAL PROPERTY: ....

In accordance with the terms and conditions of the Agreement of Purchase and Sale dated the .... day of...

20..............., regarding the above property, I/We hereby waive the condition(s) which read(s) as follows:

DRAFTING GUIDELINES

- Fully cross-reference to agreement.
- Use only if waiver provision is included in agreement.
- Does not apply with a true condition precedent.
- Insert exact clause wording being waived.
- Receipt of acknowledgement for seller can be signed by listing brokerage, but co-operating brokerage can only sign for a buyer when representing that buyer. (See Clause 3 of the *Agreement of Purchase and Sale*.)

The Faulty Waiver | RESIDENTIAL CASE LAW

A salesperson drafted an agreement of purchase and sale containing two mortgage financing conditions. The offer was conditional on obtaining a first mortgage of $50,000 (to be placed on the buyer's existing home) and a first mortgage of $122,000 on the property being purchased.

The salesperson drafted the conditions in this manner to avoid the mortgage insurance fee payable on high ratio financing. The salesperson also arranged for the buyer to meet with a mortgage broker who did arrange for $172,000 in mortgage financing, but by way of a blanket mortgage over both properties. The salesperson failed to confirm the exact financing arrangements in relation to the offer conditions and advised the buyer to waive the conditions. Upon discovering that the mortgage did not meet the terms as set out in the agreement, the buyer refused to close the transaction.

The seller sued the buyer for damages arising from breach of the agreement. The buyer then included the real estate salesperson and the brokerage in the lawsuit, claiming misrepresentation. The Court found that the salesperson's actions constituted a negligent misrepresentation. The salesperson had failed to properly review financing prior to advising the client to remove the conditions. As a consequence, the buyer was liable to the seller for contract breach, but was entitled to indemnification from the real estate salesperson and the brokerage.

Reference   Nykor v. Cil, Superior Court of Justice, July 5, 2001. Court File 96-GD-38153

Notice of Fulfillment of Condition

OREA Ontario Real Estate Association   **Notice of Fulfillment of Condition(s)**

Form 124
for use in the Province of Ontario

BUYER:...

SELLER:...

REAL PROPERTY:...

....

In accordance with the terms and conditions of the Agreement of Purchase and Sale dated the .... day of.............................,

DRAFTING GUIDELINES

- Fully cross-reference to agreement.
- Can be used if condition is fulfilled as stated in the agreement; e.g., buyer is approved by lender based on terms outlined in the mortgage condition.
- May be used in lieu of waiver (subject to above-noted provision).

- Used with a true condition precedent in which neither party can waive the condition.
- Insert exact clause wording being fulfilled.
- Seller acknowledgement can be signed by listing brokerage, but co-operating brokerage can only sign for a buyer when representing that buyer. (See Clause 3 of the *Agreement of Purchase and Sale*.)

Mutual Release

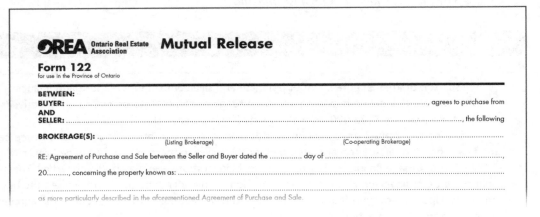

DRAFTING GUIDELINES

- Fully cross-reference to agreement.
- Insert irrevocable date.
- Release concerning all liabilities, covenants, obligations, claims and sums of money.
- Signed by all parties to the agreement and by listing brokerage and selling brokerage (if applicable).
- Confirmation of Acceptance signed and dated.
- Distribute signed copies to all signatories on the form and to the lawyers.

Termination of Agreement by Buyer

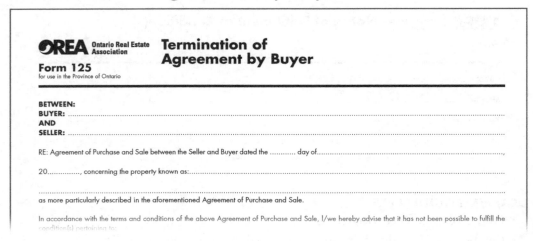

DRAFTING GUIDELINES
- Fully cross-reference to agreement.
- Detailed clause need not be cited, but be specific as to which condition(s) the termination pertains.
- Form states that parties agree to sign mutual release (attach to the termination notice).
- Acknowledgement by seller required.
- Distribute signed copies to all parties and lawyers.

Termination of Agreement by Seller

OREA Ontario Real Estate Association

Termination of Agreement by Seller

Form 126
for use in the Province of Ontario

BETWEEN:
BUYER: ....
AND
SELLER: ....

RE: Agreement of Purchase and Sale between the Seller and Buyer dated the .... day of ....,

20..............., concerning the property known as: ....

....

as more particularly described in the aforementioned Agreement of Purchase and Sale.

In accordance with the terms and conditions of the above Agreement of Purchase and Sale, I/we hereby advise that it has not been possible to fulfill the condition(s) pertaining to:

DRAFTING GUIDELINES
- Fully cross-reference to agreement.
- Detailed clause need not be cited, but be specific as to which condition(s) the termination pertains.
- Form states that parties agree to sign mutual release (attach to the termination notice).
- Acknowledgement by buyer required.
- Distribute signed copies to all parties and lawyers.

PRIVACY AND SALE DOCUMENTS

Registrants are routinely involved with confidential client information. Sellers and buyers inevitably furnish personal details; e.g., verbal disclosure of reasons for selling or providing sensitive information when buying.

Registrants must protect and promote the interest of the client including the protection of that client's confidentiality. However, beyond brokerage-specific requirements set out in REBBA 2002, broader-based privacy legislation now impacts all registrants in the collection, use and distribution of personal information.

Privacy Legislation

E-commerce has been a catalyst for increased attention on privacy matters and duties to all consumers. Privacy legislation (*Personal Information Protection and Electronic Documents Act* (PIPEDA), now envelopes many activities of private enterprises and day-to-day business dealings, including the listing and selling of real estate.

10 PRINCIPLES OF PRIVACY
CANADIAN STANDARDS ASSOCIATION INTERNATIONAL

1. ACCOUNTABILITY
An organization is responsible for personal information under its control and shall designate an individual or individuals who are accountable for the organization's compliance with the following principles.

2. IDENTIFYING PURPOSES
The purposes for which personal information is collected shall be identified by the organization at, or before the time, the information is collected.

3. CONSENT
The knowledge and consent of the individual are required for the collection, use or disclosure of personal information, except where inappropriate.

4. LIMITING COLLECTION
The collection of personal information shall be limited to that which is necessary for the purposes identified by the organization. Information shall be collected by fair and lawful means.

5. LIMITING USE, DISCLOSURE AND RETENTION
Personal information shall not be used or disclosed for purposes other than those for which it was collected, except with the consent of the individual or as required by law. Personal information shall be retained only as long as necessary for the fulfilment of those purposes.

6. ACCURACY
Personal information shall be as accurate, complete and up-to-date as is necessary for the purposes for which it is to be used.

7. SAFEGUARDS
Personal information shall be protected by security safeguards appropriate to the sensitivity of the information.

8. OPENNESS
An organization shall make readily available to individuals specific information about its policies and practices relating to the management of personal information.

9. INDIVIDUAL ACCESS
Upon request, an individual shall be informed of the existence, use and disclosure of his or her personal information and shall be given access to that information. An individual shall be able to challenge the accuracy and completeness of the information and have it amended as appropriate.

10. CHALLENGING COMPLIANCE
An individual shall be able to address a challenge concerning compliance with the above principles to the designated individual or individuals accountable for the organization's compliance.

This federal legislation identifies three information types: **personal information**, **sensitive personal information** and **personal facts**. Legislation applies to the first two, the third constitutes facts that are not readily associated with an individual. In other words, the facts are anonymized (not identifiable with an individual, as in the case of business statistics).

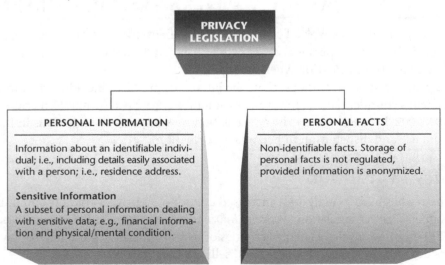

PRIVACY LEGISLATION

PERSONAL INFORMATION

Information about an identifiable individual; i.e., including details easily associated with a person; i.e., residence address.

Sensitive Information
A subset of personal information dealing with sensitive data; e.g., financial information and physical/mental condition.

PERSONAL FACTS

Non-identifiable facts. Storage of personal facts is not regulated, provided information is anonymized.

Privacy Commissioner

The Privacy Commissioner of Canada was established under PIPEDA as the ombudsman for complaints. The Commissioner is also responsible for similar duties under the *Privacy Act* which covers the federal public sector. The Commissioner not only investigates complaints, but also conducts audits, undertakes research and generally promotes privacy awareness.

 WEB LINKS
Privacy Commissioner   Go to the Privacy Commissioner's website (*www.privcom.gc.ca*) for detailed information regarding privacy legislation and guidelines for both personal and business activities.

Privacy Code

The Canadian Real Estate Association has developed a **Privacy Code** for its members based on the PIPEDA Schedule 1 (The Model Code for the Protection of Personal Information). Further, OREA and various real estate boards provide privacy guidelines on web sites. Extensive research underlies these guidelines. Three selected items are highlighted for illustration purposes.

PURPOSE/CONSENT

Reasons for collecting information must be identified; e.g., intention to include buyers' names on a mailing list. Information collected is restricted to the stated purpose, unless further consent is obtained.

Informed **consent** of the consumer is required. Explicit written consent is the best approach for most circumstances, but the legislation does contemplate oral consent or consent expressed through conduct. Consent may also be withdrawn. Generally, the more sensitive the information, the greater the need for explicit consent. Registrants should seek guidance from employing brokerages.

BROKERAGE POLICIES/FORMS

Brokerages are responsible for internal privacy policies. In particular, procedures are necessary for the handling, retention and destruction of personal information. Someone in the brokerage will be designated to be accountable for privacy compliance.

Adequate levels of security must be set up to ensure safekeeping of such data. Also, mechanisms are required for correcting or adding details and addressing access challenges to such information by consumers.

Privacy provisions are included in both the *Listing Agreement* (OREA Form 200) and the *Buyer Representation Agreement* (OREA Form 300) and corresponding commercial forms. Wordings may vary if other forms are being used by the brokerage.

SALESPERSON FILES/RECORDS

Registrants directly encounter privacy legislation through compilation of client/customer mailing lists, retention of shadow files (copies of original brokerage-held listing/sale documents in which they are involved) and gathering selected information regarding buyers and sellers, which is archived for future reference.

Privacy Code

A set of ten principles providing guidance to members of organized real estate in the collection, use and disclosure of personal information.

Consent

Consent from a privacy legislation perspective as required under the Personal Information Protection and Electronic Documents Act.

If such activity is planned, new registrants should review brokerage policies, legislative guidelines and the Privacy Code (for members of organized real estate) to ensure compliance. Essentially, privacy requirements follow four basic rules:

- Identify to consumers the uses you intend to make of their personal information.
- Collect only that information necessary for the uses identified.
- Disclose information only for the reason it was collected.
- Obtain the consent of the consumer for the collection and disclosure of information. Explicit written consent is the best.

Privacy Policies and the Brokerage MARKET PERSPECTIVE

Brokerages have instituted privacy policies that affect everything from office security to mailing lists. Many have also developed a brochure for client and customer distribution with the following statement appearing on various brokerage promotional materials:

ABC Realty Inc. complies with privacy legislation. Call us for information about our policies.

But salespersons also have responsibilities. Don't gather any information about clients or customers without their knowledge and consent.

- *Web Sites* If a personal web site asks for personal information from prospects, clearly state why the information is required and how it will be used. Most important, ask for explicit consent; i.e., add a checkbox stating: *I consent to my name being added to a mailing list for promotional materials.*

- *Open Houses* If you require buyers to sign in at open houses for security reasons, make certain that this purpose is clearly stated on the sign-in sheet. Discuss the matter openly with prospects. Don't even think about adding anyone to a mailing list without explicit consent.

- *Sales-Related Files at Home/Personal Office* Implement adequate security for all shadow files in your possession involving trades and related business. This also applies to mailing lists or other data on home computers.

- *Sale Negotiations/Deal Processing* Each of you routinely handles agency agreements, agreements of purchase and sale and sale-related forms. Respect the private nature of all documentation, just as the brokerage does when deal files are processed and stored internally.

Privacy legislation is complex. All registrants should fully investigate privacy policies established by the employing brokerage and also access the Privacy Commissioner's website for further guidance. Go to **www.privcom.gc.ca.**

AVOIDING ERRORS AND OMISSIONS

A few additional guidelines can help avoid potential errors and omissions in drafting and finalizing agreements:

- Avoid vague wordings that produce ambiguity; e.g., conditional on obtaining a satisfactory building permit (What does *satisfactory* mean?). What about obtaining an inspection? Did I include the buyer's approval? When wording the condition regarding a soil test, did I include at whose expense?
- Maintain quality control. Diligently follow acceptance procedures when handling offer documents and negotiations; e.g., presenting competing offers.
- Make certain that all disclosure requirements are met in situations involving multiple representation? Be particularly careful to ensure full and complete disclosure with competing offers.

- Ensure that all preprinted clauses are reviewed and fully understood by parties to the agreement.
- Double check offers; i.e., amounts add correctly, notice periods are appropriate, dates are sequenced, signatures and initials are inserted and details align with the listing and/or other source materials.
- Provide clear, straightforward instructions. Be in control during all negotiations.
- Take particular care when drafting any letters and consult with the brokerage regarding office policies on such matters. Make certain that words are clear, concise and to the point.
- Build a solid paper trail so that others reviewing the file can readily follow the process from initial signing to final acceptance.
- Don't let clients, customers or other salespersons rush you. Be methodical and check everything.
- When clients are signing the agreement of purchase and sale, take control of the situation. Get a signing flow going—have the wife and husband across the table from you. Give one of them the first original to sign. Watch carefully that she signs all appropriate spaces, then hand it to the spouse. Gather the first one back and double check all items. Proceed to the next. Once all are completed, sit quietly and double check each original.
- When using electronic signatures for agreements of purchase and sale, ensure all parties to the agreement have consented to use electronic signatures, the signatures can be authenticated, and are permanent and tamper-proof.
- Carefully follow privacy guidelines established by your brokerage, access the Privacy Commissioner's website for up-to-date procedures and adhere to the Privacy Code (if a member of organized real estate).

OFFER DRAFTING/PRESENTATION GUIDELINES

- The Confirmation of Acceptance is completed once the agreement has been accepted by both parties.
- An amended offer must be initialled by all parties where changes are made; i.e., ruled out. Don't forget the irrevocable clause.
- If an amendment is long; e.g., a full line of text, the parties should initial at both ends of the change.
- Signed copies are distributed to all parties to the transaction, the listing brokerage and the selling brokerage (if applicable) following acceptance.
- The signed copy with both buyer and seller acknowledgements is retained by the listing brokerage.
- Lawyers for the parties receive copies as a matter of common business practice.
- When a counter offer is made by the seller using a counter offer form, the buyer accepts by signing that form.

AFTER-SALE DOCUMENT GUIDELINES

- Ensure that the *Confirmation of Co-operation and Representation* form has appropriate disclosures and initials/signatures are complete.
- Double check trade record entries when signing. This document becomes the key business record.

- Make certain that sale-related documents, such as notices and waivers are fully cross-referenced to the agreement of purchase and sale.
- Inserting clauses in conditions such as *this offer shall become null and void and the deposit shall be returned to the buyer in full without deduction* is not sufficient for releasing a deposit. A mutual release must be signed by all parties.

PRIVACY POINTERS

- Tell the consumer why you are collecting personal information.
- Get their informed consent.
- Collect only the information requested.
- Use the information only as agreed to with the consumer.
- Protect the information within your custody and control.

THE REAL ESTATE TRANSACTION—GENERAL

KNOWLEDGE INTEGRATION

Notables

- Negotiating outcomes for buyer and seller include win-win, win-lose (or lose-win) and lose-lose.

- Negotiations can result in a no outcome, often due to lack of motivation.

- Be an informed negotiator. Always fill in the information gaps. Discover your client's wants, needs, financial abilities and housing objectives.

- The typical real estate transaction represents opposing forces. While protecting your client's interests, deal fairly and honestly with all other parties.

- The Code of Ethics provides important guidelines regarding offer presentations.

- REBBA 2002 contains requirements relating to the retention of copies of all written offers received by a seller's brokerage, regardless of whether the offer was accepted or not.

- Methods of presentation, acceptances and counter offers may vary in local marketplaces.

- Handle competing offer situations with caution. Know the rules and ensure full disclosure when multiple representation is involved.

- An acceptance must be unconditional, communicated to the offeror, made in the manner required by the offeror and made within the time required by the offeror.

- Don't let haste create unnecessary risk. Be methodical, double check documents and ensure a complete paper trail.

- Three counter offer options are available: amend/initial offer, prepare counter offer form and draft a new offer.

- A trade record sheet must be completed for all trades, regardless of whether a deposit is held or not.

- Harmonized sales tax applies to real estate commissions, regardless of whether or not the property transacted is exempted; e.g., residential resales.

- A waiver form can only be used when a waiver provision has been included in the agreement of purchase and sale.

- Notice of Fulfilment of Condition is used when the terms/wording of the condition are fulfilled, as stated in the agreement of purchase and sale.

- A fully completed, signed mutual release is required before a brokerage can disperse deposit funds from the statutory trust account.

Glossary

Consent

Personal Facts

Personal Information

Privacy Code

Sensitive Personal Information

Trade

Web Links

Web links are included for general interest regarding selected chapter topics.

Privacy Commissioner   Go to the Privacy Commissioner's website (*www.privcom.gc.ca*) for detailed information regarding privacy legislation and guidelines for both personal and business activities.

Strategic Thinking For Your Career

Questions are included to assist in developing your new career. No answers are provided.

1. What accepted practices are used in the local marketplace when presenting offers?

2. What books are available at the bookstore that can advance my knowledge of effective negotiations?

3. Are counter offer forms used at my intended employing brokerage?

4. How are trade record sheets completed at my intended employing brokerage and do they use a transaction report or similar document?

5. What additional sale-related forms are used by my intended employing brokerage?

6. How will I handle a situation in which the buyer as a client wants to waive a condition, solely on the basis that he or she will lose the property otherwise? For example, the seller issues a Notice to Remove Condition and the buyer has not had time to obtain financing or sell the home but insists on waiving the condition.

7. What information about buyer clients do I want to track and what system will I establish for information collection/storage to fully comply with privacy legislation?

Chapter Mini-Review

Solutions are located in the Appendix.

1. From a buyer's perspective, power in negotiations tends to increase as motivation decreases.

    ◯ True   ◯ False

2. Generally, the more you know about the buyer's needs and wants, the more productive the negotiations.

    ◯ True   ◯ False

3. The parties who sign the *Confirmation of Acceptance* are usually the first to sign the Acknowledgement.

    ◯ True   ◯ False

4. The salesperson should always discuss the offered price with the seller when making an appointment to present an offer.

    ◯ True   ◯ False

5. The listing brokerage retains the signed copy of the agreement that has both the buyer's and seller's acknowledgements.

    ◯ True   ◯ False

6. An accepted business practice is to provide lawyers, for the buyer and seller, with signed copies of the agreement.

    ◯ True   ◯ False

7. The seller would typically sign the Confirmation of Acceptance in a counter offer made by the seller and accepted by the buyer.

    ◯ True   ◯ False

8. In a competing offer situation, one of the options that a seller has is to refuse to sign any of the offers.

    ◯ True   ◯ False

9. A transaction report can replace a trade record sheet provided that the brokerage has developed a specific office policy to that effect.

    ◯ True   ◯ False

10. Where the right to commission is contingent on sale completion, HST is due and payable on the date of completion.

    ◯ True   ◯ False

11. Employed salespersons (as differentiated from independent contractors) need not register for HST purposes and are not required to charge HST to their employers for commissions earned.

    ◯ True   ◯ False

12. When using a waiver, registrants should insert the complete clause wording that is being waived.

    ◯ True   ◯ False

13. The Privacy Code developed by The Canadian Real Estate Association applies to all RECO registrants.

    ◯ True   ◯ False

14. Explicit written consent is the best form of informed consent from a privacy legislation perspective.

    ◯ True   ◯ False

Active Learning Exercises

Solutions are located in the Appendix.

■ Exercise 1   Competing Offers

In your own words, briefly describe three options for a seller when presented with competing offers and identify one disadvantage of each.

Option 1

Option 2

Option 3

■ Exercise 2   Fill-in-the-Blanks

Insert the most appropriate words in the following discussion between the listing salesperson and her manager concerning a recent offer presentation.

2.1   That offer presentation really went smoothly. First of all, the salesperson from the _____ brokerage called to inform me of the offer made by a young couple. He referred to this as _____ the offer. We met at the seller's house later in the afternoon and I presented the _____ salesperson's offer.

2.2   The seller asked that he and I discuss the offer in private. He agreed to the terms, signed and dated his signature, and next completed the _____ to confirm the time when the offer was finally agreed upon.

2.3   I gave a copy of the agreement to him and he signed and dated his signature under the _____ section of the Agreement. I then went outside to meet with the other salesperson. He had waited in his car while the seller and I discussed the agreement. I handed him sufficient signed copies for the _____ and the _____ brokerage.

2.4   Of course, I have the original signed copy with Acknowledgements and also the other salesperson's signature and mine concerning the _____ .

■ Exercise 3   Drafting Offer/Counter Offer

Charles M. Leung is interested in a property located at 1381 Pathfinder Road in Anycity. Draft an offer for this property owned by Alexandra Vujovic. Hans Vujovic, her spouse, is not a registered owner of this matrimonial home. Various information is described below. Insert any additional details necessary to complete the offer. A blank *Agreement of Purchase and Sale* (OREA Form 100) is provided.

THE OFFER

The property, located on the south side of Pathfinder Road, has a frontage of 72.55 feet and a depth of 118.50 feet and is described as Lots 11 and 12, Registered Plan 496, City of Anycity, Regional Municipality of Anyregion. The property has a mutual rear drive.

The offered price is $290,000 with a deposit of $10,000, a supplemental deposit of $10,000 payable 16 days from the offer date, with the balance due on completion date. The deposit is due upon acceptance of the agreement and payable to the listing brokerage, ABC Realty Inc. An existing mortgage with Anycity Financial is being assumed for approximately $150,000.00, interest rate of 5.75%, $936.50 monthly including principal, interest and taxes and expiring on January 31st, 20xx. No prepayment or other privileges exist. The assumption is conditional on the lender's approval. Allow until August 20th for that approval.

The chandelier in the dining room is excluded. Draperies and associated decorator rods in the living room and family room are included. A rental hot water tank from Anycity Energy @ $33.50 per quarter (plus tax) is assumable.

The offer, dated at Anycity on August 10th, 20xx will be irrevocable for two days and expire at 6 p.m. on that day. Allow a title search period of approximately 60 days from the offer date. Completion will be December 1st, 20xx which is a normal business day. The present use is single-family residential. Notices can be delivered to the seller by fax at 905 666–2121 and the buyer at 905 777–2121. HST is deemed to be included in the purchase price. Cliff Kuppers is the listing salesperson with ABC Realty Inc., representing the seller and Claire Rodgers is the selling salesperson with XYZ Real Estate Limited representing the buyer. Insert any additional information for a fully completed offer ready for presentation.

COUNTER OFFER: AMEND ORIGINAL OFFER

Alexandra Vujovic counters the buyer's offer on August 12th at $305,000, amends the closing date to November 1st, which is a normal business day, and extends the irrevocable period until 11:59 on August 13th. The buyer accepts the countersign at 7:00 p.m. on August 13th. Insert all additional information required for a fully completed, signed agreement including *Acknowledgements* and the *Commission Trust Agreement*.

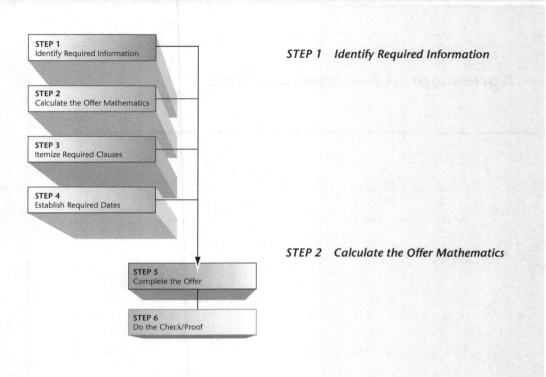

STEP 1   *Identify Required Information*

STEP 2   *Calculate the Offer Mathematics*

STEP 3   *Itemize Required Clauses*

STEP 4   *Establish Required Dates*

 **Ontario Real Estate Association**

Agreement of Purchase and Sale

Form 100
for use in the Province of Ontario

This Agreement of Purchase and Sale dated this .... day of .... 20...........

BUYER, ..., agrees to purchase from
(Full legal names of all Buyers)

SELLER, ..., the following
(Full legal names of all Sellers)

REAL PROPERTY:

Address ....

fronting on the .... side of ....

in the ....

and having a frontage of .... more or less by a depth of .... more or less

and legally described as ....

.... (the "property")
(Legal description of land including easements not described elsewhere)

PURCHASE PRICE: Dollars (CDN$) ....

.... Dollars

DEPOSIT: Buyer submits ....
(Herewith/Upon Acceptance/as otherwise described in this Agreement)

.... Dollars (CDN$) ....

by negotiable cheque payable to .... "Deposit Holder" to be held
in trust pending completion or other termination of this Agreement and to be credited toward the Purchase Price on completion. For the purposes of this
Agreement, "Upon Acceptance" shall mean that the Buyer is required to deliver the deposit to the Deposit Holder within 24 hours of the acceptance of
this Agreement. The parties to this Agreement hereby acknowledge that, unless otherwise provided for in this Agreement, the Deposit Holder shall place
the deposit in trust in the Deposit Holder's non-interest bearing Real Estate Trust Account and no interest shall be earned, received or paid on the deposit.

Buyer agrees to pay the balance as more particularly set out in Schedule A attached.

SCHEDULE(S) A..**attached hereto form(s) part of this Agreement.**

1.   IRREVOCABILITY: This offer shall be irrevocable by .... until .... a.m./p.m. on the ....
(Seller/Buyer)

day of .... 20 ...., after which time, if not accepted, this offer shall be null and void and the deposit
shall be returned to the Buyer in full without interest.

2.   COMPLETION DATE: This Agreement shall be completed by no later than 6:00 p.m. on the .... day of ....

20 .... Upon completion, vacant possession of the property shall be given to the Buyer unless otherwise provided for in this Agreement.

INITIALS OF BUYER(S): (   )   INITIALS OF SELLER(S): (   )

Form 100   Revised 2015   **Page 1 of 6**

3. **NOTICES:** The Seller hereby appoints the Listing Brokerage as agent for the Seller for the purpose of giving and receiving notices pursuant to this Agreement. Where a Brokerage (Buyer's Brokerage) has entered into a representation agreement with the Buyer, the Buyer hereby appoints the Buyer's Brokerage as agent for the purpose of giving and receiving notices pursuant to this Agreement. **Where a Brokerage represents both the Seller and the Buyer (multiple representation), the Brokerage shall not be appointed or authorized to be agent for either the Buyer or the Seller for the purpose of giving and receiving notices.** Any notice relating hereto or provided for herein shall be in writing. In addition to any provision contained herein and in any Schedule hereto, this offer, any counter-offer, notice of acceptance thereof or any notice to be given or received pursuant to this Agreement or any Schedule hereto (any of them, "Document") shall be deemed given and received when delivered personally or hand delivered to the Address for Service provided in the Acknowledgement below, or where a facsimile number or email address is provided herein, when transmitted electronically to that facsimile number or email address, respectively, in which case, the signature(s) of the party (parties) shall be deemed to be original.

FAX No.: ....   FAX No.: ....
      (For delivery of Documents to Seller)   (For delivery of Documents to Buyer)

Email Address: ....   Email Address: ....
      (For delivery of Documents to Seller)   (For delivery of Documents to Buyer)

4. **CHATTELS INCLUDED:**..

....

....

....

....

Unless otherwise stated in this Agreement or any Schedule hereto, Seller agrees to convey all fixtures and chattels included in the Purchase Price free from all liens, encumbrances or claims affecting the said fixtures and chattels.

5. **FIXTURES EXCLUDED:**..

....

....

....

....

6. **RENTAL ITEMS (Including Lease, Lease to Own):** The following equipment is rented and **not** included in the Purchase Price. The Buyer agrees to assume the rental contract(s), if assumable:

....

....

....

The Buyer agrees to co-operate and execute such documentation as may be required to facilitate such assumption.

7. **HST:** If the sale of the Property (Real Property as described above) is subject to Harmonized Sales Tax (HST), then such tax shall be

.... the Purchase Price. If the sale of the Property is not subject to HST, Seller agrees to certify on or before
      (included in/in addition to)
closing, that the sale of the Property is not subject to HST. Any HST on chattels, if applicable, is not included in the Purchase Price.

INITIALS OF BUYER(S): ( )   **INITIALS OF SELLER(S):** ( )

8. **TITLE SEARCH:** Buyer shall be allowed until 6:00 p.m. on the .... day of ...., 20..........., (Requisition Date) to examine the title to the Property at Buyer's own expense and until the earlier of: (i) thirty days from the later of the Requisition Date or the date on which the conditions in this Agreement are fulfilled or otherwise waived or; (ii) five days prior to completion, to satisfy Buyer that there are no outstanding

work orders or deficiency notices affecting the Property, and that its present use (...) may be lawfully continued and that the principal building may be insured against risk of fire. Seller hereby consents to the municipality or other governmental agencies releasing to Buyer details of all outstanding work orders and deficiency notices affecting the property, and Seller agrees to execute and deliver such further authorizations in this regard as Buyer may reasonably require.

9. **FUTURE USE:** Seller and Buyer agree that there is no representation or warranty of any kind that the future intended use of the property by Buyer is or will be lawful except as may be specifically provided for in this Agreement.

10. **TITLE:** Provided that the title to the property is good and free from all registered restrictions, charges, liens, and encumbrances except as otherwise specifically provided in this Agreement and save and except for (a) any registered restrictions or covenants that run with the land providing that such are complied with; (b) any registered municipal agreements and registered agreements with publicly regulated utilities providing such have been complied with, or security has been posted to ensure compliance and completion, as evidenced by a letter from the relevant municipality or regulated utility; (c) any minor easements for the supply of domestic utility or telephone services to the property or adjacent properties; and (d) any easements for drainage, storm or sanitary sewers, public utility lines, telephone lines, cable television lines or other services which do not materially affect the use of the property. If within the specified times referred to in paragraph 8 any valid objection to title or to any outstanding work order or deficiency notice, or to the fact the said present use may not lawfully be continued, or that the principal building may not be insured against risk of fire is made in writing to Seller and which Seller is unable or unwilling to remove, remedy or satisfy or obtain insurance save and except against risk of fire (Title Insurance) in favour of the Buyer and any mortgagee, (with all related costs at the expense of the Seller), and which Buyer will not waive, this Agreement notwithstanding any intermediate acts or negotiations in respect of such objections, shall be at an end and all monies paid shall be returned without interest or deduction and Seller, Listing Brokerage and Co-operating Brokerage shall not be liable for any costs or damages. Save as to any valid objection so made by such day and except for any objection going to the root of the title, Buyer shall be conclusively deemed to have accepted Seller's title to the property.

11. **CLOSING ARRANGEMENTS:** Where each of the Seller and Buyer retain a lawyer to complete the Agreement of Purchase and Sale of the property, and where the transaction will be completed by electronic registration pursuant to Part III of the Land Registration Reform Act, R.S.O. 1990, Chapter L4 and the Electronic Registration Act, S.O. 1991, Chapter 44, and any amendments thereto, the Seller and Buyer acknowledge and agree that the exchange of closing funds, non-registrable documents and other items (the "Requisite Deliveries") and the release thereof to the Seller and Buyer will (a) not occur at the same time as the registration of the transfer/deed (and any other documents intended to be registered in connection with the completion of this transaction) and (b) be subject to conditions whereby the lawyer(s) receiving any of the Requisite Deliveries will be required to hold same in trust and not release same except in accordance with the terms of a document registration agreement between the said lawyers. The Seller and Buyer irrevocably instruct the said lawyers to be bound by the document registration agreement which is recommended from time to time by the Law Society of Upper Canada. Unless otherwise agreed to by the lawyers, such exchange of the Requisite Deliveries will occur in the applicable Land Titles Office or such other location agreeable to both lawyers.

12. **DOCUMENTS AND DISCHARGE:** Buyer shall not call for the production of any title deed, abstract, survey or other evidence of title to the property except such as are in the possession or control of Seller. If requested by Buyer, Seller will deliver any sketch or survey of the property within Seller's control to Buyer as soon as possible and prior to the Requisition Date. If a discharge of any Charge/Mortgage held by a corporation incorporated pursuant to the Trust And Loan Companies Act (Canada), Chartered Bank, Trust Company, Credit Union, Caisse Populaire or Insurance Company and which is not to be assumed by Buyer on completion, is not available in registrable form on completion, Buyer agrees to accept Seller's lawyer's personal undertaking to obtain, out of the closing funds, a discharge in registrable form and to register same, or cause same to be registered, on title within a reasonable period of time after completion, provided that on or before completion Seller shall provide to Buyer a mortgage statement prepared by the mortgagee setting out the balance required to obtain the discharge, and, where a real-time electronic cleared funds transfer system is not being used, a direction executed by Seller directing payment to the mortgagee of the amount required to obtain the discharge out of the balance due on completion.

13. **INSPECTION:** Buyer acknowledges having had the opportunity to inspect the Property and understands that upon acceptance of this offer there shall be a binding agreement of purchase and sale between Buyer and Seller. **The Buyer acknowledges having the opportunity to include a requirement for a property inspection report in this Agreement and agrees that except as may be specifically provided for in this Agreement, the Buyer will not be obtaining a property inspection or property inspection report regarding the Property.**

14. **INSURANCE:** All buildings on the property and all other things being purchased shall be and remain until completion at the risk of Seller. Pending completion, Seller shall hold all insurance policies, if any, and the proceeds thereof in trust for the parties as their interests may appear and in the event of substantial damage, Buyer may either terminate this Agreement and have all monies paid returned without interest or deduction or else take the proceeds of any insurance and complete the purchase. No insurance shall be transferred on completion. If Seller is taking back a Charge/Mortgage, or Buyer is assuming a Charge/Mortgage, Buyer shall supply Seller with reasonable evidence of adequate insurance to protect Seller's or other mortgagee's interest on completion.

INITIALS OF BUYER(S): ⬭   INITIALS OF SELLER(S): ⬭

Exercise 3   Agreement of Purchase and Sale—Page 4 of 6

15. PLANNING ACT: This Agreement shall be effective to create an interest in the property only if Seller complies with the subdivision control provisions of the Planning Act by completion and Seller covenants to proceed diligently at Seller's expense to obtain any necessary consent by completion.

16. DOCUMENT PREPARATION: The Transfer/Deed shall, save for the Land Transfer Tax Affidavit, be prepared in registrable form at the expense of Seller, and any Charge/Mortgage to be given back by the Buyer to Seller at the expense of the Buyer. If requested by Buyer, Seller covenants that the Transfer/Deed to be delivered on completion shall contain the statements contemplated by Section 50(22) of the Planning Act, R.S.O.1990.

17. RESIDENCY: (a) Subject to (b) below, the Seller represents and warrants that the Seller is not and on completion will not be a non-resident under the non-residency provisions of the Income Tax Act which representation and warranty shall survive and not merge upon the completion of this transaction and the Seller shall deliver to the Buyer a statutory declaration that Seller is not then a non-resident of Canada; (b) provided that if the Seller is a non-resident under the non-residency provisions of the Income Tax Act, the Buyer shall be credited towards the Purchase Price with the amount, if any, necessary for Buyer to pay to the Minister of National Revenue to satisfy Buyer's liability in respect of tax payable by Seller under the non-residency provisions of the Income Tax Act by reason of this sale. Buyer shall not claim such credit if Seller delivers on completion the prescribed certificate.

18. ADJUSTMENTS: Any rents, mortgage interest, realty taxes including local improvement rates and unmetered public or private utility charges and unmetered cost of fuel, as applicable, shall be apportioned and allowed to the day of completion, the day of completion itself to be apportioned to Buyer.

19. PROPERTY ASSESSMENT: The Buyer and Seller hereby acknowledge that the Province of Ontario has implemented current value assessment and properties may be re-assessed on an annual basis. The Buyer and Seller agree that no claim will be made against the Buyer or Seller, or any Brokerage, Broker or Salesperson, for any changes in property tax as a result of a re-assessment of the property, save and except any property taxes that accrued prior to the completion of this transaction.

20. TIME LIMITS: Time shall in all respects be of the essence hereof provided that the time for doing or completing of any matter provided for herein may be extended or abridged by an agreement in writing signed by Seller and Buyer or by their respective lawyers who may be specifically authorized in that regard.

21. TENDER: Any tender of documents or money hereunder may be made upon Seller or Buyer or their respective lawyers on the day set for completion. Money shall be tendered with funds drawn on a lawyer's trust account in the form of a bank draft, certified cheque or wire transfer using the Large Value Transfer System.

22. FAMILY LAW ACT: Seller warrants that spousal consent is not necessary to this transaction under the provisions of the Family Law Act, R.S.O.1990 unless Seller's spouse has executed the consent hereinafter provided.

23. UFFI: Seller represents and warrants to Buyer that during the time Seller has owned the property, Seller has not caused any building on the property to be insulated with insulation containing ureaformaldehyde, and that to the best of Seller's knowledge no building on the property contains or has ever contained insulation that contains ureaformaldehyde. This warranty shall survive and not merge on the completion of this transaction, and if the building is part of a multiple unit building, this warranty shall only apply to that part of the building which is the subject of this transaction.

24. LEGAL, ACCOUNTING AND ENVIRONMENTAL ADVICE: The parties acknowledge that any information provided by the brokerage is not legal, tax or environmental advice.

25. CONSUMER REPORTS: The Buyer is hereby notified that a consumer report containing credit and/or personal information may be referred to in connection with this transaction.

26. AGREEMENT IN WRITING: If there is conflict or discrepancy between any provision added to this Agreement (including any Schedule attached hereto) and any provision in the standard pre-set portion hereof, the added provision shall supersede the standard pre-set provision to the extent of such conflict or discrepancy. This Agreement including any Schedule attached hereto, shall constitute the entire Agreement between Buyer and Seller. There is no representation, warranty, collateral agreement or condition, which affects this Agreement other than as expressed herein. For the purposes of this Agreement, Seller means vendor and Buyer means purchaser. This Agreement shall be read with all changes of gender or number required by the context.

27. TIME AND DATE: Any reference to a time and date in this Agreement shall mean the time and date where the property is located.

INITIALS OF BUYER(S): ⬭   INITIALS OF SELLER(S): ⬭

THE REAL ESTATE TRANSACTION—GENERAL

28. SUCCESSORS AND ASSIGNS: The heirs, executors, administrators, successors and assigns of the undersigned are bound by the terms herein.

SIGNED, SEALED AND DELIVERED in the presence of: IN WITNESS whereof I have hereunto set my hand and seal:

.... ⬤ DATE ....
(Witness)   (Buyer)   (Seal)

.... ⬤ DATE ....
(Witness)   (Buyer)   (Seal)

I, the Undersigned Seller, agree to the above offer. I hereby irrevocably instruct my lawyer to pay directly to the brokerage(s) with whom I have agreed to pay commission, the unpaid balance of the commission together with applicable Harmonized Sales Tax (and any other taxes as may hereafter be applicable), from the proceeds of the sale prior to any payment to the undersigned on completion, as advised by the brokerage(s) to my lawyer.

SIGNED, SEALED AND DELIVERED in the presence of: IN WITNESS whereof I have hereunto set my hand and seal:

.... ⬤ DATE ....
(Witness)   (Seller)   (Seal)

.... ⬤ DATE ....
(Witness)   (Seller)   (Seal)

SPOUSAL CONSENT: The Undersigned Spouse of the Seller hereby consents to the disposition evidenced herein pursuant to the provisions of the Family Law Act, R.S.O.1990, and hereby agrees with the Buyer that he/she will execute all necessary or incidental documents to give full force and effect to the sale evidenced herein.

.... ⬤ DATE ....
(Witness)   (Spouse)   (Seal)

CONFIRMATION OF ACCEPTANCE: Notwithstanding anything contained herein to the contrary, I confirm this Agreement with all changes both typed and written was finally accepted by all parties at .... a.m./p.m. this .... day of.., 20...........

....
(Signature of Seller or Buyer)

INFORMATION ON BROKERAGE(S)

Listing Brokerage .... Tel.No.(...............)...

....
(Salesperson / Broker Name)

Co-op/Buyer Brokerage .... Tel.No.(...............)...

....
(Salesperson / Broker Name)

ACKNOWLEDGEMENT

I acknowledge receipt of my signed copy of this accepted Agreement of Purchase and Sale and I authorize the Brokerage to forward a copy to my lawyer.

.... DATE ....
(Seller)

.... DATE ....
(Seller)
Address for Service ....

.... Tel.No.(..........).....................

Seller's Lawyer ....

Address ....

Email ....

(..........)....................................... (..........) ....
     Tel.No.   FAX No.

I acknowledge receipt of my signed copy of this accepted Agreement of Purchase and Sale and I authorize the Brokerage to forward a copy to my lawyer.

.... DATE ....
(Buyer)

.... DATE ....
(Buyer)
Address for Service ....

.... Tel.No.(..........).....................

Buyer's Lawyer ....

Address ....

Email ....

(..........)....................................... (..........) ....
     Tel.No.   FAX No.

FOR OFFICE USE ONLY   **COMMISSION TRUST AGREEMENT**

To: Co-operating Brokerage shown on the foregoing Agreement of Purchase and Sale:
In consideration for the Co-operating Brokerage procuring the foregoing Agreement of Purchase and Sale, I hereby declare that all moneys received or receivable by me in connection with the Transaction as contemplated in the MLS® Rules and Regulations of my Real Estate Board shall be receivable and held in trust. This agreement shall constitute a Commission Trust Agreement as defined in the MLS® Rules and shall be subject to and governed by the MLS® Rules pertaining to Commission Trust.
DATED as of the date and time of the acceptance of the foregoing Agreement of Purchase and Sale.   Acknowledged by:

....
(Authorized to bind the Listing Brokerage)   (Authorized to bind the Co-operating Brokerage)

Form 100   Revised 2015   **Page 5 of 6**

Exercise 3   Agreement of Purchase and Sale—Page 6 of 6

 **Ontario Real Estate Association**

Form 100
for use in the Province of Ontario

Schedule A
Agreement of Purchase and Sale

This Schedule is attached to and forms part of the Agreement of Purchase and Sale between:

BUYER, ..., and

SELLER, ...

for the purchase and sale of ....

.... dated the .... day of ...., 20...............

Buyer agrees to pay the balance as follows:

This form must be initialed by all parties to the Agreement of Purchase and Sale.

INITIALS OF BUYER(S):   INITIALS OF SELLER(S):

Form 100   Revised 2015   **Page 6 of 6**

◼ Exercise 4   Identify Errors and Omissions

Identify all errors, omissions and other concerns in the following agreement of purchase and sale prepared for Mr. and Mrs. Chisolm and countered by the sellers regarding 3291 Forest View Parkway in Anycity.

Exercise 4   Agreement of Purchase and Sale—Page 1 of 6

OREA Ontario Real Estate Association   **Agreement of Purchase and Sale**

Form 100
for use in the Province of Ontario

This Agreement of Purchase and Sale dated this ......**1st**...... day of ....**May**.................................... 20..**XX**....

BUYER, ...**Sylvia B. Chisolm and Wayne T. Chisolm**.................., agrees to purchase from
(Full legal names of all Buyers)

SELLER, ...**Roberts K. Mostofi and Marilyn C. Mostofi**.................., the following
(Full legal names of all Sellers)

REAL PROPERTY:

Address .... **3291 Forest View Parkway** ....

fronting on the .... **West** .... side of .... **Forest View Parkway** ....

in the .... **City of Anycity, Regional Municipality of Anyregion** ....

and having a frontage of .... **32.15 feet** .... more or less by a depth of .... **124.62 feet** .... more or less

and legally described as .... **Pt Lot 9, Plan 99M-245 subject to mutual side drive** ....

.... (the "property")
(Legal description of land including easements not described elsewhere)

PURCHASE PRICE: *RM MM* **Fifty** *SW WC*   Dollars (CDN$) .... *RM MM* **$250,000.00** *SW WC*
~~$244,000.00~~

......Two Hundred and ~~Forty-Four~~ Thousand--- Dollars

DEPOSIT: Buyer submits .... **Upon Acceptance**
Ten Thousand *RM MM*   (Herewith/Upon Acceptance/as otherwise described in this Agreement)   *RM MM* **$10,000.00**
~~Two Thousand~~--- Dollars (CDN$) .... ~~$2,000.00~~

by negotiable cheque payable to .... **ABC Realty and XYZ Real Estate Ltd.** .... "Deposit Holder" to be held
in trust pending completion or other termination of this Agreement and to be credited toward the Purchase Price on completion. For the purposes of this
Agreement, "Upon Acceptance" shall mean that the Buyer is required to deliver the deposit to the Deposit Holder within 24 hours of the acceptance of
this Agreement. The parties to this Agreement hereby acknowledge that, unless otherwise provided for in this Agreement, the Deposit Holder shall place
the deposit in trust in the Deposit Holder's non-interest bearing Real Estate Trust Account and no interest shall be earned, received or paid on the deposit.

Buyer agrees to pay the balance as more particularly set out in Schedule A attached.

SCHEDULE(S) A..**attached hereto form(s) part of this Agreement.**

1. **IRREVOCABILITY:** This offer shall be irrevocable by .... *RM MM* **Buyer** *SW WC* / **Seller** .... until **11:59** ~~a.m.~~/p.m. on the *RM MM* **3rd** *SW WC* / **2nd**
(Seller/Buyer)

day of .... **May** .... 20 **XX**...., after which time, if not accepted, this offer shall be null and void and the deposit
shall be returned to the Buyer in full without interest.

2. **COMPLETION DATE:** This Agreement shall be completed by no later than 6:00 p.m. on the **15th** day of .... **July** ....

20 **XX**........ Upon completion, vacant possession of the property shall be given to the Buyer unless otherwise provided for in this Agreement.

INITIALS OF BUYER(S): (*RM MM*)   **INITIALS OF SELLER(S):** (*SC WC*)

Form 100   Revised 2015   Page 1 of 6

3. NOTICES: The Seller hereby appoints the Listing Brokerage as agent for the Seller for the purpose of giving and receiving notices pursuant to this Agreement. Where a Brokerage (Buyer's Brokerage) has entered into a representation agreement with the Buyer, the Buyer hereby appoints the Buyer's Brokerage as agent for the purpose of giving and receiving notices pursuant to this Agreement. **Where a Brokerage represents both the Seller and the Buyer (multiple representation), the Brokerage shall not be appointed or authorized to be agent for either the Buyer or the Seller for the purpose of giving and receiving notices.** Any notice relating hereto or provided for herein shall be in writing. In addition to any provision contained herein and in any Schedule hereto, this offer, any counter-offer, notice of acceptance thereof or any notice to be given or received pursuant to this Agreement or any Schedule hereto (any of them, "Document") shall be deemed given and received when delivered personally or hand delivered to the Address for Service provided in the Acknowledgement below, or where a facsimile number or email address is provided herein, when transmitted electronically to that facsimile number or email address, respectively, in which case, the signature(s) of the party (parties) shall be deemed to be original.

FAX No.: .... **(416) 555-2121** ....
(For delivery of Documents to Seller)

FAX No.: .... **(416) 444-2121** ....
(For delivery of Documents to Buyer)

Email Address: .... **admin@abcrealty.com** ....
(For delivery of Documents to Seller)

Email Address: .... **notices@xyzrealestate.com** ....
(For delivery of Documents to Buyer)

4. CHATTELS INCLUDED: SunRay patio set including four chairs, umbrella, and table; MaxAir ceiling fan in kitchen; all decorator drapery tracks and draperies; security system; and lower family room furnishings.

Unless otherwise stated in this Agreement or any Schedule hereto, Seller agrees to convey all fixtures and chattels included in the Purchase Price free from all liens, encumbrances or claims affecting the said fixtures and chattels.

5. FIXTURES EXCLUDED: Dining room chandelier; liviing room drapes; SteelMake utility shed; and EasyCook barbecue affixed to rear patio wall.

6. RENTAL ITEMS (Including Lease, Lease to Own): The following equipment is rented and **not** included in the Purchase Price. The Buyer agrees to assume the rental contract(s), if assumable:

None

The Buyer agrees to co-operate and execute such documentation as may be required to facilitate such assumption.

7. HST: If the sale of the Property (Real Property as described above) is subject to Harmonized Sales Tax (HST), then such tax shall be .... included in .... the Purchase Price. If the sale of the Property is not subject to HST, Seller agrees to certify on or before
(included in/in addition to)
closing, that the sale of the Property is not subject to HST. Any HST on chattels, if applicable, is not included in the Purchase Price.

INITIALS OF BUYER(S): *RM MM*

INITIALS OF SELLER(S): *SC WC*

Form 100   Revised 2015   **Page 2 of 6**

Exercise 4 Agreement of Purchase and Sale—Page 3 of 6

8. **TITLE SEARCH:** Buyer shall be allowed until 6:00 p.m. on the ..20th.. day of ....May............................., 20..xx...., (Requisition Date) to examine the title to the Property at Buyer's own expense and until the earlier of: (i) thirty days from the later of the Requisition Date or the date on which the conditions in this Agreement are fulfilled or otherwise waived or; (ii) five days prior to completion, to satisfy Buyer that there are no outstanding

   work orders or deficiency notices affecting the Property, and that its present use (................single family residential...........................) may be lawfully continued and that the principal building may be insured against risk of fire. Seller hereby consents to the municipality or other governmental agencies releasing to Buyer details of all outstanding work orders and deficiency notices affecting the property, and Seller agrees to execute and deliver such further authorizations in this regard as Buyer may reasonably require.

9. **FUTURE USE:** Seller and Buyer agree that there is no representation or warranty of any kind that the future intended use of the property by Buyer is or will be lawful except as may be specifically provided for in this Agreement.

10. **TITLE:** Provided that the title to the property is good and free from all registered restrictions, charges, liens, and encumbrances except as otherwise specifically provided in this Agreement and save and except for (a) any registered restrictions or covenants that run with the land providing that such are complied with; (b) any registered municipal agreements and registered agreements with publicly regulated utilities providing such have been complied with, or security has been posted to ensure compliance and completion, as evidenced by a letter from the relevant municipality or regulated utility; (c) any minor easements for the supply of domestic utility or telephone services to the property or adjacent properties; and (d) any easements for drainage, storm or sanitary sewers, public utility lines, telephone lines, cable television lines or other services which do not materially affect the use of the property. If within the specified times referred to in paragraph 8 any valid objection to title or to any outstanding work order or deficiency notice, or to the fact the said present use may not lawfully be continued, or that the principal building may not be insured against risk of fire is made in writing to Seller and which Seller is unable or unwilling to remove, remedy or satisfy or obtain insurance save and except against risk of fire (Title Insurance) in favour of the Buyer and any mortgagee, (with all related costs at the expense of the Seller), and which Buyer will not waive, this Agreement notwithstanding any intermediate acts or negotiations in respect of such objections, shall be at an end and all monies paid shall be returned without interest or deduction and Seller, Listing Brokerage and Co-operating Brokerage shall not be liable for any costs or damages. Save as to any valid objection so made by such day and except for any objection going to the root of the title, Buyer shall be conclusively deemed to have accepted Seller's title to the property.

11. **CLOSING ARRANGEMENTS:** Where each of the Seller and Buyer retain a lawyer to complete the Agreement of Purchase and Sale of the property, and where the transaction will be completed by electronic registration pursuant to Part III of the Land Registration Reform Act, R.S.O. 1990, Chapter L4 and the Electronic Registration Act, S.O. 1991, Chapter 44, and any amendments thereto, the Seller and Buyer acknowledge and agree that the exchange of closing funds, non-registrable documents and other items (the "Requisite Deliveries") and the release thereof to the Seller and Buyer will (a) not occur at the same time as the registration of the transfer/deed (and any other documents intended to be registered in connection with the completion of this transaction) and (b) be subject to conditions whereby the lawyer(s) receiving any of the Requisite Deliveries will be required to hold same in trust and not release same except in accordance with the terms of a document registration agreement between the said lawyers. The Seller and Buyer irrevocably instruct the said lawyers to be bound by the document registration agreement which is recommended from time to time by the Law Society of Upper Canada. Unless otherwise agreed to by the lawyers, such exchange of the Requisite Deliveries will occur in the applicable Land Titles Office or such other location agreeable to both lawyers.

12. **DOCUMENTS AND DISCHARGE:** Buyer shall not call for the production of any title deed, abstract, survey or other evidence of title to the property except such as are in the possession or control of Seller. If requested by Buyer, Seller will deliver any sketch or survey of the property within Seller's control to Buyer as soon as possible and prior to the Requisition Date. If a discharge of any Charge/Mortgage held by a corporation incorporated pursuant to the Trust And Loan Companies Act (Canada), Chartered Bank, Trust Company, Credit Union, Caisse Populaire or Insurance Company and which is not to be assumed by Buyer on completion, is not available in registrable form on completion, Buyer agrees to accept Seller's lawyer's personal undertaking to obtain, out of the closing funds, a discharge in registrable form and to register same, or cause same to be registered, on title within a reasonable period of time after completion, provided that on or before completion Seller shall provide to Buyer a mortgage statement prepared by the mortgagee setting out the balance required to obtain the discharge, and, where a real-time electronic cleared funds transfer system is not being used, a direction executed by Seller directing payment to the mortgagee of the amount required to obtain the discharge out of the balance due on completion.

13. **INSPECTION:** Buyer acknowledges having had the opportunity to inspect the Property and understands that upon acceptance of this offer there shall be a binding agreement of purchase and sale between Buyer and Seller. **The Buyer acknowledges having the opportunity to include a requirement for a property inspection report in this Agreement and agrees that except as may be specifically provided for in this Agreement, the Buyer will not be obtaining a property inspection or property inspection report regarding the Property.**

14. **INSURANCE:** All buildings on the property and all other things being purchased shall be and remain until completion at the risk of Seller. Pending completion, Seller shall hold all insurance policies, if any, and the proceeds thereof in trust for the parties as their interests may appear and in the event of substantial damage, Buyer may either terminate this Agreement and have all monies paid returned without interest or deduction or else take the proceeds of any insurance and complete the purchase. No insurance shall be transferred on completion. If Seller is taking back a Charge/Mortgage, or Buyer is assuming a Charge/Mortgage, Buyer shall supply Seller with reasonable evidence of adequate insurance to protect Seller's or other mortgagee's interest on completion.

INITIALS OF BUYER(S): (RM MM)   **INITIALS OF SELLER(S):** (SC WC)

Form 100 Revised 2015 **Page 3 of 6**

15. **PLANNING ACT:** This Agreement shall be effective to create an interest in the property only if Seller complies with the subdivision control provisions of the Planning Act by completion and Seller covenants to proceed diligently at Seller's expense to obtain any necessary consent by completion.

16. **DOCUMENT PREPARATION:** The Transfer/Deed shall, save for the Land Transfer Tax Affidavit, be prepared in registrable form at the expense of Seller, and any Charge/Mortgage to be given back by the Buyer to Seller at the expense of the Buyer. If requested by Buyer, Seller covenants that the Transfer/Deed to be delivered on completion shall contain the statements contemplated by Section 50(22) of the Planning Act, R.S.O.1990.

17. **RESIDENCY:** (a) Subject to (b) below, the Seller represents and warrants that the Seller is not and on completion will not be a non-resident under the non-residency provisions of the Income Tax Act which representation and warranty shall survive and not merge upon the completion of this transaction and the Seller shall deliver to the Buyer a statutory declaration that Seller is not then a non-resident of Canada; (b) provided that if the Seller is a non-resident under the non-residency provisions of the Income Tax Act, the Buyer shall be credited towards the Purchase Price with the amount, if any, necessary for Buyer to pay to the Minister of National Revenue to satisfy Buyer's liability in respect of tax payable by Seller under the non-residency provisions of the Income Tax Act by reason of this sale. Buyer shall not claim such credit if Seller delivers on completion the prescribed certificate.

18. **ADJUSTMENTS:** Any rents, mortgage interest, realty taxes including local improvement rates and unmetered public or private utility charges and unmetered cost of fuel, as applicable, shall be apportioned and allowed to the day of completion, the day of completion itself to be apportioned to Buyer.

19. **PROPERTY ASSESSMENT:** The Buyer and Seller hereby acknowledge that the Province of Ontario has implemented current value assessment and properties may be re-assessed on an annual basis. The Buyer and Seller agree that no claim will be made against the Buyer or Seller, or any Brokerage, Broker or Salesperson, for any changes in property tax as a result of a re-assessment of the property, save and except any property taxes that accrued prior to the completion of this transaction.

20. **TIME LIMITS:** Time shall in all respects be of the essence hereof provided that the time for doing or completing of any matter provided for herein may be extended or abridged by an agreement in writing signed by Seller and Buyer or by their respective lawyers who may be specifically authorized in that regard.

21. **TENDER:** Any tender of documents or money hereunder may be made upon Seller or Buyer or their respective lawyers on the day set for completion. Money shall be tendered with funds drawn on a lawyer's trust account in the form of a bank draft, certified cheque or wire transfer using the Large Value Transfer System.

22. **FAMILY LAW ACT:** Seller warrants that spousal consent is not necessary to this transaction under the provisions of the Family Law Act, R.S.O.1990 unless Seller's spouse has executed the consent hereinafter provided.

23. **UFFI:** Seller represents and warrants to Buyer that during the time Seller has owned the property, Seller has not caused any building on the property to be insulated with insulation containing ureaformaldehyde, and that to the best of Seller's knowledge no building on the property contains or has ever contained insulation that contains ureaformaldehyde. This warranty shall survive and not merge on the completion of this transaction, and if the building is part of a multiple unit building, this warranty shall only apply to that part of the building which is the subject of this transaction.

24. **LEGAL, ACCOUNTING AND ENVIRONMENTAL ADVICE:** The parties acknowledge that any information provided by the brokerage is not legal, tax or environmental advice.

25. **CONSUMER REPORTS: The Buyer is hereby notified that a consumer report containing credit and/or personal information may be referred to in connection with this transaction.**

26. **AGREEMENT IN WRITING:** If there is conflict or discrepancy between any provision added to this Agreement (including any Schedule attached hereto) and any provision in the standard pre-set portion hereof, the added provision shall supersede the standard pre-set provision to the extent of such conflict or discrepancy. This Agreement including any Schedule attached hereto, shall constitute the entire Agreement between Buyer and Seller. There is no representation, warranty, collateral agreement or condition, which affects this Agreement other than as expressed herein. For the purposes of this Agreement, Seller means vendor and Buyer means purchaser. This Agreement shall be read with all changes of gender or number required by the context.

27. **TIME AND DATE:** Any reference to a time and date in this Agreement shall mean the time and date where the property is located.

INITIALS OF BUYER(S): (RM MM)   INITIALS OF SELLER(S): (SC WC)

Form 100   Revised 2015   **Page 4 of 6**

Exercise 4   Agreement of Purchase and Sale—Page 5 of 6

28. SUCCESSORS AND ASSIGNS: The heirs, executors, administrators, successors and assigns of the undersigned are bound by the terms herein.

SIGNED, SEALED AND DELIVERED in the presence of: IN WITNESS whereof I have hereunto set my hand and seal:

Andrew Kaiser ....   *Sylvia Chisolm* ....   ● ...... DATE ..... *May 1/xx*
(Witness)   (Buyer)   (Seal)

Andrew Kaiser ....   *Wayne Chisolm* ....   ● ...... DATE ..... *May 1/xx*
(Witness)   (Buyer)   (Seal)

I, the Undersigned Seller, agree to the above offer. I hereby irrevocably instruct my lawyer to pay directly to the brokerage(s) with whom I have agreed to pay commission, the unpaid balance of the commission together with applicable Harmonized Sales Tax (and any other taxes as may hereafter be applicable), from the proceeds of the sale prior to any payment to the undersigned on completion, as advised by the brokerage(s) to my lawyer.

SIGNED, SEALED AND DELIVERED in the presence of: IN WITNESS whereof I have hereunto set my hand and seal:

Mike Sandler ....   *Robert Mostofi* ....   ● ...... DATE ..... *May 2/xx*
(Witness)   (Seller)   (Seal)

....   ● ...... DATE ....
(Witness)   (Seller)   (Seal)

SPOUSAL CONSENT: The Undersigned Spouse of the Seller hereby consents to the disposition evidenced herein pursuant to the provisions of the Family Law Act, R.S.O.1990, and hereby agrees with the Buyer that he/she will execute all necessary or incidental documents to give full force and effect to the sale evidenced herein.

Mike Sandler ....   *Marilyn Mostofi* ....   ● ...... DATE ..... *May 2/xx*
(Witness)   (Spouse)   (Seal)

CONFIRMATION OF ACCEPTANCE: Notwithstanding anything contained herein to the contrary, I confirm this Agreement with all changes both typed and written was finally accepted by all parties at *3:30* a.m./p.m. this *3rd* day of .... *May* ...., 20 *xx*.

Andrew Kaiser
(Signature of Seller or Buyer)

INFORMATION ON BROKERAGE(S)

Listing Brokerage .... **ABC Realty Inc.** .... Tel.No.(**416**) **555-1212**
       328 Main Street, Anycity   **Mike Sandler**
                                       (Salesperson / Broker Name)

Co-op/Buyer Brokerage .... **XYZ Real Estate Ltd.** .... Tel.No.(**416**) **444-1212**
       28 Norfolk Drive, Anycity   **Andrew Kaiser**
                                       (Salesperson / Broker Name)

ACKNOWLEDGEMENT

I acknowledge receipt of my signed copy of this accepted Agreement of Purchase and Sale and I authorize the Brokerage to forward a copy to my lawyer.	I acknowledge receipt of my signed copy of this accepted Agreement of Purchase and Sale and I authorize the Brokerage to forward a copy to my lawyer.
Robert Mostofi .... DATE *May 3/xx* (Seller)	*Sylvia Chisholm* .... DATE *May 3/xx* (Buyer)
Marilyn Mostofi .... DATE *May 3/xx* (Seller)	.... DATE .... (Buyer)
Address for Service *3291 Forest View Pkwy., Anycity*	Address for Service *Apt. 32, 17 Springboard Dr.*
K9R 8J3 .... Tel.No.(*416*) *333-1212*	*Distant City P2V 3C7* ..... Tel.No.(*613*) *888-1212*
Seller's Lawyer *J. Robert Munro*	Buyer's Lawyer *Ms E. McKay c/o Moore and Morrison*
Address *32 Eastgate Avenue, Anycity K9Y 3C3*	Address *34 Central Square, Distant City P7H 3B2*
Email	Email ....
(*416*) *222-1212* (*416*) *222-2121* Tel.No. FAX No.	(*613*) *777-1212* (*613*) *777-2121* Tel.No. FAX No.

FOR OFFICE USE ONLY   **COMMISSION TRUST AGREEMENT**

To: Co-operating Brokerage shown on the foregoing Agreement of Purchase and Sale:
In consideration for the Co-operating Brokerage procuring the foregoing Agreement of Purchase and Sale, I hereby declare that all moneys received or receivable by me in connection with the Transaction as contemplated in the MLS® Rules and Regulations of my Real Estate Board shall be receivable and held in trust. This agreement shall constitute a Commission Trust Agreement as defined in the MLS® Rules and shall be subject to and governed by the MLS® Rules pertaining to Commission Trust.

DATED as of the date and time of the acceptance of the foregoing Agreement of Purchase and Sale.   Acknowledged by...

Mike Sandler ....   *Andrew Kaiser*
(Authorized to bind the Listing Brokerage)   (Authorized to bind the Co-operating Brokerage)

Form 100   Revised 2015   **Page 5 of 6**

Schedule A
Agreement of Purchase and Sale

Form 100
for use in the Province of Ontario

This Schedule is attached to and forms part of the Agreement of Purchase and Sale between:

BUYER, ... Sylvia B. Chisolm and Wayne T. Chisolm ...., and

SELLER, ... Robert K. Mostofi and Marilyn C. Mostofi ....

for the purchase and sale of .... Pt Lot 9, Plan 99M-245 subject to mutual side drive ....

.... dated the ...1st... day of .... May ...., 20..XX...

Buyer agrees to pay the balance as follows:

The Buyer agrees to pay a further sum of Two Hundred and Forty-Two Thousand Dollars ($242,000.00), subject to adjustments, to the Seller on completion of this transaction, with funds drawn on a lawyer's trust account in the form of a bank draft, certified cheque, or wire transfer using the Large Value Transfer System.

This Offer is conidtional upon the Buyer arranging, at the Buyer's own expense, a new first charge/mortgage for not less than One Hundred and Seventy-Five Thousand Dollars ($175,000.00), bearing interest at a rate of not more than 5.0% per annum, calculated semi-annually not in advance, repayable in blended monthly payments of about One Thousand and Seventeen Dollars and Eighty-One Cents ($1,017.81), including principal and interest, and to run for a term of not less than 3 years from the date of completion of this transaction. Unless the Buyer gives notice in writing, delivered to the Seller personally or in accordance with any other provisions for the delivery of notice in this Agreement of Purchase and Sale or any Schedule thereto not later than 5:00 p.m. on the 24th day of May, 20xx, that this condition is fulfilled, this Offer shall be null and void and the deposit shall be returned to the Buyer in full without deduction. This condition is included for the benefit of the Buyer and may be waived at the Buyer's sole option by notice in writing to the Seller, as aforesaid, within the time period stated herein.

The Seller agrees to take back a second Charge/Mortgage in the amount of Fifteen Thousand Dollars ($15,000.00) bearing interest at a rate of 6.5% per annum, calculated semi-annually not in advance, repayable in blended monthly payments of One Hundred and Thirty-One Dollars and Ninety-Six Cents ($131.96), including both principal and interest, and to run for a term of 2 years from the date of completion of this transaction.

This Charge/Mortgage shall contain a clause permitting the Chargor/Mortgagor, when not in default, the privilege of prepaying all or part of the principal sum on any payment date or dates without notice of bonus, provided that any partial repayment shall equal the sum of the principal amounts of the payment(s) next falling due under the Charge/Mortgage.

The Seller represents and warrants that there is no known damage as a result of a minor roof leakage that occurred and was repaired approximately two months ago.

The Buyer agrees to accept a 20-foot drainage easement crossing the property.

This form must be initialed by all parties to the Agreement of Purchase and Sale.

INITIALS OF BUYER(S): (RM MM)   INITIALS OF SELLER(S): (SC WC)

Form 100   Revised 2015   **Page 6 of 6**

■ Exercise 5   Drafting Sale-Related Documents

Complete various documents relating to the offer drafted by A. Fernandes, a salesperson (independent contractor) with XYZ Real Estate Limited (for the offer and associated forms). William Palm of ABC Realty Inc. has exclusively listed 3291 Golf Course Drive. XYZ is the co-operating brokerage who will receive 50% of the 5.0% commission paid on successful completion of the sale. The buyers' offer is presented at the Norton home. Insert additional information as required for a fully completed form. All required forms for this exercise are included following these instructions.

5.1   *Confirmation of Co-operation and Representation*

The confirmation form is signed by the buyers and Fernandes. Insert any details necessary to fully complete that form.

5.2   *Offer/Counter Offer*

The next day, following signing of the *Confirmation of Co-operation and Representation* by the listing salesperson and the sellers, the offer is presented to the Nortons. The sellers, when speaking privately with the listing salesperson W. Palm of ABC Realty Inc., decide to increase the purchase price by $15,500, remove the warranty clause and add a further day for the buyers' consideration of this counter offer.

Ellen and David Shantz, the buyers, review the counter offer on the following day and accept the terms. The sellers' lawyer is Jane Pierce of Pierce & Lyons, 327 Centre Avenue in Anycity. The buyers' lawyer is Thomas Rowley of Steward, Millard, & Stoltz, 291 Westside Drive in Anycity. Fully complete the accepted counter offer including all signatures, witnessing and related details by amending the original offer on the following pages.

5.3   *Trade Record Sheet*

Complete the trade record sheet for ABC Realty Inc. including commission distribution to the co-operating brokerage and the listing salesperson. William Palm is on a 65/35 split with ABC Realty Inc. No referral or board fees apply. Leave the balance of the form blank; i.e., deposit particulars. Such items are completed by brokerage staff.

5.4   *Waiver*

The condition on financing is waived by the buyers on the final date as set out in the agreement. Prepare the waiver.

5.5   *Amendment*

The buyers and sellers agree to amend the agreement on July 5th. The new completion date will be August 30, 20xx and the sellers have permitted access by the buyers to inspect the property before closing. The amendment is completed and signed by all parties on the 5th. Complete the *Amendment to Agreement*.

OREA Ontario Real Estate Association

Confirmation of Co-operation and Representation

Form 320
for use in the Province of Ontario

BUYER: ....

SELLER: ....

For the transaction on the property known as: ....

For the purposes of this Confirmation of Co-operation and Representation, "Seller" includes a vendor, a landlord, or a prospective, seller, vendor or landlord and "Buyer" includes a purchaser, a tenant, or a prospective, buyer, purchaser or tenant, "sale" includes a lease, and "Agreement of Purchase and Sale" includes an Agreement to Lease.

The following information is confirmed by the undersigned salesperson/broker representatives of the Brokerage(s). If a Co-operating Brokerage is involved in the transaction, the brokerages agree to co-operate, in consideration of, and on the terms and conditions as set out below.

DECLARATION OF INSURANCE: The undersigned salesperson/broker representative(s) of the Brokerage(s) hereby declare that he/she is insured as required by the Real Estate and Business Brokers Act, 2002 (REBBA 2002) and Regulations.

1. LISTING BROKERAGE

   a) ☐   The Listing Brokerage represents the interests of the Seller in this transaction. It is further understood and agreed that:

      1) ☐   The Listing Brokerage is not representing or providing Customer Service to the Buyer.
          (If the Buyer is working with a Co-operating Brokerage, Section 3 is to be completed by Co-operating Brokerage)

      2) ☐   The Listing Brokerage is providing Customer Service to the Buyer.

   b) ☐   **MULTIPLE REPRESENTATION:** The Listing Brokerage has entered into a Buyer Representation Agreement with the Buyer and represents the interests of the Seller and the Buyer, with their consent, for this transaction. The Listing Brokerage must be impartial and equally protect the interests of the Seller and the Buyer in this transaction. The Listing Brokerage has a duty of full disclosure to both the Seller and the Buyer, including a requirement to disclose all factual information about the property known to the Listing Brokerage. However, the Listing Brokerage shall not disclose:

- That the Seller may or will accept less than the listed price, unless otherwise instructed in writing by the Seller;
- That the Buyer may or will pay more than the offered price, unless otherwise instructed in writing by the Buyer;
- The motivation of or personal information about the Seller or Buyer, unless otherwise instructed in writing by the party to which the information applies, or unless failure to disclose would constitute fraudulent, unlawful or unethical practice;
- The price the Buyer should offer or the price the Seller should accept;
- And; the Listing Brokerage shall not disclose to the Buyer the terms of any other offer.

However, it is understood that factual market information about comparable properties and information known to the Listing Brokerage concerning potential uses for the property will be disclosed to both Seller and Buyer to assist them to come to their own conclusions.

Additional comments and/or disclosures by Listing Brokerage: (e.g. The Listing Brokerage represents more than one Buyer offering on this property.)

....

....

....

2. PROPERTY SOLD BY BUYER BROKERAGE – PROPERTY NOT LISTED

   ☐   The Brokerage .... represent the Buyer and the property is not listed with any real estate brokerage. The Brokerage will be paid
       (does/does not)

            ☐   by the Seller in accordance with a Seller Customer Service Agreement

      or: ☐   by the Buyer directly

Additional comments and/or disclosures by Buyer Brokerage: (e.g. The Buyer Brokerage represents more than one Buyer offering on this property.)

....

....

....

....

INITIALS OF BUYER(S)/SELLER(S)/BROKERAGE REPRESENTATIVE(S) (Where applicable)

   ◯   ◯   ◯   ◯

   BUYER   **CO-OPERATING/BUYER BROKERAGE**   **SELLER**   **LISTING BROKERAGE**

Form 320   Revised 2015   **Page 1 of 2**

Exercise 5   Confirmation of Co-operation and Representation—Page 2 of 2

3. **Co-operating Brokerage completes Section 3 and Listing Brokerage completes Section 1.**

CO-OPERATING BROKERAGE- REPRESENTATION:

a) ☐ The Co-operating Brokerage represents the interests of the Buyer in this transaction.

b) ☐ The Co-operating Brokerage is providing Customer Service to the Buyer in this transaction.

c) ☐ The Co-operating Brokerage is not representing the Buyer and has not entered into an agreement to provide customer service(s) to the Buyer.

CO-OPERATING BROKERAGE- COMMISSION:

a) ☐ The Listing Brokerage will pay the Co-operating Brokerage the commission as indicated in the MLS® information for the property

.... to be paid from the amount paid by the Seller to the Listing Brokerage.
(Commission As Indicated In MLS® Information)

b) ☐ The Co-operating Brokerage will be paid as follows:

....

....

....

Additional comments and/or disclosures by Co-operating Brokerage: (e.g., The Co-operating Brokerage represents more than one Buyer offering on this property.)

....

....

....

Commission will be payable as described above, plus applicable taxes.

COMMISSION TRUST AGREEMENT: If the above Co-operating Brokerage is receiving payment of commission from the Listing Brokerage, then the agreement between Listing Brokerage and Co-operating Brokerage further includes a Commission Trust Agreement, the consideration for which is the Co-operating Brokerage procuring an offer for a trade of the property, acceptable to the Seller. This Commission Trust Agreement shall be subject to and governed by the MLS® rules and regulations pertaining to commission trusts of the Listing Brokerage's local real estate board, if the local board's MLS® rules and regulations so provide. Otherwise, the provisions of the OREA recommended MLS® rules and regulations shall apply to this Commission Trust Agreement. For the purpose of this Commission Trust Agreement, the Commission Trust Amount shall be the amount noted in Section 3 above. The Listing Brokerage hereby declares that all monies received in connection with the trade shall constitute a Commission Trust and shall be held, in trust, for the Co-operating Brokerage under the terms of the applicable MLS® rules and regulations.

SIGNED BY THE BROKER/SALESPERSON REPRESENTATIVE(S) OF THE BROKERAGE(S) (Where applicable)

.... | ....
(Name of Co-operating/Buyer Brokerage) | (Name of Listing Brokerage)

.... | ....

Tel.: .... Fax: .... | Tel.: .... Fax: ....

.... Date:................ | .... Date:................
(Authorized to bind the Co-operating/Buyer Brokerage) | (Authorized to bind the Listing Brokerage)

.... | ....
(Print Name of Broker/Salesperson Representative of the Brokerage) | (Print Name of Broker/Salesperson Representative of the Brokerage)

CONSENT FOR MULTIPLE REPRESENTATION (To be completed only if the Brokerage represents more than one client for the transaction)

The Buyer/Seller consent with their initials to their Brokerage representing more than one client for this transaction.

◯ **BUYER'S INITIALS**   ◯ **SELLER'S INITIALS**

ACKNOWLEDGEMENT

I have received, read, and understand the above information.

.... Date: .... | .... Date: ....
(Signature of Buyer) | (Signature of Seller)

.... Date: .... | .... Date: ....
(Signature of Buyer) | (Signature of Seller)

Form 320   Revised 2015   **Page 2 of 2**

OREA Ontario Real Estate Association   # Agreement of Purchase and Sale

Form 100
for use in the Province of Ontario

This Agreement of Purchase and Sale dated this ...... **14th** ..... day of .... **June** .... 20 **XX** ......

BUYER, ... **Ellen Marie Shantz and David Charles Shantz** ...., agrees to purchase from
(Full legal names of all Buyers)

SELLER, ... **Leslie C. Norton and James P. Norton** ...., the following
(Full legal names of all Sellers)

REAL PROPERTY:

Address .... **3291 Golf Course Drive** ....

fronting on the .... **West** .... side of .... **Golf Course Drive** ....

in the .... **City of Anycity, Regional Municipality of Anyregion** ....

and having a frontage of .... **64.55 feet** .... more or less by a depth of .... **157.29 feet** .... more or less

and legally described as ... **Lot 231, Registered Plan 99M-891 subject to a 15-foot service easement**

.... **on the northeasterly corner of the rear yard** .... (the "property")
(Legal description of land including easements not described elsewhere)

PURCHASE PRICE: Dollars (CDN$) **$339,000.00**

.. **Three-Hundred and Thirty-Nine Thousand**-- Dollars

DEPOSIT: Buyer submits .... **Upon Acceptance** ....
(Herewith/Upon Acceptance/as otherwise described in this Agreement)

.. **Twenty-Five Thousand**-- Dollars (CDN$) **$25,000.00**

by negotiable cheque payable to .... **ABC Realty Inc.** .... "Deposit Holder" to be held
in trust pending completion or other termination of this Agreement and to be credited toward the Purchase Price on completion. For the purposes of this
Agreement, "Upon Acceptance" shall mean that the Buyer is required to deliver the deposit to the Deposit Holder within 24 hours of the acceptance of
this Agreement. The parties to this Agreement hereby acknowledge that, unless otherwise provided for in this Agreement, the Deposit Holder shall place
the deposit in trust in the Deposit Holder's non-interest bearing Real Estate Trust Account and no interest shall be earned, received or paid on the deposit.

Buyer agrees to pay the balance as more particularly set out in Schedule A attached.

SCHEDULE(S) A.. **attached hereto form(s) part of this Agreement.**

1. **IRREVOCABILITY:** This offer shall be irrevocable by .... **Buyer** .... until **11:59** ~~a.m.~~/p.m. on the **15th**
                                                        (Seller/Buyer)

    day of .... **June** .... 20 **XX** ..., after which time, if not accepted, this offer shall be null and void and the deposit
    shall be returned to the Buyer in full without interest.

2. **COMPLETION DATE:** This Agreement shall be completed by no later than 6:00 p.m. on the ...... **30th** ... day of .... **July** ....

    20 **XX** .... Upon completion, vacant possession of the property shall be given to the Buyer unless otherwise provided for in this Agreement.

INITIALS OF BUYER(S): (*ES DS*)   **INITIALS OF SELLER(S):** ( )

Exercise 5   Agreement of Purchase and Sale—Page 2 of 6

3. **NOTICES:** The Seller hereby appoints the Listing Brokerage as agent for the Seller for the purpose of giving and receiving notices pursuant to this Agreement. Where a Brokerage (Buyer's Brokerage) has entered into a representation agreement with the Buyer, the Buyer hereby appoints the Buyer's Brokerage as agent for the purpose of giving and receiving notices pursuant to this Agreement. **Where a Brokerage represents both the Seller and the Buyer (multiple representation), the Brokerage shall not be appointed or authorized to be agent for either the Buyer or the Seller for the purpose of giving and receiving notices.** Any notice relating hereto or provided for herein shall be in writing. In addition to any provision contained herein and in any Schedule hereto, this offer, any counter-offer, notice of acceptance thereof or any notice to be given or received pursuant to this Agreement or any Schedule hereto (any of them, "Document") shall be deemed given and received when delivered personally or hand delivered to the Address for Service provided in the Acknowledgement below, or where a facsimile number or email address is provided herein, when transmitted electronically to that facsimile number or email address, respectively, in which case, the signature(s) of the party (parties) shall be deemed to be original.

FAX No.: .... **(519) 555-2121** .... FAX No.: .... **(519) 666-2121** ....
    (For delivery of Documents to Seller)   (For delivery of Documents to Buyer)

Email Address: .... **admin@abcrealty.com** .... Email Address: .... **notices@xyzrealestate.com** ....
    (For delivery of Documents to Seller)   (For delivery of Documents to Buyer)

4. **CHATTELS INCLUDED:** Satellite dish, 2 remotes and receiver, storage shed, and SpaTime hot tub

     including enclosure and all attachments

     ....

     ....

Unless otherwise stated in this Agreement or any Schedule hereto, Seller agrees to convey all fixtures and chattels included in the Purchase Price free from all liens, encumbrances or claims affecting the said fixtures and chattels.

5. **FIXTURES EXCLUDED:** Glass decorator shelves in living room, and dining room chandelier

     ....

     ....

     ....

6. **RENTAL ITEMS (Including Lease, Lease to Own):** The following equipment is rented and **not** included in the Purchase Price. The Buyer agrees to assume the rental contract(s), if assumable:

     Hot water tank, Anycity Energy @ $36.25 quarterly (plus applicable taxes)

     ....

     ....

The Buyer agrees to co-operate and execute such documentation as may be required to facilitate such assumption.

7. **HST:** If the sale of the Property (Real Property as described above) is subject to Harmonized Sales Tax (HST), then such tax shall be

     .... included in .... the Purchase Price. If the sale of the Property is not subject to HST, Seller agrees to certify on or before
                (included in/in addition to)

     closing, that the sale of the Property is not subject to HST. Any HST on chattels, if applicable, is not included in the Purchase Price.

INITIALS OF BUYER(S): (*ES DS*)   INITIALS OF SELLER(S): ( )

Form 100   Revised 2015   **Page 2 of 6**

8. **TITLE SEARCH:** Buyer shall be allowed until 6:00 p.m. on the ....15th... day of ....July.............................., 20XX....., (Requisition Date) to examine the title to the Property at Buyer's own expense and until the earlier of: (i) thirty days from the later of the Requisition Date or the date on which the conditions in this Agreement are fulfilled or otherwise waived or; (ii) five days prior to completion, to satisfy Buyer that there are no outstanding

work orders or deficiency notices affecting the Property, and that its present use (....................single family residential........................) may be lawfully continued and that the principal building may be insured against risk of fire. Seller hereby consents to the municipality or other governmental agencies releasing to Buyer details of all outstanding work orders and deficiency notices affecting the property, and Seller agrees to execute and deliver such further authorizations in this regard as Buyer may reasonably require.

9. **FUTURE USE:** Seller and Buyer agree that there is no representation or warranty of any kind that the future intended use of the property by Buyer is or will be lawful except as may be specifically provided for in this Agreement.

10. **TITLE:** Provided that the title to the property is good and free from all registered restrictions, charges, liens, and encumbrances except as otherwise specifically provided in this Agreement and save and except for (a) any registered restrictions or covenants that run with the land providing that such are complied with; (b) any registered municipal agreements and registered agreements with publicly regulated utilities providing such have been complied with, or security has been posted to ensure compliance and completion, as evidenced by a letter from the relevant municipality or regulated utility; (c) any minor easements for the supply of domestic utility or telephone services to the property or adjacent properties; and (d) any easements for drainage, storm or sanitary sewers, public utility lines, telephone lines, cable television lines or other services which do not materially affect the use of the property. If within the specified times referred to in paragraph 8 any valid objection to title or to any outstanding work order or deficiency notice, or to the fact the said present use may not lawfully be continued, or that the principal building may not be insured against risk of fire is made in writing to Seller and which Seller is unable or unwilling to remove, remedy or satisfy or obtain insurance save and except against risk of fire (Title Insurance) in favour of the Buyer and any mortgagee, (with all related costs at the expense of the Seller), and which Buyer will not waive, this Agreement notwithstanding any intermediate acts or negotiations in respect of such objections, shall be at an end and all monies paid shall be returned without interest or deduction and Seller, Listing Brokerage and Co-operating Brokerage shall not be liable for any costs or damages. Save as to any valid objection so made by such day and except for any objection going to the root of the title, Buyer shall be conclusively deemed to have accepted Seller's title to the property.

11. **CLOSING ARRANGEMENTS:** Where each of the Seller and Buyer retain a lawyer to complete the Agreement of Purchase and Sale of the property, and where the transaction will be completed by electronic registration pursuant to Part III of the Land Registration Reform Act, R.S.O. 1990, Chapter L4 and the Electronic Registration Act, S.O. 1991, Chapter 44, and any amendments thereto, the Seller and Buyer acknowledge and agree that the exchange of closing funds, non-registrable documents and other items (the "Requisite Deliveries") and the release thereof to the Seller and Buyer will (a) not occur at the same time as the registration of the transfer/deed (and any other documents intended to be registered in connection with the completion of this transaction) and (b) be subject to conditions whereby the lawyer(s) receiving any of the Requisite Deliveries will be required to hold same in trust and not release same except in accordance with the terms of a document registration agreement between the said lawyers. The Seller and Buyer irrevocably instruct the said lawyers to be bound by the document registration agreement which is recommended from time to time by the Law Society of Upper Canada. Unless otherwise agreed to by the lawyers, such exchange of the Requisite Deliveries will occur in the applicable Land Titles Office or such other location agreeable to both lawyers.

12. **DOCUMENTS AND DISCHARGE:** Buyer shall not call for the production of any title deed, abstract, survey or other evidence of title to the property except such as are in the possession or control of Seller. If requested by Buyer, Seller will deliver any sketch or survey of the property within Seller's control to Buyer as soon as possible and prior to the Requisition Date. If a discharge of any Charge/Mortgage held by a corporation incorporated pursuant to the Trust And Loan Companies Act (Canada), Chartered Bank, Trust Company, Credit Union, Caisse Populaire or Insurance Company and which is not to be assumed by Buyer on completion, is not available in registrable form on completion, Buyer agrees to accept Seller's lawyer's personal undertaking to obtain, out of the closing funds, a discharge in registrable form and to register same, or cause same to be registered, on title within a reasonable period of time after completion, provided that on or before completion Seller shall provide to Buyer a mortgage statement prepared by the mortgagee setting out the balance required to obtain the discharge, and, where a real-time electronic cleared funds transfer system is not being used, a direction executed by Seller directing payment to the mortgagee of the amount required to obtain the discharge out of the balance due on completion.

13. **INSPECTION:** Buyer acknowledges having had the opportunity to inspect the Property and understands that upon acceptance of this offer there shall be a binding agreement of purchase and sale between Buyer and Seller. **The Buyer acknowledges having the opportunity to include a requirement for a property inspection report in this Agreement and agrees that except as may be specifically provided for in this Agreement, the Buyer will not be obtaining a property inspection or property inspection report regarding the Property.**

14. **INSURANCE:** All buildings on the property and all other things being purchased shall be and remain until completion at the risk of Seller. Pending completion, Seller shall hold all insurance policies, if any, and the proceeds thereof in trust for the parties as their interests may appear and in the event of substantial damage, Buyer may either terminate this Agreement and have all monies paid returned without interest or deduction or else take the proceeds of any insurance and complete the purchase. No insurance shall be transferred on completion. If Seller is taking back a Charge/Mortgage, or Buyer is assuming a Charge/Mortgage, Buyer shall supply Seller with reasonable evidence of adequate insurance to protect Seller's or other mortgagee's interest on completion.

INITIALS OF BUYER(S): (*ES DS*)   INITIALS OF SELLER(S): (   )

15. PLANNING ACT: This Agreement shall be effective to create an interest in the property only if Seller complies with the subdivision control provisions of the Planning Act by completion and Seller covenants to proceed diligently at Seller's expense to obtain any necessary consent by completion.

16. DOCUMENT PREPARATION: The Transfer/Deed shall, save for the Land Transfer Tax Affidavit, be prepared in registrable form at the expense of Seller, and any Charge/Mortgage to be given back by the Buyer to Seller at the expense of the Buyer. If requested by Buyer, Seller covenants that the Transfer/Deed to be delivered on completion shall contain the statements contemplated by Section 50(22) of the Planning Act, R.S.O.1990.

17. RESIDENCY: (a) Subject to (b) below, the Seller represents and warrants that the Seller is not and on completion will not be a non-resident under the non-residency provisions of the Income Tax Act which representation and warranty shall survive and not merge upon the completion of this transaction and the Seller shall deliver to the Buyer a statutory declaration that Seller is not then a non-resident of Canada; (b) provided that if the Seller is a non-resident under the non-residency provisions of the Income Tax Act, the Buyer shall be credited towards the Purchase Price with the amount, if any, necessary for Buyer to pay to the Minister of National Revenue to satisfy Buyer's liability in respect of tax payable by Seller under the non-residency provisions of the Income Tax Act by reason of this sale. Buyer shall not claim such credit if Seller delivers on completion the prescribed certificate.

18. ADJUSTMENTS: Any rents, mortgage interest, realty taxes including local improvement rates and unmetered public or private utility charges and unmetered cost of fuel, as applicable, shall be apportioned and allowed to the day of completion, the day of completion itself to be apportioned to Buyer.

19. PROPERTY ASSESSMENT: The Buyer and Seller hereby acknowledge that the Province of Ontario has implemented current value assessment and properties may be re-assessed on an annual basis. The Buyer and Seller agree that no claim will be made against the Buyer or Seller, or any Brokerage, Broker or Salesperson, for any changes in property tax as a result of a re-assessment of the property, save and except any property taxes that accrued prior to the completion of this transaction.

20. TIME LIMITS: Time shall in all respects be of the essence hereof provided that the time for doing or completing of any matter provided for herein may be extended or abridged by an agreement in writing signed by Seller and Buyer or by their respective lawyers who may be specifically authorized in that regard.

21. TENDER: Any tender of documents or money hereunder may be made upon Seller or Buyer or their respective lawyers on the day set for completion. Money shall be tendered with funds drawn on a lawyer's trust account in the form of a bank draft, certified cheque or wire transfer using the Large Value Transfer System.

22. FAMILY LAW ACT: Seller warrants that spousal consent is not necessary to this transaction under the provisions of the Family Law Act, R.S.O.1990 unless Seller's spouse has executed the consent hereinafter provided.

23. UFFI: Seller represents and warrants to Buyer that during the time Seller has owned the property, Seller has not caused any building on the property to be insulated with insulation containing ureaformaldehyde, and that to the best of Seller's knowledge no building on the property contains or has ever contained insulation that contains ureaformaldehyde. This warranty shall survive and not merge on the completion of this transaction, and if the building is part of a multiple unit building, this warranty shall only apply to that part of the building which is the subject of this transaction.

24. LEGAL, ACCOUNTING AND ENVIRONMENTAL ADVICE: The parties acknowledge that any information provided by the brokerage is not legal, tax or environmental advice.

25. CONSUMER REPORTS: The Buyer is hereby notified that a consumer report containing credit and/or personal information may be referred to in connection with this transaction.

26. AGREEMENT IN WRITING: If there is conflict or discrepancy between any provision added to this Agreement (including any Schedule attached hereto) and any provision in the standard pre-set portion hereof, the added provision shall supersede the standard pre-set provision to the extent of such conflict or discrepancy. This Agreement including any Schedule attached hereto, shall constitute the entire Agreement between Buyer and Seller. There is no representation, warranty, collateral agreement or condition, which affects this Agreement other than as expressed herein. For the purposes of this Agreement, Seller means vendor and Buyer means purchaser. This Agreement shall be read with all changes of gender or number required by the context.

27. TIME AND DATE: Any reference to a time and date in this Agreement shall mean the time and date where the property is located.

INITIALS OF BUYER(S): (*ES DS*)   INITIALS OF SELLER(S): (   )

Form 100   Revised 2015   **Page 4 of 6**

28. SUCCESSORS AND ASSIGNS: The heirs, executors, administrators, successors and assigns of the undersigned are bound by the terms herein.

SIGNED, SEALED AND DELIVERED in the presence of: IN WITNESS whereof I have hereunto set my hand and seal:

A. Fernandes .... *Ellen Shantz* .... ●   DATE *June 14/xx*
(Witness)   (Buyer)   (Seal)

A. Fernandes .... *David Shantz* .... ●   DATE *June 14/xx*
(Witness)   (Buyer)   (Seal)

I, the Undersigned Seller, agree to the above offer. I hereby irrevocably instruct my lawyer to pay directly to the brokerage(s) with whom I have agreed to pay commission, the unpaid balance of the commission together with applicable Harmonized Sales Tax (and any other taxes as may hereafter be applicable), from the proceeds of the sale prior to any payment to the undersigned on completion, as advised by the brokerage(s) to my lawyer.

SIGNED, SEALED AND DELIVERED in the presence of: IN WITNESS whereof I have hereunto set my hand and seal:

.... ●   DATE ....
(Witness)   (Seller)   (Seal)

.... ●   DATE ....
(Witness)   (Seller)   (Seal)

SPOUSAL CONSENT: The Undersigned Spouse of the Seller hereby consents to the disposition evidenced herein pursuant to the provisions of the Family Law Act, R.S.O.1990, and hereby agrees with the Buyer that he/she will execute all necessary or incidental documents to give full force and effect to the sale evidenced herein.

.... ●   DATE ....
(Witness)   (Spouse)   (Seal)

CONFIRMATION OF ACCEPTANCE: Notwithstanding anything contained herein to the contrary, I confirm this Agreement with all changes both typed and written was finally accepted by all parties at .... a.m./p.m. this .... day of.., 20..........

....
(Signature of Seller or Buyer)

INFORMATION ON BROKERAGE(S)

Listing Brokerage .... Tel.No.(...............)....................

....
(Salesperson / Broker Name)

Co-op/Buyer Brokerage .... Tel.No.(...............)....................

....
(Salesperson / Broker Name)

ACKNOWLEDGEMENT

I acknowledge receipt of my signed copy of this accepted Agreement of Purchase and Sale and I authorize the Brokerage to forward a copy to my lawyer.	I acknowledge receipt of my signed copy of this accepted Agreement of Purchase and Sale and I authorize the Brokerage to forward a copy to my lawyer.
.... DATE .... (Seller)	.... DATE .... (Buyer)
.... DATE .... (Seller) Address for Service	.... DATE .... (Buyer) Address for Service ....
.... Tel.No.(..........).........	.... Tel.No.(..........).........
Seller's Lawyer	Buyer's Lawyer ....
Address	Address ....
Email	Email ....
(..........)................... (..........)......... Tel.No. - FAX No.	(..........)................... (..........)......... Tel.No. FAX No.

FOR OFFICE USE ONLY   **COMMISSION TRUST AGREEMENT**

To: Co-operating Brokerage shown on the foregoing Agreement of Purchase and Sale:
In consideration for the Co-operating Brokerage procuring the foregoing Agreement of Purchase and Sale, I hereby declare that all moneys received or receivable by me in connection with the Transaction as contemplated in the MLS® Rules and Regulations of my Real Estate Board shall be receivable and held in trust. This agreement shall constitute a Commission Trust Agreement as defined in the MLS® Rules and shall be subject to and governed by the MLS® Rules pertaining to Commission Trust.
DATED as of the date and time of the acceptance of the foregoing Agreement of Purchase and Sale.   Acknowledged by:

....
(Authorized to bind the Listing Brokerage)   (Authorized to bind the Co-operating Brokerage)

Form 100   Revised 2015   **Page 5 of 6**

Exercise 5   Agreement of Purchase and Sale—Page 6 of 6

 **Ontario Real Estate Association**

Form 100
for use in the Province of Ontario

Schedule A
Agreement of Purchase and Sale

This Schedule is attached to and forms part of the Agreement of Purchase and Sale between:

BUYER, ... Ellen Marie Shantz and David Charles Shantz ...., and

SELLER, ... Leslie C. Norton and James P. Norton ....

for the purchase and sale of ... 3291 Golf Course Drive, City of Anycity, Regional Municipality of Anyregion

.... dated the ... 14th day of .... June ...., 20.. XX ...

Buyer agrees to pay the balance as follows:

The Buyer agrees to pay a further sum of Three Hundred and Fourteen Thousand Dollars ($314,000.00), subject to adjustments, to the Seller on completion of this transaction, with funds drawn on a lawyer's trust account in the form of a bank draft, certified cheque, or wire transfer using the Large Value Transfer System.

This Offer is conditional upon the Buyer arranging, at the Buyer's own expense, a new first Charge/ Mortgage for not less than Two Hundred Thousand Dollars ($200,000.00), bearing interest at a rate of not more than 5.75% per annum, calculated semi-annually not in advance, repayable in blended bi-weekly payments of about Five Hundred and Seventy-Six Dollars and Twenty-One Cents ($576.21), including principal and interest, and to run for a term of not less than four years from the date of completion of this transaction. Unless the Buyer gives notice in writing, delivered to the Seller personally or in accordance with any other provisions for the delivery of notice of this Agreement of Purchase and Sale or any Schedule thereto not later than 11:59 p.m. on the 30th day of June, 20xx, that this condition is fulfilled, this Offer shall be null and void and the deposit shall be returned to the Buyer in full without deduction. This condition is included for the benefit of the Buyer and may be waived at the Buyer's sole option by notice in writing to the Seller as aforesaid within the time period state herein.

The Seller represents and warrants that all mechanical equipment, including furnace, water softener and air conditioner, all electrical wiring and fixtures, and all plumbing systems are in good working order and in full compliance with current construction code standards. The Parties agree that these representations and warranties shall survive and not merge on completion of this transaction.

The Buyer acknowledges that there is no express or implied warranty by the Seller on the chattels included in the agreement of purchase and sale.

This form must be initialed by all parties to the Agreement of Purchase and Sale.

INITIALS OF BUYER(S): (*ES DS*)   **INITIALS OF SELLER(S):** ( )

 Form 100   Revised 2015   **Page 6 of 6**

Ontario Real Estate Association

Trade Record Sheet

Form 640
for use in the Province of Ontario

	Sale No:
	MLS® No:

.... Dated: ...., 20..............
(Name of Brokerage)

I, ..., have today sold (leased or rented, exchanged, optioned):
(Name of Broker/Salesperson)

Property ....

SELLER/LANDLORD:	BUYER/TENANT:
....	....
....	....
Address	Address ....
....	....
Tel	Tel ....
Fax	Fax ....
Lawyer	Lawyer ....
....	....
....	....
Tel	Tel ....
Fax	Fax ....

CO-OPERATING/LISTING BROKERAGE (If applicable):   ☐ Listing Brokerage   ☐ Co-operating Brokerage

....

Address ....

Tel ....   Fax ....

Co-op Brokerage HST Number...

REFERRAL BROKERAGE   Tel ....

Address .... Fax ....

REFERRAL BROKERAGE   Tel ....

Address .... Fax ....

Total Consideration For Transaction $ ....
(sale price, rent, exchange value, option price, fee (other))

Completion Date ....

Deposit $...   ☐ cash   ☐ cheque

If cheque, payable to ...., in trust.

Additional Deposit $ ....   ☐ cash   ☐ cheque

If cheque, payable to ...., in trust.

Property Other Than Money Held In Trust ....

....

Total	**Total**	**Total**
Commission $	HST $	Receivable Comm $ ....

....
(Broker/Salesperson)   (Broker/Salesperson)

The trademarks REALTOR®, REALTORS® and the REALTOR® logo are controlled by The Canadian Real Estate Association (CREA) and identify real estate professionals who are members of CREA. Used under license.

Form 640   Revised 2015   **Page 1 of 2**

Exercise 5   Trade Record Sheet—Page 2 of 2

Property ....

Sale No.:

Seller/Landlord ....

MLS® No.:

Buyer/Tenant ....

THE FOLLOWING TO BE COMPLETED BY THE BROKERAGE:

Total Receivable Commission:	COMMISSION	HST	TOTAL	DATE PAID	CHEQUE NO.
Listing Brokerage:					
Listing #1 Salesperson/ Broker #2					
Co-op Brokerage:					
Selling #1 Salesperson/ Broker #2					
Referral Fee:					
Referral Fee:					
Real Estate Board:					
Other:					

Received deposit from (Salesperson/Broker)... DATE ....

Additional deposit from (Salesperson/Broker)... DATE ....

Deposited in Real Estate Trust Acc. (Amount)... DATE ....

Additional deposit to Real Estate Trust Acc. (Amount)................................... DATE ....

Statement to Seller DATE...

Interest bearing deposit transferred to ....

Instrument #... DATE .... Cheque # ....

Interest bearing deposit returned

to Real Estate Trust Acc. (Amount)..................... DATE .... Cheque # ....

If applicable, Interest earned (Amount) ....

If applicable, interest paid to ....

Cheque # ....

If applicable, SIN of interest recipient ....

If applicable, Business # of Corporation ....

Remitted to Seller/Buyer (Amount) .... DATE .... Cheque # ....

Transferred to Commission Trust (Amount) .... DATE .... Cheque # ....

Transferred Commission to Gen. Acct. (Amount) ... DATE .... Cheque # ....

Additional Necessary Information ....

....

....

To the best of my knowledge and belief the above information is correct.

DATED at .... Ontario, this .... day of ...., 20..................

....
(Signature of Broker of Record)

FOR OFFICE USE ONLY   **COMMISSION TRUST AGREEMENT**
To: The Salesperson(s) shown on the foregoing Trade Record Sheet:
In consideration of the Salesperson(s) having successfully completed a trade in real estate on behalf of the Brokerage with respect to the property more particularly dened in the foregoing Trade Record Sheet, I hereby declare that all moneys received or receivable by me in connection with the transaction as contemplated in the Office Policy shall be receivable and held in trust. This agreement shall constitute a Commission Trust Agreement as defined in the Office Policy and shall be subject to and governed by the Office Policy pertaining to Commission Trust. DATED as of the date and time of the acceptance of the foregoing Trade Record Sheet.   Acknowledged by:

....
(Signature of Broker of Record/Manager)   (Signature of Broker/Salesperson)

Form 640   Revised 2015   **Page 2 of 2**

OREA Ontario Real Estate Association **Waiver**

Form 123
for use in the Province of Ontario

BUYER: ....

SELLER: ....

REAL PROPERTY: ....

....

In accordance with the terms and conditions of the Agreement of Purchase and Sale dated the .... day of...,

20.............., regarding the above property, I/We hereby waive the condition(s) which read(s) as follows:

All other terms and conditions in the aforementioned Agreement of Purchase and Sale to remain unchanged.

For the purposes of this Waiver, "Buyer" includes purchaser, tenant, and lessee, and "Seller" includes vendor, landlord, and lessor, and "Agreement of Purchase and Sale" includes an Agreement to Lease.

WAIVED at..., Ontario, at .... a.m./p.m., this .... day of .... 20........

SIGNED, SEALED AND DELIVERED in the presence of: IN WITNESS whereof I have hereunto set my hand and seal:

....   ● DATE ....
(Witness)   (Buyer/Seller)   (Seal)

....   ● DATE ....
(Witness)   (Buyer/Seller)   (Seal)

Receipt acknowledged at .... a.m./p.m., this .... day of .... 20.................... by:

Print Name: ....   Signature:...

Form 123 Revised 2008 **Page 1 of 1**

Exercise 5   Amendment to Agreement—Page 1 of 2

OREA Ontario Real Estate Association

Amendment to Agreement of Purchase and Sale

Form 120
for use in the Province of Ontario

BETWEEN BUYER, ...

AND SELLER, ...

RE: Agreement of Purchase and Sale between the Seller and Buyer, dated the .... day of ...., 20..........,

concerning the property known as...

.... as more particularly described in the aforementioned Agreement.

The Buyer(s) and Seller(s) herein agree to the following Amendments to the aforementioned Agreement:

Delete:

Insert:

INITIALS OF BUYER(S):   INITIALS OF SELLER(S):

Form 120   Revised 2014   **Page 1 of 2**

IRREVOCABILITY: This Offer to Amend the Agreement shall be irrevocable by .... until .... a.m./p.m.

(Seller/Buyer)

on the .... day of ...., 20......., after which time, if not accepted, this Offer to Amend the Agreement shall be null and void.

For the purposes of this Amendment to Agreement, "Buyer" includes purchaser and "Seller" includes vendor.

Time shall in all respects be of the essence hereof provided that the time for doing or completing of any matter provided for herein may be extended or abridged by an agreement in writing signed by Seller and Buyer or by their respective solicitors who are hereby expressly appointed in this regard.

All other Terms and Conditions in the aforementioned Agreement to remain the same.

SIGNED, SEALED AND DELIVERED in the presence of: IN WITNESS whereof I have hereunto set my hand and seal:

.... ● DATE ....
(Witness)   (Buyer/Seller)   (Seal)

.... ● DATE ....
(Witness)   (Buyer/Seller)   (Seal)

I, the Undersigned, agree to the above Offer to Amend the Agreement.

SIGNED, SEALED AND DELIVERED in the presence of: IN WITNESS whereof I have hereunto set my hand and seal:

.... ● DATE ....
(Witness)   (Buyer/Seller)   (Seal)

.... ● DATE ....
(Witness)   (Buyer/Seller)   (Seal)

The Undersigned Spouse of the Seller hereby consents to the Amendments hereinbefore set out.

.... ● DATE ....
(Witness)   (Spouse)   (Seal)

CONFIRMATION OF ACCEPTANCE: Notwithstanding anything contained herein to the contrary, I confirm this Agreement with all changes both typed and written was finally accepted by all parties at .... a.m./p.m. this .... day of ...., 20..........

....
(Signature of Seller or Buyer)

ACKNOWLEDGEMENT

I acknowledge receipt of my signed copy of this accepted Amendment to Agreement and I authorize the Brokerage to forward a copy to my lawyer.	I acknowledge receipt of my signed copy of this accepted Amendment to Agreement and I authorize the Brokerage to forward a copy to my lawyer.
.... DATE .... (Seller)	.... DATE .... (Buyer)
.... DATE .... (Seller)	.... DATE .... (Buyer)
Address for Service	Address for Service ....
.... Tel.No.(..........).....................	.... Tel.No.(..........).....................
Seller's Lawyer	Buyer's Lawyer ....
Address	Address ....
Email	Email ....
(..........)..................... (..........)..................... Tel.No. FAX No.	(..........)..................... (..........)..................... Tel.No. FAX No.

Form 120   Revised 2014   **Page 2 of 2**

CHAPTER 11

Closing The Transaction

Introduction

Salespeople are not directly involved with closings, but should understand the underlying fundamentals. In this Chapter, conveyancing is highlighted from initial searches to final registration in one of Ontario's land registry offices. Key topics include title searches, non-title searches, requisitions, undertakings and final steps including the preparation of a statement of adjustments.

E-registration procedures are also briefly addressed followed by information regarding title insurance, with particular emphasis on risks covered and listing/selling benefits from a real estate perspective.

The chapter then focuses on brokerage activities. Once the transaction is closed, the real estate brokerage processes commissions and updates internal records. Commissions are paid as per salespersons' contracts and applicable brokerage policies.

For salespersons, the closing process is the culmination of concerted effort and the opportunity to develop long-standing client relationships. At the same time, receipt of commission dollars sets in motion needed record keeping and personal financial discipline to ensure a well organized, rewarding career.

Learning Outcomes

At the conclusion of this chapter, students will be able to:

- Describe the closing process from the buyer's perspective including title searching, non-title searches, requisitions, closing and final reporting letters.
- Describe the closing process from the seller's perspective including draft deed responses to requisitions, undertakings if needed, statement of adjustments preparation, closing and the final reporting letter.
- Discuss E-registration and identify the associated operating components.
- Discuss how title insurance has evolved, basic policy coverages and benefits from a real estate perspective.
- Outline steps involved in brokerage commission processing following closing, including disbursements involving a commission trust account.
- Identify ongoing salesperson responsibilities concerning record keeping, taxation (income and HST), cash advances, fees/dues and independent contractor status (if applicable).

TITLE CONVEYANCE

Conveyancing is broadly defined as the creation of transfer documents and the associated transferral of rights or interests from one party to another. Conveyances are not limited strictly to transfers of ownership, but extend to any interest or right ranging from a **freehold estate** to assignment or limitation on use. For registrants, a **conveyance** typically involves transferring a freehold, leasehold or fractional interest in real estate.

Title conveyance for freehold property is accomplished using a **Transfer/Deed** of Land. The document is registered in either registry or land titles. For a review of registration procedures, see *Land, Structures and Real Estate Trading.* As discussed in that course, Ontario is undergoing a massive conversion from manual to electronic registration (e-registration) systems, along with conversion of registry to land titles. Electronic registration provides all functionality contained within its manual counterpart, but with the many added advantages of electronic creation, submission and storage of title documents.

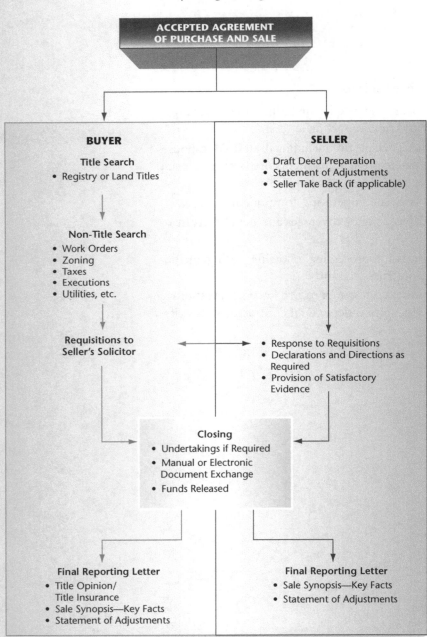

Title Conveyancing/Closing Process

ACCEPTED AGREEMENT OF PURCHASE AND SALE

BUYER

Title Search
• Registry or Land Titles

Non-Title Search
• Work Orders
• Zoning
• Taxes
• Executions
• Utilities, etc.

Requisitions to Seller's Solicitor

SELLER
• Draft Deed Preparation
• Statement of Adjustments
• Seller Take Back (if applicable)

• Response to Requisitions
• Declarations and Directions as Required
• Provision of Satisfactory Evidence

Closing
• Undertakings if Required
• Manual or Electronic Document Exchange
• Funds Released

Final Reporting Letter
• Title Opinion/ Title Insurance
• Sale Synopsis—Key Facts
• Statement of Adjustments

Final Reporting Letter
• Sale Synopsis—Key Facts
• Statement of Adjustments

Closing Process

Closing is the procedural, investigative process by which the parties, through legal counsel, carry out conveyancing requirements and satisfy terms and conditions set out in the agreement of purchase and sale. With manual registration, the process culminates in the exchange of documents and funds at the land registry office. With e-registration, the online process leads from electronic creation to final release for registration, once solicitors confirm that all documents are satisfactory.

BUYER'S PERSPECTIVE
A title search of the purchased property is necessary to ensure good and **marketable title.** In registry, a 40-year search is completed to examine the **chain of title**, together with any gap or error in that chain, traditionally referred to as a **cloud on title.** In land titles, the search is restricted to current entries for the particular property parcel.

The solicitor is looking for items such as outstanding encumbrances, restrictive covenants, non-resident parties, expropriations and matrimonial home status. He/she will also investigate adjoining lands to ensure compliance with the *Planning Act*. The date of the search is recorded in anticipation of a sub-search at point of closing. The solicitor will report to the client on title, conditions and other matters significant to the title. The buyer's solicitor also searches non-title records that can affect property title.

Non-Title Searches

The buyer's solicitor will search various non-title records including, but not limited to, the following:

- Zoning (to ensure that the present use conforms to zoning by-laws).
- Work orders or deficiency notices.
- Executions.
- Unregistered easements; e.g., hydro easements.
- Personal property pursuant to the registration system established under the *Personal Property Security Act.*
- Outstanding amounts relating to a local utility company owed by the owner of the property.
- Status of real property taxes including any special assessments/local improvements and surcharges.
- Survey documentation concerning setbacks, encroachments and related matters.
- Compliance with subdivision or site plan agreements and registered restrictive covenants.
- Status concerning Ontario New Home Warranty Program (if applicable).

The range of non-title searches varies by property and individual circumstance. For example, a rural property may require searches involving the local health unit and/or municipal records concerning the waste disposal system, conservation authority requirements for properties within regulated areas, approvals required from the Ministry of Natural Resources under the *Public Lands Act* and, in some instances, Parks Canada in relation to federally-controlled canals concerning waterfront improvements.

Requisition Date/Requisitions

The *Agreement of Purchase and Sale* (OREA Form 100) provides for a specified date (requisition date) to complete the search. The buyer may examine the title to the property at his/her own expense until a stipulated requisition date and the earlier of (i) 30 days from the later of the requisition date or the date on which the conditions in the agreement are fulfilled or otherwise waived; or (ii) five days prior to completion, to ensure that no outstanding work orders or deficiency notices exist affecting the property, to verify the property is insurable and to confirm the present use is legal.

Following searches, a **requisition letter** or similar document is transmitted to the sellers' solicitor regarding any problems, defects or general matters affecting title. Requisitions can be wide ranging; e.g., evidence that the seller is not a non-resident, declaration that the seller has occupied the premises, the seller's undertaking to pay all tax levies, charges and penalties prior to closing and provision of satisfactory evidence that all buildings have been built in accordance with municipal by-laws and provincial statutes.

> **Requisition Letter**
>
> An inquiry (typically referred to as a requisition letter) prepared by the buyer's solicitor to the seller's solicitor concerning title matters.

Final Reporting

Upon successful resolution of matters requisitioned, the sale progresses to the scheduled closing. A **final reporting letter** is prepared following closing, setting out transaction particulars from the buyer's perspective; e.g., statement of adjustments, opinion regarding title, adjustments and mortgage details (if applicable).

Final Reporting Letter

A letter prepared after closing by a buyer's or seller's solicitor setting out pertinent details regarding a real estate transaction following closing.

SELLER'S PERSPECTIVE

The seller's solicitor completes the draft deed (to be forwarded to the buyer's solicitor), prepares other documentation (e.g., seller take back mortgage), resolves issues and performs other tasks that arise as a consequence of the requisitions.

Response to Requisitions

The seller's lawyer will respond to requisitions from the buyer's solicitor provided that such are consistent with the agreement of purchase and sale and within the time limits specified. Requisition items may include:

- Statutory declaration concerning not being a non-resident;
- Declaration of possession covering the seller's period of ownership;
- Direction for payment of funds on closing;
- Seller's undertaking to pay tax levies, charges, penalties, utility accounts and provide vacant possession;
- Evidence of no executions, no contravention of the *Planning Act,* and no unregistered liens, rights-of-way, tax arrears, expropriations and construction liens;
- Discharges of any liens, mortgages or encumbrances other than those to be assumed by the buyer;
- Compliance of buildings and other improvements with zoning by-laws; and
- A statement certifying that the sale of the land and premises is exempt from harmonized sales tax, or otherwise, depending on the circumstances.

Undertakings

Undertakings may be necessary to resolve last minute issues arising at closing and can be broadly grouped under:

Undertakings

An assurance given by a client and/or a solicitor regarding unresolved items at closing of a real estate transaction.

CLIENT'S	BEST EFFORTS	PERSONAL
An assurance by the client (typically given through the lawyer). **NOTE:** The solicitor's personal liability attaches unless specifically excluded.	The lawyer will diligently take the necessary steps to ensure that specific assurances are carried through.	A personal assurance by the solicitor that something will be done.

Undertakings can involve issues such as an unanswered requisition concerning outstanding **liens**, an **encumbrance** or an **encroachment**, evidence that no tax arrears exist concerning the property and that all chattels remaining with the property are not encumbered. Another frequently encountered undertaking involves assurances that existing financing will be discharged following closing (using funds provided at closing).

Encroachment

The unauthorized intrusion onto the lands and property of another.

Statement of Adjustments

The lawyer prepares a **statement of adjustments** itemizing the financial history of the transaction. The statement sets out in balance sheet form, all credits to the seller (e.g., purchase price, prepaid taxes and prepaid utilities), all credits to the buyer (e.g., deposits and arrears in taxes prior to the date of closing) and the balance due on closing. The statement of adjustments provides all parties to the transaction with a financial breakdown, as of the closing date.

Adjustments, as detailed in *Real Estate as a Professional Career*, involve those items requiring apportionment as of the date of closing. Such adjustments for purposes of residential transactions typically include rent, mortgage interest, realty tax, local improvement rates, unmetered public or private utility charges and non-metered cost of fuel. Adjustments are apportioned and allowed to the day of completion, the day of completion itself to be charged to the buyer. As a reminder, insurance is not pro-rate, as the buyer must secure his or her own coverage.

Final Reporting

The seller's solicitor reviews all draft documents provided by the buyer's lawyer to ensure compliance with the terms of the agreement and discusses any items requiring clarification and/or resolution with the buyer's solicitor. He or she also prepares a final reporting letter following closing setting out transaction particulars from the seller's perspective; e.g., statement of adjustments, details of any seller take back, discharge of existing financing and payment of real estate commission.

TYPICAL RESIDENTIAL DISBURSEMENTS

Salespersons should be generally aware of typical disbursements involved with a residential transaction. An illustration is provided on the following page identifying typical fees and disbursements, but caution is advised. Significant cost variations are found in the marketplace depending on the property, its location (i.e., properties in Toronto are also subject to municipal land transfer tax) and other circumstances associated with a particular transaction.

COST GUIDE—FEES AND DISBURSEMENTS
Urban Residential Transaction

ITEM	ESTIMATED COST
REALTOR® Fee/Commission	*
Survey (Range for typical location survey)	$500.00–$950.00
Title Insurance (Range for average condo/single family)	$150.00–$350.00
Mortgage Financing	*

Land Transfer Tax
(Four examples are provided for illustration purposes)

Sale Price of Home	Tax Payable
$ 40,000	$ 200.00
200,000	1,725.00
400,000	4,475.00
500,000	6,475.00

Legal Fees	*

Typical List of Disbursements

City Tax Certificate	$ 20.00
Zoning Reports	70.00
Engineering Reports	40.00
Sheriff's Certificates	154.00
Registry Office Searches	125.00
Utility Searches	20.00
Register Deed	50.00
Register Mortgage	50.00
Copies, Fax, Postage, Courier	45.00
Total Disbursements	$574.00

Add (as required)

Adjustment for Municipal Taxes
Fuel (i.e., Oil: $350.00 for 910 litres)
Ontario New Home Warranty Plan Fee
Mortgage Interest Adjustment
Mortgage Holdbacks (Repairs or Taxes)
Home Inspection Fee
Fire Insurance Premium

Applicable Taxes (HST)

*Indicates estimate unavailable due to wide variances resulting from unique factors and local market practices.

EXPLANATION/NOTES

Only selected costs have been itemized. The range of fees and disbursements is by no means exhaustive and is limited to expenses usual to a typical urban residential transaction. Costs can vary significantly.

Survey cost varies according to size, type and location of property.

Insurance coverage regarding title. Survey cost may be avoided.

Mortgage financing cost varies and may include application fee, mortgage insurance fee, mortgage broker's fee and discharge costs for existing financing.

Land transfer tax is computed as follows:

.005 x the first $55,000,
plus   .01 x from $55,000.00 to $250,000,
plus   .015 x remainder of purchase price,
plus   .005 surcharge on single family homes and duplexes for the amount over $400,000

Lawyer's statement of account will normally include fee plus disbursements listed below.

Title Search   Title search fees and sheriff's office search.

Letter Searches   Building clearance, tax certificate, water and hydro certificate, natural gas status, subdivision agreement clearance, *Personal Property Security Act* searches.

Registration Costs   Transfer/deed, charge/mortgage and other documents requiring registration.

Pro-rated Adjustments   Property taxes, fuel, mortgage interest adjustments, holdbacks (taxes, repairs), any special assessments/levies.

Miscellaneous   Photocopies, fax transmissions, courier, long distance telephone, travelling costs, subsearch on closing, inspection fees.

Harmonized sales tax, as applicable.

E-REGISTRATION

The traditional system of registration at closing, now largely relegated to historical fact, involved manual submission of prescribed forms over the registration counter at the land registry office. The provincial government, recognizing inherent weaknesses and the ever-expanding needs concerning land registration, began the process of electronic land registration during the mid-1980s. At time of printing, either mandatory or optional e-registration is in place for well over 90% of the province.

For those involved with closings, the automation process eliminates the need for signatures on documents and permits remote access to electronic records by solicitors for the buyer and the seller. Consequently, the traditional requirement to attend the land registry office is eliminated, subject to some qualifiers. Persons involved can create, amend or retrieve information as required. Recent initiatives have further broadened this perspective to include links (e.g., assessment, planning and building departments) thereby allowing access to various documents involving requisitions and other needed information in pre-closing activities.

Registrants require general knowledge of automated records both to appreciate the types of procedures used in real estate closings as well as the benefits for listing, marketing and appraising functions.

POLARIS/Teranet

Electronic conversion is primarily driven by two systems: POLARIS and Teraview. POLARIS (an acronym for Province of Ontario LAnd Registration and Information System) is an automated land registration system based on title index (description of property ownership) and property mapping (surveys and plans) databases. The province-wide conversion, now largely completed, involves the lengthy reorganization of documents and data under individual parcels with unique identifiers, referred to as property identification numbers (PINs). Teranet Inc. is responsible for enhancements to the POLARIS system as well as providing an electronic, user gateway called Teraview. The process of electronic conversion is complemented by the land titles conversion project in which records are not only automated, but also moved from the cumbersome registry system into land titles.

WEB LINKS
Teranet   Go to *www.teranet.ca* for details about the scope of services offered by Teranet, over and above land registry automation. Current endeavours include geospatial services as well as security, transaction and risk management.

WEB LINKS
Teraview   The Teraview website (*www.teraview.ca*) provides a wide range of information concerning the software, including full descriptions of functionalities and steps to follow in the e-registration process.

Teraview Access

Teraview users must be registered with Teranet. Each user must have a removable computer storage device with individual security credentials. The user creates a unique password and establishes an account for access charges and other disbursements; e.g., land transfer tax can be electronically calculated, deducted at closing and forwarded to the Ministry of Finance. Teranet requires that a sufficient balance remain in the user's account at all times to handle charges and disbursements.

From a lawyer's perspective, Teraview operates on four levels:

Search	Allows the lawyer to view documents registered under POLARIS.
Create/Update	The lawyer can create, view or alter documents for registration; e.g., transfers, mortgages and mortgage discharges. The system contains data entry fields that parallel information required in the manual system.
Complete/Approve	The lawyers confirm that documents are acceptable for registration by means of an electronic complete signature.
Release/Registration	The lawyers then provide a release electronic signature and the document is released for registration. Both complete and release signatures must occur before acceptance by the land registration office. Teraview provides various levels of security that may be assigned by the lawyer to others; e.g., legal assistant and/or conveyancer.

TITLE INSURANCE

Title insurance originated in the United States given deficiencies in local and regional land registration systems. However, its ultimate real growth came as a result of mortgages, not real estate transactions. In the mid-1900s, national loan programs were developed to fund the expanding US residential marketplace. A major player was the Federal National Mortgage Association (FNMA) (also known as Fannie Mae).

To assist small banks, Fannie Mae would purchase mortgages arranged within the local marketplace. Lenders could then more aggressively pursue residential mortgages, use FNMA as a reliable purchase vehicle for such business and expand home ownership throughout the country.

To ensure marketability, FNMA required title insurance for purchased mortgages to protect the mortgagee's interests against title defects regarding the underlying property security. Ultimately, by standardizing this approach throughout the United States, a secondary mortgage market now flourishes where mortgage portfolios are bought and sold.

Title Insurance in Ontario

Title insurance in Ontario is relatively new, but expanding rapidly. During the past decade, the secondary mortgage market has grown dramatically due to lender policies, in similar fashion to the US. Extensive consumer marketing has now led to wide acceptance of owner policies as well.

The owner policy is patterned after its loan policy counterpart, but with a narrower title coverage range given higher risk associated with owner policies. With loan policies, protection is extended only to the mortgagee's interest. With owner policies, title coverage encompasses the entire property value including owner's equity.

Many reasons lie behind the success of owner policies in Ontario.

Consumer Acceptance

Consumers readily accepted the widely-marketed concept given high awareness of insurance products; e.g., life, auto, mortgage and home.

Straightforward Claim Procedures

Claim procedures are relatively straightforward. For example, if a buyer relies on a lawyer's title opinion and this opinion proves faulty, he/she must pursue legal action and obtain a judgement against that lawyer for title errors. With title insurance, a claim is submitted and paid, assuming that the defect falls within policy coverage.

Scope of Coverage

From a risk perspective, Ontario consumers quickly realized that insurers not only provided title defect coverages, but insured over certain known or contemplated defects and assumed selected risks; e.g., the possibility of minor encroachments. With a lawyer's title opinion, the client would be informed regarding the risk (i.e., the possibility of an encroachment), requiring a decision regarding whether or not to accept such risk.

Existing Surveys

From a financial perspective, title insurance simply makes good dollar sense for many real estate transactions. For example, certain insurers will accept an existing survey, thereby saving the consumer the cost of a new one. Further, by not requiring an up-to-date survey, certain losses are covered that might appear in a new survey.

Value-Added Service

Title insurance policies also received a boost from the real estate community. Registrants view such products as value-added, consumer friendly and a positive force in the closing process, as problems/delays can often be avoided. Given such popularity, insurers are now bundling other products and closing services, while streamlining procedures to align with the new e-registration system.

Policy Coverages

Two primary coverages are provided: the *duty to indemnify* (actual loss incurred) and the *duty to defend* (legal expense associated with a claim). Registrants should avoid discussing any matters regarding title coverage and refer clients to legal counsel. No standardized policy wordings currently exist and the extent of coverage, along with exclusions, must be carefully analyzed.

The structure and form of title policies, whether for lender or owner, are more or less standardized, keeping in mind that separate policies are targeted to commercial and residential properties. Commercial policies follow one of several more or less standard wordings. In the case of residential, basic policy wordings have given way to various extended coverage policies making direct comparison more complex. Title insurers may offer combined policies with coverage for both the lender and the owner.

Most title policies include a general statement of coverages, specific types of title risks covered, exclusions and exceptions from coverage and policy conditions/stipulations. Beyond pre-printed policy wording, individual policies are also subject to specific terms set out in attached schedules; e.g., amount of insurance for a particular property, along with any endorsements attached to the policy that modify the preprinted wording of the basic policy. Obviously, any title policy should be carefully read to fully appreciate the scope of insurance provided. Further, any review must include the total policy along with all attachments as exclusions, exceptions, conditions, stipulations and endorsements can affect any general coverage statement found at the start of the title policy.

TYPICAL RISKS COVERED

Any detailed comparison of either owner or lender policies, as well as residential or commercial packages, goes well beyond the scope of this text. For descriptive purposes, title risks for residential property (owner's policy) provide some indication of the scope of such coverage. The following is not an exhaustive list, but includes the typical risks that are covered when the condition of title is other than that stated in the title documents.

- A document relating to the title is not properly signed or is otherwise defective; e.g., not sealed or delivered.
- A document was defectively registered on title; e.g., a defect in a lien, charge or other encumbrance.
- Some form of forgery or fraud in documents affects title to the property.
- An inability to access the property is uncovered; i.e., the legal right for pedestrian or vehicular access.
- The title is unmarketable for a number of reasons that result in a person refusing to perform a contract, lease or make a loan.
- A contravention of a municipal by-law occurs; e.g., the owner is forced to move, or otherwise remedy a structure (or any part thereof), due to a violation of zoning by-laws.

- A contravention of a subdivision, development agreement or other agreement relating to the development of the property.
- Construction liens are discovered on title (that had not been previously agreed to be paid).
- Other individuals claim rights over the property not identified in the title documents arising from leases, contracts, options or some other possessory right.
- A lien on title is discovered that may have a priority; e.g., arising from a judgment, a mortgage or a public utility account.
- Certain restrictive covenants may exist that affect the use of the land.
- Someone else owns an interest in the title.

A detailed review of any specific policy is required along with expert advice. Registrants should also be aware that title insurance is a relatively new concept in the Canadian marketplace. Consequently, many policy wordings and issues surrounding title insurance lack interpretation through Canadian courts.

Listing/Selling Benefits

Registrants should be aware that title insurance may provide certain benefits from both a listing and selling perspective. Traditionally, buyers relied on a letter of opinion from a lawyer as assurance that the title was good and marketable. A lawyer's letter of opinion was typically qualified, at least to some degree, concerning such marketability. If a subsequent problem arose, the onus rested with the buyer to prove that the lawyer failed to do something and/or that legal services failed to meet an acceptable standard.

Title insurance provides a means to not only address qualifications within a reporting letter, but also to protect against various errors that could potentially occur through fraudulent activity, or simply errors made in documents prepared by others. Lenders, in particular, take great comfort in the value of title insurance to address issues that might be missed, despite the diligent efforts of the solicitor. Once again, prudence is advised as title policies do not solve all issues given exclusions, conditions and stipulations affecting the scope of coverage.

- **Survey** An attractive aspect of title insurance is the possible avoidance of a new survey. The elimination of the survey requirement can represent significant savings as well as eliminate a possible delay in the closing process. Coverages vary and any policy should be read carefully. Registrants should NOT in any way lead buyers to believe that the survey cost will be avoided, but rather that it might be avoided depending on specific property circumstances and the policy under consideration,

- **Title Problems at Listing** Sellers can take advantage of title insurance at the point of listing. For example, a problem relating to title may crop up in the listing process when a registrant identifies a circumstance, such as a deck that extends beyond the approved setback in the municipal zoning by-laws. The seller may be able to secure title insurance and confirm that the property will be insured against any losses that may occur due to this problem. The seller is then in a position to assure any potential buyer that this situation has been resolved through insurance coverage.

- **Marketing Incentive** The seller may agree to purchase title insurance as an incentive in the marketing of his/her property. The seller's commitment translates into cost savings at the point of negotiations with a potential buyer. Even during negotiations, the seller may offer to pay this cost.

- **Title Problems at Closing** Title policies have proven particularly effective by insuring over certain title problems that crop up at or near closing. As an example, a minor encroachment may exist that could otherwise delay or cancel a sale. Alternatively, a minor issue regarding final inspection of an addition or improvement to the property may not have been completed by the municipality. The title insurer, after an investigation of the risk involved, may elect to insure over the problem allowing the transaction to close on time.

Legal Disclosure Requirements

The Law Society of Upper Canada (LSUC) sets out various disclosure requirements for lawyers concerning title insurance pursuant to the Rules of Professional Conduct (Sec. 2.02).

2.02 QUALITY OF SERVICE
Title Insurance in Real Estate Conveyancing

(10) A lawyer shall assess all reasonable options to assure title when advising a client about a real estate conveyance and shall advise the client that title insurance is not mandatory and is not the only option available to protect the client's interests in a real estate transaction.

(11) A lawyer shall not receive any compensation, whether directly or indirectly, from a title insurer, agent or intermediary for recommending a specific title insurance product to his or her client.

(12) A lawyer shall disclose to the client that no commission or fee is being furnished by any insurer, agent or intermediary to the lawyer with respect to any title insurance coverage.

(13) If discussing *TitlePlus* insurance with the client, a lawyer shall fully disclose the relationship between the legal profession, the Society and the Lawyers' Professional Indemnity Company (LPIC).

What potential situations give rise to title claims? Registrants can best understand the merits of title insurance by example. Scenarios are provided for illustration purposes. Coverages available and settlements vary by insurer.

SCENARIO 1   Set Back Requirement

Seller Williams obtained owner and lender policies for a resale home purchase. An up-to-date survey was not required by the insurer. Two years later, Williams sells the property and the new buyers undertake a title search. The search reveals that an addition to the main structure does not comply with zoning setback provisions. The insurer investigates the problem by searching municipal records and confirms that a problem exists. The title insurer pays the cost of a minor variance application, along with the insured's legal costs to obtain the variance.

SCENARIO 2   Wrong Condominium Unit

A registrant drafted an agreement of purchase and sale for a specific condominium unit with a lake view and identified it as Unit 7, Level 18, with an address of Unit 732. However, this description was for a unit facing the opposite direction. Neither the seller, the salesperson or the buyer knew of the faulty description. During a review of the status certificate, the lawyer discovered that Unit 7, Level 18 was in fact Unit 718. Assuming an error (i.e., that Unit 732 was correct), the lawyer closed the sale. Consequently, the client purchased the wrong unit (732) and the lake view unit (718) was sold to someone else. The title insurer negotiated a settlement to compensate the owner for the loss of the lakefront view.

SCENARIO 3   Lack of Permits

New owners purchased title insurance for a home. They discovered after closing that parts of the property were shifting and that the house had been built without proper building permits. Further, the septic system was incorrectly placed on the property. The insurance company paid to correct the deficiencies.

SCENARIO 4   Encroachment

The buyers acquired a rural property and secured title insurance. A new survey was not required by the insuring company. The building encroached approximately 4 feet onto a neighbour's property, due to renovation and the addition of two rooms. An up-to-date survey would have revealed the problem. The insurance company paid for alterations to correct the situation, along with associated legal costs.

DISBURSING COMMISSION

Real estate brokerages must receive written notification from the solicitor that the transaction has closed prior to funds disbursement. *Notification of Completion of Sale* (OREA Form 642) is provided for this purpose (see *Appendix*). Typically, a direction is signed by the seller authorizing the seller's solicitor to forward commission, assuming that total commission exceeds the deposit held in the statutory real estate trust account.

Real Estate Trust Account

When a sale closes, a cheque is issued from the real estate trust account, payable to the commission trust account (assuming that the deposit is equal to or less than the total commission). If surplus exists, this amount is paid to the appropriate party, typically the seller. Commission earned is one of six possible disbursements from the real estate trust account.

Real Estate Trust Account Disbursements

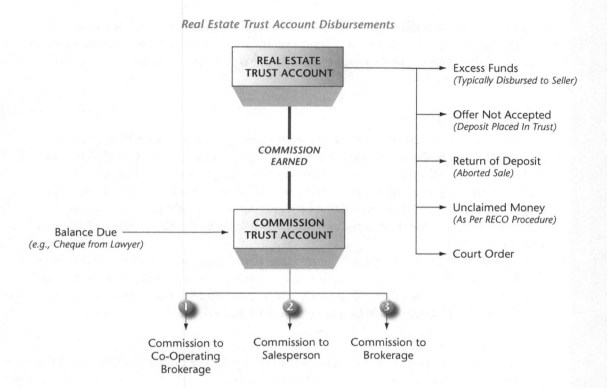

Commission Trust Account

This account is used solely for receipt and disbursement of commission funds, and is kept separate and apart from the statutory real estate trust account. This trust arrangement provides greater protection in the event of brokerage bankruptcy or misappropriation of funds.

INSURANCE PROVISION

A further consideration involves a provision from the mandatory RECO Insurance Program, with specific reference to commission protection coverage under that policy:

SECTION III – EXCLUSIONS

This POLICY does not apply to any Claim:

1. *on account of acts by any Registrant while acting as executor, administrator, trustee, guardian, conservator or in any fiduciary capacity other than as a Salesperson or Broker for a person other than himself/herself;*

2. *on account of acts by any Registrant through whose acts Loss was sustained by a Claimant and was reported to the Named Insured prior to the beginning of this Policy Period;*

3. ***by any Salesperson employed by or contracted to a Broker where the Broker fails to set up and maintain a Commission Trust Account unless the Salesperson has used his/her best efforts to determine that the Broker has set up and maintained a Commission Trust Account;***

If a brokerage does not set up a commission trust account, salespeople can still be employed by that brokerage However, they may not be able to make a claim for commission under the RECO Insurance Program; e.g., if a loss is caused by the brokerage and the salesperson knew that no commission trust was established, or did not use his/her best efforts to determine that the brokerage set up and maintained a commission trust account. *Salespeople are well advised to include reference to this requirement within their employment contracts.*

ORGANIZED REAL ESTATE

A commission trust plan, developed by the Ontario Real Estate Association, has been adopted by most real estate boards in the province. This plan ensures that brokerage to brokerage commissions are held in a trust account (designated as a commission trust account) and are protected should a member firm become insolvent or bankrupt. The commission trust plan is not mandated by legislation and should not be confused with the statutory real estate trust account required, pursuant to the *Real Estate and Business Brokers Act, 2002.*

The plan provides for a separate commission trust ledger to account for all deposits and disbursements from the commission trust account. To ensure that the trust relationship is maintained when disbursing funds to salespersons, a separate trust arrangement must be established between brokerage (employer) and salesperson (employee).

Four Step Procedure

- Brokerage adopts and enforces a section in the brokerage's office policy manual that specifically sets out the commission trust concept.
- Brokerage includes clauses in an employment agreement that reinforce the commission trust concept, as set out in the office policy manual.
- A commission trust agreement is entered into between the employer and employee for each and every transaction (either by way of a separate form or in a section added to the trade record sheet).
- A commission trust agreement is entered into between the listing and co-operating brokerages for each transaction.

Agreements of Purchase and Sale

All OREA agreements of purchase and sale provide for a commission trust agreement following the acknowledgement. The pre-printed wording includes space for the signatures of listing and co-operating brokerages, or their duly authorized representatives.

The clause states that the listing brokerage, in consideration of the co-operating brokerage procuring the agreement, declares that all monies received or receivable in connection with the transaction shall be held in trust and shall constitute a commission trust agreement. This commission trust agreement, as defined in the MLS® rules, is then subject to and governed by the MLS® rules pertaining to commission trust.

Commission Disbursement

The commission cheque from the real estate trust account is deposited in the commission trust account. The balance due, received from the lawyer, is also deposited. Funds are disbursed from this account in the following order: co-operating brokerage, brokers and salespeople and lastly the listing brokerage.

EXAMPLE   *Commission Disbursement*

Salesperson Bauer, of ABC Realty Inc,. is awaiting her listing commission following the closing of 2816 Daimler Ave. Her brokerage is holding a $7,000 deposit in trust. The balance due of $9,300 has been received from the solicitor. The co-operating brokerage, XYZ Real Estate Ltd., will participate on a 50/50 basis. Bauer is an HST-registered, independent contractor with an 80/20 split.

Total Commission Plus 13% HST	($16,300 + 2,119)		$18,419.00
	CHEQUE FROM	**CHEQUE TO**	**AMOUNT**
Step 1	Real Estate Trust	Commission Trust	7,000.00
Step 2	Lawyer	Commission Trust	11,419.00
	$9,300 balance of commission +		
	$2,119 HST (13%) on total commission		
			$18,419.00
Step 3	Commission Trust	XYZ Real Estate Ltd.	9,209.50
	50/50 distribution of ($16,300 + 13% HST)		
Step 4	Commission Trust	Salesperson Bauer	7,367.60
	80/20 distribution of ($8,150 + 13% HST)		
Step 5	Commission Trust	ABC Realty Inc.	1,841.90
	20/80 distribution of ($8,150 + 13% HST)		
			$18,419.00

Closing the Trade File

The brokerage updates the trade record sheet noting disbursements from the statutory trust, including funds transferred to the commission trust account. Appropriate notations are also made on the sale file, which is then transferred from Pending Sales to Closed/Cancelled Sales. Typically, closed sales are filed in trade number order, but archiving procedures vary by brokerage.

AFTER CLOSING

A successful real estate career requires discipline and commitment that extends beyond the closing. Most salespersons intuitively understand customer satisfaction, follow through, and keep in touch with buyers and sellers to build a clientele. Unfortunately, many registrants successful in sales fall victim to needless financial or related problems, simply due to poor organization and planning.

Personal Diary	Invest in a time management product (paper-based or electronic) that provides for detailed day-to-day notes on appointments, action lists and income/expenses. The appointments keep you on time, the action list on focus and the expenses on track.
File Records	Set up a systematic filing system for all documents.
Expert Advice	When consumers need real estate guidance, they seek out registered real estate professionals. When you need financial, investment or taxation counselling, seek out appropriate professionals. It's money well spent.
Income Tax	Don't let tax problems mar an otherwise expanding, rewarding career. The following guidelines relate particularly to independent contractors. • Make appropriate remittances on a timely basis. • Get expert advice on expense deductibility, particularly regarding home offices. • Avoid a tax backlog. The problem doesn't usually arise in the first year given partial year activity, high expenses and time lag for initial commissions. However, salespersons often mistakenly use this low year tax obligation as a future benchmark. Increased earnings and more stabilized expenses, typically result in higher tax remittances. • If taxes are not paid, Canada Revenue Agency will issue a Requirement to Pay to the brokerage. On such notice, the brokerage must remit money on your behalf out of future commissions received.
Harmonized Sales Tax	Independent contractors with annual gross revenues exceeding $30,000 must be registered and submit HST collected, less input tax credits. Make all scheduled remittances as required. In some instances, brokerages may provide HST services for independent contractors. Ensure that such activities do not adversely affect your independent contractor status.
Cash Advances	Salespeople may require funds in advance of scheduled closings. Third party companies now provide cash advance services. The salesperson typically assigns all rights to the commission in return for immediate payment (usually up to 80% of total commission owed). Carefully review the commission assignment agreement, particularly concerning transaction fees and interest charged.

Fees, Dues and Services	When budgeting for your new career, make certain to set aside funds for:
	• Initiation fees when joining a real estate board or other professional organization.
	• Annual fees; e.g., CREA, OREA and real estate board dues (if applicable).
	• RECO—registration and insurance fees.
	• Monthly board MLS® access, office fees and franchise fees (if applicable).
IC Status (if applicable)	Don't compromise your independent contractor status. Ensure that all activities and service contracts confirm that status. Canada Revenue Agency has established criteria that generally align with well-documented common law principles. For a review of independent contractor status, go to *Real Estate as a Professional Career.*

After Sale Service—Building Your Career   PERSPECTIVE

Success is not measured by one sale, one satisfied customer or one commission. Success is the never-ending pursuit of personal fulfillment, customer satisfaction and a job well done. Success is elusive, but always within your grasp.

Jacqueline wasn't the perfect fit when she began real estate sales. With a young family, her schedules were demanding. Few leads would come from friends or business associates. She and her husband had only recently arrived in Ontario. Her only employment experience was piecework in a manufacturing firm.

No flashy car, just a seven-year old van. No social clubs, just a membership at the 20-minute workout gym. No expensive clothes, but always neat as a pin. No real strategy, just a commitment to succeed.

The first few years weren't easy. Fix-me-ups were the only bright spot. She discovered others just like herself trying to build a better life. Young couples were attracted to Jacqueline and followed her lead. Buy what you can afford, fix it up, make it homey and look to move up. That's what she and her husband did. That's what others could do.

Jacqueline quickly became Jackie and her impact was being felt. It didn't matter whether it was down by the tracks, hidden on a 20' sidestreet lot or passed over by others. Jackie would take it on. It didn't matter whether it was a rental or a buy. Some said that these older properties were overpriced, but Jackie didn't know any better. She just saw demand and young families wanting to get on with their lives. No sophisticated marketing strategy…just hard work.

Today, Jackie laughs about the past with a twinkle in her eyes. Those were the good old days. Her clients have grown older with her. They moved up to bigger houses. Some, now close to retirement, seek condominium units in highrises where many of those small homes once stood. Jackie is even dealing with the children of her first clients and customers.

Someone recently said to her: "*Jackie, you sure have been lucky in real estate.*" Jackie's response: "*You're absolutely right. The harder I work, the luckier I get!*"

KNOWLEDGE INTEGRATION

Notables

- Title conveyancing involves the creation of transfer documents and associated transferral of rights or interests from one party to another.

- The buyer's solicitor is typically involved in title searches, non-title searches, requisitions directed to the seller's solicitor, registration and final reporting.

- The seller's solicitor is typically involved in the draft deed, statement of adjustments preparation, response to requisitions, registration and final reporting.

- A requisition letter typically follows the title search in which the buyer's solicitor addresses problems, defects or general matters regarding title.

- Undertakings are personal assurances given by clients or solicitors, usually to resolve last minute issues at closing.

- E-registration (optional or mandatory) is now available in almost all areas of the province.

- Title insurance is broadly grouped under loan and owner policies.

- Policy coverages vary but generally involve unmarketability of title, fraud and forgery, title defects, authenticity of title documents, access problems and other claims or rights not identified in title documentation.

- Title insurance provides two primary coverages: duty to indemnify and duty to defend.

- Commission disbursement involves both a statutory real estate trust account and a commission trust account.

- When seeking employment with a brokerage, establish if a commission trust account is being used for commission disbursements.

- Maintain accurate personal records and seek expert advice as necessary.

- Don't let tax problems spoil a worthwhile career. Adhere to all income and HST tax requirements.

Glossary

Chain of Title

Cloud on Title

Conveyance

Encroachment

Encumbrance

Final Reporting Letter

Freehold Estate

Lien

Marketable Title

Requisition Letter

Restriction

Statement of Adjustments

Transfer/Deed

Undertaking

Web Links

Web links are included for general interest regarding selected chapter topics.

Teranet   Go to *www.teranet.ca* for details about the scope of services offered by Teranet, over and above land registry automation. Current endeavours include geospatial services as well as security, transaction and risk management.

Teraview   The Teraview website (*www.teraview.ca*) provides a wide range of information concerning the software, including full descriptions of functionalities and steps to follow in the e-registration process.

Strategic Thinking For Your Career

Questions are included to assist in developing your new career. No answers are provided.

1. Do I (or a friend or relative) have a complete set of documents for the purchase or sale of a property that will help in better understanding the closing process?

2. What types of new electronic innovations (e.g., personal digital assistants) and software could assist me in organizing my new career, while ensuring accurate personal and financial records?

3. If contemplating independent contractor status, how will I handle income tax and HST remittances?

4. What expert advice do I need to ensure that my records are properly structured?

5. What fees, dues and services must be paid within the next six months and how do I intend on funding those expenses?

6. Have I set up a proper time management and file record system for my new career?

7. What guidance can my brokerage provide regarding my new career to avoid common pitfalls encountered by new salespersons?

Chapter Mini-Review

Solutions are located in the Appendix.

1. Restrictive covenants and outstanding encumbrances are part of the non-title search process.

   ◯ True   ◯ False

2. Outstanding work orders and zoning compliance are two possible non-title searches undertaken by the buyer's solicitor.

   ◯ True   ◯ False

3. A requisition can involve a request to verify that the seller is not a non-resident pursuant to the *Income Tax Act*.

   ◯ True   ◯ False

4. The gateway software used to access electronic land registration information is called POLARIS (Province of Ontario Land Registration and Information System).

   ◯ True   ◯ False

5. The statement of adjustments is normally prepared by the buyer's solicitor, unless otherwise specifically agreed.

   ◯ True   ◯ False

6. If a mortgage is taken back, the mortgage document is usually prepared by the seller's solicitor.

   ◯ True   ◯ False

7. If a residential seller has existing home insurance, the seller's solicitor will pro-rate the premium between the buyer and the seller, based on the closing date.

   ◯ True   ◯ False

8. Title insurance policies for lenders commonly include the *duty to defend* and the *duty to indemnify*, but owner policies are limited to the *duty to defend*.

   ◯ True   ◯ False

9. A typical risk covered by title insurance involves fraud or document forgery that impacts title.

   ◯ True   ◯ False

10. A survey cost might be avoided when securing title insurance based on the title insurer's policy provisions and specific property considerations.

    ◯ True   ◯ False

11. A commission trust account is a statutory requirement set out in the *Real Estate and Business Brokers Act, 2002*.

    ◯ True   ◯ False

12. A salesperson should use his/her best efforts to determine whether or not an intended employing brokerage has set up and maintains a commission trust account.

    ◯ True   ◯ False

13. HST remittances must be made by all commission salespeople.

    ◯ True   ◯ False

14. Real estate brokerages must provide cash advances on commission owing, if requested by the salesperson.

    ◯ True   ◯ False

Active Learning Exercises

Solutions are located in the Appendix.

▪ Exercise 1   Multiple Choice

1.1   Undertakings can generally be grouped under several main categories. Which is NOT one of them?

    a.   Client Assurance.

    b.   Solicitor Personal Assurance.

    c.   Guaranteed Assurance.

    d.   Best Efforts Assurance.

1.2   The seller's solicitor typically prepares a final reporting letter which:

    a.   Sets out transaction particulars from the buyer's perspective.

    b.   Might include, if applicable, details about a seller take back mortgage.

    c.   Provides evidence that the seller is not a non-resident.

    d.   Is forwarded to the buyer's solicitor prior to completion of a title search.

1.3   Which of the following is NOT correct about title insurance in Ontario?

    a.   Has certain benefits to home owners, one of which involves title problems at point of listing the property.

    b.   Typically includes both loan and owner policies.

    c.   Usually insures over minor encroachment problems.

    d.   Usually provides broader coverage with owner policies than with lender policies.

1.4   Commission disbursements to brokerages:

    a.   Follow a specific order beginning first with payment to the listing brokerage.

    b.   Is usually paid directly from the statutory real estate trust account.

    c.   Follow a specific order beginning first with payment to the co-operating brokerage.

    d.   Must occur no later than 48 hours following receipt of any balance received from a solicitor involved with the applicable transaction.

1.5   The OREA *Agreement of Purchase and Sale* (OREA Form 100) includes:

    a.   A requisition date relating to the title search process.

    b.   A date by which both solicitors must submit a final reporting letter.

    c.   A requirement that all conveyances must be completed using e-registration.

    d.   A requirement that a sub-search must be completed immediately before registration of the transfer/deed of land.

1.6 A requisition letter might include a request for which of the following?

    a. Satisfactory evidence that the seller will pay all water and gas accounts to closing date.

    b. Statement from the seller attesting that the property is exempt from harmonized sales tax.

    c. Seller's undertaking to deliver vacant possession of the premises.

    d. All of the above.

1.7 Assume an independent contractor registered for HST purposes, received a gross commission of $2,000 and paid an administrative fee of $500, which is viewed as a valid input credit. If these were the only transactions in the reporting period, what is the net remittance?

    a. $260

    b. $195

    c. $75

    d. $100

■ Exercise 2   Matching

Match the phrase/word in the left column with the appropriate description in the right column (not all descriptions are used).

___ Owner's Policy	a. Preparation of Requisition Letter
___ Commission Trust Account	b. An Assurance Provided by a Solicitor of the Client
___ Statutory Trust Account	c. Gateway Software Used to Access Electronic Land Registration Information
___ Buyer's Solicitor	
___ Undertaking	d. Protection Involving Bankruptcy
___ Teraview	e. Statement of Adjustments
___ Legal Disclosure Requirements	f. Title Insurance
___ Conveyance	g. REBBA 2002
	h. Law Society of Upper Canada
	i. Final Reporting Letter
	j. Transfer/Deed of Land

▦ Exercise 3   Commission Trust

The commission trust plan, originally developed by the Ontario Real Estate Association, sets out four steps to create a valid trust. Briefly outline these steps.

▦ Exercise 4   Disbursement Calculations

Broker Williams of ABC Realty Inc. has a deposit in the real estate trust account of $8,250 for a transaction involving a total commission of $15,500. The balance due is typically forwarded by the seller's solicitor on closing. Assume that Salesperson Verdun of ABC Realty Inc. is a HST-registered, independent contractor with a 70/30 split and XYZ is the co-operating brokerage on a 50/50 distribution arrangement.

Outline the exact order and amounts (including HST) of disbursements involving the real estate trust account and the commission trust account.

Total Commission Including HST

	CHEQUE FROM	CHEQUE TO	AMOUNT
STEP 1			
STEP 2			
STEP 3			
STEP 4			
STEP 5			

APPENDIX

THE REAL ESTATE TRANSACTION—GENERAL

APPENDIX

CONTENTS AT A GLANCE

GLOSSARY

KEYWORD	DESCRIPTION
Acknowledgement	An admission or affirmation that some circumstance exists, as in a fact, situation or liability. Acknowledgements are found in standard agreements (i.e., acknowledging receipt of a true copy) and in clauses where buyer and/or seller confirm certain facts.
Administrator	A traditional term referring to an individual who is appointed by the court to administer the estate of a deceased person without a will, as opposed to an executor who carries out instructions provided in a will. Administrators and executors are now referred to as Estate Trustees With a Will or Estate Trustees Without a Will respectively.
Advertising	Activities intended to inform and otherwise favourably influence an individual. Advertising is achieved through various media.
Agreement For Sale	An agreement for the purchase of real property wherein the purchase price is paid in installments and the title is not conveyed to the buyer until the purchase price is paid in full.
Agreement Of Purchase And Sale	A standard form that constitutes a contract when signed, by which one party agrees to sell and another agrees to purchase.
Agreement To Lease	A standard form that constitutes a contract when signed, by which one party agrees to rent real estate to another party for a rental fee or other compensation.
Assign	The act of assigning an interest. The noun *assigns* is found in the Agreement of Purchase and Sale referring to the recipient of an assignment.
Authority	The legal power or right given by a principal, and accepted by the agent, to act on the principal's behalf in business transactions with a third party.
Built-Ins	Items typically affixed to real property; e.g., built-in appliances.
Buyer Representation	A relationship in which the buyer is represented by a brokerage in negotiations for the purchase of property.
Buyer Representation Agreement	An agreement setting out the representation relationship between a brokerage and a buyer.
Capacity	The legal ability to enter into an enforceable contract.

APPENDIX

KEYWORD	DESCRIPTION
Caveat Emptor	Let the buyer beware. The buyer must examine the goods or property being acquired and, therefore, buys at his/her own risk.
Chain of Title	A chronological listing of all conveyances and other matters impacting title, typically referred to in relation to 40-year search requirements under registry.
Client	A person who is represented by a brokerage pursuant to a representation agreement.
Cloud On Title	An encumbrance or claim that affects title to real property, typically discovered during a title search.
Collateral Agreement	An agreement which exists independent of, but in addition to, another agreement.
Commission Trust Account	A real estate brokerage trust account separate and distinct from the trust account required by the *Real Estate and Business Brokers Act*. The commission trust account is used for commission disbursement and protects such commission should the broker become insolvent or bankrupt.
Completion Date	Date set for transfer of title.
Condition Precedent	A condition in an agreement calling for the happening of some event, or performance of some act, before the agreement becomes binding on the parties.
Condition Subsequent	A condition referring to a future event upon the happening of which the contract becomes no longer binding on the parties.
Consent	Consent from a privacy legislation perspective as required under the *Personal Information Protection and Electronic Documents Act*.
Consideration	Something given by one party to another to make a contract binding and viewed as one of six elements required in a legally binding agreement.
Contract	A legally binding agreement between two or more capable persons.

APPENDIX

KEYWORD	DESCRIPTION
Conveyance	A document (sometimes referred to as an instrument) used for the transfer of an interest in property from one person to another.
Customer	A person who has entered into some form of service agreement with a brokerage, but is not represented by that brokerage by way of a representation agreement.
Damages	Compensation or indemnity for loss owing due to a breach of contract or a tort (civil wrong).
Deposit	Payment of money or other valuable consideration as pledge for fulfillment of a contract.
Electronic Signatures	The *Electronic Commerce Act, 2000* (ECA) defines an electronic signature as "electronic information that a person creates or adopts in order to sign a document and that is in, attached to, or associated with the document."
Encroachment	The unauthorized intrusion onto the lands and property of another.
Encumbrance	Outstanding claim or lien recorded against property or any legal right to the use of the property by another person who is not the owner.
Escape Clause	A clause in an agreement permitting the seller to continue to offer the property for sale during a conditional period; e.g., an existing offer conditional on the sale of the buyer's home.
Estate Trustee	An individual either appointed by the court (*Estate Trustee Without a Will*—previously known as an administrator), or appointed in a will (*Estate Trustee With a Will*—previously known as an executor).
Exclusive Listing	The giving of the sole right to offer the described property for sale, subject to terms set out in the agency agreement.
Executor	A person appointed to carry out the provisions in a will. Now referred to as an Estate Trustee.
Final Reporting Letter	A letter prepared after closing by a buyer's or seller's solicitor setting out pertinent details regarding a real estate transaction following closing.

KEYWORD	DESCRIPTION
FINTRAC	The Financial Transactions and Reports Analysis Centre of Canada is a specialized agency that collects, analyzes and discloses financial information and intelligence on suspected money laundering and terrorist activities financing.
Fraud	A false representation of fact knowingly made by an individual that induces another person to act upon the representation.
Freehold Estate	Ownership for an indefinite period of time.
Genuine Intention	An authentic, real intention as opposed to only the outward appearance of a contract.
Heir	An individual who inherits or has the right to inherit property of another.
Holdover Provision	A provision in a listing agreement extending the broker's right to commission beyond the expiration date for persons introduced to the property during the currency of the listing.
Home Inspection	An inspection of a residential house including the physical structure and mechanical systems.
Illiterate	Unable to read or write.
Imputed Knowledge	Knowledge or notice of facts known by one party that are deemed to also be known by another. For real estate purposes, knowledge of a broker or salesperson is deemed to be known by all other salespersons/brokers and the employing brokerage.
Injunction	A judicial process or order requiring the person to whom it is directed to do, or refrain from doing, something.
Irrevocable	Incapable of being recalled or revoked.
Large Cash Transaction	For purposes of FINTRAC compliance, a large cash transaction is any cash involved in a real estate transaction of $10,000 or more (i.e., a deposit of $10,000 or more) or two transactions of $5,000 or more within a 24-hour period from the same client.
Latent Defect	A defect that is not readily observable by the untrained eye during the reasonable inspection of a property.
Lawful Object	The purpose of a contract is legal from both statutory and common law perspectives.

APPENDIX

KEYWORD	DESCRIPTION
Legal Description	A precise, written description by which property can be located and clearly differentiated from other properties.
Lien	The right of a creditor to create an interest in the real property until a debt is discharged.
Listing Price	The price at which a property is offered for sale in the marketplace.
Living Area Measurement	A measurement method, endorsed by the Alliance for Canadian Real Estate Education, setting out living area calculations for various styles of houses; e.g., one-storey, 1½ storey, bi-level and 2-storey.
Mandatary	A mandatary is an agent or representative who has a specific mandate as set out in a service agreement. A mandatory may be used for identification verification required by the Financial Transactions and Reports Analysis Centre of Canada.
Marketable Title	A title which a court considers to be so free from defects that even an unwilling buyer must accept.
Marketing	Activities involving the promotion and distribution of products/ services in the marketplace. In real estate, marketing is more narrowly focused on property features and brokerage/ salesperson services.
Marketing Plan	An action plan developed by a brokerage or a salesperson, flowing from a marketing strategy, to promote property and secure potential prospects.
Market Position	A specific, identifiable niche in the marketplace.
Matrimonial Home	A home designated as the family residence pursuant to the *Family Law Act*.
Minor	A person who is under the age of legal competence.
Misrepresentation	A false statement of fact, generally categorized under fraudulent or negligent.
MLS® Listing	An exclusive listing with extended authority to co-operating brokers within an MLS® system.
More or Less	Slight or unimportant inaccuracies that both parties are willing to accept.

KEYWORD	DESCRIPTION
Multiple Representation	Two or more clients in a real estate transaction are represented by the same real estate brokerage.
Non Est Factum	A person is not bound by a fraudulent contract that he or she unwittingly entered into.
Notice	Information or knowledge brought to a party's attention.
Offer and Acceptance	Mutual agreement of the parties to a contract in adherence with legal requirements; e.g., unconditional acceptance.
Open Listing	A listing given to any number of brokers without liability to compensate any except the one who first acquires a buyer ready, willing and able to meet the terms of the listing, or secures the acceptance by the seller of a satisfactory offer.
Parol Evidence Rule	A completed written contract can only be modified in writing, subject to certain legal exceptions.
Patent Defect	A defect that is readily observable by the untrained eye.
Personal Facts	Details about an individual but not identifiable with that individual. Personal facts are best referred to as anonymous information; e.g., business statistics that represent the culmination of personal data with no association to individuals from which the information was collected.
Personal Information (Federal)	Details about an identifiable individual, but not including the name, title or business address/telephone number of an employee as defined under the *Personal Information Protection and Electronic Documents Act.*
Postponement	The agreement by a mortgagee to maintain a subsequent priority during the refinancing or re-registration of another mortgage in higher priority.
Power of Attorney	Delegated written authority to a person to legally act on behalf of another.
Prepayment	A right given to a mortgagor to pay all or part of the mortgage debt in advance of the maturity date, on stipulated terms.
Privacy Code	A set of ten principles providing guidance to members of organized real estate in the collection, use and disclosure of personal information.

APPENDIX

KEYWORD	DESCRIPTION
Quantum Meruit	Remedy for breach of contract based on court determination of work/services performed.
Real Estate Trust Account	An account separate and apart from one's personal monies, as required by law. Real estate brokers are required to have a statutory trust account pursuant to the *Real Estate and Business Brokers Act*.
Renewal	A right given to the mortgagor to renew the mortgage at maturity date, on stipulated terms.
Representation	A statement made regarding some existing fact or event that induces a contract and could be the basis for rescinding that agreement, if found false.
Requisition	An inquiry (typically referred to as a requisition letter) prepared by the buyer's solicitor to the seller's solicitor concerning title matters.
Rescission	Setting aside a contract.
Restriction	A limitation placed on the use of property.
Seller Take Back	A mortgage taken back by the seller typically to facilitate the sale and/or further the seller's investment objectives.
Sensitive Personal Information	Personal details about an identifiable individual that is judged more sensitive than merely personal information given its delicate nature; e.g., a person's physical or mental condition and political opinions.
Service Agreement	An agreement in which the brokerage provides services to the customer, as distinct from a representation agreement with a client.
Special Assessment (Condominium)	An assessment not customarily levied but required over and above common expense payments given unexpected repairs or replacement of common elements, or other assets of the condominium corporation.
Special Assessment (Taxation)	An assessment or levy in addition to usual property taxes, typically involving the installation of special services. Also commonly referred to as local improvements.
Specific Performance	A court remedy for breach of contract compelling a defendant to carry out the terms of an agreement or contract.

APPENDIX

KEYWORD	DESCRIPTION
Statement of Adjustments	A statement in balance sheet format setting out the financial particulars of a real estate transaction.
Successor	A party that succeeds or follows another, as in an heir who inherits property.
Tender	An unconditional offer to perform, as in a buyer or seller tendering regarding a real estate agreement, by presenting the necessary documentation and funds at the Land Registry office on the date set for completion.
Time is of the Essence	A more or less standard agreement wording requiring punctual performance of a contract.
Title	The evidence that an owner has lawful ownership of property. In Ontario, a Transfer/Deed of Land is registered under land titles or registry as proof of ownership.
Title Insurance	Insurance relating to defects and/or invalidity of title.
Tort	A breach of duty involving a civil wrong (other than a breach of contract) that can lead to common law action for damages.
Trade	Disposition or acquisition of or transaction in real estate by sale, purchase, agreement for purchase and sale, exchange, option, lease, rental or otherwise and any offer or attempt to list real estate for the purpose of such a disposition, acquisition or transaction, and any act, advertisement, conduct or negotiation, directly or indirectly, in furtherance of any disposition, acquisition, transaction, offer or attempt, and the verb *trade* has a corresponding meaning; (Source: *Real Estate and Business Brokers Act*.
Transfer/Deed	To convey from one person to another. A transfer of real property is accomplished in Ontario through the registration of a Transfer/Deed of Land.
UFFI	Urea formaldehyde foam insulation (UFFI) was blown into place under pressure, but banned in 1980 due to health concerns.
Undertaking	An assurance given by a client and/or a solicitor regarding unresolved items at closing of a real estate transaction.
Unenforceable	That which cannot be imposed; e.g., not enforceable by the court.

APPENDIX

KEYWORD	DESCRIPTION
Void	Of no legal effect; a nullity.
Voidable	One party to a contract is entitled to rescind the contract at his or her option.
Waiver	The relinquishment of some right. More specifically, a wording within an agreement providing that the party may waive a condition at his/her sole option.
Warranty	A statement providing assurance or a guarantee that something is as presented.
Witness	An individual who signs a document attesting to the authenticity of signature(s) contained therein.

APPENDIX

MORTGAGE PAYMENT FACTORS

MORTGAGE PAYMENT FACTORS (per $1,000 of Loan Amount)

Weekly Payment Factors

Int. Rate	5	10	15	20	25
1.00	3.943244	2.020779	1.380489	1.060742	.869211
1.25	3.967692	2.045628	1.405768	1.086459	.895367
1.50	3.992209	2.070645	1.431313	1.112538	.921982
1.75	4.016796	2.095828	1.457122	1.138977	.949052
2.00	4.041452	2.121178	1.483194	1.165774	.976572
2.25	4.066177	2.146693	1.509426	1.192925	1.004538
2.50	4.090971	2.172373	1.536117	1.220428	1.032945
2.75	4.115832	2.198216	1.562966	1.248279	1.061789
3.00	4.140761	2.224222	1.590070	1.276476	1.091063
3.25	4.165758	2.250390	1.617428	1.305015	1.120762
3.50	4.190821	2.276719	1.645038	1.333891	1.150881
3.75	4.215952	2.303208	1.672897	1.363103	1.181413
4.00	4.241149	2.329856	1.701005	1.392645	1.212352
4.25	4.266412	2.356662	1.729358	1.422515	1.243691
4.50	4.291742	2.383625	1.757955	1.452707	1.275424
4.75	4.317136	2.410745	1.786793	1.483218	1.307543
5.00	4.342596	2.438019	1.815869	1.514043	1.340042
5.25	4.368121	2.465448	1.845183	1.545178	1.372912
5.50	4.393711	2.493030	1.874731	1.576619	1.406147
5.75	4.419364	2.520764	1.904511	1.608361	1.439739
6.00	4.445082	2.548648	1.934520	1.640399	1.473680
6.25	4.470863	2.576683	1.964756	1.672729	1.507963
6.50	4.496708	2.604866	1.995217	1.705345	1.542580
6.75	4.522615	2.633197	2.025900	1.738244	1.577522
7.00	4.548585	2.661674	2.056801	1.771419	1.612781
7.25	4.574617	2.690297	2.087920	1.804867	1.648351
7.50	4.600712	2.719064	2.119252	1.838581	1.684222
7.75	4.626867	2.747974	2.150796	1.872558	1.720386
8.00	4.653084	2.777025	2.182547	1.906791	1.756836
8.25	4.679362	2.806218	2.214505	1.941276	1.793564
8.50	4.705701	2.835550	2.246666	1.976008	1.830560
8.75	4.732100	2.865020	2.279026	2.010981	1.867818
9.00	4.758559	2.894628	2.311584	2.046190	1.905329
9.25	4.785077	2.924371	2.344336	2.081630	1.943086
9.50	4.811654	2.954249	2.377280	2.117296	1.981080
9.75	4.838291	2.984260	2.410413	2.153183	2.019304
10.00	4.864986	3.014404	2.443731	2.189285	2.057750
10.25	4.891739	3.044678	2.477232	2.225598	2.096411
10.50	4.918550	3.075082	2.510913	2.262115	2.135278
10.75	4.945419	3.105614	2.544771	2.298833	2.174345
11.00	4.972345	3.136274	2.578803	2.335746	2.213604
11.25	4.999327	3.167059	2.613007	2.372849	2.253048
11.50	5.026366	3.197969	2.647379	2.410136	2.292670
11.75	5.053461	3.229002	2.681916	2.447604	2.332463
12.00	5.080613	3.260158	2.716615	2.485246	2.372420
12.25	5.107819	3.291433	2.751474	2.523058	2.412534
12.50	5.135081	3.322829	2.786490	2.561036	2.452800
12.75	5.162397	3.354342	2.821659	2.599174	2.493209

Int. Rate	5	10	15	20	25
13.00	5.189768	3.385972	2.856979	2.637467	2.533757
13.25	5.217193	3.417718	2.892446	2.675911	2.574437
13.50	5.244671	3.449578	2.928059	2.714501	2.615243
13.75	5.272203	3.481550	2.963814	2.753233	2.656169
14.00	5.299788	3.513634	2.999707	2.792102	2.697209
14.25	5.327426	3.545829	3.035738	2.831104	2.738358
14.50	5.355116	3.578132	3.071901	2.870233	2.779610
14.75	5.382858	3.610543	3.108195	2.909487	2.820960
15.00	5.410651	3.643060	3.144617	2.948860	2.862404
15.25	5.438496	3.675683	3.181165	2.988348	2.903935
15.50	5.466392	3.708408	3.217834	3.027948	2.945549
15.75	5.494338	3.741237	3.254623	3.067655	2.987241
16.00	5.522335	3.774166	3.291529	3.107465	3.029007
16.25	5.550381	3.807195	3.328548	3.147374	3.070843
16.50	5.578477	3.840322	3.365680	3.187379	3.112743
16.75	5.606623	3.873546	3.402919	3.227475	3.154704
17.00	5.634817	3.906867	3.440265	3.267659	3.196722
17.25	5.663059	3.940281	3.477715	3.307927	3.238793
17.50	5.691350	3.973789	3.515265	3.348277	3.280912
17.75	5.719689	4.007389	3.552914	3.388703	3.323077
18.00	5.748075	4.041079	3.590658	3.429203	3.365284
18.25	5.776508	4.074859	3.628495	3.469774	3.407529
18.50	5.804988	4.108726	3.666424	3.510412	3.449809
18.75	5.833514	4.142681	3.704440	3.551115	3.492122
19.00	5.862087	4.176721	3.742543	3.591878	3.534462
19.25	5.890705	4.210845	3.780729	3.632699	3.576829
19.50	5.919368	4.245051	3.818996	3.673575	3.619219
19.75	5.948077	4.279340	3.857342	3.714503	3.661629
20.00	5.976830	4.313709	3.895764	3.755480	3.704057
20.25	6.005628	4.348157	3.934260	3.796504	3.746499
20.50	6.034469	4.382682	3.972829	3.837572	3.788954
20.75	6.063354	4.417285	4.011467	3.878681	3.831420
21.00	6.092283	4.451962	4.050172	3.919828	3.873893
21.25	6.121254	4.486714	4.088943	3.961011	3.916372
21.50	6.150269	4.521539	4.127777	4.002229	3.958855
21.75	6.179325	4.556436	4.166672	4.043477	4.001339
22.00	6.208423	4.591403	4.205627	4.084755	4.043823
22.25	6.237563	4.626439	4.244638	4.126059	4.086305
22.50	6.266745	4.661543	4.283704	4.167388	4.128783
22.75	6.295967	4.696714	4.322823	4.208739	4.171255
23.00	6.325229	4.731951	4.361994	4.250111	4.213720
23.25	6.354532	4.767253	4.401213	4.291502	4.256176
23.50	6.383875	4.802617	4.440480	4.332908	4.298622
23.75	6.413258	4.838044	4.479793	4.374330	4.341056
24.00	6.442679	4.873532	4.519149	4.415764	4.383477
24.25	6.472140	4.909080	4.558547	4.457210	4.425883
24.50	6.501639	4.944687	4.597985	4.498664	4.468273
24.75	6.531176	4.980351	4.637461	4.540127	4.510647

APPENDIX

MORTGAGE PAYMENT FACTORS (per $1,000 of Loan Amount)

Bi-Weekly Payment Factors

Int. Rate	\multicolumn{5}{c}{Amortization Period}				
	5	10	15	20	25
1.00	7.887244	4.041946	2.761243	2.121687	1.738588
1.25	7.936334	4.091746	2.811874	2.173178	1.790949
1.50	7.985566	4.141884	2.863038	2.225396	1.844230
1.75	8.034939	4.192359	2.914733	2.278337	1.898422
2.00	8.084452	4.243168	2.966955	2.331994	1.953518
2.25	8.134105	4.294310	3.019701	2.386364	2.009508
2.50	8.183896	4.345783	3.072968	2.441440	2.066384
2.75	8.233826	4.397587	3.126752	2.497215	2.124135
3.00	8.283894	4.449718	3.181051	2.553683	2.182751
3.25	8.334099	4.502175	3.235859	2.610839	2.242220
3.50	8.384440	4.554957	3.291174	2.668673	2.302531
3.75	8.434917	4.608062	3.346991	2.727180	2.363671
4.00	8.485530	4.661487	3.403306	2.786352	2.425628
4.25	8.536276	4.715231	3.460115	2.846180	2.488389
4.50	8.587157	4.769291	3.517414	2.906657	2.551940
4.75	8.638172	4.823667	3.575199	2.967775	2.616267
5.00	8.689319	4.878355	3.633464	3.029524	2.681357
5.25	8.740598	4.933354	3.692206	3.091897	2.747193
5.50	8.792008	4.988662	3.751419	3.154884	2.813762
5.75	8.843549	5.044277	3.811099	3.218476	2.881049
6.00	8.895220	5.100196	3.871241	3.282664	2.949037
6.25	8.947021	5.156417	3.931840	3.347438	3.017712
6.50	8.998950	5.212938	3.992890	3.412790	3.087058
6.75	9.051007	5.269757	4.054387	3.478708	3.157059
7.00	9.103192	5.326872	4.116326	3.545184	3.227698
7.25	9.155504	5.384281	4.178701	3.612207	3.298961
7.50	9.207942	5.441980	4.241507	3.679768	3.370830
7.75	9.260505	5.499968	4.304738	3.747856	3.443290
8.00	9.313193	5.558243	4.368390	3.816461	3.516325
8.25	9.366005	5.616802	4.432456	3.885572	3.589918
8.50	9.418941	5.675643	4.496930	3.955181	3.664053
8.75	9.472000	5.734763	4.561809	4.025276	3.738715
9.00	9.525180	5.794160	4.627085	4.095847	3.813887
9.25	9.578482	5.853832	4.692753	4.166883	3.889554
9.50	9.631905	5.913775	4.758807	4.238375	3.965699
9.75	9.685448	5.973989	4.825242	4.310311	4.042308
10.00	9.739110	6.034469	4.892052	4.382682	4.119365
10.25	9.792891	6.095214	4.959230	4.455478	4.196855
10.50	9.846790	6.156222	5.026772	4.528687	4.274762
10.75	9.900806	6.217489	5.094672	4.602300	4.353072
11.00	9.954939	6.279013	5.162923	4.676307	4.431771
11.25	10.009188	6.340792	5.231520	4.750697	4.510843
11.50	10.063552	6.402822	5.300456	4.825461	4.590275
11.75	10.118031	6.465103	5.369727	4.900588	4.670053
12.00	10.172624	6.527630	5.439326	4.976068	4.750162
12.25	10.227330	6.590401	5.509247	5.051892	4.830591
12.50	10.282149	6.653414	5.579484	5.128050	4.911325
12.75	10.337079	6.716667	5.650033	5.204533	4.992352

Int. Rate	\multicolumn{5}{c}{Amortization Period}				
	5	10	15	20	25
13.00	10.392121	6.780155	5.720886	5.281330	5.073659
13.25	10.447273	6.843878	5.792038	5.358432	5.155233
13.50	10.502535	6.907832	5.863483	5.435831	5.237064
13.75	10.557906	6.972015	5.935216	5.513516	5.319138
14.00	10.613385	7.036424	6.007231	5.591480	5.401445
14.25	10.668972	7.101057	6.079522	5.669712	5.483974
14.50	10.724667	7.165910	6.152083	5.748204	5.566713
14.75	10.780467	7.230981	6.224909	5.826947	5.649652
15.00	10.836373	7.296268	6.297994	5.905934	5.732780
15.25	10.892384	7.361768	6.371333	5.985155	5.816088
15.50	10.948500	7.427479	6.444919	6.064601	5.899566
15.75	11.004718	7.493397	6.518749	6.144266	5.983205
16.00	11.061040	7.559520	6.592815	6.224141	6.066994
16.25	11.117464	7.625845	6.667113	6.304219	6.150926
16.50	11.173989	7.692371	6.741637	6.384490	6.234992
16.75	11.230615	7.759094	6.816382	6.464949	6.319182
17.00	11.287342	7.826011	6.891342	6.545587	6.403490
17.25	11.344167	7.893121	6.966513	6.626397	6.487908
17.50	11.401092	7.960419	7.041889	6.707373	6.572427
17.75	11.458114	8.027905	7.117466	6.788507	6.657040
18.00	11.515233	8.095575	7.193237	6.869792	6.741741
18.25	11.572450	8.163427	7.269188	6.951222	6.826522
18.50	11.629762	8.231457	7.345344	7.032790	6.911377
18.75	11.687169	8.299665	7.421671	7.114490	6.996300
19.00	11.744671	8.368046	7.498172	7.196315	7.081284
19.25	11.802267	8.436598	7.574844	7.278260	7.166323
19.50	11.859956	8.505320	7.651682	7.360318	7.251412
19.75	11.917736	8.574208	7.728680	7.442885	7.336545
20.00	11.975610	8.643259	7.805835	7.524753	7.421716
20.25	12.033574	8.712472	7.883142	7.607118	7.506922
20.50	12.091629	8.781844	7.960596	7.689573	7.592156
20.75	12.149773	8.851372	8.038193	7.772115	7.677414
21.00	12.208066	8.921054	8.115928	7.854738	7.762691
21.25	12.266328	8.990888	8.193797	7.937436	7.847984
21.50	12.324738	9.060870	8.271797	8.020205	7.933287
21.75	12.383234	9.130999	8.349921	8.103041	8.018597
22.00	12.441816	9.201271	8.428168	8.185938	8.103910
22.25	12.500485	9.271686	8.506532	8.268892	8.189222
22.50	12.559238	9.342240	8.585009	8.351899	8.274530
22.75	12.618075	9.412930	8.663596	8.434954	8.359830
23.00	12.676996	9.483755	8.742288	8.518054	8.445119
23.25	12.736000	9.554713	8.821083	8.601194	8.530393
23.50	12.795086	9.625800	8.899975	8.684370	8.615651
23.75	12.854254	9.697014	8.978961	8.767580	8.700888
24.00	12.913502	9.768354	9.058039	8.850818	8.786102
24.25	12.972831	9.839816	9.137203	8.934082	8.871290
24.50	13.032239	9.911399	9.216451	9.017368	8.956450
24.75	13.091726	9.983100	9.295779	9.100672	9.041580

APPENDIX

MORTGAGE PAYMENT FACTORS (per $1,000 of Loan Amount)

Semi-Monthly Payment Factors

| Int. Rate | \multicolumn{5}{c}{Amortization Period} | | | | | Int. Rate | \multicolumn{5}{c}{Amortization Period} | | | | |

Int. Rate	5	10	15	20	25	Int. Rate	5	10	15	20	25
1.00	8.544651	4.378845	2.991394	2.298530	1.883501	13.00	11.260405	7.346652	6.198878	5.722597	5.497574
1.25	8.597867	4.432814	3.046258	2.354323	1.940234	13.25	11.320208	7.415727	6.275999	5.806163	5.585986
1.50	8.651237	4.487149	3.101699	2.410903	1.997963	13.50	11.380130	7.485053	6.353438	5.890051	5.674675
1.75	8.704760	4.541849	3.157715	2.468267	2.056681	13.75	11.440171	7.554628	6.431189	5.974250	5.763629
2.00	8.758436	4.596912	3.214304	2.526408	2.116378	14.00	11.500330	7.624448	6.509246	6.058751	5.852836
2.25	8.812263	4.652336	3.271460	2.585320	2.177045	14.25	11.560606	7.694510	6.587603	6.143544	5.942284
2.50	8.866241	4.708119	3.329181	2.644998	2.238672	14.50	11.620998	7.764812	6.666253	6.228619	6.031960
2.75	8.920369	4.764261	3.387463	2.705434	2.301247	14.75	11.681506	7.835351	6.745191	6.313968	6.121853
3.00	8.974647	4.820758	3.446303	2.766622	2.364760	15.00	11.742128	7.906125	6.824410	6.399580	6.211953
3.25	9.029073	4.877609	3.505695	2.828555	2.429197	15.25	11.802865	7.977129	6.903905	6.485446	6.302248
3.50	9.083648	4.934811	3.565636	2.891224	2.494547	15.50	11.863715	8.048362	6.983668	6.571559	6.392728
3.75	9.138371	4.992364	3.626123	2.954621	2.560796	15.75	11.924678	8.119821	7.063695	6.657908	6.483382
4.00	9.193241	5.050265	3.687149	3.018739	2.627931	16.00	11.985753	8.191502	7.143980	6.744485	6.574200
4.25	9.248256	5.108511	3.748711	3.083570	2.695937	16.25	12.046938	8.263403	7.224516	6.831282	6.665174
4.50	9.303418	5.167101	3.810804	3.149104	2.764799	16.50	12.108235	8.335522	7.305297	6.918291	6.756292
4.75	9.358724	5.226032	3.873424	3.215332	2.834503	16.75	12.169640	8.407854	7.386319	7.005502	6.847548
5.00	9.414174	5.285303	3.936565	3.282245	2.905033	17.00	12.231155	8.480398	7.467575	7.092909	6.938931
5.25	9.469767	5.344911	4.000222	3.349834	2.976373	17.25	12.292777	8.553151	7.549060	7.180503	7.030433
5.50	9.525504	5.404854	4.064391	3.418088	3.048508	17.50	12.354507	8.626109	7.630767	7.268277	7.122046
5.75	9.581382	5.465130	4.129066	3.486999	3.121420	17.75	12.416344	8.699270	7.712692	7.356222	7.213761
6.00	9.637402	5.526736	4.194242	3.557556	3.195033	18.00	12.478286	8.772632	7.794828	7.444333	7.305573
6.25	9.693562	5.586669	4.259913	3.626749	3.269511	18.25	12.540334	8.846191	7.877171	7.532601	7.397472
6.50	9.749862	5.647929	4.326075	3.697568	3.344656	18.50	12.602486	8.919944	7.959716	7.621019	7.489451
6.75	9.806302	5.709512	4.392721	3.769002	3.420511	18.75	12.664741	8.993889	8.042455	7.709580	7.581505
7.00	9.862880	5.771415	4.459845	3.841040	3.497059	19.00	12.727099	9.068023	8.125386	7.798279	7.673625
7.25	9.919595	5.833637	4.527443	3.913671	3.574282	19.25	12.789560	9.142344	8.208501	7.887107	7.765806
7.50	9.976448	5.896175	4.595508	3.986886	3.652164	19.50	12.852122	9.216848	8.291797	7.976059	7.858042
7.75	10.033437	5.959026	4.664035	4.060672	3.730686	19.75	12.914784	9.291533	8.375268	8.065129	7.950326
8.00	10.090562	6.022188	4.733017	4.135019	3.809831	20.00	12.977546	9.366395	8.458908	8.154309	8.042652
8.25	10.147821	6.085658	4.802449	4.209916	3.889582	20.25	13.040408	9.441434	8.542714	8.243595	8.135016
8.50	10.205215	6.149343	4.872325	4.285351	3.969921	20.50	13.103367	9.516644	8.626680	8.332980	8.227411
8.75	10.262742	6.213513	4.942638	4.361314	4.050831	20.75	13.166425	9.592025	8.710801	8.422459	8.319833
9.00	10.320402	6.277893	5.013383	4.437793	4.132294	21.00	13.229579	9.667573	8.795073	8.512026	8.412277
9.25	10.378194	6.342571	5.084553	4.514778	4.214294	21.25	13.292829	9.743285	8.879491	8.601676	8.504738
9.50	10.436117	6.407544	5.156142	4.592256	4.296814	21.50	13.356175	9.819160	8.964050	8.691403	8.597211
9.75	10.494170	6.472809	5.228143	4.670217	4.379836	21.75	13.419616	9.895193	9.048746	8.781203	8.689692
10.00	10.552353	6.538365	5.300552	4.748649	4.463344	22.00	13.483150	9.971383	9.133574	8.871070	8.782177
10.25	10.610666	6.604207	5.373361	4.827541	4.547322	22.25	13.546777	10.047728	9.218530	8.960999	8.874662
10.50	10.669106	6.670335	5.446564	4.906883	4.631752	22.50	13.610497	10.124223	9.303610	9.050987	8.967142
10.75	10.727674	6.736744	5.520155	4.986663	4.716620	22.75	13.674309	10.200868	9.388808	9.141027	9.059615
11.00	10.786369	6.803432	5.594127	5.066869	4.801910	23.00	13.738212	10.277659	9.474122	9.231116	9.152076
11.25	10.845190	6.870397	5.668474	5.147492	4.887604	23.25	13.802205	10.354593	9.559547	9.321250	9.244522
11.50	10.904137	6.937635	5.743191	5.228520	4.973690	23.50	13.866287	10.431669	9.645078	9.411423	9.336950
11.75	10.963208	7.005144	5.818269	5.309942	5.060150	23.75	13.930458	10.508883	9.730712	9.501633	9.429357
12.00	11.022403	7.072921	5.893704	5.391748	5.146971	24.00	13.994717	10.586234	9.816446	9.591875	9.521740
12.25	11.081721	7.140963	5.969489	5.473927	5.234138	24.25	14.059064	10.663718	9.902273	9.682145	9.614095
12.50	11.141161	7.209267	6.045617	5.556468	5.321637	24.50	14.123497	10.741333	9.988193	9.772439	9.706421
12.75	11.200723	7.277831	6.122082	5.639362	5.409453	24.75	14.188016	10.819077	10.074199	9.862755	9.798714

MORTGAGE PAYMENT FACTORS (per $1,000 of Loan Amount)

Monthly Payment Factors

Int. Rate	5	10	15	20	25
1.00	17.092853	8.759511	5.984032	4.598017	3.767784
1.25	17.200199	8.867930	6.094097	4.709868	3.881475
1.50	17.307863	8.977093	6.205330	4.823308	3.997171
1.75	17.415843	9.086996	6.317724	4.938326	4.114856
2.00	17.524137	9.197636	6.431274	5.054912	4.234512
2.25	17.632745	9.309011	6.545972	5.173052	4.356121
2.50	17.741664	9.421115	6.661811	5.292736	4.479662
2.75	17.850895	9.533946	6.778784	5.413950	4.605115
3.00	17.960435	9.647500	6.896884	5.536680	4.732455
3.25	18.070284	9.761774	7.016102	5.660911	4.861660
3.50	18.180439	9.876762	7.136432	5.786630	4.992703
3.75	18.290900	9.992462	7.257863	5.913820	5.125560
4.00	18.401665	10.108870	7.380387	6.042465	5.260202
4.25	18.512732	10.225981	7.503996	6.172548	5.396602
4.50	18.624102	10.343792	7.628681	6.304052	5.534730
4.75	18.735771	10.462297	7.754431	6.436959	5.674556
5.00	18.847739	10.581483	7.881238	6.571250	5.816050
5.25	18.960005	10.701376	8.009091	6.706908	5.959180
5.50	19.072566	10.821941	8.137981	6.843913	6.103915
5.75	19.185423	10.943184	8.267897	6.982245	6.250221
6.00	19.298572	11.065099	8.398828	7.121884	6.398066
6.25	19.412013	11.187683	8.530764	7.262811	6.547416
6.50	19.525745	11.310931	8.663695	7.405004	6.698238
6.75	19.639766	11.434838	8.797609	7.548443	6.850496
7.00	19.754075	11.559399	8.932494	7.693106	7.004158
7.25	19.868670	11.684610	9.068341	7.838973	7.159187
7.50	19.983549	11.810465	9.205137	7.986021	7.315549
7.75	20.098712	11.936960	9.342870	8.134229	7.473210
8.00	20.214157	12.064090	9.481529	8.283575	7.632135
8.25	20.329883	12.191850	9.621103	8.434037	7.792288
8.50	20.445888	12.320234	9.761579	8.585592	7.953635
8.75	20.562170	12.449238	9.902945	8.738219	8.116142
9.00	20.678729	12.578856	10.045189	8.891895	8.279774
9.25	20.795563	12.709083	10.188298	9.046598	8.444497
9.50	20.912670	12.839914	10.332261	9.202305	8.610276
9.75	21.030049	12.971344	10.477066	9.358995	8.777079
10.00	21.147698	13.103367	10.622699	9.516644	8.944872
10.25	21.262617	13.235979	10.769149	9.675231	9.113622
10.50	21.383803	13.369173	10.916402	9.834734	9.283297
10.75	21.502255	13.502944	11.064446	9.995129	9.453864
11.00	21.620972	13.637287	11.213269	10.156396	9.625292
11.25	21.739952	13.772197	11.362858	10.318512	9.797549
11.50	21.859194	13.907667	11.513201	10.481456	9.970606
11.75	21.978696	14.043693	11.664285	10.645206	10.144431
12.00	22.098457	14.180269	11.816096	10.809741	10.318996
12.25	22.218476	14.317389	11.968624	10.975039	10.494270
12.50	22.338750	14.455048	12.121854	11.141079	10.670227
12.75	22.459278	14.593241	12.275775	11.307841	10.846838

Int. Rate	5	10	15	20	25
13.00	22.580060	14.731961	12.430373	11.475304	11.024075
13.25	22.701092	14.871203	12.585637	11.643447	11.201912
13.50	22.822375	15.010961	12.741554	11.812250	11.380323
13.75	22.943906	15.151230	12.898111	11.981694	11.559282
14.00	23.065685	15.292005	13.055297	12.151759	11.738765
14.25	23.187708	15.433279	13.213098	12.322426	11.918747
14.50	23.309976	15.575047	13.371503	12.493674	12.099205
14.75	23.432486	15.717303	13.530498	12.665487	12.280116
15.00	23.555237	15.860041	13.690073	12.837844	12.461457
15.25	23.678228	16.003257	13.850215	13.010728	12.643207
15.50	23.801457	16.146944	14.010912	13.184121	12.825344
15.75	23.924922	16.291096	14.171253	13.358006	13.007848
16.00	24.048622	16.435709	14.333924	13.532364	13.190699
16.25	24.172556	16.580776	14.496215	13.707180	13.373878
16.50	24.296722	16.726291	14.659014	13.882435	13.557365
16.75	24.421119	16.872250	14.822310	14.058115	13.741144
17.00	24.545744	17.018645	14.986090	14.234202	13.925195
17.25	24.670597	17.165473	15.150344	14.410682	14.109502
17.50	24.795677	17.312727	15.315061	14.587538	14.294049
17.75	24.920981	17.460401	15.480229	14.764755	14.478820
18.00	25.046508	17.608491	15.645837	14.942319	14.663799
18.25	25.172256	17.756990	15.811874	15.120216	14.848971
18.50	25.298225	17.905892	15.978330	15.298430	15.034322
18.75	25.424413	18.055193	16.145194	15.476949	15.219837
19.00	25.550817	18.204887	16.312456	15.655759	15.405505
19.25	25.677437	18.354968	16.480104	15.834845	15.591311
19.50	25.804272	18.505431	16.648129	16.014197	15.777243
19.75	25.931319	18.656270	16.816521	16.193800	15.963289
20.00	26.058577	18.807480	16.985269	16.373642	16.149438
20.25	26.186046	18.959055	17.154364	16.553712	16.335678
20.50	26.313722	19.110990	17.323795	16.733998	16.521998
20.75	26.441605	19.263280	17.493554	16.914489	16.708389
21.00	26.569693	19.415920	17.663630	17.095172	16.894840
21.25	26.697985	19.568903	17.834015	17.276038	17.081342
21.50	26.826480	19.722225	18.004698	17.457076	17.267886
21.75	26.955175	19.875880	18.175672	17.638275	17.454462
22.00	27.084070	20.029863	18.346926	17.819625	17.641063
22.25	27.213162	20.184169	18.518453	18.001117	17.827679
22.50	27.342451	20.338793	18.690242	18.182742	18.014304
22.75	27.471935	20.493729	18.862286	18.364489	12.200930
23.00	27.601613	20.648972	19.034577	18.546351	18.387550
23.25	27.731482	20.804518	19.207105	18.728317	18.574156
23.50	27.861542	20.960361	19.379864	18.910381	18.760742
23.75	27.991791	21.116496	19.552844	19.092533	18.947302
24.00	28.122228	21.272918	19.726037	19.274765	19.133830
24.25	28.252851	21.429622	19.899437	19.457070	19.320319
24.50	28.383658	21.586603	20.073035	19.639441	19.506765
24.75	28.514649	21.743856	20.246823	19.821869	19.693162

APPENDIX

FORMS

OREA Ontario Real Estate Association   **Agreement of Purchase and Sale**

Form 100
for use in the Province of Ontario

This Agreement of Purchase and Sale dated this .... day of .... 20............

BUYER, ..., agrees to purchase from
(Full legal names of all Buyers)

SELLER, ..., the following
(Full legal names of all Sellers)

REAL PROPERTY:

Address ....

fronting on the .... side of ....

in the ....

and having a frontage of .... more or less by a depth of .... more or less

and legally described as ....

.... (the "property")
(Legal description of land including easements not described elsewhere)

PURCHASE PRICE: Dollars (CDN$) ....

.... Dollars

DEPOSIT: Buyer submits ....
(Herewith/Upon Acceptance/as otherwise described in this Agreement)

.... Dollars (CDN$) ....

by negotiable cheque payable to .... "Deposit Holder" to be held
in trust pending completion or other termination of this Agreement and to be credited toward the Purchase Price on completion. For the purposes of this
Agreement, "Upon Acceptance" shall mean that the Buyer is required to deliver the deposit to the Deposit Holder within 24 hours of the acceptance of
this Agreement. The parties to this Agreement hereby acknowledge that, unless otherwise provided for in this Agreement, the Deposit Holder shall place
the deposit in trust in the Deposit Holder's non-interest bearing Real Estate Trust Account and no interest shall be earned, received or paid on the deposit.

Buyer agrees to pay the balance as more particularly set out in Schedule A attached.

SCHEDULE(S) A..**attached hereto form(s) part of this Agreement.**

1.   **IRREVOCABILITY:** This offer shall be irrevocable by .... until .... a.m./p.m. on the ....
(Seller/Buyer)

day of .... 20 ...., after which time, if not accepted, this offer shall be null and void and the deposit
shall be returned to the Buyer in full without interest.

2.   **COMPLETION DATE:** This Agreement shall be completed by no later than 6:00 p.m. on the .... day of ....

20 .... Upon completion, vacant possession of the property shall be given to the Buyer unless otherwise provided for in this Agreement.

INITIALS OF BUYER(S): (⬭)   **INITIALS OF SELLER(S):** (⬭)

Form 100   Revised 2015   Page 1 of 6

3. **NOTICES:** The Seller hereby appoints the Listing Brokerage as agent for the Seller for the purpose of giving and receiving notices pursuant to this Agreement. Where a Brokerage (Buyer's Brokerage) has entered into a representation agreement with the Buyer, the Buyer hereby appoints the Buyer's Brokerage as agent for the purpose of giving and receiving notices pursuant to this Agreement. **Where a Brokerage represents both the Seller and the Buyer (multiple representation), the Brokerage shall not be appointed or authorized to be agent for either the Buyer or the Seller for the purpose of giving and receiving notices.** Any notice relating hereto or provided for herein shall be in writing. In addition to any provision contained herein and in any Schedule hereto, this offer, any counter-offer, notice of acceptance thereof or any notice to be given or received pursuant to this Agreement or any Schedule hereto (any of them, "Document") shall be deemed given and received when delivered personally or hand delivered to the Address for Service provided in the Acknowledgement below, or where a facsimile number or email address is provided herein, when transmitted electronically to that facsimile number or email address, respectively, in which case, the signature(s) of the party (parties) shall be deemed to be original.

FAX No.: ....   FAX No.: ....
            (For delivery of Documents to Seller)   (For delivery of Documents to Buyer)

Email Address: ....   Email Address: ....
            (For delivery of Documents to Seller)   (For delivery of Documents to Buyer)

4. **CHATTELS INCLUDED:**...

....

....

....

....

Unless otherwise stated in this Agreement or any Schedule hereto, Seller agrees to convey all fixtures and chattels included in the Purchase Price free from all liens, encumbrances or claims affecting the said fixtures and chattels.

5. **FIXTURES EXCLUDED:**...

....

....

....

....

6. **RENTAL ITEMS (Including Lease, Lease to Own):** The following equipment is rented and **not** included in the Purchase Price. The Buyer agrees to assume the rental contract(s), if assumable:

....

....

....

The Buyer agrees to co-operate and execute such documentation as may be required to facilitate such assumption.

7. **HST:** If the sale of the Property (Real Property as described above) is subject to Harmonized Sales Tax (HST), then such tax shall be

.... the Purchase Price. If the sale of the Property is not subject to HST, Seller agrees to certify on or before
        (included in/in addition to)
closing, that the sale of the Property is not subject to HST. Any HST on chattels, if applicable, is not included in the Purchase Price.

INITIALS OF BUYER(S): ( )   INITIALS OF SELLER(S): ( )

8. **TITLE SEARCH:** Buyer shall be allowed until 6:00 p.m. on the .... day of ...., 20..........., (Requisition Date) to examine the title to the Property at Buyer's own expense and until the earlier of: (i) thirty days from the later of the Requisition Date or the date on which the conditions in this Agreement are fulfilled or otherwise waived or; (ii) five days prior to completion, to satisfy Buyer that there are no outstanding

   work orders or deficiency notices affecting the Property, and that its present use (..) may be lawfully continued and that the principal building may be insured against risk of fire. Seller hereby consents to the municipality or other governmental agencies releasing to Buyer details of all outstanding work orders and deficiency notices affecting the property, and Seller agrees to execute and deliver such further authorizations in this regard as Buyer may reasonably require.

9. **FUTURE USE:** Seller and Buyer agree that there is no representation or warranty of any kind that the future intended use of the property by Buyer is or will be lawful except as may be specifically provided for in this Agreement.

10. **TITLE:** Provided that the title to the property is good and free from all registered restrictions, charges, liens, and encumbrances except as otherwise specifically provided in this Agreement and save and except for (a) any registered restrictions or covenants that run with the land providing that such are complied with; (b) any registered municipal agreements and registered agreements with publicly regulated utilities providing such have been complied with, or security has been posted to ensure compliance and completion, as evidenced by a letter from the relevant municipality or regulated utility; (c) any minor easements for the supply of domestic utility or telephone services to the property or adjacent properties; and (d) any easements for drainage, storm or sanitary sewers, public utility lines, telephone lines, cable television lines or other services which do not materially affect the use of the property. If within the specified times referred to in paragraph 8 any valid objection to title or to any outstanding work order or deficiency notice, or to the fact the said present use may not lawfully be continued, or that the principal building may not be insured against risk of fire is made in writing to Seller and which Seller is unable or unwilling to remove, remedy or satisfy or obtain insurance save and except against risk of fire (Title Insurance) in favour of the Buyer and any mortgagee, (with all related costs at the expense of the Seller), and which Buyer will not waive, this Agreement notwithstanding any intermediate acts or negotiations in respect of such objections, shall be at an end and all monies paid shall be returned without interest or deduction and Seller, Listing Brokerage and Co-operating Brokerage shall not be liable for any costs or damages. Save as to any valid objection so made by such day and except for any objection going to the root of the title, Buyer shall be conclusively deemed to have accepted Seller's title to the property.

11. **CLOSING ARRANGEMENTS:** Where each of the Seller and Buyer retain a lawyer to complete the Agreement of Purchase and Sale of the property, and where the transaction will be completed by electronic registration pursuant to Part III of the Land Registration Reform Act, R.S.O. 1990, Chapter L4 and the Electronic Registration Act, S.O. 1991, Chapter 44, and any amendments thereto, the Seller and Buyer acknowledge and agree that the exchange of closing funds, non-registrable documents and other items (the "Requisite Deliveries") and the release thereof to the Seller and Buyer will (a) not occur at the same time as the registration of the transfer/deed (and any other documents intended to be registered in connection with the completion of this transaction) and (b) be subject to conditions whereby the lawyer(s) receiving any of the Requisite Deliveries will be required to hold same in trust and not release same except in accordance with the terms of a document registration agreement between the said lawyers. The Seller and Buyer irrevocably instruct the said lawyers to be bound by the document registration agreement which is recommended from time to time by the Law Society of Upper Canada. Unless otherwise agreed to by the lawyers, such exchange of the Requisite Deliveries will occur in the applicable Land Titles Office or such other location agreeable to both lawyers.

12. **DOCUMENTS AND DISCHARGE:** Buyer shall not call for the production of any title deed, abstract, survey or other evidence of title to the property except such as are in the possession or control of Seller. If requested by Buyer, Seller will deliver any sketch or survey of the property within Seller's control to Buyer as soon as possible and prior to the Requisition Date. If a discharge of any Charge/Mortgage held by a corporation incorporated pursuant to the Trust And Loan Companies Act (Canada), Chartered Bank, Trust Company, Credit Union, Caisse Populaire or Insurance Company and which is not to be assumed by Buyer on completion, is not available in registrable form on completion, Buyer agrees to accept Seller's lawyer's personal undertaking to obtain, out of the closing funds, a discharge in registrable form and to register same, or cause same to be registered, on title within a reasonable period of time after completion, provided that on or before completion Seller shall provide to Buyer a mortgage statement prepared by the mortgagee setting out the balance required to obtain the discharge, and, where a real-time electronic cleared funds transfer system is not being used, a direction executed by Seller directing payment to the mortgagee of the amount required to obtain the discharge out of the balance due on completion.

13. **INSPECTION:** Buyer acknowledges having had the opportunity to inspect the Property and understands that upon acceptance of this offer there shall be a binding agreement of purchase and sale between Buyer and Seller. **The Buyer acknowledges having the opportunity to include a requirement for a property inspection report in this Agreement and agrees that except as may be specifically provided for in this Agreement, the Buyer will not be obtaining a property inspection or property inspection report regarding the Property.**

14. **INSURANCE:** All buildings on the property and all other things being purchased shall be and remain until completion at the risk of Seller. Pending completion, Seller shall hold all insurance policies, if any, and the proceeds thereof in trust for the parties as their interests may appear and in the event of substantial damage, Buyer may either terminate this Agreement and have all monies paid returned without interest or deduction or else take the proceeds of any insurance and complete the purchase. No insurance shall be transferred on completion. If Seller is taking back a Charge/Mortgage, or Buyer is assuming a Charge/Mortgage, Buyer shall supply Seller with reasonable evidence of adequate insurance to protect Seller's or other mortgagee's interest on completion.

INITIALS OF BUYER(S): (   )   INITIALS OF SELLER(S): (   )

15. PLANNING ACT: This Agreement shall be effective to create an interest in the property only if Seller complies with the subdivision control provisions of the Planning Act by completion and Seller covenants to proceed diligently at Seller's expense to obtain any necessary consent by completion.

16. DOCUMENT PREPARATION: The Transfer/Deed shall, save for the Land Transfer Tax Affidavit, be prepared in registrable form at the expense of Seller, and any Charge/Mortgage to be given back by the Buyer to Seller at the expense of the Buyer. If requested by Buyer, Seller covenants that the Transfer/Deed to be delivered on completion shall contain the statements contemplated by Section 50(22) of the Planning Act, R.S.O.1990.

17. RESIDENCY: (a) Subject to (b) below, the Seller represents and warrants that the Seller is not and on completion will not be a non-resident under the non-residency provisions of the Income Tax Act which representation and warranty shall survive and not merge upon the completion of this transaction and the Seller shall deliver to the Buyer a statutory declaration that Seller is not then a non-resident of Canada; (b) provided that if the Seller is a non-resident under the non-residency provisions of the Income Tax Act, the Buyer shall be credited towards the Purchase Price with the amount, if any, necessary for Buyer to pay to the Minister of National Revenue to satisfy Buyer's liability in respect of tax payable by Seller under the non-residency provisions of the Income Tax Act by reason of this sale. Buyer shall not claim such credit if Seller delivers on completion the prescribed certificate.

18. ADJUSTMENTS: Any rents, mortgage interest, realty taxes including local improvement rates and unmetered public or private utility charges and unmetered cost of fuel, as applicable, shall be apportioned and allowed to the day of completion, the day of completion itself to be apportioned to Buyer.

19. PROPERTY ASSESSMENT: The Buyer and Seller hereby acknowledge that the Province of Ontario has implemented current value assessment and properties may be re-assessed on an annual basis. The Buyer and Seller agree that no claim will be made against the Buyer or Seller, or any Brokerage, Broker or Salesperson, for any changes in property tax as a result of a re-assessment of the property, save and except any property taxes that accrued prior to the completion of this transaction.

20. TIME LIMITS: Time shall in all respects be of the essence hereof provided that the time for doing or completing of any matter provided for herein may be extended or abridged by an agreement in writing signed by Seller and Buyer or by their respective lawyers who may be specifically authorized in that regard.

21. TENDER: Any tender of documents or money hereunder may be made upon Seller or Buyer or their respective lawyers on the day set for completion. Money shall be tendered with funds drawn on a lawyer's trust account in the form of a bank draft, certified cheque or wire transfer using the Large Value Transfer System.

22. FAMILY LAW ACT: Seller warrants that spousal consent is not necessary to this transaction under the provisions of the Family Law Act, R.S.O.1990 unless Seller's spouse has executed the consent hereinafter provided.

23. UFFI: Seller represents and warrants to Buyer that during the time Seller has owned the property, Seller has not caused any building on the property to be insulated with insulation containing ureaformaldehyde, and that to the best of Seller's knowledge no building on the property contains or has ever contained insulation that contains ureaformaldehyde. This warranty shall survive and not merge on the completion of this transaction, and if the building is part of a multiple unit building, this warranty shall only apply to that part of the building which is the subject of this transaction.

24. LEGAL, ACCOUNTING AND ENVIRONMENTAL ADVICE: The parties acknowledge that any information provided by the brokerage is not legal, tax or environmental advice.

25. CONSUMER REPORTS: The Buyer is hereby notified that a consumer report containing credit and/or personal information may be referred to in connection with this transaction.

26. AGREEMENT IN WRITING: If there is conflict or discrepancy between any provision added to this Agreement (including any Schedule attached hereto) and any provision in the standard pre-set portion hereof, the added provision shall supersede the standard pre-set provision to the extent of such conflict or discrepancy. This Agreement including any Schedule attached hereto, shall constitute the entire Agreement between Buyer and Seller. There is no representation, warranty, collateral agreement or condition, which affects this Agreement other than as expressed herein. For the purposes of this Agreement, Seller means vendor and Buyer means purchaser. This Agreement shall be read with all changes of gender or number required by the context.

27. TIME AND DATE: Any reference to a time and date in this Agreement shall mean the time and date where the property is located.

INITIALS OF BUYER(S): ◯   INITIALS OF SELLER(S): ◯

28. SUCCESSORS AND ASSIGNS: The heirs, executors, administrators, successors and assigns of the undersigned are bound by the terms herein.

SIGNED, SEALED AND DELIVERED in the presence of: IN WITNESS whereof I have hereunto set my hand and seal:

....   ⬤   DATE ....
(Witness)   (Buyer)   (Seal)

....   ⬤   DATE ....
(Witness)   (Buyer)   (Seal)

I, the Undersigned Seller, agree to the above offer. I hereby irrevocably instruct my lawyer to pay directly to the brokerage(s) with whom I have agreed to pay commission, the unpaid balance of the commission together with applicable Harmonized Sales Tax (and any other taxes as may hereafter be applicable), from the proceeds of the sale prior to any payment to the undersigned on completion, as advised by the brokerage(s) to my lawyer.

SIGNED, SEALED AND DELIVERED in the presence of: IN WITNESS whereof I have hereunto set my hand and seal:

....   ⬤   DATE ....
(Witness)   (Seller)   (Seal)

....   ⬤   DATE ....
(Witness)   (Seller)   (Seal)

SPOUSAL CONSENT: The Undersigned Spouse of the Seller hereby consents to the disposition evidenced herein pursuant to the provisions of the Family Law Act, R.S.O.1990, and hereby agrees with the Buyer that he/she will execute all necessary or incidental documents to give full force and effect to the sale evidenced herein.

....   ⬤   DATE ....
(Witness)   (Spouse)   (Seal)

CONFIRMATION OF ACCEPTANCE: Notwithstanding anything contained herein to the contrary, I confirm this Agreement with all changes both typed and written was finally accepted by all parties at .... a.m./p.m. this .... day of..., 20...........

....
(Signature of Seller or Buyer)

INFORMATION ON BROKERAGE(S)

Listing Brokerage .... Tel.No.(................)................................

....
(Salesperson / Broker Name)

Co-op/Buyer Brokerage .... Tel.No.(................)................................

....
(Salesperson / Broker Name)

ACKNOWLEDGEMENT

I acknowledge receipt of my signed copy of this accepted Agreement of Purchase and Sale and I authorize the Brokerage to forward a copy to my lawyer.	I acknowledge receipt of my signed copy of this accepted Agreement of Purchase and Sale and I authorize the Brokerage to forward a copy to my lawyer.
.... DATE .... (Seller)	.... DATE .... (Buyer)
.... DATE .... (Seller)	.... DATE .... (Buyer)
Address for Service	Address for Service ....
.... Tel.No.(...........).....................	.... Tel.No.(...........).....................
Seller's Lawyer	Buyer's Lawyer ....
Address	Address ....
Email	Email ....
(...........)................ (...........)................ Tel.No. FAX No.	(...........)................ (...........)................ Tel.No. FAX No.

FOR OFFICE USE ONLY	**COMMISSION TRUST AGREEMENT**

To: Co-operating Brokerage shown on the foregoing Agreement of Purchase and Sale:
In consideration for the Co-operating Brokerage procuring the foregoing Agreement of Purchase and Sale, I hereby declare that all moneys received or receivable by me in connection with the Transaction as contemplated in the MLS® Rules and Regulations of my Real Estate Board shall be receivable and held in trust. This agreement shall constitute a Commission Trust Agreement as defined in the MLS® Rules and shall be subject to and governed by the MLS® Rules pertaining to Commission Trust.
DATED as of the date and time of the acceptance of the foregoing Agreement of Purchase and Sale.   Acknowledged by:

....
(Authorized to bind the Listing Brokerage)   (Authorized to bind the Co-operating Brokerage)

    Form 100   Revised 2015   **Page 5 of 6**

Form 100   *(continued)*

 **Ontario Real Estate Association**

Form 100
for use in the Province of Ontario

Schedule A
Agreement of Purchase and Sale

This Schedule is attached to and forms part of the Agreement of Purchase and Sale between:

BUYER, ..., and

SELLER, ...

for the purchase and sale of ....

.... dated the .... day of ...., 20.............

Buyer agrees to pay the balance as follows:

This form must be initialed by all parties to the Agreement of Purchase and Sale.

INITIALS OF BUYER(S):   INITIALS OF SELLER(S):

APPENDIX

OREA Ontario Real Estate Association

Form 105
for use in the Province of Ontario

Schedule _____
Agreement of Purchase and Sale

This Schedule is attached to and forms part of the Agreement of Purchase and Sale between:

BUYER, ..., and

SELLER, ...

for the property known as ....

.... dated the .... day of ...., 20..........

This form must be initialed by all parties to the Agreement of Purchase and Sale.

INITIALS OF BUYER(S):   INITIALS OF SELLER(S):

Form 105   Revised 2008   **Page 1 of 1**

Counter Offer

Form 107
for use in the Province of Ontario

Attached to and forming part of Offer to Purchase between between ....
                                                                (Buyer)

and ...., for the property known as: ....
                  (Seller)

.... dated the .... day of ...., 20............
       (Description of Property)

The Seller accepts the attached offer and all its terms and conditions subject to the following amendments, exceptions and/or additions:

This Counter Offer shall be irrevocable by the Seller until the .... day of ...., 20............
after which time, if not accepted by the Buyer and a copy delivered to the Seller or the Seller's agent, this counter offer shall be null and void and all deposit monies shall be returned to the Buyer, without interest. If this Counter Offer is accepted by the Buyer, the Seller agrees, in consideration for the brokerage's services in procuring said Offer, to pay the brokerage(s) on the date of completion the commission set out in the agreement to pay commission together with applicable HST (and any other taxes as may hereafter be applicable), which commission and taxes may be deducted from the deposit. The Seller hereby irrevocably instructs the Seller's solicitor to pay directly to the brokerage(s) with whom I have agreed to pay commission, the unpaid balance of the commission and such taxes from the proceeds of the sale prior to any payment to the undersigned on completion, as advised by the brokerage(s) to the solicitor.

SIGNED, SEALED AND DELIVERED in the presence of: IN WITNESS whereof I have hereunto set my hand and seal:

....   ●   DATE ....
(Witness)   (Seller)   (Seal)

....   ●   DATE ....
(Witness)   (Seller)   (Seal)

SPOUSAL CONSENT: The Undersigned Spouse of the Seller hereby consents to the disposition evidenced herein pursuant to the provisions of the Family Law Act, R.S.O.1990, and hereby agrees with the Buyer that he/she will execute all necessary or incidental documents to give full force and effect to the sale evidenced herein.

....   ●   DATE ....
(Witness)   (Spouse)   (Seal)

APPROVED FAX No. ....   APPROVED FAX No. ....
               (For delivery of notices to Seller)   (For delivery of notices to Buyer)

The above Counter Offer of the Seller to my Offer dated..is hereby accepted

SIGNED, SEALED AND DELIVERED in the presence of: IN WITNESS whereof I have hereunto set my hand and seal:

....   ●   DATE ....
(Witness)   (Buyer)   (Seal)

....   ●   DATE ....
(Witness)   (Buyer)   (Seal)

SELLER SIGNING THIS FORM SHOULD NOT SIGN THE ORIGINAL OFFER.

APPENDIX

 Ontario Real Estate Association

Amendment to Agreement of Purchase and Sale

Form 120
for use in the Province of Ontario

BETWEEN BUYER, ...

AND SELLER, ...

RE: Agreement of Purchase and Sale between the Seller and Buyer, dated the .... day of ...., 20...........,

concerning the property known as..

.... as more particularly described in the aforementioned Agreement.

The Buyer(s) and Seller(s) herein agree to the following Amendments to the aforementioned Agreement:

Delete:

Insert:

INITIALS OF BUYER(S):   INITIALS OF SELLER(S):

Form 120   Revised 2014   **Page 1 of 2**

IRREVOCABILITY: This Offer to Amend the Agreement shall be irrevocable by .... until .... a.m./p.m.

(Seller/Buyer)

on the .... day of ...., 20......., after which time, if not accepted, this Offer to Amend the Agreement shall be null and void.

For the purposes of this Amendment to Agreement, "Buyer" includes purchaser and "Seller" includes vendor.
Time shall in all respects be of the essence hereof provided that the time for doing or completing of any matter provided for herein may be extended or abridged by an agreement in writing signed by Seller and Buyer or by their respective solicitors who are hereby expressly appointed in this regard.

All other Terms and Conditions in the aforementioned Agreement to remain the same.

SIGNED, SEALED AND DELIVERED in the presence of: IN WITNESS whereof I have hereunto set my hand and seal:

.... ● DATE ....
(Witness)   (Buyer/Seller)   (Seal)

.... ● DATE ....
(Witness)   (Buyer/Seller)   (Seal)

I, the Undersigned, agree to the above Offer to Amend the Agreement.

SIGNED, SEALED AND DELIVERED in the presence of: IN WITNESS whereof I have hereunto set my hand and seal:

.... ● DATE ....
(Witness)   (Buyer/Seller)   (Seal)

.... ● DATE ....
(Witness)   (Buyer/Seller)   (Seal)

The Undersigned Spouse of the Seller hereby consents to the Amendments hereinbefore set out.

.... ● DATE ....
(Witness)   (Spouse)   (Seal)

CONFIRMATION OF ACCEPTANCE: Notwithstanding anything contained herein to the contrary, I confirm this Agreement with all changes both typed and written was finally accepted by all parties at .... a.m./p.m. this .... day of ...., 20..........

....
(Signature of Seller or Buyer)

ACKNOWLEDGEMENT

I acknowledge receipt of my signed copy of this accepted Amendment to Agreement and I authorize the Brokerage to forward a copy to my lawyer.	I acknowledge receipt of my signed copy of this accepted Amendment to Agreement and I authorize the Brokerage to forward a copy to my lawyer.
.... DATE	.... DATE ....
(Seller)	(Buyer)
.... DATE	.... DATE ....
(Seller)	(Buyer)
Address for Service	Address for Service ....
.... Tel.No.(..........)	.... Tel.No.(..........) ....
Seller's Lawyer	Buyer's Lawyer ....
Address	Address ....
Email	Email ....
(..........)........................... (..........)	(..........)........................... (..........) ....
Tel.No. FAX No.	Tel.No. FAX No.

Form 120 Revised 2014 **Page 2 of 2**

Form 121   *Notice to Remove Condition(s)*   Page 1 of 1

OREA Ontario Real Estate Association   **Notice to Remove Condition(s)**

Form 121
for use in the Province of Ontario

BETWEEN:

BUYER:..., agrees to purchase from

AND

SELLER:..., the following

RE: Agreement of Purchase and Sale between the Buyer and Seller dated the .... day of..,

20.................., concerning the property known as:..

....

as more particularly described in the aforementioned Agreement of Purchase and Sale.

In accordance with the terms and conditions of the above Agreement of Purchase and Sale, I/we hereby advise that I/we have received another offer to purchase the above mentioned property which is acceptable to me/us. This is to advise you that you now have:

until .... a.m./p.m. on the .... day of .... 20........., to remove the conditions(s) pertaining to:

....

....

....

....

....

contained therein, or the above mentioned Agreement of Purchase and Sale shall become null and void and I/we shall be at liberty to accept a new offer in which case the Agent is hereby directed to return the deposit to the Buyer in full and without interest. The parties agree to execute a mutual release form if this aforementioned Agreement of Purchase and Sale becomes null and void.

For the purposes of this Notice to Remove Condition, "Buyer" includes purchaser, tenant, and lessee, and "Seller" includes vendor, landlord, and lessor, and "Agreement of Purchase and Sale" includes an Agreement to Lease.

SIGNED, SEALED AND DELIVERED in the presence of: IN WITNESS whereof I have hereunto set my hand and seal:

.... (Seal) DATE........................
(Witness)   (Seller)

.... (Seal) DATE........................
(Witness)   (Seller)

I/we hereby acknowledge having today received a copy of the above notice.

SIGNED, SEALED AND DELIVERED in the presence of: IN WITNESS whereof I have hereunto set my hand and seal:

.... (Seal) DATE........................
(Witness)   (Buyer)

.... (Seal) DATE........................
(Witness)   (Buyer)

Form 121   Revised 2016   **Page 1 of 1**

OREA Ontario Real Estate Association   **Mutual Release**

Form 122
for use in the Province of Ontario

BETWEEN:

BUYER: ...., agrees to purchase from

AND

SELLER: ...., the following

BROKERAGE(S): ....

(Listing Brokerage)   (Co-operating Brokerage)

RE: Agreement of Purchase and Sale between the Seller and Buyer dated the .... day of ....,

20........., concerning the property known as: ....

....

as more particularly described in the aforementioned Agreement of Purchase and Sale.

We, the Buyers and the Sellers in the above noted transaction hereby acknowledge that the above described transaction is terminated and release each other and the Brokerage in the proposed transaction, from all liabilities, covenants, obligations, claims and sums of money arising out of the above Agreement of Purchase and Sale, together with any rights and causes of action that each party may have had against the other and/or the Brokerage, and we direct the deposit holder to disburse the deposit of:

.... Canadian Dollars ($Can.......................................)

payable to: ....

....

IRREVOCABILITY: This Mutual Release shall be irrevocable by .... until............a.m./p.m. on the ....

Buyer/Seller

day of ...., 20........., after which time if not fully executed by Buyer and Seller, this Mutual Release shall become null and void. For the purposes of this Mutual Release, "Buyer" includes purchaser, tenant, and lessee, "Seller" includes vendor, landlord, and lessor, Brokerage includes Listing Brokerage, Co-operating Brokerage (if applicable) and the registrants and employees of the Brokerage(s), and "Agreement of Purchase and Sale" includes an Agreement to Lease.

This release shall be binding upon the heirs, executors, administrators and assigns of all the parties executing same.

SIGNED, SEALED AND DELIVERED in the presence of: IN WITNESS whereof I have hereunto set my hand and seal:

....   ● DATE ....
(Witness)   (Buyer/Seller)   (Seal)

....   ● DATE ....
(Witness)   (Buyer/Seller)   (Seal)

I, the Undersigned, agree to the above offer to Mutual Release.

SIGNED, SEALED AND DELIVERED in the presence of: IN WITNESS whereof I have hereunto set my hand and seal:

....   ● DATE ....
(Witness)   (Buyer/Seller)   (Seal)

....   ● DATE ....
(Witness)   (Buyer/Seller)   (Seal)

CONFIRMATION OF ACCEPTANCE: Notwithstanding anything contained herein to the contrary, I confirm this Mutual Release with all changes both typed and written was finally accepted by all parties at .... a.m./p.m. this .... day of ...., 20...........

....
(Signature of Seller or Buyer)

The Brokerage hereby releases all parties from any claim that the Brokerage may have had for commission or other remuneration in the above transaction, except as may be hereinbefore specifically provided

SIGNED, SEALED AND DELIVERED in the presence of: IN WITNESS whereof I have hereunto set my hand and seal:

....   ● DATE ....
(Witness)   (Listing Brokerage's Broker of Record/Manager)   (Seal)

....   ● DATE ....
(Witness)   (Co-operating Brokerage's Broker of Record/Manager)   (Seal)

Form 122   Revised 2015   **Page 1 of 1**

OREA Ontario Real Estate Association **Waiver**

Form 123
for use in the Province of Ontario

BUYER: ....

SELLER: ....

REAL PROPERTY: ....

....

In accordance with the terms and conditions of the Agreement of Purchase and Sale dated the .... day of...,

20..............., regarding the above property, I/We hereby waive the condition(s) which read(s) as follows:

All other terms and conditions in the aforementioned Agreement of Purchase and Sale to remain unchanged.

For the purposes of this Waiver, "Buyer" includes purchaser, tenant, and lessee, and "Seller" includes vendor, landlord, and lessor, and "Agreement of Purchase and Sale" includes an Agreement to Lease.

WAIVED at..., Ontario, at .... a.m./p.m., this .... day of .... 20........

SIGNED, SEALED AND DELIVERED in the presence of: IN WITNESS whereof I have hereunto set my hand and seal:

.... ● DATE ....
(Witness)   (Buyer/Seller)   (Seal)

.... ● DATE ....
(Witness)   (Buyer/Seller)   (Seal)

Receipt acknowledged at .... a.m./p.m., this .... day of .... 20.................... by:

Print Name: ....   Signature:..

OREA Ontario Real Estate Association   **Notice of Fulfillment of Condition(s)**

Form 124
for use in the Province of Ontario

BUYER:...

SELLER:..

REAL PROPERTY:..

....

In accordance with the terms and conditions of the Agreement of Purchase and Sale dated the .... day of..,

20..............., regarding the above property, I/We hereby confirm that I/We have fulfilled the condition(s) which read(s) as follows:

All other terms and conditions in the aforementioned Agreement of Purchase and Sale to remain unchanged.

For the purposes of this Notice of Fulfillment of Condition, "Buyer" includes purchaser, tenant, and lessee, and "Seller" includes vendor, landlord, and lessor, and "Agreement of Purchase and Sale" includes an Agreement to Lease.

DATED at..., Ontario, at ....a.m./p.m., this.......................day of.................................... 20.......... .

SIGNED, SEALED AND DELIVERED in the presence of: IN WITNESS whereof I have hereunto set my hand and seal:

.... ● DATE.............................
(Witness)   (Buyer/Seller)   (Seal)

.... ● DATE.............................
(Witness)   (Buyer/Seller)   (Seal)

Receipt acknowledged at.......................a.m./p.m., this.. day of.. 20..................... by:

Print Name:...   Signature:...

     Form 124   Revised 2016   **Page 1 of 1**

OREA Ontario Real Estate Association

Form 125
for use in the Province of Ontario

Termination of Agreement by Buyer

BETWEEN:

BUYER: ....

AND

SELLER: ....

RE: Agreement of Purchase and Sale between the Seller and Buyer dated the .... day of..,

20..............., concerning the property known as:..

....

as more particularly described in the aforementioned Agreement of Purchase and Sale.

In accordance with the terms and conditions of the above Agreement of Purchase and Sale, I/we hereby advise that it has not been possible to fulfill the condition(s) pertaining to:

....

....

....

....

contained therein, and I/we hereby terminate the said Agreement.

The Buyer also agrees to execute the Mutual Release form attached hereto.

For the purposes of this Termination of Agreement by Buyer, "Buyer" includes purchaser, tenant, and lessee, and "Seller" includes vendor, landlord, and lessor, and "Agreement of Purchase and Sale" includes an Agreement to Lease.

SIGNED, SEALED AND DELIVERED in the presence of: IN WITNESS whereof I have hereunto set my hand and seal:

.... ● DATE ....

(Witness)   (Buyer)   (Seal)

.... ● DATE ....

(Witness)   (Buyer)   (Seal)

The Seller hereby acknowledges having today received a copy of the above Termination of Agreement.

The Seller also agrees to execute the Mutual Release form attached hereto.

SIGNED, SEALED AND DELIVERED in the presence of: IN WITNESS whereof I have hereunto set my hand and seal:

.... ● DATE ....

(Witness)   (Seller)   (Seal)

.... ● DATE ....

(Witness)   (Seller)   (Seal)

Form 125   Revised 2008   **Page 1 of 1**

OREA Ontario Real Estate Association

Form 126
for use in the Province of Ontario

Termination of Agreement by Seller

BETWEEN:

BUYER: ....

AND

SELLER: ....

RE: Agreement of Purchase and Sale between the Seller and Buyer dated the .... day of ....,

20.............., concerning the property known as: ....

....

as more particularly described in the aforementioned Agreement of Purchase and Sale.

In accordance with the terms and conditions of the above Agreement of Purchase and Sale, I/we hereby advise that it has not been possible to fulfill the condition(s) pertaining to:

....

....

....

....

....

contained therein, and I/we hereby terminate the said Agreement.

The Seller also agrees to execute the Mutual Release form attached hereto.

For the purposes of this Termination of Agreement by Seller, "Buyer" includes purchaser, tenant, and lessee, and "Seller" includes vendor, landlord, and lessor, and "Agreement of Purchase and Sale" includes an Agreement to Lease.

SIGNED, SEALED AND DELIVERED in the presence of: IN WITNESS whereof I have hereunto set my hand and seal:

....   ● DATE ....
(Witness)   (Seller)   (Seal)

....   ● DATE ....
(Witness)   (Seller)   (Seal)

The Buyer hereby acknowledges having today received a copy of the above Termination of Agreement.

The Buyer also agrees to execute the Mutual Release form attached hereto.

SIGNED, SEALED AND DELIVERED in the presence of: IN WITNESS whereof I have hereunto set my hand and seal:

....   ● DATE ....
(Witness)   (Buyer)   (Seal)

....   ● DATE ....
(Witness)   (Buyer)   (Seal)

Form 126   Revised 2008   **Page 1 of 1**

APPENDIX

 **Ontario Real Estate Association**

Offer Summary Document
For use with Agreement of Purchase and Sale

Form 801
for use in the Province of Ontario

For Brokerage submitting the offer on behalf of the Buyer:

When sent to the Listing Brokerage this form can be used as evidence that you have a written signed offer from a Buyer to the Seller.

REAL PROPERTY ADDRESS: .... (the "property")
(municipal address and/or legal description)

for an Agreement of Purchase and Sale dated: the .... day of .... , 20............... ("offer")

This offer was submitted by: **BROKERAGE:** ....

SALES REPRESENTATIVE/BROKER: ....

I/We, ..., have signed an offer for the property.
Name of Buyer(s)

....
Buyer signature   Dated   Buyer signature   Dated

This offer was submitted, ... to the Listing Brokerage at .... a.m./p.m. on the .... day of
(by fax, by email or in person)

...., 20............   Irrevocable until .... a.m./p.m. on the .... day of ...., 20............

(For Buyer counter offer - complete the following)

I/We, ..., have signed an offer for the property.
Name of Buyer(s)

....
Buyer signature   Date   Buyer signature   Date

An offer was submitted, ... to the Listing Brokerage at .... a.m./p.m. on the .... day of
(by fax, by email or in person)

...., 20............   Irrevocable until .... a.m./p.m. on the .... day of ...., 20............

For Listing Brokerage receiving the offer:

SELLER(S): ....

SELLER(S) CONTACT: ....
(ie. phone / email / fax)

LISTING BROKERAGE: ....

SALES REPRESENTATIVE/BROKER: ....

This offer was received, ... by the Listing Brokerage at .... a.m./p.m. on the .... day of ...., 20......
(by fax, by email or in person)

This offer was presented, ... to the Seller(s) at .... a.m./p.m. on the .... day of ...., 20......
(by fax, by email or in person)

Offer was: ☐ Accepted   ☐ Signed Back/Countered   ☐ Expired/Declined

Comments: ....

Form 200   *Listing Agreement—Authority to Offer for Sale*   Page 1 of 3

 **Ontario Real Estate Association**

Listing Agreement
Authority to Offer for Sale

Form 200
for use in the Province of Ontario

This is a Multiple Listing Service® Agreement ( ) **OR**   **Exclusive Listing Agreement**   **EXCLUSIVE** ( )

(Seller's Initials)   (Seller's Initials)

BETWEEN:

BROKERAGE: ....

....(the "Listing Brokerage") Tel.No. (.............)...................................

SELLER(S): ....(the "Seller")

In consideration of the Listing Brokerage listing the real property **for sale** known as...

....(the "Property")

the Seller hereby gives the Listing Brokerage the **exclusive and irrevocable** right to act as the Seller's agent, **commencing** at 12:01 a.m. on the .... day

of ...., 20..........., **until** 11:59 p.m. on the .... day of ...., 20.......... (the "Listing Period"),

{ Seller acknowledges that the length of the Listing Period is negotiable between the Seller and the Listing Brokerage and, if an MLS® listing, may be subject to minimum requirements of the real estate board, however, in accordance with the Real Estate and Business Brokers Act (2002), **if the Listing Period exceeds six months, the Listing Brokerage must obtain the Seller's initials.** } ( )

(Seller's Initials)

to offer the property **for sale** at a price of: Dollars (CDN$) ....

....Dollars

and upon the terms particularly set out herein, or at such other price and/or terms acceptable to the Seller. It is understood that the price and/or terms set out herein are at the Seller's personal request, after full discussion with the Listing Brokerage's representative regarding potential market value of the Property.

The Seller hereby represents and warrants that the Seller is not a party to any other listing agreement for the Property or agreement to pay commission to any other real estate brokerage for the sale of the property.

1. **DEFINITIONS AND INTERPRETATIONS:** For the purposes of this Listing Agreement ("Authority" or "Agreement"), "Seller" includes vendor, a "buyer" includes a purchaser, or a prospective purchaser and a "real estate board" includes a real estate association. A purchase shall be deemed to include the entering into of any agreement to exchange, or the obtaining of an option to purchase which is subsequently exercised. This Agreement shall be read with all changes of gender or number required by the context. For purposes of this Agreement, anyone introduced to or shown the Property shall be deemed to include any spouse, heirs, executors, administrators, successors, assigns, related corporations and affiliated corporations. Related corporations or affiliated corporations shall include any corporation where one half or a majority of the shareholders, directors or officers of the related or affiliated corporation are the same person(s) as the shareholders, directors, or officers of the corporation introduced to or shown the Property.

2. **COMMISSION:** In consideration of the Listing Brokerage listing the Property, the Seller agrees to pay the Listing Brokerage a commission of

..............% of the sale price of the Property or .... for any valid offer to purchase the Property from any source whatsoever obtained during the Listing Period and on the terms and conditions set out in this Agreement **OR** such other terms and conditions as the Seller may accept.

The Seller further agrees to pay such commission as calculated above if an agreement to purchase is agreed to or accepted by the Seller or anyone

on the Seller's behalf within .... days after the expiration of the Listing Period **(Holdover Period)**, so long as such agreement is with anyone who was introduced to the Property from any source whatsoever during the Listing Period or shown the Property during the Listing Period.

If, however, the offer for the purchase of the Property is pursuant to a new agreement in writing to pay commission to another registered real estate brokerage, the Seller's liability for commission shall be reduced by the amount paid by the Seller under the new agreement.

The Seller further agrees to pay such commission as calculated above even if the transaction contemplated by an agreement to purchase agreed to or accepted by the Seller or anyone on the Seller's behalf is not completed, if such non-completion is owing or attributable to the Seller's default or neglect, said commission to be payable on the date set for completion of the purchase of the Property.

Any deposit in respect of any agreement where the transaction has been completed shall first be applied to reduce the commission payable. Should such amounts paid to the Listing Brokerage from the deposit or by the Seller's solicitor not be sufficient, the Seller shall be liable to pay to the Listing Brokerage on demand, any deficiency in commission and taxes owing on such commission.

All amounts set out as commission are to be paid plus applicable taxes on such commission.

3. **REPRESENTATION:** The Seller acknowledges that the Listing Brokerage has provided the Seller with information explaining agency relationships, including information on Seller Representation, Sub-agency, Buyer Representation, Multiple Representation and Customer Service. The Seller authorizes the Listing Brokerage to co-operate with any other registered real estate brokerage (co-operating brokerage), and to offer to pay the co-operating

brokerage a commission of................% of the sale price of the Property or..

.... out of the commission the Seller pays the Listing Brokerage.

INITIALS OF LISTING BROKERAGE: ( )   **INITIALS OF SELLER(S):** ( )

Form 200   Revised 2015   **Page 1 of 3**

APPENDIX

The Seller understands that unless the Seller is otherwise informed, the co-operating brokerage is representing the interests of the buyer in the transaction. The Seller further acknowledges that the Listing Brokerage may be listing other properties that may be similar to the Seller's Property and the Seller hereby consents to the Listing Brokerage listing other properties that may be similar to the Seller's Property without any claim by the Seller of conflict of interest. The Seller hereby appoints the Listing Brokerage as the Seller's agent for the purpose of giving and receiving notices pursuant to any offer or agreement to purchase the property. Unless otherwise agreed in writing between Seller and Listing Brokerage, any commission payable to any other brokerage shall be paid out of the commission the Seller pays the Listing Brokerage, said commission to be disbursed in accordance with the Commission Trust Agreement.

MULTIPLE REPRESENTATION: The Seller hereby acknowledges that the Listing Brokerage may be entering into buyer representation agreements with buyers who may be interested in purchasing the Seller's Property. In the event that the Listing Brokerage has entered into or enters into a buyer representation agreement with a prospective buyer for the Seller's Property, the Listing Brokerage will obtain the Seller's written consent to represent both the Seller and the buyer for the transaction at the earliest practicable opportunity and in all cases prior to any offer to purchase being submitted or presented.

The Seller understands and acknowledges that the Listing Brokerage must be impartial when representing both the Seller and the buyer and equally protect the interests of the Seller and buyer. The Seller understands and acknowledges that when representing both the Seller and the buyer, the Listing Brokerage shall have a duty of full disclosure to both the Seller and the buyer, including a requirement to disclose all factual information about the Property known to the Listing Brokerage.

However, the Seller further understands and acknowledges that the Listing Brokerage shall not disclose:
- that the Seller may or will accept less than the listed price, unless otherwise instructed in writing by the Seller;
- that the buyer may or will pay more than the offered price, unless otherwise instructed in writing by the buyer;
- the motivation of or personal information about the Seller or buyer, unless otherwise instructed in writing by the party to which the information applies or unless failure to disclose would constitute fraudulent, unlawful or unethical practice;
- the price the buyer should offer or the price the Seller should accept; and
- the Listing Brokerage shall not disclose to the buyer the terms of any other offer.

However, it is understood that factual market information about comparable properties and information known to the Listing Brokerage concerning potential uses for the Property will be disclosed to both Seller and buyer to assist them to come to their own conclusions.

Where a Brokerage represents both the Seller and the Buyer (multiple representation), the Brokerage shall not be entitled or authorized to be agent for either the Buyer or the Seller for the purpose of giving and receiving notices.

MULTIPLE REPRESENTATION AND CUSTOMER SERVICE: The Seller understands and agrees that the Listing Brokerage also provides representation and customer service to other sellers and buyers. If the Listing Brokerage represents or provides customer service to more than one seller or buyer for the same trade, the Listing Brokerage shall, in writing, at the earliest practicable opportunity and before any offer is made, inform all sellers and buyers of the nature of the Listing Brokerage's relationship to each seller and buyer.

4. **FINDERS FEES:** The Seller acknowledges that the Brokerage may be receiving a finder's fee, reward and/or referral incentive, and the Seller consents to any such benefit being received and retained by the Brokerage in addition to the commission as described above.

5. **REFERRAL OF ENQUIRIES:** The Seller agrees that during the Listing Period, the Seller shall advise the Listing Brokerage immediately of all enquiries from any source whatsoever, and all offers to purchase submitted to the Seller shall be immediately submitted to the Listing Brokerage before the Seller accepts or rejects the same. If any enquiry during the Listing Period results in the Seller accepting a valid offer to purchase during the Listing Period or within the Holdover Period after the expiration of the Listing Period, the Seller agrees to pay the Listing Brokerage the amount of commission set out above, payable within five (5) days following the Listing Brokerage's written demand therefor.

6. **MARKETING:** The Seller agrees to allow the Listing Brokerage to show and permit prospective buyers to fully inspect the Property during reasonable hours and the Seller gives the Listing Brokerage the sole and exclusive right to place "For Sale" and "Sold" sign(s) upon the Property. The Seller consents to the Listing Brokerage including information in advertising that may identify the Property. The Seller further agrees that the Listing Brokerage shall have sole and exclusive authority to make all advertising decisions relating to the marketing of the Property for sale during the Listing Period. The Seller agrees that the Listing Brokerage will not be held liable in any manner whatsoever for any acts or omissions with respect to advertising by the Listing Brokerage or any other party, other than by the Listing Brokerage's gross negligence or wilful act.

7. **WARRANTY:** The Seller represents and warrants that the Seller has the exclusive authority and power to execute this Authority to offer the Property for sale and that the Seller has informed the Listing Brokerage of any third party interests or claims on the Property such as rights of first refusal, options, easements, mortgages, encumbrances or otherwise concerning the Property, which may affect the sale of the Property.

8. **INDEMNIFICATION AND INSURANCE:** The Seller will not hold the Listing Brokerage and representatives of the Brokerage responsible for any loss or damage to the Property or contents occurring during the term of this Agreement caused by the Listing Brokerage or anyone else by any means, including theft, fire or vandalism, other than by the Listing Brokerage's gross negligence or wilful act. The Seller agrees to indemnify and save harmless the Listing Brokerage and representatives of the Brokerage and any co-operating brokerage from any liability, claim, loss, cost, damage or injury, including but not limited to loss of the commission payable under this Agreement, caused or contributed to by the breach of any warranty or representation made by the Seller in this Agreement or the accompanying data form. The Seller warrants the Property is insured, including personal liability insurance against any claims or lawsuits resulting from bodily injury or property damage to others caused in any way on or at the Property and the Seller indemnifies the Brokerage and all of its employees, representatives, salespersons and brokers (Listing Brokerage) and any co-operating brokerage and all of its employees, representatives, salespersons and brokers (co-operating brokerage) for and against any claims against the Listing Brokerage or co-operating brokerage made by anyone who attends or visits the Property.

9. **FAMILY LAW ACT:** The Seller hereby warrants that spousal consent is not necessary under the provisions of the Family Law Act, R.S.O. 1990, unless the Seller's spouse has executed the consent hereinafter provided.

10. **VERIFICATION OF INFORMATION:** The Seller authorizes the Listing Brokerage to obtain any information affecting the Property from any regulatory authorities, governments, mortgagees or others and the Seller agrees to execute and deliver such further authorizations in this regard as may be reasonably required. The Seller hereby appoints the Listing Brokerage or the Listing Brokerage's authorized representative as the Seller's attorney to execute such documentation as may be necessary to effect obtaining any information as aforesaid. The Seller hereby authorizes, instructs and directs the above noted regulatory authorities, governments, mortgagees or others to release any and all information to the Listing Brokerage.

11. **USE AND DISTRIBUTION OF INFORMATION:** The Seller consents to the collection, use and disclosure of personal information by the Brokerage for the purpose of listing and marketing the Property including, but not limited to: listing and advertising the Property using any medium including the Internet; disclosing Property information to prospective buyers, brokerages, salespersons and others who may assist in the sale of the Property; such other use of

INITIALS OF LISTING BROKERAGE: (⬭)   **INITIALS OF SELLER(S):** (⬭)

the Seller's personal information as is consistent with listing and marketing of the Property. The Seller consents, if this is an MLS® Listing, to placement of the listing information and sales information by the Brokerage into the database(s) of the MLS® System of the appropriate Board, and to the posting of any documents and other information (including, without limitation, photographs, images, graphics, audio and video recordings, virtual tours, drawings, floor plans, architectural designs, artistic renderings, surveys and listing descriptions) provided by or on behalf of the Seller into the database(s) of the MLS® System of the appropriate Board. The Seller hereby indemnifies and saves harmless the Brokerage and/or any of its employees, servants, brokers or sales representatives from any and all claims, liabilities, suits, actions, losses, costs and legal fees caused by, or arising out of, or resulting from the posting of any documents or other information (including, without limitation, photographs, images, graphics, audio and video recordings, virtual tours, drawings, floor plans, architectural designs, artistic renderings, surveys and listing descriptions) as aforesaid. The Seller acknowledges that the database, within the board's MLS® System is the property of the real estate board(s) and can be licensed, resold, or otherwise dealt with by the board(s). The Seller further acknowledges that the real estate board(s) may: during the term of the listing and thereafter, distribute the information in the database, within the board's MLS® System to any persons authorized to use such service which may include other brokerages, government departments, appraisers, municipal organizations and others; market the Property, at its option, in any medium, including electronic media; during the term of the listing and thereafter, compile, retain and publish any statistics including historical data within the board's MLS® System and retain, reproduce and display photographs, images, graphics, audio and video recordings, virtual tours, drawings, floor plans, architectural designs, artistic renderings, surveys and listing descriptions which may be used by board members to conduct comparative analyses; and make such other use of the information as the Brokerage and/or real estate board(s) deem appropriate, in connection with the listing, marketing and selling of real estate during the term of the listing and thereafter. The Seller acknowledges that the information, personal or otherwise ("information"), provided to the real estate board or association may be stored on databases located outside of Canada, in which case the information would be subject to the laws of the jurisdiction in which the information is located.

In the event that this Agreement expires or is cancelled or otherwise terminated and the Property is not sold, the Seller, by initialling:	( )	( )
consent to allow other real estate board members to contact the Seller after expiration or other termination of this Agreement to discuss listing or otherwise marketing the Property.	**Does**	**Does Not**

12. SUCCESSORS AND ASSIGNS: The heirs, executors, administrators, successors and assigns of the undersigned are bound by the terms of this Agreement.

13. CONFLICT OR DISCREPANCY: If there is any conflict or discrepancy between any provision added to this Agreement (including any Schedule attached hereto) and any provision in the standard pre-set portion hereof, the added provision shall supersede the standard pre-set provision to the extent of such conflict or discrepancy. This Agreement, including any Schedule attached hereto, shall constitute the entire Agreement between the Seller and the Listing Brokerage. There is no representation, warranty, collateral agreement or condition which affects this Agreement other than as expressed herein.

14. ELECTRONIC COMMUNICATION: This Listing Agreement and any agreements, notices or other communications contemplated thereby may be transmitted by means of electronic systems, in which case signatures shall be deemed to be original. The transmission of this Agreement by the Seller by electronic means shall be deemed to confirm the Seller has retained a true copy of the Agreement.

15. SCHEDULE(S): .... and data form attached hereto form(s) part of this Agreement.

THE LISTING BROKERAGE AGREES TO MARKET THE PROPERTY ON BEHALF OF THE SELLER AND REPRESENT THE SELLER IN AN ENDEAVOUR TO OBTAIN A VALID OFFER TO PURCHASE THE PROPERTY ON THE TERMS SET OUT IN THIS AGREEMENT OR ON SUCH OTHER TERMS SATISFACTORY TO THE SELLER.

....   DATE...................................   ....
(Authorized to bind the Listing Brokerage)   (Name of Person Signing)

THIS AGREEMENT HAS BEEN READ AND FULLY UNDERSTOOD BY ME AND I ACKNOWLEDGE THIS DATE I HAVE SIGNED UNDER SEAL. Any representations contained herein or as shown on the accompanying data form respecting the Property are true to the best of my knowledge, information and belief.

SIGNED, SEALED AND DELIVERED I have hereunto set my hand and seal:

....   ● DATE ....
(Signature of Seller)   (Seal)   (Tel. No.)

....   ● DATE ....
(Signature of Seller)   (Seal)

SPOUSAL CONSENT: The undersigned spouse of the Seller hereby consents to the listing of the Property herein pursuant to the provisions of the Family Law Act, R.S.O. 1990 and hereby agrees that he/she will execute all necessary or incidental documents to further any transaction provided for herein.

....   ● DATE ....
(Spouse)   (Seal)

DECLARATION OF INSURANCE

The broker/salesperson...
(Name of Broker/Salesperson)
hereby declares that he/she is insured as required by the Real Estate and Business Brokers Act (REBBA) and Regulations.

....
(Signature(s) of Broker/Salesperson)

ACKNOWLEDGEMENT

The Seller(s) hereby acknowledge that the Seller(s) fully understand the terms of this Agreement and have received a true copy of this Agreement

on the .... day of ...., 20 ....

....   Date: ....
(Signature of Seller)

....   Date: ....
(Signature of Seller)

 **Ontario Real Estate Association**

Form 201
for use in the Province of Ontario

Seller Customer Service Agreement
Commission Agreement For Property Not Listed

This Is A Non-Exclusive Seller Customer Service Agreement
BETWEEN:
BROKERAGE: ....

....(the "Brokerage") Tel.No. (.............)..............................

SELLER(S): .... (the "Seller")

....

for the property known as: .... (the "Property")

and for the following Buyer: .... (the "Buyer")
The Brokerage agrees to provide customer service to the Seller for the sale or lease of the above described property to the Buyer and the Seller acknowledges and agrees to the terms as stated in this Agreement. **This non-exclusive Seller Customer Service Agreement:**

commences at .... a.m./p.m. on the .... day of ...., 20............,

and expires at 11:59 p.m. on the .... day of ...., 20............ [Expiry Date].

{ Seller acknowledges that the time period for this Agreement is negotiable between the Seller and the Brokerage, however, in accordance with the Real Estate and Business Brokers Act of Ontario; **If the time period for this Agreement exceeds six months, the Brokerage must obtain the Seller's initials.** }   ⬭
(Seller's Initials)

The Seller hereby represents and warrants that the Property is not listed for sale or lease with any other registered real estate brokerage and that the Seller has the sole and exclusive authority to execute this Agreement and to offer the property for sale or lease.

1. **DEFINITIONS AND INTERPRETATIONS:** For the purposes of this Agreement, "Seller" includes Vendor and Landlord and "Buyer" includes a purchaser, a tenant, or a prospective purchaser or tenant. A purchase shall be deemed to include the entering into of any agreement to exchange, or the obtaining of an option to purchase which is subsequently exercised, and a lease includes any rental agreement, sub-lease or renewal of a lease. For purposes of this Agreement, anyone introduced to or shown the Property shall be deemed to include any spouse, heirs, executors, administrators, successors, assigns, related corporations and affiliated corporations. Related corporations or affiliated corporations shall include any corporation where one half or a majority of the shareholders, directors or officers of the related or affiliated corporation are the same person(s) as the shareholders, directors, or officers of the corporation introduced to or shown the Property.
    This Agreement shall be read with all changes of gender or number required by the context.

2. **COMMISSION:** In consideration of the Brokerage showing the Property to the Buyer and/or introducing the Buyer to the Seller for the purpose of

    discussing the sale or lease of the Property, the Seller agrees to pay the Brokerage a commission of .... % of the sale price of the

    Property or ....
    for any valid offer to purchase or lease the Property entered into between the Seller and the Buyer during the term of this Agreement.
    Seller acknowledges that the commission as described above is payable to the Brokerage even if the Seller enters into an agreement to pay commission to another registered real estate brokerage during the currency of this Agreement or any extension thereof.

    The Seller agrees to pay such commission as calculated above if an agreement with the Buyer to purchase or lease the Property is agreed to or

    accepted by the Seller or anyone on the Seller's behalf within .... days after the expiration of this Agreement.
    If, however, the offer from the Buyer for the purchase or lease of the Property is pursuant to a new agreement in writing to pay commission to another registered real estate brokerage, and if the new agreement was entered into after the expiration of this Agreement, the Seller's liability for commission shall be reduced by the amount paid by the Seller under the new agreement.

INITIALS OF BROKERAGE: ⬭   **INITIALS OF SELLER(S):** ⬭

APPENDIX

Form 201   *(continued)*   Page 2 of 3

The Seller agrees to pay such commission as described above even if the transaction contemplated by an agreement to purchase or lease agreed to or accepted by the Seller or anyone on the Seller's behalf is not completed, if such non-completion is owing or attributable to the Seller's default or neglect. The commission as described above shall be payable on the date set for completion of the purchase of the Property or, in the case of a lease or tenancy, the earlier of the date of occupancy by the tenant or the execution of the lease or the date set for commencement of the lease or tenancy. Any deposit in respect of any agreement where the transaction has been completed shall first be applied to reduce the commission payable. Should such amounts paid to the Brokerage from the deposit or by the Seller's solicitor not be sufficient, the Seller shall be liable to pay to the Brokerage on demand, any deficiency in commission and taxes owing on such commission. All amounts set out as commission are to be paid plus applicable taxes on such commission.

3. **REPRESENTATION AND CUSTOMER SERVICE:** The Seller acknowledges that the Brokerage has provided the Seller with written information explaining agency relationships, including information on Seller Representation, Sub-Agency, Buyer Representation, Multiple Representation and Customer Service. The Seller acknowledges that the Brokerage will be providing customer service to the Seller and will not be representing the interests of the Seller in a transaction.
    The Brokerage may be representing the interests of the Buyer for the transaction. When the Brokerage is representing the Buyer, the Buyer is considered to be the Brokerage's client, and the Brokerage's primary duties are to protect and promote the interests of the Buyer/client. The Brokerage will disclose all pertinent information to a Buyer/client obtained from or about the Seller.
    Even though the Brokerage's primary duties may be to the Buyer, the Brokerage may provide many valuable customer services to the Seller.
    When providing customer service to the Seller, the Brokerage's duties to the Seller include:
    - the **Ethical** duty to deal fairly, honestly and with integrity;
    - the **Legal** duty to exercise due care when answering questions and providing information; and
    - the **Legal** duty to avoid misrepresentation.
    The Seller further acknowledges and agrees that the payment of commission by the Seller to the Brokerage will not create or constitute representation by the Brokerage of the Seller as a client.
    The Seller understands and agrees that the Brokerage also provides representation and customer service to other sellers and buyers.
    If the Brokerage represents or provides customer service to more than one seller or buyer for the same trade, the Brokerage shall, in writing, at the earliest practicable opportunity and before any offer is made, inform all sellers and buyers of the nature of the Brokerage's relationship to each seller and buyer.

4. **DEPOSIT:** The Seller and Brokerage agree that the deposit for a transaction shall be held in trust by the Brokerage.
    Any deposit in respect of any agreement where the transaction has been completed shall be first applied to reduce the commission payable. Should such amounts paid to the Brokerage from the deposit or by the Seller's solicitor not be sufficient, the Seller shall be liable to pay the Brokerage on demand, any deficiency in commission and taxes owing on such commission.

5. **FINDERS FEES:** The Seller acknowledges that the Brokerage may be receiving a finder's fee, reward and/or referral incentive, and the Seller consents to any such benefit being received and retained by the Brokerage in addition to the commission as described above.

6. **INSURANCE:** The Seller warrants the Property is insured, including personal liability insurance against any claims or lawsuits resulting from bodily injury or property damage to others caused in any way on or at the Property and the Seller indemnifies the Brokerage and all of its employees, representatives, salespersons and brokers for and against any claims against the Brokerage made by anyone who attends or visits the Property.

7. **VERIFICATION OF INFORMATION:** The Seller authorizes the Brokerage to obtain any information from any regulatory authorities, governments, mortgagees or others affecting the Property and the Seller agrees to execute and deliver such further authorizations in this regard as may be reasonably required.

8. **USE AND DISTRIBUTION OF INFORMATION:** The Seller consents to the collection, use and disclosure of personal information by the Brokerage for the purpose of compiling, retaining and publishing any statistics including data which may be used by the Brokerage to conduct comparative market analyses; and make such other use of information as the Brokerage deems appropriate in connection with the listing, marketing, selling or leasing of real estate.

9. **FAMILY LAW ACT:** The Seller hereby warrants that spousal consent is not necessary under the provisions of the Family Law Act, R.S.O. 1990, unless the Seller's spouse has executed the consent hereinafter provided.

10. **SUCCESSORS AND ASSIGNS:** The heirs, executors, administrators, successors and assigns of the undersigned are bound by the terms of this Agreement.

11. **CONFLICT OR DISCREPANCY:** If there is any conflict or discrepancy between any provision added to this Agreement (including any Schedule attached hereto) and any provision in the standard pre-set portion hereof, the added provision shall supersede the standard pre-set provision to the extent of such conflict or discrepancy. This Agreement, including any Schedule attached hereto, shall constitute the entire Agreement between the Seller and the Brokerage. There is no representation, warranty, collateral agreement or condition, which affects this Agreement other than as expressed herein.

INITIALS OF BROKERAGE: ⬭   INITIALS OF SELLER(S): ⬭

APPENDIX

Form 201   *Seller Customer Service Agreement—Commission Agreement for Property Not Listed*   Page 3 of 3

12. ELECTRONIC COMMUNICATION: This Agreement and any agreements, notices or other communications contemplated thereby may be transmitted by means of electronic systems, in which case signatures shall be deemed to be original. The transmission of this Agreement by the Seller by electronic means shall be deemed to confirm the Seller has retained a true copy of the Agreement.

13. SOLD SIGN: The Seller hereby agrees and consents by the Seller initialling this term of the Agreement that, upon the Seller entering into a binding Agreement to sell or lease the property with the Buyer, the Brokerage is authorized to place the Brokerage's Sold/Leased sign on the property.

(Seller's Initials)

14. SCHEDULE(S) .... attached hereto form(s) part of this Agreement.

THE BROKERAGE AGREES TO PROVIDE CUSTOMER SERVICE TO THE SELLER IN AN ENDEAVOUR TO OBTAIN THE ACCEPTANCE OF AN AGREEMENT TO PURCHASE OR LEASE BETWEEN THE SELLER AND THE BUYER.

.... DATE..................................... ....
(Authorized to bind the Brokerage)   (Name of Person Signing)

THIS AGREEMENT HAS BEEN READ AND FULLY UNDERSTOOD BY ME AND I ACKNOWLEDGE THIS DATE I HAVE SIGNED UNDER SEAL.
SIGNED, SEALED AND DELIVERED I have hereunto set my hand and seal:

.... (Seal)   DATE ....
(Signature of Seller)   (Tel. No.)

.... (Seal)   DATE ....
(Signature of Seller)

SPOUSAL CONSENT: The undersigned spouse of the Seller hereby consents to the listing of the Property herein pursuant to the provisions of the Family Law Act, R.S.O. 1990 and hereby agrees that he/she will execute all necessary or incidental documents to further any transaction provided for herein.

.... (Seal)   DATE ....
(Spouse)

DECLARATION OF INSURANCE

The broker/salesperson ....
(Name of Broker/Salesperson)
hereby declares that he/she is insured as required by the Real Estate and Business Brokers Act (REBBA) and Regulations.

....
(Signature(s) of Broker/Salesperson)

ACKNOWLEDGEMENT

The Seller(s) hereby acknowledge that the Seller(s) fully understand the terms of this Agreement and have received a true copy

of this Agreement on the .... day of ...., 20 ....

.... Date: ....
(Signature of Seller)

.... Date: ....
(Signature of Seller)

Form 201   Revised 2013   **Page 3 of 3**

 **Ontario Real Estate Association**

Form 210
for use in the Province of Ontario

Listing Agreement
Authority to Offer for Lease

This is a Multiple Listing Service® Agreement (MLS®) **OR** **Exclusive Listing Agreement** (EXCLUSIVE)

(Landlord's Initials)   (Landlord's Initials)

BETWEEN

BROKERAGE: ....

.... (the "Listing Brokerage")

LANDLORD: .... (the "Landlord")

In consideration of the Listing Brokerage listing the real property **for lease** known as ....

.... (the "Property")

the Landlord hereby gives the Listing Brokerage the **exclusive and irrevocable** right to act as the Landlord's agent, **commencing** at 12:01 a.m. on the ....

day of ...., 20.........., **until** 11:59 p.m. on the .... day of ...., 20......... (the "Listing Period"),

{ Landlord acknowledges that the length of the Listing Period is negotiable between the Landlord and the Listing Brokerage and, if an MLS® listing, may be subject to minimum requirements of the real estate board, however, in accordance with the Real Estate and Business Brokers Act (2002), **if the Listing Period exceeds six months, the Listing Brokerage must obtain the Landlord's initials.** }   (Landlord's Initials)

to offer the property **for lease** at a rent of: Dollars (CDN$) ....

....Dollars
and upon the terms particularly set out herein, or at such other rent and/or terms acceptable to the Landlord. It is understood that the rent and/or terms set out herein are at the Landlord's personal request, after full discussion with the Listing Brokerage's representative regarding potential market rent of the Property.

The Landlord hereby represents and warrants that the Landlord is not a party to any other listing agreement for the Property or agreement to pay commission to any other real estate brokerage for the lease of the property.

1. **DEFINITIONS AND INTERPRETATIONS:** For the purposes of this Listing Agreement ("Authority" or "Agreement"), "Landlord" includes lessor and a "tenant" includes a lessee, or a prospective lessee or tenant. A lease includes any rental agreement, sub-lease or renewal of a lease. The "Property" shall be deemed to include any part thereof or interest therein. A "real estate board" includes a real estate association. This Agreement shall be read with all changes of gender or number required by the context. For purposes of this Agreement, anyone introduced to or shown the Property shall be deemed to include any spouse, heirs, executors, administrators, successors, assigns, related corporations and affiliated corporations. Related corporations or affiliated corporations shall include any corporation where one half or a majority of the shareholders, directors or officers of the related or affiliated corporation are the same person(s) as the shareholders, directors, or officers of the corporation introduced to or shown the Property.

2. **COMMISSION:** In consideration of the Listing Brokerage listing the Property, the Landlord agrees to pay the Listing Brokerage a commission of:

....

for any valid offer to lease the Property from any source whatsoever obtained during the Listing Period and on the terms and conditions set out in this Agreement **OR** such other terms and conditions as the Landlord may accept. Said commission to be payable on the earlier of occupancy by the Tenant or execution of the Lease.

The Landlord further agrees to pay such commission as calculated above if an agreement to lease is agreed to or accepted by the Landlord or anyone

on the Landlord's behalf within .... days after the expiration of the Listing Period (**Holdover Period**), so long as such agreement is with anyone who was introduced to the Property from any source whatsoever during the Listing Period or shown the Property during the Listing Period. If, however, the offer to lease the Property is pursuant to a new agreement in writing to pay commission to another registered real estate brokerage, the Landlord's liability for commission shall be reduced by the amount paid by the Landlord under the new agreement.

The Landlord further agrees to pay such commission as calculated above even if the transaction contemplated by an agreement to lease agreed to or accepted by the Landlord or anyone on the Landlord's behalf is not completed, if such non-completion is owing or attributable to the Landlord's default or neglect, said commission to be payable on the earlier of the date of occupancy by the tenant or the execution of the lease or the date set for commencement of the lease or tenancy.

If a lease the Listing Brokerage arranges contains an option to extend or renew, the Landlord agrees to notify the Listing Brokerage of the exercising of said option and to pay the Listing Brokerage upon the exercising of the said option or any future option, a further commission of:

....

of the total rent for the term of such lease extension or renewal. It is understood and agreed that the said further commission is to be paid on the earlier of the date of execution of the extension or renewal or the date the extension or renewal commences. If a tenant to whom the Listing Brokerage rented or leased the Property effects an offer to purchase the Property during the tenancy period or any renewal of the tenancy agreement, the Landlord

agrees to pay the Listing Brokerage a commission of .... % of the sale price of the Property or ....

.... for the purchase of the Property.

Any deposit in respect of any agreement where the transaction has been completed shall first be applied to reduce the commission payable. Should such amounts paid to the Listing Brokerage from the deposit or by the Landlord's solicitor not be sufficient, the Landlord shall be liable to pay to the Listing Brokerage on demand, any deficiency in commission and taxes owing on such commission.

All amounts set out as commission are to be paid plus applicable taxes on such commission.

INITIALS OF LISTING BROKERAGE: ( )   **INITIALS OF LANDLORD(S):** ( )

3. **REPRESENTATION:** The Landlord acknowledges that the Listing Brokerage has provided the Landlord with written information explaining agency relationships, including information on Landlord Representation, Sub-agency, Tenant Representation, Multiple Representation and Customer Service. The Landlord authorizes the Listing Brokerage to co-operate with any other registered real estate brokerage (co-operating brokerage), and to offer to

pay the co-operating brokerage a commission of ....

....
out of the commission the Landlord pays the Listing Brokerage. The Landlord understands that unless the Landlord is otherwise informed, the co-operating brokerage is representing the interests of the tenant in the transaction. The Landlord further acknowledges that the Listing Brokerage may be listing other properties that may be similar to the Landlord's Property and the Landlord hereby consents to the Listing Brokerage acting as an agent for more than one landlord without any claim by the Landlord of conflict of interest. Unless otherwise agreed in writing between Landlord and Listing Brokerage, any commission payable to any other brokerage shall be paid out of the commission the Landlord pays the Listing Brokerage, said commission to be disbursed in accordance with the Commission Trust Agreement. The Landlord hereby appoints the Listing Brokerage as the Landlord's agent for the purpose of giving and receiving notices pursuant to any offer or agreement to lease the Property.

MULTIPLE REPRESENTATION: The Landlord hereby acknowledges that the Listing Brokerage may be entering into tenant representation agreements with tenants who may be interested in leasing the Landlord's Property. In the event that the Listing Brokerage has entered into or enters into a tenant representation agreement with a prospective tenant for the Landlord's Property, the Listing Brokerage will obtain the Landlord's written consent to represent both the Landlord and the tenant for the transaction at the earliest practical opportunity and in all cases prior to any offer to lease being submitted or presented.

The Landlord understands and acknowledges that the Listing Brokerage must be impartial when representing both the Landlord and the tenant and equally protect the interests of the Landlord and tenant. The Landlord understands and acknowledges that when representing both the Landlord and the tenant, the Listing Brokerage shall have a duty of full disclosure to both the Landlord and the tenant, including a requirement to disclose all factual information about the Property known to the Listing Brokerage.

However, the Landlord further understands and acknowledges that the Listing Brokerage shall not disclose:
- that the Landlord may or will accept less than the listed rent, unless otherwise instructed in writing by the Landlord;
- that the tenant may or will pay more than the offered rent, unless otherwise instructed in writing by the tenant;
- the motivation of or personal information about the Landlord or tenant, unless otherwise instructed in writing by the party to which the information applies or unless failure to disclose would constitute fraudulent, unlawful or unethical practice;
- the rent the tenant should offer or the rent the Landlord should accept; and
- the Listing Brokerage shall not disclose to the tenant the terms of any other offer.

However, it is understood that factual market information about comparable properties and information known to the Listing Brokerage concerning potential uses for the Property will be disclosed to both Landlord and tenant to assist them to come to their own conclusions.

Where a Brokerage represents both the Landlord and the Tenant (multiple representation), the Brokerage shall not be entitled or authorized to be agent for either the Tenant or the Landlord for the purpose of giving and receiving notices.

MULTIPLE REPRESENTATION AND CUSTOMER SERVICE: The Landlord understands and agrees that the Listing Brokerage also provides representation and customer service to other landlords and tenants. If the Listing Brokerage represents or provides customer service to more than one landlord or tenant for the same trade, the Listing Brokerage shall, in writing, at the earliest practicable opportunity and before any offer is made, inform all landlords and tenants of the nature of the Listing Brokerage's relationship to each landlord and tenant.

4. **REFERRAL OF ENQUIRIES:** The Landlord agrees that during the Listing Period, the Landlord shall advise the Listing Brokerage immediately of all enquiries from any source whatsoever, and all offers to lease submitted to the Landlord shall be immediately submitted to the Listing Brokerage by the Landlord before the Landlord accepts or rejects the same. If any enquiry during the Listing Period results in the Landlord accepting a valid offer to lease during the Listing Period or within the Holdover Period after the expiration of the Listing Period described above, the Landlord agrees to pay the Listing Brokerage the amount of commission set out above, payable within five (5) days following the Listing Brokerage's written demand therefor.

5. **MARKETING:** The Landlord agrees to allow the Listing Brokerage to show and permit prospective tenants to fully inspect the Property during reasonable hours and the Landlord gives the Listing Brokerage the sole and exclusive right to place "For Lease" and "Leased" sign(s) upon the Property. The Landlord consents to the Listing Brokerage including information in advertising that may identify the Property. The Landlord further agrees that the Listing Brokerage shall have sole and exclusive authority to make all advertising decisions relating to the marketing of the Property for lease during the Listing Period. The Landlord agrees that the Listing Brokerage will not be held liable in any manner whatsoever for any acts or omissions with respect to advertising by the Listing Brokerage or any other party, other than by the Listing Brokerage's gross negligence or wilful act.

6. **WARRANTY:** The Landlord represents and warrants that the Landlord has the exclusive authority and power to execute this Authority to offer the Property for lease and that the Landlord has informed the Listing Brokerage of any third party interests or claims on the Property such as rights of first refusal, options, easements, mortgages, encumbrances or otherwise concerning the Property, which may affect the leasing of the Property.

7. **INDEMNIFICATION AND INSURANCE:** The Landlord will not hold the Listing Brokerage and representatives of the Brokerage responsible for any loss or damage to the Property or contents occurring during the term of this Agreement caused by the Listing Brokerage or anyone else by any means, including theft, fire or vandalism, other than by the Listing Brokerage's gross negligence or wilful act. The Landlord agrees to indemnify and save harmless the Listing Brokerage and representatives of the Brokerage and any co-operating brokerage from any liability, claim, loss, cost, damage or injury, including but not limited to loss of the commission payable under this Agreement, caused or contributed to by the breach of any warranty or representation made by the Landlord in this Agreement or the accompanying data form. The Landlord warrants the Property is insured, including personal liability insurance against any claims or lawsuits resulting from bodily injury or property damage to others caused in any way on or at the Property and the Landlord indemnifies the Brokerage and all of its employees, representatives, salespersons and brokers (Listing Brokerage) and any co-operating brokerage and all of its employees, representatives, salespersons and brokers (co-operating brokerage) for and against any claims against the Listing Brokerage or co-operating brokerage made by anyone who attends or visits the Property.

8. **FAMILY LAW ACT:** The Landlord hereby warrants that spousal consent is not necessary under the provisions of the Family Law Act, R.S.O. 1990, unless the Landlord's spouse has executed the consent hereinafter provided.

9. **VERIFICATION OF INFORMATION:** The Landlord authorizes the Listing Brokerage and representatives of the Brokerage to obtain any information from any regulatory authorities, governments, mortgagees or others affecting the Property and the Landlord agrees to execute and deliver such further authorizations in this regard as may be reasonably required. The Landlord hereby appoints the Listing Brokerage or the Listing Brokerage's authorized representative as the Landlord's attorney to execute such documentation as may be necessary to effect obtaining any information as aforesaid. The Landlord hereby authorizes, instructs and directs the above noted regulatory authorities, governments, mortgagees or others to release any and all information to the Listing Brokerage.

INITIALS OF LISTING BROKERAGE: ( )   **INITIALS OF LANDLORD(S):** ( )

10. **USE AND DISTRIBUTION OF INFORMATION:** The Landlord consents to the collection, use and disclosure of personal information by the Brokerage for the purpose of listing and marketing the Property including, but not limited to: listing and advertising the Property using any medium including the Internet; disclosing Property information to prospective tenants, brokerages, salespersons and others who may assist in the leasing of the Property; such other use of the Landlord's personal information as is consistent with listing and marketing of the Property. The Landlord consents, if this is an MLS® Listing, to placement of the listing information and leasing information by the Brokerage into the database(s) of the MLS® System of the appropriate Board, and to the posting of any documents and other information (including, without limitation, photographs, images, graphics, audio and video recordings, virtual tours, drawings, floor plans, architectural designs, artistic renderings, surveys and listing descriptions) provided by or on behalf of the Landlord into the database(s) of the MLS® System of the appropriate Board. The Landlord hereby indemnifies and saves harmless the Brokerage and/or any of its employees, servants, brokers or sales representatives from any and all claims, liabilities, suits, actions, losses, costs and legal fees caused by, or arising out of, or resulting from the posting of any documents or other information (including, without limitation, photographs, images, graphics, audio and video recordings, virtual tours, drawings, floor plans, architectural designs, artistic renderings, surveys and listing descriptions) as aforesaid. The Landlord acknowledges that the database, within the board's MLS® System is the property of the real estate board(s) and can be licensed, resold, or otherwise dealt with by the board(s). The Landlord further acknowledges that the real estate board(s) may: during the term of the listing and thereafter, distribute the information in the database, within the board's MLS® System to any persons authorized to use such service which may include other brokerages, government departments, appraisers, municipal organizations and others; market the Property, at its option, in any medium, including electronic media; during the term of the listing and thereafter, compile, retain and publish any statistics including historical data within the board's MLS® System and retain, reproduce and display photographs, images, graphics, audio and video recordings, virtual tours, drawings, floor plans, architectural designs, artistic renderings, surveys and listing descriptions which may be used by board members to conduct comparative analyses; and make such other use of the information as the Brokerage and/or real estate board(s) deem appropriate, in connection with the listing, marketing and leasing of real estate during the term of the listing and thereafter. The Landlord acknowledges that the information, personal or otherwise ("information"), provided to the real estate board or association may be stored on databases located outside of Canada, in which case the information would be subject to the laws of the jurisdiction in which the information is located.

> In the event that this Agreement expires or is cancelled or otherwise terminated and the Property is not leased, the Landlord, by initialling:
>
> consent to allow other real estate board members to contact the Landlord after expiration or other termination of this Agreement to discuss listing or otherwise marketing the Property.   **Does**   **Does Not**

11. **SUCCESSORS AND ASSIGNS:** The heirs, executors, administrators, successors and assigns of the undersigned are bound by the terms of this Agreement.

12. **CONFLICT OR DISCREPANCY:** If there is any conflict or discrepancy between any provision added to this Agreement (including any Schedule attached hereto) and any provision in the standard pre-set portion hereof, the added provision shall supersede the standard pre-set provision to the extent of such conflict or discrepancy. This Agreement, including any Schedule attached hereto, shall constitute the entire Authority from the Landlord to the Brokerage. There is no representation, warranty, collateral agreement or condition which affects this Agreement other than as expressed herein.

13. **ELECTRONIC COMMUNICATION:** This Listing Agreement and any agreements, notices or other communications contemplated thereby may be transmitted by means of electronic systems, in which case signatures shall be deemed to be original. The transmission of this Agreement by the Landlord by electronic means shall be deemed to confirm the Landlord has retained a true copy of the Agreement.

14. **SCHEDULE(S):** .... and data form attached hereto form(s) part of this Agreement
THE LISTING BROKERAGE AGREES TO MARKET THE PROPERTY ON BEHALF OF THE LANDLORD AND REPRESENT THE LANDLORD IN AN ENDEAVOUR TO OBTAIN A VALID OFFER TO LEASE THE PROPERTY ON THE TERMS SET OUT IN THIS AGREEMENT OR ON SUCH OTHER TERMS SATISFACTORY TO THE LANDLORD.

....   DATE..................   ....
(Authorized to bind the Listing Brokerage)   (Name of Person Signing)

THIS AUTHORITY HAS BEEN READ AND FULLY UNDERSTOOD BY ME AND I ACKNOWLEDGE THIS DATE I HAVE SIGNED UNDER SEAL. Any representations contained herein or as shown on the accompanying data form respecting the Property are true to the best of my knowledge, information and belief.
SIGNED, SEALED AND DELIVERED I have hereunto set my hand and seal:

....
(Name of Landlord)

....   (Seal)   DATE ....
((Signature of Landlord/Authorized Signing Officer)   (Tel. No.)

....   (Seal)   DATE ....
((Signature of Landlord/Authorized Signing Officer)

SPOUSAL CONSENT: The undersigned spouse of the Landlord hereby consents to the listing of the Property herein pursuant to the provisions of the Family Law Act, R.S.O. 1990 and hereby agrees that he/she will execute all necessary or incidental documents to further any transaction provided for herein.

....   (Seal)   DATE ....
(Spouse)

DECLARATION OF INSURANCE

The broker/salesperson..
                                                (Name of Broker/Salesperson)
hereby declares that he/she is insured as required by the Real Estate and Business Brokers Act (REBBA) and Regulations.

....
(Signature(s) of Broker/Salesperson)

ACKNOWLEDGEMENT

The Landlord(s) hereby acknowledge that the Landlord(s) fully understand the terms of this Agreement and have received a true copy of this Agreement

on the .... day of ...., 20 ....

....   Date: ....
(Signature of Landlord)

....   Date: ....
(Signature of Landlord)

APPENDIX

 **Ontario Real Estate Association**

Form 220
for use in the Province of Ontario

Seller Property Information Statement
Residential

ANSWERS MUST BE COMPLETE AND ACCURATE This statement is designed in part to protect Sellers by establishing that correct information concerning the property is being provided to buyers. All of the information contained herein is provided by the Sellers to the brokerage/broker/salesperson. Any person who is in receipt of and utilizes this Statement acknowledges and agrees that **the information is being provided for information purposes only and is not a warranty as to the matters recited hereinafter even if attached to an Agreement of Purchase and Sale.** The brokerage/broker/salesperson shall not be held responsible for the accuracy of any information contained herein.

BUYERS MUST STILL MAKE THEIR OWN ENQUIRIES Buyers must still make their own enquiries notwithstanding the information contained on this statement. Each question and answer must be considered and where necessary, keeping in mind that the Sellers' knowledge of the property may be inaccurate or incomplete, additional information can be requested from the Sellers or from an independent source such as the municipality. Buyers can hire an independent inspector to examine the property to determine whether defects exist and to provide an estimate of the cost of repairing problems that have been identified. **This statement does not provide information on psychological stigmas that may be associated with a property.**

For the purposes of this Seller Property Information Statement, a "Seller" includes a landlord or a prospective landlord and a "buyer" includes a tenant, or a prospective tenant.

PROPERTY:	SELLER(S) TO **INITIAL** EACH APPLICABLE BOX			
SELLER(S):				
GENERAL: (Provide Applicable ADDITIONAL COMMENTS)	**YES**	**NO**	**UNKNOWN**	**NOT APPLICABLE**
1. I have occupied the property from...............................to...............................				
2. Does any other party have an ownership or spousal interest in the property?				
3. Is the property a condominium or a freehold property that includes an interest in a common elements condominium, (POTL)? (If yes, Schedule 221 to be completed.)				
4. Does ownership of this property require membership in an Association and payment of Association fees? If yes, specify..				
5. Is the property subject to first right of refusal, option, lease, rental agreement or other listing?				
6. Are there any encroachments, registered easements, or rights-of-way?				
7. Is there a plan of survey? Date of survey...				
8. Are there any disputes concerning the boundaries of the property?				
9. Are you aware of any non-compliance with zoning regulations?				
10. Are you aware of any pending developments, projects or rezoning applications in the neighbourhood?				
11. Are there any public projects planned for the neighbourhood? eg: road widenings, new highways, expropriations etc.				
12. Are there any restrictive covenants that run with the land?				
13. Are there any drainage restrictions?				
14. Are there any local levies or unusual taxes being charged at the present time or contemplated? If so, at what cost? .... Expiry date..				
15. Have you received any notice, claim, work order or deficiency notice affecting the property from any person or any public body?				
16. (a) Is the property connected to municipal water? (If not, Schedule 222 to be completed.)				
(b) Is the property connected to municipal sewer? (If not, Schedule 222 to be completed.)				
17. Are there any current or pending Heritage restrictions for the property or the area?				

INITIALS OF BUYER(S): ( )

Form 220   *(continued)*   Page 2 of 3

GENERAL (cont'd): (Provide Applicable ADDITIONAL COMMENTS)	YES	NO	UNKNOWN	NOT APPLICABLE
18. Are there any conditional sales contracts, leases, rental agreements or service contracts? eg: furnace, alarm system, hot water tank, propane tank, etc. Specify.. Are they assignable or will they be discharged?..				
19. Are there any defects in any appliances or equipment included with the property?				
20. Do you know the approximate age of the building(s)?Age................................ Any additions: Age..				
21. Are you aware of any past or pending claims under the Tarion Warranty Corporation (formerly ONHWP)? Tarion Warranty Corporation/ONHWP Registration No......................................				
22. Will the sale of this property be subject to HST?				

ADDITIONAL COMMENTS:...

....

....

....

ENVIRONMENTAL: (Provide Applicable ADDITIONAL COMMENTS)	YES	NO	UNKNOWN	NOT APPLICABLE
1. Are you aware of possible environmental problems or soil contamination of any kind on the property or in the immediate area? eg: radon gas, toxic waste, underground gasoline or fuel tanks etc.				
2. Are there any existing or proposed waste dumps, disposal sites or land fills in the immediate area?				
3. Are there any hydro generating projects planned for the immediate area? eg: Wind Turbines				
4. Is the property subject to flooding?				
5. Is the property under the jurisdiction of any Conservation Authority or Commission?				
6. Are you aware of any excessive erosion, settling, slippage, sliding or other soil problems?				
7. Does the property have any abandoned or de-commissioned ☐ well ☐ septic system ☐ swimming pool ☐ foundation ☐ other, specify.......................................				
8. (a) Is there a fuel oil tank on the property? If yes, complete the following: ☐ Underground. Date for required upgrading or removal................................... ☐ Aboveground. Age of tank........................... Date of last inspection...........................				
(b) Does the fuel oil tank comply with the Technical Standards and Safety Authority requirements and any other requirements for fuel to be delivered?				
9. Has the use of the property ever been for the growth or manufacture of illegal substances?				

ADDITIONAL COMMENTS:...

....

....

....

....

INITIALS OF BUYER(S): ⬭

Form 220   Revised 2016   **Page 2 of 3**

APPENDIX

IMPROVEMENTS AND STRUCTURAL: (Provide Applicable ADDITIONAL COMMENTS)	YES	NO	UNKNOWN	NOT APPLICABLE
1. Are you aware of any structural problems?				
2. (a) Have you made any renovations, additions or improvements to the property?				
(b) Was a building permit obtained?				
(c) Has the final building inspection been approved or has a final occupancy permit been obtained?				
3. To the best of your knowledge have the building(s) ever contained ureaformaldehyde insulation?				
4. Is there vermiculite insulation on the property? If yes, has it been tested for asbestos?..				
5. (a) Are you aware of any deficiencies or non-compliance with the Ontario Fire Code?				
(b) Is your property equipped with operational smoke detectors?				
(c) Is the property equipped with operational carbon monoxide detectors?				
6. (a) Is the woodstove(s)/chimney(s)/fireplace(s)/insert(s) in good working order?				
(b) Has the wood energy system been **WETT** inspected? (Wood Energy Technology Transfer)				
7. Are you aware of any problems with the central air conditioning system?				
8. Are you aware of any problems with the heating system?				
9. (a) Are you aware of any moisture and/or water problems?				
(b) Are you aware of any roof leakage or unrepaired damage? Age of roof covering				
(c) Are you aware of any damage due to wind, fire, flood, insects, termites, rodents, pets or wood rot?				
(d) Have any repairs been carried out to correct any past or present problems related to (a), (b) and/or (c)? If yes, explain in additional comments below.				
10. (a) Are you aware of any problems with the electrical system? Size of service..................................				
(b) Type of wiring: ☐ copper ☐ aluminium ☐ knob-and-tube ☐ other..................................				
11. Are you aware of any problems with the plumbing system?				
12. Is there any lead, galvanized metal, cast iron or Kitec plumbing on the property?				
13. Are you aware of any problems with the swimming pool, sauna, hot tub, jet bathtub or lawn sprinkler system?				

ADDITIONAL COMMENTS: ....

....

....

....

Schedule(s) attached hereto and forming part of this Statement include:...

The Sellers state that the above information is true, based on their current actual knowledge as of the date below. Any important changes to this information known to the Sellers will be disclosed by the Sellers prior to closing. Sellers are responsible for the accuracy of all answers. Sellers further agree to indemnify and hold the Brokerage/Broker/Salesperson harmless from any liability incurred as a result of any buyer relying on this information. The Sellers hereby authorize the Brokerage to post a copy of this Seller Property Information Statement into the database(s) of the appropriate MLS® system and that a copy of this Seller Property Information Statement be delivered by their agent or representative to prospective buyers or their agents or representatives. The Sellers hereby acknowledge receipt of a true copy of this statement.

.... DATE.............................   .... DATE..................................
(Signature of Seller)   (Signature of Seller)

I acknowledge that the information provided herein is not warranted and hereby acknowledge receipt of a copy of the above information including any applicable Schedule(s).

....   DATE..
(Signature of Buyer or Authorized Representative)

....   DATE..
(Signature of Buyer)

Form 220   Revised 2016   **Page 3 of 3**

Seller Property Information Statement
Schedule for Condominium

Form 221
for use in the Province of Ontario

This Schedule is attached to and forms part of the Seller Property Information Statement (Form 220) for:

PROPERTY:	SELLER(S) TO INITIAL EACH APPLICABLE BOX
SELLER(S):	

CONDOMINIUM CORPORATION: (Provide Applicable ADDITIONAL COMMENTS)	YES	NO	UNKNOWN	NOT APPLICABLE
1. (a) Condominium fee $..				
(b) Condominium fee includes:				
(c) Cost for amenities not included in Condominium fee $.............................. Details				
2. Are there any special assessments approved or contemplated?				
3. Have you received any written notice of lawsuit(s) pending?				
4. Have you been informed of any notices, claims, work orders or deficiency notices affecting the common elements received from any person or any public body?				
5. (a) Has a reserve fund study been completed? Date of Study...........................				
(b) Approximate amount of reserve fund as of last notification $........................				
6. (a) Are there any restrictions on pets?				
(b) Are there any restrictions on renting the property?				
(c) Are there any other restrictions on the use of the property?				
7. (a) If any renovations, additions or improvements were made to the unit and/or common elements, was approval of the Condominium Corporation obtained?				
(b) Is approval of any prospective buyer required by the Condominium Corporation?				
(c) Are any other approvals required by the Condominium Corporation or Property Manager? If yes, specify:				
(d) Name of Property Management Company				
8. Are there any pending rule or by-law amendments which may alter or restrict the uses of the property?				
9. Is the Condominium registered?				
10. Parking: Number of Spaces .... ☐ Owned ☐ Exclusive Use ☐ Leased or Licensed Parking space number(s)..				
11. Locker:.. ☐ Owned ☐ Exclusive Use Locker number(s)...				
12. (a) Amenities: ☐ Pool ☐ Sauna ☐ Exercise ☐ Room ☐ Meeting/Party Room ☐ Boat Docking ☐ Guest Parking ☐ Other.........................				
(b) Are you aware of any problems with any of the common element amenities? If yes, specify:				

ADDITIONAL COMMENTS:..
....
....

INITIALS OF BUYER(S): ⬭

Form 221 Revised 2014 **Page 1 of 1**

Form 222 *Seller Property Information Statement—Schedule for Water Supply, Waste Disposal, Access, Shoreline, Utilities*   Page 1 of 1

Seller Property Information Statement
Schedule for Water Supply, Waste Disposal, Access,
Shoreline, Utilities

Form 222
for use in the Province of Ontario

This Schedule is attached to and forms part of the Seller Property Information Statement (Form 220) for:

PROPERTY:	SELLER(S) TO **INITIAL** EACH APPLICABLE BOX			
SELLER(S):				

WATER SUPPLY AND WASTE DISPOSAL: (Provide Applicable ADDITIONAL COMMENTS)	YES	NO	UNKNOWN	NOT APPLICABLE
1. **(a)** What is your water source? ☐ Municipal ☐ Drilled ☐ Bored ☐ Dug ☐ Cistern ☐ Lake ☐ Community ☐ Shared ☐ Other..				
(b) If your water source is Community/Shared, is there a transferrable written agreement?				
(c) Are you aware of any problem re: quantity of water? (If yes, explain below)				
(d) Are you aware of any problems re: quality of water? (If yes, explain below)				
(e) Do you have any water treatment devices?..				
(f) Is your water system operable year round? Heated lines? ☐ Yes ☐ No				
(g) Date and result of most recent water test..				
(h) Are any documents available for the well? If yes, specify				
(i) Does the property have any abandoned well(s)?				
2. **(a)** What kind of sewage disposal system services the property? ☐ Municipal ☐ Septic tank with tile bed ☐ Holding tank ☐ Other (Explain below)				
(b) Are you aware of any problems with the sewage system? Date septic/holding tank last pumped........................... Age of system...............................				
(c) What documentation for the sewage system is available? ☐ Use Permit ☐ Location Sketch ☐ Maintenance Records ☐ Inspection Certificate ☐ Other				
3. Are all the well(s), water line(s) and waste disposal system(s) within the boundaries of the subject property?				

ACCESS, SHORELINE, UTILITIES: (Provide Applicable ADDITIONAL COMMENTS)	YES	NO	UNKNOWN	NOT APPLICABLE
1. **(a)** Is property access by municipal road? If yes; ☐ Open all year ☐ Seasonally open				
(b) Is the property serviced by a private road? Cost $.. per year.				
2. If your access is across private property, access is: ☐ Right of way ☐ Deeded ☐ Other .... Cost $............................... per year.				
3. **(a)** If water access only, access is: ☐ Deeded ☐ Leased ☐ Other (Explain below)				
(b) Water access cost of: Parking $............................... Dock $....................... per year.				
4. **(a)** Is the original Shore Road Allowance owned?				
(b) Are there any pending applications for shoreline improvement?				
(c) Are there any disputes concerning the shoreline or improvements on the shoreline?				
(d) Are there any structures or docks on the original Shore Road Allowance?				
(e) Is the original Road Allowance included in the lot size?				
5. Does the boundary of the property extend beyond the water line? If yes, explain below.				
6. **(a)** Is hydro available to the property?				
(b) Is the owner responsible for the installation, replacement/maintenance of any utility poles/ equipment?				

ADDITIONAL COMMENTS:...

....

....

INITIALS OF BUYER(S): ( )

Form 222   Revised 2011   **Page 1 of 1**

 **Ontario Real Estate Association**

Seller Property Information Statement
Important Information for Sellers

Form 225
for use in the Province of Ontario

TO SELLER(S): ....

....

BROKERAGE: ....

....

Form 220 - The Seller Property Information Statement "SPIS" is intended to provide information to a prospective buyer, based on the fact that the owner of the property will likely have information that a typical buyer would consider to be important.

As stated on the form, the seller is providing information as known to the seller but is not warranting the information provided. For this reason, OREA recommends that the SPIS not be attached as a Schedule to the Agreement of Purchase and Sale. There is a clause included in the standard OREA Agreement of Purchase and Sale that states "there is no representation, warranty, collateral agreement or condition which affects this Agreement other than expressed in the Agreement in writing.".

The Seller Property Information Statement, when properly completed, can be of benefit to both the sellers and the buyers. However, care must be taken when the form is completed. Sellers should answer the questions on the form as fully and accurately as possible. There is space on the form to add "Additional Comments" and this feature should be used to explain items on the form that could be claimed to be incomplete or misleading by a buyer. If there is some question as to whether a particular item should be mentioned on the form, it is better to err on the side of caution and provide the information along with an explanation, e.g. a defect that has been repaired. Also, if the information on the form becomes outdated or incorrect before the property sells or before a sale is completed, the information should be updated and given to the buyer.

With the high volume of property transactions that take place, there will inevitably be disputes between seller and buyers, whether or not an SPIS has been completed. The SPIS, when completed, may become an issue in such a dispute. There have been cases where a court has determined the sellers completed the SPIS accurately, honestly and to the best of their ability and the evidence provided by the SPIS is favourable to the sellers. There have been other cases where a court has determined that a seller has not been forthcoming with important information on the SPIS or has provided misleading information to the buyers.

Whether or not the seller completes an SPIS, the law requires a seller to disclose known hidden material defects to a property. In addition, the Real Estate and Business Brokers Act, 2002 requires registrants to determine and disclose "material facts" when a buyer is purchasing a property. The Seller Property Information Statement can be useful in fulfilling these obligations.

This information statement is provided to clarify the purpose and use of the Seller Property Information Statement.

I/We acknowledge receipt of this information:

Property ....

Seller .... Date ....

Seller .... Date ....

APPENDIX

Form 240   *Amendment to Listing Agreement*

 **Ontario Real Estate Association**

Form 240
for use in the Province of Ontario

Amendment to Listing Agreement
Price Change/Extension/Amendment(s)

RE: LISTING AGREEMENT FOR:
PROPERTY ADDRESS: ....
....

BETWEEN
SELLER: ....
AND
LISTING BROKERAGE: ....

....

MLS® NUMBER(S): ....   **L/BR ID. #** ....

INTERBOARD MLS® NUMBER: ....   **BOARD:** ....

LISTING EXPIRY DATE: ....

The Seller and the Listing Brokerage hereby agree that the above described Listing Agreement is amended as stated below:

1. LISTING PRICE:	
Former Listing Price... **New** Listing Price...	(Seller's Initials)

2. EXPIRY DATE:	
Former Expiry Date.. **New** Expiry Date..	(Seller's Initials)
Seller acknowledges that the length of the Listing Period is negotiable between the Seller and the Listing Brokerage, however, in accordance with the Real Estate and Business Brokers Act of Ontario (2002), **if the Listing Period exceeds six months from the date of this Amendment, the Listing Brokerage must obtain the Seller's initials.**	(Seller's Initials)

3. OTHER AMENDMENTS:	
a)	(Seller's Initials)
....	
b)	(Seller's Initials)
....	

All other terms and provisions of the Listing Agreement remain in full force and effect.

An extension of the expiry date must be signed and dated prior to expiration of the listing, and, if an MLS® Listing, notification of the extension must be delivered to the Real Estate Board(s) (or Brokerageloaded, if applicable) within 48 hours of receipt of the extension and prior to the expiry date of the listing.

The Listing Brokerage agrees to immediately notify the Real Estate Board(s) of the amendment(s) in accordance with the MLS® Rules and Regulations, provided that this is an MLS® listing.

This Amendment to Listing Agreement shall not take effect unless signed by all parties set out below, and initialled where applicable.

For the purposes of this Amendment to Listing Agreement, "Seller" includes vendor, landlord and lessor and Real Estate Board(s) includes Real Estate Association(s).

I hereby acknowledge receipt of a copy of this Amendment to Listing Agreement.

SIGNED, SEALED AND DELIVERED I have hereunto set my hand and seal:

....   ●   DATE..........................   ....
(Seller)   (Seal)   (Print Name of Person Signing)

....   ●   DATE..........................   ....
(Seller)   (Seal)   (Print Name of Person Signing)

SPOUSAL CONSENT: The undersigned spouse of the Seller hereby consents to the Amendment to the listing of the Property herein pursuant to the provisions of the Family Law Act, R.S.O. 1990 and hereby agrees that he/she will execute all necessary or incidental documents to further any transaction provided for herein.

....   ●   DATE..........................   ....
(Spouse)   (Seal)

....
(Name of Listing Brokerage)

....   DATE..........................   ....
(Authorized to bind the Listing Brokerage)   (Print Name of Person Signing)

Form 240   Revised 2014   **Page 1 of 1**

 **OREA** Ontario Real Estate Association   **Suspension of Listing Agreement**

Form 241
for use in the Province of Ontario

RE: LISTING AGREEMENT FOR:

PROPERTY ADDRESS: ....

....

BETWEEN

SELLER: ....

and:

LISTING BROKERAGE: ....

MLS® NUMBER(S): .... **L/BR ID. #** ....

INTERBOARD MLS® NUMBER: .... **BOARD:** ....

LISTING EXPIRY DATE: ....

The Seller and the Listing Brokerage, by mutual consent, hereby agree that the above described Listing Agreement is suspended as of:

.... until ....
              (Date of Suspension)   (Date)

and all activities and negotiations by the Listing Brokerage and co-operating brokerages shall immediately cease. No showings or marketing of the property will be permitted during the period the Listing Agreement is suspended.

The Listing Brokerage agrees to immediately notify the Real Estate Board(s) of the suspension in accordance with the MLS® Rules and Regulations, provided that this is an MLS® listing.

The Seller and the Listing Brokerage agree that the said Listing Agreement shall remain in full force and effect for all other purposes, including the payment of commission and/or other compensation. **THIS IS NOT A CANCELLATION OF THE LISTING AGREEMENT.**

This Suspension of Listing Agreement shall not take effect unless signed by all parties set out below.

For the purposes of this Suspension of Listing Agreement, "Seller" includes vendor, landlord and lessor and Real Estate Board(s) includes Real Estate Association(s).

This Agreement shall be binding upon the heirs, executors, administrators and assigns of all of the parties executing the Agreement.

SIGNED, SEALED AND DELIVERED in the presence of: IN WITNESS whereof I have hereunto set my hand and seal:

.... ● DATE ....
(Witness)   (Seller)   (Seal)

.... ● DATE ....
(Witness)   (Seller)   (Seal)

SIGNED, SEALED AND DELIVERED in the presence of: IN WITNESS whereof I have hereunto set my hand and seal:

                                                         ....
                                                         (Name of Listing Brokerage)

.... ● DATE ....
(Witness)   (Signature of Listing Brokerage's Broker of Record/Manager) (Seal)

Form 241   Revised 2008   **Page 1 of 1**

APPENDIX

Cancellation of Listing Agreement

Form 242
for use in the Province of Ontario

RE: LISTING AGREEMENT FOR:
PROPERTY ADDRESS: ....

....

BETWEEN
SELLER: ....

AND:

LISTING BROKERAGE: ....

MLS® NUMBER(S): .... **L/BR ID. #** ....

INTERBOARD MLS® NUMBER: .... **BOARD:** ....

LISTING EXPIRY DATE: ....

The Seller and the Listing Brokerage, by mutual consent, hereby release each other from the above described Listing Agreement on the following terms:

The Seller releases the Listing Brokerage from any and all liabilities, covenants, obligations and claims arising out of the Listing Agreement.

The Listing Brokerage releases the Seller from any claims of remuneration or compensation with respect to this Listing Agreement, **save and except** that:

If an offer to purchase or lease, obtained from anyone who was introduced to the property from any source whatsoever while the Listing Agreement was in effect or was shown the property while the Listing Agreement was in effect, is agreed to or accepted by the Seller or anyone on behalf of the Seller within the Listing Period or the Holdover Period provided for in the above described Listing Agreement, the Seller agrees to immediately notify the Listing Brokerage of the sale/lease and to pay the Listing Brokerage the commission agreed to in the Listing Agreement.

If, however, the offer for the purchase or lease of the Property is pursuant to a new agreement in writing to pay commission to another registered real estate brokerage, the Seller's liability for commission shall be reduced by the amount paid by the Seller under the new agreement.

The Listing Brokerage agrees to immediately notify the Real Estate Board(s) of the cancellation in accordance with the MLS® Rules and Regulations, provided that this is an MLS® listing.

This Cancellation of Listing Agreement shall not take effect unless signed by all parties set out below.

For the purposes of this Cancellation of Listing Agreement, "Seller" includes vendor, landlord and lessor. and Real Estate Board(s) includes Real Estate Association(s).

This Agreement shall be binding upon the heirs, executors, administrators and assigns of all of the parties executing the Agreement.

SIGNED, SEALED AND DELIVERED in the presence of: IN WITNESS whereof I have hereunto set my hand and seal:

.... ● DATE ....
(Witness)   (Seller)   (Seal)

.... ● DATE ....
(Witness)   (Seller)   (Seal)

SIGNED, SEALED AND DELIVERED in the presence of: IN WITNESS whereof I have hereunto set my hand and seal:

                                           ....
                                           (Name of Listing Brokerage)

.... ● DATE ....
(Witness)   (Signature of Listing Brokerage's Broker of Record/Manager)   (Seal)

Form 242   Revised 2008   **Page 1 of 1**

Assignment of Listing Agreement

Form 243
for use in the Province of Ontario

RE: LISTING AGREEMENT FOR:
PROPERTY ADDRESS: ....
....

BETWEEN
SELLER: ....
AND:
LISTING BROKERAGE: ....

MLS® NUMBER(S): ....　**L/BR ID. #** ....

INTERBOARD MLS® NUMBER: ....　**BOARD:** ....

LISTING EXPIRY DATE: ....
The Listing Brokerage for the above described Listing Agreement assigns, transfers and sets over to:

....(the "Assignee")
any and all interest in the Listing Agreement, including all rights, duties and obligations pursuant to the Agreement. The Listing Brokerage releases the Seller
from any claims of remuneration or compensation with respect to this Listing Agreement.
The Listing Brokerage agrees to immediately notify the Real Estate Board(s) of the assignment in accordance with the MLS® Rules and Regulations, provided
that this is an MLS® listing. For the purposes of this Assignment of Listing Agreement, "Seller" includes vendor, landlord and lessor and Real Estate Board(s)
includes Real Estate Association(s).
This Assignment of Listing Agreement is to be effective at 12:01 a.m., the .... day of ...., 20...........
(Effective Date) **provided that this Assignment of Listing Agreement has been executed by both the Seller and the Assignee and a
copy of the signed Agreement is returned to the Listing Brokerage prior to the Effective Date.** The above described Listing Agreement
remains in full force with the Listing Brokerage until this Assignment of Listing Agreement becomes effective.

SIGNED, SEALED AND DELIVERED in the presence of:　　IN WITNESS whereof I have hereunto set my hand and seal:

　　　　　　　　　　　　　　　　　　　　　　..
　　　　　　　　　　　　　　　　　　　　　　(Name of Listing Brokerage)

....　..　● DATE ....
(Witness)　　　　　　　　　　　　(Listing Brokerage's Broker of Record/Manager)　(Seal)

The Seller hereby consents to the Assignment and releases the Listing Brokerage from any and all liabilities, covenants, obligations and claims arising out
of the Listing Agreement.

SIGNED, SEALED AND DELIVERED in the presence of:　　IN WITNESS whereof I have hereunto set my hand and seal:

....　..　● DATE ....
(Witness)　　　　　　　　　　　　(Seller)　　　　　　　　　　(Seal)

....　..　● DATE ....
(Witness)　　　　　　　　　　　　(Seller)　　　　　　　　　　(Seal)

The Assignee hereby agrees to assume responsibility for and perform any and all duties and obligations of the Listing Brokerage pursuant to the said Listing
Agreement.

....
(Name of Assignee Brokerage)

....
(Name of Salesperson/Broker)

SIGNED, SEALED AND DELIVERED in the presence of:　　IN WITNESS whereof I have hereunto set my hand and seal:

....　..　● DATE ....
(Witness)　　　　　　　　　　　　(Assignee Brokerage's Broker of Record/Manager)　(Seal)

OREA Ontario Real Estate Association   **Residential Market Comparison Guide**

Form 260
for use in the Province of Ontario

SUBJECT PROPERTY: ....

PREPARED FOR: ....

PREPARED BY: .... DATE : ....

COMPARABLES FOR SALE NOW:

Address	Price	Features/Comments

(Use back of form for additional features/comments if required)

COMPARABLES SOLD PAST 12 MONTHS:

Address	Price	Features/Comments

(Use back of form for additional features/comments if required)

COMPARABLES EXPIRED PAST 12 MONTHS:

Address	Price	Features/Comments

(Use back of form for additional features/comments if required)

ESTIMATED SELLING COSTS :

Brokerage Fee	$	
Mortgage Payout Penalty	$	
Mortgage Discount	$	
Approximate Legal Costs	$	
Miscellaneous	$	
Total	$	

Recommendations: as of ....

I recommend a maximum list price of: $ ....

With estimated selling price of: $ ....

With estimated outstanding mortgage balance of: $ ....

With estimated selling costs of: $ ....

Anticipated net proceeds would be: $ ....

Signature ....

NB: The recipient of the above information acknowledges by reading, reviewing or receiving such information that the information may not be accurate or current or correct and agrees to indemnify, save harmless and release, the Brokerage, sales representative or broker by whom the information was prepared, from all manner of actions, causes of action, suits or claims of any kind whatsoever.

NB: The above information is the property of the Brokerage, sales representative or broker by whom it was prepared and is not to be shared, distributed, published, transmitted, assigned, communicated or transferred in any way whatsoever without the prior written consent of the Brokerage, sales representative or broker named above.

NB: The above information is NOT an appraisal and is to be used for marketing purposes only.

Form 260   Revised 2012   **Page 1 of 1**

OREA Ontario Real Estate Association   **Mortgage Verification**

Form 261
for use in the Province of Ontario

TO: ....
(Name of Mortgagee)

Date: ...., 20.............

....
(Address)

RE: Mortgage No. ....

....

The mortgage on the following property is held by you.

Address ....

Owners. ....

This property has been listed for sale and it would be appreciated if you would give my agent, ...
(Name of Brokerage)

....
(Address)

the current Mortgage information related thereto. Your assistance will be very helpful ....
(Mortgagor)

Principal Outstanding .... as of ...., 20 ....

Interest Rate .... Payments ....

Amortization Period .... Maturity Date ....

Are Property Taxes Collected?   Yes ☐   No ☐   If yes, amount of Tax Credit $ ....

Special Payment Privileges ....

May this Mortgage be paid out and discharged?   Yes ☐   No ☐   If yes, give details and costs ....

....

Is this Mortgage assumable?   Yes ☐   No ☐   Approval Necessary?   Yes ☐   No ☐   Is the Mortgage Portable?   Yes ☐   No ☐

May this Mortgage be Increased?   Yes ☐   No ☐   If yes, give details and costs ....

....

Other Special Privileges ....

Are there any other Special Clauses that could affect a Sale?   Yes ☐   No ☐   If yes, give details ....

....

Is the Mortgage in Good Standing?   Yes ☐   No ☐   If no, give details ....

....

....
(Mortgagee)

N.B.: Please return in enclosed stamped, self-addressed envelope.

Form 261   Revised 2008   **Page 1 of 1**

APPENDIX

Co-Brokerage Agreement
Between Multiple Listing Brokerages

Form 650
for use in the Province of Ontario

BETWEEN: ....
(Listing Brokerage)

SALES REPRESENTATIVE/BROKER: ....

AND: ....
(Co-Listing Brokerage)

SALES REPRESENTATIVE/BROKER: ....

RE: REAL PROPERTY FOR SALE/LEASE: ....

....

SELLER/LANDLORD: ....

This will confirm an agreement that the Listing Brokerage will pay:

.... of the total commission .... to the Co-Listing Brokerage.
     (% / $)   (% / $)

Details of service	Listing Brokerage	Co-Listing Brokerage
Upload the Listing on .... MLS® System (if applicable)	❏	❏
Upload the Listing on .... MLS® System (if applicable)	❏	❏
Presentation of Offers	❏	❏
Market/Promote the Property Listing Sale/Lease	❏	❏
Place sign on the Property	❏	❏
Send Sale Invoice Letter to Seller's Solicator	❏	❏
Deposit Holder	❏	❏
Other	❏	❏
Other	❏	❏
Other	❏	❏

Schedule(s) .... hereto attached shall form part of this Co-Brokerage Agreement.

We agree to the terms and conditions as set out herein and acknowledge having received a copy of this Co-Brokerage Agreement.

DATED at .... this .... day of .... 20....................

....
(Listing Brokerage)

....
(Authorized to bind the Listing Brokerage)   (Date)

....
(Co-Listing Brokerage)

....
(Authorized to bind the Co-Listing Brokerage)   (Date)

....
(Seller/Landlord)   (Date)

....
(Seller/Landlord)   (Date)

OREA Ontario Real Estate Association

Residential Information Checklist

Form 820
for use in the province of Ontario

PROPERTY:				
DATE:				

GENERAL: (Provide Applicable ADDITIONAL COMMENTS)	YES	NO	UNKNOWN	NOT APPLICABLE
1. I have occupied the property from.........................to.............................				
2. Does any other party have an ownership or spousal interest in the property?				
3. Is the property a condominium or a freehold property that includes an interest in a common elements condominium, (POTL)? (If yes, Schedule 821 to be completed.)				
4. Does ownership of this property require membership in an Association and payment of Association fees? If yes, specify..				
5. Is the property subject to first right of refusal, option, lease, rental agreement or other listing?				
6. Are there any encroachments, registered easements, or rights-of-way?				
7. Is there a plan of survey? Date of survey..				
8. Are there any disputes concerning the boundaries of the property?				
9. Are you aware of any non-compliance with zoning regulations?				
10. Are you aware of any pending developments, projects or rezoning applications in the neighbourhood?				
11. Are there any public projects planned for the neighbourhood? eg: road widenings, new highways, expropriations etc.				
12. Are there any restrictive covenants that run with the land?				
13. Are there any drainage restrictions?				
14. Are there any local levies or unusual taxes being charged at the present time or contemplated? If so, at what cost? .... Expiry date...........................				
15. Have you received any notice, claim, work order or deficiency notice affecting the property from any person or any public body?				

APPENDIX

Form 820   *(continued)*

GENERAL (CONT'D): (Provide Applicable ADDITIONAL COMMENTS)	YES	NO	UNKNOWN	NOT APPLICABLE
16. **a)** Is the property connected to municipal water? (If not, Schedule 822 to be completed.)				
b) Is the property connected to municipal sewer? (If not, Schedule 822 to be completed.)				
17. Are there any current or pending Heritage restrictions for the property or the area?				
18. Are there any conditional sales contracts, leases, rental agreements or service contracts? eg: furnace, alarm system, hot water tank, propane tank, etc. Specify... Are they assignable or will they be discharged?..				
19. Are there any defects in any appliances or equipment included with the property?				
20. Do you know the approximate age of the building(s)? Age............................... Any additions: Age...				
21. Are you aware of any past or pending claims under the Tarion Warranty Corporation (formerly ONHWP)? Tarion Warranty Corporation/ONHWP Registration No.................................				
22. Will the sale of this property be subject to HST?				

ADDITIONAL COMMENTS: ....
....
....
....
....
....

ENVIRONMENTAL: (Provide Applicable ADDITIONAL COMMENTS)	YES	NO	UNKNOWN	NOT APPLICABLE
1. Are you aware of possible environmental problems or soil contamination of any kind on the property or in the immediate area? eg: radon gas, toxic waste, underground gasoline or fuel tanks etc.				
2. Are there any existing or proposed waste dumps, disposal sites or land fills in the immediate area??				
3. Are there any hydro generating projects planned for the immediate area? eg: Wind Turbines				

Form 820   Revised 2016   **Page 2 of 4**

Form 820   *(continued)*

ENVIRONMENTAL (CONT'D): (Provide Applicable ADDITIONAL COMMENTS)	YES	NO	UNKNOWN	NOT APPLICABLE
4. Is the property subject to flooding?				
5. Is the property under the jurisdiction of any Conservation Authority or Commission?				
6. Are you aware of any excessive erosion, settling, slippage, sliding or other soil problems?				
7. Does the property have any abandoned or de-commissioned ☐ well ☐ septic system ☐ swimming pool ☐ foundation ☐ other, specify..				
8. **a)** Is there a fuel oil tank on the property? If yes, complete the following: ☐ Underground. Date for required upgrading or removal................................. . ☐ Aboveground. Age of tank.......................... Date of last inspection...........................				
b) Does the fuel oil tank comply with the Technical Standards and Safety Authority requirements and any other requirements for fuel to be delivered?				
9. Has the use of the property ever been for the growth or manufacture of illegal substances?				

ADDITIONAL COMMENTS: ....
....
....
....
....

IMPROVEMENTS AND STRUCTURAL: (Provide Applicable ADDITIONAL COMMENTS)	YES	NO	UNKNOWN	NOT APPLICABLE
1. Are you aware of any structural problems?				
2. **a)** Have you made any renovations, additions or improvements to the property?				
b) Was a building permit obtained?				
c) Has the final building inspection been approved or has a final occupancy permit been obtained?				
3. To the best of your knowledge have the building(s) ever contained ureaformaldehyde insulation?				
4. Is there vermiculite insulation on the property? If yes, has it been tested for asbestos?..				

APPENDIX

Form 820   *(continued)*

IMPROVEMENTS AND STRUCTURAL (CONT'D): (Provide Applicable ADDITIONAL COMMENTS)	YES	NO	UNKNOWN	NOT APPLICABLE
5. **a)** Are you aware of any deficiencies or non-compliance with the Ontario Fire Code?				
b) Is your property equipped with operational smoke detectors?				
c) Is the property equipped with operational carbon monoxide detectors?				
6. **a)** Is the woodstove(s)/chimney(s)/fireplace(s)/insert(s) in good working order?				
b) Has the wood energy system been **WETT** inspected? (Wood Energy Technology Transfer)				
7. Are you aware of any problems with the central air conditioning system?				
8. Are you aware of any problems with the heating system?				
9. **a)** Are you aware of any moisture and/or water problems?				
b) Are you aware of any roof leakage or unrepaired damage? Age of roof covering				
c) Are you aware of any damage due to wind, fire, flood, insects, termites, rodents, pets or wood rot?				
d) Have any repairs been carried out to correct any past or present problems related to (a), (b) and/or (c)? If yes, explain in additional comments below..				
10. **a)** Are you aware of any problems with the electrical system? Size of service...................................				
b) Type of wiring: ☐ copper ☐ aluminium ☐ knob-and-tube ☐ other..				
11. Are you aware of any problems with the plumbing system?				
12. Is there any lead, galvanized metal, cast iron or Kitec plumbing on the property?				
13. Are you aware of any problems with the swimming pool, sauna, hot tub, jet bathtub or lawn sprinkler system?				

ADDITIONAL COMMENTS: ....

....

....

....

....

....

Schedule(s) attached hereto and forming part of this Statement include: ....

Residential Information Checklist
Condominium

Form 821
for use in the Province of Ontario

Schedule is attached to and forms part of the Residential Information Checklist (Form #820) for:

PROPERTY:

DATE:

CONDOMINIUM CORPORATION: (Provide Applicable ADDITIONAL COMMENTS)	YES	NO	UNKNOWN	NOT APPLICABLE
1. **a)** Condominium fee $...				
b) Condominium fee includes:				
c) Cost for amenities not included in Condominium fee $ .... Details				
2. Are there any special assessments approved or contemplated?				
3. Have you received any written notice of lawsuit(s) pending?				
4. Have you been informed of any notices, claims, work orders or deficiency notices affecting the common elements received from any person or any public body?				
5. **a)** Has a reserve fund study been completed? Date of Study				
b) Approximate amount of reserve fund as of last notification $...........				
6. **a)** Are there any restrictions on pets?				
b) Are there any restrictions on renting the property?				
c) Are there any other restrictions on the use of the property?				
7. **a)** If any renovations, additions or improvements were made to the unit and/or common elements, was approval of the Condominium Corporation obtained?				
b) Is approval of any prospective buyer required by the Condominium Corporation?				
c) Are any other approvals required by the Condominium Corporation or Property Manager? If yes, specify:				
d) Name of Property Management Company				
8. Are there any pending rule or by-law amendments which may alter or restrict the uses of the property?				
9. Is the Condominium registered?				
10. Parking: Number of Spaces .... ☐ Owned ☐ Exclusive Use ☐ Leased or Licensed Parking space number(s)..				
11. Locker:.. ☐ Owned ☐ Exclusive Use Locker number(s)				
12. a) Amenities: ☐ Pool ☐ Sauna ☐ Exercise Room ☐ Meeting/Party Room ☐ Boat Docking ☐ Guest Parking ☐ Other......................				
b) Are you aware of any problems with any of the common element amenities? If yes, specify:				

ADDITIONAL COMMENTS: ....
....
....
....

APPENDIX

 **Ontario Real Estate Association**

Form 822
for use in the Province of Ontario

Residential Information Checklist
Water Supply, Waste Disposal, Access, Shoreline, Utilities

This Schedule is attached to and forms part of the Residential Information Checklist (Form #820) for:

PROPERTY:

DATE:

WATER SUPPLY AND WASTE DISPOSAL: (Provide Applicable ADDITIONAL COMMENTS)	YES	NO	UNKNOWN	NOT APPLICABLE
1. a) What is your water source? ☐ Municipal ☐ Drilled ☐ Bored ☐ Dug ☐ Cistern ☐ Lake ☐ Community ☐ Shared ☐ Other				
b) If your water source is Community/Shared, is there a transferrable written agreement?				
c) Are you aware of any problem re: quantity of water? (If yes, explain below)				
d) Are you aware of any problems re: quality of water? (If yes, explain below)				
e) Do you have any water treatment devices?				
f) Is your water system operable year round?　Heated lines?　☐ Yes　☐ No				
g) Date and result of most recent water test..................................				
h) Are any documents available for the well?				
If yes, specify				
i) Does the property have any abandoned well(s)?				
2. a) What kind of sewage disposal system services the property? ☐ Municipal ☐ Septic tank with tile bed ☐ Holding tank ☐ Other (Explain below)				
b) Are you aware of any problems with the sewage system? Date septic/holding tank last pumped.................. Age of system				
c) What documentation for the sewage system is available? ☐ Use Permit ☐ Location Sketch ☐ Maintenance Records ☐ Inspection Certificate ☐ Other				
3. Are all the well(s), water line(s) and waste disposal system(s) within the boundaries of the subject property?				

ACCESS, SHORELINE, UTILITIES: (Provide Applicable ADDITIONAL COMMENTS)	YES	NO	UNKNOWN	NOT APPLICABLE
1. a) Is property access by municipal road? If yes;　☐ Open all year　☐ Seasonally open				
b) Is the property serviced by a private road?　Cost $............................ per year.				
2. If your access is across private property, access is:　☐ Right of way　☐ Deeded ☐ Other ....　Cost $........................... per year.				
3. a) If water access only, access is:　☐ Deeded　☐ Leased　☐ Other (Explain below)				
b) Water access cost of: Parking $............................ Dock $............................ per year.				
4. a) Is the original Shore Road Allowance owned?				
b) Are there any pending applications for shoreline improvement?				
c) Are there any disputes concerning the shoreline or improvements on the shoreline?				
d) Are there any structures or docks on the original Shore Road Allowance?				
e) Is the original Road Allowance included in the lot size?				
5. Does the boundary of the property extend beyond the water line? If yes, explain below.				
6. a) Is hydro available to the property?				
b) Is the owner responsible for the installation, replacement/maintenance of any utility poles/equipment?				

ADDITIONAL COMMENTS: ....

....

....

....

Form 822　New 2015　**Page 1 of 1**

Form 823   *Residential Information Checklist—Rental or Lease—Fixture(s)/Chattel(s) Included*   Page 1 of 1

Form 823
for use in the Province of Ontario

Residential Information Checklist
Rental or Lease - Fixture(s)/Chattel(s) Included

REAL PROPERTY:

DATE:

FIXTURE/CHATTEL	OWNED	RENTED	LEASED	Amount $	ASSUMABLE	N/A	TERMS OF CONTRACT
1. Water Tank	☐	☐	☐		☐	☐	
2. Furnace	☐	☐	☐		☐	☐	
3. Water Softener	☐	☐	☐		☐	☐	
4. Alarm System	☐	☐	☐		☐	☐	
5. Air Conditioner	☐	☐	☐		☐	☐	
6. Heat Pump	☐	☐	☐		☐	☐	
7. Other.....................	☐	☐	☐		☐	☐	
8. Other.....................	☐	☐	☐		☐	☐	
9. Other.....................	☐	☐	☐		☐	☐	
10. Other...................	☐	☐	☐		☐	☐	

Terms of Contract details (provide fixture/chattel number) ....

....

....

....

ADDITIONAL COMMENTS ....

....

....

....

Form 823   New 2016   **Page 1 of 1**

 **Ontario Real Estate Association**

Green Information Checklist
Residential

Form 824
for use in the Province of Ontario

PROPERTY:	
DATE:	

ENERGY RATING / CERTIFICATE
(Check all that apply, certificate required)

	Rate / Certificate	Date
☐ EnerGuide	....	.... / .... / ....
☐ R-2000	....	.... / .... / ....
☐ LEED (Certified, Silver, Gold, Platinum)	....	.... / .... / ....
☐ Energy Star	....	.... / .... / ....
☐ BOMA Go Green	....	.... / .... / ....
☐ Green Globes	....	.... / .... / ....
☐ Green Standard	....	.... / .... / ....
☐ Other:..	....	.... / .... / ....

APPLIANCES AND COMPONENTS INCLUDED
(The Energy/Guide Label does not indicate an Energy Star Rated Efficient Appliance)

☐ Energy Star-rated Dishwasher　　　　☐ Energy Star-rated Room Air Conditioner
☐ Energy Star-rated Refrigerator　　　　☐ Energy Star-rated Dehumidifier
☐ Energy Star-rated Microwave　　　　　☐ Energy Star-rated Clothes Washer
☐ Energy Star-rated Stove/Oven　　　　　☐ Energy Star-rated Clothes Dryer
☐ Energy Star-rated Freezer　　　　　　　☐ Clothesline Internal/External (where permitted)

☐ Other: ....

ENERGY SOURCE

☐ Electric On-The-Grid　　　　　　☐ Solar Photovoltaic System
☐ Electric Partial-Grid　　　　　　☐ Wind Turbine
☐ Electric Off-The-Grid　　　　　　☐ FIT (Ontario Power Authority program)
　　　　　　　　　　　　　　　　　☐ micro FIT (Ontario Power Authority program)

☐ Other: ....

LIGHTING

☐ Automatic control system for lighting　　☐ Solar powered walkway or outdoor lighting area
☐ Natural day lighting　　　　　　　　　　☐ Solar / Sun tubes(s)
☐ Skylights　　　　　　　　　　　　　　　☐ Compact Fluorescent Lighting
　　　　　　　　　　　　　　　　　　　　☐ LED Lighting

☐ Other: ....

Form 824　New 2015　**Page 1 of 4**

Form 824   *(continued)*

VENTILATION (specify quantity where appropriate)

☐ Ventilation System
☐ Whole House Fan
☐ Heat Recovery Ventilator

☐ Other: ....

____ No. of Ceiling Fan(s)
☐ HEPA Air Filtration Unit
☐ Natural Ventilation System
☐ Solar Attic Fan

SPACE COOLING & HEATING

☐ Geothermal Heat Pump
☐ Heat Pump, Energy Star Rated
☐ Passive cooling & heating
☐ Cooling - Evaporative cooling (swamp cooler)
☐ Cooling - High SEER air conditioner (13 or higher)
☐ Overhangs above south-facing windows
☐ Heating - 90% or higher energy efficiency furnace

☐ Other: ....

☐ Heating - 90% or higher energy efficiency boiler
☐ Heating - Active solar heating
☐ Heating - Baseboard hot water heat
☐ Heating - Radiant floor heating
☐ Heating - Solar water heating
☐ HVAC zones
☐ Programmable Thermostats
☐ Heat Recovery Ventilator

WATER CONSERVATION (specify quantity where appropriate)

☐ On Demand Hot Water Heater
☐ Hot Water Heat Recovery
____ No. of Low Flush Toilet(s)
____ No. of Dual Flush Toilet(s)
☐ Waterless Urinals
____ No. of Low Flow Faucets

☐ Other: ....

____ No. of Infrared No-Touch Faucets
____ No. of Low Flow Shower Heads
☐ Solar Heated Hot Water
☐ Grey Water Recovery System
☐ Rainwater Collection and Purification System
☐ Hot Water Recirculation Pump
☐ Solar Pool Heating Collectors

INSULATION

Basement

☐ R-Value:____ (Minimum R13) (Higher Number = Better Insulation Value)

☐ Cellulose - Post Consumer Recycled Content
☐ Formaldehyde-Free Insulation
☐ Natural Fibre
☐ Structural Insulated Panels

Ceiling and Attic

☐ R-Value:____ (Minimum R38) (Higher Number = Better Insulation Value)

☐ Cellulose - Post Consumer Recycled Content
☐ Formaldehyde-Free Insulation
☐ Natural Fibre
☐ Soy Based Spray Foam
☐ Spray Foam
☐ Hatch To Attic Space (weather stripped and insulated)

Floors

☐ R-Value:____ (Higher Number = Better Insulation Value)

☐ Cellulose - Post Consumer Recycled Content
☐ Foam Board
☐ Sub-Floor Modular Insulated Panel
☐ Cork Board
☐ Rigid Board Insulation

APPENDIX

Walls

☐ R-Value:____ (Minimum R11) (Higher Number = Better Insulation Value)
   ☐ Cellulose - Post Consumer Recycled Content
   ☐ Formaldehyde-Free Insulation
   ☐ Natural Fibre
   ☐ Cork Board
   ☐ Rigid Board Insulation
   ☐ Soy Based Spray Foam
   ☐ Spray Foam
   ☐ Structural Insulated Panels (SIPs)
   ☐ Thermal Mass Construction

☐ Other : ....

ROOF

☐ Reflective Roof Coating   ☐ Reflective Roofing - Energy Star
☐ Green Roof - Vegetation/Garden   ☐ Radiant Roof Barriers
☐ Living Roof   ☐ EPDM   ☐ TPO
☐ Metal Roofing - Recycled Content   ☐ Insulated Protective Membrane
                                             ☐ Solar Shingles

☐ Other: ....

WINDOWS & DOORS

☐ Energy Star Windows, Climate Zone _B_   ☐ Energy Star Doors, Climate Zone _B_
☐ Energy-efficient Window Coatings   ☐ Low-E Window Coating
☐ Window Frames Highest Insulation   ☐ Spectrally Selective Glass
                                             ☐ Space Filling Foam

☐ Other: ....

FINISHES

☐ Flooring Alternatives: ☐ Salvaged Wood Flooring
   ☐ Locally Sourced   ☐ Green Carpet
   ☐ Bamboo Flooring   ☐ Marmoleum
   ☐ Cork Flooring   ☐ Refaced Cupboards
☐ Recycled Content Countertops   ☐ Low VOC Paint (Green Seal Certified Product)
                                             ☐ Organic Based Clay (Used as an alternative to paint)

☐ Other: ....

BUILDING MATERIALS AND TECHNIQUES

☐ Advanced Framing Techniques   ☐ Sustainable Harvested Certified Wood
☐ Building Material Reuse/Exchange   ☐ High-Ash Content Concrete Flooring
☐ Cement Board Siding   ☐ Insulating Concrete Forms
☐ House/Building Wraps - Radiant System   ☐ Straw Bale Construction
☐ Natural Fibre Insulation   ☐ Earthen Built/Rammed Earth
   (Recycled Blue Jean Material or Other Recycled Natural Content)   ☐ Straw Bale Construction
☐ Recycled Building Materials   ☐ Adobe
☐ Recycled Content Dry Wall   ☐ Reclaimed Metal Construction

☐ Other: ....

RECYCLING

☐ Built In Recycling (storage)   ☐ Outdoor Recycling Storage
☐ Built In Composting Centre (green storage) ☐ Composting Box

LANDSCAPING

☐ Bioswale for storm water
☐ Composite & plastic decking material-recycled content
☐ Composite & plastic fencing material-recycled content
☐ Restore and enhance natural vegetation & native plants
☐ Integrated pest management (NON CHEMICAL)

☐ Other: ....

☐ Mulch - locally produced "green waste"
☐ Natural water / drainage features
☐ Permeable Paving Stones
☐ Rain Garden Feature for Run Off
☐ Rainwater Barrel Collection

SURROUNDING ENVIRONMENT & MISC.

☐ Cover for wildlife
☐ Curb side recycling
☐ Parks and public lands within 2 kilometres

☐ Other: ....

☐ Deciduous Shade Trees
☐ Recycling facilities within 2 kilometres
☐ Public transportation designated stop within 500 metres

ORIENTATION AND SITE PLACEMENT

☐ Earth bermed

☐ Other: ....

☐ Passive solar design

ADDITIONAL COMMENTS:

....
....
....
....
....
....
....
....
....
....
....
....
....
....

Schedule(s) attached hereto and forming part of this Statement include: ....

APPENDIX

Buyer Representation Agreement
Authority for Purchase or Lease

Form 300
for use in the Province of Ontario

This is an Exclusive Buyer Representation Agreement

BETWEEN:

BROKERAGE: ...., Tel.No. (..........)..................................

ADDRESS: ....

.... Fax.No. (..........)..................................

hereinafter referred to as the Brokerage.

AND:

BUYER(S):..., hereinafter referred to as the Buyer,

ADDRESS: ....

Street Number   Street Name

MUNICIPALITY: .... **POSTAL CODE:** ....

The Buyer hereby gives the Brokerage the **exclusive and irrevocable authority** to act as the Buyer's agent

commencing at .... a.m./p.m. on the .... day of ...., 20.................,

and expiring at 11:59 p.m. on the .... day of ...., 20.................(Expiry Date),

{ Buyer acknowledges that the time period for this Agreement is negotiable between the Buyer and the Brokerage, however, in accordance with the Real Estate and Business Brokers Act of Ontario (2002), **if the time period for this Agreement exceeds six months, the Brokerage must obtain the Buyer's initials.** } ⬭ *(Buyer's Initials)*

for the purpose of locating a real property meeting the following general description:

Property Type (Use): ....

....

Geographic Location: ....

....

The Buyer hereby warrants that the Buyer is not a party to a buyer representation agreement with any other registered real estate brokerage for the purchase or lease of a real property of the general description indicated above.

1. **DEFINITIONS AND INTERPRETATIONS:** For the purposes of this Buyer Representation Agreement ("Authority" or "Agreement"), "Buyer" includes purchaser and tenant, a "seller" includes a vendor, a landlord or a prospective seller, vendor or landlord and a "real estate board" includes a real estate association. A purchase shall be deemed to include the entering into of any agreement to exchange, or the obtaining of an option to purchase which is subsequently exercised, and a lease includes any rental agreement, sub-lease or renewal of a lease. This Agreement shall be read with all changes of gender or number required by the context. For purposes of this Agreement, Buyer shall be deemed to include any spouse, heirs, executors, administrators, successors, assigns, related corporations and affiliated corporations. Related corporations or affiliated corporations shall include any corporation where one half or a majority of the shareholders, directors or officers of the related or affiliated corporation are the same person(s) as the shareholders, directors, or officers of the corporation introduced to or shown the property.

2. **COMMISSION:** In consideration of the Brokerage undertaking to assist the Buyer, the Buyer agrees to pay commission to the Brokerage as follows: If, during the currency of this Agreement, the Buyer enters into an agreement to purchase or lease a real property of the general description indicated above, the Buyer agrees the Brokerage is entitled to receive and retain any commission offered by a listing brokerage or by the seller. The Buyer understands that the amount of commission offered by a listing brokerage or by the seller may be greater or less than the commission stated below. The Buyer understands that the Brokerage will inform the Buyer of the amount of commission to be paid to the Brokerage by the listing brokerage or the seller at the earliest practical opportunity. The Buyer acknowledges that the payment of any commission by the listing brokerage or the seller will not make the Brokerage either the agent or sub-agent of the listing brokerage or the seller.

INITIALS OF BROKERAGE: ⬭   INITIALS OF BUYER(S): ⬭

Form 300   *(continued)*   Page 2 of 3

If, during the currency of this Agreement, the Buyer enters into an agreement to purchase any property of the general description indicated above,

the Buyer agrees that the Brokerage is entitled to be paid a commission of .... % of the sale price of the property

or ....

or for a lease, a commission of ....

The Buyer agrees to pay directly to the Brokerage any deficiency between this amount and the amount, if any, to be paid to the Brokerage by a listing brokerage or by the seller. The Buyer understands that if the Brokerage is not to be paid any commission by a listing brokerage or by the seller, the Buyer will pay the Brokerage the full amount of commission indicated above.

The Buyer agrees to pay the Brokerage such commission if the Buyer enters into an agreement within .... days after the expiration of this Agreement (Holdover Period) to purchase or lease any real property shown or introduced to the Buyer from any source whatsoever during the term of this Agreement, provided, however, that if the Buyer enters into a new buyer representation agreement with another registered real estate brokerage after the expiration of this Agreement, the Buyer's liability to pay commission to the Brokerage shall be reduced by the amount paid to the other brokerage under the new agreement.

The Buyer agrees to pay such commission as described above even if a transaction contemplated by an agreement to purchase or lease agreed to or accepted by the Buyer or anyone on the Buyer's behalf is not completed, if such non-completion is owing or attributable to the Buyers default or neglect. Said commission, plus any applicable taxes, shall be payable on the date set for completion of the purchase of the property or, in the case of a lease or tenancy, the earlier of the date of occupancy by the tenant or the date set for commencement of the lease or tenancy. All amounts set out as commission are to be paid plus applicable taxes on such commission.

This Agreement applies for the purchase or lease of one real property. Notwithstanding the foregoing, in the event that the Buyer leases a property, this agreement remains in force as set out herein for the purchase of the leased property or a property of the general description indicated above. The leasing of a property by the Buyer does not terminate this Agreement with respect to the purchase of a property.

3.   **REPRESENTATION:** The Buyer acknowledges that the Brokerage has provided the Buyer with written information explaining agency relationships, including information on Seller Representation, Sub-Agency, Buyer Representation, Multiple Representation and Customer Service. The Brokerage shall assist the Buyer in locating a real property of the general description indicated above and shall represent the Buyer in an endeavour to procure the acceptance of an agreement to purchase or lease such a property.

The Buyer acknowledges that the Buyer may not be shown or offered all properties that may be of interest to the Buyer. The Buyer hereby agrees that the terms of any buyer's offer or agreement to purchase or lease the property will not be disclosed to any other buyer. The Buyer further acknowledges that the Brokerage may be entering into buyer representation agreements with other buyers who may be interested in the same or similar properties that the Buyer may be interested in buying or leasing and the Buyer hereby consents to the Brokerage entering into buyer representation agreements with other buyers who may be interested in the same or similar properties without any claim by the Buyer of conflict of interest. The Buyer hereby appoints the Brokerage as agent for the purpose of giving and receiving notices pursuant to any offer or agreement to purchase or lease a property negotiated by the Brokerage.

MULTIPLE REPRESENTATION: The Buyer hereby acknowledges that the Brokerage may be entering into listing agreements with sellers of properties the Buyer may be interested in buying or leasing. In the event that the Brokerage has entered into or enters into a listing agreement with the seller of a property the Buyer may be interested in buying or leasing, the Brokerage will obtain the Buyer's written consent to represent both the Buyer and the seller for the transaction at the earliest practicable opportunity and in all cases prior to any offer to purchase or lease being submitted or presented.

The Buyer understands and acknowledges that the Brokerage must be impartial when representing both the Buyer and the seller and equally protect the interests of the Buyer and the seller in the transaction. The Buyer understands and acknowledges that when representing both the Buyer and the seller, the Brokerage shall have a duty of full disclosure to both the Buyer and the seller, including a requirement to disclose all factual information about the property known to the Brokerage.

However, The Buyer further understands and acknowledges that the Brokerage shall not disclose:
- that the seller may or will accept less than the listed price, unless otherwise instructed in writing by the seller;
- that the Buyer may or will pay more than the offered price, unless otherwise instructed in writing by the Buyer;
- the motivation of or personal information about the Buyer or seller, unless otherwise instructed in writing by the party to which the information applies or unless failure to disclose would constitute fraudulent, unlawful or unethical practice;
- the price the Buyer should offer or the price the seller should accept; and
- the Brokerage shall not disclose to the Buyer the terms of any other offer.

However, it is understood that factual market information about comparable properties and information known to the Brokerage concerning potential uses for the property will be disclosed to both Buyer and seller to assist them to come to their own conclusions.

Where a Brokerage represents both the Seller and the Buyer (multiple representation), the Brokerage shall not be entitled or authorized to be agent for either the Buyer or the Seller for the purpose of giving and receiving notices.

MULTIPLE REPRESENTATION AND CUSTOMER SERVICE: The Buyer understands and agrees that the Brokerage also provides representation and customer service to other buyers and sellers. If the Brokerage represents or provides customer service to more than one seller or buyer for the same trade, the Brokerage shall, in writing, at the earliest practicable opportunity and before any offer is made, inform all sellers and buyers of the nature of the Brokerage's relationship to each seller and buyer.

4.   **REFERRAL OF PROPERTIES:** The Buyer agrees that during the currency of this Buyer Representation Agreement the Buyer will act in good faith and work exclusively with the Brokerage for the purchase or lease of a real property of the general description indicated above. The Buyer agrees that, during the currency of this Agreement, the Buyer shall advise the Brokerage immediately of any property of interest to the Buyer that came to the Buyer's attention from any source whatsoever, and all offers to purchase or lease submitted by the Buyer shall be submitted through the Brokerage to the seller. If the Buyer arranges a valid agreement to purchase or lease any property of the general description indicated above that came to the attention of the Buyer during the currency of this Agreement and the Buyer arranges said agreement during the currency of this Agreement or within the Holdover Period after expiration of this Agreement, the Buyer agrees to pay the Brokerage the amount of commission set out above in Paragraph 2 of this Agreement, payable within (5) days following the Brokerage's written demand therefor.

INITIALS OF BROKERAGE: (⬭)   **INITIALS OF BUYER(S):** (⬭)

Form 300   Revised 2015   **Page 2 of 3**

5. **INDEMNIFICATION:** The Brokerage and representatives of the Brokerage are trained in dealing in real estate but are not qualified in determining the physical condition of the land or any improvements thereon. The Buyer agrees that the Brokerage and representatives of the Brokerage will not be liable for any defects, whether latent or patent, to the land or improvements thereon. All information supplied by the seller or landlord or the listing brokerage may not have been verified and is not warranted by the Brokerage as being accurate and will be relied on by the Buyer at the Buyer's own risk. The Buyer acknowledges having been advised to make their own enquiries to confirm the condition of the property.

6. **FINDERS FEE:** The Buyer acknowledges that the Brokerage may be receiving a finder's fee, reward and/or referral incentive, and the Buyer consents to any such benefit being received and retained by the Brokerage in addition to the commission as described above.

7. **CONSUMER REPORTS:** The Buyer is hereby notified that a Consumer Report containing credit and/or personal information may be referred to in connection with this Agreement and any subsequent transaction.

8. **USE AND DISTRIBUTION OF INFORMATION:** The Buyer consents to the collection, use and disclosure of personal information by the Brokerage for such purposes that relate to the real estate services provided by the Brokerage to the Buyer including, but not limited to: locating, assessing and qualifying properties for the Buyer; advertising on behalf of the Buyer; providing information as needed to third parties retained by the Buyer to assist in a transaction (e.g. financial institutions, building inspectors, etc...); and such other use of the Buyer's information as is consistent with the services provided by the Brokerage in connection with the purchase or prospective purchase of the property.

    The Buyer agrees that the sale and related information regarding any property purchased by the Buyer through the Brokerage may be retained and disclosed by the Brokerage and/or real estate board(s) (if the property is an MLS® Listing) for reporting, appraisal and statistical purposes and for such other use of the information as the Brokerage and/or board deems appropriate in connection with the listing, marketing and selling of real estate, including conducting comparative market analyses.

    The Buyer acknowledges that the information, personal or otherwise ("information"), provided to the real estate board or association may be stored on databases located outside of Canada, in which case the information would be subject to the laws of the jurisdiction in which the information is located.

9. **CONFLICT OR DISCREPANCY:** If there is any conflict or discrepancy between any provision added to this Agreement and any provision in the standard pre-set portion hereof, the added provision shall supersede the standard pre-set provision to the extent of such conflict or discrepancy. This Agreement, including any provisions added to this Agreement, shall constitute the entire Agreement between the Buyer and the Brokerage. There is no representation, warranty, collateral agreement or condition, which affects this Agreement other than as expressed herein.

10. **ELECTRONIC COMMUNICATION:** This Buyer Representation Agreement and any agreements, notices or other communications contemplated thereby may be transmitted by means of electronic systems, in which case signatures shall be deemed to be original. The transmission of this Agreement by the Buyer by electronic means shall be deemed to confirm the Buyer has retained a true copy of the Agreement.

11. **SCHEDULE(S):**.. attached hereto form(s) part of this Agreement.

THE BROKERAGE AGREES TO REPRESENT THE BUYER IN LOCATING A REAL PROPERTY OF THE GENERAL DESCRIPTION INDICATED ABOVE IN AN ENDEAVOUR TO OBTAIN THE ACCEPTANCE OF AN AGREEMENT TO PURCHASE OR LEASE A PROPERTY ON TERMS SATISFACTORY TO THE BUYER.

....   DATE...................................   ....
(Authorized to bind the Brokerage)   (Name of Person Signing)

THIS AGREEMENT HAS BEEN READ AND FULLY UNDERSTOOD BY ME AND I ACKNOWLEDGE THIS DATE I HAVE SIGNED UNDER SEAL. Any representations contained herein are true to the best of my knowledge, information and belief.

SIGNED, SEALED AND DELIVERED I have hereunto set my hand and seal:

....   ● DATE...................................   ....
(Signature of Buyer)   (Seal)   (Tel. No.)

....   ● DATE...................................   ....
(Signature of Buyer)   (Seal)

DECLARATION OF INSURANCE

The broker/salesperson ....
(Name of Broker/Salesperson)
hereby declares that he/she is insured as required by the Real Estate and Business Brokers Act (REBBA) and Regulations.

....
(Signature(s) of Broker/Salesperson)

ACKNOWLEDGEMENT

The Buyer(s) hereby acknowledge that the Buyer(s) fully understand the terms of this Agreement and have received a true copy of this Agreement

on the .... day of ...., 20 ....

....   Date:...
(Signature of Buyer)

....   Date:...
(Signature of Buyer)

 **Ontario Real Estate Association**

Form 301
for use in the Province of Ontario

Cancellation of
Buyer Representation Agreement

TO:

BROKERAGE: ....

FROM:

BUYER: ....

RE: Buyer Representation Agreement between the Buyer and the Brokerage signed by the Buyer on the .... day of ....,

20............ and that was to continue in effect until the.................day of ....,20...............

I hereby request the cancellation of this Buyer Representation Agreement for the following reasons:

....

....

....

....

....

The cancellation of this Agreement will take effect only when approved and signed below by the Broker of Record/Manager of the Brokerage Firm.

This Cancellation Agreement shall be null and void if, prior to the expiry of the Authority and Holdover Period of the Buyer Representation Agreement, the Buyer enters into an agreement to purchase or lease a property that came to the attention of the Buyer after the commencement and before the cancellation of the Buyer Representation Agreement. Subject to this restriction, and the requirement for the signature of the Broker of Record/Manager below, the Buyer and the Brokerage are released from the remaining term of the Buyer Representation Agreement.

....
(Signature of Buyer)   (Date)

....
(Signature of Buyer)   (Date)

The Brokerage hereby agrees to the cancellation of the Buyer Representation Agreement:

....
(Signature of Broker of Record/Manager)   (Date)

....
(Name of Brokerage)   (Address)

APPENDIX

 **Ontario Real Estate Association**

Assignment of Buyer Representation Agreement

Form 302
for use in the Province of Ontario

RE: BUYER REPRESENTATION AGREEMENT BETWEEN:

BUYER: ....

AND:

BROKERAGE: ....

AGREEMENT EXPIRY DATE: ....

The Brokerage for the above described Buyer Representation Agreement assigns, transfers and sets over to:

.... (the "Assignee")
any and all interest in the Buyer Representation Agreement, including all rights, duties and obligations pursuant to the Agreement. The Brokerage releases the Buyer from any claims of remuneration or compensation with respect to this Buyer Representation Agreement.

For the purposes of this Assignment of Buyer Representation Agreement, "Buyer" includes purchaser, tenant and lessee.

This Assignment of Buyer Representation Agreement is to be effective at 12:01 a.m., the .... day of ....,20..........
(Effective Date) **provided that this Assignment of Buyer Representation Agreement has been executed by both the Buyer and the Assignee and a copy of the signed Agreement is returned to the Brokerage prior to the Effective Date.** The above described Buyer Representation Agreement remains in full force with the Brokerage until this Assignment of Buyer Representation Agreement becomes effective.

SIGNED, SEALED AND DELIVERED in the presence of: IN WITNESS whereof I have hereunto set my hand and seal:

....
(Name of Brokerage Firm)

.... ● DATE ....
(Witness)   (Signature of Broker of Record/Manager)   (Seal)

The Buyer hereby consents to the Assignment and releases the Brokerage from any and all liabilities, covenants, obligations and claims arising out of the Buyer Representation Agreement

SIGNED, SEALED AND DELIVERED in the presence of: IN WITNESS whereof I have hereunto set my hand and seal:

.... ● DATE ....
(Witness)   (Buyer)   (Seal)

.... ● DATE ....
(Witness)   (Buyer)   (Seal)

The Assignee hereby agrees to assume responsibility for and perform any and all duties and obligations of the Brokerage pursuant to the said Buyer Representation Agreement.

SIGNED, SEALED AND DELIVERED in the presence of: IN WITNESS whereof I have hereunto set my hand and seal:

....
(Name of Assignee Brokerage)

.... ● DATE ....
(Witness)   (Signature of Assignee Broker of Record/Manager) (Seal)

Form 302   Revised 2008   **Page 1 of 1**

APPENDIX

OREA Ontario Real Estate Association

Amendment to Buyer Representation Agreement

Form 305
for use in the Province of Ontario

RE: BUYER REPRESENTATION AGREEMENT

BETWEEN:

BUYER: ....
AND
BROKERAGE: ....

BUYER REGISTRATION NUMBER(S) (if applicable): ....

EXPIRY DATE: ....

The Buyer and the Brokerage hereby agree that the above described Buyer Representation Agreement is amended as stated below:

---

1. EXPIRY DATE:

    New Expiry Date .... **Former** Expiry Date ....

    Buyer acknowledges that the length of the Agreement is negotiable between the Buyer and the Brokerage, however, in accordance with the Real Estate and Business Brokers Act of Ontario (2002), **if the Agreement exceeds six months from the date of this Amendment, the Brokerage must obtain the Buyer's initials.**

    (Buyer's Initials)

---

2. OTHER AMENDMENTS: ....

....

....

....

....

All other terms and provisions of the Buyer Representation Agreement remain in full force and effect.

An extension of the expiry date must be signed and dated prior to expiration of the Agreement.

The Brokerage agrees to immediately notify the Real Estate Board(s) of the amendment(s) in accordance with the Real Estate Board Rules and Regulations, provided that this Agreement is registered with the Real Estate Board.

This Amendment to Agreement shall not take effect unless signed by all parties set out below.

For the purposes of this Amendment to Buyer Representation Agreement, "Buyer" includes purchaser, tenant and lessee and Real Estate Board(s) includes Real Estate Association(s).

SIGNED, SEALED AND DELIVERED I have hereunto set my hand and seal:

.... ● DATE ....
(Buyer)   (Seal)

.... ● DATE ....
(Buyer)   (Seal)

....
(Name of Brokerage)

.... DATE ....
(Authorized to bind the Brokerage)   (Print Name of Person Signing)

Form 305   Revised 2008   **Page 1 of 1**

OREA Ontario Real Estate Association

Form 310
for use in the Province of Ontario

Buyer Customer Service Agreement
For Use When the Buyer is Not Represented
By the Brokerage

This Is A Non-Exclusive Buyer Customer Service Agreement

BETWEEN:

BROKERAGE:.., Tel.No. (...........)..................................

ADDRESS:...

.... Fax.No. (...........)..................................

hereinafter referred to as the Brokerage.

AND:

BUYER(S):.., hereinafter referred to as the

Buyer, for the purpose of locating a real property meeting the following general description:

Property Type (Use):...

....

Geographic Location:..

....

In consideration of the Brokerage providing customer service to the Buyer for the purchase or lease of a real property of the general description indicated above, the Buyer acknowledges and agrees to the terms as stated in this Agreement.

This non-exclusive Buyer Customer Service Agreement:

commences at..........................a.m./p.m. on the.................................day of.., 20..............,

and expires at 11:59 p.m. on the..............................day of.., 20..............(Expiry Date).

{ Buyer acknowledges that the time period for this Agreement is negotiable between the Buyer and the Brokerage, however, in accordance with the Real Estate and Business Brokers Act of Ontario (2002), **if the time period for this Agreement exceeds six months, the Brokerage must obtain the Buyer's initials.** }

( ) (Buyer's Initials)

The Buyer hereby warrants that the Buyer is not a party to a buyer representation agreement with any other registered real estate brokerage for the purchase or lease of a real property of the general description indicated above.

1. **DEFINITIONS AND INTERPRETATIONS:** For the purposes of this Buyer Customer Service Agreement ("Authority" or "Agreement"), "Buyer" includes purchaser and tenant, a "seller" includes a vendor, a landlord or a prospective seller, vendor or landlord and a "real estate board" includes a real estate association. A purchase shall be deemed to include the entering into of any agreement to exchange, or the obtaining of an option to purchase which is subsequently exercised, and a lease includes any rental agreement, sub-lease or renewal of a lease. This Agreement shall be read with all changes of gender or number required by the context.

2. **COMMISSION:** For a Buyer Customer Service Agreement between Buyer and Brokerage, there is no requirement for the Buyer to pay the Brokerage compensation for the customer service provided by the Brokerage, unless otherwise agreed to in writing.

3. **REPRESENTATION AND CUSTOMER SERVICE:** The Buyer acknowledges that the Brokerage has provided the Buyer with written information explaining agency relationships, including information on Seller Representation, Sub-Agency, Buyer Representation, Multiple Representation and Customer Service. The Buyer acknowledges that the Brokerage will be providing customer service to the Buyer and will not be representing the interests of the Buyer in a transaction. The Brokerage may be representing the interests of the seller as an agent or sub-agent. When the Brokerage is representing the seller, the seller is considered to be the Brokerage's client, and the Brokerage's primary duties are to protect and promote the interests of the seller/client. The Brokerage will disclose all pertinent information to a seller/client obtained from or about the Buyer.

   Even though the Brokerage's primary duties may be to the seller, the Brokerage may provide many valuable customer services to the Buyer.

   When providing customer service to the Buyer, the Brokerage's duties to the Buyer include:
   - the **Ethical** duty to deal fairly, honestly and with integrity;
   - the **Legal** duty to exercise due care when answering questions and providing information; and
   - the **Legal** duty to avoid misrepresentation.

   The Buyer acknowledges that the Buyer may not be shown or offered all properties that may be of interest to the Buyer. The Buyer hereby agrees that the terms of any buyer's offer or agreement to purchase or lease the property will not be disclosed to any other buyer.

   The Buyer understands and agrees that the Brokerage also provides representation and customer service to other buyers and sellers. If the Brokerage represents or provides customer service to more than one seller or buyer for the same trade, the Brokerage shall, in writing, at the earliest practicable opportunity and before any offer is made, inform all sellers and buyers of the nature of the Brokerage's relationship to each seller and buyer.

INITIALS OF BROKERAGE: ( )   **INITIALS OF BUYER(S):** ( )

Form 310 Revised 2015 **Page 1 of 2**

Form 310   *(continued)*   Page 2 of 2

4. **INDEMNIFICATION:** The Brokerage and representatives of the Brokerage are trained in dealing in real estate but are not qualified in determining the physical condition of the land or any improvements thereon. The Buyer agrees that the Brokerage and representatives of the Brokerage will not be liable for any defects, whether latent or patent, to the land or improvements thereon. All information supplied by the seller or landlord or the listing brokerage may not have been verified and is not warranted by the Brokerage as being accurate and will be relied on by the Buyer at the Buyer's own risk. The Buyer acknowledges having been advised to make their own enquiries to confirm the condition of the property.

5. **FINDERS FEE:** The Buyer acknowledges that the Brokerage may be receiving a finder's fee, reward and/or referral incentive, and the Buyer consents to any such benefit being received and retained by the Brokerage in addition to the commission as described above.

6. **CONSUMER REPORTS: The Buyer is hereby notified that a Consumer Report containing credit and/or personal information may be referred to in connection with this Agreement and any subsequent transaction.**

7. **USE AND DISTRIBUTION OF INFORMATION:** The Buyer consents to the collection, use and disclosure of personal information by the Brokerage for such purposes that relate to the real estate services provided by the Brokerage to the Buyer including, but not limited to: locating, assessing and qualifying properties for the Buyer; advertising on behalf of the Buyer; providing information as needed to third parties retained by the Buyer to assist in a transaction (e.g., financial institutions, building inspectors, etc...); and such other use of the Buyer's information as is consistent with the services provided by the Brokerage in connection with the purchase or prospective purchase of the property.

    The Buyer agrees that the sale and related information regarding any property purchased by the Buyer through the Brokerage may be retained and disclosed by the Brokerage and/or real estate board(s) (if the property is an MLS® Listing) for reporting, appraisal and statistical purposes and for such other use of the information as the Brokerage and/or board deems appropriate in connection with the listing, marketing and selling of real estate, including conducting comparative market analyses.

    The Buyer acknowledges that the information, personal or otherwise ("information"), provided to the real estate board or association may be stored on databases located outside of Canada, in which case the information would be subject to the laws of the jurisdiction in which the information is located.

8. **CONFLICT OR DISCREPANCY:** If there is any conflict or discrepancy between any provision added to this Agreement and any provision in the standard pre-set portion hereof, the added provision shall supersede the standard pre-set provision to the extent of such conflict or discrepancy. This Agreement, including any provisions added to this Agreement, shall constitute the entire Agreement between the Buyer and the Brokerage. There is no representation, warranty, collateral agreement or condition, which affects this Agreement other than as expressed herein.

9. **ELECTRONIC COMMUNICATION:** This Buyer Customer Service Agreement and any agreements, notices or other communications contemplated thereby may be transmitted by means of electronic systems, in which case signatures shall be deemed to be original. The transmission of this Agreement by the Buyer by electronic means shall be deemed to confirm the Buyer has retained a true copy of the Agreement.

10. **SCHEDULE(S):** .... attached hereto form(s) part of this Agreement.

THE BROKERAGE AGREES TO ASSIST THE BUYER IN LOCATING A REAL PROPERTY OF THE GENERAL DESCRIPTION INDICATED ABOVE AND TO PROVIDE CUSTOMER SERVICE TO THE BUYER IN AN ENDEAVOUR TO PROCURE THE ACCEPTANCE OF AN AGREEMENT TO PURCHASE OR LEASE A PROPERTY ACCEPTABLE TO THE BUYER.

....   DATE....................................   ....
(Authorized to bind the Brokerage)   (Name of Person Signing)

THIS AGREEMENT HAS BEEN READ AND FULLY UNDERSTOOD BY ME AND I ACKNOWLEDGE THIS DATE I HAVE SIGNED UNDER SEAL. Any representations contained herein are true to the best of my knowledge, information and belief.

SIGNED, SEALED AND DELIVERED I have hereunto set my hand and seal:

....   (Seal)   DATE...
(Signature of Buyer)

....   (Seal)   DATE...
(Signature of Buyer)

Address...

(..............)...   (..............)...
   Tel. No.   FAX No.

DECLARATION OF INSURANCE

The broker/salesperson...
                                                          (Name of Broker/Salesperson)
hereby declares that he/she is insured as required by the Real Estate and Business Brokers Act (REBBA) and Regulations.

....
                                        (Signature(s) of Broker/Salesperson)

ACKNOWLEDGEMENT

The Buyer(s) hereby acknowledge that the Buyer(s) fully understand the terms of this Agreement and have received a true copy of this Agreement

on the .... day of ...., 20 ....

....   Date:...
(Signature of Buyer)

....   Date:...
(Signature of Buyer)

APPENDIX

OREA Ontario Real Estate Association

Confirmation of Co-operation and Representation

Form 320
for use in the Province of Ontario

BUYER: ....

SELLER: ....

For the transaction on the property known as: ....

For the purposes of this Confirmation of Co-operation and Representation, "Seller" includes a vendor, a landlord, or a prospective, seller, vendor or landlord and "Buyer" includes a purchaser, a tenant, or a prospective, buyer, purchaser or tenant, "sale" includes a lease, and "Agreement of Purchase and Sale" includes an Agreement to Lease.

The following information is confirmed by the undersigned salesperson/broker representatives of the Brokerage(s). If a Co-operating Brokerage is involved in the transaction, the brokerages agree to co-operate, in consideration of, and on the terms and conditions as set out below.

DECLARATION OF INSURANCE: The undersigned salesperson/broker representative(s) of the Brokerage(s) hereby declare that he/she is insured as required by the Real Estate and Business Brokers Act, 2002 (REBBA 2002) and Regulations.

1.   LISTING BROKERAGE

   a) ☐   The Listing Brokerage represents the interests of the Seller in this transaction. It is further understood and agreed that:

      1) ☐   The Listing Brokerage is not representing or providing Customer Service to the Buyer.
              (If the Buyer is working with a Co-operating Brokerage, Section 3 is to be completed by Co-operating Brokerage)

      2) ☐   The Listing Brokerage is providing Customer Service to the Buyer.

   b) ☐   **MULTIPLE REPRESENTATION:** The Listing Brokerage has entered into a Buyer Representation Agreement with the Buyer and represents the interests of the Seller and the Buyer, with their consent, for this transaction. The Listing Brokerage must be impartial and equally protect the interests of the Seller and the Buyer in this transaction. The Listing Brokerage has a duty of full disclosure to both the Seller and the Buyer, including a requirement to disclose all factual information about the property known to the Listing Brokerage. However, the Listing Brokerage shall not disclose:

      • That the Seller may or will accept less than the listed price, unless otherwise instructed in writing by the Seller;
      • That the Buyer may or will pay more than the offered price, unless otherwise instructed in writing by the Buyer;
      • The motivation of or personal information about the Seller or Buyer, unless otherwise instructed in writing by the party to which the information applies, or unless failure to disclose would constitute fraudulent, unlawful or unethical practice;
      • The price the Buyer should offer or the price the Seller should accept;
      • And; the Listing Brokerage shall not disclose to the Buyer the terms of any other offer.

      However, it is understood that factual market information about comparable properties and information known to the Listing Brokerage concerning potential uses for the property will be disclosed to both Seller and Buyer to assist them to come to their own conclusions.

Additional comments and/or disclosures by Listing Brokerage: (e.g. The Listing Brokerage represents more than one Buyer offering on this property.)

....

....

....

....

2.   PROPERTY SOLD BY BUYER BROKERAGE – PROPERTY NOT LISTED

   ☐   The Brokerage ....represent the Buyer and the property is not listed with any real estate brokerage. The Brokerage will be paid
              (does/does not)

         ☐   by the Seller in accordance with a Seller Customer Service Agreement

   or: ☐   by the Buyer directly

Additional comments and/or disclosures by Buyer Brokerage: (e.g. The Buyer Brokerage represents more than one Buyer offering on this property.)

....

....

....

....

INITIALS OF BUYER(S)/SELLER(S)/BROKERAGE REPRESENTATIVE(S) (Where applicable)

                  ⬭   ⬭

   BUYER   **CO-OPERATING/BUYER BROKERAGE**   **SELLER**   **LISTING BROKERAGE**

Form 320   *(continued)*   Page 2 of 2

3. **Co-operating Brokerage completes Section 3 and Listing Brokerage completes Section 1.**

    CO-OPERATING BROKERAGE- REPRESENTATION:

    a) ☐   The Co-operating Brokerage represents the interests of the Buyer in this transaction.

    b) ☐   The Co-operating Brokerage is providing Customer Service to the Buyer in this transaction.

    c) ☐   The Co-operating Brokerage is not representing the Buyer and has not entered into an agreement to provide customer service(s) to the Buyer.

    CO-OPERATING BROKERAGE- COMMISSION:

    a) ☐   The Listing Brokerage will pay the Co-operating Brokerage the commission as indicated in the MLS® information for the property

    .... to be paid from the amount paid by the Seller to the Listing Brokerage.

    (Commission As Indicated In MLS® Information)

    b) ☐   The Co-operating Brokerage will be paid as follows:

    ....

    ....

    Additional comments and/or disclosures by Co-operating Brokerage: (e.g., The Co-operating Brokerage represents more than one Buyer offering on this property.)

    ....

    ....

    ....

    Commission will be payable as described above, plus applicable taxes.

    COMMISSION TRUST AGREEMENT: If the above Co-operating Brokerage is receiving payment of commission from the Listing Brokerage, then the agreement between Listing Brokerage and Co-operating Brokerage further includes a Commission Trust Agreement, the consideration for which is the Co-operating Brokerage procuring an offer for a trade of the property, acceptable to the Seller. This Commission Trust Agreement shall be subject to and governed by the MLS® rules and regulations pertaining to commission trusts of the Listing Brokerage's local real estate board, if the local board's MLS® rules and regulations so provide. Otherwise, the provisions of the OREA recommended MLS® rules and regulations shall apply to this Commission Trust Agreement. For the purpose of this Commission Trust Agreement, the Commission Trust Amount shall be the amount noted in Section 3 above. The Listing Brokerage hereby declares that all monies received in connection with the trade shall constitute a Commission Trust and shall be held, in trust, for the Co-operating Brokerage under the terms of the applicable MLS® rules and regulations.

SIGNED BY THE BROKER/SALESPERSON REPRESENTATIVE(S) OF THE BROKERAGE(S) (Where applicable)

.... (Name of Co-operating/Buyer Brokerage)	.... (Name of Listing Brokerage)
....	....
Tel:. .... Fax:	Tel:. .... Fax: ....
.... Date:................... (Authorized to bind the Co-operating/Buyer Brokerage)	.... Date:................... (Authorized to bind the Listing Brokerage)
.... (Print Name of Broker/Salesperson Representative of the Brokerage)	.... (Print Name of Broker/Salesperson Representative of the Brokerage)

CONSENT FOR MULTIPLE REPRESENTATION (To be completed only if the Brokerage represents more than one client for the transaction)

The Buyer/Seller consent with their initials to their Brokerage representing more than one client for this transaction.

⬭ **BUYER'S INITIALS**   ⬭ **SELLER'S INITIALS**

ACKNOWLEDGEMENT

I have received, read, and understand the above information.

.... Date: .... (Signature of Buyer)	.... Date: .... (Signature of Seller)
.... Date: .... (Signature of Buyer)	.... Date: .... (Signature of Seller)

APPENDIX

Ontario Real Estate Association

Agreement To Co-Operate
(to be used Prior to Showing)

Form 651
for use in the Province of Ontario

BETWEEN: .... Listing Brokerage

AND: .... Co-operating Brokerage

RE: PROPERTY: ....

....

OWNED BY: .... as Seller/Landlord

This will confirm our Agreement that the Listing Brokerage will co-operate with listing information and will pay:

.... % of the selling price ....

As a full co-operating fee on the completion of the transaction plus applicable taxes on such commission, all in accordance with the MLS® Rules and Policies of the Real Estate Board/Association (if applicable).

This Agreement shall be subject to the following conditions:

....

....

....

MLS® No. / Excl. Listing .... with ....

Name of Board

Listing Price: $ .... Expiry Date of Listing ....

This Agreement shall expire: ....

COMMISSION TRUST AGREEMENT

To: Co-operating Brokerage shown on the foregoing Agreement to Cooperate:
Upon the Co-operating Brokerage procuring an Agreement of Purchase and Sale, and in consideration thereof, I hereby declare that all moneys received or receivable by me in connection with the Transaction as contemplated in the MLS® Rules and Regulations of my Real Estate Board/Association (if applicable) shall be receivable and held in trust. This agreement shall constitute a Commission Trust Agreement as defined in the MLS® Rules and shall be subject to and governed by the MLS® Rules pertaining to Commission Trust.
We agree to the terms and conditions as set out herein and acknowledge this date having received a true copy of this Agreement.

DATED at .... this .... day of .... 20 ....

....
Witness   Authorized to bind the Listing Brokerage   Date

....
Witness   Authorized to bind the Co-operating Brokerage   Date

Form 651   New 2015   Page 1 of 1

APPENDIX

Form 811   *Working with a REALTOR® Brochure*   Page 1 of 2

Working with a REALTOR®

The Agency Relationship

OREA Ontario Real Estate Association

When working with a REALTOR®, it is important to understand who the REALTOR® works for. To whom is the REALTOR® legally obligated?

REALTORS® are governed by the legal concept of "agency". An agent is legally obligated to look after the best interests of the person he or she represents. The agent must be loyal to that person.

A real estate brokerage may be your agent — if you have clearly established an agency relationship with that REALTOR® with a representation agreement. But often, you may assume such an obligation exists when it does not.

REALTORS® believe it is important that the people they work with understand when an agency relationship exists and when it does not — and understand what it means.

Honesty and Integrity

Most real estate professionals in our province are members of the Ontario Real Estate Association (OREA) and only members of OREA can call themselves REALTORS®.

When you work with a REALTOR®, you can expect strict adherence to provincial laws, which include a Code of Ethics. That code assures you will receive the highest level of service, honesty and integrity.

Highest Professional Standards

Before receiving a real estate registration, candidates must successfully complete an extensive course of study developed by OREA on behalf of the Real Estate Council of Ontario. That is only the beginning: in the first two years of practice, registrants are required to successfully complete three additional courses as part of their articling with an experienced broker. In addition, all registrants must continue to attend courses throughout their careers in order to maintain their registration.

Want More Information?

- Visit wedothehomework.ca
- Visit www.orea.com
- Check out homes for sale at www.realtor.ca

Other pamphlets available:
- Buying a Home
- Home Ownership Incentives
- Selling a Home

OREA

Ontario Real Estate Association

Promoting Professionalism

99 Duncan Mill Road,
Don Mills, Ontario M3B 1Z2
Telephone: 416-445-9910
Fax: 416-445-2644
Toll Free: 1-800-265-OREA (6732)
www.orea.com
info@orea.com

Form 811   for use in the Province of Ontario   Revised 2016

The REALTOR®-Consumer Relationship

In Ontario, the real estate profession is governed by the *Real Estate and Business Brokers Act, 2002*, and Associated Regulations (REBBA 2002 or Act), administered by the Real Estate Council of Ontario (RECO). All Ontario REALTORS® are registered under the Act and governed by its provisions. REBBA 2002 is consumer protection legislation, regulating the conduct of real estate brokerages and their salespeople/brokers. The Act provides consumer protection in the form of deposit insurance and requires every salesperson/broker to carry errors & omission (E&O) insurance.

When you choose to use the services of a REALTOR®, it is important to understand that this individual works on behalf of a real estate brokerage, usually a company. The brokerage is operated by a Broker of Record, who has the ultimate responsibility for the employees registered with the brokerage. When you sign a contract, it is with the brokerage, not with the salesperson/broker employee.

The Act also requires that the brokerage (usually through its REALTORS®) explain the types of service alternatives available to consumers and the services the brokerage will be providing. The brokerage must document the relationship being created between the brokerage and the consumer, and submit it to the consumer for his/her approval and signature. The most common relationships are "client" and "customer", but other options may be available in the marketplace.

Client

A "client" relationship creates the highest form of obligation for a REALTOR® to a consumer. The brokerage and its salespeople/brokers have a fiduciary (legal) relationship with the client and represent the interests of the client in a real estate transaction. The REALTOR® will establish this relationship with the use of a representation agreement, called a Listing Agreement with the seller and a Buyer Representation Agreement with the buyer. The agreement contains an explanation of the services the brokerage will be providing, the fee arrangement for those services, the obligations the client will have under the agreement, and the expiry date of the agreement.

Ensure that you have read and fully understand any such agreement before you sign the document.

Once a brokerage and a consumer enter into a client relationship, the brokerage must protect the interests of the client and do what is best for the client. A brokerage must strive for the benefit of the client and must not disclose a client's confidential information to others. Under the Act, the brokerage must also make reasonable efforts to determine any material facts relating to the transaction that would be of interest to the client and must inform the client of those facts. Although they are representing the interests of their client, they must still treat all parties to the transaction with fairness, honesty, and integrity.

Customer

A buyer or seller may not wish to be under contract as a client with the brokerage but would rather be treated as a customer. A REALTOR® is obligated to treat every person in a real estate transaction with honesty, fairness, and integrity, but unlike a client, provides a customer with a restricted level of service. Services provided to a customer may include showing the property or properties, drafting the offer, presenting the offer, etc. Brokerages use a Customer Service Agreement to document the services they are providing to a buyer or seller customer.

Under the Act, the REALTOR® has disclosure obligations to a customer and must disclose material facts known to the brokerage that relate to the transaction.

What happens when...

Buyer(s) and the seller(s) are sometimes under contract with the same brokerage when properties are being shown or an offer is being contemplated. There can also be instances when there is more than one offer on a property and more than one buyer and seller are under a representation agreement with the same brokerage. This situation is referred to as multiple representation. Under the Act, the REALTORS® and their brokerage must make sure all buyers, sellers, and their REALTORS® confirm in writing that they

acknowledge, understand, and consent to the situation before their offer is made. REALTORS® typically use what is called a Confirmation of Co-operation and Representation form to document this situation.

In offer negotiations, nerves may become frayed, so if you have any questions when reference is made to multiple representation or multiple offers, please ask your REALTOR® for an explanation.

Critical information

REALTORS® are obligated to disclose facts that may affect a buying or selling decision. It may be difficult for a REALTOR® to judge what facts are important. They also may not be in a position to know a fact. You should communicate to your REALTOR® what information and facts about a property are important to you in making a buying or selling decision, and document this information to avoid any misunderstandings and/or unpleasant surprises.

Similarly, services that are important to you and are to be performed by the brokerage, or promises that have been made to you, should be documented in your contract with the brokerage and its salesperson/broker.

To ensure the best possible real estate experience, make sure all your questions are answered by your REALTOR®. You should read and understand every contract before you finalize it.

Please note that Federal legislation requires REALTORS® to verify the identity of sellers and buyers with whom they are working.

This brochure is for information only and is not a contract. For the purposes of this information, the term "seller" can be interpreted as "landlord" and "buyer" can mean "tenant".

Acknowledgement by

_____
(Names)

I/we have read, understand, and have received a copy of the *Working with a REALTOR®* – *The Agency Relationship* brochure:

Buyers

As buyer(s), I/we understand that:

_____
(Name of Brokerage)

Initial one:

____ Is representing my interests, to be documented in a separate written agency representation agreement, and I understand the brokerage may represent and/or provide customer service to other buyers and sellers.

____ Is not representing my interests, to be documented in a separate written customer service agreement, but will act in a fair, ethical and professional manner.

_____   _____
Signature(s)   Date

Sellers

As seller(s), I/we understand that:

_____
(Name of Brokerage)

Initial one:

____ Is representing my interests, to be documented in a separate written agency representation agreement, and I understand the brokerage may represent and/or provide customer service to other sellers and buyers.

____ Is not representing my interests, to be documented in a separate written customer service agreement, but will act in a fair, ethical and professional manner.

_____   _____
Signature(s)   Date

OREA Ontario Real Estate Association

Form 500
for use in the Province of Ontario

Agreement of Purchase and Sale
Commercial

This Agreement of Purchase and Sale dated this .... day of ...., 20.......................

BUYER, ..., agrees to purchase from
(Full legal names of all Buyers)

SELLER, ..., the following
(Full legal names of all Sellers)

REAL PROPERTY:

Address ....

fronting on the .... side of ....

in the ....

and having a frontage of .... more or less by a depth of .... more or less

and legally described as ....

.... (the "property")
(Legal description of land including easements not described elsewhere)

PURCHASE PRICE: Dollars (CDN$) ....

.... Dollars

DEPOSIT: Buyer submits ....
(Herewith/Upon Acceptance/as otherwise described in this Agreement)

.... Dollars (CDN$) ....

by negotiable cheque payable to.. .... "Deposit Holder"
to be held in trust pending completion or other termination of this Agreement and to be credited toward the Purchase Price on completion. For the purposes
of this Agreement, "Upon Acceptance" shall mean that the Buyer is required to deliver the deposit to the Deposit Holder within 24 hours of the acceptance
of this Agreement. The parties to this Agreement hereby acknowledge that, unless otherwise provided for in this Agreement, the Deposit Holder shall place
the deposit in trust in the Deposit Holder's non-interest bearing Real Estate Trust Account and no interest shall be earned, received or paid on the deposit.

Buyer agrees to pay the balance as more particularly set out in Schedule A attached.

SCHEDULE(S) A ....**attached hereto form(s) part of this Agreement.**

1.   **IRREVOCABILITY:** This offer shall be irrevocable by .... until .... a.m./p.m. on
(Seller/Buyer)

     the .... day of ...., 20......................, after which time, if not accepted, this
     offer shall be null and void and the deposit shall be returned to the Buyer in full without interest.

2.   **COMPLETION DATE:** This Agreement shall be completed by no later than 6:00 p.m. on the .... day of ....

     ...., 20............................. Upon completion, vacant possession of the property shall be given to the Buyer
     unless otherwise provided for in this Agreement.

INITIALS OF BUYER(S): (   )   INITIALS OF SELLERS(S): (   )

3. **NOTICES:** The Seller hereby appoints the Listing Brokerage as agent for the Seller for the purpose of giving and receiving notices pursuant to this Agreement. Where a Brokerage (Buyer's Brokerage) has entered into a representation agreement with the Buyer, the Buyer hereby appoints the Buyer's Brokerage as agent for the purpose of giving and receiving notices pursuant to this Agreement. **Where a Brokerage represents both the Seller and the Buyer (multiple representation), the Brokerage shall not be appointed or authorized to be agent for either the Buyer or the Seller for the purpose of giving and receiving notices.** Any notice relating hereto or provided for herein shall be in writing. In addition to any provision contained herein and in any Schedule hereto, this offer, any counter-offer, notice of acceptance thereof or any notice to be given or received pursuant to this Agreement or any Schedule hereto (any of them, "Document") shall be deemed given and received when delivered personally or hand delivered to the Address for Service provided in the Acknowledgement below, or where a facsimile number or email address is provided herein, when transmitted electronically to that facsimile number or email address, respectively, in which case, the signature(s) of the party (parties) shall be deemed to be original.

    FAX No.: ....   FAX No.: ....
    　　　　　　(For delivery of Documents to Seller)　　　　　　　　　　(For delivery of Documents to Buyer)

    Email Address: ....   Email Address: ....
    　　　　　　(For delivery of Documents to Seller)　　　　　　　　　　(For delivery of Documents to Buyer)

4. **CHATTELS INCLUDED:** ....

    ....

    ....

    ....

    ....

    Unless otherwise stated in this Agreement or any Schedule hereto, Seller agrees to convey all fixtures and chattels included in the Purchase Price free from all liens, encumbrances or claims affecting the said fixtures and chattels.

5. **FIXTURES EXCLUDED:** ....

    ....

    ....

    ....

    ....

6. **RENTAL ITEMS (Including Lease, Lease to Own):** The following equipment is rented and **not** included in the Purchase Price. The Buyer agrees to assume the rental contract(s), if assumable:

    ....

    ....

    ....

    ....

    The Buyer agrees to co-operate and execute such documentation as may be required to facilitate such assumption.

7. **HST: If the sale of the property (Real Property as described above) is subject to Harmonized Sales Tax (HST), then such tax shall be in addition to the Purchase Price.** The Seller will not collect HST if the Buyer provides to the Seller a warranty that the Buyer is registered under the Excise Tax Act ("ETA"), together with a copy of the Buyer's ETA registration, a warranty that the Buyer shall self-assess and remit the HST payable and file the prescribed form and shall indemnify the Seller in respect of any HST payable. The foregoing warranties shall not merge but shall survive the completion of the transaction. If the sale of the property is not subject to HST, Seller agrees to certify on or before closing, that the transaction is not subject to HST. Any HST on chattels, If applicable, is not included in the Purchase Price.

              INITIALS OF BUYER(S): ◯   **INITIALS OF SELLERS(S):** ◯

8. **TITLE SEARCH:** Buyer shall be allowed until 6:00 p.m. on the .... day of..., 20................, (Requisition Date) to examine the title to the property at his own expense and until the earlier of: (i) thirty days from the later of the Requisition Date or the date on which the conditions in this Agreement are fulfilled or otherwise waived or; (ii) five days prior to completion, to satisfy himself that there

   are no outstanding work orders or deficiency notices affecting the property, that its present use (...) may be lawfully continued and that the principal building may be insured against risk of fire. Seller hereby consents to the municipality or other governmental agencies releasing to Buyer details of all outstanding work orders and deficiency notices affecting the property, and Seller agrees to execute and deliver such further authorizations in this regard as Buyer may reasonably require.

9. **FUTURE USE:** Seller and Buyer agree that there is no representation or warranty of any kind that the future intended use of the property by Buyer is or will be lawful except as may be specifically provided for in this Agreement.

10. **TITLE:** Provided that the title to the property is good and free from all registered restrictions, charges, liens, and encumbrances except as otherwise specifically provided in this Agreement and save and except for (a) any registered restrictions or covenants that run with the land providing that such are complied with; (b) any registered municipal agreements and registered agreements with publicly regulated utilities providing such have been complied with, or security has been posted to ensure compliance and completion, as evidenced by a letter from the relevant municipality or regulated utility; (c) any minor easements for the supply of domestic utility or telephone services to the property or adjacent properties; and (d) any easements for drainage, storm or sanitary sewers, public utility lines, telephone lines, cable television lines or other services which do not materially affect the use of the property. If within the specified times referred to in paragraph 8 any valid objection to title or to any outstanding work order or deficiency notice, or to the fact the said present use may not lawfully be continued, or that the principal building may not be insured against risk of fire is made in writing to Seller and which Seller is unable or unwilling to remove, remedy or satisfy or obtain insurance save and except against risk of fire (Title Insurance) in favour of the Buyer and any mortgagee, (with all related costs at the expense of the Seller), and which Buyer will not waive, this Agreement notwithstanding any intermediate acts or negotiations in respect of such objections, shall be at an end and all monies paid shall be returned without interest or deduction and Seller, Listing Brokerage and Co-operating Brokerage shall not be liable for any costs or damages. Save as to any valid objection so made by such day and except for any objection going to the root of the title, Buyer shall be conclusively deemed to have accepted Seller's title to the property.

11. **CLOSING ARRANGEMENTS:** Where each of the Seller and Buyer retain a lawyer to complete the Agreement of Purchase and Sale of the property, and where the transaction will be completed by electronic registration pursuant to Part III of the Land Registration Reform Act, R.S.O. 1990, Chapter L4 and the Electronic Registration Act, S.O. 1991, Chapter 44, and any amendments thereto, the Seller and Buyer acknowledge and agree that the exchange of closing funds, non-registrable documents and other items (the "Requisite Deliveries") and the release thereof to the Seller and Buyer will (a) not occur at the same time as the registration of the transfer/deed (and any other documents intended to be registered in connection with the completion of this transaction) and (b) be subject to conditions whereby the lawyer(s) receiving any of the Requisite Deliveries will be required to hold same in trust and not release same except in accordance with the terms of a document registration agreement between the said lawyers. The Seller and Buyer irrevocably instruct the said lawyers to be bound by the document registration agreement which is recommended from time to time by the Law Society of Upper Canada. Unless otherwise agreed to by the lawyers, such exchange of the Requisite Deliveries will occur in the applicable Land Titles Office or such other location agreeable to both lawyers.

12. **DOCUMENTS AND DISCHARGE:** Buyer shall not call for the production of any title deed, abstract, survey or other evidence of title to the property except such as are in the possession or control of Seller. If requested by Buyer, Seller will deliver any sketch or survey of the property within Seller's control to Buyer as soon as possible and prior to the Requisition Date. If a discharge of any Charge/Mortgage held by a corporation incorporated pursuant to the Trust And Loan Companies Act (Canada), Chartered Bank, Trust Company, Credit Union, Caisse Populaire or Insurance Company and which is not to be assumed by Buyer on completion, is not available in registrable form on completion, Buyer agrees to accept Seller's lawyer's personal undertaking to obtain, out of the closing funds, a discharge in registrable form and to register same, or cause same to be registered, on title within a reasonable period of time after completion, provided that on or before completion Seller shall provide to Buyer a mortgage statement prepared by the mortgagee setting out the balance required to obtain the discharge, and, where a real-time electronic cleared funds transfer system is not being used, a direction executed by Seller directing payment to the mortgagee of the amount required to obtain the discharge out of the balance due on completion.

13. **INSPECTION:** Buyer acknowledges having had the opportunity to inspect the property and understands that upon acceptance of this offer there shall be a binding agreement of purchase and sale between Buyer and Seller.

14. **INSURANCE:** All buildings on the property and all other things being purchased shall be and remain until completion at the risk of Seller. Pending completion, Seller shall hold all insurance policies, if any, and the proceeds thereof in trust for the parties as their interests may appear and in the event of substantial damage, Buyer may either terminate this Agreement and have all monies paid returned without interest or deduction or else take the proceeds of any insurance and complete the purchase. No insurance shall be transferred on completion. If Seller is taking back a Charge/ Mortgage, or Buyer is assuming a Charge/Mortgage, Buyer shall supply Seller with reasonable evidence of adequate insurance to protect Seller's or other mortgagee's interest on completion.

INITIALS OF BUYER(S): ( )   **INITIALS OF SELLERS(S):** ( )

15. PLANNING ACT: This Agreement shall be effective to create an interest in the property only if Seller complies with the subdivision control provisions of the Planning Act by completion and Seller covenants to proceed diligently at his expense to obtain any necessary consent by completion.

16. DOCUMENT PREPARATION: The Transfer/Deed shall, save for the Land Transfer Tax Affidavit, be prepared in registrable form at the expense of Seller, and any Charge/Mortgage to be given back by the Buyer to Seller at the expense of the Buyer. If requested by Buyer, Seller covenants that the Transfer/Deed to be delivered on completion shall contain the statements contemplated by Section 50(22) of the Planning Act, R.S.O.1990.

17. RESIDENCY: (a) Subject to (b) below, the Seller represents and warrants that the Seller is not and on completion will not be a non-resident under the non-residency provisions of the Income Tax Act which representation and warranty shall survive and not merge upon the completion of this transaction and the Seller shall deliver to the Buyer a statutory declaration that Seller is not then a non-resident of Canada;
(b) provided that if the Seller is a non-resident under the non-residency provisions of the Income Tax Act, the Buyer shall be credited towards the Purchase Price with the amount, if any, necessary for Buyer to pay to the Minister of National Revenue to satisfy Buyer's liability in respect of tax payable by Seller under the non-residency provisions of the Income Tax Act by reason of this sale. Buyer shall not claim such credit if Seller delivers on completion the prescribed certificate.

18. ADJUSTMENTS: Any rents, mortgage interest, realty taxes including local improvement rates and unmetered public or private utility charges and unmetered cost of fuel, as applicable, shall be apportioned and allowed to the day of completion, the day of completion itself to be apportioned to Buyer.

19. TIME LIMITS: Time shall in all respects be of the essence hereof provided that the time for doing or completing of any matter provided for herein may be extended or abridged by an agreement in writing signed by Seller and Buyer or by their respective lawyers who may be specifically authorized in that regard.

20. PROPERTY ASSESSMENT: The Buyer and Seller hereby acknowledge that the Province of Ontario has implemented current value assessment and properties may be re-assessed on an annual basis. The Buyer and Seller agree that no claim will be made against the Buyer or Seller, or any Brokerage, Broker or Salesperson, for any changes in property tax as a result of a re-assessment of the property, save and except any property taxes that accrued prior to the completion of this transaction.

21. TENDER: Any tender of documents or money hereunder may be made upon Seller or Buyer or their respective lawyers on the day set for completion. Money shall be tendered with funds drawn on a lawyer's trust account in the form of a bank draft, certified cheque or wire transfer using the Large Value Transfer System.

22. FAMILY LAW ACT: Seller warrants that spousal consent is not necessary to this transaction under the provisions of the Family Law Act, R.S.O.1990 unless Seller's spouse has executed the consent hereinafter provided.

23. UFFI: Seller represents and warrants to Buyer that during the time Seller has owned the property, Seller has not caused any building on the property to be insulated with insulation containing ureaformaldehyde, and that to the best of Seller's knowledge no building on the property contains or has ever contained insulation that contains ureaformaldehyde. This warranty shall survive and not merge on the completion of this transaction, and if the building is part of a multiple unit building, this warranty shall only apply to that part of the building which is the subject of this transaction.

24. LEGAL, ACCOUNTING AND ENVIRONMENTAL ADVICE: The parties acknowledge that any information provided by the brokerage is not legal, tax or environmental advice, and that it has been recommended that the parties obtain independent professional advice prior to signing this document.

25. CONSUMER REPORTS: The Buyer is hereby notified that a consumer report containing credit and/or personal information may be referred to in connection with this transaction.

26. AGREEMENT IN WRITING: If there is conflict or discrepancy between any provision added to this Agreement (including any Schedule attached hereto) and any provision in the standard pre-set portion hereof, the added provision shall supersede the standard pre-set provision to the extent of such conflict or discrepancy. This Agreement including any Schedule attached hereto, shall constitute the entire Agreement between Buyer and Seller. There is no representation, warranty, collateral agreement or condition, which affects this Agreement other than as expressed herein. For the purposes of this Agreement, Seller means vendor and Buyer means purchaser. This Agreement shall be read with all changes of gender or number required by the context.

27. TIME AND DATE: Any reference to a time and date in this Agreement shall mean the time and date where the property is located.

INITIALS OF BUYER(S): ( )   INITIALS OF SELLERS(S): ( )

28. SUCCESSORS AND ASSIGNS: The heirs, executors, administrators, successors and assigns of the undersigned are bound by the terms herein.

SIGNED, SEALED AND DELIVERED in the presence of: IN WITNESS whereof I have hereunto set my hand and seal:

....
....   ●   DATE ....
(Witness)   (Buyer/Authorized Signing Officer)   (Seal)

....   ●   DATE ....
(Witness)   (Buyer/Authorized Signing Officer)   (Seal)

I, the Undersigned Seller, agree to the above offer. I hereby irrevocably instruct my lawyer to pay directly to the brokerage(s) with whom I have agreed to pay commission, the unpaid balance of the commission together with applicable Harmonized Sales Tax (and any other taxes as may hereafter be applicable), from the proceeds of the sale prior to any payment to the undersigned on completion, as advised by the brokerage(s) to my lawyer.

SIGNED, SEALED AND DELIVERED in the presence of: IN WITNESS whereof I have hereunto set my hand and seal:

....
....   ●   DATE ....
(Witness)   (Seller/Authorized Signing Officer)   (Seal)

....   ●   DATE ....
(Witness)   (Seller/Authorized Signing Officer)   (Seal)

SPOUSAL CONSENT: The Undersigned Spouse of the Seller hereby consents to the disposition evidenced herein pursuant to the provisions of the Family Law Act, R.S.O.1990, and hereby agrees with the Buyer that he/she will execute all necessary or incidental documents to give full force and effect to the sale evidenced herein.

....   ●   DATE ....
(Witness)   (Spouse)   (Seal)

CONFIRMATION OF ACCEPTANCE: Notwithstanding anything contained herein to the contrary, I confirm this Agreement with all changes both typed and written was finally accepted by all parties at .... a.m./p.m. this .... day of.., 20...........

....
(Signature of Seller or Buyer)

INFORMATION ON BROKERAGE(S)

Listing Brokerage .... Tel.No.(...............)...

....
(Salesperson / Broker Name)

Co-op/Buyer Brokerage .... Tel.No.(...............)...

....
(Salesperson / Broker Name)

ACKNOWLEDGEMENT

I acknowledge receipt of my signed copy of this accepted Agreement of Purchase and Sale and I authorize the Brokerage to forward a copy to my lawyer.

.... DATE .... (Seller)	.... DATE .... (Buyer)
.... DATE .... (Seller)	.... DATE .... (Buyer)
Address for Service	Address for Service ....
.... Tel.No.(...........)...........................	.... Tel.No.(...........)...........................
Seller's Lawyer	Buyer's Lawyer ....
Address	Address ....
Email	Email ....
(...........)..................................... (...........)................	(...........)..................................... (...........)................
Tel.No. FAX No.	Tel.No. FAX No.

I acknowledge receipt of my signed copy of this accepted Agreement of Purchase and Sale and I authorize the Brokerage to forward a copy to my lawyer.

FOR OFFICE USE ONLY   **COMMISSION TRUST AGREEMENT**

To: Co-operating Brokerage shown on the foregoing Agreement of Purchase and Sale:
In consideration for the Co-operating Brokerage procuring the foregoing Agreement of Purchase and Sale, I hereby declare that all moneys received or receivable by me in connection with the Transaction as contemplated in the MLS® Rules and Regulations of my Real Estate Board shall be receivable and held in trust. This agreement shall constitute a Commission Trust Agreement as defined in the MLS® Rules and shall be subject to and governed by the MLS® Rules pertaining to Commission Trust.

DATED as of the date and time of the acceptance of the foregoing Agreement of Purchase and Sale.   Acknowledged by:

....
(Authorized to bind the Listing Brokerage)   (Authorized to bind the Co-operating Brokerage)

Form 500   *(continued)*

 **Ontario Real Estate Association**

Form 500
for use in the Province of Ontario

Schedule A
Agreement of Purchase and Sale – Commercial

This Schedule is attached to and forms part of the Agreement of Purchase and Sale between:

BUYER, ..., and

SELLER, ...

for the purchase and sale of ....

.... dated the .... day of ...., 20...................

Buyer agrees to pay the balance as follows:

This form must be initialed by all parties to the Agreement of Purchase and Sale.

INITIALS OF BUYER(S):   INITIALS OF SELLERS(S):

Form 500   Revised 2015   **Page 6 of 6**

Form 520   *Listing Agreement—Commercial—Authority to Offer for Sale*   Page 1 of 4

Ontario Real Estate Association

Form 520
for use in the Province of Ontario

Listing Agreement – Commercial
Authority to Offer for Sale

This is a Multiple Listing Service® Agreement   ◯ (Seller's Initials)   **OR**   **This Listing is Exclusive**   ◯ (Seller's Initials)

BETWEEN:

BROKERAGE: ....

.... (the "Listing Brokerage")

SELLER(S): ....(the "Seller")

In consideration of the Listing Brokerage listing the real property **for sale** known as ....

.... (the "Property")

the Seller hereby gives the Listing Brokerage the **exclusive and irrevocable** right to act as the Seller's agent,

commencing at 12:01 a.m. on the .... day of ...., 20............,

until 11:59 p.m. on the .... day of ...., 20................ (the "Listing Period"),

{ Seller acknowledges that the length of the Listing Period is negotiable between the Seller and the Listing Brokerage and, if an MLS® listing, may be subject to minimum requirements of the real estate board, however, in accordance with the Real Estate and Business Brokers Act of Ontario (2002), **if the Listing Period exceeds six months, the Listing Brokerage must obtain the Seller's initials.** }   ◯ (Seller's Initials)

to offer the Property **for sale** at a price of:

.... Dollars ($Cdn ....)

and upon the terms particularly set out herein, or at such other price and/or terms acceptable to the Seller. It is understood that the price and/or terms set out herein are at the Seller's personal request, after full discussion with the Listing Brokerage's representative regarding potential market value of the Property.

The Seller hereby represents and warrants that the Seller is not a party to any other listing agreement for the Property or agreement to pay commission to any other real estate brokerage for the sale of the property.

1. **DEFINITIONS AND INTERPRETATIONS:** For the purposes of this Listing Agreement ("Authority" or "Agreement"), "Seller" includes vendor and a "buyer" includes a purchaser or a prospective purchaser. A purchase shall be deemed to include the entering into of any agreement to exchange, or the obtaining of an option to purchase which is subsequently exercised, or the causing of a First Right of Refusal to be exercised, or an agreement to sell or transfer shares or assets. "Real property" includes real estate as defined in the Real Estate and Business Brokers Act (2002). The "Property" shall be deemed to include any part thereof or interest therein. A "real estate board" includes a real estate association. This Agreement shall be read with all changes of gender or number required by the context. For purposes of this Agreement, anyone introduced to or shown the Property shall be deemed to include any spouse, heirs, executors, administrators, successors, assigns, related corporations and affiliated corporations. Related corporations or affiliated corporations shall include any corporation where one half or a majority of the shareholders, directors or officers of the related or affiliated corporation are the same person(s) as the shareholders, directors, or officers of the corporation introduced to or shown the Property.

2. **COMMISSION:** In consideration of the Listing Brokerage listing the Property for sale, the Seller agrees to pay the Listing Brokerage a commission

   of .... % of the sale price of the Property or ....

   ....

   for any valid offer to purchase the Property from any source whatsoever obtained during the Listing Period and on the terms and conditions set out in this Agreement **OR** such other terms and conditions as the Seller may accept.

INITIALS OF LISTING BROKERAGE: ◯   **INITIALS OF SELLER(S):** ◯

Form 520   Revised 2015   **Page 1 of 4**

APPENDIX

The Seller further agrees to pay such commission as calculated above if an agreement to purchase is agreed to or accepted by the Seller or anyone on

the Seller's behalf within .... days after the expiration of the Listing Period (**Holdover Period**), so long as such agreement is with anyone who was introduced to the Property from any source whatsoever during the Listing Period or shown the Property during the Listing Period. If, however, the offer for the purchase of the Property is pursuant to a new agreement in writing to pay commission to another registered real estate brokerage, the Seller's liability for commission shall be reduced by the amount paid by the Seller under the new agreement.

The Seller further agrees to pay such commission as calculated above even if the transaction contemplated by an agreement to purchase agreed to or accepted by the Seller or anyone on the Seller's behalf is not completed, if such non-completion is owing or attributable to the Seller's default or neglect, said commission to be payable on the date set for completion of the purchase of the Property.

Any deposit in respect of any agreement where the transaction has been completed shall first be applied to reduce the commission payable. Should such amounts paid to the Listing Brokerage from the deposit or by the Seller's solicitor not be sufficient, the Seller shall be liable to pay to the Listing Brokerage on demand, any deficiency in commission and taxes owing on such commission.

In the event the buyer fails to complete the purchase and the deposit or any part thereof becomes forfeited, awarded, directed or released to the Seller, the Seller then authorizes the Listing Brokerage to retain as commission for services rendered, fifty (50%) per cent of the amount of the said deposit forfeited, awarded, directed or released to the Seller (but not to exceed the commission payable had a sale been consummated) and to pay the balance of the deposit to the Seller.

All amounts set out as commission are to be paid plus applicable taxes on such commission.

3. **REPRESENTATION:** The Seller acknowledges that the Listing Brokerage has provided the Seller with written information explaining agency relationships,including information on Seller Representation. Sub-agency, Buyer Representation, Multiple Representation and Customer Service. The Seller authorizes the Listing Brokerage to co-operate with any other registered real estate brokerage (co-operating brokerage), and to offer to pay

the co-operating brokerage a commission of .... % of the sale price of the Property or ....

....

out of the commission the Seller pays the Listing Brokerage. The Seller understands that unless the Seller is otherwise informed, the co-operating brokerage is representing the interests of the buyer in the transaction. The Seller further acknowledges that the Listing Brokerage may be listing other properties that may be similar to the Seller's Property and the Seller hereby consents to the Listing Brokerage acting as an agent for more than one seller without any claim by the Seller of conflict of interest. Unless otherwise agreed in writing between Seller and Listing Brokerage, any commission payable to any other brokerage shall be paid out of the commission the Seller pays the Listing Brokerage.

The Seller hereby appoints the Listing Brokerage as the Seller's agent for the purpose of giving and receiving notices pursuant to any offer or agreement to purchase the Property.

MULTIPLE REPRESENTATION: The Seller hereby acknowledges that the Listing Brokerage may be entering into buyer representation agreements with buyers who may be interested in purchasing the Seller's Property. In the event that the Listing Brokerage has entered into or enters into a buyer representation agreement with a prospective buyer for the Seller's Property, the Listing Brokerage will obtain the Seller's written consent to represent both the Seller and the buyer for the transaction at the earliest practical opportunity and in all cases prior to any offer to purchase being submitted or presented.

The Seller understand and acknowledges that the Listing Brokerage must be impartial when representing both the Seller and the buyer and equally protect the interests of the Seller and buyer. The Seller understands and acknowledges that when representing both the Seller and the buyer, the Listing Brokerage shall have a duty of full disclosure to both the Seller and the buyer, including a requirement to disclose all factual information about the Property known to the Listing Brokerage.

However, the Seller further understands and acknowledges that the Listing Brokerage shall not disclose:

- that the Seller may or will accept less than the listed price, unless otherwise instructed in writing by the Seller;
- that the buyer may or will pay more than the offered price, unless otherwise instructed in writing by the buyer;
- the motivation of or personal information about the Seller or buyer, unless otherwise instructed in writing by the party to which the information applies or unless failure to disclose would constitute fraudulent, unlawful or unethical practice;
- the price the buyer should offer or the price the Seller should accept; and
- the Listing Brokerage shall not disclose to the buyer the terms of any other offer.

However, it is understood that factual market information about comparable properties and information known to the Listing Brokerage concerning potential uses for the Property will be disclosed to both Selle r and buyer to assist them to come to their own conclusions.

Where a Brokerage represents both the Seller and the Buyer (multiple representation), the Brokerage shall not be entitled or authorized to be agent for either the Buyer or the Seller for the purpose of giving and receiving notices.

MULTIPLE REPRESENTATION AND CUSTOMER SERVICE: The Seller understands and agrees that the Listing Brokerage also provides representation and customer service to other sellers and buyers. If the Listing Brokerage represents or provides customer service to more than one seller or buyer for the same trade, the Listing Brokerage shall, in writing, at the earliest practicable opportunity and before any offer is made, inform all sellers and buyers of the nature of the Listing Brokerage's relationship to each seller and buyer.

INITIALS OF LISTING BROKERAGE: **INITIALS OF SELLER(S):**

4. **REFERRAL OF ENQUIRIES:** The Seller agrees that during the Listing Period, the Seller shall advise the Listing Brokerage immediately of all enquiries from any source whatsoever, and all offers to purchase submitted to the Seller shall be immediately submitted to the Listing Brokerage by the Seller before the Seller accepts or rejects the same. If any enquiry during the Listing Period results in the Seller's accepting a valid offer to purchase during the Listing Period or within the Holdover Period after the expiration of the Listing Period described above, the Seller agrees to pay the Listing Brokerage the amount of commission set out above, payable within five (5) days following the Listing Brokerage's written demand therefor.

5. **MARKETING:** The Seller agrees to allow the Listing Brokerage to show and permit prospective buyers to fully inspect the Property during reasonable hours and the Seller gives the Listing Brokerage the sole and exclusive right to place "For Sale" and "Sold" sign(s) upon the Property. The Seller consents to the Listing Brokerage including information in advertising that may identify the Property. The Seller further agrees that the Listing Brokerage shall have sole and exclusive authority to make all advertising decisions relating to the marketing of the Property during the Listing Period. The Seller agrees that the Listing Brokerage will not be held liable in any manner whatsoever for any acts or omissions with respect to advertising by the Listing Brokerage or any other party, other than by the Listing Brokerage's gross negligence or wilful act.

6. **WARRANTY:** The Seller represents and warrants that the Seller has the exclusive authority and power to execute this Authority to offer the Property for sale and that the Seller has informed the Listing Brokerage of any third party interests or claims on the Property such as rights of first refusal, options, easements, mortgages, encumbrances or otherwise concerning the Property, which may affect the sale of the Property.

7. **INDEMNIFICATION AND INSURANCE:** The Seller will not hold the Listing Brokerage and representatives of the Brokerage responsible for any loss or damage to the Property or contents occurring during the term of this Agreement caused by the Listing Brokerage or anyone else by any means, including theft, fire or vandalism, other than by the Listing Brokerage's gross negligence or wilful act. The Seller agrees to indemnify and save harmless the Listing Brokerage and representatives of the Brokerage and any co-operating brokerage from any liability, claim, loss, cost, damage or injury, including but not limited to loss of the commission payable under this Agreement, caused or contributed to by the breach of any warranty or representation made by the Seller in this Agreement or the accompanying data form. The Seller agrees to indemnify and save harmless the Listing Brokerage and representatives of the Brokerage and any co-operating brokerage from any liability, claim, loss, cost, damage or injury as a result of the Property being affected by any contaminants or environmental problems.
The Seller warrants the Property is insured, including personal liability insurance against any claims or lawsuits resulting from bodily injury or property damage to others caused in any way on or at the Property and the Seller indemnifies the Brokerage and all of its employees, representatives, salespersons and brokers (Listing Brokerage) and any co-operating brokerage and all of its employees, representatives, salespersons and brokers (co-operating brokerage) for and against any claims against the Listing Brokerage or co-operating brokerage made by anyone who attends or visits the Property.

8. **FAMILY LAW ACT:** The Seller hereby warrants that spousal consent is not necessary under the provisions of the Family Law Act, R.S.O. 1990, unless the Seller's spouse has executed the consent hereinafter provided.

9. **FINDERS FEES:** The Seller acknowledges that the Brokerage may be receiving a finder's fee, reward and/or referral incentive, and the Seller consents to any such benefit being received and retained by the Brokerage in addition to the commission as described above.

10. **VERIFICATION OF INFORMATION:** The Seller authorizes the Listing Brokerage to obtain any information from any regulatory authorities, governments, mortgagees or others affecting the Property and the Seller agrees to execute and deliver such further authorizations in this regard as may be reasonably required. The Seller hereby appoints the Listing Brokerage or the Listing Brokerage's authorized representative as the Seller's attorney to execute such documentation as may be necessary to effect obtaining any information as aforesaid. The Seller hereby authorizes, instructs and directs the above noted regulatory authorities, governments, mortgagees or others to release any and all information to the Listing Brokerage.

11. **USE AND DISTRIBUTION OF INFORMATION:** The Seller consents to the collection, use and disclosure of personal information by the Brokerage for the purpose of listing and marketing the Property including, but not limited to: listing and advertising the Property using any medium including the Internet; disclosing Property information to prospective buyers, brokerages, salespersons and others who may assist in the sale of the Property; such other use of the Seller's personal information as is consistent with listing and marketing of the Property. The Seller consents, if this is an MLS® Listing, to placement of the listing information and sales information by the Brokerage into the database(s) of the MLS® System of the appropriate Board, and to the posting of any documents and other information (including, without limitation, photographs, images, graphics, audio and video recordings, virtual tours, drawings, floor plans, architectural designs, artistic renderings, surveys and listing descriptions) provided by or on behalf of the Seller into the database(s) of the MLS® System of the appropriate Board. The Seller hereby indemnifies and saves harmless the Brokerage and/or any of its employees, servants, brokers or sales representatives from any and all claims, liabilities, suits, actions, losses, costs and legal fees caused by, or arising out of, or resulting from the posting of any documents or other information (including, without limitation, photographs, images, graphics, audio and video recordings, virtual tours, drawings, floor plans, architectural designs, artistic renderings, surveys and listing descriptions) as aforesaid.
The Seller acknowledges that the database, within the board's MLS® System is the property of the real estate board(s) and can be licensed, resold, or otherwise dealt with by the board(s). The Seller further acknowledges that the real estate board(s) may: during the term of the listing and thereafter, distribute the information in the database, within the board's MLS® System to any persons authorized to use such service which may include other brokerages, government departments, appraisers, municipal organizations and others; market the Property, at its option, in any medium, including electronic media; during the term of the listing and thereafter, compile, retain and publish any statistics including historical data within the board's MLS® System and retain, reproduce and display photographs, images, graphics, audio and video recordings, virtual tours, drawings, floor plans, architectural designs, artistic renderings, surveys and listing descriptions which may be used by board members to conduct comparative analyses; and make such other use of the information as the Brokerage and/or real estate board(s) deem appropriate, in connection with the listing, marketing and

INITIALS OF LISTING BROKERAGE: **INITIALS OF SELLER(S):**

APPENDIX

selling of real estate during the term of the listing and thereafter. The Seller acknowledges that the information, personal or otherwise ("information"), provided to the real estate board or association may be stored on databases located outside of Canada, in which case the information would be subject to the laws of the jurisdiction in which the information is located.

In the event that this Agreement expires or is cancelled or otherwise terminated and the Property is not sold, the Seller, by initialling:

consent to allow other real estate board members to contact the Seller after expiration or other termination of this Agreement to discuss listing or otherwise marketing the Property.

(Does)   **(Does Not)**

12. SUCCESSORS AND ASSIGNS: The heirs, executors, administrators, successors and assigns of the undersigned are bound by the terms of this Agreement.

13. CONFLICT OR DISCREPANCY: If there is any conflict or discrepancy between any provision added to this Agreement (including any Schedule attached hereto) and any provision in the standard pre-set portion hereof, the added provision shall supersede the standard pre-set provision to the extent of such conflict or discrepancy. This Agreement, including any Schedule attached hereto, shall constitute the entire Authority from the Seller to the Brokerage. There is no representation, warranty, collateral agreement or condition, which affects this Agreement other than as expressed herein.

14. ELECTRONIC COMMUNICATION: This Listing Agreement and any agreements, notices or other communications contemplated thereby may be transmitted by means of electronic systems, in which case signatures shall be deemed to be original. The transmission of this Agreement by the Seller by electronic means shall be deemed to confirm the Seller has retained a true copy of the Agreement.

15. SCHEDULE(S) .... and data form attached hereto form(s) part of this Agreement.

THE LISTING BROKERAGE AGREES TO MARKET THE PROPERTY ON BEHALF OF THE SELLER AND REPRESENT THE SELLER IN AN ENDEAVOUR TO OBTAIN A VALID OFFER TO PURCHASE THE PROPERTY ON THE TERMS SET OUT IN THIS AGREEMENT OR ON SUCH OTHER TERMS SATISFACTORY TO THE SELLER.

....   DATE ....
(Authorized to bind the Listing Brokerage)   (Name of Person Signing)

THIS AUTHORITY HAS BEEN READ AND FULLY UNDERSTOOD BY ME AND I ACKNOWLEDGE THIS DATE I HAVE SIGNED UNDER SEAL. Any representations contained herein or as shown on the accompanying data form respecting the Property are true to the best of my knowledge, information and belief.

SIGNED, SEALED AND DELIVERED I have hereunto set my hand and seal:

....
(Name of Seller)

....   ● DATE ....
(Signature of Seller/Authorized Signing Officer)   (Seal)   (Tel. No.)

....   ● DATE ....
(Signature of Seller/Authorized Signing Officer)   (Seal)

SPOUSAL CONSENT: The undersigned spouse of the Seller hereby consents to the listing of the Property herein pursuant to the provisions of the Family Law Act, R.S.O. 1990 and hereby agrees that he/she will execute all necessary or incidental documents to further any transaction provided for herein.

....   ● DATE ....
(Spouse)   (Seal)

DECLARATION OF INSURANCE

The broker/salesperson ....
                                                        (Name of Broker/Salesperson)

hereby declares that he/she is insured as required by the Real Estate and Business Brokers Act (REBBA) and Regulations.

....
(Signature(s) of Broker/Salesperson)

ACKNOWLEDGEMENT

The Seller(s) hereby acknowledge that the Seller(s) fully understand the terms of this Agreement and have received a true copy of this Agreement on the .... day of ...., 20 ....

....   Date: ....
(Signature of Seller)

....   Date: ....
(Signature of Seller)

Listing Agreement – Commercial
Authority to Offer for Lease

Form 525
for use in the Province of Ontario

This is a Multiple Listing Service® Agreement (Landlord's Initials)   **OR**   **This Listing is Exclusive** (Landlord's Initials)

BETWEEN:

BROKERAGE: ....

.... (the "Listing Brokerage")

LANDLORD (Lessor),:...(the "Landlord")

In consideration of the Listing Brokerage listing the property **for lease** known as...

.... (the "Property")

the Landlord hereby gives the Listing Brokerage the **exclusive and irrevocable** right to act as the Landlord's agent,

commencing at 12:01 a.m. on the .... day of ...., 20............,

until 11:59 p.m. on the .... day of ...., 20............ (the "Listing Period"),

{ Landlord acknowledges that the length of the Listing Period is negotiable between the Landlord and the Listing Brokerage and, if an MLS® listing, may be subject to minimum requirements of the real estate board, however, in accordance with the Real Estate and Business Brokers Act of Ontario (2002), **if the Listing Period exceeds six months, the Listing Brokerage must obtain the Landlord's initials.** }   (Landlord's Initials)

to offer the property **for lease** at a rent of: ....

....

....

herein are at the Landlord's personal request, after full discussion with the Listing Brokerage's representative regarding potential market rent of the Property.

The Landlord hereby represents and warrants that the Landlord is not a party to any other listing agreement for the Property or agreement to pay commission to any other real estate brokerage for the lease of the property.

1. **DEFINITIONS AND INTERPRETATIONS:** For the purposes of this Listing Agreement ("Authority" or "Agreement"), "Landlord" includes lessor and a "tenant" includes a lessee, or a prospective lessee or tenant. A lease includes any rental agreement, sub-lease or renewal of a lease. The "Property" shall be deemed to include any part thereof or interest therein. A "real estate board" includes a real estate association. This Agreement shall be read with all changes of gender or number required by the context. For purposes of this Agreement, anyone introduced to or shown the Property shall be deemed to include any spouse, heirs, executors, administrators, successors, assigns, related corporations and affiliated corporations. Related corporations or affiliated corporations shall include any corporation where one half or a majority of the shareholders, directors or officers of the related or affiliated corporation are the same person(s) as the shareholders, directors, or officers of the corporation introduced to or shown the Property.

2. **COMMISSION:** In consideration of the Listing Brokerage listing the Property, the Landlord agrees to pay the Listing Brokerage a commission of

    ....

    ....

    ....

    for any valid offer to lease the Property from any source whatsoever obtained during the Listing Period and on the terms and conditions set out in this Agreement **OR** such other terms and conditions as the Landlord may accept. Said commission to be payable on the earlier of occupancy by the Tenant or execution of the Lease.

    The Landlord further agrees to pay such commission as calculated above if an agreement to lease is agreed to or accepted by the Landlord or anyone

INITIALS OF LISTING BROKERAGE: ( )   **INITIALS OF LANDLORD(S):** ( )

APPENDIX

Form 525   *(continued)*

on the Landlord's behalf within .... days after the expiration of the Listing Period **(Holdover Period)**, so long as such agreement is with anyone who was introduced to the Property from any source whatsoever during the Listing Period or shown the Property during the Listing Period. If, however, the offer to lease the Property is pursuant to a new agreement in writing to pay commission to another registered real estate brokerage, the Landlord's liability for commission shall be reduced by the amount paid by the Landlord under the new agreement.

The Landlord further agrees to pay such commission as calculated above even if the transaction contemplated by an agreement to lease agreed to or accepted by the Landlord or anyone on the Landlord's behalf is not completed, if such non-completion is owing or attributable to the Landlord's default or neglect, said commission to be payable on the earlier of the date of occupancy by the tenant or the execution of the lease or the date set for commencement of the lease or tenancy.

The Landlord acknowledges and agrees that, for any lease the Listing Brokerage arranges, any provisions for a period of free rent, abatement of rent, or rent inducement will not affect the calculation of the commission or other remuneration payable hereunder. The commission or other remuneration will be calculated on the basis of rent that, but for such free rent, abatement or rent inducement, would otherwise be payable.

If a lease the Listing Brokerage arranges contains an option to extend or renew, the Landlord agrees to notify the Listing Brokerage of the exercising of said option and to pay the Listing Brokerage upon the exercising of the said option or any future option, a further commission

of .... of the total rent for the term of such lease extension or renewal. It is understood and agreed that the said further commission is to be paid on the earlier of the date of execution of the extension or renewal or the date the extension or renewal commences. If a tenant to whom the Listing Brokerage rented or leased the Property effects an offer to purchase the Property during the tenancy period or any renewal of the tenancy agreement, the Landlord

agrees to pay the Listing Brokerage a commission of .... % of the sale price of the Property or ....

.... for the purchase of the Property. Any deposit in respect of any agreement where the transaction has been completed shall first be applied to reduce the commission payable. Should such amounts paid to the Listing Brokerage from the deposit or by the Landlord's solicitor not be sufficient, the Landlord shall be liable to pay to the Listing Brokerage on demand, any deficiency in commission and taxes owing on such commission.

In the event the tenant fails to complete the lease and the deposit or any part thereof becomes forfeited, awarded, directed or released to the Landlord, the Landlord then authorizes the Listing Brokerage to retain as commission for services rendered, fifty (50%) per cent of the amount of the said deposit forfeited, awarded, directed or released to the Landlord (but not to exceed the commission payable had a lease been consummated) and to pay the balance of the deposit to the Landlord.

All amounts set out as commission are to be paid plus applicable taxes on such commission.

3. **REPRESENTATION:** The Landlord acknowledges that the Listing Brokerage has provided the Landlord with written information explaining agency relationships, including information on Landlord Representation, Sub-agency, Tenant Representation, Multiple Representation and Customer Service. The Landlord authorizes the Listing Brokerage to co-operate with any other registered real estate brokerage (co-operating brokerage), and to offer to

pay the co-operating brokerage a commission of ....

.... out of the commission the Landlord pays the Listing Brokerage. The Landlord understands that unless the Landlord is otherwise informed, the co-operating brokerage is representing the interests of the tenant in the transaction. The Landlord further acknowledges that the Listing Brokerage may be listing other properties that may be similar to the Landlord's Property and the Landlord hereby consents to the Listing Brokerage acting as an agent for more than one landlord without any claim by the Landlord of conflict of interest. Unless otherwise agreed in writing between Landlord and Listing Brokerage, any commission payable to any other brokerage shall be paid out of the commission the Landlord pays the Listing Brokerage. The Landlord hereby appoints the Listing Brokerage as the Landlord's agent for the purpose of giving and receiving notices pursuant to any offer or agreement to lease the Property.

MULTIPLE REPRESENTATION: The Landlord hereby acknowledges that the Listing Brokerage may be entering into tenant representation agreements with tenants who may be interested in leasing the Landlord's Property. In the event that the Listing Brokerage has entered into or enters into a tenant representation agreement with a prospective tenant for the Landlord's Property, the Listing Brokerage will obtain the Landlord's written consent to represent both the Landlord and the tenant for the transaction at the earliest practical opportunity and in all cases prior to any offer to lease being submitted or presented.

The Landlord understands and acknowledges that the Listing Brokerage must be impartial when representing both the Landlord and the tenant and equally protect the interests of the Landlord and tenant. The Landlord understands and acknowledges that when representing both the Landlord and the tenant, the Listing Brokerage shall have a duty of full disclosure to both the Landlord and the tenant, including a requirement to disclose all factual information about the Property known to the Listing Brokerage.

However, the Landlord further understands and acknowledges that the Listing Brokerage shall not disclose:

*   that the Landlord may or will accept less than the listed rent, unless otherwise instructed in writing by the Landlord;
*   that the tenant may or will pay more than the offered rent, unless otherwise instructed in writing by the tenant;
*   the motivation of or personal information about the Landlord or tenant, unless otherwise instructed in writing by the party to which the information applies or unless failure to disclose would constitute fraudulent, unlawful or unethical practice;
*   the rent the tenant should offer or the rent the Landlord should accept; and
*   the Listing Brokerage shall not disclose to the tenant the terms of any other offer.

INITIALS OF LISTING BROKERAGE: ⬭   **INITIALS OF LANDLORD(S):** ⬭

Form 525   Revised 2015   **Page 2 of 4**

Form 525   *(continued)*

However, it is understood that factual market information about comparable properties and information known to the Listing Brokerage concerning potential uses for the Property will be disclosed to both Landlord and tenant to assist them to come to their own conclusions.

Where a Brokerage represents both the Landlord and the Tenant (multiple representation), the Brokerage shall not be entitled or authorized to be agent for either the Tenant or the Landlord for the purpose of giving and receiving notices.

MULTIPLE REPRESENTATION AND CUSTOMER SERVICE: The Landlord understands and agrees that the Listing Brokerage also provides representation and customer service to other landlords and tenants. If the Listing Brokerage represents or provides customer service to more than one landlord or tenant for the same trade, the Listing Brokerage shall, in writing, at the earliest practicable opportunity and before any offer is made, inform all landlords and tenants of the nature of the Listing Brokerage's relationship to each landlord and tenant.

4. **REFERRAL OF ENQUIRIES:** The Landlord agrees that during the Listing Period, the Landlord shall advise the Listing Brokerage immediately of all enquiries from any source whatsoever, and all offers to lease submitted to the Landlord shall be immediately submitted to the Listing Brokerage by the Landlord before the Landlord accepts or rejects the same. If any enquiry during the Listing Period results in the Landlord accepting a valid offer to lease during the Listing Period or within the Holdover Period after the expiration of the Listing Period described above, the Landlord agrees to pay the Listing Brokerage the amount of commission set out above, payable within five (5) days following the Listing Brokerages written demand therefor.

5. **MARKETING:** The Landlord agrees to allow the Listing Brokerage to show and permit prospective tenants to fully inspect the Property during reasonable hours and the Landlord gives the Listing Brokerage the sole and exclusive right to place "For Lease" and "Leased" sign(s) upon the Property. The Landlord consents to the Listing Brokerage including information in advertising that may identify the Property. The Landlord further agrees that the Listing Brokerage shall have sole and exclusive authority to make all advertising decisions relating to the marketing of the Property during the Listing Period. The Landlord agrees that the Listing Brokerage will not be held liable in any manner whatsoever for any acts or omissions with respect to advertising by the Listing Brokerage or any other party, other than by the Listing Brokerage's gross negligence or wilful act.

6. **WARRANTY:** The Landlord represents and warrants that the Landlord has the exclusive authority and power to execute this Authority to offer the Property for lease and that the Landlord has informed the Listing Brokerage of any third party interests or claims on the Property such as rights of first refusal, options, easements, mortgages, encumbrances or otherwise concerning the Property, which may affect the leasing of the Property.

7. **INDEMNIFICATION AND INSURANCE:** The Landlord will not hold the Listing Brokerage and representatives of the Brokerage responsible for any loss or damage to the Property or contents occurring during the term of this Agreement caused by the Listing Brokerage or anyone else by any means, including theft, fire or vandalism, other than by the Listing Brokerage's gross negligence or wilful act. The Landlord agrees to indemnify and save harmless the Listing Brokerage and representatives of the Brokerage and any co-operating brokerage from any liability, claim, loss, cost, damage or injury, including but not limited to loss of the commission payable under this Agreement, caused or contributed to by the breach of any warranty or representation made by the Landlord in this Agreement or the accompanying data form. The Landlord agrees to indemnify and save harmless the Listing Brokerage and representatives of the Brokerage and any co-operating brokerage from any liability, claim, loss, cost, damage or injury as a result of the Property being affected by any contaminants or environmental problems.

   The Landlord warrants the Property is insured, including personal liability insurance against any claims or lawsuits resulting from bodily injury or property damage to others caused in any way on or at the Property and the Landlord indemnifies the Brokerage and all of its employees, representatives, salespersons and brokers (Listing Brokerage) and any co-operating brokerage and all of its employees, representatives, salespersons and brokers (co-operating brokerage) for and against any claims against the Listing Brokerage and representatives of the Brokerage or co-operating brokerage made by anyone who attends or visits the Property.

8. **VERIFICATION OF INFORMATION:** The Landlord authorizes the Listing Brokerage to obtain any information from any regulatory authorities, governments, mortgagees or others affecting the Property and the Landlord agrees to execute and deliver such further authorizations in this regard as may be reasonably required. The Landlord hereby appoints the Listing Brokerage or the Listing Brokerage's authorized representative as the Landlord's attorney to execute such documentation as may be necessary to effect obtaining any information as aforesaid. The Landlord hereby authorizes, instructs and directs the above noted regulatory authorities, governments, mortgagees or others to release any and all information to the Listing Brokerage.

9. **USE AND DISTRIBUTION OF INFORMATION:** The Landlord consents to the collection, use and disclosure of personal information by the Brokerage for the purpose of listing and marketing the Property including, but not limited to: listing and advertising the Property using any medium including the Internet; disclosing Property information to prospective tenants, brokerages, salespersons and others who may assist in the leasing of the Property; such other use of the Landlord's personal information as is consistent with listing and marketing of the Property. The Landlord consents, if this is an MLS® Listing, to placement of the listing information and leasing information by the Brokerage into the database(s) of the MLS® System of the appropriate Board, and to the posting of any documents and other information (including, without limitation, photographs, images, graphics, audio and video recordings, virtual tours, drawings, floor plans, architectural designs, artistic renderings, surveys and listing descriptions) provided by or on behalf of the Landlord into the database(s) of the MLS® System of the appropriate Board. The Landlord hereby indemnifies and saves harmless the Brokerage and/or any of its employees, servants, brokers or sales representatives from any and all claims, liabilities, suits, actions, losses, costs and legal fees caused by, or arising out of, or resulting from the posting of any documents or other information (including, without limitation, photographs, images, graphics, audio and video recordings, virtual tours, drawings, floor plans, architectural designs, artistic renderings, surveys and listing descriptions) as aforesaid. The Landlord acknowledges that the database, within the board's MLS® System is the property of the real estate board(s) and can be licensed, resold, or otherwise dealt with by the board(s). The Landlord further acknowledges that the real estate board(s) may: during the term of the listing and thereafter, distribute the information in the database, within the board's MLS® System to any persons authorized to use such service which may include other brokerages, government departments, appraisers, municipal organizations and others; market the Property, at its option, in any medium, including electronic media; during the term of the listing and thereafter, compile,

INITIALS OF LISTING BROKERAGE: ◯   **INITIALS OF LANDLORD(S):** ◯

APPENDIX

retain and publish any statistics including historical data within the board's MLS® System and retain, reproduce and display photographs, images, graphics, audio and video recordings, virtual tours, drawings, floor plans, architectural designs, artistic renderings, surveys and listing descriptions which may be used by board members to conduct comparative analyses; and make such other use of the information as the Brokerage and/or real estate board(s) deem appropriate, in connection with the listing, marketing and leasing of real estate during the term of the listing and thereafter. The Landlord acknowledges that the information, personal or otherwise ("information"), provided to the real estate board or association may be stored on databases located outside of Canada, in which case the information would be subject to the laws of the jurisdiction in which the information is located.

In the event that this Agreement expires or is cancelled or otherwise terminated and the Property is not leased, the Landlord, by initialling: consent to allow other real estate board members to contact the Landlord after expiration or other termination of this Agreement to discuss listing or otherwise marketing the Property.	⬭ **(Does)** ⬭ **(Does Not)**

10. **SUCCESSORS AND ASSIGNS:** The heirs, executors, administrators, successors and assigns of the undersigned are bound by the terms of this Agreement.

11. **CONFLICT OR DISCREPANCY:** If there is any conflict or discrepancy between any provision added to this Agreement (including any Schedule attached hereto) and any provision in the standard pre-set portion hereof, the added provision shall supersede the standard pre-set provision to the extent of such conflict or discrepancy. This Agreement, including any Schedule attached hereto, shall constitute the entire Authority from the Landlord to the Brokerage. There is no representation, warranty, collateral agreement or condition, which affects this Agreement other than as expressed herein.

12. **ELECTRONIC COMMUNICATION:** This Listing Agreement and any agreements, notices or other communications contemplated thereby may be transmitted by means of electronic systems, in which case signatures shall be deemed to be original. The transmission of this Agreement by the Landlord by electronic means shall be deemed to confirm the Landlord has retained a true copy of the Agreement.

13. **SCHEDULE(S)** .... and data form attached hereto form(s) part of this Agreement.

THE LISTING BROKERAGE AGREES TO MARKET THE PROPERTY ON BEHALF OF THE LANDLORD AND REPRESENT THE LANDLORD IN AN ENDEAVOUR TO OBTAIN A VALID OFFER TO LEASE THE PROPERTY ON THE TERMS SET OUT IN THIS AGREEMENT OR ON SUCH OTHER TERMS SATISFACTORY TO THE LANDLORD.

....   DATE ....
(Authorized to bind the Listing Brokerage)   (Name of Person Signing)

THIS AUTHORITY HAS BEEN READ AND FULLY UNDERSTOOD BY ME AND I ACKNOWLEDGE THIS DATE I HAVE SIGNED UNDER SEAL.
Any representations contained herein or as shown on the accompanying data form respecting the Property are true to the best of my knowledge, information and belief.

SIGNED, SEALED AND DELIVERED I have hereunto set my hand and seal:

....
(Name of Landlord)

....   ● DATE...........................   ....
(Signature of Landlord/Authorized Signing Officer)   (Seal)   (Tel. No.)

....   ● DATE...........................   ....
(Signature of Landlord/Authorized Signing Officer)   (Seal)

SPOUSAL CONSENT: The undersigned spouse of the Landlord hereby consents to the listing of the Property herein pursuant to the provisions of the Family Law Act, R.S.O. 1990 and hereby agrees that he/she will execute all necessary or incidental documents to further any transaction provided for herein.

....   ● DATE...........................   ....
(Spouse)   (Seal)

DECLARATION OF INSURANCE

The broker/salesperson ....
                                            (Name of Broker/Salesperson)
hereby declares that he/she is insured as required by the Real Estate and Business Brokers Act (REBBA) and Regulations.

....
                                            (Signature(s) of Broker/Salesperson)

ACKNOWLEDGEMENT

The Landlord(s) hereby acknowledge that the Landlord(s) fully understand the terms of this Agreement and have received a true

copy of this Agreement on the .... **day of** ....**, 20** ....

....   Date: ....
(Signature of Landlord)

....   Date: ....
(Signature of Landlord)

 **Ontario Real Estate Association**

Buyer Representation Agreement – Commercial
Mandate for Purchase or Lease

Form 540
for use in the Province of Ontario

This is an Exclusive Buyer Representation Agreement

BETWEEN:

BROKERAGE: ...., Tel.No. (.........)................................

ADDRESS: ....

.... Fax.No. (.........)................................

hereinafter referred to as the Brokerage.

AND:

BUYER(S) ...., hereinafter referred to as the Buyer,

ADDRESS: ....

The Buyer hereby gives the Brokerage the **exclusive and irrevocable authority** to act as the Buyer's agent

commencing at .... a.m./p.m. on the .... day of ...., 20............,

and expiring at 11:59 p.m. on the .... day of ...., 20.............(Expiry Date).

{ Buyer acknowledges that the time period for this Agreement is negotiable between the Buyer and the Brokerage,
however, in accordance with the Real Estate and Business Brokers Act of Ontario (2002),
If the time period for this Agreement exceeds six months, the Brokerage must obtain the Buyer's initials. } (Buyer's Initials)

for the purpose of locating a real property meeting the following general description:

Property Type (Use): ....

....

Geographic Location: ....

....

The Buyer hereby warrants that the Buyer is not a party to a buyer representation agreement with any other registered real estate brokerage for the purchase or lease of a real property of the general description indicated above.

1. **DEFINITIONS AND INTERPRETATIONS:** For the purposes of this Buyer Representation Agreement ("Mandate"), "Buyer" includes purchaser, lessee and tenant and a "seller" includes a vendor, a lessor, a landlord or a prospective seller, vendor, lessor or landlord. A "real property" includes real estate as defined in the Real Estate and Business Brokers Act (2002). A purchase shall be deemed to include the entering into of any agreement to exchange, or the obtaining of an option to purchase which is subsequently exercised, or an agreement to purchase or transfer shares or assets, and a lease includes any rental agreement, sub-lease or renewal of a lease. A "real estate board" includes a real estate association. This Agreement shall be read with all changes of gender or number required by the context. For the purposes of this Agreement, the definition of "Buyer" in the phrase "any property of interest to the Buyer that came to the Buyer's attention from any source whatsoever" shall be deemed to include any spouse, heirs, executors, administrators, successors, assigns, related corporations and affiliated corporations. Related corporations or affiliated corporations shall include any corporation where one half or a majority of the shareholders, directors or officers of the related or affiliated corporation are the same person(s) as the shareholders, directors, or officers of the corporation introduced to or shown the property.

2. **SERVICES PROVIDED BY THE BROKERAGE:** It is understood that the Brokerage may assist the Buyer with any or all of the following services, and any other services, as agreed to between the Buyer and the Brokerage:
   - to identify the needs of the Buyer.
   - to locate available properties that may meet the Buyer's needs.
   - to assist the Buyer in negotiations for the purchase or lease of any property of interest to the Buyer (subject to the special provisions for Multiple Representation described below).
   - Other: (Attach Schedule if additional space is required) ....

INITIALS OF BROKERAGE: ( )   **INITIALS OF BUYER(S):** ( )

Form 540 *(continued)*

3. **RESPONSIBILITIES OF THE BUYER:** In consideration of the Brokerage undertaking to assist the Buyer, the Buyer agrees to:
    • co-operate with the Brokerage with respect to the Brokerage providing any or all of the services described above, as agreed to between the Buyer and the Brokerage.
    • work exclusively with the Brokerage for the purchase or lease of a real property that meets the Buyer's needs.
    • advise the Brokerage immediately of any property of interest to the Buyer that came to the Buyer's attention from any source whatsoever during the currency of this Agreement.
    • submit through the Brokerage all offers by the Buyer during the currency of this Agreement to purchase or lease a real property of the general description indicated above.
    • submit through the Brokerage all offers by the Buyer within .... days after expiration of this Agreement for the purchase or lease of any property that came to the Buyer's attention from any source whatsoever during the currency of this Agreement.

    The Buyer agrees the Brokerage is entitled to be paid a commission of ....
    ....
    ....
    The Buyer authorizes the Brokerage to receive payment of commission from the seller of the property or the seller's agent. Should the Brokerage be unable to obtain an agreement in writing from the seller or the seller's agent to pay the full commission described above, the Buyer will be so informed in writing prior to submitting an offer to purchase or lease and the Buyer will pay the commission for the transaction, or any deficiency in the amount of commission described above, directly to the Brokerage.
    The Buyer agrees to pay such commission as described above even if a transaction contemplated by an agreement to purchase or lease agreed to or accepted by the Buyer or anyone on the Buyer's behalf is not completed, if such non-completion is owing or attributable to the Buyer's default or neglect. The Buyer understands that a failure to negotiate and submit offers through the Brokerage as described herein will make the Buyer liable for payment of commission to the Brokerage. The payment of commission by the seller to the Brokerage will not make the Brokerage the agent for the seller. All amounts set out as commission are to be paid plus applicable taxes on such commission.

4. **REPRESENTATION:** The Buyer acknowledges that the Brokerage has provided the Buyer with written information explaining agency relationships, including information on Seller Representation, Sub-Agency, Buyer Representation, Multiple Representation and Customer Service.
    The Brokerage shall assist the Buyer in locating a real property of the general description indicated above and shall represent the Buyer in an endeavour to procure the acceptance of an agreement to purchase or lease such a property.
    The Buyer acknowledges that the Buyer may not be shown or offered all properties that may be of interest to the Buyer.
    The Buyer hereby agrees that the terms of any buyer's offer or agreement to purchase or lease the property will not be disclosed to any other buyer. The Buyer further acknowledges that the Brokerage may be entering into buyer representation agreements with other buyers who may be interested in the same or similar properties that the Buyer may be interested in buying or leasing and the Buyer hereby consents to the Brokerage entering into buyer representation agreements with other buyers who may be interested in the same or similar properties without any claim by the Buyer of conflict of interest. The Buyer hereby appoints the Brokerage as agent for the purpose of giving and receiving notices pursuant to any offer or agreement to purchase or lease a property negotiated by the Brokerage.

    MULTIPLE REPRESENTATION: The Buyer hereby acknowledges that the Brokerage may be entering into listing agreements with sellers of properties the Buyer may be interested in buying or leasing. In the event that the Brokerage has entered into or enters into a listing agreement with the seller of a property the Buyer may be interested in buying or leasing, the Brokerage will obtain the Buyer's written consent to represent both the Buyer and the seller for the transaction at the earliest practicable opportunity and in all cases prior to any offer to purchase or lease being submitted or presented. The Buyer understands and acknowledges that the Brokerage must be impartial when representing both the Buyer and the seller and equally protect the interests of the Buyer and the seller in the transaction. The Buyer understands and acknowledges that when representing both the Buyer and the seller, the Brokerage shall have a duty of full disclosure to both the Buyer and the seller, including a requirement to disclose all factual information about the property known to the Brokerage.
    However, The Buyer further understands and acknowledges that the Brokerage shall not disclose:
    • that the seller may or will accept less than the listed price, unless otherwise instructed in writing by the seller;
    • that the Buyer may or will pay more than the offered price, unless otherwise instructed in writing by the Buyer;
    • the motivation of or personal information about the Buyer or seller, unless otherwise instructed in writing by the party to which the information applies or unless failure to disclose would constitute fraudulent, unlawful or unethical practice;
    • the price the Buyer should offer or the price the seller should accept; and
    • the Brokerage shall not disclose to the Buyer the terms of any other offer.
    However, it is understood that factual market information about comparable properties and information known to the Brokerage concerning potential uses for the property will be disclosed to both Buyer and seller to assist them to come to their own conclusions.

    Where a Brokerage represents both the Seller and the Buyer (multiple representation), the Brokerage shall not be entitled or authorized to be agent for either the Buyer or the Seller for the purpose of giving and receiving notices.

    MULTIPLE REPRESENTATION AND CUSTOMER SERVICE: The Buyer understands and agrees that the Brokerage also provides representation and customer service to other buyers and sellers. If the Brokerage represents or provides customer service to more than one seller or buyer for the same trade, the Brokerage shall, in writing, at the earliest practicable opportunity and before any offer is made, inform all sellers and buyers of the nature of the Brokerage's relationship to each seller and buyer.

    INITIALS OF BROKERAGE: ⬭   INITIALS OF BUYER(S): ⬭

APPENDIX

5. **FINDERS FEES:** The Buyer acknowledges that the Brokerage may be receiving a finder's fee, reward and/or referral incentive, and the Buyer consents to any such benefit being received and retained by the Brokerage in addition to the commission as described above.

6. **INDEMNIFICATION:** The Brokerage and representatives of the Brokerage are trained in dealing in real estate but are not qualified in determining the physical condition of the land or any improvements thereon. The Buyer agrees that the Brokerage and representatives of the Brokerage will not be liable for any defects, whether latent or patent, to the land or improvements thereon. All information supplied by the seller or landlord or the listing brokerage may not have been verified and is not warranted by the Brokerage as being accurate and will be relied on by the Buyer at the Buyer's own risk. The Buyer acknowledges having been advised to make their own enquiries to confirm the condition of the property.

7. **ENVIRONMENTAL INDEMNIFICATION:** The Buyer agrees to indemnify and save harmless the Brokerage and representatives of the Brokerage from any liability, claim, loss, cost, damage or injury as a result of any property of interest to the Buyer being affected by any contaminants or environmental problems.

8. **USE AND DISTRIBUTION OF INFORMATION:** The Buyer consents to the collection, use and disclosure of personal information by the Brokerage for such purposes that relate to the real estate services provided by the Brokerage to the Buyer including, but not limited to: locating, assessing and qualifying properties for the Buyer; advertising on behalf of the Buyer; providing information as needed to third parties retained by the Buyer to assist in a transaction (e.g. financial institutions, building inspectors, etc...); and such other use of the Buyer's information as is consistent with the services provided by the Brokerage in connection with the purchase or prospective purchase of the property.
    The Buyer agrees that the sale and related information regarding any property purchased by the Buyer through the Brokerage may be retained and disclosed by the Brokerage and/or real estate board(s) (if the property is an MLS® Listing) for reporting, appraisal and statistical purposes and for such other use of the information as the Brokerage and/or board deems appropriate in connection with the listing, marketing and selling of real estate, including conducting comparative market analyses.
    The Buyer acknowledges that the information, personal or otherwise ("information"), provided to the real estate board or association may be stored on databases located outside of Canada, in which case the information would be subject to the laws of the jurisdiction in which the information is located.

9. **CONFLICT OR DISCREPANCY:** If there is any conflict or discrepancy between any provision added to this Agreement and any provision in the standard pre-set portion hereof, the added provision shall supersede the standard pre-set provision to the extent of such conflict or discrepancy. This Agreement, including any provisions added to this Agreement, shall constitute the entire Authority from the Buyer to the Brokerage. There is no representation, warranty, collateral agreement or condition, which affects this Agreement other than as expressed herein.

10. **ELECTRONIC COMMUNICATION:** This Buyer Representation Agreement and any agreements, notices or other communications contemplated thereby may be transmitted by means of electronic systems, in which case signatures shall be deemed to be original. The transmission of this Agreement by the Buyer by electronic means shall be deemed to confirm the Buyer has retained a true copy of the Agreement.

11. **SCHEDULE(S)** .... attached hereto form(s) part of this Agreement.

THE BROKERAGE AGREES TO REPRESENT THE BUYER IN LOCATING A REAL PROPERTY OF THE GENERAL DESCRIPTION INDICATED ABOVE IN AN ENDEAVOUR TO OBTAIN THE ACCEPTANCE OF AN AGREEMENT TO PURCHASE OR LEASE A PROPERTY ON TERMS SATISFACTORY TO THE BUYER.

....   DATE ....
(Authorized to bind the Brokerage)   (Name of Person Signing)

THIS AGREEMENT HAS BEEN READ AND FULLY UNDERSTOOD BY ME AND I ACKNOWLEDGE THIS DATE I HAVE SIGNED UNDER SEAL.

Any representations contained herein are true to the best of my knowledge, information and belief.

SIGNED, SEALED AND DELIVERED I have hereunto set my hand and seal:

....
(Name of Buyer)

....   ● DATE ....
(Signature of Buyer/Authorized Signing Officer)   (Seal)   (Tel. No.)

....   ● DATE ....
(Signature of Buyer/Authorized Signing Officer)   (Seal)   (Tel. No.)

DECLARATION OF INSURANCE

The broker/salesperson ....
                                                    (Name of Broker/Salesperson)
hereby declares that he/she is insured as required by the Real Estate and Business Brokers Act (REBBA) and Regulations.

....
                                (Signature(s) of Broker/Salesperson)

ACKNOWLEDGEMENT

The Buyer(s) hereby acknowledge that the Buyer(s) fully understand the terms of this Agreement and have received a true copy

of this Agreement on the .... day of ...., 20 ....

....   Date: ....
(Signature of Buyer/Authorized Signing Officer)

....   Date: ....
(Signature of Buyer/Authorized Signing Officer)

Amendment to Buyer Representation Agreement — Commercial

Form 541
for use in the Province of Ontario

RE: BUYER REPRESENTATION AGREEMENT— COMMERCIAL BETWEEN:

BUYER: ....
AND
BROKERAGE: ....

BUYER REGISTRATION NUMBER(S) (if applicable): ....

EXPIRY DATE: ....

The Buyer and the Brokerage hereby agree that the above described Buyer Representation Agreement— Commercial is amended as stated below:

1. EXPIRY DATE:

New Expiry Date .... **Former** Expiry Date ....

Buyer acknowledges that the length of the Agreement is negotiable between the Buyer and the Brokerage, however, in accordance with the Real Estate and Business Brokers Act of Ontario (2002), **if the Agreement exceeds six months from the date of this Amendment, the Brokerage must obtain the Buyer's initials.**

⬭
(Buyer's Initials)

2. OTHER AMENDMENTS: ....

....

....

....

....

All other terms and provisions of the Buyer Representation Agreement— Commercial remain in full force and effect.
An extension of the expiry date must be signed and dated prior to expiration of the Agreement.
The Brokerage agrees to immediately notify the Real Estate Board(s) of the amendment(s) in accordance with the Real Estate Board Rules and Regulations, provided that this Agreement is registered with the Real Estate Board.

This Amendment to Agreement shall not take effect unless signed by all parties set out below.

For the purposes of this Amendment to Buyer Representation Agreement— Commercial, "Buyer" includes purchaser, tenant and lessee and Real Estate Board(s) includes Real Estate Association(s).

SIGNED, SEALED AND DELIVERED I have hereunto set my hand and seal:

.... ●   DATE ....
(Buyer)   (Seal)

.... ●   DATE ....
(Buyer)   (Seal)

....
(Name of Brokerage)

....   DATE ....
(Authorized to bind the Brokerage)   (Print Name of Person Signing)

Form 541   Revised 2008   **Page 1 of 1**

 **Individual Identification Information Record**

Form 630
for use in the Province of Ontario

NOTE: An Individual Identification Information Record is required by the *Proceeds of Crime (Money Laundering) and Terrorist Financing Act*. This Record must be completed by the REALTOR® member whenever they act in respect to the purchase or sale of real estate.

It is recommended that the Individual Identification Information Record be completed:

(i) for a buyer when the offer is submitted and/or a deposit made, and

(ii) for a seller when the seller accepts the offer.

Transaction Property Address: ....

....

....

Sales Representative/Broker Name: ....

Date: ....

A. Verification of Individual

NOTE: This section must be completed for clients that are individuals or unrepresented individuals who are not clients, but are parties to the transaction (e.g. unrepresented buyer or seller). Where an unrepresented individual refuses to provide identification after reasonable efforts are made to verify that identification, a REALTOR® member must keep a record of that refusal and consider sending a Suspicious Transaction Report to FINTRAC if there are reasonable grounds to suspect that the transaction involves property from the proceeds of crime, or terrorist activity. Where you are using an agent or mandatary to verify an individual, see procedure described in CREA's FINTRAC Compliance manual.

1. **Full legal name of individual:** ....

2. **Address:** ....

....

....

....

3. **Date of Birth:** ....

4. **Nature of Principal Business or Occupation:** ....

5. **Type of Identification Document*:** ....
   (must view the original, see below for list of acceptable documents)

6. **Document Identifier Number:** ....

7. **Issuing Jurisdiction:** ....
   (insert name of the applicable Province, Territory, Foreign Jurisdiction or "Federal Government of Canada")

8. **Document Expiry Date:** ....
   (must be valid and not expired)

*Acceptable identification documents: birth certificate, driver's licence, provincial health insurance card (not acceptable if from Ontario, Nova Scotia, Manitoba or Prince Edward Island), passport, record of landing, permanent resident card, old age security card, a certificate of Indian status, or SIN card (although SIN numbers are not to be included on any report sent to FINTRAC). Other acceptable identification documents: provincial or territorial identification card issued by the Insurance Corporation of British Columbia, Alberta Registries, Saskatchewan Government Insurance, the Department of Service Nova Scotia and Municipal Relations, the Department of Transportation and Infrastructure Renewal of the Province of Prince Edward Island, Service New Brunswick, the Department of Government Services and Lands of the Province of Newfoundland and Labrador, the Department of Transportation of the Northwest Territories or the Department of Community Government and Transportation of the Territory of Nunavut. If identification document is from a foreign jurisdiction, it must be equivalent to one of the above identification documents.

 This document has been prepared by The Canadian Real Estate Association to assist members in complying with requirements of Canada's *Proceeds of Crime (Money Laundering) and Terrorist Financing Regulations.* © 2014-2015.

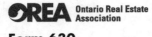

Individual Identification
Information Record

Form 630
for use in the Province of Ontario

B. Verification of Third Parties *(if applicable)*

NOTE: Complete this section of the form when a client *or* unrepresented individual is acting on behalf of a third party. Where you cannot determine if there is a third party, but there are reasonable grounds to suspect the individual is acting on behalf of a third party, you must keep a record of that fact.

1. **Name of third party:** ....

2. **Address:** ....

   ....

   ....

   ....

3. **Date of Birth:** ....

4. **Nature of Principal Business or Occupation:** ....

5. **Incorporation number and place of issue** *(if applicable)***:** ....

6. **Relationship between third party and client:** ....

   ....

   ....

   ....

2
of 4

 **Ontario Real Estate Association**

Individual Identification Information Record

Form 630
for use in the Province of Ontario

Only complete Sections C and D for your clients.

C. Client Risk *(ask your Compliance Officer if this section is applicable)*

Determine the level of risk of a money laundering or terrorist financing offence for this client by determining the appropriate cluster of client in your policies and procedures manual this client falls into and checking one of the checkboxes below:

Low Risk

☐ Canadian Citizen or Resident Physically Present

☐ Canadian Citizen or Resident Not Physically Present

☐ Canadian Citizen or Resident – High Crime Area – No Other Higher Risk Factors Evident

☐ Foreign Citizen or Resident that does not Operate in a High Risk Country (physically present or not)

☐ Other, explain:

Medium Risk

☐ Explain:

High Risk

☐ Foreign Citizen or Resident that operates in a High Risk Country (physically present or not)

☐ Other, explain:

If you determined that the client's risk was high, tell your brokerage's Compliance Officer. They will want to consider this when conducting the overall brokerage risk assessment, which occurs every two years. It will also be relevant in completing Section D below. Note that your brokerage may have developed other clusters not listed above. If no cluster is appropriate, the agent will need to provide a risk assessment of the client, and explain their assessment, in the relevant space above.

REALTOR®

This document has been prepared by The Canadian Real Estate Association to assist members in complying with requirements of Canada's *Proceeds of Crime (Money Laundering) and Terrorist Financing Regulations.* © 2014-2015.

3
of 4

APPENDIX

⭕REA Ontario Real Estate Association

Individual Identification Information Record

Form 630
for use in the Province of Ontario

D. Business Relationship

(ask your Compliance Officer when this section is applicable if you don't know)

D.1. Purpose and Intended Nature of the Business Relationship

Check the appropriate boxes.

Acting as an agent for the purchase or sale of:

☐ Residential property   ☐ Residential property for income purposes

☐ Commercial property   ☐ Land for Commercial Use

☐ Other, please specify:. . . . .

D.2. Measures Taken to Monitor Business Relationship and Keep Client Information Up-To-Date

D.2.1. Ask the Client if their name, address or principal business or occupation has changed and if it has include the updated information on page one.

D.2.2 Keep all relevant correspondence with the client on file in order to maintain a record of the information you have used to monitor the business relationship with the client. Optional - if you have taken measures beyond simply keeping correspondence on file, specify them here:

D.2.3. If the client is high risk you must conduct enhanced measures to monitor the brokerage's business relationship and keep their client information up to date. Optional - consult your Compliance Officer and document what enhanced measures you have applied:

D.3 Suspicious Transactions

Don't forget, if you see something suspicious during the transaction report it to your Compliance Officer. Consult your policies and procedures manual for more information.

 Ontario Real Estate Association

Corporation/Entity Identification Information Record

Form 631
for use in the Province of Ontario

NOTE: A Corporation/Entity Identification Information Record is required by the *Proceeds of Crime (Money Laundering) and Terrorist Financing Act*. This Record must be completed by the REALTOR® member whenever they act in respect to the purchase or sale of real estate.

It is recommended that the Corporation/Entity Identification Information Record be completed:

    (i) for a buyer when the offer is submitted and/or a deposit made, and

    (ii) for a seller when the seller accepts the offer.

Transaction Property Address: ....

....

....

Sales Representative/Broker Name: ....

Date: ....

A.1. Verification of Corporation

1. **Name of corporation:** ....

2. **Corporate Address:** ....

....

....

3. **Nature of Principal Business:** ....

4. **Name of Directors:** As set out in certificate of corporate status or other record confirming corporation's existence.

....

....

5. **Type and Source of Verification Record:**

Must confirm existence of the corporation (e.g., certificate of corporate status, published annual report, government notice of assessment). If record is in paper format, a copy must be kept. If record is an electronic version, a record of the corporation's registration number and type and source of record (e.g., Corporations Canada website) must be kept.

....

....

6. **Registration number of corporation:** ....

7. **Copy of corporate record showing authority to bind corporation regarding transaction:**

(e.g., certificate of incumbency, articles of incorporation, by-laws setting out officers duly authorized to sign on behalf of corporation)

....

....

 1 of 4

 **Ontario Real Estate Association**

Corporation/Entity Identification Information Record

Form 631
for use in the Province of Ontario

A.2. Verification of Other Entity *(if applicable)*

1. **Name of other entity:** ....

2. **Address:** ....

   ....

   ....

3. **Nature of Principal Business:** ....

4. **Type of Verification Record:** Must confirm existence of other entity (e.g., partnership agreement, articles of association).

   ....

5. **Source of Record:** ....

   Record may be paper or an electronic version. If record is in paper format, a copy must be kept. If record is an
   electronic version, a record of the entity's registration number and type and source of record must be kept.

6. **Registration number:** ....

B. Verification of Third Parties *(if applicable)*

NOTE: Complete this section of the form when a client is acting on behalf of a third party. Where you cannot determine if
there is a third party, but there are reasonable grounds to suspect the client is acting on behalf of a third party, you must
keep a record of that fact.

1. **Name of other entity:** ....

2. **Address:** ....

   ....

   ....

3. **Date of Birth:** ....

4. **Nature of Principal Business or Occupation:** ....

   ....

5. **Incorporation number and place of issue** *(if applicable):* ....

   ....

6. **Relationship between third party and client:** ....

   ....

   ....

 This document has been prepared by The Canadian Real Estate Association to assist members in complying with requirements
of Canada's *Proceeds of Crime (Money Laundering) and Terrorist Financing Regulations*. © 2014-2015.   **2** of 4

Form 631   *(continued)*   Page 3 of 4

 **Ontario Real Estate Association**

Corporation/Entity Identification Information Record

Form 631
for use in the Province of Ontario

Only complete Sections C and D for your clients.

C. Client Risk *(ask your Compliance Officer if this section is applicable)*

Determine the level of risk of a money laundering or terrorist financing offence for this client by determining the appropriate cluster of client in your policies and procedures manual this client falls into and checking one of the checkboxes below:

Low Risk

☐ Canadian Corporation or Entity

☐ Foreign Corporation or Entity that does not operate in a High Risk Country

☐ Other, explain:

Medium Risk

☐ Explain:

High Risk

☐ Foreign Corporation or Entity that operates in a High Risk Country

☐ Other, explain:

If you determined that the client's risk was high, tell your brokerage's Compliance Officer. They will want to consider this when conducting the overall brokerage risk assessment, which occurs every two years. It will also be relevant in completing Section D below. Note that your brokerage may have developed other clusters not listed above. If no cluster is appropriate, the agent will need to provide a risk assessment of the client, and explain their assessment, in the relevant space above.

3 of 4

APPENDIX

 **Ontario Real Estate Association**   **Corporation/Entity Identification Information Record**

Form 631
for use in the Province of Ontario

D. Business Relationship
(ask your Compliance Officer when this section is applicable if you don't know)

D.1. Purpose and Intended Nature of the Business Relationship

Check the appropriate boxes.

Acting as an agent for the purchase or sale of:

☐ Land for Commercial Use

☐ Commercial property

☐ Other, please specify: . . . .

D.2. Measures Taken to Monitor Business Relationship and Keep Client Information Up-To-Date

D.2.1. If the client is a corporation, ask if its name and address and name of its directors have changed and if they have include the updated information on page one. If the client is an entity other than a corporation, ask if its name, address and principal place of business has changed and if they have include the updated information on page one.

D.2.2 Keep all relevant correspondence with the client on file in order to maintain a record of the information you have used to monitor the business relationship with the client. Optional - if you have taken measures beyond simply keeping correspondence on file, specify them here:

D.2.3. If the client is high risk you must conduct enhanced measures to monitor the brokerage's business relationship and keep their client information up to date. Optional - consult your Compliance Officer and document what enhanced measures you have applied:

D.3 Suspicious Transactions

Don't forget, if you see something suspicious during the transaction report it to your Compliance Officer. Consult your policies and procedures manual for more information.

 This document has been prepared by The Canadian Real Estate Association to assist members in complying with requirements of Canada's *Proceeds of Crime (Money Laundering) and Terrorist Financing Regulations.* © 2014-2015.

APPENDIX

 **Ontario Real Estate Association**

Form 632
for use in the Province of Ontario

Identification Mandatary/ Agent Agreement

BETWEEN:
REAL ESTATE BROKER: _____ , having its principal office at _____ (the "**Broker**");
_____
_____
_____

and
IDENTIFICATION AGENT: _____ , having its principal office at _____
_____
_____
_____

The parties agree to the terms and conditions set out in this agreement as of _____, 20___ (the "**Effective Date**").

1. Purpose

This agreement constitutes a written agreement as required by Section 64.1 of the Regulations under the Proceeds of Crime (Money Laundering) and Terrorist Financing Act.

2. Services

(a) On request, the Agent will provide the Broker with the identification services described in Schedule A in respect of an individual and/or the identification services described in Schedule B in respect of a corporation or other entity (the "**Services**"). The Broker will make available to the Agent all reasonable information required to enable the Agent to perform the Services.

(b) The Broker will compensate the Agent as follows: _____

3. Approvals and Authority

The Agent will obtain Broker's prior written approval for all Services it performs on the Broker's behalf.

4. Termination

Either party may terminate this agreement at any time on written notice to the other, provided that the Agent is required to complete any Services requested at the time of termination, and the Broker is required to pay for such Services.

5. Indemnification

The Agent will indemnify the Broker against any claims, liability, costs and reasonable expenses arising directly from the Agent's negligent acts or omissions in the performance of the Services.

6. Confidentiality

The Agent acknowledges that any information received from the Broker and/or the individuals from whom the Agent may obtain information under this Agreement is proprietary and confidential, and constitutes "personal information" within the meaning of the *Personal Information Protection and Electronic Documents Act* (PIPEDA) (collectively, "Confidential Information"). The Agent will not reveal to any third party any information provided by the Broker, except as required by the Regulations or as necessary to perform the Services, either during or subsequent to the term of this Agreement, and will at all times comply with the provisions of PIPEDA or any applicable provincial privacy legislation as well as any privacy policies of the Broker. Upon termination of this Agreement, the Agent will return to the Broker all Confidential Information in the possession of the Agent.

7. Regulatory Compliance

The parties acknowledge that the Broker is subject to a number of regulatory regimes, including regulations and regulatory requirements, decisions, rulings and guidelines issued by the Financial Transactions and Reports Analysis Centre of Canada ("FINTRAC"). The Agent will provide its reasonable assistance to the Broker in order to facilitate the Broker's compliance with FINTRAC requirements.

The Agent will abide by the policies and procedures designated by Broker and lawfully issued by Broker in accordance with the *Proceeds of Crime (Money Laundering) and Terrorist Financing Act*, regulations and regulatory requirements, decisions, rulings and guidelines issued by FINTRAC.

 1 of 4

 **Ontario Real Estate Association**

Identification Mandatary/ Agent Agreement

Form 632
for use in the Province of Ontario

8. Non-Assignable

This Agreement is not assignable by either party without mutual consent, which consent will not be unreasonably withheld.

9. Audit

The Agent grants to the Broker the right, at all reasonable times, to examine and audit all records in its possession or under its control which directly pertain to the Services provided to the Broker under this Agreement or as otherwise may be required under the Regulations.

10. Applicable Law

This Agreement will be construed in accordance with the laws of the [Insert name of Province/Territory]
_____ and the laws of Canada applicable therein.

11. Severability

The obligations and agreements of the Broker and Agent under this Agreement will be treated as separate and severable.

12. Complete Agreement

This Agreement, including the attached Schedules, constitutes the entire Agreement between the Broker and the Agent. The terms cannot be changed, except by an instrument in writing signed by the parties.

The Agent's authority to act on behalf of the Broker is limited to the rights, duties and responsibilities set out in this Agreement.

IN WITNESS WHEREOF the parties have executed this agreement the _____ day of _____, 20____ .

BROKER   **AGENT**

Per: _____   Per: _____

Title: Authorized Signing Officer   Title: Authorized Signing Officer

Date: _____   Date: _____

_____   _____

_____   _____

_____   _____

_____   _____

_____   _____

_____   _____

2 of 4

 **OREA** Ontario Real Estate Association

Form 632
for use in the Province of Ontario

Identification Mandatary/ Agent Agreement

Schedule A - Services with respect to individuals

1. Agent will take the necessary steps to verify and provide the following information to the Broker when dealing with an individual:

(a) Full legal name of individual: _____

(b) Address: _____

_____

(c) Date of Birth: _____

(d) Nature of Principal Business or Occupation: _____

(e) Type of Identification Document (e.g. drivers permit, passport, or government issued ID)[1]

_____

(Note: provide photocopy of Identification Document)

(f) Document Identifier Number: _____

(g) Issuing Jurisdiction: _____

(h) Document Expiry: _____

2. Agent will take necessary steps to verify whether or not the individual is acting on behalf of a third party and provide the following information to the Broker:

(a) Is Client acting on behalf of a third party?

Yes ☐   No ☐   Reasonable suspicion[2] ☐

(b) Name of third party: _____

(c) Address: _____

(d) Date of Birth: _____

(e) Nature of Principal Business or Occupation: _____

(f) Incorporation number and place of issue (if applicable): _____

(g) Relationship between third party and client: _____

_____

_____

_____

_____

_____

_____

_____

[1] List of Acceptable Identification Documents is subject to change at the sole discretion of the Broker upon notice to agent. The following may apply: birth certificate, driver's licence, provincial health insurance card (not acceptable if from Ontario, Manitoba, Nova Scotia or Prince Edward Island), passport, record of landing, permanent resident card, old age security card, a certificate of Indian status, or SIN card (although SIN numbers are not to be included on any report sent to FINTRAC). Other acceptable identification documents: provincial or territorial identification card issued by the Insurance Corporation of British Columbia, Alberta Registries, Saskatchewan Government Insurance, the Department of Service Nova Scotia and Municipal Relations, the Department of Transportation and Infrastructure Renewal of the Province of Prince Edward Island, Service New Brunswick, the Department of Government Services and Lands of the Province of Newfoundland and Labrador, the Department of Transportation of the Northwest Territories or the Department of Community Government and Transportation of the Territory of Nunavut. If identification document is from a foreign jurisdiction, it must be equivalent to one of the above identification documents.

[2] Reasonable suspicion would arise when circumstances indicate the possibility of a third party but the individual will not confirm.

 This document has been prepared by The Canadian Real Estate Association to assist members in complying with requirements of Canada's *Proceeds of Crime (Money Laundering) and Terrorist Financing Regulations*. © 2008-2015.

 **Ontario Real Estate Association**

Form 632
for use in the Province of Ontario

Identification Mandatary/ Agent Agreement

Schedule B - Services in respect of corporations/other entities

Corporation

1. Agent will take the necessary steps to verify and provide the following information to the Broker when dealing with a corporation (with a copy of the actual record, where indicated):

(a) Name of corporation: _____

(b) Corporate address: _____
_____

(c) Nature of Principal Business: _____

(d) Names of Directors[3]: _____

(e) Copy of record confirming existence of corporation: _____

(i) Type of verification record[4]: _____

(ii) Source of verification record[5]: _____

(f) Registration number of corporation: _____

(g) Copy of corporate record showing authority to bind corporation regarding transaction[6]:
_____

Other entity (e.g., partnership)

2. Agent will take the necessary steps to verify and provide the following information to the Broker when dealing with an entity (with a copy of the actual record, where indicated):

(a) Name of entity: _____

(b) Entity address: _____
_____

(c) Nature of Principal Business: _____

(d) Copy of record confirming existence of entity: _____

(i) Type of verification record[7]: _____

(ii) Source of verification record[8]: _____

(e) Registration number of entity: _____

3. Agent will take the necessary steps to verify whether or not the corporation or entity is acting on behalf of a third party.

(a) Is Client acting on behalf of a third party?

Yes ☐   No ☐   Reasonable suspicion[9] ☐

(b) Name of third party: _____

(c) Address: _____
_____

(d) Date of Birth: _____

(e) Nature of Principal Business or Occupation: _____

(f) Incorporation number and place of issue (if applicable): _____

(g) Relationship between third party and client: _____

---

[3] As set out in certificate of corporate status or other record confirming corporation's existence.

[4] For example, certificate of corporate status, published annual report, government notice of assessment.

[5] If record is in paper format, a copy must be sent by the Agent to the Broker. If the record is an electronic version, a record of the corporation's registration number and type and source of record (e.g., Corporations Canada website) must be indicated above.

[6] For example, certificate of incumbency, articles of incorporation, by-laws setting out officers duly authorized to sign on behalf of corporation. A copy must be sent by the Agent to the Broker.

[7] For example, partnership agreement, articles of association.

[8] If record is in paper format, a copy must be sent by the Agent to the Broker. If the record is an electronic version, a record of the entity's registration number and type and source of record must be indicated above.

[9] Reasonable suspicion would arise when circumstances indicate the possibility of a third party but the entity's representative will not confirm.

---

 4 of 4

Consent Agreement

OREA Ontario Real Estate Association

Form 633
for use in the Province of Ontario

_____
[date]

VIA _____
[means of communication]

_____
[address]

_____

_____

Attention: _____
[name of lawyer or representative]

Dear Sir or Madam:

Re: Identification Information Record - _____
[details of transaction (e.g., address)]

Real estate agents/brokers are subject to the *Proceeds of Crime (Money Laundering) and Terrorist Financing Act* and its associated Regulations. As such, we are required to confirm the existence of, and ascertain the name and address of, every corporation or other entity (e.g., partnership) on whose behalf we conduct a transaction, as well as the names of its directors. We are also required to confirm that the person entering into the transaction on behalf of the corporation has the power to bind the corporation regarding the transaction. We therefore request your assistance in completing our Identification Information Record

with respect to the above-noted transaction for _____
[name of corporation]

We enclose a form which lists the information we are required to include in our records. Please complete the form, attach the requested documents and return the materials to

_____ at _____
[name]   *[refer to mailing address or email address]*

We also enclose a consent from _____ to the release
of this information.   *[name of corporation]*

We are required to confirm the existence of _____
[name of corporation]

and complete the information record within 30 days of the closing of this transaction or, where the corporation is the buyer, within 30 days of the deposit being made. We would

therefore appreciate receiving the documents listed above no later than _____
[date]

If you have any questions please do not hesitate to contact us.

Yours very truly,

APPENDIX

Form 633   *(continued)*

OREA Ontario Real Estate Association   **Consent Agreement**

Form 633
for use in the Province of Ontario

Information Form Respecting Corporations/Other Entities

If you act for a corporation

1. Please provide the following information:

(a) Name of corporation:	
(b) Corporate address:	
(c) Nature of Principal Business:	
(d) Names of Directors:	

2. Please provide the following records:

   (a) Copy of a corporate record showing authority to bind corporation regarding transaction[1]

   (b) Copy of record confirming existence of corporation[2]:

   (c) If the records are in paper format, please enclose a copy with this form. In the event that you provide an electronic version of a record which is publically accessible, please provide the following information:

i.	Registration number of corporation:	
ii.	Type of verification record[3]:	
iii.	Source of verification record[4]:	

---

[1] For example, certificate of incumbency, articles of incorporation or by-laws setting out the officers duly authorized to sign on behalf of corporation.

[2] For example, certificate of corporate status or other record confirming corporation's existence.

[3] For example, certificate of corporate status, published annual report, government notice of assessment.

[4] For example, Corporations Canada website.

2 of 5

ØREA Ontario Real Estate Association   **Consent Agreement**

Form 633
for use in the Province of Ontario

If you act for an entity other than a corporation (e.g., partnership)

1. Please provide the following information:

(a) Name of entity:	
(b) Entity address:	
(c) Nature of Principal Business:	

2. Please provide the following records:

   (a) Copy of record confirming existence of entity[5]:

   If the record is in paper format, please enclose a copy with this form. In the event that you provide an electronic version of a record which is publically accessible, please provide the following information:

i.	Registration number of entity:	
ii.	Type of verification record:	
iii.	Source of verification record:	

Whether you act for a corporation or an entity other than a corporation

Please indicate whether or not the corporation or entity is acting on behalf of a third party with respect to this real estate transaction.

   (a) Is corporation or entity acting on behalf of a third party?

Yes		No		Reasonable suspicion[6]	

---

[5] For example, partnership agreement, articles of association.
[6] Reasonable suspicion would arise when circumstances indicate the possibility of a third party but the entity's representative will not confirm.

Consent Agreement

Form 633
for use in the Province of Ontario

(b) Name of third party:	
(c) Address:	
(d) Date of Birth:	
(e) Nature of Principal Business or Occupation:	
(f) Incorporation number and place of issue (if applicable):	
(g) Relationship between third party and corporation or entity:	

OREA Ontario Real Estate Association   **Consent Agreement**

Form 633
for use in the Province of Ontario

Consent

I, _____ as a duly authorized representative of _____ ,
    [name of individual]   *[name of corporation]*

hereby authorize _____ to release and communicate to_____
                          [lawyer]   *[name]*

the corporation information set out in the attached Information Form Respecting Corporations/Other Entities

for the sole purpose of enabling_____ to comply with his/her obligations
                                          [name]

under the *Proceeds of Crime (Money Laundering) and Terrorist Financing Act* and its associated Regulations.

Name in print:	
Signature:	
Date:	

APPENDIX

 **Receipt of Funds Record**

Form 635
for use in the Province of Ontario

NOTE: A Receipt of Funds record is required by the *Proceeds of Crime (Money Laundering) and Terrorist Financing Act* for every amount of funds that a REALTOR® member receives in the course of a single purchase or sale real estate transaction.
A REALTOR® does NOT have to complete a Receipt of Funds Record if:
  (i)   the funds are received from a financial entity or a public body that is buying or selling; or,
  (ii) a Large Cash Transaction Record must be completed; or,
  (iii) the deposit does not go into the trust account of a licensed practitioner. In other words, if the deposit goes directly into the account of a builder, lawyer or notary, or developer, a Receipt of Funds Record does not have to be completed by a member acting as the buyers' agent.

When this Record is completed, it is the responsibility of the broker to ensure that a record is kept for five years from the date it was created.
  (i)   When a REALTOR® member completes a Receipt of Funds Record, they must also complete an Identification Information Record at the same time, unless the Identification Information Record was completed prior to the receipt of funds.
  (ii) When both the buyer and seller are represented, it is the agent of the buyer who is required to complete and retain a Receipt of Funds Record in respect of the deposit made, regardless of who retains the deposit.

Transaction Property Address: ....

....

....

Sales Representative/Broker Name: ....

Date: ....

1. Amount of Funds Received: .... **Currency:** ....

  ☐ Cheque ☐ Certified Cheque ☐ Cash ☐ Bank Draft

  ☐ Other, explain: ....

(a) If cash, indicate method of receipt *(in person, mail, courier, other (explain))* ....

(b) If cheque, indicate: Number of account: ....

  Financial Institution: .... **Name of account holder:** ....

2. Date of receipt of funds: ....

3. Account where funds were deposited *(eg. Broker's trust account):* ....
Where there are two agents involved in a transaction and the funds are deposited in the listing agent's account the buyer's agent is responsible for completing the receipt of funds record. However, the buyer's agent is not required to include the number and type of the listing agent's account or the name of the person or entity that is the holder of that account if, after taking reasonable measures, they are unable to do so. Further, if dealing with trust accounts, although the buyer's agent must indicate that the funds were deposited into the listing agent's trust account, the buyer's agent would not be required to include the number of the trust account or the name or entity that holds the trust account.

Note that if multiple accounts are affected, information on all accounts affected needs to be recorded. For example, assuming the buyer's agent transfers funds from their account into the listing agent's account, both accounts are affected by the transaction and therefore both numbers are to be recorded on the Receipt of Funds Record. However, the features noted in the previous paragraph with respect to the listing agent's accounts still apply.

  Indicate type of account where deposit has been made: ☐ Trust ☐ Other

  Number of account: .... **Name of account holder:** ....

4. Purpose of funds (e.g., deposit for purchase): ....

5. Other details concerning receipt of funds: ....

....

 This document has been prepared by The Canadian Real Estate Association to assist members in complying with requirements of Canada's *Proceeds of Crime (Money Laundering) and Terrorist Financing Regulations.* © 2014-2015.

Form 640   *Trade Record Sheet*   Page 1 of 2

OREA Ontario Real Estate Association   **Trade Record Sheet**

Form 640
for use in the Province of Ontario

| Sale No: |
| MLS® No: |

.... Dated: ...., 20...........
(Name of Brokerage)

I, ..., have today sold (leased or rented, exchanged, optioned):
(Name of Broker/Salesperson)

Property ....

SELLER/LANDLORD:	**BUYER/TENANT:**
....	....
....	....
Address	Address ....
....	....
Tel	Tel ....
Fax	Fax ....
Lawyer	Lawyer ....
....	....
....	....
Tel	Tel ....
Fax	Fax ....

CO-OPERATING/LISTING BROKERAGE (If applicable):   ☐ Listing Brokerage   ☐ Co-operating Brokerage

Address ....
Tel .... Fax ....
Co-op Brokerage HST Number..

REFERRAL BROKERAGE   Tel ....
Address .... Fax ....

REFERRAL BROKERAGE   Tel ....
Address .... Fax ....

Total Consideration For Transaction $ ....
(sale price, rent, exchange value, option price, fee (other))

Completion Date ....

Deposit $... ☐ cash   ☐ cheque

If cheque, payable to ...., in trust.

Additional Deposit $ .... ☐ cash   ☐ cheque

If cheque, payable to ...., in trust.

Property Other Than Money Held In Trust ....
....

Total	**Total**	**Total**
Commission $	HST $	Receivable Comm $ ....

(Broker/Salesperson)   (Broker/Salesperson)

   Form 640   Revised 2015   **Page 1 of 2**

Form 640   *(continued)*   Page 2 of 2

Property ....   Sale No.: _____

Seller/Landlord ....   MLS® No.: _____

Buyer/Tenant ....

THE FOLLOWING TO BE COMPLETED BY THE BROKERAGE:

Total Receivable Commission:	COMMISSION	HST	TOTAL	DATE PAID	CHEQUE NO.
Listing Brokerage:					
Listing #1 Salesperson/ Broker #2					
Co-op Brokerage:					
Selling #1 Salesperson/ Broker #2					
Referral Fee:					
Referral Fee:					
Real Estate Board:					
Other:					

Received deposit from (Salesperson/Broker) ....   DATE ....

Additional deposit from (Salesperson/Broker) ....   DATE ....

Deposited in Real Estate Trust Acc. (Amount)..   DATE ....

Additional deposit to Real Estate Trust Acc. (Amount)................................   DATE ....

Statement to Seller DATE...

Interest bearing deposit transferred to ....

Instrument #...   DATE ....   Cheque # ....

Interest bearing deposit returned

to Real Estate Trust Acc. (Amount).....................................   DATE ....   Cheque # ....

If applicable, Interest earned (Amount) ....

If applicable, interest paid to ....

Cheque # ....

If applicable, SIN of interest recipient ....

If applicable, Business # of Corporation ....

Remitted to Seller/Buyer (Amount) ....   DATE ....   Cheque # ....

Transferred to Commission Trust (Amount) ....   DATE ....   Cheque # ....

Transferred Commission to Gen. Acct. (Amount) ....   DATE ....   Cheque # ....

Additional Necessary Information ....

....

....

To the best of my knowledge and belief the above information is correct.

DATED at .... Ontario, this .... day of ...., 20...............

....
(Signature of Broker of Record)

FOR OFFICE USE ONLY   **COMMISSION TRUST AGREEMENT**
To: The Salesperson(s) shown on the foregoing Trade Record Sheet:
In consideration of the Salesperson(s) having successfully completed a trade in real estate on behalf of the Brokerage with respect to the property more particularly dened in the foregoing Trade Record Sheet, I hereby declare that all moneys received or receivable by me in connection with the transaction as contemplated in the Office Policy shall be receivable and held in trust. This agreement shall constitute a Commission Trust Agreement as defined in the Office Policy and shall be subject to and governed by the Office Policy pertaining to Commission Trust. DATED as of the date and time of the acceptance of the foregoing Trade Record Sheet.   Acknowledged by:

....
(Signature of Broker of Record/Manager)   (Signature of Broker/Salesperson)

Form 640   Revised 2015   **Page 2 of 2**

OREA Ontario Real Estate Association

Notification of Completion of Sale

Form 642
for use in the Province of Ontario

LAWYER: ....

....

....

Fax# ....

PLEASE COMPLETE AND RETURN THIS FORM TO:

.... (Real Estate Brokerage)

....

....

Fax# ....

This is to advise you that the transaction concerning the property known as:

....

between .... (Seller(s))

and .... (Buyer(s))

was completed on .... (date)

DATED at .... this .... day of ...., 20.................

....
(Lawyer)

Form 642   Revised 2008   **Page 1 of 1**

APPENDIX

CLAUSES

RESIDENTIAL AND COMMERCIAL CLAUSES

Introduction

The Ontario Real Estate Association can best fulfil its responsibility and role in organized real estate by ensuring that all persons engaged in real estate brokerage business, either as brokers or salespersons, have an opportunity to be properly trained and well informed, and thereby better serve the public in a professional manner. To this end, this series of clauses is provided to complement the growing list of educational programs, reference materials, standard forms, and video instruction available to the general membership.

General Disclaimer and Caution to User

The Ontario Real Estate Association has developed these clauses for the use of its members in drafting Agreements of Purchase and Sale. The clauses which are contained herein are provided solely for the purpose of guidance and do not in any way constitute required wording.

Take note that every real estate transaction is unique and the Ontario Real Estate Association does not warrant and is not responsible in any way for the adequacy, sufficiency, applicability, accuracy or suitability of any of the clauses or provisions hereinafter set out. Further, the Ontario Real Estate Association assumes no liability for the utilization of any of the clauses or provisions hereinafter set out.

The real estate professional is encouraged to seek expert advice in the drafting of agreements.

Important Instructions To Users

(a) Typed Supersedes Printed: Any clauses added to the body of the Offer will supersede any information in the pre-printed form. Therefore, care must be taken with any inclusions.

(b) Conditions versus Warranties/Representations: The decision to utilize a condition, warranty, or other representation will depend largely on circumstances. The vast majority of clauses are presented in "condition" format. However, various warranty examples have been included. The reader should note that most warranties included in the handbook are made "to the best knowledge and belief," survive the closing, and do not extend beyond completion of the transaction. Many variations exist in the marketplace and caution is advised when using warranties and representations. A limited number of such clauses has been included for information purposes only.

(c) Alternative Wordings: In select instances, alternative wordings are provided for the same general topic area (i.e., road access to a recreational property might address rights-of-way, unregistered easements, public road access, privately maintained road, etc.). Users should carefully read all possibilities and revise as required to meet individual circumstances.

(d) Capitalized Words: The first letter of selected words has been capitalized for emphasis only (i.e., Buyer, Seller, Agreement of Purchase and Sale, Lease) and should not be viewed as a required format.

(e) Use of Pronouns: This text should be read with all changes of gender and number as the reader may feel are required.

TABLE OF CONTENTS

APPENDIX

APPENDIX

APPENDIX

APPENDIX

APPENDIX

APPENDIX

APPENDIX

APPENDIX

ACCESS

ACC–1

Condition—Obtaining
Right-of-way

This Offer is conditional upon the Buyer obtaining an Agreement to create an easement with (name of persons), for the purpose of (insert specific use), located and more particularly described as (outline planned location). Unless the Buyer gives notice in writing delivered to the Seller personally or in accordance with any other provisions for the delivery of notice in this Agreement of Purchase and Sale or any Schedule thereto not later than _____ p.m. on the day of _____, 20_____, that this condition is fulfilled, this Offer shall become null and void and the deposit shall be returned to the Buyer in full without deduction. This condition is included for the benefit of the Buyer and may be waived at the Buyer's sole option by notice in writing to the Seller as aforesaid within the time period stated herein.

NOTE: This condition must be used with caution, as further approvals will be required for the right-of-way to be legal (i.e., Committee of Adjustments).

ACC–2

Condition—Road Access
by Open Public Road

This Offer is conditional upon the Buyer determining, at the Buyer's own expense, that access by automobile to the property is by a public road which is maintained at public expense throughout the year. Unless the Buyer gives notice in writing delivered to the Seller personally or in accordance with any other provisions for the delivery of notice in this Agreement of Purchase and Sale or any Schedule thereto not later than _____ p.m. on the _____ day of _____, 20_____, that this condition has been fulfilled, this Offer shall become null and void and the deposit shall be returned to the Buyer in full without deduction. This condition is included for the benefit of the Buyer and may be waived at the Buyer's sole option by notice in writing to the Seller as aforesaid within the time period stated herein.

ACC–3

Condition—Road Access
to Public Highways

This Offer is conditional upon the Buyer determining, at the Buyer's own expense, that all vehicular entrances to and exits from the property onto public highways have been approved under the Public Transportation and Highways Improvement Act or any predecessor thereof. Unless the Buyer gives notice in writing delivered to the Seller personally or in accordance with any other provisions for the delivery of notice in this Agreement of Purchase and Sale or any Schedule thereto not later than _____ p.m. on the _____ day of _____, 20_____, that his condition has been fulfilled, this Offer shall become null and void and the deposit shall be returned to the Buyer in full without deduction. This condition is included for the benefit of the Buyer and may be waived at the Buyer's sole option by notice in writing to the Seller as aforesaid within the time period stated herein.

ACC–4

Road Access—Alternatives

The Seller represents and warrants, to the best of the Seller's knowledge and belief, that the property fronts on: [choose appropriate statement]

> (a) a road which is maintained on a year round basis at public expense; OR
> > OR
> (b) a road which is maintained on a seasonal basis at public expense; OR
> > OR
> (c) a road which is not maintained at public expense.

The Parties agree that this representation and warranty shall survive and not merge on completion of this transaction, but apply only to the state of the property existing at completion of this transaction.

ACC–5

Road Access—Privately
Maintained Road

The Buyer acknowledges that the private road accessing the said property is maintained by the [insert appropriate local cottage association or other relevant group], at an annual cost of $_____ for each property.

ACC–6

Road Access—Unregistered Easement (Trespass Access)

The Buyer acknowledges that the [road/path/lane], to the said property may be an unregistered easement. The Seller shall provide to the Buyer, on or before completion, a statutory declaration or declarations establishing that the existing [road/path/lane], has been used by the Seller and/or predecessors in title to gain access to the said property for a period of _____ years.

NOTE: In situations involving unregistered easements, legal advice should be sought.

....

ACC–7

Water Access

The Buyer acknowledges that the property is only accessible by water.

....

ACC–8

Water Access— Fluctuating Water Levels

The Buyer acknowledges that the water levels in the area where the property is situated may fluctuate between a low and high water level and may be extremely low or extremely high from time to time. Therefore, access to the property through means of water and/or access to the water from the property may be difficult or not available. The Buyer agrees that no claim will be made against the Seller, or any Brokerage, Broker or Salesperson, respecting the levels of the water including without limitation matters of access whether to the property by water or from the property to the water.

ASSIGNMENT OF AGREEMENT

ASSIGN–1

Right to Assign Agreement

The Buyer shall have the right at any time prior to closing, to assign the within Offer to any person, persons or corporation, either existing or to be incorporated, and upon delivery to the Seller of notice of such assignment, together with the assignee's covenant in favour of the Seller to be bound hereby as Buyer, the Buyer hereinbefore named shall stand released from all further liability hereunder.

NOTE: Do not use when the Agreement includes a STB Charge/Mortgage.

....

ASSIGN–2

Right to Assign— Seller's Consent

The Buyer covenants and agrees that the Buyer will in no way directly or indirectly assign, rent, lease, convey, list or in any way advertise for sale, sell, or otherwise transfer the Buyer's rights under this Agreement prior to completion to any other person or entity without the express written consent of the Seller. Such consent may be granted or withheld at the Seller's sole option.

ASSOCIATION FEES

ASSOC–1

Association Fees on Title

The Buyer acknowledges that there are agreements, restrictions and covenants registered on the title pertaining to an association and that there is an association fee payable in respect thereof. The Seller warrants that the said fee payable to the association in respect of the property is approximately $ _____ per _____ [year/month] and includes but is not limited to_____.
The Buyer agrees to accept the title subject to the said agreements, restrictions and covenants and assume payment of the association fee, to be adjusted as of completion.

BUILDINGS/CONSTRUCTION

This Offer is conditional upon the Buyer determining, at the Buyer's own expense, that a building permit for the structure indicated on Schedule "_____" attached hereto is available with respect to the property. Unless the Buyer gives notice in writing to the Seller personally or in accordance with any other provisions for the delivery of notice in this Agreement of Purchase and Sale or any Schedule thereto not later than _____ p.m. on the _____ day of _____, 20_____ , that this condition has been fulfilled, this Offer shall become null and void and the deposit shall be returned to the Buyer in full without deduction. This condition is included for the benefit of the Buyer and may be waived at the Buyer's sole option by notice in writing to the Seller as aforesaid within the time period stated herein.

BUILD/CONST–1

Condition—Obtaining Building Permit

CHATTELS/EQUIPMENT/FIXTURES

This offer is conditional upon the Buyer reviewing the terms of any rental agreements, rental contracts, lease contracts or lease to own agreements ("Rental Agreements") with respect to the rental items not included in the purchase price but to be assumed by the Buyer and finding such terms to be satisfactory to the Buyer in the Buyer's sole and absolute discretion. The Seller will provide copies of such rental agreements within _____ days of acceptance of this offer. Unless the Buyer gives notice in writing to the Seller personally or in accordance with any other provisions for delivery of notice in this Agreement of Purchase and Sale or any Schedule thereto not later than 5 p.m. on the _____ day of _____, 20_____, that this condition is fulfilled, this offer shall be null and void and the deposit shall be returned to the Buyer in full without deduction. This condition is included for the sole benefit of the Buyer and may be waived at the Buyer's sole option by notice in writing to the Seller as aforesaid within the time period stated herein.

CHATT–1

Condition— Rental Contracts

The Seller represents and warrants that the chattels and fixtures as included in this Agreement of Purchase and Sale will be in good working order and free from all liens and encumbrances on completion. The Parties agree that this representation and warranty shall survive and not merge on completion of this transaction, but apply only to the state of the property at completion of this transaction.

CHATT–2

Chattels and Fixtures— Good Working Order

The Buyer acknowledges that there is no express or implied warranty by the Seller on the chattels included in this Agreement of Purchase and Sale.

CHATT–3

Chattels—No Warranty

The Seller warrants that all the mechanical, electrical, heating, ventilation, air conditioning systems, air compressors, elevators, conveyor systems, sprinkler systems, boilers, and all other equipment on the real property shall be in good working order on completion. The Parties agree that this warranty shall survive and not merge on completion of this transaction, but apply only to those circumstances existing at the completion of this transaction.

CHATT–4

Equipment— Good Working Order

The Seller agrees to give the Buyer the first right to negotiate for the purchase of any equipment to be sold by the Seller upon a price to be mutually agreed upon. In the event that the parties cannot agree to a price at least _____ days prior to the date of completion, then said first right shall become null and void.

CHATT–5

Equipment— Purchase of Additional

APPENDIX

CHATT–6
Equipment—Removal

The Seller agrees to remove, at the expense of the Seller, any machinery or equipment, including mountings protruding from walls and floors, and to repair any damage caused by said removal.

CHATT–7
Lighting Fixtures

All lighting fixtures on the premises are included in the purchase price and are to be in good working order on completion.

CHATT–8
Rental Items

The following equipment is rented and not included in the Purchase Price. The Buyer agrees to assume the rental contract(s) if assumable: _____ [item] having a payment of $ _____, _____[monthly, quarterly, etc.].

NOTE: A variety of items may be rentals, e.g. hot water tank, air conditioner, water softener, furnace, furnace burner, etc. Care must be taken to ensure all rentals are documented.

COMPLETION DATE

COMP–1
Change of Completion Date by Buyer

Notwithstanding the completion date set out in this Offer, the Buyer may _____ [advance/postpone] the completion date of the transaction by not more than _____ days, by giving written notice of the amended completion date to the Seller or the Seller's Solicitor at least _____ days in advance of the earlier of the completion date set out herein and the amended completion date.

COMP–2
Change of Completion Date by Seller

Notwithstanding the completion date set out in this Offer, the Seller may _____ [advance/postpone] the completion date of the transaction by not more than _____ days, by giving written notice of the amended completion date to the Buyer or the Buyer's Solicitor at least _____ days in advance of the earlier of the completion date set out herein and the amended completion date.

COMP–3
Change of Completion Date—Mutual Agreement

Notwithstanding the completion date set out in this Agreement, the Buyer and Seller may, by mutual agreement in writing, advance or extend the date of completion of this transaction.

COMP–4
Change of Completion Date—Probate Trustee

The Buyer and Seller agree that the Seller, upon giving a minimum of _____ days written notice to the Buyer (excluding, Saturday, Sunday or Statutory Holidays), may unilaterally extend the date set for completion, one or more times, not to exceed _____ days in total, for the purpose of obtaining a Certificate of Appointment of Estate Trustee.

CONDOMINIUM

This offer is conditional upon the Buyer's lawyer reviewing the Status Certificate and Attachments and finding the Status Certificate and Attachments satisfactory in the Buyer's Lawyer's sole and absolute discretion. The _____ [Buyer/Seller] agrees to request at the _____ [Buyer's/Seller's] expense, the Status Certificate and attachments within _____ days of acceptance of this Offer. Unless the Buyer gives notice in writing to the Seller personally or in accordance with any other provisions for the delivery of notice in this Agreement of Purchase and Sale or any Schedule thereto not later than 5 p.m. on the _____ day of _____, 20_____, that this condition is fulfilled, this Offer shall be null and void and the deposit shall be returned to the Buyer in full without deduction.

    This condition is included for the benefit of the Buyer and may be waived at the Buyer's sole option by notice in writing to the Seller as aforesaid within the time period stated herein.

CONDO–1

Condition—
Review of Condominium
Documents—
By Specific Date

This offer is conditional upon the Buyer's lawyer reviewing the Status Certificate and Attachments and finding the Status Certificate and Attachments satisfactory in the Buyer's Lawyer's sole and absolute discretion. The _____ [Buyer/Seller] agrees to request at the _____ [Buyer's/Seller's] expense, the Status Certificate and attachments within _____ days after acceptance of this Offer. Unless the Buyer gives notice in writing to the Seller personally or in accordance with any other provisions for the delivery of notice in this Agreement of Purchase and Sale or any Schedule thereto not later than 5 p.m. on the fifth day (excluding Saturdays, Sundays and Statutory Holidays) following receipt by the Buyer of the Status Certificate and attachments, that this condition is fulfilled, this Offer shall be null and void and the deposit shall be returned to the Buyer in full without deduction. This condition is included for the benefit of the Buyer and may be waived at the Buyer's sole option by notice in writing to the Seller as aforesaid within the time period stated herein.

CONDO–2

Condition—
Review of Condominium
Documents—
Within _____ Days

The Seller represents and warrants that, with respect to the unit, the Condominium Act, Declaration, Bylaws and Rules of the Condominium Corporation have been complied with, and that no improvements, additions, alterations or repairs that require the consent of the Condominium Corporation have been carried out in the said unit, the exclusive use areas or the common elements, unless the required consent has been obtained from the Condominium Corporation. This warranty shall survive and not merge on the completion of this transaction.

CONDO–3

Alterations By Owner

The Buyer covenants and agrees that no alterations will be made to the unit during the term of interim occupancy. Upon completion of the transaction, the Buyer agrees to abide by the Bylaws and Rules relating to alterations and changes within the unit.

CONDO–4

Alterations/Changes to Unit
During Interim Occupancy

The Buyer hereby covenants with the Seller and with the Condominium Corporation that the Buyer, members of the household, and guests, will comply with the Condominium Act, the Declaration, the Bylaws and all Rules and Regulations, in using the unit and the common elements, and will be subject to the same duties imposed by the above as those applicable to other individual unit owners.

CONDO–5

Compliance by Buyers,
Guests and Family Members

The Buyer acknowledges that any default in payment of occupancy fees shall be deemed to be a default under the terms and conditions of the Agreement of Purchase and Sale, and subject to the remedies provided herein for the Seller.

CONDO–6

Default by New Buyers
During Interim Occupancy

APPENDIX

CONDO-7

Occupancy by Buyer Prior to Completion of Construction

The Buyer acknowledges that the unit being acquired is currently under construction. The Buyer shall take occupancy of the unit provided that the interior of the unit has been substantially completed, notwithstanding that the common areas have not been substantially finished. The Seller agrees to complete same in a good and workmanlike manner in a reasonable period of time. The Buyer further acknowledges that failure to complete either the unit or the common areas by the occupancy date in no way relieves the Buyer from completing the transaction.

CONDO-8

Occupancy by Buyer Prior to Completion—Payment of Occupancy Fee

The Buyer shall be entitled to occupy the property from the _____ day of _____, 20_____, until the date of completion at a monthly fee hereinafter referred to as an occupancy fee. The occupancy fee shall be calculated based on the proportionate share of the common expenses, the estimated realty taxes, and mortgage interest as detailed herein (or designated as Schedule "_____" attached to and forming part of this Agreement). Said occupancy fee shall be due and payable on a monthly basis, in advance, commencing on the 1st day of each month following the date of occupancy. Partial charges prior to the 1st day of the initial month shall be pro-rated accordingly. The Buyer further agrees to provide the Seller with post-dated cheques to cover the occupancy cost for a period of twelve months, or such period to be established by the Seller whichever is the lesser.

CONDO-9

Permission to Access Unit

The Buyer agrees to allow the Seller access to the unit for the purpose of inspection, maintenance, or completion of uncompleted work for a period of six (6) months following the date of completion, provided that reasonable notice is given to the Buyer. Any subsequent access shall be pursuant to the Bylaws, Rules and Regulations as established by the Board of Directors of the Condominium Corporation.

CONDO-10

Tenant to Occupy Property

The Buyer agrees to abide by the Declaration, Bylaws, Rules and Regulations of the Condominium Corporation and, if the property is to be rented, the Buyer agrees to inform all tenants of the Rules and Regulations and receive written acknowledgement of the tenants regarding their willingness to abide by same within the rental document. It is clearly understood that all rental agreements shall conform with the Rules and Regulations as passed from time to time by the Board of Directors of the Condominium Corporation.

APPENDIX

DEPOSITS/PAYMENTS

The Buyer agrees to pay a further sum of _____ ($ _____), subject to adjustments, to the Seller on completion of this transaction, with funds drawn on a lawyer's trust account in the form of a bank draft, certified cheque or wire transfer using the Large Value Transfer System.

DEP/PAY–1

A Further Sum of

....

The Buyer agrees to pay the balance of the purchase price, subject to adjustments, to the Seller on completion of this transaction, with funds drawn on a lawyer's trust account in the form of a bank draft, certified cheque or wire transfer using the Large Value Transfer System.

DEP/PAY–2

Balance of Purchase Price

....

The Buyer agrees to pay a further sum of _____ ($ _____), to _____, by negotiable cheque, not later than _____ p.m. on the _____ day of _____, 20_____, as a supplementary deposit to be held in trust in the same manner as the initial deposit pending completion or other termination of this Agreement. This amount is to be credited towards the purchase price on completion of this transaction.

DEP/PAY–3

Deposit Increase—
Additional Payment

....

The Buyer agrees to pay the following supplementary deposits in the amounts stated not later than: [List Appropriate Times, Dates and Amounts] to _____, by negotiable cheque, to be held in trust pending completion or other termination of this Agreement. Such payments are to be credited towards the purchase price on completion of this transaction.

DEP/PAY–4

Deposit Increase—
Multiple Payments

....

The Buyer agrees to pay a further sum of _____ ($ _____), to _____, by negotiable cheque, at the time of notification of fulfilment or removal of the condition pertaining to _____, as an additional deposit to be held in trust pending completion or other termination of this Agreement. This amount is to be credited towards the purchase price on completion of this transaction.

DEP/PAY–5

Deposit Increase—On
Removal of Condition(s)

....

The parties to this Agreement hereby acknowledge that the Deposit Holder shall place the deposit in trust in the Deposit Holder's interest bearing real estate trust account, which earns interest at _____, and the Deposit Holder shall pay any interest it earns or receives on the deposit to _____ at the same rate of interest the Deposit Holder earns or receives on the Deposit Holder's real estate trust account.

NOTE: The Listing Brokerage is required to have Social Insurance Number(s) before paying interest on deposits.

DEP/PAY–6

Deposit Interest—Payment
of All Interest Earned

....

The parties to this Agreement hereby acknowledge and agree that the Deposit Holder shall place the deposit in the Deposit Holder's interest bearing real estate trust account, which earns interest at _____, and the Deposit Holder shall pay interest at a rate of _____ on the deposit to _____. The parties to this Agreement hereby acknowledge and agree that the Deposit Holder shall be entitled to retain the difference between the interest earned on the deposit and the agreed rate of interest payable.

DEP/PAY–7

Deposit Interest—
Payment of Interest at a
Rate Less Than Earned

APPENDIX

DEP/PAY-8

Deposit Interest—Payment of Interest Earned Provided Minimum Amount Earned

The parties to this Agreement hereby acknowledge and agree that the Deposit Holder shall place the deposit in the Deposit Holder's interest bearing real estate trust account, which earns interest at _____, and the Deposit Holder shall pay any interest it earns or receives on the deposit to _____, provided the amount of the interest that the Deposit Holder earns or receives on the deposit is equal to or greater than _____. The parties to this Agreement hereby acknowledge and agree that the Deposit Holder shall be entitled to retain any interest earned or retained on the deposit, which is less than _____.

....

DEP/PAY-9

Deposit Interest—Term Deposit Bearing Interest

The parties to this Agreement hereby acknowledge that the Deposit Holder shall place all deposit monies in an interest bearing security with any accrued interest on the deposit to be paid to the Buyer as soon as possible after completion or other termination of this Agreement. The deposit holder will immediately inform the person depositing the trust money as to the interest rate received on the deposit. In the event that the closing date is advanced or the transaction is terminated, the party receiving the interest agrees to accept the short-term rate for deposits withdrawn before maturity.

DEVELOPMENT/SEVERANCE/SUBDIVISION

NOTE: The sale of large parcels of land and vacant land can be subject to capital gains and/or HST. This can depend upon present and future use, who is selling, and who is buying. Expert advice should be sought.

DEV-1

Condition—Services—Hydro/Telephone

This Offer is conditional upon the Buyer determining, at the Buyer's own expense, that the provision of service by hydro and telephone to the said property shall not exceed a cost of _____ ($ _____). Unless the Buyer gives notice in writing delivered to the Seller personally or in accordance with any other provisions for the delivery of notice in this Agreement of Purchase and Sale or any Schedule thereto not later than _____ p.m. on the _____ day of _____, 20_____, that this condition is fulfilled, this Offer shall become null and void and the deposit shall be returned to the Buyer in full without deduction. This condition is included for the benefit of the Buyer and may be waived at the Buyer's sole option by notice in writing to the Seller as aforesaid within the time period stated herein.

....

DEV-2

Condition—Severance—Seller Undertakes Expense and Completion

This Offer is conditional upon the Buyer obtaining, at the Seller's expense, a consent to sever the property as follows: (provide description of proposed severance). Unless the Buyer gives notice in writing delivered to the Seller personally or in accordance with any other provisions for the delivery of notice in this Agreement of Purchase and Sale or any Schedule thereto not later than _____ p.m. on the _____ day of _____, 20_____, that this condition is fulfilled, this Offer shall become null and void and the deposit shall be returned to the Buyer in full without deduction. The Seller agrees to sign any requisite documents required for the above condition and do all things reasonably necessary in support of the satisfaction of the condition.

The Seller understands and acknowledges that the Seller shall be responsible for satisfying any conditions imposed for approval of the severance, and if such conditions give the Seller options in the manner of compliance, the Buyer shall determine which option will be selected. The Seller shall obtain a reference plan prepared by an Ontario Land Surveyor suitable for registration purposes in the Land Registry Office in which the said property is located.

NOTE: Additional wording may be inserted concerning the extension of the completion date if the severance is not completed and limits of cost relating to obtaining said severance.

This Offer is conditional upon the Buyer determining, at the Buyer's own expense, the cost of constructing roads, installing necessary services, and generally ascertaining if the terrain will permit development at a reasonable price. Unless the Buyer gives notice in writing delivered to the Seller personally or in accordance with any other provisions for the delivery of notice in this Agreement of Purchase and Sale or any Schedule thereto not later than _____ p.m. on the _____ day of _____, 20_____, that this condition is fulfilled, this Offer shall become null and void and the deposit shall be returned to the Buyer in full without deduction. This condition is included for the benefit of the Buyer and may be waived at the Buyer's sole option by notice in writing to the Seller as aforesaid within the time period stated herein.

DEV–3

Condition—Suitability for Roads/Services

The Seller acknowledges that it is the intention of the Buyer to develop and/or renovate and resell the property.

DEV–4

Intention of Buyer to Develop

The Seller warrants that the lands are not subject to a Site Plan Development Agreement.

DEV–5

No Site Plan Development Agreement

The Seller acknowledges that the Buyer is acquiring the property for development, and the purchase price is calculated on the basis of _____ ($_____) per acre. In the event of a discrepancy in area, the purchase price will be adjusted accordingly at time of completion.

NOTE: Survey or other acceptable confirmation of exact acreage is required.

DEV–6

Price Based Upon Acreage

The Seller agrees to co-operate with the Buyer in the application for and registration of any plan or plans of subdivision on the said property and the Seller agrees to execute any requisite documents for the application and registration of any plan of subdivision, provided that the Buyer pay all costs for the application, requirements for approval and registration of the plan of subdivision.

DEV–7

Seller Consents to Subdivide

The Seller shall be permitted the right to remain upon and continue the Seller's use of the real property, free of any payment of rent for a period of _____ after the date of completion, provided that the Seller agrees to vacate the property at the end of the period and provided that the Seller shall, during the period, maintain the lands and buildings in good repair and not permit waste upon the property. The Seller shall pay taxes, insurance and utilities during this period. The Buyer shall have free access to the lands during this period and reasonable access to the buildings. The Seller shall be permitted to remove all personal property from the said property either during this period or upon vacating the property. These provisions, where applicable, shall not lapse or merge on completion of this transaction.

DEV–8

Seller Permitted to Remain on Property

The Seller warrants that municipal services to the subject property include _____ and _____ are available for use by the Buyer, Buyer to pay any usual connection charges.

DEV–9

Services—Warranty

APPENDIX

DOCKS/BOATHOUSES

DOCKS–1

Condition—Docks/ Boathouses (Including Reference to Conservation and/or Canal Authorities)

This Offer is conditional upon the Buyer determining, at the Buyer's own expense, that the [boathouse, dock, pier, etc.], used in conjunction with the property, and passing to the Buyer on completion, [has/have] received all necessary approvals and permits from the Ministry of Natural Resources, the Federal Government under the *Navigable Waters Protection Act*, Canada, from [insert appropriate conservation or canal authority as required], and from all other relevant authorities. Unless the Buyer gives notice in writing delivered to the Seller personally or in accordance with any other provisions for the delivery of notice in this Agreement of Purchase and Sale or any Schedule thereto not later than _____ p.m. on the _____ day of _____, 20_____, that this condition has been fulfilled, this Offer shall become null and void and the deposit shall be returned to the Buyer in full without deduction. This condition is included for the benefit of the Buyer and may be waived at the Buyer's sole option by notice in writing to the Seller as aforesaid within the time period stated herein.

DOCKS–2

Docks/Boathouses— Warranty (Including Reference to Conservation and/or Canal Authorities)

The Seller represents and warrants to the best of his knowledge and belief that the [boathouse, dock, pier, etc.], used in conjunction with the property, and passing to the Buyer on completion, [has/have] received all necessary approvals and permits from the Ministry of Natural Resources, the Federal Government under the *Navigable Waters Protection Act*, Canada, from [insert appropriate conservation or canal authority as required], and from all other relevant authorities. The Parties agree that these representations and warranties shall survive and not merge on completion of this transaction, but apply only to those circumstances existing at completion of this transaction.

ELECTRONIC

ELEC–1

Electronic Signature

The parties hereto consent and agree to the use of electronic signature pursuant to the *Electronic Commerce Act 2000*, S.O. 2000, c17 as amended from time to time with respect to this Agreement and any other documents respecting this transaction.

ENVIRONMENTAL

This Offer is conditional upon the Buyer determining, at the Buyer's own expense that all environmental laws and regulations have been complied with, no hazardous conditions or substances exist on the land, no limitations or restrictions affecting the continued use of the property exist, other than those specifically provided for herein, no pending litigation respecting Environmental matters, no outstanding Ministry of Environment Orders, investigation, charges or prosecutions respecting Environmental matters exist, there has been no prior use as a waste disposal site, and all applicable licences are in force. The Seller agrees to provide to the Buyer upon request, all documents, records, and reports relating to environmental matters in possession of the Seller. The Seller further authorizes (insert appropriate Ministry), to release to the Buyer, the Buyer's Representative or Solicitor, any and all information that may be on record in the Ministry office with respect to the said property.

Unless the Buyer gives notice in writing delivered to the Seller personally or in accordance with any other provisions for the delivery of notice in this Agreement of Purchase and Sale or any Schedule thereto not later than _____ p.m. on the _____ day of _____, 20_____, that the preceding condition has been fulfilled, this Offer shall become null and void and the deposit shall be returned to the Buyer in full without deduction. This condition is included for the benefit of the Buyer and may be waived at the Buyer's sole option by notice in writing to the Seller as aforesaid within the time period stated herein.

ENV-1

Condition—All Environmental Laws Complied With

. . . .

This Offer is conditional upon the Buyer determining, at the Buyer's own expense, that the property does not contain a habitat or critical habitat as defined in the *Species at Risk Act*, SC 2002, C29, nor a habitat as defined in the *Endangered Species Act*, 2007 S.O. 2007, C6. Unless the Buyer gives notice in writing delivered to the Seller personally or in accordance with any other provisions for the delivery of notice in this Agreement of Purchase and Sale or any Schedule thereto not later than _____ p.m. on the _____ day of _____, 20_____, that this condition has been fulfilled, this Offer shall become null and void and the deposit shall be returned to the Buyer in full without deduction. This condition is included for the benefit of the Buyer and may be waived at the Buyer's sole option by notice in writing to the Seller as aforesaid within the time period stated herein.

ENV-2

Condition— Endangered Species

. . . .

This Offer is conditional upon the approval of the terms hereof by the Buyer's Solicitor. Unless the Buyer gives notice in writing delivered to the Seller personally or in accordance with any other provisions for the delivery of notice in this Agreement of Purchase and Sale or any Schedule thereto not later than _____ p.m. on the _____ day of _____, 20_____, that this condition is fulfilled, this Offer shall be null and void and the deposit shall be returned to the Buyer in full without deduction. This condition is included for the benefit of the Buyer and may be waived at the Buyer's sole option by notice in writing to the Seller as aforesaid within the time period stated herein. The Buyer and Seller hereby acknowledge that enactments and proposed enactments by the Federal, Provincial and Municipal Governments may have an impact on the use of land. The Buyer and Seller hereby acknowledge that the foregoing condition is inserted specifically to allow the Buyer to obtain legal advice as to the potential impact of Federal, Provincial and Municipal laws and enactments and Regulations made thereto that may affect the subject property, presently or in the immediate future. The Buyer and Seller further acknowledge that such opinions fall outside the qualifications and ability of the Brokerage and accordingly, the Buyer and Seller hereby agree that they shall hold harmless and indemnify the Brokerage from any claims, actions or causes of action that may be the result of such Legislation or future enactments.

ENV-3

Condition— Environmental Legislation— Lawyer's Approval and Acknowledgement

APPENDIX

ENV–4

Condition— Environmentally Protected Zone, Flood Plain, Hazard Land

This Offer is conditional upon the Buyer determining, at the Buyer's own expense, that no portion of the property has been designated as hazard land, flood plain, or an environmentally protected zone. Unless the Buyer gives notice in writing delivered to the Seller personally or in accordance with any other provisions for the delivery of notice in this Agreement of Purchase and Sale or any Schedule thereto not later than _____ p.m. on the _____ day of _____, 20_____, that this condition has been fulfilled, this Offer shall become null and void and the deposit shall be returned to the Buyer in full without deduction. This condition is included for the benefit of the Buyer and may be waived at the Buyer's sole option by notice in writing to the Seller as aforesaid within the time period stated herein.

ENV–5

Condition— Oil Tank—Aboveground or Underground

This Agreement is conditional upon the Buyer obtaining a report from a fuel oil distributor registered under the Technical Standards and Safety Act, 2002, and any Regulations thereto as amended from time to time stating the tank system in, on or about the property is in a safe operating condition and complies with the requirements of the *Technical Standards and Safety Act, 2002*, and any Regulations thereto as amended from time to time. Seller agrees to allow access to the property by the fuel oil distributor for purpose of obtaining a report. Unless the Buyer gives notice in writing delivered to the Seller personally or in accordance with any other provisions for the delivery of notice in this Agreement of Purchase and Sale or any Schedule thereto not later than _____ p.m. on the _____ day of _____, 20_____, that this condition has been fulfilled, this Offer shall be null and void and the deposit shall be returned to the Buyer in full without deduction. This condition is included for the benefit of the Buyer and may be waived at the Buyer's sole option by notice in writing to the Seller as aforesaid within the time period stated herein.

ENV–6

Agricultural Activities Acknowledgement

The Buyer acknowledges that the property lies within, partially within, adjacent to or within two kilometres of an area zoned, used or identified for agricultural and food production activities and that such activities occur in the area. These activities may include intensive operations that cause discomfort and inconveniences that involve, but not limited to dust, noise, flies, light, odour, smoke, traffic, vibration, operating of machinery during any 24 hour period, storage and utilization of manure and the application by spraying or otherwise of chemical fertilizers, soil amendments, herbicides and pesticides. One or more of these inconveniences have protection in Ontario under the *Farming and Food Production Protection Act*.

ENV–7

Endangered Species— Acknowledgement

The Buyer acknowledges that the property may contain a habitat or critical habitat as defined in the *Species at Risk Act*, SC 2002, C29, and/or a habitat as defined in the *Endangered Species Act*, 2007 S.O. 2007, C6.

ENV–8

Environmental Issues— Release of Documents from Appropriate Ministries

The Seller authorizes the [insert appropriate Ministry], to release to the Buyer, or the Buyer's Representative or Solicitor, any and all information that may be on record in the Ministry's office with respect to the said property.

APPENDIX

The Seller represents and warrants to the best of the Seller's knowledge and belief that during the period of his ownership of the property, that all environmental laws and regulations have been complied with, no hazardous conditions or substances exist on the land, no limitations or restrictions affecting the continued use of the property exist, other than those specifically provided for herein, no pending litigation respecting Environmental matters, no outstanding Ministry of Environment Orders, investigations, charges or prosecutions regarding Environmental matters exist, there has been no prior use as a waste disposal site, and all applicable licences are in force. The Seller agrees to provide to the Buyer upon request, all documents, records, and reports relating to environmental matters that are in the possession of the Seller. The Seller further authorizes [insert appropriate Ministry], to release to the Buyer, the Buyer's Agent or Solicitor, any and all information that may be on record in the Ministry office with respect to the said property.

The Parties agree that this representation and warranty shall form an integral part of this Agreement and survive the completion of this transaction, but apply only to circumstances existing at completion of this transaction.

ENV-9

Environmental Warranty— All Laws Complied With

....

The Buyer acknowledges that the use of the property and buildings and structures thereon may have been for the growth or manufacture of illegal substances and acknowledges that the Seller makes no representations and/or warranties with respect to the state of repair of the premises and the Buyer accepts the property and the buildings and structures thereon in their present state and in an "as is" condition.

ENV-10

Growth or Manufacture of Illegal Substances— Acknowledgment

....

The Seller represents and warrants that during the time the Seller has owned the property, the use of the property and the buildings and structures thereon has not been for the growth or manufacture of any illegal substances, and that to the best of the Seller's knowledge and belief, the use of the property and the buildings and structures thereon has never been for the growth or manufacture of illegal substances. This warranty shall survive and not merge on the completion of this transaction.

ENV-11

No Growth or Manufacture of Illegal Substances— Warranty

....

The Seller represents and warrants that the fuel oil tank in, on or about the property is in compliance with the requirements of the *Technical Standards and Safety Act, 2002*, and any Regulations thereto as amended from time to time and has been registered with the Technical Standards and Safety Authority. Seller agrees to provide Buyer with the Registration number and all relevant documents prior to closing. This warranty shall survive and not merge upon the completion of this transaction.

ENV-12

Underground Tank— Compliance Warranty

....

The Buyer acknowledges that there was an underground fuel tank on the property that has been removed and the Seller agrees to provide to the Buyer at the Seller's own expense by no later than _____ p.m. on the _____ day of _____, 20_____, evidence that a contractor registered under the *Technical Standards and Safety Act, 2002*, and any Regulations thereto as amended from time to time, has removed the said fuel oil tank, assessed the soil surrounding the underground fuel oil tank for contamination and cleaned and removed any contamination.

ENV-13

Underground Tank—Seller Has Removed

....

The Seller agrees that the Seller will, at the Seller's expense, have the underground fuel oil tank on the property removed from the property by a contractor registered under the *Technical Standards and Safety Act, 2002*, and any Regulations thereto as amended from time to time by no later than _____ p.m. on the _____ day of _____, 20_____, and thereafter to have the soil surrounding the underground fuel oil tank assessed for contamination and any contamination cleaned and removed by a contractor registered under the *Technical Standards and Safety Act, 2002*, and any Regulations thereto as amended from time to time, and on or before closing to provide evidence of the said testing, cleaning and removal from the said contractor and to restore the grading and landscaping on the property to the existing or a comparable condition to which it was prior to the removal of the said fuel oil tank.

ENV-14

Underground Tank—Seller to Remove

APPENDIX

FRANCHISE

FRANCH–1

Condition—Buyer to
Approve Documentation

This offer is conditional upon the Buyer reviewing the terms of any agreements, contracts, between the Seller and _____("Franchisor") with respect to the purchase of the business and finding such terms to be satisfactory to the Buyer in the Buyer's sole and absolute discretion. The Seller will provide copies of such Franchise Agreement within _____ days of acceptance of this offer. Unless the Buyer gives notice in writing to the Seller personally or in accordance with any other provisions for delivery of notice in this Agreement of Purchase and Sale or any Schedule thereto not later than 5 p.m. on the _____ day of _____, 20_____, that this condition is fulfilled, this offer shall be null and void and the deposit shall be returned to the Buyer in full without deduction. This condition is included for the sole benefit of the Buyer and may be waived at the Buyer's sole option by notice in writing to the Seller as aforesaid within the time period stated herein.

FRANCH–2

Condition—Buyer to be
Approved

This offer is conditional upon the Buyer being approved by _____("Franchisor") with respect to the purchase of the business and the assumption of any agreements or contracts between the Seller and the Franchisor. Unless the Buyer gives notice in writing to the Seller personally or in accordance with any other provisions for delivery of notice in this Agreement of Purchase and Sale or any Schedule thereto not later than 5 p.m. on the _____ day of _____, 20_____, that this condition is fulfilled, this offer shall be null and void and the deposit shall be returned to the Buyer in full without deduction.

FUEL TANK

FUEL–1

Acknowledgement—
Adjustment Clause

The Seller and Buyer agree that there shall be no adjustment on completion for the unmetered cost of fuel.

GREEN ENERGY

GREEN–1

Condition—MicroFIT
Contract

This offer is conditional upon the Buyer reviewing all requisite documentation relating to the Seller's MicroFIT contract with the Ontario Power Authority and determining the terms of the contract are satisfactory to the Buyer in the Buyer's sole and absolute discretion. Unless the Buyer gives notice in writing delivered to the Seller personally or in accordance with any other provisions for the delivery of notice in this Agreement of Purchase and Sale or any Schedule thereto not later than _____ p.m. on the _____ day of _____, 20_____, that this condition is fulfilled, this offer shall become null and void and the deposit shall be returned to the Buyer in full without deduction. This condition is included for the benefit of the Buyer and may be waived at the Buyer's sole option by notice in writing to the Seller as aforesaid within the time period stated herein.

The Seller agrees to provide the Buyer with a copy of the requisite documentation within _____ days of the acceptance of this offer.

GREEN–2

Acknowledgement—
MicroFIT Contract

The Buyer acknowledges the Buyer has reviewed all requisite documents relating to the Seller's MicroFIT contract with the Ontario Power Authority and understands the Buyer must take the necessary steps to obtain the assignment of the contract to the Buyer, and understands that failure to obtain the required assignment will result in termination of the MicroFIT contract.

The Buyer acknowledges that any decommissioning of the renewable energy facility will require that all governmental, legislative and contractual requirements must be complied with at the expense of the property owner, and may include, without limitation, the requirements that the facility must be dismantled and removed, the site and any lands and water negatively affected by the facility must be restored to and left in a safe and clean condition.

GREEN–3

Decommissioning Renewable Energy Facility

The Buyer acknowledges and accepts that the subject property is located in an area where renewable energy producing equipment is proposed or already in operation, including, but not limited to Wind Turbines and Solar Energy Collectors.

GREEN–4

Renewable Energy Projects

The Seller represents and warrants to the Buyer that to the best of the Seller's knowledge and belief there are no wind turbine(s) installed or proposed to be installed within _____ of the boundaries of the subject property. The parties agree that this representation and warranty shall survive and not merge on completion of this transaction.

GREEN–5

Wind Turbines—Warranty

CAUTION: The topic of Green Energy and Renewable Energy can be very complicated and Members must be prepared to create specific clauses to deal with unique circumstances, as required.

NOTE: Members should also be aware that Renewable Energy installations can affect the insurability of a property and clauses may be required to verify the insurability of a property and the costs of insurance.

HERITAGE

The parties hereto acknowledge that the subject property is/may be designated as a Heritage Property and is subject to the provisions of the *Ontario Heritage Act, 1974*. The Buyer acknowledges that the Seller has made this disclosure. The Buyer accepts the property with this designation and agrees to continue with this transaction.

HERIT–1

Ontario Heritage Act **Designation**

HST

NOTE 1: HST is applicable to new properties, substantially renovated properties, properties where input tax credits have been claimed.

NOTE 2: The sale of large parcels of land and vacant land can be subject to capital gains and/or HST. This can depend upon present and future use, who is selling, and who is buying. EXPERT ADVICE SHOULD BE SOUGHT.

The Buyer shall deliver to the Seller on closing:

HST–1

HST Buyer is Registrant (Commercial Component)

1. a statutory declaration that the Buyer is a registrant within the meaning of Part IX of the *Excise Tax Act of Canada* (the "Act") and that the Buyer's registration is in full force and effect;

2. reasonable evidence of the Buyer's registration under the Act; and

3. an undertaking by the Buyer to remit any tax eligible under the Act in respect of this transaction and to indemnify the Seller against all loss, costs and damages resulting from the Buyer's failure to do so.

APPENDIX

INSPECTION OF PROPERTY

INSP-1

Condition— Inspection of Property by a Home Inspector— General Inspection

This Offer is conditional upon the inspection of the subject property by a home inspector at the Buyer's own expense, and the obtaining of a report satisfactory to the Buyer in the Buyer's sole and absolute discretion. Unless the Buyer gives notice in writing delivered to the Seller personally or in accordance with any other provisions for the delivery of notice in this Agreement of Purchase and Sale or any Schedule thereto not later than _____ p.m. on the _____ day of _____, 20_____, that this condition is fulfilled, this Offer shall be null and void and the deposit shall be returned to the Buyer in full without deduction. The Seller agrees to co-operate in providing access to the property for the purpose of this inspection. This condition is included for the benefit of the Buyer and may be waived at the Buyer's sole option by notice in writing to the Seller as aforesaid within the time period stated herein.

INSP-2

Condition—Inspection of Property by a Home Inspector—General Inspection—Condo

This Offer is conditional upon the inspection of the unit and common elements by a home inspector at the Buyer's own expense and the obtaining of a report satisfactory to the Buyer in the Buyer's sole and absolute discretion. Unless the Buyer gives notice in writing delivered to the Seller personally or in accordance with any other provisions for the delivery of notice in this Agreement of Purchase and Sale or any Schedule thereto not later than _____ p.m. on the _____ day of _____, 20_____, that this condition is fulfilled, this Offer shall be null and void and the deposit shall be returned to the Buyer in full without deduction. The Seller agrees to co-operate in providing access to the unit for the purpose of this inspection. This condition is included for the benefit of the Buyer and may be waived at the Buyer's sole option by notice in writing to the Seller as aforesaid within the time period stated herein.

INSP-3

Condition— Inspection of Property— Limited Inspection

This Offer is conditional upon the Buyer, at the Buyer's own expense, having the relevant building(s) inspected by a bona fide home inspection firm to determine that the building(s) are in sound structural and mechanical condition and that the electrical system is safe and adequate, and that, in the written opinion of the home inspection firm, all deficiencies can be remedied at a cost not greater than _____ ($ _____). Unless the Buyer gives notice in writing delivered to the Seller personally or in accordance with any other provisions for the delivery of notice in this Agreement of Purchase and Sale or any Schedule thereto not later than _____ p.m. on the _____ day of _____ 20_____, that this condition is fulfilled, this Offer shall be null and void and the deposit shall be returned to the Buyer in full without deduction. The Seller agrees to co-operate in providing access to the property for the purpose of this inspection. The Seller agrees this condition is included for the benefit of the Buyer and may be waived at the Buyer's sole option by notice in writing to the Seller as aforesaid within the time period stated herein.

INSP-4

Condition— Inspection of Property— Seller Allowed to Remedy

This Offer is conditional upon the inspection of the subject property by a home inspector at the Buyer's own expense and the obtaining of a report satisfactory to the Buyer or, if not satisfactory to the Buyer, a report revealing deficiencies in the property which the Seller is willing and able to remedy. Unless the Buyer gives notice in writing delivered to the Seller personally or in accordance with any other provisions for the delivery of notice in this Agreement of Purchase and Sale or any Schedule thereto not later than _____ p.m. on the _____ day of _____, 20_____, that this condition is fulfilled, this Offer shall be null and void and the deposit shall be returned to the Buyer in full without deduction. The Seller agrees to co-operate in providing access to the property for the purpose of this inspection. This condition is included for the benefit of the Buyer and may be waived at the Buyer's sole option by notice in writing to the Seller as aforesaid within the time period stated herein.

This Offer is conditional upon the inspection of the subject unit by a home inspector at the Buyer's own expense and the obtaining of a report satisfactory to the Buyer or, if not satisfactory to the Buyer, a report revealing deficiencies in the unit which the Seller is willing and able to remedy. Unless the Buyer gives notice in writing to the Seller personally or in accordance with any other provisions for the delivery of notice in this Agreement of Purchase and Sale or any Schedule thereto not later than _____ p.m. on the _____ day of _____, 20_____, that this condition is fulfilled, this Offer shall be null and void and the deposit shall be returned to the Buyer in full without deduction. The Seller agrees this condition is included for the benefit of the Buyer and may be waived at the Buyer's sole option by notice in writing to the Seller as aforesaid within the time period stated herein.

INSP–5

Condition—
Inspection—Seller Allowed
to Remedy—Condo

This Offer is conditional upon the Buyer or the Buyer's appointed representative inspecting the subject property for termites and obtaining a report satisfactory to the Buyer at the Buyer's own expense. Unless the Buyer gives notice in writing delivered to the Seller personally or in accordance with any other provisions for the delivery of notice in this Agreement of Purchase and Sale or any Schedule thereto not later than _____ p.m. on the _____ day of _____, 20_____, that this condition is fulfilled, this Offer shall be null and void and the deposit shall be returned to the Buyer in full without deduction. The Seller agrees to co-operate in providing access to the property for the purpose of this inspection. This condition is included for the benefit of the Buyer and may be waived at the Buyer's sole option by notice in writing to the Seller as aforesaid within the time period stated herein.

INSP–6

Condition—
Inspection of Property—
Termites

This Offer is conditional upon the inspection of the subject property by _____ and the obtaining of a report satisfactory to the Buyer at the Buyer's own expense. Unless the Buyer gives notice in writing delivered to the Seller personally or in accordance with any other provisions for the delivery of notice in this Agreement of Purchase and Sale or any Schedule thereto not later than _____ p.m. on the _____ day of _____, 20_____, that this condition is fulfilled, this Offer shall be null and void and the deposit shall be returned to the Buyer in full without deduction. The Seller agrees to co-operate in providing access to the property for the purpose of this inspection. This condition is included for the benefit of the Buyer and may be waived at the Buyer's sole option by notice in writing to the Seller as aforesaid within the time period stated herein.

INSP–7

Condition—
Inspection of Property—
Third Party

This Offer is conditional upon the inspection of the unit and common elements by _____ and the obtaining of a report satisfactory to the Buyer at the Buyer's own expense. Unless the Buyer gives notice in writing delivered to the Seller personally or in accordance with any other provisions for the delivery of notice in this Agreement of Purchase and Sale or any Schedule thereto not later than _____p.m. on the _____ day of _____, 20_____, that this condition is fulfilled, this Offer shall be null and void and the deposit shall be returned to the Buyer in full without deduction. The Seller agrees to cooperate in providing access to the unit for the purpose of this inspection. This condition is included for the benefit of the Buyer and may be waived at the Buyer's sole option by notice in writing to the Seller as aforesaid within the time period stated herein.

INSP–8

Condition—
Inspection of Property
by a Third Party—Condo

APPENDIX

INSP-9

Condition—
Retrofit Inspection of
Property Fire—General
Inspection

This Offer is conditional upon the inspection of the subject property at the Buyer's own expense, and the obtaining of a report satisfactory to the Buyer in the Buyer's sole and absolute discretion respecting retrofitting pursuant to and in compliance with the *Fire Protection and Prevention Act, 1997*, and its regulations as amended from time to time. Unless the Buyer gives notice in writing delivered to the Seller personally or in accordance with any other provisions for the delivery of notice in this Agreement of Purchase and Sale or any Schedule thereto not later than _____ p.m. on the _____ day of _____, 20_____, that this condition is fulfilled, this Offer shall be null and void and the deposit shall be returned to the Buyer in full without deduction. The Seller agrees to co-operate in providing access to the property for the purpose of this inspection. This condition is included for the benefit of the Buyer and may be waived at the Buyer's sole option by notice in writing to the Seller as aforesaid within the time period stated herein.

INSP-10

Condition—
Retrofit Inspection of
Property Electricity—
General Inspection

This Offer is conditional upon the inspection of the subject property at the Buyer's own expense, and the obtaining of a report satisfactory to the Buyer in the Buyer's sole and absolute discretion respecting retrofitting pursuant to and in compliance with the *Electricity Act, 1998*, and its regulations as amended from time to time. Unless the Buyer gives notice in writing delivered to the Seller personally or in accordance with any other provisions for the delivery of notice in this Agreement of Purchase and Sale or any Schedule thereto not later than _____ p.m. on the _____ day of _____, 20_____, that this condition is fulfilled, this Offer shall be null and void and the deposit shall be returned to the Buyer in full without deduction. The Seller agrees to co-operate in providing access to the property for the purpose of this inspection. This condition is included for the benefit of the Buyer and may be waived at the Buyer's sole option by notice in writing to the Seller as aforesaid within the time period stated herein.

NOTE: Both conditions, INSP–9 and INSP–10, are required to be fulfilled for a Retrofit Certificate of Compliance.

INSP-11

Condition—
WETT Inspection

This offer is conditional upon the Buyer obtaining at the Buyer's expense a Wood Energy Technology Transfer (WETT) inspection, and obtaining a report satisfactory to the Buyer in the Buyer's sole and absolute discretion. Unless the Buyer gives notice in writing delivered to the Seller personally or in accordance with any other provisions for the delivery of notice in this Agreement of Purchase and Sale or any Schedule thereto not later than _____ p.m. on the _____ day of _____, 20_____ , that this condition is fulfilled, this offer shall be null and void and the deposit shall be returned to the Buyer in full without deduction. The Seller agrees to co-operate in providing access to the property for the purpose of this inspection. This condition is included for the benefit of the Buyer and may be waived at the Buyer's sole option by notice in writing to the Seller as aforesaid within the time period stated herein.

INSP-12

Delivery of Report

In the event the foregoing condition is not fulfilled or waived by the Buyer, the Buyer agrees to provide the Seller with a true copy of the Inspection Report and all estimates related thereto prior to the return of the deposit herein.

INSP-13

Inspection of Systems

Upon acceptance of this Offer, the Buyer shall be allowed to enter the premises, from time to time, after permission from the Seller, for the purpose of obtaining information about heating and electrical systems, maintenance, and any other related utility service for the building.

APPENDIX

The Buyer shall have the right to inspect the property prior to completion for the purpose of inspection for _____

_____

[e.g., financing, insurance, estimate(s) from contractor(s) etc.] to a maximum of _____ time(s), at a mutually agreed upon time(s). The Seller agrees to provide access to the property for the purpose of the inspection(s).

INSP-14

Right of Inspection Prior to Completion

· ·

The Buyer shall have the right to inspect the property one further time prior to completion, at a mutually agreed upon time, provided that written notice is given to the Seller. The Seller agrees to provide access to the property for the purpose of this inspection.

INSP-15

Right of Re-inspection Prior to Completion

· ·

The Seller(s) acknowledge(s) and consent(s) to a third party taking photographs/videos of the property as required for the purpose of an inspection with respect to the above.

NOTE: This clause may be added to an inspection condition (e.g., appraisal, home inspection, when there is an expectation that photos/videos will be taken by the third party).

INSP-16

Seller's Consent for Photos/Videos

INSURANCE

This offer is conditional on the Buyer arranging insurance for the property satisfactory to the Buyer in the Buyer's sole and absolute discretion. Unless the Buyer gives notice in writing delivered to the Seller personally or in accordance with any other provisions for the delivery of notice in this Agreement of Purchase and Sale or any Schedule thereto not later than _____ p.m. on the _____ day of _____, 20_____, that this condition is fulfilled, this offer shall be null and void and the deposit shall be returned to the Buyer in full without deduction. The Seller agrees to co-operate in providing access to the property, if necessary, for any inspection of the property required for the fulfillment of this condition. This condition is included for the benefit of the Buyer and may be waived at the Buyer's sole option by notice in writing to the Seller as aforesaid within the time period stated herein.

NOTE: Due to the nature of this clause, a short time frame should be chosen for this condition.

INSUR-1

Condition— Arranging Insurance

· ·

This offer is conditional upon the Buyer arranging insurance on the property for the following named perils: _____ at a yearly cost not to exceed _____, excluding applicable taxes. Unless the Buyer gives notice in writing delivered to the Seller personally or in accordance with any other provisions for the delivery of notice in this Agreement of Purchase and Sale or any Schedule thereto not later than _____ p.m. on the _____ day of _____, 20_____, that this condition is fulfilled, this Offer shall be null and void and the deposit shall be returned to the Buyer in full without deduction. The Seller agrees to co-operate in providing access to the property, if necessary, for any inspection of the property required for the fulfillment of this condition. This condition is included for the benefit of the Buyer and may be waived at the Buyer's sole option by notice in writing to the Seller as aforesaid within the time period stated herein.

INSUR-2

Condition— Arranging Insurance— Cost Not to Exceed

APPENDIX

KITEC/PLUMBING

KIT–1

Seller Warrants and Represents—No Kitec Plumbing on Property

The Seller represents and warrants to the Buyer that during the time the Seller owned the property, the Seller has not installed in any building on the property Kitec plumbing, any fittings for Kitec plumbing nor any Kitec Plumbing Systems ("Kitec") and that to the best of the undersigned's knowledge, no building on the property contains or has ever contained Kitec. This representation and warranty shall survive and not merge on the completion of the above transaction, and if the building is part of a multiple unit building, this warranty shall only apply to the part of the building, which is subject to this transaction.

KIT–2

Buyer Acknowledges—Kitec Plumbing on Property

The Buyer acknowledges that the property and buildings and structures has had installed therein or thereon Kitec plumbing, fittings for Kitec plumbing or Kitec Plumbing Systems ("Kitec") and acknowledges that the Seller makes no representations and/or warranties with respect to the state of repair of the premises respecting the said Kitec and the Buyer accepts the property and the buildings and structures thereon in their present state and in an "as is" condition.

LANDLEASE

LAND/LSE–1

Condition— Landlease— Landlord's Approval

This Offer is conditional upon the Landlord consenting to the assignment of the landlease to the Buyer. Unless the Buyer gives notice in writing delivered to the Seller personally or in accordance with any other provisions for the delivery of notice in this Agreement of Purchase and Sale or any Schedule thereto not later than _____ p.m. on the _____ day of _____, 20_____, that this condition has been fulfilled, this Offer shall become null and void and the deposit shall be returned to the Buyer in full without deduction. The Buyer hereby agrees to proceed immediately to make an application and provide such material as may be required by the Landlord for approval of the Buyer as Tenant.

NOTE: This clause is a true Condition Precedent and neither a Seller nor a Buyer is entitled to waive this condition.

LAND/LSE–2

Landlease— Buyer to Assume

The Seller agrees to assign, and the Buyer agrees to assume, the existing landlease on the property, with [insert name of Tenant], a copy of which is attached as Schedule "_____".

NOTE: See also LAND/LSE–3 Option to Purchase and LAND/LSE–1 Condition—Landlease—Landlord's Approval.

LAND/LSE–3

Landlease— Option to Purchase

During the currency of this landlease, the Buyer shall have the option of purchasing the land for a sum of _____ ($ _____), which is not included in the above purchase price.

NOTE: See also LAND/LSE–2 Buyer to Assume and LAND/LSE–1 Condition—Landlease—Landlord's Approval.

LAWYER'S APPROVAL

This Offer is conditional upon the approval of the terms hereof by the Buyer's Solicitor. Unless the Buyer gives notice in writing delivered to the Seller personally or in accordance with any other provisions for the delivery of notice in this Agreement of Purchase and Sale or any Schedule thereto not later than _____ p.m. on the _____ day of _____, 20_____, that this condition is fulfilled, this Offer shall be null and void and the deposit shall be returned to the Buyer in full without deduction. This condition is included for the benefit of Buyer and may be waived at the Buyer's sole option by notice in writing to the Seller as aforesaid within the time period stated herein.

LAW-1

Condition—
Lawyer's Approval—Buyer

....

This Offer is conditional upon the approval of the terms hereof by the Seller's Solicitor. Unless the Seller gives notice in writing delivered to the Buyer or to the Buyer's address as hereinafter indicated personally or in accordance with any other provisions for the delivery of notice in this Agreement of Purchase and Sale or any Schedule thereto not later than _____ p.m. on the _____ day of _____, 20_____, that this condition is fulfilled, this Offer shall be null and void and the deposit shall be returned to the Buyer in full without deduction. This condition is included for the benefit of Seller and may be waived at the Seller's sole option by notice in writing to the Buyer as aforesaid within the time period stated herein.

LAW-2

Condition—
Lawyer's Approval—Seller

....

The Parties to this Agreement acknowledge that the real estate Broker(s) so named in this Agreement has recommended that the Parties obtain independent professional advice prior to signing this document. The Parties further acknowledge that no information provided by such real estate Broker(s) is to be construed as legal, tax or environmental advice.

LAW-3

Legal, Accounting or
Environmental Advice

LEASE APPROVAL

Upon acceptance of this Offer, the Seller agrees to provide the Buyer with copies of all leases on the property. Upon review by the Buyer, if the terms of said leases are unacceptable to the Buyer, in the Buyer's sole and absolute discretion, the Buyer shall have the right to terminate this Agreement by notice in writing delivered to the Seller personally or in accordance with any other provisions for the delivery of notice in this Agreement of Purchase and Sale or any Schedule thereto not later than _____ p.m. on the _____ day of _____, 20_____, and the deposit shall be returned to the Buyer in full without deduction.

LEASE/APP-1

Condition—Buyer's Right
to Review Leases
(Condition Subsequent)

LEASE/APP–2

Condition—Inspection of
Leases and Real Property
(Condition Subsequent)

This Agreement is conditional upon the Buyer inspecting and approving the real property, the Leases (or Offers to Lease if no Leases are available), and improvements. Unless the Buyer notifies the Seller in writing delivered to the Seller personally or in accordance with any other provisions for the delivery of notice in this Agreement of Purchase and Sale or any Schedule thereto not later than _____ p.m. on the _____ day of _____, 20_____, that the Buyer is not satisfied with any of the above inspections, the Buyer shall be deemed to have waived this condition and this Agreement shall remain valid and binding.

The Seller agrees to:

a) Supply the Buyer not later than _____ p.m. on the _____ day of _____, 20_____, with all Leases and/or Offers to Lease which are in force at the time of acceptance of this Offer and a set of "as built" building plans for the development of the site (if such are in its possession);

b) Allow the Buyer, its agents and employees, to inspect the land and improvements at mutually convenient time or times; and

c) Authorize all governmental and other authorities having jurisdiction over the real property to release to the Buyer all information such authorities have on file respecting the property.

Should the Buyer hire agents, the cost and responsibility of such work shall be for the account of the Buyer. The Buyer covenants and agrees to restore the property forthwith after inspection to its pre-existing physical condition prior to the time of the first such inspection.

If the Buyer is not satisfied with the results of the Buyer's inspection, the Buyer shall so notify the Seller, who may elect to remedy such results. If the Seller does not remedy such results to the satisfaction of the Buyer, the Buyer may terminate this Agreement by notice in writing delivered to the Seller personally or in accordance with any other provisions for the delivery of notice in this Agreement of Purchase and Sale or any Schedule thereto not later than _____ p.m. on the _____ day of _____, 20_____, and the deposit shall be returned to the Buyer in full without deduction.

The Buyer agrees to treat the results of such inspections in a strictly confidential manner and not to disclose the results to a third party except where required by law. There shall be no compulsory requirement to disclose the result to the Seller.

APPENDIX

LEASE/COMMERCIAL

This Offer is conditional upon the approval of the terms hereof by the Landlord's Board of Directors. Unless the Landlord gives notice in writing delivered to the Tenant personally or in accordance with any other provisions for the delivery of notice in this Agreement to Lease or any Schedule thereto not later than _____ p.m. on the _____ day of _____, 20_____, that this condition is fulfilled, this Offer shall be null and void and the deposit shall be returned to the Tenant in full without deduction.

NOTE: This Clause is a true condition precedent and neither Landlord nor Tenant is entitled to waive this condition.

LEASE/COMM–1

Condition—
Approval from Board of
Directors—Landlord

. . . .

This Offer is conditional upon the approval of the terms hereof by the Tenant's Board of Directors. Unless the Tenant gives notice in writing delivered to the Landlord personally or in accordance with any other provisions for the delivery of notice in this Agreement to Lease or any Schedule thereto not later than _____ p.m. on the _____ day of _____, 20_____, that this condition is fulfilled, this Offer shall be null and void and the deposit shall be returned to the Tenant in full without deduction.

NOTE: This Clause is a true condition precedent and neither Landlord nor Tenant is entitled to waive this condition.

LEASE/COMM–2

Condition—
Approval from Board of
Directors—Tenant

. . . .

The Landlord shall have until not later than _____ p.m. on the _____ day of _____, 20_____, to verify that the financial covenant of the Tenant is satisfactory to the Landlord. If the Tenant's covenant is not acceptable to the Landlord, the Landlord may terminate this Agreement by notice in writing delivered to the Tenant personally or in accordance with any other provisions for the delivery of notice in this Agreement to Lease or any Schedule thereto within the time period stated above and the Tenant's deposit shall be returned in full without deduction.

LEASE/COMM–3

Condition—Financial
Covenant of Tenant
(Condition Subsequent)

. . . .

This Offer is conditional upon the approval of the terms hereof by the Landlord's Solicitor. Unless the Landlord gives notice in writing delivered to the Tenant personally or in accordance with any other provisions for the delivery of notice in this Agreement to Lease or any Schedule thereto not later than _____ p.m. on the _____ day of _____, 20_____, that this condition is fulfilled, this Offer shall be null and void and the deposit shall be returned to the Tenant in full without deduction. This condition is included for the benefit of the Landlord and may be waived at the Landlord's sole option by notice in writing to the Tenant as aforesaid within the time period stated herein.

LEASE/COMM–4

Condition—
Lawyer's Approval—
Landlord

. . . .

This Offer is conditional upon the approval of the terms hereof by the Tenant's Solicitor. Unless the Tenant gives notice in writing delivered to the Landlord personally or in accordance with any other provisions for the delivery of notice in this Agreement to Lease or any Schedule thereto not later than _____ p.m. on the _____ day of _____, 20_____, that this condition is fulfilled, this Offer shall be null and void and the deposit shall be returned to the Tenant in full without deduction. This condition is included for the benefit of the Tenant and may be waived at the Tenant's sole option by notice in writing to the Landlord as aforesaid within the time period stated herein.

LEASE/COMM–5

Condition—
Lawyer's Approval—Tenant

LEASE/COMM–6

Condition—
Occupancy Permit
(Condition Subsequent)

The Tenant shall obtain an occupancy permit from the relevant municipality prior to taking occupancy. If the Tenant gives notice in writing delivered to the Landlord personally or in accordance with any other provisions for the delivery of notice in this Agreement to Lease or any Schedule thereto not later than _____ p.m. on the _____ day of_____, 20_____, that an occupancy permit is not obtainable prior to the date set for occupancy, this Agreement, and the Lease, if signed, shall be terminated and the Tenant's deposit shall be returned in full without deduction. The Landlord agrees to provide the Tenant with all of the plans and drawings required for said permit, at the Landlord's expense.

LEASE/COMM–7

Condition—Zoning
Satisfaction (Condition
Subsequent))

The Tenant shall have until not later than _____ p.m. on the _____ day of _____, 20_____, to satisfy itself that the property is zoned in final and binding form under the relevant zoning bylaws and official plan to permit it to develop or use the property for the purpose of _____. If the Tenant is not so satisfied at the Tenant's sole and arbitrary discretion, the Tenant may terminate this Agreement by notice in writing delivered to the Landlord personally or in accordance with any other provisions for the delivery of notice in this Agreement to Lease or any Schedule thereto within the time period stated above and the deposit shall be returned to the Tenant in full without deduction.

LEASE/COMM–8

Agreement to Sign Lease

Prior to the Tenant taking possession of the demised premises, the parties shall execute the Lease in the form attached hereto, as Schedule "_____" of the Agreement to Lease.

LEASE/COMM–9

Alterations and
Improvements

The Tenant may make any necessary alterations and improvements to said premises, at the Tenant's own expense, subject to the Landlord's written consent, and such consent shall not be unreasonably withheld. The Tenant may, however, make any necessary minor internal improvements to said premises, at the Tenant's own expense, without the Landlord's consent and in compliance with all applicable governmental bylaws and codes governing the use of the demised premises.

LEASE/COMM–10

Arbitration

All disputes or differences arising in regard to the contract shall be settled by arbitration in accordance with the *Arbitration Act of Ontario, 1991*, or any subsequent legislation in effect at the date of commencement of such arbitration.

NOTE: Care must be taken not to create a conflict with this clause and clauses providing for settlement of disputes or differences by alternate means.

LEASE/COMM–11

Area Defined

The Landlord and Tenant agree that the rentable area of the leased premises is about _____ square feet, with the actual area to be adjusted accordingly, should the actual measurement differ. The area shall be measured by using the current Building Owners and Managers Association Standards.

LEASE/COMM–12

Area Measurement

The Landlord and the Tenant agree that, should the actual square footage differ from the area stated herein, the annual rental rate shall be adjusted to reflect the actual square footage of the demised premises.

LEASE/COMM–13

Assign or Sub-lease

The Lease shall contain a clause permitting the Tenant to assign or sub-lease the demised premises, in whole or part, at any time or times, with consent of the Landlord, and such consent shall not be unreasonably withheld or delayed. Provided that consent as aforesaid shall be required if the Tenant is a corporation and there has been a change of control in the corporation, notwithstanding, the Tenant shall remain on covenant.

APPENDIX

The Tenant shall have the right to assign its interests under this Lease to a limited company, partnership, or person. The Tenant agrees to send written notice to the Landlord of its intention to assign to the Landlord and obtain the Landlord's written approval prior to any assignment. Such approval shall not be arbitrarily or unreasonably withheld or delayed.

LEASE/COMM-14

Assignment— Approval by Landlord

It is understood and agreed between the Parties that the Tenant may assign the Lease to an individual, company, partnership or joint venture in which it has a financial interest without consent of the Landlord, provided that the Tenant shall not be relieved of any liability under this Agreement.

LEASE/COMM-15

Assignment Without Approval

The Tenant's use of the premises is to comply with all requirements of the municipal zoning bylaws, the requirements of the Ministry of the Environment and the rules and regulations of the *Environmental Protection Act* and any amendments thereto.

The Tenant agrees to indemnify and hold harmless the Landlord from and against any claims, demands, losses, costs, damages, actions, suits or proceedings which may be brought or commenced by anyone or any group including any environmental agency or group as a result of the Tenant's use of the premises or any breach by the Tenant of any rules, bylaws, and regulations.

The Tenant warrants that no noxious or environmentally unfriendly chemicals or products shall be allowed to enter the drains throughout the lease term, and upon vacating the premises, no such chemicals or products shall be left on the premises.

LEASE/COMM-16

Chemicals— Compliance with Regulations

The Tenant covenants to comply with all applicable governmental bylaws and codes governing the use of the demised premises.

LEASE/COMM-17

Compliance with By-laws and Codes

The Tenant hereby covenants and agrees that the contents, terms and conditions of this Agreement and the Lease to be executed shall be kept strictly confidential. It is understood that the Tenant will not, without written permission of the Landlord, discuss or reveal the terms of this Agreement with other Parties including, but not limited to other tenants, prospective tenants, real estate agents, suppliers or customers, save and except for the legal and financial advisors of the Tenant.

LEASE/COMM-18

Confidentiality

The Landlord may require that all mechanical, electrical, roofing and structural work to be done with respect to the leased premises, by the Tenant at any time, be carried out by the Landlord's contractors and employees at the Tenant's costs, such costs to be competitive with the prices obtained by the Tenant from its contractors.

LEASE/COMM-19

Contractors to be Used

At any time after the _____ day of _____, 20_____, should the Landlord undertake to proceed with full or partial demolition of the building, then upon_____ full calendar months written notice from the Landlord to the Tenant, of the Landlord's undertaking to demolish, the Tenant agrees to vacate the premises, and surrender the unexpired portion of the term, at the expiry of the above notice period. Upon surrender of the premises, the Landlord shall pay to the Tenant by way of compensation for improvements an amount standing in the same proportion to the cost to the Tenant of leasehold improvements made by the Tenant pursuant to the provisions of the Lease or with the consent of the Landlord as the unexpired portion of the term stands to the period of time from the Tenant's payment of such cost to the end of the unexpired portion of the term.

LEASE/COMM-20

Demolition Clause

APPENDIX

LEASE/COMM-21

**Early Occupancy—
Gross Rent Free**

It is understood and agreed that, provided a formal lease has been executed by both the Landlord and the Tenant, and upon Tenant providing evidence of Tenant's insurance satisfactory to the Landlord, the Tenant shall be granted possession of the demised premises on the _____ day of _____, 20_____, gross rent free to the Lease Commencement Date, in order to prepare the premises for the operation of its business, provided that, during the said rent-free period, the Tenant shall comply with all the terms and conditions of the lease.

NOTE: This Clause should be used in conjunction with an Insurance Clause specifically outlining insurance requirements.

LEASE/COMM-22

**Early Occupancy—
Net Rent Free**

It is understood and agreed that, provided a formal lease has been executed by both the Landlord and the Tenant, and upon Tenant providing evidence of Tenant's insurance satisfactory to the Landlord, the Tenant shall be granted possession of the demised premises on the _____ day of _____, 20_____, net rent free to the Lease Commencement Date, in order to prepare the premises for the operation of its business, provided that, during the said rent-free period, the Tenant shall comply with all the terms and conditions of the lease, and be responsible for the Tenant's proportionate share of all expenses of the property, save and except for payment of minimum rent.

LEASE/COMM-23

**Electrical and Mechanical
Equipment in Good
Working Order**

The Landlord warrants that all mechanical, heating, ventilating, air conditioning equipment (HVAC), and electrical equipment will be in good working order, normal wear and tear excepted, on or before the occupancy date set herein.

LEASE/COMM-24

Entire Agreement

It is understood and agreed that the contract resulting from the acceptance of this Offer shall be as expressly set out herein and in the schedules attached hereto and, except as expressly set out herein and in the attached schedules hereto, there are no collateral or other representations, warranties, conditions or agreements between the Landlord and Tenant, and none shall be implied.

LEASE/COMM-25

**Escalation Clause for
Property Taxes**

The Tenant shall pay its proportionate share of any increase in property taxes and local improvement levies over the base year of 20_____.

LEASE/COMM-26

**First Right of Refusal on
Vacant Space—Lease**

The Tenant shall have the first right of refusal on adjacent space if and when such space becomes available. In the event that the Landlord receives an Offer which it finds acceptable, it shall so notify the Tenant in writing, and the Tenant shall have 72 hours to match the Offer, by notice in writing delivered to the Landlord, failing which the Tenant shall have lost its first right of refusal. For purposes herein, adjacent space shall be deemed to be space on the first floor above, the first floor below, and/or adjoining space on the same floor as the subject unit.

The Landlord covenants and agrees with the Tenant that, during the term of the lease or any renewal thereof, the Landlord will give the Tenant three (3) business days to submit an Offer upon the same terms and conditions as any bona fide Offer to purchase the leased property that the Landlord has received and is willing to accept, and any Lease executed by the Landlord and Tenant shall include this first right of refusal. The Landlord shall give the Tenant written notice of such bona fide Offer and a copy of such Offer to the Tenant. In the event that the Tenant submits to the Landlord, within the time period described above, a written and signed Offer to purchase the property upon the same terms and conditions as the Offer initially received by the Landlord, the Landlord shall accept the Offer submitted by the Tenant. In the event that the Tenant fails to deliver to the Landlord, within the time limit described above, a written and signed Offer to purchase the property on the same terms and conditions as the initial Offer, the Landlord shall be at liberty to sell the property to the Buyer who submitted the initial Offer. Should the Tenant exercise the said first right of refusal, the Landlord agrees to pay the Agents so named in this Agreement, (or their successor companies) a fee of _____.

LEASE/COMM-27

First Right of Refusal to Purchase

It is agreed that the lease arising from this Offer shall be based on a rental rate which includes the Landlord paying realty taxes, outside maintenance, building insurance, heat, hydro and water rates that pertain to the subject leased premises.

LEASE/COMM-28

Gross Lease

It is understood and agreed that any lease arising from this Offer shall be based on a rental rate which shall include the Tenant's proportionate share of realty taxes, outside maintenance, building insurance, heat, hydro, water rates, and management fees, if any. All inclusions have a base year of 20_____, and are subject to yearly adjustments according to actual increases. Such increases above the base year shall be paid proportionately by the Tenant.

LEASE/COMM-29

Gross Lease with Escalations

The Tenant acknowledges that HST will be collectable by the Landlord on the rent paid and on common area expenses as defined herein.

LEASE/COMM-30

HST—Lease

The obligations created by the Tenant so named herein shall be jointly and severally assumed by the guarantor, whose name is identified at the end of this Agreement, and the guarantor agrees to be bound by the terms herein. In the enforcement of its rights under this guarantee, the Landlord may proceed against the guarantor as if the guarantor were named as Tenant under this Lease.

LEASE/COMM-31

Guarantor

The Lease shall contain a clause requiring the Tenant to obtain insurance, at the expense of the Tenant, as required by the Landlord and which may include insurance on the property and operations of the Tenant, including insurance for fire and such additional perils as are normally insured against, liability insurance, boiler and machinery insurance, plate glass insurance and any other insurance as may be reasonably required by the Landlord.

LEASE/COMM-32

Insurance— Tenant to Obtain

The Tenant shall have the option to cancel the Lease at any time during the Lease, provided that the Tenant gives the Landlord at least _____ days written notice of the Tenant's intention to cancel, and provided that the Tenant is not in default at the time of giving of such notice, or at the time of termination itself. The payment for this option shall be a cancellation fee of _____, payable at the time of giving notice of intention to cancel.

LEASE/COMM-33

Lease Cancellation Privilege

APPENDIX

LEASE/COMM–34

Lease Form

Attached hereto as Schedule "_____" is a copy of the Landlord's standard Lease form, which the Landlord will alter to reflect the business terms defined herein, and the Tenant agrees to sign same subject to minor adjustments as negotiated between the Landlord's and the Tenant's Solicitors, both acting reasonably. In the event of a difference or contradiction between this Offer and the standard Lease form, the terms of the Lease as so negotiated shall prevail, save for manifest error.

LEASE/COMM–35

Net Lease

The rent is to be on an absolutely net basis to the Landlord, and the Tenant agrees to pay as additional rent, its proportionate share of the cost of operation and maintenance for the site, to include but not limited to water, heat, hydro, administrative costs, garbage disposal, realty taxes, outside maintenance and building insurance, (except for structural repairs and items of a capital nature) including all costs of maintaining, repairing, replacing, upkeep, servicing and including, without limiting the generality of the foregoing, other costs and expenses which are defined in the Landlord's lease. These common area costs are currently estimated to be $ _____ per square foot per year, and will be adjusted annually according to actual costs. At the end of the calendar year the Landlord will itemize the common area costs, should the Tenant so request.

LEASE/COMM–36

Option to Purchase

In consideration of the sum of _____ ($ _____) paid by the Tenant to the Landlord, the receipt of which is hereby acknowledged, and in consideration of the terms and conditions herein recited, the Landlord gives to the Tenant an option irrevocable within the time limit herein for acceptance, to purchase, free and clear of all encumbrances, the lands and premises situated at _____ in the _____ of _____ in the _____ of _____. The option shall be open for acceptance by notice in writing delivered to the Landlord not later than _____ p.m. on the _____ day of _____, 20_____. The terms of the purchase shall be the following: _____.

LEASE/COMM–37

Option to Renew— Appraisal

Provided that the Tenant is not in default under the terms of the lease, the Tenant shall have the option to renew said Lease for a further term of _____ (_____) years, on the same terms and conditions, save and except for a further renewal, and the rental rate, which shall be the then current rent for similar location, and on similar lease terms at the time of renewal, provided that the Tenant advises the Landlord in writing _____ (_____) months prior to the end of the term that the Tenant wishes to exercise the Tenant's option to renew. If the Landlord and Tenant do not agree by one month prior to the end of the term on the rental rate for the renewal term, the matter shall be determined by appraisal. The cost of these appraisals shall be shared equally by Landlord and Tenant. Either the Landlord or the Tenant (the "Notifying Party") may by notice (the "First Notice") to the other (the "Other Party") designate an appraiser. The Other Party may within 10 days following the giving of the First Notice designate a second appraiser by notice (the "Second Notice") to the Notifying Party, failing which the first appraiser shall be the sole appraiser. Within 10 days following the giving of the Second Notice (if given), the two appraisers shall appoint a third appraiser, failing which either party may apply to a judge of the Ontario Court (General Division) as persona designata to appoint the third appraiser. The sole appraiser, or if there are three appraisers, the three appraisers, independently of each other, shall proceed to determine the fair market rental rate for the renewal term. If there is a sole appraiser, the rate determined by the sole appraiser shall be the rate for the renewal term. If there are three appraisers, the two rental rates determined by the appraisers which are closest to each other in amount shall be averaged, or, if the highest and lowest rate differ from the other rate by the same amount, all three rates shall be averaged, and the average rate shall be the rate for the renewal term. Any appraiser appointed pursuant hereto shall be a person with the qualifications and experience requisite to appraise property of the type and location of the demised premises.

Provided that the Tenant is not at any time in default of any covenants within the lease, the Tenant shall be entitled to renew this lease for additional term(s) of _____ (_____) year(s) _____ (_____) month(s) (each) on written notice to the Landlord given not less than _____ months prior to the expiry of the current term at a rental rate to be negotiated. In the event the Landlord and Tenant cannot agree on the fixed minimum rent at least two months prior to expiry of the current lease, the fixed minimum rent for the renewal period shall be determined by arbitration in accordance with the Arbitration Act or any successor or replacement act.

LEASE/COMM-38

Option to Renew—Arbitration

....

The Landlord will provide the Tenant with a minimum of _____ (_____) parking spaces, included in the rent, during the term of the Lease, and the Tenant and the customers, representatives and agents of the Tenant shall have the sole and exclusive right to use these parking spaces set out in Schedule "_____" attached.

LEASE/COMM-39

Parking

....

It is understood and agreed that the Tenant may utilize the existing partitions in the demised premises and may re-locate such partitions and build additional partitions, as required by the Tenant.

LEASE/COMM-40

Partitions

....

The Tenant may build additional partitions, as required, subject to approval by the Landlord, provided that such approval shall not be unreasonably withheld.

LEASE/COMM-41

Partitions with Approval

....

The Tenant's proportionate share of such common area shall be defined as the Tenant's area defined herein, divided by the total rentable area, expressed as a percentage. For purposes herein, the rentable area is defined as _____ and the Tenant's area shall be defined as _____.

LEASE/COMM-42

Proportionate Share

....

Notwithstanding the Lease Commencement Date, the Tenant shall not be obliged to pay minimum rent during the first _____ month(s) of the term, provided, however, that the Tenant shall be responsible to pay for all additional rent from the Lease Commencement Date.

LEASE/COMM-43

Rent Free Period

....

The rent paid by the Tenant to the Landlord shall be _____ per annum, paid 1/12 monthly in advance. This rate shall be on a _____ basis to the Landlord.

NOTE: For use when the Clause is not included in the pre-printed Agreement to Lease.

LEASE/COMM-44

Rental Amount

....

The Tenant may, at the Tenant's own expense, subject to the written approval of the Landlord, install any fittings, fixtures, and partitions that may be necessary for the operation of the Tenant's business, from time to time during the lease term, provided that upon termination of the lease term or renewal thereof, the Tenant shall, at the option of the Landlord, restore the premises to its original condition, at no cost to the Landlord.

LEASE/COMM-45

Restoring Premises to Original Condition

....

The Lease shall contain a clause providing that the Tenant shall have full access at all times from _____ for the purpose of shipping and receiving.

LEASE/COMM-46

Shipping and Receiving Access

APPENDIX

LEASE/COMM–47

Signs

The Tenant may install in, upon, or about the said premises any signs and advertising material which shall remain the property of the Tenant, which the Tenant may remove upon the expiration of the Lease, provided that all damage caused is repaired and the premises left in good repair. All signs and location(s) are to be approved beforehand in writing by the Landlord (such consent not to be unreasonably withheld) and must conform with all applicable governmental bylaws and codes.

LEASE/COMM–48

Space Layout Sketch

The Tenant shall provide the Landlord, within three (3) days of acceptance of this Offer, a layout sketch showing the area that the Landlord is to improve for the Tenant.

LEASE/COMM–49

Structural Penetration

It is agreed and understood that no openings may be made in the floors, walls and roof of the demised premises without the prior written consent of the Landlord. Should the Landlord consent to such work, it shall be done and maintained in a professional manner, at the sole cost of the Tenant.

LEASE/COMM–50

Use of Common Areas

It is understood and agreed that the Tenant shall have the right to use, in common with all others entitled thereto, the common areas of the property, including lobbies, hallways, common rooms, entrances, driveways, parking lots and common lands appurtenant to the building containing the demised premises, and the Tenant covenants that the Tenant will not obstruct these common areas.

LEASE/COMM–51

Work by Landlord

As an inducement for the Tenant to enter into a Lease contract with the Landlord, the Landlord covenants that it will carry out the following work prior to the Tenant taking possession, at no cost to the Tenant: [insert as needed].

LEASE/COMM–52

Workmanlike Manner

Any work carried out by the Landlord, or the Tenant, their employees, agents or contractors shall be done in a workmanlike and professional manner and in compliance with all applicable governmental bylaws and codes governing the use of the demised premises.

LEASE/RESIDENTIAL

NOTE: For the purpose of these clauses "Tenant" and "Landlord" have been used.
Tenant = Lessee and Landlord = Lessor. Either term may be used.

NOTE: In all cases please refer to the *Residential Tenancies Act*.

NOTE: It is not lawful for a Landlord to "demand" post-dated cheques for rent as a requirement when
leasing residential premises.

This Offer to Lease is conditional upon the Landlord satisfying the Landlord concerning the personal and/or credit worthiness of the Tenant. The Tenant hereby consents to having the Landlord conduct or cause to be conducted a personal and/or credit investigation in respect to the Tenant. Unless the Landlord gives notice in writing delivered to the Tenant personally or in accordance with any other provisions for the delivery of notice in this Agreement to Lease or any Schedule thereto not later than _____p.m. on the _____ day of _____, 20_____, that this condition is fulfilled, this Offer shall be null and void and the deposit shall be returned to the Tenant in full without deduction. This condition is included for the benefit of the Landlord and may be waived at the Landlord's sole option by notice in writing to the Tenant as aforesaid within the time period stated herein.

NOTE: To comply with the *Consumer Reporting Act*, if the Landlord refuses to grant a lease due to information
contained in a Consumer Report, the Landlord must give Notice that:

A) Refusal was due to information received from a consumer reporting agency or other person; and

B) Upon written request of the Tenant (within 60 days of notice) the Landlord is obligated to inform
the Tenant of the nature and source of the information.

LEASE/RES–1
Condition—Credit Check

- -

Tenant and Landlord agree that an accepted Agreement to Lease shall form a completed lease and no other lease will be signed between the Parties.

NOTE: If using this clause, delete the reference to a lease being drawn from the Agreement to Lease.

LEASE/RES–2
**Agreement to Lease Only/
No Lease to be Signed**

- -

Landlord shall provide alterations and improvements as detailed on Schedule "_____" attached hereto, at the Landlord's own expense, in a good and workmanlike manner prior to the commencement of the lease.

LEASE/RES–3
Alterations/Improvements

- -

The following appliances belonging to the Landlord are to remain on the premises for the Tenant's use: (include itemized list with description: make, model, and serial number).

LEASE/RES–4
Appliances Included

- -

Landlord represents and warrants that the appliances as listed in this Agreement to Lease will be in good working order at the commencement of the lease term. Tenant agrees to maintain said appliances in a state of ordinary cleanliness at the Tenant's cost.

LEASE/RES–5
**Appliances and Landlord/
Tenant Responsibilities**

- -

Tenant agrees that any chattels left on the rented premises, and not specifically mentioned herein, may remain and be stored on the premises at no cost to, and shall remain at the risk of, the Landlord.

LEASE/RES–6
Chattels Left by Owner

- -

Landlord agrees to have the carpets professionally cleaned prior to the commencement of the lease at the Landlord's cost, and Tenant shall have the carpets professionally cleaned at end of lease term at Tenant's cost.

LEASE/RES–7
Cleaning of Carpets

APPENDIX

LEASE/RES-8

Condo By-law Compliance

Tenant shall comply with all the Bylaws of the Condominium Corporation.

....

LEASE/RES-9

Consent to Decorate

Tenant agrees not to make any decorating changes to the premises without the express written consent of the Landlord or his authorized agent.

....

LEASE/RES-10

Increase in Rent

Tenant agrees that an increase of _____ % will be in effect on the second year of this lease, in accordance with the guidelines established under the applicable rent review legislation.

NOTE: The increase inserted must not take the rent above the legal maximum.

....

LEASE/RES-11

Maintenance of Grounds

The Tenant shall keep the lawns in good condition and shall not injure or remove the shade trees, shrubbery, hedges or any other tree or plant which may be in, upon or about the premises, and shall keep the sidewalks in front and at the sides of the premises free of snow and ice.

....

LEASE/RES-12

Maintenance of Swimming Pool

Tenant agrees to provide general maintenance for the swimming pool located on the premises, including cleaning, use of chemicals, opening and winterizing of pool. The Landlord shall be responsible for the upkeep of the equipment, including both chattels and fixtures associated with the operation of the pool.

NOTE: The Landlord may wish to reserve the right to open and/or winterize the pool.

....

LEASE/RES-13

Option to Purchase

In consideration of the sum of _____ ($_____) paid by the Tenant to the Landlord, the receipt of which is hereby acknowledged, and in consideration of the terms and conditions herein recited, the Landlord gives to the Tenant an option irrevocable within the time limit herein for acceptance, to purchase, free and clear of all encumbrances, the lands and premises situated at _____ in the _____ of_____ in the _____ of _____. The option shall be open for acceptance by notice in writing delivered to the Landlord not later than _____ p.m. on the _____ day of _____, 20_____. The terms of the purchase shall be the following: _____.

....

LEASE/RES-14

Permission to Sublet— Subject to Landlord's Approval

Landlord shall permit Tenant to sublet during the lease term, subject to approval of the Landlord, which shall not be unreasonably withheld.

....

LEASE/RES-15

Pets

Tenant agrees to be responsible for any repair or replacement cost due to the presence of any pets on the premises. Tenant further agrees that if pets are kept on the premises, Tenant shall, at lease termination, have the carpets professionally cleaned and make any repairs that may be necessary to restore any damages caused by pets.

....

LEASE/RES-16

Renewal Options

Tenant, if not in default hereunder, shall have the option, by written notice, given to the Landlord at least _____ days before the end of the lease term, to renew the lease for a further year term on the following terms and conditions: [Itemize tenancy particulars as agreed by the Parties.].

The Tenant agrees to allow the Landlord or his agent to show the property at all reasonable hours to prospective Buyers or Tenants, after giving the Tenant at least twenty four (24) hours written notice of such showing, and to allow the Landlord to affix a For Sale or For Rent sign on the property.

LEASE/RES-17
Showing of Rental Property

....

Landlord shall pay real estate taxes, [condominium fees and parking *if applicable*] and maintain fire insurance on the premises. Tenant acknowledges the Landlord's fire insurance on the premises provides no coverage on Tenant's personal property.

LEASE/RES-18
Taxes/Fire Insurance

....

Tenant agrees to pay the cost of all utilities required on the premises during the term of the lease and any extension thereof, including but not limited to electricity, water, sewer and gas or other fuel. Tenant further agrees to provide proof to the Landlord on or before the date of possession that the services have been transferred to the Tenant's name.

LEASE/RES-19
Tenant Pays Utilities

....

The Landlord covenants and agrees with the Tenant that, during the term of the lease or any renewal thereof, the Landlord will give the Tenant three (3) business days to submit an Offer upon the same terms and conditions as any bona fide Offer to purchase the leased property that the Landlord has received and is willing to accept, and any Lease executed by the Landlord and Tenant shall include this first right of refusal.

LEASE/RES-20
Tenant's First Right of Refusal

The Landlord shall give the Tenant written notice of such bona fide Offer and a copy of such Offer to the Tenant. In the event that the Tenant submits to the Landlord, within the time period described above, a written and signed Offer to purchase the property upon the same terms and conditions as the Offer initially received by the Landlord, the Landlord shall accept the Offer submitted by the Tenant. In the event that the Tenant fails to deliver to the Landlord, within the time limit described above, a written and signed Offer to purchase the property on the same terms and conditions as the initial Offer, the Landlord shall be at liberty to sell the property to the Buyer who submitted the initial Offer. Should the Tenant exercise the said first right of refusal, the Landlord agrees to pay the Agents so named in this Agreement, (or their successor companies) a fee of _____.

MAINTENANCE

The Seller agrees to leave the premises, including the floors, in a clean and broom swept condition.

MAINT-1
Cleaning

....

The Seller agrees to repair at the expense of the Seller, prior to the date of completion, any openings or holes in walls, floors, ceilings or window areas resulting from the removal of equipment, as requested after discussion with the Buyer and more particularly as hereinafter set out: _____ _____ [list where] and permit the Buyer the right to inspect the premises to ensure that said repairs have been completed.

MAINT-2
Equipment—Seller to Repair Damage on Removal

....

The Seller agrees to clean, repair or replace any damaged floor covering in the sections of the building as indicated by the Buyer and more particularly as hereinafter set out: _____ _____ [list where] and permit the Buyer the right to inspect the premises to ensure that said cleaning, repairing or replacing has been completed.

MAINT-3
Floors

MORTGAGES

MORT-1

**Condition—
Approval to Assume
Existing Mortgage
(Condition Precedent)**

The Buyer agrees to assume the existing _____ Charge/Mortgage held by _____ for approximately _____ , ($_____), bearing interest at the rate of _____ % per annum, calculated semi-annually not in advance, repayable in blended monthly payments of _____ ($ _____), including both principal and interest, and due on the _____ day of _____, 20_____. This Offer is conditional upon the Buyer obtaining the approval of the Chargee/Mortgagee to assume the existing Charge/Mortgage. Unless the Buyer gives notice in writing delivered to the Seller personally or in accordance with any other provisions for the delivery of notice in this Agreement of Purchase and Sale or any Schedule thereto not later than _____ p.m. on the _____ day of _____, 20_____, that this condition is fulfilled, this Offer shall be null and void and the deposit shall be returned to the Buyer in full without deduction. The Buyer hereby agrees to proceed immediately to make an application and provide such material as may be required by the Chargee/Mortgagee for approval of the Buyer as the Chargor/Mortgagor.

NOTE: This clause is a true Condition Precedent and neither a Seller nor a Buyer is entitled to waive this condition.

. . . .

MORT-2

**Condition—
Arranging a New Mortgage**

This Offer is conditional upon the Buyer arranging, at the Buyer's own expense, a new _____ Charge/Mortgage for not less than _____ ($ _____), bearing interest at a rate of not more than ___ % per annum, calculated semi-annually not in advance, repayable in blended monthly payments of about _____ ($ _____), including principal and interest, and to run for a term of not less than _____ years from the date of completion of this transaction. Unless the Buyer gives notice in writing delivered to the Seller personally or in accordance with any other provisions for the delivery of notice in this Agreement of Purchase and Sale or any Schedule thereto not later than _____ p.m. on the _____ day of _____, 20_____, that this condition is fulfilled, this Offer shall be null and void and the deposit shall be returned to the Buyer in full without deduction. This condition is included for the benefit of the Buyer and may be waived at the Buyer's sole option by notice in writing to the Seller as aforesaid within the time period stated herein.

NOTE 1: A waiver for the Buyer is included unless the Charge/Mortgage is to be arranged with specific Chargee/Mortgagee (i.e., if it is to be arranged through the Seller's Chargee/ Mortgagee then so state in the description and DO NOT provide a waiver, otherwise the Seller could suffer a substantial monetary penalty to discharge an existing Charge/Mortgage) – or see **MORT-11** below).

NOTE 2: If a Seller Take Back Charge/Mortgage is also being arranged, include **MORT-15** with **MORT-14** to prevent an Oklahoma offer (otherwise the property could be over financed to the detriment of the Seller's security).

NOTE 3: In the event a Finder's Fee is received from a lending institution or Mortgage Broker, it is wise to include an acknowledgement such as the following:

> *"The Seller acknowledges that the agent will receive a Finder's Fee of $_____ in connection with the arranging of financing for the Buyer".*

. . . .

MORT-3

**Condition—
Arranging a New Mortgage
as Percentage of Purchase
Price**

This Offer is conditional upon the Buyer arranging, at the Buyer's own expense, a new _____ Charge/Mortgage for not less than _____ % of the purchase price, bearing interest at a rate of not more than _____ % per annum, calculated semi-annually not in advance, repayable in equal blended monthly payments, amortized over a period of not less than _____ years and to run for a term of not less than _____ years from the date of completion of this transaction. Unless the Buyer gives notice in writing delivered to the Seller personally or in accordance with any other provisions for the delivery of notice in this Agreement of Purchase and Sale or any Schedule thereto not later than _____ p.m. on the _____ day of _____, 20 _____, that this condition is fulfilled, this Offer shall be null and void and the deposit shall be returned to the Buyer in full without deduction. This condition is included for the benefit of the Buyer and may be waived at the Buyer's sole option by notice in writing to the Seller as aforesaid within the time period stated herein.

This Offer is conditional upon the Buyer arranging, at the Buyer's own expense, a new _____ Charge/Mortgage satisfactory to the Buyer in the Buyer's sole and absolute discretion. Unless the Buyer gives notice in writing delivered to the Seller personally or in accordance with any other provisions for the delivery of notice in this Agreement of Purchase and Sale or any Schedule thereto not later than _____ p.m. on the _____ day of _____, 20_____, that this condition is fulfilled, this Offer shall be null and void and the deposit shall be returned to the Buyer in full without deduction. This condition is included for the benefit of the Buyer and may be waived at the Buyer's sole option by notice in writing to the Seller as aforesaid within the time period stated herein.

MORT–4

Condition—
Arranging New Mortgage Satisfactory to Buyer

NOTE: Sellers should be aware that this condition does not contain any specific terms of the proposed financing Buyers wish to arrange and thus provides Buyers with more latitude in declining financing.

Buyers using this clause should be advised they have an obligation to make a "good faith" effort to arrange the necessary financing, and should not use this clause inappropriately as a means to cancel the transaction.

The Buyer may terminate this Agreement through written notice delivered to the Seller personally or in accordance with any other provisions for the delivery of notice in this Agreement of Purchase and Sale or any Schedule thereto not later than _____ p.m. on the _____ day of _____, 20_____, if a new first Charge/Mortgage cannot be arranged by the Buyer, at the Buyer's expense. This Charge/Mortgage is to be for a sum of not less than _____ ($ _____) bearing interest at a rate of not more than _____% per annum, calculated semi-annually, not in advance, repayable in blended monthly payments of about _____, ($ _____), including both principal and interest, and to run for a term of not less than _____ year(s) from the date of completion of this transaction. Upon receipt of the above notice, this Agreement shall be null and void and the deposit shall be returned to the Buyer in full without deduction. If no such notice is received within the above time limit, then this term of contract shall be deemed waived by the Buyer and this Agreement shall remain valid and binding whether or not such Charge/Mortgage has been arranged.

MORT–5

Condition—
Arranging New Mortgage (Condition Subsequent)

This Offer is conditional upon the Seller being satisfied concerning the personal and/or credit worthiness of the Buyer. Unless the Seller gives notice in writing to the Buyer personally or in accordance with any other provisions for the delivery of notice in this Agreement of Purchase and Sale or any Schedule thereto not later than _____ p.m. on the _____ day of _____, 20_____, that this condition is fulfilled, this Offer shall be null and void and the deposit shall be returned to the Buyer in full without deduction. This condition is included for the benefit of the Seller and may be waived at the Seller's sole option by notice in writing to the Buyer as aforesaid within the time period stated herein.

MORT–6

Condition—Credit Check

This Offer is conditional upon the Seller being satisfied that the cost to discharge the _____ Charge(s)/Mortgage(s) shall not exceed the sum of _____, ($_____). Unless the Seller gives notice in writing delivered to the Buyer personally or in accordance with any other provisions for the delivery of notice in this Agreement of Purchase and Sale or any Schedule thereto not later than _____ p.m. on the _____ day of _____, 20_____, that this condition is fulfilled, this Offer shall be null and void and the deposit shall be returned to the Buyer in full without deduction. This condition is included for the benefit of the Seller and may be waived at the Seller's sole option by notice in writing to the Buyer as aforesaid within the time period stated herein.

MORT–7

Condition—
Discharge of Mortgage(s)—Cost

NOTE: Most discharges are covered in the printed Agreement.

APPENDIX

MORT–8

Condition—
Overleveraged Property

The Seller hereby acknowledges that the real property is subject to registered encumbrances that may, given the Seller's obligation to pay commissions and other related closing costs, exceed the available proceeds of sale from this transaction. This Offer shall, therefore, be conditional upon the Seller obtaining the written approval of all Chargees/Mortgagees and other registered encumbrancers as to the final acceptance of this Offer and their agreement to discharge their encumbrances without payment in the aggregate of more than the available proceeds from this transaction. Unless the Seller gives notice in writing delivered to the Buyer personally or in accordance with any other provisions for the delivery of notice in this Agreement of Purchase and Sale or any Schedule thereto not later than _____ p.m. on the _____ day of _____, 20_____, that this condition is fulfilled, this Offer shall be null and void and the deposit shall be returned to the Buyer in full without deduction. This condition is included for the benefit of the Seller and may be waived at the Seller's sole option by notice in writing to the Buyer as aforesaid within the time period stated herein.

....

MORT–9

Condition—
Paydown of Existing
Mortgage by Seller

The Seller agrees to pay the existing _____ Chargee/Mortgagee the sum required to reduce the interest rate by _____% for the term of _____ year(s) of this Charge/Mortgage. This Offer is conditional upon the Seller being satisfied that the cost to reduce the interest rate to _____% shall not exceed the sum of _____ ($ _____). Unless the Seller gives notice in writing delivered to the Buyer personally or in accordance with any other provisions for the delivery of notice in this Agreement of Purchase and Sale or any Schedule thereto not later than _____ p.m. on the _____ day of _____, 20_____, that this condition is fulfilled, this Offer shall be null and void and the deposit shall be returned to the Buyer in full without deduction. This condition is included for the benefit of the Seller and may be waived at the Seller's sole option by notice in writing to the Buyer as aforesaid within the time period stated herein.

....

MORT–10

Condition—
Sale of Mortgage by Seller

This Offer is conditional upon the Seller obtaining at the Seller's own expense, a commitment for the sale of the aforementioned _____Charge/Mortgage [for an amount of not less than _____($_____)] OR [at a discount of not more than _____% of the amount of said Charge/Mortgage]. Unless the Seller gives notice in writing delivered to the Buyer personally or in accordance with any other provisions for the delivery of notice in this Agreement of Purchase and Sale or any Schedule thereto not later than _____ p.m. on the _____ day of _____, 20_____, that this condition is fulfilled, this Offer shall be null and void and the deposit shall be returned to the Buyer in full without deduction. This condition is included for the benefit of the Seller and may be waived at the Seller's sole option by notice in writing to the Buyer as aforesaid within the time period stated herein.

....

MORT–11

Discharge of Existing
Mortgage—Buyer to Pay
Prepayment Charges

If the Charge/Mortgage being arranged by the Buyer is not obtained through the existing Chargee/Mortgagee, _____, the Buyer will pay to the Seller, in addition to the purchase price, all prepayment and bonus charges which the existing Chargee/Mortgagee lawfully charges the Seller.

....

MORT–12

Discharge of Existing
Mortgage—Seller to Pay
Prepayment Charges

The Seller acknowledges that there may be a penalty to discharge the existing Charge/Mortgage and agrees to pay any costs, expenses or penalties incurred in discharging the existing Charge/Mortgage.

APPENDIX

The Buyer agrees to assume the existing _____ Charge/Mortgage held by _____ for approximately _____ ($_____), bearing interest at the rate of _____ % per annum, calculated semi-annually not in advance, repayable in blended monthly payments of _____ ($_____), including both principal and interest, and due on the _____ day of _____, 20_____.

NOTE: The personal covenant of the original Chargor/Mortgagor still applies following the assumption of the Charge/Mortgage by the Buyer.

MORT–13

Existing Mortgage—
Buyer to Assume
(No Approval)

The Seller agrees to take back a _____ Charge/Mortgage in the amount of _____ ($_____), bearing interest at the rate of _____% per annum, calculated semi-annually not in advance, repayable in blended monthly payments of _____ ($_____), including both principal and interest, and to run for a term of _____ years from the date of completion of this transaction. (See Prepayment Privileges, Clauses **MORT–23**, **MORT–24**, **MORT–25** & **MORT–26**.)

NOTE: Without a prepayment privilege, the borrower does not have any automatic right to early discharge of the Charge/Mortgage or prepayment of principal.

MORT–14

Seller Take Back Mortgage

In the event that the first mortgage arranged by the Buyer has a principal amount in excess of _____ ($_____), the principal amount of the second mortgage will be reduced by the excess amount, with a corresponding reduction in the payment for the second mortgage. The Buyer agrees to provide the Seller or the Seller's lawyer with a confirmation of the principal amount of the first mortgage to be registered.

NOTE: To be used with MORT–14 when the offer is conditional on arranging a prior mortgage.

MORT–15

Seller Take Back Mortgage—
Second Mortgage Clause
to Prevent Overfinancing
(Oklahoma)

The Seller agrees to take back a _____ Charge/Mortgage [for the balance of the Purchase price] OR [in the amount of _____ ($_____)] bearing interest at the rate of _____% per annum, repayable interest only _____ [state payment interval; e.g., monthly, quarterly, etc.] and maturing on the _____ day of _____, 20____. (See Prepayment Privileges, Clauses **MORT–23**, **MORT–24**, **MORT–25** & **MORT–26**.)

NOTE: Without a prepayment privilege, the borrower does not have any automatic right to early discharge of the Charge/Mortgage or prepayment of principal.

MORT–16

Seller Take Back Mortgage—
Simple Interest Only

The Buyer acknowledges that the Charge/Mortgage being taken back by the Seller may be sold. The Buyer agrees to co-operate fully with the Seller in connection with the sale of this Charge/Mortgage, and shall provide such personal and financial information, together with such documents as the Assignee of the Charge/Mortgage may reasonably require, forthwith upon request by the Seller, in order that the sale of the Charge/Mortgage may be completed.

MORT–17

Seller Take Back—To Be Sold
By Seller Prior to Closing
(Buyer to Co-operate)

The Buyer warrants that the down payment stated in this transaction shall be at least _____ % of the purchase price and does not incur any payment obligations or indebtedness.

MORT–18

Seller Take Back—
Source of Downpayment

The Buyer shall deliver to the Chargee/Mortgagee on the closing of this transaction, and on each anniversary of the closing, a series of post-dated cheques to cover all Charge/Mortgage payments due during the next twelve months.

MORT–19

Term—Post Dated Cheque
Requirement

APPENDIX

MORT–20

Term—Postponement–1

This Charge/Mortgage shall contain a clause permitting the renewal or replacement of the existing first Charge/Mortgage at any time, provided that any increase in the principal amount of the new first Charge/ Mortgage over the amount of principal owing under the first Charge/Mortgage at the time of renewal or replacement shall be applied in reduction of the principal amount of this Charge/Mortgage; and the Chargee/Mortgagee hereunder shall execute and deliver to the Chargor/Mortgagor such postponement agreement, Charge/Mortgage Statement, or other documents as the new first Chargee/Mortgagee may reasonably require, forthwith upon request.

NOTE: If Charge/Mortgage being arranged is a third, etc., change clause to read: "replacement of the first and/or second Charge(s)/Mortgage(s)" and "principal owing under the first and/or second Charge(s)/Mortgage(s)".

MORT–21

Term—Postponement–2

The Chargor/Mortgagor shall have the privilege of renewing or replacing the existing first Charge/Mortgage at any time provided that any increase in the principal of the new first Charge/Mortgage over the amount of principal owing under the first Charge/Mortgage at the time of renewal or replacement shall be applied without penalty in reduction of the principal amount of this Charge/Mortgage and the Chargee/Mortgagee will execute and deliver to the Chargor/Mortgagor a postponement agreement in favour of the new first Chargee/Mortgagee.

MORT–22

Term—Postponement–3

The Chargee/Mortgagee will execute and deliver to the Chargor/Mortgagor a postponement agreement in favour of the new first Chargee/Mortgagee, provided that such replacement Charge/Mortgage shall not bear interest in excess of _____% per annum and if such financing is for an amount greater than the outstanding principal balance of the existing first Charge/Mortgage at the date of registration of the new first Charge/Mortgage, such increase shall be paid towards the reduction of the principal balance outstanding on this Charge/Mortgage.

MORT–23

Term—Prepayment—
Fully Open

This Charge/Mortgage shall contain a clause permitting the Chargor/Mortgagor, when not in default, the privilege of prepaying all or part of the principal sum outstanding at any time or times without notice or bonus.

MORT–24

Term—Prepayment—Open
in Accordance with Principal
Amounts Falling Due

This Charge/Mortgage shall contain a clause permitting the Chargor/Mortgagor, when not in default; the privilege of prepaying all or part of the principal sum on any payment date or dates without notice or bonus, provided that any partial prepayment shall equal the sum of the principal amounts of the payment(s) next falling due under the Charge/Mortgage.

MORT–25

Term—Prepayment—
Open on Anniversary Date

This Charge/Mortgage shall contain a clause permitting the Chargor/Mortgagor, when not in default, the privilege of prepaying on each anniversary date a sum not to exceed _____% of the original principal amount, without notice or bonus.

MORT–26

Term—Prepayment—
Subject to Bonus

This Charge/Mortgage shall contain a clause permitting the Chargor/Mortgagor, when not in default, the privilege of prepaying on any payment date a sum not to exceed _____% of the original principal amount, subject to a bonus of _____ month's interest on the amount of principal being repaid.

MORT–27

Term—Renewal—
Same Terms Except for
Further Renewal

This Charge/Mortgage shall contain a clause permitting the Chargor/Mortgagor, when not in default, the privilege of renewing this Charge/Mortgage on its maturity, for a further term of _____ year(s) on the same terms and conditions save and except for the right to any further renewal.

APPENDIX

This Charge/Mortgage shall contain a clause permitting the Chargor/Mortgagor, when not in default, the privilege of renewing this Charge/Mortgage upon its maturity, for a further term of _____ year(s) at the rate of interest charged by _____, on the date thirty days preceding the maturity date of the Charge/Mortgage, to credit worthy borrowers for _____ year Charge/Mortgage loans, and otherwise on the same terms and conditions save and except for the right of a further renewal.

MORT–28

Term—Renewal—
At Current Rate of Interest

. . . .

This Charge/Mortgage shall contain a clause providing that the Chargor/Mortgagor shall have the right to alter or demolish any or all of the existing buildings now on the property without such activity constituting waste under the terms of this Charge/Mortgage, provided that such alteration or demolition shall comply with all applicable bylaws, building codes or other applicable laws or regulations.

MORT–29

Term—Right to Demolish

. . . .

This Charge/Mortgage shall contain a clause providing that if the Chargor/Mortgagor sells, assigns, or otherwise transfers title to the property or places a Charge/Mortgage on the property without the express consent of the Chargee/Mortgagee then, at the sole option of the Chargee/Mortgagee, all monies secured thereby shall become due and payable immediately, together with interest accrued to the date thereof.

MORT–30

Term—Transfer/
Acceleration Provision—
At Option of Mortgagee

MORTGAGES/DEVELOPMENT

This Charge/Mortgage shall contain a clause permitting the dedication of all roads and other lands required by municipal and provincial authorities on any proposed plan or plans of sub-division and providing for a discharge of such lands, as may be required for such purposes, from the Charge/Mortgage, without additional payment by the Chargor/Mortgagor other than the normal legal costs of the Chargee/Mortgagee.

MORT/DEV–1

Mortgagee's Consent—
Dedication of Road

. . . .

This Charge/Mortgage shall contain a clause requiring the Chargee/Mortgagee to postpone the Charge/ Mortgage in favour of the granting of any easements to municipal or other governmental authorities or Public Utilities Commission or Corporation, required for the supply and/or installation of gas, telephone, electricity, water, sewer, railroad, or other similar services, without additional payment by the Chargor/ Mortgagor other than the normal legal costs of the Chargee/ Mortgagee.

MORT/DEV–2

Mortgagee's Consent—
Granting of Easements

. . . .

This Charge/Mortgage shall contain a clause permitting the Chargor/Mortgagor to apply to register the lands, or any part or parts, under the Land Titles System, and the Chargee/Mortgagee agrees to execute any and all documents required by the Chargor/Mortgagor with respect thereto, provided that the Chargor/Mortgagor pay all costs of said registration.

MORT/DEV–3

Mortgagee's Consent—
Registration in Land Titles

. . . .

This Charge/Mortgage shall contain a clause requiring the Chargee/Mortgagee, upon written notice, to execute applications and all other documents required for the Chargor/Mortgagor to change the Official Plan, if necessary, and to re-zone the lands to a zoning suitable to the Chargor/ Mortgagor, or to amend any bylaws, and to support such application or applications for re-zoning or amending of bylaws and to co-operate with the Chargor/Mortgagor in all reasonable respects, provided that the Chargor/Mortgagor pay all costs of said re-zoning.

MORT/DEV–4

Mortgagee's Consent—
Re-zoning

APPENDIX

MORT/DEV–5

Mortgagee's Consent—
Subdivide

This Charge/Mortgage shall contain a clause permitting the Chargor/Mortgagor to register a plan or plans of sub-division on the Charged/Mortgaged lands and the Chargee/Mortgagee agrees to cooperate with the Chargor/Mortgagor and execute any required documents for the application and registration of any plan of sub-division, provided that the Chargor/Mortgagor pay all costs for the application, requirements for approval and registration of the plan of sub-division.

MORTGAGES/POWER OF SALE

MORT/POS–1

Power of Sale (General
Provision)

It is further understood that on the date of acceptance of this Offer there is default under the terms of the Charge/Mortgage which entitles the Seller to exercise the Power of Sale. The only evidence of the default which the Buyer may require shall be a statutory declaration by the Seller setting forth the facts entitling the Seller to sell under the Power of Sale, including the particulars of the notice of exercising the Power of Sale, the names of the persons upon whom service of the notice has been effected, and declaring that default under the Charge/Mortgage entitling the Seller to exercise the Power of Sale has continued up to and including the date of acceptance of this Offer and to the time of closing. The Buyer understands and agrees that the Chargor/Mortgagor has the right to redeem the property up to the time of waiver or expiration of all rights of termination or fulfillment of all conditions and this Agreement is subject to that right. In the event of redemption by the Chargor/Mortgagor, this Agreement shall be null and void and any deposit monies paid will be refunded in full without deduction.

Where a court of competent jurisdiction prevents the completion of the within sale by an interim, interlocutory or permanent injunction or otherwise, then the Seller (Chargee/Mortgagee) is not obliged to complete the said transaction and the Agreement shall be terminated and the deposit shall be returned to the Buyer in full without deduction. In no event shall the Seller be responsible for any costs, expenses, loss or damages incurred or suffered by the Buyer and the Seller shall not have any further liability to the Buyer whatsoever.

Notwithstanding other provisions of this Agreement, the Seller shall not be required either on or before closing to discharge its own Charge/Mortgage or any existing Charges/Mortgages, liens or other encumbrances subsequent in priority to the Seller's Charge/Mortgage, which may be registered against the Property.

The Buyer also acknowledges that the Seller makes no representation and/or warranties with respect to the state of repair of the premises, inclusions of chattels or fixtures, or ownership of fixtures or appliances, and the Buyer agrees to accept the property "as is". Chattels and fixtures on the premises may or may not be included with the premises but the Seller shall not be obliged to remove any chattels or fixtures. All the provisions of the *Mortgages Act* shall supersede any part of this Agreement which may be in variance thereof or in conflict therewith.

NOTE: Most Chargee(s)/Mortgagee(s) have their own specific clauses concerning Power of Sale. Each situation should be carefully analyzed prior to the drafting of an Agreement of Purchase and Sale.

NEW HOMES

NEW–1

Builder Registered

The Seller represents and warrants, to the best of the Seller's knowledge and belief, that the said home and its builder are both registered under the Ontario New Home Warranty Program. The Parties agree that this representation and warranty shall form an integral part of this Agreement and survive the completion of this transaction. Documents attesting to these registrations are attached as Schedule "_____" and form part of this Agreement of Purchase and Sale.

APPENDIX

The Seller agrees to complete the house, the (itemize any other structures), and grounds in a good and workmanlike manner, in accordance with all the specifications outlined in Schedule "_____" attached hereto and forming part of this Agreement of Purchase and Sale.

NEW–2

Completion of Construction

....

The Buyer and the Seller acknowledge and agree that the HST payable in connection with the purchase and sale transaction contemplated by this Agreement of Purchase and Sale is included in the purchase price subject to the provisions hereinafter set out.

NEW–3

HST—New Homes

Notwithstanding that the purchase price payable by the Buyer includes HST, the Buyer hereby assigns and transfers to the Seller all of the Buyer's rights, title and interest in any rebates, refunds or credits available, including Federal Sales Tax rebates and HST rebates to which the Buyer is entitled in connection with the payment of HST payable on the transfer to the Buyer of ownership or possession of the property. The Buyer further appoints and authorizes the Seller or the Seller's agents to be the Buyer's authorized representative and attorney for the purposes of applying for and collecting such tax rebates. The Buyer agrees to execute, at no cost to the Seller, any and all documents required to give effect to this provision.

The Buyer represents and warrants to the Seller that the Buyer shall personally occupy the property or cause one or more of the Buyer's relations to occupy the property as the Buyer's or the Buyer's relation's primary place of residence upon completion and agrees to deliver to the Seller on closing a Statutory Declaration in the Seller's form in which the Buyer declares that the property being purchased by the Buyer is for use as the Buyer's or the Buyer's relation's primary place of residence and will be so occupied forthwith upon completion.

In the event that the Buyer breaches the warranty or any of the provisions referred to above which results in the Buyer being ineligible or the Seller being unable to obtain the rebates referred to herein then the Buyer shall pay to the Seller forthwith an amount equal to the amount which the Buyer would have been eligible to obtain were it not for such breach or failure to carry out the Buyer's obligations.

NOTE: Definition of Relation as set out in the *Excise Tax Act*.

> *Relation*—A relation means an individual related to you by blood, marriage, common-law partnership, or adoption within the meaning of the *Income Tax Act*. "Blood relation" is limited to parents, children, or other descendants or siblings. "Marriage relation" includes your spouse or a person who is connected to your spouse by blood or adoption. A relation includes a common-law partner, a former spouse or a former common-law partner.

....

NOTE: In Ontario, Tarion requires that when a new home is sold, the Agreement must include the standard Tarion form of Addendum, exactly as published by Tarion and complete the form without any revisions or deletions. The required Addendum (Schedule) is statutorily deemed to be part of the Agreement of Purchase and Sale. To obtain the Tarion forms, go to the Tarion website at **http://www.tarion.com**.

NEW–4

Link to TARION Schedules

PARKING

The Seller agrees to remove all equipment, storage containers and any other materials, including refuse and debris, from the property and to leave the parking area in a clean and vacant condition.

PARK–1

Parking Area

APPENDIX

RENT/SALE OF PROPERTY

NOTE: The following rental clauses have been developed for the sale of small rental properties (e.g., duplexes and triplexes etc.). For large multi-unit complexes special conditions will apply and expert assistance should be sought.

NOTE: Since rental properties fall within the definition of a "business" in the *Real Estate and Business Brokers Act,* the appropriate financial statements or Form 503 must be delivered to the Buyer.

RENT–1

Adjustment of Purchase Price Due to Shortfall in Rental Income

The Parties agree that if the actual rent, including any planned increases as declared in this Agreement, is less than the rent warranted, including any planned increases by the Seller, then the Parties agree that the Seller shall pay the Buyer as liquidated damages, the amount of the difference times a factor of _____, as either an adjustment on the purchase price of the property or as a separate payment at the sole discretion of the Buyer.

NOTE: The factor is negotiable between the Parties, but is often based on the ratio between the overall purchase price and gross rent (gross rental multiplier).

RENT–2

Confidentiality of Disclosed Rental Information

The Buyer will hold in strict confidence any knowledge about the rent review situations of the property, financial documents, leases, and such other records of the property which the Buyer obtains from this Agreement or any other source, subject only to the use of such information in order to obtain professional advice and in the application or appeal process concerning rent review.

RENT–3

Increase of Rent with Notices Prior to Completion of Sale

The Seller shall, at the earliest legally permitted time to completion, give notices of rent increases, at the statutory rate or as otherwise agreed between the Buyer and the Seller, and provide the Buyer with proof of proper service thereof.

RENT–4

No Rent Increases Pending Completion of Sale

Pending completion, the Seller shall not give any notices of rent increases.

RENT–5

Notices to Tenants of New Owner

Upon completion, the Seller shall provide the Buyer with a notice to all tenants advising them of the new owner and requiring all future rents to be paid as the Buyer directs. The Seller will pay to the Buyer any rent paid to the Seller in error or in violation of the direction for a period of _____ months following completion, after which period the Seller may refuse to accept rent from tenants or return it to them.

NOTE: Lawyers for parties will treat rent deposits and interest thereon as part of the adjustment process.

The Seller represents and warrants, to the best of the Seller's knowledge and belief, that the current actual rents are:

Unit	Current Rent	Last Increase (Date/Amount)

RENT–6

Rent—No Warranty Re Legality of Rents

The Parties agree that this representation and warranty shall survive and not merge on completion of this transaction, but apply only to those circumstances existing at completion of this transaction. The Parties also agree that the warranty given is as to actual rents only, and does not extend to the legality of the rents.

NOTE: Additional categories may be used to expand tenancy information: Apartment #, Tenant Name, Type of Tenancy, Expiry Date, Rent Due Date, Prepaid Rent, and Tenancy Particulars (Items included in Rent).

NOTE: The actual lease documents should be attached as a Schedule to the Agreement. If too many documents, consider making Offer conditional upon inspection of tenancy agreement.

The Seller represents and warrants, to the best of the Seller's knowledge and belief that, during the period of the Seller's ownership, the property has been rented in accordance with Landlord and Tenant legislation and that any rent increase has been effected in accordance with relevant rent review legislation. The Parties agree that this representation and warranty shall survive and not merge on completion of this transaction, but apply only to those circumstances existing at completion of this transaction.

RENT–7

Rent— General Warranty by Seller

The Seller represents and warrants, to the best of the Seller's knowledge and belief, that there are no disputes between the Seller as landlord and any tenant as to the state of repair of the leased premises, the payment of rents, contravention of applicable rent review legislation for residential tenancies, or other material items concerning the tenants' lease agreements other than as specifically set out in this Agreement of Purchase and Sale. The Parties agree that these representations and warranties shall survive and not merge on completion of this transaction, but apply only to those circumstances existing at completion of this transaction.

RENT–8

Rent—Seller Warranty Regarding Disputes

Unless otherwise agreed between the Buyer and the Seller, the Seller shall not renegotiate any leases after this Agreement becomes unconditional.

RENT–9

Seller Not to Renegotiate Leases Prior to Completion without Buyer Instruction

The Seller shall make reasonable attempts to renegotiate leases with current tenants [for terms not to exceed _____ years] as agreed between the Buyer and Seller.

RENT–10

Seller to Renegotiate Leases

APPENDIX

RENT REVIEW

RENT/REV–1

Rent Review Application Pending—Buyer to Pay/Buyer to Control

The Parties agree that the Seller will allow the pending rent review application, and any appeal thereof, to be continued in the Seller's name, in the control of the Buyer and at the expense of the Buyer including the payment of any liability for costs in the Divisional Court or a higher court. Provided further, that if an appeal is brought to, or defended in, the Divisional Court or a higher court the Buyer shall provide the Seller's Solicitor with the amount of _____ ($ _____), at each level of court to which the appeal is taken, to a maximum amount of _____ ($ _____), to be held in trust as security for the Seller's liability for costs.

NOTE: Buyers using this clause should seek legal advice as to potential amounts involved.

RENT/REV–2

Rent Review Application Pending—Seller to Pay/Buyer to Control

The Parties agree that the Seller will co-operate with the Buyer in completing all pending rent review applications and appeals thereof which shall be at the expense of the Seller up to a maximum of _____ ($ _____), until the completion of any appeal whether to the Landlord and Tenant Board or to the Divisional Court, provided further that such application and appeals shall be in the control of the Buyer throughout.

NOTE: Buyers and Sellers using this clause should seek legal advice as to potential amounts involved.

RENT/REV–3

Rent Review Application—Seller to Provide Financial Information and Documentation Necessary for Rent Review Application

The Seller shall provide the Buyer with any and all financial information and/or documents in the Seller's possession and control, which the Buyer requires to effect or defend any rent review application or appeal.

NOTE: See confidentiality clause RENT–2.

REPRESENTATIONS/WARRANTIES

NOTE 1: Various warranty clauses are provided. Care must be taken to ensure that the correct wording is utilized to reflect the agreement of the parties.

NOTE 2: When drafting these clauses, you may wish to provide a specific time limit for the Buyer to notify the Seller. (See Warranties – Specific Time Period)

REP/WARR–1

Seller Not Liable

The Buyer acknowledges the Buyer has been informed of the following possible latent defect(s) in the property: _____. The Buyer further acknowledges it is the Buyer's sole responsibility to complete their own due diligence concerning this defect, for example, obtaining a report concerning this defect, and the Buyer releases the Seller of all liability for current and future damages resulting from this possible defect.

NOTE: This clause should be used only when a specific defect is identified and disclosed and should not be used by the Seller as a general "as is" clause.

REP/WARR–2

Seller Representations—General

The Seller represents and warrants that on completion: _____ [e.g., There is no known damage to the basement, roof, or elsewhere caused by water seepage or flooding]. The Parties agree that these representations and warranties shall survive and not merge on completion of this transaction, but apply only to the state of the property at completion of this transaction.

The Seller represents and warrants that on completion: _____
[e.g., There is no known damage to the basement, roof, or elsewhere caused by water seepage or flooding]. The Parties agree that these representations and warranties shall survive and not merge on completion of this transaction, but apply only to the state of the property at completion of this transaction. The Buyer, at the Buyer's sole option, may terminate this Agreement at any time prior to completion in the event any of the representations and warranties contained herein are incorrect, and the deposit shall be returned to the Buyer in full without deduction.

REP/WARR–3

Seller Representations—Termination Remedy

The Parties agree that the representations and warranties stated herein shall survive and not merge on completion, but shall expire at _____ p.m. on the _____ day of _____, 20_____, and be of no further force and effect unless the Buyer, prior to such expiry, has given written notice of a claim under the warranty to the Seller.

REP/WARR–4

Warranties—Specific Time Period

The Parties agree that the representations and warranties stated herein shall survive and not merge on completion of this transaction.

REP/WARR–5

Warranties—Survive Completion

The Parties agree that the representations and warranties stated herein shall survive and not merge on completion of this transaction, but apply only to the state of the property at completion of this transaction.

REP/WARR–6

Warranties—Survive Completion—Limited to Current Transaction

SALE OF BUYER'S PROPERTY

This Offer is conditional upon the sale of the Buyer's property known as _____.
Unless the Buyer gives notice in writing delivered to the Seller personally or in accordance with any other provisions for the delivery of notice in this Agreement of Purchase and Sale or any Schedule thereto not later than _____ p.m. on the _____ day of _____, 20_____, that this condition is fulfilled, this Offer shall be null and void and the deposit shall be returned to the Buyer in full without deduction. This condition is included for the benefit of the Buyer and may be waived at the Buyer's sole option by notice in writing to the Seller as aforesaid within the time period stated herein.

SBP–1

Condition—Buyer's Property

This Offer is conditional upon the Buyer receiving notification of the removal of all conditions in an existing Agreement of Purchase and Sale for the property known as _____.
Unless the Buyer gives notice in writing delivered to the Seller personally or in accordance with any other provisions for the delivery of notice in this Agreement of Purchase and Sale or any Schedule thereto not later than _____ p.m. on the _____ day of _____, 20_____, that this condition is fulfilled, this Offer shall be null and void and the deposit shall be returned to the Buyer in full without deduction. This condition is included for the benefit of the Buyer and may be waived at the Buyer's sole option by notice in writing to the Seller as aforesaid within the time period stated herein.

SBP–2

Condition—Removal of All Conditions—Buyer's Property

APPENDIX

SBP–3

Condition— Seller's Release from Previous Agreement

This Offer is conditional upon the Seller obtaining a release from a prior Agreement of Purchase and Sale. Unless the Seller gives notice in writing delivered to the Buyer personally or in accordance with any other provisions for the delivery of notice in this Agreement of Purchase and Sale or any Schedule thereto not later than _____ p.m. on the _____ day of _____, 20_____ , that this condition is fulfilled, this Offer shall be null and void and the deposit shall be returned to the Buyer in full without deduction.

NOTE: This clause is a true Condition Precedent and neither a Seller nor a Buyer is entitled to waive this condition.

SBP–4

Escape Clause— Buyer's Property

Provided further that the Seller may continue to offer the property for sale and, in the event the Seller receives another Offer satisfactory to the Seller, the Seller may so notify the Buyer in writing by delivery to the Buyer personally or in accordance with any other provisions for the delivery of notice in this Agreement of Purchase and Sale or any Schedule thereto. The Buyer shall have _____ hours from the giving of such notice to waive this condition by notice in writing delivered to the Seller personally or in accordance with any other provisions for the delivery of notice in this Agreement of Purchase and Sale or any Schedule thereto, failing which this Offer shall be null and void, and the Buyer's deposit shall be returned in full without deduction.

NOTE: The Escape Clause only requires the removal of one specific condition.

SBP–5

Escape Clause— Notices Re: Multiple Representation

If the Listing Brokerage represents both the Seller and the Buyer in this transaction in multiple representation, the Brokerage is not authorized to receive the Notice to Remove Condition on behalf of the Buyer and the Brokerage is not authorized to receive the Notice of Waiver of Condition on behalf of the Seller. Said notices will be delivered by the Brokerage either to the parties to the transaction, the address of the parties, the lawyers representing the parties, or transmitted to the fax number or email address designated by the parties other than the Brokerage's fax number or email address.

NOTE: This clause to be used with escape clause only.

SBP–6

Escape Clause— Removal of All Conditions

Provided further that the Seller may continue to offer the property for sale and, in the event the Seller receives another Offer satisfactory to the Seller, the Seller may so notify the Buyer personally or in accordance with any other provisions for the delivery of notice in this Agreement of Purchase and Sale or any Schedule thereto. The Buyer shall have _____ hours from the giving of such notice to waive any and all conditions by notice in writing delivered to the Seller personally or in accordance with any other provisions for the delivery of notice in this Agreement of Purchase and Sale or any Schedule thereto, failing which this Offer shall be null and void and the deposit shall be returned to the Buyer in full without deduction.

SEWER/WATER

NOTE: Sale of Property with a well and/or septic system involves specific knowledge of the system. (e.g., There is a difference in a well's performance depending on many variables, e.g., the amount of available water, the delivery capacity of the well system, the amount of water that can be delivered over a certain period of time, and seasonable variables. The type of well, drilled, bored, or dug can also affect performance). Expert advice should be sought.

This Offer is conditional upon the Buyer determining, at the Buyer's own expense, that:

(1) all sewage systems serving the property are wholly within the setback requirements of the said property and have received all required Certificates of Installation and Approval pursuant to the *Environmental Protection Act*;

(2) all sewage systems serving the property have been constructed in accordance with the said Certificates of Installation and Approval;

(3) all sewage systems serving the property have received all required use permits under the said Act or any other legislation; and further, that on inspection, the septic bed is in good working order.

The Buyer shall be allowed to retain at the Buyer's own expense, a professional in the septic business to make an examination of the septic system.

Seller agrees to allow access to the property for the purposes of a septic inspection and agrees to allow the Buyer to request information as outlined above from the appropriate authorities having jurisdiction.

Unless the Buyer gives notice in writing delivered to the Seller personally or in accordance with any other provisions for the delivery of notice in this Agreement of Purchase and Sale or any Schedule thereto not later than _____ p.m. on the _____ day of _____, 20_____, that these conditions have been fulfilled, this Offer shall become null and void and the deposit shall be returned to the Buyer in full without deduction. These conditions are included for the benefit of the Buyer and may be waived at the Buyer's sole option by notice in writing to the Seller as aforesaid within the time period stated herein.

NOTE: SEWER/WATER-1 does not speak to the working order of the Septic System and, therefore, should be used in conjunction with SEWER/WATER-4.

SEWER/WATER-1

Condition—
Sewage Systems—
Approvals

This Offer is conditional upon the Buyer determining, at the Buyer's own expense, that:

(1) there is an adequate water supply to meet the Buyer's household needs;

(2) the pump and all related equipment serving the property are in proper operating condition; and

(3) the Buyer can obtain a Bacteriological Analysis of Drinking Water from the authority having jurisdiction indicating that there is no significant evidence of bacterial contamination.

Unless the Buyer gives notice in writing delivered to the Seller personally or in accordance with any other provisions for the delivery of notice in this Agreement of Purchase and Sale or any Schedule thereto not later than _____ p.m. on the _____ day of _____, 20_____, that these conditions have been fulfilled, this Offer shall become null and void and the deposit shall be returned to the Buyer in full without deduction. These conditions are included for the benefit of the Buyer and may be waived at the Buyer's sole option by notice in writing to the Seller as aforesaid within the time period stated herein. The Seller agrees to allow access to the subject property to the Buyer or the Buyer's agent for the purpose of satisfying this condition.

SEWER/WATER-2

Condition—
Water Supply—
All Well Types

APPENDIX

SEWER/WATER-3

Sewage Systems—
Approvals—Warranty

The Seller represents and warrants, to the best of the Seller's knowledge and belief, that:

(1) all sewage systems serving the property are wholly within the setback requirements of the said property, and have received all required Certificates of Installation and Approval pursuant to the *Environmental Protection Act*;

(2) all sewage systems serving the property have been constructed in accordance with the said Certificates of Installation and Approval;

(3) all sewage systems serving the property have received all required Use permits under the said Act or any other legislation; and further, all sewage systems serving the property have been maintained in good working order during the Seller's occupancy and will be in good working order on closing.

Further, the Seller agrees to provide any and all documentation relating to the sewage system, within the Seller's possession, or which may be made available to the Seller by the appropriate authorities, and given to the Buyer prior to the last date set for examining title. The Parties agree that these representations and warranties shall survive and not merge on completion of this transaction, but apply only to the state of the property existing at the completion of this transaction.

SEWER/WATER-4

Sewage System—
Good Working Order—
Warranty

The Seller represents and warrants, to the best of the Seller's knowledge and belief, that, during the Seller's occupancy of the building, the sewage system has been and will be in good working order on closing. The Parties agree that this representation and warranty shall survive and not merge on completion of this transaction, but apply only to the state of the property existing at completion of this transaction.

SEWER/WATER-5

Water Supply—
All Well Types—Warranty

The Seller represents and warrants, to the best of the Seller's knowledge and belief, that, during the Seller's occupancy of the property, the pump and all related equipment serving the said property have performed adequately, and will be in good working order on closing and are currently capable of delivering not less than _____ gallons per minute (GPM) on the continuous basis of not less than _____ hours. The Parties agree that this representation and warranty shall survive and not merge on completion of this transaction, but apply only to the state of the property at completion of this transaction.

NOTE: If the Seller does not know the current status of the well, the Seller should be advised to verify through a professional well inspection as the current water supply can vary from the original well record. The supply of water is contingent on many variables, e.g. the actual amount of water in the well, the capacity of the well system to deliver the water and over what length of time will the GPM be sustained.

APPENDIX

SHORE ROAD ALLOWANCES

This Offer is conditional upon the Buyer determining at the Buyer's own expense that:

(1) the property being purchased has at least [insert appropriate frontage dimension], [metres/feet], of frontage on [name of lake or river];

(2) no road allowance, open or unopened, or other public or private lands exist which will interfere with the right of the Buyer to use and enjoy the said water frontage; and

(3) that there are no unregistered rights or easements.

Unless the Buyer gives notice in writing delivered to the Seller personally or in accordance with any other provisions for the delivery of notice in this Agreement of Purchase and Sale or any Schedule thereto not later than _____ p.m. on the _____ day of _____, 20_____, that these conditions have been fulfilled, this offer shall become null and void and the deposit shall be returned to the Buyer in full without deduction. These conditions are included for the benefit of the Buyer and may be waived at the Buyer's sole option by notice in writing to the Seller as aforesaid within the time period stated herein.

. . . .

The Buyer acknowledges that the original shore road allowance is not closed and consequently is not part of the property being sold under this Agreement of Purchase and Sale.

. . . .

The Buyer acknowledges that the original shore road allowance is not closed and consequently is not part of the property being sold under this Agreement of Purchase and Sale, and that the improvements apparently on the said property may encroach on said unowned shore road allowance.

SHORE–1

Condition—
Water Frontage—
Shore Road Allowance—
Unregistered Easements

SHORE–2

Shore Road Allowance—
Acknowledgement

SHORE–3

Shore Road Allowance—
With Encroachments

SOIL TEST

This Offer is conditional upon the Buyer obtaining at the Buyer's own expense, soil tests verifying the land is satisfactory to the Buyer, in the Buyer's sole and absolute discretion, for the construction of a _____ on the land. Unless the Buyer gives notice in writing delivered to the Seller personally or in accordance with any other provisions for the delivery of notice in this Agreement of Purchase and Sale or any Schedule thereto not later than _____ p.m. on the _____ day of _____, 20_____, that this condition is fulfilled, this Offer shall be null and void and the deposit shall be returned to the Buyer in full without deduction. The Seller agrees to co-operate in providing access to the land for the purpose of the soil tests. This condition is included for the benefit of the Buyer and may be waived at the Buyer's sole option by notice in writing to the Seller as aforesaid within the time period stated herein. If the Buyer fails to provide a notice of fulfilment of the condition or fails to waive the condition as provided above, the Buyer agrees to reasonably restore any alterations to the condition of the property caused by the soil tests.

. . . .

The Seller agrees to grant the Buyer and the Buyer's authorized agent the right to enter the property for the purpose of surveying and conducting soil tests prior to the completion of this transaction. Such permission does not extend to any alteration of the lands, servicing work, removal of trees, soil, or any other activity which would alter the current state of the property.

SOIL–1

Condition—
Satisfactory Soil Test

SOIL–2

Preliminary Work—
Access to Property

APPENDIX

SPIS

SPIS–1

Condition—
Buyer's Acceptance of SPIS

This Offer is conditional upon the Buyer receiving a Seller Property Information Statement completed by the Seller and the Buyer accepting the information on the form as satisfactory in the Buyer's sole and absolute discretion. Unless the Buyer gives notice in writing delivered to the Seller personally or in accordance with any other provisions for the delivery of notice in this Agreement of Purchase and Sale or any Schedule thereto not later than _____ p.m. on the _____ day of _____, 20_____, that this condition is fulfilled, this offer shall be null and void and the deposit shall be returned to the Buyer in full without deduction. This condition is included for the benefit of the Buyer and may be waived at the Buyer's sole option by notice in writing to the Seller as aforesaid within the time period stated herein.

The Seller hereby agrees to deliver to the Buyer upon acceptance of this Agreement a Seller Property Information Statement for the property with complete and accurate answers, to the best of the Seller's knowledge and belief, to the questions contained therein.

SPIS–2

SPIS—
Buyer's Acknowledgement

The Buyer acknowledges that the Buyer has received a completed Seller Property Information Statement from the Seller and has had an opportunity to read the information provided by the Seller on the Seller Property Information Statement prior to submitting this offer.

SURVEYS

NOTE 1: See Form 100, Clause—Documents and Discharge.

NOTE 2: Buyer should acknowledge, in the Offer, any known easements. See Form 100, Clause—Title.

NOTE 3: Allow adequate time and ensure deadline is prior to end of requisition period. Alternatively, the requirement for a survey could be "within days after waiver of all conditions (and prior to end of requisition period)".

NOTE 4: Do not use the phrase "up-to-date". This expression is subject to different interpretation by individual Buyers, Sellers and their respective Solicitors.

SURVEY–1

Buyer Acknowledges
Possible Survey
Requirement

The Buyer acknowledges that a new survey may be required for purposes of financing and also to satisfy the requirements of the Buyer's Solicitor, and agrees to obtain said survey at the Buyer's expense.

SURVEY–2

Seller to Provide Existing
Survey with Declaration

The Seller agrees to provide, at the Seller's own expense, not later than _____ p.m. on the _____ day of _____, 20_____, an existing survey of said property showing the current location of all structures, buildings, fences, improvements, easements, rights-of-way, and encroachments affecting said property. The Seller will further deliver, on completion, a declaration confirming that there have been no additions to the structures, buildings, fences, and improvements on the property since the date of this survey.

SURVEY–3

Seller to Provide
New Survey

The Seller agrees to provide, at the Seller's own expense, not later than _____ p.m. on the _____ day of _____, 20_____, a new survey of said property showing the current location of all structures, buildings, fences, improvements, easements, rights-of-way, and encroachments affecting said property.

The Seller agrees to provide, at the expense of the Seller, a survey of the property, completed by an Ontario Land Surveyor, showing the current location of all buildings, structures, additions, fences, improvements, easements, rights-of-way and encroachments affecting the property. The Seller also agrees to supply all building plans, mechanical drawings, and any other plans, and all warranties and service manuals, if available, applicable to any equipment or chattels included in the purchase price.

SURVEY–4

Survey, Building Plans, Mechanical Drawings, Warranties

SWIMMING POOL

The Seller represents and warrants to the best of the Seller's knowledge and belief that the swimming pool, its equipment, and the fencing of the said pool, comply with all applicable bylaws, regulations, and legislation. The Parties agree that this representation and warranty shall survive and not merge on completion of this transaction, but apply only to the state of the property existing at completion of this transaction.

SWIM–1

By-Law Compliance

The Seller represents and warrants that the swimming pool and equipment are now, and on the completion date shall be, in good working order. The Parties agree that this representation and warranty shall survive and not merge on completion of this transaction, but apply only to the state of the property existing at completion of this transaction.

SWIM–2

Good Working Order— Warranty

The Seller agrees to winterize the swimming pool and equipment prior to completion, and shall provide a written undertaking on completion that the Seller shall be responsible for any costs or expenses incurred by the Buyer if the swimming pool and equipment are not properly winterized, provided only that the Buyer gives written notice of any claim to the Seller not later than _____ p.m. on the _____ day of _____, 20_____, failing which the Seller accepts no responsibility for costs.

SWIM–3

Winterization

TAX/PROPERTY

The Buyer understands and acknowledges that the Buyer is taking title to the real property knowing that the Seller's tax rate is based on a calculation of a property class that will not apply to the Buyer on completion. The Buyer further acknowledges that the Buyer will have to make application to qualify for the Farmland Class tax rate defined under the *Assessment Act of Ontario*, Regulation 282, 1998, Ontario Fair Assessment System and if the property does not qualify for the Farmland Class tax rate, the Buyer's property tax rate may be substantially higher than the Seller's.

TAX–1

Farm Tax—Buyer's Acknowledgement

The Seller warrants that the lands are free and clear of any local improvement charges and will be free and clear of local improvement charges on completion and that Seller has not received any notification of future local improvement charges for the property. If local improvement charges are not paid as of completion, they will be adjusted as a benefit to the Buyer on completion.

TAX–2

Local Improvement Charges

TAX-3

**Tax Holdback—
Completion of Building
Increases Assessment**

The Buyer and Seller acknowledge that the property taxes have not been finally assessed prior to completion of the building(s) on the property. The Buyer and Seller agree that the Seller's solicitor shall hold back the amount of $ _____ for the payment of property taxes for the period prior to completion of this transaction. The Buyer or the Buyer's solicitor shall forthwith after notification by the municipality notify the Seller's solicitor of the amount of finally assessed property taxes. The Seller's solicitor shall immediately after notification pay the hold back or the amount thereof necessary to be paid in payment of the taxes accruing or owing prior to date of completion. If there has been no notification to the Seller's solicitor as aforesaid within three years after the completion of this transaction, the Seller's solicitor may release the holdback to the Seller. The Seller's solicitor shall supply a personal undertaking on completion to the Buyer to evidence the foregoing.

NOTE: This clause applies to the resale of nearly new construction, where the initial assessment was based only on land value.

TENANCY/ASSUMPTION

TEN-1

**Assume Single Tenancy—
No Lease**

The Seller represents and warrants that the _____ [property, basement, or _____ floor apartment] is occupied by _____ as a monthly tenant at the rate of _____ ($ _____) per month, payable on the _____ day of each month. The Parties agree that this representation and warranty shall survive and not merge on completion of this transaction, but apply only to those circumstances at completion of this transaction.

TEN-2

**Assume Single Tenancy—
With Lease**

The _____ [property, basement, or _____ floor apartment] is occupied by _____ pursuant to a lease expiring on the _____ day of _____, 20_____. The Seller represents and warrants that the copy of the said lease attached hereto as Appendix _____ is a true and complete copy of the said lease. The Parties agree that this representation and warranty shall survive and not merge on completion of this transaction, but apply only to those circumstances existing at completion of this transaction.

TEN-3

**Assumption of Tenancies—
Multiple Units**

Buyer agrees to assume the existing tenancies, as set out in the attached Schedule "_____", which the Seller warrants are the only tenancies affecting the property.

NOTE: Schedule should itemize categories such as: Apartment #, Tenant Name, Tenancy, Expiry Date, Rent Due Date, Prepaid Rent, and Tenancy Particulars (Items included in Rent).

NOTE: The actual lease documents should be attached as a Schedule to the Agreement. If too many documents, consider making Offer conditional upon inspection of tenancy agreement.

TITLE

The Buyer acknowledges that it has no legal or equitable interest in the Property as a result of entering into this Agreement until such time as the Buyer has completed the transaction. The Buyer covenants and agrees that the Buyer shall not cause or permit the registration of this Agreement or any memorandum or any notice (including a certificate of pending litigation or caution) thereof or with respect thereto at any time at the Land Registry Office or the Land Titles Office for _____ or in any other office of public record. If the Buyer shall be in breach of this covenant, the Seller shall, in addition to all other rights and remedies in law or in equity, be entitled to:

a) Cancel this Agreement and retain the deposit and any earned interest, free of all claims by the Buyer; and

b) A decree of order restraining or removing such registration and the Buyer shall not plead in defence thereto that there would be an adequate remedy at law, it being recognized and agreed that the injury and damage resulting from such breach would be impossible to measure monetarily.

In case of any such registration, the Buyer, on behalf of the Buyer and the Buyer's successors and assigns and on behalf of anyone claiming under the Buyer, hereby irrevocably appoints, nominates and constitutes the Seller as the Buyer's true and lawful attorney for the Buyer and in the Buyer's name and on the Buyer's behalf to execute all documents, releases, agreements and things as may be necessary or desirable to ensure that title to the Property is free of all claims of the Buyer.

TITLE–1

Agreement Not To Be Registered

. . . .

The Seller hereby declares to the Buyer, and the Buyer acknowledges, understands, and accepts that this property is subject to certain reservations of the Crown, specifically but not limited to the fact that the [describe specific limitations and reservations] have been reserved.

TITLE–2

Crown Restrictions

. . . .

The Buyer agrees to accept title to the property subject to an easement in favour of _____
_____.

TITLE–3

Easement— Acknowledgement

. . . .

The Seller acknowledges and agrees that the Buyer has entered into this Agreement as Trustee for an unnamed Principal (the "Principal") and that upon the Buyer delivering written notice to the Seller of the name of the Principal, the Seller will complete the transaction with the Principal as if the Principal had been the party who originally signed the Agreement, and the Buyer who signed the Agreement shall have no personal liability for the Agreement.

TITLE–4

In Trust for Undisclosed Principal

. . . .

The Seller agrees that the Buyer shall have the right to apply to register the lands or any part or parts under the Land Titles System, and Seller agrees to execute all documents required by the Buyer with respect thereto, provided that the Buyer pay all costs of said application and registration.

TITLE–5

Seller's Consent for Registration in Land Titles

UFFI

UFFI–1

Acknowledgement—UFFI Present in Building

The Seller discloses and the Buyer acknowledges that the building contains urea formaldehyde foam insulation. The Buyer accepts the property in that state and further acknowledges that the Seller does not warrant the quality or quantity of the insulation or the quality of its installation.

UFFI–2

Seller has No Knowledge of UFFI

The Seller has no knowledge as to whether the property has been insulated with urea formaldehyde foam insulation and specifically makes no warranty in that regard. This paragraph supersedes any other term or condition or warranty in relation to urea formaldehyde foam insulation.

NOTE: Use where Seller has no personal knowledge of UFFI (i.e. a corporation handling a company transfer, Seller selling under Power of Sale, etc.). The Buyer may consider making the Offer conditional on an inspection for UFFI.

UFFI–3

UFFI Found But Corrective Action Taken

The Seller represents and warrants that the building was insulated with urea formaldehyde foam insulation but has undergone the following corrective actions: _____
_____. The Parties agree that this representation and warranty shall survive and not merge on completion of this transaction, but apply only to the state of the property at completion of this transaction.

NOTE: Details of all corrective action should be inserted in the space provided or supporting documentation attached as a Schedule.

UFFI–4

UFFI Removed from Building

The Seller represents and warrants that, although urea formaldehyde foam insulation (UFFI) was installed in the building, such UFFI was removed in _____, _____, by _____ , and the Seller further warrants that, to the best of his knowledge, no UFFI has been installed in the building since such removal. The Parties agree that this representation and warranty shall survive and not merge on completion of this transaction, but apply only to the state of the property at completion of this transaction. As evidence of the removal, the Seller attaches the following documents as Schedule "_____" which shall form part of this Agreement of Purchase and Sale.

UFFI–5

UFFI Test Performed with Negative Result

The Seller represents and warrants that the building was tested for the presence of urea formaldehyde foam insulation (UFFI) on the _____ day of _____, 20_____, by _____, and the result of such testing indicated that no UFFI was present in the building, and on the basis of such results the Seller provides this warranty. This clause applies only to UFFI and does not, in any way, include the testing of urea formaldehyde emissions from sources other than UFFI. The Parties agree that this representation and warranty shall survive and not merge on completion of this transaction, but apply only to the state of the property at completion of this transaction. As evidence of such testing, the Seller attaches the following documents as Schedule "_____" which shall form part of this Agreement of Purchase and Sale: _____
_____ [itemize documents].

UFFI–6

UFFI Test Performed with Positive Result But Within Acceptable Limits

The Seller acknowledges that the building contains urea formaldehyde foam insulation (UFFI) and was tested for the presence of emissions from UFFI on the _____ day of _____, 20_____, by _____, and the results of such testing indicated that emission from UFFI are within the acceptable limits and no further actions have been taken. As evidence of such testing, the Seller attaches the following documents as Schedule "_____" which shall form part of this Agreement of Purchase and Sale: _____
_____.

APPENDIX

VACANT POSSESSION/NOTICES

The Buyer hereby authorizes and directs the Seller, and the Seller agrees, when this Agreement becomes unconditional, to give to the tenant(s) the requisite notices under the *Residential Tenancies Act*, requiring vacant possession of the property for use by the Buyer or the Buyer's immediate family, effective as of the _____ day of _____, 20_____, and the seller agrees to deliver copies of the requisite notices to the Buyer immediately after service of the notices upon the tenant. The Buyer and the Seller hereby agree in the event that the tenant fails to vacate the property prior to completion of the transaction, the Buyer agrees to assume the existing tenant upon completion of this transaction. Upon vacant possession being provided to the Buyer, the Buyer or the Buyer's immediate family agrees to take possession of and occupy the property forthwith thereafter. The Buyer agrees to provide the Seller with a written indemnity on completion, indemnifying the Seller from all actions, causes of action, claims and demands of any kind whatsoever, that may occur in the event that the Buyer does not take possession of and occupy the property as aforesaid.

NOTE: Due to the current state of Landlord and Tenant Law, the Seller will not be able to "guarantee" vacant possession on completion if a tenant refuses to vacate.

> **VAC–1**
> **Vacant Possession/Notices**

VERMICULITE

This Offer is conditional upon the Buyer testing the subject property for the presence of asbestos within the vermiculite insulation located upon property at the Buyer's own expense, and the obtaining of a report, respecting the said test satisfactory to the Buyer in the Buyer's sole and absolute discretion. Unless the Buyer gives notice in writing delivered to the Seller personally or in accordance with any other provisions for the delivery of notice in this Agreement of Purchase and Sale or any Schedule thereto not later than _____ p.m. on the _____ day of _____, 20_____, that this condition is fulfilled, this Offer shall be null and void and the deposit shall be returned to the Buyer in full without deduction. The Seller agrees to co-operate in providing access to the property for the purpose of this inspection. This condition is included for the benefit of the Buyer and may be waived at the Buyer's sole option by notice in writing to the Seller as aforesaid within the time period stated herein.

> **VER–1**
> **Condition— Testing of Property for Vermiculite**

The Seller has no knowledge as to whether the property has been insulated with insulation containing vermiculite and specifically makes no warranty in that regard. This paragraph supersedes any other term or condition or warranty in relation to vermiculite insulation.

> **VER–2**
> **No Knowledge of Vermiculite**

The Seller represents and warrants that the building was tested for the presence of asbestos within the vermiculite insulation located upon the property on the _____ day of _____, 20_____, by _____, and the result of such testing indicated that no asbestos was present in the vermiculite insulation in the building, and on the basis of such results the Seller provides this warranty. This clause applies only to vermiculite insulation and does not, in any way, include the testing of the presence of asbestos from sources other than the vermiculite insulation. The Parties agree that this representation and warranty shall survive and not merge on completion of this transaction, but apply only to the state of the property at completion of this transaction. As evidence of such testing, the Seller attaches the following documents as Schedule "_____" which shall form part of this Agreement of Purchase and Sale:
_____.

> **VER–3**
> **Vermiculite—Asbestos Test Performed With Negative Result**

VER–4

Vermiculite Corrective Action

The Seller represents and warrants that the building was insulated with vermiculite insulation but has undergone the following corrective actions: _____. The Parties agree that this representation and warranty shall survive and not merge on completion of this transaction, but apply only to the state of the property at completion of this transaction.

NOTE: Details of all corrective action should be inserted in the space provided or supporting documentation attached as a Schedule.

VER–5

Vermiculite Removed from the Building

The Seller represents and warrants that, although vermiculite insulation was installed in the building, such vermiculite insulation was removed in _____, _____, by _____, and the Seller further warrants that, to the best of his knowledge, no vermiculite insulation has been installed in the building since such removal. The Parties agree that this representation and warranty shall survive and not merge on completion of this transaction, but apply only to the state of the property at completion of this transaction. As evidence of the removal, the Seller attaches the following documents as Schedule "_____" which shall form part of this Agreement of Purchase and Sale.

VER–6

Vermiculite Warranty

The Seller represents and warrants to the Buyer that during the time the Seller has owned the property, Seller has not caused any building on the property to be insulated with insulation containing vermiculite, and to the best of the Seller's knowledge no building on the property contains or has ever contained insulation containing vermiculite. This warranty shall survive and not merge on the completion of this transaction, and if the building is part of a multiple unit building, this warranty shall only apply to that part of the building which is the subject of this transaction.

ZONING

ZONING–1

Condition— Re-zoning/Minor Variance

This Offer is conditional upon the [Buyer/Seller] obtaining at the [Buyer's/Seller's] expense, a [re-zoning/minor variance], to allow for [specify exact variance/use] for said property. Both Buyer and Seller agree to proceed in a diligent manner to acquire the [re-zoning/minor variance]. Unless the [Buyer/Seller] gives notice in writing delivered to the [Seller/Buyer] not later than _____ p.m. on the _____ day of _____, 20___, that this condition is fulfilled, this Offer shall become null and void and the deposit shall be returned to the Buyer in full without deduction.

NOTE: If the Buyer wishes to retain the right to purchase the property, even though the rezoning or minor variance is not approved, then a "Waiver" should be included.

ZONING–2

Condition— Re-zoning with Seller's Consent

This Offer is conditional upon the Buyer obtaining at the Buyer's expense, a re-zoning of the property to permit _____ for the said property. Both Buyer and Seller agree to proceed in a diligent manner to obtain the re-zoning. Unless the Buyer gives notice in writing delivered to the Seller personally or in accordance with any other provisions for the delivery of notice in this Agreement of Purchase and Sale or any Schedule thereto not later than _____ p.m. on the _____ day of _____, 20_____, that this condition has been fulfilled, this Offer shall become null and void and the deposit shall be returned to the Buyer in full without deduction. This condition is included for the benefit of the Buyer and may be waived at the Buyer's sole option by notice in writing to the Seller as aforesaid within the time period stated herein.

The Seller agrees, upon written notice, to execute applications and all other documents required for the Buyer to change the official plan, if necessary, and to re-zone the lands to a zoning suitable to the Buyer, or to amend any bylaws, and to support such application or applications for re-zoning or amending of bylaws, and to co-operate with the Buyer, in all reasonable respects, provided that the Buyer pay all costs of said re-zoning.

The Buyer shall have until not later than _____ p.m. on the _____ day of _____, 20_____, to satisfy the Buyer that the property is zoned in final and binding form under the relevant zoning bylaws and official plan to permit it to develop or use the property for the purpose of _____. If the Buyer is not so satisfied at the Buyer's sole and arbitrary discretion, the Buyer may terminate this Agreement by notice in writing delivered to the Seller personally or in accordance with any other provisions for the delivery of notice in this Agreement of Purchase and Sale or any Schedule thereto prior to the expiry of such period and the deposit shall be returned to the Buyer in full without deduction.

ZONING–3

Condition— Zoning Satisfaction (Condition Subsequent)

. . . .

The Seller represents and warrants, to the best of his knowledge and belief, that:

(1) the buildings now located on the property are located wholly on the property and comply with all zoning and building bylaws; and

(2) the driveways serving the property are located wholly within the limits of the property, and entrance relating to such driveways have been approved by the appropriate road authority.

The Parties agree that these representations and warranties shall survive and not merge on completion of this transaction, but apply only to the state of the property existing at completion of this transaction.

ZONING–4

Location of Buildings/Driveways

. . . .

The Buyer acknowledges that the municipality where the property is situated may have a bylaw that restricts or limits the owner's right to rent out property and the buyer agrees to purchase the property subject to that restriction or limitation.

ZONING–5

Restriction—Short Term Accommodation

. . . .

The Seller warrants that the lands are zoned as _____ under bylaw _____ for the municipality of _____.

ZONING–6

Zoning—Warranty

APPENDIX

SOLUTIONS

CHAPTER 1
UNDERSTANDING CONTRACT LAW

Chapter Mini-Review

1. A void contract has no legal status.

    ✔ **True**   ○ False

    A void contract has never legally come into existence.

2. Mistakes are commonly grouped under three categories: common, mutual and bilateral.

    ○ True   ✔ **False**

    Mistakes are grouped under common, mutual and unilateral.

3. If consideration contravenes the law, then the contract is unenforceable.

    ✔ **True**   ○ False

    Consideration must be lawful in order for the contract to be enforced.

4. If a seller counters a buyer's offer, the original buyer's offer may still be accepted by the seller (despite the counter offer) if proper notice of his/her intent is given.

    ○ True   ✔ **False**

    A buyer's offer is ended upon the rejection of that offer and subsequent counter offer by the seller.

5. Fraud not only destroys the contract, but also can give rise to damages.

    ✔ **True**   ○ False

    The injured party has the legal right to recover damages for deceit.

6. A contract cannot be binding without consideration.

    ○ True   ✔ **False**

    A contract can be made binding without consideration if a seal is used.

7. Innocent misrepresentation involves a statement by one party of a material fact that is known to be untrue.

    ○ True   ✔ **False**

    An innocent misrepresentation involves a statement that is untrue, but is honestly believed to be true.

8. Various remedies are provided for a breach of contract including rescission, damages and specific performance.

    ✔ **True**   ○ False

    These are three of five remedies for breach of contract. The others are quantum meruit and injunction.

9. The court will assess both the existence and adequacy of consideration when a dispute arises concerning contract enforceability.

    ○ True   ✔ **False**

    The court addresses only the existence of consideration, not its adequacy.

10. Privity of contract refers to the legal concept that, generally, only parties to the contract can enforce it or be bound by it.

    ✔ **True**   ○ False

    A person is said to be 'not privy to the contract,' as he or she is not a party to that contract.

APPENDIX

11. The *Statute of Frauds* requires that all contracts involving real estate must be drafted on an agreement of purchase and sale approved by the Real Estate Council of Ontario.

 True   **False**

The Statute of Frauds only states that contracts, including real estate contracts, must be in writing to be enforceable at law. The statute does not require a standardized form approved by the Real Estate Council of Ontario.

12. Tort liability is defined as a breach of duty involving a contract, such as an accepted agreement of purchase and sale.

 True   **False**

Tort liability involves a breach of duty other than under a contract, which can arise due to negligent misrepresentation and resulting in common law action for damages.

13. A contract can only be terminated by the mutual agreement of the parties.

 True   **False**

Mutual agreement is only one of five methods of terminating an agreement.

14. Non est factum can be pleaded by a person who misunderstands a contract but nevertheless signs it. However, such a pleading may not have merit if that individual was negligent in not reading the contract. Therefore, he or she has no real defence.

 True   False

An individual is not bound by a contract that is other than which he/she contemplated, but there is no defence if a person fails to read a contract and then discovers later that the contract is other than that contemplated.

15. The *Vendors and Purchasers Act* sets out provisions that are deemed statutorily to be included within an agreement of purchase and sale.

 True   False

The *Vendors and Purchasers Act* was enacted because no standard form of agreement exists in Ontario for the sale of land.

16. A seller representation agreement is a standard form approved by the Real Estate Council of Ontario.

True   **False**

The Real Estate Council of Ontario does not approve standard representation forms. However, it should be noted that REBBA 2002 does stipulate certain information that must be contained within a representation agreement.

17. Failure to disclose a material latent defect could invalidate a contract. A material latent defect is one that is readily observable to the casual observer.

True   **False**

A material latent defect is NOT readily observable to the casual observer and may significantly impact enjoyment of the property.

APPENDIX

Active Learning Exercises

■ Exercise 1   Contract Terms (Fill-in-the-Blanks)

1.1 Smith signs an agreement that amounts to price fixing, this contract has

> *no lawful object*   .

1.2 The fact that parties must be legally capable of entering into contracts is referred

to as *capacity of the parties*   .

1.3 An agreement set aside by the court is referred to as

> *rescission*   .

1.4 When an offended party can make a choice between performing or not performing

a contract, the contract is said to be   *voidable*   .

1.5 When parties misunderstand each other and are at cross purposes when it comes

to a contract, this situation is referred to as a

> *mutual mistake*   .

1.6 Compensation for losses arising from a breach of contract is referred to as

> *damages*   .

1.7 Complete the following phrase: Old consideration is

> *no consideration*   .

1.8 When a person does not act with free will, he/she is often said to be under

> *duress or undue influence*   .

■ Exercise 2   Consideration

Identify whether consideration is present or not in the following situations.

2.1 Seller Smith pays $68,750 for home renovations to Builder Anderson.

☑ **Present**   ◯ Not Present

Both parties receive something of value, the activity is lawful and no past consideration is involved.

2.2 Seller Smith agrees not to open a pizza business to compete with Buyer Jones' newly acquired pizza business that was sold by Smith to Jones. In return for this agreement, Jones pays Smith $20,000.

☑ **Present**   ◯ Not Present

Both parties receive something of value, the activity is lawful and no past consideration is involved.

2.3 Assume Jones paid Smith $1.00 rather than the $20,000 in Question 2.2. Is consideration present or not present?

☑ **Present**   ◯ Not Present

Amount of consideration does not impact contract status. The law is only concerned that some value exists, not the extent of that value.

2.4 Assume no money changed hands in Question 2.2, but the agreement was signed under seal. Is consideration present or not present?

◯ Present   ☑ **Not Present**

Consideration is not present. If a seal is used, however, no consideration is required.

2.5 Seller Smith sells his home for $225,000 to Buyer Jones, but does not include any chattels. Subsequently, Jones and Smith agree that all recreation room furniture will be included, but do not sign an agreement to that effect. Is consideration present or not present regarding the furniture?

◯ Present   ☑ **Not Present**

The agreement for furniture is verbal and beyond the contract concerning the house.

2.6 Seller Smith sells his auto for $16,400 to Jones and agrees to be paid in shares from an illegal business venture in which Jones is involved.

◯ Present   ☑ **Not Present**

No consideration is present in this scenario, as the source of money arises from an illegal business operation and both parties are aware of its illegality.

APPENDIX

CH1 EX3

■ Exercise 3   Multiple Choice

3.1 Mutual agreement in a contract requires that there must be an offer, an acceptance and a communication of that acceptance. Which of the following is NOT a requirement of acceptance? **This question requires that the *incorrect* option be identified.**

a. Unconditional.

> *This statement is correct.* The acceptance of an offer must be unconditional.

b. **Communicated by personal delivery to the offeror.**

> ✅ *THIS IS THE INCORRECT STATEMENT.* The communication can be made in various ways, not simply personal delivery.

c. Made in the manner required by offeror.

> *This is a correct statement.* The acceptance must be made in the manner required by the offeror.

d. Made within the time limit of the offeror.

> *This is a correct statement.* The acceptance must be made within the time limit of the offeror.

3.2 Which of the following does NOT result in a lack of genuine intention during a contractual undertaking? **This question requires that the *incorrect* option be identified.**

a. Duress.

> *This is a correct statement.* Duress undermines genuine intention.

b. Undue influence.

> *This is a correct statement.* Undue influence results in a lack of genuine intention.

c. Mistake.

> *This is a correct statement.* A mistake can result in a lack of genuine intention.

d. **Specific Performance.**

> ✅ *THIS IS THE INCORRECT STATEMENT.* Specific performance is a remedy concerning a breach of a contract.

3.3 If a contract has been terminated by breach and the injured party has done part of what was promised, that individual is entitled to reasonable value for what has been done. Which of the following best describes this right?

a. Right to damages.

> *Incorrect.* Right to damages is a remedy, but this term is not the appropriate response for this particular question.

b. Right to specific performance.

> *Incorrect.* Right to specific performance is a remedy, but this term is not the appropriate response for this particular question.

c. **Right to quantum meruit.**

> ✅ *CORRECT.* Quantum meruit is a remedy involving the entitlement to reasonable value for what has been done.

d. None of the above.

> *Incorrect.* One of the alternate responses is correct.

APPENDIX

3.4 Which of the following is a correct statement regarding consideration?   `CH1` `EX3`

a. Consideration is not an important element in contracting.

Incorrect. Consideration is an essential element in contracting.

b. Consideration must be equal to what is received in return.

Incorrect. Consideration need only exist, but may not be commensurate with what is received in return.

c. If a promise is made under seal, no consideration is necessary to make it binding.

✓ *CORRECT.* No consideration is required when an agreement is made under seal.

d. Consideration must always be monetary.

Incorrect. Consideration need not be monetary; e.g., a promise for a promise.

3.5 Which of the following is NOT a correct statement? **This question requires that the *incorrect* option be identified.**

a. A minor's right to avoid a contract is extinguished immediately once he/she reaches the age of majority.

✓ *THIS IS THE INCORRECT STATEMENT.* The minor's right to avoid a contract can extend beyond the age of majority under certain circumstances.

b. Contracts with infants for the sale of land are generally voidable by the infant.

This statement is correct. Contracts with minors are generally voidable.

c. Specific performance is a discretionary remedy for breach of contract and will not normally be granted if an award of damages would be adequate.

This statement is correct. Specific performance may be required in some instances, as damages may be inadequate to offset the loss or harm done.

d. An action for negligence can involve a circumstance in which a salesperson provides information to a customer and that individual relies on such information to his/her detriment.

This statement is correct. Tort liability arises from a common law action for damages, often arising from negligence.

APPENDIX

3.6 A salesperson has a prospect interested in a property. The buyer notices water stains on the basement walls. Without any further investigation, the salesperson assures the buyer that there is no problem. After closing, the buyer discovers a major leakage problem that will prove costly to repair. How is the salesperson's representation best described?

a. Innocent misrepresentation.

Incorrect. An innocent misrepresentation involves a statement made that is untrue, but honestly believed to be true.

b. **Negligent misrepresentation.**

 CORRECT. The situation is best described as negligent misrepresentation, as a misrepresentation is made negligently and the resulting harm can give rise to an action for damages under tort law.

c. Fraudulent misrepresentation.

Incorrect. Fraudulent misrepresentation involves a statement made with the knowledge of its falsity.

d. Common mistake.

Incorrect. A common mistake is one in which both parties are mistaken about some underlying fact.

▣ Exercise 4   Minors

4.1 Real estate contracts with minors (infants) are generally voidable, sometimes void and never binding on the infant. Therefore, a contract involving the young couple could not be enforced. (Note: The word generally has been emphasized as registrants are reminded that some exceptions can apply; e.g., necessities of life and the enforceability of the contract if such an agreement was clearly in that person's best interests.)

4.2 Under normal circumstances, a minor (infant) might avoid the contract for a reasonable period of time after the age of majority. If a contract is ratified after the age of majority, the right to avoid the contract has disappeared.

4.3 Whether or not the minors have purported to be over 18 is immaterial. The answer in 4.1 remains the same.

▣ Exercise 5   Scenarios

5.1 No contract exists. Acceptance must be complete and definite in its terms. A conditional acceptance is given and, therefore, does not meet acceptance criteria. Note: The salesperson could have clarified the matter by inserting a proper condition in the offer.

5.2 No contract exists. Technically, the counter offer was not accepted until one minute after the time limit set out in the agreement of purchase and sale (i.e., 11:59 pm). More importantly, the acceptance was not communicated to Smith within the allotted time period. The salesperson would have to amend the irrevocable date, counter the offer back to Smith and then communicate acceptance of the counter offer back to the buyer.

5.3 The counter offer, once rejected, is null and void. This is not to say that Smith and Jones could not renew negotiations and ultimately enter into a contract. Salespersons should carefully review the counter offer process with sellers to avoid confusion and potential problems.

APPENDIX

CHAPTER 2
REBBA 2002 AND
THE REAL ESTATE TRANSACTION

Chapter Mini-Review

1. Registrants must provide conscientious and competent service to clients, but not to customers.

   ○ True   **False**

   Conscientious and competent service must be provided to both clients and customers.

2. A registrant who offers an opinion about the value of a client's property must have appropriate education or experience to provide such an opinion.

    True ○ False

   A registrant must demonstrate reasonable knowledge, skill, judgement and competence as per the Code of Ethics, Sec. 6: Providing Opinions, Etc.

3. Brokers and salespersons must be careful not to interfere with client relationships of other registrants.

    True ○ False

   Communication with the client should be communicated through the other registrant, unless the other registrant has consented otherwise in writing.

4. A salesperson who contravenes Sec. 34: Falsifying Information can face a fine of up to $50,000.

   ✓ **True** ○ False

   The salesperson may also face a prison term of up to two years. See the applicable *Registrar's Bulletin*.

5. A seller does not have to give his or her written consent in order for a salesperson to include the following heading on a classified advertisement: New Listing: 84 Weston Court.

   ○ True   **False**

   Sec. 36 of the Code requires written consent when identifying property particulars.

6. A seller must complete a seller property information statement when offering a property for sale, failing which the registrant acting for that seller client would be in violation of Code of Ethics, Sec. 20: Seller Property Information Statement.

   ○ True   **False**

   Sec. 20 provides that the registrant must disclose the existence of a seller property information statement, not that the seller must complete this statement.

7. A salesperson must disclose the existence and substance of competing offers to every person who is making one of the competing offers.

   ○ True   **False**

   A salesperson must not disclose the substance of such offers.

8. A registrant must advise a buyer client of all significant activities undertaken on behalf of that client when representing that client.

    True ○ False

   This requirement is set out in the Code of Ethics, Sec. 23: Steps Taken by Registrant.

APPENDIX

9. A deposit received from a buyer involving a transaction must be placed in the real estate trust account within two days.

 True ✔ False

REBBA 2002 provides that deposits must be placed in the real estate trust account within five business days of receipt.

10. Trust funds need not be kept separate from other funds within a brokerage, provided that the brokerage maintains a trust ledger and carries out monthly reconciliation for such funds.

○ True ✔ False

Trust funds must be kept separate from all other monies at all times.

11. If monies are dispersed from the trust fund in error, the broker of record must ensure that sufficient funds are immediately deposited in the trust account to offset this error.

✔ True ○ False

The Act requires that any shortfall in the trust account be immediately rectified.

12. A brokerage is only permitted to have one trust account.

○ True ✔ False

A brokerage may have more than one trust account (e.g., for property management purposes), but only with the Registrar's approval. Brokerages also have a commission trust account, which is a RECO insurance policy requirement.

13. A seller's brokerage has the option to retain, for a period of one year only, either a summary document of an accepted offer that results in the purchase of real estate or an actual copy of the accepted offer.

○ True ✔ False

A seller's brokerage must retain a copy of an accepted written offer in its entirety for at least six years. Copies of an unsuccessful offer, or an equivalent summary document for that unsuccessful offer, must be retained for at least one year.

Active Learning Exercises

■ Exercise 1   Multiple Choice

1.1 A salesperson, acting on behalf of his brokerage, is representing both buyer and seller. He advises his seller client to accept an offer from his buyer client, while knowing that a competing offer will net more to his seller client. Which of the following Code of Ethics provisions best applies to this situation?

a. Sec. 3: Fairness, Honesty, Etc.

Incorrect. While fairness and honesty is owed, a more appropriate option should be selected.

b. Sec. 4: Best Interests

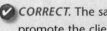 *CORRECT.* The salesperson must protect and promote the client's interests above all else.

c. Sec. 5: Conscientious and Competent Service, Etc.

Incorrect. While conscientious service must be provided, a more appropriate option should be selected.

d. Sec. 7: Dealings with Other Registrants

Incorrect. This Code provision addresses interference with other registrants. A more appropriate option should be selected.

APPENDIX

1.2   A salesperson, acting on behalf of her brokerage, represents a buyer client and has three available properties that meet the buyer's requirements. The commission rates offered to a co-operating brokerage for the sale of these properties varies; i.e., 1.5%, 2.5% and 3%. According to the Code of Ethics, she should:

CH2   EX1

a.   Introduce the client only to the property that most closely meets the buyer's requirements.

Incorrect. Doing so would limit choice and not align with the Code of Ethics requirement.

b.   Introduce the client to the property that provides the highest commission rate.

Incorrect. Doing so would limit choice and not align with the Code of Ethics requirement.

c.   **Introduce the client to all three available properties.**

✓ *CORRECT.* The client should be introduced to all properties that meet his or her requirements.

d.   Introduce the client only to the property that provides the lowest commission rate.

Incorrect. Properties should be introduced to the buyer regardless of commission rates for those properties.

1.3   A salesperson, acting on behalf of his brokerage, has received an offer for his seller client's home from a salesperson with a co-operating brokerage. The salesperson delays the presentation of this offer for one day hoping to secure a better offer from another prospective buyer.

a.   **This delay is in contravention of the Code of Ethics, Sec. 24: Conveying Offers.**

✓ *CORRECT.* An offer must be delivered to the client at the earliest practicable opportunity.

b.   This delay is acceptable, as the salesperson may obtain a better offer from another prospective buyer.

Incorrect. An offer must be delivered to the client at the earliest practicable opportunity.

c.   This situation is not addressed in the Code of Ethics

Incorrect. This situation is addressed in the Code of Ethics.

d.   This delay is acceptable provided that the delay is not more than 24 hours.

Incorrect. Delivery must be at the earliest practicable opportunity. The Code makes no reference to a specific permissible delay period for offer presentation.

1.4   Which of the following statements is correct?

a.   A registrant must ensure that the client receives a copy of the signed agreement of purchase and sale at the earliest practicable opportunity, but this requirement does not extend to customers.

Incorrect. The requirement for prompt delivery applies to both clients and customers.

b.   A registrant is permitted to make an inaccurate representation provided that no damages arise from that representation.

Incorrect. A registrant must not make an inaccurate representation, regardless of whether damages result or not.

c.   A registrant may offer services even though he or she does not have the necessary skills and knowledge, provided that a written consent is obtained from the person receiving those services.

Incorrect. The Code specifically states that services should not be offered without appropriate skill and knowledge. Written consent is irrelevant to the basic requirement.

d.   **A registrant must disclose known or ought to be known material facts to a customer.**

✓ *CORRECT.* Material facts must be disclosed to both clients and customers.

1.5 According to the Code of Ethics, a Seller Property Information Statement:

a. Must be completed by the registrant when preparing a seller representation agreement for a prospective client.

Incorrect. The Code of Ethics has no such requirement.

b. **Is intended to provide information to buyers about the real estate that is being offered for sale.**

✓ *CORRECT.* The seller property information statement provides information about the listed property.

c. Must be attached to any agreement for the conveyance of an interest in real estate to which it applies.

Incorrect. The Code of Ethics has no such requirement.

d. Is a confidential document that must not be disclosed to prospective buyers.

Incorrect. The Code of Ethics requires that, if such a document is prepared, it must be disclosed to every buyer who expresses an interest in the applicable real estate.

1.6 A listing salesperson is presenting two offers, one for $397,000 that he obtained from a buyer and a second offer for $399,000 obtained by a salesperson from a co-operating brokerage. The listing salesperson agrees to reduce commission by $4,000 to make his offer more attractive, but does not disclose this fact to the other brokerage or its respective buyer.

a. The listing salesperson does not have to disclose this commission reduction, as it is a private matter between the salesperson and the seller client.

Incorrect. The Code of Ethics requires disclosure of this fact to other parties who have made a written offer.

b. The listing salesperson, by not disclosing this fact, is in violation of Sec. 24: Conveying Offers.

Incorrect. Sec. 24 does not specifically address the issue in this particular question.

c. **The listing salesperson, by not disclosing this fact, is in violation of Sec. 25: Agreement Relating to Commission.**

✓ *CORRECT.* Sec. 25: Agreement Relating to Commission requires that a commission reduction be disclosed to other parties who have made a written offer.

d. The listing salesperson cannot reduce commission during negotiations.

Incorrect. Commission may be renegotiated at any time, subject to the agreement of the applicable parties.

APPENDIX

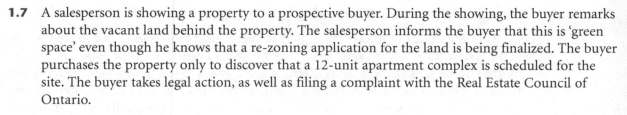

1.7 A salesperson is showing a property to a prospective buyer. During the showing, the buyer remarks about the vacant land behind the property. The salesperson informs the buyer that this is 'green space' even though he knows that a re-zoning application for the land is being finalized. The buyer purchases the property only to discover that a 12-unit apartment complex is scheduled for the site. The buyer takes legal action, as well as filing a complaint with the Real Estate Council of Ontario.

a. The salesperson is not responsible for inaccurate statements concerning matters that exist beyond the specific property being shown.

Incorrect. Salespersons must not provide inaccurate representations and this requirement is not limited strictly to matters concerning the home being shown, but rather to all representations made.

b. The salesperson innocently made a mistake and would not be subject to any disciplinary action.

Incorrect. The Code addresses inaccurate representations regardless of whether such representations were innocent or not.

c. The salesperson would not be subject to disciplinary action, as the matter is being addressed by the Courts.

Incorrect. Registrants can face both legal remedies, as well as disciplinary action by the Real Estate Council of Ontario.

d. **The salesperson has made an inaccurate representation and, more particularly, is in violation of Sec. 37 of the Code of Ethics.**

✅ *CORRECT.* Sec. 37 of the Code is quite clear that 'a registrant must not knowingly make an inaccurate representation.'

1.8 A salesperson places a classified advertisement for a listed property and includes his registered name and telephone number, but fails to also include the registered name of the brokerage in the ad. Which of the following options best addresses this situation?

a. The salesperson is in violation of Sec. 38: Error, Misrepresentation, Fraud, Etc.

Incorrect. The salesperson is in violation of the Code of Ethics, but this is not the correct section reference.

b. The salesperson made an innocent mistake and is not in violation of the Code of Ethics.

Incorrect. The Code requires mandatory compliance. Making an innocent mistake is not an adequate defence, as all registrants must be aware of regulatory requirements.

c. **The salesperson is in violation of Sec. 36: Advertising.**

✅ *CORRECT.* More specifically, the salesperson is in violation of Sec. 36(3) which states that the salesperson must prominently identify the employing brokerage.

d. The salesperson is not required to include the brokerage name within the ad, as long as the brokerage telephone number is inserted in the ad.

Incorrect. The name of the employing brokerage must be prominently displayed within the ad.

APPENDIX

▣ Exercise 2   The Countered Counter Offer

Sec. 27 of the Code of Ethics requires that any agreement that deals with a conveyance of an interest in real estate must be legible. In the scenario, parts of the offer became illegible given numerous changes. A registrant is well advised to have a new agreement signed by the parties that includes all changes to ensure that there is no confusion. Alternatively, a counter offer form should be used rather than amending the original offer. This topic is addressed in more detail in Chapter 10.

▣ Exercise 3   The Incentive

The salesperson has violated Sec. 34 and 35 of the *Real Estate and Business Brokers Act, 2002*, which is a serious offence in which a registrant falsifies or counsels others to falsify any information or document. From a Code of Ethics perspective, the registrant is also in violation of Sec. 38: Error, Misrepresentation, Fraud, Etc. and Sec. 39: Unprofessional Conduct, Etc.

▣ Exercise 4   The Commission

Sec. 19: Properties That Meet Buyer's Criteria.

▣ Exercise 5   The Presentation

Sec. 7: Dealings with Other Registrants.

APPENDIX

CHAPTER 3
DOCUMENTING SELLER REPRESENTATION

Chapter Mini-Review

1. A data input form establishes the legal relationship between seller and brokerage, while also setting out property details.

    True   **False**

   The representation agreement (listing authority) establishes the legal relationship, not the data input form.

2. The amount payable to a co-operating brokerage must be included in a seller representation agreement, according to requirements set out in REBBA 2002.

    True   False

   These requirements, as well as others, are set out in Sec. 11 of the Code of Ethics.

3. Listing salespersons are well advised to suggest that sellers remove excluded fixtures prior to showings to avoid misunderstandings.

    True   False

   Confusion as to what is included and excluded can cause significant problems in the negotiating process.

4. The OREA *Listing Agreement* requires a holdover provision not to exceed 60 days.

    True   **False**

   The OREA *Listing Agreement* does not set a maximum holdover period. A holdover period should be realistic given particular circumstances. Most residential holdover periods are 60–90 days, but commercial agreements may include longer periods.

5. According to the Code of Ethics, if a listing exceeds three months, the listing brokerage must have the seller's initials in close proximity to the expiry date set out in the representation agreement.

    True   **False**

   The time limit set out in the Code of Ethics, Sec. 11 is six months, not three months.

6. A registrant authorized to bind the listing brokerage must sign and date his or her signature on the representation agreement.

    True   False

   This requirement is set out in Sec. 13 of the Code of Ethics. Note: The seller is not obligated to sign a written agreement, but the registrant is required to prepare and sign the document before any buyer makes an offer regarding the seller's property.

7. According to REBBA 2002, a brokerage cannot collect a commission based on the difference between the asking and selling prices.

    True   False

   This is a correct statement. See REBBA, Sec. 36 for selected commission calculation requirements.

8. Brokerages are permitted to pay commission or other remuneration to salespersons employed by another brokerage, provided that consent is obtained from that other brokerage pursuant to requirements set out in REBBA 2002.

    True   **False**

Brokerages are not permitted to pay commission or other remuneration to salespersons employed by another brokerage. Any payment made would be to the employing brokerage and that brokerage would, in turn, pay the applicable brokers or salespersons.

9. The seller must complete a Seller Property Information Statement (SPIS) at the time that a representation agreement is signed with a brokerage.

 True   **False**

Completion of an SPIS is not mandatory.

10. The OREA SPIS Schedule for condominium can also be used for access and shoreline issues.

 True   **False**

The OREA SPIS schedule for condominium is developed solely for use with condominiums. The appropriate schedule for access and shoreline issues is Form 222: *Schedule for Water Supply, Waste Disposal, Access and Shoreline.*

11. Transposing information from an original source document to the representation agreement (including the data input form) is a potential source for error in the listing process.

 **True**   False

Transposition problems are easy to make and often difficult to find when proofing. Always double check information being recorded to ensure accuracy.

12. According to errors and omissions claims experience involving rural property, problems with wells and septic systems have been a significant issue over the past few years.

 **True**   False

Based on statistics provided in this chapter, approximately one out of four claims for rural properties have involved wells or septic systems.

Active Learning Exercises

■ Exercise 1   Matching

Match the words in the left column with the appropriate description in the right column (not all descriptions are used).

c.	Broker Load	Electronic Transmission to Real Estate Board
d.	SPIS	Not a Warranty Even if Attached to an Agreement
f.	Family Law Act	Spousal Consent
b.	Cancellation of Listing Agreement	Seller and Listing Brokerage Release Each Other by Agreement
g.	Amendment to Listing Agreement	Extend the Expiry Date
a.	Mortgage Verification	Written Confirmation of Principal Outstanding
k.	Express Authority	A Precise Instruction
i.	Exclusive Listing	Sole Right to Sell Property

No Match: e., h. and j.

APPENDIX

Exercise 2   The Home at 36 Longmore Drive

OREA Ontario Real Estate Association

Listing Agreement
Authority to Offer for Sale

Form 200
for use in the Province of Ontario

This is a **Multiple Listing Service® Agreement** 🅼🅻🆂 (WJ JJ)   **OR**   **Exclusive Listing Agreement**   **EXCLUSIVE** ◯
(Seller's Initials)   (Seller's Initials)

BETWEEN:
BROKERAGE: .... ABC Realty Inc. ....

....(the "Listing Brokerage") Tel.No. (..905..) 555-1212

SELLER(S): ...... Wilma Jane Johnson and John Henry Johnson ......(the "Seller")

In consideration of the Listing Brokerage listing the real property **for sale** known as...... 36 Longmore Drive

City of Westville ....(the "Property")

the Seller hereby gives the Listing Brokerage the **exclusive and irrevocable** right to act as the Seller's agent, **commencing** at 12:01 a.m. on the ..30th.. day

of ...... March ......, 20..XX..., **until** 11:59 p.m. on the ..30th.. day of ...... June ......, 20..XX... (the "Listing Period"),

{ Seller acknowledges that the length of the Listing Period is negotiable between the Seller and the Listing Brokerage and, if an MLS® listing, may be subject to minimum requirements of the real estate board, however, in accordance with the Real Estate and Business Brokers Act (2002), **if the Listing Period exceeds six months, the Listing Brokerage must obtain the Seller's initials.** } ◯
(Seller's Initials)

to offer the property **for sale** at a price of: Dollars (CDN$) $297,900.00

...Two Hundred and Ninety-Seven Thousand Nine Hundred--Dollars

and upon the terms particularly set out herein, or at such other price and/or terms acceptable to the Seller. It is understood that the price and/or terms set out herein are at the Seller's personal request, after full discussion with the Listing Brokerage's representative regarding potential market value of the Property.

The Seller hereby represents and warrants that the Seller is not a party to any other listing agreement for the Property or agreement to pay commission to any other real estate brokerage for the sale of the property.

1. **DEFINITIONS AND INTERPRETATIONS:** For the purposes of this Listing Agreement ("Authority" or "Agreement"), "Seller" includes vendor, a "buyer" includes a purchaser, or a prospective purchaser and a "real estate board" includes a real estate association. A purchase shall be deemed to include the entering into of any agreement to exchange, or the obtaining of an option to purchase which is subsequently exercised. This Agreement shall be read with all changes of gender or number required by the context. For purposes of this Agreement, anyone introduced to or shown the Property shall be deemed to include any spouse, heirs, executors, administrators, successors, assigns, related corporations and affiliated corporations. Related corporations or affiliated corporations shall include any corporation where one half or a majority of the shareholders, directors or officers of the related or affiliated corporation are the same person(s) as the shareholders, directors, or officers of the corporation introduced to or shown the Property.

2. **COMMISSION:** In consideration of the Listing Brokerage listing the Property, the Seller agrees to pay the Listing Brokerage a commission of
..6.0..% of the sale price of the Property or ...... N/A ...... for any valid offer to purchase the Property from any source whatsoever obtained during the Listing Period and on the terms and conditions set out in this Agreement **OR** such other terms and conditions as the Seller may accept.

The Seller further agrees to pay such commission as calculated above if an agreement to purchase is agreed to or accepted by the Seller or anyone
on the Seller's behalf within ......90...... days after the expiration of the Listing Period (**Holdover Period**), so long as such agreement is with anyone who was introduced to the Property from any source whatsoever during the Listing Period or shown the Property during the Listing Period.

If, however, the offer for the purchase of the Property is pursuant to a new agreement in writing to pay commission to another registered real estate brokerage, the Seller's liability for commission shall be reduced by the amount paid by the Seller under the new agreement.

The Seller further agrees to pay such commission as calculated above even if the transaction contemplated by an agreement to purchase agreed to or accepted by the Seller or anyone on the Seller's behalf is not completed, if such non-completion is owing or attributable to the Seller's default or neglect, said commission to be payable on the date set for completion of the purchase of the Property.

Any deposit in respect of any agreement where the transaction has been completed shall first be applied to reduce the commission payable. Should such amounts paid to the Listing Brokerage from the deposit or by the Seller's solicitor not be sufficient, the Seller shall be liable to pay to the Listing Brokerage on demand, any deficiency in commission and taxes owing on such commission.

All amounts set out as commission are to be paid plus applicable taxes on such commission.

3. **REPRESENTATION:** The Seller acknowledges that the Listing Brokerage has provided the Seller with information explaining agency relationships, including information on Seller Representation, Sub-agency, Buyer Representation, Multiple Representation and Customer Service. The Seller authorizes the Listing Brokerage to co-operate with any other registered real estate brokerage (co-operating brokerage), and to offer to pay the co-operating

brokerage a commission of......3......% of the sale price of the Property or...... N/A ......

.... out of the commission the Seller pays the Listing Brokerage.

INITIALS OF LISTING BROKERAGE: (AL)   **INITIALS OF SELLER(S):** (WJ JJ)

Form 200   Revised 2015   **Page 1 of 3**

The Seller understands that unless the Seller is otherwise informed, the co-operating brokerage is representing the interests of the buyer in the transaction. The Seller further acknowledges that the Listing Brokerage may be listing other properties that may be similar to the Seller's Property and the Seller hereby consents to the Listing Brokerage listing other properties that may be similar to the Seller's Property without any claim by the Seller of conflict of interest. The Seller hereby appoints the Listing Brokerage as the Seller's agent for the purpose of giving and receiving notices pursuant to any offer or agreement to purchase the property. Unless otherwise agreed in writing between Seller and Listing Brokerage, any commission payable to any other brokerage shall be paid out of the commission the Seller pays the Listing Brokerage, said commission to be disbursed in accordance with the Commission Trust Agreement.

MULTIPLE REPRESENTATION: The Seller hereby acknowledges that the Listing Brokerage may be entering into buyer representation agreements with buyers who may be interested in purchasing the Seller's Property. In the event that the Listing Brokerage has entered into or enters into a buyer representation agreement with a prospective buyer for the Seller's Property, the Listing Brokerage will obtain the Seller's written consent to represent both the Seller and the buyer for the transaction at the earliest practicable opportunity and in all cases prior to any offer to purchase being submitted or presented.

The Seller understands and acknowledges that the Listing Brokerage must be impartial when representing both the Seller and the buyer and equally protect the interests of the Seller and buyer. The Seller understands and acknowledges that when representing both the Seller and the buyer, the Listing Brokerage shall have a duty of full disclosure to both the Seller and the buyer, including a requirement to disclose all factual information about the Property known to the Listing Brokerage.

However, the Seller further understands and acknowledges that the Listing Brokerage shall not disclose:
- that the Seller may or will accept less than the listed price, unless otherwise instructed in writing by the Seller;
- that the buyer may or will pay more than the offered price, unless otherwise instructed in writing by the buyer;
- the motivation of or personal information about the Seller or buyer, unless otherwise instructed in writing by the party to which the information applies or unless failure to disclose would constitute fraudulent, unlawful or unethical practice;
- the price the buyer should offer or the price the Seller should accept; and
- the Listing Brokerage shall not disclose to the buyer the terms of any other offer.

However, it is understood that factual market information about comparable properties and information known to the Listing Brokerage concerning potential uses for the Property will be disclosed to both Seller and buyer to assist them to come to their own conclusions.

Where a Brokerage represents both the Seller and the Buyer (multiple representation), the Brokerage shall not be entitled or authorized to be agent for either the Buyer or the Seller for the purpose of giving and receiving notices.

MULTIPLE REPRESENTATION AND CUSTOMER SERVICE: The Seller understands and agrees that the Listing Brokerage also provides representation and customer service to other sellers and buyers. If the Listing Brokerage represents or provides customer service to more than one seller or buyer for the same trade, the Listing Brokerage shall, in writing, at the earliest practicable opportunity and before any offer is made, inform all sellers and buyers of the nature of the Listing Brokerage's relationship to each seller and buyer.

4. **FINDERS FEES:** The Seller acknowledges that the Brokerage may be receiving a finder's fee, reward and/or referral incentive, and the Seller consents to any such benefit being received and retained by the Brokerage in addition to the commission as described above.

5. **REFERRAL OF ENQUIRIES:** The Seller agrees that during the Listing Period, the Seller shall advise the Listing Brokerage immediately of all enquiries from any source whatsoever, and all offers to purchase submitted to the Seller shall be immediately submitted to the Listing Brokerage before the Seller accepts or rejects the same. If any enquiry during the Listing Period results in the Seller accepting a valid offer to purchase during the Listing Period or within the Holdover Period after the expiration of the Listing Period, the Seller agrees to pay the Listing Brokerage the amount of commission set out above, payable within five (5) days following the Listing Brokerage's written demand therefor.

6. **MARKETING:** The Seller agrees to allow the Listing Brokerage to show and permit prospective buyers to fully inspect the Property during reasonable hours and the Seller gives the Listing Brokerage the sole and exclusive right to place "For Sale" and "Sold" sign(s) upon the Property. The Seller consents to the Listing Brokerage including information in advertising that may identify the Property. The Seller further agrees that the Listing Brokerage shall have sole and exclusive authority to make all advertising decisions relating to the marketing of the Property for sale during the Listing Period. The Seller agrees that the Listing Brokerage will not be held liable in any manner whatsoever for any acts or omissions with respect to advertising by the Listing Brokerage or any other party, other than by the Listing Brokerage's gross negligence or wilful act.

7. **WARRANTY:** The Seller represents and warrants that the Seller has the exclusive authority and power to execute this Authority to offer the Property for sale and that the Seller has informed the Listing Brokerage of any third party interests or claims on the Property such as rights of first refusal, options, easements, mortgages, encumbrances or otherwise concerning the Property, which may affect the sale of the Property.

8. **INDEMNIFICATION AND INSURANCE:** The Seller will not hold the Listing Brokerage and representatives of the Brokerage responsible for any loss or damage to the Property or contents occurring during the term of this Agreement caused by the Listing Brokerage or anyone else by any means, including theft, fire or vandalism, other than by the Listing Brokerage's gross negligence or wilful act. The Seller agrees to indemnify and save harmless the Listing Brokerage and representatives of the Brokerage and any co-operating brokerage from any liability, claim, loss, cost, damage or injury, including but not limited to loss of the commission payable under this Agreement, caused or contributed to by the breach of any warranty or representation made by the Seller in this Agreement or the accompanying data form. The Seller warrants the Property is insured, including personal liability insurance against any claims or lawsuits resulting from bodily injury or property damage to others caused in any way on or at the Property and the Seller indemnifies the Brokerage and all of its employees, representatives, salespersons and brokers (Listing Brokerage) and any co-operating brokerage and all of its employees, representatives, salespersons and brokers (co-operating brokerage) for and against any claims against the Listing Brokerage or co-operating brokerage made by anyone who attends or visits the Property.

9. **FAMILY LAW ACT:** The Seller hereby warrants that spousal consent is not necessary under the provisions of the Family Law Act, R.S.O. 1990, unless the Seller's spouse has executed the consent hereinafter provided.

10. **VERIFICATION OF INFORMATION:** The Seller authorizes the Listing Brokerage to obtain any information affecting the Property from any regulatory authorities, governments, mortgagees or others and the Seller agrees to execute and deliver such further authorizations in this regard as may be reasonably required. The Seller hereby appoints the Listing Brokerage or the Listing Brokerage's authorized representative as the Seller's attorney to execute such documentation as may be necessary to effect obtaining any information as aforesaid. The Seller hereby authorizes, instructs and directs the above noted regulatory authorities, governments, mortgagees or others to release any and all information to the Listing Brokerage.

11. **USE AND DISTRIBUTION OF INFORMATION:** The Seller consents to the collection, use and disclosure of personal information by the Brokerage for the purpose of listing and marketing the Property including, but not limited to: listing and advertising the Property using any medium including the Internet; disclosing Property information to prospective buyers, brokerages, salespersons and others who may assist in the sale of the Property; such other use of

INITIALS OF LISTING BROKERAGE: (AL)   INITIALS OF SELLER(S): (WJ JJ)

Form 200 Revised 2015 **Page 2 of 3**

the Seller's personal information as is consistent with listing and marketing of the Property. The Seller consents, if this is an MLS® Listing, to placement of the listing information and sales information by the Brokerage into the database(s) of the MLS® System of the appropriate Board, and to the posting of any documents and other information (including, without limitation, photographs, images, graphics, audio and video recordings, virtual tours, drawings, floor plans, architectural designs, artistic renderings, surveys and listing descriptions) provided by or on behalf of the Seller into the database(s) of the MLS® System of the appropriate Board. The Seller hereby indemnifies and saves harmless the Brokerage and/or any of its employees, servants, brokers or sales representatives from any and all claims, liabilities, suits, actions, losses, costs and legal fees caused by, or arising out of, or resulting from the posting of any documents or other information (including, without limitation, photographs, images, graphics, audio and video recordings, virtual tours, drawings, floor plans, architectural designs, artistic renderings, surveys and listing descriptions) as aforesaid. The Seller acknowledges that the database, within the board's MLS® System is the property of the real estate board(s) and can be licensed, resold, or otherwise dealt with by the board(s). The Seller further acknowledges that the real estate board(s) may: during the term of the listing and thereafter, distribute the information in the database, within the board's MLS® System to any persons authorized to use such service which may include other brokerages, government departments, appraisers, municipal organizations and others; market the Property, at its option, in any medium, including electronic media; during the term of the listing and thereafter, compile, retain and publish any statistics including historical data within the board's MLS® System and retain, reproduce and display photographs, images, graphics, audio and video recordings, virtual tours, drawings, floor plans, architectural designs, artistic renderings, surveys and listing descriptions which may be used by board members to conduct comparative analyses; and make such other use of the information as the Brokerage and/or real estate board(s) deem appropriate, in connection with the listing, marketing and selling of real estate during the term of the listing and thereafter. The Seller acknowledges that the information, personal or otherwise ("information"), provided to the real estate board or association may be stored on databases located outside of Canada, in which case the information would be subject to the laws of the jurisdiction in which the information is located.

In the event that this Agreement expires or is cancelled or otherwise terminated and the Property is not sold, the Seller, by initialling:

Does   **Does Not**

consent to allow other real estate board members to contact the Seller after expiration or other termination of this Agreement to discuss listing or otherwise marketing the Property.

12. SUCCESSORS AND ASSIGNS: The heirs, executors, administrators, successors and assigns of the undersigned are bound by the terms of this Agreement.

13. CONFLICT OR DISCREPANCY: If there is any conflict or discrepancy between any provision added to this Agreement (including any Schedule attached hereto) and any provision in the standard pre-set portion hereof, the added provision shall supersede the standard pre-set provision to the extent of such conflict or discrepancy. This Agreement, including any Schedule attached hereto, shall constitute the entire Agreement between the Seller and the Listing Brokerage. There is no representation, warranty, collateral agreement or condition which affects this Agreement other than as expressed herein.

14. ELECTRONIC COMMUNICATION: This Listing Agreement and any agreements, notices or other communications contemplated thereby may be transmitted by means of electronic systems, in which case signatures shall be deemed to be original. The transmission of this Agreement by the Seller by electronic means shall be deemed to confirm the Seller has retained a true copy of the Agreement.

15. SCHEDULE(S): ......N/A.. and data form attached hereto form(s) part of this Agreement.

THE LISTING BROKERAGE AGREES TO MARKET THE PROPERTY ON BEHALF OF THE SELLER AND REPRESENT THE SELLER IN AN ENDEAVOUR TO OBTAIN A VALID OFFER TO PURCHASE THE PROPERTY ON THE TERMS SET OUT IN THIS AGREEMENT OR ON SUCH OTHER TERMS SATISFACTORY TO THE SELLER.

Albert Lee..   DATE...*March 30/xx*......   Albert Lee...............................
(Authorized to bind the Listing Brokerage)   (Name of Person Signing)

THIS AGREEMENT HAS BEEN READ AND FULLY UNDERSTOOD BY ME AND I ACKNOWLEDGE THIS DATE I HAVE SIGNED UNDER SEAL. Any representations contained herein or as shown on the accompanying data form respecting the Property are true to the best of my knowledge, information and belief.

SIGNED, SEALED AND DELIVERED I have hereunto set my hand and seal:

Wilma Jane Johnson.................   ● (Seal)   DATE *March 30/xx*......   905-444-1212.........
(Signature of Seller)   (Tel. No.)

John Henry Johnson...................   ● (Seal)   DATE *March 30/xx*......   ....
(Signature of Seller)

SPOUSAL CONSENT: The undersigned spouse of the Seller hereby consents to the listing of the Property herein pursuant to the provisions of the Family Law Act, R.S.O. 1990 and hereby agrees that he/she will execute all necessary or incidental documents to further any transaction provided for herein.

....   ● (Seal)   DATE.............................
(Spouse)

DECLARATION OF INSURANCE

The broker/salesperson.............................   Albert Lee.............................
                                                    (Name of Broker/Salesperson)
hereby declares that he/she is insured as required by the Real Estate and Business Brokers Act (REBBA) and Regulations.

Albert Lee.............................
(Signature(s) of Broker/Salesperson)

ACKNOWLEDGEMENT

The Seller(s) hereby acknowledge that the Seller(s) fully understand the terms of this Agreement and have received a true copy of this Agreement

on the ....*30th*.... day of ....*March*...................., 20 ...*XX*...............................

Wilma Jane Johnson..   Date: *March 30/xx*......
(Signature of Seller)

John Henry Johnson..   Date: *March 30/xx*......
(Signature of Seller)

ONTARIO REAL ESTATE ASSOCIATION

OREA
Ontario
Real Estate
Association

RESIDENTIAL/RECREATIONAL

MLS #_____

☑ EXISTING ☐ TO BE BUILT ☐ NEW ☐ UNDER CONSTRUCTION

Effective Date: March 30/xx Expiry Date: June 30/xx Completion/Possession Date: 90 Days Price $297,900.00 Terms Cash to Mortgage

Commission to Selling Broker: 3% Matrimonial Home: ☑ Yes ☐ No Easement and/or Encroachment: ☐ Yes ☐ No ☑ Unk

Holdover Period 90 days SPIS Completed: ☑ Yes ☐ No Listing Authority Modification: ☐ Yes ☑ No

Special Provisions:_____ Applicable Schedules:_____

Property Address: 36 Longmore Drive Municipality/Township: City of Westville, Region of Postal Code: M1K 1V3

Roll #: 61314-49034-0000 PIN #: 3392-4100 Legal Description: /Plan, Lot #, County, Town]: Anyregion Lot 22 Plan 470

Side of Road: West Area/Map Locator: 115 B 4 Near: Main and Elm Streets Property Size: 50 ft x 120 ft

Seller/Owners [s]: Wilma Jane Johnson and John Henry Johnson Phone: 905-444-1212

Assessment: $265,000 Taxes: $4,482.81 Year 20xx Local Improvement: ☐ Yes ☑ No

Directions:_____

Broker: 1) ABC Realty Inc. ID#_____ Phone # 905-555-1212 Fax #: 905-555-1213 email:_____
        2)_____ ID#_____ Phone #_____ Fax #:_____ email:_____

Salesperson: 1) Albert Lee ID#_____ Phone # 905-555-1214 Fax #: 905-555-1215 email:_____
            2)_____ ID#_____ Phone #_____ email:_____

Occupant: (Select ___ only)	Indicate whether Property is: (Select ___ only)	Water Meter: ☑ yes ☐ no	UFFI: ☐ yes ☐ no	☐ removed ☑ unknown

Occupant: (Select ___ only)
☑ Owner
☐ Tenant
☐ Vacant

Showings: (Select ___ only)
☐ Direct
☐ Lock Box
☑ Call LBO

Indicate whether Property is: (Select ___ only)
☐ For Lease Only
☑ For Sale Only
☐ For Sale or Lease
☐ Exchange

Age of Dwelling: 25 yrs
(Use NE for New Construction or indicate the age in years or use Unk for unknown)

Zoning R1

Water Meter: ☑ yes ☐ no
Water Supply: (Select ___ only)
(Indicate in remarks section if supply is not connected)
☐ cistern   ☑ municipal
☐ drilled well   ☐ well
☐ river/lake   ☐ none
☐ dug-well   ☐ other_____

Sewer Type:
☑ Sanitary Connected   ☐ Sanitary Not Connected
☐ Septic Installed   ☐ Storm Connected
☐ See Remarks   ☐ Storm Not Connected

UFFI: ☐ yes ☐ no
Building Location Survey: ☑ yes ☐ no
Single Family ☑ yes ☐ no
Multi-Unit - 2 units ☐ yes ☐ no
Comments:_____

Room Sizes and Levels: all room sizes are approximate and are to be verified by the Purchaser. Use only the abbreviation listed below to describe each room. Insert the level abbreviation and insert the room size. Please indicate if measurement is in ☑ imperial or ☐ metric.

Foyer	FO	Recreation Room	RR	Utility	UT	Great Room	GR	4 pce. Bathroom	B4
Living Room	LR	Recreation Room w/FP	RF	Fruit Cellar	FC	Great Room w/FP	GF	5 pce. Bathroom	B5
Living Room/Dining Room	LD	Play Room	PR	Games Room	GR	Cold Room	CR	6 pce. Bathroom	B6
Living Room w/FP	LF	Family Room	FR	Sunroom	SR	Porch Enclosed	PE	2 pce. Ensuite	E2
Dining Room	DR	Family Room w/FP	FF	Attic	AT	Other	OT	3 pce. Ensuite	E3
Kitchen	K1	Master Bedroom	MB	Hobby Room	HR	1 pce. Bathroom	B1	4 pce. Ensuite	E4
Lower Kitchen	K2	Bedroom	BR	Workshop	WK	2 pce. Bathroom	B2	5 pce. Ensuite	E5
Eating Area	EA	Laundry	LA	Media Room	MR	3 pce. Bathroom	B3		
Den	DE								

1-2pc +
# of Bedrooms 3 # of Kitchens 1 # of Baths 1-4pc R-In Baths: ☐ yes ☑ no Ensuite Baths: ☐ yes ☑ no

LEVEL	ROOM	DIMENSIONS			LEVEL	ROOM	DIMENSIONS	
M	LR	14'8"	x	19'				x
M	DR	13'6"	x	11'8"				x
M	K1	17'	x	12'3"				x
M	MB	14'10"	x	13'9"				x
M	BR2	13'	x	13'8"				x
M	BR3	11'	x	12'				x
B	RR	16'	x	10'				x
			x					x
			x					x

BATHROOMS	LEVEL
B2	M
B4	M

Levels	
Main	M
2nd Level	2
3rd Level	3
4th Level	4
Lower	L
Basement	B
Other	O

Water Front
☐ yes ☑ no
Type of Dwelling (Select ___ only)
☐ Carriage House
☐ Cottage
☑ Detached
☐ Link
☐ Mobile/Modular
☐ Row
☐ Semi Detached
☐ Stacked
☐ Townhouse
☐ Townhouse End-unit
☐ See Remarks
☐ Other
Style (Select ___ only)
☐ 1 ½ Storey
☐ 1 ¾ Storey
☑ 1 Storey
☐ 1 Storey Raised
☐ 2 ½ Storey
☐ 2 Storey
☐ 3 Level Back Split
☐ 3 Level Side Split
☐ 3 Storey
☐ 4 Level Back Split
☐ 4 Level Side Split
☐ 5 Level Back Split
☐ 5 Level Side Split
☐ Bi-Level
☐ See Remarks
Rental Equipment (Select ___ only)
☐ Conversion Burner
☐ Conversion Burner & Water Heater
☐ Conversion Burner, Water Heater & Water Softener
☐ Fireplace
☑ Water Filter
☑ Water Heater
☐ Water Softener
☐ See Remarks
Fireplace & Type (Select ___ only)
☐ yes ☑ no
☐ # of units_____
☐ Electric
☐ Gas (natural)
☐ Propane
☐ Rough-in
☐ Wood
☐ Woodstove
☐ Other
☐ See Remarks

Garage (Select ___ only)
☐ Attached
☐ Auto. Gar.Opener
☐ Carport
☐ Detached
☐ Double
☐ Inside Entry
☐ One one-half
☐ Single
☐ Triple
☐ See Remarks
Parking (Select ___ only)
☐ Double
☐ Front Drive
☐ Gravel
☐ Mutual
☐ No Drive
☐ Rear Drive
☑ Side Drive
☐ Single
☐ Surfaced
☐ See Remarks
Foundation (Select ___ only)
☑ Block
☐ Concrete (Poured)
☐ Pillar/Piers
☐ Stone/Brick
☐ Wood
☐ None
☐ See Remarks
Insulation (Select ___ only)
☑ Basement
☑ Ceilings
☐ Floors
☑ Perimeter Walls
☐ Walls
Basement (Select ___ only)
☐ Crawl
☑ Full
☐ Partial
☐ Slab
☐ See Remarks
☐ None
Basement Develop. (Select ___ only)
☑ Finished
☐ Partly Finished
☐ Unfinished
☐ See Remarks

Fuel (Select ___ only)
☐ Electricity
☑ Gas (natural)
☐ Oil
☐ Pellets
☐ Propane
☐ Solar
☐ Wood
☐ Other
☐ See Remarks
Heating and Cooling (Select ___ only)
☐ Baseboard
☐ Central Air Cond.
☐ Electric Air Cleaner
☐ Energy Efficient
☑ Forced Air
☐ Fresh Air Exchange
☐ Furnace
☐ Gravity
☐ Heat Pump
☐ Hot Water/Steam
☐ Radiant
☐ Solar
☐ Space Heater
☐ Wall Furnace
☐ Other
☐ See Remarks
Square Footage (Select ___ only)
☐ 0-750
☐ 751-1000
☐ 1001-1200
☑ 1201-1500
☐ 1501-2000
☐ over 2000
Est. Sq. Ft:_____

Indoor Features (Select ___ only)
☐ Alarm System
☑ Cable TV connected
☐ Cable TV not connected
☐ Central vacuum
☐ Compactor
☐ Dishwasher
☐ Dryer
☐ Electric Air Cleaner
☐ Freezer
☐ Garburetor
☐ In-Law Suite
☐ Intercom
☐ Microwave
☐ Oven built-in
☐ Refrigerator
☐ Stove
☐ Washer
☐ Water Filter
☐ Water Softener
☐ Whirlpool tub
☐ Window A/Conditioner
☐ See Remarks
Other Features (Select ___ only)
☐ Above Ground Pool
☐ Balcony
☐ Barbeque Equipment
☐ Boat House
☐ Boat Lift
☐ Dock
☐ Greenhouse
☐ Hot Tub Pool
☐ Indoor Pool
☐ Inground Pool
☐ Patio
☐ Satellite Dish
☐ Sauna
☐ Skylight
☐ Sleeping Cabin
☐ Smoke Detector
☐ Solarium
☐ Sprinkler System
☐ Storage Shed
☑ Storm Doors
☑ Storm Windows
☐ Sundeck
☐ TV Antenna
☐ Wet Bar
☐ Workbench

Roof (Select ___ only)
☑ Asphalt
☐ Wood Shingle
☐ Metal
☐ Tar & Gravel
☐ Tile
☐ Concrete
☐ Other
Flooring (Select ___ only)
☑ Carpet w/w
☐ Ceramic
☐ Hardwood
☐ Lino/Vinyl
☐ Softwood
☐ Other_____
☐ See Remarks
Exterior Finish (Select ___ only)
☐ Aluminum
☑ Brick
☐ Concrete Block
☐ Hard Bd.
☐ Insulbrick
☐ Log
☐ Stone
☐ Stucco
☐ Vinyl
☐ Wood
☐ Other_____
☐ See Remarks
Acreage (Select ___ only)
☑ .99 or less
☐ 1-1.99 acres
☐ 2-4.99 acres
☐ 5-9.99 acres
☐ 10-24.99 acres
☐ 25 + acres
Water Access (Select ___ only)
☐ Waterfront Owned
☐ Waterfront Not Owned
☐ Deeded Access
☐ Public Access Nearby
☐ Island
☐_____

Topography (Select ___ only)
☐ Cons./Green Belt
☐ Escarpment
☑ Fenced
☐ Flood Plain
☐ Golf Course
☐ Hardwood Bush
☐ Level
☐ Open Space
☐ Partially cleared
☐ Pond
☐ Ravine
☐ Rolling
☐ Sand Beach
☐ Sea Wall
☐ Sloping/Terraced
☐ Softwood Bush
☐ Stream/River
☐ Waterfront
☐ Wooded/Treed
☐ Other
Road Access (Select ___ only)
☐ Private
☐ Private-Mtnce Fee
☑ Public
☐ Right of Way
☐ Seasonal
☐ Water Access
☐ Year Round
Right of Way
☐ Yes ☐ No ☑ Unk
☐ subject to
☐ benefit of
Advertising
For Sale Sign
☑ Yes ☐ No
Listing Broker Only
☐ Yes ☑ No
_____
Broker Loaded
☐ Yes ☐ No
Broker Load #:_____

Seller[s] Initials WJ JJ

ONTARIO REAL ESTATE ASSOCIATION

OREA
Ontario
Real Estate
Association

RESIDENTIAL/RECREATIONAL

Page 2

1ˢᵗ Mortgage Information:

❏ Clear

Mortgagee	Amount	Rate	Due Date	Pmt (P&I)	Additional Information
Lender Inc.	$73,600.00	7.75%	June 1/xx 2 yrs hence	$469.97	

[Select all applicable options]

☑ May be assumed with approval ❏ May be paid off without penalty ❏ Must be paid off
❏ May be assumed without approval ❏ May be paid off with penalty ❏ Seller may buy down
❏ May be increased ❏ Seller may take back ❏ Mortgage information verified
❏ Must be assumed ❏ Buyer to arrange own financing ❏ See remarks

2nd Mortgage Information:

❏ Clear

Mortgagee	Amount	Rate	Due Date	Pmt (P&I)	Additional Information

[Select all applicable options]

❏ May be assumed with approval ❏ May be paid off without penalty ❏ Must be paid off
❏ May be assumed without approval ❏ May be paid off with penalty ❏ Seller may buy down
❏ May be increased ❏ Seller may take back ❏ Mortgage information verified
❏ Must be assumed ❏ Buyer to arrange own financing ❏ See remarks

Other Mortgage Information:
❏ Clear

Mortgagee	Amount	Rate	Due Date	Pmt (P&I)	Additional Information

[Select all applicable options]

❏ May be assumed with approval ❏ May be paid off without penalty ❏ Must be paid off
❏ May be assumed without approval ❏ May be paid off with penalty ❏ Seller may buy down
❏ May be increased ❏ Seller may take back ❏ Mortgage information verified
❏ Must be assumed ❏ Buyer to arrange own financing ❏ See remarks

Chattels Included:[___ characters including spaces are available] [The MLS® reserves the right to abbreviate if content exceeds space allowed]

Garden Shed

Fixtures Excluded:[___ characters including spaces are available] [The MLS® reserves the right to abbreviate if content exceeds space allowed]

Musical Door Chimes, dining room chandelier.

REMARKS:[The MLS® reserves the right to abbreviate if content exceeds space allowed]

Heating costs approximately $1,450 per annum.

I ACKNOWLEDGE HAVING CAREFULLY READ THIS ENTIRE FORM AND, AS OF THIS DATE, CONFIRM THE ACCURACY OF THE ABOVE INFORMATION CONCERNING MY PROPERTY. I AGREE TO ALLOW CHANGES TO ITEMS SUCH AS TAXES, ASSESSMENT, LEGAL DESCRIPTION AND LOT SIZE AS MAY BE NECESSARY. I FURTHER AGREE THAT THE LISTING BROKER, AS DEEMED APPROPRIATE, MAY AMEND THE ADVERTISEMENT COPY FOR THE INTERNET.

Wilma Jane Johnson   *March 30/xx*
[SIGNATURE OF SELLER]   [DATE]

John Henry Johnson   *March 30/xx*
[SIGNATURE OF SELLER]   [DATE]

■■■

PLEASE COMPLETE THE APPROPRIATE SPACE[S]
❏ Photo Attached   ❏ Take Photo #1-View _____
❏ Sketch Attached
❏ New Picture   ❏ Take Photo #2-View _____
❏ Use Previous Picture
                                     MLS# _____
If special photographic instructions are required, please indicate:

Page 2 of 2

CH3   EX3

■ **Exercise 3   Regulatory Requirements**

3.1   An unexpired listing agreement existed at the time that a different registrant had the seller sign a second listing agreement. The registrant then attempted to collect commission pursuant to this second agreement. The seller did not agree in writing to pay two commissions, but forgot that the first agreement had not expired.

REBBA ✔   CODE ◯

Subsec. 33(3)

3.2   The Anycity market is slow and the salesperson requires a nine-month listing period for the seller's residential property. The listing is completed and signed by the seller, but no initials are included regarding the extended listing period, as required under the Act and Regulations.

REBBA ◯   CODE ✔

Subsec. 11(2)

3.3   The salesperson had a listing signed on March 14th, but forgot to provide copies. Realizing his mistake several days later, he called the sellers. Unconcerned, the sellers told him not to bother. The salesperson took no further action.

REBBA ◯   CODE ✔

Sec. 12

3.4   The seller requests that the expiry date on a representation agreement be July 31st, or alternatively June 30th, if he elects to take holidays during July. The salesperson agrees and inserts the two dates in the agreement.

REBBA ◯   CODE ✔

Subsec. 11(3)

3.5   The brokerage receives a finder's fee relating to arranging a mortgage for the buyer, but does not disclose this fact to the seller client.

REBBA ◯   CODE ✔

Subsec. 18(4)

3.6   The salesperson completes a representation agreement that includes both the payment of a commission based on a percentage of sale price, along with a flat fee of $2,000.

REBBA ✔   CODE ◯

Subsec. 36(1)

APPENDIX

■ Exercise 4   SPIS: 287 Westvale Crescent

SECTION	LINE	CONCERN	BRIEF EXPLANATION
General	2	Ownership Interest	Who is the other party and what is the extent of ownership? The other party's signature will be required on a listing agreement and an agreement of purchase and sale.
	4	Rental Agreement	Various matters including: what is legal rent, are students occupying a self-contained apartment or rooms, does the *Residential Tenancies Act* apply, and can vacant possession be given at closing?
	8	Fence Dispute	Was it concluded amicably? Do unsettled matters remain? Was a survey obtained to resolve the dispute?
	14	Local Improvements (Local Levies)	What costs are involved and when is the expiry? Students should note Question 10, as it appears that improvements are ongoing. What impact does this have on a potential buyer?
	17	Heritage	Older property may be within heritage district. What restrictions impact housing in the district and specifically, what is the current status of this house in that regard?
Environmental	8	Fuel Tank	All underground tanks must be upgraded or removed within specified dates. Information and guidance required from the Technical Standards and Safety Authority.
Improvements and Structural	2	Renovations	What minor changes were made? Was a building permit required?
	3	UFFI	Seller did not complete this item. Was UFFI present?
	5	Fire Code	Is the building in compliance with the Building Code, particularly given upper-level rental arrangements?
	6	Fireplace	Was the gas fireplace installed by an authorized technician or was this part of seller's work?
	9	Leakage	General condition of roof; extent of damage requiring repair.
	10	Wiring	Out-of-date knob and tube wiring can cause problems when acquiring house insurance; 60-amp service is inadequate given current household demands, particularly given rental situation.
	12	Plumbing	High probability of lead or galvanized piping given age of structure.

APPENDIX

■ **Exercise 5   The Basement Apartment**

a. The salesperson failed to provide conscientious and competent service (Code of Ethics, Sec. 5) and did not use his best efforts to prevent misrepresentation (Code of Ethics, Sec. 38). Note: The Panel hearing this case under the previous Act found the salesperson in violation of several Rules under the previous Code of Ethics, assessed an administrative penalty of $500 and costs of $1,650.

b. The Panel found that a salesperson should be aware of a by-law prohibiting basement apartments in single-family homes. Further, the salesperson was careless by not making inquiries about the legality of the basement apartment, particularly since other MLS® listings raised the issue.

The advertisements were misleading, as they did not warn prospective tenants regarding the matter. The omission of this pertinent information caused considerable inconvenience and disruption to the tenant and her best interests were not protected.

CHAPTER 4
DOCUMENTING BUYER REPRESENTATION

Chapter Mini-Review

1. The OREA *Buyer Representation Agreement* provides for commission payment either by the listing brokerage or the seller.

    True   False

   The form also clearly states that such payment by a seller does not create a representation relationship with that seller.

2. A buyer representation agreement must prominently display the date and provide space for the buyer's initials if the term of the agreement exceeds four months.

   ◯ True   **False**

   The requirement relates to listings exceeding six months, not four. See Sec. 11 of the Code of Ethics.

3. The *Consumer Reporting Act* requires that every person be notified if a consumer report may be referred to in connection with a transaction.

    True   ◯ False

   Notification must be provided. See Clause 7 in the OREA *Buyer Representation Agreement*.

4. The residential OREA *Buyer Representation Agreement* contains an expanded definition of *purchase* to include the transfer of shares or assets.

   ◯ True   **False**

   The OREA *Buyer Representation Agreement* —*Commercial* contains this expanded definition.

5. Indemnification involves the obligation to pay a commission to a real estate brokerage.

   ◯ True   **False**

   Indemnification involves the obligation to compensate a real estate brokerage for loss or damage when carrying out lawful acts.

6. A registrant authorized to bind the brokerage must sign and date his or her signature on the buyer representation agreement.

    True   ◯ False

   This requirement is set out in Sec. 14 of the Code of Ethics. Note: The buyer is not obligated to sign a written agreement, but the registrant is required to prepare and sign the document before the buyer makes an offer.

7. According to REBBA 2002, no legal action can be taken to claim commission or other remuneration unless the person bringing such action was either registered or exempt.

    True   ◯ False

   This is a correct statement. REBBA, Sec. 9 sets out this requirement.

8. If a buyer is introduced to a property by a brokerage during the listing period, but buys the property following expiration of the holdover period, a commission is due and payable according to the wording of the OREA *Buyer Representation Agreement*.

   ◯ True   **False**

The OREA *Buyer Representation Agreement* provides for a holdover provision that is effective for a period stated within that holdover clause and not beyond.

9. A brokerage cannot receive money from anyone other than the client regarding services being provided to that client without his or her consent.

 True   ◯ False

Additional fees must be disclosed pursuant to Sec. 18 of the Code of Ethics.

10. In the commercial court case involving tenant representation outlined in this chapter, the Judge awarded a commission of 6% for the first year and 2 ½% for subsequent years, based on his determination that these were commission rates generally in effect for the local market.

 True   ◯ False

Courts typically look for prevailing rates in the marketplace when determining such issues. See REBBA, Subsec. 36(1).

11. Registrants are well advised to avoid making any statements to a buyer client that involve making a prediction or giving absolute assurance.

 True   ◯ False

Making predictions and giving absolute assurances increase risk.

12. Failure to disclose the known existence of a past grow operation, within a property being seriously considered by a client, would be a violation of the Code of Ethics.

 True   False

As highlighted in one of two RECO Discipline Decisions included in this chapter, the non-disclosure of a material fact would be a violation of the Code of Ethics.

Active Learning Exercises

▣ Exercise 1   Matching

Match the phrase/word in the left column with the appropriate description in the right column (not all descriptions are used).

c.	*Buyer Registry Service*	*Toronto Real Estate Board*
d.	*Consumer Report*	*Notification Required if Report May be Referred to*
f.	*Change Expiry Date*	*Amendment to Representation Agreement*
b.	*Cancellation of Buyer Representation Agreement*	*Buyer and Brokerage Release Each Other by Agreement*
g.	*Holdover*	*Remains After Expiration of Agreement*
a.	*Caveat Emptor*	*Let the Buyer Beware*
k.	*Express Authority*	*A Precise Instruction*
i.	*Exclusive Buyer Representation Agreement*	*Sole Right to Locate Suitable Property*

No Match: e., h. and j.

■ Exercise 2 The Altered Buyer Representation Agreement

- The first alteration (change made to exclusive authority) permits any other brokerage to seek out property on behalf of the buyer.
- The geographic area is limited to Ridgewood. If the Howells buy out of that area, the agreement might not be enforceable. Regardless, the provision appears too limiting given their initial instructions.
- While the 2.5% commission is intact, the obligation to pay a deficiency has now been eliminated and the brokerage may not get paid for work done.
- The holdover clause has been reduced from 60 to 10 days. Further, the buyers have added a clause giving them the right to purchase directly from a seller and not pay a commission. These factors significantly limit commission rights and should be carefully evaluated from a brokerage perspective.
- The form now implies that every possible property will be shown to the buyers. This poses problems if a suitable property is inadvertently overlooked. Further, the instruction is not practical and may involve extensive time commitment over properties that are of no interest to the client.
- The provision for multiple representation has been removed. This eliminates the possibility of selling any property listed with the brokerage, and conflicts with the earlier amendment to see all properties.
- Indemnification clause is removed which directly affects liability from the broker's perspective.

■ Exercise 3 SPIS—36 Windward Avenue, Gateway Estates

This case study highlights selected problem areas and is intended for education purposes only. Registrants are reminded that properties are unique and issues impacting the land, the main structure and other improvements will vary significantly.

SECTION	LINE	CONCERN	BRIEF EXPLANATION
General	6	Right-of-way	Will it affect property usage and enjoyment? Buyer should determine size and relevant facts.
	7	1986 Survey	Is survey up-to-date? Check further with seller/listing broker.
	8		Not Answered. Check with seller (or listing salesperson if applicable).
	10 11		Property at rear will be a park. Check with local planning department to assess impact.
	14	Local Levies	Main road upgrade. Establish what costs are involved. Check with seller (through listing salesperson) or tax department.
	16(a)	Municipal Water	Answered 'yes' but contradicts Schedule.
	16(b)	Municipal Sewer	Answered 'yes' but contradicts Schedule.
	18	Water Softener	Rental or owned. Further details required; e.g., if owned, is there any warranty? If rented, what obligations must be assumed? Check further with listing broker.

APPENDIX

	20		Life expectancy of major components: roof, furnace, etc. Suggest home inspection.
Environmental	1	Possible Environmental	Buyer may want to investigate further; e.g., soil contamination. Contact Ministry of the Environment for additional information.
	2	Dump Site	Establish old waste dump location/size. Check with Ministry of the Environment.
	3	Wind Turbines	Unknown status. Further details required.
	5	Jurisdiction	Check with the local Conservation Authority.
Structural	1	Cracks in Exterior	Cause and scope of problem. Recommend home inspection.
	2a 2b	Renovations	Moved support post in basement without permit. Has structural integrity been compromised? Recommend home inspection.
	3	UFFI	Unknown status. Further details required. Suggest home inspection.
	6	Woodstove/ Fireplace	Was installation correct? Confirm further with seller. Home inspection recommended.
	6b		Not Answered. Check with seller (or listing salesperson if applicable).
	9a	Water Problems	Sump pump installed. Was there a moisture problem? Cause of leakage. Specific inspection required.
	9b	Roof Covering	Fourteen years old. Replacement probably needed soon. Suggest home inspection.
	10b	Electrical System	Type of wiring unknown. Home inspection recommended.
	11	Well Repaired	Is further information available? Check with seller (through listing salesperson).
	13	Swimming Pool	See above (Structural #9a). Moisture problem may relate to pool.
Form 222 **Water Supply & Waste Disposal**	1 abc	Water Source	Need up-to-date information. What is quality/quantity of water? Make offer conditional on water test. Have seller warranty condition of well and equipment. Seek other source documentation in seller's possession.
	2 abc	Sewage Disposal	Need current information. Does it work properly? Make offer conditional if adequate source documentation not available. Is Certificate of Installation (for increased bed) available? Seller warranty in offer may be required.

APPENDIX

CHAPTER 5
MULTIPLE REPRESENTATION AND CUSTOMER SERVICE AGREEMENTS

Chapter Mini-Review

1. The issue of competing interests is a major source of conflict for a brokerage when attempting to represent more than one client.

    True   False

   Multiple representation places the brokerage in an awkward position of trying to serve two masters.

2. Under multiple representation, as set out in the OREA *Listing Agreement* (OREA Form 200), the listing brokerage can disclose what the seller may or will accept, if written instruction to do so is given by the seller.

    True   False

   The wording specifically provides for this possibility when an appropriate instruction is given by the seller/client.

3. A key question should litigation arise over multiple representation is: *Did the salesperson's actual conduct align with the stated procedure as set out in the representation form?*

    True   False

   The substance of representation is focused on the actions of the registrant and the facts of the case, not judged primarily on the forms and the words within such forms.

4. According to the Code of Ethics, a brokerage need only disclose to a client the services provided to that client when discussing a representation agreement.

    True   **False**

   Section 10 of the Code of Ethics requires that disclosure involve types of service alternatives, including a representation agreement or another type of agreement.

5. *Working with a REALTOR®* (OREA Form, 810) published by the Ontario Real Estate Association, provides a description of services potentially provided by a brokerage, but does not include an acknowledgement.

   True   **False**

   The *Working with a REALTOR®* form contains an acknowledgement that can be retained by the brokerage as confirmation that various services were explained to the client or customer.

6. The *Confirmation of Co-operation and Representation* (OREA Form 320) is typically signed at the time that the listing agreement or buyer representation agreement is signed.

    True   **False**

   The *Confirmation of Co-operation and Representation* (OREA Form 320) is typically signed prior to the presentation of an offer.

APPENDIX

7. The OREA *Listing Agreement* (OREA Form 200) contains a provision relating to the seller's consent to obtaining a finder's fee, but such a provision is not included in the *Buyer Representation Agreement* (OREA Form 300).

 True   False

A finder's fee provision involving consent of the client to such a fee is included in both forms.

8. A seller customer service agreement does not typically include any reference to the payment of commission to the brokerage.

 True   False

A seller customer service agreement typically includes a commission payment provision. The payment of commission, in itself, does not create a representation relationship between the seller and the brokerage.

9. A customer service agreement with a buyer may require that the brokerage protect and promote the interests of that customer.

 True   False

Service agreements do not involve any activities on the part of the brokerage that would require promoting the interests of the customer. Representation agreements, not service agreements, involve promotion of the client's best interests.

10. Minimum content requirements for agreements apply equally to representation agreements and service agreements.

 True   False

Those requirements are set out in the Code of Ethics, Sec. 11: Contents of Written Agreements.

11. The *Confirmation of Co-operation and Representation* (OREA Form 320) can be used for situations involving multiple representation or co-operating brokerages, but does not apply to circumstances involving single representation.

 True   False

The *Confirmation of Co-operation and Representation* (OREA Form 320) is designed to address most common situations involving representation including, single representation.

12. The *Buyer Customer Service Agreement* (OREA Form 310) provides that the buyer must pay compensation to the brokerage for services rendered.

True   False

The form wording does not include a requirement for compensation, but does contemplate that such an arrangement could be made if agreed to by the parties.

APPENDIX

Active Learning Exercises

▣ Exercise 1   Fill-in-the-Blanks

1.1 Salesperson James provides a *Working with a REALTOR®* form to the seller client and receives written acknowledgement of [*client*] status.

1.2 Salesperson James then has Watson sign a (an) [*listing*] agreement, which sets out the agreement between them and details such things as representation procedures and commission payment.

1.3 Salesperson Janson provides a (an) [*Working With A REALTOR® Form*] to the buyer to comply with the Code of Ethics, Sec 10 regarding the types of service alternatives available to the buyer.

1.4 Salesperson Janson, who drafts the agreement of purchase and sale, also completes a (an) [*Confirmation of Co-operation and Representation*] to confirm the roles of both listing and co-operating brokerages.

1.5 The form, prepared under 1.4, is then signed by

[*Janson*] ,
[*Williams*] ,
[*James*] and
[*Watson*] .

1.6 The signing of this form meets requirements as set out in this chapter under [*Step 2: Disclosure Before Offer*] .

▣ Exercise 2   Questions, Questions

2.1 Sec. 10 of the Code of Ethics requires that a written disclosure of the types of services being offered by a brokerage is provided. The form contains a straightforward explanation of representation and customer service options and sets the stage for all subsequent disclosures as mandated by the Code.

APPENDIX

2.2 The signing of an acknowledgement does not in itself create any contractual obligations. The purpose of the form is two-fold. First, buyers such as the Joneses will receive a general understanding of representation and customer service options. Second, the acknowledgement provides written evidence that the broker or salesperson, on behalf of the brokerage, has complied with REBBA 2002 disclosure procedures. The acknowledgement is kept on file with other documents, if and when such documents are signed. The signature merely acknowledges that the form has been read and understood, and is not intended to obligate the buyer in any way.

2.3 A prompt decision is best, as potential conflict can arise immediately. For example, the buyer may wish to discuss certain financial matters that impact his or her house buying ability with the salesperson. In a customer relationship, the salesperson owes a duty to his seller client to disclose such facts. In a buyer client relationship, such details would be kept confidential, unless otherwise agreed in writing. While buyers and sellers are not obligated to sign written agreements, registrants are reminded that they are obligated to prepare such agreements ready for signature.

■ Exercise 3   The Listing Agreement

3.1 The seller agrees to pay a commission on any sale effected from any source whatsoever within the terms set out in this agreement. This clause applies, as the sale would occur on the final day of the listing period. It should be noted that even if the sale occurred several weeks later, the holdover provision would apply, as the showing took place within the listing period.

3.2 Based on the wording detailed in Clause 2 of the *Listing Agreement*, it is highly unlikely that the listing brokerage (ABC Realty Inc.) will be able to successfully claim a commission from the sellers given that the sellers were not responsible for the fact that the transaction did not close (i.e., the transaction in fact did not close as a result of the buyer's financial difficulties).

3.3 The brokerage is to be advised of all enquiries from any source whatsoever during the currency of the listing.

3.4 The seller has already acknowledged that multiple representation could occur (as described in the listing agreement). However, the existence of a competing buyer client now requires that the written consent of both clients be obtained. Further, disclosure of this situation must also include the other buyer working with the co-operating brokerage.

3.5 If the seller refuses to consent to the multiple representation, the brokerage must divest itself of one of the clients and return to single representation. Typically, the brokerage would retain the first client (i.e., the seller, in this instance) and not continue representing the buyer client.

■ Exercise 4   The Confirmation of Co-operation and Representation

4.1   Total Sale Price: $495,000

Commission: 3.25% x $495,000 = $16,087.50

ABC Realty Inc. receives $8,043.75 and disburses $5,228.44 to Salesperson Lee and retains the balance of $2,815.31.

XYZ Real Estate Ltd. receives $8,043.75 and disburses $4,826.25 to Salesperson Ward and retains the balance of $3,217.50.

4.2   See the following page for the completed *Confirmation of Co-operation and Representation* (OREA Form 320).

4.3   If the form is not signed, XYZ Real Estate Ltd. could possibly have difficulty collecting the commission if ABC Realty Inc. refused to forward the appropriate funds following receipt. If the sale was an MLS® transaction, real estate board by-laws/ rules and regulations normally provide for the immediate payment of co-operating brokerages within the jurisdiction. However, the collecting of commission between brokerages from different boards can cause some difficulties should the listing brokerage, for example, be unco-operative regarding payment. The *Confirmation of Co-operation and Representation* (OREA Form 320) is often used between boards given the inability to enforce real estate board by-laws/rules and regulations concerning the payment of commission beyond that particular board's jurisdictional area. The form is also used for exclusively-listed property.

 **Confirmation of Co-operation and Representation**

Ontario Real Estate Association

Form 320
for use in the Province of Ontario

BUYER: .... Donald Reed ....

SELLER: .... John Michael Smith and Mary Rose Smith ....

For the transaction on the property known as: .... 789 Main Street, Anycity, Anyregion ....

For the purposes of this Confirmation of Co-operation and Representation, "Seller" includes a vendor, a landlord, or a prospective, seller, vendor or landlord and "Buyer" includes a purchaser, a tenant, or a prospective, buyer, purchaser or tenant, "sale" includes a lease, and "Agreement of Purchase and Sale" includes an Agreement to Lease.

The following information is confirmed by the undersigned salesperson/broker representatives of the Brokerage(s). If a Co-operating Brokerage is involved in the transaction, the brokerages agree to co-operate, in consideration of, and on the terms and conditions as set out below.

DECLARATION OF INSURANCE: The undersigned salesperson/broker representative(s) of the Brokerage(s) hereby declare that he/she is insured as required by the Real Estate and Business Brokers Act, 2002 (REBBA 2002) and Regulations.

1. **LISTING BROKERAGE**
   a) ☑ The Listing Brokerage represents the interests of the Seller in this transaction. It is further understood and agreed that:
       1) ☑ The Listing Brokerage is not representing or providing Customer Service to the Buyer.
              (If the Buyer is working with a Co-operating Brokerage, Section 3 is to be completed by Co-operating Brokerage)
       2) ☐ The Listing Brokerage is providing Customer Service to the Buyer.

   b) ☐ **MULTIPLE REPRESENTATION:** The Listing Brokerage has entered into a Buyer Representation Agreement with the Buyer and represents the interests of the Seller and the Buyer, with their consent, for this transaction. The Listing Brokerage must be impartial and equally protect the interests of the Seller and the Buyer in this transaction. The Listing Brokerage has a duty of full disclosure to both the Seller and the Buyer, including a requirement to disclose all factual information about the property known to the Listing Brokerage. However, the Listing Brokerage shall not disclose:

   - That the Seller may or will accept less than the listed price, unless otherwise instructed in writing by the Seller;
   - That the Buyer may or will pay more than the offered price, unless otherwise instructed in writing by the Buyer;
   - The motivation of or personal information about the Seller or Buyer, unless otherwise instructed in writing by the party to which the information applies, or unless failure to disclose would constitute fraudulent, unlawful or unethical practice;
   - The price the Buyer should offer or the price the Seller should accept;
   - And; the Listing Brokerage shall not disclose to the Buyer the terms of any other offer.

   However, it is understood that factual market information about comparable properties and information known to the Listing Brokerage concerning potential uses for the property will be disclosed to both Seller and Buyer to assist them to come to their own conclusions.

   Additional comments and/or disclosures by Listing Brokerage: (e.g. The Listing Brokerage represents more than one Buyer offering on this property.)

   ....
   ....
   ....
   ....

2. **PROPERTY SOLD BY BUYER BROKERAGE – PROPERTY NOT LISTED**
   ☐ The Brokerage .... represent the Buyer and the property is not listed with any real estate brokerage. The Brokerage will be paid
                    (does/does not)
                              ☐ by the Seller in accordance with a Seller Customer Service Agreement
           or: ☐ by the Buyer directly

   Additional comments and/or disclosures by Buyer Brokerage: (e.g. The Buyer Brokerage represents more than one Buyer offering on this property.)

   ....
   ....
   ....
   ....

INITIALS OF BUYER(S)/SELLER(S)/BROKERAGE REPRESENTATIVE(S) (Where applicable)

DR	*LW*	*JS MS*	*AL*
BUYER	**CO-OPERATING/BUYER BROKERAGE**	**SELLER**	**LISTING BROKERAGE**

Form 320   Revised 2015   Page 1 of 2

APPENDIX

3.   Co-operating Brokerage completes Section 3 and Listing Brokerage completes Section 1.

CO-OPERATING BROKERAGE- REPRESENTATION:

a)   ☑   The Co-operating Brokerage represents the interests of the Buyer in this transaction.

b)   ☐   The Co-operating Brokerage is providing Customer Service to the Buyer in this transaction.

c)   ☐   The Co-operating Brokerage is not representing the Buyer and has not entered into an agreement to provide customer service(s) to the Buyer.

CO-OPERATING BROKERAGE- COMMISSION:

a)   ☑   The Listing Brokerage will pay the Co-operating Brokerage the commission as indicated in the MLS® information for the property

.............................1.625%.............................. to be paid from the amount paid by the Seller to the Listing Brokerage.

(Commission As Indicated In MLS® Information)

b)   ☐   The Co-operating Brokerage will be paid as follows:

....

....

Additional comments and/or disclosures by Co-operating Brokerage: (e.g., The Co-operating Brokerage represents more than one Buyer offering on this property.)

....

....

....

Commission will be payable as described above, plus applicable taxes.

COMMISSION TRUST AGREEMENT: If the above Co-operating Brokerage is receiving payment of commission from the Listing Brokerage, then the agreement between Listing Brokerage and Co-operating Brokerage further includes a Commission Trust Agreement, the consideration for which is the Co-operating Brokerage procuring an offer for a trade of the property, acceptable to the Seller. This Commission Trust Agreement shall be subject to and governed by the MLS® rules and regulations pertaining to commission trusts of the Listing Brokerage's local real estate board, if the local board's MLS® rules and regulations so provide. Otherwise, the provisions of the OREA recommended MLS® rules and regulations shall apply to this Commission Trust Agreement. For the purpose of this Commission Trust Agreement, the Commission Trust Amount shall be the amount noted in Section 3 above. The Listing Brokerage hereby declares that all monies received in connection with the trade shall constitute a Commission Trust and shall be held, in trust, for the Co-operating Brokerage under the terms of the applicable MLS® rules and regulations.

SIGNED BY THE BROKER/SALESPERSON REPRESENTATIVE(S) OF THE BROKERAGE(S) (Where applicable)

XYZ Real Estate Ltd.
(Name of Co-operating/Buyer Brokerage)

15 Centre Street, Anycity, Anyregion M5E 6G8

Tel:. *416-333-1212*   Fax:. *416-333-2121*

Linda Ward   Date: *Nov. 16/xx*
(Authorized to bind the Co-operating/Buyer Brokerage)

Linda Ward
(Print Name of Broker/Salesperson Representative of the Brokerage)

ABC Realty Inc.
(Name of Listing Brokerage)

123 Main Street, Anycity, Anyregion M3X 3C1

Tel:. *416-444-1212*   Fax:. *416-444-2121*

Albert Lee   Date: *Nov. 16/xx*
(Authorized to bind the Listing Brokerage)

Albert Lee
(Print Name of Broker/Salesperson Representative of the Brokerage)

CONSENT FOR MULTIPLE REPRESENTATION (To be completed only if the Brokerage represents more than one client for the transaction)

The Buyer/Seller consent with their initials to their Brokerage representing more than one client for this transaction.

BUYER'S INITIALS   SELLER'S INITIALS

ACKNOWLEDGEMENT

I have received, read, and understand the above information.

Donald Reed   Date: *Nov. 16/xx*
(Signature of Buyer)

....   Date: ....
(Signature of Buyer)

John M. Smith   Date: *Nov. 16/xx*
(Signature of Seller)

Mary R. Smith   Date: *Nov. 16/xx*
(Signature of Seller)

CHAPTER 6
MARKETING THE PROPERTY

Chapter Mini-Review

1. Two characteristics of a saleable listing are exclusivity and a reasonable listing time period.

    True   ◯ False

   The other characteristics are accurate information, price, rapport with the seller and knowledge of the property.

2. A comparative market analysis is used to establish market value when listing a property for sale.

   ◯ True   False

   A comparative market analysis is used to establish a listing price, not a market value.

3. The seller's motivation for selling is not highly relevant when preparing for a listing presentation.

   ◯ True   False

   Motivation is an important aspect in the listing process. Motivated sellers realistically price their properties to make them attractive to prospective buyers.

4. A property that is frequently shown to prospective buyers is the most likely property to sell in a short period of time.

   ◯ True   False

   While greater frequency of showings can lead to a sale, such frequency can sometimes be misunderstood. For example, if the property is overpriced, registrants may be showing it solely for comparison purposes to sell other more realistically priced properties.

5. A brokerage is always responsible for deceitful statements made by a seller client regarding his or her property that result in litigation.

   ◯ True   False

   While the possibility of liability can arise, the Court will judge the case based on specific circumstances. In one case cited in this chapter (Accurate Details a Must), the seller was found negligent but not the brokerage listing the property.

6. If a seller states that he has installed new shingles on a residential structure within the last six months, the salesperson listing the property should investigate further to substantiate this statement.

    True   ◯ False

   Substantiation can be accomplished in various ways, but requesting a receipt for the particular work done is the best strategy.

7. Rail access, cranes and sprinkler systems are three of many factors that should be taken into consideration when listing property used for industrial purposes.

    True   ◯ False

   Some other factors include key measurements, unique features and availability of financial information.

APPENDIX

CH6   MR

8. The *Competition Act* sets out various guidelines concerning advertising, one of which relates to the use of abbreviations when promoting property through print and electronic media.

 True   False

The Competition Bureau is concerned that abbreviations can be confusing or misleading.

9. Based on the requirements of the *Competition Act*, a disclaimer cannot be included in the fine print for an advertisement, but must be prominently displayed within the ad instead.

 True   **False**

A disclaimer in the fine print will not normally arouse concern provided that the disclaimer is complementary to the main message and not contradictory to it.

10. The Registrar cannot only order the cessation of false advertising, but can also require the registrant to retract statements or publish corrections.

 True   False

In addition to these powers granted under REBBA 2002, the Registrar can also require pre-approval of the registrant's advertising for a period up to one year.

11. Advertising, for purposes of guidelines published by the Registrar, can include print as well as electronic media.

 True   False

Advertising guidelines relate to print as well as electronic media (e.g., Internet, radio and television).

12. A registrant cannot make an advertising claim regarding volume of business conducted, as such is not in keeping with the Code of Ethics.

 True   **False**

Claims regarding business volume can be made provided that such comply with advertising guidelines established by the Registrar.

APPENDIX

Active Learning Exercises

▣ Exercise 1   Multiple Choice

1.1 A brokerage advertises that the organization is 'Number One'. This is acceptable to the Registrar provided that:

a. The brokerage places the advertisement in all local papers.

Incorrect. No such requirement exists.

b. The brokerage refers only to transactions and does not address dollar volume.

Incorrect. Brokerages may refer to transactions (or transaction sides or ends).

c. **The brokerage discloses the basis upon which the comparison or claim is made.**

✔ *CORRECT.* Advertising claims must be substantiated by way of details as to how the claim was determined.

d. The brokerage seeks the permission of the local real estate board to publish this information.

Incorrect. Negotiating acceptable terms is one of several services provided to buyers.

1.2 A brokerage, when advertising a commission rate:

a. Must include a statement in the advertisement that the rate advertised is not fixed, set or mandated by law.

Incorrect. The requirement is not that such a statement be included, but rather that a statement within an ad cannot state or suggest that the rate advertised is fixed, set or mandated by law.

b. **Must include a description of any situation in which the commission rate advertised is not in fact charged.**

✔ *CORRECT.* Brokerages need not include any further description, if in fact the commission charged is the only one charged by that brokerage.

c. Must include the phrase 'as low as' to indicate that higher rates may apply.

Incorrect. This phrase is not required, but if used, then the brokerage must explain under what circumstances a higher rate would apply.

d. Must include the amount of commission paid to co-operating brokerages.

Incorrect. The amount of commission paid to a co-operating brokerage must be set out in a written agreement (e.g., representation agreements) but is not required in an advertisement.

APPENDIX

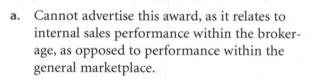

1.3   A registrant receives an award for outstanding sales performance by her employing brokerage. The registrant:

a.   Cannot advertise this award, as it relates to internal sales performance within the brokerage, as opposed to performance within the general marketplace.

Incorrect. Registrants are permitted to advertise awards, provided that such ads meet guidelines set out by the Registrar.

b.   Can only advertise this award if the award was purchased by the registrant or her employing brokerage.

Incorrect. An award that is purchased by a registrant, by someone else on behalf of the registrant or by the employing brokerage cannot be advertised.

c.   Must include the phrase '*Award available for inspection upon request.*'

Incorrect. No such requirement exists.

d.   **Must include the source and date of that award in any advertising.**

✔ *CORRECT.* The source and date of the award must be included in any advertisement.

1.4   A registrant may use property 'sold' cards to advertise a seller client's property that has just sold, provided that:

a.   **The seller gives his or her written consent and is the owner of the property at the time of the consent.**

✔ *CORRECT.* The seller's written consent must be obtained and the seller must still own the property.

b.   The transaction has closed and the seller gives his or her written consent.

Incorrect. The buyer's written consent must be obtained after the transaction has closed.

c.   The buyer and seller give written consent regardless of whether the sale has closed or not.

Incorrect. Whether the seller's or buyer's consent is required depends on whether the transaction has closed or not.

d.   The sold card used includes the terms of the agreement under which the property was sold.

Incorrect. No terms of the agreement can be included without the written consent of both parties.

1.5   Which of the following statements is correct regarding guidelines set out under the *Competition Act*?

a.   **Disclaimers and limiting conditions must be consistent with the overall impression given in advertising.**

✔ *CORRECT.* Guidelines provided by the Competition Bureau emphasize that disclaimers and limiting conditions must be consistent with the overall impression given.

b.   With contests, the advertiser need only disclose the closing date and where contest rules can be obtained.

Incorrect. The two disclosures are valid, but several other key facts must be disclosed regarding contests.

c.   Five point print size is acceptable for fine print.

Incorrect. Seven point print size is acceptable for fine print.

d.   Only registrants in organized real estate need to comply with Competition Bureau guidelines.

Incorrect. Guidelines provided by the Competition Bureau apply to many businesses providing products and services in the marketplace.

APPENDIX

1.6 Which of the following is a correct statement?

a. A model home pictured in an advertisement doesn't necessarily have to resemble the actual home or homes being offered at the construction site.

Incorrect. No erroneous impressions can be conveyed when using pictures or illustrations.

b. With a promotional claim, the actual text and the general impression need not agree.

Incorrect. Actual text and general impression should agree.

c. Promotional claims can be used in print advertising, but not Internet marketing.

Incorrect. Promotional claims can be used in both print and electronic marketing media.

d. **All MLS® listings are viewed as advertisements for purposes of the *Competition Act*.**

✓ *CORRECT.* All MLS® listings are viewed as advertisements and consequently fall under the *Competition Act*.

1.7 According to guidelines provided under the *Competition Act*:

a. Brokerages should not use the terms: *best*, *first*, *largest* or *most popular* when describing real estate.

Incorrect. Brokerages may use such terms, but the onus rests on the brokerage to substantiate their usage. Each case will be viewed by the Competition Bureau on its own merits.

b. **Abbreviations found in the local trading place are generally acceptable provided that they do not confuse or mislead.**

✓ *CORRECT.* Locally acceptable abbreviations can be used, provided that they do not confuse or mislead.

c. A property cannot sell above the advertised price.

Incorrect. The *Competition Act* specifically permits the sale of real estate above the advertised price.

d. Disclaimers are not permitted when including property details in a seller representation agreement.

Incorrect. Disclaimers can be used but must not contradict or materially limit information included in the seller representation agreement.

  ■ Exercise 2   The CMA

2.1 Maximum Suggested Listing Price: $200,000–$205,000

Estimated Selling Price: $192,000–$197,000

Notes regarding market activity as per CMA:

- A similar property at 39 Springdale Road sold 8 months ago for $189,900.
- 196 Falcon Street sold for $208,700. The sale tends to support the price of $192,000 to $197,000 after adjusting for extensive landscaping and some upgrades.
- At a list price of $200,000 to $205,000, this property is competitively priced below similar homes at 132 Springdale Road and 39 Cedar Avenue.
- A listing price of $200,000 to $205,000 makes the property competitive with similar homes listed in the area.
- Answers may vary based on market assumptions.

APPENDIX

2.2   Calculations leading to anticipated net proceeds:

Commission	Sale price $197,000 x 5.25%	= $10,342.50
HST	$10,342.50 x 13%	= 1,344.53
		$11,687.03

Mortgage Penalty (Rough approximation is acceptable):

3 months' interest	$127,300 x 6.5% x 3/12	= $2,068.63

Form calculations are based on a listing price of $205,000 and a selling price of $197,000. Student answers will vary based on assumptions made. The HP 10BII calculates interest penalties. Formulae for penalties, bonuses and related calculations are covered in *Principles of Mortgage Financing*.

Exercise 2   Residential Market Comparison Guide—Bottom

(Use back of form for additional features/comments if required)

ESTIMATED SELLING COSTS:

Brokerage Fee:	$ 11,687
Mortgage Payout Penalty	$ 2,068 (Est.)
Mortgage Discount	$ N/A
Approximate Legal Costs	$ 650
Miscellaneous	$ N/A
Total	$ 14,405

Recommendations: as of June 16, 20xx

I recommend a maximum list price of:	$ 205,000
With estimated selling price of:	$ 197,000
With estimated outstanding mortgage balance of	$ 127,300
With estimated selling costs of:	$ 14,405
Anticipated net proceeds would be:	$ 55,295

Signature: *A. Salesperson*

NB: The recipient of the above information acknowledges by reading, reviewing or receiving such information that the information may not be accurate or current or correct and agrees to indemnify, save harmless and release, the Brokerage, sales representative or broker by whom the information was prepared, from all manner of actions, causes of action, suits or claims of any kind whatsoever.

◼ Exercise 3   The Overpriced Property

Ten possible answers are included:

- Qualified buyers who might otherwise have purchased the property do not seriously consider the home, as it is beyond their price range.
- Property may become stale as motivated buyers pass on the property. Showings which do occur are usually for comparative shopping (i.e., to demonstrate attractive pricing of other listings).
- Staleness can lead to buyers thinking that something is possibly wrong with the property (over and above the unrealistic listing price).
- The seller may have to reduce the price below fair market value to revive interest in the property.
- If the price is reduced, bargain hunters are attracted hoping the seller is under pressure to sell.
- The property may sit on the market for a long time and not attract any offers. If the seller has committed himself/herself to another property, he/she may feel pressured into accepting the first offer that appears even if it is below market value.
- If the property does not sell, the advertising expenses paid by the brokerage may be wasted.
- If the property does not sell, the image of the brokerage, the broker or salesperson are potentially affected.
- If the home remains unsold, the seller may blame the broker or salesperson for not working hard enough even though the real reason involves overpricing.

- If the salesperson can't get the seller to reduce the price, the broker or salesperson may lose interest in trying to sell the property.

▣ Exercise 4   The Anxious Seller

REBBA 2002 and the Competition Act

Ad may be judged false and misleading based on the following:

- Is this vacant land or a building lot; i.e., is a building permit available?
- *Best building site:* If representations are made, these must be fully supportable.
- *Seller take back:* What constitutes easy terms? Seller's instruction about 50% down is not an easy term.
- See Sec. 47 of the *Competition Act* and Sec. 37 of the Code of Ethics.

Other Comments

The salesperson is not working in the best interests of the client by advertising other than the listed price (Code of Ethics, Sec. 4). The salesperson must include the full registered name of the employing brokerage (Code of Ethics, Sec. 36).

APPENDIX

CHAPTER 7
ANALYZING THE AGREEMENT

Chapter Mini-Review

1. An agreement for sale provides that title is retained by the seller until some future stipulated date or until some future event occurs.

    True   False

   An agreement for sale typically requires sequential payments over a period of time before title is transferred.

2. A non-owner, for purposes of an agreement of purchase and sale, could be an individual having power of attorney or a person being an estate trustee (executor) to an estate.

    True   False

   A non-owner could also include an *in trust* arrangement.

3. A Certificate of Appointment is required by a corporation in order to sign an agreement of purchase and sale when acquiring or disposing of real property.

    True   **False**

   A Certificate of Appointment relates to an estate sale, not to the signing of documents by a corporation.

4. A survey can be attached as a schedule to an agreement of purchase and sale only if a proper legal description is not available.

    True   **False**

   A survey can be attached as a schedule to any agreement of purchase and sale depending on the circumstances.

5. Minor variations in lot dimensions might be tolerated by the courts if such were slight and unimportant.

    True   False

   While this statement is true, the challenge rests in determining what is insignificant and appropriate caution is advised.

6. All deposits relating to the *Agreement of Purchase and Sale* (OREA Form 100) must be deposited within two banking days of receipt.

    True   **False**

   The deposit must be made within five business days of receipt.

7. A seller has the right to remove all chattels, while all fixtures remain with the land (unless otherwise specified in the agreement).

    True   False

   The seller has this right, but remember that problems can arise if items on the property are not correctly identified as included or excluded.

8. Rental equipment located on the property must be assumed by the buyer according to the *Agreement of Purchase and Sale* (OREA Form 100).

    True   **False**

   The wording in the offer regarding rental equipment only applies to such items that can be assumed, not *all* rental items located on the property would be included.

APPENDIX

9. The term *irrevocable* broadly refers to any instruction that is incapable of being recalled or revoked.

 True   False

Make certain that parties signing an agreement of sale are aware that they are signing under seal. If a dispute arises regarding this issue, seek legal counsel.

10. The fax number and/or email address of the co-operating brokerage should be inserted in the appropriate space under *Notices* when that co-operating broker is not representing the buyer.

 True   **False**

The fax number and/or email address of the co-operating brokerage is inserted when that co-operating brokerage is representing the buyer.

11. Most residential resale transactions do not attract harmonized sales tax.

 True   False

This is a true statement, but registrants should always be mindful that the vast majority are exempt, but not all.

12. The requisition period in the *Agreement of Purchase and Sale* (OREA Form 100) provides the opportunity to examine title, including matters that go to the root of that title.

 True   False

Root of title issues must be reported by legal counsel within the requisition period.

13. A lawyer's personal undertaking may be required to delay discharging a mortgage until after the completion date.

 True   False

In some instances, mortgages may not be discharged for several days following closing.

14. No right of reinspection is included in the *Agreement of Purchase and Sale* (OREA Form 100), but a buyer may negotiate such a right with the seller.

 True   False

The pre-printed clause only states that the buyer has had the opportunity to inspect the property. A separate clause is necessary for reinspection.

15. If substantial damage occurs to a house prior to the completion date, the agreement will be automatically terminated.

 True   **False**

The buyer may elect to take any insurance proceeds and complete the transaction.

16. The deed in a real estate transaction is typically prepared at the buyer's cost.

 True   **False**

The deed is typically prepared at the seller's cost.

17. Section 116 of the *Income Tax Act* imposes a tax liability on the buyer.

 True   False

The Act also has procedures to alleviate that liability.

18. If a property is a matrimonial home, the non-owner spouse must sign both the spousal consent and also sign as one of the sellers.

 True   **False**

The non-owner spouse only signs the spousal consent.

APPENDIX

19. Contracts are generally assignable at common law.

 True   ◯ False

Contracts are assignable, but the obligations under that contract remain with the person who originally signed the contract.

20. The salesperson who drafts the agreement of purchase and sale must witness all signatures affixed to that agreement.

◯ True   ✔ **False**

Any competent person can witness a signature.

21. Commission to a co-operating brokerage is the first disbursement made from the commission trust account when a listing brokerage processes commission funds received relating to a closed transaction.

 True   ◯ False

The co-operating brokerage is paid first, followed by salespersons within the brokerage and, lastly, to the brokerage general account.

Active Learning Exercises

■ **Exercise 1   Scenarios**

1.1 The Jones' are signing an offer concerning their home in Westville. Jim is the owner and Ruth, his spouse, is not on title but paid for half of the home when they were married. *James R. Jones and Ruth B. Jones* has been inserted on the line for Seller.

◯ Acceptable   ✔ **Not Acceptable**

Ruth Jones should not be identified on the Seller line. She should sign under *Spousal Consent*.

1.2 Mary Sanchez intends to act as a trustee for her sister's estate. The salesperson inserts the following on the Seller line: *Mary Sanchez—Estate Trustee Status Pending*.

◯ Acceptable   ✔ **Not Acceptable**

Problems can arise if a Certificate of Appointment is not obtained.

1.3 Salesperson Sanjay attaches a schedule to the offer dated October 3, 20xx between Seller Wellington and Buyer Chin. He writes the following at the top of the schedule: *Schedule B Attached and Forming Part of an Agreement of Purchase and Sale dated October 3, 20xx; Seller: Wellington; Buyer: Chin.* He has both parties affix their initials.

✅ **Acceptable**   ◯ Not Acceptable

Schedule is properly labelled, cross-referenced and initialed.

1.4 Salesperson Smith describes chattels included with the sale as follows: *Fridge, stove and dishwasher.*

◯ Acceptable   ✅ **Not Acceptable**

Description vague. Buyer has no protection should appliances be switched.

1.5 Salesperson Lee prepares an offer with a condition expiring on March 15th and a requisition date of March 12th.

◯ Acceptable   ✅ **Not Acceptable**

The time to search title should extend beyond the expiry of any condition.

1.6 Neither the buyer nor the seller are certain whether HST applies. The salesperson in a multiple representation inserts the following in Clause 7: *Included In.*

◯ Acceptable   ✅ **Not Acceptable**

Including HST in the purchase price could impact the seller, if HST does apply. The salesperson should seriously consider including a condition in the offer to further investigate HST status.

1.7 The salesperson insists that the buyers and sellers initial at the bottom of page 1 of the *Agreement of Purchase and Sale* (OREA Form 100).

✅ **Acceptable**   ◯ Not Acceptable

Initialing confirms that both parties reviewed Page 1.

1.8 The buyer signs an agreement on April 23, 200x with an irrevocable date of April 25th. The agreement is subsequently accepted verbally by Mr. Chung, the seller on April 23rd at 2 p.m.. However, his spouse (also an owner) cannot be reached until the following day. At 3 p.m. on April 24th, she signs acceptance and Mr. Chung is reached at his office where he signs an hour later confirming his verbal acceptance of April 23rd. The Confirmation of Acceptance reads as follows: …*was finally executed by all parties at 3 p.m. on this 24th day of April, 200x.*

◯ Acceptable   ✅ **Not Acceptable**

The agreement was finally executed at 4:00 p.m. by Mr. Chung.

APPENDIX

1.9 The buyer hears from a friend that the seller has no intention of moving out of the home, despite the fact that only three days remain until completion date. Firmly believing that the property will not close, the buyer drops by the seller's house and demands access to see if the rumours are true. If so, he will instruct the lawyer to tender documents the next morning.

◯ Acceptable   ✔ **Not Acceptable**

The buyer cannot demand access to the property prior to closing under the terms of the *Agreement of Purchase and Sale* (unless some authority was granted by way of a clause). The buyer is also instructing the lawyer in error. Tendering cannot occur until the date set for completion.

1.10 The salesperson drafts an agreement including a seller take back mortgage. He advises the seller that the buyer must provide evidence of adequate insurance relating to the mortgagee's (seller's) interest on completion.

✔ **Acceptable**   ◯ Not Acceptable

The salesperson is correctly describing the buyer's obligation pursuant to Clause 14—Insurance.

1.11 The seller is married but her spouse does not have joint ownership in the matrimonial home, which is now being sold. When presenting an offer on OREA Form 100, the buyer representative insists that a clause be inserted in the agreement. The clause would provide a warranty by the seller to the buyer that the consent of the seller's spouse is not required.

◯ Acceptable   ✔ **Not Acceptable**

Such a clause is not required, as this wording is already contained in Clause 22—*Family Law Act*.

1.12 The sellers insist that the OREA *Agreement of Purchase and Sale* is technically wrong and wants the salesperson to stroke out all references to '*I*' and insert '*We*'. The salesperson agrees.

◯ Acceptable   ✔ **Not Acceptable**

Clause 26—Agreement in Writing already contemplates this situation.

1.13 The buyer has not yet selected a lawyer and the salesperson inserts the words '*To be Advised*' in the acknowledgement space, but emphasizes that the buyer make the selection as soon as possible.

✔ **Acceptable**   ◯ Not Acceptable

Buyers and sellers are not obligated to have a lawyer in order to sign the acknowledgement. However, a salesperson should take appropriate steps to obtain this information as soon as possible. It should be noted that only a lawyer can register title under the electronic registration system. Therefore, both the buyer and seller will require a lawyer in order to close a transaction

APPENDIX

CH7 EX2 ■ **Exercise 2   Multiple Choice**

2.1 Which one of the following statements is correct with respect to the *Notices* clause in OREA's Agreement of Purchase and Sale?

a. **A Listing Brokerage's fax number must not be entered into the *Notices* clause if the brokerage also represents the buyer.**

✔ *CORRECT.* Entering the listing brokerage's fax number in a multiple representation situation could result in a serious conflict of interest.

b. Fax numbers must always be entered into the *Notices* clause in OREA's Agreement of Purchase and Sale.

Incorrect. The section for fax numbers may be left blank as it is up to the parties to the transaction to decide whether they want to use fax numbers or not. Of course, buyers and/or sellers are free to decide that they wish to have their own fax number (home/business) put into the *Notices* clause irrespective of whether they are represented or not.

c. A co-operating brokerage's fax number can only be entered into the *Notices* clause if the buyer is a customer of that brokerage.

Incorrect. A co-operating brokerage that has the buyer as a customer should not enter that brokerage's fax number into the *Notices* clause as this would imply a representation relationship where one did not exist.

d. A brokerage's fax number must never be entered into the *Notices* clause since the clause specifically states that only the buyer/seller's fax number can be entered.

Incorrect. There is nothing in the *Notices* clause that prohibits a brokerage from entering their fax numbers in certain situations i.e. where the listing brokerage only represents the seller, the brokerage's fax number may be entered into the seller section; where the co-operating brokerage represents the buyer, the co-operating brokerage's fax number may be entered into the buyer section.

2.2 An irrevocable instruction regarding how long an offer remains open for acceptance is:

a. **Generally binding if signed under seal.**

✔ *CORRECT.* An irrevocable instruction is generally binding if signed under seal, notwithstanding some legal debate on the issue.

b. Established by legal counsel for the buyer and seller after offer acceptance.

Incorrect. The irrevocable instruction is established at point of making an offer.

c. Not applicable for most offers involving residential property.

Incorrect. The irrevocable offer is an integral part of residential and commercial negotiations.

d. Mandated to be no more than 48 hours from signing of the agreement.

Incorrect. No such mandate exists.

APPENDIX

2.3 According to the *Agreement of Purchase and Sale* (OREA Form 100) the buyer accepts title subject to certain exceptions. Which is NOT one of them? **This question requires that the *incorrect* option be identified.**

CH7   EX2

a. Relevant items specifically set out in the agreement.

This option is correct. The form does provide that certain exceptions can be set out in the agreement.

b. **Ownership issues that go to the root of title.**

✓ *THIS IS THE INCORRECT STATEMENT.* Ownership issues that go to the root of title are not permissible exceptions.

c. Registered restrictions or covenants which are complied with.

This option is correct. The form does provide for exceptions involving registered restrictions or covenants which are complied with.

d. Minor utility easements.

This option is correct. Minor utility easements are valid exceptions.

2.4 Which of the following statements is correct?

a. Root of title issues and matters of title are the same thing and the terms can be used interchangeably.

Incorrect. The terms *root of title* and *matters of title* cannot be used interchangeably.

b. The current zoning must always be inserted under present use in Clause 8 of the *Agreement of Purchase and Sale.*

Incorrect. This line can be left blank. The agreement provides that if nothing is inserted, its present use may be lawfully continued.

c. **Inserting the word *included* in Clause 7 (HST) places the risk on the seller should the property be subject to HST.**

✓ *CORRECT.* The seller would then be responsible should the property be subject to HST and, consequently, added to the selling price.

d. The preprinted wording of the OREA *Agreement of Purchase and Sale* provides for a completion no later than 11:59 p.m. on the completion date set out.

Incorrect. The preprinted wording of the *Agreement of Purchase and Sale* (OREA Form 100) provides for a completion no later than 6 p.m. on the completion date set out in the agreement.

APPENDIX

2.5 In setting out details concerning buyers and sellers in an agreement of purchase and sale, which of the following is NOT correct? **This question requires that the *incorrect* option be identified.**

a. Insert full identity of all partners when including a partnership as a buyer or seller.

This option is correct. The full identity of all partners should be included.

b. Use legal names for buyers and sellers when completing the offer.

This option is correct. Legal names for buyers and sellers should be used. Initials are acceptable as part of the legal name; e.g., middle name(s).

c. Use the corporate seal or insert the words: I/We have the authority to bind the corporation.

This option is correct. Use the corporate seal or insert the applicable words.

d. **Always include both spouses as sellers when dealing with a married couple.**

✔ *THIS IS THE INCORRECT STATEMENT.* One of the spouses may not be an owner and should not be included as such in the agreement of purchase and sale.

2.6 Clause 3–Notices generally provides:

a. **Authority for the listing brokerage and co-operating brokerage to give and receive notices on behalf of their respective clients.**

✔ *CORRECT.* Clause 3 involves notices on behalf of clients.

b. Authority for the listing brokerage and co-operating brokerage to give and receive notices on behalf of their respective customers.

Incorrect. Clause 3 involves notices on behalf of clients, not customers.

c. Authority for the listing brokerage and co-operating brokerage to sign agreements of purchase and sale on behalf of their clients.

Incorrect. Clause 3 does not refer to such an authority.

d. Authority for the listing brokerage and co-operating brokerage to amend agreements on behalf of their clients.

Incorrect. Clause 3 does not refer to such an authority.

APPENDIX

2.7   Which of the following statements is NOT correct? **This question requires that the** *incorrect* **option be identified.**

a.   A person signing in trust is not generally liable for contracts signed under seal.

This is correct. A person signing in trust is not generally liable for contracts signed under seal, but legal advice is strongly recommended regarding such matters.

b.   All legally authorized estate trustees of a property should sign the agreement of purchase and sale when selling that property.

This is correct. Legal as well as practical issues can arise if an agreement does not have all legally authorized estate trustees.

c.   The deposit is typically held by the listing brokerage.

This is correct. The listing brokerage typically holds the deposit.

d.   The title search clause in the *Agreement of Purchase and Sale* (OREA Form 100) provides only one time period for title and related searches.

✅ *THIS IS THE INCORRECT STATEMENT.* Two time periods are provided, the first concerning the title search and the second regarding such matters as work orders.

🔲 Exercise 3   Errors and Omissions

- Only one witness signature, but two buyers' signatures.
- One of the buyers does not date the signature.
- The seller's signature is beyond the irrevocable date.
- The seller's signature is not witnessed.
- The Confirmation of Acceptance is signed before the seller accepts and after the irrevocable date has expired.
- The wrong person is signing the Confirmation of Acceptance. If Sandhu accepted the initial Metzger offer, then the seller should execute the accepted agreement.
- Only one buyer signed the acknowledgement.
- The Acknowledgement section is signed after the expiry of the offer.
- The Commission Trust section is not signed.

🔲 Exercise 4   The Fine Print

- Clause 8 (Title Search) makes the offer conditional on title examination regarding work orders, deficiencies, continuation of present use and building insurability.
- Clause 10 (Title) further provides that title must be good and free from all registered restrictions, charges, liens and encumbrances subject to various provisos set out in the wording.
- Clause 14 (Insurance), while not creating a specific condition, does provide for agreement termination in the event of substantial damage before closing.
- Clause 15 (Planning Act) provides for compliance with the subdivision control provisions of the *Planning Act.*

APPENDIX

CHAPTER 8
DRAFTING OFFERS: PART 1

Chapter Mini-Review

1. All brokerages in Ontario must use the *Agreement of Purchase and Sale* (OREA Form 100).

    True   **False**

   The *Agreement of Purchase and Sale* (OREA Form 100) is widely used, but not mandatory.

2. Cheat sheets are seldom used and have been discouraged by the Real Estate Council of Ontario and real estate boards.

    True   **False**

   Cheat sheets (or their electronic counterparts) are widely used, as they provide a consistent approach to offer drafting within brokerages.

3. When two brokerages are involved with respective clients in a real estate transaction, the *Individual Identification Information Form* must be completed by the co-operating brokerage, but not by the listing brokerage.

    True   **False**

   Each brokerage must complete the applicable form (i.e., individual or corporate/entity) for their respective clients.

4. The Receipt of Funds Record must be prepared for every amount of funds received by a real estate brokerage.

    True   **False**

   While this record is required in most instances, there are exceptions including funds received from a government agency.

5. A mandatary is required for identification verification of a buyer client from another country, when a face-to-face meeting is not possible.

    True   False

   A mandatary is required and a contractual agreement must be established with the mandatary.

6. The deposit is always the difference between the agreed price and the amount inserted in the *pay the balance as follows* line.

    True   **False**

   This formula is correct for an all cash offer, but does not apply in other circumstances such as when the buyer is assuming an existing mortgage.

7. The completion date normally follows the title search date by two or three days.

    True   **False**

   Sufficient time must be allowed to properly complete a search. Recall that root of title and matters of title issues must both be addressed. Search periods are typically 30 days or more, depending on circumstances involving a specific property and associated negotiations.

8. Deposit increases can be accomplished through multiple payments provided that times, dates and amounts are stated in the agreement.

 True   False

The use of multiple deposit payments will vary based on locale and current market conditions. Typically, these are not commonly found in lower priced properties, but are more prevalent when dealing with expensive properties.

9. A buyer who deliberately withholds a deposit may be in breach of the contract.

 True   False

The decision by a Court will depend on circumstances, but generally if a deliberate decision was made not to pay the deposit, a breach of the contract would occur.

10. The decision to use a representation/ warranty or other clause; e.g., acknowledgement or statement of agreed facts, is typically dictated by circumstances.

 True   False

Exact wordings will vary by circumstance to meet specific needs.

11. A delay in the delivery of a deposit by a co-operating brokerage can jeopardize the listing brokerage's ability to satisfy depositing requirements set out in the *Real Estate and Business Brokers Act, 2002*.

 True   False

The maximum permissible time is five business days following receipt, regardless of delays between the co-operating brokerage and listing brokerage.

12. A right to access clause must always include a provision that such access by the buyer shall be at reasonable times and only upon sufficient notice to the seller.

 True   False

A right to access clause can vary depending on circumstances, as well as the express wishes of the person making the offer.

13. An acknowledgement clause cannot be inserted that overrides the preprinted portion of an agreement of purchase and sale.

 True   False

An acknowledgement clause can override the preprinted portion of the agreement. Registrants should always be cautious in doing so.

14. In drafting any action to be taken, the words *authorizes* and *directs* must always be inserted.

 True   False

As with most clauses, wordings can be adjusted to suit circumstances.

15. The order of acknowledgements, representations and agreed facts clauses within an agreement of purchase and sale is normally at the option of the person drafting the offer.

 True   False

Ordering of clauses is a matter of personal preference, but the order should be logical and sequential.

APPENDIX

16. FINTRAC deems that a business relationship is effectively established whenever a brokerage conducts three or more transactions with a client within a two-year period.

 True **False**

A business relationship is effectively established whenever a brokerage conducts two or more transactions with a client within a five-year period. The business relationship expires if there are less than two transactions within a five-year period. Transactions relate to a purchase and/or sale.

17. Real estate brokerages have an obligation to conduct a risk assessment of all corporate clients with respect to the possibility of money laundering or terrorist financing. The obligation to conduct a risk assessment does not extend to clients who are private individuals.

 True **False**

This obligation applies to every client, including individuals, corporations, and other entities. Other entities could include a trust, a partnership, a fund, or an unincorporated association or organization.

Active Learning Exercises

▣ Exercise 1   Matching

Match the words in the right column with the appropriate descriptions in the left column (not all descriptions are used).

h.	Represents/Warrants Clause	Survive Closing
e.	Admission or Affirmation That Something Exists	Acknowledgement
f.	Purchase Price Minus Deposit, Mortgage Assumptions and Seller Take Backs	Pay the Balance as Follows: Amount
a.	It is Understood and Agreed	Agreed Facts
b.	Potential Basis for Rescinding a Contract	False Representation
c.	Offer Plan	Offer Mathematics
d.	Co-operating Brokerage	Deposit Receipt

No Match: g., and i.

▣ Exercise 2   Six Components

1.	By Whom?
2.	Amount?
3.	Adjustments?
4.	To Whom?
5.	When to be Paid?
6.	How to be Paid?

APPENDIX

◼ Exercise 3   Clause Analysis

3.1 The buyer agrees to pay a further sum of Ten Thousand Dollars to ABC Realty Inc., by cheque, at the time of notification or fulfillment or removal of the condition pertaining to arranging a new first mortgage, as an additional deposit to be held in trust pending completion of this agreement. This amount is to be credited toward the deposit on completion of this transaction.

◯ Acceptable   ✔ Not Acceptable

Suggested Wording: The buyer agrees to pay a further sum of Ten Thousand Dollars **($10,000.00)** to ABC Realty Inc. by **negotiable** cheque, at the time of notification or fulfillment or removal of the condition pertaining to arranging a new first mortgage, as an additional deposit to be held in trust pending completion or **other termination** of this agreement. Such payments are to be credited towards the **purchase price** on completion of this transaction.

3.2 The buyer represents and warrants that on completion, the satellite receiver and associated equipment, as further detailed under Chattels in this agreement, shall be in good working order. The parties agree that this representation and warranty shall survive and not merge on completion of this transaction, but apply only to the state of the property existing at completion of this transaction.

◯ Acceptable   ✔ Not Acceptable

Suggested Wording: The **seller** represents and warrants …

The cross-reference wording regarding further description under Chattels is acceptable, as equipment specifics (e.g., model/serial number and accessory descriptions) should be detailed under that pre-printed clause.

3.3 The buyer and seller agree that the representations and warranties stated herein shall survive and merge on completion of this transaction.

◯ Acceptable   ✔ Not Acceptable

Suggested Wording: The buyer and seller agree that the representations and warranties stated herein shall survive and **not** merge on completion of this transaction.

3.4 The buyer shall have the right to inspect the property one further time at completion, provided that notice is given to the seller. The seller agrees to provide access to the property for the purpose of this inspection.

◯ Acceptable   ✔ Not Acceptable

Suggested Wording: The buyer shall have the right to inspect the property one further time **prior to** completion, provided that **written** notice is given to the seller. The seller agrees to provide access to the property for the purpose of this inspection.

◼ Exercise 4   The Jones/Brown All Cash Offer

See the following pages for the completed offer. A solution is not provided regarding completion of the *Individual Identification Information Record* and the *Receipt of Funds*, as various fictitious details must be provided by the student.

APPENDIX

OREA Ontario Real Estate Association

Agreement of Purchase and Sale

Form 100
for use in the Province of Ontario

This Agreement of Purchase and Sale dated this ......**16th**...... day of ....**July**........................ 20...**XX**...

BUYER, ...**Ronald A. Jones and Cathy W. Brown**........................, agrees to purchase from
(Full legal names of all Buyers)

SELLER, ...**Yvonne J. Racine and Scott P. Racine**........................, the following
(Full legal names of all Sellers)

REAL PROPERTY:

Address ....**224 Stevenson Avenue**........................

fronting on the ....**South**................ side of ....**Stevenson Avenue**................

in the ....**City of Anycity, Regional Municipality of Anyregion**................

and having a frontage of ....**39.55 feet**............ more or less by a depth of ....**120.20 feet**............ more or less

and legally described as ....**Lot 12, Registered Plan 4332 subject to a mutual rear drive**............

.... (the "property")
(Legal description of land including easements not described elsewhere)

PURCHASE PRICE:　　　　　　　　　　　　　　　Dollars (CDN$) ......**$231,000.00**......

......**Two Hundred and Thirty-One Thousand**-- Dollars

DEPOSIT: Buyer submits ....**Upon Acceptance**........................
(Herewith/Upon Acceptance/as otherwise described in this Agreement)

......**Ten Thousand**-- Dollars (CDN$) ......**$10,000.00**......

by negotiable cheque payable to ....**ABC Realty Inc.**........................ "Deposit Holder" to be held in trust pending completion or other termination of this Agreement and to be credited toward the Purchase Price on completion. For the purposes of this Agreement, "Upon Acceptance" shall mean that the Buyer is required to deliver the deposit to the Deposit Holder within 24 hours of the acceptance of this Agreement. The parties to this Agreement hereby acknowledge that, unless otherwise provided for in this Agreement, the Deposit Holder shall place the deposit in trust in the Deposit Holder's non-interest bearing Real Estate Trust Account and no interest shall be earned, received or paid on the deposit.

Buyer agrees to pay the balance as more particularly set out in Schedule A attached.

SCHEDULE(S) A..**attached hereto form(s) part of this Agreement.**

1. **IRREVOCABILITY:** This offer shall be irrevocable by ....**Buyer**................ until ....**6:00**.... ~~a.m.~~/p.m. on the ....**18th**....
   (Seller/Buyer)

   day of ....**July**................ 20 ..**XX**.., after which time, if not accepted, this offer shall be null and void and the deposit shall be returned to the Buyer in full without interest.

2. **COMPLETION DATE:** This Agreement shall be completed by no later than 6:00 p.m. on the ....**16th**.... day of ....**September**............

   20 ..**XX**...... Upon completion, vacant possession of the property shall be given to the Buyer unless otherwise provided for in this Agreement.

INITIALS OF BUYER(S): (*RJ CB*)　　　　INITIALS OF SELLER(S): (　　)

Form 100　Revised 2015　**Page 1 of 6**

APPENDIX

3. **NOTICES:** The Seller hereby appoints the Listing Brokerage as agent for the Seller for the purpose of giving and receiving notices pursuant to this Agreement. Where a Brokerage (Buyer's Brokerage) has entered into a representation agreement with the Buyer, the Buyer hereby appoints the Buyer's Brokerage as agent for the purpose of giving and receiving notices pursuant to this Agreement. **Where a Brokerage represents both the Seller and the Buyer (multiple representation), the Brokerage shall not be appointed or authorized to be agent for either the Buyer or the Seller for the purpose of giving and receiving notices.** Any notice relating hereto or provided for herein shall be in writing. In addition to any provision contained herein and in any Schedule hereto, this offer, any counter-offer, notice of acceptance thereof or any notice to be given or received pursuant to this Agreement or any Schedule hereto (any of them, "Document") shall be deemed given and received when delivered personally or hand delivered to the Address for Service provided in the Acknowledgement below, or where a facsimile number or email address is provided herein, when transmitted electronically to that facsimile number or email address, respectively, in which case, the signature(s) of the party (parties) shall be deemed to be original.

FAX No.: ....   FAX No.: ....
            (For delivery of Documents to Seller)   (For delivery of Documents to Buyer)

Email Address: ....   Email Address: ....
            (For delivery of Documents to Seller)   (For delivery of Documents to Buyer)

4. **CHATTELS INCLUDED:** Draperies and decorator rods in the master bedroom, living room, and dining room; swimming pool accessories including PoolClean vacuum, hoses, and hand skimmer

Unless otherwise stated in this Agreement or any Schedule hereto, Seller agrees to convey all fixtures and chattels included in the Purchase Price free from all liens, encumbrances or claims affecting the said fixtures and chattels.

5. **FIXTURES EXCLUDED:** Built-in bookcases located on north wall of the family room

6. **RENTAL ITEMS (Including Lease, Lease to Own):** The following equipment is rented and **not** included in the Purchase Price. The Buyer agrees to assume the rental contract(s), if assumable:

Rental hot water tank, Anycity Energy payable $33.50 quarterly (plus taxes)

The Buyer agrees to co-operate and execute such documentation as may be required to facilitate such assumption.

7. **HST:** If the sale of the Property (Real Property as described above) is subject to Harmonized Sales Tax (HST), then such tax shall be
.... included in .... the Purchase Price. If the sale of the Property is not subject to HST, Seller agrees to certify on or before
     (included in/in addition to)
closing, that the sale of the Property is not subject to HST. Any HST on chattels, if applicable, is not included in the Purchase Price.

INITIALS OF BUYER(S): (RJ CB)   INITIALS OF SELLER(S): ( )

Form 100   Revised 2015   **Page 2 of 6**

8. **TITLE SEARCH:** Buyer shall be allowed until 6:00 p.m. on the ....1st.... day of ....September...................., 20..XX...., (Requisition Date) to examine the title to the Property at Buyer's own expense and until the earlier of: (i) thirty days from the later of the Requisition Date or the date on which the conditions in this Agreement are fulfilled or otherwise waived or; (ii) five days prior to completion, to satisfy Buyer that there are no outstanding

work orders or deficiency notices affecting the Property, and that its present use (..................single family residential..................) may be lawfully continued and that the principal building may be insured against risk of fire. Seller hereby consents to the municipality or other governmental agencies releasing to Buyer details of all outstanding work orders and deficiency notices affecting the property, and Seller agrees to execute and deliver such further authorizations in this regard as Buyer may reasonably require.

9. **FUTURE USE:** Seller and Buyer agree that there is no representation or warranty of any kind that the future intended use of the property by Buyer is or will be lawful except as may be specifically provided for in this Agreement.

10. **TITLE:** Provided that the title to the property is good and free from all registered restrictions, charges, liens, and encumbrances except as otherwise specifically provided in this Agreement and save and except for (a) any registered restrictions or covenants that run with the land providing that such are complied with; (b) any registered municipal agreements and registered agreements with publicly regulated utilities providing such have been complied with, or security has been posted to ensure compliance and completion, as evidenced by a letter from the relevant municipality or regulated utility; (c) any minor easements for the supply of domestic utility or telephone services to the property or adjacent properties; and (d) any easements for drainage, storm or sanitary sewers, public utility lines, telephone lines, cable television lines or other services which do not materially affect the use of the property. If within the specified times referred to in paragraph 8 any valid objection to title or to any outstanding work order or deficiency notice, or to the fact the said present use may not lawfully be continued, or that the principal building may not be insured against risk of fire is made in writing to Seller and which Seller is unable or unwilling to remove, remedy or satisfy or obtain insurance save and except against risk of fire (Title Insurance) in favour of the Buyer and any mortgagee, (with all related costs at the expense of the Seller), and which Buyer will not waive, this Agreement notwithstanding any intermediate acts or negotiations in respect of such objections, shall be at an end and all monies paid shall be returned without interest or deduction and Seller, Listing Brokerage and Co-operating Brokerage shall not be liable for any costs or damages. Save as to any valid objection so made by such day and except for any objection going to the root of the title, Buyer shall be conclusively deemed to have accepted Seller's title to the property.

11. **CLOSING ARRANGEMENTS:** Where each of the Seller and Buyer retain a lawyer to complete the Agreement of Purchase and Sale of the property, and where the transaction will be completed by electronic registration pursuant to Part III of the Land Registration Reform Act, R.S.O. 1990, Chapter L4 and the Electronic Registration Act, S.O. 1991, Chapter 44, and any amendments thereto, the Seller and Buyer acknowledge and agree that the exchange of closing funds, non-registrable documents and other items (the "Requisite Deliveries") and the release thereof to the Seller and Buyer will (a) not occur at the same time as the registration of the transfer/deed (and any other documents intended to be registered in connection with the completion of this transaction) and (b) be subject to conditions whereby the lawyer(s) receiving any of the Requisite Deliveries will be required to hold same in trust and not release same except in accordance with the terms of a document registration agreement between the said lawyers. The Seller and Buyer irrevocably instruct the said lawyers to be bound by the document registration agreement which is recommended from time to time by the Law Society of Upper Canada. Unless otherwise agreed to by the lawyers, such exchange of the Requisite Deliveries will occur in the applicable Land Titles Office or such other location agreeable to both lawyers.

12. **DOCUMENTS AND DISCHARGE:** Buyer shall not call for the production of any title deed, abstract, survey or other evidence of title to the property except such as are in the possession or control of Seller. If requested by Buyer, Seller will deliver any sketch or survey of the property within Seller's control to Buyer as soon as possible and prior to the Requisition Date. If a discharge of any Charge/Mortgage held by a corporation incorporated pursuant to the Trust And Loan Companies Act (Canada), Chartered Bank, Trust Company, Credit Union, Caisse Populaire or Insurance Company and which is not to be assumed by Buyer on completion, is not available in registrable form on completion, Buyer agrees to accept Seller's lawyer's personal undertaking to obtain, out of the closing funds, a discharge in registrable form and to register same, or cause same to be registered, on title within a reasonable period of time after completion, provided that on or before completion Seller shall provide to Buyer a mortgage statement prepared by the mortgagee setting out the balance required to obtain the discharge, and, where a real-time electronic cleared funds transfer system is not being used, a direction executed by Seller directing payment to the mortgagee of the amount required to obtain the discharge out of the balance due on completion.

13. **INSPECTION:** Buyer acknowledges having had the opportunity to inspect the Property and understands that upon acceptance of this offer there shall be a binding agreement of purchase and sale between Buyer and Seller. **The Buyer acknowledges having the opportunity to include a requirement for a property inspection report in this Agreement and agrees that except as may be specifically provided for in this Agreement, the Buyer will not be obtaining a property inspection or property inspection report regarding the Property.**

14. **INSURANCE:** All buildings on the property and all other things being purchased shall be and remain until completion at the risk of Seller. Pending completion, Seller shall hold all insurance policies, if any, and the proceeds thereof in trust for the parties as their interests may appear and in the event of substantial damage, Buyer may either terminate this Agreement and have all monies paid returned without interest or deduction or else take the proceeds of any insurance and complete the purchase. No insurance shall be transferred on completion. If Seller is taking back a Charge/Mortgage, or Buyer is assuming a Charge/Mortgage, Buyer shall supply Seller with reasonable evidence of adequate insurance to protect Seller's or other mortgagee's interest on completion.

INITIALS OF BUYER(S): (*RJ CB*)   INITIALS OF SELLER(S): ( )

Form 100   Revised 2015   **Page 3 of 6**

15. PLANNING ACT: This Agreement shall be effective to create an interest in the property only if Seller complies with the subdivision control provisions of the Planning Act by completion and Seller covenants to proceed diligently at Seller's expense to obtain any necessary consent by completion.

16. DOCUMENT PREPARATION: The Transfer/Deed shall, save for the Land Transfer Tax Affidavit, be prepared in registrable form at the expense of Seller, and any Charge/Mortgage to be given back by the Buyer to Seller at the expense of the Buyer. If requested by Buyer, Seller covenants that the Transfer/Deed to be delivered on completion shall contain the statements contemplated by Section 50(22) of the Planning Act, R.S.O.1990.

17. RESIDENCY: (a) Subject to (b) below, the Seller represents and warrants that the Seller is not and on completion will not be a non-resident under the non-residency provisions of the Income Tax Act which representation and warranty shall survive and not merge upon the completion of this transaction and the Seller shall deliver to the Buyer a statutory declaration that Seller is not then a non-resident of Canada; (b) provided that if the Seller is a non-resident under the non-residency provisions of the Income Tax Act, the Buyer shall be credited towards the Purchase Price with the amount, if any, necessary for Buyer to pay to the Minister of National Revenue to satisfy Buyer's liability in respect of tax payable by Seller under the non-residency provisions of the Income Tax Act by reason of this sale. Buyer shall not claim such credit if Seller delivers on completion the prescribed certificate.

18. ADJUSTMENTS: Any rents, mortgage interest, realty taxes including local improvement rates and unmetered public or private utility charges and unmetered cost of fuel, as applicable, shall be apportioned and allowed to the day of completion, the day of completion itself to be apportioned to Buyer.

19. PROPERTY ASSESSMENT: The Buyer and Seller hereby acknowledge that the Province of Ontario has implemented current value assessment and properties may be re-assessed on an annual basis. The Buyer and Seller agree that no claim will be made against the Buyer or Seller, or any Brokerage, Broker or Salesperson, for any changes in property tax as a result of a re-assessment of the property, save and except any property taxes that accrued prior to the completion of this transaction.

20. TIME LIMITS: Time shall in all respects be of the essence hereof provided that the time for doing or completing of any matter provided for herein may be extended or abridged by an agreement in writing signed by Seller and Buyer or by their respective lawyers who may be specifically authorized in that regard.

21. TENDER: Any tender of documents or money hereunder may be made upon Seller or Buyer or their respective lawyers on the day set for completion. Money shall be tendered with funds drawn on a lawyer's trust account in the form of a bank draft, certified cheque or wire transfer using the Large Value Transfer System.

22. FAMILY LAW ACT: Seller warrants that spousal consent is not necessary to this transaction under the provisions of the Family Law Act, R.S.O.1990 unless Seller's spouse has executed the consent hereinafter provided.

23. UFFI: Seller represents and warrants to Buyer that during the time Seller has owned the property, Seller has not caused any building on the property to be insulated with insulation containing ureaformaldehyde, and that to the best of Seller's knowledge no building on the property contains or has ever contained insulation that contains ureaformaldehyde. This warranty shall survive and not merge on the completion of this transaction, and if the building is part of a multiple unit building, this warranty shall only apply to that part of the building which is the subject of this transaction.

24. LEGAL, ACCOUNTING AND ENVIRONMENTAL ADVICE: The parties acknowledge that any information provided by the brokerage is not legal, tax or environmental advice.

25. CONSUMER REPORTS: The Buyer is hereby notified that a consumer report containing credit and/or personal information may be referred to in connection with this transaction.

26. AGREEMENT IN WRITING: If there is conflict or discrepancy between any provision added to this Agreement (including any Schedule attached hereto) and any provision in the standard pre-set portion hereof, the added provision shall supersede the standard pre-set provision to the extent of such conflict or discrepancy. This Agreement including any Schedule attached hereto, shall constitute the entire Agreement between Buyer and Seller. There is no representation, warranty, collateral agreement or condition, which affects this Agreement other than as expressed herein. For the purposes of this Agreement, Seller means vendor and Buyer means purchaser. This Agreement shall be read with all changes of gender or number required by the context.

27. TIME AND DATE: Any reference to a time and date in this Agreement shall mean the time and date where the property is located.

INITIALS OF BUYER(S): (*RJ CB*)   INITIALS OF SELLER(S): (   )

Form 100   Revised 2015   **Page 4 of 6**

28. SUCCESSORS AND ASSIGNS: The heirs, executors, administrators, successors and assigns of the undersigned are bound by the terms herein.

SIGNED, SEALED AND DELIVERED in the presence of: IN WITNESS whereof I have hereunto set my hand and seal:

Linda Ward ....   *Cathy Brown* ....   ● .... DATE *July 16/xx*
(Witness)   (Buyer)   (Seal)

Linda Ward ....   *Ronald Jones* ....   ● .... DATE *July 16/xx*
(Witness)   (Buyer)   (Seal)

I, the Undersigned Seller, agree to the above offer. I hereby irrevocably instruct my lawyer to pay directly to the brokerage(s) with whom I have agreed to pay commission, the unpaid balance of the commission together with applicable Harmonized Sales Tax (and any other taxes as may hereafter be applicable), from the proceeds of the sale prior to any payment to the undersigned on completion, as advised by the brokerage(s) to my lawyer.

SIGNED, SEALED AND DELIVERED in the presence of: IN WITNESS whereof I have hereunto set my hand and seal:

....   ● .... DATE ....
(Witness)   (Seller)   (Seal)

....   ● .... DATE ....
(Witness)   (Seller)   (Seal)

SPOUSAL CONSENT: The Undersigned Spouse of the Seller hereby consents to the disposition evidenced herein pursuant to the provisions of the Family Law Act, R.S.O.1990, and hereby agrees with the Buyer that he/she will execute all necessary or incidental documents to give full force and effect to the sale evidenced herein.

....   ● .... DATE ....
(Witness)   (Spouse)   (Seal)

CONFIRMATION OF ACCEPTANCE: Notwithstanding anything contained herein to the contrary, I confirm this Agreement with all changes both typed and written was finally accepted by all parties at .... a.m./p.m. this .... day of..., 20...........

....
(Signature of Seller or Buyer)

INFORMATION ON BROKERAGE(S)

Listing Brokerage .... ABC Realty Inc. .... Tel.No.(416) 444-1212

123 Main Street, Anycity   Albert Lee
                                  (Salesperson / Broker Name)

Co-op/Buyer Brokerage .... XYZ Real Estate Limited .... Tel.No.(416) 333-1212

15 Centre Street, Anycity   Linda Ward
                                  (Salesperson / Broker Name)

ACKNOWLEDGEMENT

I acknowledge receipt of my signed copy of this accepted Agreement of Purchase and Sale and I authorize the Brokerage to forward a copy to my lawyer.   I acknowledge receipt of my signed copy of this accepted Agreement of Purchase and Sale and I authorize the Brokerage to forward a copy to my lawyer.

.... DATE .... DATE ....
(Seller)   (Buyer)

.... DATE .... DATE ....
(Seller)   (Buyer)

Address for Service ....   Address for Service ....

.... Tel.No.(.........)...........   .... Tel.No.(.........)...........

Seller's Lawyer ....   Buyer's Lawyer ....

Address ....   Address ....

Email ....   Email ....

(.........)...........   (.........)...........   (.........)...........   (.........)...........
       Tel.No.   FAX No.   Tel.No.   FAX No.

FOR OFFICE USE ONLY   **COMMISSION TRUST AGREEMENT**

To: Co-operating Brokerage shown on the foregoing Agreement of Purchase and Sale:
In consideration for the Co-operating Brokerage procuring the foregoing Agreement of Purchase and Sale, I hereby declare that all moneys received or receivable by me in connection with the Transaction as contemplated in the MLS® Rules and Regulations of my Real Estate Board shall be receivable and held in trust. This agreement shall constitute a Commission Trust Agreement as defined in the MLS® Rules and shall be subject to and governed by the MLS® Rules pertaining to Commission Trust.

DATED as of the date and time of the acceptance of the foregoing Agreement of Purchase and Sale.   Acknowledged by:

....
(Authorized to bind the Listing Brokerage)   (Authorized to bind the Co-operating Brokerage)

Form 100   Revised 2015   **Page 5 of 6**

 **Ontario Real Estate Association**

Schedule A

Agreement of Purchase and Sale

Form 100
for use in the Province of Ontario

This Schedule is attached to and forms part of the Agreement of Purchase and Sale between:

BUYER, ... Ronald A. Jones and Cathy W. Brown ...., and

SELLER, ... Yvonne J. Racine and Scott P. Racine ....

for the purchase and sale of .... 224 Stevenson Avenue, City of Anycity, Regional Municipality of Anyregion

.... dated the ..16th.. day of .... July ...., 20.. xx ..

Buyer agrees to pay the balance as follows:

The Buyer agrees to pay a further sum of Ten Thousand Dollars ($10,000.00) to ABC Realty Inc. by negotiable cheque not later than 5:00 p.m. on the 28th day of July, 20xx, as a supplementary deposit to be held in trust in the same manner as the initial deposit pending completion or other termination of this Agreement. This amount is to be credited towards the purchase price on completion of this transaction.

The Buyer agrees to pay a further sum of Two Hundred and Eleven Thousand Dollars ($211,000.00), subject to adjustments, to the Seller on completion of this transaction, with funds drawn on a lawyer's trust account in the form of a bank draft, a certified cheque, or wire transfer using the Large Value Transfer System.

The Seller represents and warrants to the best of the Seller's knowledge and belief, that the swimming pool, its equipment, and the fencing of the said pool comply with all applicable bylaws, regulations, and legislation; and that the swimming pool and equipment are now and on the completion date shall be in good working order. The Parties agree that this representation and warranty shall survive and not merge on completion of this transaction, but apply only to the state of the property existing at completion of this transaction.

The Seller agrees to repair any damage caused by the removal of the built-in bookcases in the family room, and repaint the entire applicable family room wall prior to completion at the Seller's expense.

This form must be initialed by all parties to the Agreement of Purchase and Sale.

INITIALS OF BUYER(S): *RJ CB*   **INITIALS OF SELLER(S):**

Form 100 Revised 2015   **Page 6 of 6**

CHAPTER 9
DRAFTING OFFERS: PART 2

Chapter Mini-Review

1. A condition precedent would normally include a reference as to who is to perform the condition and at whose expense?

 True   False

Who is to perform the condition and at whose expense are two of several requirements in a properly structured condition precedent.

2. In a condition precedent, neither party has the right to waive the condition, unless a waiver provision is included.

 True   False

The law has established that neither party has the automatic and unilateral right to waive a condition, unless such is provided for in the agreement.

3. An escape clause may result in a buyer waiving a condition before it is fulfilled.

 True   False

The waiver allows the party with the condition to give up his or her conditional protection and proceed with the agreement.

4. A waiver provision can be used with condition subsequent.

 True   **False**

No waiver provision is necessary as a binding contract is in place (unless terminated in accordance with the condition).

5. Any condition relating to a home inspection must not include a waiver provision.

 True   **False**

A waiver provision can be used, as the party requesting the home inspection may wish to waive the condition, even if it has not been met.

6. An escape clause allows the seller to continue to offer the property for sale following acceptance of a conditional offer.

 True   False

The escape clause is commonly associated with conditions relating to the sale of the buyer's property.

7. A typical residential home inspection takes between two and three hours to complete.

 True   False

Two to three hours is typical, but length of time will vary based on the specific property.

8. A pre-listing home inspection can be helpful as it provides the seller with information to remedy potential problem areas prior to offering the property for sale.

 True   False

The pre-listing inspection can be helpful, but is not widely found in the marketplace.

9. A stacked multiple condition can potentially avoid lengthy and cumbersome individual conditions, each with its respective time period and waiver provision.

 ✔ **True**   ◯ False

Multiple conditions can be an effective way to handle complex situations involving several conditions.

11. If the purchase price is $300,000, the deposit is $30,000 and a mortgage taken back by the seller is $200,000, the *pay the balance as follows* amount is $70,000.

✔ **True**   ◯ False

The answer is arrived at by subtracting the deposit and mortgage take back from the purchase price.

10. Mortgage assumptions for residential property do not typically require the mortgagee's approval.

 ◯ True   ✔ **False**

Most mortgage assumptions in today's market require mortgagee approval.

12. A postponement provision in a second mortgage is normally included if the expiry date of the second mortgage precedes the expiry of the first mortgage.

◯ True   ✔ **False**

A postponement is normally included if the expiry date of the first mortgage precedes the expiry date of the second.

Active Learning Exercises

 Exercise 1   Multiple Choice

1.1 Which of the following statements is correct?

a. With condition subsequent, a binding contract is created if the condition is fulfilled or waived.

Incorrect. A condition subsequent is binding unless terminated in accordance with the condition wording. A waiver does not apply.

b. A condition precedent involving a land severance is typically a true condition precedent.

 CORRECT. The condition must be fulfilled for the contract to be binding.

c. In an agreement, the title search period must be shorter than the longest conditional period.

Incorrect. The reverse is true. The title search period must be longer than the longest conditional period.

d. The waiver provision provides that the seller may continue to offer the property for sale.

Incorrect. An escape clause provides for this possibility.

APPENDIX

1.2 One of the most notable benefits of a professional home inspection is:

a. The determination of the presence or absence of hazardous substances.

Incorrect. Items such as hazardous substances and other environmental issues are typically excluded in a home inspection report.

b. The assistance given in estimating market value.

Incorrect. The home inspection report is not involved with estimating market value.

c. The assessment of the strength of internal structural components.

Incorrect. The inspection report does not address structural strength, but concentrates on a visual inspection relating to the present condition of visible housing components.

d. **A report including systems or components in need of immediate repair.**

✔ *CORRECT.* A professional home inspection provides a report that includes systems or components in need of immediate repair.

1.3 Based on legal issues reviewed in this chapter, which of the following is NOT correct? **This question requires that the *incorrect* option be identified.**

a. Clear words are vital when developing conditional clauses.

This option is correct. Clear words are essential.

b. Buyers should act honestly in performing conditions and not in a capricious manner.

This option is correct. Honesty is necessary.

c. Terms of a condition should be diligently performed.

This option is correct. Terms of a condition need to be diligently performed.

d. **The Court has little regard for specific condition wordings if a dispute arises.**

✔ *THIS IS THE INCORRECT OPTION.* Wordings are carefully scrutinized should a dispute arise.

1.4 An escape clause:

a. Must be inserted if the conditional period exceeds 30 days.

Incorrect. The decision regarding number of days is a matter of judgement and negotiations.

b. Must have a 48-hour time limit for waiving condition(s) after receiving notice.

Incorrect. The decision regarding the time limit is a matter of judgement and negotiations.

c. Is always used with a condition precedent involving the sale of the buyer's property.

Incorrect. The decision to use or not use an escape clause is a matter of judgement and negotiations.

d. **Might be included with a condition based on market circumstances and the length of the conditional period.**

✔ *CORRECT.* An escape clause might be included with a condition based on market circumstances and the length of the conditional period.

APPENDIX

1.5 A mortgage condition requiring that the buyer be approved for a mortgage, through the same lender who currently has a first mortgage on the property:

CH9 EX1

a. Would include a waiver provision.

Incorrect. A waiver would not be used, as this scenario is a true condition precedent.

b. **Would not include a waiver provision.**

✔ *CORRECT.* No waiver provision is needed, as the condition must be fulfilled in order to make the contract binding.

c. Must include both a waiver provision and an escape clause.

Incorrect. A waiver would not be used and an escape clause is not a '*must*' and, in fact, would not be typically used.

d. None of the above.

Incorrect. One of the alternate responses is correct.

1.6 Which of the following is a correct statement?

a. **A typical postponement clause provides that if additional monies are advanced by way of a new first mortgage, the excess must be paid to reduce the second mortgage.**

✔ *CORRECT.* This provision protects the interests of the second mortgage.

b. A renewal clause must only provide for a single renewal of a mortgage.

Incorrect. A renewal clause can provide for one or more renewals and also include stipulations.

c. Seller take backs require the same approval process, as would be undertaken had the buyer secured financing through a lending institution.

Incorrect. A typical seller would not normally apply mortgage underwriting rules usual to a conventional lender.

d. A seller who decides to take back a mortgage is not typically required to report interest received on that mortgage until the mortgage term has ended.

Incorrect. Interest is typically deemed to be income for the year in which it was received.

▣ Exercise 2   Offer Drafting

CH9 EX2

See the following pages for the completed offer.

Clause   *SPB-3: Condition—Seller's Release from Previous Offer*

APPENDIX

CH9 **EX2**

OREA Ontario Real Estate Association   # Agreement of Purchase and Sale

Form 100
for use in the Province of Ontario

This Agreement of Purchase and Sale dated this ......**1st**...... day of ....**September**.......................... 20...**XX**...

BUYER, ...**Douglas M. Huber and Ella C. Huber**.............., agrees to purchase from
(Full legal names of all Buyers)

SELLER, ...**Betty W. Favreau and Denise B. Strauss**.............., the following
(Full legal names of all Sellers)

REAL PROPERTY:

Address ....**832 Wentworth Drive**.......................................

fronting on the ....**South**.............. side of ....**Wentworth Drive**..............

in the ....**City of Anycity, Regional Municipality of Anyregion**..............

and having a frontage of ....**46.50 feet**.......... more or less by a depth of ....**109.30 feet**.......... more or less

and legally described as ......**Pt. Lot 7, Concession IV, more specifically described as Part 1,**......

..............**Reference Plan 99R 3816**.............. (the "property")
(Legal description of land including easements not described elsewhere)

PURCHASE PRICE: Dollars (CDN$) ......**$289,500.00**......

Two Hundred Eighty-Nine Thousand Five Hundred-- Dollars

DEPOSIT: Buyer submits ....**Upon Acceptance**..............
(Herewith/Upon Acceptance/as otherwise described in this Agreement)

Fifteen Thousand-- Dollars (CDN$) ......**$15,000.00**......

by negotiable cheque payable to ....**ABC Realty Inc.**.............. "Deposit Holder" to be held
in trust pending completion or other termination of this Agreement and to be credited toward the Purchase Price on completion. For the purposes of this
Agreement, "Upon Acceptance" shall mean that the Buyer is required to deliver the deposit to the Deposit Holder within 24 hours of the acceptance of
this Agreement. The parties to this Agreement hereby acknowledge that, unless otherwise provided for in this Agreement, the Deposit Holder shall place
the deposit in trust in the Deposit Holder's non-interest bearing Real Estate Trust Account and no interest shall be earned, received or paid on the deposit.

Buyer agrees to pay the balance as more particularly set out in Schedule A attached.

SCHEDULE(S) A..**attached hereto form(s) part of this Agreement.**

1. **IRREVOCABILITY:** This offer shall be irrevocable by ....**Buyer**.............. until ......**6:00**...... a.m./p.m. on the ......**3rd**......
(Seller/Buyer)

    day of ....**September**.............. 20 ..**XX**.., after which time, if not accepted, this offer shall be null and void and the deposit
shall be returned to the Buyer in full without interest.

2. **COMPLETION DATE:** This Agreement shall be completed by no later than 6:00 p.m. on the ......**1st**...... day of ....**December**..........

    20 ..**XX**...... Upon completion, vacant possession of the property shall be given to the Buyer unless otherwise provided for in this Agreement.

INITIALS OF BUYER(S): (*DH EH*)   **INITIALS OF SELLER(S):** ( )

Form 100   Revised 2015   **Page 1 of 6**

APPENDIX

3.   NOTICES: The Seller hereby appoints the Listing Brokerage as agent for the Seller for the purpose of giving and receiving notices pursuant to this Agreement. Where a Brokerage (Buyer's Brokerage) has entered into a representation agreement with the Buyer, the Buyer hereby appoints the Buyer's Brokerage as agent for the purpose of giving and receiving notices pursuant to this Agreement. **Where a Brokerage represents both the Seller and the Buyer (multiple representation), the Brokerage shall not be appointed or authorized to be agent for either the Buyer or the Seller for the purpose of giving and receiving notices.** Any notice relating hereto or provided for herein shall be in writing. In addition to any provision contained herein and in any Schedule hereto, this offer, any counter-offer, notice of acceptance thereof or any notice to be given or received pursuant to this Agreement or any Schedule hereto (any of them, "Document") shall be deemed given and received when delivered personally or hand delivered to the Address for Service provided in the Acknowledgement below, or where a facsimile number or email address is provided herein, when transmitted electronically to that facsimile number or email address, respectively, in which case, the signature(s) of the party (parties) shall be deemed to be original.

FAX No.: ....   FAX No.: ....
           (For delivery of Documents to Seller)   (For delivery of Documents to Buyer)

Email Address: ....   Email Address: ....
           (For delivery of Documents to Seller)   (For delivery of Documents to Buyer)

4.   CHATTELS INCLUDED: DigiScan satellite receiver Model 5000, including two converters
....
....
....
....

Unless otherwise stated in this Agreement or any Schedule hereto, Seller agrees to convey all fixtures and chattels included in the Purchase Price free from all liens, encumbrances or claims affecting the said fixtures and chattels.

5.   FIXTURES EXCLUDED: None
....
....
....
....
....

6.   RENTAL ITEMS (Including Lease, Lease to Own): The following equipment is rented and **not** included in the Purchase Price. The Buyer agrees to assume the rental contract(s), if assumable:

    Hot water tank, Anycity Energy, $33.50 per qtr. (plus taxes); AquaClean Model 2200 water

      softener, $18.00/mo. (plus taxes)

The Buyer agrees to co-operate and execute such documentation as may be required to facilitate such assumption.

7.   HST: If the sale of the Property (Real Property as described above) is subject to Harmonized Sales Tax (HST), then such tax shall be

.... included in .... the Purchase Price. If the sale of the Property is not subject to HST, Seller agrees to certify on or before
       (0included in/in addition to)

closing, that the sale of the Property is not subject to HST. Any HST on chattels, if applicable, is not included in the Purchase Price.

INITIALS OF BUYER(S): (*DH EH*)   INITIALS OF SELLER(S): (   )

Form 100   Revised 2015   **Page 2 of 6**

8. **TITLE SEARCH:** Buyer shall be allowed until 6:00 p.m. on the ......15th..... day of ....November.................., 20..XX...., (Requisition Date) to examine the title to the Property at Buyer's own expense and until the earlier of: (i) thirty days from the later of the Requisition Date or the date on which the conditions in this Agreement are fulfilled or otherwise waived or; (ii) five days prior to completion, to satisfy Buyer that there are no outstanding

work orders or deficiency notices affecting the Property, and that its present use (...............single family residential...............) may be lawfully continued and that the principal building may be insured against risk of fire. Seller hereby consents to the municipality or other governmental agencies releasing to Buyer details of all outstanding work orders and deficiency notices affecting the property, and Seller agrees to execute and deliver such further authorizations in this regard as Buyer may reasonably require.

9. **FUTURE USE:** Seller and Buyer agree that there is no representation or warranty of any kind that the future intended use of the property by Buyer is or will be lawful except as may be specifically provided for in this Agreement.

10. **TITLE:** Provided that the title to the property is good and free from all registered restrictions, charges, liens, and encumbrances except as otherwise specifically provided in this Agreement and save and except for (a) any registered restrictions or covenants that run with the land providing that such are complied with; (b) any registered municipal agreements and registered agreements with publicly regulated utilities providing such have been complied with, or security has been posted to ensure compliance and completion, as evidenced by a letter from the relevant municipality or regulated utility; (c) any minor easements for the supply of domestic utility or telephone services to the property or adjacent properties; and (d) any easements for drainage, storm or sanitary sewers, public utility lines, telephone lines, cable television lines or other services which do not materially affect the use of the property. If within the specified times referred to in paragraph 8 any valid objection to title or to any outstanding work order or deficiency notice, or to the fact the said present use may not lawfully be continued, or that the principal building may not be insured against risk of fire is made in writing to Seller and which Seller is unable or unwilling to remove, remedy or satisfy or obtain insurance save and except against risk of fire (Title Insurance) in favour of the Buyer and any mortgagee, (with all related costs at the expense of the Seller), and which Buyer will not waive, this Agreement notwithstanding any intermediate acts or negotiations in respect of such objections, shall be at an end and all monies paid shall be returned without interest or deduction and Seller, Listing Brokerage and Co-operating Brokerage shall not be liable for any costs or damages. Save as to any valid objection so made by such day and except for any objection going to the root of the title, Buyer shall be conclusively deemed to have accepted Seller's title to the property.

11. **CLOSING ARRANGEMENTS:** Where each of the Seller and Buyer retain a lawyer to complete the Agreement of Purchase and Sale of the property, and where the transaction will be completed by electronic registration pursuant to Part III of the Land Registration Reform Act, R.S.O. 1990, Chapter L4 and the Electronic Registration Act, S.O. 1991, Chapter 44, and any amendments thereto, the Seller and Buyer acknowledge and agree that the exchange of closing funds, non-registrable documents and other items (the "Requisite Deliveries") and the release thereof to the Seller and Buyer will (a) not occur at the same time as the registration of the transfer/deed (and any other documents intended to be registered in connection with the completion of this transaction) and (b) be subject to conditions whereby the lawyer(s) receiving any of the Requisite Deliveries will be required to hold same in trust and not release same except in accordance with the terms of a document registration agreement between the said lawyers. The Seller and Buyer irrevocably instruct the said lawyers to be bound by the document registration agreement which is recommended from time to time by the Law Society of Upper Canada. Unless otherwise agreed to by the lawyers, such exchange of the Requisite Deliveries will occur in the applicable Land Titles Office or such other location agreeable to both lawyers.

12. **DOCUMENTS AND DISCHARGE:** Buyer shall not call for the production of any title deed, abstract, survey or other evidence of title to the property except such as are in the possession or control of Seller. If requested by Buyer, Seller will deliver any sketch or survey of the property within Seller's control to Buyer as soon as possible and prior to the Requisition Date. If a discharge of any Charge/Mortgage held by a corporation incorporated pursuant to the Trust And Loan Companies Act (Canada), Chartered Bank, Trust Company, Credit Union, Caisse Populaire or Insurance Company and which is not to be assumed by Buyer on completion, is not available in registrable form on completion, Buyer agrees to accept Seller's lawyer's personal undertaking to obtain, out of the closing funds, a discharge in registrable form and to register same, or cause same to be registered, on title within a reasonable period of time after completion, provided that on or before completion Seller shall provide to Buyer a mortgage statement prepared by the mortgagee setting out the balance required to obtain the discharge, and, where a real-time electronic cleared funds transfer system is not being used, a direction executed by Seller directing payment to the mortgagee of the amount required to obtain the discharge out of the balance due on completion.

13. **INSPECTION:** Buyer acknowledges having had the opportunity to inspect the Property and understands that upon acceptance of this offer there shall be a binding agreement of purchase and sale between Buyer and Seller. **The Buyer acknowledges having the opportunity to include a requirement for a property inspection report in this Agreement and agrees that except as may be specifically provided for in this Agreement, the Buyer will not be obtaining a property inspection or property inspection report regarding the Property.**

14. **INSURANCE:** All buildings on the property and all other things being purchased shall be and remain until completion at the risk of Seller. Pending completion, Seller shall hold all insurance policies, if any, and the proceeds thereof in trust for the parties as their interests may appear and in the event of substantial damage, Buyer may either terminate this Agreement and have all monies paid returned without interest or deduction or else take the proceeds of any insurance and complete the purchase. No insurance shall be transferred on completion. If Seller is taking back a Charge/Mortgage, or Buyer is assuming a Charge/Mortgage, Buyer shall supply Seller with reasonable evidence of adequate insurance to protect Seller's or other mortgagee's interest on completion.

INITIALS OF BUYER(S): (*DH EH*)   INITIALS OF SELLER(S): ( )

Form 100   Revised 2015   **Page 3 of 6**

15. **PLANNING ACT:** This Agreement shall be effective to create an interest in the property only if Seller complies with the subdivision control provisions of the Planning Act by completion and Seller covenants to proceed diligently at Seller's expense to obtain any necessary consent by completion.

16. **DOCUMENT PREPARATION:** The Transfer/Deed shall, save for the Land Transfer Tax Affidavit, be prepared in registrable form at the expense of Seller, and any Charge/Mortgage to be given back by the Buyer to Seller at the expense of the Buyer. If requested by Buyer, Seller covenants that the Transfer/Deed to be delivered on completion shall contain the statements contemplated by Section 50(22) of the Planning Act, R.S.O.1990.

17. **RESIDENCY:** (a) Subject to (b) below, the Seller represents and warrants that the Seller is not and on completion will not be a non-resident under the non-residency provisions of the Income Tax Act which representation and warranty shall survive and not merge upon the completion of this transaction and the Seller shall deliver to the Buyer a statutory declaration that Seller is not then a non-resident of Canada; (b) provided that if the Seller is a non-resident under the non-residency provisions of the Income Tax Act, the Buyer shall be credited towards the Purchase Price with the amount, if any, necessary for Buyer to pay to the Minister of National Revenue to satisfy Buyer's liability in respect of tax payable by Seller under the non-residency provisions of the Income Tax Act by reason of this sale. Buyer shall not claim such credit if Seller delivers on completion the prescribed certificate.

18. **ADJUSTMENTS:** Any rents, mortgage interest, realty taxes including local improvement rates and unmetered public or private utility charges and unmetered cost of fuel, as applicable, shall be apportioned and allowed to the day of completion, the day of completion itself to be apportioned to Buyer.

19. **PROPERTY ASSESSMENT:** The Buyer and Seller hereby acknowledge that the Province of Ontario has implemented current value assessment and properties may be re-assessed on an annual basis. The Buyer and Seller agree that no claim will be made against the Buyer or Seller, or any Brokerage, Broker or Salesperson, for any changes in property tax as a result of a re-assessment of the property, save and except any property taxes that accrued prior to the completion of this transaction.

20. **TIME LIMITS:** Time shall in all respects be of the essence hereof provided that the time for doing or completing of any matter provided for herein may be extended or abridged by an agreement in writing signed by Seller and Buyer or by their respective lawyers who may be specifically authorized in that regard.

21. **TENDER:** Any tender of documents or money hereunder may be made upon Seller or Buyer or their respective lawyers on the day set for completion. Money shall be tendered with funds drawn on a lawyer's trust account in the form of a bank draft, certified cheque or wire transfer using the Large Value Transfer System.

22. **FAMILY LAW ACT:** Seller warrants that spousal consent is not necessary to this transaction under the provisions of the Family Law Act, R.S.O.1990 unless Seller's spouse has executed the consent hereinafter provided.

23. **UFFI:** Seller represents and warrants to Buyer that during the time Seller has owned the property, Seller has not caused any building on the property to be insulated with insulation containing ureaformaldehyde, and that to the best of Seller's knowledge no building on the property contains or has ever contained insulation that contains ureaformaldehyde. This warranty shall survive and not merge on the completion of this transaction, and if the building is part of a multiple unit building, this warranty shall only apply to that part of the building which is the subject of this transaction.

24. **LEGAL, ACCOUNTING AND ENVIRONMENTAL ADVICE:** The parties acknowledge that any information provided by the brokerage is not legal, tax or environmental advice.

25. **CONSUMER REPORTS: The Buyer is hereby notified that a consumer report containing credit and/or personal information may be referred to in connection with this transaction.**

26. **AGREEMENT IN WRITING:** If there is conflict or discrepancy between any provision added to this Agreement (including any Schedule attached hereto) and any provision in the standard pre-set portion hereof, the added provision shall supersede the standard pre-set provision to the extent of such conflict or discrepancy. This Agreement including any Schedule attached hereto, shall constitute the entire Agreement between Buyer and Seller. There is no representation, warranty, collateral agreement or condition, which affects this Agreement other than as expressed herein. For the purposes of this Agreement, Seller means vendor and Buyer means purchaser. This Agreement shall be read with all changes of gender or number required by the context.

27. **TIME AND DATE:** Any reference to a time and date in this Agreement shall mean the time and date where the property is located.

INITIALS OF BUYER(S): (*DH EH*)   INITIALS OF SELLER(S): (   )

28. SUCCESSORS AND ASSIGNS: The heirs, executors, administrators, successors and assigns of the undersigned are bound by the terms herein.

SIGNED, SEALED AND DELIVERED in the presence of: IN WITNESS whereof I have hereunto set my hand and seal:

Mike Sandler   *Doug Huber*   ⬤ (Seal)   DATE ..... *Sept. 1/xx* .....
(Witness)   (Buyer)

Mike Sandler   *Ella Huber*   ⬤ (Seal)   DATE ..... *Sept. 1/xx* .....
(Witness)   (Buyer)

I, the Undersigned Seller, agree to the above offer. I hereby irrevocably instruct my lawyer to pay directly to the brokerage(s) with whom I have agreed to pay commission, the unpaid balance of the commission together with applicable Harmonized Sales Tax (and any other taxes as may hereafter be applicable), from the proceeds of the sale prior to any payment to the undersigned on completion, as advised by the brokerage(s) to my lawyer.

SIGNED, SEALED AND DELIVERED in the presence of: IN WITNESS whereof I have hereunto set my hand and seal:

....   ⬤ (Seal)   DATE ....
(Witness)   (Seller)

....   ⬤ (Seal)   DATE ....
(Witness)   (Seller)

SPOUSAL CONSENT: The Undersigned Spouse of the Seller hereby consents to the disposition evidenced herein pursuant to the provisions of the Family Law Act, R.S.O.1990, and hereby agrees with the Buyer that he/she will execute all necessary or incidental documents to give full force and effect to the sale evidenced herein.

....   ⬤ (Seal)   DATE ....
(Witness)   (Spouse)

CONFIRMATION OF ACCEPTANCE: Notwithstanding anything contained herein to the contrary, I confirm this Agreement with all changes both typed and written was finally accepted by all parties at .... a.m./p.m. this .... day of ...., 20..........

....
(Signature of Seller or Buyer)

INFORMATION ON BROKERAGE(S)

Listing Brokerage ..... **ABC Realty Inc.** ..... Tel.No.(**416**) **555-1212** .....
..... **123 Main Street, Anycity M3X 3C1** ..... **Albert Lee** .....
                                  (Salesperson / Broker Name)

Co-op/Buyer Brokerage ..... **XYZ Realty Inc.** ..... Tel.No.(**416**) **555-2121** .....
..... **28 Norfield Drive, Anycity M3X 4C6** ..... **Mike Sandler** .....
                                  (Salesperson / Broker Name)

ACKNOWLEDGEMENT

I acknowledge receipt of my signed copy of this accepted Agreement of Purchase and Sale and I authorize the Brokerage to forward a copy to my lawyer. | I acknowledge receipt of my signed copy of this accepted Agreement of Purchase and Sale and I authorize the Brokerage to forward a copy to my lawyer.

.... DATE .... | .... DATE ....
(Seller) | (Buyer)

.... DATE .... | .... DATE ....
(Seller) | (Buyer)
Address for Service .... | Address for Service ....
.... Tel.No.(..........). | .... Tel.No.(..........).
Seller's Lawyer .... | Buyer's Lawyer ....
Address .... | Address ....
Email .... | Email ....
(..........)................. (..........)................. | (..........)................. (..........).................
   Tel.No.   FAX No. | Tel.No.   FAX No.

FOR OFFICE USE ONLY   **COMMISSION TRUST AGREEMENT**

To: Co-operating Brokerage shown on the foregoing Agreement of Purchase and Sale:
In consideration for the Co-operating Brokerage procuring the foregoing Agreement of Purchase and Sale, I hereby declare that all moneys received or receivable by me in connection with the Transaction as contemplated in the MLS® Rules and Regulations of my Real Estate Board shall be receivable and held in trust. This agreement shall constitute a Commission Trust Agreement as defined in the MLS® Rules and shall be subject to and governed by the MLS® Rules pertaining to Commission Trust.
DATED as of the date and time of the acceptance of the foregoing Agreement of Purchase and Sale.   Acknowledged by:

....
(Authorized to bind the Listing Brokerage)   (Authorized to bind the Co-operating Brokerage)

Form 100   Revised 2015   **Page 5 of 6**

 **Ontario Real Estate Association**

Schedule A
Agreement of Purchase and Sale

Form 100
for use in the Province of Ontario

This Schedule is attached to and forms part of the Agreement of Purchase and Sale between:

BUYER, ... Douglas M. Huber and Ella C. Huber .... , and

SELLER, ... Betty W. Favreau and Denise B. Strauss ....

for the purchase and sale of ..... 832 Wentworth Drive, City of Anycity, Regional Municipality of Anyregion .....

.... dated the ...1st... day of .... September .... , 20 **xx** .....

Buyer agrees to pay the balance as follows:

The Buyer agrees to pay a further sum of Ten Thousand Dollars ($10,000.00) to ABC Realty Inc. by negotiable cheque not later than 5:00 p.m. on the 15th day of September, 20xx, as a supplementary deposit to be held in trust in the same manner as the initial deposit pending completion or other termination of this Agreement. This amount is to be credited towards the purchase price on completion of this transaction.

The Buyer agrees to pay a further sum of Two Hundred and Sixty-Four Thousand Five Hundred Dollars ($264,500.00), subject to adjustments, to the Seller on completion of this transaction, with funds drawn on a lawyer's trust account in the form of a bank draft, certified cheque, or wire transfer using the Large Value Transfer System.

This offer is conditional upon:
* The inspection of the subject property by a home inspector at the Buyer's own expense, and the obtaining of a report satisfactory to the Buyer in the Buyer's sole and absolute discretion.
* The sale of the Buyer's property known as 320 Maple Lane, West City.

Unless the Buyer gives notice in writing delivered to the Seller personally or in accordance with any other provisions for the delivery of notice in this Agreement of Purchase and Sale or any Schedule thereto not later than 5:00 p.m. on the 1st day of November, 20xx, that these conditions are fulfilled, this Offer shall be null and void and the deposit shall be returned to the Buyer in full without deduction. The Seller agrees to co-operate in providing access to the property for the purpose of this inspection. These conditions are included for the benefit of the Buyer and may be waived at the Buyer's sole option by notice in writing to the Seller as aforesaid within the time period stated herein.

Provided further that the Seller may continue to offer the property for sale and in the event the Seller receives another Offer satisfactory to the Seller, the Seller may so notify the Buyer in writing by delivery to the Buyer personally or in accordance with any other provisions for the delivery of notice in this Agreement of Purchase and Sale or any Schedule thereto. The Buyer shall have 48 hours from the giving of such notice to waive all conditions by notice in writing delivered to the Seller personally or in accordance with any other provisions for the delivery of notice in this Agreement of Purchase and Sale or any Schedule thereto, failing which this Offer shall be null and void, and the Buyer's deposit shall be returned in full without deduction.

The Seller represents and warrants that the damage to the garage doors shall be repaired at the Seller's expense and both doors shall be operating smoothly and in good working order on the completion date. The Parties agree that this representation and warranty shall survive and not merge on completion of this transaction, but apply only to the state of the property existing at completion of this transaction.

This form must be initialed by all parties to the Agreement of Purchase and Sale.

INITIALS OF BUYER(S):   **INITIALS OF SELLER(S):** ( )

Form 100   Revised 2015   **Page 6 of 6**

■ **Exercise 3   Identifying Errors and Omissions**

Buyer Name	Not correctly identified.
Legal Description	Upper tier municipality is missing; i.e., Regional Municipality of Anyregion.
Legal Description	Plan number is missing.
Deposit	Amount generally viewed as inadequate given offer price.
Irrevocable	Should read buyer, not seller.
HST	Incorrect entry: should read in addition to or included in.
Title Search	Title search time period ends prior to conditional period. The buyer may incur legal costs prior to removal of the condition.
Initials	Buyers' initials in wrong location.
Witness	Both signatures should be witnessed.
Pay a further sum clause	Amount should read as $237,000.
Pay a further sum clause	Missing *subject to adjustments* phrase.
Conditional Clause	Missing *at the buyer's own expense* phrase.
Conditional Clause	Missing *in full without deduction* phrase.
Conditional Clause	Conditional period is too long.

■ **Exercise 4   Critically Analyze Clauses**

Condition/Escape Clause

BUYER'S PERSPECTIVE	SELLER'S PERSPECTIVE
Limited time period to remove condition (should another offer appear) may not provide the buyer reasonable time to waive the condition; i.e., 18 hours. No provision for return of deposit, if condition not waived.	Extended conditional period (approx. 5 months) impacts marketability of seller's home. Market conditions are strong. Seller should seriously consider his or her options; i.e., not accepting this offer or limiting conditional period.

Represents/Warrants Clause

BUYER'S PERSPECTIVE	SELLER'S PERSPECTIVE
Wording is too vague. What does satisfactorily mean? Clause wording is incomplete.	Hot tub warranty clause is incomplete, as it should only apply to the state of the property on closing.

APPENDIX

Home Inspection Clause

BUYER'S PERSPECTIVE	SELLER'S PERSPECTIVE
Seller will be arranging an inspection. No assurances as to what will be provided. Buyer has no option should report prove unsatisfactory. Appropriate condition required permitting buyer to obtain report.	Seller will not likely be willing to provide an inspection report.

Right to Re-Inspect Clause

BUYER'S PERSPECTIVE	SELLER'S PERSPECTIVE
The buyer could technically re-inspect the property on numerous occasions and still not ultimately waive the condition.	Right has no limitation, except for reasonable notice and would not be advisable from the seller's perspective.

◼ Exercise 5   Clause Order

2	Chattels Included
4	First Mortgage Condition Clause
6	Postponement Clause
1	Purchase Price
5	Seller Take Back Clause
3	Title Search Period

NOTE: The first mortgage clause must not contain a waiver otherwise the buyer could waive the condition and arrange a mortgage for a higher amount, possibly resulting in the property being over financed to the detriment of the seller's security. In the alternative, MORT-15 could be included in the Seller Take Back mortgage.

◼ Exercise 6   Amending the Offer

Seller Take Back   Rule out last two sentences in the seller take back clause.

Prepayment   Insert more precise privilege that aligns with the amortization schedule. This clause avoids the payments of insignificant amounts that do not correctly align with payment dates. Further, such payments are easily tracked by the mortgagee.

Renewal   The renewal clause included in the offer is unacceptable, as it provides for mortgage renewal on the same terms and conditions (including the further right of renewal). The revised clause limits renewal to one additional three-year term.

Credit   Insert condition concerning credit worthiness. The Fergusons can then fully investigate the buyer prior to making a final decision.

APPENDIX

OREA Ontario Real Estate Association

Form 100
for use in the Province of Ontario

Schedule A
Agreement of Purchase and Sale

This Schedule is attached to and forms part of the Agreement of Purchase and Sale between:

BUYER, ... Mary J. O'Hara and Christopher P. O'Hara ...., and

SELLER, ... William C. Ferguson and Darlene P. Ferguson ....

for the purchase and sale of .... 3281 River Parkway, City of Anycity, Regional Municipality of Anyregion ....

.... dated the ...15th... day of .... April ...., 20.XX...

Buyer agrees to pay the balance as follows:

The Buyer agrees to pay a further sum of Seventy Thousand Dollars ($70,000.00), subject to adjustments, to the Seller on completion of this transaction, with funds drawn on a lawyer's trust account in the form of a bank draft, certified cheque, or wire transfer using the Large Value Transfer System.

The Seller agrees to take back a first Charge/Mortgage in the amount of Two Hundred Thousand Dollars ($200,000.00), bearing interest at the rate of 5.00% per annum, calculated semi-annually not in advance, repayable in blended monthly payments of One Thousand One Hundred and Sixty-Three Dollars and Twenty-One Cents ($1,163.21), including both principal and interest, and to run for a term of not less than three years from the date of completion of this transaction. ~~This Charge/Mortgage shall contain a clause permitting the prepaying of any or all of the principal sum outstanding at any time of times without notice or bonus. Said Charge/Mortgage shall be renewable at the sale option of the Buyer on the same terms and conditions.~~ *WF DF*

This Charge/Mortgage shall contain a clause permitting the Chargor/Mortgagor, when not in default, the privilege of prepaying all or part of the principal sum on any payment date or dates without notice or bonus, provided that any partial prepayment shall equal the sum of the principal amounts of the payment(s) next falling due under the Charge/Mortgage. *WF DF*

This Charge/Mortgage shall contain a clause permitting the Chargor/Mortgagor, when not in default, the privilege of renewing this Charge/Mortgage upon maturity, for a further term of three years at the rate of interest charged by Anycity Financial inc. on the date 30 days preceding the maturity date of the Charge/Mortgage, to credit worthy borrowers for three-year Charge/Mortgage loans, and otherwise the same terms and conditions save and except for the right of a further renewal. *WF DF*

This Offer is conditional upon the Seller being satisfied concerning the personal and/or credit worthiness of the Buyer. Unless the Seller gives notice in writing to the Buyer personally or in accordance with any other provisions for the delivery of notice in this Agreement of Purchase and Sale or any Schedule thereto not later than 11:59 p.m. on the 23rd day of April, 20xx, that this condition is fulfilled, this Offer shall be null and void and the deposit shall be returned to the Buyer in full without deduction. This condition is included for the benefit of the Seller and may be waived at the Seller's sole option by notice in writing to the Buyer as aforesaid within the time period state herein. *WF DF*

This form must be initialed by all parties to the Agreement of Purchase and Sale.

INITIALS OF BUYER(S): *MO CO*

INITIALS OF SELLER(S): *WF DF*

Form 100   Revised 2015   **Page 6 of 6**

CHAPTER 10
NEGOTIATING AGREEMENTS

Chapter Mini-Review

1. From a buyer's perspective, power in negotiations tends to increase as motivation decreases.

    True   False

   The buyer who doesn't have to make a decision wields the power.

2. Generally, the more you know about the buyer's needs and wants, the more productive the negotiations.

    True   False

   Productive negotiations and solutions typically lie within the prospect's needs and wants.

3. The parties who sign the Confirmation of Acceptance are usually the first to sign the Acknowledgement.

   True   False

   The Confirmation of Acceptance confirms agreement between the parties and, consequently, would receive a copy first.

4. The salesperson should always discuss the offered price with the seller when making an appointment to present an offer.

    True   **False**

   Discussing the offered price will overshadow other important terms and considerations. Negotiations regarding price are best done at the time of offer presentation in person.

5. The listing brokerage retains the signed copy of the agreement that has both the buyer's and seller's acknowledgements.

    True   False

   The original copy (i.e., the copy with buyer and seller signatures) is retained by the listing brokerage.

6. An accepted business practice is to provide lawyers, for the buyer and seller, with signed copies of the agreement.

    True   False

   This is a customary procedure throughout Ontario.

7. The seller would typically sign the Confirmation of Acceptance in a counter offer made by the seller and accepted by the buyer.

    True   **False**

   The buyer would sign the confirmation, not the seller.

8. In a competing offer situation, one of the options that a seller has is to refuse to sign any of the offers.

    True   False

   This might occur in a strong seller market, in which many buyers are competing for few properties.

APPENDIX

9. A transaction report can replace a trade record sheet provided that the brokerage has developed a specific office policy to that effect.

○ True   ✓ **False**

A transaction report, as commonly referred to in brokerages, is an office document that precedes the issuance of a trade record sheet.

10. Where the right to commission is contingent on sale completion, HST is due and payable on the date of completion.

✓ **True**   ○ False

HST is due and payable on the date of completion.

11. Employed salespersons (as differentiated from independent contractors) need not register for HST purposes and are not required to charge HST to their employers for commissions earned.

✓ **True**   ○ False

Conversely, most independent contractors must charge HST, unless income is below the minimum level, currently set at $30,000.

12. When using a waiver, registrants should insert the complete clause wording that is being waived.

✓ **True**   ○ False

This is done to avoid any possible confusion as to what is being waived.

13. The Privacy Code developed by The Canadian Real Estate Association applies to all RECO registrants.

○ True   ✓ **False**

The Privacy Code applies to members of organized real estate only. Other registrants can obtain relevant information directly from the Privacy Commissioner's office.

14. Explicit written consent is the best form of informed consent from a privacy legislation perspective.

✓ **True**   ○ False

Registrants should always seek explicit written consent.

APPENDIX

Active Learning Exercises

▣ Exercise 1   Competing Offers

- **Accept one offer.** Remaining buyers look for other properties. If the accepted offer falls through, the seller may have lost all interested buyers.
- **Counter one offer.** The buyer involved in the counter offer may wait until the last minute, not accept the counter and leave the seller with the possibility of no other offers.
- **Reject all offers.** Some or all buyers may not participate in further negotiations.

▣ Exercise 2   Fill-in-the-Blanks

2.1   That offer presentation really went smoothly. First of all, the salesperson from the `co-operating (or selling)` brokerage called to inform me of the offer made by a young couple. He referred to this as `registering` the offer. We met at the seller's house later in the afternoon and I presented the `co-operating` salesperson's offer.

2.2   The seller asked that he and I discuss the offer in private. He agreed to the terms, signed and dated his signature, and next completed the `Confirmation of Acceptance` to confirm the time when the offer was finally agreed upon.

2.3   I gave a copy of the agreement to him and he signed and dated his signature under the `Acknowledgement` section of the Agreement. I then went outside to meet with the other salesperson. He had waited in his car while the seller and I discussed the agreement. I handed him sufficient signed copies for the `buyers` and the `co-operating (or selling)` brokerage.

2.4   Of course, I have the original signed copy with Acknowledgements and also the other salesperson's signature and mine concerning the `Commission Trust Agreement` .

▣ Exercise 3   Drafting Offer/Counter Offer

See the following pages for the completed offer.

APPENDIX

OREA Ontario Real Estate Association   **Agreement of Purchase and Sale**

Form 100
for use in the Province of Ontario

This Agreement of Purchase and Sale dated this ......10th...... day of ....August.............. 20..XX..

BUYER, ...**Charles M. Leung**.............................., agrees to purchase from
(Full legal names of all Buyers)

SELLER, ...**Alexandra Vujovic**..............................., the following
(Full legal names of all Sellers)

REAL PROPERTY:

Address ....**1381 Pathfinder Road**........................

fronting on the ....**South**............ side of ....**Pathfinder Road**............

in the ....**City of Anycity, Regional Municipality of Anyregion**............

and having a frontage of ....**72.55 feet**........ more or less by a depth of ....**118.50 feet**........ more or less

and legally described as ....**Lots 11 and 12, Registered Plan 496 subject to a mutual drive**........

.... (the "property")
(Legal description of land including easements not described elsewhere)

                                                                    CL **$305,000.00** AV
PURCHASE PRICE: Dollars (CDN$) ~~$290,000.00~~
    Three Hundred and Five Thousand *CL* AV
    ~~Two-Hundred and Ninety Thousand~~--- Dollars

DEPOSIT: Buyer submits ....**Upon Acceptance**..................
                        (Herewith/Upon Acceptance/as otherwise described in this Agreement)

    Ten Thousand--- Dollars (CDN$) **$10,000.00**

by negotiable cheque payable to ....**ABC Realty Inc.**.................. "Deposit Holder" to be held
in trust pending completion or other termination of this Agreement and to be credited toward the Purchase Price on completion. For the purposes of this
Agreement, "Upon Acceptance" shall mean that the Buyer is required to deliver the deposit to the Deposit Holder within 24 hours of the acceptance of
this Agreement. The parties to this Agreement hereby acknowledge that, unless otherwise provided for in this Agreement, the Deposit Holder shall place
the deposit in trust in the Deposit Holder's non-interest bearing Real Estate Trust Account and no interest shall be earned, received or paid on the deposit.

Buyer agrees to pay the balance as more particularly set out in Schedule A attached.

SCHEDULE(S) A..**attached hereto form(s) part of this Agreement.**
                            CL **Seller** AV   *CL* **11:59** AV   *CL* **13th** AV
1. **IRREVOCABILITY:** This offer shall be irrevocable by ....~~Buyer~~............ until ~~6:00~~ ~~a.m.~~/p.m. on the ~~12th~~
                                                    (Seller/Buyer)

day of ....**August**................ 20 **XX**..., after which time, if not accepted, this offer shall be null and void and the deposit
shall be returned to the Buyer in full without interest.

                                                        CL **November** AV
2. **COMPLETION DATE:** This Agreement shall be completed by no later than 6:00 p.m. on the ...**1st**... day of ....~~December~~............

20 **XX**......... Upon completion, vacant possession of the property shall be given to the Buyer unless otherwise provided for in this Agreement.

INITIALS OF BUYER(S): (*CL*)   **INITIALS OF SELLER(S):** (AV)

                                            Form 100   Revised 2015   **Page 1 of 6**

3. NOTICES: The Seller hereby appoints the Listing Brokerage as agent for the Seller for the purpose of giving and receiving notices pursuant to this Agreement. Where a Brokerage (Buyer's Brokerage) has entered into a representation agreement with the Buyer, the Buyer hereby appoints the Buyer's Brokerage as agent for the purpose of giving and receiving notices pursuant to this Agreement. **Where a Brokerage represents both the Seller and the Buyer (multiple representation), the Brokerage shall not be appointed or authorized to be agent for either the Buyer or the Seller for the purpose of giving and receiving notices.** Any notice relating hereto or provided for herein shall be in writing. In addition to any provision contained herein and in any Schedule hereto, this offer, any counter-offer, notice of acceptance thereof or any notice to be given or received pursuant to this Agreement or any Schedule hereto (any of them, "Document") shall be deemed given and received when delivered personally or hand delivered to the Address for Service provided in the Acknowledgement below, or where a facsimile number or email address is provided herein, when transmitted electronically to that facsimile number or email address, respectively, in which case, the signature(s) of the party (parties) shall be deemed to be original.

FAX No.: ......**(905) 666-2121**...... FAX No.: ......**(905) 777-2121**......
(For delivery of Documents to Seller)   (For delivery of Documents to Buyer)

Email Address: .... Email Address: ....
(For delivery of Documents to Seller)   (For delivery of Documents to Buyer)

4. CHATTELS INCLUDED: Existing draperies and decorator rods in the living room and family room

....

....

....

....

Unless otherwise stated in this Agreement or any Schedule hereto, Seller agrees to convey all fixtures and chattels included in the Purchase Price free from all liens, encumbrances or claims affecting the said fixtures and chattels.

5. FIXTURES EXCLUDED: Dining room chandelier

....

....

....

....

6. RENTAL ITEMS (Including Lease, Lease to Own): The following equipment is rented and **not** included in the Purchase Price. The Buyer agrees to assume the rental contract(s), if assumable:

Rental hot water tank, Anycity Energy, payable $33.50 quarterly (plus applicable taxes)

....

....

The Buyer agrees to co-operate and execute such documentation as may be required to facilitate such assumption.

7. HST: If the sale of the Property (Real Property as described above) is subject to Harmonized Sales Tax (HST), then such tax shall be

.........**included in**......... the Purchase Price. If the sale of the Property is not subject to HST, Seller agrees to certify on or before
(included in/in addition to)
closing, that the sale of the Property is not subject to HST. Any HST on chattels, if applicable, is not included in the Purchase Price.

INITIALS OF BUYER(S): (CL)   INITIALS OF SELLER(S): (AV)

Form 100   Revised 2015   **Page 2 of 6**

8. **TITLE SEARCH:** Buyer shall be allowed until 6:00 p.m. on the ......10th.... day of ....October......................., 20..XX...., (Requisition Date) to examine the title to the Property at Buyer's own expense and until the earlier of: (i) thirty days from the later of the Requisition Date or the date on which the conditions in this Agreement are fulfilled or otherwise waived or; (ii) five days prior to completion, to satisfy Buyer that there are no outstanding

work orders or deficiency notices affecting the Property, and that its present use (.........single family residential................) may be lawfully continued and that the principal building may be insured against risk of fire. Seller hereby consents to the municipality or other governmental agencies releasing to Buyer details of all outstanding work orders and deficiency notices affecting the property, and Seller agrees to execute and deliver such further authorizations in this regard as Buyer may reasonably require.

9. **FUTURE USE:** Seller and Buyer agree that there is no representation or warranty of any kind that the future intended use of the property by Buyer is or will be lawful except as may be specifically provided for in this Agreement.

10. **TITLE:** Provided that the title to the property is good and free from all registered restrictions, charges, liens, and encumbrances except as otherwise specifically provided in this Agreement and save and except for (a) any registered restrictions or covenants that run with the land providing that such are complied with; (b) any registered municipal agreements and registered agreements with publicly regulated utilities providing such have been complied with, or security has been posted to ensure compliance and completion, as evidenced by a letter from the relevant municipality or regulated utility; (c) any minor easements for the supply of domestic utility or telephone services to the property or adjacent properties; and (d) any easements for drainage, storm or sanitary sewers, public utility lines, telephone lines, cable television lines or other services which do not materially affect the use of the property. If within the specified times referred to in paragraph 8 any valid objection to title or to any outstanding work order or deficiency notice, or to the fact the said present use may not lawfully be continued, or that the principal building may not be insured against risk of fire is made in writing to Seller and which Seller is unable or unwilling to remove, remedy or satisfy or obtain insurance save and except against risk of fire (Title Insurance) in favour of the Buyer and any mortgagee, (with all related costs at the expense of the Seller), and which Buyer will not waive, this Agreement notwithstanding any intermediate acts or negotiations in respect of such objections, shall be at an end and all monies paid shall be returned without interest or deduction and Seller, Listing Brokerage and Co-operating Brokerage shall not be liable for any costs or damages. Save as to any valid objection so made by such day and except for any objection going to the root of the title, Buyer shall be conclusively deemed to have accepted Seller's title to the property.

11. **CLOSING ARRANGEMENTS:** Where each of the Seller and Buyer retain a lawyer to complete the Agreement of Purchase and Sale of the property, and where the transaction will be completed by electronic registration pursuant to Part III of the Land Registration Reform Act, R.S.O. 1990, Chapter L4 and the Electronic Registration Act, S.O. 1991, Chapter 44, and any amendments thereto, the Seller and Buyer acknowledge and agree that the exchange of closing funds, non-registrable documents and other items (the "Requisite Deliveries") and the release thereof to the Seller and Buyer will (a) not occur at the same time as the registration of the transfer/deed (and any other documents intended to be registered in connection with the completion of this transaction) and (b) be subject to conditions whereby the lawyer(s) receiving any of the Requisite Deliveries will be required to hold same in trust and not release same except in accordance with the terms of a document registration agreement between the said lawyers. The Seller and Buyer irrevocably instruct the said lawyers to be bound by the document registration agreement which is recommended from time to time by the Law Society of Upper Canada. Unless otherwise agreed to by the lawyers, such exchange of the Requisite Deliveries will occur in the applicable Land Titles Office or such other location agreeable to both lawyers.

12. **DOCUMENTS AND DISCHARGE:** Buyer shall not call for the production of any title deed, abstract, survey or other evidence of title to the property except such as are in the possession or control of Seller. If requested by Buyer, Seller will deliver any sketch or survey of the property within Seller's control to Buyer as soon as possible and prior to the Requisition Date. If a discharge of any Charge/Mortgage held by a corporation incorporated pursuant to the Trust And Loan Companies Act (Canada), Chartered Bank, Trust Company, Credit Union, Caisse Populaire or Insurance Company and which is not to be assumed by Buyer on completion, is not available in registrable form on completion, Buyer agrees to accept Seller's lawyer's personal undertaking to obtain, out of the closing funds, a discharge in registrable form and to register same, or cause same to be registered, on title within a reasonable period of time after completion, provided that on or before completion Seller shall provide to Buyer a mortgage statement prepared by the mortgagee setting out the balance required to obtain the discharge, and, where a real-time electronic cleared funds transfer system is not being used, a direction executed by Seller directing payment to the mortgagee of the amount required to obtain the discharge out of the balance due on completion.

13. **INSPECTION:** Buyer acknowledges having had the opportunity to inspect the Property and understands that upon acceptance of this offer there shall be a binding agreement of purchase and sale between Buyer and Seller. **The Buyer acknowledges having the opportunity to include a requirement for a property inspection report in this Agreement and agrees that except as may be specifically provided for in this Agreement, the Buyer will not be obtaining a property inspection or property inspection report regarding the Property.**

14. **INSURANCE:** All buildings on the property and all other things being purchased shall be and remain until completion at the risk of Seller. Pending completion, Seller shall hold all insurance policies, if any, and the proceeds thereof in trust for the parties as their interests may appear and in the event of substantial damage, Buyer may either terminate this Agreement and have all monies paid returned without interest or deduction or else take the proceeds of any insurance and complete the purchase. No insurance shall be transferred on completion. If Seller is taking back a Charge/Mortgage, or Buyer is assuming a Charge/Mortgage, Buyer shall supply Seller with reasonable evidence of adequate insurance to protect Seller's or other mortgagee's interest on completion.

INITIALS OF BUYER(S): (CL)   INITIALS OF SELLER(S): (AV)

15. **PLANNING ACT:** This Agreement shall be effective to create an interest in the property only if Seller complies with the subdivision control provisions of the Planning Act by completion and Seller covenants to proceed diligently at Seller's expense to obtain any necessary consent by completion.

16. **DOCUMENT PREPARATION:** The Transfer/Deed shall, save for the Land Transfer Tax Affidavit, be prepared in registrable form at the expense of Seller, and any Charge/Mortgage to be given back by the Buyer to Seller at the expense of the Buyer. If requested by Buyer, Seller covenants that the Transfer/Deed to be delivered on completion shall contain the statements contemplated by Section 50(22) of the Planning Act, R.S.O.1990.

17. **RESIDENCY:** (a) Subject to (b) below, the Seller represents and warrants that the Seller is not and on completion will not be a non-resident under the non-residency provisions of the Income Tax Act which representation and warranty shall survive and not merge upon the completion of this transaction and the Seller shall deliver to the Buyer a statutory declaration that Seller is not then a non-resident of Canada; (b) provided that if the Seller is a non-resident under the non-residency provisions of the Income Tax Act, the Buyer shall be credited towards the Purchase Price with the amount, if any, necessary for Buyer to pay to the Minister of National Revenue to satisfy Buyer's liability in respect of tax payable by Seller under the non-residency provisions of the Income Tax Act by reason of this sale. Buyer shall not claim such credit if Seller delivers on completion the prescribed certificate.

18. **ADJUSTMENTS:** Any rents, mortgage interest, realty taxes including local improvement rates and unmetered public or private utility charges and unmetered cost of fuel, as applicable, shall be apportioned and allowed to the day of completion, the day of completion itself to be apportioned to Buyer.

19. **PROPERTY ASSESSMENT:** The Buyer and Seller hereby acknowledge that the Province of Ontario has implemented current value assessment and properties may be re-assessed on an annual basis. The Buyer and Seller agree that no claim will be made against the Buyer or Seller, or any Brokerage, Broker or Salesperson, for any changes in property tax as a result of a re-assessment of the property, save and except any property taxes that accrued prior to the completion of this transaction.

20. **TIME LIMITS:** Time shall in all respects be of the essence hereof provided that the time for doing or completing of any matter provided for herein may be extended or abridged by an agreement in writing signed by Seller and Buyer or by their respective lawyers who may be specifically authorized in that regard.

21. **TENDER:** Any tender of documents or money hereunder may be made upon Seller or Buyer or their respective lawyers on the day set for completion. Money shall be tendered with funds drawn on a lawyer's trust account in the form of a bank draft, certified cheque or wire transfer using the Large Value Transfer System.

22. **FAMILY LAW ACT:** Seller warrants that spousal consent is not necessary to this transaction under the provisions of the Family Law Act, R.S.O.1990 unless Seller's spouse has executed the consent hereinafter provided.

23. **UFFI:** Seller represents and warrants to Buyer that during the time Seller has owned the property, Seller has not caused any building on the property to be insulated with insulation containing ureaformaldehyde, and that to the best of Seller's knowledge no building on the property contains or has ever contained insulation that contains ureaformaldehyde. This warranty shall survive and not merge on the completion of this transaction, and if the building is part of a multiple unit building, this warranty shall only apply to that part of the building which is the subject of this transaction.

24. **LEGAL, ACCOUNTING AND ENVIRONMENTAL ADVICE:** The parties acknowledge that any information provided by the brokerage is not legal, tax or environmental advice.

25. **CONSUMER REPORTS: The Buyer is hereby notified that a consumer report containing credit and/or personal information may be referred to in connection with this transaction.**

26. **AGREEMENT IN WRITING:** If there is conflict or discrepancy between any provision added to this Agreement (including any Schedule attached hereto) and any provision in the standard pre-set portion hereof, the added provision shall supersede the standard pre-set provision to the extent of such conflict or discrepancy. This Agreement including any Schedule attached hereto, shall constitute the entire Agreement between Buyer and Seller. There is no representation, warranty, collateral agreement or condition, which affects this Agreement other than as expressed herein. For the purposes of this Agreement, Seller means vendor and Buyer means purchaser. This Agreement shall be read with all changes of gender or number required by the context.

27. **TIME AND DATE:** Any reference to a time and date in this Agreement shall mean the time and date where the property is located.

INITIALS OF BUYER(S): (*CL*)   INITIALS OF SELLER(S): (AV)

Form 100   Revised 2015   **Page 4 of 6**

28. SUCCESSORS AND ASSIGNS: The heirs, executors, administrators, successors and assigns of the undersigned are bound by the terms herein.

SIGNED, SEALED AND DELIVERED in the presence of:　　IN WITNESS whereof I have hereunto set my hand and seal:

Clair Rodgers ....　*Charles Leung* ....●........ DATE *August 10/xx*
(Witness)　　　　　　　　　　　　　　　(Buyer)　　　　　　　　　　(Seal)

....　...●........ DATE ....
(Witness)　　　　　　　　　　　　　　　(Buyer)　　　　　　　　　　(Seal)

I, the Undersigned Seller, agree to the above offer. I hereby irrevocably instruct my lawyer to pay directly to the brokerage(s) with whom I have agreed to pay commission, the unpaid balance of the commission together with applicable Harmonized Sales Tax (and any other taxes as may hereafter be applicable), from the proceeds of the sale prior to any payment to the undersigned on completion, as advised by the brokerage(s) to my lawyer.

SIGNED, SEALED AND DELIVERED in the presence of:　　IN WITNESS whereof I have hereunto set my hand and seal:

Cliff Kuppers ....　*Alexandra Vujovic* ....●........ DATE *August 12/xx*
(Witness)　　　　　　　　　　　　　　　(Seller)　　　　　　　　　　(Seal)

....　...●........ DATE ....
(Witness)　　　　　　　　　　　　　　　(Seller)　　　　　　　　　　(Seal)

SPOUSAL CONSENT: The Undersigned Spouse of the Seller hereby consents to the disposition evidenced herein pursuant to the provisions of the Family Law Act, R.S.O.1990, and hereby agrees with the Buyer that he/she will execute all necessary or incidental documents to give full force and effect to the sale evidenced herein.

Cliff Kuppers ....　*Hans Vujovic* ....●........ DATE *August 13/xx*
(Witness)　　　　　　　　　　　　　　　(Spouse)　　　　　　　　　　(Seal)

CONFIRMATION OF ACCEPTANCE: Notwithstanding anything contained herein to the contrary, I confirm this Agreement with all changes both typed and written was finally accepted by all parties at ...*7:00*... a.m./p.m. this ...*13th*... day of.........*August*........., 20.*XX*...

　　　　　　　　　　　　　　　　　　　　　　Charles Leung
　　　　　　　　　　　　　　　　　　　　(Signature of Seller or Buyer)

INFORMATION ON BROKERAGE(S)

Listing Brokerage .... ABC Realty Inc. ....　Tel.No.(... 905 ...) 666-1212

　328 Main Street, Anycity　　　Cliff Kuppers
　　　　　　　　　　　　　　　(Salesperson / Broker Name)

Co-op/Buyer Brokerage .... XYZ Real Estate Limited ....　Tel.No.(...905...) 777-1212

　28 Norfield Drive, Anycity　　　Clair Rodgers
　　　　　　　　　　　　　　　(Salesperson / Broker Name)

ACKNOWLEDGEMENT

I acknowledge receipt of my signed copy of this accepted Agreement of Purchase and Sale and I authorize the Brokerage to forward a copy to my lawyer.	I acknowledge receipt of my signed copy of this accepted Agreement of Purchase and Sale and I authorize the Brokerage to forward a copy to my lawyer.
Alexandra Vujovic .... DATE *Aug. 13/xx* (Seller)	*Charles Leung* .... DATE *Aug. 13/xx* (Buyer)
.... DATE .... (Seller)	.... DATE .... (Buyer)
Address for Service *1381 Pathfinder Road, Anycity K0C 2TC*	Address for Service *302 Crescent Court, Anycity K2B 3C7*
Tel.No.(.*905*.)*888-1212*	Tel.No.(.*905*.) *333-1212*
Seller's Lawyer *James Millcraft c/o Millcraft & James*	Buyer's Lawyer *Michelle Lyons c/o Lyons & MacDonald*
Address *3270 Centre Street, Anycity K0D 3B7*	Address *1 City Centre Square, Suite 402, Anycity K4T 3Y8*
Email	Email ....
(.*905*.) *444-1212* (.*905*.) *444-2121* Tel.No. FAX No.	(..*905*.) *222-1212* (..*905*.) *222-2121* Tel.No. FAX No.

FOR OFFICE USE ONLY　　COMMISSION TRUST AGREEMENT

To: Co-operating Brokerage shown on the foregoing Agreement of Purchase and Sale:
In consideration for the Co-operating Brokerage procuring the foregoing Agreement of Purchase and Sale, I hereby declare that all moneys received or receivable by me in connection with the Transaction as contemplated in the MLS® Rules and Regulations of my Real Estate Board shall be receivable and held in trust. This agreement shall constitute a Commission Trust Agreement as defined in the MLS® Rules and shall be subject to and governed by the MLS® Rules pertaining to Commission Trust.

DATED as of the date and time of the acceptance of the foregoing Agreement of Purchase and Sale.　Acknowledged by:

Cliff Kuppers ....　*Clair Rodgers* ....
(Authorized to bind the Listing Brokerage)　　　　(Authorized to bind the Co-operating Brokerage)

Form 100　Revised 2015　**Page 5 of 6**

OREA Ontario Real Estate Association

Form 100
for use in the Province of Ontario

Schedule A
Agreement of Purchase and Sale

This Schedule is attached to and forms part of the Agreement of Purchase and Sale between:

BUYER, Charles M. Leung , and

SELLER, Alexandra Vujovic

for the purchase and sale of 1381 Pathfinder Road, City of Anycity, Regional Municipality of Anyregion

dated the 10th day of August , 20 xx

Buyer agrees to pay the balance as follows:

The Buyer agrees to pay a further sum of Ten Thousand Dollars ($10,000.00) to ABC Realty Inc. by negotiable cheque not later than 5:00 p.m. on the 26th day of August, 20xx, as a supplementary deposit to be held in trust in the same manner as the initial deposit pending completion or other termination of this Agreement. This amount is to be credited towards the purchase price on completion of this transaction.

CL   AV

One Hundred and Thirty-Five Thousand Dollars ($135,000.00)
The Buyer agrees to pay a further sum of ~~One Hundred and Twenty Thousand Dollars ($120,000.00)~~, subject to adjustments, to the Seller on completion of this transaction, with funds drawn on a lawyer's trust account in the form of a bank draft, certified cheque, or wire transfer using the Large Value Transfer System.

The Buyer agrees to assume the existing first Charge/Mortgage held by Anycity Financial for approximately One Hundred and Fifty Thousand Dollars ($150,000.00) bearing interest at the rate of 5.75% per annum, calculated semi-annually not in advance, repayable in blended monthly payments of Nine Hundred and Thirty-Six Dollars and Fifty Cents ($936.50), including principal, interest and taxes, and due on January 31, 20xx. This Offer is conditional upon the Buyer obtaining the approval of the Chargee/Mortgagee to assume the existing Charge/Mortgage. Unless the Buyer gives notice in writing, delivered to the Seller personally or in accordance with any other provisions for the delivery of notice in this Agreement of Purchase and Sale or any Schedule thereto not later than 5:00 p.m. on the 26th day of August, 20xx, that this condition is fulfilled, this Offer shall be null and avoid and the deposit shall be returned to the Buyer in full without deduction. The Buyer hereby agrees to proceed immediately to make an application and provide such material as may be required by the Chargee/Mortgagee for approval of the Buyer as the Chargor/Mortgagor

This form must be initialed by all parties to the Agreement of Purchase and Sale.

INITIALS OF BUYER(S): *CL*

INITIALS OF SELLER(S): AV

■ Exercise 4   Identify Errors and Omissions

PAGE 1

Price/Deposit	Initials required for both price and deposit.
Deposit	Deposit typically held by listing broker. Cannot be held jointly by two brokerages.
Irrevocable	Should have been irrevocable by buyer initially and then amended to read as seller.
Initials	Initials are reversed at the bottom of the page.

PAGE 2

Chattels	Incomplete description of security system and lower family room furnishings.
Fixtures Excl.	Clause 1 shows all drapes included. Clause 2 excludes living room drapes as fixtures.
Initials	Initials are reversed at the bottom of the page.

PAGE 3

Title Search	Title search period earlier than mortgage condition.
Initials	Initials are reversed at the bottom of the page.

PAGE 5

Spouse	Marilyn Mostofi's signature in wrong location. Should be as seller, not under spousal consent.
Confirmation	Co-operating salesperson signing *Confirmation of Acceptance*. Should be last person signing counter offer. In this instance, Silvia or Wayne Chisolm should sign.
Acknowledgment	Wayne Chisolm's signature and required date are missing.

PAGE 6

Property	Cross reference for property should include address.
Pay Further Sum	Should be $225,000 ($250,000 − $10,000 − $15,000).
First Mortgage	Wording should be changed to "not more than" and the waiver provision should be deleted to prevent a possible Oklahoma offer. As an alternative, MORT-15 could be added to the agreement.
Seller Take Back	Should be conditional on credit check of buyer.
Leakage	Clause does not adequately protect the buyer. See *Appendix: Clauses—Rep/Warr-1*.

APPENDIX

Easement	Easement description poses problems, as it is indefinite regarding location. Further, no reference to easement appears in the legal description. Issue should have been addressed prior to drafting agreement, attach a survey showing easement, or insert appropriate condition to investigate further if unable to clearly establish location. Legal advice should be sought.	
Initials	Initials are reversed at the bottom of the page.	

■ Exercise 5   Drafting Sale-Related Documents

See the following pages for all completed forms.

 **Ontario Real Estate Association**

Confirmation of Co-operation and Representation

Form 320
for use in the Province of Ontario

BUYER: .... Ellen Marie Shantz and David Charles Shantz ....

SELLER: .... Leslie C. Norton and James P. Norton ....

For the transaction on the property known as: ...... 3291 Golf Course Drive, City of Anycity, Regional Municipality of Anyregion .....

For the purposes of this Confirmation of Co-operation and Representation, "Seller" includes a vendor, a landlord, or a prospective, seller, vendor or landlord and "Buyer" includes a purchaser, a tenant, or a prospective, buyer, purchaser or tenant, "sale" includes a lease, and "Agreement of Purchase and Sale" includes an Agreement to Lease.

The following information is confirmed by the undersigned salesperson/broker representatives of the Brokerage(s). If a Co-operating Brokerage is involved in the transaction, the brokerages agree to co-operate, in consideration of, and on the terms and conditions as set out below.

DECLARATION OF INSURANCE: The undersigned salesperson/broker representative(s) of the Brokerage(s) hereby declare that he/she is insured as required by the Real Estate and Business Brokers Act, 2002 (REBBA 2002) and Regulations.

1. LISTING BROKERAGE

   a) ☑ The Listing Brokerage represents the interests of the Seller in this transaction. It is further understood and agreed that:

   1) ☑ The Listing Brokerage is not representing or providing Customer Service to the Buyer.
   (If the Buyer is working with a Co-operating Brokerage, Section 3 is to be completed by Co-operating Brokerage.)

   2) ☐ The Listing Brokerage is providing Customer Service to the Buyer.

   b) ☐ **MULTIPLE REPRESENTATION:** The Listing Brokerage has entered into a Buyer Representation Agreement with the Buyer and represents the interests of the Seller and the Buyer, with their consent, for this transaction. The Listing Brokerage must be impartial and equally protect the interests of the Seller and the Buyer in this transaction. The Listing Brokerage has a duty of full disclosure to both the Seller and the Buyer, including a requirement to disclose all factual information about the property known to the Listing Brokerage. However, the Listing Brokerage shall not disclose:

   • That the Seller may or will accept less than the listed price, unless otherwise instructed in writing by the Seller;
   • That the Buyer may or will pay more than the offered price, unless otherwise instructed in writing by the Buyer;
   • The motivation of or personal information about the Seller or Buyer, unless otherwise instructed in writing by the party to which the information applies, or unless failure to disclose would constitute fraudulent, unlawful or unethical practice;
   • The price the Buyer should offer or the price the Seller should accept;
   • And; the Listing Brokerage shall not disclose to the Buyer the terms of any other offer.

   However, it is understood that factual market information about comparable properties and information known to the Listing Brokerage concerning potential uses for the property will be disclosed to both Seller and Buyer to assist them to come to their own conclusions.

Additional comments and/or disclosures by Listing Brokerage: (e.g. The Listing Brokerage represents more than one Buyer offering on this property.)

....

....

....

2. PROPERTY SOLD BY BUYER BROKERAGE – PROPERTY NOT LISTED

   ☐ The Brokerage .... represent the Buyer and the property is not listed with any real estate brokerage. The Brokerage will be paid
   (does/does not)

   ☐ by the Seller in accordance with a Seller Customer Service Agreement

   or: ☐ by the Buyer directly

Additional comments and/or disclosures by Buyer Brokerage: (e.g. The Buyer Brokerage represents more than one Buyer offering on this property.)

....

....

....

INITIALS OF BUYER(S)/SELLER(S)/BROKERAGE REPRESENTATIVE(S) (Where applicable)

ES DS	*AJ*	*LN JN*	*WP*
BUYER	**CO-OPERATING/BUYER BROKERAGE**	**SELLER**	**LISTING BROKERAGE**

Form 320   Revised 2015   **Page 1 of 2**

APPENDIX

Exercise 5 Confirmation of Co-operation and Representation—Page 2 of 2

3. Co-operating Brokerage completes Section 3 and Listing Brokerage completes Section 1.

CO-OPERATING BROKERAGE- REPRESENTATION:

a) ☑ The Co-operating Brokerage represents the interests of the Buyer in this transaction.

b) ☐ The Co-operating Brokerage is providing Customer Service to the Buyer in this transaction.

c) ☐ The Co-operating Brokerage is not representing the Buyer and has not entered into an agreement to provide customer service(s) to the Buyer.

CO-OPERATING BROKERAGE- COMMISSION:

a) ☐ The Listing Brokerage will pay the Co-operating Brokerage the commission as indicated in the MLS® information for the property

.... to be paid from the amount paid by the Seller to the Listing Brokerage.
(Commission As Indicated In MLS® Information)

b) ☑ The Co-operating Brokerage will be paid as follows:

The listing brokerage will pay 2.5% of the sale price to the co-operating brokerage

Additional comments and/or disclosures by Co-operating Brokerage: (e.g., The Co-operating Brokerage represents more than one Buyer offering on this property.)

Commission will be payable as described above, plus applicable taxes.

COMMISSION TRUST AGREEMENT: If the above Co-operating Brokerage is receiving payment of commission from the Listing Brokerage, then the agreement between Listing Brokerage and Co-operating Brokerage further includes a Commission Trust Agreement, the consideration for which is the Co-operating Brokerage procuring an offer for a trade of the property, acceptable to the Seller. This Commission Trust Agreement shall be subject to and governed by the MLS® rules and regulations pertaining to commission trusts of the Listing Brokerage's local real estate board, if the local board's MLS® rules and regulations so provide. Otherwise, the provisions of the OREA recommended MLS® rules and regulations shall apply to this Commission Trust Agreement. For the purpose of this Commission Trust Agreement, the Commission Trust Amount shall be the amount noted in Section 3 above. The Listing Brokerage hereby declares that all monies received in connection with the trade shall constitute a Commission Trust and shall be held, in trust, for the Co-operating Brokerage under the terms of the applicable MLS® rules and regulations.

SIGNED BY THE BROKER/SALESPERSON REPRESENTATIVE(S) OF THE BROKERAGE(S) (Where applicable)

XYZ Real Estate Limited	*ABC Realty Inc.*
(Name of Co-operating/Buyer Brokerage)	(Name of Listing Brokerage)
886 West Heights Boulevard, Anycity K9J 1B3	*8738 Water St., Anycity K9B 3C2*
Tel:. *(519) 666-1212* Fax: *(519) 666-2121*	Tel:. *(519) 333-1212* Fax: *(519) 333-2121*
A. Fernandes Date: *June 14/xx*	*William Palm* Date: *June 14/xx*
(Authorized to bind the Co-operating/Buyer Brokerage)	(Authorized to bind the Listing Brokerage)
A. Fernandes	**William Palm**
(Print Name of Broker/Salesperson Representative of the Brokerage)	(Print Name of Broker/Salesperson Representative of the Brokerage)

CONSENT FOR MULTIPLE REPRESENTATION (To be completed only if the Brokerage represents more than one client for the transaction)

The Buyer/Seller consent with their initials to their Brokerage representing more than one client for this transaction.

BUYER'S INITIALS   SELLER'S INITIALS

ACKNOWLEDGEMENT

I have received, read, and understand the above information.

Ellen Shantz Date: *June 14/xx*	*Leslie Norton* Date: *June 15/xx*
(Signature of Buyer)	(Signature of Seller)
David Shantz Date: *June 14/xx*	*James Norton* Date: *June 15/xx*
(Signature of Buyer)	(Signature of Seller)

Form 320 Revised 2015 **Page 2 of 2**

OREA Ontario Real Estate Association

Agreement of Purchase and Sale

Form 100
for use in the Province of Ontario

This Agreement of Purchase and Sale dated this ...... 14th ...... day of .... June .... 20 .. XX ..

BUYER, ... Ellen Marie Shantz and David Charles Shantz ...., agrees to purchase from
(Full legal names of all Buyers)

SELLER, ... Leslie C. Norton and James P. Norton ...., the following
(Full legal names of all Sellers)

REAL PROPERTY:

Address .... 3291 Golf Course Drive ....

fronting on the .... West .... side of .... Golf Course Drive ....

in the .... City of Anycity, Regional Municipality of Anyregion ....

and having a frontage of .... 64.55 feet .... more or less by a depth of .... 157.29 feet .... more or less

and legally described as .. Lot 231, Registered Plan 99M-891 subject to a 15-foot service easement

.... on the northeasterly corner of the rear yard .... (the "property")
(Legal description of land including easements not described elsewhere)

PURCHASE PRICE: *ES DS*   *LN JN*   Dollars (CDN$)   *ES DS* **$354,500.00** *LN JN*
                                                              ~~$339,000.00~~

Three Hundred and Fifty-Four Thousand Five Hundred
~~Three Hundred and Thirty-Nine Thousand~~-- Dollars

DEPOSIT: Buyer submits .... Upon Acceptance ....
(Herewith/Upon Acceptance/as otherwise described in this Agreement)

Twenty-Five Thousand-- Dollars (CDN$) .. $25,000.00

by negotiable cheque payable to .... ABC Realty Inc. .... "Deposit Holder" to be held
in trust pending completion or other termination of this Agreement and to be credited toward the Purchase Price on completion. For the purposes of this Agreement, "Upon Acceptance" shall mean that the Buyer is required to deliver the deposit to the Deposit Holder within 24 hours of the acceptance of this Agreement. The parties to this Agreement hereby acknowledge that, unless otherwise provided for in this Agreement, the Deposit Holder shall place the deposit in trust in the Deposit Holder's non-interest bearing Real Estate Trust Account and no interest shall be earned, received or paid on the deposit.

Buyer agrees to pay the balance as more particularly set out in Schedule A attached.

SCHEDULE(S) A .... **attached hereto form(s) part of this Agreement.**

1. **IRREVOCABILITY:** This offer shall be irrevocable by .... *ES DS* **Seller** *LN JN* .... until ..11:59.. ~~a.m.~~/p.m. on the .... *ES DS* **16th** *LN JN* ....
                                         ~~Buyer~~   ~~15th~~
                                    (Seller/Buyer)

   day of .... June .... 20 .. XX .., after which time, if not accepted, this offer shall be null and void and the deposit shall be returned to the Buyer in full without interest.

2. **COMPLETION DATE:** This Agreement shall be completed by no later than 6:00 p.m. on the ..30th.. day of .... July ....

   20 .. XX ...... Upon completion, vacant possession of the property shall be given to the Buyer unless otherwise provided for in this Agreement.

INITIALS OF BUYER(S): (*ES DS*)   **INITIALS OF SELLER(S):** (*LN JN*)

Form 100   Revised 2015   **Page 1 of 6**

3. **NOTICES:** The Seller hereby appoints the Listing Brokerage as agent for the Seller for the purpose of giving and receiving notices pursuant to this Agreement. Where a Brokerage (Buyer's Brokerage) has entered into a representation agreement with the Buyer, the Buyer hereby appoints the Buyer's Brokerage as agent for the purpose of giving and receiving notices pursuant to this Agreement. **Where a Brokerage represents both the Seller and the Buyer (multiple representation), the Brokerage shall not be appointed or authorized to be agent for either the Buyer or the Seller for the purpose of giving and receiving notices.** Any notice relating hereto or provided for herein shall be in writing. In addition to any provision contained herein and in any Schedule hereto, this offer, any counter-offer, notice of acceptance thereof or any notice to be given or received pursuant to this Agreement or any Schedule hereto (any of them, "Document") shall be deemed given and received when delivered personally or hand delivered to the Address for Service provided in the Acknowledgement below, or where a facsimile number or email address is provided herein, when transmitted electronically to that facsimile number or email address, respectively, in which case, the signature(s) of the party (parties) shall be deemed to be original.

FAX No.: ..... **(519) 555-2121** .....
(For delivery of Documents to Seller)

FAX No.: ..... **(519) 666-2121** .....
(For delivery of Documents to Buyer)

Email Address: ..... **admin@abcrealty.com** .....
(For delivery of Documents to Seller)

Email Address: ..... **notices@xyzrealestate.com** .....
(For delivery of Documents to Buyer)

4. **CHATTELS INCLUDED:** ..... Satellite dish, 2 remotes and receiver, storage shed, and SpaTime hot tub including enclosure and all attachments .....

Unless otherwise stated in this Agreement or any Schedule hereto, Seller agrees to convey all fixtures and chattels included in the Purchase Price free from all liens, encumbrances or claims affecting the said fixtures and chattels.

5. **FIXTURES EXCLUDED:** ..... Glass decorator shelves in living room, and dining room chandelier .....

6. **RENTAL ITEMS (Including Lease, Lease to Own):** The following equipment is rented and **not** included in the Purchase Price. The Buyer agrees to assume the rental contract(s), if assumable:

..... Hot water tank, Anycity Energy @ $36.25 quarterly (plus applicable taxes) .....

The Buyer agrees to co-operate and execute such documentation as may be required to facilitate such assumption.

7. **HST:** If the sale of the Property (Real Property as described above) is subject to Harmonized Sales Tax (HST), then such tax shall be ..... **included in** ..... the Purchase Price. If the sale of the Property is not subject to HST, Seller agrees to certify on or before
(included in/in addition to)
closing, that the sale of the Property is not subject to HST. Any HST on chattels, if applicable, is not included in the Purchase Price.

INITIALS OF BUYER(S): (*ES DS*)   **INITIALS OF SELLER(S):** (*LN JN*)

8. **TITLE SEARCH:** Buyer shall be allowed until 6:00 p.m. on the ....15th.... day of ....July........................., 20..XX...., (Requisition Date) to examine the title to the Property at Buyer's own expense and until the earlier of: (i) thirty days from the later of the Requisition Date or the date on which the conditions in this Agreement are fulfilled or otherwise waived or; (ii) five days prior to completion, to satisfy Buyer that there are no outstanding

    work orders or deficiency notices affecting the Property, and that its present use (.................single family residential..................) may be lawfully continued and that the principal building may be insured against risk of fire. Seller hereby consents to the municipality or other governmental agencies releasing to Buyer details of all outstanding work orders and deficiency notices affecting the property, and Seller agrees to execute and deliver such further authorizations in this regard as Buyer may reasonably require.

9. **FUTURE USE:** Seller and Buyer agree that there is no representation or warranty of any kind that the future intended use of the property by Buyer is or will be lawful except as may be specifically provided for in this Agreement.

10. **TITLE:** Provided that the title to the property is good and free from all registered restrictions, charges, liens, and encumbrances except as otherwise specifically provided in this Agreement and save and except for (a) any registered restrictions or covenants that run with the land providing that such are complied with; (b) any registered municipal agreements and registered agreements with publicly regulated utilities providing such have been complied with, or security has been posted to ensure compliance and completion, as evidenced by a letter from the relevant municipality or regulated utility; (c) any minor easements for the supply of domestic utility or telephone services to the property or adjacent properties; and (d) any easements for drainage, storm or sanitary sewers, public utility lines, telephone lines, cable television lines or other services which do not materially affect the use of the property. If within the specified times referred to in paragraph 8 any valid objection to title or to any outstanding work order or deficiency notice, or to the fact the said present use may not lawfully be continued, or that the principal building may not be insured against risk of fire is made in writing to Seller and which Seller is unable or unwilling to remove, remedy or satisfy or obtain insurance save and except against risk of fire (Title Insurance) in favour of the Buyer and any mortgagee, (with all related costs at the expense of the Seller), and which Buyer will not waive, this Agreement notwithstanding any intermediate acts or negotiations in respect of such objections, shall be at an end and all monies paid shall be returned without interest or deduction and Seller, Listing Brokerage and Co-operating Brokerage shall not be liable for any costs or damages. Save as to any valid objection so made by such day and except for any objection going to the root of the title, Buyer shall be conclusively deemed to have accepted Seller's title to the property.

11. **CLOSING ARRANGEMENTS:** Where each of the Seller and Buyer retain a lawyer to complete the Agreement of Purchase and Sale of the property, and where the transaction will be completed by electronic registration pursuant to Part III of the Land Registration Reform Act, R.S.O. 1990, Chapter L4 and the Electronic Registration Act, S.O. 1991, Chapter 44, and any amendments thereto, the Seller and Buyer acknowledge and agree that the exchange of closing funds, non-registrable documents and other items (the "Requisite Deliveries") and the release thereof to the Seller and Buyer will (a) not occur at the same time as the registration of the transfer/deed (and any other documents intended to be registered in connection with the completion of this transaction) and (b) be subject to conditions whereby the lawyer(s) receiving any of the Requisite Deliveries will be required to hold same in trust and not release same except in accordance with the terms of a document registration agreement between the said lawyers. The Seller and Buyer irrevocably instruct the said lawyers to be bound by the document registration agreement which is recommended from time to time by the Law Society of Upper Canada. Unless otherwise agreed to by the lawyers, such exchange of the Requisite Deliveries will occur in the applicable Land Titles Office or such other location agreeable to both lawyers.

12. **DOCUMENTS AND DISCHARGE:** Buyer shall not call for the production of any title deed, abstract, survey or other evidence of title to the property except such as are in the possession or control of Seller. If requested by Buyer, Seller will deliver any sketch or survey of the property within Seller's control to Buyer as soon as possible and prior to the Requisition Date. If a discharge of any Charge/Mortgage held by a corporation incorporated pursuant to the Trust And Loan Companies Act (Canada), Chartered Bank, Trust Company, Credit Union, Caisse Populaire or Insurance Company and which is not to be assumed by Buyer on completion, is not available in registrable form on completion, Buyer agrees to accept Seller's lawyer's personal undertaking to obtain, out of the closing funds, a discharge in registrable form and to register same, or cause same to be registered, on title within a reasonable period of time after completion, provided that on or before completion Seller shall provide to Buyer a mortgage statement prepared by the mortgagee setting out the balance required to obtain the discharge, and, where a real-time electronic cleared funds transfer system is not being used, a direction executed by Seller directing payment to the mortgagee of the amount required to obtain the discharge out of the balance due on completion.

13. **INSPECTION:** Buyer acknowledges having had the opportunity to inspect the Property and understands that upon acceptance of this offer there shall be a binding agreement of purchase and sale between Buyer and Seller. **The Buyer acknowledges having the opportunity to include a requirement for a property inspection report in this Agreement and agrees that except as may be specifically provided for in this Agreement, the Buyer will not be obtaining a property inspection or property inspection report regarding the Property.**

14. **INSURANCE:** All buildings on the property and all other things being purchased shall be and remain until completion at the risk of Seller. Pending completion, Seller shall hold all insurance policies, if any, and the proceeds thereof in trust for the parties as their interests may appear and in the event of substantial damage, Buyer may either terminate this Agreement and have all monies paid returned without interest or deduction or else take the proceeds of any insurance and complete the purchase. No insurance shall be transferred on completion. If Seller is taking back a Charge/Mortgage, or Buyer is assuming a Charge/Mortgage, Buyer shall supply Seller with reasonable evidence of adequate insurance to protect Seller's or other mortgagee's interest on completion.

INITIALS OF BUYER(S): (*ES DS*)   **INITIALS OF SELLER(S):** (*LN JN*)

15. **PLANNING ACT:** This Agreement shall be effective to create an interest in the property only if Seller complies with the subdivision control provisions of the Planning Act by completion and Seller covenants to proceed diligently at Seller's expense to obtain any necessary consent by completion.

16. **DOCUMENT PREPARATION:** The Transfer/Deed shall, save for the Land Transfer Tax Affidavit, be prepared in registrable form at the expense of Seller, and any Charge/Mortgage to be given back by the Buyer to Seller at the expense of the Buyer. If requested by Buyer, Seller covenants that the Transfer/Deed to be delivered on completion shall contain the statements contemplated by Section 50(22) of the Planning Act, R.S.O.1990.

17. **RESIDENCY:** (a) Subject to (b) below, the Seller represents and warrants that the Seller is not and on completion will not be a non-resident under the non-residency provisions of the Income Tax Act which representation and warranty shall survive and not merge upon the completion of this transaction and the Seller shall deliver to the Buyer a statutory declaration that Seller is not then a non-resident of Canada; (b) provided that if the Seller is a non-resident under the non-residency provisions of the Income Tax Act, the Buyer shall be credited towards the Purchase Price with the amount, if any, necessary for Buyer to pay to the Minister of National Revenue to satisfy Buyer's liability in respect of tax payable by Seller under the non-residency provisions of the Income Tax Act by reason of this sale. Buyer shall not claim such credit if Seller delivers on completion the prescribed certificate.

18. **ADJUSTMENTS:** Any rents, mortgage interest, realty taxes including local improvement rates and unmetered public or private utility charges and unmetered cost of fuel, as applicable, shall be apportioned and allowed to the day of completion, the day of completion itself to be apportioned to Buyer.

19. **PROPERTY ASSESSMENT:** The Buyer and Seller hereby acknowledge that the Province of Ontario has implemented current value assessment and properties may be re-assessed on an annual basis. The Buyer and Seller agree that no claim will be made against the Buyer or Seller, or any Brokerage, Broker or Salesperson, for any changes in property tax as a result of a re-assessment of the property, save and except any property taxes that accrued prior to the completion of this transaction.

20. **TIME LIMITS:** Time shall in all respects be of the essence hereof provided that the time for doing or completing of any matter provided for herein may be extended or abridged by an agreement in writing signed by Seller and Buyer or by their respective lawyers who may be specifically authorized in that regard.

21. **TENDER:** Any tender of documents or money hereunder may be made upon Seller or Buyer or their respective lawyers on the day set for completion. Money shall be tendered with funds drawn on a lawyer's trust account in the form of a bank draft, certified cheque or wire transfer using the Large Value Transfer System.

22. **FAMILY LAW ACT:** Seller warrants that spousal consent is not necessary to this transaction under the provisions of the Family Law Act, R.S.O.1990 unless Seller's spouse has executed the consent hereinafter provided.

23. **UFFI:** Seller represents and warrants to Buyer that during the time Seller has owned the property, Seller has not caused any building on the property to be insulated with insulation containing ureaformaldehyde, and that to the best of Seller's knowledge no building on the property contains or has ever contained insulation that contains ureaformaldehyde. This warranty shall survive and not merge on the completion of this transaction, and if the building is part of a multiple unit building, this warranty shall only apply to that part of the building which is the subject of this transaction.

24. **LEGAL, ACCOUNTING AND ENVIRONMENTAL ADVICE:** The parties acknowledge that any information provided by the brokerage is not legal, tax or environmental advice.

25. **CONSUMER REPORTS: The Buyer is hereby notified that a consumer report containing credit and/or personal information may be referred to in connection with this transaction.**

26. **AGREEMENT IN WRITING:** If there is conflict or discrepancy between any provision added to this Agreement (including any Schedule attached hereto) and any provision in the standard pre-set portion hereof, the added provision shall supersede the standard pre-set provision to the extent of such conflict or discrepancy. This Agreement including any Schedule attached hereto, shall constitute the entire Agreement between Buyer and Seller. There is no representation, warranty, collateral agreement or condition, which affects this Agreement other than as expressed herein. For the purposes of this Agreement, Seller means vendor and Buyer means purchaser. This Agreement shall be read with all changes of gender or number required by the context.

27. **TIME AND DATE:** Any reference to a time and date in this Agreement shall mean the time and date where the property is located.

INITIALS OF BUYER(S): (ES DS)   INITIALS OF SELLER(S): (LN JN)

Form 100   Revised 2015   **Page 4 of 6**

APPENDIX

28. SUCCESSORS AND ASSIGNS: The heirs, executors, administrators, successors and assigns of the undersigned are bound by the terms herein.

SIGNED, SEALED AND DELIVERED in the presence of: IN WITNESS whereof I have hereunto set my hand and seal:

A. Fernandes ....   *Ellen Shantz* ....   ● .... DATE *June 14/xx*
(Witness)   (Buyer)   (Seal)

A. Fernandes ....   *David Shantz* ....   ● .... DATE *June 14/xx*
(Witness)   (Buyer)   (Seal)

I, the Undersigned Seller, agree to the above offer. I hereby irrevocably instruct my lawyer to pay directly to the brokerage(s) with whom I have agreed to pay commission, the unpaid balance of the commission together with applicable Harmonized Sales Tax (and any other taxes as may hereafter be applicable), from the proceeds of the sale prior to any payment to the undersigned on completion, as advised by the brokerage(s) to my lawyer.

SIGNED, SEALED AND DELIVERED in the presence of: IN WITNESS whereof I have hereunto set my hand and seal:

W. Palm ....   *Leslie Norton* ....   ● .... DATE *June 15/xx*
(Witness)   (Seller)   (Seal)

W. Palm ....   *Jim Norton* ....   ● .... DATE *June 15/xx*
(Witness)   (Seller)   (Seal)

SPOUSAL CONSENT: The Undersigned Spouse of the Seller hereby consents to the disposition evidenced herein pursuant to the provisions of the Family Law Act, R.S.O.1990, and hereby agrees with the Buyer that he/she will execute all necessary or incidental documents to give full force and effect to the sale evidenced herein.

....   ● .... DATE ....
(Witness)   (Spouse)   (Seal)

CONFIRMATION OF ACCEPTANCE: Notwithstanding anything contained herein to the contrary, I confirm this Agreement with all changes both typed and written was finally accepted by all parties at ... *6:00* ... a.m./p.m. this ... *16th* ... day of .... *June* ...., 20 *XX* ...

                                                           Ellen Shantz
                                                           (Signature of Seller or Buyer)

INFORMATION ON BROKERAGE(S)		
Listing Brokerage .... ABC Realty Inc.		Tel.No.(519) 555-1212
328 Main Street, Anycity	William Palm	
	(Salesperson / Broker Name)	
Co-op/Buyer Brokerage .... XYZ Real Estate Ltd.		Tel.No.(519) 666-1212
28 Norfield Drive, Anycity	A. Fernandes	
	(Salesperson / Broker Name)	

ACKNOWLEDGEMENT

I acknowledge receipt of my signed copy of this accepted Agreement of Purchase and Sale and I authorize the Brokerage to forward a copy to my lawyer.

Leslie Norton .... DATE *June 16/xx*
(Seller)
Jim Norton .... DATE *June 16/xx*
(Seller)
Address for Service *3291 Golf Course Dr., Anycity KOL 3B3*
.... Tel.No.(*519*) *777-1212*
Seller's Lawyer ... *Jane Pierce c/o Pierce and Lyons*
Address ... *327 Centre Avenue, Anycity KOT 3B2*
Email ....
(*519*) *888-1212*   (*519*) *888-2121*
     Tel.No.   FAX No.

I acknowledge receipt of my signed copy of this accepted Agreement of Purchase and Sale and I authorize the Brokerage to forward a copy to my lawyer.

Ellen Shantz .... DATE *June 16/xx*
(Buyer)
David Shantz .... DATE *June 16/xx*
(Buyer)
Address for Service ... *3271 Vista Parkway, Anycity K9B 3C3*
.... Tel.No.(*519*) *222-1212*
Buyer's Lawyer *Thomas Rowley c/o Steward Millard and Stoltz*
Address ... *291 Westside Drive, Anycity K9C 4B2*
Email ....
(*519*) *333-1212*   (*519*) *333-2121*
     Tel.No.   FAX No.

FOR OFFICE USE ONLY   **COMMISSION TRUST AGREEMENT**

To: Co-operating Brokerage shown on the foregoing Agreement of Purchase and Sale:
In consideration for the Co-operating Brokerage procuring the foregoing Agreement of Purchase and Sale, I hereby declare that all moneys received or receivable by me in connection with the Transaction as contemplated in the MLS® Rules and Regulations of my Real Estate Board shall be receivable and held in trust. This agreement shall constitute a Commission Trust Agreement as defined in the MLS® Rules and shall be subject to and governed by the MLS® Rules pertaining to Commission Trust.

DATED as of the date and time of the acceptance of the foregoing Agreement of Purchase and Sale.   Acknowledged by:

W. Palm ....   *A. Fernandes* ....
(Authorized to bind the Listing Brokerage)   (Authorized to bind the Co-operating Brokerage)

Form 100   Revised 2015   **Page 5 of 6**

 **Ontario Real Estate Association**

Form 100
for use in the Province of Ontario

Schedule A
Agreement of Purchase and Sale

This Schedule is attached to and forms part of the Agreement of Purchase and Sale between:

BUYER, ... Ellen Marie Shantz and David Charles Shantz ...., and

SELLER, ... Leslie C. Norton and James P. Norton ....

for the purchase and sale of .. 3291 Golf Course Drive, City of Anycity, Regional Municipality of Anyregion

.... dated the ..14th.. day of .... June ...., 20..xx..

ES DS   LN JN

Buyer agrees to pay the balance as follows:

Three Hundred and Twenty-Nine Thousand Five Hundred

ES DS The Buyer agrees to pay a further sum of ~~Three Hundred and Fourteen Thousand~~ Dollars

($329,500.00)

LN JN ~~($314,000.00)~~, subject to adjustments, to the Seller on completion of this transaction, with funds drawn on a lawyer's trust account in the form of a bank draft, certified cheque, or wire transfer using the Large Value Transfer System.

This Offer is conditional upon the Buyer arranging, at the Buyer's own expense, a new first Charge/Mortgage for not less than Two Hundred Thousand Dollars ($200,000.00), bearing interest at a rate of not more than 5.75% per annum, calculated semi-annually not in advance, repayable in blended bi-weekly payments of about Five Hundred and Seventy-Six Dollars and Twenty-One Cents ($576.21), including principal and interest, and to run for a term of not less than four years from the date of completion of this transaction. Unless the Buyer gives notice in writing, delivered to the Seller personally or in accordance with any other provisions for the delivery of notice in this Agreement of Purchase and Sale or any Schedule thereto not later than 11:59 p.m. on the 30th day of June, 20xx, that this condition is fulfilled, this Offer shall be null and void and the deposit shall be returned to the Buyer in full without deduction. This condition is included for the benefit of the Buyer and may be waived at the Buyer's sole option by notice in writing to the Seller as aforesaid within the time period stated herein.

ES DS ~~The Seller represents and warrants that all mechanical equipment, including furnace, water~~
LN JN ~~softener and air conditioner, all electrical wiring and fixtures, and all plumbing systems are in good~~ ~~working order and in full compliance with current construction code standards. The Parties agree~~ ~~that this warranty shall survive and not merge on completion of this transaction.~~

The Buyer acknowledges that there is no express or implied warranty by the Seller on the chattels included in the agreements of purchase and sale.

This form must be initialed by all parties to the Agreement of Purchase and Sale.

INITIALS OF BUYER(S): (*ES DS*)   **INITIALS OF SELLER(S):** (*LN JN*)

Form 100   Revised 2015   **Page 6 of 6**

OREA Ontario Real Estate Association   **Trade Record Sheet**

Form 640
for use in the Province of Ontario

Sale No:	3296
MLS® No:	22873

ABC Realty Inc.
(Name of Brokerage)   Dated: .... **June 16** .... , 20.**XX** ....

I, ... **William Palm** .... , have today sold (leased or rented, exchanged, optioned):
(Name of Broker/Salesperson)

Property .... **3291 Gold Course Drive, Anycity** ....

SELLER/LANDLORD:

Leslie Norton and James Norton

Address 3291 Golf Course Drive, Anycity K0L 3B3

Tel   (519) 777-1212

Fax

Lawyer   Jane Pierce
Pierce & Lyons
327 Centre Avenue, Anycity K0T 3B2

Tel (519) 888-1212
Fax (519) 888-2121

BUYER/TENANT:

Ellen Shantz and David Shantz

Address 3271 Vista Parkway, Anycity K9B 3C3

Tel   (519) 222-1212

Fax

Lawyer   Thomas Rowley
Steward, Millard and Stoltz
291 Westside Drive, Anycity K9C 4B2

Tel (519) 333-1212
Fax (519) 333-2121

CO-OPERATING/LISTING BROKERAGE (If applicable):   ☐ Listing Brokerage   ☑ Co-operating Brokerage

XYZ Real Estate Limited

Address   886 West Heights Boulevard, Anycity K9T 1B3

Tel (519) 666-1212   Fax (519) 666-2121

Co-op Brokerage HST Number 0879332511 RT

REFERRAL BROKERAGE   Tel
Address   Fax

REFERRAL BROKERAGE   Tel
Address   Fax

Total Consideration For Transaction $ **$354,500.00**
(sale price, rent, exchange value, option price, fee (other))

Completion Date **July 30, 20xx**

Deposit $ **$25,000**   ☐ cash ☑ cheque

If cheque, payable to   **ABC Realty Inc.**   , in trust.

Additional Deposit $ **N/A**   ☐ cash ☐ cheque

If cheque, payable to   , in trust.

Property Other Than Money Held In Trust

Total Commission $ 17,725.00	**Total HST $** 2,304.25	**Total Receivable Comm $** 20,209.25

William Palm
(Broker/Salesperson)   (Broker/Salesperson)

Exercise 5   Trade Record Sheet—Page 2 of 2   **CH10** **EX5**

Property	3291 Gold Course Drive, Anycity			Sale No.: 3296	
Seller/Landlord	Leslie Norton and James Norton			MLS® No.: 22873	
Buyer/Tenant	Ellen Shantz and David Shantz				

THE FOLLOWING TO BE COMPLETED BY THE BROKERAGE:

	COMMISSION	HST	TOTAL	DATE PAID	CHEQUE NO.
Total Receivable Commission:	$17,725.00	$2,304.25	$20,029.25		
Listing Brokerage: ABC Realty Inc.	$3,101.87	$403.24	$3,505.11		
Listing Salesperson/ #1 William Palm Broker #2	$5,760.63	$748.88	$6,509.51		
Co-op Brokerage: XYZ Real Estate Limited	$8,862.50	$1,152.13	$10,014.63		
Selling #1 Salesperson/ Broker #2					
Referral Fee:					
Referral Fee:					
Real Estate Board:					
Other:					

Received deposit from (Salesperson/Broker) .... DATE ....

Additional deposit from (Salesperson/Broker) .... DATE ....

Deposited in Real Estate Trust Acc. (Amount) .... DATE ....

Additional deposit to Real Estate Trust Acc. (Amount) .... DATE ....

Statement to Seller DATE..................................

Interest bearing deposit transferred to ....

Instrument #.. DATE .... Cheque # ....

Interest bearing deposit returned

to Real Estate Trust Acc. (Amount).. DATE .... Cheque # ....

If applicable, Interest earned (Amount) ....

If applicable, interest paid to ....

Cheque # ....

If applicable, SIN of interest recipient ....

If applicable, Business # of Corporation ....

Remitted to Seller/Buyer (Amount) .... DATE .... Cheque # ....

Transferred to Commission Trust (Amount) .... DATE .... Cheque # ....

Transferred Commission to Gen. Acct. (Amount) .... DATE .... Cheque # ....

Additional Necessary Information ....

....

To the best of my knowledge and belief the above information is correct.

DATED at .... Ontario, this .... day of ...., 20..............

....
(Signature of Broker of Record)

FOR OFFICE USE ONLY   **COMMISSION TRUST AGREEMENT**
To: The Salesperson(s) shown on the foregoing Trade Record Sheet:
In consideration of the Salesperson(s) having successfully completed a trade in real estate on behalf of the Brokerage with respect to the property more particularly dened in the foregoing Trade Record Sheet, I hereby declare that all moneys received or receivable by me in connection with the transaction as contemplated in the Office Policy shall be receivable and held in trust. This agreement shall constitute a Commission Trust Agreement as defined in the Office Policy and shall be subject to and governed by the Office Policy pertaining to Commission Trust. DATED as of the date and time of the acceptance of the foregoing Trade Record Sheet.   Acknowledged by:

R. A. Johnson   Jennifer Lancaster
....
(Signature of Broker of Record/Manager)   (Signature of Broker/Salesperson)

Form 640   Revised 2015   **Page 2 of 2**

OREA Ontario Real Estate Association   **Waiver**

Form 123
for use in the Province of Ontario

BUYER: .... Ellen Marie Shantz and David Charles Shantz ....

SELLER: .... Leslie C. Norton and James P. Norton ....

REAL PROPERTY: .... 3291 Golf Course Drive, City of Anycity, Regional Municipality of Anyregion ...

....

In accordance with the terms and conditions of the Agreement of Purchase and Sale dated the ...14th.. day of............ June ....,

20.XX........., regarding the above property, I/We hereby waive the condition(s) which read(s) as follows:

This Offer is conditional upon the Buyer arranging, at the Buyer's own expense, a new first Charge/ Mortgage for not less than Two Hundred Thousand Dollars ($200,000.00), bearing interest at a rate of not more than 5.75% per annum, calculated semi-annually not in advance, payable in blended bi-weekly payments of about Five Hundred and Seventy-Six Dollars and Twenty-One Cents ($576.21), including principal and interest, and to run for a term of not less than four years from the date of completion of this transaction. Unless the Buyer gives notice in writing, delivered to the Seller personally or in accordance with any other provisions for the delivery of notice in this Agreement of Purchase and Sale or any Schedule thereto not later than 11:59 p.m. on the 30th day of June, 20xx, that this condition is fulfilled, this Offer shall be null and void and the deposit shall be returned to the Buyer in full without deduction. This condition is included for the benefit of the Buyer and may be waived at the Buyer's sole option by notice in writing to the Seller as aforesaid within the time period stated herein.

All other terms and conditions in the aforementioned Agreement of Purchase and Sale to remain unchanged.

For the purposes of this Waiver, "Buyer" includes purchaser, tenant, and lessee, and "Seller" includes vendor, landlord, and lessor, and "Agreement of Purchase and Sale" includes an Agreement to Lease.

WAIVED at............ *Anycity* ...., Ontario, at *12:30* a.m./p.m., this *30th* day of .... *June* .... 20.XX....

SIGNED, SEALED AND DELIVERED in the presence of: IN WITNESS whereof I have hereunto set my hand and seal:

..... *A. Fernandes* .... *Ellen Shantz* ....   ● DATE .... *June 30/xx* ....
(Witness)   (Buyer/Seller)   (Seal)

..... *A. Fernandes* .... *David Shantz* ....   ● DATE .... *June 30/xx* ....
(Witness)   (Buyer/Seller)   (Seal)

Receipt acknowledged at .. *2:30* . a.m./p.m., this *30th* day of .... *June* .... 20.XX............ by:

Print Name: .... **Leslie Norton** ....   Signature:...... *Leslie Norton* ....

APPENDIX

OREA Ontario Real Estate Association

Amendment to Agreement of Purchase and Sale

Form 120
for use in the Province of Ontario

BETWEEN BUYER, ... Ellen Marie Shantz and David Charles Shantz ....

AND SELLER, ... Leslie C. Norton and James P. Norton ....

RE: Agreement of Purchase and Sale between the Seller and Buyer, dated the ...14th... day of .... June ...., 20..XX..,

concerning the property known as ...3291 Golf Course Drive, City of Anycity, Regional Municipality of Anyregion...

.... as more particularly described in the aforementioned Agreement.

The Buyer(s) and Seller(s) herein agree to the following Amendments to the aforementioned Agreement:

Delete:

This Agreement shall be completed no later than 6:00 p.m. on the 30th day of July, 20xx.

Insert:

This Agreement shall be completed no later than 6:00 p.m. on the 30th day of August, 20xx.

This buyer shall have the right to inspect the property one further time prior to completion, at a mutually agreed upon time, provided that written notice is given to the Seller. The Seller agrees to provide access to the property for the purpose of this inspection.

INITIALS OF BUYER(S): (*ES DS*)   **INITIALS OF SELLER(S):** (*LN JN*)

Form 120   Revised 2014   **Page 1 of 2**

IRREVOCABILITY: This Offer to Amend the Agreement shall be irrevocable by .... Buyer .... until 11:59 ~~a.m.~~/p.m.
                                                       (Seller/Buyer)

on the 5th day of .... July ...., 20 XX , after which time, if not accepted, this Offer to Amend the Agreement shall be null and void.

For the purposes of this Amendment to Agreement, "Buyer" includes purchaser and "Seller" includes vendor.
Time shall in all respects be of the essence hereof provided that the time for doing or completing of any matter provided for herein may be extended or abridged by an agreement in writing signed by Seller and Buyer or by their respective solicitors who are hereby expressly appointed in this regard.

All other Terms and Conditions in the aforementioned Agreement to remain the same.

SIGNED, SEALED AND DELIVERED in the presence of: IN WITNESS whereof I have hereunto set my hand and seal:

A. Fernandes   *Ellen Shantz* .... ● DATE *July 5/xx*
(Witness)   (Buyer/Seller)   (Seal)

A. Fernandes   *David Shantz* .... ● DATE *July 5/xx*
(Witness)   (Buyer/Seller)   (Seal)

I, the Undersigned, agree to the above Offer to Amend the Agreement.

SIGNED, SEALED AND DELIVERED in the presence of: IN WITNESS whereof I have hereunto set my hand and seal:

W. Palm   **Leslie Norton**   ● DATE *July 5/xx*
(Witness)   (Buyer/Seller)   (Seal)

W. Palm   **Jim Norton**   ● DATE *July 5/xx*
(Witness)   (Buyer/Seller)   (Seal)

The Undersigned Spouse of the Seller hereby consents to the Amendments hereinbefore set out.

....   ● DATE ....
(Witness)   (Spouse)   (Seal)

CONFIRMATION OF ACCEPTANCE: Notwithstanding anything contained herein to the contrary, I confirm this Agreement with all changes both typed and written was finally accepted by all parties at 5:00 ~~a.m.~~/p.m. this 5th day of .... July ...., 20 XX .

                                       Leslie Norton
                                       (Signature of Seller or Buyer)

ACKNOWLEDGEMENT

I acknowledge receipt of my signed copy of this accepted Amendment to Agreement and I authorize the Brokerage to forward a copy to my lawyer.

Leslie Norton .... DATE *July 5/xx*
(Seller)

Jim Norton .... DATE *July 5/xx*
(Seller)

Address for Service *3291 Golf Course Dr., Anycity*
KOL 3B3 .... Tel.No.(*519*) *777-1212*

Seller's Lawyer *Jane Pierce c/o Pierce and Lyons*

Address *327 Centre Avenue, Anycity KOT 3B2*

Email ....

(*519*) *888-1212*   (*519*) *888-2121*
     Tel.No.   FAX No.

I acknowledge receipt of my signed copy of this accepted Amendment to Agreement and I authorize the Brokerage to forward a copy to my lawyer.

Ellen Shantz .... DATE *July 5/xx*
(Buyer)

David Shantz .... DATE *July 5/xx*
(Buyer)

Address for Service *3271 Vista Parkway, Anycity K9B 3C3*
.... Tel.No.(*519*) *222-1212*

Buyer's Lawyer *Thomas Rowley c/o Steward Millard and Stoltz*

Address *291 Westside Drive, Anycity K9C 4B2*

Email ....

(*519*) *333-1212*   (*519*) *333-2121*
     Tel.No.   FAX No.

                                               Form 120   Revised 2014   **Page 2 of 2**

CHAPTER 11
CLOSING THE TRANSACTION

CH11 MR

Chapter Mini-Review

1. Restrictive covenants and outstanding encumbrances are part of the non-title search process.

    True   **False**

   Such items directly affect title and are viewed as part of the title search process, as distinct from non-title search items such as property taxes and executions.

2. Outstanding work orders and zoning compliance are two possible non-title searches undertaken by the buyer's solicitor.

    True   False

   Other non-title items could involve outstanding utility amounts and unregistered easements.

3. A requisition can involve a request to verify that the seller is not a non-resident pursuant to the *Income Tax Act*.

    True   False

   Requisitions can be wide ranging as they can relate to various problems, defects or other matters concerning title.

4. The gateway software used to access electronic land registration information is called POLARIS (Province of Ontario Land Registration and Information System).

    True   **False**

   The gateway software is called Teraview.

5. The statement of adjustments is normally prepared by the buyer's solicitor, unless otherwise specifically agreed.

    True   **False**

   The statement of adjustments is usually prepared by the seller's solicitor, unless otherwise specifically agreed.

6. If a mortgage is taken back, the mortgage document is usually prepared by the seller's solicitor.

    True   False

   The seller's solicitor prepares documents concerning any seller take back mortgage and also prepares the draft deed.

7. If a residential seller has existing home insurance, the seller's solicitor will pro-rate the premium between the buyer and the seller, based on the closing date.

    True   **False**

   Insurance is not pro-rated. The buyer must secure his or her own coverage.

8. Title insurance policies for lenders commonly include the *duty to defend* and the *duty to indemnify*, but owner policies are limited to the *duty to defend*.

    True   **False**

   Title policies for both lenders and owners typically include both duties.

APPENDIX

9. A typical risk covered by title insurance involves fraud or document forgery that impacts title.

✓ True   ○ False

Fraud and document forgery are typically covered. The full scope of coverage will vary by insurer.

10. A survey cost might be avoided when securing title insurance based on the title insurer's policy provisions and specific property considerations.

✓ True   ○ False

The cost may be avoided, but policies regarding this issue will vary by insurer.

11. A commission trust account is a statutory requirement set out in the *Real Estate and Business Brokers Act, 2002*.

○ True   **✓ False**

A commission trust account is not mandatory under the Act.

12. A salesperson should use his/her best efforts to determine whether or not an intended employing brokerage has set up and maintains a commission trust account.

✓ True   ○ False

A salesperson may not be able to make a claim, regarding commission under the RECO insurance program, if he was aware that the brokerage did not have a commission trust account.

13. HST remittances must be made by all commission salespeople.

○ True   **✓ False**

HST remittances must be made by independent contractors who meet HST requirements, but not by other employed salespersons.

14. Real estate brokerages must provide cash advances on commission owing, if requested by the salespeople.

○ True   **✓ False**

The brokerage has no obligation to provide cash advances on commission owing.

APPENDIX

Active Learning Exercises

■ Exercise 1   Multiple Choice

1.1 Undertakings can generally be grouped under several main categories. Which is NOT one of them? **This question requires that the** *incorrect* **option be identified.**

a. Client Assurance.

This option is correct. Client assurance is one of three undertakings described in this chapter.

b. Solicitor Personal Assurance.

This option is correct. Solicitor personal assurance is one of three undertakings described in this chapter.

c. **Guaranteed Assurance.**

✔ *THIS IS THE INCORRECT OPTION.* A guaranteed assurance is not one of the three undertakings described in this chapter.

d. Best Efforts Assurance.

This option is correct. Best efforts assurance is one of three undertakings described in this chapter.

1.2 The seller's solicitor typically prepares a final reporting letter which:

a. Sets out transaction particulars from the buyer's perspective.

Incorrect. The buyer's lawyer would detail transaction particulars from the buyer's perspective.

b. **Might include, if applicable, details about a seller take back mortgage.**

✔ *CORRECT.* A final reporting letter from the seller's solicitor would, if applicable, include details about a seller take back mortgage.

c. Provides evidence that the seller is not a non-resident.

Incorrect. This information would typically be associated with an undertaking arising out of a requisition by the buyer's solicitor.

d. Is forwarded to the buyer's solicitor prior to completion of a title search.

Incorrect. The final reporting letter is the final stage and would not be issued prior to the title search.

1.3 Which of the following is NOT correct about title insurance in Ontario? **This question requires that the** *incorrect* **option be identified.**

a. Has certain benefits to home owners, one of which involves title problems at point of listing the property.

This option is correct. The title policy for an owner covers the entire property (mortgage plus equity) and typically less coverages are provided given greater risk.

b. Typically includes both loan and owner policies.

This option is correct. Insurers typically offer both loan and owner policies.

c. Usually insures over minor encroachment problems.

This option is correct. Policies usually insure over minor encroachment problems.

d. **Usually provides broader coverage with owner policies than with lender policies.**

✔ *THIS IS THE INCORRECT OPTION.* Typically, coverage for lenders is greater than for owners as the risk is less; i.e., a lender policy only covers the mortgage while an owner's policy covers both mortgage and equity.

APPENDIX

1.4   Commission disbursements to brokerages:

a.   Must follow a specific order beginning first with payment to the listing brokerage.

Incorrect. Commission disbursement to the co-operating brokerage precedes payment to the listing brokerage.

b.   Is usually paid directly from the statutory real estate trust account.

Incorrect. The vast majority of brokerages have commission trust accounts for commission disbursement.

c.   **Must follow a specific order beginning first with payment to the co-operating brokerage.**

✔ *CORRECT.* Disbursement to a co-operating brokerage is the first payment, followed by commission to employed salespeople and then commission to the brokerage.

d.   Must occur no later than 48 hours following receipt of any balance received from a solicitor involved with the applicable transaction.

Incorrect. No such time limit exists, but prompt payment is expected.

1.5   The OREA *Agreement of Purchase and Sale* (OREA Form 100) includes:

a.   **A requisition date relating to the title search process.**

✔ *CORRECT.* A requisition date is provided in Clause 8 of the *Agreement of Purchase and Sale* (OREA Form 100).

b.   A date by which both solicitors must submit a final reporting letter.

Incorrect. The *Agreement of Purchase and Sale* (OREA Form 100) does not address final reporting letters.

c.   A requirement that all conveyances must be completed using e-registration.

Incorrect. The *Agreement of Purchase and Sale* (OREA Form 100) provides for both manual and electronic registration, as electronic conversion is not yet finalized.

d.   A requirement that a sub-search must be completed immediately before registration of the transfer/deed of land.

Incorrect. The *Agreement of Purchase and Sale* (OREA Form 100) does not specifically address sub-searches within the preprinted wording.

1.6   A requisition letter might include a request for which of the following?

a.   Satisfactory evidence that the seller will pay all water and gas accounts to closing date.

Incorrect. This is a correct statement, but a more suitable answer option is available.

b.   Statement from the seller attesting that the property is exempt from harmonized sales tax.

Incorrect. This is a correct statement, but a more suitable answer option is available.

c.   Seller's undertaking to deliver vacant possession of the premises.

Incorrect. This is a correct statement, but a more suitable answer option is available.

d.   **All of the above.**

✔ *CORRECT.* Options a., b. and c. are correct statements.

APPENDIX

1.7 Assume an independent contractor registered for HST purposes, received a gross commission of $2,000 and paid an administrative fee of $500, which is viewed as a valid input credit. If these were the only transactions in the reporting period, what is the net remittance?

a. $260

Incorrect. Check math. The administration fee is subtracted from the gross commission income.

b. $195

✔ *CORRECT.* HST calculation ($2,000–$500 x .13 (13%) = $195.

c. $75

Incorrect. Check math. The current HST rate is 13%.

d. $100

Incorrect. Check math.

■ Exercise 2   Matching

Match the words in the left column with the appropriate descriptions in the right column (not all descriptions are used).

f.	*Owner's Policy*	*Title Insurance*
d.	*Commission Trust Account*	*Protection Involving Bankruptcy*
g.	*Statutory Trust Account*	*REBBA 2002*
a.	*Buyer's Solicitor*	*Preparation of Requisition Letter*
b.	*Undertaking*	*An Assurance Provided by a Solicitor of the Client*
c.	*Teraview*	*Gateway Software Used to Access Electronic Land Registration Information*
h.	*Legal Disclosure Requirements*	*Law Society of Upper Canada*
j.	*Conveyance*	*Transfer/Deed of Land*

No Match: e., and i.

■ Exercise 3   Commission Trust

- Brokerage office policy clearly sets out the commission trust concept.
- Clauses in employment agreements reinforce the commission trust concept.
- A commission trust agreement is entered into with every transaction by way of a separate document, or a section added to the trade record sheet.
- A commission trust agreement is entered into between listing and co-operating brokerages (i.e., agreement of purchase and sale) for each transaction.

APPENDIX

■ Exercise 4   Disbursement Calculations

Total Commission Including HST	($15,500 + 2,015)		**$17,515.00**
	CHEQUE FROM	CHEQUE TO	AMOUNT
Step 1	Real Estate Trust	Commission Trust	8,250.00
Step 2	Lawyer *$7,250 balance of commission +* *$2,015 HST on total commission*	Commission Trust	9,265.00
			$17,515.00
Step 3	Commission Trust *50/50 distribution of ($15,500 + HST)*	XYZ Real Estate Ltd.	8,757.50
Step 4	Commission Trust *70/30 distribution of ($7,750 + HST)*	Salesperson Verdun	6,130.25
Step 5	Commission Trust *30/70 distribution of ($7,750 + HST)*	ABC Realty Inc.	2,627.25
			$17,515.00

APPENDIX